I0833802

THE VISIONS OF Anne Catherine Emmerich

BOOK II

THE VISIONS OF Anne Catherine Emmerich

BOOK II

The Journeys of Jesus
Continue Till Just Before the Passion
With a Day-by-Day Chronicle
August AD 30 to February AD 33

From the Notes of
CLEMENS BRENTANO

Revised and Supplemented
by James Richard Wetmore
General Editor

Chronology and Daily Summaries
by Robert Powell, Ph.D.

Angelico Press

First published in the USA
by Angelico Press 2015
Revised Text, New Text, Supplements,
Translations, and Layout

For information, address:
Angelico Press
169 Monitor St.
Brooklyn, NY 11222
www.angelicopress.com

Book I: ISBN 978-1-59731-146-5 (pbk)
Book I: ISBN 978-1-59731-467-1 (hbk)
Book II: ISBN 978-1-59731-147-2 (pbk)
Book II: ISBN 978-1-59731-468-8 (hbk)
Book III: ISBN 978-1-59731-148-9 (pbk)
Book III: ISBN 978-1-59731-469-5 (hbk)

Cover Images:
J. James Tissot (French, 1836–1902)
Front: *Jesus Goes in the Evening to Bethany* (detail)
Back: *Jesus Goes Up Alone onto a Mountain to Pray* (detail)
Brooklyn Museum, purchased by
public subscription: 00.159.201, 00.159.137
Reproduced by permission
of the Brooklyn Museum
Cover Design: Michael Schrauzer

CONTENTS

Day-by-Day Chronicle of the Life, Travels, and Teaching of Jesus During His Public Ministry

Year 2: AD 30

ILLUSTRATIONS

MAPS

YEARS 2–4

Day-by-Day

CHRONICLE

OF THE LIFE, TRAVELS, & TEACHING OF JESUS

⊕

Jesus's Teaching Mission in the Country of
Northern Galilee and on the Banks of the Jordan
August 3–September 28, AD 30

From the Second Feast of Tabernacles
to the First Conversion of Magdalene
September 29–November 8, AD 30

Preaching and Miracles of Jesus in
Capernaum and the Surrounding Districts
November 9–December 24, AD 30

From the Second Conversion
of Magdalene to the Delivery of the
Keys to Peter—Travels in Northern Galilee
December 25, AD 30–March 22, AD 31

From the Second
Passover to the Return from Cyprus
March 23, AD 31–July 8, AD 31

Period Missing from the
Record of Anne Catherine's Visions
July 9, AD 31–May 16, AD 32

The Raising of Lazarus
Jesus in the Land of the Three Kings
May 17, AD 32–February 18, AD 33

The Sea of Tiberias

JESUS'S TEACHING MISSION IN THE COUNTRY OF NORTHERN GALILEE AND ON THE BANKS OF THE JORDAN

The Messengers of the Centurion of Capernaum

Thursday, August 3, AD 30 (Ab 15)

This morning Jesus arrived at Cana. He stayed near the synagogue with a doctor of the Law. While he was teaching those who had gathered in the forecourt of the house where he was staying, a messenger from Zorobabel, a high-ranking official of Capernaum, arrived with a message saying that his son was dying. There then occurred, at a distance, the miraculous healing of the boy, as described in John 4:46–54. This was the second sign that Jesus did upon coming up from Judea to Galilee (the first being the turning of water into wine at the wedding at Cana).

FROM Nain, Jesus, leaving Nazareth on the left, journeyed past Tabor to Cana, where he put up near the synagogue with a doctor of the Law. The forecourt of the house was soon full of people who had anticipated his coming from Engannim, and were here awaiting him. He had been teaching the whole morning, when a servant of the centurion of Capernaum with several companions mounted on mules arrived.[C5] He was in a great hurry and wore an air of anxiety and solicitude. He vainly sought on all sides to press his way through the throng around Jesus, but could not succeed. After several fruitless attempts, he began to cry out lustily: "Venerable Master, let thy servant approach thee! I come as the messenger of my lord of Capernaum. In his name and as the father of his son, I implore thee to come with me at once, for my son is very sick and nigh unto death." Jesus appeared not to hear him; but encouraged at seeing that some were directing Jesus's attention to him, the man again sought to press through the crowd. But not succeeding, he cried out anew: "Come with me at once, for my son is dying!" When he cried so impatiently, Jesus turned his head toward him and said loud enough for the people to hear: "If you see not signs and wonders, you do not believe. I know your case well. You want to boast of a miracle and glory over the Pharisees, though you have the same need of being humbled as they. My mission is not to work miracles in order to further your designs. I stand in no need of your approbation. I shall reserve my miracles until it is my Father's will that I should perform them, and I shall perform them when my mission calls for it!" And thus Jesus went on for a long time, humbling the man before all the people. He said that that man had been waiting long for him to cure his son, that he might boast of it before the Pharisees. But miracles, Jesus continued, should not be desired in order to triumph over others, and he exhorted his hearers to believe and be converted.

The man listened to Jesus's reproaches without being at all disturbed. Not at all diverted from his design, he again tried to approach nearer, crying out: "Of what use is all that, Master? My son is in the agony of death! Come with me at once, he may perhaps be already dead!" Then Jesus said to him: "Go, thy son liveth!" The man asked: "Is that really true?" Jesus answered: "Believe me, he has in this very hour been cured." Thereupon the man believed and, no longer importuning Jesus to accompany him, mounted his mule and hastened back to Capernaum. Jesus remarked that he had yielded this time; at another time he

I saw this man not as invested with the royal commission, but as himself the father of the sick boy. He was the chief officer of the centurion of Capernaum. The latter had no children, but had long desired to have one. He had, consequently, adopted as his own a son of this his confidential servant and his wife. The boy was now fourteen years old. The man came in quality of messenger, though he was himself the true father and almost indeed the master. I saw the whole affair, all the circumstances were clear to me. It was perhaps on account of them that Jesus permitted the man to importune him so long. The details I have just given were not publicly known.

The boy had long sighed after Jesus. The sickness was at first slight and the desire for Jesus's presence arose from the feeling entertained against the Pharisees. But for the last fourteen days, the case becoming aggravated, the boy had constantly said to his physicians: "All these medicines do me no good. Jesus, the prophet of Nazareth, alone can help me!" When the danger had become imminent, messages had been dispatched to Samaria by means of the holy women, while Andrew and Nathaniel had been sent to Engannim; and at last the father and steward himself rode to Cana, where he found Jesus. Jesus had delayed to grant his prayer in order to punish what was evil in his intentions.

It was a day's journey from Cana to Capernaum, but the man rode with such speed that he reached home before night. A couple of hours from Capernaum, some of his servants met him and told him that the boy was cured. They had come after him to tell him that if he had not found Jesus, he should give himself no further trouble, for the boy had been suddenly cured at the seventh hour. Then he repeated to them the words of Jesus. They were filled with astonishment, and hurried home with him. I saw the centurion Zorobabel and the boy coming to the door to meet him. The boy embraced him. He repeated all that Jesus had said, the servants that accompanied him confirming his words. There was great joy, and I saw a feast made ready. The youth sat between his adopted father and his real father, the mother being nearby. He loved his real father as much as he did the supposed one, and the former exercised great authority in the house.

After Jesus had dismissed the man of Capernaum, he cured several sick persons, who had been brought into a court of the house. There were some possessed among them, though not of the vicious kind. The possessed were often brought to Jesus's instructions. At first sight of him, they fell into frightful raging and threw themselves on the ground, but as soon as he commanded them to be at peace, they became quiet. After some time, however, they seemed no longer able to restrain themselves, and began again to move convulsively. Jesus made them a sign with his hand, and they again recovered themselves. The instruction over, he commanded Satan to go out of them. They lay, as was usual on such occasions, for about two minutes as if unconscious, and then, coming to themselves, thanked Jesus joyfully, not exactly knowing what had happened to them. There are such good, possessed people of whom the demon has taken possession by no fault of their own. I cannot clearly explain it, but I saw on this occasion, as well as upon others, how it happens that a guilty person may, by the mercy and long-sufferance of God, be spared, while Satan takes possession of one of his weak, innocent relatives. It is as if the innocent took upon himself a part of the other's punishment. I cannot make it clear, but it is certain that we are all members of one body. It is as if a healthy member, in consequence of a secret, intimate bond between them, suffers for another that is not sound. Such were the possessed of this place. The wicked are much more terrible and they cooperate with Satan, but the others merely suffer the possession and are meanwhile very pious.

Jesus afterward taught in the synagogue. There were present from Nazareth several doctors of the Law, and they invited him to return with them. They said that his native city was ringing with the great miracles he had wrought in Judea, Samaria, and Engannim; that he knew very well the opinion prevalent in Nazareth that whoever had not studied in the school of the Pharisees could not know much; therefore they desired him to come and teach them better. They thought by these arguments to seduce Jesus. But he replied that he would not yet go to Nazareth, and that when he did, they would not obtain what they were now demanding.

After the instruction in the synagogue, Jesus was present at a great feast in the house of the father of the bride of Cana. The bride and bridegroom with the widowed aunt of the latter were there. Nathaniel the bridegroom had joined Jesus as a disciple on his coming to Cana, and had helped to keep order during the instruction and the curing of the sick. The bridegroom and bride dwelt alone. They carried on no housekeeping, for they received their meals from the parents of the latter. Her father limped a little. They were good people. Cana was a clean, beautiful city on a lofty plateau. Several highways ran through it, and one straight to Capernaum, about seven hours distant. The road inclined a little before reaching Capernaum.

After the feast, Jesus returned to his abode and again healed several sick persons who were patiently awaiting him. He did not always cure in the same way. Sometimes it was by a word of command, sometimes he laid his hands upon the sick, again he bowed himself over them, again he ordered them to bathe, and sometimes he mixed dust with his saliva and smeared their eyes with it. To some he gave admonitions, to others he declared their sins, and others again he sent away without being cured.

Jesus in Capernaum

Friday, August 4, AD 30 (*Ab 16*)

Jesus and the three disciples made their way to Capernaum, where they were greeted by Zorobabel and members of his family. Jesus laid his hand on the child's head and gave him the name Jesse (before he had been called Joel). After visiting his mother, Jesus went to the synagogue for the start of the sabbath. Afterward, he healed the sick.

WHEN Jesus, with the disciples who had accompanied him to Cana, left for Capernaum, he was followed by Nathaniel, whose wife with her aunt and others had already gone on before. The road, about seven hours in length, was tolerably straight. It ran by a little lake like that of Ainon, around which lay country seats and gardens. The magnificently fruitful region of Galilee began here, and in many places there were watchtowers.

When Jesus approached the environs of Capernaum, several possessed began to rage outside the gate and to call into the city: "The prophet is coming! What does he want here? What business has he with us?" But when he reached the city, they ran away. A tent had been erected outside. The centurion and the father of the boy came out to meet Jesus, the child walking between them. They were followed by the entire family, all the relatives, servants, and slaves. These last were pagans who had been sent to Zorobabel by Herod. It was a real procession, and all cast themselves down before Jesus giving thanks. They washed his feet and offered him a little luncheon, a mouthful to eat and a glass of wine. Jesus spoke some words of admonition to the boy, laying his hand on his head as he knelt before him. He now received the name of Jesse, whereas he had before been called Joel. The centurion's name was Zorobabel. He earnestly besought Jesus to stay with him while at Capernaum and to accept a feast in his honor. But Jesus refused, still reproaching him with his desire to see a miracle in order to vex others. He said: "I should not have cured the boy, had not the faith of the messenger been so strong and urgent." And thereupon Jesus went on his way.

But Zorobabel had a great banquet prepared to which all the servants and laborers of his numerous gardens around the city were called. The miracle had been related to them, and all deeply moved believed in Jesus. During the entertainment the domestics and many of the poor, to whom presents had been made, intoned a song of praise and thanksgiving in the entrance porch.

The news of the miracle soon spread throughout Capernaum. Zorobabel sent an account of it to the mother of Jesus and the apostles. I saw the latter again busy at their fisheries. I saw the news taken also to Peter's mother-in-law, who was then lying sick.

Jesus went around Capernaum to his mother's dwelling, where about five women together with Peter, Andrew, James, and John were assembled. They went out to meet him, and there were great rejoicings at his coming and his miracles. He took a meal here and then went back to Capernaum for the sabbath. The women remained at home.

A great concourse of people and many sick were gathered at Capernaum.[C6] The possessed ran crying about the streets as Jesus approached. He commanded them to be silent, and passed along through them to the synagogue. After the prayer, a stiff-necked Pharisee by the name of Manasseh was called upon, for it was his turn to read the scriptures aloud. But Jesus told them to give him the roll, that he would do the reading. They obeyed, and he read from the beginning of the First Book of Moses down to the account of the murmuring of the children of Israel. He spoke of the ingratitude of their fathers, of the mercy of God toward them, and of the nearness of the kingdom, warning them to beware of acting as their fathers had done. He explained all the errors and crooked ways of their fathers by a comparison with their own erroneous notions, drawing a parallel between the Promised Land of those far-off times and the kingdom now so near. Then he read the first chapter of Isaiah, which he interpreted as referring to the present. He spoke of crime and its punishment, of their long waiting for a prophet, and of how they would treat him now that they had him. He cited the various animals, all of which knew their master, although they, his hearers, knew him not. He spoke of the one that longed to help them, picturing to them the woeful appearance he would present in consequence of their outrages upon him, also of the punishment in store for Jerusalem, and of the small number of the elect when all this would take place. The Lord would, nevertheless, multiply them while the wicked would be destroyed. He called upon them to be converted, saying that even were they all covered with blood, if they cried to God and turned from their evil ways, they would become clean. Again he referred to Manasseh who had given so much scandal, who had committed so much iniquity before the Lord; therefore had God permitted him in punishment to be led away captive to Babylon, where he had been converted, had cried to God for pardon, and had received a share in the Promise. Jesus then opened the scriptures as if by accident at Isaiah, and read the passage: "Behold a virgin shall conceive," which he applied to himself and the coming of the Messiah.

He had given the same explanation at Nazareth some time before his baptism, whereupon his hearers had mocked, saying: "We never saw him eating much butter and honey when with his father, the poor carpenter."

The Pharisees and many others of Capernaum were not well satisfied at Jesus's having spoken to them so severely about ingratitude; they had expected some pleasant, flattering words on the score of the good reception they had extended to him. The instruction lasted tolerably long and, when Jesus was going out of the synagogue, I heard two of the Pharisees whispering to each other: "They have brought some sick. Let us see whether he will dare to heal them on the sabbath." The streets had been lighted with torches, and many of the houses illuminated with lamps. Some, however, were dark; they were the homes of the evil-minded. Wherever Jesus passed, he found sick in front of the houses and lights by them; some had been carried to the door in the arms of their relatives, while near them stood others bearing torches. There was great bustling to and fro in the streets, and shouts of joy were heard on all sides. Many of the possessed cried after Jesus, and he delivered them with a word of command. I saw one of them with a fearful countenance and bristling hair springing toward him in rage and fury, and crying out: "Thou! What dost thou want here? What business hast thou here?" Jesus repulsed him, saying: "Withdraw, Satan!" And I saw the man dashed to the ground as if his neck and every bone in his body were broken. When he rose up, he was quite changed, quite gentle, and he knelt at Jesus's feet weeping and thanking. Jesus commanded him to be converted. I saw him curing many as he thus passed along.

After that Jesus went with the disciples to his mother's. It was night. On the way Peter spoke of his household affairs: he had neglected many things connected with his fishery, from which he had been so long absent; he must provide for his wife, his children, and his mother-in-law. John replied that he and James had to take care of their parents, and that was more important than the care of a mother-in-law. And so they bandied words freely and jocosely. Jesus observed that the time would soon come when they would give up their present fishing, in order to catch fish of another kind. John was much more childlike and familiar with Jesus than the others. He was so affectionate, so submissive in all things, without solicitude or contradiction. Jesus returned to his mother's; the others, to their homes.

Saturday, August 5, AD 30 (*Ab 17*)

On the way to the synagogue, Jesus healed many. After the morning service, two adulterous women approached him, wanting to repent publicly of their sins. Jesus forgave them. And for this, and for healing on the sabbath, he was called to account by the Pharisees. That evening the Pharisees met with the town elders, including Zorobabel, to discuss what to do about Jesus. Zorobabel was able to exert a calming influence.

Early next day Jesus left his mother's, which was about three-quarters of an hour from Capernaum in the direction of Bethsaida, and went to the first-named city with his disciples. The road was at first somewhat of an ascent, but near Capernaum it began to decline. Before reaching the gate of the city, the traveler came to a house belonging to Peter, who had allotted it to Jesus and the disciples and placed in it a pious old man as steward. It was about an hour and a half from the lake. All the disciples from Bethsaida and the country around were gathered in Capernaum, whither also Mary and the holy women had come. Numbers of sick were ranged along the streets by which Jesus was to pass. They had been brought the day before, but had not been cured. Jesus healed a great many on his way to the synagogue in which, during his instruction, he related a parable. When he left the synagogue, he still continued teaching, and several persons threw themselves at his feet begging pardon for their sins. Two of them were adulteresses who had been put away by their husbands, and there were four men, among them the seducers of those women. They burst into tears and wanted to confess their sins before the multitude. But Jesus replied that their sins were already known to him, that a time would come when the open confession of them would be necessary, but at present it would only scandalize their neighbor and attract upon them persecution. He exhorted them to watch over themselves that they might not relapse into sin, but if they should be so unhappy as to do so, not to despair, but to turn to God and do penance. He forgave them their sins, and when the men asked to which baptism they should go, to that of John's disciples, or wait for his own, he told them to go to the former.

The Pharisees present wondered very much that Jesus should undertake to forgive sins, and called him to account for it. But Jesus silenced them by his answer, that it was easier for him to forgive sins than to heal, for to him that sincerely repents, sin is forgiven, and he will not lightly sin again; but the sick who are cured in body often remain sick in soul, and make use of their body to relapse into sin. Then they asked him whether the husbands of those women whose sins had been forgiven should take back their once-repudiated wives. Jesus answered that time did not permit him to discuss that point, but later on he would instruct them upon it. They questioned him also upon his curing on the sabbath. Jesus defended himself with the query: "If one of you had an animal that should fall into a well on the sabbath, would you not draw it out?"

In the afternoon Jesus retired with all his disciples to the house outside Capernaum, where the holy women were already assembled. They partook of an entertainment, which the centurion Zorobabel had provided. He and Salathiel, the father of the boy, reclined at table with Jesus and the disciples, while Jesse, the boy, served. The women sat at a separate table. Jesus taught. They brought the sick to him, making their way into the house, yes, even crowding with cries for help into the dining hall. He cured many. The meal over, Jesus returned to the synagogue, and I heard him discoursing, among other things, of Isaiah and his prophecy to King Achaz: "Behold, a virgin shall conceive and give birth to a son," etc. (Isa. 7:14).

When he left the synagogue, he cured numbers on the streets, and that until night had closed. Among them were many women afflicted with an issue of blood. Sad and mournful, they stood at a distance enveloped in their veils, not daring to approach Jesus or the crowd around him. Jesus knew their suffering, turned toward them, and healed them with a glance. He never touched such sufferers. There was some mystery in the prohibition to that effect which I cannot now express. A fast day began on that evening.

When Jesus returned with his disciples to his mother's, the question arose as to whether they should go with him next morning to the lake, and I heard Peter excusing himself on account of the bad state of his boat.

The people whose sins Jesus had forgiven were clothed in penitential garb and enveloped in large veils. From the last sabbath but one, the Jews wore black and the whole time was a season of penance commemorative of the destruction of Jerusalem, hence the severity of Jesus's words when speaking of the chastisement awaiting that city. On leaving Capernaum, the road ran by a large building surrounded by water. Here the dangerous possessed were shut up at night. As Jesus went by, they raged and cried: "There he goes! What does he want? Is it that he thinks to drive us out?" When Jesus responded: "Be silent, and remain until I come again. Then it will be your time to retire," they became quiet.

When Jesus left the city, the Pharisees and magistrates held a meeting at which the centurion Zorobabel was present. They deliberated upon all they had seen, upon what they should do, what line of conduct they should pursue with respect to Jesus. They said: "What commotion, what agitation this man creates! Peace is no longer found in the land! The people leave their daily avocations and follow his menacing speeches. He is constantly talking of his Father, but is he not from Nazareth? Is he not the son of a poor carpenter? Whence comes it that he has so great assurance and audacity? Upon what does he rest his titles? He heals on the sabbath, thus disturbing its peace! He forgives sins! Is his power from on high? Has he some secret arts? How has he become so familiar with the scriptures, so ready in explaining them? Was he not reared in the school of Nazareth? Perhaps he is connected in some way with foreigners, with a strange nation! He is always speaking of the approaching establishment of a kingdom, of the nearness of the Messiah, of the destruction of Jerusalem. Joseph, his father, was of illustrious birth; but perhaps he is not Joseph's son, or he may be the supposititious child of some other, of some powerful man who wants to get a foothold in our country, and thus become master in Judea. He must have some great protector, some secret resources upon which to count, else he could never be so bold, so audacious, he would never act with such disregard of legitimate authority and established customs, just as if he had a perfect right to do so. He absents himself for long periods at a time. Where and among whom is he then? Whence has he his knowledge and his skill in working miracles? What must we do about him?" And so they went on discharging their wrath and interchanging conjectures. The centurion Zorobabel alone remained calm; he even had some influence in pacifying the rest. He urged them to patience. "Wait," said he. "If his power is from God, he will certainly triumph; but if not, he will come to naught. So long as he cures our sick and labors to make us better, we have reason to love him and to thank him who sent him."

Sunday, August 6, AD 30 (Ab 18)

Today, Jesus walked to the Sea of Galilee, where he met with Peter and Andrew. He taught at their fishery and then—together with Peter—visited the latter's home.

Early next day Jesus went with about twenty of his disciples toward the lake, not by the direct road, but off to the south around the height upon which Mary's house stood toward the west. That elevation, though separated from it by a valley, was only a projection from the foot of a mountain chain running northward. Jesus chose this route as being better suited to teaching. There were many beautiful brooks running down from the height into the lake, and the little river near Capernaum flowed along in this direction. This part of the country was watered and fertilized by the numerous streams that flowed around Bethsaida. Jesus paused several times with his disciples to rest in those pleasant spots, and often stood still to teach of the tithes. The disciples complained of the great severity with which the tithes were levied at Jerusalem, and asked whether it would not be well to suppress them. Jesus answered that God had commanded the tenth part of all the fruits of the earth to be given to the temple and its servers, in order to remind men that they had not the propriety, but only the usufruct of them; even of vegetables and green things, the tenth part ought to be given by abstaining from their use. Then the disciples spoke of Samaria, expressing their regret for having perhaps hurried his departure thence. They did not know, they said, that the people of Samaria were so anxious to receive his teaching, so disposed to receive him well; had it not been for their importunity, he might have remained longer among them. To this Jesus replied that the two days he had spent in Shechem were sufficient, that the Shechemites were hot-blooded and quickly roused, but of all that had been converted, it was likely that only about twenty would remain steadfast. The coming great harvest he would resign to them, the disciples.

Touched by Jesus's last instructions, the disciples spoke compassionately of the Samaritans, recalling to their praise the history of the man that had fallen among robbers near Jericho. Priest and Levite had passed by, the Samaritan alone had taken him up and poured wine and oil into his wounds. This fact was generally known. It had really happened in the neighborhood of Jericho. From their compassion for the wounded man and their rejoicing over the kind dispositions of the Samaritans, Jesus took occasion to relate to them another parable of the same kind. He began with Adam and Eve, and recounted their Fall in simple words, as given in the Bible. They had, he said, been driven from Paradise, had sought refuge with their children in a desert full of robbers and murderers, and like the poor man of the parable, lay there struck and wounded by sin. Then did the king of heaven and earth make use of all means in his power to procure help for poor humanity. He had given them his Law, had sent them chosen priests and prophets with all that was necessary to cure their ills. But suffering humanity had been helped by none of these aids; it had even at times rejected them with contempt. At last the king sent his own son in the guise of a poor man, to help the fallen race. And then Jesus described his own poverty, no shoes, no covering for the head, no girdle, etc., and yet he pours oil and wine into the poor traveler's wounds in order to heal them. But they who with full power had been sent to cure the wounds of the sufferer, had not had pity on him; they had seized the king's son and put him to death, killed him who had poured oil and wine into the sufferer's wounds. Jesus related this parable to his disciples that, reflecting upon it, they might express their thoughts, and he might clear up any misconceptions they might have concerning it. But they did not understand him. Noticing that he had described the king's son under characteristics that belonged to himself, they began to entertain all kinds of thoughts and to whisper among themselves: "Who can that Father of his be of whom he is always speaking?" Then Jesus touched upon the solicitude they had expressed on the preceding day for the loss experienced by the neglect of their fisheries, and compared it with the disposition of the king's son. He had abandoned all things and, when others in their abundance had left the wounded man to die, he had anointed him with oil and wine. And he went on: "The Father will not abandon the servants of his Son. They shall receive all back with a rich reward when he gathers them around him in his kingdom."

Fishing Boat on the Sea of Galilee

In the midst of these and similar instructions, they reached the lake a little below Bethsaida, where lay the boats of Peter and Zebedee. A part of the shore was entirely fenced in, and up on the bank were little mud cabins for the fishermen's use. Jesus went down to it with his disciples. On the ships were the pagan slaves, but no Jews were engaged in fishing because of the fast day. Zebedee was in one of the huts on the shore. Jesus told those in the ships to discontinue their fishing and come to land. He was at once obeyed, and then he gave them an instruction.

Jesus afterward proceeded up the lake toward Bethsaida, a half-hour distant. Peter's license to fish embraced about an hour's distance along the shore. Between the harbor and Bethsaida was a little bay into which emptied several streams, branches of that which flowed from Capernaum through the valley, and which received in its course other rivulets and creeks. It formed a great pool outside Capernaum. Jesus did not go to Bethsaida. He went to the west and then by the north side of the valley to Peter's house, which stood on the eastern side of that high ground upon whose opposite side was Mary's dwelling.

Jesus entered with Peter. Mary and the other holy women were already there. The other disciples did not go in. They waited nearby in the garden, or went on ahead to Mary's. As Peter entered the house with Jesus, he said: "Master, we have had a fast day, but thou hast fed us." Peter's house was very neatly built with forecourt and garden. It was very long, and on the roof, one could promenade and enjoy a beautiful view toward the lake. I saw neither Peter's step-daughter nor his wife's sons. They may have been at school. His wife was with the holy women. Peter had no children by her. His mother-in-law was a tall, thin woman, so weak and sickly that, in going around the house, she had to lean against the walls for support.

Jesus held a long conference with the women on the subject of the house they had hired up on the borders of the lake, where he intended often to be. He warned them against extravagance and indiscretion, though they were to guard likewise against anxiety and solicitude. As for himself, he said, he needed very little, it was chiefly for the disciples and for the poor they should provide. Leaving Peter's, he crossed with his disciples to his mother's. There he conversed for some time and then went out alone to pray.

The stream of Capernaum flowed along by Peter's house. He could in his little boat, in the middle of which was a seat, sail down to the lake with his fishing tackle. When the holy women heard from Jesus that he was going to Nazareth for the coming sabbath, a distance of nine or ten hours, they did not like the idea. They begged him to remain where he was, or at least to come back soon. Jesus replied that he did not think he would stay long at Nazareth, since the inhabitants would not be very well pleased with him for not complying with their wishes. He mentioned several points upon which they would reproach him, and drew his mother's attention to them, adding that he would let her know if things turned out as he said.

Jesus in Bethsaida

Monday, August 7, AD 30 (Ab 19)

This morning, Jesus taught in the synagogue at Bethsaida. Afterward, he went with Saturnin and another disciple to a home for lepers and simpletons. Jesus consoled and healed many of them, then returned to Andrew's home to dine.

FROM Mary's, Jesus went with the disciples along the north side of the valley to the declivity of the mountain that stretched on to Bethsaida, distant not quite an hour. The holy women also left Peter's house and went to that of Andrew at the northern extremity of Bethsaida. It was in good condition, though not so large as Peter's.

Bethsaida was a little fishing place. Only the central part of the city extended some distance inland; the two extremities stretched around the lake like slender arms. From Peter's fishery one could see it lying off toward the north. The inhabitants were made up for the most part of fishermen, blanket weavers, and tentmakers. They were people, simple and untutored, reminding me of our turfcutters. The blankets were made of goats' and camels' hair. The long hairs from the camel's neck and breast fell over the edges and shone so beautifully that they looked like fringe and lace.

The old centurion Zorobabel had not come to Bethsaida. He was too infirm for so long a walk. He might indeed have gone on horseback, but then he would have missed Jesus's instructions on the way; besides, he was not yet baptized. Bethsaida was full of people from the surrounding towns and villages, along with strangers from the other side of the lake, from the country of Chorazin and Bethsaida-Julias.

Jesus taught in the synagogue, which was not a very large building. He spoke of the nearness of God's kingdom, saying in very plain words that he himself was the monarch of that kingdom, and arousing the usual amount of wonder in his disciples and hearers. As on the preceding days, he taught in general terms and cured many sick who had been brought and laid outside the synagogue. Several possessed cried after him: "Jesus of Nazareth! Prophet, king of the Jews!" He commanded them silence, for the time had not yet come to make him known.

When Jesus had finished teaching and healing, he went with his disciples to Andrew's to get something to eat. But he did not go in—he said that he had another kind of hunger. Taking with him Saturnin and another of the disciples, they went up the shores of the lake about seven minutes' walk from Andrew's. There in a lonely hospital were some poor lepers, simpletons, and other miserable, forlorn creatures languishing, quite forgotten by the rest of the world; some of them were entirely nude. No one from Bethsaida had followed Jesus, for fear of contracting impurity. The cells of these poor creatures were built around a court. They never left them, their food being given them through an aperture in the door. Jesus commanded the superintendent of the hospital to bring out the miserable patients. The disciples covered all in need with the clothing they had brought. Then Jesus instructed and consoled them, going from one to another around the circle, and healing many by the imposition of his sacred hands. He passed some in silence, others he commanded to bathe or fulfill different prescriptions. The cured sank on their knees before him, giving thanks with abundant tears. It was truly touching. These people were utterly neglected. Jesus took the superintendent back to Andrew's to dine with him. As they were leaving the hospital, the relatives of some of the cured presented themselves from Bethsaida bringing them clothes. They took them joyfully first to their homes and next to the synagogue, to give thanks to God.

There was a grand dinner prepared at Andrew's consisting of fine, large fish. They ate in an open hall, the women at a separate table. Andrew himself served. His wife was very active and industrious, rarely leaving the house. She carried on a kind of trade in net weaving, employing a number of poor girls for the work. The greatest system and order reigned throughout her establishment. Among those so employed were some poor, fallen women, once honorable wives, but afterward repudiated for misconduct. They had no place of refuge, and so the good mistress, pitying their distress, gave them work, instructed them in their duty, and prevailed upon them to implore the mercy of God.

That evening Jesus taught in the synagogue, and then recommenced his journeying with the disciples. He passed many sick, but without curing them, for, as he said, their time had not yet come. After taking leave of his mother, he returned with all his disciples to the house near Capernaum that Peter had placed at his service. Jesus conversed there a long time with his disciples, and then left them to go spend the night in prayer on a hill, which tapered to a point and was covered with cypresses.

Capernaum lay in a half-circle up on a mountain. It had numerous vineyards and terraced gardens. On the top of the mountain grew wheat, thick and stout as rushes. It was a large and pleasant place. It had once been still more extensive, or another city had stood in the vicinity, for not far off I saw all kinds of ruins like tokens of a destructive war.

(Follow Map 19)

Jesus in and around Little Sepphoris • His Different Ways of Curing the Sick

Tuesday, August 8, AD 30 (Ab 20)

Accompanied by Tharzissus and Aristobolus, Jesus made his way to Little Sepphoris.

JESUS went from Capernaum to Nazareth, the Galilean disciples accompanying him for about five hours. He instructed them on the way concerning their future vocation. He counseled Peter to leave the borders of the lake, take up his abode in his house near Capernaum, and give up his business. They passed several cities, also the little lake with the country seats around it. In a shepherd field two possessed men came running to Jesus and implored to be cured. They were the owners of the herds browsing around, and were only now and then tormented by the devil. Just at that time they were free from his influence. Jesus would not cure them, but commanded them first to amend their ways. He made use of an example: If a man was sick from overloading his stomach, and wanted to get well in order to indulge in new excesses, what would they think of him? The men turned away quite ashamed. The disciples left Jesus a couple of hours from Sepphoris and returned to Peter's, Saturnin among them. There were only two with him now. They were from Jerusalem, and were on their way home. Jesus went to Little Sepphoris, or Lesser Sepphoris, and put up with the relatives of St. Anne. It was not, however, at Anne's paternal home, for that was between this Sepphoris and Greater Sepphoris, the latter distant about an hour. There were many houses lying around in a circle of five hours, all belonging to the city of Sepphoris. Jesus did not go at this time to Greater Sepphoris, where were schools of the various sects and tribunals of justice.

There were not many rich people in Little Sepphoris. They manufactured cloth and the rich women made silk tassels and laces for the service of the temple. The whole region was like an enchanting garden, consisting of many little hamlets with country seats, gardens, and walks scattered among them. Greater Sepphoris was a far more important place; it was very large and possessed many castles. The country around was lovely and abounded in springs. The cattle were of extraordinary size.

Jesus's relatives had three sons, one of whom, by name Kolaya, was his disciple. The mother wanted Jesus to admit the others also into the number of his disciples, and brought forward the sons of Mary Cleophas as an argument in her own favor. Jesus gave her room to hope. After the death of Christ, these sons were ordained to the priesthood at Eleutheropolis by Joseph Barsabbas, the bishop of that place.

Wednesday, August 9, AD 30 (Ab 21)

This evening, Jesus spoke at the synagogue in Little Sepphoris concerning marriage and divorce.

Jesus taught in the synagogue before a great concourse assembled from the country around. He went also with his cousins out of the city, and gave instructions here and there to little crowds of people that followed him or were waiting for him. On his return he cured many sick persons outside the synagogue; then entering, he taught of marriage and divorce. He reproached the doctors with having made additions to the Law. He pointed to a certain place in a roll of parchment, accused one of the oldest among them of having inserted it, convicted him of fraud, and commanded him to erase the passage. The old man humbled himself before Jesus, even prostrating at his feet in presence of all the others, acknowledged his fault, and thanked for the lesson just received.

Thursday, August 10, AD 30 (Ab 22)

Jesus went to a house between Little and Greater Sepphoris where he cured an old woman of edema and healed a boy—about eight years old—who had been blind from birth. Saturnin was with him now, and when they proceeded to the valley of Zebulon they were joined by Jesus's childhood companion, Parmenas.

Jesus spent the night in prayer. From the house of his relatives in Little Sepphoris he went to that which had in former times belonged to Anne's father. It was situated between Little Sepphoris and Greater Sepphoris. There was now only one disciple with him. The present occupants of the house were, in consequence of frequent marriages, no longer related to Jesus. There was only one old woman who could still claim relationship. She was dropsical and bedridden. Her usual companion was a little blind boy, who sat by her bedside. Jesus prayed with the old woman, making her repeat after him. He laid his hand for an instant on her head, then on the region of the stomach. She began to grow faint, remained unconscious for about a minute, and then found herself quite relieved. Jesus ordered her to rise. The edema had not entirely disappeared, but the woman could walk, and soon after, without difficulty, through copious perspiration and the healthful action of nature, she was entirely freed from her trouble. She interceded with Jesus for the blind boy. He was about eight years old, and had never seen nor spoken, although he could hear. The old woman praised his piety and obedience. Jesus put his forefinger into the child's mouth, then breathing upon his thumbs or moistening them with saliva, he held them upon the closed eyes of the boy while he prayed, his eyes raised to heaven. Suddenly the child opened his eyes, and the first object he beheld was Jesus his Redeemer! Out of himself with joy and amazement, he threw himself into Jesus's arms, stammering his thanks, and then fell weeping at his feet. Jesus admonished him affectionately to be obedient and to love his parents. He told him that if, when blind, he had exercised those virtues, he should more faithfully practice them now that he could see, and never use his eyes to sin. Then in came the parents and the whole family, and there was intense joy and thanksgiving.

Jesus did not always operate his cures in the same manner, though performing them in much the same way as the apostles, the saints, and the priests after them down to our own day. He laid hands upon and prayed with the sick, but his action was quicker than that of the apostles. He performed his cures and other miracles as models for his followers and disciples. He always made the manner of their performance conform to the evil and the special needs of those that had recourse to him. He touched the lame, their muscles were loosened, and they stood upright. The broken parts of fractured members he placed together, and they united. He touched the leprous, and immediately at the touch of his divine hand, I saw the blisters drying and peeling off, leaving behind the red scars. These, little by little, though more quickly than was usual in ordinary cures, disappeared. The greater or less merit of the invalid often determined the rapidity of his cure. I never saw a humpback instantly become straight, nor a crooked bone suddenly become a perfectly formed one. Not that Jesus could not have produced such effects, but his miracles were not intended as spectacles for a gazing multitude. They were works of mercy, they were symbolical images of his mission, a releasing, a reconciliation, an instruction, a development, a redeeming. As he desired man's cooperation in the work of his own redemption, so too did he demand from those that asked of him a miraculous cure their own cooperation by faith, hope, love, contrition, and reformation of life. Every state had its own manner of treatment. As every malady of the body symbolized some malady of the spiritual order, some sin or the chastisement due to it, so did every cure symbolize some grace, some conversion, or the cure of some particular spiritual evil. It was only in presence of pagans that I saw Jesus sometimes operating more astonishing, more prodigious miracles. The miracles of the apostles and of saints that came after them were far more striking than those of our Lord and far more contrary to the usual course of nature, for the pagans needed to be strongly affected, while the Jews needed only to be freed from their bonds. Jesus often cured by prayer at a distance, and often by a glance, especially in the case of women afflicted with an issue of blood. They did not venture to approach him, nor dared they do so according to the Jewish laws. Such laws as carried with them some mysterious signification he followed, others he ignored. Jesus went afterward to a school situated at an equal distance from Nazareth and from Little Sepphoris. Parmenas, the disciple from Nazareth, went thither to meet him. He had been one of the companions of Jesus's boyhood, and he would have joined the disciples at once, were it not for his aged parents at Nazareth. He supported them by executing commissions.

Friday, August 11, AD 30 (Ab 23)

This morning, Pharisees from Greater and Little Sepphoris drew Jesus into a great dispute concerning the strict teaching on marriage and divorce that he had recently expounded in Little Sepphoris (Matthew 19:3–9). That afternoon, Jesus went to Nazareth and taught in the synagogue at the start of the sabbath. He spoke of the passage in Isaiah 61:1–2 and of its fulfillment, as narrated in Luke 4:16–22.

Map 19: The Healings at Capernaum

August 8–26, AD 30

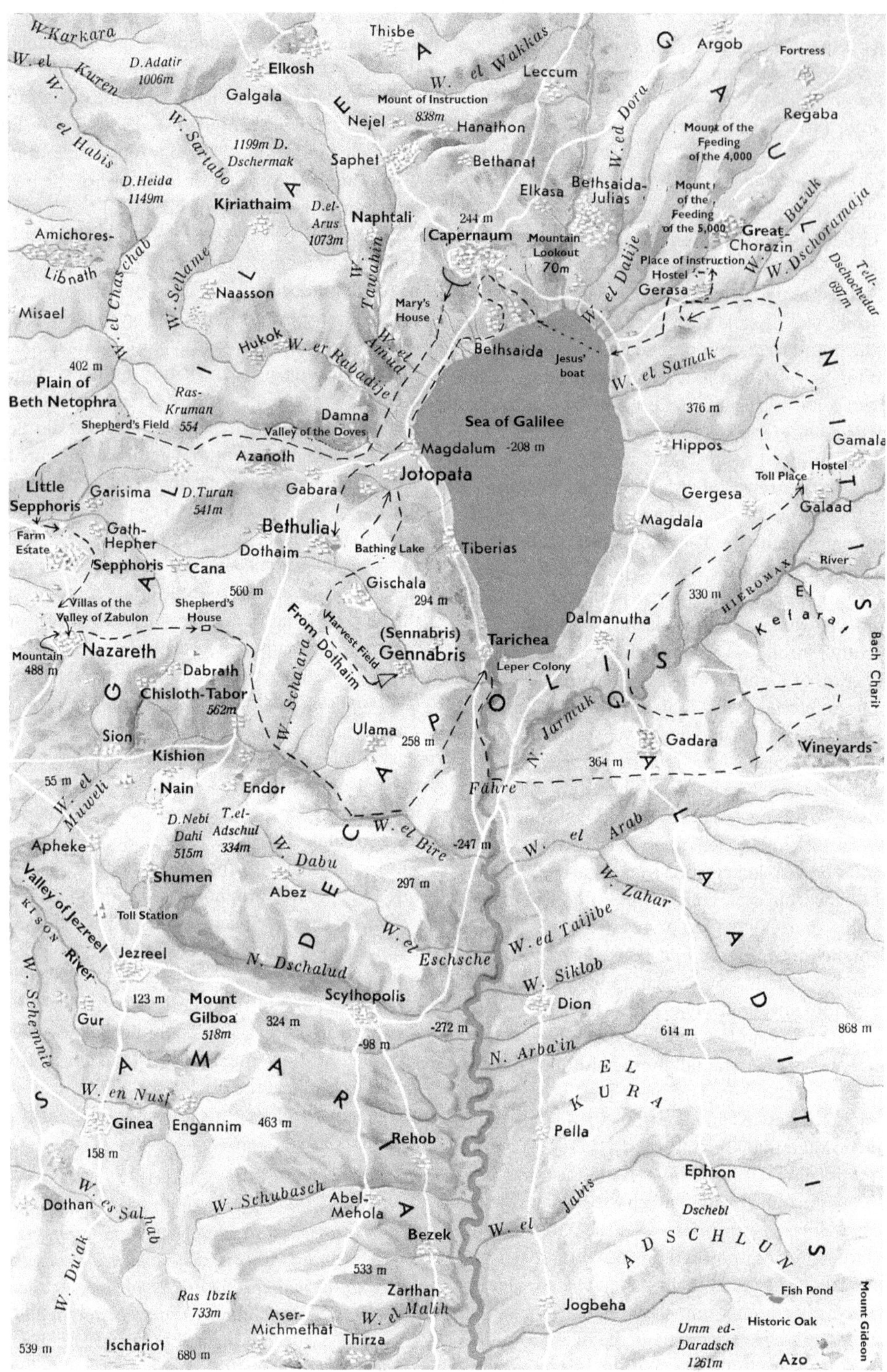

Capernaum—Little Sepphoris—Zebulon Valley—Nazareth—Tarichea—Publican's Place near Gilead
Gerasa—Bethsaida—Capernaum—Bethulia—Jotopata—Gennabris

There were many doctors and Pharisees in the school of Little Sepphoris and Greater Sepphoris, also some people who had assembled to argue with Jesus on that passage relating to divorce which he had declared unlawful, and for the insertion of which passage he had reprehended the doctor in the synagogue. That reprehension of Jesus had been very badly received in Greater Sepphoris, for the addition made to the Law on that point was in keeping with the teaching of the Pharisees. In this city divorces were obtained on most insignificant pretexts, and there was even an asylum for the reception of repudiated wives. The doctor who had been guilty of the interpolation had transcribed a roll of the Law and inserted little false interpretations here and there. They disputed a long time with Jesus, affirming that they could not understand how he could presume to expunge that passage. He reduced them to silence, though not to the acknowledgment of their error, as he had done the first. He showed them the prohibition against any interpolation, and consequently the obligation of expunging such a passage. He demonstrated to them the falsity of their explanations, and sharply rebuked them for the facility with which the marriage bond was dissolved in their city. He enumerated some cases in which it would be quite unlawful for the husband to put away his wife, but said that if one party could not live in peace with the other, they might with permission separate. The stronger party, however, ought not without cause drive away the weaker one against the will of the latter.

But Jesus's words did not effect much among his opponents. They were vexed and proud, but they could not gainsay his arguments. The doctor of the Law who had been reprimanded and converted by Jesus in Little Sepphoris separated entirely from the Pharisees and made known to the people that he would for the future teach the Law without addition. If they were unwilling to retain him on those conditions, he would withdraw. The interpolated passage in the Law of divorce ran as follows: "If before marriage one of the parties has had illicit communication with a third person, the marriage is invalid. The third person has the right to claim the one with whom he or she has sinned, even though the parties of the present marriage desire to remain united." Jesus inveighed against this, and declared the law of divorce to have been given to a barbarous people only. Two of the most distinguished Pharisees engaged in the dispute were precisely in that predicament. They were preparing to avail themselves of that interpolation with regard to divorce, and therefore had they been zealous in proclaiming that part of their so-called law. This fact was not publicly known, but Jesus knew it and therefore he said to them: "In defending this distortion of the Law, are you not perhaps defending your own case also?" at which words they fell into a fury.

Jesus in Nazareth • The Pharisees Want to Cast Him down a Mountain

JESUS went from this place to Nazareth, the distance being about two hours. He taught outside the city in the dwelling belonging to the children of his deceased friend, Eliud the Essene. They washed his feet, gave him some refreshment, and remarked how rejoiced the Nazarenes would be at his coming. Jesus replied that their joy would be of short duration, since they would not care to hear what he must say to them, and then he went into the city. Someone had been appointed to wait for him at the gate. Scarcely had he made his appearance when several Pharisees and a crowd of people came forward to meet him. They received him very ceremoniously and wanted to conduct him to a public inn where they had prepared for him a feast of welcome before the sabbath. But Jesus refused to partake of it, saying that he had just now other work on hand. He went immediately to the synagogue, whither he was followed by the Pharisees and a concourse of people. The hour of the sabbath had not yet sounded.

Jesus taught of the coming of the kingdom and the fulfillment of the prophecies. Asking for the Book of Isaiah, he unrolled it and read as follows: "The Spirit of the Lord is upon me, because the Lord hath anointed me: he hath sent me to preach to the meek, to heal the contrite of heart, and to preach a release to the captives, and deliverance to them that are shut up." The manner in which Jesus read this text gave his hearers to understand that it was spoken of himself, that the Spirit of God had descended upon himself, that he himself had come to announce salvation to poor, suffering humanity, that all wrong should be made right, widows should be consoled, the sick cured, sinners forgiven. His words were so beautiful, so loving that, wondering and full of joy, they said one to another: "He speaks as if he himself were the Messiah!" They were so carried away with admiration for him that they became quite vain of the fact that he belonged to their own city. Jesus went on teaching after the sabbath began. He spoke of the voice of the precursor in the desert, and said that all things should be made even, the crooked ways straight, etc.

The instructions over, Jesus accepted a meal that had been prepared for him. The people behaved toward him in a very friendly manner, and told him that they had many sick whom he must cure. Jesus excused himself. But they thought that he meant: "Not today. Wait till tomorrow." After the meal, he returned to the Essenes outside the city.

As they were congratulating him upon the kind reception he had received, he told them to wait till the following day when they would have another story to tell.

Saturday, August 12, AD 30 (Ab 24)

Jesus taught again in the synagogue at Nazareth and sharply reproached the Pharisees for their misinterpretation of the Law. At midday, he dined with an Essene family. He then returned to teach at the synagogue again (Luke 4:23–28). At the close of the sabbath, when Jesus came out of the synagogue, he was immediately surrounded by about twenty Pharisees. They began to lead him out of the town toward a nearby hill, for they intended to cast him down from the brow of the hill. Suddenly, however, Jesus stopped, stood still, and with the help of angelic beings passed—as if invisible—through the midst of the crowd to his escape (Luke 4:29–30).

When Jesus went next morning to the synagogue, a Jew whose turn it was to read was about to take the roll of scriptures. But Jesus desired them to hand it to him.[C7] He taught from Deuteronomy, chapter 4, of the obedience due to the commandments, from which nothing must be taken and to which nothing must be added. He reminded them that, although Moses had zealously repeated to the children of Israel all that God commanded, yet they had frequently violated his ordinances. The Ten Commandments presented themselves in the course of the reading, and Jesus explained the first, that on the love of God. He spoke very severely, reproaching them with the additions they made to the Law, laying burdens upon the poor people, and not fulfilling the Law itself. He assailed them so sharply on this point that they became angry, for they could not say that he was uttering falsehood. But they murmured and said one to another: "How does he dare all at once to speak so boldly! He has been away from his native city only a short time, and now he wants to pass himself off for some extraordinary personage. He speaks as if he were the Messiah. But we know his father, the poor carpenter, well, and we know him too. Where did he learn the scriptures? How can he dare presume to interpret for us?" And so they went on, growing more and more excited against him, for they were mortified to have been thus convicted before all the people.

But Jesus quietly continued his teaching, and went when it suited him out to the Essene family. Here he was visited by the sons of the rich man, the youths who some time previously had so earnestly asked to be received among the disciples, and whose parents were aiming only at worldly renown and science for them. They pressed Jesus to dine with them, but he declined. Then they renewed their entreaties to be received among his followers, saying that they had fulfilled all that he had on a former occasion commanded them. Jesus replied: "If ye have done that, there is no need of becoming my pupils. You are yourselves masters," and with these words he dismissed them.

Jesus ate and taught in the family circle of the Essenes, who told him in how many ways they were annoyed by their neighbors. He counseled them to remove to Capernaum, where he himself would dwell in the future.

Meantime the Pharisees had consulted together, had incited one another against Jesus, and had come to the determination that, if he spoke so boldly again that evening, they would show him that he had no right to do so in Nazareth, and would perpetrate upon him what had so long been desired in Jerusalem. Still they were not without hope that he would yield to their wishes and, through respect for them, work some miracle in their presence. When he returned to the synagogue for the close of the sabbath, he found lying in front of it some sick who had been brought there by order of the Pharisees. But he passed through them without curing any. He went on with his discourse in the synagogue, speaking of the plenitude of time, of his own mission, of the last chance of grace, of the depravity of the Pharisees and the punishment in store for them if they did not reform, and impressed upon them the fact of his own coming to help, to heal, and to teach. They became more and more displeased, especially when he said: "But ye say to me, 'Physician, cure Thyself! In Capernaum and elsewhere, thou hast wrought miracles. Do the same here in thy native city!' But I say to you no prophet is accepted in his own country." Then comparing the present to a time of famine and the different cities to poor widows, he said: "There was great famine throughout the land in the time of Elijah, and there were many widows in those days, but the prophet was sent to none but the widow of Sarepta. And there were many lepers in the days of Elisha, but he cleansed none but Naaman the Syrian," and so Jesus compared their city to a leper who was not healed. They became terribly furious at being likened unto lepers, and, rising up from their seats, they stormed against him and made as if they would seize him. But he said: "Observe your own laws and break not the sabbath! When it is over do what you propose to do." They allowed him to proceed with his discourse, though they kept up the murmuring among themselves and addressed scornful words to him. Soon after they left their places and went down to the door.

Jesus, however, continued to teach and explain his last words, after which he, too, left the synagogue. Outside the door, he found himself surrounded by about twenty angry

Pharisees who laid hands on him, saying: "Come on up with us to a height from which thou canst advance some more of thy doctrines! There we can answer thee as thy teaching ought to be answered." Jesus told them to take their hands off, that he would go with them. They surrounded him like a guard, the crowd following. The moment the sabbath ended, jeers and insults arose on all sides. They raged and hooted, each trying to outdo his neighbor in the number and quality of his scoffing attacks upon Jesus. "We will answer thee!" they cried. "Thou shalt go to the widow of Sarepta! Thou shalt cleanse Naaman the Syrian! Art thou Elijah? And art thou going to drive up to heaven? Well, we'll show thee a good starting place! Who art thou? Why didst thou not bring thy followers with thee? Ah, thou wast afraid. Was it not here that thou, like thy poor parents, gained thy daily bread? And now that thou hast whereon to live, wilt thou turn us to scorn! But we will listen to thee! Thou shalt speak in the open air before all the people, and we will answer thee!" and thus shouting and raging they led Jesus up the mountain. He, meanwhile, quietly went on teaching as usual, answering their vain talk with passages from holy scripture and significant words that sometimes put them to shame, and at others threw them into greater rage.

The synagogue was in the western part of Nazareth. It was already dark and two of the crowd bore torches. They led Jesus around by the eastern side of the synagogue, then turned into a broad street that ran westward out of the city. Ascending the mountain, they reached a lofty spur which on the northern side overlooked a marshy pool, and on the south formed a rocky projection over a steep precipice. It was from this point they were in the habit of precipitating malefactors. Here they intended once more to call Jesus to account, and then to hurl him down.[c8] The abyss ended in a narrow ravine. They were not far from the scene of action when Jesus, who had been led as a prisoner among them, stood still, while they continued their way mocking and jeering. At that instant I saw two tall figures of light near Jesus, who took a few steps back through the hotly pursuing crowd, reached the city wall on the mountain ridge of Nazareth, and followed it till he came to the gate by which he had entered the evening before. He went straight to the house of the Essene. The good people had not been anxious about his safety. They believed in him and were expecting his return. He spoke to them of the late occurrence, reminded them that he had foretold it, again bade them go to Capernaum and, after about half an hour, left the city in the direction of Capernaum.

Nothing was more laughable than the perplexity, the alarm, the silly plight of the Pharisees when, all of a sudden, they found Jesus no more among them. The cry was raised: "Halt! Where is he? Halt!" The crowd came rushing on, the Pharisees pressed back upon them, the narrow path became a scene of confusion and uproar. They laid hold of one another, they squabbled and shouted, they ran to all the ravines, and poked their torches into the caves, thinking that he had hidden therein. They endangered neck and limb in their fruitless search, and one upbraided the other for having allowed him to slip away. Quiet was not restored until long after Jesus had left the city, and then they set guards upon and around the whole mountain. Returning to the city, the Pharisees said: "Now we have seen what he is—a magician. The devil has helped him. He will soon spring up again in some other place, and throw all around him into confusion."

Sunday, August 13, AD 30 (Ab 25)

This morning Jesus met up with four disciples—Saturnin, Parmenas, and the Greek brothers Tharzissus and Aristobolus—on their way from Nazareth to Tarichea. They walked together, arriving around four o'clock that afternoon. Here in Tarichea Jesus healed five lepers. He and the four disciples then proceeded on to the Jordan, which they crossed that night.

Jesus had ordered his disciples to leave Nazareth at the close of the exercises in the synagogue, and await him at a certain place on the road to Tarichea. Saturnin and other disciples from Capernaum had received the same directions. All met Jesus at dawn and with him took a little rest in a retired valley. Saturnin had brought some bread and honey. Jesus told them of what had taken place at Nazareth, and bade them be calm and obedient, in order not to interfere with his work by stirring up too great excitement among the populace of different cities. Then they took a retired route through the valleys and past cities toward the effluence of the Jordan from the Sea of Galilee. A large, fortified city lay at the southern extremity on a tongue of land not far from the outlet of the Jordan. A large bridge and a dam led to it. Between the city and the lake was a gently sloping plain covered with verdure. The city was called Tarichea.

Cure of Lepers at Tarichea • Jesus Instructs His Disciples in Similitudes

JESUS did not go into the city. Taking a bypath, he drew near the southern wall not far from the gate. On the exterior side of this wall was a row of huts built purposely for the leprous. As Jesus approached them, he said to the disciples: "Stand at some distance and call out the lepers. Tell them to follow me, and I will cleanse them! When they come out, do ye stand at a distance that ye may not be alarmed nor contract stain. Moreover do not speak of what ye shall see, for ye remember the fury of the Nazarenes. Ye must not scandalize anyone." Then Jesus went on a little toward the Jordan while the disciples called to the sick: "Come out and follow the prophet of Nazareth! He will help you!" When the disciples saw the poor sufferers coming out of their huts, they hurried away. Jesus, turning out of the road that led to the city, walked slowly toward the region of the Jordan. Five men of different ages answered the disciples' invitation and issued from the cells in the city wall. They were clothed in white garments long and wide, but wore no girdle. On their head was a cowl from which fell over the face a black flap with holes in it for the eyes. They followed Jesus in single file to a retired spot, where he paused. There the first threw himself at his feet and kissed the hem of his robe. Jesus turned, laid his hand upon the leper's head, prayed over him, blessed him, and bade him step aside. He did in like manner to the second, and so on even to the fifth and last. They now removed their masks, uncovered their hands, and the crust of the leprosy peeled entirely off. Jesus warned them against the sins by which they had brought upon themselves that sickness, told them how they should henceforth conduct themselves, and commanded them not to say anything about his having cured them. But they replied: "Lord, thou didst come so suddenly to us! So long have we hoped for thee, so long sighed for thee, and we had no one to tell thee of our misery, no one to bring thee to us! Lord, thou didst come to us so unexpectedly! How can we restrain our joy? How can we be silent about thy miracle!" Jesus repeated that they must not speak of it until they had fulfilled the Law. They should show themselves to the priests that they might see they were clean, offer the prescribed sacrifices, and perform the prescribed purifications; then they might proclaim their cure. At these words the five men again fell on their knees giving thanks, and then went back to their cells. Jesus continued his way to the Jordan and there rejoined the disciples. These five lepers were not closely confined. There was a certain space marked out for them around which they could go. No one went near them, and it was only from a distance that anyone spoke to them. Their food was deposited in a certain place on platters, which were not used a second time. The lepers broke and buried them. A new dish of little value was given them with every fresh supply of food.

Jesus walked with the disciples some distance toward the Jordan through delightful groves and avenues, and in a retired spot rested and took some refreshment. After that they crossed the river in a little boat. Boats of this kind lay at intervals along the shore for the accommodation of travelers, who could by that means ferry themselves over. The workmen, living at different distances along the shore, saw that the boats were taken back to where they belonged. Jesus, with the four disciples, did not journey close to the lake, but up toward the east, to the city of Gilead. The four disciples with him were Parmenas of Nazareth, Saturnin, and two brothers: one called Tharzissus, the other Aristobolus. Tharzissus afterward became the bishop of Athens. Aristobolus later on was associated to Barnabas. I heard that with the word "brother"; but he was his spiritual brother only. He was a great deal with Paul and Barnabas, and I think he became a bishop of Britany. Lazarus had brought the two brothers to Jesus. They were foreigners, I think Greeks, whose father had settled lately in Jerusalem. They were shipping merchants. Some of their slaves, or servants, when journeying with a caravan, had gone with their beasts of burden to hear John's teaching and had been baptized by him. It was by means of these servants that the young men's parents heard of John and Jesus. Taking their sons, they went themselves to John, and both father and sons were baptized and circumcised, after which the whole family removed to Jerusalem. They were not without means, but later on they relinquished all their wealth in favor of the rising community of Christians. Both the young men were tall, dark-complexioned, and clever; both had received a refined education. They were fine-looking young men, active and skillful at arranging things and making all comfortable on journeys.

Monday, August 14, AD 30 (Ab 26)

Jesus and the four disciples made their way to Gilead, where they stayed at an inn on the outskirts of town.

A little river watered the country up which Jesus was now journeying, and at a certain place he crossed it. The prophet Elijah had once been in these parts. Jesus recalled the fact and, during the whole journey, instructed the disciples in simple similitudes borrowed from various conditions of life, from the several professions, from the groves and stones and plants and places that presented themselves on the road. The disciples questioned him upon all that had happened to him in Sepphoris and Nazareth. He spoke to them of marriage in connection with the dispute he had had with the Pharisees, at Sepphoris, upon the question of divorce. The conjugal bond is indissoluble. Divorce was granted by Moses in favor of a barbarous, sinful people only.

The disciples questioned Jesus also upon the reproach made him by the Nazarenes, that he had no love for his neighbor, and in his own city, which ought to be the nearest and dearest to him, he would work no cures. They asked if one's fellow townsmen should not be looked upon as neighbors. Then Jesus gave them a long instruction upon the love of the neighbor, proposing to them all kinds of similitudes and questions, the former of which he drew from different states of life in the world. He dwelt long upon them and pointed out place after place that rose up in the distance, and said in which such or such an industry was especially pursued. He spoke, too, of those that were to follow him. They were, he said, to leave father and mother, and yet obey the Fourth Commandment. They must treat their native city as he had done Nazareth, if so it deserved of them, and still exercise the love of the neighbor. God, their heavenly Father, and he who had been sent by him, had the first claim to their love. Then he spoke of the love of the neighbor such as the world understands it, and of the publicans of Gilead (which city they were then passing), who loved those most that paid them the highest tax. He pointed afterward to Dalmanutha, which lay to the left, and said: "Those tentmakers and carpet-weavers love as their neighbor those that buy many tents from them, but their own poor they leave without shelter."

He then borrowed a comparison from the sandalmakers, which had reference to the vain curiosity of the people of Nazareth. "I have no need," he said, "of their homage, which they clothe in beautiful colors like the variegated sandals in the workshop of the sandalmaker, but which will afterward be trodden underfoot in the mud." And again, pointing to a certain city, he said: "They are like the sandalmaker of that city. They slight and disparage their own children, and so the latter are forced to go abroad. But when among strangers they have learned a new style of making beautiful, green sandals, their fellow citizens recall them through desire to see their work. They boast of the new-fashioned articles which, like the glory attached to them, are soon to be trodden underfoot." Then Jesus put the question: "Suppose a traveler tears one of his sandals and goes to a sandalmaker's to buy one. Will the latter present him with the other one, also?" In this way Jesus drew comparisons from fishermen, architects, and other avocations.

The disciples asked him where he intended to fix his abode, whether he would build a house in Capernaum. He answered that he would not build upon sand, and he mentioned another city that he had to found. I could not so well understand the conversation between Jesus and the disciples when they were walking; when they were seated I could hear better. I remember this much, however, that Jesus expressed his desire for a little boat, that he might go here and there upon the lake. He wanted to teach on water as well as on land.

They now went into the country of Gileaditis. Abraham and Lot had sojourned here, and even at that early period had divided the country between them. Jesus referred to that circumstance. He told the disciples also that in order to avoid scandalizing anyone, they should not speak of the lepers who had lately been cleansed. He warned them to be particularly circumspect now to cause no excitement, for the Nazarenes would certainly stir up alarm and hatred. He told them that on the sabbath he would again teach in Capernaum. They should then have a chance to see the love of the neighbor and the gratitude of men exemplified, for the welcome extended to him this time would be very different from that received on the occasion of the cure of the centurion's son.

They may have been journeying for some hours to the northeast around a curve of the lake, when they arrived near Gilead to the south of Gamala. As in most of the cities in this district, the population was made up of pagans and Jews. The disciples were disposed to enter the city. But Jesus told them that, if he went to the Jews of the place, they would neither welcome him nor give him anything; and if to the pagans, the Jews would be scandalized and would pursue him with calumny. He predicted the entire destruction of the city, saying that iniquity abounded in it.

The disciples spoke of a certain Agabus, a prophet living at that time in Argob, a city of that region. For a long time, he had had numerous visions of Jesus and his doings, and had lately uttered some prophecies regarding him. Later on Agabus joined the disciples. Jesus informed them that Agabus was the son of Herodian parents, who had reared him in the errors of their sect, but he had afterward rejected them. He called the sects beautifully covered sepulchers full of corruption.

The Herodians were numerous on the west side of the Jordan in Perea, Trachonitis, and especially in Ituraea. They lived very privately and had some kind of mysterious organization by which they secretly helped one another. Many poor people applied to them, and received immediate relief. These Herodians were outwardly great sticklers for the prescriptions of the Pharisees; in secret they aimed at freeing Judea from the Roman yoke, and consequently were closely attached to Herod. They were something like the modern freemasons. I understood from Jesus's words that they feigned to be very holy and magnanimous, but in reality they were hypocrites.

Jesus and the disciples remained at some distance from Gilead at an inn resorted to by publicans. Quite a number of them were gathered there at the time, to whom the pagans paid taxes on their imported goods. They did not appear to know Jesus, and he did not address them. He taught, however, of the nearness of the kingdom, and of the father who had sent his son into the vineyard. He gave them very clearly to understand that he himself was the

Son, adding that all who do his will are children of the Father. But these last words perplexed them. Jesus exhorted them to baptism. Many were converted, and asked whether or not they should be baptized by John's disciples. He answered that they should wait patiently until his own disciples baptized in those parts. The disciples also asked their Master today whether his baptism was different from that of John, because they had received the latter. Jesus, in his answer, made a distinction between the two, calling John's a baptism of penance.

In Jesus's instruction to the publicans, something entered relating to the Trinity, something about the Father, the Son, and the Holy Spirit in their Unity, though expressed in other terms. The disciples were not at all reserved before the publicans of this place.

As Jesus when in Nazareth had stopped with the Essenes, a circumstance that drew upon him the reproaches of the Pharisees, the disciples put questions to him concerning that sect. I heard Jesus answering in sentences expressive of praise, though interrogative in form. Mentioning various ways by which justice and fraternal love might be wounded, he asked after each: "Do the Essenes do this? Do the Essenes do that?" etc.

Near Gilead some possessed, who were running around in a desolate region outside the city, began to cry after Jesus. They were perfectly abandoned. They robbed and killed anyone that ventured within their reach, and committed diverse kinds of excesses. Jesus looked back after them and gave them his blessing. They instantly ceased to rave, were freed from the evil spirit and, hurrying to him, fell at his feet. He exhorted them to penance and baptism, though bidding them wait for the latter until his disciples should go to Ainon to baptize. The country about Gilead was rocky, of a white, brittle formation.

Tuesday, August 15, AD 30 (Ab 27)

Today they went northward to the town of Gerasa, where they arrived that evening. Here he received a message sent by the holy Virgin on behalf of a widow of Nain who was possessed. This widow was an acquaintance of Maroni, the widow of Nain whom Jesus had visited there on Ab 14. Receiving the message, Jesus healed the possessed woman from a distance.

Jesus and the disciples went from here across the mountain, to the south of which lay Gamala, and took a northwesterly direction to the lake. He passed Gerasa which, at about one hour's distance, lay between two ridges of the mountain. Nearby was a kind of swamp formed from a brook whose waters were dammed up, and whose only outlet into the lake was through a ravine. Jesus related to the disciples some incidents connected with this place: The people of Gerasa had once upon a time ridiculed a prophet, on account of his misshapen form, whereupon he had said to them: "Listen, O ye that insult my misfortune! Your children shall remain obdurate when one greater than I shall teach and heal in this place. Troubled at the loss of their unclean herds, they will not rejoice at the salvation that is offered them." This was a prophecy regarding Jesus Christ and the driving of Satan into the swine.

Jesus told the disciples what awaited him in Capernaum: that the Pharisees of Sepphoris, exasperated by his teaching upon divorce, had sent their emissaries to Jerusalem; that the Nazarenes had joined their complaints to theirs; and that a whole troop of Pharisees from Jerusalem, Nazareth, and Sepphoris was now dispatched to Capernaum, to be on the watch for him and to dispute against him.

Just at this moment they encountered several immense caravans of pagans with mules and oxen. The latter had great, thick jaws, broad, heavy horns, and went along with lowered head. It was a trading caravan going from Syria into Egypt. They had come over into the country of Gerasa partly in ships and partly over the bridge of the Jordan higher up. There were many among them who had joined the caravan for the purpose of hearing the prophet. A company waited upon Jesus to know whether the prophet would teach in Capernaum. But he told them that they should not now go to Capernaum, but encamp on the declivity of the mountain to the north of Gerasa, whither the prophet would soon go. There was something in Jesus's tone and manner that made them respond: "Master, thou too art a prophet!" and his glance roused in them the doubt as to whether he might not himself be the one for whom they were in search.

When Jesus entered the inn outside Gerasa with his disciples there to lodge, the crowd of pagans and travelers was so great that he left at once, but the disciples stayed with the pagans, talking to them of the prophet and instructing them.

Gerasa lay on the declivity of a valley about an hour and a half from the lake. It was larger and cleaner than Capernaum and, like almost all the cities of these parts, it had a mixed population of pagans and Jews. The former had their own temples. The latter formed the poor and oppressed portion of the inhabitants, although they had their synagogue and rabbi. There was much business carried on and the trades were numerous, for the caravans from Syria and Asia passed through Gerasa going down into Egypt. I saw before the city gate a long building, seven and a half minutes in length, wherein were manufactured long iron bars and pipes. They forged the bars flat, and then soldered them together into a circular form. Leaden pipes also were made. The furnaces at which they worked were not fed with wood, but with some kind of a black mass dug out of the earth. The iron they used came from Argob.

The pagans of the caravan had encamped to the north of Gerasa and on the southern side of the rising mountain.

To the same place some pagans belonging to the city had come, also some Jews; but these latter stood apart by themselves. The pagans were differently clad from the Jews, their tunics reaching only halfway down the lower limbs. Some of them must have been rich, for I saw women who had their hair so braided with pearls as to form a perfect cap. Some wore it on the top of the head above their veil, braided with pearls into a little basket.

Wednesday, August 16, AD 30 (Ab 28)

After teaching some unbelievers on a mountainside near Gerasa, Jesus journeyed to a place on the northeast side of the Sea of Galilee, where a boat sent by Peter and Andrew was waiting to collect him. He traveled across the lake and landed near Bethsaida. Peter, Andrew, John, James the Greater, James the Less, and Philip met him there. They all went with him to Peter's house, where the holy Virgin and some of the holy women were waiting. All expressed their concern about the vehemence of the Pharisees directed toward Jesus, and said it would be better for him not to teach in Capernaum, where fifteen Pharisees had been sent to investigate the new prophet. Jesus, however, dismissed their worries with a few words.

Jesus ascended the mountainside, where walking about he taught the crowds. He went among them, here and there, and at times he stood still, keeping up a kind of conversation with the travelers. He addressed them with questions, which he answered himself in words full of instruction. He asked, for instance: "Whence are ye? What impelled you to take this journey? What do ye expect from the prophet?" and then he taught them what they must become, in order to share in salvation. He said: "Blessed are they that have journeyed so long and so toilsome a way, to seek salvation! But woe to them among whom it arises and who will not receive it!" He explained the prophecy of the Messiah and the call of the Gentiles, told of that of the three kings (of whom these people knew) and also of their expedition in obedience to it.

In the caravan were some people from that country and city where the envoy of Abgar of Edessa had stayed overnight near the brick kilns, on his return journey with Jesus's picture and letter. Jesus did not cure any sick here. The strangers were for the most part well-disposed, but there were some among them who regretted having undertaken such a journey. They had expected to hear something very different from the prophet's words, something more flattering to the senses.

After these instructions, into which Jesus introduced many similitudes, he went with his four disciples to dine with a Jewish doctor of the Law, a Pharisee, who dwelt outside the city. He had invited Jesus to be his guest, though his pride prevented his appearing at the instruction given the Gentiles. There were present at table some other Pharisees from the city. They received Jesus in a friendly manner which, however, was only feigned, for they were hypocrites. A circumstance occurred during the course of the meal that gave Jesus a suitable opportunity for telling them the truth. A pagan slave, or servant, laid upon the table a beautiful dish of many colors filled with confectionery, made of spices kneaded together in the shape of birds and flowers. One of the guests raised the alarm. There was, he said, something unclean on the dish, and he pushed the poor slave back, called him opprobrious names, and put him last among the other servants. Jesus interposed: "Not the dish, but what is in it is full of uncleanness." The master of the house replied: "Thou mistakest, those sweetmeats are perfectly clean and very costly." Jesus responded in words like these: "They are truly unclean! They are nothing else than sensual pleasures made of the sweat, the blood, the marrow, and the tears of widows, orphans, and the poor," and he read them a severe lesson upon their manner of acting, their prodigality, their covetousness, and their hypocrisy. They grew wrathful, but could make no reply. They quitted the house, leaving Jesus alone with the host. This latter was very smooth and affable toward Jesus, but it was all hypocrisy. He was hoping in this way to entrap him and get something at last to report against him to the committee at Capernaum.

Toward evening Jesus again taught the pagans on the mountain. When they asked him whether they should be baptized by John and expressed a wish to settle in Palestine, Jesus counseled them to put off their baptism until better instructed. He told them, moreover, to go first of all across the Jordan to Upper Galilee and into the region of Adama, where they would find good people and pagans already instructed, and where he himself would again teach. It was dark and Jesus taught by torchlight.

The instruction over, he left his hearers, and went to the shore of the lake and down to the spot where Peter's men were waiting for him with a boat. It was late. The three sailors made use of lights when they disembarked about half an hour below Bethsaida-Julias. Peter and Andrew, with the help of their servants, had built especially for his use the little boat in which Jesus had crossed. They were not only mariners and fishermen, but shipbuilders also.

Peter owned three vessels, one of them very large, as long as a house. Jesus's little boat held about ten men. It was oval in form, almost like an egg. In the forepart and stern were enclosed places for storing, and affording accommodations for washing the feet. In the center rose the mast with poles extended from it to the sides of the vessel for support; above and around these poles swung the sails. The seats were ranged around the mast. Jesus often taught from this little boat, which he used likewise to cross from point to point and to sail about among the other ships. The large vessels had around the lower part of the mast decks formed like terraces, or galleries, one above another. They were supported by posts placed at regular intervals, so that a view could be had through them from side to side. They were furnished with canvas curtains that could be drawn so as to form separate compartments like little cells. The poles supporting the mast had projecting rounds to facilitate climbing, and on either side of the vessel were floating chests, or barrels like wings or fins, to prevent its being overturned in a storm. They could be filled with water or emptied, according as it was necessary for the ship to ride more lightly or sink to a greater depth. The fish caught was sometimes preserved in them. At either end of the vessel were movable planks which, on being shoved out, facilitated access to the casks, to neighboring boats, or to the nets. When not in use for fishing purposes, the vessels were held in readiness to transport caravans and travelers across the lake. The sailors and servants of the fishermen were, for the most part, pagan slaves. Peter owned some.

Jesus in Peter's House • Measures Taken by the Pharisees • Cures

JESUS landed above Bethsaida not far from the house of the lepers where Peter, Andrew, John, James the Greater, James the Less, and Philip were awaiting his coming. He did not go with them through Bethsaida, but took the shorter route over the height to Peter's dwelling in the valley between that city and Capernaum, where Mary and the other women were assembled. Peter's mother-in-law was in bed sick. Jesus went to see her, but did not cure her yet. They washed the Master's feet and then sat down to a meal, during which the conversation turned principally upon the fact that, from the several most famous schools in Judea and Jerusalem, fifteen Pharisees had been sent to Capernaum to spy on Jesus's actions. From the larger places, two had been sent; from Sepphoris only one; and from Nazareth came that young man who had several times begged of Jesus to be admitted to his disciples, and whom Jesus had again rejected at his last visit to his native city. He had married lately, and was now appointed scribe of the commission. Jesus said to the disciples: "Behold, for whom you interceded! He desired to become my disciple, and yet he is now come to lay snares for me!" This young man wanted to join Jesus through a motive of vanity and, not being allowed to do so, he took part with Jesus's enemies. The Pharisees forming the commission were empowered to remain for some time in Capernaum. Of those that came in pairs, one returned to report, the second remaining to spy on Jesus's conduct and teaching. They had already held a meeting before which the centurion Zorobabel, the son, and father had to appear and answer interrogatories respecting the boy's cure and Jesus's doctrine. They could neither deny the cure nor challenge the doctrine, nevertheless they could not reconcile themselves to what had happened. They were angry because Jesus had not studied under them; they found fault with his frequenting the company of common people, such as the Essenes, fishermen, publicans, and sinners; they were indignant at his presuming to teach without a mission from Jerusalem, from the Sanhedrin; they were offended at his not having recourse to themselves for counsel and instruction; and they could not endure that he was neither Pharisee nor Sadducee, that he taught among the Samaritans, and cured on the sabbath day. They were in short furious at the thought that to render him justice would be to denounce and condemn themselves. The young man from Nazareth was a violent enemy of the Samaritans, whom he persecuted in many ways.

Jesus's friends and relatives did not want him to teach in Capernaum on the sabbath. Even his mother was full of anxiety, and she expressed her opinion that it would be more advisable for him to go to the other side of the lake. From such objections, Jesus turned aside with a few brief words and without explanations.

There were in Bethsaida and Capernaum immense numbers of sick, of pagans, and Jews. Several troops of the travelers that Jesus had lately met on the other side of the lake were here awaiting him. Near Bethsaida were large open inns covered with reeds, some for pagans, some for Jews. Above this place were the pagan baths; below were the Jewish.

Peter accommodated many of the Jewish sick in the precincts of his dwelling, and Jesus next morning healed a large number of them. Jesus had said to Peter the evening before that he should leave his fishery on the following day and help him to fish after men; soon would he call upon him to quit it entirely. Peter obeyed, though not without some inward embarrassment. He was always of the opinion that life with the Master was too high for him, he could not understand it. He believed in Jesus, he saw his miracles, he shared freely his substance with the other disciples, he did willingly all that was enjoined upon him, but yet he felt unfit for such a vocation. He thought himself too simple, too unworthy, and to this was added a secret anxiety for the welfare of his business. Sometimes also it was very vexatious to him to find himself the object of such railleries as, "He is only a poor fisherman, and yet look at him going around with the prophet! And his house is a perfect rendezvous for fanatics and seditious persons. See how he neglects his business!" All this made it a struggle for Peter since, though full of faith and love, he was not at that time so enthusiastic, so zealous as Andrew and the other disciples. He was timid and humble, attached to his ordinary occupations, and in his simplicity would have preferred being left in the peaceful discharge of them.

Thursday, August 17, AD 30 (Ab 29)

Jesus healed many people on his way to Bethsaida and in the town itself. That night he returned to Peter's house again.

Jesus went from Peter's dwelling over the mountain ridge to the north side of Bethsaida. The whole road was full of sick, pagans and Jews, separate however, the leprous far removed from all others. There were blind, lame, mute, deaf, paralytic, and an exceedingly large number of dropsical Jews. The ceremony of curing was performed with the greatest order and solemnity. The people had already been two days here, and the disciples of the place—Andrew, Peter, and the others whom Jesus had notified of his coming—had arranged them comfortably in the nooks, retired and shady, and the little gardens on the road.[C9] Jesus instructed and admonished the sick, who were carried or led and ranged around him in groups. Some desired to confess their sins to him, and he stepped with them to a more retired spot. They sank on their knees before him, confessing and weeping. Among the pagans were some that had committed murder and robbery on their journeys. Jesus passed by some, leaving them lying unnoticed for a time while he turned to others; but afterwards coming back to them, he exclaimed: "Rise! Thy sins are forgiven thee!" Among the Jews were adulterers and usurers. When Jesus saw in them proofs of repentance, he imposed on them a penance, repeated some prayers with them, laid his hands upon them, and cured them. He commanded many to purify themselves in a bath. Some of the pagans he ordered to receive baptism or to join their converted brethren in Upper Galilee. Band after band passed before him, and the disciples preserved order.

Jesus went through Bethsaida also. It was crowded with people, as if upon a great pilgrimage. He cured here in the different inns and along the streets. Refreshments had been prepared in Andrew's house. I saw some children there: Peter's stepdaughter and some other little girls of about ten years, two others between eight and ten, and Andrew's little son who wore a yellow tunic with a girdle. There were also some females of advanced age. All were standing on a kind of covered porch outside the house, speaking of the prophet, asking whether he would soon come, and running from side to side to see whether he were in sight. They had assembled here in order to get a glimpse of him, though ordinarily the children were kept under greater restraint. At last Jesus passed, turned his head toward them, and gave them his blessing. I saw him going again to Peter's and curing many. He cured about one hundred on that day, pardoned their sins, and pointed out to them what they should do in the future.

I saw again that Jesus exercised many different manners of curing, and that probably he did so in order to instruct the disciples as to how they should act, also the ministers of the church till the end of time. All the actions of Jesus, even his sufferings, appeared to be of a purely human nature. There were no sudden, no magical transformations in the cures he wrought. I saw in them a certain transition from sickness to health analogous to the nature of the malady and the sins that had given rise to it. I saw stealing upon those over whom he prayed or upon whom he laid his hand a certain stillness and inward recollection, which lasted for some moments, when they rose up as if from a slight swoon, cured. The lame rose without effort and cast themselves cured at his feet, though their full strength and agility returned to some only after a few hours, to others not for days. I saw some sick of edema who could totter toward him without assistance, and others who had to be carried. He generally laid his hand on their head and stomach and pronounced some words, after which they at once arose and walked. They felt quite relieved, the water passing from them in perspiration. The leprous, on being cured, immediately lost the scales of their disease, though still retaining the red scars. They that recovered sight, speech, or hearing, had at first a feeling of strangeness in the use of those senses. I saw some swollen with gout cured. Their pains left them, and they could walk, but the swelling did not go down at once, though it disappeared very soon. Convulsions were cured immediately and fevers vanished at his word, though their victims did not instantly become strong and vigorous. They were like drooping plants regaining freshness in the rain. The possessed usually sank into a short swoon from which they recovered with a calm expression of countenance and quite worn-out, though freed from the evil one. All was conducted quietly and methodically. Only for unbelievers and the malevolent had the miracles of Jesus anything frightful in them.

The pagans present on this occasion had been influenced to come chiefly by people that had been to the baptism and teaching of John, and by other pagans from Upper Galilee where Jesus had formerly taught and cured.

Some had already received John's baptism, and some had not. Jesus did not order them to be circumcised. When questioned on this point, he instructed them upon the circumcision of the heart and the senses, and taught them how to mortify themselves. He spoke to them of charity, temperance, frugality, ordered them to keep the Ten Commandments, taught them some parts of a prayer like the petitions of the Lord's Prayer, and promised to send them his disciples.

Jesus Teaches and Cures in Capernaum

Friday, August 18, AD 30 (Ab 30)

After healing many in Bethsaida, Jesus made his way to the synagogue in Capernaum. It was the start of the sabbath, and also the beginning of the month of Elul. In Capernaum, many Pharisees, including the fifteen newcomers who were there to investigate him, listened to Jesus's teaching. They were astounded at his interpretation of the prophet Isaiah (Chapter 49), whispering to one another: "Never before has a prophet taught like this!" (Mark 1:21–22). But they had no reply to Jesus's sermon. Then Jesus left the synagogue. Outside he healed the sick and, afterward, returned to Peter's house, where he healed more people.

ON the preceding evening, flags with knots and strings of fruit were raised on the synagogues and public buildings of Bethsaida, to herald the last day of the month Ab. With the sabbath, the first day of the month Elul began. Next morning, after Jesus had healed many sick Jews in Bethsaida, he went with the disciples to Peter's, near Capernaum. The women had preceded him thither, and crowds of sick were again awaiting him. There were two deaf men into whose ears Jesus put his finger. Two others were brought forward, who could scarcely walk, besides which their arms were perfectly stiff and their hands swollen. Jesus laid his hand on them and prayed; then grasping them by both hands, he swung their arms up and down, and they were cured. The swelling did not, however, disappear at once, but only after a couple of hours. He exhorted them for the future to use their hands for the glory of God, for it was sin that had reduced them to this state. He cured many others, and then went into the city for the sabbath.

The concourse of people at Capernaum was very great. The possessed had been released from their place of confinement and ran crying out along the streets to meet Jesus. He commanded them to be silent and delivered them; whereupon, to the astonishment of the multitude, they followed him quietly to the synagogue and listened to his instruction. The Pharisees, and among them those fifteen from the other cities, sat around his chair, forced to treat him with respect and hypocritical reverence. They gave him the scriptures, and he taught from Isaiah 49, that God had not forgotten his people. He read aloud: "If even a woman should forget her child, yet would not God forget his people"; and then explained from the following verses that the impiety of men could not restrain God, could not hinder him from realizing his thoughts of mercy. The time of which the prophet speaks, that the eyes of God are always on the walls of Zion, had now come, now should the destroyers flee and the builders commence their labor. The Lord would gather together nations to ornament his sanctuary. There will be so many good and pious souls, so many benefactors and leaders of the poor nations that the sterile synagogue will say: Who has begotten to me so many children? The Gentiles shall be converted to the church, the kings of the earth shall serve her! The God of Jacob shall snatch from the enemy, from the perverted synagogue, her children; and they that like murderers lay hands on the Savior, shall rage against one another, and choke one another. (Isaiah 50:1 *et seq.*) Jesus explained this as referring to the destruction of Jerusalem, since it would not receive the kingdom of grace. God demands whether he has separated from the synagogue, whether he has given her a bill of divorce, whether he has sold his people. Yes, on account of their sins, have they been sold! On account of her transgressions, has the synagogue been abandoned! He has called, he has warned, and no one has heeded. But he is the mighty God, he can cause heaven and earth to tremble. Jesus applied all to his own time. He showed that all had been led astray, those that had been forsaken by the synagogue. And then, as if speaking to himself, he uttered the words of this passage of Isaiah: "The Lord hath given me a learned tongue, that I should know how to uphold by word him that is weary: he hath opened his ears to him in the morning to hear his commands, and he hath not resisted." The Pharisees took these words as foolish self-praise, though they were ravished by his preaching, and said to one another at the end of it: "Never before has any prophet so taught!" They whispered, nevertheless, some malicious remarks into one another's ears. Jesus went on with the explanation of this passage: "I have given my body to the strikers, and my cheeks to them that plucked them," applying it to the persecutions that he had already endured and to what he had still to suffer. He spoke of the ill-treatment he had received at Nazareth, saying: "Let him who can condemn me, come forward!" His enemies, he said, would grow old and come to naught in their vain teachings, the Judge would come upon them. The godly would hear his voice, while the ignorant, the unenlightened, should call to God and hope in Him. The Day of Judgment would come, and they that had kindled the fire would go to ruin. This passage, of the destruction of the Jewish people and Jerusalem, Jesus also explained.

The Pharisees had not a word to reply. They listened in silence, transported by his words, though occasionally whispering a jeering remark into their neighbor's ear. Jesus then explained something from Moses as he always did at the termination of his sermons, and added a parable, which he addressed more particularly to the disciples and to the faithless young scribe of Nazareth. The parable was that of the talent put out at interest, for the young scribe was vain of his acquirements. He was humbled interiorly by it, but not improved. Jesus related the parable in terms similar to, though not quite the same as those given in the Gospel.

In front of the synagogue, Jesus cured the sick on the streets, and then went with his disciples to Peter's outside the city gate. Nathaniel Chased and the bridegroom, also Thaddeus, had come hither from Cana for this sabbath. Thaddeus was often in Capernaum, for he traveled a great deal throughout the country, dealing in fishing nets, sailcloth, and tackling. That night the house was again full of sick persons, and separated from the rest were several women afflicted with an issue of blood. Some women, completely enveloped, were brought on portable beds by their friends. They were pale and emaciated, and had already sighed long after Jesus's help. This time I saw that he imposed hands on the sufferers, and blessed them. Then he commanded those on the beds to throw off their covers and arise. They obeyed, one helping the other. Jesus exhorted them and bade them adieu. During the night, he retired to pray.

The spying Pharisees had not spoken openly in Capernaum of the object of their mission; even the centurion Zorobabel had been questioned only secretly. They had sufficient pretexts to account for their presence: The Jews were in the habit of going from one place to another for the celebration of the sabbath, especially if a distinguished doctor was expected to preside; it was customary, besides, for crowds to retire into the country of Galilee, to rest from business and enjoy the beauty and luxuriance that everywhere abounded.

ELUL (29 days):
August 18/19 to September 15/16, AD 30
Elul NewMoon: August 17 at 9:15 PM Jerusalem time

Saturday, August 19, AD 30 (Elul 1)

Jesus went again to the synagogue in Capernaum to teach. It was the sabbath. And there took place the scene, described in Mark 1:23–27 and Luke 4:31–36, where Jesus healed a man who was possessed. After further healings, around midday, Jesus went to Peter's house in Bethsaida where he healed Peter's mother-in-law, who had a raging fever. She rose immediately from her bed and helped the other women serve the next meal (Luke 4:38–39; Matthew 8:14–15; Mark 1:29–31). Jesus then healed many more people who were brought to him at Peter's house (Mark 1:32–34). Later, after teaching again in the synagogue, Jesus withdrew to a lonely place where he spent the night in prayer.

On the following day Jesus went very early to Capernaum. There was an innumerable concourse gathered before the synagogue, among them crowds of sick, of whom he healed many. When he entered the synagogue wherein the Pharisees were assembled, some possessed who were present began to cry out after him. One in particular, more noisy than his fellows, went running toward him crying: "What have we to do with thee, Jesus of Nazareth? Thou hast come to destroy us! I know that thou art the Holy One of God!" Jesus commanded the demon to be silent and to go out of the man.[C10] The latter, tearing himself, ran back among his companions, but the devil, uttering great cries, went out of him. The man then became perfectly calm, and cast himself at Jesus's feet. Many of those present, and especially the disciples, said in the hearing of the Pharisees, who were scandalized at what they saw: "What kind of a new doctrine is this? Who can this teacher be? He has power over the impure spirits!"

The crowd was so dense, there were so many sick in and around the synagogue, that Jesus had to take his stand on a spot to be seen and heard not only from within, but also from the court, which was crowded. The Pharisees stood around him inside, while Jesus turned toward the court to address the people. Sometimes he turned toward the interior of the synagogue, and again toward those outside. The halls around the building were open for the accommodation of the immense throng of hearers, who filled not only the court, but mounted the steps leading to the flat roofs of the buildings that enclosed it. Below were the cells and oratories reserved for penitents and those that came to pray. There were some places specially reserved for the sick.

Jesus again clearly and energetically expounded Isaiah, applying all to their own time and to himself. The times, he said, were fulfilled and the kingdom was near. They had always longed after the fulfillment of the prophecies, they had sighed for the prophet, the Messiah, who would relieve them of their burdens. But when he would come, they would not receive him, because he would fail to realize their erroneous notions of him. Then taking the signs of the coming of the prophet for whose accomplishment they always sighed, those signs that were still read from the scriptures in their synagogues and for which they prayed, he proved that they had all been fulfilled. He said: "The lame shall walk, the blind see, the deaf hear. Is there not something of this now? What mean these gatherings of the Gentiles to hear instruction? What do the possessed cry out? Why are the demons expelled? Why do the cured praise God? Do not the wicked persecute him? Do not spies surround him? But they will cast out and kill the son of the lord of the vineyard, and how shall it be with them? If ye will not receive salvation, yet shall it not be lost. Ye cannot prevent its being given to the poor, the sick, to sinners and publicans, to the penitent, and even to the Gentiles in whose favor it shall be taken from you." Such was the substance of Jesus's discourse. He added: "That John whom they have imprisoned ye acknowledge to be a prophet! Go to him in his prison and ask him for whom did he prepare the ways and of whom did he bear witness?" While Jesus spoke, the rage of the Pharisees increased, and they whispered and muttered together.

During Jesus's discourse, four distinguished men of Capernaum, sick of an unclean malady, were carried by eight others less sick to the synagogue and placed in such a position in the court that Jesus could see them and they could hear his teaching. On account of their sickness, they were allowed to enter only by one particular gate, but that being just at present obstructed by the crowd, the eight semi-invalids had to lift them in their beds to a place over a wall and force their own way through the crowd, which at once retreated before the unclean sickness. When the Pharisees saw the newcomers, they became angry and began to snarl at them as public sinners suffering from an unclean malady. They spoke aloud against them, asking what kind of irregularity was this, that such people should venture into their vicinity? When their remarks ran through the crowd and reached the objects of them, the poor sick men became sad and frightened lest Jesus, being informed of their sins, should refuse to cure them. They were full of contrition, and had long sighed for Jesus's assistance. But when Jesus heard the murmuring of the Pharisees, he turned on the instant to where the sick men were lying in fear and anxiety, addressed his discourse to the crowd in the court and, casting a look full of earnestness and love on the sufferers, cried out to them: "Your sins are forgiven you!" At this the poor men burst into tears, while the Pharisees, highly exasperated, growled out: "How does he dare say so? How can he forgive sins!" Jesus said: "Follow me down there, and see what I am going to do! Why are ye offended at my doing the will of my Father? If ye do not want salvation yourselves, yet should you not grudge it to the repentant! Ye are angry that I cure on the sabbath? Does the hand of the Almighty rest on the sabbath day from doing good and punishing evil? Does he not feed the hungry, cure the sick, and shed around his blessings on the sabbath? Can he not send sickness on the sabbath? May he not let you die on the sabbath? Be not vexed that the Son does the will and the works of his Father on the sabbath!" When he reached the sick men, he ordered the Pharisees to stand in a row at some distance, saying: "Stay here, for to ye these men are unclean, though to me not, since their sins have been forgiven them! And now, tell me. Is it harder to say to a contrite sinner, 'Thy sins are forgiven thee,' than to say to a sick man, 'Arise, and carry thy bed hence'"? The Pharisees had not a word to answer. Then Jesus approached the sick men, laid his hands on them one after the other, uttered a few words of prayer over them, raised them up by the hand, and commanded them to render thanks to God, to sin no more, and to carry away their beds. All four arose. The eight who had carried them and who were themselves half-sick, had become quite vigorous, and they helped the others to throw off the covers in which they were wrapped. These latter appeared to be only a little fatigued and embarrassed. Putting together the poles of their portable beds, they shouldered them, and all twelve went off through the wondering and exulting crowd joyfully intoning the song of thanksgiving: "Praised be the Lord God of Israel! He has done great things to us. He has had mercy on his people, and has cured us by his prophet!"

But the Pharisees, full of wrath and deeply mortified, hurried away without taking leave of the Savior. Everything about Jesus exasperated them: his actions and his manner of performing them, that he was not of the same opinion with them, that he did not esteem them just, wise, and holy, that he associated with people whom they despised. They had a thousand objections to make to him; namely, that he did not keep the fasts strictly, he associated with sinners, pagans, Samaritans, and the rabble at large, that he was himself of mean extraction, that he gave too much liberty to his disciples and did not keep them in proper respect—in a word, everything in him displeased them. Still they could bring no special charge against him. His wisdom and his astonishing miracles they could not deny; consequently, they took refuge in ever-increasing rage and calumny. When one considers the life of Jesus in detail, the priests and people of his time are found to be pretty much the same as they are nowadays. If Jesus actually returned to earth, from many doctors of the Law, from many politicians, he would have to endure still worse things.

The sickness of the lately cured consisted in a discharge of impure humors. They were, before their cure, quite exhausted and motionless, as if they had had an apoplectic stroke. The eight others were partially lame on one side. The beds consisted of two poles with feet, a crosspiece in the middle, on which a mat was stretched. They rolled the whole together, and carried them on their shoulders like a couple of poles. It was a touching sight—those men going through the crowd singing!

Jesus Cures Peter's Mother-In-Law • Peter's Great Humility

JESUS now went without delay with the disciples out of the city gate and along the mountain to Peter's in Bethsaida. They had urged him to do so, for they thought that Peter's mother-in-law was dying. Her sickness had very much increased, and now she had a raging fever. Jesus went straight into her room. [C11] He was followed by some of the family; I think Peter's daughter was among them. He stepped to that side of the bed to which the sick woman's face was turned, and leaned against the bed, half-standing, half-sitting, so that his head approached hers. He spoke to her some words, and laid his hand upon her head and breast. She became perfectly still. Then standing before her, he took her hand and raised her into sitting posture, saying: "Give her something to drink!" Peter's daughter gave her a drink out of a vessel in the form of a little boat. Jesus blessed the drink and commanded the invalid to rise. She obeyed and arose from her low couch. Her limbs were bandaged, and she wore a wide nightdress. Disengaging herself from the bandages, she stepped to the floor and rendered thanks to the Lord, the entire household uniting with her.

At the meal that followed, she helped with the other women and, perfectly recovered, served at table. After that, Jesus, with Peter, Andrew, James, John, and several of the other disciples, went to Peter's fishery on the lake. In the instruction he gave them, he spoke principally of the fact that they would soon give up their present occupations and follow him. Peter became quite timid and anxious. He fell on his knees before Jesus, begging him to reflect upon his ignorance and weakness, and not to insist on his undertaking anything so important, that he was entirely unworthy, and quite unable to instruct others. Jesus replied that his disciples should have no worldly solicitude, that he who gave health to the sick would provide for their subsistence and furnish them with ability for what they had to do. All were perfectly satisfied, excepting Peter who, in his humility and simplicity, could not comprehend how he was for the future to be, not a fisherman, but a teacher of men. This, however, is not the call of the apostles related in the Gospel. That had not yet taken place. Peter had nevertheless already given over a great part of his business to Zebedee. After this walk by the lake, Jesus again went to Capernaum and found an unusual number of sick around Peter's house outside the city. He cured many, and taught again in the synagogue.

As the concourse of people continued to increase, Jesus, without being noticed, disengaged himself from the crowd, and went alone to a wild but very pleasant ravine which extended to the south of Capernaum, from Zorobabel's mansion to the dwellings of his servants and workmen. In it were grottoes, bushes, and springs, numerous birds, and all kinds of tame, rare animals. It was a skillfully cared-for solitude belonging to Zorobabel, besides being a part of that garden of pleasure, Galilee, thrown open to the public. Jesus spent the night alone and in prayer, the disciples being ignorant of his whereabouts.

Sunday, August 20, AD 30 (Elul 2)

Early this morning Peter and the other disciples came to Jesus and told him that many sick people were waiting for him (Mark 1:36–37). Jesus replied that he would return another time and took leave of the disciples. Later he met up again with Saturnin, Parmenas, Tharzissus, and Aristobolus and they continued together to Bethulia. That evening, he put up at an inn, where he taught.

Early next morning, he left the wilderness, but not to return to Capernaum. He ordered Peter and another of the disciples who had come to seek him to send Parmenas, Saturnin, Aristobolus, and Tharzissus to a certain place where he would meet them, and thence go to the baths of Bethulia. He went around the height of the valley on which lay Magdalum, which he passed a couple of hours eastward to the left. On the south side of this height was the city of Jotopata.

Jesus at the Baths of Bethulia and in Jotopata

AT first I thought that Jesus was going to Gennabris, situated among the mountains, about three hours west of Tiberias. But he did not go there, but to the north side of the valley where was the fountain of Bethuel. A great many wealthy and distinguished people from Galilee and Judea owned villas and gardens here, which they occupied in the beautiful season of the year. On the south side of the lake, formed by the northern declivity of the heights of Bethuel, were rows of houses and warm baths, those toward the east being the warmer. The baths had one large reservoir in common, around which were private apartments formed by tents; in them were tubs sunk to a greater or lesser depth in the water, according to the convenience of the bathers. These private apartments communicated with the reservoir. There were many inns in the neighborhood of the baths. A private house and garden could also be hired for the season with everything else free. The revenues belonged to the city of Bethulia, and were used principally to keep up the baths. The waters of the lake were uncommonly pure, clear as a mirror to the very bottom, which was paved with beautiful, little white pebbles. It was fed by a stream from the east which flowed from the baths in the valley of Magdalum. The lake swarmed with little pleasure boats, which in the distance looked like ducks. On the north side of the lake, but facing south, were dwellings for the accommodation of female visitors at the baths. Their walks and pleasure grounds, however, were near the brook that flowed through those of the men. Both sides of the valley formed a gentle declivity toward the lake. From the dwellings and baths there ran around the lake, crossing and opening into one another, shady avenues, embowered walks with wide-stretching trees and luxuriant foliage, among which lay meadows of very high and beautiful grass, orchards, vegetable gardens, and grounds for riding and games. The view was enchantingly beautiful—hills and mountains, all teeming with the most exuberant fertility, rich especially in grapes and fruits. The second harvest of the year was now ripe.

Jesus remained on the side of the lake by which he had come, and put up at a traveler's inn. People soon gathered around him, and he taught them with great sweetness outside the inn. Many women were among his hearers.

Monday, August 21, AD 30 (Elul 3)

Jesus taught in Bethulia today.

Next morning I saw a number of little boats coming over from the south side of the lake where the bathers were. It was a deputation of the most distinguished men, come to invite Jesus courteously to return with them and preach. Jesus ferried across with them and went to an inn where they presented him with a little luncheon. He taught in the cool of the morning and evening under shady trees, on a hill not far from the inn. Most of his hearers stood around him, the women on one side veiled. The order observed was truly pleasing. The people were, for the most part, well-bred and well-inclined, cheerful and good-humored. As there were no factions among them, one did not fear to give vent to his feelings before the others, consequently they were all most reverential and attentive to Jesus. They were perfectly carried away and rejoiced by his very first discourse. He taught of purification by water, of the union, equality, and the feeling of confidence that reigned among them, of the mystery of water, of the washing away of sin, of the bath of baptism as administered by John, of the charity and good understanding that ought to unite the baptized, the converted, etc. He borrowed, moreover, subject matter and graceful similitudes from the lovely season, from the country around, the mountains, trees, fruit, and herds, in short from everything they saw about them. I saw his audience around Jesus in a circle, and at times exchanging places with newcomers to whom he repeated the substance of his last discourse.

I saw some gouty invalids moving slowly about. They were mostly government officials and officers who were enjoying a vacation. I recognized them by the uniforms they wore when leaving for their different garrisons around the country. During their stay at the baths, all were dressed alike with nothing to distinguish them from other people. The men wore fine, yellow woolen stuff made into tunics of four separate skirts, one above the other, the lower one wrapped into a kind of trousers down to the knees; some went barefoot, others wore sandals. The upper part of the body was covered with a scapular open at the sides and bound at the waist by a broad girdle. The shoulders were covered with an armflap that reached halfway to the elbow; the head was uncovered. They played at games, fighting with little sticks and armed with shields made of leaves. They attacked one another in rows and also singly, aiming at pushing their opponents from their places. They ran toward a goal for a wager, jumped over ropes, sprang through hoops upon which all sorts of glittering things were hanging. These they were not to touch in passing through, otherwise they tinkled and fell off. The contestant for the prize lost in proportion to the number thus displaced. The prizes consisted of fruit which I saw lying ready for the winners. I saw some playing on reed flutes; others had long, thick reeds through which they gazed into the distance and into the lake. Sometimes they blew balls or little arrows through them, as if they were shooting after fishes. I saw that these reeds were flexible; they could be bent to form a ring and then hung on the arm. I saw them also sticking glass globes of different colors on the ends of the reeds and waving them to and fro, thus reflecting the light of the sun. The whole landscape was mirrored in the globes, but in an inverted position. When the globes were revolved, the whole lake appeared to be passing overhead. This greatly diverted the beholders.

The fruits, and especially the grapes, were truly magnificent. I saw some persons very respectfully and courteously bringing some of the finest to Jesus.

The dwellings of the women were on the opposite side of the valley; but their baths were on this side, more toward the east and out of sight of those of the men. On the banks of the stream that flowed into the lake I saw little boys in short, white woolen tunics with willow switches of various colors in their hands, driving flocks of different kinds of aquatic birds. The water from the stream and lake was conducted up to the inns on the height and also to the baths. It was received in channels from which it was raised to higher reservoirs, and from them to others, and so on. I saw the women also playing at different games on the green. They were very modestly clothed in fine, white woolen wrappers that fell around them in numerous folds and were girded twice, over the breast and again at the waist. The wide sleeves could be raised or lowered by means of buckles. Around the wrists they had large, stiff frills with many folds, like the tail of a peacock. Their headdress consisted of a cap of circular puffs graduated lower and narrower, wound with silk or small feathers of natural whiteness. It looked like a snail's shell made of feathers. It was tied behind and a long point made of tassels hung down the back. They wore no veil, but over the face were two sections of finely plaited, white, transparent stuff like half fans, which reached to below the nose, and had holes for the eyes. They could lower them in part if they wished to guard against the sun, or throw them entirely back. Before men they were lowered.

I saw the women amusing themselves lustily at the following game. Each had a girdle ending in a ring, or a loop, around her waist. They formed a circle, each holding her neighbor fast by the loop with one hand, the other being free. A trinket was concealed in the grass and they turned round here and there in a circle until one of the players spied it. When she stopped to pick it up, the others in the circle gave a sudden jerk; those following likewise stooped after the treasure, each one trying not to fall. Sometimes they tumbled over one another amid shouts of laughter.

Bethulia was situated on a plateau in a mountainous region, solitary and wild. It was an hour and a half south of the lake. Above it was a great, rough-looking tower and many ruined walls and towers. Once upon a time, the city must have extended much further and been very strongly fortified. Trees were now growing on those walls, upon which vehicles could be driven, and I saw the visitors at the baths promenading on them. The city lay high up around the mountain. Here it was that Judith became illustrious. The camp of Holofernes stretched from the lake through the ravine of Jotopata around to Dothaim, a couple of hours to the south of Bethulia. From Jotopata also there were visitors at the baths. They did not wait to hear Jesus's instructions but, returning to Jotopata, spread the news of his presence in Bethulia. Jotopata was situated about an hour and a half to the southeast, built in the bosom of the mountains as in an immense cave. Before it rose a mountain from which the descent into the city was over deep, wild ditches. It appeared to be built in a deep quarry, the mountain hanging high over it. To the north of

Old Roman Aqueduct

this mountain, not quite two hours distant, was Magdalum, on the edge of a deep dale, with its surroundings of avenues, gardens, and towers of all kinds stretching off into the middle of it. Between the mountain and Magdalum were still standing the remains of the channel of an aqueduct through whose arches one could look far off into the country. The channel was now overgrown by vines and foliage. Southward from Jotopata rose another wild mountain pierced right and left by broad ravines. It was a region full of wonderful hiding places. There were numerous Herodians in Jotopata. In a wall of the fortifications they had a secret meeting place. The sect was composed of shrewd, intelligent people ranged under a secret superior. They had signs whereby they recognized one another, and the chiefs could also tell (how, I do not now know) if a member had betrayed anything. Secret enemies of the Romans, they were plotting a revolution in favor of Herod. Although in reality followers of the Sadducees, yet in the exterior they conformed to the Pharisees, thinking in this way to draw over both parties to their designs. They knew indeed that the time had come for the appearance of the Messiah, the king of the Jews, and they resolved to make use of the general belief for the furtherance of their ends. Exteriorly and through motives of cunning, they were very bland and tolerant, though really treacherous sneaks. They had, properly speaking, no religion at all; but under the cloak of piety they labored at the founding of an independent kingdom of this world, and Herod supported them in their intrigues.

When the synagogue of Jotopata heard of Jesus's presence in the neighborhood, they sent two Herodians to the baths of Bethulia, to find out what sort of a person he was and to invite him to Jotopata. Jesus, however, gave them no decided answer as to whether he would go or not. About seven of the disciples that had journeyed with him a couple of weeks before met him here again. Two of them were John's disciples, some relatives of his who also were disciples, from the country of Hebron, and one was a cousin from Little Sepphoris. They had been seeking him in Galilee, and had now found him. During those days I saw Jesus speaking confidentially with several of the guests at the baths. There must have been some of his own followers among them.

When the Herodians returned to Jotopata, one of them set about preparing the people in case Jesus should come to their city. He told them that Jesus, the prophet of Nazareth, who was now nearby at the baths of Bethulia, would probably visit their city for the coming sabbath. He was the one who had made a great uproar in Capernaum on the preceding sabbath and on the sabbath before that in Nazareth. He warned them not to be seduced by him, not to applaud him, not even to let him speak for any length of time, but to interrupt him with murmurs and contradictions whenever he said anything singular or unintelligible; and so the people were prepared for Jesus's coming.

Tuesday, August 22, AD 30 (Elul 4)

This morning, Jesus taught and healed in Bethulia. And in the afternoon he and his disciples went to the nearby town of Jotopata. Here there were many Herodians. (The Herodians were a secret brotherhood opposed to Roman rule; they had the support of Herod Antipas.) Jesus taught in the synagogue. The Herodians tried to trap him into saying that he was the Messiah, but Jesus exposed them, and proclaimed their secrets to the assembled people.

Jesus delivered at the baths of Bethulia another discourse full of beauty and simplicity. Numbers of men formed around him a circle in which he moved about among them. At a distance in the background, several men lame with the gout were timidly standing. They had come to make use of the baths, but had not yet ventured to approach Jesus. Jesus repeated what he had taught yesterday and the day before, exhorting his audience to purification from sin. All hearts were touched and turned to him. Many exclaimed: "Lord, who could hear thee and resist thy words!" Jesus replied: "Ye have heard much about me, and now ye listen to my words. Who do ye think I am?" Some said: "Lord, thou art a prophet!" Others answered: "Thou art more than a prophet! No prophet ever taught such things as thou dost teach. None has ever done the things that thou hast done!" But others, again, kept silence. Jesus, penetrating the thoughts of these last, pointing to them, said: "These men's thoughts are the right ones." Someone then said: "Lord, thou canst do all things! Is it not so? They said that thou hast even raised the dead, the daughter of Jairus. Is it so?" The speaker alluded to that Jairus who dwelt in a city not far from Gibeah, where Jesus had at an earlier period instructed the poor, depraved inhabitants. Jesus answered the question addressed to him by a simple "Yes!" and then his questioner went on to inquire why Jairus still remained in so disreputable a place. Thereupon Jesus began to speak of fountains in the desert, applying the similitude to the necessity of the weak for a powerful leader. Jesus's hearers were full of confidence and they questioned him with simplicity. Then he asked them: "What do ye know of me? What evil do men say of me?" Some answered: "They complain that thou dost not discontinue thy works on the sabbath day and that thou healest the sick on that day." Then Jesus, pointing to a little neighboring field near a pond, in which shepherd boys were guarding tender lambs and other young cattle, said: "See those young shepherd boys and their tender lambs! If one of the little animals should fall into the pond on the sabbath and bleat for help, would not all the others stand around the brink bleating piteously also? Now, the poor little shepherds could not help the lamb out. But supposing the son of the master of the flocks were passing by—supposing he had been charged to look after the lambs and see to their pasture—would he not be touched with pity at the sound of the poor little thing's bleating? Would he not hasten to draw it out of the mire?" Here all raised their hands like children at catechism, and cried out: "Yes, yes! He would!" Jesus went on: "And if it were not a lamb, if it were the fallen children of the heavenly Father, if it were your own brethren, yes, if it were yourselves! Should not the Son of the heavenly Father help you on the sabbath?" All cried out again: "Yes! Yes!" Then Jesus pointed to the men sick of the gout standing afar off, and said: "Behold your sick brethren! Shall I not help them if they implore my assistance on the sabbath day? Shall they not receive pardon of their sins, if they bewail them on the sabbath day? If they confess them on the sabbath and cry to their Father in heaven?" With uplifted hands, they all cried out: "Yes, yes!"

Then Jesus motioned to the gouty patients, and they moved slowly and heavily into the circle. He spoke a few words to them on faith, prayed for awhile, and said: "Stretch out your arms!" They stretched out their afflicted arms toward him. Jesus passed his hand down them, breathed for an instant on their hands, and they were cured, were able to use their limbs. Jesus commanded them to bathe, and warned them to abstain from certain drinks. They cast themselves at his feet giving thanks, while the whole assembly sang canticles of praise and glory.

Jesus wanted to depart, but they begged him to remain with them. They were full of love and good intentions, they were very much impressed. He told them that he had to proceed further and fulfill his mission. They accompanied him a part of the way with the disciples. He dismissed them with his blessing, and went on to Jotopata about an hour and a half to the east.

It was afternoon when Jesus arrived at his destination. He washed his feet and took a luncheon at an inn outside the city. The disciples went before him into Jotopata to the chief of the synagogue, and requested the key for their Master, who wished to teach. The people hurriedly gathered in crowds, and the doctors of the Law and the Herodians were all expectancy to ensnare him in his doctrine. When he had taken his place in the synagogue, they put to him questions upon the approach of the kingdom, the computation of time, the fulfilling of the weeks of Daniel, and the coming of the Messiah. Jesus answered in a long discourse, showing that the prophecies were now fulfilled. He spoke, too, of John and his prophecies, whereupon they took occasion to warn him hypocritically to be careful as to what he said in his instructions, not to set aside the Jewish customs, and to take a lesson from John's imprisonment! What he said of the fulfillment of the weeks of Daniel, of the near coming of the Messiah, and of the king of the Jews, was excellent and quite in accordance with their own ideas. But, as he told them, they might seek where they would, they would still nowhere find the Messiah. Jesus had, though rather vaguely, applied the prophecies to himself. They understood him well enough, but they pretended that such things could not happen to anyone, and that they had failed to catch his meaning. In reality they wanted to force him to speak out more clearly, so that they might get something of which to accuse him. Jesus said to them: "How ye play the hypocrite! What turns ye away from me? Why do ye despise me? Ye lay snares for me, and ye seek to form new plots with the Sadducees, as ye did in Jerusalem at Passover! Why do ye caution me, citing John and Herod?" Then he cast into their face Herod's shameful deeds, his murders, his dread of the newborn king of the Jews, his cruel massacre of the Innocents, and his frightful death, the crimes of his successors, the adultery of Antipas, and the imprisonment of John. He spoke of the hypocritical, secret sect of the Herodians who were in league with the Sadducees, and showed them what kind of a Messiah and what sort of a kingdom of God they were awaiting. He pointed to different places in the distance, saying: "They will be able to do nothing against me until my mission is fulfilled. I shall twice traverse Samaria, Judea, and Galilee. Ye have witnessed great signs wrought by me, and seeing still greater, ye shall remain blind." Then he spoke of judgment, of the death of the prophets, and of the chastisement that was to overtake Jerusalem. The Herodians, that secret society, seeing themselves discovered, blanched with rage when Jesus referred to Herod's misdeeds and laid open the secrets of the sect before the people. They were silent and, one by one, left the synagogue, as did also the Sadducees who here had charge of the schools. There were no Pharisees in Jotopata.

Jesus now found himself alone with his seven disciples and the people. He continued to teach some time longer, and many were very much impressed. They declared that they had never listened to such instructions, and that he taught better than their own teachers. They reformed their lives, and followed him later. But a large part of the people, instigated by the Sadducees and Herodians, murmured against him and raised a tumult. Jesus therefore left the city with the disciples and went southward through the valley, and then up for a couple of hours into a harvest field between Bethulia and Gennabris. Here he put up at a large farmhouse, whose occupants were well known to him. The holy women had often stayed here overnight on their journeys to Bethany, and the messengers between them and the Savior used to put up at the same place.

Jesus in the Harvest Field of Dothaim and in Gennabris

Wednesday, August 23, AD 30 (Elul 5)

It was harvest time. Jesus and the disciples walked from field to field. Here and there, he held a discourse with the workers.

JESUS in the harvest field of Dothaim taught of reaping, gleaning, and binding into sheaves. This was the field in which later on he and the disciples plucked the ears of wheat. He went around the field, here and there, talking of seeds and stony soil, for such was the character of this region. He said that he was come to gather the good ears, and explained the parable of rooting up the tares at the harvest. He likened the harvest to the kingdom of God. He instructed at intervals during the work and while going from one field to another.

The stalks remained standing high, the ears only having been cut off and bound together in the form of a cross. In the evening after the harvest, Jesus from a hilltop delivered a long discourse before the laborers. Borrowing a similitude from a brook that flowed in their vicinity, he applied it to the life, gentle and beneficent, of some men; he spoke of the flowing waters of grace, and of the conducting of those waters to our own field, etc. He sent John's two disciples to Ainon with a commission to say to his own disciples there that they should go to Machaerus and calm the people, for he knew that an insurrection had broken out in that place. Aspirants to baptism had crowded to Ainon; immense caravans had arrived. But when they found out that the prophet had been arrested, they proceeded to Machaerus, their numbers increasing on the way. They raged and shouted, crying for John to be released, that he might instruct and baptize them. They even threw stones at Herod's palace, all the approaches to which the guards hastily closed. Herod pretended that he was not at home.

Thursday, August 24, AD 30 (Elul 6)

Today, Jesus continued on his way toward Gennabris.

That evening Jesus put up near Gennabris in another farmhouse, and taught again of the grain of mustard seed. The master of the house complained to him of a neighbor who for a long time had encroached upon his field and in many ways infringed his rights. Jesus went to the field with the owner, that he might point out to him the injury done. As the present state of affairs had lasted some time, the damage was considerable, and the owner complained that he could not do anything with the trespasser. Jesus asked whether he still had sufficient for the support of himself and his family. The man answered, yes, that he enjoyed competency. Upon hearing this, Jesus told him that he had lost nothing, since properly speaking nothing belongs to us, and so long as we have sufficient to support life, we have enough. The owner of the field should resign still more to his importunate neighbor, in order to satisfy the latter's greed after earthly goods. All that one cheerfully gives up here below for the sake of peace, will be restored to him in the kingdom of his Father. That hostile neighbor, viewed from his own standpoint, acted rightly, for his kingdom was of this world, and he sought to increase in earthly goods. But in Jesus's kingdom, he should have nothing. The owner of the field should take a lesson from his neighbor in the art of enriching himself, and should strive to acquire possessions in the kingdom of God. Jesus drew a similitude from a river which wore away the land on one side and deposited the debris on the other. The whole discourse was something like that upon the unjust steward, in which worldly artifice and earthly greed after enrichment should furnish an example for one's manner of acting in spiritual affairs. Earthly riches were contrasted with heavenly treasures. Some points of the instruction seemed a little obscure to me, though to the Jews, on account of their notions, their religion, and the standpoint from which they viewed things, all was quite plain and intelligible. To them all was symbolical.

The field in which lay Joseph's well was in this neighborhood, and Jesus took occasion from the circumstance just related to refer to a somewhat similar struggle recorded in the Old Testament. Abraham had given far more land to Lot than the latter had demanded. After relating the fact, Jesus asked what had become of Lot's posterity, and whether Abraham had not recovered full propriety. Ought we not to imitate Abraham? Was not the kingdom promised to him, and did he not obtain it? This earthly kingdom, however, was merely a symbol of the kingdom of God, and Lot's struggle against Abraham was typical of the struggle of man with man. But, like Abraham, man should aim at acquiring the kingdom of God. Jesus quoted the text of holy scripture in which the strife alluded to is recorded, and continued to talk of it and of the kingdom before all the harvest laborers.

The unjust husbandman likewise was present with his followers. He listened in silence and at a distance. He had engaged his friends to interrupt Jesus from time to time with all kinds of captious questions. One of them asked him what would be the end of his preaching, what would come of it all. Jesus answered so evasively that they could make nothing out of his words. They were, however, something to this effect: If his preaching seemed too long to some, to others it was short. He spoke in parables of the harvest, of sowing, of reaping, of separating the tares from the good grain, of the bread and nourishment of eternal life, etc. The good husbandman, the host of Jesus, listened to his teaching with a docile heart. He ceased to accuse his enemy, later on gave over all he possessed into the treasury of the rising church, and his sons joined the disciples.

There was much talk here of the Herodians. The people complained of their spying into everything. They had recently accused and arrested here at Dothaim and also in Capernaum several adulterers, and taken them to Jerusalem where they were to be judged. The people of Dothaim were well pleased that such persons should be removed from among them, but the feeling of being continually watched was very distasteful to them. Jesus spoke of the

Herodians with perfect freedom. He told the people to beware of sin, also of hypocrisy and criticizing others. One should confess his own delinquencies before sitting in judgment upon his neighbor. Then Jesus painted the ordinary manner of acting among the Herodians, applying to them the passage from the prophet Isaiah read in the synagogue on the preceding sabbath, which treats of mute dogs that do not bark, that do not turn away from evil, and that tear men in secret. He reminded them that those adulterers were delivered over to justice while Herod, the patron of their accusers, lived in the open commission of the same crime, and he gave them signs by which they might recognize the Herodians.

There were in several of the huts nearby some men who had received injuries during their labor. Jesus visited them, cured the poor creatures, and told them to go to the instruction and resume their work. They did so, singing hymns of praise.

Jesus sent some shepherds from Dothaim to Machaerus with directions to John's disciples to induce the people to disperse, for their rebellion, he said, might render John's imprisonment more rigorous, or even give occasion for his death.

Herod and his wife were in Machaerus. I saw that Herod caused the Baptist to be summoned to his presence in a grand hall near the prison. There he was seated surrounded by his guard, many officers, doctors of the Law, and numerous Herodians and Sadducees. John was led through a passage into the hall and placed in the midst of guards before the large, open doors. I saw Herod's wife insolently and scornfully sweeping past John as she entered the hall and took an elevated seat. Her physiognomy was different from that of most Jewish women. Her whole face was sharp and angular, even her head was pointed, and her countenance was in constant motion. She had developed a very beautiful figure, and in her dress she was loud and extreme, also very tightly laced. To every chaste mind she must have been an object of scandal, as she did everything in her power to attract all eyes upon her.

Herod began to interrogate John, commanding him to tell him in plain terms what he thought of Jesus who was making such disturbance in Galilee. Who was he? Was he come to deprive him (Herod) of his authority? He (Herod) had heard indeed that he (John) had formerly announced Jesus, but he had paid little attention to the fact. Now, however, John should disclose to him his candid opinion on the subject, for that man (Jesus) held wondrous language on the score of a kingdom, and uttered parables in which he called himself a king's son, etc., although he was only the son of a poor carpenter. Then I heard John in a loud voice, and as if addressing the multitude, giving testimony to Jesus. He declared that he himself was only to prepare his ways; that compared with him, he was nobody; that never had there been a man, not even among the prophets, like unto Jesus, and never would there be one; that he was the Son of the Father; that he was the Christ, the King of Kings, the Savior, the Restorer of the kingdom; that no power was superior to his; that he was the Lamb of God who was to bear the sins of the world, etc. So spoke John of Jesus, crying in a loud voice, calling himself his precursor, the preparer of his ways, his most insignificant servant. It was evident that his words were inspired. His whole bearing was stamped with the supernatural, so much so that Herod, becoming terrified, stopped his ears. At last he said to John: "Thou knowest that I wish thee well. But thou dost excite sedition against me amongst the people by refusing to acknowledge my marriage. If thou wilt moderate thy perverse zeal and recognize my union as lawful before the people, I shall set thee free, and thou canst go around teaching and baptizing." Thereupon John again raised up his voice vehemently against Herod, rebuking his conduct before all the assistants, and saying to him: "I know thy mind! I know that thou recognizest the right and tremblest before the judgment! But thou hast sunk thy soul in guilty pleasures, thou liest bound in the snares of debauchery!" The rage of the wife at these words is simply indescribable, and Herod became so agitated that he hastily ordered John to be led away. He gave directions for him to be placed in another cell which, having no communication outside, would prevent his being heard by the people.

Herod was induced to hold that judicial examination because of his anxiety, excited by the tumult raised by the aspirants to baptism and the news brought him by the Herodians of the wonders wrought by Jesus.

The whole country was discussing the execution in Jerusalem of certain adulterers from Galilee who had been denounced by the Herodians. They dwelt upon the fact that sinners in humble life were brought to justice while the great ones went free; and that the accusers themselves, the Herodians, were adherents of the adulterous Herod who had imprisoned John for reproaching him with his guilt. Herod became dispirited. I saw the execution of the adulterers mentioned above. Their crimes were read to them, and then they were thrust into a dungeon in which was a small pit. They were placed at its edge. They fell upon a knife which cut off their heads. In a vault below waited some jailers to drag away the lifeless trunks. It was some kind of a machine into which the condemned were precipitated. It was in this same place that James the Greater was executed at a later period.

Friday, August 25, AD 30 (Elul 7)

Andrew, James, and John came to Jesus to conduct him to Gennabris. They arrived in Gennabris at the start of the sabbath. Jesus taught in the synagogue, which was very full. Afterward, he was invited to a meal by a Pharisee.

On the following day Jesus was again teaching among the harvesters when Andrew, James, and John arrived. Nathaniel was at his house in the suburbs of Gennabris. Jesus informed his disciples that he would next go through Samaria to the place of baptism on the Jordan. The well of Dothaim, at which Joseph was sold, was not far from the field in which Jesus was then teaching.

The people of the place asked whether or not they did rightly in supporting the poor, crippled laborers that could no longer work. Jesus answered that in acting thus they acquitted themselves of a duty, but they should not pride themselves upon it, otherwise they would lose their reward. Then he entered the huts of the sick, cured many of them, bade them attend the instruction and return to their work. They obeyed, praising God.

Jesus then went to the synagogue in Gennabris for the sabbath. Gennabris was as large as Münster, and about one hour's distance from the mountain upon whose heights lay the harvest field in which Jesus had last taught. It was situated toward the east on a slope covered with gardens, baths, and pleasure resorts. On the side by which Jesus arrived it was defended by deep ditches of standing water. After half an hour Jesus and the disciples reached the walls and tower gates of the city precincts, where were gathered many disciples from the country around. With about twelve of them, Jesus entered the city, where numbers of Pharisees, Sadducees, and especially Herodians had assembled for the sabbath. They had undertaken with crafty words to entrap Jesus in his speech. They said among themselves that such a project would be more difficult to carry out in small places, since in such Jesus was more daring, but among them the thing could be easily managed. They congratulated themselves beforehand, quite sure of the success of their plans. The crowd present, having been intimidated by these enemies of Jesus, held their peace and made no manifestation upon Jesus's arrival. He entered the city quietly, and the disciples washed his feet outside the synagogue. The doctors of the Law and the people were already assembled inside. They received him coolly, though with some hypocritical demonstrations of respect, and permitted him to read aloud and interpret the scriptures. He opened at Isaiah 54–56, from which he read and explained some sentences, treating of God's establishing his church, of what it cost him to build it, of the obligation of all to drink of her waters and, though without money, to go and eat of her bread. Men, said Jesus, sought earnestly to satisfy their hunger in the synagogue, but no bread was there to be found. The Word come forth from the mouth of God—namely, the Messiah—should accomplish his work. In the kingdom of God, that is, in the church, strangers and Gentiles should, if they had faith, labor and bear fruit; Jesus called the Gentiles eunuchs because, unlike the patriarchs, they had not concurred in the lineage of the Messiah. He applied numerous texts of the prophet to his kingdom, to the church, and to heaven. He compared the Jewish teachers of his own day to mute dogs which, instead of keeping guard, think but of fattening themselves, of eating and drinking immoderately. By these words he meant the Herodians and Sadducees who, lurking in secret, attack people without barking, yes, even assault the pastors of the flock. Jesus's words were very sharp and incisive.

Toward the close of his discourse, he read from Deuteronomy 11:29, of the blessing upon Gerizim and the curse upon Hebal, and of many other things connected with the commandments and the Promised Land. These different passages Jesus applied to the kingdom of God.

One of the Herodians stepped up to him and very respectfully begged him to say a word upon the number of those that would enter his kingdom. They thought to entrap him by this question, because on the one side, all by circumcision had a share in the kingdom; and on the other, while rejecting many of the Jews, he had spoken even of Gentiles and eunuchs as having a part in it. Jesus did not give them a direct answer. He beat around and at last struck upon a point that made them forget their former question. To another question put to him, his answer consisted of a series of interrogations: How many of those that had wandered in the desert entered the land of Canaan? Nevertheless, had not all gone through the Jordan? How many really entered into possession of the land? Had they conquered it entirely, or were they not obliged to share it with the Gentiles? Would they not one day be chased out of it? Jesus added, moreover, that no one should enter into his kingdom excepting by the narrow way and the gate of the Spouse. I understood that by this were signified Mary and the church. In the church we are regenerated by baptism; from Mary was the Bridegroom born, in order that through her he might lead us into the church, and through the church to God. He contrasted entrance by the gate of the Spouse with entrance through a side door. It was a similitude like unto that of the Good Shepherd and the hireling (John 10:1, *et seq.*). He added that entrance is permitted only by the door. The words of Jesus on the cross before he died, when he called Mary the mother of John and John the son of Mary, have a mysterious connection with this regeneration of man through his death.

Not having succeeded that evening in ensnaring Jesus, his enemies resolved to postpone further attempts until the close of the sabbath. It is indeed wonderful! When Jesus's enemies were concocting their schemes, they could boast of how they would catch him and pin him down in his doctrine; but as soon as he presented himself before them, they could bring nothing against him; they were amazed and almost persuaded of the truth of his words, though at the same time full of rage.

Jesus quietly left the synagogue. They conducted him to a repast with one of the Pharisees, where, too, they could neither attack nor surprise him. He spoke here a parable of a feast to which the master of the house had invited the guests at a certain hour, after which the doors were closed and tardy comers were not admitted.

The repast over, Jesus went with the disciples to sleep at the house of another Pharisee, an upright man and an acquaintance of Andrew. He had honestly defended those disciples, among them Andrew, who, in consequence of what had happened at Passover, had been brought before the court of justice. He had lately become a widower. He was still young, and soon after he joined the disciples. His name was Dinocus, or Dinotus. His son, twelve years old, was called Josaphat. His house was to the west and outside the city. Jesus had come to Gennabris from the south. He had descended the cultivated neighboring heights of Dothaim, which lay more to the south than Gennabris, and then secretly turned back to the latter city. The Pharisee's house was on the west side, as I have said, while Nathaniel's was on the north toward Galilee.

I saw today that Herod, after John's judicial hearing, sent officers to the tumultuous people. They were commissioned to deal very gently with them, to tell them not to be disquieted on John's account, but peaceably to return to their homes. The officers assured them that John was very well and kindly treated. They said, moreover, that Herod had indeed changed his prisoner's cell, but it was only that he might have him nearer to himself. In disobeying the orders given them to disperse quietly, they might cast suspicion upon their master and render his imprisonment more painful. They should therefore go home at once, for he would soon resume his work of baptizing. The messengers from Jesus and John arrived just as Herod's officers were haranguing the crowd, and they too having delivered similar messages, the people scattered by degrees. But Herod was a prey to the greatest anxiety. The execution of the adulterers in Jerusalem had reminded the public of his own adulterous marriage. They murmured loudly over John's imprisonment for having spoken the truth and maintained the Law, according to which those poor criminals had been put to death in Jerusalem. Herod had moreover heard of Jesus's miracles and discourses in Galilee, and it had also reached his ears that he was now coming down to the Jordan to teach. He was in great dread lest the excited populace might thereby be still more stirred up. Under the influence of these feelings, I saw him calling a meeting of the Pharisees and Herodians, to deliberate upon some means of restraining Jesus. The result of the conference was that he sent eight of the members to give Jesus to understand in the most delicate manner possible that he should confine himself, his miracles, and his teaching to Upper Galilee and the far side of the lake; that he should not enter Herod's dominions in Galilee, and still less that part of the country around the Jordan under his jurisdiction. They were to intimidate him with the example of John, since Herod might easily feel himself constrained to make him share John's captivity. This commission started for Galilee that same day.

Saturday, August 26, AD 30 (*Elul 8*)

Jesus taught again this morning in the synagogue. Herod Antipas had sent some spies to Galilee to hear what Jesus was preaching. Jesus referred to them in these words: "When they come, you may tell the foxes (*spies*) *to take word back to that other fox* (*Herod*) *not to trouble himself about me. He may continue his wicked course and fulfill his designs with regard to John the Baptist. For the rest, I shall not be constrained by him. I shall continue to teach wherever I am sent in every region, and even in Jerusalem itself when the time comes. I shall fulfill my mission and account for it to my Father in heaven." That evening, after the close of the sabbath, Jesus was invited to a banquet to celebrate the completion of the harvest. He spoke of Isaiah 58:7* (*"Share your bread with the hungry, and bring the poor and homeless into your house. . . ."*) *and asked whether it was not customary to invite the poor to such feasts of thanksgiving. Jesus expressed this by saying: "Where are the poor?" Then he sent his disciples out to bring in the poor from the streets.*

Next morning Jesus again taught in the synagogue and without much contradiction, for his enemies had resolved to wait for the afternoon instruction, when they might attack him all together. He again chose his texts alternately from Isaiah and Deuteronomy. Occasion offered to speak of the worthy celebration of the sabbath, and he dwelt upon it at length. The sick of Gennabris had been so intimidated by the threats of the Herodians that they did not dare to implore Jesus to help them.

Jesus spoke also in the synagogue of the embassy sent by Herod to lie in wait to catch him in his speech. "When they come," said he, "ye may tell the foxes to take word back to that other fox not to trouble himself about me. He may continue his wicked course and fulfill his designs in John's regard. For the rest, I shall not be restrained by him. I shall continue to teach wherever I am sent in every region, and even in Jerusalem itself when the time comes. I shall fulfill my mission and account for it to my Father in heaven." His enemies were very much incensed at his words.

In the afternoon Jesus and the disciples left the house of Dinotus the Pharisee, to take a walk. When they reached the gate near which was Nathaniel's house, Andrew went in and called him out. He came and presented to Jesus his cousin, a very young man to whom he intended to resign his business in order to follow Jesus uninterruptedly. I think he attached himself to Jesus irrevocably at that time.

After their walk, they entered the city at the side upon which the synagogue was situated. About twelve poor day laborers, sick from hard work and privation, having heard of the cure of cases like their own effected by Jesus in the harvest field, had dragged themselves from the country to the city in the hope of receiving a similar favor. They had stationed themselves in a row outside the synagogue, ready to cry to Jesus for help as he passed. Jesus approached, and said to them in passing some words of comfort. To their entreaties to help them, he bade them have patience. Close behind him followed the doctors of the Law, who were enraged that these strangers had dared petition Jesus for a cure, since up to this time they had succeeded in restraining the sick of the city from a similar proceeding. They roughly repulsed the poor, miserable creatures, telling them under cloak of a good intention that they must not excite trouble and disturbance in the city; that they must take themselves off right away, for Jesus had important questions to treat with themselves; there was now no time for him to busy himself with them. And as the poor men could not retire quickly enough to suit their wishes, they had them removed by force.

In the synagogue Jesus taught chiefly of the sabbath and its sanctification. The commandment to that effect was contained in the passage from Isaiah read on that day. After teaching some time, he pointed to the deep moats around the city near which their asses were grazing, and asked: "If one of those asses should fall into a moat on the sabbath day, would ye venture to draw it out on the sabbath day in order to save its life?" They were silent. "Supposing it was a human being that fell in, would ye venture to help him out?" Still they were silent. "Would ye allow salvation of body and soul to be meted out to yourselves on the sabbath day? Would ye permit a work of mercy to be performed on the sabbath day?" Again they were silent. Then said Jesus: "Since ye are silent, I must take it for granted that ye have nothing to oppose to my doctrine. Where are those poor men who implored my help outside the synagogue? Bring them hither!" As they whom he addressed showed no inclination to obey, Jesus said: "Since ye will not execute my orders, I shall have recourse to my disciples." At these words, his enemies changed their minds, and sent messengers to seek for the sick men. Soon the poor creatures made their appearance, dragging in slowly. It was a pitiful sight. There were about twelve of them, some lame, and some so frightfully swollen with edema that even their puffed-up fingers stood wide apart from one another. They entered rejoicing and full of hope, although they had shortly before departed very sad, on account of the rebuff received from the doctors of the Law.

Jesus commanded them to stand in a line, and it was touching to see the less afflicted placing those worse than themselves in front, that Jesus might cure them first. Jesus descended a couple of steps and called the first up to him. Most of them were paralyzed in the arms. Jesus silently prayed over them, his eyes raised to heaven, and touched their arms, gently stroking them downward. Then he moved their hands up and down, and ordered them to step back and give thanks to God. They were cured. The dropsical could scarcely walk. Jesus laid his hand on their head and breast. Their strength instantly returned, they were able to retire briskly, and in a few days the water had entirely disappeared.

During this miraculous healing the people began to press forward in crowds, among them many other poor, sick creatures who, uniting their voices with those of the cured, proclaimed aloud the praises of God. The concourse was so great that the doctors of the Law, filled with shame and rage, had to give place to the people, and some of them even left the synagogue. Jesus went on instructing the multitude until the close of the sabbath. He spoke to them of the nearness of the kingdom, of penance and conversion. The scribes with all their opposition and cunning had not another word to say. It was extremely ridiculous to see those men, who had so loudly boasted to one another, not once daring to open their mouths. They could not in even the least thing carry their point against Jesus, they could not answer even his simplest question.

After the sabbath, a great banquet was spread in one of the public pleasure resorts of the city. It was intended to celebrate the close of the harvest, and Jesus with his disciples was invited. The guests were made up of the most distinguished citizens of the place, also many visitors to the city, and even some rich peasants. At several tables, laden with the products of the harvest, all kinds of fruit and grain and even poultry were eaten. Whatever had yielded an abundant crop was here represented with profusion. The flocks also yielded their share to the entertainment. Some of the animals were roasted ready to be eaten, while others were slaughtered and ready for cooking, as symbols of abundance.

The first places had been assigned to Jesus and his disciples, notwithstanding which a haughty Pharisee had put himself foremost. When Jesus went to the table, he asked him in a low voice how he had come by the place that he occupied. The Pharisee replied: "I am here because it is the praiseworthy custom of this city for the learned and distinguished to sit first." Jesus responded: "They that strive after the first places upon earth, shall have no place in the kingdom of my Father." The Pharisee, quite ashamed, resigned the seat for a lower one, though at the same time he tried to make it appear that he did so on an inspiration of his own. During the repast Jesus spoke of some things regarding the sabbath, especially of that passage of Isaiah 58:7: "Deal thy bread to the hungry, and bring the needy and the harborless into thy house," and asked whether it was not customary at such feasts, feasts of thanksgiving for a plentiful harvest, to invite the poor as guests and let them take part. He expressed his surprise at their having omitted that custom. "Where," he asked, "are the poor?" "Since," he continued, "ye have invited me, have given me the first place, have made me the Master of your feast, it behooves me to see about the guests that have a right to be present. Go, call in those people that I cured, and bring all the rest of the poor!" But as they were in no hurry to fulfill Jesus's commands, his disciples hastened out and collected the poor in all the streets. They soon came trooping in, and Jesus and the disciples gave up their seats to them, while the scribes, one by one, slipped out of the hall. Jesus, the disciples, and some right-minded people among the guests served the poor at table. When their meal was over, they divided among them all that was left, to the great joy of the recipients. Then Jesus and his followers returned to the house of Dinotus the Pharisee on the west side of the city, and there rested.

Sunday, August 27, AD 30 (Elul 9)

This morning, Jesus healed many people in Gennabris. In the afternoon, he and his disciples set off in a southerly direction and stayed overnight in an empty shed not far from Ulama.

The next day crowds of sick from Gennabris itself and from the country around came to the house at which Jesus was staying, and he devoted the whole morning to their cure. They were mostly paralyzed in their hands and dropsical. The son of the Pharisee Dinotus, at whose house Jesus was stopping, was about twelve years old, and was named Josaphat. When his father gave up all to follow Jesus, he accompanied him. The Jewish boys wore a long tunic pierced on both sides, buttoned in front and laced down to the feet. When more grown, they exchanged the long tunic for a shorter one like those of their elders, and bound their limbs in something like pantaloons. When the boys' tunic was girded at the waist, it hung in gathers; but it was usually worn flowing like a loose shirt, though often it was tucked up a little. When Jesus took leave of Dinotus, he pressed him to his heart, and the man shed many tears.

Jesus with Nathaniel, Andrew, James, Saturnin, Aristobulus, Tharzissus, Parmenas, and about four other disciples, went between two to three hours southward through the valleys. They spent the night under an empty shed belonging to the harvesters, on a declivity between two cities. The one on the left was called Ulama; that to the right was, I think, named Japhia. The distance between Ulama and Tarichea was about the same as between Gennabris and Tiberias. The city to the right was less elevated than Bethulia, and was at a good distance from it, but to one far away, the mountain between them not being visible, Bethulia appeared to rise above and directly behind Japhia. The locality seemed to lie quite near to Jesus's route as he journeyed along, but the road soon made a bend that hid it from sight.

That field in which Jesus instructed the harvesters was the very same in which Joseph met his brethren with their herds, and the long four-cornered well the same into which he was let down.

(Follow Map 20)

Jesus in Abel-Mehola

Monday, August 28, AD 30 (Elul 10)

Continuing southward, Jesus and the disciples arrived around two o'clock this afternoon at Abel-Mehola. Here he healed many sick people. This was frowned upon by the disapproving Pharisees.

NEXT morning, Jesus left the shed under which he had passed the night, and journeyed with his disciples about five hours to the south. It was almost two o'clock when they reached the little city Abel-Mehola, where the prophet Elisha was born. It lay on one of the heights of Mount Hermon, its towers rising to the summit of the mountain ridge. It was only a couple of hours from Scythopolis, and to the west ran the valley of Jezreel. With the city of Jezreel itself, Abel-Mehola lay in a straight line. Not far from Abel-Mehola, and nearer the Jordan, was the town of Bezek.

Samaria was several hours to the southwest. Abel-Mehola was in or upon the confines of Samaria, but inhabited by Jews.

Jesus and his disciples sat down on the resting place outside the city, as travelers in Palestine were accustomed to do. Hospitable people from the city used then to take them to their houses for entertainment. And thus it happened now. Some people going by recognized Jesus. They had seen him once before when he was journeying through these parts at the Feast of Tabernacles. They hurried into the city and spread the news. Soon out came a well-to-do peasant with his servants, bringing to Jesus and the disciples bread and honey and something to drink. He invited them into his house, and they followed him. They having arrived there, he washed their feet and provided them with fresh garments while their own were being shaken and brushed. Then he ordered a repast straightaway to be prepared, and to it he invited several Pharisees with whom he was on good terms. They soon made their appearance. The host showed himself hospitable and friendly to a degree, though he was a rascal in disguise. He wanted to be able to boast before the people of the city that he had entertained the prophet in his house, and to offer to the Pharisees an opportunity to probe Jesus. They thought they could do that better when alone with him at table than in the synagogue before the people.

But hardly was the table set when all the sick of the place, all that were able to be moved, appeared before the house and gathered together in the courtyard—to the great displeasure of the owner, as well as of the Pharisees. The former hurried out to drive them away, but Jesus, turning from the table with the words: "I have other food after which my soul hungers," followed, his disciples after him, and began curing the sick. There were among them several possessed who set up a shout after Jesus. He cured them with a glance and a word of command. Many others were lame in one or both hands.

Jesus passed his hand down their arms and raised them up and down. On the head and breast of the dropsical he laid his hand. Others were consumptive, others were covered with small, though not infectious sores. Some he ordered to bathe. To others he commanded certain works, and told them that they would be perfectly well in a few days. Far in the background, and leaning against the wall for support, stood several women afflicted with an issue of blood. They were veiled and, in their shame, ventured only now and then to cast a sidelong glance toward Jesus. When they raised a fold of their veil for this purpose, the countenance disclosed bore signs of suffering. At last Jesus approached them, touched and cured them, and they cast themselves at his feet.

The whole crowd set up shouts of joy and intoned hymns of thanksgiving. The Pharisees inside had closed all the doors and windows of the house. They sat down to table vexed and disappointed, but jumped up from time to time to peep through the lattice. The work of healing went on for so long that, when they wanted to go home, they were forced to pass through the courtyard filled with the sick, the cured, and the exulting crowd. The sight stabbed them to the very heart. The crowd became at last so great that Jesus had to take refuge in the house until they had dispersed.

It was already dusk when five Levites presented themselves to invite Jesus and the disciples to pass the night in the schoolhouse over which they presided. The guests of the pharisaical peasant took leave of him with thanks for his hospitality. Jesus gave him a short exhortation before leaving, and made use of an expression similar to those he had used among the Herodians, something about foxes. But the man preserved his friendly exterior. Jesus and the disciples partook of a little luncheon in the schoolhouse. They slept in a long corridor on which carpets had been spread, their couches separated from one another by movable screens. There was a boys' school in one part of the building, and in another, young pagan girls desirous of embracing Judaism received thorough instruction. This school was in existence even in Jacob's time.

When Jacob was persecuted in diverse ways by Esau, Rebecca sent him secretly to Abel-Mehola where he owned herds and servant, and dwelt in tents. Rebecca established there a school for the young Canaanite girls and other Gentile maidens. Like Esau, his children, his servants, and others of Isaac's family intermarried with these Gentiles. Rebecca, who held such alliances in abhorrence, had the young girls that desired it instructed in this school in the customs and religion of Abraham. The ground on which the school was built belonged to her.

Jacob long remained hidden at Abel-Mehola. When Rebecca was questioned as to his whereabouts, she used to answer that he was far away herding flocks for strangers. At times he returned secretly to see her, but on Esau's account she had to keep him hidden. Jacob dug a well near Abel-Mehola, the same by which Jesus had been seated before entering the city. The people held it in great reverence and always kept it covered. He had also made a cistern in the neighborhood. It was long, four-cornered, and had a flight of steps leading down into it. Later on, Jacob's abode became known. Rebecca noticed that, like Esau, her younger son was likely to espouse a Canaanite wife, so she and Isaac sent him to her native place to his Uncle Laban, where he served for Rachel and Leah.

Rebecca had established the school so far from her own

Map 20: Journeys in Perea and Gileaditis

August 27–September 27, AD 30

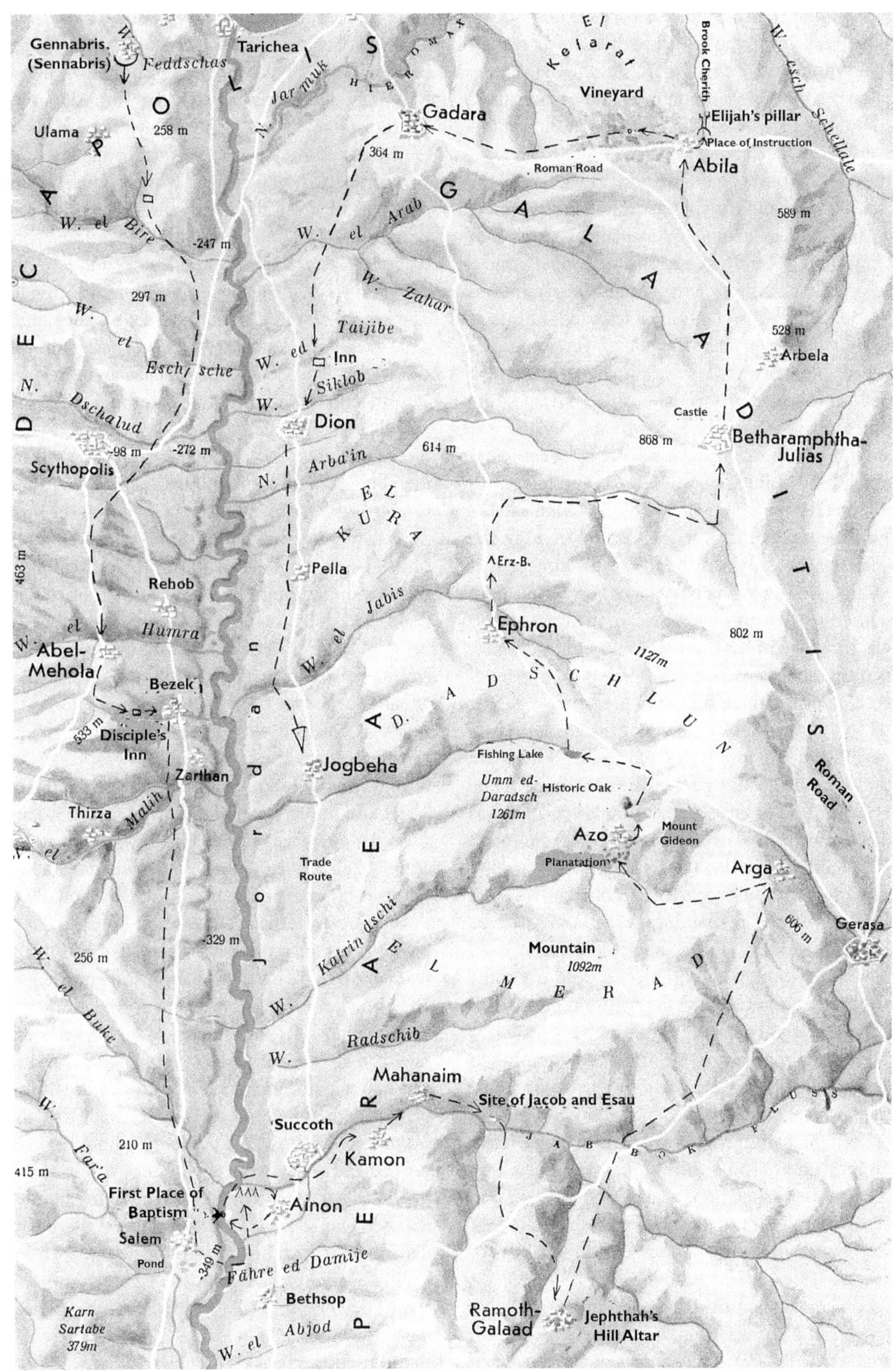

Gennabris—Abel-Mehola—Bezeck—Ainon—Mahanaim—Ramoth-Gilead—Arga—Azo-Ephron
Betharamphtha-Julias—Abila—Gadara—Dion—Jogbeha

home in the land of Heth because Isaac had so many quarrels with the Philistines, who did all in their power to ruin him. She had confided the direction of the school to a man from her own country, Mesopotamia, and to her nurse who, I think, was his wife. The young girls dwelt in tents and were instructed in all that a wife in a migratory household of the pastoral times ought to know. They learned the religion of Abraham and the special duties of wives of his race. They had gardens in which they planted all kinds of running vines, such as gourds, melons, cucumbers, and a kind of grain. They had very large sheep whose milk was used for food. They were taught also to read, but this as well as writing came very hard to them. The writing of those days was done in a very strange way on thick brown tablets, not on rolls of skin as in later times, but upon the bark of trees. I saw them peeling it off, and burning the letters into it. They had a little box full of zigzag compartments, which I saw shining on the surface, and filled with all kinds of metal signs. These the writer heated in a flame and burnt one after another into the bark tablet. I saw the fire in which they heated the metal. It was the same as that used for boiling, roasting, and baking, also for giving light. Upon seeing it used in this last way, I thought: "They do indeed place their light here under a bushel." In a vessel, whose form reminded me of the headdress that many of the pagan idols wore, there burned a black mass. A hole was bored in the middle of it, for the passage of air, perhaps. The little round towers encircling the vessel were hollow, and into them some part of the cooking could be placed. Over the pan of coals, something like a cover was turned upside down. It was tapering toward the top and pierced by a number of holes. On this, too, was a circle of little towers in which things could be warmed. All around this bushel-like cover were openings with sliding screens. When they wanted light, all they had to do was to open one of these little windows and the glare from the flame shone forth. They always opened them toward the quarter from which no draught came, a precaution very necessary in tents. Below the coal pan, was a little place for ashes in which they could bake flat cakes, and on top of the whole arrangement water could be boiled in shallow vessels. This they drew off for bathing, washing, and cooking. They could also broil and roast on these stoves. They were thin and light, could be carried on journeys, and easily moved from place to place. It was over such stoves that the metal letters were heated before being burnt into the tablets of bark.

The people of Canaan had black hair and were darker than Abraham and his countrymen, who were of a ruddy, olive complexion. The costume of the Canaanite women was different from that of the daughters of Israel. They wore a wide tunic of yellow wool down to the knee. It consisted of four pieces which could be drawn together by a running string below the knee, thus forming a kind of wide pantalet. It was not bound around the upper part of the limbs like that of the Jewish women, but its wide folds fell front and back from the waist to the knee. The upper part of the body was covered with a similarly doubled lappet that fell over the breast and back. The pieces were bound together on the shoulders, forming a sort of wide scapular, likewise open on both sides and fastened around the waist with a belt, above which it hung loose like a sack. The whole costume from shoulder to knee looked like a wide sack bound at the waist and ending abruptly below the latter. The feet were sandaled and the lower limbs wound crosswise with straps, through the openings of which the skin could be seen. The arms were covered with pieces of fine, transparent stuff which, by several shining metal rings, were formed into a sleeve. They wore on the head a pointed cap of little feathers, from the top of which hung something like the crest of a helmet ending in a large tuft. These people were beautiful and well-made, but much more ignorant than the children of Israel. Some of them had long mantles also, narrow above and wide below. The women of Israel wore over a kind of bandage wrapped around the body a long tunic, and lastly a long gown fastened in front with buttons. They wound their heads in a veil or with several rows of ruffs, such as are worn nowadays around the neck.

I saw that they studied in Rebecca's time the religion of Abraham: the creation of the world, about Adam and Eve and their entrance into Paradise, Eve's seduction by Satan, and the Fall of the first man and woman by their violation of the abstinence commanded them by God. By the eating of the forbidden fruit arose sinful appetites in man. The young girls were taught also that Satan had promised our first parents a divine illumination and knowledge, but that after sin they were blinded. A film was drawn over their eyes; they lost the gift of vision they had possessed. Now they had to labor in the sweat of their brow, bring forth children in pain, and with difficulty acquire the knowledge of which they had need. They learned, too, that to the woman a son was promised who should crush the serpent's head. They were taught about Abel and Cain and the latter's descendants, who became degenerate and wicked. The sons of God, seduced by the beauty of the daughters of men, formed unions with them from which sprang a mighty, godless race of giants, powerful in enchantment and the art of magic, a race that discovered and taught to others all kinds of pleasure and false wisdom, all that buried the soul in sin and tore it away from God, a race that had so seduced and corrupted men that God resolved to destroy them all with the exception of Noah and his family. This people had fixed their principal abode on a high mountain range up which they ever pressed higher and higher. But in the Deluge that mountain was submerged, and a sea now covers its site. They (the scholars of Rebecca's school) learned also all about the Deluge, about Noah's escape in the ark, about Shem, Ham, and Japhet, about Ham's sin, and the reiterated wickedness of men at the Tower of Babel. They were told of the building of that Tower, of its destruction, of the confusion of tongues, and of the dispersion of men now become enemies to one another. All this recalled to the youthful minds of the scholars the impiety of the giants on that high mountain, those wicked, powerful men, those dealers in witchcraft, and they saw the fatal consequences of unions forbidden by the Law of God. Necromancy and idolatry were practiced likewise at the Tower of Babel.

By such teachings were the converted Gentile maidens warned against alliances with idolaters, idle efforts after necromancy and the hidden arts, against the seductions of the world, sensual delights, vain adornments—in a word, against all that did not lead to God. They were taught to look upon such things as tending to those sins on whose account God had once destroyed humankind. They were, on the other hand, instructed in the fear of God, obedience, subjection, and in the faithful, simple exercise of all duties devolving upon the pastoral life. They were also taught the Commandments that God gave to Noah, for instance, abstinence from uncooked meat. They learned of God's having made choice of the race of Abraham, to make of his descendants his chosen people from whom the Redeemer was to be born. For this purpose he had called Abraham from the land of Ur, and had set him apart from the infidel races. They were told of God's sending white men to Abraham, that is, men who appeared white and luminous. These men had confided to Abraham the mystery of God's Blessing, owing to which his posterity was to be great above all the nations of the earth. The transmitting of that mystery they referred to only in general terms, as of a Blessing from which Redemption should spring. They were told also about Melchizedek's being a white man like those sent to Abraham, of his sacrifice of bread and wine, and of his blessing Abraham. The chastisement inflicted by God upon Sodom and Gomorrha formed a part of the instruction given.

Tuesday, August 29, AD 30 (Elul 11)

Jesus and his disciples visited a school for orphans in Abel-Mehola, where he told the children the story of Job as it actually took place. (According to Anne Catherine, Job was Abraham's great-great-great-grand-father.) Jesus spent the whole day with the children and took an evening walk with them. In the house at which Jesus put up there was also a boys' school. It was a kind of orphanage, an institution for the education of children abandoned by their parents.

When Jesus visited the school, the young girls were computing a chronological table upon the coming of the Messiah. All agreed in their reckoning, which brought the result down to their own time. Just at that moment, in stepped Jesus and his disciples, a circumstance that produced a very powerful impression upon the scholars. Jesus took up the subject then engrossing their attention, and explained to them with the utmost clearness that the Messiah was already come, though not yet recognized. He spoke of the unknown Messiah, and of the signs that were to herald his coming, and that had already been fulfilled. Of the words: "A virgin shall bring forth a son," Jesus spoke only in veiled terms, since those children were too young to comprehend them. He exhorted them to rejoice that they lived in a time after which the patriarchs and prophets had so long sighed. He dwelt upon the persecutions and sufferings the Messiah was to endure, and explained some texts of prophecy to that effect. He told them to be on the watch for what would take place in Jericho at the approaching Feast of Tabernacles. He spoke of miracles, and particularly of the curing of the blind. He made for them also a chronology of the Messiah, spoke of John and of the baptism, asked whether they too wanted to be baptized, and, lastly, related to them the parable of the lost drachma.

The girls sat in school cross-legged, sometimes with one knee raised. Each was provided with a kind of table and bench combined. She leaned sideways against the one, and when writing, supported her roll on the other. They often stood while listening to the instruction given them.

There were some of Jewish parentage who had been rescued from slavery, in which they had grown up without instruction in the religion of their forefathers. Both Pharisees and Sadducees taught in the school. Little girls also were received, the youngest of whom received instruction from the older ones.

At the moment of Jesus's entrance into this school, the boys were making some calculation connected with Job. As they could not readily do it, Jesus explained it and wrote it down for them in letters. He also explained to them something relating to measure, two hours of distance or time, I do not now know which. He explained much of the Book of Job. Some of the rabbis at this period attacked the truth of the history therein contained, since the Edomites, to which race Herod belonged, bantered and ridiculed the Jews for accepting as true the history of a man of the land of Edom, although in that land no such man was ever known to exist. They looked upon the whole story as a mere fable, gotten up to encourage the Israelites under their afflictions in the desert. Jesus related Job's history to the boys as if it had really happened. He did so in the manner of a prophet and catechist, as if he saw all passing before him, as if it were his own history, as if he heard and saw everything connected with it, or as if Job himself had told it to him. His hearers knew not what to think. Who was this man that now addressed them? Was he one of Job's contemporaries? Or was he an angel of God? Or was he God himself? But the boys did not wonder long about it, for they soon felt that Jesus was a prophet, and they associated him with Melchizedek, of whom they had heard and of whose origin man knows not. Jesus spoke likewise of the signification of salt. He made it clear by a parable, and related that of the prodigal son. The Pharisees arrived during Jesus's instructions, and were highly displeased to find him applying to himself all the signs and prophecies quoted by him in reference to the Messiah.

That evening Jesus went with the Levites and the children to take a walk outside the city. The little girls followed last, in the charge of the older ones. Jesus, letting the boys go on ahead, stood still from time to time until these little ones came up, and then instructed them in examples drawn from nature, from all the objects around them, the trees, fruits, flowers, bees, birds, sun, earth, water, flocks, and field labors. In indescribably beautiful words, he next taught the boys about Jacob and the well that he had dug in that locality. He told them that now the living water was about to be poured upon them, and how perfidious a thing it was to fill up, choke up the well, as the enemies of Abraham and Jacob had done. He applied it to those that wanted to suppress the doctrine and miracles of the prophets, namely, the Pharisees.

Wednesday, August 30, AD 30 (Elul 12)

This morning, Jesus taught in the synagogue. Here some Pharisees and Sadducees disputed with him. He also healed a man whose arms and hands were paralyzed. During the afternoon and evening, Jesus performed more cures.

When on the following morning Jesus went to the synagogue, he found there all the Pharisees and Sadducees of the place, as also a great concourse of people. He opened the scriptures and expounded the prophets. Some of the Pharisees and Sadducees obstinately disputed with him, but he put them all to shame. A man whose arms and hands were paralyzed had meantime been slowly making his way to the door of the synagogue. He had been so long trying, and had at last succeeded in getting a position by which Jesus must pass on going out. One of the Pharisees eyed the poor creature with displeasure, and ordered him away. As he refused to obey, they tried to push him out. But he supported himself as well as he could against the door and looked piteously at Jesus, who was on a high seat at a considerable distance from the entrance and separated from him by an immense crowd. Jesus turned toward him and said: "What do you desire of me?" The man answered: "Master, I implore thee to cure me. Thou canst do it, if thou wilt!" Jesus replied: "Thy faith hath saved thee. Stretch forth thy hands above the people," and in that moment the man was healed at a distance. He raised up his hands praising God. Then Jesus said: "Go home, and raise no excitement!" But the man replied: "Master, how can I be silent on so great a benefit?" and he went out and told it to all that he met. And now crowds of sick gathered before the synagogue, and Jesus cured them as he passed out. After that he dined with the Pharisees who, in spite of their inward displeasure, always treated him courteously. This was part of their policy, that they might the more easily entrap him. He performed more cures that evening.

Jesus Goes from Abel-Mehola to Bezek

Thursday, August 31, AD 30 (Elul 13)

After revisiting the children at the school in Abel-Mehola, Jesus and his disciples made their way to Bezek. Many disciples from Ainon and Jerusalem met up with Jesus in Bezek. Altogether about thirty disciples were present.

NEXT morning found Jesus still at the school of Abel-Mehola. He was quite surrounded by the little girls who crowded close upon him, holding on to his garments and clasping his hand. He was unspeakably kind to them, and exhorted them to obedience and the fear of God. The larger ones stood back. The disciples present were somewhat annoyed and uneasy. They were anxious for their Master to take his departure. According to their Jewish notions, such familiarity with children was not becoming in a prophet, and they feared it would injure his reputation.

Jesus did not trouble himself about their thoughts. After he had instructed all the children, addressed some exhortations to the larger ones, and encouraged their teachers in their good resolutions, he directed one of the disciples to give the little girls a present, and each in effect received two small coins fastened together. I think they were two drachmas. Then Jesus blessed them all in general and left the place with the disciples, starting eastward toward the Jordan.

During the journey Jesus taught in a field before some huts where a crowd of laborers and shepherds had gathered. About four o'clock that afternoon they reached the neighborhood of Bezek about two hours east of Abel-Mehola and near the Jordan. It was like two distinct cities, lying as it did on both sides of a stream that flowed into the Jordan. The country around was hilly and rugged; the houses stood somewhat scattered. Bezek was less a city than two united villages. The inhabitants lived to themselves with very little contact with strangers. They were chiefly engaged in husbandry, and they leveled their rugged and hilly farmlands with great labor. They also manufactured agricultural implements for sale, and wove coarse carpets and canvas for tents.

About an hour and a half from this place, the Jordan made a bend toward the west, as if about to flow straight to the Mount of Olives. It turned back, however, thus forming a kind of peninsula on its eastern bank, upon which stood a row of houses. In coming from Galilee to Abel-Mehola, Jesus had to cross a little river. Ainon was on the opposite side of the Jordan, about four hours, perhaps, from Bezek.

Jesus taught in an inn outside the city, the first of those erected for his and the disciples' accommodation that he had met on this journey since leaving Bethany. It was in the charge of a pious, upright man, who went out to meet the travelers, washed their feet and gave them refreshments, after which Jesus entered the city. The superintendents of the school came out into the street to receive him, and he visited several houses and cured the sick.

There were now thirty disciples with Jesus. Those from Jerusalem and its environs had arrived with Lazarus, and several of John's disciples had come. Some of the latter were just from Machaerus with a message to Jesus from their master, a pressing request to reveal himself more clearly and to say only that he was the Messiah. Among these messengers of John was the son of the widower Cleophas. I think he was Cleophas of Emmaus, a relative of Cleophas, the husband of Mary's eldest sister. Another of these disciples was Joseph Barsabbas, related to Zechariah of Hebron. His parents, though living now in Cana, had once dwelt in Nazareth. Among these disciples of John I still recall others. The sons of Mary Heli, the eldest sister of the blessed Virgin, were John's disciples. They were born so long after their sister Mary Cleophas that they were scarcely older than her sons. They clung to the Baptist until he was beheaded, and then joined the disciples of Jesus.

The married couple who directed the inn at Bezek were good, devout people. They observed continence by virtue of a vow, although they were not Essenes. They were distant relatives of the holy family. During his stay here, Jesus had several private interviews with these good people.

All the friends and disciples ate and slept with Jesus in the newly erected inn. They found ready for them, thanks to the forethought of Lazarus and the holy women, table furniture, covers, carpets, beds, screens, and even sandals and other articles of clothing. Martha had near the desert of Jericho a house full of women whom she kept busy preparing all these things. She had gathered together many poor widows and penniless girls, who were striving to lead a good life. There they lived and worked together. All was carried on quietly and unknown to the public. It was no little thing to provide for so many inns and so many people and to superintend them constantly—above all, to send messengers around to them, or give them personal attention.

Friday, September 1, AD 30 (Elul 14)

In the morning, Jesus taught on a hill in the middle of Bezek and, later in the day, he healed many people. That evening, he taught in the synagogue as the sabbath began.

Next morning Jesus delivered a long and magnificent discourse on a hill in the middle of the city, where the inhabitants had erected for him a teacher's chair. The crowd was great, and among them were about ten Pharisees who had come from the places around with the intention of catching Jesus in his words. His teaching here was mild and full of love, for the people, who were well disposed, had profited by John's visit and instructions, and especially by the baptism which many of them had received. Jesus exhorted them to remain contented with their humble condition, to be industrious, and to show mercy to their neighbor. He spoke of the reign of grace, of the kingdom, of the Messiah, and more significantly than ever of himself. He alluded to John and his testimony, to his imprisonment and the persecution directed against him. He spoke likewise of the royal adulterer for the denunciation of whom John had been cast into prison, though in Jerusalem certain men guilty of the same crime, but who had carried on their evil doings less openly than Herod, had been condemned and executed. Jesus spoke significantly and to the point. He gave particular admonitions to each condition, age, and sex. A Pharisee having asked whether he was going to take John's place, or whether he was the one of whom John had spoken, Jesus answered indirectly and reproached the questioner with his evil intention to entrap him.

After that Jesus gave a very touching instruction to the boys and girls. He counseled the boys to bear with one another. If one should strike a companion or throw him down, the ill-treated party should bear it patiently and think not of retaliating. He should turn away in silence, forgiving his enemy, and his love should become twice as great as it was before, yes, for they should show affection even to enemies. They should not covet the goods of others. If a boy wanted the pen, the writing materials, the plaything, the fruit belonging to his neighbor, the latter should relinquish not only the object coveted, but give him still more if allowed to do so. They should fully satisfy their neighbor's cupidity if permitted to give the things away, for only the patient, the loving, and the generous should have a seat in his kingdom. This seat Jesus described to them in childlike terms as a beautiful throne.

He spoke of earthly goods which a man must give up in order to attain those of heaven. Among other admonitions to the girls, he warned them not to seek to excel others, not to envy others for their fine clothes, but to be gentle and obedient, to love their parents and fear God.

At the close of the public instruction, Jesus turned to his disciples, consoled them with more than ordinary tenderness, and exhorted them to bear all things with him and not to be preoccupied with the cares of this world. He promised that they should be richly rewarded by their Father in heaven and, with himself, should possess the kingdom. He spoke to them of the persecutions that he and they would have to suffer, and said plainly: "If the Pharisees, the Sadducees, or the Herodians should love or praise ye, it would be a sign that ye had wandered from my teachings and were no longer my disciples." He mentioned those sects with significant nicknames. Then he praised the people of the place, particularly for their charitable compassion, for they often took poor orphans from the school at Abel-Mehola into their service. He congratulated them on the new synagogue they had built by contribution, in which some of the devout souls of Capernaum also had joined. Then he cured many of their sick, took a repast with all the disciples at the inn, and in the evening when the sabbath began, went to the synagogue.

Jesus taught in the synagogue from Isaiah 51:12, "I myself will comfort you." He spoke against merely human respect, telling them that they should not fear the Pharisees and other oppressors, but remember that God had created them and preserved them till the present. He explained the words: "I have put my words in thy mouth," to mean that God had sent the Messiah, that this Messiah was God's Word in the mouth of his people, that this Messiah gave utterance to God's Word, and that they themselves were God's people. Jesus applied all this so clearly to himself that the Pharisees whispered among themselves that he was palming himself off for the Messiah. Then he said that Jerusalem should awaken from her intoxication, for the hour of wrath had passed and that of grace had dawned. The unfruitful synagogue had given birth to not one that could lead and raise up the poor people, but now should sinners, hypocrites, and oppressors be chastised and oppressed in their turn. Jerusalem should arise, Zion should awaken! Jesus applied all in a spiritual sense to the pious and holy, to the penitent, to those that through the Jordan—that is, through baptism—should go into the Promised Land of Canaan, into the kingdom of his Father. The uncircumcised, the impure, the licentious, the sinful should no longer corrupt the people. He taught of Redemption and of the Name of God, which should now be announced among them. Then from Deuteronomy 16, 17, and 18, he spoke of judges and public officers, of prevarication and bribery, and inveighed vehemently against the Pharisees. After that he cured many sick outside the synagogue.

Saturday, September 2, AD 30 (*Elul 15*)

Jesus taught in the synagogue until the close of the sabbath. That evening he healed many who were sick, and then dined with his disciples.

The next day Jesus again taught in the synagogue, taking his texts from Isaiah 51 and 52, and from Deuteronomy 16–21. He spoke of John and the Messiah. He gave signs by which the latter might be recognized, and they were different from those by which he usually designated him. He said plainly that he himself was the Messiah, for many of his hearers were already, through the teaching of John, well prepared for the announcement. Jesus based this part of his discourse upon Isaiah 52:13–15. He said: "The Messiah will gather ye together. He will be full of wisdom, he will be exalted and glorified. Many of ye have shuddered at the thought of Jerusalem's being laid waste and desolate under the rule of the Gentiles, and in like manner will your Redeemer be persecuted and despised by men. He will be a man without repute among other men. And yet he will baptize, will purify the Gentiles. He will teach kings, who will be silent before him, and they to whom he has not been announced will both hear of him and see him." Then Jesus recounted all that he had done, all the miracles he had wrought since his baptism, the persecution he had undergone at Jerusalem and Nazareth, the contempt he had endured, the spying and scornful laughter of the Pharisees. He alluded to the miracle at Cana, to the healing of the blind, the mute, the deaf, the lame, and to the raising from the dead of the daughter of Jairus of Phasael. Pointing in the direction of Phasael, he said: "It is not very far from here. Go and ask whether I say the truth!" Then he continued: "Ye have seen and known John. He proclaimed himself the precursor of the Messiah, the preparer of his ways! Was John an effeminate man, one given to the softness and delicacy of high life? Was he not rather reared in the wilderness? Did he dwell in palaces? Did he eat of costly dishes? Did he wear fine clothing? Did he make use of flattering words? But he called himself the precursor—then did not the servant wear the livery of his Lord? Would a king, a rich, a glorious, a powerful king such as ye expect your Messiah to be, have such a precursor? And yet ye have the Redeemer in your midst, and ye will not recognize him. He is not such as your pride would have him, he is not such as ye are yourselves, therefore ye will not acknowledge him!"

Jesus then turned to Deuteronomy 18:18–19: "I will raise them up a prophet out of the midst of their brethren.... And he that will not hear his words, which he shall speak in my name, I will be the revenger," and he delivered a powerful discourse upon these texts. No one dared oppose a word to his teaching. He said: "John lived solitary in the desert. He mingled not with men, and ye blamed the life he led. I go from place to place, I teach, I heal, and that too ye blame! What kind of a Messiah do ye want? Each one would like to have a Messiah according to his own ideas! Ye resemble children running in the streets. Each makes for himself the instrument he likes best. One brings forth low, bass notes from the horn he has twisted out of bark, and another screeches high on his flute of reeds." Then Jesus named all kinds of playthings used by children, saying that his hearers were like the owners of those toys. Each wanted to sing upon his own note, each was pleased with his own toy alone.

Toward evening, when Jesus left the synagogue, he found a great crowd of sick waiting for him outside. Some were lying on litters over which awnings had been stretched. Jesus, followed by his disciples, went from one to the other, curing them. Here and there appeared some poor possessed, raging and crying after him. He delivered them as he passed, and commanded them to be silent. There were paralytics, consumptives, the deaf, the mute, and the dropsical with tumors or scrofulous swellings on their neck. Jesus healed all, one after the other, by the imposition of hands, though his manner and touch were different in different cases. Some were entirely cured at once, a little weakness alone remaining; others were greatly relieved, the perfect cure following quickly according to the nature of the malady and the dispositions of the invalid. The cured moved away chanting a psalm of David. But there were so many sick that Jesus could not go around among them all. The disciples lent their aid in raising, supporting, and extricating them from their wrappings and covers. At last Jesus laid his hands on the head of Andrew, of John, and of Joseph Barsabbas, took their hands into his own, and commanded them to go and, in his name, do to some of the sick as he had done. They instantly obeyed and cured many.

After that, Jesus and the disciples returned to the inn, where they took a repast at which no stranger was present. Jesus blessed the food. A great part of it was left, and this he sent to the poor pagans encamped outside Bezek and to the other poor. The disciples had instructed the pagans belonging to the caravans.

Immense multitudes had assembled in Bezek from both shores of the Jordan. All that had heard John were now eager to hear Jesus. The pagan caravans, though on their way to Ainon, had come hither to hear him. Bezek was about three-quarters of an hour from the Jordan, on a swiftly flowing stream which divided the city into two parts.

Jesus Leaves Bezek and Goes to Ainon • Mara of Suphan

Sunday, September 3, AD 30 (Elul 16)

Jesus and the disciples made their way to the Jordan, which they crossed with the ferry near Salem. They stayed the night in tents between Succoth and Ainon.

JESUS still taught and cured in the country around the inn. The neophytes, the pagan caravan, and many others took their way to the Jordan with the intention of crossing. The ferry was an hour and a half to the south of Bezek, below a city called Zarthan, which was one hour's distance from the first named, and lower down on the Jordan. On the opposite side of the river, between Bezek and Zarthan, was a place called Adam. It was near that city of Zarthan that the Jordan had ceased to flow while the children of Israel were crossing. Solomon once had some vases cast here. That industry was still carried on. West of the bend that the Jordan makes in this neighborhood was a mountain extending off to Samaria, and in it was a mine from which was obtained a metal something like that which we call brass. Jesus taught all along the route. When questioned as to whether he intended to teach in Zarthan, he answered: "There are other localities that need it more. John was often there, so ye may ask the people whether he feasted and lived on dainty fare." The Jordan was here crossed by a great ferry, just below which began the detour of the river toward the west. After crossing, Jesus and his followers went on for about two hours eastward and along the northern bank of a little stream that flowed into the Jordan somewhere below the ferry. Then they crossed another stream near which lay Succoth to their left, looking as if they had just stepped over it. They rested under tents between Succoth and Ainon, which places may have been about four hours apart. If they had again crossed the river and gone up a little distance, they could have seen Salem, which was hidden from them by the hilly bank. It was opposite Ainon, and somewhat below the middle of another bend of the Jordan westward.

Monday, September 4, AD 30 (Elul 17)

This morning, in Ainon, Jesus healed many people. Then, toward midday, he went to the place of baptism, where he taught and also prepared those waiting to be baptized. Around three o'clock in the afternoon he returned to Ainon and went to the home of Mara the Suphanite, to exorcise her (she was possessed) and to forgive her sins. After, at a festive meal held in honor of Jesus, Mara the Suphanite and her three children entered and presented Jesus with costly spices.

Crowds innumerable were collected at Ainon. The pagans were encamped between the hill upon which it was built, and the Jordan. There were ten Pharisees present, some from Ainon, some from other places, among them the son of Simeon of Bethany. Some of them were reasonable enough and animated by upright intentions.

The little city of Ainon lay on the north side of the hill, as if built up entirely of beautiful villas. On this side and beyond the city was the source of the basin destined for baptism, which was on the east side of the hill. The stream was conducted through the hill in metal pipes, which could be closed and opened when needed. There was a springhouse over the source.

The Pharisees, among them the son of Simon the leper, came out to this place to meet Jesus and the disciples. They welcomed them cordially and politely, led them into a tent, washed their feet, brushed their garments, and presented them refreshments of honey, bread, and wine. Jesus congratulated them on the good dispositions of many among them though, as he said, it grieved him that they belonged to that sect. He accompanied them to the city, where he soon came to a court in which a crowd of sick of all kinds, some natives of the city, some strangers, were awaiting his arrival. Some were lying under tents, others were in the halls that opened into the court. Many could walk, and Jesus helped them one after another with imposition of hands and words of admonition. The disciples assisted in bringing the sick forward, in raising them and freeing them from their covers, etc. The Pharisees and many others were present. Several women stood at a distance, pale and enveloped in their mantles. They were afflicted with an issue of blood. When Jesus had finished with the rest, he approached them, laid his hands upon them, and cured them. Among the sick were paralytics and edemic; consumptives, some with abscesses on their necks and other parts of the body (though not such as to render them unclean); the deaf and the mute; in a word, sufferers of all kinds.

At the extremity of this court was a large portico opening into the city. I saw in it many spectators, Pharisees and women. To the Pharisees of Ainon, since there were upright souls among them and also because they had received him frankly and respectfully, Jesus showed a certain indulgence that he had not exhibited in other places. He wished thereby to make void the reproach that he associated only with publicans, sinners, and vagrants. He wanted to show them that he would pay them due honor if they demeaned themselves properly and with upright intentions. They showed great activity in preserving order among the people on this occasion, and Jesus allowed them to do it.

While Jesus was busy curing the sick, a beautiful woman of middle age and in the garb of a stranger entered the large portico by the gate leading from the city. Her head and hair were wound in a thin veil woven with pearls. She wore a bodice in shape somewhat like a heart, and open at the sides, something like a scapular thrown over the head and fastened together around the body by straps reaching from the back. Around the neck and breast it was ornamented with cords and pearls. From it fell, in folds to the ankle, two deep skirts, one shorter than the other. Both were of fine white wool embroidered with large, colored flowers. The sleeves were wide and fastened with armlets. To the shoulder straps that connected the front and back of the bodice was attached the upper part of a short mantle that fell over the arms. Over this flowed a long veil, of the whiteness of wool.

The woman, ashamed and anxious, entered slowly and timidly, her pale countenance bespeaking confusion and her eyes red from weeping. She wanted to approach Jesus, but the crowd was so great that she could not get near him. The Pharisees keeping order went to her, and she at once addressed them: "Lead me to the prophet, that he may forgive my sins and cure me!" The Pharisees stopped her with the words: "Woman, go home! What do you want here? The prophet will not speak to you. How can he forgive you your sins? He will not busy himself with you, for you are an adulteress." When the woman heard these words, she grew pale, her countenance assumed a frightful expression, she threw herself on the ground, rent her mantle from top to bottom, snatched her veil from her head and cried: "Ah, then I am lost! Now they lay hold of me! They are tearing me to pieces! See, there they are!" and she named five devils who were raging against her, one of her husband, the other four of her paramours. It was a fearful spectacle. Some of the women standing around raised her from the ground, and bore her wailing to her home. Jesus knew well what was going on, but he would not put the Pharisees of this place to shame. He did not interfere, but quietly continued his work of healing, for her hour had not yet come.

Soon after, accompanied by the disciples and Pharisees, and followed by the people, Jesus went through the city to the hill upon which John had formerly taught. It was in the center of moss-covered ramparts and there were some buildings around. On the side by which they approached was a half-ruined castle, in one of whose towers Herod took up his abode during John's teaching. The whole hill was already covered with the expectant crowd. Jesus mounted to the place where John had taught. It was covered with a large awning open on all sides. Here he delivered a long discourse in which he spoke of the mercy of God to men, particularly to his own people. He ran through the entire scriptures, showed God's guidance of his chosen nation, his promises to them, and proved that they were all being realized in the present. Jesus did not, however, say so openly at Ainon as he had done at Bezek that he was himself the Messiah. He spoke also of John, his imprisonment and his mission. One crowd of listeners was at intervals supplanted by another, that all might hear his words. Jesus questioned some of them as to why they wanted to receive baptism, why they had put it off till the present, and what they thought the ceremony to be. He divided them into classes, some of which were to be baptized at once, and others only after further instruction. I remember the answer of one group of neophytes to the question why they had delayed till now. One of the number said: "Because John constantly taught that a man was to come who would be greater than himself. We waited consequently in order to receive still greater grace." At these words, all that approved the response raised their hands. They formed a special class to receive more particular instructions as preparation for baptism.

The discourse ended at about three o'clock in the afternoon. Then Jesus and the disciples went with the Pharisees down the hill and into the city, where a great entertainment had been prepared for him in one of the public halls. But when he drew near the hall, he stopped short, saying: "I have another kind of hunger," and he asked (though he already knew) where that woman lived whom they had sent away from him in the morning. They pointed out the house. It was near the hall of entertainment. Jesus left his companions standing where they were, while he went forward and entered the house through the courtyard.

As Jesus approached, I saw the fearful torture and affliction of the woman inside. The devil, who had possession of her, drove her from one corner to another. She was like a timorous animal that would hide itself. As Jesus was traversing the court and drawing near to where she was, she fled through a corridor and into a cellar in the side of the hill upon which her house was built. In it was a vessel like a great cask, narrow above and wide below. She wanted to hide herself in it, but when she tried to do so, it burst with a loud crash. It was an immense earthen vessel. Jesus meantime halted and cried: "Mara of Suphan, wife of. . . ." (here he pronounced her husband's name, which I have forgotten) "I command thee in the Name of God to come to me!" Then the woman, enveloped from head to foot, as if the demon forced her still to hide in her mantle, came creeping to Jesus's feet on all fours, like a dog awaiting the whip. But Jesus said to her: "Stand up!" She obeyed, but drew her veil tightly over her face and around her neck as if she wanted to strangle herself. Then said the Lord to her: "Uncover thy face!" and she unwound her veil, but lowering her eyes and averting them from Jesus as if forced to do so by an interior power. Jesus, approaching his head to hers, said: "Look at me!" and she obeyed. He breathed upon her, a black vapor went out of her on all sides, and she fell unconscious before him. Her servant maids, alarmed by the loud bursting of the cask, had hurried thither and were standing nearby. Jesus directed them to take their mistress upstairs and lay her on a bed. He soon followed with two of the disciples that had accompanied him, and found her weeping bitter tears. He went to her, laid his hand on her head, and said: "Thy sins are forgiven thee!" She wept vehemently and sat up. And now her three children entered the room, a boy about twelve years old, and two little girls of about nine and seven. The girls wore little short-sleeved tunics embroidered in yellow. Jesus stepped forward to meet the children, spoke to them kindly, asked them some questions, and gave them some instruction. Their mother said: "Thank the prophet! He has cured me!" whereupon the little ones fell on the ground at Jesus's feet. He blessed them, led them one by one to their mother, in order of age, and put their little hands into hers. It seemed to me that, by this action, Jesus removed from the children the disgrace, and thus legitimized them, for they were the fruits of adulterous unions. Jesus still consoled the woman, telling her that she would be reconciled with her husband, and counseling her thenceforth to live righteously in contrition and penance. After that he went with the disciples to the entertainment of the Pharisees.

This woman was from Suphan in the land of Moab. She was a descendant of Orpah, the widow of Chilion, and daughter-in-law of Naomi, who upon the latter's advice did not go with her to Bethlehem, though Ruth, the widow of Orpah's other son Mahlon, accompanied Naomi thither. Orpah, the widow of Chilion, who was the son of Elimelech of Bethlehem, married again in Moab, and from that union sprang the family of Mara the Suphanite. She was a Jewess and rich, but an adulteress. The three children that she had with her at the time of her conversion were illegitimate. Her legitimate children had been retained by their father when he repudiated his unfaithful wife, their mother. She was living at this time in a house of her own at Ainon. For a long time she had conceived sentiments of sorrow for her disorders and had done penance, her conduct being so reserved and proper that she had won the esteem of even the most respectable women of Ainon. The Baptist's preaching against Herod's unlawful connection had strongly affected her. She was often possessed by five devils. They had again seized upon her when, as a last resource, she had gone to the court where Jesus was curing the sick. The rebuff of the Pharisees and their words, which in her deep dejection she had taken as true, had driven her to the brink of despair. Through her descent from Orpah, Ruth's sister-in-law, she was connected with the House of David, the ancestral line of Jesus. It was shown me how this stream, deviating in her from its course and troubled by her abominable sins, was purified anew in her by the grace of Jesus and flowed once more in its direct course toward the church.

Jesus went into the entertainment hall in which were the Pharisees and the rest of the disciples, and took his place with them at table. The Pharisees were somewhat displeased that Jesus had left them and gone to seek the woman whom they had so harshly repulsed that morning before so many people. But they said nothing, fearing to receive a reproof themselves. Jesus treated them with much consideration during the meal, and taught in numerous similitudes and parables. Toward the middle of the entertainment, the three children of the Suphanite entered in their holiday dresses. One of the little girls bore an urn full of fragrant water, the other had a similar one of nard, and the boy carried a vessel. They entered the hall by the door opposite the unoccupied side of the table, cast themselves down before Jesus, and set their presents on the table in front of him. Mara herself followed with her maids, but she dared not approach. She was veiled, and carried a shining crystal vase with colored veins like marble in which, surrounded by upright sprays of delicate green foliage, were various kinds of costly aromatics. Her children had offered similar vases, but smaller. The Pharisees cast forbidding glances upon the mother and children. But Jesus said: "Draw near, Mara!" and she stepped humbly behind him, while her children, to whom she had handed it, deposited her offering beside the others on the table. Jesus thanked her. The Pharisees murmured as later on they did at Magdalene's present to Jesus. They thought it a great waste, quite opposed to economy and compassion for the needy; however, they only wanted something to bring against the poor woman. Jesus spoke to her very kindly, as also to the children, to whom he presented some fruit which they took away with them. The Suphanite remained veiled and standing humbly behind Jesus. He said to the Pharisees: "All gifts come from God. For precious gifts, gratitude gives in return what it has the most precious, and that is no waste. The people that gather and prepare these spices must live." Then he directed one of the disciples to give the value of them to the poor, spoke some words upon the woman's conversion and repentance, restored her to the good opinion of all, and called upon the inhabitants of the city to treat her affectionately. Mara spoke not a word, but wept quietly under her veil the whole time. At last she cast herself in silence at Jesus's feet, rose, and left the dining hall.

Jesus took this occasion to give some instruction against adultery. Which among them, he asked, felt himself free from spiritual adultery. He remarked that John had not been able to convert Herod, but that this poor woman had of her own accord turned away from her evil life, and then he related the parable of the sheep lost and found. He had already consoled the woman in her own house, assuring her that her children would turn out well, and holding out to her the hope that she should one day join the women under Martha's supervision and work for the benefit of the inns. I saw the disciples after the entertainment giving abundantly of what was left to the poor. Jesus then went down to the west side of the hill of Ainon where the camp of the pagans lay at some distance. There was also, I think, a tent inn on this side. There Jesus instructed the pagans. Ainon was in the dominion of Herod, but it belonged, like a property across the boundary, to the Tetrarch Philip. Many soldiers of Herod were again there trying to find out news for their master.

Jesus in Ramoth-Gilead

Tuesday, September 5, AD 30 (Elul 18)

Jesus instructed Andrew, James, and John and some other disciples to remain at Ainon to baptize those who came there for baptism. Meanwhile, accompanied by about twelve disciples, Jesus went to Kamon. Here he taught and healed. Then he crossed the Jabbok where the patriarch Jacob had once been (Genesis 32:2), and entered the town of Mahanaim. Here he held a discourse on Jacob. Afterward, he went on to Ramoth-Gilead where, that evening, he taught in the synagogue on commemorating the sacrifice of Jephthah's daughter (Judges 11:29–40).

FROM Ainon, Jesus went with twelve disciples to the Jabbok and the neighboring places. Andrew, James, John, and some other disciples remained at Ainon, in order to baptize at the pool of baptism east of the hill. The water ran from the hill into the baptismal basin, formed a little lake behind it, watered some meadows as a little brook, and then fell into a reservoir on the north of Ainon from which it could be turned at pleasure into the Jordan.

I saw Jesus with the disciples teaching in a city about one hour east of Succoth and on the south side of the Jabbok. Among the numerous sick that he healed was a man who since his birth had one eye closed. Jesus moistened it with his saliva. The eye opened, and the man enjoyed perfect sight.

Jesus crossed the Jabbok, which flows through a valley, and turned to the east until he came into the vicinity of Mahanaim, a nice, clean city in two sections. He sat down by the well outside, and soon out came the elders of the synagogues and the chief men of the city with goblets, food, and drink. They bade Jesus welcome, washed his and the disciples' feet, poured ointment on Jesus's head, gave him and the disciples a little luncheon, and conducted him with great love and simplicity into the city. Jesus delivered a short discourse upon the patriarch Jacob and of all that had happened to him in those parts. Most of these people had been baptized by John. A patriarchal simplicity reigned in all the cities around this region, and many of the ancient customs were still observed. Jesus did not tarry long here, only time enough to receive the honors paid him on his route.

From Mahanaim he went along the northern bank of the Jabbok for about an hour eastward to the place where Jacob and Esau met. The valley here sinks deep. During the whole way Jesus taught his disciples. After some time they crossed again to the southern bank not far from where two little streams united to form the Jabbok. Then they continued their journey for about a mile to the east with the desert of Ephron on their right.

After traversing the valley they found, upon a mountain ridge to the east of the forest of Ephron, Ramoth-Gilead, a beautiful city, clean and regularly built. In it the pagans had their own quarter and temple. The sacred services were celebrated by Levites. One of the disciples went on ahead to announce Jesus's approach. The Levites and others of distinction were already awaiting him in a tent near the well outside the city. They washed the newcomers' feet, gave them the usual refreshments as a pledge of hospitality, and conducted them into the city. There they found a crowd of poor sick gathered on an open square to implore Jesus's help. He cured many of them. That evening he taught in the synagogue, for it was the beginning of the sabbath that commemorated the sacrifice of Jephthah's daughter, which in this city was celebrated as a mourning and national festival. There were crowds of young maidens and other people from the country around.

Jesus and the disciples took a repast with the Levites and stayed overnight in a house near the synagogue. There were in these parts no special inns prepared for Jesus. In Ainon, Kamon, and Mahanaim they were hired in advance, and the number of guests limited. Ramoth was built in terraces on a hill behind which, in a little valley flanked by a steep, rocky wall, was the quarter of the city inhabited by the pagans. They had a temple. One could always recognize their abodes by the figures erected on the roofs. On the roof of this temple was a whole group. The central figure wore a crown and stood in a reservoir or fountain, holding a basin in its hand. Around it were several figures of children dipping up the water and pouring it from one to another until at last it fell into the basin held by the middle figure.

The cities in this region were more beautiful, more neatly built than the old Jewish ones. The streets were laid off in the form of a star, all verging to a central point, and the extremities were rounded, thus making the circumference assume something of a zigzag form, as did also the city walls. Ramoth-Gilead was formerly a city of refuge for criminals. There was a large solitary building in which they were lodged, but at the time of Jesus's visit it had fallen to ruin and appeared to be no longer used. They made tapestry here, embroidered with figures of all kinds of animals and flowers, partly for trade, and partly for the use of the temple. I saw numbers of women and young maidens working at it in long tents. The costume of the people resembled more the patriarchal style, and they were very clean. Their clothing was of fine wool.

Wednesday, September 6, AD 30 (Elul 19)

Jesus attended the festival to commemorate the sacrifice of Jephthah's daughter. This lasted until late afternoon. That evening, Jesus healed many sick people and taught in the synagogue about the sale of Joseph by his brothers.

Jesus assisted at a solemn memorial feast of the sacrifice of Jephthah's daughter. He went with his disciples and the Levites to a beautiful open square outside the city to the east where preparations for the festival had been made. The inhabitants of Ramoth-Gilead were already assembled and ranged in large circles. Here were still the hill and the altar upon which Jephthah's daughter was immolated. In front of it was a semicircle of grassy seats for the maidens, and nearby were seats for the Levites and magistrates of the city. All went in a long and orderly procession to their places. The young girls of Ramoth and many from the neighboring cities assisted at the feast in robes of mourning. One young girl, clothed in white and veiled, personated Jephthah's daughter herself. A troop of others clad in somber robes, their faces veiled to the chin and wearing black, fringed sashes on the forearm, represented her lamenting companions. Tiny girls scattering flowers and playing on little flutes mournfully headed the procession, in which three lambs were led. The ceremonies were long and of the most touching nature. They comprehended different parts, chanting, religious instructions, and representations of the sad drama, while psalms and songs commemorative of it were sung. The maiden that personated Jephthah's daughter was comforted and lamented in chorus by her companions, though she herself was sighing only after death. Among the Levites also in some of the choirs of singers, there seemed to be held a conference upon the heroine's fate; but she presented herself before them and in earnest words begged to be allowed to accomplish the vow. They made use of different rolls of writing in the different scenes, some parts being recited from memory, others read from the rolls.

Jesus took an active part in the celebration. He personated the supreme judge, or high priest, and besides the speeches assigned his role, he delivered instructions before and during the ceremonies. Three lambs were sacrificed in memory of Jephthah's daughter, their blood sprinkled around the altar, and the roasted flesh given to the poor. Jesus gave the young maidens some words of instruction on the danger of yielding to vanity. I understood from it that Jephtias would have been liberated had she not been so vain.

The feast lasted until afternoon. During the whole celebration, the maidens successively replaced one another in personating Jephtias. As soon as one finished her part, the next in order rose from the stone seat upon which she had been sitting in the midst of the circle, retired with her into a tent nearby, and assumed the costume of the victim, that worn by her at the moment of immolation.

The tomb of the young heroine was on a neighboring hill, and on it the lambs were sacrificed. It was a four-cornered sarcophagus opening on top. When the fat of the lambs and the other portions to be sacrificed were almost consumed, what was left of the victims was introduced slantingly into the opening, that with the ashes it might fall into the tomb. When the lambs were slaughtered, I saw the blood sprinkled around the altar, and the maidens putting, with a little rod, a drop of it on the end of the long, narrow veil hanging over their shoulder. Jesus said: "Jephtias! Thou shouldst have thanked God in the retirement of thine own home for the victory he had granted thy people. But becoming vain and seeking praise as a hero's daughter, thou didst with frivolous ornaments and festive sounds go forth boasting before the other daughters of the land."

When the festive ceremonies were ended, all retired to a pleasure garden nearby where arbors and tents had been erected and an entertainment prepared. Jesus took part in it. He placed himself at the table at which the poor were fed, and related a parable. The maidens ate in the same tent, but separated from the others by a screen about three feet high. Lying at table, one could not see over it, though to one standing, it did not obstruct the view. After the meal Jesus with the Levites, the disciples, and many others returned to the city, where numbers of sick were patiently awaiting his coming. He cured them, as well as some lunatics and others afflicted with melancholy. He taught in the synagogue, taking for his subject Jacob and Joseph and the selling of the latter to the Egyptians. He said: "One day another also shall be sold by one of his brethren. But he will pardon his penitent brethren and in the time of famine feed them with the Bread of Eternal Life." On that same evening, some of the pagans outside the city accosted the disciples very humbly, asking them whether they too might hope to share in the great prophet's teachings. The disciples informed Jesus of their desire, and he promised to go to them in the morning.

Jephthah was the natural son of an idolatrous mother. Driven by his father's legitimate children from Ramoth, called also Mizpah, he lived in the neighboring land of Tob. He joined some military adventurers and led a life of brigandage. His pagan wife died young, leaving him an only daughter, who was beautiful and extraordinarily talented, but rather given to vanity. Jephthah was an exceedingly rash, absolute, and determined man, eager for victory, and strongly wedded to his own word. He was more like a pagan hero than a Jew. He was an instrument in the hand of God. Fired with desire to conquer and rule the land from which he had been expelled, he made that solemn vow to offer to the Lord as a holocaust the first one that should come out of his own house on his victorious return. He dreamed not that it would be his only daughter; as for the rest of his family, he had no love for them.

Jephthah's vow was not pleasing to God; nevertheless he permitted it, decreeing that its fulfillment should be a chastisement upon both father and daughter and cut off the posterity of the former from Israel. His daughter would perhaps have been perverted by the success and elevation of her father; but as it was, she did penance during two months and died for God. It is probable that she also influenced her father to a better way of thinking and made him more faithful to God. The daughter went out followed by a long train of maidens with songs and flutes and timbals to meet her father. It was at a whole hour's distance from the city that she met him, still she was the first whom he saw belonging to his own family. When she discovered her misfortune, she entered into herself and asked for a reprieve of two months, that she might retire into solitude to prepare by penance for her sacrifice, and to mourn with her companions over her virginal death, which would deprive her father of posterity in Israel. With several of her young companions she went into the mountains opposite the valley of Ramoth, where for two months she dwelt under a tent in prayer, fasting, and sackcloth. The maidens of Ramoth took turns in staying with her. She mourned especially her vanity and thirst for glory. The rulers held council as to whether she could be freed from death, but it was not possible since her father had sworn a solemn oath. It was consequently a vow that could in nowise be commuted. I saw too that the daughter herself desired its fulfillment, and petitioned for it in words both wise and touching.

Her sacrifice was accompanied by every mark of grief, her companions chanting songs of mourning around her. She was seated on the same spot upon which the memorial feast was celebrated. Here again a council was held for the purpose of delivering her from death, but stepping forward, she expressed her wish to die, just as I had seen at the feast. She was clothed in a long, white garment that closely enveloped her from the breast to the feet; but from her head to her breast she wore a transparent, white veil through which could be seen her face, neck, and shoulders. She walked courageously to the altar. Her father hurried from the scene without bidding her adieu. Then she drank something red from a vessel presented her. I think it was something to render her unconscious. One of Jephthah's warriors was deputed to give the deathblow. His eyes were bandaged as a sign that he did not incur the guilt of murder, since he would not see the blow that was to kill the victim. She was then laid on his left arm, and he pierced her throat with a short, sharp weapon. She had no sooner drunk the red liquid than it produced its effect, for she was perfectly unconscious when laid on the warrior's arm. Two of her young companions, who also were in white and appeared to act as bridesmaids, caught the blood in a dish and poured it on the altar. She was afterward enveloped by her companions in a winding sheet and laid at full length on the altar, the upper surface of which was grated. A fire was kindled below and, when her garments were burned and the whole looked like a blackened mass, some men raised the grate with the corpse upon it. They rested the grate upon the edge of an open tomb nearby, and then gently raising the grate, let the body slide down into it. The tomb was then closed. It was still to be seen even in Jesus's time.

The companions of Jephtias and many of the assistants steeped their veils and handkerchiefs in her blood, while others gathered up the ashes of the holocaust. Before Jephtias made her appearance in her sacrificial habiliments, her young companions had retired with her into a tent where she bathed and was prepared for the ceremony.

It was to the north of Ramoth, over two hours' distance in the mountains, that Jephtias and her companions met her father. They were mounted upon little asses adorned with ribbons and hung with tinkling bells. One rode in front of Jephtias, one on either side, and the rest followed with songs and music. They sang the canticle of Moses upon the defeat of the Egyptians. As soon as Jephthah descried his daughter, he rent his garments and became inconsolable. Jephtias herself did not give way to grief, but learned with calmness the fate that awaited her.

When she and her companions left her father's house for the wilderness, taking with them such food as was allowed for a fast, Jephthah spoke to his daughter for the last time. This was in a certain manner the beginning of the sacrifice. At the moment of parting, he laid his hand, as was customary in offering sacrifice, upon his daughter's head with the simple words: "Go forth! Thou wilt never have a spouse!"—to which she responded: "No, I shall never have a spouse!"—and he never again spoke to her. After his daughter's death, Jephthah had a beautiful monument erected in Ramoth and a little temple built over it. He ordered a memorial festival to be annually celebrated on the anniversary of his daughter's immolation as a remembrance of his sad vow and a warning to others against such rashness. (Judg. 11:39–40)

Jephthah's mother was a pagan who had been converted to Judaism. His wife was the daughter of a man born from the illicit union of a Jew with an idolatress. On his expulsion from his native place, his daughter did not accompany him. She remained in Ramoth where, meanwhile, her mother died. When, in time of danger, Jephthah was recalled to Tob by his compatriots, he did not return into the city of his birth. He assembled the people and concerted measures with them in the camp outside of Mizpah. His own home and his only daughter he did not see. When he made that vow, he never thought of her, but of his other relatives who had repudiated him, and therefore God punished him.

Thursday, September 7, AD 30 (Elul 20)

This morning Jesus preached in the non-Jewish quarter of Ainon. Several pagans immediately decided to become baptized. In the afternoon, Jesus taught again in the synagogue. Then, following a meal with some Levites, Jesus left the town and went to an inn near the town of Arga.

The feast lasted four days. Jesus with his disciples visited also the pagan quarters in Ramoth. The people met him with marks of reverence at the head of their street. Not far from their temple was an open-air space used for public discourses. Several of the sick and aged had been brought thither, the former of whom Jesus healed. They that had solicited a visit from him appeared to be learned men, priests, and philosophers. They knew about the journey of the three kings, and of their having seen the birth of the king of the Jews in the stars, for they, too, had a similar expectation and were likewise engaged in the observation of the stars. Not far from here was a kind of observatory similar to that in the land of the holy three kings, and from it they gazed at the stars. They had long sighed for instruction, and now they received it from Jesus himself. He spoke to them of very profound mysteries, even of the most holy Trinity. I heard these words that especially astonished me: "There are three that give testimony: the water, the spirit, and the blood, and these three are one." He spoke of the Fall of man, of the promised Redeemer, of the guidance of humankind, of the Deluge, of the passage through the Red Sea and the Jordan, and of baptism. He told them that the Jews had not obtained entire possession of the Promised Land, that many pagans still dwelt therein, but that he was now come to take possession of all that remained and unite it to his kingdom—not, however, by the sword, but by charity and grace. His words made so deep an impression upon many of his hearers that he sent them to Ainon to be baptized. Seven aged men that could no longer travel Jesus allowed to be baptized at once by two of the disciples. A basin was brought and placed before them while they stood up to the knees in the water in a bathing cistern near at hand. Above the basin was placed a railing upon which they could lean. Two of the disciples laid their hands on the neophyte's shoulders while Matthias, a disciple of John, poured on their heads, one after another, water from a shell at the end of which was a handle. Jesus dictated to the disciples the form of words they should use. The old men were clothed in beautiful white garments, all very neat and clean.

Then Jesus gave an instruction to the people in general, taking for his subject chastity and marriage. To the women he spoke especially of obedience, of humility, and the education of their children. These people were well-disposed. They conducted Jesus most affectionately back to the Jewish quarter, where he went to the synagogue and healed the sick that he found before it. The Levites were not well pleased at Jesus's having visited the pagans. In the synagogue, where Jephthah's festival was still being celebrated, Jesus taught of the call of the Gentiles. He said that many of them would rank higher in his kingdom than the children of Israel, and that he was come to unite with the rightful possessors of the Promised Land, by grace, instruction, and baptism, the idolaters whom the Israelites had not expelled. He spoke also of Jephthah's victory and vow.

While Jesus was preaching in the synagogue, the maidens were celebrating their feast at the monument that Jephthah had erected to his daughter. It had been rebuilt, and every year at the recurrence of the festival was beautified by the contributions of the young girls. It stood in a round temple with an opening in the roof. In the center of this temple was a smaller one of the same form. It consisted of a kind of cupola supported by columns, in one of which was concealed a staircase leading up to it. Around the cupola wound a spiral walk upon which was a representation of the triumphal procession of Jephtias, the figures being the height of a child. This piece of workmanship was of light material, but shining like polished metal. The base supporting it was of open work, through which the figures appeared to be gazing down into the little temple. The top of the cupola was crowned by a circular, metal platform from which a kind of ladder, consisting of a pole with projecting rods on either side, led up to the roof of the exterior temple. From this roof the view over the city and surrounding country was very extended. The platform at the top of the ladder was wide enough to allow two girls holding on to the pole to make a turn around it hand in hand. A pedestal in the center of the smaller temple supported a white marble figure of Jephthah's daughter seated on a chair of the same material, just as she appeared before her immolation. Her head reached to the first coil of the spiral-shaped cupola. Around the base of the statue, there was space enough for three men to walk abreast.

The columns surrounding the little temple were connected together by beautiful grates. The exterior was of stone veined in different colors. The coils of the cupola varied in degrees of whiteness from bottom to top, the upper ones of the purest white.

In the temple around this monument, the young girls now celebrated Jephtias's feast. The maiden's statue held a handkerchief to the eyes with one hand as if shedding tears, while the other hanging listlessly at her side held a flower or broken branch. The young girls' celebration was conducted with order. Sometimes they stretched curtains from the outer circle of the temple to the interior of the monument and took their places in little groups apart to pray and sigh and mourn in silence, their eyes fixed on the statue. Sometimes they sang together in chorus, sometimes in alternate choirs. Again, they passed two by two before the statue, strewing flowers, adorning it with wreaths and, as if to console Jephtias, chanting hymns on the shortness of life. I remember the expressions: "Today for me! Tomorrow for thee!" Then they sang the praises of Jephtias's fortitude and resignation, lauding her highly as the price of their victory. Then they mounted in groups by the serpentine walk up to the top of the cupola where they sang triumphal songs. Some went up to the roof of the exterior temple, looked out over the country as if to catch a glimpse of the conquering hero, and pronounced the fearful vow. The procession then returned lamenting to the monument, mourned over the young virgin, and consoled her on the privation of the privileges of maternity. The exercises were interspersed with canticles of thanksgiving to God and reflections upon his justice, the various scenes being accompanied by very touching pantomimes, expressive by turns of joy, grief, and devotion. A grand entertainment was prepared for the young girls in the temple. I saw them not reclining at one table, but sitting in tiers of three, one above another, all around the temple, with little round tables at their side. They sat cross-legged. They had all kinds of wonderful dishes and delicacies made up into figures—for instance, that of a lamb lying on its back and filled with fruit and other eatables.

Jesus Leaves Ramoth and Goes to Arga, Azo, and Ephron

AFTER assisting at an entertainment given him by the Levites, Jesus with seven disciples and some people belonging to Ramoth went northward and crossed the Jabbok. After climbing the mountains westward for about three hours, they arrived at the ancient kingdom of Basan and reached a city with two very steep mountains on one side and a long one on the other. It was called Arga and belonged to the district Argob, in the half-tribe Manasseh. An hour and a half or two hours eastward from Arga, near the source of the brook Og, was situated a great city named Gerasa. To the southeast of this and on an elevated site one could see Jabesh-Gilead. The country around was stony. At a distance one might think there were no trees in these parts, but many sections were covered with low, green bushes. The kingdom of Basan commenced here, and Arga was its first city. The family of the half-tribe of Manasseh extended a little farther to the south. About an hour northward of the Jabbok, I saw a boundary marked off by stakes.

Jesus stayed overnight with his companions about half an hour from the city in a public inn situated on a grand highway that ran from the east toward Arga. The disciples had food with them. In the night, when all were asleep, Jesus arose and went alone into the open air to pray.

Arga was a large, populous, and extraordinarily clean city. Like most of the cities in these parts where pagans form a portion of the population, it was built in the form of a star, the streets wide and straight. The mode of life was quite different from that observed in Judea and Galilee, the customs being much better. Levites were sent hither from Jerusalem and other localities to teach in the synagogue. They were changed from time to time, for if those sent did not give satisfaction, the people had the right to complain, and thus get others. People of bad conduct were not allowed to go at large. They were sent to a place of punishment and there detained. The inhabitants did not carry on private housekeeping, that is, they did not prepare their food in their own houses. They had large public kitchens where all was cooked and whither they went either to get their food and carry it to their homes, or to partake of it in halls adjoining. They slept on the roofs of their houses under tents. There were large dyeing establishments in this city, for they were skillful in the art of coloring, producing especially beautiful violets. The manufacture and embroidery of large carpets were also carried on here with more skill and to a greater extent than in Ramoth. Between the city and the wall ran tent after tent where women sat and worked at long strips of stuff stretched before them. On account of the delicate nature of their employments, the people of Arga were famed of old for their exceedingly great cleanliness. Quantities of oil of superior quality were produced around Arga. The olive trees grew in long rows neatly tied to trellises. Down in the valleys toward the Jordan, the people had numbers of camels and excellent pasture grounds. There grew also in this region a precious wood, which was used in the building of the Ark of the Covenant and the table of showbread. The bark of the tree that produced it was smooth and beautiful, the branches hung like those of the willow, the leaves were like pear leaves, though very much larger, green on one side and on the other covered with some gray-colored stuff. It bore berries like the fruit of the dogrose, though larger. The wood was exceedingly hard and tough, and could be split into very fine strips like bark. When dry and bleached, it became firm and beautiful and almost indestructible. The tree contained a very fine pith, which was extracted by incisions so as to leave in the center of the inmost plank only a delicate, reddish vein. The wood was made into little tables, and used for all kinds of inlaid work. They dealt also in myrrh and other spices, although these did not grow there. They obtained them from the caravans that often unloaded their camels and rested here for weeks at a time. They pressed the spices into balls and prepared them to be used by the Jews in embalming the dead. The cows and sheep of Arga were very large.

When on the following morning Jesus and his disciples went toward Arga, the Levites and chief men of the city met him with every mark of respect, conducted him to a tent, washed his feet, and presented him refreshments. Some of the disciples had gone on before Jesus to apprise the townspeople of his coming. He taught in the synagogue, after which he cured a great many sick, among them numbers of consumptives. He went likewise to many of the sick in their homes. Toward three o'clock a dinner was spread. Jesus dined with the Levites in a public hall, the dishes having been brought thither from the eating house. In the evening, he taught again in the synagogue, for it was the commencement of the sabbath. Next morning he gave another discourse, speaking at length of Moses in the wilderness on Mounts Sinai and Horeb, of the construction of the Ark of the Covenant, of the table of showbread, etc. As the ancestors of his hearers had sent offerings for the same, Jesus alluded to them as symbolical. He exhorted them now, in the time of their fulfillment, to bring heart and soul as an offering by penance and conversion, and he showed them the connection between that offering of their forefathers and their own present condition. But I do not remember it. The substance of this discourse was as follows:

While Jesus was speaking, I had an extended and circumstantial vision of the departure of the Israelites from Egypt. I saw that Jethro, the father-in-law, and Sephora, the wife of Moses, dwelt in Arga with the two sons and a daughter of the latter. I saw Jethro with the wife and children of Moses journeying to join him on Mount Horeb. Moses received them most joyfully, and related all the miracles wrought by God for the deliverance of his people from Egypt, whereupon Jethro offered sacrifice. I saw too that Moses at this time settled the disputes of all the Israelites himself, but Jethro counseled him to nominate subordinate judges. He then returned home, leaving Sephora and her sons with Moses. I saw Jethro recounting in Arga all the wonders he had seen, and many were thereby roused to great reverence for the God of the Israelites. Then Jethro sent Moses presents and offerings on camels, to which the Argites had contributed. The presents consisted of fine oil, which was afterward burned before the tabernacle; very fine, long strands of camel's hair for spinning and weaving into covers and curtains; and most beautiful setim wood, which was afterward made into the poles of the Ark of the Covenant and the table for the showbread. I think, too, they sent a kind of grain out of which the showbread was made. It was made from the pith of a reedlike plant, from which long before I saw Mary making pap.

***Friday, September 8, AD 30** (**Elul 21**)*

Jesus taught in the synagogue at Arga today and again this evening at the beginning of the sabbath. He spoke of the slaying of Zimri and the Midianite woman by Phinehas the grandson of Aaron. (*Numbers 25:6–15*)

On the sabbath Jesus taught in the synagogue from Isaiah and from Deuteronomy 21:26. He spoke also of Balak and the prophet Balaam. I saw many things connected with both, but I cannot now recall them. That evening in the sabbath instructions, he related from the Law of Moses, which had previously been read, the history of Zimri and the Midianite stabbed by Phinehas (Num. 25:7).

(Here Anne Catherine repeated in an admirable manner, although she had never heard nor read them, a number of the Laws of Moses as set forth in Deuteronomy 21:26. They were those that especially corresponded to her own position in childhood and the ideas peculiar to the occupations connected with it; for instance, the law forbidding one that has found a bird's nest to take the parent birds as well as the young; that which commands the gleanings of the harvest to be left for the poor; that which prohibits pledges to be taken from the poor, or borrowing from them, etc. Jesus touched upon all these points, dwelling at length upon the law that forbids defrauding laborers of their wages, because the people of Arga lived by labor. Sister Emmerich was rejoiced when told that all those laws could be found in the Bible, and she wondered at having heard them so correctly.)

***Saturday, September 9, AD 30** (**Elul 22**)*

Jesus taught morning and afternoon in the synagogue. During the day, he met with a group of pagans, who asked to be baptized.

The sabbath over, Jesus went to an inn belonging to the pagans who had sent him, by the disciples, a most pressing invitation to that effect. He was received with great humility and affection. He instructed them upon the call of the pagans, telling them that he was now come to win over those that had not been conquered by the Israelites. They questioned him upon the fulfillment of the prophecy that the scepter should be taken away from Judah at the time of the Messiah, and he gave them an answer full of instruction. They knew the story of the three kings, and begged for baptism. Jesus explained what the ceremony meant, that it was to be for them a preparation for their sharing in the kingdom of the Messiah. These good pagans were travelers, and had been a couple of weeks at Arga, awaiting the arrival of a caravan. They numbered five families, about thirty-seven souls in all. They could not go to the baptism at Ainon, for fear of missing the caravan. They asked Jesus where they should take up their future residence, and he indicated to them the place. I never heard him speaking to the pagans of circumcision, but he always insisted on continence and the obligation of having but one wife.

Sunday, September 10, AD 30 (Elul 23)

Jesus gave instruction to the pagans. They were then baptized by Saturnin and Joseph Barsabbas. In the afternoon, Jesus went to the little town of Azo, where, in the evening—with the start of Elul 24—a festival was celebrated to commemorate Gideon's victory over the Midianites. It was from Azo that Gideon set out with three hundred men to do battle (Judges 7:7–25). In the synagogue, Jesus spoke of this historical event.

These pagans were at once baptized by Saturnin and Joseph Barsabbas. They stepped into a bathing cistern, and bowed over a large basin in front of it which Jesus had blessed. The water was thrice poured over their head.

All were clothed in white. After the ceremony they presented to Jesus golden bracelets and earrings for the money box of the disciples. Those articles formed the principal part of their commerce. They were changed into money, which by Jesus's orders was distributed to the poor. Jesus taught again in the synagogue, cured the sick, and dined with the Levites.

After the meal, accompanied by several people, Jesus went a couple of hours farther on to the north to a little place named Azo, where were many people gathered for the celebration of a feast commemorative of Gideon's victory begun that evening. Jesus was received outside the city by the Levites. They washed his feet and offered him to eat, after which he went into the synagogue and taught.

In Jephthah's time, Azo was a fortified city, but was destroyed during the war that called him from the land of Tob. It was in Jesus's time a very clean little place, the houses in one long row. There were no pagans in it, and the inhabitants were singularly good, industrious, and well-behaved. They had many olive trees skillfully planted on terraces outside the city, and which they carefully tended. Stuffs were also fabricated and embroidered here. The manner of living was the same as at Arga. The people of Azo looked upon themselves as Jews of exceptional purity, since they lived entirely apart from the pagans. Everything was very clean in Azo. The road led down through a gently sloping valley, in which lay the city flanked on the west by a mountain.

When Deborah ruled in Israel and Sisera was slain by Yahel, there lived for a long time at Mizpah a woman disguised as a man. She was descended from a woman who had survived the destruction of the tribe of Benjamin to which she belonged. This descendant assumed male attire and knew so well how to conceal her sex as to arouse the suspicion of no one. She had visions, she prophesied, and often served the Israelites in quality of spy. But whenever they employed her in that way, they met with defeat. The Midianites were encamped at that time near Azo, and that woman went out to them in the dress of a distinguished military officer. She called herself Abinoahm after one of the heroes present at the defeat of Sisera. She passed unperceived through several quarters of the camp, spying as she went. At last she entered the general's tent and expressed her readiness to deliver all Israel into his hands. She had been accustomed to abstain from wine and to conduct herself with great reserve and circumspection. But upon this occasion she became intoxicated, and her sex was discovered. They nailed her hand and foot to a plank, and cast her into a pit with the words: "May even her name be here buried with her!"

It was from Azo that Gideon went out against the camp of the Midianites. Gideon was a very handsome, powerful man of the tribe of Manasseh. He dwelt with his father near Shiloh. Israel was in a critical condition at that time. The Midianites and other idolatrous tribes overran the country, laid waste the fields, and carried off the harvest. Gideon, a son of Joas the Ezrite, dwelling in Ephra, was very brave and liberal. He often threshed his wheat before his neighbors and generously divided it among the needy. I saw him going out at early morn before daybreak, while the dew still lay on the ground, to a very large tree with spreading branches under which his threshing floor lay concealed. The oak covered with its broad branches the wide rocky basin in which it stood. This basin was surrounded by a mound-like wall that reached to the branches of the tree, so that a person standing at the foot of the oak was as if in a large vaulted cave and could not be seen from without. The trunk was, as it were, formed of many single branches wound together. The soil was firm and rocky. Around in the walls were large cavities in which the grain was stored in casks of bark. The threshing was done with a cylinder that revolved on wheels around the tree, and on it were wooden hammers that fell upon the grain. High up in the tree was a seat from which one could see around. The Midianites pitched their tents from Basan down across the Jordan, and even to the very field of Esdrelon. The valley of the Jordan swarmed with grazing camels, which circumstance greatly served Gideon's purpose. He reconnoitered for several weeks, and with his three hundred men, moved slowly toward Azo. I saw him slipping unperceived into the camp of the Midianites, and listening to what was said in one of the tents. Just at that moment, a soldier exclaimed to one of his companions: "I have been dreaming that a loaf of bread fell down the mountain and crushed our tent." The other answered:

"That is a bad omen! Gideon will certainly fall upon us with his Israelites." On the following night, Gideon and his handful of warriors, with lighted torches in one hand and the trumpets upon which they were blowing in the other, pressed into the camp. Other bands did the same from opposite sides. The enemy became panic-stricken. They turned their swords against one another, while being slain and routed on all sides by the children of Israel. The mountain from which the bread rolled down, as seen in the soldier's dream, was directly back of Azo and it was from there that Gideon made his attack in person.

Monday, September 11, AD 30 (Elul 24)

This morning Jesus took part in a gathering to commemorate Gideon's victory. In the afternoon, another gathering was held, during which Jesus told the parable of the prodigal son to a group of poor people there.

The annual commemoration of Gideon's victory was now being celebrated in Azo. Outside the city was a large oak on a hill and at its foot an altar of stone. Between this tree and the mountain from which the soldier had seen the bread rolling down, the disguised prophetess lay buried. This tree was different from our oaks. It bore a large fruit with a green husk, under which was an exceedingly hard kernel in a little cup like our acorns. The Jews of Azo used these kernels for the tops of their walking sticks. For the accommodation of the large concourse of people, there was from that tree down to the city a whole row of tabernacles made of foliage and adorned with all kinds of fruit.

Jesus and the disciples went with the Levites in procession to the Ark. Five little he-goats, their necks adorned with red wreaths, were led in advance of the cortege. When they reached the oak, they were shut up in little grated caverns cut out of the side of the hill around the tree. Little cakes were also carried thither for sacrifice, and trumpets were blown. Different passages of Gideon's life were read from rolls, and canticles of victory sung. Then the goats were slaughtered and cut up, several pieces along with some of the cakes being laid upon the altar around which the blood was sprinkled. A Levite blew fire from a tube into the wood lying under the grating of the altar, in memory of the angel's having enkindled Gideon's sacrifice with a rod.

Jesus delivered a discourse to the assembled crowd, and thus the morning passed. In the afternoon he went with the Levites and the principal citizens to a valley south of the city where, around a little fountain, were a public bathing place and pleasure garden. In a garden apart were the women and maidens playing at games and enjoying themselves. An entertainment had been prepared here and, according to an ancient custom, the upper tables were assigned to the poor. Jesus took his place at one of them. He related the parable of the prodigal son and told of the calf that his father commanded to be slaughtered for him. He passed the night under a tent on the roof of the synagogue, for the people of this place were accustomed to sleep on the roofs.

Tuesday, September 12, AD 30 (Elul 25)

After teaching in the synagogue and healing many people, Jesus and the disciples—together with about thirty people from Azo—walked to a small fishing lake. Jesus and the disciples then made their way to the town of Ephron.

The feast was continued during the next day. The tabernacles of foliage were intended for the Feast of Tabernacles also, which was to begin in about fourteen days. Next morning Jesus delivered an instruction in the synagogue, and outside the school cured many blind, many consumptives, and several harmless possessed. After that he partook of a dinner and then left the city, accompanied by the Levites and others, about thirty in all.

The road led first over that mountain from which the soldier had seen the barley loaf rolling down into the camp of the Midianites. Then the travelers climbed by a defile over another mountain narrow, long, and high, on the opposite side of which they journeyed northward through the valley for about an hour. They reached at last a pleasant little lake near which rose some buildings belonging to the Levites of Azo. A brook flowed through it and down through the valley into the Jordan. About six hours northeastwardly from this point was Betharamphtha-Julias built around a mountain.

Jesus partook of a luncheon by the lake. It consisted of roasted fish, honey, bread, and a beverage of balm from a little jug, all of which the party had with them. The lake was about three hours' distance from Azo. All along the route Jesus had related parables of the sower and the stony soil, for it was over such they were then journeying. He also related another of fishes and how to catch them. There were some little boats on the lake fishing with drawnets, the capture being intended for the poor.

An hour and a half distant was Ephron. It could not be seen from here, though the high mountains in its vicinity were distinctly visible. Jesus now took leave of those that had accompanied him from Azo, and proceeded to Ephron. Azo was the best place he had met on his way in these parts. Jesus was as usual received outside of Ephron by the Levites of the place, and here too were found already waiting for him a crowd of sick.

They lay in wooden chests to which handles were attached for convenience in carrying. Jesus cured them all.

Ephron lay on the southern height of a narrow pass through which flowed a stream down into the Jordan. The latter could be seen far away through the defile. The stream of which I speak was often dried up. Opposite Ephron rose a narrow but lofty mountain. It was upon it that Jephthah's daughter with her maids awaited the signal of her father's victory, namely, the rising of a column of smoke. The moment she descried it, she hurried back to Ramoth whence with great pomp she set out to meet her father. Jesus instructed and cured many here.

Wednesday, September 13, AD 30 (Elul 26)

In Ephron there were Levites who belonged to an ancient sect called Rechabites. Jesus reproached them for the severity of their interpretation of the Law, and instructed the people not to heed their harsh interpretation.

The Levites of this place belonged to an ancient sect called Rechabites. Jesus reproached them for the hardness and severity of their opinions, and advised the people not to observe many of their prescriptions. In his instruction he alluded to the punishment of those Levites of Bethsames that had irreverently (too curiously) gazed upon the Ark of the Covenant which had been brought back by the Philistines. The Rechabites were descended from Jethro, the father-in-law of Moses. In early times they lived under tents, carried on no husbandry, and abstained from the use of wine. They exercised the office of chanters and gatekeepers in the temple. Those men that near Bethsames had, contrary to orders, gazed upon the returning Ark and had for so doing been punished with death, were Rechabites who there dwelt under tents. Jeremiah tried once, but in vain, to make them drink wine in the temple. He afterward held up to Israel as an example the obedience of these men to their laws. In Jesus's time they no longer dwelt under tents, though they still preserved many of their peculiar customs. They wore a hairy ephod (a scapular) as a cilicium [hair shirt] next their skin, and over that a garment made from the skins of beasts. Their outer robe was white, beautiful and clean, and was confined by a broad girdle. One of the points in which they differed from the Essenes was in their better mode of dressing. Their rules relating to purity were excessively strict, and they had very singular customs with regard to marriage. They passed judgment after examining blood drawn from the candidate for marriage. According to this test they decided whether he should marry or not, enjoining it upon some of their sect and forbidding it to others. In early times they were to be found in Argob, Jabesh, and in Judea. They offered no opposition to the words of Jesus, but took his instructions and his reproaches alike humbly and in good part. He reprehended them most of all for their unmerciful severity to adulterers and murderers to whom they granted no quarter.

There were on this mountain many foundries and forges. They made pots and gutters, also water pipes. These last were formed of two pieces soldered together.

Jesus in Betharamphtha-Julias • Abigail, Repudiated Wife of Philip the Tetrarch

Thursday, September 14, AD 30 (Elul 27)

After healing the sick of Ephron, Jesus and the disciples made their way to Betharamphtha.

FROM Ephron, Jesus went with his disciples and several of the Rechabites about five hours to the north to Betharamphtha-Julias, a beautiful city situated on a height. On the way he gave an instruction near a mine from which was obtained the copper that was wrought in Ephron. There were some Rechabites in Betharamphtha, and among them priests. Those of Ephron appeared to me to be under their jurisdiction.

Friday, September 15, AD 30 (E1u128)

At Betharamphtha there was a castle. Here Abigail, the divorced wife of the tetrarch Philip, lived with her five daughters. The people of Betharamphtha held Abigail in high esteem for her goodness and benevolence. Here, in Betharamphtha, Jesus too was received hospitably by the people. That evening, with the onset of the sabbath, he taught in the synagogue.

Betharamphtha was large and extended far around a mountain. The western part was inhabited by Jews, the eastern and a portion of the heights by idolaters. The two quarters were separated by a walled-in road and a pleasure garden full of shady walks. High on the mountain arose a beautiful castle with its towers, its gardens, and trees. It was occupied by a divorced wife of the tetrarch Philip, who had settled upon her all the revenues of this part of his territory. She was descended from the kings of Gessur, and had with her five daughters already well grown. She was named Abigail and, although tolerably advanced in years, was still active and beautiful. Her disposition was full of goodness and benevolence.

Philip was older than Herod of Pera and Galilee. He was a pagan of peaceable inclinations, but a lover of pleasure. He was half-brother of the other Herod, born of a different mother, and had first married a widow with one daughter. When Abigail's husband was dispatched by Philip to a war or to Rome, I know not which, he left his wife behind. She meanwhile was seduced by Philip, who married her, whereupon her husband died of grief. When after some years Philip's first wife, whom he had repudiated for the sake of Abigail, was about to die, she begged him on her deathbed to have pity at least on her daughter. Philip, who had by this time grown tired of Abigail, married his step-daughter, and banished Abigail and her five daughters to Betharamphtha, called also Julias in honor of a Roman empress. Here she occupied herself in doing good. She was favorably disposed toward the Jews, and cherished a great desire after truth and salvation. She was, however, under the watchful guardianship of some of Philip's officers, who had to render an account of her. Philip had one son, and his present wife was much younger than himself.

Jesus was received cordially and hospitably in Betharamphtha. The morning after his arrival he cured many sick Jews, and taught that evening in the synagogue, as also on the next morning, his instructions turning upon the tithes and the offering of the firstborn, and the sixtieth verse of Isaiah. (Deut. 26–30, Isaiah 60)

Saturday, September 16, AD 30 (Elul 29)

Jesus taught again in the synagogue this morning, and then cured many sick people. Abigail, having heard of Jesus's presence in the town, sent gifts from her castle so that the townspeople could all the more honorably welcome Jesus and his disciples. That evening trumpets were blown from the roof of the synagogue to mark the start of Tishri 1, signifying the beginning of the civil year (the religious year began with Nisan 1).

Abigail was held in esteem by the inhabitants of Betharamphtha. She sent gifts down from her castle to the Jews for the more honorable entertainment of Jesus and his disciples. On the first of the month of Tisri the new year was celebrated, which fact was announced from the roof of the synagogue by all kinds of musical instruments, among them harps and a number of large trumpets with several mouthpieces. I saw again one of those wonderful instruments I had formerly seen on the synagogue of Capernaum. It was filled with wind by means of a bellows. All the houses and public buildings were adorned on this feast day with flowers and fruit. The different classes of people had different customs. During the night many persons, most of them women clothed in long garments and holding lighted lanterns, prayed upon the tombs. I saw too that all the inhabitants bathed, the women in their houses and the men at the public baths. The married men bathed separate from the youths, as also the elder women from the maidens. As bathing was very frequent among the Jews and water not abundant, they made use of it sparingly. They lay on their back in tubs and, scooping up the water in a shell, poured it over themselves; it was often more like a washing than a bath. They performed their ablutions today at the baths outside the city, in water perfectly cold. Mutual gifts were interchanged, the poor being largely remembered. They commenced by giving them a good entertainment, and on a long rampart were deposited numerous gifts for them, consisting of food, raiment, and covers. Every one that received presents from his friends bestowed a part of them upon the poor. The Rechabites present superintended and directed all things. They saw what each one gave to the poor and how it was distributed. They kept three lists, in which they secretly recorded the generosity of the donors. One of these lists was called the Book of Life; another, the Middle Way; and the third, the Book of Death. It was customary for the Rechabites to exercise all such offices, while in the temple they were gatekeepers, treasurers, and above all, chanters. This last office they fulfilled on today's feast. Jesus also received presents in Betharamphtha of clothing, covers, and money, all of which he caused to be distributed among the poor.

TISHRI (30 days):
September 16/17 to October 15/16, AD 30 Tishri
New Moon: September 16 at 8:00 AM Jerusalem time

Sunday, September 17, AD 30 (Tishri 1)

The festival celebrating the start of the civil year continued today. At an open place in the town, Jesus and his disciples met Abigail, accompanied by her five daughters. She cast herself down at Jesus's feet and invited him to an entertainment she had arranged in his honor. Jesus accepted the invitation. After the meal, he talked with Abigail in the portico of her castle. She was full of anxiety because of her tragic destiny and hoped for pardon for her wrongdoings. Jesus comforted her, saying her sins would be forgiven.

During the festival Jesus went to visit the pagans. Abigail had pressed him earnestly to come to see her, and the Jews themselves, upon whom she bestowed many benefits, had begged him to have an interview with her. I saw Jesus with some of his disciples crossing the Jewish quarter of the city to that of the pagans. He reached the public pleasure grounds, pleasant and shady, that lay between the two quarters, and where the Jews and pagans usually met when necessary. Abigail was already there with her suite, her five grown daughters, many other pagan maidens, and some pagan followers. Abigail was a tall, vigorous woman of about fifty years, almost the same age as Philip. She wore an expression of sadness and anxious yearning. She sighed after instruction and conversion to a better life, but she knew not how to set about its attainment, for she was not allowed to act freely and was jealously watched by her wardens. She cast herself at Jesus's feet. He raised her up and, walking up and down, instructed her and her companions. He spoke of the fulfillment of the prophecies, of the vocation of the Gentiles, and of baptism. From all the places at which Jesus had been since he left Ainon proceeded caravans of Jews and Gentiles thither in uninterrupted succession, to receive baptism from the disciples left there for that purpose. Andrew, James the Less, John, and the disciples of John the Baptist were all busy administering baptism. Messengers were constantly going and coming between them and the imprisoned Baptist.

Jesus received from Abigail the customary marks of honor. She had appointed Jewish servants to wash his feet and to offer him the refreshments usually extended to strangers as tokens of welcome. She very humbly begged his pardon for desiring an interview with him, but, as she said, she had so long sighed after his instructions. She begged him to take part in an entertainment she had prepared in his honor. Jesus was very courteous toward all, but especially toward Abigail herself. His every word and glance made a strong impression on her soul. She was full of anxiety, and was not without some glimmering of the truth. This instruction to the pagans lasted till nearly afternoon. Then at Abigail's invitation Jesus passed to the east side of the city not far from the pagan temple. There were many baths in the vicinity and a kind of public feast going on, for the pagans also celebrated the new moon today with special magnificence. In coming hither Jesus took the road that separated the two quarters of the city, the Jewish from the pagan. In the abodes formed in the walls were many poor, sick pagans lying in chests full of straw and chaff. The destitute among the pagans were numerous. As yet Jesus cured none of their sick.

On the pleasure grounds of the pagans, where the entertainment was prepared, Jesus taught for a long time, sometimes walking around, and again during the meal. He made use of all kinds of parables relating to animals, in order to illustrate to them their own vain and fruitless lives. He spoke of the unwearied and often useless labor of the spider, of the active industry of the ant and wasp, and placed before them as a contrast the beautifully ordered work of the bee. The food offerings of the entertainment, at which Abigail assisted in person, reclining at the table, were for the most part distributed at Jesus's request to the poor. There were also on this day great solemnities in the pagan temple, a very magnificent building with large open porticos on five sides through which was afforded a view into the interior. It was capped by a high cupola. There were many idols in the different halls of the temple, the principal one being named Dagon. The upper part of its body was like a human being, the lower part like a fish. There were others in the form of animals, but none so beautiful as the idols of the Greeks and Romans. I saw young maidens hanging wreaths on and around the idols, then singing and dancing before them, while the pagan priests burnt incense on a little three-legged table. On the cupola was a very wonderful and ingenious piece of mechanism which revolved the whole night. It was a brilliant globe covered with stars. As it slowly revolved, it could be seen from the interior of the temple as well as from without. It represented something connected with the course of the stars and the new moon, or the new year. The globe revolved slowly. When it had reached one of the extreme points in its orbit, the songs and rejoicings in the temple ceased on the opposite side, to be taken up on that to which the globe had turned.

Not far from the festive scene where Jesus had been entertained was a large pleasure garden, and in it were the young girls amusing themselves at various games. Their robes were slightly raised and their lower limbs strapped with bands. They were armed with bows, arrows, and little spears wreathed with flowers. A kind of race course had been ingeniously formed of branches, flowers, and decorations of all kinds, along which the girls ran, shooting their arrows at the same time after the birds that were fastened here and there for that purpose, and darting their spears at the different animals, the kids and little asses, that were fenced in around the course. On this festal race course was a horrible idol with broad, open jaws like a beast, and hands hanging before it like a human being. It was hollow, and under it blazed a fire. The animals killed by the girls were placed in its jaws, where they were consumed, their ashes falling into the fire below. Those that had escaped the darts of the young huntresses were set aside and regarded as sacred. The priests laid upon them the sins of the people and set them free. It was something like the Jewish scapegoat. Were it not for the torture of the animals, so painful to behold, and the horrible idol, the fleetness and skill of the young girls would have been a very pleasing sight. The feast lasted till evening and, when the moon rose, animals were offered in sacrifice. When night closed, the whole temple and Abigail's castle were ablaze with torches.

Jesus taught again after the repast. Many of the pagans were converted and went to Ainon for baptism. That evening Jesus went up the mountain by torchlight and had an interview with Abigail in the portico of her castle. Near her were some of Philip's officers, who watched her constantly. Her every action was on that account one of constraint, and she gave the Lord to understand her embarrassing position by the look she cast upon those men. Jesus, however, knew her whole interior and the bonds that held her captive. He had compassion upon her.

She asked whether she might hope for pardon from God. One thing in particular constantly harassed her, namely, her infidelity to her lawful husband and his death. Jesus comforted her, saying that her sins would be forgiven her, she should continue her good works, persevere and pray. She was of the race of Jebusites. These pagans were accustomed to allow their deformed children to perish, and were very superstitious about the signs that accompanied their birth.

In all the places through which Jesus had passed lately, preparations were busily going forward for the Feast of Tabernacles. They were transporting lathwork from place to place and putting up light tents and huts made of foliage here and there on the roofs of Betharamphtha. The maidens were busied with plants and flowers which they put into water and set in the cellars to keep fresh. There were so many fast days before the feast, and so much was needed on account of the entertainments given upon it, that everything had to be prepared some time before. Such cares were entrusted to many of the poor, who received food and money in return for their services. When all was over they were entertained at a grand feast and again recompensed. In all these places no open shops were to be seen. Outside the temple in Jerusalem there were some places around upon which stood shops; in other cities, here and there, but chiefly at the gate, was a tent in which covers were sold. One never saw in Palestine people sitting together in the public houses. Here and there in the corner of a wall might be seen a man standing with a leathern bottle or pitcher. The traveler in passing got his little jug replenished, but rarely did he sit down to drink. A drunkard was never seen on the streets. The water vendors carried a pole across the shoulder on which were hung two leathern bottles, one in front, the other behind. As for dishes and vessels of iron, to procure them a man had to mount his ass and go to where they were fabricated.

Monday, September 18, AD 30 (Tishri 2)

This morning, after healing many people, Jesus spoke in the synagogue. He taught about Isaac's sacrifice (Genesis 22), which was associated with the two-day New Year festival at the start of the month of Tishri. Leaving Betharamphtha, Jesus and his disciples then proceeded to Abila, where he taught at an open place where there was a pillar erected in memory of Elijah.

On the following day Jesus cured, on the walled-in road between the Jewish and the pagan quarters, all the poor, sick pagans who were lying so miserably in the cavities of the wall, and the disciples distributed alms among them. After that until the time of his departure, Jesus taught in the synagogue. As the festival then celebrated was likewise commemorative of the sacrifice of Isaac, Jesus spoke of the true Isaac, but his hearers did not understand him. In all these places, he alluded very significantly to the Messiah, though without saying in express terms that it was himself.

Jesus in Abila and Gadara

JESUS, with the disciples and accompanied by the Levites, went three hours to the northwest toward a deep dale through which the brook Kerith flowed to the Hieromax. In this dale lay the beautiful city of Abila, built around the source of the brook Kerith. The Levites accompanied him to a mountain that stood halfway on the road, and then went back to Betharamphtha. It was three o'clock in the afternoon when the Levites of Abila, among whom were several Rechabites, received Jesus outside the city. Three of the disciples from Galilee were with the Levites awaiting his arrival. They conducted him at once into the city and to a very lovely fountain, the source of the brook Kerith. The beautiful little edifice, supported by columns that had been built over the source, formed the central point, to which ran colonnades connecting it with the synagogue and other public buildings. The city was built on both sides of the gently rising height. The streets ran from these central buildings in the form of a star so that from every one of them the fountain could be seen. It was at this fountain that the Levites washed the feet of Jesus and the disciples, and offered them the customary refreshments. In the neighboring gardens and on the buildings around were men and maidens busily preparing for the Feast of Tabernacles.

From here Jesus accompanied the Levites northward about half an hour outside the city into the valley to where a broad, stone bridge was built over the stream. On it, in memory of Elijah, was a low pedestal, or column, surmounted by a cupola resting on eight pillars. The pedestal supported a pulpit to which the teacher mounted by steps. Both banks of the narrow stream were cut in tiers to afford seats for the audience, and both were now crowded with people. In addressing them Jesus turned from side to side that all might hear.

Today was a feast in this city commemorative of Elijah, of something that had happened to him here by the stream. The instruction was followed by a banquet at the baths and pleasure garden outside the city. The festival ended with the sabbath, because on the following day a fast was kept in remembrance of the murder of Godolias. The sound of trumpets was still heard during the day.

On the declivity of the mountain west of the city of Abila I saw a very beautiful sepulcher in front of which was a little garden. In the latter were assembled the women belonging to three families of Abila. They were celebrating a solemnity in honor of the dead. They sat on the ground closely veiled, wept, uttered lamentations, and frequently prostrated with the face to the earth. They killed several birds of very beautiful plumage, plucked them, and burned the lovely, shining feathers on the tomb. The flesh was afterward given to the poor. The tomb was that of an Egyptian woman from whom the mourners had descended. Before the departure of the children of Israel, there lived in Egypt an illegitimate relative of the Pharaoh then reigning. She was very favorably disposed toward Moses, and rendered great services to the Israelites. She was a prophetess, and she it was that had discovered Joseph's mummy to Moses on the last night of his stay in Egypt. Her name was Segola, and she was the mother of Aaron's wife, from whom, however, he separated and married Elizabeth, the daughter of Aminadab of the tribe of Judah. The repudiated wife also was connected in some way with Aminadab, but how I do not now know. She had by her mother Segola, as well as by Aaron himself, been richly dowered. Taking with her large treasure, she accompanied the Israelites on their departure and married a second time during their stay in the desert. She afterward attached herself to the Midianites, especially to the family of Jethro. Her descendants settled near Abila where they dwelt under tents, and it was here that she was buried. After the time of the prophet Elijah, Abila was built, and it was then that those descendants settled there. I did not see the city in Elijah's time; it may have been destroyed before him. There were still three families of those descendants in Abila, and they were celebrating today the anniversary of the death of their ancestress, Segola's daughter, whose mummy had been transported hither from the desert and entombed. The women made an offering of their earrings and other trinkets to the Levites in memory of their deceased relative. Jesus praised her from the pulpit of Elijah and spoke of the goodness of Segola, her mother. The women listened attentively from where they stood behind the men. There were numbers of poor at the banquet in the bathing garden, and every guest was obliged before partaking of the meal to give something from his own plate to his poor neighbor.

Tuesday, September 19, AD 30 (Tishri 3)

This morning Jesus was conducted by Levites to a home for the blind and the deaf and mute, whom he healed, causing great jubilation in Abila. Afterward, he taught again from the pillar of Elijah and spoke about the prophet's life.

I saw the Levites conducting Jesus next day into a great court all around which were cells. Here were found about twenty patients, some of them deaf and mute, others blind from their birth, who were cared for by attendants and two physicians. It was a kind of hospital. The deaf and mute were exactly like children. Each had a little garden in which he amused himself and raised flowers. Soon all gathered around Jesus, laughing and pointing with their finger to their mouth. Jesus stooped and wrote all kinds of signs in the sand with his finger. They watched him attentively and, at every mark he made, pointed around them to this or that object. It was in this way that he made them understand something about God. I know not whether he formed letters or figures, or whether the mutes had ever before been instructed in that way. After that Jesus put his finger into their ears and touched them under the tongue with his thumb and forefinger. They shuddered as if a shock thrilled through their whole being, they gazed around, they heard, they wept, they stammered, they talked, they cast themselves down at Jesus's feet, and broke forth into a most touching, monotone chant of a few words. It sounded almost like that sweet singing I heard in the caravan of the holy three kings.

Then Jesus turned to the blind men who were standing still in a row. He prayed and laid his two thumbs on their eyes. They opened their eyes, fixed them upon their Savior and Redeemer, and mingled their songs of praise with those of the once deaf and mute, but who could now extol his goodness and listen to his words. Oh, what a charming, what a joyous scene! No words can describe it! The whole city crowded in joy and jubilation to hail Jesus as he came forth from the court surrounded by the miraculously cured, whom he had ordered to bathe.

After that, Jesus, with the disciples and Levites, traversed the city to the pulpit of Elijah. The excitement throughout the city was great. At the news of the miracles just wrought, several possessed had been set at large. On a corner of one of the streets some women, poor simpletons, ran after Jesus, chattering and repeating the words: "Jesus of Nazareth! Prophet! Thou art a prophet! Thou art Jesus! Thou art the Christ! The prophet!" They were harmless fools. Jesus commanded them to be silent, and they became quiet. He laid his hand on their heads, and they fell on their knees in tears. Silent and confused, they allowed themselves to be quietly led away by their friends. Then several possessed pressed raging through the crowd as if to tear Jesus to pieces. He cast upon them a single glance, and they fell like whining dogs at his feet. With a word of command, he drove the devil forth. They sank down unconscious, a dark vapor escaped from them, and then they arose weeping and thanking and were led to their homes by their friends. Jesus generally ordered such persons to perform certain purifications. He again taught from the pulpit on the brook, alluding in the course of his instruction to Elijah, to Moses, and to the departure of the Israelites from Egypt. He spoke of the cures that had just been effected in their midst, and of the prophecies which declared that in the Messiah's time the mute would speak and the blind see. He also made allusion to those that saw these signs and yet would not acknowledge them.

I saw on that occasion many things connected with Elijah. He was a tall, spare man with hollow, reddish cheeks, a bright, piercing glance, a long, thin beard, and a bald head with only a circle of hair around the back. On the top of his head were three large protuberances almost of the form of bulbs, one in the middle, two somewhat toward the forehead. He wore a garment made of two skins fastened together on the shoulder, open at the sides, and bound around the waist with a cord. Over his shoulders and around his knees hung the hair of the beast's skin. He carried a staff in his hand. His shins were far darker than his face. He was nine months in Abila, and two years and three months in Sarepta with the widow. While at Abila, he dwelt in a cave on the eastern slope of the valley not far from the brook. I saw how the bird brought him food. At first there arose a little dark figure like a shadow out of the earth, holding in its hand a thin cake. It was neither man nor beast, it was the evil one come to tempt the prophet. Elijah would not touch the bread, but bade the tempter begone. Then I saw a bird coming to the vicinity of his cave with bread and other food, which it hid under the leaves, as if for itself. It must have been a waterfowl, for it was web-footed. Its head was somewhat broad, and by the side of the beak hung bags something like pockets, and under the beak hung a craw. It made a cracking noise with its bill, like a stork. I saw that this bird was quite at home with Elijah, so much so that on a sign from the prophet it came and went. I saw him pointing to it right and left. I have often seen the same kind of bird with the hermits, also with Zosimus and Mary of Egypt. When Elijah was with the widow of Sarepta, besides the oil and meal that never decreased, other food was sometimes brought him by ravens.

Jesus went with the Levites to the cave of Elijah. On the eastern declivity of the valley under a broad, overhanging cliff was a narrow rocky bank upon which Elijah, under shelter of the upper rock, used to sleep on a couch overgrown with moss. When the sabbath, on the fourth of the month Tisri, began, and the fast was over, there was an entertainment in the bathing gardens, at which again the poor were fed.

Wednesday, September 20, AD 30 (Tishri 4)

After teaching in the synagogue and healing a number of people, Jesus and his disciples—accompanied by some Levites and Rechabites and other inhabitants of the town—went for a walk, passing through some vineyards on the way. As they walked, Jesus interpreted several passages from the prophets concerning the Messiah.

Next morning, after Jesus had again taught and cured the sick in the synagogue, he went with the disciples, the Levites, the Rechabites, and some of the citizens to the western heights of the mountain. There making a circuit of about an hour, he went through the vineyards giving instructions. On this mountain range, as far as Gadara, were numerous rocky projections like mounds. Some had been raised by nature, others formed by the hand of man, and around them vines were planted, the vinestocks as thick as one's arm. They were planted far apart and threw out their branches to a great distance. The bunches of fruit were often as long as one's arm, while the single grapes were large as plums. The leaves were larger than those of our vines, though small when compared with the fruit. The Levites put many questions to Jesus upon different portions of the Psalms that treated of the Messiah. They said: "Thou art certainly the greatest prophet after the Messiah! Thou canst explain these points to us." Among other things there was question of the words: "Dixit Dominus Domino meo" ["The Lord said unto my Lord," Psalm 110:1], and of him that with blood-besprinkled garments trod the wine press alone. Jesus explained all to them with its profound signification and applied it to himself. During this little instruction they sat around one of the vine hills eating grapes. The Rechabites, however, would not touch the fruit, because they were forbidden to drink wine. But Jesus challenged them upon their abstinence and commanded them to eat, saying that if they sinned by so doing, he would take the guilt upon himself. When they brought forward their Law as an excuse for not complying, I heard them saying that Jeremiah, on the command of God, had once forbidden it and they had obeyed. But now that Jesus ordered otherwise, they hearkened to his word. Toward evening they returned to the city, and assisted at another entertainment to which the poor were admitted. Then Jesus taught in the synagogue and afterward went to the house of the Levites, where he passed the night on the roof under a tent.

Thursday, September 21, AD 30 (Tishri 5)

Again Jesus taught in the synagogue and healed. Then he and the disciples made their way to Gadara, arriving there that evening.

Attended by the Levites, Jesus went from Abila to Gadara and reached the small Jewish quarter of the city in the evening. It was separate from the larger pagan quarter which had as many as four idolatrous temples. I knew at once that Gadara was a pagan city from seeing the idol of Baal standing under a large tree. Jesus was well received here. There were Pharisees and Sadducees among the inhabitants, also a Sanhedrin for the country around, although the male Jews of the place numbered from three to four hundred only. Jesus found some Galilean disciples awaiting him in Gadara. They were Nathaniel (Chased), Jonathan, Peter's half-brother, and, I think, Philip. Jesus put up at the inn outside the Jewish quarter, where already a great number of arbors had been erected for the Feast of Tabernacles.

Friday, September 22, AD 30 (Tishri 6)

Jesus taught in the synagogue at Gadara for much of the day. As the sabbath began that evening, he taught about the renewal of God's covenant through Moses (Deuteronomy 29ff.).

Next morning when Jesus went to the synagogue to preach he was met by a great crowd of sick, who had assembled outside to wait for him, and also by several raging possessed. The Pharisees and Sadducees, though apparently well-disposed, wanted to drive these people away. They should not be so importunate, they said, it was not the time for that. But Jesus very graciously interposed. "Let them remain," he said, "for it was for them that I came," and he cured many of them.

The Jewish Sanhedrin of Gadara was meantime deliberating whether or not they should allow Jesus to teach, since so much was said against him. They unanimously resolved to permit him to do so, for they had heard him very well spoken of, especially after the cure of the son of the centurion of Capernaum.

The disciples lately arrived spoke to Jesus of another person at Capernaum who greatly needed his assistance.

In the synagogue Jesus taught of Elijah, of Ahab and Jezebel, and of the idol of Baal erected in Samaria. In speaking of Elijah, Jesus said that he had not received bread from ravens, because he had been disobedient. There was also some allusion made to King Balthasar of Babylon, who had desecrated the sacred vessels and had seen the writing on the wall. Jesus taught long and earnestly from Isaiah, most strikingly applying the prophet's words to himself and uttering profound thoughts upon his own approaching Passion and victory. He spoke of the wine press, of the red, bloody garments, of the lonely worker, of the nations trodden down in wrath. He had previously spoken of the rebuilding of Zion, of the watchmen upon the walls of the Holy City, and I felt that he was alluding to the church. To me his teaching, though so profound and earnest, was so clear, and yet the Jewish doctors, though surprised and deeply affected, failed to understand him. That night they met together, consulted the scriptures, weighed and compared various passages. They thought that he must surely be allied to some neighboring nation, and that he would soon return with a powerful army and conquer Judea.

The idol Baal, under a wide-spreading tree outside the entrance of the pagan quarter, was of metal. It had a broad head and an immense mouth. The head went up in a point like a sugarloaf, and around it was a wreath of leaves like a crown. The idol, short, broad, and chunky, looked like an ox sitting upright. In one hand it held a bunch of corn, and in the other some kind of plant, perhaps grapes, or something similar. There were seven openings in its body, and it sat in a kind of cauldron in which a fire could be lighted under it. On its feasts, the idol was clothed.

Gadara was a stronghold. The pagan quarter was tolerably large and somewhat sheltered by the highest peak of the mountain, at whose northern base were warm baths and beautiful buildings.

Saturday, September 23, AD 30 (Tishri 7)

This morning, after healing the sick, Jesus taught again in the synagogue. In the afternoon, at the request of a pagan priestess whose child had just died, he went to her house in the pagan quarter of the town and raised the child from the dead. Then he healed many other pagan children, who were all suffering because of their parents' worship of Moloch. Jesus exorcised the priestess and then revealed to the assembled people the nature of their idolatry. The people believed; they determined to renounce the worship of Moloch and turn to the God of Israel. That evening, with the start of Tishri 8, there began a day of fasting in penance for the worship in ancient days of the golden calf (this fast-day normally fell on Tishri 7, but was shifted to Tishri 8 this year as Tishri 7 coincided with the sabbath).

On the following morning as Jesus was curing numbers of sick outside the city, the priests approached to salute him. "Why," said he addressing them, "Why were ye so disturbed last night over my teaching of yesterday? Why should ye tremble before an army, since God protects the just? Fulfill the Law and the prophets! Why then should ye fear?" Jesus again taught in the synagogue as on the preceding day.

Toward noon a pagan woman timidly approached the disciples and implored them to bring Jesus to her house that he might cure her child. Jesus went with several of his disciples into the pagan quarter. The woman's husband met him at the gate and led him into the house.

The wife cast herself at Jesus's feet, saying: "Master, I have heard of thy wonders and that thou canst perform greater prodigies than Elijah. Behold, my only boy is dying, and our wise lady cannot help him. Do thou have pity on us!" The boy, about three years old, lay in a little crib in the corner. The evening before, the father had taken the child into the vineyard and he had eaten a few grapes. Soon after, the boy became sick, and the father had to take him back home whimpering loudly. The mother had held him all night in her arms, vainly trying to relieve him. He already wore the appearance of death, indeed he looked as if he might really be dead. At this point the mother had hastened to the Jewish quarter to implore Jesus's aid, for the pagans had heard of the cures wrought by him on the day before. Jesus said to her: "Leave me alone with the child, and send to me two of my disciples!" Then came Joseph Barsabbas and Nathaniel the bridegroom. Jesus took the boy from his crib into his arms, laid him on his breast, breast to breast, pressed him to himself, bowed his face upon the face of the child, and breathed upon him. The child opened his eyes and rose up. Then Jesus held him out in his arms and commanded the two disciples to lay their hands upon the child's head and to bless him. They obeyed, and the child was cured. Jesus then took him to the anxiously waiting parents who, embracing the child, cast themselves down at Jesus's feet. The mother cried out: "Great is the God of Israel! He is far above all the gods! My husband has already told me that, and henceforth I will serve no other god!" A crowd soon gathered and several other children were brought to the Lord. He cured one little boy of a year old by the imposition of hands. Another of seven years was a simpleton and subject to convulsions arising from possession by the evil one. The child did not endure any violent assaults, but he was often paralyzed and speechless. Jesus blessed him and ordered him a bath of three different waters: some from the warm spring of Amathus north of the base of the mountain of Gadara, some from the brook Kerith near Abila, and lastly some from the river Jordan. The Jews of these parts kept on hand some of the water of the Jordan taken from the point over which Elijah had crossed. They preserved it in leathern bottles, and used it in cases of leprosy.

The pagan mothers complained of the frequent illness of their children and of the little assistance they derived from their priestess in such trials. Jesus commanded the priestess to be summoned before him. She obeyed reluctantly, for she did not want to enter Jesus's presence. She was closely enveloped in veils. Jesus ordered her to draw near. But she would not look at him, she turned her face away and behaved exactly like the possessed. She was irresistibly forced to turn away from the glance of Jesus, though at his command she approached. Jesus, addressing the pagan men and women before him, said: "I will show you now what wisdom you reverence in this woman and what is her skill," and he commanded the spirits to leave her. Thereupon a black vapor issued from her and all kinds of figures: noxious insects, snakes, toads, rats, dragons withdrew from her like shadows. It was a horrible sight. Jesus exclaimed: "Behold what doctrine ye follow!" The woman fell upon her knees weeping and sobbing. She was now quite changed, quite tractable, and Jesus ordered her to disclose by what means she had tried to cure the children. With many tears and half reluctantly she obeyed. She told that she had been taught to make the children sick by charms and witchcraft, that she might afterward cure them for the honor of the gods. Jesus then commanded her to accompany him and the disciples to where the god Moloch was kept, and he directed several of the pagan priests to be called. A crowd had gathered, for the news of the child's cure was soon spread. The place to which Jesus now went was not a temple, but a hill surrounded by tombs. The god was in a subterranean vault in the midst of them. The vault was closed on top by a cover. Jesus told the pagan priests to call forth their god. When by means of machinery they had caused the idol to rise into sight, Jesus expressed to them his regret that they had a god that was unable to help himself.

Then turning to the priestess, he commanded her to rehearse the praises of her god, tell how she served him, and what reward he gave her. Like Balaam the prophet, the woman began to repeat aloud before all the people the horrors of Moloch's worship and the wonders of the God of Israel. Jesus then directed the disciples to upset the idol and to shake it violently. They did as commanded. Jesus said to the pagans: "Behold the god that ye serve! Behold the spirits that ye adore!" and in the sight of all present, there appeared all kinds of diabolical figures issuing from the idol. They trembled convulsively, crept around for awhile, and vanished into the earth among the tombs. The idolaters gazed at the scene in affright and confusion. Jesus said: "If we cast your god down again into his den, he will surely go to pieces." The priests implored Jesus not to destroy their idol, whereupon he allowed them to raise it as before and lower it into its place. Most of the idolaters were deeply touched and ashamed, especially the priests, although some were very indignant. The people were, however, on Jesus's side. He gave them a beautiful instruction and many were converted.

Moloch was seated like an ox on his hind legs, his forepaws stretched out like the arms of one who is going to receive something upon them, but by means of machinery he could be made to draw them in. His gaping mouth disclosed an enormous throat, and on his forehead was one crooked horn. He was seated in a large basin. Around the body were several projections like outside pockets. On festival days long straps were hung around his neck. In the basin under him fire was made when sacrifices were to be offered. Around the rim of the basin numbers of lamps were kept constantly burning before the god. Once upon a time it was customary to sacrifice children to him, but now they dared no longer do so, and animals of all kinds were offered in their stead. They were consumed in the openings of his body or cast into his yawning jaws. The sacrifice most agreeable to him was an Angora goat. There was also a machine by which the priests and others could descend to the idol in the subterranean vault among the tombs. The worship of Moloch was, however, no longer in great repute. He was invoked chiefly for purposes of sorcery and especially by the mothers of sick children. Each pocket around his person was consecrated to special sacrifices. Children used to be laid on his arms and consumed by the fire under him and in him, for he was hollow. He drew his arms in when the victim was deposited upon them, and pressed it tightly that its screams might not be heard. There was machinery in the hind legs by which he could be made to rise. He was surrounded with rays.

Jesus in Dion and Jogbeha

THE PAGANS whose children Jesus had cured asked him whither they should remove, for they were determined to renounce idolatry. Jesus spoke to them of baptism, exhorting them in the meantime to remain tranquil and persevere in their good resolutions. He spoke to them of God as of a father to whom we must sacrifice our evil inclinations, and who asks no other offering from us than that of our own heart. When addressing the pagans, Jesus always said to them, more plainly than he did to the Jews, that God has no need of our offerings. He exhorted them to contrition and penance, to thanksgiving for benefits received, and to compassion toward the suffering. Returned to the Jewish quarter, he terminated the exercises of the sabbath and took a repast, after which began a fast in atonement for the adoration of the golden calf. It was celebrated on the 8th of Tisri because the 7th, the fast day proper, fell this year on the sabbath.

Sunday, September 24, AD 30 (Tishri 8)

After further teaching and healing this morning in Gadara, Jesus and his disciples left, traveling southward toward Dion. They stayed overnight at an inn some distance north of the town.

Jesus left the city the next afternoon. The pagans whose children he had cured thanked him again outside their own quarter. He blessed them, and with twelve disciples went down through the valley to the south of Gadara. He crossed a mountain and reached a little stream flowing from the range below Betharamphtha-Julias where the mines were. It was three hours from Gadara to the inn near the stream at which Jesus and the disciples put up. The Jews dwelling around that part of the country were engaged in gathering in the fruits. Jesus instructed them. There was also a band of pagans near the stream busy gathering white flowers from a blooming hedge, but it was not the flowers alone that they gathered, but also great, ugly beetles and other insects. When Jesus approached them, they drew back as if in fear. It was shown me that these insects were intended for the idol Beelzebub at Dion. I saw the idol outside the gate of the city, sitting under a large willow. It had a figure something like a monkey with short arms and slender legs, and it was seated like a human being. Its head was pointed and furnished with two little horns bent like a crescent, and the face with its extremely long nose was horrible. The chin was short but projecting, the mouth large and like that of a beast, the body lank, the legs long and thin with clawed toes. It wore an apron. In one hand it grasped a vessel by the stem, and in the other held a butterfly just escaping the larva cocoon. The butterfly, which was something like a bird and something like a disgusting insect, shone with variegated colors.

Around the head of the idol and just above the forehead was a wreath of loathsome beetles and flying vermin, forming as it were a compact mass, one appearing to hold the other fast. Above the forehead and in the center of the pointed head between the horns sat one of those disgusting things larger and more hideous than the others. They were glittering, and they radiated all the colors, but they were horrible, venomous things with long bodies, horns, feelers, and stings. When Jesus drew near to the pagans that were seeking these insects for the idol, the whole crown flew asunder like a dark swarm and hid in the holes and corners around the country, while all kinds of frightful black spirits crept with them, frightened, into the holes. They were the wicked spirits that were honored in Beelzebub with those beetles.

Monday, September 25, AD 30 (Tishri 9)

Jesus and the disciples arrived at Dion about ten o'clock this morning. He began immediately to heal the sick, continuing to do so for much of the afternoon. Great jubilation broke out on account of these healings. The people sang: "Blessed is he who considers the poor. . . ." (Psalm 41). Jesus and those with him then went to the synagogue and thanked God. Afterward, they ate a meal together. That evening, everyone returned to the synagogue in mourning garments for the great Feast of Atonement then starting (Tishri 10).

On the following forenoon, Jesus reached Dion, that is, the Jewish quarter, which was much smaller than that of the pagans. The latter was beautifully situated on the declivity of a mountain and had several temples. The Jewish quarter was entirely distinct from it. Where Jesus arrived outside the city the arbors were, for the most part, finished. Under one of them he was ceremoniously received by the priests and magistrates of the place, his feet washed, and the customary refreshments offered. Immediately after, he went out among the sick, numbers of whom were lying and standing under the arbors that had been erected from this spot to the city. The disciples assisted and kept order. There were sick of all kinds: lame, mute, blind, dropsical, and paralyzed. Jesus cured and exhorted many. There were some that stood upright on three-legged crutches, and there were other crutches upon which the invalid could rest without using the feet. These latter were almost like go-carts. At last Jesus came to the sick women. They were lying, leaning, and sitting nearer the city under a long arbor that had been erected over a terraced bank. This bank was covered with beautiful, fine grass that hung like soft, silky hair, and over it was spread a carpet. There were several women afflicted with an issue of blood. They were closely veiled and remained at a distance. Others were hypochondriacal, their faces wan and sallow, their countenance sad and gloomy. Jesus addressed them graciously and cured them one after another. He gave each at the same time hints and admonitions suited to her case for correcting her several imperfections, for avoiding such and such sins, and he instructed all as to what penances to perform. He also blessed and cured several children presented to him by their mothers. This work lasted until the afternoon and ended amid general rejoicings. The cured went away singing canticles of thanksgiving, joyously and merrily carrying their beds and crutches. They returned to the city processionally in beautiful order as they had been cured, accompanied by their rejoicing relatives, friends, and attendants. Jesus with the disciples and Levites walked in their midst. The humility and gravity of Jesus on such occasions are inexpressible. The women and children led the procession chanting the fortieth Psalm of David: "Blessed is he that understandeth concerning the needy and the poor." They went to the synagogue and thanked God, after which they took a meal under an arbor. It consisted of fruit, birds, honeycomb, and toasted bread. When the sabbath began, all went in mourning garments to the synagogue, for the great Feast of Atonement then commenced for the Jews.

Tuesday, September 26, AD 30 (Tishri 10)

Today, for the Feast of Atonement, Jesus taught in the synagogue regarding penance. He spoke against those who practiced only bodily purification and did not restrain those desires of the soul that were evil.

Jesus delivered in the synagogue a discourse on penance. He spoke against those that limit themselves to corporal purification without restraining the evil desires of the soul. Some of the Jews disciplined themselves under their wide mantles around the thighs and legs. The pagans of Dion also celebrated a feast with an enormous quantity of incense. The very seats upon which they sat were placed over burning perfumes.

I saw, too, the celebration of the Feast of Atonement in Jerusalem, the numerous purifications of the high priest, his arduous preparations and mortification, the sacrifices, the sprinkling of blood, the burning of incense, also the scapegoat, and the casting of lots for the two goats. One was for sacrifice, the other was chased away into the desert with something containing fire tied to its tail. It ran wildly through the wilderness, and at last plunged down a precipice. This desert, which was once traversed by David, commenced above the Mount of Olives. The high priest was today violently agitated and troubled; he would have been glad if another could have performed the duties of his office instead of himself. He was full of dread at the moment of entering the Holy of Holies, and he earnestly begged the people to pray for him. The people thought he must have committed some sin, and felt very anxious lest some calamity might befall him in the Holy of Holies. The truth was, his conscience smote him for the share he had had in the murder of Zechariah, the father of John. This sin was chastised with interest in the person of his son-in-law, who passed sentence of death on Jesus. I do not think this high priest was Caiaphas, but his father-in-law.

The holy mystery was no longer in the Ark of the Covenant. There were in it only some little linen napkins and the various compartments. This Ark of the Covenant was new and quite different in form from the first. The angels were different. They were seated and surrounded by a triple scarf; one foot was raised, the other hung at the side of the Ark, and the crown was still between them. There were all kinds of sacred things in the Ark, such as oil and incense. I remember that the high priest burned incense and sprinkled blood, that he took one of the little linen cloths from the Ark, that he mixed some blood (which he either drew from his finger or had on his finger) with water, and then presented it to a row of priests to drink. It was a kind of figure of Holy Communion. I saw also that the high priest, chastised by God, was become very miserable and was struck with leprosy. There was great consternation in the temple. I heard a most impressive lesson read in the temple from Jeremiah and at the same time I saw many scenes in the life of the prophet and much of the horrors of idolatry in Israel.

I saw also during another reading in the temple that Elijah, after his death, wrote a letter to King Jehoram. The Jews would not believe it. They explained it in this way: They said that Elisha, who brought the letter to Jehoram, had given it to him as a prophetical letter bequeathed to himself by Elijah. I began myself to think it very strange, when suddenly I was transported to the East and, in my journey, passed the Mountain of the Prophets, which I saw covered with ice and snow. It was crowned with towers, presenting perhaps the appearance it wore in the time of Jehoram. I went on then eastwardly to Paradise, and saw therein the beautiful, wonderful animals walking and gamboling around. There, too, were the glistening walls and, lying asleep on either side of the gate, Enoch and Elijah. Elijah was in spirit gazing upon all that was then going on in Palestine. An angel laid before him a roll of fine, white parchment and a reed pen. Elijah sat up and wrote, resting the parchment on his knees. I saw a little chariot something like a chair, or throne, coming over an eminence, or around by some steps from the inside of the garden. It was drawn by three marvelously beautiful white animals. I saw Elijah mount it and, as if on a rainbow, journey quickly to Palestine. The chariot stood still over a house of Samaria. I saw Elisha inside praying, his eyes raised to heaven. I saw Elijah letting the letter fall before him, and Elisha bearing the same to King Jehoram. The animals were harnessed to Elijah's chariot, one in front and two behind. They were indescribably lovely, delicately formed animals of the size perhaps of a large roe, snow-white, with long, white, silken hair. Their limbs were very slender, their head always in motion, and on their forehead was an elegant horn bent somewhat toward the front. On the day that Elijah was taken up to heaven, I saw his chariot drawn by the same kind of animals.

I saw also the history of Elisha and the Sunamitess. Elisha performed prodigies even more wonderful than those of Elijah, and in his dress and manners there was something more elegant and refined. Elijah was wholly a man of God with nothing in his manners modelled after other men. He was something like John the Baptist; they were men of the same stamp. I saw also how Gehazi, the servant of Elisha, ran after the man whom his master had cured of leprosy (Naaman). It was night and Elisha was asleep. Gehazi overtook Naaman at the Jordan and demanded presents from him in the name of his master.

On the next day Gehazi was pursuing his work as if nothing had happened (he was making light wooden screens to be used as partitions between sleeping apartments) when Elisha asked him: "Where hast thou been?" and exposed to him all that had taken place the previous night. The servant was punished with leprosy, which he transmitted to his posterity.

As the idolatry practiced by the human race, the adoration of animals and idols in the early times, the repeated lapsing of the Israelites into the same, and the great mercy of God in sending them the prophets were shown me, and I was wondering how men could adore such abomination, I had a vision in which I saw that the same abomination still exists on the earth, though in a form less material, more spiritual. I saw innumerable visions throughout the whole world of idolatry infecting even Christianity, and I saw it indeed in almost all the forms in which it was formerly practiced. I saw priests adoring serpents in presence of the most blessed sacrament, their different passions assuming the various forms of those serpents. I saw all kinds of similar animals by the side of learned and distinguished men. They adored them while at the same time they thought themselves above all religion! I saw toads and all kinds of hateful creatures near poor, low, depraved people. I saw also entire churches in the practice of idolatry, namely, a dark, reformed church in the North with empty, horrible altars upon which stood ravens receiving the adoration of the congregation. The people saw not indeed such animals, but they were adoring them in their own conceits and haughty self-sufficiency. I saw ecclesiastics for whom little distorted figures, little pugs, etc., were turning the leaves of their breviary while they recited the Holy Office. Yes, I saw with some even the idols of ancient times, such as Moloch and Baal. They were placed on the table among their books, and held sway over them. I have seen them even presenting morsels of food to those men who despised the holy simplicity of the children of God, and made a mockery of it.

I saw that such horrors are as rife in our own day as in the past, and that the visions of idolatry vouchsafed me were not accidental. If the ungodliness and idolatry of men of our own day could assume a corporeal form, if their thoughts and sentiments could be reduced to exterior acts, we should find the same idols existing now as in days gone by.

Wednesday, September 27, AD 30 (Tishri 11)

This morning, after teaching in the synagogue, Jesus and the disciples left Dion. They went southward to Jogbeha, where members of the Karaites sect, descended from Jethro, the father-in-law of Moses, lived. They led a plain, simple life. Because they rejected all oral traditions relating to the Law, the Karaites were the sworn enemies of the Pharisees. They lived in expectation of the coming of the Messiah, and regarded Jesus as a prophet. They received Jesus with great reverence. During his instruction, Jesus commended them for their charitable way of life.

When Jesus again left Dion, several pagans from the pagan quarter approached him very timidly. They had heard of the wonderful cures he had effected in Gadara, and they now brought their children to him. Jesus cured them and induced the parents to determine to receive baptism. After that he went with twelve disciples five hours to the south and over the brook that flowed down from the valley of Ephron. One half-hour to the south of this brook lay Jogbeha, a little, unknown place, quite hidden away in a hollow behind a forest. It was founded by a prophet, a spy of Moses and Jethro, whose name sounds like Malachi. He is not, however, one and the same with the last prophet, Malachi. Jethro, the father-in-law of Moses, employed him as a servant. He was exceedingly faithful and prudent, on which account Moses sent him to explore this country. He had come two years before Moses arrived himself, had explored the country for miles around even as far as the borders of the lake, and had given an account of all that he saw. Jethro at that time dwelt near the Red Sea, but upon Malachi's report he went with the wife and sons of Moses to Arga. Malachi was at last pursued as a spy. They hunted him to kill him. There was no city here in those times, only a few people living in tents. Malachi took refuge in a swamp, or cistern, and an angel appeared and helped him. He brought him upon a long strip of parchment the command to continue three years longer reconnoitering the country. The inhabitants, that is those who lived in the tents, provided him with clothes such as they themselves wore, long, red tunics and jackets of the same color. Malachi also explored the country around Betharamphtha. He lived for some time among the tent-dwellers of Jogbeha, and by his superior intelligence rendered them great assistance.

In the hollow in which Jogbeha was hidden was a ditch filled with water and quite covered with reeds, and on the spot in which Malachi lay concealed was a well that had been filled up. It began later on to bubble and cast out quantities of sand with occasional columns of vapor and sometimes pebbles. By degrees was formed around the well a hill, which was soon clothed with verdure. The swamp was filled up by earth brought from a neighboring mountain, and buildings were erected upon it. Thus arose around the well, which was covered by a beautiful spring house, the city of Jogbeha, which name signifies: "It will be elevated." The marshy cistern must have been built around in far earlier times, for lying near were the moss-covered ruins of walls in which were still discernible the holes destined probably for fish. There were other ruins in this locality like the foundation of an ancient tent castle. Malachi taught the inhabitants to use black mineral pitch in building.

Jesus was very graciously received in the isolated city of Jogbeha. Living apart from the other inhabitants was a sect called Karaites. They wore long, yellow scapulars, white garments, and aprons of rough skin. The youths wore shorter clothes and had their limbs wound with strips of stuff. There were about four hundred of these men. Once upon a time they were of far more importance, but suffered much from the oppression of enemies. They were of the race of Esra and a descendant of Jethro. One of their teachers had a great dispute once with a distinguished pharisaical doctor. They clung strictly to the letter of the Law and rejected oral additions, led a life very simple and plain, and had all their goods in common. If a member withdrew from the community, he had to abandon whatever goods or property he had brought to it. There were no poor among them, for they mutually assisted one another; even strangers were supported by them. They reverenced old age, and among them were many aged persons, whom the young treated with the greatest deference. They called those holding a distinguished position "ancients." The Karaites were sworn enemies of the Pharisees, who added all sorts of oral traditions to the Law, though in some points they were somewhat similar to the Sadducees. In their manners and customs, however, they were different, being far stricter. One of them belonging to this place had married a woman of the tribe of Benjamin and on that account had been driven from the community. It was at the time of the great strife with that tribe. They suffered nothing in the least resembling an image, and they believed that the souls of the deceased passed into other bodies, even into those of the lower animals. They delighted in the thought of the beautiful animals in Paradise. They were in expectation of the Messiah, after whom they earnestly prayed, but they looked for him to come as a worldly monarch. They regarded Jesus as a prophet. They observed great cleanliness, but did not adhere to the numerous purifications, the throwing away of dishes, and similar annoying observances not in the Law. They followed the Law religiously, though interpreting it much more freely than did the Pharisees.

They lived here quietly, having little communication with other people, permitting neither luxury nor vanity, and supporting themselves by their modest labor. A great many willow trees grew in these parts, from which they wove baskets and beehives, for there were many bees around here. They also made coarse covers, and light wooden vessels, all working together under long tents. Their arbors for the Feast of Tabernacles now at hand stood already prepared outside the city. They entertained Jesus with honey and bread baked in the ashes. Jesus taught here. He instructed them in all things, and they listened to him very reverently. He expressed to them the wish that they should live in Judea, and praised the reverence of their children toward their parents, of the scholars for their teachers, and the regard they entertained for age. He also commended their attention to the poor and the sick, for whom they provided in well-arranged hospitals.

***Thursday, September 28, AD 30** (**Tishri 12**)*

Today Jesus taught in Jogbeha, and healed many sick people. He and the disciples then went to Succoth, where they stayed overnight.

FROM THE SECOND FEAST OF TABERNACLES TO THE FIRST CONVERSION OF MAGDALENE

(Follow Map 21)

Jesus in Ainon and Succoth • Mara of Suphan • Conversion of an Adulteress

***Friday, September 29, AD 30** (**Tishri 13**)*

Jesus and his disciples proceeded from Succoth to Ainon, where Mara the Suphanite, whom he had healed on Elul 17, had prepared a festive welcome for him. After conversing with Mara at her home, Jesus went to the place of baptism and met with Andrew, James, and John, who had stayed there baptizing since Elul 18. Jesus addressed the assembled people. Among those present were Lazarus, Joseph of Arimathea, and some other disciples from Jerusalem, who had traveled there for the special sabbath preceding the Feast of Tabernacles. That evening, as the sabbath began, Jesus taught in the synagogue at Ainon. Afterward, there was a banquet at the public hall arranged by Mara the Suphanite in honor of Jesus.

FROM Jogbeha, Jesus went through Succoth to Ainon, a distance of about an hour along a pleasant road, enlivened by the camps of the caravans and the pilgrims going to baptism. It was already lined with long rows of tents covered with foliage, and the people were still busied with preparations, because with the close of the coming sabbath, the Feast of Tabernacles began. Jesus taught at intervals on the way. Just outside Ainon they had erected a beautiful tent, and a solemn reception was prepared for Jesus by Mara the Suphanite. The most distinguished personages of the city were present, also the priests, and Mara with her children. The men washed the feet of Jesus and his disciples, and costly refreshments were offered them, according to custom. Mara's children and others of their age presented the dishes of food. The women, closely veiled, prostrated before Jesus, their faces on the ground. He saluted and blessed them graciously. Mara, with tears of joy and gratitude, invited Jesus to repair to her house. When he entered the city, Mara's children, two girls and a boy, and others of their age with long garlands of flowers and scarfs of woolen stuff, walked before him and at his side.

Jesus, accompanied by his disciples, entered the courtyard of Mara's house, passing under a flowery arch erected for the occasion. Mara again cast herself at his feet, weeping and thanking, her children following her example. Jesus caressed the little ones. Mara told him that Dinah the Samaritan had been there, and that the man with whom she had been living up to that time had received baptism. Mara knew Dinah, since her own husband and three legitimate children lived in Damascus. She and the Samaritan had together sounded Jesus's praises. She was radiant with joy, and showed Jesus many costly robes for the use of the priests, and a high miter which she herself had made for the temple, for she was incredibly skillful at such work, and rich in money and property. Jesus was very gracious toward her. He spoke to her of her husband, advising her to go back to him, to be reconciled with him, for her presence near him would prove of use, and her illegitimate children could be provided for elsewhere. He directed her also to send a messenger to her husband to request him to come to her. On leaving her house Jesus went to the place of baptism, where he mounted the pulpit and taught the people.

Lazarus, Joseph of Arimathea, Veronica, Simeon's sons, and some disciples from Jerusalem had come hither for the sabbath. Andrew, John, and some of the Baptist's disciples were still here, but James the Less had gone back. The Baptist had again sent messengers to Jesus urging him to go to Jerusalem and to say openly before the whole world who he was. John was now so impatient, so anxious, because though so powerfully impelled to announce Jesus, he was unable to do so.

Map 21: Travels in Samaria

September 28–November 1, AD 30

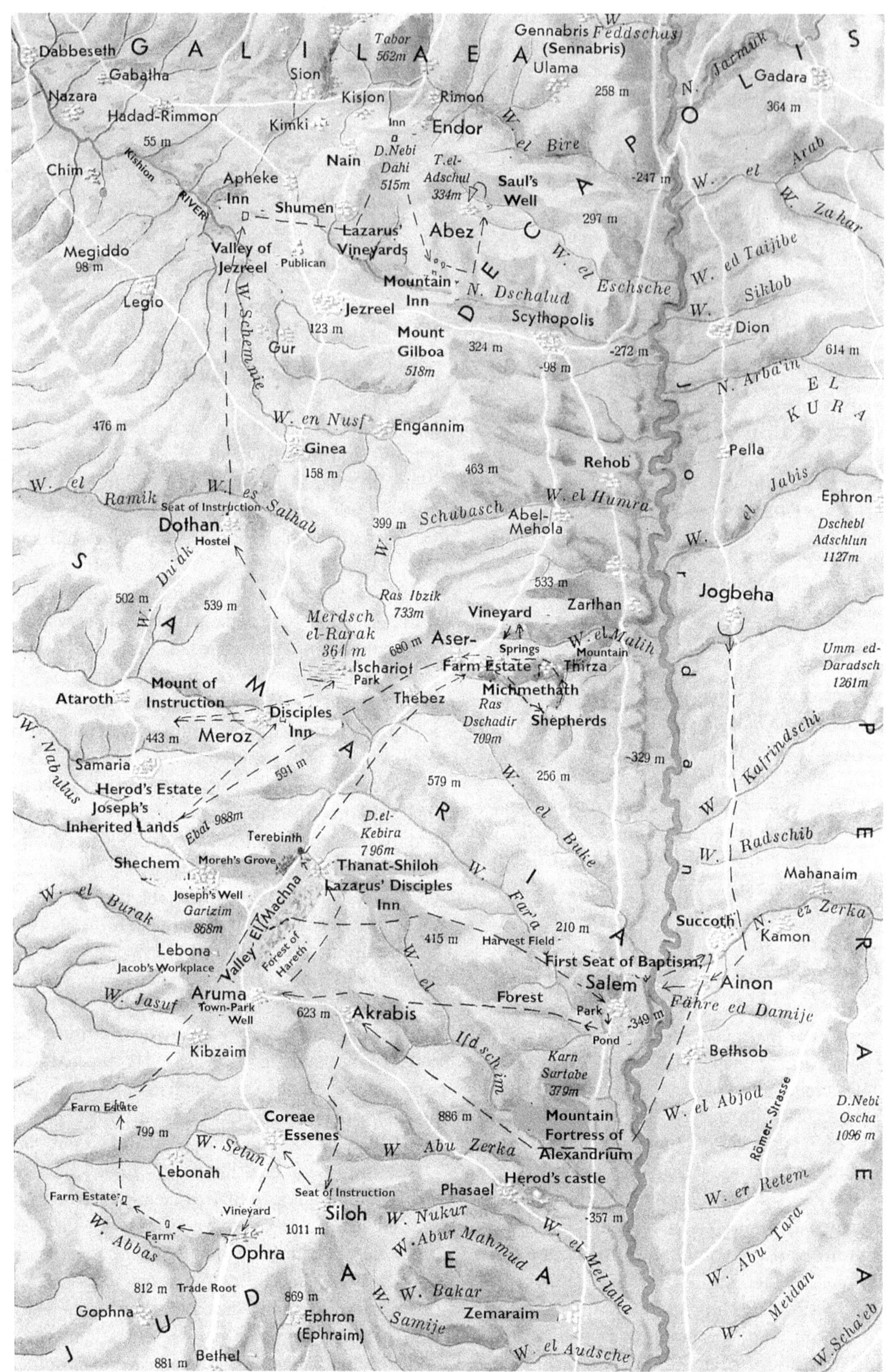

Jogbeha—Ainon—Succoth—Ainon—Akrabis—Shiloh—Coreae—Ophra—Salem—Aruma
Thanat-Shiloh—Aser-Michmethat—Meroz—Ischariot—Dothan—Abez

When the sabbath began, Jesus taught in the synagogue, taking for his subjects the creation of the world, the waters, and the Fall of man. He alluded very significantly to the Messiah, commenting in the most striking manner upon Isaiah 42:5–43, and applying the same to himself and the Jewish people. After the sabbath, there was an entertainment given to Jesus at the public banqueting hall. It had been prepared by Mara of Suphan. The tables, as well as the hall, were beautifully decorated with foliage and flowers and lamps. The guests were numerous and among them were many whom Jesus had cured. The women sat on one side behind a screen. During the meal Mara went forward with her children and placed costly perfumes on the table. She then poured a flask of fragrant balm over Jesus's head, and cast herself down before him. Jesus received these attentions graciously, and related parables. No one found fault with Mara, for all loved her on account of her munificence.

Saturday, September 30, AD 30 (Tishri 14)

Jesus taught in the synagogue, healed many of the sick, and then told the parable of the prodigal son (Luke 15:11–32). That evening, after the close of the sabbath, everyone gathered at a place on the outskirts of the town. Here tabernacles had been erected, for it was the commencement of the Feast of Tabernacles (Tishri 15), which was to last for seven days (Leviticus 23:33–43). The meal lasted until late that night. Jesus went from table to table instructing the guests.

Next morning Jesus cured several sick persons, and taught in the synagogue. He also taught in a place to which those pagans that had received baptism and those still in expectation of the same were admitted. In his latter instruction he spoke so feelingly, so naturally, of the lost son, that one would have thought him the father who had found his son. He stretched out his arms, exclaiming: "See! See! He returns! Let us make ready a feast for him!" It was so natural that the people looked around, as if all that Jesus was saying were a reality. When he mentioned the calf that the father had slaughtered for the newly found son, his words were full of mysterious significance. It was as if he said: "But what would not be that love which would lead the heavenly Father to give his own Son as a sacrifice, to save his lost children." The instruction was addressed principally to penitents, to the baptized, and to the pagans present, who were depicted as the lost son returning to his home. All were excited to joy and mutual charity. The fruit of Jesus's teaching was soon apparent at the celebration of the Feast of Tabernacles, in the good will and hospitality shown by the Jews to their pagan brethren. In the afternoon Jesus with his disciples and a crowd of the inhabitants took a walk outside the city and along by the Jordan, through the beautiful meadows and flowery fields in which the tents of the pagans stood. The parable they had just heard, that of the prodigal son, formed the subject of conversation, and all were cheerful and happy, full of love toward one another.

The exercises of the sabbath were today brought to a close at an earlier hour than usual. Jesus again taught and cured some sick before its close. Then all went out of the city, or rather to a quarter somewhat remote, for it was built very irregularly, the streets broken up by open squares and gardens. And now was celebrated a great feast. The tabernacles were arranged in three rows and adorned with flowers, green branches, all kinds of devices formed of fruit, streamers, and innumerable lamps. The middle row was occupied by Jesus, the disciples, the priests, and the chief men of the city disposed in numerous groups. In one of the side rows were the women, and in the other the school children, the youths, and the maidens forming three distinct bands. The teachers sat with their pupils, and every class had its own chanters. Soon the children, crowned with flowers, surrounded the tables with flutes and chimes and harps, playing and singing. I saw also that the men held in one hand palm branches on which were little tinkling balls, and branches of willow with fine, narrow leaves, also the branches of a kind of bush such as we cultivate in pots. It was myrtle. In the other they held the beautiful yellow Etrog apple.

They waved their branches as they sang. This was done three times: at the commencement, in the middle, and at the end of the feast. That kind of apple is not indigenous to Palestine; it comes from a warmer clime. It may indeed be found here and there in the sunny regions, but it is not so vigorous nor does it ripen to maturity. It was transported hither by caravans from warm countries. The fruit is yellow and like a small melon; it has a little crown on top, is ribbed and somewhat flat. The pulp in the center of the fruit is streaked with red, and in it closely packed together are five little kernels, but no seed vessel. The stalk is rather curved, and the blossoms form a large, white cluster like our elderberry. The branches below the large leaves strike root again in the earth, whence new ones spring up and thus an arbor is formed. The fruit rises from the axil of the leaves.

The pagans also took part in this feast. They, too, had their tabernacles of green branches, and those that had received baptism took their places next to the Jews, by whom they were cordially and hospitably entertained. All were still influenced by the impressions received at the instruction upon the prodigal son. The meal lasted until late into the night. Jesus went up and down along the tables instructing the guests, and wherever anything was needed supplying the want through one of the disciples. Joyous sounds of conversation and merriment arose from all sides, occasionally interrupted by prayer and canticles. The whole place was ablaze with lights. The roofs of Ainon were covered with tents and tabernacles, and there the occupants of the houses slept at night. In the tabernacles outside the city many poor people and servants, after the feast was over and all had gone to rest, passed the night as guards.

Sunday, October 1, AD 30 (Tishri 15)

After teaching and healing this morning in Ainon, Jesus and the disciples made their way slowly to Succoth, arriving there around five in the afternoon. In the large synagogue at Succoth an adulteress pressed through the crowd listening to Jesus and begged for mercy. She confessed her shame. Jesus said: "Your sins are forgiven! Arise, child of God!" Then he reconciled her with her husband.

Jesus, accompanied by the disciples and many others, returned from Ainon to Succoth, which was at no great distance. The greater part of the way was covered with tabernacles and tents, for many from the surrounding districts celebrated the feast here, and the caravans, which were constantly coming and going, were now resting for the feast. The whole length of the road was like one triumphal march. Behind the tabernacles were stands covered with awnings at which provisions could be purchased. It took Jesus several hours to traverse this road, for he was everywhere saluted and from time to time he stood still to instruct. He did not reach the synagogue of Succoth till toward evening. Succoth, on the north bank of the Jabbok, was a beautiful city, and had a very magnificent synagogue. Besides the Feast of Tabernacles, there was another celebrated today in Succoth, that of the reconciliation of Jacob and Esau. The whole day was devoted to it, and there were visitors from all the country around. Among the school children at Ainon were some of the orphans from the school of Abel-Mehola, who were now in Succoth, having come for the feast of today. It was the real anniversary of Jacob and Esau's reconciliation, which, according to the Jewish tradition, had taken place on this day.

The synagogue, one of the most beautiful that I have ever seen, was rendered still more gorgeous today by its festal decorations of countless crowns, flowery garlands, and lovely, sparkling lamps. It was lofty and supported by eight columns. On both sides of the edifice ran corridors communicating with the buildings that comprised the dwellings of the Levites and the schools. One end of the synagogue was more elevated than the rest, and here toward the center rose an ornamented pillar with little cases and projections running up around it, in which were kept the rolls of the Law. Behind the pillar was a table, and near it a curtain that could be drawn to cut off the neighboring space from the rest of the synagogue. A couple of steps farther back was a row of seats for the priests, with one more elevated in the middle for the preacher. Back of these seats stood an altar of incense above which, in the roof of the synagogue, was an opening; and behind this altar, at the far end of the edifice, were tables upon which the offerings were deposited. The men, ranged according to their classes, stood in the center of the synagogue. To the left, on a slight elevation and separated by a grating, was the place for the women; and on the right was that of the school children grouped in classes, the boys and girls separate.

The feast of today celebrated the reconciliation between God and man. There was a general confession of sin made either in public or private, according to individual desire. All gathered round the altar of incense, offered gifts of expiation, received a penance from the priests, and made voluntary vows. This ceremony bore a striking resemblance to our sacrament of Penance. The priest from the teacher's chair spoke of Jacob and Esau, who had today been reconciled with God and each other, also of Laban and Jacob who had again become friends and offered a sacrifice to the Lord, and he earnestly exhorted his hearers to penance. Many of those present had by John's teaching and that of Jesus during the past days been very much touched, and were waiting only for this great festival to do penance. Some men, whose consciences reproached them with grave faults, went through the door in the grating near the teacher's chair around behind the altar, and laid on the tables their offerings, which a priest received. Then, returning to the priests in front of the pillar containing the Law, they confessed their sins either publicly to the assembled priests, or privately to one of their own choice. In the latter case, both priest and penitent retired behind the curtain, the confession was made in a low voice, a penance imposed, and at the same time incense was cast upon the altar. If the smoke arose in a certain way, the people took it as a sign of the genuineness of the penitent's contrition and of the pardon accorded his sins. The rest of the Jews chanted and prayed during the confessions. The penitents made a kind of profession of faith, promising fidelity to the Law, to Israel, and to the Holy of Holies. Then they prostrated and confessed their sins, often with abundant tears. The female penitents followed after the men, and their offerings were received by the priests. Then retiring behind a grating, they called for a priest and confessed.

The Jews accused themselves of sins against the Ten Commandments and of all violations of established usages. There was something singular in their confession, which I hardly know how to repeat. They bemoaned the sins of their forefathers. They spoke of a soul prone to sin received from their progenitors, and of another, a holy one, received from God. They appeared indeed to speak of two distinct souls. The priests in their exhortation likewise said something to the same effect, namely, "May their" (the ancestors') "sinful soul remain not in us, but may our holy soul remain in us!" I cannot now recall what was said of the influence mutually exerted by these two souls upon, and by, and in, each other. Jesus next spoke. He touched upon this same point, but treated it differently from the doctors. He said that it should indeed be so no longer. The sinful soul received from their forefathers should not remain in them. It was a touching instruction, clearly signifying that Jesus himself was about to make satisfaction for all souls. They also lamented the sins of their parents, as if knowing that all kinds of evils had descended to them through their progenitors, as if through them they were still in possession of the sad heritage of sin.

The penitential exercises had already begun when Jesus arrived. He was received at the entrance of the synagogue, and for awhile he remained standing at one side on the platform among the doctors, one of whom was preaching. It was about five o'clock when he arrived. The offerings of the penitents consisted of all sorts of fruits, money, articles of clothing for the priests, pieces of fabric, silken tassels and knots, girdles, etc., and principally of frankincense, some of which was burned at once.

And now I witnessed a touching spectacle. While the confessions were going on and the offerings were being made by the penitents, I noticed a distinguished-looking lady in a private seat near the secluded place of penance. Her seat was cut off from the rest by a grating. I noticed her troubled and agitated appearance. Her maidservant was nearby, having just deposited on a stool at her mistress' side a basket containing the gifts intended for the offering. The lady was impatient for her turn to come, and when at last she could no longer restrain her agitation and desire for reconciliation, she arose, drew her veil and, preceded by her maid with the offerings, passed through the grating and straight to the priests, into a place to which entrance was forbidden to women. The wardens tried to prevent her, but the maid would not be stopped. She forced her way in, exclaiming: "Make way! Make way for my mistress! She wants to make her offering, she wants to do penance! Make way for her! She wants to purify her soul!" The lady, agitated and bowed down by sorrow, advanced toward the priests, threw herself on her knees, and begged to be reconciled. But they told her to withdraw, they could not hear her there. One of them however, younger than his brethren, took her by the hand, saying: "I will reconcile thee! If thy corporal presence belongs not here, not so thy soul, since thou art penitent!" Then turning with her toward Jesus, he said: "Rabbi, what sayest thou?" The lady fell on her face before Jesus, and he answered: "Yes, her soul has a right to be here! Permit this daughter of Adam to do penance!" and the priest retired with her into the curtained enclosure. When she reappeared, she prostrated in tears upon the ground, exclaiming: "Wipe your feet on me, for I am an adulteress!" and the priests touched her lightly with the foot. Her husband, who knew nothing of what was transpiring, was sent for. At his entrance, Jesus occupied the teacher's chair, and his words sank deep into the man's heart. He wept, and his wife, veiled and prostrate on the ground before him, confessed her guilt.

Her tears flowed abundantly, and she appeared to be more dead than alive. Jesus addressed her: "Thy sins are forgiven thee! Arise, child of God!" and the husband, deeply moved, reached out his hand to his penitent wife. Their hands were then bound together with the wife's veil and the long, narrow scarf of the husband, and loosened again after they had received a benediction. It was like a second nuptial ceremony. The lady was now, after her reconciliation, quite inebriated with joy. At the moment her offerings were presented, she had cried out: "Pray! Pray! Burn incense, offer sacrifices, that my sins may be forgiven!" and she falteringly repeated various passages from the Psalms, while being conducted to her place by the priests.

Her offering consisted of many costly fruits such as they were accustomed to use at the Feast of Tabernacles. They had been carefully arranged in the basket, so that they would not injure one another by pressure. There were also borders, silk tassels, and fringes for priestly vestments. She at the same time committed to the flames several magnificent silk robes in which her vanity had arrayed itself for the gaze of her paramour. She was a tall, robust, beautifully formed woman of an ardent and vivacious temperament. Her deep contrition and voluntary avowal of guilt had won for her forgiveness, and her husband was heartily reconciled with her. She had had no children by her illicit connection, had been the first to dissolve her sinful bonds, and had won over her paramour to penance. She did not, however, make him known either to the priests or to her husband. It was forbidden to the latter to make inquiries, and to her to name the guilty one. The husband was a pious man; he forgave and forgot with all his heart. The multitude present did not indeed catch the details of the scene. Still they saw the interruption, they saw that something extraordinary was transpiring, and they heard the lady's cry for prayer and sacrifice. All prayed earnestly for her, and rejoiced over a soul doing penance. The people of this place were very good, as they generally were on the east side of the Jordan, for they had retained more of the manners and customs of the ancient patriarchs.

Jesus continued teaching in beautiful and touching language. I recall distinctly his allusion to the sins of our forefathers and our own share in the same, and he rectified the ideas of some of his auditors on that subject. Once he used the expression: "Your fathers have eaten grapes, and your teeth have been set on edge."

The schoolteachers were then questioned upon the faults of their pupils, while the latter were reminded that if they accused themselves and were sorry, they would be forgiven.

There were many sick outside the synagogue and, although it was not customary for them to enter on the Feast of Tabernacles, yet Jesus directed the disciples to bring them into the corridor between the sacred building and the dwellings of the doctors. At the close of the feast, the whole synagogue having long before been lighted up with lamps, he went out into the corridor and cured many of them. At the moment Jesus entered the corridor, a messenger appeared from the lately reconciled lady, begging Jesus to grant her a few words. Jesus went to her and retired apart with her a few instants. She threw herself at his feet and exclaimed: "Master, he with whom I sinned implores thee to reconcile him to God!" and Jesus promised to see him there in that same place after the repast.

The curing of the sick was followed by an entertainment in honor of the feast, and given on one of the open squares of the city. Jesus, the disciples, the Levites, and the most distinguished personages of the city took their places under a large and beautiful bower that formed the center of many others, the men and women separate. The poor were not forgotten. Everyone sent the best from his own table to them. Jesus went around from table to table, not excepting that of the women. The reconciled sinner was full of joy, as were also her female friends. They gathered around her, heartily wishing her every happiness. As Jesus was making the rounds of the tables, she seemed to be very uneasy about something, and frequently cast anxious glances toward him, hoping that he would not forget his promise to reconcile the partner of her guilt, for she knew that he was already waiting at the place designated. When Jesus drew near to where she sat, he quieted her anxiety, telling her that he knew what was troubling her and bidding her rest assured that all would be well in its own good time. When the guests separated for their homes, Jesus started for his lodgings near the synagogue. He was met by the man who had been waiting in the corridor for him, and who now threw himself at his feet and confessed his sin. Jesus exhorted him to sin no more and imposed on him as penance to give the priests every week for a certain time something for a charitable purpose. He was not obliged to make public offerings, but to mourn his sin in private.

Monday, October 2, AD 30 (Tishri 16)

This morning Jesus returned from Succoth to the place of baptism near Ainon, where he healed the sick. He received the confessions of many people, granting them absolution from their sins.

When Jesus returned from Succoth to Ainon, he gave instructions at the place of baptism, cured the sick, and visited the Gentiles. Several little parties of neophytes were baptized. There were still standing here some of the arrangements John had made when baptizing for the first time at the Jordan near Ono, a tent and the baptismal stone. The neophytes leaned over a railing, their heads over the baptismal pool. Jesus received the confessions of many and granted them absolution from their sins, a power which he had imparted to some of the older disciples—for instance, to Andrew. John the Evangelist did not yet baptize. He acted as witness and sponsor.

Tuesday, October 3, AD 30 (Tishri 17)

This morning, after talking with Mara at her house in Ainon, Jesus left the town and proceeded to the shepherds' settlement called Akrabis.

Before Jesus again left Ainon with his disciples, he had an interview with Mara the Suphanite in her own house. He gave her salutary advice. Mara was entirely changed. She was full of love, zeal, humility, and gratitude; she busied herself with the poor and the sick. When journeying after her cure through Ramoth and Basan, Jesus had sent a disciple to Bethany to inform the holy women of it and of her reconciliation, in consequence of which announcement Veronica, Johanna Chusa, and Martha had been to visit her.

On his departure from Ainon, Jesus received rich presents from Mara and many other people, all of which were at once distributed to the poor. The gateway by which he left the city was decorated with an arch of flowers and garlands. The assembled crowd saluted him with songs of praise, and he was met outside the city by women and children who presented him with wreaths. This was one of the customs at the Feast of Tabernacles. Many of the citizens accompanied him beyond the city limits. For two hours his road ran to the south, through the valley of the Jordan, and on this side of the river. Then it wound for about half an hour to the west, then turned again to the south and led to the city of Akrabis, which was situated upon a ridge of the mountain.

Jesus in Akrabis, Shiloh, and Coreae

JESUS was received in ceremony outside of Akrabis, for the inhabitants were expecting his coming. The tabernacles of green branches were ranged for some distance beyond the city, and into one of the largest and most beautiful they conducted Jesus for the customary washing of feet and offering of refreshments. Akrabis was rather a large place, about two hours from the Jordan. It had five gates, and was traversed by the highway between Samaria and Jericho. Travelers in this direction had to pass through Akrabis, consequently it was well supplied with provisions and other necessaries. Outside the gate at which Jesus arrived were inns for the accommodation of caravans. Tabernacles were erected before each of the five gates, for each quarter of the city had its own gate.

Wednesday, October 4, AD 30 (Tishri 18)

Jesus walked around Akrabis, pausing at each entrance gate, where tabernacles had been erected. He healed many people as he went. After a festive meal, he and the disciples went on to Shiloh, arriving there toward evening. He taught in the open air from a teacher's chair carved from stone.

Next day Jesus made the rounds of the city, visited all the tabernacles, and gave instructions here and there. The people observed many customs peculiar to this festival; for instance, they took only a mouthful in the morning, the rest of the repast being reserved for the poor. Their employment during the day was interrupted by canticles and prayers, and instructions were given by the elders. These instructions were now delivered by Jesus. On his coming and going he was received and escorted by little boys and girls carrying around him garlands of flowers. This, too, was one of their customs. The residents of the different quarters sometimes went from their own tabernacles to those of their neighbors, either to listen to the instructions or to assist at an entertainment. On such occasions they went processionally, carrying garlands such as were borne by Jesus's escort.

The women were busied with all sorts of occupations in the tabernacles. Some were sitting embroidering flowers on long strips of stuff, others were making sandals out of the coarse, brown hair of goats and camels. They attached their work to their girdle as we do our knitting. The soles were furnished with a support like a heel both before and behind, also with sharp points, in order to aid in climbing the mountains. The people gave Jesus a very cordial reception, but the doctors of the Law were not so simple-hearted as their confreres at Ainon and Succoth. They were indeed courteous in their manner, but somewhat reserved.

From Akrabis Jesus went to Shiloh, distant only one hour in a direct line toward the southwest; but as the road winds first down into the valley and then over the mountain, it makes the distance a good two hours. The inhabitants of Shiloh, like those of Akrabis, were assembled in the tabernacles outside the gates of the city. They, too, knew of Jesus's coming and were waiting for him. They saw him and his companions from afar, climbing up the winding road that led to their city. When they perceived that he was not directing his steps to the gate nearest to Akrabis, but was going around the city more to the northwest, to that which led from Samaria, they sent messengers to announce the fact to the people of that quarter. These latter received him into their tabernacles, washed his feet, and presented the customary refreshments. He went immediately to the central height of the city, where once the Ark of the Covenant had rested, and taught in the open air from a teacher's chair very beautifully wrought in stone. Here, too, were tabernacles and houses of entertainment, in which latter everything needed in the former was cooked in common. Men were performing this duty, but they appeared to me to be slaves and not real Jews.

Thursday, October 5, AD 30 (Tishri 19)

This morning Jesus taught again in Shiloh from the stone teacher's chair. He spoke of God's mercy to the people of Israel, the destruction of the temple, and the present time of grace, whereby he made it quite clear that it was he himself who was to bring salvation.

The day following was one of the most solemn of the feast, though I do not know whether what I saw here was a purely local custom or one practiced generally. One of the doctors of the Law annually on this day delivered from the teacher's chair a castigatory sermon, to which not one of his hearers dared offer the least contradiction. It was principally for the purpose of delivering this sermon that Jesus had come here today. All the Jews, men, women, youths, maidens, and children had assembled to hear him. They had come processionally from their different tabernacles, carrying festoons and garlands of leaves between the various divisions and classes. The teacher's chair, under an awning decorated with foliage, crowned a terraced eminence. Jesus taught until midday. He spoke of the mercy of God toward his people, of Israel's revolts and turpitude, of the chastisements awaiting Jerusalem, of the destruction of the temple, of the present time of grace, the last that would be offered them. He said that if the Jews rejected this last grace, never to the end of time should they as a nation receive another, and that a much more frightful chastisement should fall upon Jerusalem than it had ever yet experienced. The whole discourse was calculated to inspire fear. All listened silent and terrified, for Jesus very clearly signified, as he explained the prophecies, that he himself was the one who was to bring salvation. The Pharisees of the place, who were not of much account and who, like those of Akrabis, had received Jesus with a show of hypocritical reverence, kept silence, though filled with wonder and irritation. The people, however, applauded Jesus and sang his praises. Jesus spoke likewise of the scribes, their misrepresentations of the holy scriptures, their false interpretations and additions.

That evening a public entertainment was given in the tabernacles on the eminence. But Jesus was not present at it. He went down to the tabernacles of the poor, where he consoled and instructed. Wherever there were no Pharisees to spy their actions, the people pressed around Jesus, cast themselves at his feet, paid him homage, confessed their sins, and made known their needs. He consoled them and gave them advice. It was a touching sight to see all this going on in the darkness of night among the tabernacles, from which shone forth a faint and trembling glimmer. No lights were to be seen for, on account of the draught, the lamps had been covered with screens, and the yellow glare they cast lit up the green foliage, the fruits, and the people in a manner quite strange to behold. From the height of Shiloh, many places around could be distinctly seen, and everywhere shone the glimmering light of the tabernacle-feast, while the sound of singing came from far and near. Jesus did not perform any cures here. The Pharisees kept the sick back, and the people appeared to be afraid. Here as in Akrabis, the song of the Pharisees, when they heard of Jesus's coming, was: "What new doctrine is he now going to bring us? What design has he in coming here?"

Friday, October 6, AD 30 (Tishri 20)

Jesus went this morning from Shiloh to Coreae. There he healed the blind youth Manahem, who had the gift of prophecy. That evening, with the beginning of the sabbath, he spoke in the synagogue about Noah, the ark, and the rainbow as the sign of God's mercy.

From Shiloh Jesus took a southwestwardly direction and went down for one and a half hours to Coreae, a place that could be seen from the height of the former city. It had neither walls nor ramparts. The Pharisees of Coreae went out some distance beyond the city to meet Jesus, taking with them one of their fellow citizens who had been blind from his birth. They thought to tempt Jesus. The blind man had over his garments, around his shoulder, and over his head a wide scarf like a linen cloth. He was a tall, handsome man. As Jesus drew near, to the astonishment of the bystanders, the blind man turned toward him and cast himself at his feet. Jesus raised him and questioned him on his religion, the Ten Commandments, the Law, and the prophecies. The blind man answered more intelligently than any had dared to hope, yes, he even seemed to utter prophecies. He spoke of the persecution awaiting Jesus, saying that he must not yet go to Jerusalem, because there his enemies would put him to death. All present were struck with fear. The crowd gathered around was great. Jesus asked him whether he desired to see the tabernacles of Israel, the mountains and the Jordan, his own parents and friends, the temple, the Holy City, and lastly himself, Jesus, who was then standing before him. The blind man answered that he already saw him, that he had seen him as soon as he drew near, and he described his appearance and dress. "But," he continued, "I do desire to see all other things, and I know that, if thou wilt, thou canst give me sight." Then Jesus laid his hand on the man's forehead, prayed, and with his thumb made the sign of the cross on his closed eyelids, raising them at the same time. Thereupon the man cast off the scarf from his head and shoulders, looked gladly and wonderingly around, and exclaimed: "Great are the works of the Almighty!" He fell at Jesus's feet, who blessed him. The Pharisees looked on in silence, the relatives of the blind man gathered around him, the crowd intoned psalms, while the blind man himself in a prophetic strain spoke and chanted alternately of Jesus and the fulfillment of the Promise. Jesus went on into the city, where he healed many sick and restored sight to others that were blind, whom he found in the space between the houses and the earthen mounds. The usual courtesies of washing the feet and offering refreshments had already been tendered to him in one of the tabernacles outside the city. The blind man, who accompanied Jesus the whole way, continued to speak under prophetic inspiration of the Jordan, of the Holy Spirit who had descended upon him, and of the voice from heaven.

That evening Jesus preached in the synagogue for the sabbath. He spoke of the family of Noah, of the building of the ark, of the vocation of Abraham, and expounded the passages of Isaiah in which mention is made of God's covenant with Noah, and of the rainbow as a sign in the heavens. As he spoke I saw all very distinctly: the whole life and all the generations of the patriarchs, the branches that separated from the parent stock, and the idolatry that arose from them. When I am actually gazing upon such things, all seems clear and natural, but when out of vision, when returned to the routine of daily life, I am saddened by its weary interruptions and can no longer comprehend what I have seen with the eye of the spirit. Jesus spoke likewise of the erroneous interpretation of the scripture and of false computation of time. He proved by his own reckoning, which was quite simple and clear, that all things in the scriptures could be made accurately to accord. I cannot understand how such things could have been thrown into confusion, while others had been totally forgotten.

One section of Coreae lay upon a terraced mountain; the other, connected with the first by a row of small houses, extended eastward into a deep mountain dale. Some Pharisees and many sick from Shiloh were here awaiting Jesus. Although Coreae lay a little more to the west than Akrabis, yet it was still nearer to the Jordan as the river made a bend in this locality. It was not a large place and the people were not rich. They did cheap basketwork, made beehives and long strips of straw matting, some coarse, some fine. The straw or reeds were bleached and of the best. They made also whole screens like entire walls of this matting for separating sleeping chambers one from another. There were in the neighborhood many other little places. The mountains of this region are steep and rugged. Across the Jordan from Akrabis was the region traversed by Jesus the preceding year at the Feast of Tabernacles when he went through the valley to Dibon.

Saturday, October 7, AD 30 (Tishri 21)

Jesus taught in the synagogue and healed many sick people. This evening, with the close of the sabbath, the Feast of Tabernacles also drew to a close.

Next morning Jesus preached in the synagogue and, while the Jews took their sabbath promenade, cured many sick who had been brought to a large hall nearby. At the close of the sabbath, while assisting at the entertainment given in the tabernacles, Jesus had a dispute with the Pharisees. The subject under discussion was the prophecies uttered lately by the man born blind and to whom Jesus had given sight. The Pharisees maintained that the same man had already predicted many things that had never come to pass, to which Jesus replied that the Spirit of God had not then descended upon him. During the conversation mention was made of Ezekiel as if his early prophecies relating to Jerusalem had not been fulfilled, to which Jesus responded that the Spirit of God had not come upon him until he was in Babylon near the river Chobar, when something was given him to swallow. Jesus's response reduced the Pharisees to silence.

The man restored to sight went around the city, praising God, singing psalms, and prophesying. The day before he had been to the synagogue, where he was invested with a broad girdle and was admitted by vow among the Nazarites. A priest performed over him the ceremony of consecration. I think he afterward joined the disciples.

Sunday, October 8, AD 30 (Tishri 22)

After visiting Manahem's parents, Jesus and about seven disciples went to Ophra. During the afternoon Jesus visited several houses in Ophra and healed the sick. That evening, in the synagogue, a celebration took place in connection with the "day of joy" following on from the Feast of Tabernacles.

Jesus visited the parents of the man restored to sight, he himself having prayed him to do so. He conducted him to their home, which was in a retired part of the city. They were Essenes, of the grade that lived in marriage, distant relatives of Zechariah, and connected in some way with the Essene community of Mizpah. They had several sons and daughters, the one restored to sight being the youngest child. There were several other Essene families, all related to them, living in their neighborhood. They owned beautiful fields on a declivity just outside their quarter of the city, and cultivated wheat and barley. They retained for their own use only a third part of the produce, one being given to the poor, the other to the community at Mizpah. These Essenes came out hospitably to meet Jesus and welcome him in front of their dwellings. The father of the blind man restored to sight presented him to Jesus with the request that he would receive him as the least of the servants and messengers of his disciples, the one to go before him and prepare the inns for his reception. Jesus accepted him and sent him at once to Bethany with Silas and one of the disciples from Hebron. I think he intended to give Lazarus a joyful surprise by means of the man restored to sight, for he had known the latter as one born blind. The young man's father was named Cyrus, Sirius, or Syrus, the name of a king who reigned during the Jewish Captivity. The son's name was Manahem. He had always worn a girdle under his garments, but after his cure he put it outside and made a formal vow for a time. He possessed the gift of prophecy. Even when blind he had always been present at John's preaching, and had received baptism. He often gathered many of the youths of Coreae around him, instructed them and, inspired by the Spirit, prophesied to them of Jesus. His parents loved him on account of his piety and zeal, and provided him with clothing of the best. When Jesus gave him sight, he said: "I give thee a double gift, sight of soul and of body." The Pharisees of Coreae treated Manahem with contempt on account of his prophecies. They called them troubled fancies, foolish reveries, and said that he was vain of his fine clothes. They had brought him out themselves to meet Jesus, being firmly convinced that he could not cure him since no one had ever seen any pupil in his eyes. And now that he was restored to sight, the most wicked among them dared to affirm that he had never been blind, that being an Essene, he had very likely made a vow to feign blindness.

The Pharisees who spoke with Jesus of Ezekiel had expressed their contempt for the prophet. He was, they said, only a servant of Jeremiah and he had, in the school of the prophet, very preposterous, very gloomy reveries. Things had fallen out quite differently from his predictions. Manahem also had uttered very profound prophecies of Melchizedek, Malachi, and Jesus.

Jesus in Ophra, Salem, and Aruma

ONE hour to the southwest of Coreae was the city of Ophra, hidden among the mountains. Starting from Coreae the traveler had first to ascend and then to descend the mountain road. An hour and a half at most westward from it, and on the north side of the desert to Beth-Horon toward the west, stood the mountain fortress of Alexandrium. Mount Garizim lay on the northwest, to the south and west the plain just mentioned and the mountains of the tribe of Benjamin. Mary often traversed this plain. Many lonely shepherd huts were scattered over it, and the city of Bethel was built on its confines.

Three highroads ran through Ophra. Caravans from Hebron were constantly passing this way, consequently the whole place was made up of public inns and mercantile houses. The people were somewhat rude and greedy for gain. Once during the preceding year they had received a visit from some of Jesus's disciples, and since that they had improved a little. At the moment of Jesus's arrival, the men of the place were busy gathering grapes in the vineyards that lined the road on either side, for a solemn festival was to begin that evening. The tabernacles were deserted excepting by the children, the youths, and the maidens, who with banners were going through them processionally. The priests also were engaged removing the prayer rolls and other holy things from the tabernacles to the synagogue, where they laid a prayer roll on every seat. I saw the women in their homes. They were dressed in their holiday robes, and were praying from rolls of parchment.

Jesus was espied by some men outside the gate. They went to him and conducted him into the city. They washed his feet and he took a little luncheon at an inn near the synagogue. After that he visited several houses, healing the sick and giving instruction. That evening the roll of the Law was carried around in the school, and everyone read a little out of it. This ceremony was followed by a grand entertainment given in the public festive hall. I saw lambs on the table, and the Esrog apples also that had been procured for the Feast of Tabernacles were eaten. These apples were prepared with some ingredients. Each was cut into five parts, and these were again tied into one by a red thread. Five persons ate of one apple. The dishes had all been prepared by sabbath servants, that is, by pagans who appeared to be in a kind of slavery.

Monday, October 9, AD 30 (Tishri 23)

In the synagogue Jesus spoke about Adam and Joshua. He taught concerning worldly cares and referred to the lilies of the field (Matthew 6:25–34). Then he spoke of Daniel and Job. That evening he received a visit from a messenger of the pagan Cyrinus of Cyprus inviting Jesus to Cyprus.

Next morning Jesus went from house to house, exhorting the people to turn away from their avarice and love of gain, and engaging them to attend the instruction to be given in the synagogue. He saluted all with a congratulatory word on the close of the feast. The people of Ophra were so usurious and unpolished that they were held in the same low esteem as the publicans. But they had now improved a little. That afternoon the branches of which the tabernacles had been formed were brought processionally by the boys to the square in front of the synagogue, there piled in a heap, and burned. The Jews watched with interest the rising of the flames, presaging from their various movements good or bad fortune. Jesus preached afterward in the synagogue, taking for his subjects the happiness of Adam, his Fall, the Promise, and some passages from Joshua. He spoke also of too great solicitude for the things of life, of the lilies that do not spin, of the ravens that do not sow, etc., and brought forward examples in the person of Daniel and Job. They, he said, were men of piety, engrossed in occupations, but still without worldly solicitude.

Jesus was not entertained *gratis* in Ophra. The disciples had to pay all expenses at the inn. While he and they were still there a man from Cyprus came to see him. He had been to see John at Machaerus, ten hours from Ophra, and had been conducted hither by a servant of Zorobabel, the centurion of Capernaum. He had been commissioned by an illustrious man of Cyprus to bring him some reliable news of Jesus, also of John, of whom he had heard so much.

The messenger did not tarry long at Ophra. He left as soon as he had executed his commission, for a ship was in waiting to carry him home. He was a pagan, but of a most amiable and humble disposition. The centurion's servant had, at his request, conducted him from Capernaum to John, at Machaerus, and from the latter to Jesus, at Ophra. Jesus conversed with him a long time, and the disciples put in writing before his departure all that he desired to know. One of the ancestors of his master had been king of

Cyprus. He had received many Jews fleeing from persecution and had even entertained them at his own table. This work of mercy bore its fruit in one of his descendants, obtaining for him the grace to believe in Jesus Christ. In this vision I had a glimpse of Jesus retiring after the coming Passover to Tyre and Sidon, and thence sailing over to the island of Cyprus to announce his doctrine.

Tuesday, October 10, AD 30 (Tishri 24)

Today Jesus and the disciples left Ophra. On the way they visited some farms. They stayed overnight at a farmhouse where some shepherds were living.

Wednesday, October 11, AD 30 (Tishri 25)

Jesus and the disciples continued on, arriving at the town of Salem early in the afternoon. After healing the sick, Jesus taught at the synagogue. He spoke of Melchizedek of Salem, and also of the prophet Malachi, who had once stayed there.

Jesus journeyed on through the valley between Alexandrium and Lebona to Salem. He descended through the forest of Hareth into the plain of Salem. Gardens and beautiful walks lay around the outskirts of the city, which was most delightfully situated. It was not very large, but cleaner and more regular than many others in this region, laid out in the form of a star, the points radiating from a fountain in the center. All the streets ran toward the fountain, and were broken up by beautiful walks. The city at this period, however, had something in its appearance that bespoke decline. The fountain was regarded as sacred. It was once tainted like that near Jericho, but Elisha had, like the one alluded to, purified it by casting into it salt and water in which the holy mystery had been immersed. The little edifice erected over it was very beautiful. In the center of the city and not far from the fountain arose a lofty castle, then in ruins, the large window casements destitute of windows. Nearby stood a high, round tower. On its flat top, which was surrounded by a gallery, a flag was waving. At about two-thirds of the height of the tower projected four beams toward the four quarters of the world, upon which hung large polished globes that glittered in the sun. They faced four different cities, and were a sort of memorial of David's time. He had once sojourned here with Michol and, when obliged to flee into the land of Gilead, had by means of these globes received information from Jonathan concerning Saul and his movements against himself. The globes, by previous agreement, were hung sometimes this way, sometimes that, thus indicating by signs what was transpiring in those parts.

Jesus was very well received. People whom he met near the harvest ricks accompanied him to the city, from which others were coming to meet him. They conducted him and the disciples to a house, in which they washed their feet and provided them with sandals and garments until their own were dusted and cleaned. Travelers were often presented with the dress thus provided, but Jesus never accepted it as a gift. He generally had a change with him, of which one of the disciples took charge. The Salemites

Descent through the Forest of Lebanon

then took Jesus to their beautiful fountain and tendered to him the customary refreshments. There were gathered around the fountain numbers of sick of all kinds, so numerous that even the streets were lined with them. Jesus at once began to cure, passing quietly from one to another until nearly four o'clock, when he assisted at a dinner given at an inn, and thence proceeded to the synagogue to preach. During the discourse he spoke of Melchizedek, also of Malachi who had once sojourned here and who had prophesied the sacrifice according to the order of Melchizedek. Jesus told them that the time for that sacrifice was drawing near, and that those ancient prophets would have been happy to have seen and heard what they now saw and heard.

The people of Salem were of the middle class, neither poor nor rich, but well inclined and charitable toward one another. The doctors of the synagogue likewise were well-intentioned, but they were often visited by Pharisees from the neighborhood—to their own great annoyance and that of the citizens. Salem enjoyed certain privileges. It had under its jurisdiction the district in its immediate vicinity and other neighboring places. Jesus was especially kind to these people and confirmed them in their good sentiments.

Thursday, October 12, AD 30 (Tishri 26)

Jesus was a guest at a festive meal in his honor at one of the inns in Salem. Some Pharisees from the neighboring town of Aruma were present at the banquet, and they invited Jesus to Aruma for the sabbath.

On the morning of the next day Jesus went about an hour southeast of Salem to a nook between the Jordan and the little river that flows into it from Akrabis. There was a pleasure garden in this hilly region, also three fish ponds, one above another, each fed by the waters of the little river. There were also baths that could be warmed. Jesus was followed thither by many from the city. From this garden Ainon could be distinctly seen across the Jordan, whose opposite bank was full of promenaders. Toward noon all returned to the city and found assembled some of the Pharisees from Aruma. This city was situated on a mountain two hours west of Salem and about one hour northwest of the newly built city of Phasael, which lay almost hidden in a corner of the mountains. It was there the devout Jairus dwelt, whose daughter Jesus had not long ago raised to life. Among those Pharisees was a brother of Simon the Leper, of Bethany. He was one of the most distinguished Pharisees of Aruma. There were also some Sadducees present. They had all come as guests, for it was customary for the doctors of the Law to visit one another during the days immediately following the Feast of Tabernacles. Some from other places besides Aruma were present also. A banquet was given in one of the public houses of Salem, at which Jesus and all the doctors assisted. The latter feared that Jesus was going to preach in Salem on the coming sabbath. They did not relish the idea, since the inhabitants were already unfavorably disposed toward themselves; therefore Simon's brother invited Jesus to go to Aruma for the sabbath, and Jesus accepted the invitation. Phasael was a new place at which Herod stopped when in that part of the country. The city was surrounded by palm trees, and a little stream took its rise in the neighborhood, thence flowing into the Jordan almost opposite Succoth. The inhabitants appeared to be colonists. The city was built by Herod.

Friday, October 13, AD 30 (Tishri 27)

Jesus and the disciples traveled to Aruma. That evening, with the onset of the sabbath, he spoke at the synagogue about the sacred Hebrew language, Abraham's ancestors, and God's call to Abraham (Gen. 12).

On Jesus's arrival at Aruma, he was not received by the Pharisees outside the city gate. Consequently, with his seven disciples, all like himself with girded garments, he passed through into the city. There he was received according to the custom of the place by some of the well-disposed citizens, and as was always done to travelers that entered the gate with their garments girded. The fact of their entering in that style indicated that they had not yet received hospitality. Jesus and the disciples were taken to a house where their feet were washed, their clothes dusted, and refreshments offered them. After that Jesus went to the priests' house near the synagogue, where was Simon's brother together with several other Pharisees and Sadducees who had come hither from Thebez and other places.

Providing themselves with rolls of the scriptures, they went with Jesus to the public baths outside the city. There they deliberated upon the passages of holy scripture that occurred in the lesson of the present sabbath. It was like a preparation for a sermon. They were very courteous, very polished in their manner toward Jesus, whom they pressed to preach that evening, begging him at the same time not to say anything that could make the people mutinous. They did not say this in plain terms, but they made themselves understood thus. Jesus replied sternly and unhesitatingly that he would teach what was in the scripture, namely, the truth, and he went on to speak of wolves in sheep's clothing.

In the synagogue Jesus taught of Abraham's vocation and his journey to Egypt, of the Hebrew tongue, of Noah, Heber, Peleg, and Job. The lessons were from Genesis 12 and Isaiah. Jesus said that already in Heber's time God had separated the Israelites from the rest of humankind, for he had given Heber a new language, the Hebrew, which had nothing in common with other tongues then existing. This was done in order the more effectually to separate his race from all others. Before that, Heber, like Adam, Seth, and Noah, had spoken that first mother tongue. But at the building of the Tower of Babel this had been confused and broken up into numerous dialects. In order to separate Heber entirely from the rest of men, God had given him a language of his own, the holy, ancient Hebrew, without which he and his descendants would never have been able to keep themselves pure and a distinct race.

While at Aruma, Jesus received hospitality at the house of Simon the Leper's brother. Simon himself, though now living in Bethany, was originally from Aruma. He was a person of little importance, though with aspirations to the contrary, but his brother of Aruma was well versed in the lore of the day. All things were perfectly regulated in this Pharisee's house. If Jesus was not received with the reverence that faith inspires, still he was treated conformably to the best laws of hospitality. He was given a separate oratory, the toilet linen and vessels were beautiful, and the master of the house himself paid the customary honors to his guest. The wife and children did not make their appearance.

Jairus of Phasael, whose daughter Jesus had raised from the dead, was also here for the sabbath and had an interview with Jesus. He then went to see the disciples and took them around through the city. His daughter was not in Phasael, but at the girls' school up at Abel-Mehola. On this day many young girls came here in a body, as I had previously seen the men visiting different places in parties. Abel-Mehola may have been something over six hours from Phasael.

Saturday, October 14, AD 30 (Tishri 28)

Jesus taught again in the synagogue, and later visited a home for old people, whom he comforted and consoled. After a banquet given in his honor, he taught again that evening in the synagogue, where the festival of the consecration of Solomon's temple was being commemorated (1 Kings 8:65–66). He referred to the destruction of the temple, and that it would be rebuilt in three days.

Outside of Aruma and to the east stood an immense old building occupied by aged men and widows. They were not Essenes, though they were clothed in long, white robes and lived according to a certain rule. Jesus taught among them. When invited to a dinner or an entertainment, Jesus usually went from table to table and gave instructions.

The Feast of the Dedication of Solomon's temple was being celebrated in Aruma. The synagogue was brilliantly illuminated. In the middle of it stood a pyramid of lights. The feast proper was already past. I think it was immediately after the Feast of Tabernacles. The present nocturnal celebration was a continuation of it. Jesus preached on the dedication. He told of God's appearing to Solomon and saying to him that he would preserve the Israelites and the temple as long as they remained faithful to him, and that he would even dwell among them in the sacred edifice; but that he would destroy it if they fell away from him. Jesus used severe language when alluding to this. He applied it to the present, to his own day, in which evil had reached its height. If, he said, they were not converted, the temple would be destroyed. Then the Pharisees began to dispute with him. They declared that God had not made use of such threats, that it was all a fable, an imagination of Solomon. The discussion became very lively, and I saw Jesus speaking with great animation. There was something in his appearance that affected them strongly and they could scarcely rest their eyes upon him. He spoke to them upon the passages met today in the sabbath lessons, of distorting and corrupting the eternal truths, of the history and chronology of ancient pagan nations, the Egyptians, for instance. He demanded of the Pharisees how they could venture to reproach these pagans, they themselves being even then in so miserable a condition, since what had been handed over to them as something so peculiarly theirs, something so sacred, the Word of the Almighty upon which his covenant with their holy temple was founded, they could whimsically and capriciously reject as imaginations and fables. He affirmed and repeated God's promises to Solomon, and told them that in consequence of their false interpretations and sinful explanations Jehovah's menaces were about to be fulfilled, for when faith in his most holy promises was wavering, the foundation of his temple also began to totter. He said: "Yes, the temple will be overturned and destroyed, because ye do not believe in the promises, because ye do not know that which is holy, because ye treat it as a thing profane! You yourselves are laboring at its downfall. No part of it shall escape destruction. It will go to pieces on account of your sins!" In this wise spoke Jesus, and with such significance that he appeared to allude to himself under the name of the temple, as before his Passion he said still more plainly: "I will build it up again in three days." His words on this occasion were not so significant, though sufficiently so to fill his hearers with fury not unmixed with dread, and make them feel that there was something extraordinary and mysterious in his speech. They expressed their indignation in loud mutterings. Jesus paid no attention to them. He coolly continued his discourse in language they could not gainsay, for though against their will, they were interiorly convinced of the truth of his words. As he left the synagogue, the Pharisees offered him their hand, as if desirous of apologizing for their violence. They wished to maintain an appearance of friendliness. Jesus gently addressed to them some earnest words, and left the synagogue, which was then closed.

I had a vision of Solomon. He was standing upon a column in the court of the temple and near the altar of incense, addressing the people and praying aloud to God. The column was high enough for him to be distinctly seen. There was an interior ascent to the top upon which was a broad platform with a chair. It was movable and could be transported from place to place. I afterward saw Solomon in the fortress of Zion, for he did not yet occupy his new palace. It was there also that at an earlier period I saw God communicating with David, especially at the time of Nathan's embassy. There was also a terrace sheltered by a tent, upon which David slept. I saw Solomon praying on that terrace. A supernatural light of intense brilliancy shone around him, and from the light a voice proceeded.

Solomon was a handsome man. He was tall and his limbs were rounded, not spare and angular like those of most people of that place. His hair was brown and straight, his beard short and well trimmed, his brown eyes full of penetration, his face round and full with rather prominent cheekbones. He had not at that time devoted himself to his harem of pagan women.

To avoid scandalizing his enemies, Jesus did not publicly cure in Aruma. The people were besides intimidated by the Pharisees, and dared not make their appearance by day. It was an exceedingly touching sight to see Jesus, as I did, going on two successive nights through the moonlit streets and seeking admittance at some of the poorest gates where people were humbly awaiting him. With the two disciples that accompanied him he entered the courtyards and cured many sick. They were pious souls who believed in him and had implored his help through the intervention of the disciples. All this could be easily done without observation, since the streets in that quarter were very quiet. They were lined by the walls of the forecourt in which were little entrance gates; the windows of the houses were in the back, opening into the courtyards and little gardens. The people were patiently waiting for Jesus. I remember seeing a woman afflicted with an issue of blood. She was closely enveloped in a long veil, and was led by two young girls into the court. Jesus did not remain long by the sick when he cured at night. To arouse their faith, he usually put to them the question: "Dost thou believe that God can cure thee, and that he has given that power to one on earth?" These were the words, or something to the same effect, for I cannot clearly recall them. Then he presented his girdle to the sick woman to kiss and spoke some words that sounded like the following: "I heal thee through the mystery" (or it may have been: I heal thee in the intention) "in which this girdle has been worn from the beginning and will be worn till the end." In curing others Jesus laid the ends of the girdle on their heads. It was a long, wide strip like a towel. It was worn sometimes unfolded, sometimes folded into a narrow band, and again with long, hanging ends ornamented with fringe.

The valley to the east of Aruma, which extended from east to west in the direction of Sichar and northward to the mountain northeast of Shechem, was woody. To the east of this mountain, which rose in the midst of the plain of Shechem, was the little wood known as the grove of Mamre. It was there that Abraham had first pitched his tent, there also that God appeared to him and made to him the promise of a numerous posterity. A large tree stood nearby. Its bark was not so rough as that of the oak and it bore flowers and fruit at the same time. The latter were used for the knobs of pilgrim staffs. It was near this tree that the Lord appeared.

The highroad ran from Shechem to the left of the wood and around Mount Garizim. In the plain to the north of the forest was a city that recalled Abraham's sojourn in those parts. Some vestiges of it must still exist. It was three hours north of Aruma and two northwest of Phasael. It was called Thanat-Shiloh.

Jesus Leaves Aruma and Goes to Thanat-Shiloh and Aser-Michmethath

Sunday, October 15, AD 30 (*Tishri 29*)

This morning Jesus exchanged words with the Pharisees, who defended their adherence to outer customs and forms. Jesus pointed out to them that this was of no use because they had in fact lost the inner spirit of their religion. He and the disciples then proceeded to an inn near Thanat-Shiloh, which Lazarus had put at their disposal.

AFTER Jesus had once more earnestly addressed the Pharisees, telling them that they had lost the spirit of their religion, that they now held only to empty forms and customs which, however, the devil had managed to fill with himself, as they might see if they looked around on the pagans.

He left Aruma and went to the city Thanat-Shiloh, outside of which stood one of the inns established by Lazarus. He instructed the men and women whom he found at work on the immense corn ricks in the field. He introduced into his discourse parables relating to agriculture and the various kinds of land. These people were slaves and followers of the Samaritan creed.

Monday, October 16, AD 30 (*Tishri 30*)

This evening, with the New Moon festival celebrating the start of the month of Heshvan, Jesus taught in the synagogue at Thanat-Shiloh.

That evening Jesus taught in the synagogue. It was the Feast of the New Moon, consequently the synagogue and other public buildings were hung with wreaths of fruit.

A great many sick had assembled in front of the synagogue. They were mostly afflicted with paralysis, gout, or issue of blood, and some were possessed. Jesus blessed numbers of children, both sick and well. Many of those that were paralyzed in their hands and on one side owed their sickness in most cases to their labors in the field and to lying on the damp earth at night or in the daytime when in a profuse perspiration. I saw such cases in the fields outside of Gennabris, in Galilee.

Approach to Shechem

HESHVAN (30 days): October 16/17 to November 14/15, AD 30 Heshvan New Moon: October 15 at 6:45 PM Jerusalem time

Tuesday, October 17, AD 30 (Heshvan 1)

Jesus healed the sick in Thanat-Shiloh and then went into the fields, which were being harvested. There he taught again referring to unnecessary and exaggerated concern for the cares of life (Matthew 6:25–34).

Jesus went next day into the harvest field and cured many whom he found there. Some people brought out from the city baskets of provisions, and a great entertainment was spread in one of the tabernacles that still remained standing. Jesus afterward delivered a long discourse, in which he spoke against unnecessary and extravagant care for the preservation of life. He brought forward the example of the lilies. They do not spin, and yet they are clothed more beautifully than Solomon in all his glory. Jesus said many beautiful things to the same effect of the different animals and objects around. He also taught that they should not profane the sabbath and feasts by working for gain. Works of mercy, such as delivering a man or a beast from danger, were allowable; but as for the harvest, they should commit the care of its fruits to God's providence and not on account of threatening weather gather them in on the sabbath. Jesus's words on this subject were very beautiful and detailed. It was almost the same kind of a sermon as that on the Mount, for he often repeated the words: "Blessed are these! Blessed are those!"

Such instructions were much needed by the people of this place, for they were extraordinarily covetous and greedy for gain in trade and agriculture. They were wholly engrossed in their calling, and their servants were overburdened. They were charged with the collection of the tithes from the surrounding country. The sums thus coming into their possession they used to hold back for a considerable time, in order to put them out at usury. The products of their fields they sold. The old people worked in wood, for which they often betook themselves to the neighboring forest. I saw them cutting in large numbers the wooden heels worn under the sandals. There were many fig orchards around the city. There were no Pharisees here. The people were rather coarse, but very proud of their descent from Abraham. The sons of Abraham, however, whom the patriarch had settled here, had soon degenerated. They intermarried with the Shechemites, and when Jacob returned to that region the law of circumcision was already forgotten. Jacob had intended to fix his residence there, but was deterred from doing so by Dinah's seduction. He knew the children of Abraham who dwelt in those parts, and sent them presents. Dinah had gone to take a walk by the well of Salem. Some of the people in the fields, those to whom her father had sent presents, invited her to visit them. She was accompanied by her maids, but leaving them, she ventured alone into the fields, desirous of gratifying her curiosity. It was then that the Shechemite saw and ensnared her.

Wherever Jesus went, the sick were collected in crowds. We shall not be surprised at this when we remember that, as soon as his presence became known in any place, they were hurried thither from the huts and villages around the whole country.

Wednesday, October 18, AD 30 (Heshvan 2)

This morning Jesus healed again in Thanat-Shiloh. He left the town around midday, proceeding on to Aser-Michmethath. That night he stayed with the family of Obed, who owned a large estate outside of the town.

Here in Thanat the Jews and Samaritans lived separate, the former being the more numerous. Jesus preached to the Samaritans also, though remaining the while on Jewish territory. His hearers were gathered on the boundary of their own quarter at the head of one of the streets. He also cured their sick. The Jews of Thanat were not so hostile toward them as were those of other places, since here they held not so rigorously to the Law, and especially to the observance of the sabbath.

Jesus cured here in diverse ways. Some cures were effected at a distance by a glance and a word, some by a mere touch, some by imposition of hands; over some of the sick he breathed, others he blessed, and the eyes of some he moistened with saliva. Many of the sick happening to touch him were cured, and others at a distance were cured without his even turning to them. Toward the close of his career, he seemed to be more rapid in his movements than in the beginning. I thought that he made use of these different forms of healing to show that he was bound to no single one, but could produce a similar effect by the use of varied means. But he once said himself in the Gospel that one kind of devil was to be expelled in one way, another in a different way. He cured each in a manner analogous to his malady, his faith, and his natural temperament, as in our own time we behold him chastising some sinners and converting others. He did not interrupt the order of nature, he merely loosened the bonds that bound the sufferer. He cut no knots, he untied them, and he did everything so easily for he possessed the key to all. Inasmuch as he had become the God-Man, he treated those that he cured in a human manner. I had already been told that Jesus had healed in these different forms in order to instruct the disciples how to act in similar cases. The various forms of blessings, consecrations, and sacraments made use of by the church find their models in those then observed by Jesus.

Toward noon Jesus left the city accompanied by several persons. He proceeded along a tolerably broad highway toward the northeast. It led to Scythopolis with Doch upon the right and Thebez on the left at the eastern extremity of the mountain upon which Samaria was built. He descended toward the Jordan and into a valley through which a stream flowed to the river. Here he encountered a crowd of people, most of them Samaritan laborers who, eager to receive instruction, had hurried thither in advance of him. He found them waiting for him, and he stopped to address them. To the left of the valley and upon a height stood a little place consisting of one long row of houses. It was called Aser-Michmethath, and into it Jesus entered toward evening. Abel-Mehola may have been seven hours distant. Mary and the holy women passed by Aser on their journeys to Judea when they did not take the mountainous road past Samaria. The blessed Virgin and Joseph took this route on their flight into Egypt. That same evening Jesus went to the well of Abraham and to the pleasure gardens outside of Aser-Michmethath, and there cured many sick. Among them were two Samaritans who had been brought thither. Jesus was very affectionately received by the people of this place. They were very good and each one coveted the honor of showing him hospitality. But he put up outside the place with a family whose mode of life was patriarchal in its simplicity. The father was named Obed. Jesus and all the disciples were very lovingly entertained by him. The road through the country from Thanat-Shiloh to this place was far wider and better than that through Akrabis to Jericho. The latter was so very narrow, so uneven and rocky that beasts of burden could with difficulty traverse it with their loads of merchandise.

It was under the tree near Abraham's well that, in the

time of the Judges, the false prophetess carried on her sorcery and gave advice that always turned out disastrously. She used to perform all kinds of ceremonies there at night by the light of torches, calling up by her incantations singular figures of animals, etc. She was nailed to a board by the Midianites at Azo. This took place under the same tree beneath which Jacob buried the idols plundered from the Shechemites.

Joseph with the blessed Virgin and Jesus had lain concealed a day and a night near that tree on their flight into Egypt, for Herod's persecution had been proclaimed and it was very unsafe to travel in these parts. I think too that, on the journey to Bethlehem when Mary was so chilled by the cold, it was near this tree she suddenly became warm.

Aser-Michmethath lay across a mountain ridge that descends toward the valley of the Jordan. The southern side of the mountain belonged to Ephraim; the northern, to Manasseh. On the former stood Michmethath, on the latter Aser, the two forming but one city called Aser-Michmethath. The boundary ran between them. The synagogue was in Aser. The inhabitants of the two quarters were dissimilar in their customs, and had little communication. Michmethath, the quarter belonging to the tribe of Ephraim, extended up the mountain in one long line of houses; below in the valley was the little stream by which Jesus had instructed the Samaritans who had preceded him thither. A little beyond this point and nearer to the entrance of the city was the beautiful well surrounded by baths and pleasure gardens. The well, access to which was by a flight of steps, consisted of a solid basin in whose terraced center rose the tree to which I have more than once alluded. From this reservoir the surrounding bathing cisterns were fed. It was here that Jesus cured the two Samaritan women.

Obed's house was on his large estate outside of Michmethath. He was a kind of chief, or head magistrate of the place. The inhabitants of this quarter were for the most part related to one another, and several of the families were either those of Obed's own children or those of his other relatives. In his character of eldest and chief, Obed managed their business, directed their agricultural and pastoral affairs. His wife, with her housekeeping and the female portion of the family, occupied a separate part of the house. She was still quite a vigorous old Jewess. She had a kind of school, and taught the young girls of the other families all sorts of handiwork. Charity, wise counsels, and industry reigned throughout the whole house. Obed had eighteen children, some of whom were still unmarried. Two of his daughters had wedded husbands from Aser, the quarter belonging to Manasseh. This was a cause of regret to Obed, as I learned from his conversation with Jesus, for the people of Aser were not the best in the world and their customs were very different from those of their sister city.

Thursday, October 19, AD 30 (Heshvan 3)

This morning about four hundred people gathered to hear Jesus on a grass terrace, near a well at the entrance to the town. Jesus spoke of his mission and also about baptism and repentance. He then prepared some of those in the audience for baptism. He spent much of the rest of the day with Obed, who had eighteen children, and who modeled his life after Job.

Next morning Jesus preached near the well to an audience of about four hundred people, all ranged around on the grass of the terraced declivity. He spoke in significant terms of the approach of the kingdom, of his own mission, of penance, and of baptism. He also prepared some for the last-named ceremony, among whom were Obed's children. After that, accompanied by Obed, he went to some dwellings in the fields where he consoled and instructed the servants and aged persons who had had to remain at home while the others repaired to his sermon. Obed conversed long with Jesus of Abraham and Jacob, who had once sojourned in this region, and of Dinah's misfortune. The inhabitants of Michmethath looked upon themselves as descendants from Judah. Holofernes, the Midian adventurer, had at his invasion quite ruined this place, and after that the ancestors of these people settled here with the firm determination to live together according to their ancient, pious customs. This they had done down to the present. Obed followed the ancient usages of the pious Hebrews, and reverenced Job in an especial manner. He amply provided for his sons and daughters on their settlement in life, and at every marriage in his family he gave large offerings to the poor and to the temple.

Jesus blessed numbers of children everywhere presented to him by their mothers.

That afternoon there was a grand entertainment given in the open space around Obed's house and in the courtyard under the tabernacles which were still standing everywhere. Almost all the inhabitants of Michmethath took part in it, especially the poor of the whole region. Jesus went around to all the tables, blessing and teaching and lovingly helping with the various dishes. He related many parables. The women were seated in a separate tabernacle. Afterward Jesus visited and cured some sick in their homes, and again blessed many little ones presented to him by their mothers, who stood ranged in a row. There were a great many children present, especially around Obed's wife, for she had many pupils. Obed had a little son of about seven years, and with him Jesus exchanged many words. The boy lived in the field at the house of one of his elder brothers. He was an exceedingly pious child, and often knelt out in the field at night to pray. This did not please the elder brother, and Obed himself felt a little anxiety about the boy. But Jesus's words restored peace to their anxious hearts. After his death, the boy joined the disciples.

In the war of the Maccabees, Michmethath remained true and rendered much help to the Jews. Judas Maccabeus himself sojourned here at different times. Obed took Job for his model in all things, and led in the bosom of his large family a life altogether patriarchal.

Friday, October 20, AD 30 (Heshvan 4)

After confessing their sins to Jesus, a number of people were baptized by Saturnin and Joseph Barsabbas. That evening, as the sabbath began, Jesus taught in the synagogue about the miraculous deeds of the prophet Elisha.

When Jesus went into the other part of the city, the quarter belonging to the tribe of Manasseh, he found near the synagogue some Pharisees (not the best disposed toward himself) and many arrogant citizens. They were friends and supporters of those that collected the taxes and imposts for the Romans, which they afterward put out at usury. Jesus taught, and then cured the sick. The Pharisees and proud citizens treated Jesus with coldness and indifference. They were displeased at his having visited the simple, rustic people of Michmethath before honoring their own city with his presence. They had no love for him. And yet they were ambitious for his first visit as a learned doctor to be to themselves, rather than to their unsophisticated neighbors, upon whom they looked down.

Jesus, accompanied by a crowd of people, went back to the well outside Michmethath and began preparations for the ceremony of baptism. Many confessed their sins in general terms, while many others, going in private to Jesus, made them known in detail, and asked for penance and pardon. Saturnin and Joseph Barsabbas performed the ceremony of baptism, the other disciples acting as sponsors. It took place in an immense bathing cistern. After the baptism, Jesus returned to Aser for the sabbath. He preached from Genesis 18:23ff, of the destruction of Sodom and Gomorrha, and then, taking up the miracles recorded of Elisha, he spoke in strong language on the necessity of penance. His words were not pleasing to the Pharisees, for he reproached them with their contempt for the publicans while they themselves were secretly practicing usury, though hiding the fact under their sanctimonious exterior.

Saturday, October 21, AD 30 (Heshvan 5)

Jesus taught again in the synagogue and then healed the sick. At a meal held in his honor, he told the Pharisees the parable of the unjust steward (Luke 16:1–15). That evening, a fast-day began to commemorate the blinding of Zedekiah by Nebuchadnezzar (2 Kings 25:7).

After he had again taught in the synagogue at Aser, his subjects being Abraham and Elisha, he cured many sick, some of them demoniacs and others possessed by the spirit of melancholy. That afternoon a dinner was given in the public house. The Pharisees had issued invitations; but ignoring that fact, Jesus invited many poor people, as also the inhabitants of Michmethath, and ordered the disciples to defray all expenses. While at table he had a warm discussion with the Pharisees, whereupon he related the parable of the unjust debtor who desired the remission of his own debts, though oppressing others on account of theirs. Jesus applied the parable to themselves. They extorted taxes from the poor and at the same time deceived the Romans by pocketing the proceeds and declaring the people unable to pay; or again, by levying high taxes, only a third part of which was delivered over to the Romans. The Pharisees tried to justify themselves, but Jesus silenced them with the words: "Render unto Caesar that which is Caesar's, and to God that which is God's." In their fury they exclaimed: "What's that to him?"

Sunday, October 22, AD 30 (Heshvan 6)

As usual on a fast-day, the people went for a walk. Jesus went, too, and taught as he walked. When he reached the town well, he said that the kingdom of God would pass from the Jews to the world. Later, he recounted the parable of the talents (Matthew 25:14–30) to Obed. Toward evening, he instructed a group of women, recounting the parable of the wise and foolish virgins (Matthew 25:1–13).

A fast day commemorative of the putting out of Zedekiah's eyes by Nebuchadnezzar having begun, Jesus preached in the fields among the shepherds, also at Abraham's well. He spoke of the kingdom of God, declaring that it would pass from the Jews to the Gentiles, the latter of whom would even attain preeminence over the former. Obed afterward remarked to Jesus that if he preached to the Gentiles in that strain, they might possibly become proud. Jesus replied very graciously, and explained that it was just on account of their humility that they should reach the first place. He warned Obed and his people against the feeling of conscious rectitude and self-complacency to which they were predisposed. They in a measure distinguished themselves from their neighbors, and on account of their well-regulated life, their temperance, and the fruits of salvation amassed thereby, they esteemed themselves good and pleasing in the sight of God. Such sentiments might very easily end in pride. To guard against such a consequence, Jesus related the parable of the day laborers. He instructed the women also in their own separate pleasure garden, in which was a beautiful bower. To them he related the parable of the wise and the foolish virgins. While so engaged, Jesus stood, and they sat around him in a terraced circle, one above another. They sat on the ground with one knee slightly raised, and on it resting their hands. All the women on such occasions wore long mantles or veils that covered them completely; the rich had fine, transparent ones, while those of the poor were of coarse, thick stuff. At first these veils were worn closed, but during the sermon they were opened for the sake of comfort.

About thirty men were here baptized. Most of them were servants and people from a distance who had come hither after John's imprisonment.

Jesus took a walk with the people through the vineyards, the fruits of which were ripening for the second time that year.

Monday, October 23, AD 30 (Heshvan 7)

This morning Jesus left Aser-Michmethath, accompanied by five disciples. Teaching as he walked, Jesus arrived at Meroz during the afternoon. In the evening, he taught in the synagogue. Afterward, he and the disciples went to an inn belonging to Lazarus outside—to the east—of the town. There he was visited by Bartholomew, Simon, Judas Thaddeus, and Philip. They stayed the night with him. Bartholomew and Simon recommended that Jesus accept Judas Iscariot as a disciple, whereupon Jesus sighed and appeared to be troubled.

Jesus left Michmethath with five disciples (the two disciples of John had gone back to Machaerus) and descended the road by which he had come. The little stream in the valley to the south of Aser-Michmethath had its source in the fountain at which Jesus had given baptism by means of the disciples. He proceeded about three hours westward along the valley at the southern foot of the mountain upon which Thebez and Samaria lay. He gave instructions to the shepherds whom he met along the way, and toward noon reached the field that Jacob had destined for the special inheritance of Joseph. It lay in a valley to the south of Samaria and extended from east to west, one hour long and a half broad. A brook flowed westward through that valley. From the vineyards on the heights around could be seen Shechem a couple of hours to the south. It had everything to make it desirable: vineyards, pasture lands, grain, orchards, and water, besides the necessary buildings, all in good order. The landlord of this property was leaseholder, for it now belonged to Herod. It was the house at which the blessed Virgin and the holy women awaited the coming of Jesus from Shechem, and in which he cured the boy. The people here were very good. They assembled in crowds to hear Jesus's instructions, after which they tendered to him a dinner in the open air which he graciously accepted. This special patrimony of Joseph was not the field near Shechem which Jacob had purchased from Haor. It was another property upon which the Amorites had a footing along with the rightful occupants. They were dwelling on it at the time of purchase, and Jacob was obliged to drive them off. He did not relish their proximity, fearing lest his own people would intermarry among them. A kind of single combat or amicable contention took place between the two parties. It had been agreed upon that the one who broke his opponent's sword, or shield, or struck it out of his hand, should take possession of the land, the other having to retire. They decided the question in another way also, namely, by shooting at a certain boundary with the bow and arrow. Jacob and the Amorite leader took their places opposite each other, each attended by a certain number of his own followers standing in the rear. The struggle began. Jacob conquered his adversary, and the latter had to remove. After the contest they made a treaty. All this took place soon after the purchase of the field. Jacob dwelt eleven years near Shechem.

From this place Jesus again ascended the mountain northwestwardly to Meroz, a city on the southern side of a mountain on whose northern side stood Ataroth. Meroz was built on a higher elevation than Samaria, as well as Thebez off to the north and Aser-Michmethath to the east.

Jesus Teaches in Meroz and Receives Judas Iscariot to the Number of His Disciples • Ancestry and Character of Judas Iscariot

JESUS had never before been in Meroz. It was surrounded by a dry moat, which at times received some water from the mountain streams. The place had a bad name in Israel on account of the perfidy of its inhabitants. It had been peopled by the descendants of Aser and Gad, sons of Jacob and the handmaiden Zilpah, some of whom had intermarried with the Gentiles of Shechem. The other tribes refused to acknowledge the offspring of these mixed marriages, and they were despised likewise on account of their faithlessness and perfidy. Meroz, in consequence, became an isolated place, and its inhabitants, being thus cut off from much good, were likewise shielded from much evil. They had fallen into oblivion, perished, as it were, from among men. Their chief occupations consisted in dressing skins, making leather, preparing furs and garments of the same, and manufacturing leather sandals, straps, girdles, shields, and military jerkins. They brought the skins from afar on asses and dressed them partly near Meroz, using for that purpose a cistern supplied with water from their fountain in the city. But because this itself was fed from an aqueduct and had not always a full supply, they tanned the skins near Iscariot, a marshy region, a couple of hours to the west of Meroz and northward from Aser-Michmethath. It was a desolate little place of only a few dwellings. Nearby was a ravine through which a little stream flowed to the valley of the Jordan. It was on its banks that the people of Meroz prepared their skins. Judas and his parents had for some time dwelt in this locality, hence the surname borne by the former.

Jesus was very joyfully received at some distance from their city by the poor citizens of Meroz. They knew of his approach and went out to meet him, carrying sandals and garments for his use while they cleaned and brushed his own. Jesus thanked them and went with the disciples into the city, where they washed his feet and offered the customary refreshments. The Pharisees came to salute him. Toward evening he taught in the synagogue before a large audience, taking for his subject the slothful servant and the buried talent. By this parable Jesus designated the inhabitants themselves. Born of the maidservant, they had received one talent only, which they should have put out at interest; but instead of that they had buried it. The Master was coming and they should hasten to gain something. Jesus rebuked them also for their little love for their neighbor and their hatred of the Samaritans.

The Pharisees were not well pleased with Jesus, but the people so much the more, as they were very greatly oppressed by them. They rejoiced likewise at Jesus's visit because their whole region seemed to lie forgotten by all the world, and no one ever came to help or instruct them in any way.

After the sermon, Jesus went with his disciples to an inn that stood outside the western gate of the city. Lazarus had erected it for their use on some ground that he owned in these parts. Bartholomew, Simon the Zealot, Judas Thaddeus, and Philip came here to see Jesus, by whom they were cordially received. They had already spoken with the disciples. They dined with Jesus and remained overnight. Jesus had often before seen Bartholomew, had given him an interior call to his service and had even spoken of him to the disciples. Simon and Thaddeus were his cousins. Philip also was related to him and, like Thaddeus, was already among the disciples. Jesus had called all these to follow him when, upon his last visit to Capernaum at Peter's fishery on the lake, he had spoken of their soon being summoned to do so. It was then that Peter had expressed himself so desirous of being allowed to remain at home as unfit for such a calling. Then it was that Peter uttered the words that later on were recorded in the Gospel.

Judas Iscariot likewise had come with the above named disciples to Meroz. He did not, however, spend the evening with Jesus, but at a house in the city where he had often before stayed. Bartholomew and Simon spoke with Jesus of Judas. They said that they knew him to be an active, well-informed man, very willing to be of service, and very desirous of a place among the disciples. Jesus sighed as they spoke and appeared troubled. When they asked him the cause of his sadness, he answered: "It is not yet time to speak, but only to think of it." He taught during the whole meal, and all slept at the inn.

The newly arrived disciples had come from Capernaum, where they had met Peter and Andrew. They had messages from there and had also brought Jesus some money for the expenses of the journey, the charitable gift of the women. Judas, having met them at Nain, accompanied them to Meroz. Even at this early period he was already known to all the disciples, and he had recently been in Cyprus. His manifold accounts of Jesus, of his miracles, of the various opinions formed of him, namely, that some looked upon him as the son of David, others called him the Christ, and the majority esteemed him the greatest of the prophets, had made the Jews and pagans of the island very inquisitive with regard to him. They had heard, too, many wonderful things of his visit to Tyre and Sidon. The Cyprian pagan, the officer who visited Jesus in Ophra, had in consequence of all these marvelous accounts been sent thither by his master, who was very much impressed by them. Judas had accompanied the officer back to Cyprus. On his return journey he stopped at Ornithopolis where the parents of Saturnin, originally from Greece, then dwelt.

When Judas learned on the way that Jesus was going into the region of Meroz, where he himself was well-known, he went to seek Bartholomew in Debbaseth. He was already acquainted with him and he invited him to go with him to Meroz and present him to Jesus. Bartholomew expressed his willingness to do so. But he went first to Capernaum with Judas Thaddeus to see the disciples there, thence with Thaddeus and Philip to Tiberias, where Simon the Zealot joined them, and then stopped at Nain for Judas who had journeyed thither to meet them. He begged them again to present him to Jesus as one desirous of becoming a disciple. They were well pleased to do so, for they took delight in his cleverness, his readiness to render service, and his courteous manner.

Judas Iscariot may have been at that time twenty-five years old. He was of middle height and by no means ugly. His hair was of a deep black, his beard somewhat reddish. In his attire he was perfectly neat and more elegant than the majority of Jews. He was affable in address, obliging, and fond of making himself important. He talked with an air of confidence of the great or of persons renowned for holiness, affecting familiarity with such when he found himself among those that did not know him. But if anyone who knew better convicted him of untruth, he retired confused. He was avaricious of honors, distinctions, and money. He was always in pursuit of good luck, always longing for fame, rank, a high position, wealth, though not seeing clearly how all this was to come to him. The appearance of Jesus in public greatly encouraged him to hope for a realization of his dreams. The disciples were provided for; the wealthy Lazarus took part with Jesus, of whom everyone thought that he was about to establish a kingdom; he was spoken of on all sides as a king, as the Messiah, as the prophet of Nazareth. His miracles and wisdom were on every tongue. Judas consequently conceived a great desire to be numbered as his disciple and to share his greatness which, he thought, was to be that of this world. For a long time previously he had picked up, wherever he could, information of Jesus and had in turn carried around tidings of him. He had sought the acquaintance of several of the disciples, and was now nearing the object of his desires. The chief motive that influenced him to follow Jesus was the fact that he had no settled occupation and only a half-education. He had embarked on trade and commerce, but without success, and had squandered the fortune left him by his natural father. Lately he had been executing all kinds of commissions, carrying on all kinds of business and brokerage for other people. In the discharge of such affairs he showed himself both zealous and intelligent. A brother of his deceased father, named Simeon, was engaged in agriculture in Iscariot, the little place of about twenty houses that belonged to Meroz and from which it lay only a short distance toward the east. His parents had lived there a long time, and even after their death he had generally made it his home, hence his appellation of Iscariot. His parents at one time led a wandering life, for his mother was a public dancer and singer. She was of the race of Jephthah, or rather that of his wife, and from the land of Tob. She was a poetess. She composed songs and anthems, which she sang with harp accompaniment. She taught young girls to dance, and carried with her from place to place all sorts of feminine finery and new fashions. Her husband, a Jew, was not with her; he lived at Pella. Judas was an illegitimate child whose father was an officer in the army near Damascus. He was born at Ascalon on one of his mother's professional journeys, but she soon freed herself from the encumbrance by exposing the child. Shortly after his birth, he was abandoned on the water's edge. But being found by some rich people with no children of their own, they cared for the child and bestowed upon him a liberal education. Later on, however, he turned out to be a bad boy and, through some kind of knavery, fell again to the care of his mother, who assumed the charge for pay. It is in my mind that the husband of his mother, becoming acquainted with the boy's origin, had cursed him. Judas received some wealth from his illegitimate father. He was possessed of much wit. After the death of his parents, he lived mostly in Iscariot with his uncle Simeon, the tanner, and helped him in his business. He was not as yet a villain, but loquacious, greedy for wealth and honor, and without stability. He was neither a profligate nor a man without religion, for he adhered strictly to all the prescriptions of the Jewish Law. He comes before me as a man that could be influenced as easily to the best things as to the worst. With all his cleverness, courteousness, and obligingness, there was a shade of darkness, of sadness, in the expression of his countenance, proceeding from his avarice, his ambition, his secret envy of even the virtues of others.

He was not, however, exactly ugly. There was something bland and affable in his countenance, though at the same time, something abject and repulsive. His father had something good in him, and thence came that possessed by Judas. When as a boy he was returned to his mother, and she on his account was embroiled in a quarrel with her husband, she cursed him. Both she and her husband were jugglers. They practiced all kinds of tricks; they were sometimes in plenty and as often in want.

The disciples in the beginning were favorably inclined toward Judas on account of his obliging ways, for he was ready even to clean their shoes. As he was an excellent walker, he made at first long journeys in the service of the little community. I never saw him work a miracle. He was always full of envy and jealousy and, toward the close of Jesus's career, he had become weary of obedience, of the wandering life of the disciples, and of the—to him—inexplicable mystery that surrounded the divine Master.

Tuesday, October 24, AD 30 (Heshvan 8)

This morning Jesus and the disciples went to the town well and healed the sick who had gathered there. Afterward, he healed some of those who were possessed and visited the leper-house to cure the lepers. That afternoon, Bartholomew and Simon introduced Judas Iscariot to Jesus. Jesus was friendly, but filled with indescribable sorrow. Judas bowed and said: "Master, I pray thee allow me to join your teaching." Jesus replied gently and with the prophetic words: "You may have a place among my disciples, unless you would prefer to leave it to another." Later, Jesus taught from a mountain located between Meroz and Ataroth, for it had been announced to the people in both towns that he would teach here today.

In the center of Meroz was a beautifully constructed fountain, the water of which was conducted through pipes from the neighboring mountain, at a little distance to the north of the city. There were five galleries around the well, each of which contained a reservoir. Into these reservoirs the water of the well could be pumped. In the outer gallery of all were little bathing houses, and the whole place could be closed. Here to these galleries around the well had numbers of very sick persons belonging to the city, some of them considered incurable, been brought on beds. The worst were placed in the little bathing houses in the outside circle. Meroz, abandoned, despised, and helpless, possessed an astonishing number of sick, dropsical old people, paralytics, and sufferers of all kinds. Jesus, accompanied by the disciples, Judas excepted (he had not yet been presented to Jesus), went into the city. The Pharisees of the place and some strangers who had come from a distance were present. They took their stand at the center of the fountain where they could see all that went on. They appeared astonished and even somewhat scandalized at the miracles of Jesus. They were old people grounded in their own opinion, who had listened to previous accounts of such wonders with wise shakes of the head, smiles, and shrugs, giving credence to none of it. But now they beheld with surprise and vexation those seriously affected, those incurables of their own city, by whose deep-seated maladies they hoped to see Jesus's healing power set at naught, taking up their beds and going off to their homes with songs of praise for their perfect cure. Jesus preached, instructed and consoled the sick, and gave himself no trouble about the Pharisees. The whole city resounded with joy and thanksgiving. This lasted from early morn till nearly noon.

Jesus and the disciples now returned to their inn by the western gate of the city. On their way through the streets, some furious possessed, that had been allowed to leave their place of confinement, cried after Jesus. He commanded them to be silent. They instantly ceased their cries and threw themselves humbly at his feet. Jesus cured them and admonished them to purify themselves. From the inn he went to the hospital of the lepers a short distance from the city, entered, called the lepers before him, touched them, healed them, and commanded them to present themselves before the priests for the customary purifications. Jesus did not allow the disciples to follow him into the leprous hospital. He sent them up to the mountain where, after healing the lepers, he was to deliver an instruction.

On the way the disciples were met by Judas Iscariot, and when Jesus again joined them, Bartholomew and Simon the Zealot presented him to Jesus with the words: "Master, here is Judas of whom we have spoken to thee." Jesus looked at him graciously, but with indescribable sorrow. Judas, bowing, said: "Master, I pray thee allow me to share thy instructions." Jesus replied sweetly and in words full of prophetic meaning: "Thou mayst have a place among my disciples, unless thou dost prefer to leave it to another." These were his words or at least their purport. I felt that Jesus was prophesying of Matthias, who was to fill Judas's place among the twelve, and alluding also to his own betrayal. The expression was more comprehensive, but I felt that such was the allusion.

They now continued the ascent of the mountain, Jesus teaching all the while. On the summit was gathered a great crowd from Meroz, from Ataroth off to the north, and from the whole region around. There were also many Pharisees from these places. Jesus had some days previously announced the sermon by means of the disciples. He preached in vigorous terms of the kingdom, of penance, of the abandonment in which the people of Meroz lived, and he earnestly exhorted them to arise from their sluggishness. There was no teacher's chair up here. The preacher took his stand on an eminence, surrounded by a trench and a low wall, upon which the listeners leaned or stood.

The view from this point was very beautiful and extended. One could see over Samaria, Meroz, Thebez, Michmethath, and away over the whole country around. Mount Garizim, however, was not in view, though the towers of its ancient temple were visible. Toward the southeast, the horizon stretched off to the Dead Sea and eastward over the Jordan to Gilead. To the north in an oblique direction rose the heights of Tabor, the view further extending in the direction of Capernaum.

When evening closed, Jesus informed his hearers that he would teach there again in the morning. A great many of the people slept on the mountain under tents as they were at so great a distance from home. Jesus and the disciples went back to the inn near Meroz. All along the way Jesus taught of the good employment of time, of salvation so long looked for and now so near, of abandoning their relatives in order to follow him, and of helping the needy. Arrived at the inn, he dined with the disciples. While on the mountain he had caused to be distributed to the poor the money that the disciples had brought with them from Capernaum. Judas regarded that distribution with a covetous eye. During the meal at the inn, Jesus continued his instructions, and indeed after it far into the night. Today, for the first time, Judas sat at table with the Savior and spent the night under the same roof with him.

Sermon on the Mountain near Meroz • The Daughters of Lais

Wednesday, October 25, AD 30 (Heshvan 9)

Today Jesus continued his teaching from the mountain. Disputing with the Pharisees, he referred to the two commandments: Love of God and love of neighbor (Matthew 22:36–40). Later in the day, while healing the sick, he was approached by a rich pagan widow from Nain, called Lais. She sought Jesus's aid on behalf of her two daughters, Sabia and Athalia, both of whom had stayed in Nain because they were possessed. Jesus exorcised Lais's daughters from afar and told her to purify herself, saying: "The sins of the parents are on these children." After this healing, Manahem, the blind youth whose sight Jesus had restored in Coreae, returned from delivering a message to Lazarus in Bethany and came to Jesus. Manahem was accompanied by the nephews of Joseph of Arimathea, Aram and Themani.

NEXT morning Jesus went again to the mountain and there during the whole forenoon delivered a grand discourse similar to that known as the Sermon on the Mount. The multitude present was great, and food was distributed: bread and honey, along with fish taken from the ponds fed by the little brooks that watered the region. Jesus had by means of the disciples procured provisions for the poor. Toward the end of the discourse he alluded again to the one talent that, as children of the handmaid, they had received and buried, and he inveighed severely against the Pharisees for their hatred toward them, asking why they had not long ago led these people back to the truth. His words vexed the Pharisees, and they began to retort. They reproached Jesus for allowing his disciples so much liberty, especially on the score of fasting, washing, purifications, the sabbath, the shunning of publicans and the different sects. It was not in this way, they said, the children of the prophets and the scribes used to live.

Jesus replied in the words of the commandment of fraternal love: "Love God above all things and thy neighbor as thyself. That is the first commandment!" and he told the disciples that they should learn to practice it, instead of covering up its abuse by means of exterior practices. Jesus spoke somewhat figuratively; consequently, Philip and Thaddeus said to him: "Master, they have not understood thee." Then Jesus explained himself quite significantly. He had compassion for the poor, ignorant, sinful people whom they, the Pharisees, with all their outward observance of the Law, had allowed to go to destruction, and he ended by boldly declaring that they who acted so should have no part in his kingdom. He then went down the mountain to his inn, which was one-half hour from the scene of the sermon and another from the city. He met all along the way, on litters under tents, a great number of sick of all kinds patiently awaiting his coming. Many of them had come too late for the first cures. They belonged to the country far around. Jesus cured them, addressing to them at the same time words of consolation and exhortation to a change of life.

A pagan widow of Nain, called Lais, was also here waiting for Jesus. She had come to implore his aid in behalf of her two daughters, Sabia and Athalia. They were in a fearful manner possessed by the devil, and were at home in Nain confined to their respective apartments. They were perfectly furious. They dashed themselves here and there, they bit their own flesh, and struck wildly around them; no one ventured to approach them. At other times their members were contracted by cramps, and they fell to the ground pale and unconscious. Their mother, accompanied by handmaids and menservants, had come to Jesus for help. She was waiting at a distance eagerly desirous of his approach, but to her disappointment she saw him always turning to others. The poor mother could not restrain her eagerness, but cried out from time to time as he drew near: "Ah, Lord, have mercy on me!" but Jesus appeared not to hear her. The women near her suggested that she should say: "Have mercy on my daughters!" since she herself was not a sufferer. She replied: "They are my own flesh. In having mercy on me, he will have mercy on them also!" and again she uttered the same cry. At last Jesus turned and addressed her: "It is proper that I should break bread to the children of my own household before attending to strangers."

The mother replied: "Lord, thou art right. I will wait or even come again, if thou canst not help me today, for I am not worthy of thy assistance!" Jesus had, however, finished his work of healing, and the cured, singing canticles of praise, were going off with their beds. Jesus had turned away from the disconsolate mother and appeared about to retire. Seeing this, the poor woman grew desperate. "Ah!" she thought, "He is not going to help me!" But as the words flashed through her mind, Jesus turned toward her and said: "Woman, what askest thou of me?" She cast herself veiled at his feet and answered: "Lord, help me! My two daughters at Nain are tormented by the devil. I know that thou canst help them if thou wilt, for all things are possible to thee." Jesus responded: "Return to thy home! Thy daughters are coming to meet thee. But purify thyself! The sins of the parents are upon these children." These last words Jesus spoke to her privately. She replied: "Lord, I have already long wept my sin. What shall I do?" Then Jesus told her that she should get rid of her unjustly acquired goods, mortify her body, pray, fast, give alms, and comfort the sick. She promised with many tears to do all that he suggested, and then went away full of joy. Her two daughters were the fruit of an illicit connection. She had three sons born in lawful wedlock, but they lived apart from their mother, who still retained property belonging to them. She was very rich and, notwithstanding her repentance, lived, like most people of her class, a life of luxury. The daughters were confined in separate chambers. While Jesus was speaking with their mother, they fell unconscious, and Satan went out of them in the form of a black vapor. Weeping vehemently and quite changed, they called their female attendants and informed them that they were cured. When they learned that their mother had gone to the prophet of Nazareth, they set out to meet her, accompanied by many of their acquaintances. They met her at about an hour's distance from Nain and related all that had happened to them.

The mother then went on to the city, but the daughters with their maids and servants proceeded straight forward to Meroz. They wished to present themselves to Jesus who, they had heard, was going to teach there again the next morning.

During the healing of the sick, Manahem, the blind disciple of Coreae, who had been restored to sight and whom Jesus had sent with a message to Lazarus, returned from Bethany with the two nephews of Joseph of Arimathea. Jesus gave them an interview. The holy women had sent by them money and gifts of various kinds to Jesus. Dinah the Samaritan had visited the holy women at Capernaum, bringing with her a rich contribution. Veronica and Johanna Chusa had also visited Mary. On their return journey they called to see Magdalene, whom they found very much changed. She was depressed in spirits, her folly apparently undergoing a struggle with her good inclinations. The holy women took Dinah with them to Bethany. There was at this epoch a rich, aged widow who joined Martha's little band and gave all she possessed for the benefit of the young community.

When the Pharisees invited Jesus to a dinner, they asked him whether his disciples, young, inexperienced men, some of them quite rustic and unaccustomed to the society of the learned, should also be invited. Jesus answered: "Yes! For whoever invites me, invites the members of my household also; and he that rejects them likewise rejects me." At these words, they bade him bring the disciples with him. All repaired to the public house in the city, where Jesus still taught and explained parables.

The property upon which Lazarus had established the inn near Meroz consisted of a beautiful field and numerous orchards interspersed with charming groves. Some of his servants lived there to attend to the fruit and provide for its sale. At this time they had charge also of the inn. At the last meeting of Jesus with Lazarus at Ainon it had been agreed that Jesus should tarry for some time in these parts. The holy women had, in consequence, come thither to get the inn in order, and the people around the country had been notified to expect Jesus.

Thursday, October 26, AD 30 (Heshvan 10)

Jesus continued his teaching from the mountain. Later, as he was coming down from there, he was approached by Lais and her two healed daughters, whom she had brought from Nain. They cast themselves down at Jesus' feet and gave thanks. He commanded them to rise and told them that they now belonged to the community of his heavenly Father.

On the following morning, before going again to the mountain, Jesus taught at the fountain in Meroz, and again reproached the Pharisees for the little care they took of the people. After that he ascended the mountain and delivered an instruction similar to that known as the Sermon on the Mount. Before taking leave of the people, he once more gave an explanation of the buried talent. Some of his hearers had already been three days encamped on the mountain. Those in need had been placed apart from the rest and were provided with food and other necessaries by the disciples. Judas's uncle, Simeon of Iscariot, a devout, old man, dark complexioned and vigorous, entreated Jesus to go to Iscariot, and Jesus promised to do so. When he went down the mountain he found some sick awaiting him. They were still able to walk. Jesus cured them. This took place on the road between the inn and Lazarus's property, at a little distance below the place where the disciples had distributed food to the people.

On the same spot upon which the pagan woman Lais of Nain had knelt yesterday at Jesus's feet praying for her sick daughters, were today those daughters, now both cured, awaiting the coming of Jesus. They were named Athalia and Sabia, and were accompanied by their maids and menservants. With all their attendants, they cast themselves down before Jesus, saying: "Lord, we esteemed ourselves unworthy to listen to thy instructions, therefore we waited here to thank thee for freeing us from the power of the evil one." Jesus commanded them to rise. He commended their mother's patience, humility, and faith, for as a stranger she had waited until he had broken bread to his own household. But now, he continued, she too belonged to his household, for she had recognized the God of Israel in his mercy. The heavenly Father had sent him to break bread to all that believed in his mission and brought forth fruits of penance. Then he ordered the disciples to bring food, which he gave to the maidens and all their attendants—to each a piece of bread and a piece of fish—delivering to them at the same time an instruction thereon full of deep significance. After that he went on with the disciples to the inn. One of the maidens was twenty, the other five and twenty years old. Their sickness and the confinement in which they lived had made them pale and wan.

A Tannery

Jesus in Iscariot and Dothan • Cure of Issachar

Friday, October 27, AD 30 (Heshvan 11)

After visiting Simon of Iscariot, the uncle of Judas, in Iscariot, Jesus and the disciples made their way to Dothan for the sabbath. Here he was joined by some other disciples, including Nathaniel the bridegroom. That evening, he taught in the synagogue.

NEXT morning, Jesus left the inn with the disciples and journeyed eastward to Iscariot, distant not quite an hour. On the swampy ground of a deep ravine stood a row of houses, about twenty-five, near a stream of water black and full of reeds. Here and there it was dammed so as to form pools for tanning. Very frequently this water failed, and then they had to let in other sources. The cattle for slaughter belonging to Meroz were pastured around these parts. When needed in Meroz, they were slaughtered here, then flayed, and the hide handed over to the tanners of Iscariot. The ravine in which the little place lay was directly to the north of Michmethath. The tanner's trade, on account of the odors attending it, was held in detestation by the Jews. Although for tanning the hides of the slaughtered cattle pagan slaves and others of the most despised races were needed, yet in Meroz they dwelt apart from the other inhabitants. In Iscariot no calling was carried on but tanning, and it seemed to me that most of the houses of this place belonged to old Simeon, the uncle of Judas.

Judas was very dear and quite useful to his old uncle in his leather trade. Sometimes he dispatched him with asses to purchase raw hides, sometimes with prepared leather to the seaport towns, for he was a clever and cunning broker and commission merchant. Still he was not at this time a villain, and had he overcome himself in little things, he would not have fallen so low. The blessed Virgin very often warned him, but he was extremely vacillating. He was susceptible of very vehement, though not lasting repentance.

His head was always running on the establishment of an earthly kingdom, and when he found that not likely to be fulfilled, he began to appropriate the money entrusted to his care. He was therefore greatly vexed that the worth of Magdalene's ointment had not passed as alms through his hands. It was at the last Feast of Tabernacles in Jesus's lifetime that Judas began to go to the bad. When he betrayed Jesus for money, he never dreamed of his being put to death. He thought his Master would soon be released; his only desire was to make a little money.

Judas was, here in Iscariot, very obliging and ready to serve; he was perfectly at home. His uncle, the tanner Simeon, a very busy and active man, received Jesus and the disciples at some distance from the place, washed their feet, and offered the customary refreshments. Jesus and the disciples visited his house where were his family, consisting of his wife, his children, and his servants.

Jesus paid a visit to the opposite side of the place where, in the midst of a field, was a kind of pleasure garden in which the tabernacles were still standing. All the inhabitants of the place were here assembled. Jesus taught upon the parable of the sower and the different kinds of soil. He exhorted the people to let the instructions they had heard from him on the mountain near Meroz find good soil in their hearts.

Jesus afterward, with the disciples and Simeon's family, took a little repast standing. During it old Simeon begged him to admit Judas his nephew, whom he praised in many ways, to a participation in his teachings and his kingdom. Jesus responded in pretty much the same terms as he had used toward Judas himself: "Everyone may have a share therein, provided he is resolved not to relinquish his portion to another." Jesus performed no cures here, for the sick had already been healed on the mountain.

Jesus and the disciples went from Iscariot back toward the west almost as far as the inn. Then turning to the north, they traversed the valley having the mountain upon which Jesus had taught to the left, turned somewhat northwestwardly, then again to the north, and journeyed along a low mountain terrace toward Dothan, which could be seen lying low in the eastern valley of the plain of Esdrelon. To the east rose the mountains above, and to the west lay the valley below it.

Jesus was accompanied by three troops of men who, having been present at his instructions on the mountain, were now returning in bands to their homes for the sabbath. When one party left him, another came up to bear him company. It was almost three hours from the inn to Dothan, a place as large as Münster. I had a vision in which I saw that it was here that the soldiers sent by Jeroboam to seize Elisha were struck blind. Dothan had five gates and as many principal streets; it was traversed likewise by two highways. One of the latter led from Galilee down to Samaria and Judea; the other came from the opposite side of the Jordan and ran through the valley of Apheke and Ptolomais on the sea. Trade in wood was carried on in Dothan. On the mountain chain around here and near Samaria there was still much wood; but across the Jordan near Hebron, and at the Dead Sea, the mountains are quite bare. I saw in the neighborhood of Dothan much work going on under tents in the preparation of wood. All sorts of beams for the different parts of ships were put into shape, and long, thin slats were prepared for wicker partitions. Outside the gates on the highways that crossed each other in Dothan were several inns.

Jesus went with the disciples to the synagogue, where a crowd was already assembled, among them many Pharisees and doctors. They must have had some intimation of Jesus's coming, for they were so polite as to receive him in the court outside the synagogue, wash his feet, and present to him the customary refection. Then they conducted him in and handed him the roll of the Law. The sermon was on the death of Sarah, Abraham's second marriage with Keturah, and the dedication of Solomon's temple.

The sabbath instructions over, Jesus went to an inn outside the city. There he found Nathaniel the bridegroom, two sons of Cleophas and his mother's eldest sister, and a couple of the other disciples who had come hither for the sabbath. There were now about seventeen disciples with him. The people from the house on Lazarus's estate near Ginea, where Jesus stopped recently when he went to Ataroth, were also here to celebrate the sabbath.

Saturday, October 28, AD 30 (Heshvan 12)

This morning, after teaching in the synagogue, Jesus visited Issachar of Dothan, a rich man of about fifty, who had recently married his brother's widow, Salome, who was twenty-five years old. Issachar lay ill with edema, and Jesus healed him. That evening, Issachar and Salome held a banquet at their home for Jesus and the disciples. Thomas, the future disciple, who was well known to Issachar, attended the banquet. Bartholomew, Judas Iscariot, and James the Less were also present.

Dothan was a beautiful, well-built old city, very agreeably situated. In the rear, though at a considerable distance, arose a mountain chain, and in front it looked out upon the delightful plain of Esdrelon. The mountains of this region are not so steep and rugged. Peak rises above peak, and the roads are better. The houses were of the old style, like those in David's time. Many had little turrets on the corners of the flat roofs capped by large domes, or cupolas, in which an observer could sit and view the surrounding locality. It was from such a cupola that David saw Bathsheba. There were also on the roofs galleries of roses and even of trees.

Jesus entered many of the forecourts of the dwellings, where he found sick whom he cured. The occupants standing at their doors implored him to come in, which he did accompanied by two of the disciples. They also in different places begged the disciples to intercede for them, which they accordingly did. Jesus went likewise to the place in which the lepers abode, separated from all others, and there he healed the sufferers. There were many lepers in this city. It may have been on account of their frequent communication with strangers for trading purposes, for besides the trade in wood, the inhabitants of Dothan carried on other branches of industry. They imported carpets, raw silk, and similar goods which they unpacked and again exported.

I saw goods like the above at the house of the sick man whom Jesus was entreated by Nathaniel to visit. Nathaniel lived at his house. It was a very elegant looking dwelling surrounded by courtyards and open colonnades, and situated not far from the synagogue. The occupant was a wealthy man of about fifty years named Issachar, who was suffering from edema. Notwithstanding his miserable condition, Issachar had a few days previously to the coming of Jesus espoused a young woman named Salome, aged twenty-five years. This union was according to legal prescription analogous to that of Ruth and Boaz—it gave Salome the right to inherit Issachar's property. The evil tongues of the city, especially the Pharisees, found great fault with this marriage, which at once became the general talk. But Issachar and Salome put their trust in Jesus, for at his last visit to this part of the country, they had recommended their affairs to him.

The family had been long acquainted with Jesus, even during the lifetime of Salome's parents, for Mary and Joseph when journeying from Nazareth to visit Elizabeth had found hospitality with them. This happened shortly before the Passover solemnity. Joseph went with Zechariah from Hebron to Jerusalem for the feast, after which he returned to Hebron and then went home leaving Mary there. Thus had Jesus, while still in his mother's womb, received hospitality in this house, to which he now came thirty-one years later as the Savior of humankind, to discharge in the person of their sick son the debt of gratitude he owed to the goodness of the parents.

Salome was the child of this house and the widow of Issachar's brother, Issachar himself being the widower of Salome's sister. The house and all the property were to revert to Salome, for neither she nor Issachar had had children by the previous union. They were childless and the only descendants of an illustrious race. They had espoused each other trusting to the merciful healing power of Jesus. Salome was allied to Joseph's family. She was originally from Bethlehem, and Joseph's father was accustomed to call her grandfather by the title of brother, although he was not really his brother. They had a descendant of the family of David among their forefathers who, I think, was also a king. His name sounds like Ela. It was through respect to this ancient friendship that Mary and Joseph were there entertained. Issachar was of the tribe of Levi.

Upon his entrance into the house Jesus was met by Salome, her maids, and the other servants of the household. Salome cast herself at Jesus's feet and begged her husband's cure. Jesus went with her into the chamber of the sick man, who lay covered up on his couch, for he was dropsical as well as paralyzed on one side. Jesus saluted him and spoke to him words full of kindness. The sick man was very much touched and gratefully acknowledged the salutation, though he could not rise. Then Jesus prayed, touched the sufferer, and gave him his hand. Instantly the sick man arose, threw another garment around him, and left his bed, when he and his wife cast themselves at Jesus's feet. The Lord addressed them a few words of exhortation, blessed them, promised them posterity, and then led them out of the chamber to their assembled household, who were all filled with joy. The miraculous cure was kept a secret all that day.

Issachar invited Jesus and all his followers to stay that night at his house and, after the exercises of the synagogue, to dine with him. Jesus accepted the invitation, and then went to preach in the synagogue. Toward the end of his discourse the Pharisees and Sadducees began to strive against him. From the explanation of Abraham's marriage with Keturah, he had come to speak of marriage itself. The Pharisees broached that of Issachar and Salome. They declared it insane in a man so sick and old to marry a young woman. Jesus replied that the couple had married in obedience to the Law, and he asked how could they, who held so strictly to the same, blame them. They answered by asking how he could look upon such a union as prescribed by the Law, since so old and sick a man could hope for no blessing on his marriage, consequently such an affair was no other than a scandal. Jesus responded: "His faith has preserved to him the fruit of wedlock. Do ye set limits to the almighty power of God? Has not the sick man married in obedience to the Law? In trusting in God and believing that he will help him, he has done excellently well. But this is not the cause of your indignation. Ye hoped that this family would die out for want of heirs, and then ye would get their property into your own hands." Then he cited the example of many devout old people whose faith had been rewarded with posterity, and said many other things upon the subject of matrimony. The Pharisees were furious, but had not a word in reply.

The sabbath over, Jesus left the synagogue and, accompanied by the disciples, went to Issachar's, where a grand banquet had been prepared for him. Jesus, the disciples related to him, and Issachar himself sat at one table, while Salome, the wife, came and went doing the honors of the same. The other disciples ate in a side hall. Previously to sitting down Jesus had healed several sick. It was dusk, and the miracles were performed by torchlight outside the synagogue and near Issachar's dwelling, where the sick had gathered. I saw among the disciples Judas Iscariot, Bartholomew, and Thomas, also an own brother and a stepbrother of the last named. Thomas had two stepbrothers. They had come thither for the sabbath from Apheke, seven hours distant, and they put up at Issachar's, Thomas being well-known to him on account of his commercial pursuits. Though he had acquaintances among the disciples, he had never yet spoken to Jesus, for he was anything but obtrusive. James the Less also had come from Capernaum for the sabbath, likewise Nathaniel, the son of the widow Anna, eldest daughter of Cleophas, who was now living with Martha. Nathaniel was the youngest of her sons engaged at Zebedee's fishery. He was about twenty years old, gentle and amiable, with something of the appearance of John. He had been reared in the house of his grandfather, and was nicknamed "Little Cleophas," in order to distinguish him from the other Nathaniels. I learned that on this sabbath when I heard Jesus say: "Call little Cleophas to me!"

The entertainment consisted of birds, fish, honey, and bread. There were in this city numbers of pigeons, turtledoves, and colored birds which ran like hens around the houses, and often took flight to the beautiful plain of Jezreel. During the meal, Issachar spoke of Mary. He recalled the fact of her having been in that house in her youth, and said that his wife's parents had often related the circumstance, telling how young and beautiful and pious she was. He expressed the hope that God, who had cured him through Joseph's son (he guessed not his Savior's origin), would likewise give him posterity. All the disciples found hospitality at this house. There were large, open porticos around it on which beds were prepared for them, separated from one another by movable partitions.

Of the Dothanites, some were very good, and some very bad. On account of the antique style of its houses, Dothan compared with the other cities in its neighborhood as Cologne with our other German towns.

Sunday, October 29, AD 30 (Heshvan 13)

This morning, while Jesus was walking with the disciples, Thomas asked Jesus if he could become a disciple. Then two of John the Baptist's disciples approached him. They had been sent by John, who was in prison at Machaerus (see Matthew 11:2–6 and Luke 7:18–23). After teaching again in the synagogue, Jesus and the disciples left Dothan and went to stay the night at an inn near Shunem.

Next morning, when Jesus and the disciples went to walk outside the city, Thomas approached and begged Jesus to admit him to the number of his disciples. He promised to follow him and fulfill all his commands for, as he said, by his preaching and by the miracles he had witnessed, he was convinced of the truth of what John and all the disciples of his acquaintance had said about him. He begged, also, to be allowed a part in his kingdom. Jesus replied that he was no stranger to him and that he knew that he, Thomas, would come to him. But Thomas would not subscribe to that. He asserted that he had never before thought of taking such a step, for he was no friend of novelty, and had only now determined upon it since he was convinced of his truth by his miracles. Jesus responded: "Thou speakest like Nathaniel. Thou dost esteem thyself wise, and yet thou talkest foolishly. Shall not the gardener know the trees of his garden? The vinedresser, his vines? Shall he set out a vineyard, and not know the servants whom he sends into it?" Then he related a similitude of the cultivation of figs upon thorns.

Two of John's disciples who had been sent to Jesus by the Baptist had an interview here with Jesus and then returned to Machaerus. They had been present at the sermon on the mountain near Meroz and had witnessed the miracles there performed. They belonged to the disciples that had followed their master to the place of his imprisonment and had received his instructions outside his prison. They were warmly attached to him. As they had never witnessed any of Jesus's actions, John had sent them to him that they might be convinced of the truth of what he himself had told them of him. He commissioned them to beg Jesus in his name to declare openly and precisely who he was and to establish his kingdom on earth. These disciples told Jesus that they were now convinced of all that John had announced of him, and they inquired whether he would not soon go to free John from prison. John, they said, hoped to be released through him, and they themselves were longing for him to establish his kingdom and set their master at liberty. They thought that would be a more profitable miracle than even his curing the sick. Jesus replied that he knew that John was longing and hoping soon to be freed from imprisonment, and that he should indeed be released, but that he should go to Machaerus and deliver John who had prepared his ways, John himself never even dreamed. Jesus ended by commanding them to announce to John all that they had seen and say to him that he would fulfill his mission.

I do not know whether John was aware that Jesus was to be crucified and that his kingdom was not to be an earthly one. I think that he thought Jesus, after converting and freeing the people, would establish a holy kingdom upon earth.

Toward noon Jesus and the disciples returned to the city and to Issachar's, where many people were already assembled. The mistress and domestics were busy preparing the noonday meal. Back of the house was a charming spot in the center of which was a beautiful fountain surrounded by summerhouses. The fountain was regarded as sacred, for it had been blessed by Elisha. There was a handsome chair nearby for the preacher's use and around it an enclosed space with shade trees, in which quite a number might assemble for instructions. Several times in the year, especially at Pentecost, public instructions were given here. There were besides, in the region of the fountain, places with long, stone stalls or narrow terraces, where caravans and the crowds going to Jerusalem at Passover time could rest and take refreshments. Issachar's house stood near enough to command a view of the fountain and its surroundings. The arrangements of the resting place and the customs observed there were also superintended from Issachar's, where a kind of freight business was carried on. The caravans unloaded and unpacked their goods here for Issachar to forward to other places, and very frequently the merchants and their servants received hospitality at his house, although it was not a public inn. Issachar's business was like that of the father of the bride of Cana in Galilee. The beautiful fountain had one inconvenience. It was so deep that the water could be pumped only with great fatigue. When pumped up, it ran into basins standing around.

There were crowds assembled around the fountain on the invitation of Jesus and Issachar. Jesus, from the teacher's chair, delivered a discourse to the people on the fulfillment of the Promise, the nearness of the kingdom, on penance and conversion, and of the way to implore the mercy of God and to receive his graces and miracles. He alluded to Elisha, who had formerly taught in this same place. The Syrians sent to take him prisoner were struck with blindness. Then Elisha conducted them to Samaria into the hands of their enemies, but far from allowing them to be put to death, he entertained them hospitably, restored their sight, and sent them back to their king. Jesus applied this to the Son of Man and the persecution he endured from the Pharisees. He spoke also for a long time of prayer and good works, related the parable of the Pharisee and the Publican, and told his hearers that they ought to adorn and perfume themselves on their fast days instead of parading their piety before the people. The inhabitants of this place, who were very much oppressed by the Pharisees and Sadducees, were greatly encouraged by Jesus's teaching. But the Pharisees and Sadducees, on the contrary, were enraged upon seeing the joyous multitude and hearing the words of Jesus. Their rage increased when they beheld Issachar in perfect health going around among the people, joyfully helping the disciples and his own servants to distribute food to them as they seated themselves along the stone benches. This sight so exasperated them that they stormed violently against Jesus. It looked as if they were about to take him into custody. They began again to rail at his curing on the sabbath. Jesus bade them listen to him calmly. He placed them in a circle around him and, making use of his customary argument, said to the chief among them: "If on the sabbath you should happen to fall into the well here, would you not wish to be drawn out at once?" And so he continued to speak until they slunk back, covered with confusion. After this Jesus left the city with several of his disciples and descended into the valley that runs from south to northwest of Dothan.

Issachar had distributed large alms in Dothan, and sent also to the inn of the little community asses with various necessaries. The provisions and beverages provided by the disciples, and which had become somewhat stale, he caused to be exchanged for better. He gave to each of them a cup like those used at Cana, and a flat jug, or pitcher, made of white material with a ring by which it could hang. The stoppers were a kind of sponge tightly compressed. The jugs contained a refreshing drink made of balm. He gave likewise to each disciple a sum of money for alms and other things they might require.

Judas Iscariot and many other disciples returned from Dothan to their own homes. Jesus kept with him only nine, among whom were Thomas, James the Less, Joseph Barsabbas, Simon, Thaddeus, little Cleophas (Nathaniel), Manahem, and Saturnin.

After Jesus's departure, the Pharisees recommenced their mockery and insults. They said to the people: "One can easily see who he is. He has allowed himself to be sumptuously entertained by Issachar. His disciples are a set of lazy vagrants whom he supports and feasts at the expense of others. If he did right, he would stay at home and support his poor mother. His father was a poor carpenter. But that respectable calling does not suit him, and so he goes wandering around disturbing the whole country."

While Issachar was distributing his alms, he constantly repeated: "Help yourselves freely! Take freely! It is not mine. It belongs to the Father in heaven. Thank him, for it is only lent to me!"

Jesus Goes from Dothan to Endor • Cure of a Pagan Boy

AFTER a journey of about five hours, and night having set in, Jesus and the disciples arrived at a lonely inn where only sleeping accommodations were to be found. Nearby was a well that owed its origin to Jacob. The disciples gathered wood and made a fire. On the way Jesus had had a long conversation with them, intended principally for the instruction of Thomas, Simon, Manahem, "Little Cleophas," and the others newly received. He spoke of their following him, and through the deep conviction of the worthlessness of earthly goods, of their leaving their relatives without regret and without looking back. He promised that what they had left should be restored to them in his kingdom a thousandfold. But they should reflect maturely whether or not they could break their earthly ties.

To some of the disciples, and especially to Thomas, Judas Iscariot was not particularly pleasing. He did not hesitate to say plainly to Jesus that he did not like Judas because he was too ready to say yes and no. Why, he asked, had he admitted that man among his disciples, since he had been so difficult to please in others. Jesus answered evasively that from eternity it was decreed by God for Judas, like all the others, to be of the number of his disciples.

When the disciples had retired to rest, Jesus went alone into the mountains to pray.

Monday, October 30, AD 30 (Heshvan 14)

Jesus did not enter Shunem but, passing by Endor, went on to an inn in the valley between Abez and Mount Gilboa. Here he was met by a group of about fifteen elderly people, family relatives. Jesus spoke much with these pious, simple-hearted people, who expressed their concern on account of the Pharisees' hostility toward Jesus.

Early the next morning some inhabitants of Shunem came to Jesus at the inn earnestly begging him to go with them, for they had some children seriously sick whom they wished him to cure. Shunem was a couple of hours to the east of where Jesus then was. The poor people had long been vainly expecting Jesus's coming. But Jesus replied that he could not go then, because others were awaiting him, but that he would send his disciples to them. They rejoined that they had already had some of them in their town, but the cure of their children had not followed. They insisted upon his coming himself. Jesus exhorted them to patience, and they left him.

He now went with his disciples to Endor. On the road from Dothan to Endor were two wells of Jacob, to which his herds used to be led, and for which he often had to struggle with the Amorites.

Lazarus owned a field near Jezreel at some distance from Endor. Joachim and Anne owned another two hours to the northeast of Endor, and it was to it that the latter accompanied Mary on her journey to Bethlehem. It was from this field that the little she-ass, that ran on so gaily before the holy travelers, had been taken to be presented to Joseph. Joachim owned another field on the opposite side of the Jordan on the confines of the desert and forest of Ephron, and not far from Gaser. Thither had he retired to pray when he returned sad from the temple, and there, too, had he received the command to go to Jerusalem, where Anne would meet him under the Golden Gate.

Jesus paused at a row of houses outside of Endor and taught. At the earnest request of the people, he entered some of them and cured the sick, several of whom had been carried thither from Endor. Among the sufferers were some pagans, but they remained at a distance. One pagan however, a citizen of Endor, approached Jesus. He had with him a boy of seven years possessed of a mute devil, and he was often so violent that he could not be restrained. As the man drew near Jesus, the boy became quite unmanageable, broke loose from his father, and crept into a hole in the mountain. The father cast himself at Jesus's feet, bewailing his misery. Jesus went to the hole and commanded the boy to come forth before his Master. At these words, the boy came out meekly and fell on his knees before Jesus, who laid his hands upon him and commanded Satan to withdraw. The boy became unconscious for a few moments, while a dark vapor issued from him. Then he arose and ran full of talk to his father, who embraced him, and both went and fell on their knees before Jesus, giving thanks. Jesus addressed some words of admonition to the father, and commanded him to go to Ainon to be baptized. Jesus did not enter Endor.

The suburb in which he found himself had more beautiful edifices than the city itself. There was something about Endor that spoke of death. Part of the city was a waste, its walls in ruins, its streets overgrown with grass. Many of the inhabitants were pagans under the power of the Jews, and were obliged to labor at all kinds of public works. The few rich Jews found in Endor used to peep timidly out of their doors and quickly draw in their heads, as if they feared that someone was stealing their money behind their back.

From here Jesus went two hours to the northeast into a valley that ran from the Plain of Esdrelon to the Jordan, north of Mount Gilboa. In this valley lay on a hill, like an island, the city of Abez, a place of moderate grandeur surrounded by gardens and groves. A little river flowed before it, and eastward in the valley was a beautiful fountain, called Saul's well because Saul was once wounded there. Jesus did not go into the city, but to a row of houses on the northern declivity of Mount Gilboa between the gardens and fields, on the latter of which were high heaps of grain. Here he went into an inn in which a crowd of old men and women, his own relatives, were awaiting him. They washed his feet and showed him every mark of genuine confidence and reverence. They were in number about fifteen, nine men and six women, who had sent him word that they would meet him here. Several of them were accompanied by their servants and children. They were mostly very aged persons, relatives of Anne, Joachim, and Joseph. One was a young half-brother of Joseph, who dwelt in the valley of Zebulon. Another was the father of the bride of Cana. Anne's relatives from the region of Sepphoris, where at his last visit to Nazareth Jesus had restored sight to the blind boy, were among them. All had journeyed hither in a body and on asses in order to see and speak with Jesus. Their desire was that he would fix his abode somewhere and cease wandering about. They wanted him to seek a place where he could teach in peace and where there were no Pharisees. They set before him the great danger he ran, since the Pharisees and other sects were so embittered against him. "We are well aware," they said, "of the miracles and graces that proceed from thee. But we beg thee to have some settled home where thou canst quietly teach, that we may not be in constant anxiety on thy account." They even began to propose to him different places which they thought suitable.

These pious, simple-hearted people made this proposal to Jesus out of their great love for him. The bitter taunts uttered in their hearing against him by the evil-minded gave them pain. Jesus replied in affectionate, but vigorous terms, very different from those he was accustomed to use when addressing the multitude or the disciples. He spoke in plain words, explained the Promise, and showed them that it was his part to fulfill the will of his Father in heaven. He told them moreover that he had not come for rest, not for any particular persons, nor for his own relatives, but for all humankind. All indiscriminately were his brethren, all were his relatives. Love rests not. Whoever dreams of succoring misery, must seek out the poor. After the comforts of this life he did not aim, for his kingdom was not of this world. Jesus took a great deal of trouble with these good old people, who listened with ever increasing astonishment to his words, whose deep significance gradually unfolded to their understanding. Their earnestness and their love for Jesus grew at each moment. He took them separately for a walk on the shady part of the mountain, where he instructed and comforted them, each according to his or her special needs, and after that he spoke to them again all together. And so the day closed, and they took together a simple repast of bread, honey, and dried fruits which they had brought with them.

That evening the disciples presented to Jesus a young man from the environs of Endor, the son of a school-master. He was a student preparing to hold a position similar to that of his father. He begged Jesus to receive him among his disciples. He had been informed, he said, that Jesus might perhaps have some need of him, that he might possibly give him some office. Jesus replied that he had no need of him, that the knowledge he came to bring upon earth was different from that which he had acquired, that he was too attached to material things, and so he sent him away.

Tuesday, October 31, AD 30 (Heshvan 15)

Jesus began the morning talking with his elderly relatives, then he traveled with his disciples to Abez. Here, after teaching at the well (Saul's well) east of the town, Jesus blessed a number of children, and then taught in the synagogue.

About noon on the following day, Jesus's relatives started for Mount Tabor, where they separated and returned to their homes in different directions. Jesus had quite consoled and enlightened the good, old people, and had infused new life into them. Although they may not have understood all that he told them, yet they felt a great calm fall upon their soul, and they journeyed home with the firm conviction that he had spoken divine words and that he knew better what to do and how to shape his course than they could tell him. Still more touching than their meeting was their departure when, with tears and smiles and gracious nods, their demeanor expressive of confidence mingled with respectful reserve, they took their way down through the valley. Some rode on asses, others went on foot leaning on their long staves, and all with their garments girded for traveling. Jesus and the disciples, after helping them to mount their asses and arrange their bundles, accompanied them a part of the way.

Jesus in Abez and Dabrath on Tabor

JESUS and the disciples now went through the valley to a beautiful well, about a quarter of an hour east of Abez. Several women were standing by it, having come out of the city to draw water. When they saw Jesus coming, some of them hurried into the neighboring houses and soon came back accompanied by several men and women. They brought basins and towels, bread and small fruits in baskets; they washed his feet, and gave him and the disciples to eat. Many others had joined the little group, and Jesus delivered to them an instruction. Then they conducted him into the city where he was met at the gate by children, little girls and boys, bearing wreaths and festoons of flowers. They surrounded him in triumph, and at every step, at every street corner their numbers increased. The disciples, thinking the throng too great, wanted to send the children away. But Jesus exclaimed: "Do ye fall back, and let the little ones come forward!" At these words the children pressed around him more closely than before. He embraced them, pressed them to his heart, and blessed them. The mothers and fathers were looking on from the doors and vestibules of their courtyards. At last he reached the synagogue, where he preached to a crowded assembly. That evening he cured some invalids at their own homes. A repast was laid under an arbor still standing from the Feast of Tabernacles, and of it many people of the city partook.

Thomas had gone back from Endor to Apheke. I saw here in Abez some women afflicted with an issue of blood. They mingled with the crowd, slipped behind Jesus, kissed the hem of his robe, and were cured. In large cities such women would have remained at a distance; in smaller places they were not so punctilious.

A messenger from Cana came to Jesus in Abez. The chief magistrate of the city implored him to come to see his son, who was seriously sick. Jesus calmed him and told him to wait yet a little while. Then two Jewish messengers arrived from Capernaum. They had been dispatched to him by a pagan who had already, through the disciples, implored Jesus's aid in behalf of his sick servant. They begged him earnestly to return at once with them to Capernaum, for the servant was nigh unto death. Jesus replied that he would go in his own good time, that the man was not dying. The messengers, hearing this, remained for the instruction.

The inhabitants of Abez were chiefly Gileadites of Jabes. They had settled here in the time of the high priest Heli in consequence of a struggle that had arisen among the people of Gilead. The judge ruling at that time was consulted in the affair, and he decided that some of the Gileadites should remove to Abez.

Saul was wounded near the well of Abez and, on one of the heights to the south, breathed his last. From this circumstance the well was called Saul's well. The people of Abez belonged to the middle class of society. They made baskets and mats of reeds that grew abundantly in the neighboring marshes formed by the streams running down from the mountains. They prepared also wicker work for putting light huts together, and gave some attention to agriculture and grazing.

Saul and the Witch of Endor

THE ISRAELITES were drawn up before Endor near Jezreel, and the Philistines were marching against them from Shunem. The struggle had already begun when Saul, with two companions—all three in the garb of prophets—went in the darkness of evening to the witch of Endor, who dwelt in some old ruins outside the city. She was a poor, despised creature still somewhat young. Her husband went around the country with a puppet show upon his back, practicing sorcery and exhibiting his wonders to the soldiers of the garrisons and other idlers. When Saul

Cave of the Witch of Endor

resolved to consult the witch, he was already half-desperate. The witch at first was unwilling to satisfy his desire. She was afraid of its coming to the ears of King Saul, who had strictly prohibited all dealing in witchcraft. But Saul assured her with a solemn oath that that should not happen. Then she led him from the room in which they were, and which had nothing extraordinary in its appearance, to an obscure cellar. Saul demanded that Samuel's spirit should be evoked. The witch drew a circle around Saul and his companions, traced signs around the circle, and spun threads of colored wool in all sorts of figures before and around Saul. She stood at some distance in front of him, a basin of water on the ground before her, and plates like metallic mirrors in her hands. These latter she waved toward each other and over the water, muttering some words and at times calling something aloud. She had previously directed Saul through which part of the crossed threads he was to gaze. By her diabolical skill, she was able to bring up before the eyes of her interrogators scenes of whole campaigns, battles, and the figures of those engaged in them. Such a delusion she was now preparing to evoke for Saul, when suddenly she beheld near her an apparition. Out of herself with astonishment and dread, she let the mirror fall into the basin and cried out:

"Thou hast deceived me! Thou art Saul!" Saul bade her fear nothing, but say to him what she then saw. She replied: "I see a saint rising out of the earth." Saul beheld nothing, and again he questioned: "What does he look like?" The woman, trembling with fear, answered: "An old man in priestly robes!" and with these words she rushed past Saul and out of the cave. When Saul beheld Samuel, he fell prostrate on his face. Samuel spoke: "Why hast thou troubled my repose? The chastisement of God will soon fall upon thee! Tomorrow thou wilt be with me among the dead, the Philistines shall conquer Israel, and David will be king." At these words Saul, overcome by grief and horror, lay on the ground like one dead. His companions raised him and placed him leaning against the wall. They tried to rouse him, the woman brought bread and meat, but he refused to eat. The witch advised him not to engage in the battle, but to retire to Abez where the inhabitants, being Gileadites, would give him a good reception. Saul went thither next morning at dawn. The Israelites were routed beyond Mount Gilboa. Saul was attacked not by the whole army of Philistines, but only by a roving party. He was at the moment seated in his chariot, with an officer standing behind him. The Philistines, rushing by, shot spears and arrows at him, though not dreaming that it was Saul himself. He was grievously wounded, and his attendants led the chariot to the plain south of the valley and out of the road upon which Jesus had yesterday been with his relatives. When Saul felt himself mortally wounded, he requested his officer to kill him at once, but the latter refused. Then Saul, supporting himself in the chariot, which had a railing in front, tried to fall on the point of his own sword, but he could not succeed. The officer, seeing his determination, opened that swinging railing in front of the chariot, thus enabling Saul to fall on his sword, while at the same instant he pierced himself with his own. An Amalecite passing at the moment recognized Saul, possessed himself of his regal ornament, and carried it to David. After the battle, Saul's body was laid beside his sons, who had fallen to the east of the scene of slaughter. They had been killed before their father's death. The Philistines used to hack the bodies of their enemies to pieces.

The brook flowing through this valley was called Kadumin. It is mentioned in Deborah's Canticle. The prophet Malachi once sojourned here for a time and prophesied. Abez was about three hours from the pagan city Scythopolis.

Wednesday, November 1, AD 30 (Heshvan 16)

Jesus taught again at Saul's well. That afternoon, he and the disciples walked to Dabrath, where they stayed overnight at an inn outside town.

On leaving the well, Jesus and the disciples proceeded some distance to the east, then turning, pursued their journey northward. He crossed the height that closed in the valley on the north and, after about three hours, reached another at the foot of Mount Tabor to the east.

Brook Kishon in the Plain of Esdrelon

The brook Kishon, which rises to the north of the mountain, here flowed around it and off to the Plain of Esdrelon. Here lay the city Dabrath in an angle of the first plateau of Tabor. The view from the city takes in the high plain of Saron and extends to the region in which the Jordan flows from the Sea of Galilee. The brook Kishon ran through the whole of this quarter.

(Follow Map 22)

Thursday, November 2, AD 30 (Heshvan 17)

In Dabrath, Jesus visited his relative Jesse, who requested that his two sons—Caleb and Aaron—be taken as disciples. Later, Jesus healed the sick and taught in the synagogue.

Map 22: Travels in Southern Galilee
November 1–18, AD 30

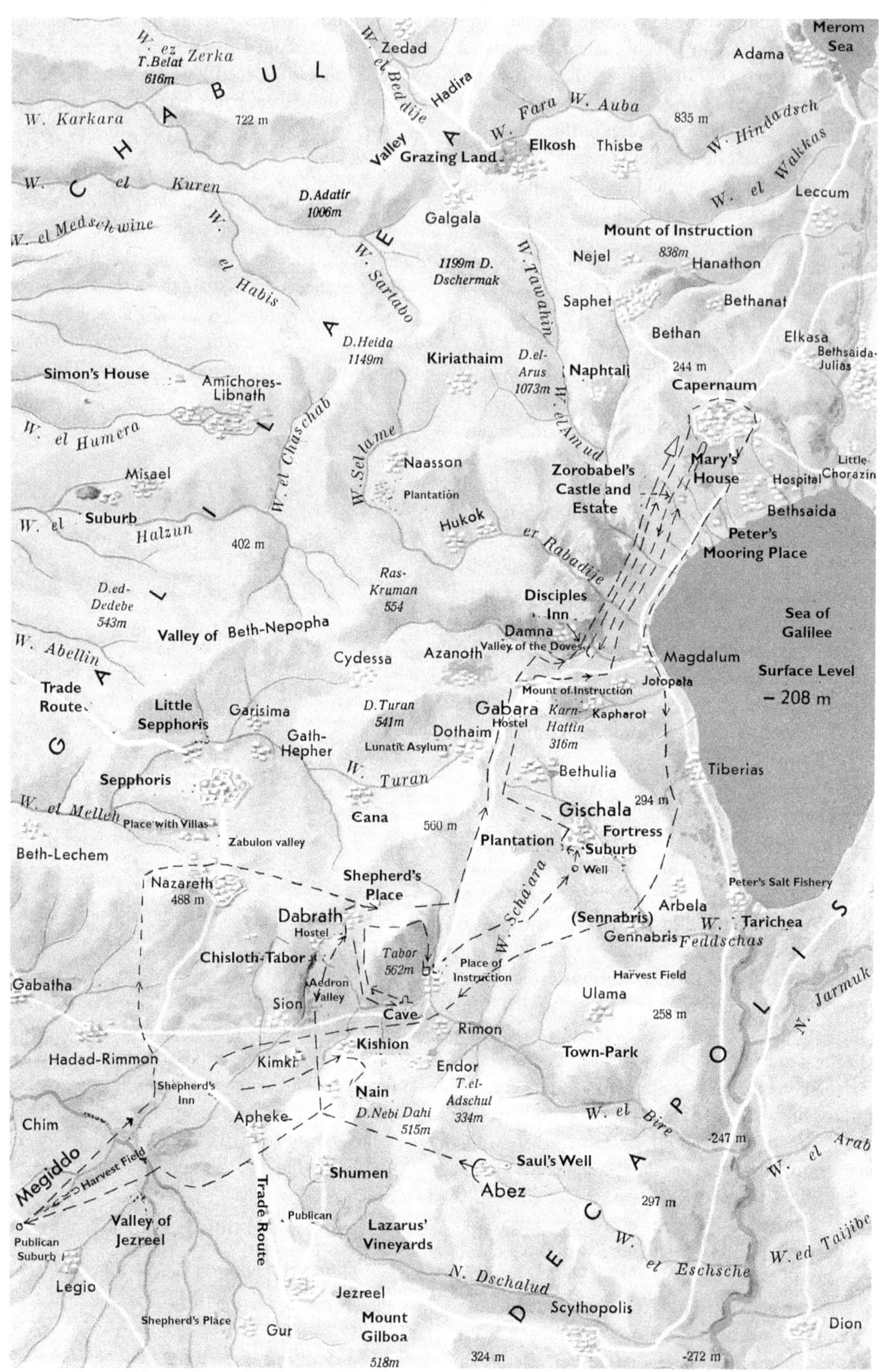

Abez—Dabrath—Malachi's Cave—Dabrath—Place of Instruction on Mount Tabor—Gischala
Gabara—Mount of Instruction—Gabara—Zorobabel—Capernaum—Valley of the Doves
Capernaum—Plain of Jezreel—Nain—Suburb of Megiddo—Capernaum

Jesus remained at an inn outside the city until the following day, when he went into Dabrath. A crowd instantly pressed around him. He cured some sick, of whom, however, there were not many, as the air of this place was very pure.

The city of Dabrath was very beautifully built. I still remember one of the houses. It was surrounded by a large courtyard and porticos, from which two flights of steps led up to the roof. Behind the city rose an eminence projecting from the foot of Tabor, and around it wound serpentine paths. It took about two hours to reach the top. All along inside the city walls dwelt Roman soldiers. Dabrath was one of the cities named for the collection of taxes. It had five large streets, each of which was occupied by the workmen belonging to one trade. It was not exactly on the highroad, for the nearest was at a distance of half an hour; nevertheless, all kinds of business was carried on in it. It was a Levitical city, and the imposts raised in it were devoted to the support of sacred worship. The boundary posts that marked the limits of the tribe of Issachar were scarcely a quarter of an hour distant. The synagogue stood upon an open space, also that house mentioned above. Jesus went into the latter, for its occupant was a nephew of his foster father, Joseph.

Joseph's brother, the father of this nephew, was called Elia. He had had five sons—of whom one named Jesse, now an old man, dwelt in that house. His wife was still living, and they had a family of six children, three sons and three daughters. Two of the sons were already between eighteen and twenty years old. Their names were Caleb and Aaron. Their father begged Jesus to receive them as disciples, which he did. They were to join the band when he should again pass through that part of the country. Jesse collected the taxes destined for the support of the Levites. He superintended also a cloth factory in which the wool that he purchased was cleansed, spun, and woven. Fine cloth was manufactured there, and a whole street was in Jesse's employ. He had also, in a long building, a machine for expressing the juice from various herbs, some of which were found on Tabor, and others were brought hither from a distance. The juice of some was used in dyeing; others, for beverages; and others, again, were made into perfumery. I saw hollow cylinders standing in troughs, in which by means of a heavy pounder the herbs were pressed. The pipes through which the expressed juice flowed ran outside of the building and were provided with spigots. When the pounders were not in use, they were kept in place by means of wedges. They prepared also the oil of myrrh. Jesse and his whole family were very pious. His children went daily, and he often accompanied them, to pray on Tabor. Jesus and the disciples made their home with them while at Dabrath.

There were both Pharisees and Sadducees in this city. They formed a kind of consistory, and held council together as to how they could contradict Jesus. That evening Jesus went with the disciples to Mount Tabor, whither a multitude had preceded him. There he taught by moonlight until far into the night.

Friday, November 3, AD 30 (Heshvan 18)

Jesus was teaching before the synagogue when he was approached by a rich widow—Naomi of Dabrath—who had deceived her husband by committing adultery, causing him to die of grief. She cast herself at Jesus's feet and confessed her sins. Jesus said: "Arise! Your sins are forgiven!" With the start of the sabbath, Jesus entered the synagogue and taught there. He stayed overnight in the house of Jesse.

On the southeastern side of Tabor lay a cave with a little garden in front. There the prophet Malachi had often sojourned. Farther up the mountain were another cave and garden where Elijah and his disciples sometimes lived retired, as upon Carmel. These caves were now held as shrines by pious Jews, and thither they used to go to pray.

Looking toward Mount Tabor

To the north of Mount Tabor was situated the city of Tabor, whence the mountain derived its name, and about an hour westward in the direction of Sepphoris was another fortified place. Casaloth was in the valley on the south side of the mountain, northward from Nain, and in the direction of Apheke. The tribe of Zebulon extends farthest to the north on this side. I have heard a more modern name given to this place, and I saw that relatives of Jesus once dwelt there, namely, a sister of Elizabeth, who, like the maidservant of Mary Mark, bore the name of Rhoda. She had three daughters and two sons. One of the daughters was one of the three widows, friends of Mary, and her two sons were among the disciples. One of Rhoda's sons married Maroni, and died without issue. His widow, in obedience to the Law, entered into a second marriage with one of her first husband's family named Eliud, a nephew of Mother Anne. She lived at Nain and by her second husband had one son, who was called Martialis. She was now a widow for the second time, and she is the so-called widow of Nain whose son Martialis was raised from the dead by the Lord.

Jesus taught on the open space in front of the synagogue. Numerous sick had collected there from the neighborhood around, and the Pharisees were greatly irritated. There was a rich woman in Dabrath named Naomi. She had been unfaithful to her husband, and he had died of grief. For a long time she had promised to marry the agent that attended to her business, but he, too, was being deceived by her. Naomi had heard Jesus's instructions in Dothan and had been, in consequence, very much changed. She was full of repentance and desired only to beg of him pardon and penance. She attended Jesus's teaching here in Dabrath, was present at the cures he wrought, and tried by every means to approach him, but he always turned away from her. She was a person of distinction and well-known in the city, and as her disorders were not public, she had not fallen into general disesteem. While she was trying to approach Jesus, she encountered the Pharisees, who asked her whether she was not ashamed of herself and bade her return to her home. Their words, however, did not restrain her; she was as if out of herself in her eager desire for pardon. At last she succeeded in breaking through the crowd. She threw herself down on the ground before Jesus, crying out: "Lord, is there grace, is there pardon still for me? Lord, I can no longer live so! I sinned grievously against my husband, and I have deceived the man that now has charge of my affairs!" And thus she confessed her sins before all. All, however, did not hear her, for Jesus had stepped aside, and the Pharisees pressing forward had made a great uproar. Jesus said to Naomi: "Arise! Thy sins are forgiven thee!" She obeyed, begging at the same time for a penance, but Jesus put her off till another time. Then she divested herself of her rich ornaments: the strings of pearls around her headdress, her rings, her bracelets, and the golden cords around her arms and neck. She handed them all over to the Pharisees with the request that they should be given to the poor, and then she drew her veil closely around her.

Jesus now went into the synagogue, for the sabbath had begun. The infuriated Pharisees and Sadducees followed him. The reading for the day was about Jacob and Esau. Jesus applied the details connected with the birth of the two brothers to his own time. Esau and Jacob struggled in their mother's womb, thus did the synagogue struggle against the piously disposed. The Law was harsh and severe, the firstborn like Esau, but it had sold its birthright to Jacob for a mess of pottage, for the redolent odors arising from all kinds of unimportant usages and exterior ceremonies. Jacob, who had now received the Blessing, would become a great nation whom Esau would have to serve. The whole explanation was very beautiful, and the Pharisees could bring nothing forward against it, although they disputed long with Jesus. They reproached him upon several heads: that he attached to himself followers, that he established private inns throughout the country, employing for the same the money and property of rich widows which should have been given for the use of the synagogue and the doctors. And so, they said, would it now be with Naomi; besides, how could he forgive her her sins?

Saturday, November 4, AD 30 (Heshvan 19)

This morning, Jesus visited the school in Dabrath. He addressed the children and blessed them. At the close of the sabbath he taught again in the synagogue, speaking of the patriarchs Isaac and Jacob and referring to the prophet Malachi's prophecy (1:11). That night, back at Jesse's house, he was visited by Cyrinus of Cyprus and talked with him until dawn.

Next morning Jesus did not go to the synagogue, but to the school for the boys and girls. The children followed him even into Jesse's court while he was taking dinner there, and Jesus instructed and blessed them again. The woman lately converted was likewise there with her steward. Jesus spoke with each alone and then to both together. On account of her present sentiments, Jesus advised the woman not to marry again, especially as her suitor was of low origin. She was to deliver to him a part of her fortune and, after reserving sufficient for her own support, distribute the rest to the poor.

After the sabbath day repast, when the Jews were taking their customary promenade, some Jewish women came to visit Jesse's wife. There, in Jesus's presence, they engaged in an instructive game such as was usual on the sabbath. The converted Naomi was present. The game consisted of a combination of parables, enigmas, or questions, calculated to instruct and edify. For example, such questions as the following were proposed: Where had each one her treasure? Did she put it out at high interest? Did she hide it? Did she share it with her husband? Did she leave it to her domestics? Did she carry it with her to the synagogue? Was her heart attached to it? Many of these questions turned upon the care of children and servants, etc. Jesus spoke also of oil and the lamp, of the burning of a well-filled lamp, of the spilling of the oil, applying all these things in a spiritual sense. One of the women was questioned on one of these points. She answered promptly and graciously: "Yes, Master! I take great care that the sabbath lamp is always of the best." Her neighbors were very much amused at her words. They laughed at her, for she had not caught Jesus's meaning. He always gave a very striking explanation, and whoever made a wrong answer was obliged to give a present to the poor as a fine. The woman of whom I have spoken gave a piece of cloth.

Jesus wrote also, before each one, an enigma in the sand with a reed, the answer to which had likewise to be written in the same way by the one to whom it was addressed. In this manner he revealed to each her evil inclinations and defects, so that she trembled with fear, though without the necessity of blushing before her neighbor. He advised them especially of the faults of which they were guilty at the last Feast of Tabernacles, for in the greater liberty they enjoyed at that time and the merrymaking then customary, they may easily have sinned. Several of these women afterward spoke in private to Jesus, confessed their transgressions, and begged for penance and forgiveness. Jesus consoled them and reconciled them to God. During this instruction the women were ranged in a semicircle under the portico of the courtyard. They sat on rugs and cushions, their backs resting against the stone benches. The disciples and friends of the family were standing on either side at some distance. There was no loud speaking, since the loiterers on the street could, by climbing the wall, have created disturbance, for they were all out in the open air. The women had brought with them as presents for Jesus all kinds of spices, comfits, and perfumes. He gave them to the disciples with directions to distribute them to the sick poor who never could get such luxuries.

Before Jesus returned to the synagogue for the closing services of the sabbath, the Herodians sent messengers to request him to meet them at a certain place in the city, since they wanted to speak with him. Jesus replied to the messengers with a severe expression: "Say to those hypocrites that they may open their double-tongued mouths against me in the synagogue, for there shall I answer them and others." He added other hard names, and then went to the school.

The sabbath reading again treated of Jacob and Esau, of Grace and the Law, and of the children and servants of the Father. Jesus inveighed so vehemently against the Pharisees, the Sadducees, and the Herodians, that their fury increased at each moment. The necessity in which Isaac had been of removing from place to place and the filling up of the wells by the Philistines, Jesus applied to his own teaching mission and the persecution he endured from the Pharisees. Passing then to Malachi, he announced the fulfillment of his prophecy: "My name shall be magnified upon the border of Israel. From the rising of the sun even to the going down, my name is great among the Gentiles." Then he made known to them all the ways he had traversed on either side of the Jordan, in order to glorify the name of the Lord. He declared that he would continue his course to the end, and in severe language he quoted against them these other words of the prophet: "The son shall honor the father, and the servant his master." His enemies were confounded, and had nothing to reply.

When the crowd had left the synagogue and Jesus likewise had withdrawn with the disciples, he suddenly found his way blockaded in one of the courts by the Pharisees. They surrounded him in one of the halls and demanded that he should answer some questions. It was not necessary, they said, for the people to hear all that they had to say. And then they proposed to him all kinds of captious questions, especially upon their relations to the Romans who were here stationed. Jesus's answer reduced them to silence. When at last, with flattery and menaces, they demanded that he should give up traveling around with disciples, desist from preaching and curing, else they would denounce and punish him as a disturber of the peace, as a seditious character, he replied: "Until the end shall ye find upon my footsteps the ignorant, the sinful, the poor, the sick, and my own disciples—those whom ye have abandoned to their ignorance and sinfulness, whom ye have left in their poverty and misery." Seeing that they could gain nothing by their artful words, they left the synagogue with him. Outwardly they assumed a courteous demeanor, but inwardly they were full of rage, though not unmixed with admiration.

THE PAGAN CYRINUS OF CYPRUS

FROM the school, Jesus went in the evening twilight, accompanied by the disciples and the people who had awaited him outside the synagogue, up to Tabor. A multitude of others and some of his own relatives were already there assembled. Jesus sat down on the mountain, his hearers reclining or sitting below at his feet. The stars were twinkling in the sky, and the moon was shedding around her gentle radiance. Jesus taught until late into the night. He often did this even after a toilsome day's work when in the midst of a little band of pious souls. The peace was then more profound, his audience less distracted; the heavens, the stars, the wide expanse of nature, the pleasant coolness of the air, the stillness reigning around, fell like soothing balm upon men's souls. They heard their Teacher's voice more distinctly, comprehended his words more easily, were less confused at hearing their own faults laid bare, carried his instructions home with them, and pondered them with fewer distractions. This was especially the case in the magnificent region in which Jesus now was, in the wide prospect that unfolded from the heights of Tabor. The mount itself, on account of the sojourn of Elijah and Malachi upon it for a time, was held in special veneration.

When Jesus was returning home late in the night, followed by the crowd, there approached him on the way a pagan from Cyprus who had been present at the instructions. He was one of the occupants of Jesse's house and had something to do connected with the manufacture of the essential oils. Up to this time, however, he had kept aloof through a spirit of humility. But now Jesus took him into a room of the house where he sat with him alone, as he had done with Nicodemus, instructing him and answering the questions that he put so humbly, yet with so eager a desire of learning the truth.

This pagan, a man most noble and wise, was named Cyrinus. His remarks were most profound, and he received Jesus's instructions with indescribable humility and joy. Jesus, on his side, was very loving and confidential toward him. Cyrinus said that for a long time past he had been sensible of the emptiness of idolatry and had longed to become a Jew, but that there was one thing which presented an insuperable objection, namely, circumcision. He asked whether it was not possible to attain salvation without it. Jesus answered him in words both familiar and significant regarding that mystery. He might, said Jesus, circumcise his senses, his heart, and his tongue from carnal desires and pleasures, and then go to Capernaum for baptism. At these words, Cyrinus asked why he did not preach that openly, for he thought that if Jesus did so, many pagans who were longing for it would be converted. Jesus answered that if he should say such a thing to the multitude, blinded as they were by their prejudices, they would certainly put him to death, and one must not scandalize the weak. Again, abolishing circumcision might give rise to multiplied sects; besides, the law was necessary for some of the pagans as a means of trial and sacrifice. But now that the kingdom of God was drawing near, the covenant of circumcision in the flesh was fulfilled and the circumcision of the heart and the spirit must take its place. Cyrinus inquired also as to the sufficiency of John's baptism, and Jesus spoke with him upon that point. He told Jesus about many people who were sighing after him in Cyprus, and complained to him of his two sons who, though otherwise very virtuous, were fierce enemies of Judaism. Jesus consoled him and promised that, after he had fulfilled his mission, his sons would yet become zealous workers in his vineyard. These sons were, I think, called Aristarchus and Trophimus. They afterward became disciples of the apostles. This most touching nocturnal interview lasted till morning.

On the sunny side of the mountain were large reservoirs hewn out of the rocky wall, and in them were vessels belonging to Jesse, in which were prepared perfumes from herbs and other substances. The oil dropped from one vessel into another, making many a turn in its course.

Jesus Goes to Gischala, the Birthplace of Paul

Sunday, November 5, AD 30 (Heshvan 20)

Jesus and the disciples went to Gischala, a stronghold garrisoned by Roman soldiers, whom Herod had to pay for. Jesus gave instruction to his disciples in which he mentioned three "men of zeal" from Gischala. The first was the founder of the Sadducees, who had lived over two hundred years before Christ. The second was John of Gischala, who subsequently fomented an uprising in Galilee and actively resisted the Romans at the siege of Jerusalem. The third was Saul, who later became the apostle Paul, now living with his parents at Tarsus, but who had been born in Gischala.

FROM Dabrath Jesus went in the forenoon with the disciples three hours northward to the plain and city of Gischala, almost an hour from Bethulia. Just at the outset of his journey lay a place to the east, I think Japhia, and another directly opposite toward the west and northward from Tabor. Gischala was situated upon a height, but one not so elevated as that of Bethulia. It was a stronghold garrisoned by pagan soldiers in Herod's pay. The Jews dwelt in a little quarter apart, about fifteen minutes distant from the fortress. Gischala was very different from other cities. There were open squares and large buildings surrounded with palisades, as if to afford space for hitching horses, and all around the city ran a wall with towers, from whose stories troops of soldiers could defend it. All this gave Gischala a very remarkable appearance. Near one of the towers stood the pagan temple. The Jews of the little city lived on good terms with the pagan soldiers, for whom they manufactured articles of leather, harness for the horses and military equipment for the men. They were likewise partly the owners and partly the overseers and stewards of the fertile region lying around the city. Far from it, off to Capernaum, stretched the magnificent country of Galilee. The citadel stood upon a height up to which led a paved road from terrace to terrace. The little Jewish quarter lay outstretched on the declivity of that same height. Before it was a well, or rather a cistern, for drinking water, which was conducted from distant sources by means of pipes. It was by this cistern that Jesus and the disciples sat down on their arrival.

The residents of the Jewish quarter were just then celebrating a feast and all the inhabitants, young and old, were out in the gardens and fields. The pagan children from the city were present also, but they kept to themselves somewhat apart from the others. When the people spied Jesus going to the cistern, the chief men of the city, with their learned schoolmaster, approached him. They welcomed him and the disciples, washed their feet, and presented them fruit. Jesus, still at the cistern, gave an instruction in which he alluded to the harvest in a parable, for in this region at that moment they were busy gathering in their second harvest of grapes and all kinds of fruit. He next went over to where the pagan children were, spoke to the mothers, blessed them, and cured several who were sick.

The Jews of Gischala were on that day celebrating a feast commemorative of their deliverance from the yoke of a tyrant, the first founder of the Sadducees. He lived over two hundred years before Christ, but I have forgotten his name. He was one of the officers of the Sanhedrin in Jerusalem, and was charged to watch over the points of faith not found set down in the written Law. He had tormented the people horribly with his rigorous ideas, one of which was that no reward could be hoped from God, but that he was to be served by them as slaves serve their master. Gischala was his birthplace, but his townsmen held his memory in horror. Today's festival was a memorial rejoicing at his death. One of his disciples was from Samaria. Sadoch, who denied the dogma of the resurrection of the body, continued to promulgate the founder's doctrine. He was a pupil of Antigonus. Sadoch also had a Samaritan accomplice helping to propagate his errors.

Jesus and his disciples lodged with the elder of the synagogue and taught in the forecourt of the same. They brought some sick to him, whom he healed, among them a dropsical old woman. This elder of the synagogue was a very good and learned man. The people abhorred the Pharisees and Sadducees, and had taken great care to provide themselves with such a teacher. That he might acquire more knowledge, they had sent him traveling far away, even down to Egypt. Jesus conversed a long time with him. As usual, the elder turned the conversation upon John, whom he praised very highly. He asked Jesus why, powerful and enlightened as he was said to be and as he was in reality, he did not make some effort to free that man so truly grand and admirable.

During his instruction in the forecourt of the synagogue Jesus uttered prophetic words to the disciples concerning Gischala. They were as follows: Three zealots had arisen in Gischala. The first was that one in whose memory the Jews were then celebrating a feast; the second was a great villain, John of Gischala, who had raised a terrible insurrection in Galilee and at the siege of Jerusalem had committed frightful excesses; the third was living at the very time he was speaking. He would pass from hatred to love, would be zealous for the truth, and would convert many to God. This third was Paul, who was born at Gischala, but whose parents afterward removed to Tarsus.

After his conversion and when journeying to Jerusalem, Paul very zealously preached the Gospel at Gischala. His parents' house was still standing, and rented to strangers. It was situated at the extremity of the suburb of Gischala, and at some distance were squares surrounded with palisades and little buildings, like bleaching huts, that reached almost to the city itself. Paul's parents must have carried on the manufacture of linen, or perhaps they had a weaver's establishment. A pagan officer named Achias now rented and lived in the dwelling house.

CURE OF THE SON OF A PAGAN OFFICER

IT would be difficult to describe the fruitfulness of the region around Gischala. The people were now gathering the second crop of grapes, different kinds of fruits, aromatic shrubs, and cotton. A kind of reed grew in these parts, the lower leaves of which were large, the upper ones small. From it distilled a sweet juice like resin. Here, too, were seen those trees whose fruit was used for the decoration of the tabernacles. The fruit was called the apples of the patriarchs, from the fact of their having been brought hither from the warm eastern countries by the patriarchs. These trees were trained against walls forming an espalier, although their trunk was often more than a foot in diameter. Here also were found many plants producing cotton, whole fields of sweet-scented shrubs, and the aromatic herb from which nard is made. Figs, olives, and grapes were in abundance, while magnificent melons lay in countless numbers in the fields, the roads to which were lined with palms and date trees. In the midst of this luxuriance of nature were great herds of cattle grazing in the most beautiful meadows covered with grass and herbs. I saw likewise large trees with great, thick nuts, the wood of which was exceedingly tough and solid.

As Jesus was walking through the fields and gardens into which the people were fast gathering, groups collected around him here and there. He instructed them in parables taken from their ordinary circumstances and occupations. The pagan children mingled familiarly with those of their Jewish neighbors in harvest time, but they were somewhat differently clothed.

Fig Trees

Monday, November 6, AD 30 (Heshvan 21)

Today a Roman officer—named Achias—who was living in the house vacated by Saul and his parents, came to Jesus, bowed down before him, and said: "Master, reject not your servant! Have pity on my little son lying sick at home!" After exchanging a few words, Jesus said: "Your faith has saved you!" Jesus then entered the house where Saul had been born and Achias now lived and healed his son who was without speech and paralyzed. Afterward, he and the disciples left Gischala and went on to Gabara, where Jesus taught in the synagogue.

In the house in which Paul was born there lived at this period an officer in command of the pagan soldiers of the citadel. He was called Achias. He had a sick son seven years old, to whom he had given the name of Jephthah after the Jewish hero. Achias was a good man. He sighed for help from Jesus, but none of the inhabitants of Gischala would intercede for him with the Lord. The disciples were all engaged: some busy around their Master, others scattered among the harvesters to whom they were telling of Jesus and repeating his instructions, while some others had already been dispatched as messengers to Capernaum and into the neighboring districts. The townspeople had no liking for the officer, whom they did not care to have so near them. They would have been glad had he fixed his abode elsewhere. They were, besides, not very friendly in disposition, and even showed very little enthusiasm over Jesus himself. They went carelessly on with their work, listening to his words, but taking no lively, active interest. The anxious father therefore made bold to follow Jesus, but at a distance. At last he approached him, stepped before him, bowing, and said: "Master, reject not thy servant! Have pity on my little son lying sick at home!" Jesus replied: "It behooveth to break bread to the children of the household before giving it to the stranger who stands without." Achias responded: "Lord, I believe the Promise. I believe that thou hast said that such as believe in thee are not strangers but thy children. Lord, have pity on my son!" Then said Jesus: "Thy faith hath saved thee!" and followed by some of the disciples, he went into the house in which Paul was born and in which Achias now resided.

It was rather more elegant than the generality of Jewish dwellings, though its arrangements were pretty much of the same style. There was a courtyard in front, from which one entered a broad hall, on either side of which were sleeping apartments, or spaces, cut off from the main portion by movable screens. In the center of the house arose the fireplace. Around it lay large rooms and halls, provided with broad stone benches near the walls, upon which lay rugs and cushions. The windows were high up in the building. Achias conducted Jesus into the interior of the house, and some of the servants carried to him the boy in his bed. The wife of Achias followed veiled. She bowed timidly, and stood somewhat behind the rest in anxious expectation. Achias was radiant with joy. He called in all his domestics who, full of curiosity, were standing at a distance. The boy was a beautiful child of about six years. He had on a long woolen gown and a striped fur around his neck and crossed on the breast. He was without speech and paralyzed, wholly unable to move. But he looked intelligent and affectionate, and cast upon Jesus a most touching glance.

Jesus addressed to the parents and all present some words on the vocation of the Gentiles, the nearness of the kingdom, of penance, and of the entrance into the Father's house by baptism. Then he prayed, took the boy from his little bed up in his arms, laid him on his breast, bowed low over him, put his fingers under his tongue, set him down on the floor, and led him to the officer who, with the mother trembling for joy, rushed forward with heartfelt tears to meet and embrace their child. The little fellow, likewise stretching out his arms toward his parents, cried: "O father! O mother! I can walk, I can again speak!" Then Jesus said: "Take the boy! Ye know not what a treasure has been given to you in him. He is now restored to you, but he will one day be redemanded of you!" The parents led the child again to Jesus and in tears threw themselves with him at his feet, uttering thanks. Jesus blessed the boy and spoke to him most kindly. The officer begged Jesus to step with him into an adjoining apartment and take some refreshment. This he did along with the disciples. They partook, standing, of bread, honey, small fruits, and some kind of beverage. Jesus again spoke with Achias, telling him that he should go to Capernaum and there receive baptism, and that he might join Zorobabel. Achias and his domestics did this later on. The boy Jephthah afterward became a very zealous disciple of St. Thomas.

The soldiers of Gischala, in quality of guards, assisted at the crucifixion of Christ. They were on similar occasions employed as police.

Jesus bade farewell to the home of the happy Achias. He spoke with his disciples of the child and of the fruits of salvation he was destined to reap. He told them also that from that same house one had already gone out who would accomplish great things in his kingdom.

Jesus Teaches in Gabara • Magdalene's First Conversion

ON leaving Gischala, Jesus did not go to Bethulia, which was near, but leaving it on the left he traversed the valley and the plain to the somewhat important city of Gabara. It lay at the western foot of the mountain on whose southeastern slope was perched the Herodian eyrie Jotopata. The distance between the city and the fortress, that is, if one went around the mountain, was one hour. This mountain, in which steps were hewn, arose like a steep wall behind Gabara, whose inhabitants were engaged in the manufacture of cotton fine as silk, which they wove into cloth and covers. They made of it also a kind of mattress, which they stretched and fastened on hooks. This formed the whole bed. Some others were engaged in salting and exporting fish.

Tuesday, November 7, AD 30 (Heshvan 22)

Today Jesus prepared for the Sermon on the Mount that he would deliver the following day. He sent out his disciples to the neighboring places to make it known that he would give instruction on the mountain beyond Gabara. Some sixty disciples, friends, and relatives of Jesus came to Gabara in expectation of this occasion. Among them was Mary Magdalene, who had been persuaded to come by her sister Martha.

While still in Gischala, Jesus had sent some of the disciples around to the neighboring places to say that he would deliver a great instruction on the mountain beyond Gabara. There came in consequence, from a circuit of several hours, large crowds of people, who encamped around the mountain. On the summit was an enclosed space in which was a teacher's chair long out of use.

Peter, Andrew, James, John, Nathaniel Chased, and all the rest of the disciples had come, besides most of John's disciples and the sons of the blessed Virgin's eldest sister. There were altogether about sixty disciples, friends, and relatives of Jesus here assembled. The more intimate of the disciples were greeted by Jesus with clasping of both hands and pressing cheek to cheek.

Crowds of pagans came from Cydessa, one hour westward of the neighboring city of Damna, from Adama and the country around Lake Merom. The people crowding hither brought with them provisions and sick of all kinds. Cydessa was a pagan city in the heart of Zebulon. It was in ruins in the time of Alexander the Great, who bestowed it upon a man from Tyre called Livias. The latter restored it, and led thither many of his pagan countrymen from Tyre. The first pagans that came to John's baptism were from Cydessa, which was very beautifully situated and commanded a view of the luxuriantly fruitful country around.

Magdalene

MAGDALENE also wended her way to the Mount of Instruction near Gabara. Martha and Anna Cleophas had left Damna, where the holy women had an inn, and gone to Magdalum with the view of persuading Magdalene to attend the sermon that Jesus was about to deliver on the mountain beyond Gabara. Veronica, Johanna Chusa, Dinah, and the Suphanite had meanwhile remained at Damna, distant three hours from Capernaum and over one hour from Magdalum. Magdalene received her sister in a manner rather kind and showed her into an apartment not far from her room of state, but into this latter she did not take her. There was in Magdalene a mixture of true and false shame. She was partly ashamed of her simple, pious, and plainly dressed sister who went around with Jesus's followers so despised by her visitors and associates, and she was partly ashamed of herself before Martha. It was this feeling that prevented her taking the latter into the apartments that were the scenes of her follies and vices. Magdalene was somewhat broken in spirit, but she lacked the courage to disengage herself from her surroundings. She looked pale and languid. The man with whom she lived, on account of his low and vulgar sentiments, was utterly distasteful to her. Martha treated her very prudently and affectionately. She said to her: "Dinah and Mara the Suphanite, whom you know, two amiable and clever women, invite you to be present with them at the instruction that Jesus is going to give on the mountain.

It is so near, and they are so anxious for your company. You need not be ashamed of them before the people, for they are respectable, they dress with taste, and they have distinguished manners. You will behold a very wonderful spectacle: the crowds of people, the marvelous eloquence of the prophet, the sick, the cures that he effects, the hardihood with which he addresses the Pharisees! Veronica, Mary Chusa, and Jesus's mother, who wishes you so well—we all are convinced that you will thank us for the invitation. I think it will cheer you up a little. You appear to be quite forlorn here, you have no one around you who can appreciate your heart and your talents. Oh, if you would only pass some time with us in Bethany! We hear so many wonderful things, and we have so much good to do, and you have always been so full of compassion and kindness. You must at least come to Damna with me tomorrow morning. There you will find all the women of our party at the inn. You can have a private apartment and meet only those that you know," etc. In this strain Martha spoke to her sister, carefully avoiding anything that might wound her. Magdalene's sadness predisposed her to listen favorably to Martha's proposals. She did indeed raise a few difficulties, but at last yielded and promised Martha to accompany her to Damna. She took a repast with her and went several times during the evening from her own apartments to see her. Martha and Anna Cleophas prayed together that night that God would render the coming journey fruitful in good for Magdalene.

A few days previously James the Greater, impelled by a feeling of intense compassion for Magdalene, had come to invite her to the preaching soon to take place at Gabara.

She had received him at a neighboring house. James was in appearance very imposing. His speech was grave and full of wisdom, though at the same time most pleasing. He made a most favorable impression upon Magdalene, and she received him graciously whenever he was in that part of the country. James did not address to her words of reproof; on the contrary, his manner toward her was marked by esteem and kindliness, and he invited her to be present at least once at Jesus's preaching. It would be impossible, he said, to see or hear one superior to him. She had no need to trouble herself about the other auditors, and she might appear among them in her ordinary dress. Magdalene had received his invitation favorably, but she was still undecided as to whether she should or should not accept it, when Martha and Anna Cleophas arrived.

On the eve of the day appointed for the instruction, Magdalene with Martha and Anna Cleophas started from Magdalum to join the holy women at Damna. Magdalene rode on an ass, for she was not accustomed to walking. She was dressed elegantly, though not to such excess nor so extravagantly as at a later period when she was converted for the second time. She took a private apartment in the inn and spoke only with Dinah and the Suphanite, who visited her by turns. I saw them together, an affable and well-bred confidence marking their conversation. There was, however, on the part of the converted sinners, a shade of embarrassment similar to what might be experienced on a military officer's meeting a former comrade who had become a priest. This feeling soon gave way to tears and womanly expressions of mutual sympathy, and they went together to the inn at the foot of the mountain. The other holy women did not go to the instruction, in order not to annoy Magdalene by their presence. They had come to Damna with the intention of prevailing upon Jesus to remain there and not go to Capernaum, where Pharisees from various localities were again assembled.

They, the Pharisees, had taken up their abode together, determined to make Capernaum their headquarters for awhile, since it was the central point of all Jesus's journeyings. The young Pharisee from Samaria who was present the last time was not among this set; another had taken his place. At Nazareth also and in other places the Pharisees had formed similar unions against Jesus.

The holy women, and especially Mary, were very much troubled, for the Pharisees had uttered loud threats. They sent a messenger to Jesus imploring him not to go to Capernaum after this instruction, but to join them in Damna; or he might turn to the right or to the left as seemed good to him; or better perhaps would it be for him to cross the lake and preach among the pagan cities where he would run no risk. Jesus replied by sending them word not to worry about him, that he knew what was best for him to do, and that he would see them again in Capernaum.

The Mount of Instruction near Gabara • Magdalene

MAGDALENE and her companions reached the mountain in good time, and found crowds of people already encamped around it. The sick of all kinds were, according to the nature of their maladies, ranged together in different places under light canopies and arbors. High upon the mountain were the disciples, kindly ranging the people in order and rendering them every assistance. Around the teacher's chair was a low, semicircular wall, and over it an awning. The audience had here and there similar awnings erected. At a short distance from the teacher's chair, Magdalene and the other women had found a comfortable seat upon a little eminence.

Wednesday, November 8, AD 30 (Heshvan 23)

Around ten o'clock Jesus arrived at the mountain, where there was a teacher's chair. He delivered a powerful discourse, culminating with the words: "Come! Come to me, all who are weary and laden with guilt! Come to me, O sinners! Do penance, believe, and share the kingdom with me!" At these words, Mary Magdalene was deeply moved inwardly, and Jesus, perceiving her agitation, addressed his hearers with some words of consolation—words actually meant for Mary Magdalene—and she was converted. That evening, a Pharisee named Simon Zabulon invited Jesus to a banquet. During the meal, Mary Magdalene entered the room carrying a flask of ointment, with which she anointed Jesus's head. (This scene and the ensuing dispute with Simon Zabulon is described in Luke 7:36–50.)

About ten o'clock, Jesus ascended the mountain with his disciples, followed by the Pharisees, the Herodians, and the Sadducees, and took the teacher's chair. The disciples were on one side, the Pharisees on the other, forming a circle around him. Several times during his discourse Jesus made a pause to allow his hearers to exchange places, the more distant coming forward, the nearest falling back, and he likewise repeated the same instructions several times. His auditors partook of refreshments in the intervals, and Jesus himself once took a mouthful to eat and a little drink. This discourse of Jesus was one of the most powerful that he had yet delivered. He prayed before he began, and then told his hearers that they should not be scandalized at him if he called God his Father, for whosoever does the will of the Father in heaven, he is his son, and that he really accomplished the Father's will, he clearly proved. Hereupon he prayed aloud to his Father and then commenced his austere preaching of penance after the manner of the ancient prophets. All that had happened from the time of the first Promise, all the figures and all the menaces, he introduced into his discourse and showed how, in the present and in the near future, they would be accomplished. He proved the coming of the Messiah from the fulfillment of the prophecies. He spoke of John, the precursor and preparer of the ways, who had honestly fulfilled his mission, but whose hearers had remained obdurate. Then he enumerated their vices, their hypocrisy, their idolatry of sinful flesh; painted in strong colors the Pharisees, Sadducees, and Herodians; and spoke with great warmth of the anger of God and the approaching judgment, of the destruction of Jerusalem and the temple, and of the diverse woes that hung over their country. He quoted many passages from the prophet Malachi, explaining and applying them to the precursor, to the Messiah, to the pure oblation of bread and wine of the New Law (which I plainly understood to signify the Holy Sacrifice of the Mass), to the judgment awaiting the godless, to the second coming of the Messiah on the last day, and spoke of the confidence and consolation those that feared God would then experience. He added, moreover, that the grace taken from them would be given to the pagans.

Then turning to the disciples, Jesus exhorted them to confidence and perseverance, and told them that he would send them to preach salvation to all nations. He warned them to hold neither to the Pharisees, the Sadducees, nor the Herodians, whom he painted in lively colors by comparisons as just as they were striking. This was peculiarly vexatious to the last named, since no one wanted to be publicly known as an Herodian. They who adhered to this sect did so mostly in secret.

When in the course of his instruction Jesus observed that if his hearers would not accept the salvation offered them, it would be worse for them than for Sodom and Gomorrha, some of the Pharisees, taking advantage of a pause, stepped up to him with the question: "Then, will this mountain, this city, yes, even the whole country, be swallowed up along with us all? And could there happen something still worse?" Jesus answered: "The stones of Sodom were swallowed up, but not all the souls, for these latter knew not of the Promise, nor had they the Law and the prophets." He added some words that I understood of his own future descent into Limbo, and from which I gathered that many of those souls were saved. Then coming back to the Jews of his own time, he reminded them that they were a chosen race whom God had formed into one nation, that they had received instruction and warnings, the Promises and their realization, that if they rejected them and persevered in their incredulity, not the rocks, the mountains (for they obeyed the Lord), but their own stony hearts, their own souls, would be hurled into the abyss. And thus would their lot be more grievous than that of Sodom.

When Jesus had thus vehemently urged the guilty to penance, when he had so severely pronounced judgment upon the obdurate, he became once more all love, invited all sinners to come to him, and even shed over them tears of compassion. Then he implored his Father to touch their hearts that some, a few, yes, even one, though burdened with all kinds of guilt, might return to him. Could he gain but one soul, he would share all with it, he would give all that he possessed, yes, he would even sacrifice his life to purchase it. He stretched out his arms toward them, exclaiming: "Come! Come to me, ye who are weary and laden with guilt! Come to me, ye sinners! Do penance, believe, and share the kingdom with me!" Then turning to the Pharisees, to his enemies, he opened his arms to them also, beseeching all, at least one of them, to come to him.

Magdalene had taken her seat among the other women with the self-confident air of a lady of the world, but her manner was assumed. She was inwardly confused and a prey to interior struggle. At first she gazed around upon the crowd, but when Jesus appeared and began to speak, her eyes and soul were riveted upon him alone. His exhortations to penance, his lively pictures of vice, his threats of chastisement, affected her powerfully, and unable to suppress her emotions, she trembled and wept beneath her veil. When Jesus, himself shedding tears full of loving compassion, cried out for sinners to come to him, many of his hearers were transported with emotion. There was a movement in the circle and the crowd pressed around him. Magdalene also, and following her example the other women likewise, took a step nearer. But when Jesus exclaimed: "Ah! If even one soul would come to me!" Magdalene was so moved that she wanted to fly to him at once. She stepped forward; but her companions, fearing some disturbance, held her back, whispering: "Wait! Wait!" This movement of Magdalene attracted scarcely any notice among the bystanders, since the attention of all was riveted upon Jesus's words. Jesus, aware of Magdalene's agitation, uttered words of consolation meant only for her. He said: "If even one germ of penance, of contrition, of love, of faith, of hope has, in consequence of my words, fallen upon some poor, erring heart, it will bear fruit, it will be set down in favor of that poor sinner, it will live and increase. I myself shall nourish it, shall cultivate it, shall present it to my Father." These words consoled Magdalene while they pierced her inmost soul, and she stepped back again among her companions.

It was now about six o'clock, and the sun had already sunk low behind the mountain. During his discourse Jesus was turned to the west, the point toward which the teacher's chair faced, and there was no one behind him. And now he prayed, dismissed the multitude with his blessing, and commanded the disciples to buy food and distribute it to the poor and needy. Whoever had more than enough for himself was to give it or sell it for the benefit of the poor, who were to take home with them whatever they received over and above. Some of the disciples went immediately to execute their Master's commission. Most of those present gave willingly what they could spare, while others just as willingly took some indemnification for it. The disciples were well-known in this part of the country, so the poor were well cared for, and they thanked the great charity of the Lord.

Meanwhile the other disciples accompanied Jesus to the sick, numbers of whom had been brought thither. The Pharisees, scandalized, impressed, astonished, enraged, went back to Gabara. Simon Zabulon, the chief of the synagogue, reminded Jesus of the invitation to sup in his house. Jesus replied that he would be there. The Pharisees murmured against Jesus and criticized him the whole way down the mountain, finding fault with his doctrine and his manners. Each was ashamed to allow his neighbor to remark the favorable impression that had been made upon him, and so by the time they reached the city, they had again entrenched themselves in their own self-righteousness.

Magdalene and her companions followed Jesus. The former went among the people and took her place near the sick women as if to render them assistance. She was very much impressed, and the misery that she witnessed moved her still more. Jesus turned first to the men, among whom for a long time he healed diseases of all kinds. The hymns of thanksgiving from the cured and their attendants as they moved away, rang on the breeze. When he approached the sick females, the crowd that pressed around him and the need that he and his disciples had of space forced Magdalene and the holy women to fall back a little. Nevertheless, Magdalene sought by every opportunity, by every break in the crowd, to draw near to him, but Jesus constantly turned away from her.

He healed some women afflicted with a flow of blood. But how express the feelings of Magdalene, so delicate, so effeminate, whose eyes were quite unused to the sight of human suffering! What memories, what gratitude swelled the heart of Mara the Suphanite when six women, bound three and three, were forcibly led to Jesus by strong servant maids who dragged them along with cords, or long linen bands! They were possessed in the most frightful manner by unclean spirits, and they were the first possessed women that I saw brought publicly to Jesus. Some were from beyond the Sea of Galilee, some from Samaria, and among them were several pagans. They had been bound together only upon reaching this place. Ordinarily they were perfectly quiet and gentle, they offered no violence to one another. But anon, they became quite furious, screaming and hurling themselves here and there. Their custodians bound them and kept them at a distance during Jesus's discourse, and now when all was nearly over, they brought them forward. As the afflicted creatures drew near to Jesus and the disciples, they began to offer vehement resistance. Satan was tormenting them horribly. They uttered the most awful cries and fell into violent contortions. Jesus turned toward them and commanded them to be silent, to be at peace. They instantly stood still and motionless; then he went up to them, ordered them to be unbound, commanded them to kneel down, prayed, and laid his hands upon them. Under the touch of his hand they sank into a few moments' unconsciousness, during which the wicked spirits went out of them in the form of a dark vapor. Then their attendants lifted them up, and veiled and in tears they stood before Jesus, inclining low and giving thanks. He warned them to amend their lives, to purify themselves and do penance, lest their misfortune might come upon them more frightfully than before.

It was dusk before Jesus and the disciples, preceded and followed by crowds of people, started at last down the mountain for Gabara. Magdalene, obeying only her impulse without regard to appearances, followed close after Jesus in the crowd of disciples, and her four companions, unwilling to separate from her, did the same. She tried to keep as close to Jesus as she possibly could, though such conduct was quite unusual in females. Some of the disciples called Jesus's attention to the fact, remarking at the same time what I have just observed. But Jesus, turning around to them, replied: "Let them alone! It is not your affair!" And so he entered the city. When he reached the hall in which Simon Zabulon had prepared the feast, he found the forecourt filled with the sick and the poor who had crowded thither on his approach, and who were loudly calling upon him for help. Jesus at once turned to them, exhorting, consoling, and healing them. Meanwhile Simon Zabulon, with some other Pharisees, made his appearance. He begged Jesus to come in to the feast, for they were awaiting him. "Thou hast," he continued, "already done enough for today. Let these people wait till another time, and let the poor go off at once." But Jesus replied: "These are my guests. I have invited them, and I must first see to their entertainment. When thou didst invite me to thy feast, thou didst invite them also. I shall not go into thy feast until they are helped, and then even I will go in only with them." Then the Pharisees had to go and prepare tables around the court for the cured and the poor. Jesus cured all, and the disciples led those that wished to remain to the tables prepared for them, and lamps were lighted in the court.

Magdalene and the women had followed Jesus hither. They stood in one of the halls of the court adjoining the entertainment hall. Jesus, followed by some of the disciples, went to the table in the latter and from its sumptuous dishes sent various meats to the tables of the poor. The disciples were the bearers of these gifts; they likewise served and ate with the poor. Jesus continued his instructions during the entertainment. The Pharisees were in animated discussion with him when Magdalene, who with her companions had approached the entrance, all of a sudden darted into the hall. Inclining humbly, her head veiled, in her hand a little white flask closed with a tiny bunch of aromatic herbs instead of a stopper, she glided quickly into the center of the apartment, went behind Jesus, and poured the contents of her little flask over his head.[C12] Then catching up the long end of her veil, she folded it, and with both hands passed it lightly once over Jesus's head, as if wishing to smooth his hair and to arrest the overflow of the ointment. The whole affair occupied but a few instants, and after it Magdalene retired some steps. The discussion carried on so hotly at the moment suddenly ceased. A hush fell upon the company, and they gazed upon Jesus and the woman. The air was redolent with the fragrance of the ointment. Jesus was silent. Some of the guests put their heads together, glanced indignantly at Magdalene, and exchanged whispers. Simon Zabulon especially appeared scandalized. At last Jesus said to him: "Simon, I know well of what thou art thinking! Thou thinkest it improper that I should allow this woman to anoint my head. Thou art thinking that she is a sinner, but thou art wrong. She, out of love, has fulfilled what thou didst leave undone. Thou hast not shown me the honor due to guests." Then he turned to Magdalene, who was still standing there, and said: "Go in peace! Much has been forgiven thee." At these words Magdalene rejoined her companions, and they left the house together. Then Jesus spoke of her to the guests. He called her a good woman full of compassion. He censured the criticizing of others, public accusations, and remarks upon the exterior fault of others while the speakers often hid in their own hearts much greater, though secret evils. Jesus continued speaking and teaching for a considerable time, and then returned with his followers to the inn.

Magdalene was deeply touched and impressed by all she had seen and heard. She was interiorly vanquished. And because she was possessed of a certain impetuous spirit of self-sacrifice, a certain greatness of soul, she longed to do something to honor Jesus and to testify to him her emotion. She had noticed with chagrin that neither before nor during the meal had he, the most wonderful, the holiest of teachers, he, the most compassionate, the most miraculous helper of humankind, received from these Pharisees any mark of honor, any of those polite attentions usually extended to guests, and therefore she felt herself impelled to do what she had done. The words of Jesus, "If even one would be moved to come to me!" still lingered in her memory.

The little flask, which was about a hand in height, she generally carried with her as do the grand ladies of our own day. Magdalene's dress was white, embroidered with large red flowers and tiny green leaves. The sleeves were wide, gathered in and fastened by bracelets. The robe was cut wide and hung loose in the back. It was open in front to just above the knee, where it was caught by straps, or cords. The bodice, both back and front, was ornamented with cords and jewels. It passed over the shoulders like a scapular and was fastened at the sides; under it was another colored tunic. The veil that she usually wound about her neck she had, on entering the banquet hall, opened wide and thrown over her whole person. Magdalene was taller than all the other women, robust, but yet graceful. She had very beautiful, tapering fingers, a small, delicate foot, a wealth of beautiful long hair, and there was something imposing in all her movements.

When Magdalene returned to the inn with her companions, Martha took her to another about an hour distant and near the baths of Bethulia. There she found Mary and the holy women awaiting her coming. Mary conversed with her. Magdalene gave an account of Jesus's discourse, while the two other women related the circumstances of Magdalene's anointing and Jesus's words to her. All insisted on Magdalene's remaining and going back with them, at least for awhile, to Bethany. But she replied that she must return to Magdalum to make some arrangements in her household, a resolution very distasteful to her pious friends. She could not, however, cease talking of the impressions she had received and of the majesty, force, sweetness, and miracles of Jesus. She felt that she must follow him, that her own life was an unworthy one, and that she ought to join her sister and friends. She became very thoughtful, she wept from time to time, and her heart grew lighter. Nevertheless, she could not be induced to remain, so she returned to Magdalum with her maid. Martha accompanied her a part of the way, and then joined the holy women who were going back to Capernaum.

Magdalene was taller and more beautiful than the other women. Dinah, however, was much more active and dexterous, very cheerful, ever ready to oblige, like a lively, affectionate girl, and she was moreover very humble. But the blessed Virgin surpassed them all in her marvelous beauty. Although in external loveliness she may have had her equal, and may have even been excelled by Magdalene in certain striking features, yet she far outshone them all in her indescribable air of simplicity, modesty, earnestness, sweetness, and gentleness. She was so very pure, so free from all earthly impressions that in her one saw only the reflex image of God in his creature. No one's bearing resembled hers, except that of her Son. Her countenance surpassed that of all women in its unspeakable purity, innocence, gravity, wisdom, peace, and sweet, devout loveliness. Her whole appearance was noble, and yet she was like a simple, innocent child. She was very grave, very quiet, and often pensive, but never did her sadness destroy the beauty of her countenance, for her tears flowed softly down her placid face.

Magdalene was soon again in her old track. She received the visits of men who spoke in the usual disparaging way of Jesus, his journeys, his doctrine, and of all who followed him. They ridiculed what they heard of Magdalene's visit to Gabara, and looked upon it as a very unlikely story. As for the rest, they declared that they found Magdalene more beautiful and charming than ever. It was by such speeches that Magdalene allowed herself to be infatuated and her good impressions dissipated. She soon sank deeper than before, and her relapse into sin gave the devil greater power over her. He attacked her more vigorously when he saw that he might possibly lose her. She became possessed, and often fell into cramps and convulsions.

TISSOT ILLUSTRATIONS
[SECTION C]

The Public Teaching of Jesus

⊕

The Disciples of Jesus Baptize [C1]

⊕

AFTER the repast, Jesus gave an instruction in the hall opening on the court in presence of the governor and his household, all of whom were to be baptized. After that he went to the place of instruction outside the city where he found many already waiting for him, and there too he taught in preparation for baptism. The people came in bands and went by turns, proceeding from this place to the synagogue where they prayed, sprinkled their heads with ashes, and did penance. They repaired afterward to the bathing garden near the "Place of Grace," where two by two they performed their ablutions in a bathhouse separated from each other by a curtain.

When the last band had left the place of instruction, Jesus and his disciples followed. The baptismal well was that into which the water from the arm of the Jordan flowed. The basin here, as in other places, was surrounded by a canal so broad as to afford a passage for two, and from it five conduits connected with the basin.

This reservoir with its five canals had not been especially constructed for the baptism. The number five was of frequent recurrence in Palestine, and the five aqueducts leading to the pool of Bethesda, to John's fountain in the desert, and to the baptismal well of Jesus, bore reference no doubt to the five sacred wounds, or to some other mystery of religion.

Jesus here gave instructions as an immediate preparation for baptism. The neophytes were clothed in long mantles which they laid aside at the moment of stepping into the canal, retaining only the covering for the loins and the little scapular on the breast. Water from the basin had been let into the canal. On the pathways over it stood the baptizers and the sponsors. The water was thrice poured from a shallow dish over the head in the name of Jehovah and him whom he had sent. Four disciples baptized at the same time, two others imposing hands as sponsors. This ceremony, with the instructions of Jesus in preparation for it, lasted until evening. Many of the aspirants to baptism were not admitted to its reception. [471, Book I]

[JOHN 4:1–4] 1 Now when the Lord knew that the Pharisees had heard that Jesus was making and baptizing more disciples than John 2 (although Jesus himself did not baptize, but only his disciples), 3 he left Judea and departed again to Galilee. 4 He had to pass through Samaria.

The Woman (Dinah) of Samaria at the Well [C2]

⊕

SEVERAL deeply rutted roads ran from different points around the little hill and up to the octangular buildings that enclosed Jacob's well, which was surrounded by trees and grassy seats. The springhouse was encircled by an open arched gallery under which about twenty people could find standing room. Directly opposite the road that led from Sychar and under the arched roof was the door, usually kept shut, that opened into the springhouse proper. There was an aperture in the cover of the latter, which could be closed at pleasure. The interior of the little springhouse was quite roomy. The well was deep and surrounded by a stone rim high enough to afford a seat. Between it and the walls, one could walk around freely. The well had a wooden cover, which when opened disclosed a large cylinder just opposite the entrance and lying across the well. On it hung the bucket, which was unwound by means of a winch.

I saw a woman briskly ascending the hill, to get water from Jacob's well for herself and others She was called Dinah. Coming thus suddenly upon Jesus, Dinah was startled. She lowered her veil and hesitated to advance, for the Lord was sitting full in her path. He graciously drew his feet back, for the path was narrow, with the words: "Pass on, and give me to drink!" Then Dinah passed by him.

Jesus arose and followed her to the well, which she unlocked. While going thither, she said: "How canst thou, being a Jew, ask a drink from a Samaritan?" And Jesus answered her: "If thou didst know the gift of God and who he is that sayeth to thee: 'Give me to drink,' thou wouldst perhaps have asked of him, and he would have given thee living water." Then Dinah loosened the cover and the bucket, meanwhile saying to Jesus, who had seated himself on the rim of the well: "Sir, thou hast nothing wherein to draw, and the well is deep. Then, taking a little vessel made of bark and shaped like a horn, she filled it with water and handed it to Jesus, who, sitting on the rim of the well, drank it and said to her: "Whosoever drinketh of this water, shall thirst again, but he that drinks of the water that I shall give him, shall not thirst forever." [488, Book I]

[JOHN 4:4–15] 4 He had to pass through Samaria. 5 So he came to a city of Samaria, called Sychar, near the field that Jacob gave to his son Joseph. 6 Jacob's well was there, and so Jesus, wearied as he was with his journey, sat down beside the well. It was about the sixth hour. 7 There came a woman of Samaria to draw water. Jesus said to her, "Give me a drink." 8 For his disciples had gone away into the city to buy food. 9 The Samaritan woman said to him, "How is it that you, a Jew, ask a drink of me, a woman of Samaria?" For Jews have no dealings with Samaritans. 10 Jesus answered her, "If you knew the gift of God, and who it is that is saying to you, 'Give me a drink,' you would have asked him, and he would have given you living water." 11 The woman said to him, "Sir, you have nothing to draw with, and the well is deep; where do you get that living water? 12 Are you greater than our father Jacob, who gave us the well, and drank from it himself, and his sons, and his cattle?" 13 Jesus said to her, "Every one who drinks of this water will thirst again, 14 but whoever drinks of the water that I shall give him will never thirst; the water that I shall give him will become in him a spring of water welling up to eternal life." 15 The woman said to him, "Sir, give me this water, that I may not thirst, nor come here to draw."

Jesus Unrolls the Book in the Synagogue [C3]

⊕

[LUKE 4:16–24] 16 And he came to Nazareth, where he had been brought up; and he went to the synagogue, as his custom was, on the sabbath day. And he stood up to read; 17 and there was given to him the book of the prophet Isaiah. He opened the book and found the place where it was written, 18 "The Spirit of the Lord is upon me, because he has anointed me to preach good news to the poor. He has sent me to proclaim release to the captives and recovering of sight to the blind, to set at liberty those who are oppressed, 19 to proclaim the acceptable year of the Lord." 20 And he closed the book, and gave it back to the attendant, and sat down; and the eyes of all in the synagogue were fixed on him. 21 And he began to say to them, "Today this scripture has been fulfilled in your hearing." 22 And all spoke well of him, and wondered at the gracious words which proceeded out of his mouth; and they said, "Is not this Joseph's son?" 23 And he said to them, "Doubtless you will quote to me this proverb, 'Physician, heal yourself; what we have heard you did at Capernaum, do here also in your own country.'" 24 And he said, "Truly, I say to you, no prophet is acceptable in his own country." [493, Book I]

EVERY respectable male member of the community might be requested to explain the Bible. In fact, this task might be performed by any one who had reached the age of 13 years. When some Rabbi or foreign doctor happened to be present in the Synagogue, it was the custom to pay him the compliment of asking him to comment upon the Holy Scriptures. This, no doubt, often occurred in the case of Jesus Christ. We know, from the account given in the Acts of the Apostles, that later, Saint Paul, in his missionary journeys, turned this custom to account, to make his way into the Jewish Synagogues and there bear witness to Jesus.

Jesus Goes Out into a Desert Place [C4]

⊕

SEEING this confusion, Jesus disappeared in the crowd, left the city, and took a steep byway into the mountains where there was a solitary place. His three disciples followed, but after long seeking found him not till night. He was praying. [497, Book I]

[LUKE 4:42–43] 42 And when it was day he departed and went into a lonely place. And the people sought him and came to him, and would have kept him from leaving them; 43 but he said to them, "I must preach the good news of the kingdom of God to the other cities also; for I was sent for this purpose."

The Healing of the Officer's Son [C5]

⊕

FROM Nain, Jesus, leaving Nazareth on the left, journeyed past Tabor to Cana, where he put up near the synagogue with a doctor of the Law. The forecourt of the house was soon full of people who had anticipated his coming from Engannim, and were here awaiting him. He had been teaching the whole morning, when a servant of the centurion of Capernaum with several companions mounted on mules arrived. He was in a great hurry and wore an air of anxiety and solicitude. He vainly sought on all sides to press his way through the throng of Jesus, but could not succeed.

After several fruitless attempts, he began to cry out lustily: "Venerable Master, let thy servant approach thee! I come as the messenger of my lord of Capernaum. In his name and as the father of his son, I implore thee to come with me at once, for my son is very sick and nigh unto death." Jesus appeared not to hear him; but encouraged at seeing that some were directing Jesus's attention to him, the man again sought to press through the crowd. But not succeeding, he cried out anew: "Come with me at once, for my son is dying!" When he cried so impatiently, Jesus turned his head toward him and said loud enough for the people to hear: "If you see not signs and wonders, you do not believe. I know your case well. You want to boast of a miracle and glory over the Pharisees, though you have the same need of being humbled as they. And thus Jesus went on for a long time, humbling the man before all the people.

The man listened to Jesus's reproaches without being at all disturbed. Not at all diverted from his design, he again tried to approach nearer, crying out: "Of what use is all that, Master? My son is in the agony of death! Come with me at once, he may perhaps be already dead!" Then Jesus said to him: "Go, thy son liveth!" The man asked: "Is that really true?" Jesus answered: "Believe me, he has in this very hour been cured." Thereupon the man believed and, no longer importuning Jesus to accompany him, mounted his mule and hastened back to Capernaum.

It was a day's journey from Cana to Capernaum, but the man rode with such speed that he reached home before night. A couple of hours from Capernaum, some of his servants met him and told him that the boy was cured. They had come after him to tell him that if he had not found Jesus, he should give himself no further trouble, for the boy had been suddenly cured at the seventh hour. Then he repeated to them the words of Jesus. They were filled with astonishment, and hurried home with him.

I saw the centurion Zorobabel and the boy coming to the door to meet him. The boy embraced him. He repeated all that Jesus had said, the servants that accompanied him confirming his words. There was great joy, and I saw a feast made ready. The youth sat between his adopted father and his real father, the mother being nearby. He loved his real father as much as he did the supposed one, and the former exercised great authority in the house. [1]

[JOHN 4:46–54] 46 So he came again to Cana in Galilee, where he had made the water wine. And at Capernaum there was an official whose son was ill. 47 When he heard that Jesus had come from Judea to Galilee, he went and begged him to come down and heal his son, for he was at the point of death. 48 Jesus therefore said to him, "Unless you see signs and wonders you will not believe." 49 The official said to him, "Sir, come down before my child dies." 50 Jesus said to him, "Go; your son will live." The man believed the word that Jesus spoke to him and went his way. 51 As he was going down, his servants met him and told him that his son was living. 52 So he asked them the hour when he began to mend, and they said to him, "Yesterday at the seventh hour the fever left him." 53 The father knew that was the hour when Jesus had said to him, "Your son will live"; and he himself believed, and all his household. 54 This was now the second sign that Jesus did when he had come from Judea to Galilee.

All the City was Gathered at his Door [C6]

⊕

[MARK 1:32–34] 32 That evening, at sundown, they brought to him all who were sick or possessed with demons. 33 And the whole city was gathered together about the door. 34 And he healed many who were sick with various diseases, and cast out many demons; and he would not permit the demons to speak, because they knew him. [3]

THE streets of towns in the East, especially those of Galilee and Judea, are very narrow and tortuous. They are, moreover, very dark, on account of the way in which most of them are shut in by the arches supporting the houses. These arches, which connect the houses on either side together, add greatly to their solidity, so that when the modern public works office, with a view to letting in more light, orders their removal, recourse has to be had to props, to prevent the buildings from falling down. It is several times stated in the gospels that when Jesus drove out evil spirits, they bore witness to him and acknowledged his superhuman power. In the case under notice, Jesus rebuked the unclean spirit, saying, "Hold thy peace," because that spirit had cried out, "I know thee who thou art," that is to say, he guessed the divine character of Christ, and his mission as the Messiah, from his works. Now it did not suit our Lord to reveal before his hour was come a truth so transcendent, and one for which men, especially his fellow countrymen, were so little prepared. It was outside the house of Simon that the scene described by Saint Mark took place.

Jesus Teaches in the Synagogue [C7]

⊕

WHEN Jesus went next morning to the synagogue, a Jew whose turn it was to read was about to take the roll of scriptures. But Jesus desired them to hand it to him. He taught from Deuteronomy, chapter 4, of the obedience due to the commandments, from which nothing must be taken and to which nothing must be added. He reminded them that, although Moses had zealously repeated to the children of Israel all that God commanded, yet they had frequently violated his ordinances. The Ten Commandments presented themselves in the course of the reading, and Jesus explained the first, that on the love of God. He spoke very severely, reproaching them with the additions they made to the Law, laying burdens upon the poor people, and not fulfilling the Law itself. He assailed them so sharply on this point that they became angry, for they could not say that he was uttering falsehood. [12]

[MATTHEW 4:23–25] 23 And he went about all Galilee, teaching in their synagogues and preaching the gospel of the kingdom and healing every disease and every infirmity among the people. 24 So his fame spread throughout all Syria, and they brought him all the sick, those afflicted with various diseases and pains, demoniacs, epileptics, and paralytics, and he healed them. 25 And great crowds followed him from Galilee and the Decapolis and Jerusalem and Judea and from beyond the Jordan.

The Brow of the Hill near Nazareth [C8]

⊕

THE synagogue was in the western part of Nazareth. It was already dark and two of the crowd bore torches. They led Jesus around by the eastern side of the synagogue, then turned into a broad street that ran westward out of the city. Ascending the mountain, they reached a lofty spur which on the northern side overlooked a marshy pool, and on the south formed a rocky projection over a steep precipice. It was from this point they were in the habit of precipitating malefactors. Here they intended once more to call Jesus to account, and then to hurl him down. The abyss ended in a narrow ravine. They were not far from the scene of action when Jesus, who had been led as a prisoner among them, stood still, while they continued their way mocking and jeering. At that instant I saw two tall figures of light near Jesus. . . . Nothing was more laughable than the perplexity, the alarm, the silly plight of the Pharisees when, all of a sudden, they found Jesus no more among them. [13]

[LUKE 4:28–30] 28 When they heard this, all in the synagogue were filled with wrath. 29 And they rose up and put him out of the city, and led him to the brow of the hill on which their city was built, that they might throw him down headlong. 30 But passing through the midst of them he want away.

The Sick Awaiting the Passage of Jesus [C9]

⊕

JESUS went from Peter's dwelling over the mountain ridge to the north side of Bethsaida. The whole road was full of sick, pagans and Jews, separate however, the leprous far removed from all others. There were blind, lame, mute, deaf, paralytic, and an exceedingly large number of dropsical Jews. The ceremony of curing was performed with the greatest order and solemnity. The people had already been two days here, and the disciples of the place—Andrew, Peter, and the others whom Jesus had notified of his coming—had arranged them comfortably in the nooks, retired and shady, and the little gardens on the road. [19]

[LUKE 6:19] 19 And all the crowd sought to touch him, for power came forth from him and healed them all. [MATTHEW 14:35–36] 35 And when the men of that place recognized him, they sent round to all that region and brought to him all that were sick, 36 and besought him that they might only touch the fringe of his garment; and as many as touched it were made well.

The Possessed Man in the Synagogue [C10]

⊕

ON the following day Jesus went very early to Capernaum. There was an innumerable concourse gathered before the synagogue, among them crowds of sick, of whom he healed many. When he entered the synagogue wherein the Pharisees were assembled, some possessed who were present began to cry out after him. One in particular, more noisy than his fellows, went running toward him crying: "What have we to do with thee, Jesus of Nazareth? Thou hast come to destroy us! I know that thou art the Holy One of God!" Jesus commanded the demon to be silent and to go out of the man. The latter, tearing himself, ran back among his companions, but the devil, uttering great cries, went out of him. The man then became perfectly calm, and cast himself at Jesus' feet. [21]

[MARK 1:21–28] 21 And they went into Capernaum; and immediately on the sabbath he entered the synagogue and taught. 22 And they were astonished at his teaching, for he taught them as one who had authority, and not as the scribes. 23 And immediately there was in their synagogue a man with an unclean spirit; 24 and he cried out, "What have you to do with us, Jesus of Nazareth? Have you come to destroy us? I know who you are, the Holy One of God." 25 But Jesus rebuked him, saying, "Be silent, and come out of him!" 26 And the unclean spirit, convulsing him and crying with a loud voice, came out of him. 27 And they were all amazed, so that they questioned among themselves, saying, "What is this? A new teaching! With authority he commands even the unclean spirits, and they obey him." 28 And at once his fame spread everywhere throughout all the surrounding region of Galilee.

The Healing of Peter's Mother-in-Law [C11]

⊕

JESUS now went without delay with the disciples out of the city gate and along the mountain to Peter's in Bethsaida. They had urged him to do so, for they thought that Peter's mother-in-law was dying. Her sickness had very much increased, and now she had a raging fever. Jesus went straight into her room. He was followed by some of the family; I think Peter's daughter was among them. He stepped to that side of the bed to which the sick woman's face was turned, and leaned against the bed, half-standing, half-sitting, so that his head approached hers. He spoke to her some words, and laid his hand upon her head and breast. She became perfectly still. Then standing before her, he took her hand and raised her into sitting posture, saying: "Give her something to drink!" Peter's daughter gave her a drink out of a vessel in the form of a little boat. Jesus blessed the drink and commanded the invalid to rise. She obeyed and arose from her low couch. Her limbs were bandaged, and she wore a wide nightdress. Disengaging herself from the bandages, she stepped to the floor and rendered thanks to the Lord, the entire household uniting with her. At the meal that followed, she helped with the other women and, perfectly recovered, served at table. [23]

[MARK 1:29–31] 29 And immediately he left the synagogue, and entered the house of Simon and Andrew, with James and John. 30 Now Simon's mother-in-law lay sick with a fever, and immediately they told him of her. 31 And he came and took her by the hand and lifted her up, and the fever left her; and she served them.

The Meal in the House of the Pharisee [C12]

⊕

THE Pharisees, scandalized, impressed, astonished, enraged, went back to Gabara. Simon Zabulon, the chief of the synagogue, reminded Jesus of the invitation to sup in his house. Jesus replied that he would be there. It was dusk before Jesus and the disciples, preceded and followed by crowds of people, started at last down the mountain for Gabara. Magdalene, obeying only her impulse without regard to appearances, followed close after Jesus in the crowd of disciples.

Meanwhile Simon Zabulon, with some other Pharisees, made his appearance. He begged Jesus to come in to the feast, for they were awaiting him. "Thou hast," he continued, "already done enough for today. Let these people wait till another time, and let the poor go off at once." But Jesus replied: "These are my guests. I have invited them, and I must first see to their entertainment. When thou didst invite me to thy feast, thou didst invite them also. I shall not go into thy feast until they are helped, and then even I will go in only with them." Magdalene and the women had followed Jesus hither. They stood in one of the halls of the court adjoining the entertainment hall. The Pharisees were in animated discussion with him when Magdalene, who with her companions had approached the entrance, all of a sudden darted into the hall. Inclining humbly, her head veiled, in her hand a little white flask closed with a tiny bunch of aromatic herbs instead of a stopper, she glided quickly into the center of the apartment, went behind Jesus, and poured the contents of her little flask over his head. Then catching up the long end of her veil, she folded it, and with both hands passed it lightly once over Jesus's head, as if wishing to smooth his hair and to arrest the overflow of the ointment. The whole affair occupied but a few instants, and after it Magdalene retired some steps. The discussion carried on so hotly at the moment suddenly ceased. A hush fell upon the company, and they gazed upon Jesus and the woman. The air was redolent with the fragrance of the ointment. Jesus was silent. Some of the guests put their heads together, glanced indignantly at Magdalene, and exchanged whispers. Simon Zabulon especially appeared scandalized. At last Jesus said to him: "Simon, I know well of what thou art thinking! Thou thinkest it improper that I should allow this woman to anoint my head. Thou art thinking that she is a sinner, but thou art wrong. She, out of love, has fulfilled what thou didst leave undone. Thou hast not shown me the honor due to guests." Then he turned to Magdalene, who was still standing there, and said: "Go in peace! Much has been forgiven thee." [109]

[LUKE 7:36–39] 36 One of the Pharisees asked him to eat with him, and he went into the Pharisee's house, and took his place at table. 37
And behold, a woman of the city, who was a sinner, when she learned that he was at table in the Pharisee's house, brought an alabaster
flask of ointment, 38 and standing behind him at his feet, weeping, she began to wet his feet with her tears, and wiped them with the hair
of her head, and kissed his feet, and anointed them with the ointment. 39 Now when the Pharisee who had invited him saw it, he said to
himself, "If this man were a prophet, he would have known who and what sort of woman this is who is touching him, for she is a sinner."

LUKE 7:38 indicates with sufficient clearness how the scene referred to took place. It was possible to pass from the court or garden by way of arcades to the room in which the meal was served, without opening any door, and Mary Magdalene could thus, without troubling any of the attendants, make her way in behind Jesus, who was reclining at table with his feet raised above the ground. She had only to bend down slightly to be able to anoint the feet of the Master, after she had poured oil on his head. The table was of the form of a horseshoe, and the servants waited within the semicircle formed by it, so that the Magdalene's presence could not possibly have annoyed anyone. Moreover, in the East, access to rooms in which feasts are being held is more or less free to all.

PREACHING AND MIRACLES OF JESUS IN CAPERNAUM AND THE SURROUNDING DISTRICTS

Cornelius the Centurion

Thursday, November 9, AD 30 (Heshvan 24)

Jesus and his disciples went to the estate of Zorobabel, the high-ranking official of Capernaum, whose son Jesus had healed on Ab 15.

FROM Gabara, Jesus went to the estate of the officer Zorobabel near Capernaum. The two lepers whom at his last visit to Capernaum he had healed, here presented themselves to return him thanks. The steward, the domestics, and the cured son of Zorobabel also were here. They had already been baptized. Jesus taught and cured many sick. In the dusk of the evening, after his disciples had separated and gone to their respective families, Jesus proceeded along the valley of Capernaum to the house of his mother. All the holy women were here assembled, and there was great joy. Mary and the women renewed their petition to Jesus that he would cross to the other side of the lake early next morning because the committee of the Pharisees was so irritated against him. Jesus calmed their fears. Mary interceded for the sick slave of the centurion Cornelius, who was, she said, a very good man. Although a pagan, he had, through affection for the Jews, built them a synagogue. She begged him likewise to cure the sick daughter of Jairus, the elder of the synagogue, who lived in a little village not far from Capernaum.

Friday, November 10, AD 30 (Heshvan 25)

This morning, in Capernaum, Jesus was approached by the Roman centurion Cornelius, whose servant was desperately ill. Jesus praised Cornelius for his faith and healed the servant from afar (Matthew 8:5–13 and Luke 7:1–10). Next, Jesus went to a leper's hut and healed the leper, as described in Mark 1:40–45. Then, leaving the leper's hut, he went to an inn in the Valley of the Doves, south of Capernaum, where he met Maroni, the widow of Nain, who begged him to come and heal her twelve-year-old son. In the afternoon he returned to Capernaum and taught in the synagogue as the sabbath began. Suddenly a man who was possessed ran in and caused a great commotion. Jesus healed him (Mark 1:21–28). Seeing this, the Pharisees—utterly astounded—gave up their plan to lay hands on Jesus.

When Jesus next morning, with some of the disciples, was going to the residence of the pagan officer Cornelius, which stood on a height to the north of Capernaum, he was met in the neighborhood of Peter's house by the two Jews whom Cornelius had once before sent to him. They again begged him to have pity on his servant, for Cornelius, they said, deserved the favor. He was a friend of the Jews and had built them a synagogue, reckoning it at the same time an honor to be allowed to do so. Jesus responded that he was even then on his way to Cornelius's, and he directed them to dispatch a messenger in haste to announce his coming. Before reaching Capernaum, Jesus took, just to the right of the gate, the road running between the city and the ramparts and passed the hovel of a leper living in the city wall. A short distance farther on brought Cornelius's house in sight. Upon receiving the message sent by Jesus, Cornelius had left it as if to get a glimpse of him. He knelt down and, esteeming himself unworthy to approach him or to speak with him personally, hurried off a messenger with these words: "The centurion bids me say to thee, 'Lord, I am not worthy that thou shouldst enter under my roof! [D1] Speak but one word, and my servant shall be healed. For if I, who am only a humble man dependent upon my superior, say to my servant: Do this! Do that! and he does it, how much easier will it be for thee to command thy servant to be healed and that he should be so!'" When these words were delivered to Jesus by Cornelius's messenger, he turned to those standing around and said: "Verily, I say unto ye, I have not found such faith in Israel! Know ye then! Many shall come from the east and the west and shall take place with Abraham, Isaac, and Jacob in heaven; and many of the children of God's kingdom, the Israelites, shall be cast out into exterior darkness where there shall be weeping and gnashing of teeth!" Then, turning to the servant of the centurion, he said: "Go, and as thou hast believed, so be it done to thee!" The messenger bore the words to the kneeling centurion, who inclined to the earth, arose, and hastened back to the house. As he entered, he encountered his servant, who was coming to meet him, enveloped in a mantle, his head bound in a scarf. He was not a native of the country, as was indicated by his yellowish-brown complexion.

Jesus immediately turned back to Capernaum. As he was again passing the leper's hut, the leper himself came out and threw himself down before him. "Lord," he said, "if thou wilt, thou canst make me clean." Jesus replied: "Stretch forth thy hands!" He touched them and said: "I do will it. Be thou clean!" and the leprosy fell from the man. [D2] Jesus commanded him to present himself to the priests for inspection, to make the offering prescribed by the Law, and to speak to none other of his cure. The man went to the pharisaical priests and submitted himself to their examination as to whether he was cured or not. They became enraged, examined him rigorously, but were forced to acknowledge him cured. They had so lively a dispute with him that they almost drove him from their presence.

Jesus turned off into the street that led into the heart of the city, and for about an hour cured numbers of sick that had been brought together, also some possessed. Most of the sick were lying near a well, around which stood little huts. After that Jesus, with several of the disciples, left the city and went to a little valley beyond Magdalum not far from Damna. There they found a public inn, at which were Maroni, the widow of Nain, and the pagan Lais of Nain and her two daughters, Sabia and Athalia, both of whom Jesus, when at Meroz, had from a distance delivered from the devil. Maroni, the widow of Nain, now came beseeching Jesus to go to her son Martialis, a boy of twelve years, who was so ill that she feared to find him dead on her return. Jesus told her to go home in peace, that he would follow her—but when, he did not say. Maroni had brought with her presents for the inn. She immediately hurried back home with her servant. She had about nine hours to travel. She was a wealthy woman and very good, a mother to all the poor children in Nain.

Bartholomew also had arrived bringing with him Joses, the little son of his widowed sister, perhaps to be baptized. Thomas too was there and with him Jephthah, the little cured son of Achias, the centurion of Gischala. Achias himself was not present, but Judas Iscariot had come from Meroz. Lais and her two daughters had already embraced Judaism in Nain and renounced idolatry before the Jewish priests. At this ceremony a kind of baptism was performed by the priests which, however, consisted only of a sprinkling with water and other purifications. In such cases, the Jews baptized women, but the baptism of Jesus and of John was not conferred upon females before Pentecost.

All the future apostles were now in Capernaum, with the exception of Matthias. A great many of Jesus's disciples and relatives, among the latter many women related to him by blood, were present. Of the number was Mary Heli, Mary's elder sister. She was now perhaps seventy years old, and together with her second husband, Obed, had come bringing an ass laden with presents to Mary. She dwelt at Japha, a little place an hour at most from Nazareth, where Zebedee once lived and where his sons were born. She was greatly rejoiced at seeing again her three sons, James, Sadoch, and Heliachim, all disciples of John. This James was as old as Andrew. He is the same that with two other disciples, Cephas and John, once disputed with Paul on the subject of Jewish circumcision. After Jesus's death he became a priest, and was one of the oldest and most distinguished of the seventy disciples. Later he accompanied James the Greater to Spain, to the islands, into Cyprus, and into the idolatrous countries bordering the confines of Judea. Not this James, but James the Less, the son of Alpheus and Mary Cleophas, became the first bishop of Jerusalem.

Miraculous Cures Wrought by Jesus • His Reasons for Teaching in Parables

THE Pharisees and Sadducees determined to oppose Jesus today in the synagogue. They had laid their plans and bribed the people to raise a tumult in which Jesus was to be formally thrust out of the edifice or taken prisoner. But the affair turned out quite differently. Jesus commenced his teaching in the synagogue by a very vigorous address, like one having power and authority to speak. The rage of the exasperated Pharisees increased at each moment. It was about to be let loose upon him when suddenly a great disturbance arose in the synagogue. A man belonging to the city and possessed by the devil, and who on account of his madness had been fast bound, had while his keepers were in the synagogue broken his bonds. He came plunging like a fury into the synagogue, and with frightful cries pressed his way through the people, whom he tossed right and left, and who also began to utter screams of terror. He ran straight to the spot where Jesus was teaching, crying out: "Jesus of Nazareth! What have we to do with thee? Thou hast come to drive us out! I know who thou art! Thou art the Holy One of God!" But Jesus remained quite unmoved. He scarcely turned from his elevated position toward him, made only a menacing gesture sideways with his hand, and said quietly: "Be still, and go out of him!" Thereupon the man, becoming silent, sank down, still tossed to and fro on the ground, and Satan departed from him under the form of a thick, black vapor. The man now grew pale and calm, prostrated on the ground, and wept. All present were witness to this awful and wonderful spectacle of Jesus's power. Their terror was changed into a murmur of admiration. The courage of the Pharisees forsook them, and they huddled together, saying to one another: "What manner of man is this? He commands the spirits, and they go out of the possessed!" Jesus went on quietly with his discourse. The man that had been freed from the devil, weak and emaciated, was conducted home by his wife and relatives, who had been in the synagogue. When the sermon was over, he met Jesus and asked for some advice. Jesus warned him to refrain from his evil habits lest something worse might befall him, and exhorted him to penance and baptism. The man was a cloth weaver. He made cotton scarfs, narrow and light,

Parable of the Enemy Who Sows

[MATTHEW 13:36–40] 36 Then he left the crowds and went into the house. And his disciples came to him, saying, "Explain to us the parable of the weeds of the filed." 37 He answered, "He who sows the good seed is the Son of Man; 38 the field is the world, and the good seed means the sons of the kingdom; the weeds are the sons of the evil one, 39 and the enemy who sowed them is the devil; the harvest is the close of the age, and the reapers are angels. 40 Just as the weeds are gathered and burned with fire, so will it be at the close of the age.

such as were worn around the neck. He returned to his work perfectly cured in mind and body. Such unclean spirits often domineer over men that freely give themselves up to their passions.

After this scene, the Pharisees were afraid to assault Jesus that day, and so they remained quiet while he went on with his teaching. The lessons for the sabbath were taken from Moses and Osee. There were no more interruptions, though Jesus spoke very forcibly and severely. His appearance and his words were much more impressive than usual. He spoke as one having authority. The instruction over, he went to Mary's, where were gathered the women with many relatives and disciples.

I counted all the holy women who were associated together till the death of Jesus to help the little community. There were seventy. At this time there were already thirty-seven who took part in this duty. Sabia and Athalia also, the daughters of Lais of Nain, were toward the last admitted among the female followers. At the time of St. Stephen, they were among the Christians who settled in Jerusalem.

***Saturday, November 11, AD 30** (**Heshvan 26**)*

Today Jesus taught in parables (Matthew 13:18–30, 34–43). After the close of the sabbath, the Pharisees began to dispute with him in the forecourt of the synagogue. They accused him of blasphemy for having forgiven Mary Magdalene her sins three days before at the meal arranged by the Pharisee Simon Zabulon. Their accusations caused a great uproar, during which Jesus left quietly. He went to his mother's house and talked with her and the other women there.

The Hidden Treasure

[MATTHEW 13:44] 44 The kingdom of heaven is like treasure hidden in a field. When a man found it, he hid it again, and then in his joy went and sold all he had and bought that field..

Next morning Jesus again taught unmolested in the synagogue. The Pharisees had said to one another: "We can do nothing with him now, his adherents are too numerous. We shall contradict him now and then, we shall report all at Jerusalem, and wait till he goes up to the temple for Passover." The streets were again filled with the sick. Some had come before the sabbath, and some till now had not believed, but on the report of the possessed man's cure, they had themselves transported thither from all quarters of the city. Many of them had been there before, but had not been cured. They were weak, tepid, slothful souls, more difficult to convert than great sinners of more ardent nature. Magdalene was converted only after many struggles and relapses, but her last efforts were generous and final. Dinah the Samaritan turned at once from her evil ways, and the Suphanite, after sighing long for grace, was suddenly converted. All the great female sinners were very quickly and powerfully converted, as was also the sturdy Paul, to whom conversion came like a flash of lightning. Judas, on the contrary, was always vacillating, and at last fell into the abyss. It was the same with the great and most violent maladies which I saw Jesus, in his wisdom, cure

Mountain Way near Gabara

at once. They that were afflicted with them, like the possessed, had no will whatever to remain in the state in which they were, or again, self-will was entirely overcome by the violence of the malady. But as to those that were less grievously affected, whose sufferings only opposed an obstacle to their sinning with more facility, and whose conversion was insincere, I saw that Jesus often sent them away with an admonition to reform their lives; or that he only alleviated without curing their bodily ills, that through their pressure the soul might be cured. Jesus could have cured all that came to him, and that instantaneously, but he did so only for those that believed and did penance, and he frequently warned them against a relapse. Even those that were only slightly sick he sometimes cured at once, if such would prove beneficial to their soul. He was not come to cure the body that it might the more readily sin, but he cured the body in order to deliver and save the soul. In every malady, in every kind of bodily infirmity, I see a special design of God. Sickness is the sign of some sin. It may be his own or another's, a sin of which he may be conscious or not, that the sufferer has to expiate, or it may be a trial expressly prepared for him, which by patience and submission to God's will he may change into capital that will yield a rich return. Properly speaking, no one suffers innocently, for who is innocent, since the Son of God had to take upon himself the sins of the world that they might be blotted out? To follow him, we are all obliged to bear our cross after him.

Since joy and the highest degree of patience in suffering, since the union of pain with the Passion of Jesus Christ, belong to the perfect, it follows that a disinclination to suffer is in itself an imperfection. We are created perfect and we shall again be born to perfection, consequently the cure of sickness is an effect of pure love and mercy toward poor sinners, a favor wholly unmerited by them. They have deserved more than sickness, they have deserved death; but the Lord by his own death has delivered them that believe in him and perform works in accordance with their faith.

And so I saw Jesus on this day cure many possessed, paralyzed, dropsical, gouty, mute, blind, many afflicted with an issue of blood, in fine, violent maladies of all kinds. I saw him several times pass by some that were able to stand. They were those who had frequently received slight relief from him, but their conversion not being earnest, they had relapsed in body and soul. As Jesus was passing by them, they cried out: "Lord, Lord! Thou dost cure all that are grievously sick, and thou dost not cure us! Lord, have pity on us! We are sick—again!" Jesus responded: "Why do ye not stretch forth your hands to me?" At these words, all stretched out their hands to him, and said: "Lord, here are our hands!" Jesus replied: "Ye do indeed stretch forth these hands, but the hands of your heart I cannot seize. Ye withdraw them and lock them up, for ye are filled with darkness." Then he continued to admonish them, cured several, who were converted, slightly relieved others, and passed by some unnoticed.

That afternoon he went with all his disciples and relatives to the lake. There was on the south side of the valley a pleasure garden provided with conveniences for bathing, the water being furnished from the brook of Capernaum. Here they paused, and administered baptism in the garden.

The blessed Virgin with several of the women, among them Dinah, Mary, Lais, Athalia, Sabia, and Martha, went for a walk in the neighborhood of Bethsaida, a little beyond the lepers' asylum. A caravan of pagans was encamped thereabouts, and among them were several women from Upper Galilee. The blessed Virgin consoled and instructed them. The women sat in a circle on a little eminence, and Mary sometimes sat, sometimes walked among them. They asked her questions which she answered clearly, and told them many things about the patriarchs, the prophets, and Jesus.

Jesus meantime was instructing a crowd in parables. The disciples did not understand him. Later, when again alone with them, he explained the parable of the sower. He spoke of the tares among the wheat and of the danger of pulling up the wheat with them. It was principally James the Greater who told Jesus that he and his companions did not understand him, and he asked him why he did not speak more clearly. Jesus answered that he would make all intelligible to them, but that on account of the weak and the pagans, the mysteries of the kingdom of God could not then be exposed more plainly. As even with such precautions, these mysteries alarmed his hearers, who in their state of depravity esteemed them too sublime for them, they must at first be presented, as it were, under the cover of a similitude. They must fall into their hearts like the grain of seed. In the grain the whole ear is enclosed, but to produce it, the grain must be hidden in the earth. He explained to them likewise the parable referring to their own call to labor in the harvest. He insisted chiefly upon their following him; they would soon be with him always, and he would explain all things to them. James the Greater said also: "Master, why wilt thou explain all to us who are so ignorant? Why must we publish these things to others? Tell them rather to the Baptist, who believes so firmly who thou really art. He can publish them, he can make them known!"

That evening when Jesus was teaching again in the synagogue, the Pharisees, who could once more breathe somewhat freely, began to dispute with him on the subject of his forgiving sins. They reproached him with the fact of his having in Gabara said to Mary Magdalene that her sins were forgiven her, and they asked how he knew that. How could he do that? Such talk was blasphemy! Jesus silenced them. Then they tried to provoke him to say that he was not a man, that he was God. But Jesus again confounded them in their words. This scene took place in the forecourt of the synagogue. At last the Pharisees raised a great cry and tumult. But Jesus slipped from their hands and into the crowd, so that they could not tell where he had gone. He went by the flowery dale back of the synagogue to the garden of Zorobabel and thence by roundabout ways to the house of his mother. He tarried there a part of the night, and sent word to Peter and the other disciples to meet him next morning at the opposite side of the valley beyond Peter's fishery, as he wished them to go with him to Nain.

The centurion Cornelius and his servant asked Jesus what they should do. He answered that they and all their family should receive baptism.

The Raising of the Youth of Nain from the Dead

***Sunday, November 12, AD 30** (**Heshvan 27**)*

Jesus and his disciples walked in the direction of Nain. On the way, Jesus taught how to distinguish true teachers from false (Matthew 7:15–20). That night, he stayed with his disciples at a shepherd's inn three or four hours from Nain.

THE ROAD to Nain crossed the valley of Magdalum above Peter's fishery to the east of the mountain that looked down upon Gabara, and then ran into the valley eastward of Bethulia and Gischala. Jesus may have journeyed with the disciples nine to ten hours when they put up at a shepherd inn about three or four hours from Nain. They had crossed the brook Kishon once. Jesus taught the whole way, explaining to his disciples in particular how they would be able to detect false teachers.

Nain was a beautiful little place with well-built houses, and was sometimes known also as Engannim. It lay upon a charming hill on the brook Kishon to the south, about an hour from Mount Tabor, and facing Endor on the southwest. Jezreel was more to the south, but was hidden by intervening heights. The beautiful Plain of Esdrelon stretched out before Nain, which was almost three or four hours distant from Nazareth. The country here was uncommonly rich in grain, fruit, and wine. The widow Maroni owned a whole mountain covered with the most beautiful vineyards. Jesus had about thirty companions. The path over the hill was rather narrow, so some went on before Jesus, and others behind him.

***Monday, November 13, AD 30** (**Heshvan 28**)*

At around nine in the morning, as Jesus and the disciples were approaching Nain, they met a funeral procession emerging from the city gate. Jesus commanded the coffin bearers to stand still and set the coffin down. He raised his eyes to heaven and spoke the words recorded in Matthew 11:25–30. There then occurred the miraculous raising from the dead of the youth of Nain—the twelve-year-old Martialis, son of the widow Maroni—described in Luke 7:11–17.

It was almost nine in the morning when Jesus and his companions drew near to Nain and encountered the funeral procession at the gate. A crowd of Jews enveloped in mourning mantles passed out of the city gate with the corpse. Four men were carrying the coffin, in which reposed the remains upon a kind of frame made of crossed poles curved in the middle. The coffin was in shape something like the human form, light like a woven basket, with a cover fastened to the top. Jesus passed through the disciples who, formed into two rows on either side of the road, advanced to meet the coming procession, and said: "Stand still!" Then as he laid his hand upon the coffin, he said: "Set the coffin down." The bearers obeyed, the crowd fell back, and the disciples ranged on either side. The mother of the dead youth, with several of her female friends, was following the corpse. They too paused just as they were passing out of the gate a few feet from where Jesus was standing. They were veiled and showed every sign of grief. The mother stood in front shedding silent tears. She may indeed have been thinking: "Ah, he has come too late!" Jesus said to her most kindly and earnestly: "Woman, weep not!" The grief of all present touched him, for the widow was much loved in the city on account of her great charity to orphans and the poor. Still there were many wicked and malignant people around, and numbers of others came flocking from the city. Jesus called for water and a little branch. Someone brought to a disciple, who handed them to Jesus, a little vessel of water and a twig of hyssop. Jesus took the water and said to the bearers: "Open the coffin and loosen the bands!" While this command was being executed, Jesus raised his eyes to heaven and said: "I confess to thee, O Father, Lord of heaven and earth, because thou hast hidden these things from the wise and prudent, and hast revealed them to little ones. Yea, Father, for so it hath seemed good in thy sight. All things are delivered to me by my Father, and not one knoweth the Son but the Father; neither doth anyone know the Father but the Son, and he to whom it shall please the Son to reveal him. Come to me, all you that labor and are burdened, and I will refresh you. Take up my yoke upon you, and learn of me, because I am meek and humble of heart, and you shall find rest to your souls, for my yoke is sweet and my burden light!" When the bearers removed the cover, I saw the body wrapped like a babe in swaddling clothes and lying in the coffin. Supporting it in their arms, they loosened the bands, drew them off, uncovered the face, unbound the hands, and left about it only one linen covering. Then Jesus blessed the water, dipped the little branch into it, and sprinkled the crowd. Thereupon I saw numbers of small, dark figures like insects, beetles, toads, snakes, and little black birds issuing from many of the bystanders. The crowd became purer and brighter. Jesus then sprinkled the dead youth with the little branch, and with his hand made the sign of the cross over him, upon which I beheld a murky, black, cloud-like figure issuing from the body. Jesus said to the youth, "Arise!" He arose to a sitting posture, and gazed around him in questioning astonishment.[D3] Then Jesus said: "Give him some clothing!" and they threw round him a mantle. The youth then rose to his feet and said: "What is all this? How came I here?" The attendants put sandals upon his feet and he stepped forth from the coffin. Jesus took him by the hand and led him to the arms of his mother, who was hastening toward him. As he restored him to her, he said: "Here, thou hast thy son back, but I shall demand him of thee when he shall have been regenerated in baptism." The mother was so transported with joy, amazement, and awe, that she uttered no thanks at the moment. Her feelings found vent only in tears and embraces. The procession accompanied her to her home, the people chanting a hymn of praise. Jesus followed with the disciples. He entered the widow's house, which was very large and surrounded by gardens and courts. Friends came crowding from all quarters, all pressing eagerly to see the youth. The attendants gave him a bath, and clothed him in a white tunic and girdle. They washed the feet of Jesus and the disciples, after which the usual refreshments were presented them. Now began at once a joyous and most abundant distribution of gifts to the poor, who had gathered around the house to offer congratulations. Clothing, linen, corn, bread, lambs, birds, and money were given out plentifully. Meanwhile Jesus instructed the crowds assembled in the courtyards of the widow.

Martialis, in his white tunic, was radiant with joy. He ran here and there, showing himself to the eager throng, and helping in the distribution of gifts. He was full of childish gaiety. It was amusing to see school children brought by their teachers into the courtyard and approaching him. Many of them hung back quite timidly as if they thought Martialis a spirit. He ran after them and they retreated before him. But others played the valiant and laughed at their companions' fears. They looked with disdain upon the cowardly and gave Martialis their hand, just as a large boy touches with the tips of his fingers a horse or other animal of which the little ones are afraid.

Tables were spread both in the house and courts, and at them all were feasted. Peter, as the widow's relative, for she was the daughter of his father-in-law's brother, was especially happy and at home in the house. He discharged in a certain degree the office of father of the family. Jesus frequently addressed questions and words of instruction to the resuscitated boy. He did this in the hearing of those present, who all appeared to be touched by what he said. His words implied that death, which had entered the world by sin, had bound him, had enchained him, and would have dealt him the mortal blow in the tomb; furthermore, that Martialis with eyes closed would have been cast into the darkness and later would have opened them where neither mercy nor help could be extended to him. But at the portals of the tomb the mercy of God, mindful of the piety of the boy's parents and of some of his ancestors, had broken his bonds. Now by baptism he was to free himself from the sickness of sin, in order not to fall into a still more frightful imprisonment. Then Jesus dilated upon the virtues of parents.

Their virtues profit their children in after years. It was in consideration of the righteousness of the patriarchs that almighty God, down to the present day, had protected and spared Israel; but now, enchained in sin and covered with the veil of mental blindness, they had become like unto this youth. They were standing on the brink of the grave, and for the last time was mercy extended to them. John had prepared the way and with a powerful voice had called upon their hearts to arise from the slumber of death. The heavenly Father had now, for the last time, pity upon them. He would open to life the eyes of those that did not obstinately keep them closed. Jesus compared the people in their blindness to the youth shut up in his coffin who, though near the tomb, though outside the gate of the city, had been met by salvation. "If," he said, "the bearers had not heeded my voice, if they had not set down the coffin, had not opened it, had not freed the body from its winding sheet, if they had obstinately hurried forward with their burden, the boy would have been buried—and how terrible that would have been!" Then Jesus likened to this picture he had drawn the false teachers, the Pharisees. They kept the poor people from the life of penance, they fettered them with the bonds of their arbitrary laws, they enclosed them in the coffin of their vain observances, and cast them thus into an eternal tomb. Jesus finished by imploring and conjuring his hearers to accept the proffered mercy of his heavenly Father, and hasten to life, to penance, to baptism!

It was remarkable that Jesus blessed on this occasion with holy water, in order to drive out the evil spirits that held sway over several of the bystanders. Some of the latter were scandalized, others were envious, and some again were full of a certain malicious joy at the thought that Jesus would certainly be unable to raise the youth from the dead. When Jesus blessed with the water, I saw a little cloud, composed of the figures or shadows of noxious vermin, arise from the youth's body and disappear in the earth. At the raising of others from the dead, Jesus called back the soul of the deceased, which was separated from the body and in the abode assigned it according to its deeds. It came at the call of Jesus, hovered over the dead body, finally sank into it, and the dead arose. But with the youth of Nain, it was as if death—like a suffocating weight— had been taken away from his body.

The meal over, Jesus went with the disciples to the beautiful garden of the widow Maroni at the southern end of the city. The maimed and sick lined his whole route, and he cured them all. The streets were alive with excitement. It was already growing dark when Jesus entered the garden where Maroni with her relatives and domestics, several doctors of the Law, Martialis, and some other boys were gathered. There were several summer houses in the garden. Before one more beautiful than the others, whose roof was supported on pillars, and which might be shut in by movable screens, was a torch placed high under the palm trees. Its flames lighted up the whole hall, and glistened beautifully on the long, green leaves. Near the trees, on which fruit was still hanging, one could see as distinctly and clearly by the light of the torch as by day. At first Jesus taught and explained walking around; afterward, he entered the summer house. He often spoke to Martialis in the hearing of others. It was a wonderfully beautiful evening in that garden. The night was advanced when Jesus and his followers returned to Maroni's house, in whose side buildings all found lodgings.

Tuesday, November 14, AD 30 (*Heshvan 29*)

This morning, news of the miracle spread rapidly and many sick people came to be healed. Jesus also spoke of the sanctity of marriage, and helped to reconcile several couples whose wives were seeking divorce from their husbands. Around midday, Jesus left Nain, accompanied by his disciples, and went to Megiddo, where he stayed the night at an inn on the outskirts of the town.

At the news of Jesus's presence in Nain and the resurrection of the boy, crowds of people, among them many sick, gathered into the city from the whole country around. They completely filled the street in front of Maroni's residence, where they stood in long rows. Jesus cured part of them the next morning, and established peace in several households. Several women had come to him, asking whether he could not give them a bill of divorce. They complained of their husbands with whom, they said, they could no longer live. This was an artful device of the Pharisees. They were confounded by his miracles and could do nothing against him; but yet being full of wrath, they resolved to tempt him to say on the subject of divorce something against the Law, that they might be able to accuse him as a teacher of false doctrine. But Jesus said to the discontented wives: "Bring me a vessel of milk and another of water. Then I shall answer ye." They went into a neighboring house and returned with a bowl of milk and one of water. Jesus poured one into the other and said: "Separate the two again, so that the milk shall be again by itself, and in like manner the water. Then I shall give you a bill of divorce." The women replied that they could not do that. Then Jesus spoke of the indissolubility of marriage, and that it was only on account of the obduracy of the Jews that Moses had allowed divorce. But perfectly disunited husband and wife never could be, since they are one in the flesh; and although they might not live together, yet must the husband support the wife and children, and neither could remarry. After that Jesus accompanied the wives to their homes, where he had a private interview with the husbands. Then he saw each couple together, reproached both parties, the wives coming in for the larger share, and ended by forgiving them. The delinquents shed tears and afterward lived happily together, more faithful to each other than they had ever before been. The Pharisees were furious on seeing that their design had completely failed.

That morning Jesus restored sight to many of the blind by mixing in his hand clay and saliva and smearing it to their eyes.

Jesus in Megiddo • John's Disciples

WHEN Jesus was leaving Nain, Maroni, her boy and her domestics, all the cured, and many good people of the city accompanied him, singing psalms and bearing green branches before him. He went with the disciples westward along the north bank of the Kishon. The mountain that shut in the valley of Nazareth lay to the right. Toward evening he and the disciples arrived at the environs of Megiddo, which stood on the mountain chain whose eastern declivity leads down into the valley of Zebulon. Here he entered an inn, and soon afterward gave an instruction in front of it. When the laborers in the fields saw Jesus and his followers drawing near, they threw on the garments which at their work they had laid aside.

Megiddo stood on an eminence and was partly fallen to decay. In the very heart of the city there were ruins entirely overgrown with moss, while here and there arose a dilapidated arch. They must have belonged to a castle of the kings of Canaan. I heard that Abraham also once sojourned in this region. The suburb in which Jesus put up was more modern and more full of life than the city itself. It consisted of a long row of houses at the base of the mountain, over which ran a great commercial highway from Ptolomais. There were numerous large inns in the neighborhood, and many publicans dwelt here. They had heard Jesus's teaching and had resolved to receive penance and baptism. The Pharisees of the place were scandalized at these things. A great crowd of sick were already gathered and others were constantly coming. Jesus sent word to them by the disciples that he would go to them toward evening, and he directed how they should be arranged, which directions the disciples fulfilled. Outside the city of Megiddo was a large meadow surrounded by walls and porches wherein the sick were brought and laid in order.

Wednesday, November 15, AD 30 (Heshvan 30)

During the afternoon Jesus wandered in the fields east of Megiddo teaching the workers who were busy sowing seeds. He taught them in parables. As he was thus engaged, some disciples of John the Baptist arrived and accompanied Jesus into Megiddo. Many sick people were gathered there: lame, blind, mute, deaf, and others. Jesus cured them all and then addressed John's disciples with the words in Matthew 11:2–6 (also Luke 7:18–23). After John's disciples had left, Jesus spoke to those who remained (Matthew 11:7–15; also Luke 7:24–29). That evening, the New Moon festival to celebrate the commencement of the month of Kislev took place.

Meanwhile Jesus, with the disciples, went through the fields outside the city instructing in parables the laborers there engaged in sowing. Some of the disciples taught those at a greater distance until Jesus came up; then they turned back to those that Jesus had already instructed, explained to them whatever they had not clearly understood, and told them about the Lord's miracles. Jesus and the disciples always taught the same things to the different sets of workmen, so that on comparing notes, they all found that they had heard the same. They who had understood better could afterward explain to the others. They often discontinued their work in this hot country to rest, and it was of these intermissions, and the opportunity afforded by the time devoted to meals, that Jesus took advantage to teach.

While Jesus was thus traversing the fields with the disciples, four of John's followers arrived. They saluted the disciples and paid attention to their instructions. They had strips of fur around their necks, and leathern thongs bound their waists. They had not been sent by John, although they had constant contact with him and his disciples. They were degenerate followers of John, sworn to the Herodians, who had sent them to follow Jesus and hear what he taught concerning his kingdom. They were more austere, though at the same time more polished in their manners, than Jesus's disciples. Some hours after, another troop of John's disciples made their appearance. They were twelve in number, only two of whom had been sent by John; the rest had come through curiosity. As they approached, Jesus was returning to the city, and they followed him. Some of them had been present at the last miracles wrought by Jesus, and had hastened back to tell John what they had seen. When Jesus raised the youth of Nain, some of them were present, and they hurried off to Machaerus to inform John. They said to him: "What is it? What must we think? We have seen him perform such and such miracles! We have heard such and such words from his lips! But his disciples are much less strict than we in the observance of the Law. Whom shall we follow? Who is Jesus? Why does he cure all that appeal to him? Why does he console and help strangers, though he does not take a step toward freeing you?"

John always had trouble with his disciples, for they would not separate from him. It was for that reason that he sent them so often to Jesus, that they might learn to know him and eventually follow him. But they were so prejudiced in favor of John that what they saw and heard made little impression upon them. It was his desire that his disciples should follow Jesus that led John to urge him so frequently to manifest himself; he hoped that his followers would yield to the movement that converted the other Jews. He thought that, seeing them come again and again with their doubts, Jesus would be, as it were, necessitated to proclaim aloud that he was the Messiah, the Son of God; therefore it was that he sent those two with their usual questions to him.

On entering the city with his disciples, Jesus went to the circular enclosure where the sick from the whole country around were encamped. Among them were some from Nazareth who knew him. The lame, the blind, the mute, the deaf, the sick of all kinds were here gathered, also several possessed. Making a turn around the circle, Jesus cured the last named, many of whom were suffering from different degrees of possession. They were indeed not so violent as such poor creatures had been at other times, but they were afflicted with convulsions and their limbs were distorted. Jesus cured them with a word of command uttered as he passed and at some distance. A dark vapor issued from them, they became somewhat faint and, when returned to full consciousness, they were quite changed. The vapors, on first issuing from their bodies, appeared quite subtle; but they soon condensed and united. Sometimes they sank into the earth, or again rose in the air; on this occasion they followed the former course. The evil spirit often departs like a dark shadow in human form. Instead of vanishing immediately, I have seen him wandering around among the bystanders before disappearing.

Jesus had scarcely begun to cure when John's disciples, with a certain air of importance—as if the bearers of a commission—stepped up to him and gave signs of their desire to address him. Jesus, however, paid no attention to them, but went on with the cures. Such treatment was greatly displeasing to them, and they could not understand it. Many of John's disciples were decidedly narrow-minded and jealous. Jesus wrought miracles, John did not. John spoke so highly of Jesus, and yet Jesus made no effort to free him from confinement. Although impressed by his miracles and doctrine, yet they soon allowed themselves to be influenced again by the public voice which was asking: "Who is he? Are not his poor relatives known by everyone?" Then again, they could not understand his words relative to his kingdom. They saw no kingdom and no preparations for one. As John had been honored by so many and now lay proscribed in prison, they thought, among other things, that Jesus did not help him, that he allowed him to languish in captivity, in order to increase his own popularity. They were scandalized also at the liberty of his disciples. They esteemed it excessive humility in John to prize Jesus so highly and that he was constantly sending to implore him to manifest himself, to make an open declaration of who he was. As Jesus always spoke evasively on that point and as they had no idea that John sent them to him in order that they might know him, this knowledge was to them at the time, on account of their preconceived ideas, more difficult than it might have been to the most simple child.

As Jesus was making the circuit of the enclosure curing, he came to a sick man from Nazareth who began to speak of his acquaintance with him. "Do you remember," he said, "that you lost your grandfather when you were twenty-five years old? We were often together in those days." The man referred to the death of St. Anne's second or third husband. Jesus did not pause for many words. He answered merely: "Yes, yes, I remember," and turned at once to the man's sins and sufferings. When he found him penitent and believing, he cured him, addressed to him some words of admonition, and passed on to the next invalid.

When Jesus reached the opposite side of the enclosure, the disciples sent by John confronted him. They had, from their stand in the center, watched with amazement the miracles wrought. They now addressed him in these words: "John the Baptist has sent us to thee to ask art thou he who is to come or look we for another?" Jesus answered: "Go and relate to John what you have heard and seen. The blind see, the lame walk, the lepers are cleansed, the deaf hear, the dead rise again, widows are consoled, the poor have the Gospel preached to them. What is crooked is made straight. And blessed is he that shall not be scandalized in me." After these words Jesus turned away, and John's disciples took their departure.

Jesus could not speak more plainly of himself, for who would have understood him? His disciples were good, simple-hearted, generous, and pious souls, but as yet quite incapable of comprehending such a mystery. Many of them were related to him by ties of blood, consequently they would have been scandalized at more precise language on Jesus's part, or would have conceived erroneous ideas of him. As for the multitude at large, they were altogether unprepared for such a truth, and besides, he was surrounded by spies. Even among John's disciples, the Pharisees and Herodians had their creatures.

Mount Tabor Viewed from Megiddo

When John's messengers had departed, Jesus began to teach. The cured, crowds of people, the scribes of the place, his disciples, and the five publicans that dwelt here, formed the audience. The instruction was continued by the light of torches, and the remaining sick were afterward cured. Jesus took for the subject of his discourse his own reply to John's disciples. He spoke of how they should use the benefits received from God, and exhorted to penance and a change of life. As he knew that some of the Pharisees present had taken occasion—from the brevity of his reply to John's messengers—to say to the people that he, Jesus, made little account of John and was willing enough to see him ruined in public estimation (that he himself might be exalted), he explained the answer he had given as well as what he had said on the score of penance. He also recalled to them what they themselves had heard John say of him. Why, he asked, were they always doubting? What did they expect from John? He said: "What went ye out to see when ye went to John? Did ye go to see a reed shaken in the wind? Or a man effeminately and magnificently clothed? Listen! They that are clothed sumptuously and who live delicately are in the palaces of kings. But what did ye desire to see when ye went in quest of him? Was it to see a prophet? Yea, I tell ye, ye saw more than a prophet when ye saw him. This is he of whom it is written: 'Behold, I send my angel before thy face, who shall prepare thy way before thee. Amen, I say to you there hath not risen among them that are born of women a greater prophet than John the Baptist, and yet he that is least in the kingdom of heaven is greater than he. And from the days of John the Baptist until now the kingdom of heaven suffereth violence, and the violent bear it away. For all the prophets and the Law prophesied of it until John; and if ye will receive it, he is Elijah that is to come again. He that hath ears to hear, let him hear!'"

All present were very much impressed by Jesus's words, and wanted to receive baptism. The scribes alone murmured. They were especially scandalized at Jesus because he accepted hospitality from the publicans, who also were present at this instruction. Jesus therefore profited by this opportunity to speak of all the reports they had set afloat concerning both John and himself, particularly of the reproach made against him of frequenting the company of publicans and sinners.

After that Jesus entered the house of one of the publicans, where he found the other four, and there he taught. Among his hearers on this occasion were some that had determined to amend their lives and to receive baptism. This house was near the enclosure wherein Jesus had just cured the sick. There was another publican's house at the entrance of the city, and still some others beyond.

Debbaseth, where Bartholomew resided, could be seen from the road when first starting from Nain to Megiddo, but on a nearer approach the heights of the latter place concealed it from view. It was situated about an hour and a half to the west on the Kishon, at the entrance of the valley of Zebulon.

KISLEV (30 days): November 15/16 to December 14/15, AD 30 Kislev New Moon: November 14 at 5:30 AM, Jerusalem time

Jesus Leaves Megiddo • Cure of a Leper

Thursday, November 16, AD 30 (Kislev 1)

Today, Jesus and the disciples left Megiddo in the direction of Mount Tabor. Jesus taught as they went. Toward evening, they arrived at a small shepherds' place at the foot of the northwest side of the mountain. Here Jesus taught. They all stayed there overnight.

As the Feast of the New Moon was beginning, Jesus took the return route from Megiddo to Capernaum. He was accompanied by about twenty-four of his disciples, the four false disciples of John, and some of the publicans of Megiddo who wanted to be baptized in Capernaum. They journeyed along slowly, sometimes pausing to stand or sit in the charming spots through which they passed, for Jesus taught the whole time. The way led from Megiddo northeastward, and off to the northwest side of Tabor. Jesus's teaching was a preparation for the definitive calling and sending of the apostles, which was soon to take place. He earnestly exhorted them to lay aside all worldly cares and to abandon their possessions. His words were so touching and affectionate. Once he snapped off a flower that was growing by the wayside, and said: "These have no cares! Look at their beautiful colors, their delicate little stamens! Was Solomon the Wise in all his magnificence more beautifully clothed than they?" Jesus often made use of this similitude.

He continued his instruction in a series of parables so striking that each of the apostles could recognize the one intended for himself. He spoke also of his kingdom, telling them that they should not be so eager after high employments therein, should not picture it to themselves as something earthly. Jesus said this because John's four disciples, who were secret partisans of the Herodians, were especially interested in this part of his discourse. He warned the disciples of what people they should for the future beware, and described the Herodians in terms so exact that no one could fail to recognize them. Among other things, he said that they should beware of certain people in sheep's skins and long leathern straps!

"Beware," he said, "of the profane in sheepskins and long girdles!" By these words, Jesus signified the lurking Herodian disciples of John who, in imitation of John's true followers, wore a kind of sheepskin stole around the neck and crossed on the breast. They might know them, he said, by this, that they could not look one straight in the face; or again, if they (the disciples of Jesus), their hearts overflowing with joy and ardor, should impart something of their feelings to one of these false zealots in sheepskins and girdles, they might recognize him for what he was in reality by the agitation of his heart. It would turn this way and that way like a restless animal. Jesus named a beetle which, when confined, runs round and round, seeking some hole by which to escape. Once he bent back a thornbush, saying: "Look, and see whether you can find any fruit here or not." Some of the disciples had the simplicity to look into the bush. But Jesus said: "Do men seek figs upon thistles and grapes upon thorns?"

Toward evening they arrived at a row of houses, twenty in number, with a school on the northwestern side of the foot of Tabor. The place lay from one and a half to two hours eastward from Nazareth and one-half hour from the city of Tabor. The people here were a good-natured group. They had known Jesus in his early years when he used to wander around Nazareth with his young friends. They were for the most part shepherds. While guarding their flocks, they busied themselves in gathering cotton which, as soon as they spied Jesus coming, they packed up in their sacks and carried to their homes, after which they hurried forth to meet him. I saw them with their rough fur caps in their hands, but in the school their heads were covered. They received Jesus at the spring, washed his feet and those of the disciples, and offered them some refreshment. There was no synagogue in the place, only a school with its resident teacher. Jesus went to it, and taught in parables.

This little village belonged to a distinguished man who lived with his wife in a large house at some distance. This man had fallen into sin and was now afflicted with leprosy; consequently, he lived apart from his wife. She occupied the upper stories of the house, while he lodged in one of the side buildings. In order to escape the grievous alternative of entire separation from his fellow-men, he had not made known his malady. His case was not, however, so secret that many were not aware of its existence, but they connived at it. It was well known in the little village, and although the ordinary route ran past his dwelling, the people always managed to take another way. They informed the disciples of the circumstance. The poor leper had for a long time sincerely bewailed his transgressions and longed for the coming of Jesus. And now he called a little boy of about eight years, his slave, who supplied him with necessaries, and said to him: "Go to Jesus of Nazareth and watch your chance. When you see him at some distance from his disciples or walking apart from them, cast yourself at his feet and say: 'Rabbi, my master is sick. He thinks that thou canst help him by merely passing before our house, a way that all others shun. He humbly beseeches thee to have compassion on his misery and to walk along the street, for he is certain of being cured.'" The boy went to Jesus and very cleverly executed the commission. Jesus replied: "Tell your master that I shall go to him in the morning," and he took the boy by one hand, laying the other on his head with words of praise. This meeting took place as Jesus was leaving the school to go to the inn. Jesus knew that the boy was coming, and had designedly remained a little behind the disciples. The boy wore a yellow tunic.

Anne's property lay on a height to the west of Nazareth. It was distant about an hour, and was between the valley of Nazareth and that of Zebulon. A narrow valley planted with trees ran from it to Nazareth, and by it Anne could go to Mary's house without traversing the city.

Friday, November 17, AD 30 (Kislev 2)

This morning Jesus went to the home of a leper, whom he healed. Then Jesus and his disciples walked in the direction of Capernaum, arriving there shortly after the beginning of the sabbath. They went to the synagogue, where Jesus taught. As he was leaving the synagogue, two lepers came to him and—trembling—sank down on their knees before him. Jesus laid his hands upon them, breathed upon the face of each, and said: "Your sins are forgiven!" The Pharisees protested loudly because he had healed on the sabbath and questioned by what right he was able to forgive sins. Without uttering a word, Jesus passed through their midst. He went to his mother's house. After consoling his mother and the other women there, Jesus went out and spent the night in prayer.

Next morning at early dawn Jesus left the inn with the disciples. When he turned into the street that ran past the leper's dwelling, they told him that he ought not to go that way. But he went on and commanded them to follow. They did so, but timidly and apprehensively, for they feared being reported at Capernaum. John's disciples did not go with him by this way.

The boy, who was on the watch, notified his master of Jesus's approach. The sick man came down by a path leading to the street, paused at some distance, and cried out: "Lord, do not come nearer to me! If thou dost merely will me to be healed, I shall be saved." The disciples remained standing at a distance. Jesus replied: "I will it!" went up to the man, touched him, and spoke to him as he lay prostrate on his face at his feet. He was clean; his leprosy had fallen off. He related to Jesus all the circumstances of his case, and received for reply that he should return to his wife, and by degrees appear again among the people. Jesus admonished him of his sins, commanded him to receive the penance of baptism, and enjoined upon him a certain alms. He then went back to his disciples and spoke to them of the cure just wrought. He told them that whoever had faith and possessed a pure heart might with impunity touch even the leprous.

When the cured man had bathed and dressed, he went to his wife and told her of the miracle just effected in him by Jesus. Some spiteful people of the place sent news of the affair to the priests and Pharisees of the city of Tabor, who immediately saw fit to institute a commission of investigation. They surprised the poor man by submitting him to a close examination as to whether he was really cured or not, and sharply called him to account for keeping his malady secret. They now made a great noise over the affair which, though publicly known, they had long tolerated.

Jesus journeyed quickly with the disciples all the remainder of the day, pausing only now and again to rest a few moments and take some refreshment. He taught all along the way about the forsaking of temporal goods, and in parables instructed them upon the kingdom of God. He told them that it was impossible to make all these things clear to them just then, but a time would come when they would comprehend all. He spoke of giving up earthly care of food and raiment. They would soon see a hungry multitude with provisions far from sufficient for their wants. They, the disciples, would say to him: "Whence shall we get bread?" and a superabundance should be given unto them. They had to build houses and build them securely! Jesus said this in such a way as to intimate that it was by sacrifice and personal exertion that these houses, namely, employments and charges in his kingdom, were to be obtained. The disciples, however, understood him in a worldy sense.

Judas was very much rejoiced. He gave noisy expression to his satisfaction and said aloud in the hearing of all that he would not shirk labor, that he would do his share of the work. On hearing this, Jesus stood still and said: "We are not yet at the end of our mission. It will not always be as it is now. Ye will not always be well received and entertained, ye will not always have things in abundance. The time will come when they will persecute you and thrust you out, when ye will have neither shelter, nor food, nor clothing, nor shoes." And he went on to tell them that they should think seriously of these things and hold themselves in readiness to renounce everything, also that he had something important to propose to them. He spoke likewise of two kingdoms opposed to each other. No one can serve two masters. Whoever desired to serve in his kingdom must forsake the other. Then passing to the Pharisees and their accomplices, he said something about the masks or disguises that they wore. They taught the dead form of the Law and sought to have it observed; but the best part of it, its purport—the charity, forgiveness, and mercy that it inculcates—they wholly neglected. But he, Jesus, taught just the contrary, namely that the rind without the kernel is dead and barren. First comes the essence of the Law, and then the Law itself; the kernel must increase with the growth of the shell. He gave them also some instructions on prayer. They should, he said, pray in secret and not ostentatiously before others. Many similar things he said on this occasion.

When journeying with his disciples, Jesus generally instructed them, thus preparing them to understand better what they would hear in his next public discourse and be able to make it clear to the people. He often repeated the same things, though in different words and order. Among the disciples who accompanied Jesus today, James the Greater and Joseph Barsabbas most frequently put questions to him, though Peter did so sometimes. Judas often spoke in a loud voice. Andrew was already well acquainted with the teachings of his Master. Thomas was preoccupied, as if weighing consequences. John took everything simply and lovingly. The best instructed of the disciples were the most silent, partly through modesty, and partly because they were not always willing to show that they did not understand Jesus's words.

Thus journeying through the valleys, they arrived shortly before the beginning of the sabbath at the valley east of Magdalum. Here they encountered the pagan Cyrinus of Dabrath, and the centurion Achias of Gischala, who were going to Capernaum for baptism.

When nearing Capernaum, Jesus was instructing the disciples as to how they should exercise themselves in obedience as a preparation for their mission, and especially how they should conduct themselves when he should send them to teach the people. He gave them likewise some general rules for their deportment when in certain company. He did this in a few words before the departure of the four Herodians who had journeyed with his little party, and sufficiently loud for them to hear. He said: "If on your journeys worldly men join you—whom ye may recognize by their smooth speech and sly questions—who will not be shaken off, who always, half agreeing, half good-naturedly contradicting, question and discuss various subjects that agitate the heart, then should ye at any cost break away from them. And why? Because ye are still too weak, too simple-hearted. Ye might easily fall into the snares of such lurkers. I do not shun them, for I know them, and I wish them to hear my teaching."

Jesus Teaches in the Synagogue of Capernaum, and Heals Two Lepers

JESUS again passed by the estate of the centurion Zorobabel as he and his disciples were hurrying along, for the sabbath had already begun. In his charity, Zorobabel had permitted two young scribes of about twenty-five years, who on account of their dissolute life had been stricken with leprosy, to take up their abode in his garden. They were perfectly loathsome to look upon, and in their misery subjected to the greatest contempt. The red mantles that enveloped them hid the ulcers with which they were covered. They had once formed a part of Magdalene's gay coterie at Magdalum, had afterward carried on their excesses in other places, and fell at last into the extreme misery in which they now were. At Jesus's recent visit to these parts they were ashamed to present themselves before him, but now, convinced by the news of his miracles and great mercy, they had allowed themselves to be dragged to a place near the road by which he would pass and where they could cry to him for help. Jesus would not pause. He hurried on, but told two of Zorobabel's servants, who came running after him pleading for the unfortunate creatures, to bring them to the synagogue in Capernaum. When the people were assembled, they (the servants) were to conduct the lepers to the gallery one story high that had been built adjoining the synagogue, and from which the teaching going on inside could be heard by those from without. There they should pray and excite themselves to contrition until he should call them. The servants immediately hastened back and took the poor men by a shortcut through the flowery ravine to Capernaum. They dragged them, though not without difficulty, up the outside steps to the gallery where, leaning in at the windows of the synagogue, they could, apart from the throng and in the open air, listen to the teachings of Jesus and with penitent hearts await their Savior's call.

Jesus soon arrived with the disciples. After they had washed their feet and ungirded their garments, they entered the synagogue. When Jesus approached the pulpit, he found it occupied by one who was reading aloud. The latter, however, at once arose and yielded his place to Jesus, who immediately took the roll of scriptures and began to teach upon the passages referring to Jacob's being called to account by Laban, his struggle with the angel, his reconciliation with Esau, and the seduction of Dinah, after which he turned to the prophet Osee. When Jesus without the least hesitation took the rolls and began to read, the Pharisees smiled scornfully, as if to pronounce him wanting in courtesy. They were exasperated at Jesus's reappearance, for the raising of the youth of Nain, as well as his numerous cures in Megiddo, were already noised throughout Capernaum. They watched eagerly and with inquietude to see what new thing he was now going to undertake. Almost all of Jesus's relatives, including the women, were gathered today in the synagogue.

As the crowd was leaving the synagogue followed by Jesus, the disciples, and the Pharisees, these last thought they would still carry on the dispute with Jesus in the portico, but an unforeseen incident prevented their design. Jesus went to the door, looked up to the gallery where the two unclean men were still standing, and called to them to come down. But they were timid and ashamed. Through fear of the Pharisees, they did not venture to obey at once. Then Jesus commanded them, in a name that I cannot recall, to come down, and to their own great astonishment they found themselves able to descend the steps alone. The portico had been lighted up with torches for the convenience of the dispersing crowd. How furious were the Pharisees when they recognized by the dull glare of the torches the two poor, despised sinners in their red mantles! The lepers sank trembling on their knees before Jesus. He laid his hand on them, breathed into their faces, and said: "Your sins are forgiven you!" and admonished them to continence and the baptism of penance. He commanded them also to forsake their vain studies, for that he himself would teach them the truth and the way. They rose up. Their disfigurement had visibly decreased, their ulcers had dried, and the scales had fallen off. With tears they thanked their benefactor, and left the place with Zorobabel's servants. Many of the well-disposed among the bystanders pressed around the cured, celebrating in words of praise their penance and their healing.

The Pharisees, however, were mad with rage. They cried out to Jesus: "What! Healest thou on the sabbath! And dost thou also forgive sins! How canst thou forgive sins?" Then, turning to the people, they cried: "He has a devil who helps him! He is a madman! That is easily seen in his wandering about. Scarcely had he begun to carry on his game here, when off he goes to Nain to raise the dead, then to Megiddo, and then back here again! No good man in his senses would carry on in that way! He has a powerful, wicked spirit who helps him!" And they added: "When Herod finishes with John, this man's turn will come, unless he takes himself out of the way!" But Jesus went out through the midst of them. His female relatives, who had waited for him in a neighboring house after leaving the synagogue, wept and lamented over the violent rage of the Pharisees.

Jesus left the city and, taking the road to the northeast, directed his steps to the hill beyond the valley where Mary's house stood. On the way thither were clumps of trees and grottoes in which he stopped to pray. He arrived late at Mary's, where he consoled the women, after which he again went out and spent the whole night in prayer.

Saturday, November 18, AD 30 (Kislev 3)

After healing some people at Peter's house, Jesus instructed some fifty people waiting to be baptized. These were then baptized by Andrew and Saturnin. Later, Jesus went to the synagogue in Capernaum and healed a number of sick people who were waiting outside. Here he was approached by Jairus, the chief of the synagogue. Jairus pleaded with Jesus to come and heal his daughter, Salome, who was on the point of death (Mark 5:21–24). Jesus agreed to go with Jairus, but on the way a messenger came to relate the news that Salome was already dead. Jesus, in his mercy, performed the miracle of raising Salome from the dead. Because of her parents' attitude toward Jesus, which the girl imitated, this led again to her illness and death on Kislev 16/17. (See second raising of Salome from the dead on this date.)

Next morning, Jesus repaired to the garden in the neighborhood of Peter's house. It was enclosed by a hedge, and in it all the preparations for baptism had been made. There were several circular cisterns, formed in the ground and surrounded by a little channel, into which the water of a stream running nearby could be turned. A long arbor could, by hangings and screens, be divided into little compartments for the convenience of the neophytes when disrobing. An elevated stand had been erected for Jesus. The disciples were all present and about fifty aspirants to baptism, among the latter some relatives of the holy family, an old man and three youths from Sepphoris, the boy whom Jesus had healed at that same place, and the old woman from there, who had recently visited Jesus in Abez. There were present, moreover, Cyrinus from Cyprus; the Roman centurion Achias and his little, miraculously cured son Jephthah, of Gischala; the centurion Cornelius, his yellow slave who had been cured by Jesus, and several of his domestics; many pagans from Upper Galilee; a dark-skinned slave of Zorobabel; the five publicans of Megiddo; some boys, among whom was Joses, the nephew of Bartholomew; likewise all the cured lepers and possessed of these parts, including the two young scribes healed the preceding evening. The last mentioned were indeed free from ulcers, but their countenance was still disfigured and bore the marks of suffering.

All the neophytes were clothed in penitential robes of gray wool, a four-cornered kerchief over their heads. Jesus instructed and prepared them for baptism, after which they retired into the arbor and put on their baptismal garments, white tunics, long and wide. Their heads were uncovered, the kerchief, now thrown round their shoulders, and they stood in the channel around the basins, their hands crossed on their breasts. Andrew and Saturnin baptized, while Thomas, Bartholomew, John and others imposed hands as sponsors. The neophytes, with bared shoulders, leaned over a railing around the edge of the basin. One of the disciples carried a vessel of water that had been blessed by Jesus, from which the baptizers scooped some with the hand and poured it thrice over the heads of those being baptized. Thomas was sponsor to Jephthah, the son of Achias. Although several received baptism at the same time, yet the ceremony lasted until nearly two o'clock in the afternoon.

The Resurrection of the Daughter of Jairus, the Chief of the Synagogue

LATER on, when Jesus was curing some of the sick in the square before the synagogue of Capernaum, Jairus, the chief of the synagogue, presented himself before him. He cast himself at his feet and implored him to visit and cure his sick daughter, who was then breathing her last. Jesus was on the point of starting with Jairus when messengers hastily arrived from the house of the latter and thus addressed him: "Thy daughter has expired. There is no need further to trouble the Master." On hearing these words, Jesus said to Jairus: "Fear not! Trust in me, and thou shalt receive help!" They directed their steps to the northern quarter of the city where dwelt Cornelius, whose house was not far removed from that of Jairus. As they drew near they saw a multitude of minstrels and female mourners already assembled in the courtyard and before the door. Jesus entered, taking with him only Peter, James the Greater, and John. In passing through the court, he said to the mourners: "Why do ye thus lament and weep? Go your way! The damsel is not dead, but only sleeping." At this the crowd of mourners began to laugh him to scorn, for they knew that she was dead. But Jesus insisted on their retiring even from the court, which he ordered to be locked. Then he entered the apartment in which the grief-stricken mother was busied with her maid preparing the winding sheet; thence, accompanied by the father, the mother, and the three disciples, he passed on to the chamber in which the girl lay. Jesus stepped toward the couch, the parents standing behind him, the disciples to the right at the foot of the bed. [D4] The mother did not please me. She was cold and wanting in confidence. The father, too, was not a warm friend of Jesus. He would not willingly do anything to displease the Pharisees. It was anxiety and necessity alone that had driven him to Jesus. He was actuated by a double motive. If Jesus cured his child, she would be restored to him; if not, he would have prepared a triumph for the Pharisees. Still, the cure of Cornelius's servant had greatly impressed him and awakened in him a feeling of confidence. The little daughter was not tall, and she was very much wasted. At most, I should say she was eleven years old, and even at that small for her age, for the Jewish girls of twelve are usually full-grown. She lay on the couch enveloped in a long garment. Jesus raised her lightly in his arms, held her on his breast, and breathed upon her. Then I saw something wonderful. Near the right side of the corpse was a luminous figure in a sphere of light. When Jesus breathed upon the little girl, that figure entered her mouth as a tiny human form of light. Then he laid the body down upon the couch, grasped one of the wrists, and said: "Damsel, arise!" The girl sat up in her bed. Jesus still held her by the hand. Then she stood up, opened her eyes, and supported by the hand of Jesus, stepped from the couch to the floor. Jesus led her, weak and tremulous, to the arms of her parents. They had watched the progress of the event at first coldly, though anxiously, then trembling with agitation, and now they were out of themselves for very joy. Jesus bade them give the child to eat and to make no unnecessary noise over the affair. After receiving the thanks of the father, he went down to the city. The mother was confused and stupefied. Her words of thanks were few. The news soon spread through the mourners that the maiden was alive. They immediately returned, some confused at their former incredulity, others still uttering vulgar pleasantries, and went into the house, where they saw the damsel eating.

On the way back, Jesus spoke with his disciples on the subject of this miracle. He said that these people, namely, the father and mother, had had neither real faith nor an upright intention. If the daughter was raised from the dead, it was for her own sake and for the glory of God's kingdom. The death from which she had just been roused, that is, the death of the body, was a guiltless one, but from the death of the soul she must now preserve herself. Jesus then went to the great square of the city, cured many sick there awaiting him, and taught in the synagogue until the close of the sabbath. The Pharisees were so agitated and incensed that it would not have taken much to make them lay hands on Jesus if he had trusted himself among them. They began again to declare that he effected his miracles by the power of sorcery. Jesus, however, slipped out of the city through Zorobabel's garden, and the disciples also dispersed.

Jesus spent part of the night retired in prayer. He supplicated for the conversion of sinners and besought his heavenly Father to confound and frustrate the designs of the Pharisees, for he acted in everything as man, in order that we should imitate him. He also begged his Father to allow him to perfect his work, since according to our way of thinking, the Pharisees were ready to tear him to pieces. He withdrew from their presence, but on the following day, the sabbath itself, he again cured at the door of the synagogue and taught inside. And why did not the Pharisees drive the sick away? Why did they not forbid Jesus to teach in the synagogue? It was because prophets and doctors had at all times the right to teach, to help, and to heal. They did indeed accuse him of error and blasphemy, though they were unable to prove their accusations. As for the baptism that he gave, they did not trouble themselves about it and went not to where it was administered.

There was no public highway through the valley; only a road over the mountains led to Bethsaida. The valley was traversed by only the footpath taken by the fishermen and the peasants when on their way to the lake.

Martha and the holy women of Jerusalem, Dinah and others, after Jesus's departure went back to Nain and thence to their own homes. Maroni and her son were so beset by people desirous of seeing one raised from the dead that they were obliged to conceal themselves.

Cornelius the centurion gave a feast at his house in honor of his cured servant. Numbers of pagans were in attendance, also crowds of the poor. Immediately after the miracle, Cornelius informed Jesus of his intention to sacrifice burnt offerings of all kinds of animals. But Jesus replied that it would be better for him to invite his enemies in order to reconcile them one with another; his friends, that he might lead them to the truth; and the poor, that he might recreate and entertain them with the food he had destined for sacrifice, for God no longer delighted in burnt offerings. Multitudes of pagans went from beyond Bethsaida and the mountains to the house of Cornelius, where the feast was celebrated.

(Follow Map 23)

Sunday, November 19, AD 30 (Kislev 4)

After being present for the baptism of a number of people this morning, Jesus taught from the banks of the Sea of Galilee. As the throng of people grew, Jesus and some of his disciples climbed aboard a ship placed at his disposal, and Jesus taught from there. The other disciples boarded Peter's ship. This then hooked up Jesus's ship, towing it across the lake while Jesus continued to teach on the way. Around four o'clock that afternoon they reached the eastern shore and went to a nearby place of tax collectors where Matthew (then called Levi) lived. He cast himself down before Jesus. Jesus said: "Levi (Matthew), arise, and follow me!" (Matthew 9:9). That night, Jesus stayed at an inn in the town of Bethsaida-Julias.

Jesus was again at the place of baptism. Saturnin experienced great joy in baptizing his two younger brothers and an uncle, all of whom were pagans. Their mother also had come with them. She was already a Jewess. His father was dead. Saturnin was descended from a royal race. His parents dwelt in Patras. At the time of which I speak his father was dead, but his stepmother with two daughters and two sons still lived there. From a brown-skinned man, a relative and follower of the dark complexioned one of the three kings, and whom he had met on a journey, Saturnin heard the story of the star and the birth of Jesus. Thereupon he went to Jerusalem and, when John began his career, became one of his first disciples; but after Jesus's baptism, he went with Andrew to Jesus. His stepmother with her two little girls had removed to Jerusalem with him, while the boys remained behind with their uncle. They too were now come to their brother. They were rich.

There were about twelve other men baptized. When they stepped into the channel around the basin, they tucked up their long garments and leaned over the edge. After their baptism they retired into the arbor and reclothed themselves, putting on a baptismal garment consisting of a long white mantle. The Jews did not trouble themselves about the baptized pagans. If the latter did not present themselves before the priests for circumcision, the former took no notice of it. They did not make much account of the pagans, for they themselves were quite lukewarm and they avoided whatever could give them trouble. Cornelius, who dwelt among them and had caused a synagogue to be built, would probably have to receive circumcision if he wished to continue his relationship with them.

Jesus afterward taught on the borders of the lake, not far from Peter's fishery.[D5] He had journeyed with the

Map 23: The Sermons on the Mount

November 19–December 10, AD 30

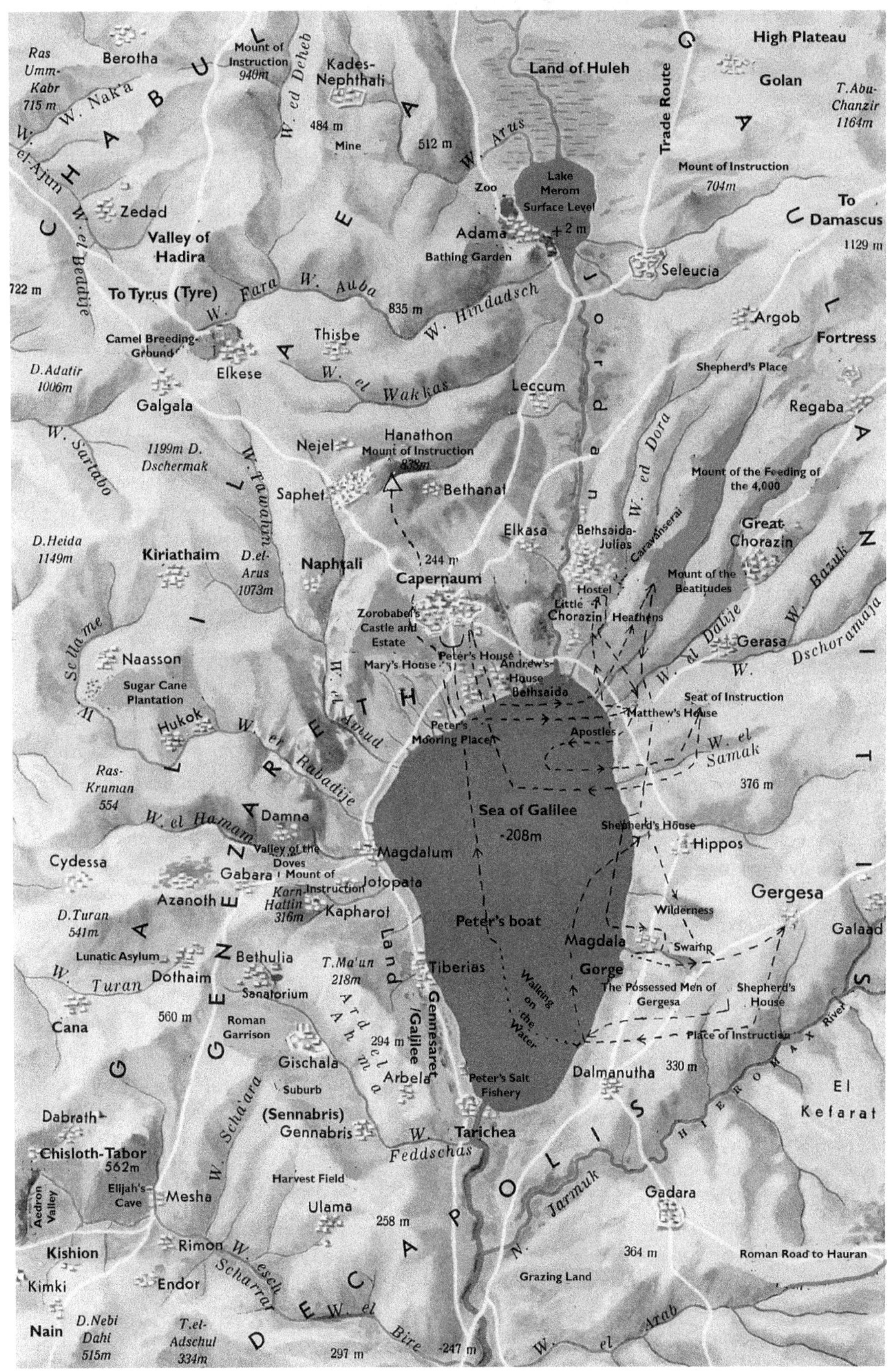

Capernaum—Matthew's House—Mount of Instruction near Gerasa—Bethsaida—Mount of Beatitudes
Magdala—Gergesa—Capernaum—Mount of Instruction near Hanathon

disciples over the mountain back of Mary's and Peter's dwellings in the direction of Bethsaida, and thence had descended to the lake. The shore near Bethsaida was steep, but at the point to which I now allude it gently sloped and afforded an easy landing place. Peter's ship and Jesus's little boat lay here. The latter was small and could at most contain fifteen men.

Jesus Instructs from His Boat • Call of Matthew

A GREAT crowd of pagans who had been at Cornelius's feast were here assembled. Jesus was instructing them and, as the throng became very great, he with some of his disciples went on board his little boat, while the rest of them and the publicans went on Peter's boat. And now from the boat he instructed the pagans on the strand,[D6] making use of the parables of the sower and the tares in the field. The instruction over, they struck out across the lake, the disciples in Peter's boat plying the oars. Jesus's boat was fastened to Peter's, and the disciples took turns to row. Jesus sat on a raised seat near the mast, the others around him and on the edge of the boat. They interrogated him upon the meaning of the parable and asked why he spoke in similitudes. Jesus gave them a satisfactory explanation. They landed at a point between the valley of Gerasa and Bethsaida-Julias. A road ran from the shore to the houses of the tax collectors, and into it the four who were with Jesus turned. Jesus meanwhile, with the disciples, continued along the shore to the right, thus passing Matthew's residence, though at a distance. A side path ran from this road to his custom office, and along it Jesus bent his steps, the disciples timidly remaining behind. Servants and publicans were out in front of the custom house, busied with all kinds of merchandise. When Matthew from the top of a little eminence beheld Jesus and the disciples coming toward him, he became confused and withdrew into his private office.[D7] But Jesus continued to approach, and from the opposite side of the road called him. Then came Matthew hurrying out, prostrated with his face on the ground before Jesus, protesting that he did not esteem himself worthy that Jesus should speak with him. But Jesus said: "Matthew, arise, and follow me!" Then Matthew arose, saying that he would instantly and joyfully abandon all things and follow him. He accompanied Jesus back to where the disciples were standing, who saluted him and extended to him their hands. Thaddeus, Simon, and James the Less were particularly rejoiced at his coming. They and Matthew were half brothers. Their father Alpheus, before his marriage with their mother Mary Cleophas, was a widower with one son, Matthew. Matthew insisted upon all being his guests. Jesus, however, assured him that they would return next morning, and then they continued on their way.

Matthew hurried back to his house, which stood in a corner of the mountains about a quarter of an hour from the lake. The little stream that flows from Gerasa into the lake ran past it at no great distance, and the view extended over lake and field. Matthew at once procured a substitute in his business, an excellent man belonging to Peter's boat, who was to discharge his duties until further arrangements could be made. Matthew was a married man with four children. He joyfully imparted to his wife the good fortune that had fallen to him, as well as his intention to abandon all and follow Jesus, and she received the announcement with corresponding joy. Then he directed her to see to the preparing of an entertainment for the next morning, he himself taking charge of the invitations and other arrangements. Matthew was almost as old as Peter. One might easily have taken him for the father of his young half brother Joseph Barsabbas. He was a man of heavy, bony frame with black hair and beard. Since his acquaintance with Jesus on the way to Sidon, he had received John's baptism and regulated his whole life most conscientiously.

On leaving Matthew, Jesus crossed the mountain at the rear of his dwelling and proceeded northward into the valley of Bethsaida-Julias, where he found encamped caravans and traveling pagans, whom he instructed.

Monday, November 20, AD 30 (Kislev 5)

Today Jesus and the disciples visited Matthew at his house and welcomed him as a disciple. Judas Thaddeus, Simon, James the Less, and Joseph Barsabbas were especially overjoyed at this—Matthew was their stepbrother—and embraced him warmly. Jesus spoke with Matthew's wife and blessed the children. Then Matthew knelt before him, and Jesus—laying his hand upon him—blessed him and gave him the name Matthew (he had been called Levi before). Following this, there was a banquet in Matthew's home at which a large number of tax collectors and Pharisees were present, as described in Luke 5:29–39. Jesus stayed overnight at Matthew's house, while the disciples slept on their boats.

Toward noon the next day Jesus returned with the disciples to Matthew's, where many publicans who had been invited were already assembled. Some Pharisees and some of John's disciples had joined Jesus on the way, but they did not enter Matthew's. They stayed outdoors, sauntering around the garden with the disciples, to whom they put the question: "How can you tolerate your Master's making himself so familiar with sinners and publicans?" They received for answer: "Ask himself why he does so!" But the

Pharisees responded: "One cannot speak with a man who always maintains that he is right."

Matthew received Jesus and his followers most lovingly and humbly, and washed their feet. His half brothers warmly embraced him, and then he presented his wife and children to Jesus. Jesus spoke to the mother and blessed the children, who then retired, to return no more. I have often wondered why the children whom Jesus blessed usually appeared no more. I saw Jesus seated, and Matthew on his knees before him. Jesus laid his hand upon him, blessed him, and addressed to him some words of instruction. Matthew had formerly been called Levi, but now he received the name of Matthew. The feast was a magnificent one. The table, in the form of a cross, was set in an open hall. Jesus sat in the midst of the publicans. In the intervals between the different courses, the guests arose and engaged in conversation with one another.[D8] Poor travelers passing by were supplied with food by the disciples, for the street on which the house stood led down to the ferry. It was on the occasion of their leaving table that the Pharisees approached the disciples, and then occurred the speeches and objections narrated in the Gospel of St. Luke 5:30–39. The Pharisees insisted particularly on the subject of fasting, because among the strict Jews a fast day began that evening in expiation of the sacrilege King Joachim committed by burning the books of the prophet Jeremiah. Among the Jews, especially in Judea, it was not customary to pluck fruit by the wayside. Now Jesus permitted it to his disciples, and this the Pharisees made a subject of reproach to him. While giving his answers to the Pharisees, Jesus was reclining at table with the publicans, whereas the disciples to whom the questions of the Pharisees were addressed were standing or walking among them. Jesus turned his head from side to side in answering.

Capernaum was much more lively now than formerly. Crowds of strangers were streaming in on account of Jesus, some of them his friends, others his enemies, and most of them pagans, the followers of Zorobabel and Cornelius.

The Final Call of Peter, Andrew, James, and John • Jesus Stills the Tempest on the Lake

Tuesday, November 21, AD 30 (Kislev 6)

This morning, from the shore of the Sea of Galilee, Jesus called to Peter and Andrew, who were casting a net into the lake, "Come and follow me, I will make you fishers of men." A little further down the shore he called also to the brothers James and John (Matthew 4:18–22). Peter and Andrew baptized today, and also Saturnin. That evening, as crowds thronged around him, Jesus and the future twelve apostles boarded Peter's boat, and Jesus gave instructions to go over to the other side of the lake in the direction of Tiberias (Matthew 8:18). In the middle of the lake a great storm arose, which Jesus calmed (Matthew 8:23–27; Luke 8:22–25). Then he commanded the disciples to sail back in the direction from which they had come, toward Chorazin (as the neighborhood was called on account of the town Great Chorazin).

NEXT morning, when Jesus went to the lake, which was about a quarter of an hour distant from Matthew's dwelling, Peter and Andrew were upon the point of launching out on the deep to let down their nets. Jesus called to them: "Come and follow me![D9] I will make you fishers of men!" They instantly abandoned their work, hove to their boat, and came on shore. Jesus went on a little farther up the shore to the ship of Zebedee, who with his sons James and John was mending his nets on the ship. Jesus called the two sons to come to him.[D10] They obeyed immediately and came to land, while Zebedee remained on the ship with his servants.

Then Jesus sent Peter and Andrew, James and John into the mountains where the pagans were encamped, with the order to baptize all that desired it. He himself had prepared them for it during the two preceding days. With Saturnin and the other disciples, Jesus went in another direction. All were to meet again that evening at Matthew's, and I saw Jesus pointing out with his finger the way they were to take. While he was calling the four disciples, the others had waited for him at a little distance up the road, but when he commissioned those four to go and baptize, they were all together.

Jesus had indeed, at an earlier period, formally called the fishermen from their occupations, but with his consent they had always returned to them. So long as they themselves were not engaged in teaching, it was not necessary for them to follow him constantly. Their means of navigation and their dealings with the pagan caravans were very advantageous, likewise, while he sojourned at Capernaum. When, after the last Passover, they had for a longer time been with Jesus, they had indeed taught here and there, and had even wrought some miraculous cures. In these latter, however, they were not always successful, on account of their want of faith. They had also suffered persecution at this early stage of their apostolic career. In Gennabris they were led bound before the Pharisees and cast into prison. They received at that time from Jesus the power to bless the water intended for baptism. This power was not imparted to them by the imposition of hands, but with a blessing.

Peter was, besides his fishery, engaged also in agriculture and cattle raising; consequently it was harder for him than for the others to break away from his business affairs. To this was added the feeling of his own unworthiness and his fancied incapacity for teaching, which made separation from his surroundings still more difficult. His house outside Capernaum was large and long, surrounded by a courtyard, side buildings, halls, and sheds. The waters of the brook of Capernaum, flowing in front of it, were dammed nearby into a beautiful pond in which fish were kept. All around were grass plots, upon which bleaching was done and nets were spread.

Andrew had followed the Lord longer, and he was already more detached from worldly affairs than his brother. James and John up to this period were accustomed to return at intervals to their parents.

It is understood that the Gospels do not contain the details of Jesus's intercourse with the disciples, but only a short statement of it. This call of the fishermen from their boats to make them fishers of men is there set down as happening at the beginning of his public life, and as the only call that Saints Peter, Andrew, John, and James received. Many of the miracles, parables, and instructions of Jesus are afterward recorded as instance of his power and wisdom, without any reference whatever to their order of time.

Peter, Andrew, James and John went to the pagan encampment, and there Andrew baptized. Water was brought from the brook in a large basin. The neophytes knelt in a circle, their hands crossed upon their breasts. Among them stood boys from three to six years. Peter held the basin, and Andrew, scooping the water up with his hand three different times, sprinkled the heads of the neophytes three at a time and repeated the words of baptism. The other disciples went around outside the circle laying their hands on the newly baptized. These latter then withdrew, and their places were immediately filled by others. The ceremony was discontinued at intervals, and then the disciples recounted the parables they had learned from their Master, spoke of Jesus, his doctrine, and his miracles, and explained to the pagans points of which they were still ignorant regarding the Law and the Promises of God. Peter was particularly animated in his delivery and accompanied his words with many gestures. John and James likewise spoke very beautifully. Jesus meantime was teaching in another valley, and with him was Saturnin, baptizing.

That evening when all were again assembled at Matthew's, the crowd was very great and pressed around Jesus. On that account, with the twelve apostles and Saturnin he went on board Peter's boat and commanded them to row toward Tiberias, which was on the opposite side of the lake in its greatest breadth. It looked as if Jesus wanted to escape from the crowd that pressed upon him, for he was worn out with fatigue. Three platforms surrounded the lower part of the mast, like steps one above the other. In the middle one, in one of the apartments used by the sentry, Jesus lay down and fell asleep,[D11] for he was very tired. The rowers were above him. From Jesus's resting place, although protected by a roof, there was an un-obstructed view over the whole lake. When the party put out from shore, the weather was calm and beautiful, but they had scarcely reached the middle of the lake before a violent tempest arose. I thought it very strange that, although the sky was shrouded in darkness, the stars were to be seen. The wind blew in a hurricane and the waves dashed over the boat, the sails of which had been furled. I saw from time to time a brilliant light glancing over the troubled waters. It must have been lightning. The danger was imminent, and the disciples were in great anxiety when they awoke Jesus with the words: "Master! Hast thou no care for us? We are sinking!" Jesus arose, looked out on the water, and said quietly and earnestly, as if speaking to the storm: "Peace! Be still!" and instantly all became calm.[D12] The disciples were struck with fear.

Fishing Boats on the Sea of Galilee

They whispered to one another: "Who is this man that can control the waves?" Jesus reproved them for their little faith and their fear. He ordered them to row back to Chorazin, for so the place of Matthew's custom house was called, on account of the city of Chorazin. The region on the other side of the lake between Capernaum and Gischala was named Galilee. Zebedee's boat also returned with them, and another filled with passengers went off to Capernaum.

There were in all about fifteen men on the boat with Jesus. We must not be surprised at the rowers' position above the sleeping place of Jesus, nor at the fact of Jesus's being able, notwithstanding, to take in the whole view of the lake. The oars rested upon the high sides of the boat and struck far out into the water. They were provided with long handles and the rowers were obliged to stand high. It was about one hour from Chorazin to the southwest and a little to the north of Gergesa, which occupied a less elevated position.

Wednesday, November 22, AD 30 (Kislev 7)

Jesus taught today from the side of a mountain about one hour southwest of Great Chorazin. He healed many people and blessed the children who were brought to him. Many Gentiles were present, and all those seeking baptism were baptized. That evening, in Matthew's house, Jesus told the disciples the parable of the hidden treasure (Matthew 13:44), which he interpreted as the Gentiles' longing for salvation.

At the place where Jesus paused to address the multitude there was a stone seat intended for the teacher. The instruction had been announced two days before, and there were in all probability two thousand listeners in attendance. Jesus healed also a great crowd of people, the blind and lame, the mute and leprous. As he began to teach, some of the possessed who had been led thither commenced to shout and to rave. Jesus commanded them to be silent and to lie down on the ground. Like frightened dogs they lay on the ground and moved not until, at the close of his discourse, he went to them and delivered them.

Among the numerous cures, I remember that of a man with an arm perfectly withered and a hand shrunken and crooked. Jesus stroked down the arm, took the hand in his own, and straightened out each finger one after the other, at the same time gently bending and pressing it. All this took place almost instantaneously, in a shorter time than one takes to say how it was done. The hand was restored to its proper shape, the blood began to circulate, and the man could move it although it was still wasted and weak. Its strength, however, momentarily increased.

There were in the crowd many women and children of all ages. Jesus had them brought to him in bands, one after another. He walked about among them, gave them his blessing, and instructed them in tones loud enough to be heard by all. I saw him during this instruction take a child by the hand and turn it here and there, to show how men, without complaint or resistance, should allow themselves to be conducted by God. He paid great attention to the children. Most of these people were pagans, others were Jews from Syria and Decapolis. At the spreading rumor of Jesus's doings, they had come in great caravans with their servants and children and sick to the teaching, healing, and baptism. Jesus came to meet them here, that the crowd in Capernaum might not become too great. Among them I saw the relatives of the woman mentioned in the Gospel, the woman afflicted with the issue of blood, who was then at Capernaum. Those relatives were an uncle of her deceased husband from Paneas, in whose house she had been married; her grown daughter; and another woman. They spoke to the disciples, begging them to conduct them to Capernaum that evening, and they inquired also after their sick relatives.

They heard Jesus's instructions.

Baptism was administered the whole day at this place. As on the preceding day, the neophytes knelt in circles. I saw again many little boys baptized. They stood in circles, their hands joined on their breasts. The water had been brought in leathern bottles from the valley of Chorazin. Present among the crowd of hearers were some Pharisees from the surrounding districts and some of John's false disciples, who acted as spies upon Jesus. In the evening he returned to Matthew's with the disciples. He related another parable, that of the treasure which a man found hidden in his neighbor's field. Without disclosing the secret, he went and sold all that he owned in order to buy that field. This parable Jesus applied to the great desire of the Gentiles to seize upon the kingdom of God. To escape the crowd that pressed upon him, Jesus again went on board a boat and there taught. He did not, however, go far out on the water, but returned and spent the night in prayer.

Thursday, November 23, AD 30 (Kislev 8)

After teaching and healing on the shore of the lake, Jesus and the twelve sailed back to Bethsaida, arriving there around four o'clock. They were met by his mother, accompanied by the widow of Nain (Maroni) and her son Martialis.

Next morning the disciples brought him the news that Mary Cleophas was lying very ill at Peter's near Capernaum, that his mother entreated him to come to her soon, and that a great multitude of sick of whom many were from Nazareth, were awaiting his arrival. Jesus again taught and cured numbers on the shore of the lake. Many possessed were brought to him, and he delivered them. The crowd of people and the pressure of the throng were constantly on the increase, and no words can say how unweariedly Jesus labored and helped all in need.

That afternoon he and all his apostles rowed over to Bethsaida. Matthew had delivered the custom house to a man belonging to the fishery. Since his reception of John's baptism, he had carried on his business in an altogether blameless manner. The other publicans also were honest in their dealings and very liberal men, who gave large alms to the poor.

Judas is still good. He is uncommonly active and ready to render service, though in his distribution of alms somewhat close and calculating. A large number of Gentiles crossed the lake today. Those that were not going on further, to Capernaum for instance, left their camels and asses on rafts towed by the boats, or led them over the bridge that crossed the Jordan above the lake.

It was approaching four o'clock when Jesus reached Bethsaida, where Mary with Maroni and her son, who had been here for two days, were awaiting his coming along with others. Jesus took some refreshments, while Mary Cleophas's sons repaired at once to their sick mother. A crowd of people was assembled in front of Andrew's house, and Jesus taught and cured until after night had closed.

Friday, November 24, AD 30 (Kislev 9)

Jesus's fame had spread, so that large crowds flocked to Capernaum hoping to see him. As a result, about twelve thousand people were now gathered there. As the sabbath began, Jesus taught in the synagogue, and healed a possessed man who had been brought there.

The throng of strangers to Capernaum at this time, both Jews and Gentiles, surpassed anything that can be imagined. Great caravans were encamped in all the country around. Very probably the number of strangers sojourning all around the country on Jesus's account amounted to twelve thousand. The valleys and nooks of the surrounding districts were alive with grazing camels and asses. The fodder was put before them at a convenient height, and then they were tied to it. They browsed also on the numerous buds of the hedges and thickets, though to the great prejudice of the same. Tents were pitched everywhere. Since Jesus's sojourn Capernaum had greatly increased in size, wealth, and importance. Many families from afar had there taken up their abode, and the throng of visitors brought money into the city. Zorobabel's house, as well as that of Cornelius, were now almost connected with the city proper.

Numerous sick were brought to Capernaum from the towns and villages lying around. All had been thrown into excitement by the raising of the youth of Nain, and the other astonishing miracles. Many sick from Nazareth, even those that were considered incurable and others nigh unto death, had been brought hither to Jesus in all confidence by their friends. Peter's house outside the city, its courtyard, outbuildings, and sheds were crowded with them. Tents and arbors of all kinds were hastily put up and provisions provided. The widow of Nain, who was related to Peter, and Mary Cleophas, likewise a connection of his through her third husband, were there. Mary Cleophas's usual residence was at Cana, but she had accompanied the widow of Nain to Capernaum. She had with her Simeon, the son of her third marriage, a boy of eight years. She was already fever-stricken on her arrival, and her sickness was on the increase. Jesus had not yet gone to her. I remarked some people from Greece among the multitudes here awaiting Jesus, some from Patras, Saturnin's native city.

John the Baptist's Message to the Synagogue • The Miraculous Draught of Fishes

SEVERAL of John's disciples, sent by their master, came from Machaerus to Capernaum before the sabbath began. They were some of the oldest and most confidential of his disciples, and among them were the brothers of Mary Cleophas, James, Sadoch, and Heliachim. They called the elders and the committee appointed by the Pharisees into the porch before the synagogue, and there presented to them a long, narrow, conical roll of parchment. It was a letter from John, and contained in strong and expressive terms his testimony of Jesus. While they were reading it and, somewhat perplexed, were discussing its contents among themselves, a numerous crowd assembled, to whom the messengers from John made known what their master had at Machaerus declared in a magnificent discourse before Herod, his own disciples, and a crowded audience. I saw the whole scene. When the disciples whom John had sent to Jesus at Megiddo had returned to their master, bringing with them the news of Jesus's miracles and teachings, as well as the persecution he endured from the Pharisees; when they repeated the various rumors afloat concerning Jesus and the complaints of many because he made no effort to release him (John), the Baptist felt himself urged once more to bear public witness to him. This he did the more readily since all his efforts to induce him to testify of himself had been fruitless. Therefore he sent a request to Herod to allow him to address his disciples and all others who might desire to hear him. He brought forward as a plea in his own favor that he should soon be reduced to silence. Herod did not hesitate to grant the favor asked. John's disciples and a crowd of people were admitted to the open square of the castle in which the precursor was confined. Herod and his wicked wife sat on elevated seats surrounded by a numerous guard of soldiers. Then John was led forth from his prison and he began his discourse. Herod was quite pleased that the affair should come off, as he was glad of the opportunity to appease the people by letting them see how light and easy was the imprisonment to which John was subjected. Under the powerful inspiration of the Holy Spirit, the Baptist spoke of Jesus. He himself, he said, was sent only to prepare the ways for him. He had never announced another than Jesus; but, stubborn as they were, the people would not acknowledge him. Had they then forgotten, he asked, what he had told them of him? He would recall it to them clearly once more, for his own end was not far distant! At these last words, the whole assembly was moved, and many of John's disciples wept. Herod grew uneasy and embarrassed, for he had by no means resolved upon John's death, while his concubine dissembled her feelings as best she could. John continued zealously to speak. He recounted the wonders that took place at Jesus's baptism and declared him the Beloved Son of God announced by the prophets. His doctrine was the same as his Father's. What he did the Father also did, and no one can go to the Father excepting by him, that is, by Jesus. And so he went on, refuting at length the reproaches of the Pharisees against him, and especially that of his healing on the sabbath day. Everyone, he said, should keep holy the sabbath, but the Pharisees profaned it, since they did not follow the teachings of Jesus, the teachings of the Son of him who had instituted the sabbath. John said many things of a similar nature, and proclaimed Jesus the one outside of whom no salvation could be found. Whoever believed not in him and followed not his doctrine, would be condemned. He exhorted his disciples to turn to Jesus, not to remain standing blindly near him on the threshold, but to enter into the temple itself.

After his discourse, John sent several of his disciples with a letter to the synagogue of Capernaum. In it he repeated all that he had said in testimony of Jesus, namely, that he was the Son of God and the fulfillment of the Promise, and that all his acts and teachings were right and holy. He refuted their objections, threatened them with God's judgments, and earnestly entreated them not to turn away from salvation. He commanded the disciples to read to the people another letter containing the same things, and to repeat to them all that he had just said. And now I saw John's disciples doing in Capernaum what had been commanded them. An unusually large crowd was assembled, for the city was actually swarming with people on this sabbath. There were here Jews from all quarters, and they listened with great joy to John's testimony of Jesus. Many gave utterance to loud acclamations, and their faith gained new strength.

The Pharisees had to give way to the multitude; they could not say a word. They shrugged their shoulders, shook their heads, and feigned to be well-disposed. They, however, asserted their own authority and told John's disciples that they would place no obstacle in Jesus's way if he refrained from violating the laws and disturbing the public peace. He was, it was true, very wonderfully endowed; but it was theirs to maintain order, and there should be moderation in all things. John too was a good man, but shut up as he was in prison, he might easily form a wrong estimate of things; besides, he had never been much with Jesus.

And now the hour for the sabbath struck, and all betook themselves to the synagogue, among them Jesus and the disciples. All listened with the greatest admiration to Jesus's words. He spoke of Joseph, sold by his brethren, and explained some passages from Amos that contained the menaces of God against the prevarications of Israel. No one interrupted him. The Pharisees listened with secret envy and astonishment that they could not repress. John's testimony, proclaimed so boldly to the public, had somewhat intimidated them.

But suddenly there arose fearful cries in the synagogue. Some people had brought in a man, violently possessed, belonging to Capernaum. All of a sudden he made an assault on those around him, and attempted to tear them with his teeth. Jesus turned to the side whence the noise proceeded and said: "Silence! Take him!" The man became perfectly calm. They led him out of the synagogue, and he threw himself on the ground, looking quite intimidated. When Jesus had finished the sabbath instructions and was about to withdraw, he went to where the man was lying and delivered him from the devil. After that he repaired with the disciples to Peter's near the lake, because there he could be more at peace. That night he went off by himself to pray. Among all those that Jesus cured, I never saw any such as we call insane. They were all demoniacs and possessed.

The Pharisees were still together. They ran through all kinds of ancient writings relative to the prophets, their manner of life, their teachings, and their actions. They dwelt especially upon Malachi, of whom many traditions were still extant, and compared what they found with the doctrine of Jesus. They were obliged to give Jesus the preference and admire his gifts, though they continued to criticize his teachings.

Saturday, November 25, AD 30 (Kislev 10)

Mary Cleophas lay desperately ill at Peter's house. After teaching at the synagogue in Capernaum, Jesus went to Peter's house and healed her.

Next morning Jesus again taught in the synagogue before an immense crowd. Meanwhile Mary Cleophas had become so sick that the blessed Virgin sent to Jesus to implore his help. Jesus then went to Peter's near the city where Mary, the widow of Nain, and the sons and brothers of the sick woman were. The sorrow of little Simeon, then about eight years old, was quite remarkable. He was the youngest son of Mary Cleophas by her third husband, Jonah. Jonah was the young brother of Peter's father-in-law, who had been associated with him in the fishery, and who had died about half a year previously. Jesus went to the sick woman's bed, prayed, and laid his hands upon her. She was quite exhausted by fever. Then he grasped her by the hand and told her that she should no longer be sick. He directed them to give her to eat, and I saw them bringing her a cup of something, after which she had to eat a little. This he ordered to almost all the sick whom he cured, and I heard that it bore some signification to the most blessed sacrament. As a general thing, Jesus blessed the food thus ordered. The joy of her sons, and especially that of little Simeon, was indescribable when their mother arose cured and began to serve the other sick. As for Jesus, he went out immediately and began to cure the crowds of sick awaiting his coming in the sheds and buildings around the house. The sick of all kinds were gathered here, some of long duration looked upon as incurable, others apparently at the point of death. They had been brought from far and wide; some were even from Nazareth and had known Jesus in his early youth. I saw some carried to him on the shoulders of others, looking more like corpses than creatures with life.

Some of John's disciples, they that had brought the writings, came here to Jesus to amuse themselves and tell him how indignant they were against him because he made no effort to deliver their master from imprisonment. They told him how rigorously they had fasted to obtain that God would move him to free their master. Jesus comforted them and again praised John as the holiest of men. After that I heard them speaking with Jesus's disciples. They inquired why Jesus did not himself baptize. Their master, as they said, labored so zealously in that way. The disciples of Jesus answered in words like these: "John baptized, because he is the Baptist; but Jesus heals, because he is the Savior," adding that John had never effected a miraculous cure.

And now there came to Jesus some scribes from Nazareth. They were very courteous, and besought him once more to visit Nazareth. It looked as if they wanted to make him forget what had happened there. But Jesus replied that no prophet is esteemed in his own native city. He went then to the synagogue, where he delivered the sabbath instructions till its close. On leaving the synagogue, he cured a blind man.

Peter's wife presided over the domestic affairs of his house outside the city, while those of the other near the lake were directed by his mother-in-law and step-daughter.

Jesus went away to pray. Some of the disciples, they that had formerly been engaged in fishing, asked and obtained their Master's permission to go on board their boats and pass the night at their old occupation, since there was great need of fish to supply the stupendous multitude of strangers then present in Capernaum.

There were also many desirous of crossing to the other side of the lake.

Sunday, November 26, AD 30 (Kislev 11)

After he and the disciples had distributed gifts and alms to the poor, Jesus taught on the shore of the lake. As the crowd grew very large, he and the disciples boarded a boat moored close by. From there, Jesus continued to teach the crowds on the shore. A scribe—Saraseth of Nazareth—came up and declared his readiness to follow him. Jesus replied: "Foxes have holes, and birds of the air have nests; but the Son of Man has nowhere to lay his head" (Matthew 8:19–20). As evening approached, Jesus instructed Peter to row his boat out upon the lake and to cast out the nets. A great shoal of fish filled them (Luke 5:4–5) so that it was not until the early hours of the following morning, between three and four o'clock, that Peter and his helpers were able to land the fish. Jesus was waiting on the shore, where the exchange of words given in Luke 5:6–10 took place.

The disciples spent the whole night in fishing, and next morning rowed many passengers across. Jesus meanwhile, with the rest of the disciples, busied himself in distributing alms to the poor, to the sick that had been cured, and to needy travelers. This distribution was accompanied by instruction. With his own hands Jesus presented to each one that of which he had need, giving him at the same time words of consolation and advice. The alms consisted of clothing, various materials and covers, bread, and money. The holy women also gave alms from their own stock of provisions, as well as from the gifts bestowed upon them by certain benevolent persons. The disciples carried the bread and clothing in baskets, and made the distribution of them according to Jesus's orders.

Later in the day Jesus gave at Peter's fishery a discourse, which was attended by an immense crowd. The boats of Peter and Zebedee were lying not far from the shore. The disciples who had been fishing the night before were on the shore a little distant from the crowd, busy cleaning their nets. Jesus's little boat was lying near the larger ones. When the press became too great—for the level shore was very narrow at this point, a rocky mountain wall rising in the rear—Jesus made a sign to the fishermen, and they rowed his boat to where he was standing. While it was approaching, a scribe from Nazareth [Saraseth], who had come hither with some of the sick whom Jesus had cured yesterday, said: "Master, I will follow thee whithersoever thou goest!" Jesus replied: "The foxes have holes, and the birds of the air nests, but the Son of Man has not where to lay his head."

The Sea of Galilee from Ain et-Tin

The little boat pushed up to the shore, and Jesus entered it with some of his disciples. They rowed out a short distance from the land and then up and down, pausing sometimes here, sometimes there, while Jesus instructed the crowd on the shore. He related to them several parables of the kingdom of God, among them that in which the kingdom of heaven is compared to a net cast into the sea, and that of the enemy who sowed cockle among the wheat.

Evening was now closing. Jesus told Peter to row his boat out on the lake and to cast his nets to the fish. Peter, slightly vexed, replied: "We have labored all night and have taken nothing, but at thy word I will let down the net," and he with the others entered their boats with their nets and rowed out on the lake. Jesus bade adieu to the crowd, and in his own little boat wherein were Saturnin, Veronica's son, who had arrived the day before, and some of the other disciples—he followed after Peter's. He continued to instruct them, explaining similitudes, and when out on the deep water told them where to let down the nets. Then he left them and rowed over in his little boat to the landing place near Matthew's.

By this time it was night, and on the edge of the boats near the nets, torches were blazing. The fishers cast out the net, and rowed toward Chorazin, but soon they were unable to raise it. When at last, continuing to row eastward, they dragged it out of the deep into shallow water, it was so heavy that it gave way here and there.[D13] They inserted scoops formed like little boats into the net, seized the fish with their hands, and put them into smaller nets and into the casks that floated at the sides of their boats. Then they called to their companions on Zebedee's boat, who came and emptied a part of the net. They were actually terrified at the sight of the draught of fishes. Never before had such a thing happened to them. Peter was confounded. He felt how vain were all the cares they had hitherto bestowed upon their fishing, how fruitlessly they had labored, notwithstanding their trouble—and here, at a word from him, they had caught at one draught more than they had ever done in months together.

When the net was relieved of part of its weight, they rowed to the shore, dragged it out of the water, and gazed awestruck at the multitude of fish it still contained. Jesus was standing on the shore. Peter, humbled and confused, fell at his feet and said: "Lord, depart from me, for I am a sinful man!" But Jesus said: "Fear not, Peter! From henceforth thou shalt catch men!" Peter, however, was quite overcome by sadness at the sight of his own unworthiness and vain solicitude for the things of this life. It was now between three and four in the morning, and it began to grow light.

Monday, November 27, AD 30 (Kislev 12)

Today Jesus went up a mountainside with Saturnin and Amandor. He taught them about prayer. Meanwhile the disciples, selling the fish in Capernaum and elsewhere recounted the miracle of the huge shoal of fish.

The disciples, having put the fish into a place of safety, retired to their boats for a short sleep. Jesus, with Saturnin and Veronica's son, turned off to the east, and climbed the northern end of the mountain ridge upon whose southern extremity stood Gamala. Little hills and thickets were here scattered around. Jesus instructed Saturnin and Veronica's son how to pray and gave them several points upon which to reflect. Then he withdrew from them into solitude, while they rested, walked about, and prayed.

The disciples spent the next day in transporting their fish, a great portion of which was distributed to the poor, and to all they recounted the wonderful circumstances attending their labor. The pagans bought a great many, and many more were taken to Capernaum and Bethsaida. All were now firmly convinced of the folly of solicitude for the nourishment of the body; for as the sea obeyed Jesus in the time of tempest, so did the fish obey him. They were caught at his word.

Toward evening they went again to the landing place on the east side of the lake, and Jesus with the two disciples went with them toward Capernaum. He repaired to Peter's house outside the city, and there until after night he cured by the light of torches many sick, both men and women, who were quite abandoned on account of their maladies, which were considered unclean. Their friends had not dared to bring them openly with the other sick. Jesus cured them secretly by night in Peter's yard. There were some among them who for years had been separated from their friends, and who were in a most pitiable condition. All the rest of the night Jesus spent in prayer.

The Sermon on the Mount • Cure of a Paralytic

Tuesday, November 28, AD 30 (Kislev 13)

Jesus and the disciples sailed across the Sea of Galilee. After disembarking, they went to a mountain near Bethsaida-Julias, where many people were gathered to hear Jesus teach. Here began the "Sermon on the Mount" referred to in Matthew 5 and Luke 6. This sermon lasted some fourteen days, but its conclusion was not delivered until three months later, on Nisan 2. To begin with, Jesus spoke of the first beatitude (Matthew 5:3). The instruction lasted the whole day.

JESUS rowed with several of the disciples over the lake and landed one hour to the north of Matthew's. Already many pagans, as well as those whom Jesus had cured and the newly baptized, had repaired to the mountain east of Bethsaida-Julias where Jesus was to teach. All around stood the camps of the pagans. The disciples who had been fishing on the night of the miraculous draught asked Jesus whether they too should go with him, for their recent success had freed them from anxiety upon the score of provisions, and they felt that all was in his hands. Jesus replied that they should baptize those that were still in Capernaum, and after that employ their time at their accustomed occupations, as the immense number of strangers then in and around the city rendered extra supplies necessary.

Before crossing the lake, Jesus delivered to his disciples a comprehensive instruction. In it he gave them an idea of the whole plan of the discourses upon which he intended to dwell for a long time. He told them that they (the disciples) were the salt of the earth destined to vivify and preserve others, consequently that they themselves must not lose their savor. Jesus explained all this to them at full length, making use of numerous examples and parables. After that he rowed across the lake.

The disciples (the fishermen) and Saturnin began their work of baptizing in the valley of Capernaum. The son of the widow of Nain was here baptized and named Martialis, Saturnin imposing hands upon him. The holy women did not follow Jesus to the instructions, but remained behind to celebrate with the widow of Nain the baptismal feast of her son.

There were with Jesus, Joseph of Arimathea's nephews, who had come from Jerusalem; Nathaniel; Manahem of Coreae; and many other disciples. In these last days I saw about thirty of them gathered together in Capernaum.

On landing at the east side of the lake just below the mouth of the Jordan, the traveler ascended the mountain to the east and then, turning westward, went on to the spot upon which the instruction was to be given. Another way could be taken, namely, that over the Jordan bridge to the north of the lake. But this latter way, on account of the wild character of the country and its numerous ravines, was rather a difficult road to the mountain. Bethsaida-Julias was situated on the eastern bank of the mouth of the Jordan, the river there forming a bend. The western shore was high, and to it ran a road.

There was no teacher's chair on the mountain, only an eminence surrounded by a mound of earth and covered by an awning. The view from the west and southwest extended over the lake and to the opposite mountains. One could even descry Mount Tabor. Crowds of people, most of them pagans that had received baptism, were encamped around. There were Jews also present. Separation between them was not so rigorously observed here, since communication between the Jews and Gentiles was greater in these parts, and on this side of the lake the latter enjoyed certain privileges.

Jesus began by enumerating the eight beatitudes,[D14] and then went on to explain the first: "Blessed are the poor in spirit, for theirs is the kingdom of heaven." He related examples and parables, spoke of the Messiah, and especially of the conversion of the Gentiles. Now was accomplished what the prophet foretold of the Desired of Nations: "And I will move all nations. And the Desired of all nations shall come, and I will fill this house with glory, saith the Lord of hosts." There was no curing on this day, for the sick had been healed on the preceding days. The Pharisees had come over in one of their own boats and they listened to Jesus's words with chagrin and jealousy. The people had brought with them food, which they ate during the pauses of the instruction. Jesus and the disciples had fish, bread, and honey, also little flasks of some kind of juice, or balm, a few drops of which were mixed with the water they drank.

Toward evening the people from Capernaum, Bethsaida, and other neighboring places returned to their homes in the boats that awaited them on the lake. Jesus and his disciples went down toward the valley of the Jordan and into a shepherd inn, where they passed the night. Jesus still continued to teach the disciples, thus to prepare them for their future mission.

Jesus devoted fourteen days to instructions on the eight beatitudes, and spent the intervening sabbath in Capernaum.

Wednesday, November 29, AD 30 (Kislev 14)

Today Jesus began to teach concerning the second beatitude (Matthew 5:4). Five holy women were present, including the holy Virgin Mary, Mary Cleophas, and Maroni of Nain, and also all the twelve disciples who later became apostles. After the sermon, Jesus taught the disciples as indicated in Matthew 5:14–20.

On the following day he continued his preaching on the mountain. Mary, Mary Cleophas, Maroni of Nain, and two other women were present. When Jesus with the apostles and disciples went back to the lake, he spoke of their vocation in these words: "Ye are the light of the world!" He illustrated by the similitude of the city seated on a mountain, the light on the candlestick, and the fulfilling of the Law. Then he rowed to Bethsaida, and put up at Andrew's.

Among the neophytes whom Saturnin baptized on those days near Capernaum were some Jews from Achaia whose ancestors had fled thither at the time of the Babylonian Captivity.

The recently-built city of Bethsaida-Julias was inhabited mostly by pagans. There were, however, some Jews, and the city possessed a famous school in which all kinds of knowledge were taught. Jesus had not yet visited it, but the inhabitants went out to the instruction and also to Capernaum, where their sick were cured. Bethsaida-Julias was beautifully situated in the narrow valley of the Jordan, built a little up on the eastern side of the mountain, one-half hour from the point where the river flows into the lake. One hour northward, a stone bridge spanned the Jordan.

Thursday, November 30, AD 30 (Kislev 15)

Jesus continued to teach the second beatitude. He also explained many teachings of the prophets.

While going down from the mountain whereon he had been teaching, Jesus again instructed the disciples, and spoke of the sufferings and sharp persecutions in store for them. He slept that night in Peter's boat.

Friday, December 1, AD 30 (Kislev 16)

Jesus preached today concerning the third beatitude. But because the sabbath was approaching, he broke off early and sailed back toward Capernaum. There he taught near the south gate, in a house that Peter had rented. It was here that the healing of the paralytic described in Mark 2:1–2, Luke 5:17–26, and Matthew 9:1–9 occurred. After this, Jesus went to the synagogue, where he taught—this time without disruption. Jairus, whose daughter (Salome) Jesus had raised from the dead on Kislev 3, was there. As Jesus left, Jairus approached him to ask help for Salome, who was again close to death. Jesus agreed to go. On their way, the message of Salome's death reached them. But they continued on. Then occurred the healing of the widow Enue from Caesarea Philippi, who had been suffering from a flow of blood for twelve years (Matthew 9:20–22, Mark 5:25–34, and Luke 8:43–48). Reaching Jairus's home Jesus then repeated the raising of Salome from the dead (Matthew 9:23–25, Mark 5:35–43, and Luke 8:49–56). Afterward, Jesus left the house. On his way through the streets of Capernaum he was approached by two blind men, whom he healed (Matthew 9:27–30). Following this, Jesus healed Joas the Pharisee, who was possessed (Matthew 9:32–34).

When Jesus next day went down from the mountain to Capernaum, he found a crowd of people assembled to bid him welcome. He repaired to Peter's house near the city. It stood outside the gate to the right on entering the city from the valley. When it was known that Jesus and the disciples were in the house, a crowd soon gathered around him. The scribes and Pharisees also hastened out to hear him. The whole court around the open hall in which Jesus sat and taught with the disciples and scribes was full. He spoke of the Ten Commandments and, coming to the words recorded in the Gospel of the Sermon on the Mount: "You have heard that it was said to them of old: thou shalt not kill," he based upon them his instruction on the forgiveness of injuries and the love of one's enemies. Just at this moment a loud noise arose on the roof of the hall, and through the usual opening in the ceiling a paralytic on his bed was lowered by four men, who cried out: "Lord, have pity upon a poor sick man!"

He was let down by two cords into the midst of the assembly before Jesus.[D15] The friends of the sick man had tried in vain to carry him through the crowd into the courtyard, and had at last mounted the outside steps to the roof of the hall, whose trap door they opened. All eyes were fixed upon the invalid, and the Pharisees were vexed at what appeared to them a great misdemeanor, a piece of unheard-of impertinence. But Jesus, who was pleased at the faith of the poor people, stepped forward and addressed the paralytic, who lay there motionless: "Be of good heart, son, thy sins are forgiven thee!" words which were, as usual, particularly distasteful to the Pharisees. They thought within themselves: "That is blasphemy! Who but God can forgive sins?" Jesus saw their thoughts and said: "Wherefore have ye such thoughts of bitterness in your heart? Which is easier to say to the paralytic: Thy sins are forgiven thee; or to say: Arise, take up thy bed, and walk? But that you may know that the Son of Man has power on earth to forgive sins, I say to thee" (here Jesus turned to the paralytic): "Arise! Take up thy bed, and go into thy house!" And immediately the man arose cured, rolled up the coverlets of his bed, laid the laths of the frame together, took them under his arm and upon his shoulder, and accompanied by those that had brought him and some other friends went off singing canticles of praise while the whole multitude shouted for joy. The Pharisees, full of rage, slipped away, one by one. It was now the sabbath, and Jesus, followed by the multitude, repaired to the synagogue.

Jairus and his Daughter • Her Relapse • Cure of a Woman Afflicted with an Issue of Blood, of Two Blind Men, and of a Pharisee

JAIRUS, the chief of the synagogue, was also present at that last miracle in the synagogue. He was very sad and full of remorse. His daughter was again near death, and truly a frightful death, as it had fallen upon her in punishment of her own and her parents' sins. Since the preceding sabbath she had lain ill of a fever. The mother and her sister together with Jairus's mother, who all lived in the same house, had, along with the daughter herself, taken Jesus's miraculous healing in a very frivolous way, without gratitude and without in any way altering their life. Jairus, weak and yielding, entirely under the control of his vain and beautiful wife, had let the women have their own way. Their home was the theater of female vanity, and all the latest pagan styles of finery were brought into requisition for their adornment. When the little girl was well again, these women laughed among themselves at Jesus and turned him into ridicule. The child followed their example. Until very recently she had retained her innocence, but now it was no longer so. A violent fever seized upon her. The burning and thirst that she had endured were something extraordinary; the last week was spent in a state of constant delirium, and she now lay near death. The parents suspected that it was a punishment of their frivolity, though they would not acknowledge it to themselves. At last the mother became so ashamed and so frightened that she said to Jairus: "Will Jesus again have pity on us?" and she commissioned her husband once more humbly to implore his assistance. But Jairus was ashamed to appear again before the Lord, so he waited till the sabbath instructions were over. He had full faith that Jesus could help him at any time, if he would. He was too ashamed to be seen by the people again asking for help.

When Jesus was leaving the synagogue, a great crowd pressed around him, for there were many, both sick and well, who wanted to speak to him. Jairus approached with trouble on his countenance. He threw himself at Jesus's feet, and begged him again to have pity on his daughter whom he had left in a dying state. Jesus promised that he would return with him. And now there came someone from Jairus's house looking for him, because he stayed so long, and the mother of the girl thought that Jesus would not come. The messenger told Jairus that his daughter was already dead. Jesus comforted the father and told him to have confidence. It was already dark, and the crowd around Jesus was very great. Just then a woman afflicted with an issue of blood, taking advantage of the darkness, made her way through the crowd, leaning on the arms of her nurses. She dwelt not far from the synagogue. The women afflicted with the same malady, though not so grievously as herself, had told her of their own cure some hours earlier. They had that day at noon, when Jesus was passing in the midst of the crowd, ventured to touch his garments, and were thereby instantly cured. Their words roused her faith. She hoped in the dusk of evening and in the throng that would gather round Jesus on leaving the synagogue, to be able to touch him unnoticed. Jesus knew her thoughts and consequently slackened his pace. The nurses led her as close to him as possible. Standing near her were her daughter, her husband's uncle, and Lea. The sufferer knelt down, leaned forward supporting herself on one hand, and with the other reaching through the crowd she touched the hem of Jesus's robe.[D16] Instantly she felt that she was healed. Jesus at the same moment halted, glanced around at the disciples, and inquired: "Who hath touched me?"

To which Peter answered: "Thou askest, 'Who touched me?' The people throng and press upon thee, as thou seest!" But Jesus responded: "Someone hath touched me, for I know that virtue is gone out from me." Then he looked around and, as the crowd had fallen back a step, the woman could not longer remain hidden. Quite abashed, she approached him timidly, fell on her knees before him, and acknowledged in hearing of the whole crowd what she had done. Then she related how long she had suffered from an issue of blood, and that she believed herself healed by the touch of his garment. Turning to Jesus, she begged him to forgive her. Then Jesus addressed to her these words: "Be comforted, my daughter, thy faith hath made thee whole! Go in peace, and remain free from thy infirmity!" and she departed with her friends.

She was thirty years old, very thin and pale, and was named Enue. Her deceased husband was a Jew. She had only one daughter, who had been taken charge of by her uncle. He had now come to the baptism, accompanied by his niece and a sister-in-law named Lea. The husband of the latter was a Pharisee and an enemy of Jesus. Enue had, in her widowhood, wished to enter into a connection which to her rich relatives appeared far below her position; therefore they had opposed her.

Jesus with rapid steps accompanied Jairus to his house. Peter, James, John, Saturnin, and Matthew were with him. In the forecourt were again gathered the mourners and weepers, but this time they uttered no word of mockery, nor did Jesus say as he did before: "She is only sleeping," but passed on straight through the crowd. Jairus's mother, his wife, and her sister came timidly forth to meet him. They were veiled and in tears; their robes, the garments of mourning. Jesus left Saturnin and Matthew with the people in the forecourt, while, accompanied by Peter, James, and John, the father, the mother, and the grandmother, he entered the room in which the dead girl lay. It was a different room from the first time. Then she lay in a little chamber; now she was in the room behind the fireplace. Jesus called for a little branch from the garden and a basin of water, which he blessed. The corpse lay stiff and cold. It did not present so agreeable an appearance as on the former occasion. Then I had seen the soul hovering in a sphere of light close to the body, but this time I did not see it at all. On the former occasion, Jesus said: "She is sleeping," but now he said nothing. She was dead. With the little branch Jesus sprinkled her with the blessed water, prayed, took her by the hand, and said: "Little maid, I say to thee, arise!" As Jesus was praying, I saw the girl's soul in a dark globe approaching her mouth, into which it entered. She suddenly opened her eyes, obeyed the touch of Jesus's hand, arose and stepped from her couch. Jesus led her to her parents who, receiving her with hot tears and choking sobs, sank at Jesus's feet. He ordered them to give her something to eat, some bread and grapes. His order was obeyed. The girl ate and began to speak. Then Jesus earnestly exhorted the parents to receive the mercy of God thankfully, to turn away from vanity and worldly pleasure, to embrace the penance preached to them, and to beware of again compromising their daughter's life now restored for the second time. He reproached them with their whole manner of living, with the levity they had exhibited at the reception of the first favor bestowed upon them, and their conduct afterward, by which in a short time they had exposed their child to a much more grievous death than that of the body, namely, the death of the soul. The little girl herself was very much affected and shed tears. Jesus warned her against concupiscence of the eyes and sin. While she partook of the grapes and the bread that he had blessed, he told her that for the future she should no longer live according to the flesh, but that she should eat of the Bread of Life, the Word of God, should do penance, believe, pray, and perform works of mercy. The parents were very much moved and completely transformed. The father promised to break the bonds that bound him to worldliness, and to obey Jesus's orders, while the mother and the rest of the family, who had now come in, expressed their determination to reform their lives. They shed tears and gave thanks to Jesus. Jairus, entirely changed, immediately made over a great part of his possessions to the poor. The daughter's name was Salome.

As a crowd had gathered before the house, Jesus told Jairus that they should make no unnecessary reports concerning what had just taken place. He often gave this command to those whom he cured, and that for various reasons. The chief was that the divulging and boasting of such favors troubles the recollection of the soul and prevents its reflection upon the mercy of God. Jesus desired that the cured should enter into themselves instead of running about enjoying the new life that had been given them, and thereby falling an easy prey to sin. Another reason for enjoining silence was that Jesus wanted to impress upon the disciples the necessity of avoiding vainglory and of performing the good they did through love and for God alone. Sometimes again, he made use of this prohibition in order not to increase the number of the inquisitive, the importunate, and the sick who came to him not by the impulse of faith. Many indeed came merely to test his power, and then they fell back into their sins and infirmities, as Jairus's daughter had done.

Jesus and his five disciples left Jairus's house by the rear, in order to escape the crowd that pressed around the door. The first miracle here was performed in clear daylight; that of today was after the sabbath and by the light of lamps. Jairus's house was in the northern part of the city. Jesus, on leaving it, turned to the northwest off toward the ramparts. Meanwhile two blind men with their guides were on the lookout for his coming. It seemed almost as if they scented his presence, for they followed after him, crying: "Jesus, thou Son of David, have pity on us!" At that moment Jesus went into the house of a good man who was devoted to him. The house was built in the rampart and had on the other side a door opening into the country beyond the city precincts. The disciples sometimes stopped at this house. Its owner was one of the guards in this section of the city. The blind men, however, still followed Jesus, and even into the house, crying in beseeching tones: "Have mercy on us, Son of David!" At last Jesus turned to them and said: "Do you believe that I can do this unto you?" and they answered: "Yea, Lord!" Then he took from his pocket a little flask of oil, or balsam, and poured some into a small dish, brown and shallow. Holding it and the flask in his left hand, with the right he put into the dish a little earth, mixed it up with the thumb and forefinger of the right hand, touched the eyes of the blind men with the same, and said: "May it be done unto you according to your desire!" [D17] Their eyes were opened, they saw, they fell on their knees and gave thanks. To them also Jesus recommended silence as to what had just taken place. This he did to prevent the crowd from following him and to avoid exasperating the Pharisees. The cries of the blind men as they followed him had, however, already betrayed his presence in this part of the country, and besides this, the two men could not forbear imparting their happiness to all whom they met. A crowd was in consequence soon gathered around Jesus.

Some people from the region of Sepphoris, distant relatives of Anne, brought hither a man possessed of a mute devil. [D18] His hands were bound, and they led him and pulled him along by cords tied around his body, for he was perfectly furious and oftentimes scandalous in his behavior. He was one of those Pharisees that had formed a committee to spy on the actions of Jesus. He was named Joas, and belonged to the number of those that had disputed with Jesus in an isolated school between Sepphoris and Nazareth. When Jesus returned from Nain, that is about fourteen days before, the demon seized upon Joas, because, silencing his own interior convictions, he had, through sheer adulation of the other Pharisees, joined in the calumnious cry against Jesus: "He is possessed by the devil! He runs like a madman about the country!" It was on the subject of divorce that Jesus had disputed with him at Sepphoris. The man was in grievous sin. As he was led up, he made an attempt to rush upon Jesus, but he, with a motion of the hand, commanded the devil to withdraw. The man shuddered, and a black vapor issued from his mouth. Then he sank on his knees before Jesus, confessed his sins, and begged forgiveness. Jesus pardoned him, and enjoined certain fasts and alms as a penance. He had likewise to abstain for a long time from several kinds of food of which the Jews were exceedingly fond, garlic for instance. The excitement produced by this cure was very great, for it was considered a most difficult thing to drive out mute devils. The Pharisees had already put themselves to much trouble on Joas's account. Were it not that he was brought by his friends, he never would have appeared before Jesus, for the Pharisees would not have permitted it. Now indeed were they indignant that one of their own number had been helped by Jesus and had openly avowed his sins, in which they themselves had had a share. As the cured man was returning to his home, the news of his deliverance was spread throughout Capernaum, and the people everywhere proclaimed that such wonders had never before been heard in Israel. But the Pharisees in their fury retorted: "By the prince of devils he casteth out devils."

Jesus now left the house by the back door, and with him the disciples. They went around to Peter's on the west side and a little distant from the city, and here Jesus spent the night.

During these days Jesus repeated to his disciples his testimony of John the Baptist. "He is," he said, "as pure as an angel. Nothing unclean has ever entered his mouth, nor has an untruth or anything sinful ever come forth from it." When the disciples asked Jesus whether John had long to live, Jesus answered that he would die when his time came, and that was not far off. This information made them very sad.

Cure of a Man with a Withered Hand • "Blessed is the Womb that Bore Thee!"

Saturday, December 2, AD 30 (Kislev 17)

Today Jesus visited the centurion Cornelius. Then he went to Jairus's house and cautioned Salome to follow the word of God. At the close of the sabbath, he taught in the synagogue. The Pharisees left early, and Jesus continued teaching the disciples, as indicated in Matthew 5:27–37. The Pharisees then returned with a man whose hand was withered, whom Jesus healed.

WHEN Jesus went to the synagogue to teach, the Pharisees laid a snare for him. In a corner of the synagogue was a poor creature with a withered hand. He had not ventured to appear before Jesus, and now held back, intimidated by the presence of the Pharisees. These latter were reproaching Jesus, asking him how he could make his appearance with a publican like Matthew. To this Jesus responded that he had come to console and convert sinners, but that no Pharisee should ever be numbered among his disciples. The Pharisees mockingly retorted: "Master, here is one for whom thou hast come. Perhaps, thou wilt heal him also." Thereupon Jesus commanded the man with the withered hand to come forward and stand in the midst of the assembly. He did so, and Jesus said to him: "Thy sins are forgiven thee!" [D19] The Pharisees, who scorned the poor man—whose reputation was not of the best—cried out: "His withered hand has never hindered him from sinning." Then Jesus grasped the hand, straightened the fingers, and said: "Use thy hand!" The man stretched out his hand, found it cured, and went away giving thanks. Jesus justified him against the calumnies of the Pharisees, expressed compassion for him, and declared him a good-hearted fellow. The Pharisees were covered with confusion and filled with wrath. They declared Jesus a sabbath-breaker against whom they would lodge an accusation, and then took their departure. In the neighborhood of the synagogue they met some Herodians with whom they consulted as to how they should lie in wait for Jesus on the next feast in Jerusalem. [D20]

Sunday, December 3, AD 30 (Kislev 18)

Jesus taught again in the house near the south gate of Capernaum and spoke of the beatitudes. Among the hearers was Lea, the sister-in-law of Enue, whom he had healed two days before. As Jesus was saying the sixth beatitude, "Blessed are the pure in heart, for they shall see God," Mary and four holy women entered the room. Lea called out: "Blessed is the womb that bore you, and the breasts that you sucked!" Jesus replied: "Blessed rather are those who hear the word of God and keep it!" (Luke 11:27–28). Later, Jesus taught again from a boat at the shore of the lake. It was here that he spoke the words in Luke 9:59–62. He then sailed across to the region of Great Chorazin.

When Jesus later on addressed the people in Peter's house, among the other women present was Lea, the sister-in-law of Enue, recently cured of the issue of blood. Her husband was a Pharisee and a zealous opponent of Jesus, but Lea herself was profoundly impressed by the instructions she had heard. I saw her at first, calm and sorrowful, often changing her place among the crowd, as if looking for someone, but I found out that she was in this way obeying the impulse that prompted her to proclaim aloud her reverence for Jesus. Then approached the mother of Jesus accompanied by several women, namely, Martha, Susanna of Jerusalem, Dinah the Samaritan, and Susanna Alpheus, a daughter of Mary Cleophas and sister of the apostles. She was about thirty and had grown children. Her husband lived in Nazareth, and it was there that she had joined the holy women. Susanna Alpheus desired to be admitted among the community of women that rendered service to Jesus and his disciples. Mary and her companions entered the court that led to the hall in which Jesus was teaching. He had been reproaching the Pharisees with their hypocrisy and impurity and, because he always interwove some of the beatitudes with his other teachings, he just at that moment exclaimed: "Blessed are the pure of heart, for they shall see God!" Lea, meanwhile, seeing Mary coming in, could no longer restrain herself and, as if intoxicated with joy, she cried out from among the crowd: "More blessed" (these are the exact words that I heard) "more blessed the womb that bore thee and the breasts that gave thee suck!" To which I saw Jesus quietly replying: "And far more blessed are they that hear the word of God and keep it!" [D21] and he went on with his discourse. Lea went to Mary, saluted her, spoke of Enue's cure and of her own resolve to give her wealth to the community, and requested Mary to intercede with her Son for her husband's conversion. He was a Pharisee of Paneas. Mary conversed with her in a low voice. She had not heard Lea's sudden exclamation nor Jesus's reply, and soon she withdrew with the women.

Mary was possessed of admirable simplicity. Jesus never showed her any marks of distinction before others, excepting that he treated her with reverence. She never had much to do with any, unless with the sick and the ignorant, and her demeanor was always marked by humility, recollection, and simplicity. All, even the enemies of Jesus, honored her; and yet she never sought after anyone, but was always quiet and alone.

Jesus went next to Peter's fishery where, before a great crowd of people, he taught in parables of the kingdom of God. Then he mounted his little boat and taught from the lake. A scribe from Nazareth named Saraseth proposed himself as a disciple, when Jesus repeated to him the words: "The foxes have their holes, etc." Saraseth afterward married Salome, the daughter of Jairus. After Jesus's death, both husband and wife joined the community.

Besides this scribe, there were two others who for some time followed Jesus as disciples. One of them asked him whether he would not soon take possession of his kingdom, for he had already sufficiently proved his mission. Would he not soon seat himself upon the throne of David? Jesus having reprimanded him and ordered him to follow him with docility, he replied that he would first go and take leave of his family. To this Jesus responded: "Whoever puts his hands to the plough, etc." A third, who had joined Jesus at Sepphoris, expressed his wish to go and bury his father. Jesus replied: "Let the dead bury their dead." These words were not spoken literally, for his father was not yet dead. It was an expression which meant receiving one's share of the patrimony and providing for one's parents.

Monday, December 4, AD 30 (Kislev 19)

Today Jesus continued the Sermon on the Mount near Bethsaida-Julias. He spoke on the fourth beatitude. Afterward, he went with the twelve to a place on the east shore of the lake. There he gave the twelve authority to cast out unclean spirits (Matthew 10:1–4). Jesus then sailed with the twelve and about five other disciples to Magdala, where he exorcised some people who were possessed. Peter, Andrew, James, and John also cast out unclean spirits. Jesus and the disciples then spent the night on board the boat.

Jesus spent that night on the mountain near Chorazin with two of the disciples, under a tent and in prayer. The other disciples came next morning to the sermon. Jesus explained today the fourth beatitude and this passage from Isaiah: "Behold my servant, I will uphold him: My elect, my soul delighteth in him. I have given my Spirit upon him, he shall bring forth judgment to the Gentiles." The multitude was very great.

There was present a troop of Roman soldiers from the different garrisons around the country. They had been sent to hear Jesus's doctrines, to note his bearing, and to give information on the same. From Gaul and other provinces of the Empire they had written to Rome for news of the prophet of Judea, because this last named country was under the Roman sway. Rome had in consequence made inquiries of the officers of the different garrisons, and these latter had now sent about a hundred of their trusty soldiers, who stood where they could both see and hear well.

The instruction over, Jesus went with the disciples down the mountain to the valley on the south. Here there was a spring, and here too had bread and fish been prepared by the holy women who devoted themselves to such services. The multitude had encamped on the mountainside. Many of them were without provisions, and they sent some of their number to beg food of the disciples. The bread and fish were arranged in baskets on a grassy mound. Jesus blessed the baskets and helped the disciples to distribute their contents to all that asked. It was apparently far from enough, and yet all received what they needed. I heard the people saying: "It is multiplied in his hands." The Roman soldiers also asked for some of the blessed bread, for they wanted to send it to Rome as a testimony of what they had seen and heard. Jesus ordered what remained to be given to them, and there was still enough for all the leaders. They wrapped it up carefully and took it away with them.

Jesus in Magdala and Gergesa • The Demon Driven into the Swine

IN the intervals of his public teaching and curing, Jesus, whenever he found himself alone with his apostles and disciples, prepared them for their mission. Today he led the twelve to a retired spot near the lake, placed them in the order mentioned in the Gospel, and conferred upon them the power of healing and of casting out devils. To the other disciples he gave only the power to baptize and impose hands. At the same time, he addressed to them a touching discourse in which he promised to be with them always and to share with them all that he possessed.[D22] The power to heal and to drive out the devil, Jesus bestowed in the form of a blessing. All wept, and Jesus himself was very much moved. At the close he said that there was still much to be done and then they would go to Jerusalem, for the fullness of time was drawing near. The apostles were glowing with enthusiasm. They expressed their readiness to do all that he would command and to remain true to him. Jesus replied that there were afflictions and hardships in store for them, and that evil would glide in among them. By these words he alluded to Judas. With discourses such as the above, they reached their little boats. Jesus and the twelve, with about five of the disciples, among them Saturnin, rowed to the east bank of the lake, down past Hippos, and landed near the little village of Magdala. This place lay close to the lake and north of the dark ravine into which flowed the waters from the pool near Gergesa, higher up the country. To the east of Magdala rose a mountain. The village was built so near to it that it enjoyed the benefit of only the midday and evening sun; it was consequently damp and foggy, especially in the neighborhood of the ravine.

Jesus and his disciples did not at once enter Magdala. Peter's boat was lying near a sandbank to which extended a bridge. As soon as Jesus stepped on shore, several possessed came running toward him with loud cries. They asked what he wanted there, and cried out for him to leave them in peace. This they did of their own accord. Jesus delivered them. They gave thanks, and went into the village. And now others came, bringing with them other possessed. Some of the disciples, Peter, Andrew, John, James and his cousins then went into Magdala, where they delivered the possessed and cured many sick, among others some women attacked by convulsions. They drove out devils and commanded sickness to disappear in the name of Jesus of Nazareth. I heard some of them adding the words, "Whom the storm of the sea obeyed." Some of those that were cured by the disciples went to Jesus to hear his admonitions and instructions. He explained to them and to the disciples why the possessed were so very numerous in these parts. It was because the inhabitants were so intent upon the things of this world and so given up to the indulgence of their passions. Several of these possessed were from Gergesa, which lay up on the mountain about one hour to the east of Magdala. They infested the surrounding country, hiding in the caves and tombs. Jesus continued the cures until after twilight, and then spent the night on the boat with the disciples.

From the region of Gergesa, which had a circumference of about four hours, none had attended Jesus's instructions on the mountain.

Tuesday, December 5, AD 30 (Kislev 20)

On an incline east of Magdala, Jesus healed two possessed youths from Gergesa. Later, he and the disciples boarded their boat and sailed out upon the lake, where they spent the night.

On the following day Jesus climbed the mountain, and encountered two Jewish youths who had come from Gergesa to meet him. They were possessed by the devil. They were not furious, though the attacks of the evil one were frequent, and they roved restlessly about. When Jesus some time before had crossed the Jordan from Tarichea and passed Gerasa, these young men were not yet possessed. They had then come out to meet him and begged to be received among his disciples, but Jesus sent them away. Now again, after Jesus had delivered them, they desired to be received by him. They told him that the misfortune from which he had just freed them never would have overtaken them if he had yielded to their first request. Jesus exhorted them to amendment of life, and bade them return home and announce by what means their deliverance had been effected. The youths obeyed. As Jesus went along, pausing here and there to teach before the huts and homes of the shepherds, many possessed and simpletons ran hiding behind the hedges and hills, crying after him and making signs for him to keep off and not disturb their peace. But Jesus called them to him, and delivered them. Many of those thus freed cried out, imploring him not to drive them into the abyss! Some of the apostles also performed cures by the imposition of hands, and engaged the people to repair to the mountain beyond Magdala to the south, where Jesus was going to deliver an instruction.

Wednesday, December 6, AD 30 (Kislev 21)

Today there occurred the healing of the two possessed men from Gergesa whose demons Jesus drove out into a great herd of swine, which then plunged down into the lake (Mark 5:1–20).

A great crowd assembled at the place designated. Jesus exhorted them to penance, spoke of the near approach of the kingdom of God, and reproached them with clinging to the goods of this world. He spoke also of the value of the soul. They should know, he said, that God prizes the soul more highly than man's great, worldly possessions.

By these last words Jesus made reference to the herd of swine which was soon to be precipitated into the lake, for the people had invited Jesus to go again to Gergesa. To this invitation Jesus replied that he would indeed accept it, but that his coming would be an untimely one for them, and that they would not give him a very warm welcome. They begged him not to traverse the ravine on his return to them, for there were two furious possessed roaming about in it who had broken their chains and had already strangled some people.[D23] But Jesus responded that on that very account he would, when it was time, go that way, for he had been sent upon earth for the sake of the miserable. It was at this conjuncture that he uttered the passage in which it is said, "If Sodom and Gomorrha had heard and seen the things that have taken place here in Galilee, they would have done penance."

When Jesus was about to depart, the people prayed him to tarry awhile longer, for never had they heard so pleasing a discourse. It was, they said, like the morning sunbeams shining upon their gloomy, foggy home. They begged him to remain, for it was already dark. To this Jesus replied in a similitude on the darkness: he feared not this darkness, but they should dread remaining in eternal darkness, and that at a time in which the light of the Word of God had shone upon them. Then he retired to the ships with the disciples. They rowed at first as if directing their course across to Tiberias, but then turned again to the east, lay to about one hour south of the ravine, and spent the night on their ships.

Magdala was an unimportant place, smaller than Bethsaida. It was only a landing place for boats, and derived its subsistence from Hippos, which was largely engaged in trade and commerce. A highroad ran past Gerasa and down to Hippos, and was the scene of constant traffic. The country of Magdala was known also as the country of Dalmanutha, from the town that lay a couple of hours further to the south and on the other side of the ravine.

When Jesus landed next morning, several demoniacs were presented to him, and he cured them by laying his hands upon them. The people of this region practiced sorcery. They ate of a certain herb that grew abundantly in the ravine and on the mountain, and thus became intoxicated and fell into convulsions. They had another plant of which they made use to counteract the effects of the first, but for some time past it had lost its virtue and now the poor creatures were left in their misery. The country of the Gergeseans was a tract of land from four to five hours in length, and about a half-hour in breadth. It was distinguished from the surrounding districts by its history and the character of its inhabitants, which latter was not of the best. It began with the ravine between Dalmanutha and Magdala, included the ravine, and on the south began with and comprised ten villages scattered in a row along the narrow strip of land, with Gergesa and Gerasa at either end. Beyond Gerasa it was bounded by the region of Chorazin, the land of Zin, and a district containing many deserts. On the east it was bounded by the long mountain ridge on whose southern extremity stood the citadel of Gamala; on the south, by the ravine; and on the west, the valley on the shore of the lake. In this valley lay Dalmanutha, Magdala, and Hippos, which did not belong to the country of Gergesa, no more than the rest of the lakeshore, excepting the ravine to the south of Magdala. On the north it ended with Chorazin. This district with its ten villages must not be confounded with the Decapolis, or that of the ten cities, which extended far around it and from which it was wholly distinct. In Gideon's struggle against the Midianites, the inhabitants of the ten villages supported the pagans who since that time had acquired the upper hand and kept the Jews in great subjection. They raised in all these places, to the scandal of the Jews that dwelt there, immense numbers of swine, which in herds of several thousands were turned out to fatten in a great marsh on the northern height of the ravine. They were attended by a hundred pagan herdsmen and their boys. The marsh, which was about three quarters of an hour southeast of Gergesa, at the foot of the mountain of Gamala, discharged its boggy waters southward into the ravine over a dam of logs and heavy planks that changed the brook above it into a swamp. The superfluous waters flowed through the ravine into the Sea of Galilee. Numbers of huge oaks grew near the marsh and on the sides of the ravine. No part of this region was very fertile, and only in a few sunny places grew some vines. They had also a kind of reed from which sugar can be made, but they exported it in its crude state.

It was not so much their idolatrous worship that subjected the people of this region to the power of the devil, as the depth to which they were sunk in sorcery. Gergesa and the surrounding places were full of wizards and witches who carried on their disorders by means of cats, dogs, toads, snakes, and other animals. They conjured up these creatures, and even went around in their form injuring and killing men. They were like werewolves that can hurt people even at a distance, that take revenge after a long time upon those whom they hate, and that can raise storms at sea. The women used to brew some kind of a magical beverage. Satan had entirely conquered this region, which possessed innumerable demoniacs, raging lunatics, and victims of convulsions.

It was approaching ten in the morning when Jesus with some of the disciples mounted a little boat, crossed the brook some distance up to the stream, and rowed into the ravine. This was a shorter way than that by land. Jesus climbed the northern side of the ravine, and the disciples joined him one after another. While he was ascending, two raging possessed higher up on the mountain were running about, darting in and out of the sepulchers, casting themselves on the ground, and beating themselves with the bones of the dead. They uttered horrible cries and appeared to be under the spell of some secret influence, for they could not flee. As Jesus drew nearer, they cried out from behind the bushes and rocks that lay a little higher up on the mountain: "Ye Powers! Ye Dominations! Come to our aid! Here comes one stronger than we!" Jesus raised his hand toward them and commanded them to lie down.

They fell flat on their faces, but raising their heads again, cried out: "Jesus! Thou Son of God the Most High, what have we to do with thee? Why art thou come to torment us before the time? We conjure thee in the name of God to leave us in peace!" By this time Jesus and the disciples had reached them as they lay trembling, their whole persons horribly agitated. Jesus ordered the disciples to give them some clothing, and commanded the possessed to cover themselves. The disciples threw to them the scarfs they wore around their necks and in which they were accustomed to muffle their heads. The possessed, trembling and writhing convulsively, covered themselves, as if constrained to do so against their will, arose, and cried out to Jesus not to torture them. Jesus asked: "How many are ye?" They answered, "Legion." The wicked spirits spoke always in the plural by the mouth of these two possessed. They said that the evil desires of these men were innumerable. This time the devil spoke the truth. For seventeen years these men had lived in communication with him, and in the practice of sorcery. Now and then they had suffered assaults like the present, but for the last two years they had been running, frantic, around the desert. They had been entangled in all the abominations of magic.

Nearby was a vineyard on a sunny slope, and in it an immense wooden vat formed of great beams. It was not quite the height of a man, but so broad that twenty men could stand in it. The Gergeseans used to press in it grapes mixed with the juice of that intoxicating herb of which I have spoken. The juice ran into little troughs and thence into large, earthen vessels with narrow necks which, when full, were buried underground in the vineyard. This was that intoxicating beverage which produced effects so fatal upon all that drank of it. The herb was about the length of one's arm, with numerous thick green leaves one above the other, and it terminated in a bud. The people of these parts used the juice in order to rouse in themselves diabolical ecstasies. On account of its inebriating vapors, the drink was prepared in the open air, though during the operation a tent was erected over the vat. The pressmen were just coming to their work when Jesus commanded the possessed, or rather the legion in them, to overturn the vat. The two men seized the great, full vat, turned it upside down without the least difficulty, the contents streamed around, and the workmen fled with cries of terror. The possessed, trembling and shuddering, returned to Jesus, and the disciples also were very much frightened. The devil now cried out by the mouth of the possessed, begging Jesus not yet to cast them into the abyss, not yet to drive them from this region, and ended by the request: "Let us go into yonder swine!" Jesus replied: "Ye may go!" At these words the two miserable possessed sank down in violent convulsions, and a whole cloud of vapors issued from their bodies in numberless forms of insects, toads, worms, and chiefly mole-crickets.

A few moments after, there arose from the herds of swine sounds of grunting and raging, and from the herdsmen shouts and cries. The swine, some thousands in number, came rushing from all quarters and plunged down through the bushes on the mountainside.[D24] It was like a furious tempest, mingled with the cries and bellowings of animals. This scene was not the work of a few minutes only. It lasted a couple of hours, for the swine rushed here and there, plunging headlong and biting one another. Numbers precipitated themselves into the marsh and were swept down over the waterfall, and all went raging toward the lake.

The disciples looked on disquieted, fearing lest the waters in which they fished, as well as the fish themselves, would be rendered impure. Jesus divined their thoughts, and told them not to fear, since the swine would all go down into the whirlpool at the end of the ravine. There was at this place a great pool of stagnant water completely separated from the lake by a sandbank, or strip of shore. It was overgrown with reeds and bushes, and at high water was frequently submerged. This pool was a deep abyss which, through the sandbank, had an inlet from the lake, but no outlet into the same, and in it was a whirlpool. It was into this caldron the swine plunged. The herdsmen who had, at first, run after the animals, now came back to Jesus, saw the possessed who had been delivered, heard all that had happened, and then began to complain loudly of the injury done them. But Jesus replied that the salvation of these two souls was worth more than all the swine in the world. Then he bade them go to the owners of the swine and say that the devil, whom the godlessness of the inhabitants of this country sent into men, had by him been driven out of the men, and that they had gone into the swine! The possessed who had been delivered, Jesus sent to their homes to procure clothing, while he himself with the disciples went up toward Gergesa. Several of the herdsmen had already run to the city and, in consequence of the reports they spread, people came pouring out from all sides. They that had been cured at Magdala, as well as the two Jewish youths cured the day before, and most of the Jews of the city, had assembled to wait for Jesus's coming. The two possessed, now cured, came back in a short time decently clothed, to hear Jesus's preaching. They were distinguished pagans belonging to the city, relatives of some of the pagan priests.

The people employed in preparing the wine mentioned above, and whose full vat had been overturned, were also running about the city, letting be known everywhere the loss they had sustained at the hands of the possessed. This gave rise to great alarm and uproar. Many ran to see whether they could rescue some of the swine, while others hurried out to the wine cask. The confusion lasted until after nightfall.

Jesus meanwhile was instructing on a hill about one-half hour from Gergesa. But the chief men of the city and the pagan priests sought to keep the people from him by telling them that Jesus was a mighty sorcerer through whom great evils would come upon them. When they had taken counsel together, they sent out a deputation to Jesus with instructions to hasten and beg him not to tarry in those parts and not to do them still greater injury. The deputies added that they recognized in him a great magician, but begged him to withdraw from their boundaries. They sorely lamented their swine and the overturning of their brewing vat. Their fright and amazement were extreme when they beheld the two possessed, cured and clothed, sitting among the listeners at Jesus's feet. Jesus bade them dismiss their fears, because he would not trouble them long. He had come for the sake of the poor sick and possessed alone, since he knew well that the unclean swine and the infamous beverage were of more value to them than the salvation of their souls. But the Father in heaven, who had given to him the power to rescue the poor people before him and to destroy the swine, judged otherwise. Then he held up to them all their infamy, their sinful dealing in sorcery, their dishonest gains, and their demonolatry. He called them to penance, to baptism, and offered them salvation. But they had the injury done them, the loss of the swine, in their heads, and so persisted in their pressing, though half-frightened request, that he would go away. After that they returned to the city. Judas Iscariot was particularly busy and active among the Gergeseans, for he was well-known in these parts. His mother had dwelt here with him for some time when he was still young, and just after he had run away from the family in which he had been secretly reared. The two possessed were acquaintances of his youth.

The Jews rejoiced in secret over the loss sustained by the Gentiles in their swine, for they were very much oppressed by them and greatly scandalized on account of the unclean animals. Still there were many among them who lived on easy terms with the pagans and defiled themselves with their superstitious practices.

All that had been cured on that day and the day before, as also the two possessed, were baptized by the disciples. They were very much impressed and thoroughly changed. The two possessed last delivered and the two Jewish youths entreated Jesus to allow them to remain with him and be his disciples. To the two last delivered, Jesus replied that he would give them a commission, namely, they should go through the ten villages of the Gergeseans, show themselves everywhere, and everywhere relate what had happened to them, what they had heard and seen, call the inhabitants to penance and baptism, and send them to him. He added that they should not be troubled if they were greeted by a shower of stones from those whom they addressed. If they executed this commission properly, they should receive in recompense the spirit of prophecy. Then they would always know where to find him, in order to send thither those that desired to hear his teachings, and they should impose hands on the sick, who would thereby be healed. Having thus spoken, Jesus blessed the two young men, who on the next day began their mission, and later on became disciples.

The apostles in baptizing here used water that they had brought with them in leathern bottles. The people knelt in a circle around them, and they baptized three at a time out of the basin that one held, sprinkling each three times with water scooped up in the hand.

That evening Jesus and the disciples entered Gergesa, and went to the house of the ruler of the synagogue. Then came the magistrates of the city urging the ruler to make Jesus depart as soon as possible, and threatening to hold him responsible for any further injury the city might sustain at his hands. Jesus told the disciples that he had permitted the demons to overturn the vat and to enter into the swine, that the proud pagans might see that he was the prophet of the Jews whom they so shamefully despised and oppressed. He wished at the same time, as he said, by the loss of the swine—in which so many of them bore a share—to draw the attention of these people to the danger that threatened their souls and to arouse them from the sleep of sin that they might hearken to his teaching. The beverage he had allowed to be wasted, as it was the principal cause of their vices and demoniacal possession.

Thursday, December 7, AD 30 (Kislev 22)

Jesus taught and healed for much of the day. Then he instructed the disciples to sail back to Bethsaida, while he withdrew into the hills alone to pray. That night, the disciples saw Jesus walking across the water toward them. (This was not the walking on the water described in Matthew 14:22–33, which took place later, on Shebat 16/17).

On the following day a great crowd again gathered around Jesus, for his miracles had become known throughout the whole country, and many Jews who had been converted left Gergesa at once.

The apostles, who had been healing in the villages nearby, returned in time for Jesus's discourse, bringing with them those they had cured. There were some women among them carrying baskets of provisions, which they gave to the apostles. Once when Jesus was closely pressed by the crowd, a woman from Magdala approached him. She was afflicted with an issue of blood. Though long unable to walk, she had gathered up strength to slip alone through the crowd and to kiss his garment, whereupon she was healed. Jesus went on with his discourse, but after a little while he said: "I have healed someone. Who is it?" At these words, the woman drew near, giving thanks. She had heard of Enue's cure, and had imitated her example. That evening Jesus, the disciples, and the two Jewish youths lately delivered from demoniacal possession, left Gergesa, journeyed around Magdala, and climbed the mountain north of Hippos. This last named place was not situated on the lake, but on a mountain some distance inland. Jesus and his followers descended on the opposite side and put up at a shepherd's house.

Here Jesus reminded the disciples that the birthday of Herod would soon be celebrated, and told them that he intended going to Jerusalem. They tried to dissuade him from doing so, saying that Passover was now not far off, and then they should be obliged to go. But Jesus replied in such a way as to give them to understand that he did not intend to show himself openly at the feast. The two Gergesean disciples again begged to be allowed to accompany him. Jesus replied that he had another mission in reserve for them, namely, to go around among the ten cities between Kedar and Paneas and announce to the Jews of those places all that they had seen and heard. He gave them his benediction and made them the same promises as to the other two. If they fulfilled their commission well, the spirit of prophecy should be given to them, they should always know his whereabouts, and should be able to heal the sick in his name. As with the others, so too with them, a certain time had to elapse before these promises would be realized. The two others had first to announce him in the ten Gergesean villages, and afterward to the pagans of the Decapolis. The youths bade farewell to Jesus, who directed the disciples to go to Bethsaida and, in spite of their entreaties, he himself remained behind. He retired into a wilderness near the shore to pray. I saw him walking about among the steep, rocky hills, some of which looked black and like human figures amid the darkness of night.

It was already quite dark when I saw Jesus walking straight over the waves. It was almost opposite Tiberias, a little eastward of the middle of the lake. He appeared as if intending to pass within a little distance of the disciples' boat. The high wind was contrary, and the disciples weary of rowing. When they saw the figure on the waves, they were affrighted, for they knew not whether it was Jesus or his spirit, and they cried aloud from fear. But Jesus called out: "Fear not! It is I!" Then Peter cried: "Lord, if it be thou, bid me come to thee upon the waters." And Jesus said: "Come!"

Peter, in his ardor, leaped on the little ladder and out of the boat. He hurried along for a short distance on the troubled waters toward Jesus, as if on level ground. It seemed to me that he hovered over the surface, for the inequality of the waves appeared to be no obstacle to his progress. But when he began to wonder, and to think more of the sea, its winds and its waves, than of the words of Jesus, he grew frightened and commenced to sink. Crying out, "Lord, save me!" He sank up to the breast and stretched out his hand. Instantly Jesus was at his side. He seized his hand and said: "O thou of little faith, why didst thou doubt?" Then they entered the boat, and Jesus reproached Peter and the others for their fear. The wind lulled immediately and they steered toward Bethsaida. A ladder was always in readiness to be thrown over the side of the boat for the convenience of those about to enter.

Jesus Cures in Bethsaida and again Returns to Capernaum

Friday, December 8, AD 30 (*Kislev 23*)

Soon after Jesus and the disciples landed at Bethsaida, two blind men approached him. Jesus healed them. The people knew that Jesus had come for the sabbath. Indeed, so many came to him that he did not have time even to eat (*Mark 3:20–21*). *Not far from Capernaum, a person who was blind and mute and filled with demons was brought to Jesus. Jesus healed him, evoking the crowd's astonishment* (*Matthew 12:22–23*). *But the Pharisees said that Jesus drove out demons with the help of the devil* (*Matthew 12:24*). *That evening, as the sabbath began, Jesus taught undisturbed in the synagogue, answering the Pharisees' accusation with the words reported in Matthew 12:25–30. That night, again, he stayed at Peter's house.*

TWO blind men came to meet Jesus on his arrival in Bethsaida, crying out to him for help and, as if to disprove the old saying, they were leading each other. Jesus restored their sight, cured also the lame and gave speech to the mute. Wherever he appeared, crowds pressed around him bringing to him their sick. Many touched him, and were cured. The people were everywhere expecting him, because they knew that he was coming again for the sabbath. The story of the two possessed and of the swine was already well-known here, and had excited great comment and astonishment. Some of the disciples baptized the cured at Peter's house. But as Jesus continued his labors and took no time either to eat or to rest, the disciples sought him out and tried to induce him to take some repose and refreshment.

When he went back to Capernaum, a man mute, blind, and possessed by the demon came to meet him, and Jesus cured him instantaneously. This miracle created intense astonishment, for even when approaching Jesus, the man had recovered his speech and cried out: "Jesus, thou Son of David, have mercy on me!" Jesus touched his eyes, and he saw.[D25] He was possessed of many devils, having been wholly perverted by the pagans on the other side of the lake. The sorcerers and soothsayers of the land of Gergesa had seized upon him. They dragged him around with them by a cord and exhibited him in other places, where they showed off his strength in all kinds of skillful feats. They showed how he, though blind and mute, still could accomplish everything, could know and understand all, could go everywhere, could bring everything and know everything by virtue of certain incantations, for all this the demon performed in him. These pagan sorcerers from Gergesa, who were ever wandering through the Decapolis and other cities, used the devil by means of that poor creature to help them earn their bread. If they journeyed over the sea, their miserable victim was not allowed to go on board a ship, but at the command of his masters, he was obliged to swim like a dog at its side. No one any longer troubled himself about him, for he was looked upon as forever lost. Most of the time he had no place of shelter. He lay in tombs and caves and endured all manner of ill-treatment from his cruel masters. The poor wretch had long been in Capernaum, and yet no one had led him to Jesus. Now, however, he went to him himself and was cured.

While Jesus was teaching in Peter's house near the city gate just before the sabbath began, a great tumult arose in Capernaum. The miracle of the swine and the deliverance of the mute and blind possessed had created great excitement. Several boats of Jews from Gergesa had crossed the lake to spread far and wide the report that Jesus cast out devils by the power of the devil. This irritated the people, and they gathered in large numbers outside the synagogue. As Jesus drew near to the city, the man possessed of the devil, as well as blind and mute, ran out through the streets to meet him. He was without a keeper and was followed by a crowd of people who became witnesses of his miraculous cure. They were so transported by it that they gave loud expression to their indignation against the Pharisees, who never wearied inveighing against Jesus, repeating again as they were now doing that he healed through the power of the devil. Among the crowd here assembled were many armed with a crossbow. These men called out to the Pharisees to desist from slandering Jesus, to recognize his power and acknowledge that never before had such things been done in Israel, and that no prophet before him had ever wrought such wonders. If they did not cease from obstinately opposing Jesus, they might depart from Capernaum, for that they (the people) could no longer support such abuse and ingratitude.

On hearing this, the Pharisees pretended to be quite subdued. One of them, a great, broad fellow, stepped out before the rest and craftily addressed the crowd. He said it was indeed true that never had such doctrines been heard, never had such doings, such wonders been seen in Israel, no prophet had ever performed the like. But he begged them to consider the circumstances attending the driving out of the demon from the man of Gergesa, as also those connected with the similar wonders wrought among them that very day. The man whom they had just seen delivered from the power of the devil, owing to his relations with the Gergeseans, just as good as belonged to them. In the critical examination of such things, one could not be too circumspect, etc., etc. Then he went on to give them a lengthy description of the kingdom of darkness. He described its orders and hierarchies, and showed how one is subordinate to another. Jesus, he said, had now a powerful spirit in league with him. If not, why had he not long ago delivered that furious demoniac? Why, if he were the Son of God, was he not able to banish the demons from the land of Gergesa, without going there in person? No! He was obliged first to go into that country, and conclude an agreement with the chief of the Gergesean demons. He had to make a bargain with that demon prince and give him the swine as his booty, for although inferior to Beelzebub, that prince was still of some consequence. And now since he had freed that man at Gergesa, he had, by virtue of the same agreement, delivered the one here in Capernaum through the power of Beelzebub. With much cunning and eloquence the Pharisee advanced the above and similar stuff. Then he begged his hearers to be calm and attend to the conclusion, for their own doings would show forth the fruit of all this excitement. The laborer no longer performed his task on working days, but ran around after the new teacher and his miracles, and the sabbath was turned into a day of din and uproar. Then he exhorted them to reflect, to go home at once and take some rest in preparation for the coming feast. By such persuasions he succeeded in inducing the people to disperse, and many of the light-minded were half convinced by his empty babble.

It was the eve of the Feast of the Dedication of the Temple. In the houses and schools stood pyramids of lighted lamps, while in the gardens and courtyards and at the fountains were lights and torches arranged in all kinds of figures. Jesus, followed by his disciples, entered the synagogue and taught unmolested, for his enemies were afraid of him. He knew their thoughts and in what terms they had addressed the people, and he made allusion to it in these words: "Every kingdom divided against itself shall not stand. And if Satan cast out Satan, he is divided against himself. How then shall his kingdom stand? And if I by Beelzebub cast out devils, by whom do your children cast them out?" With words like these Jesus silenced them and, without further contradiction, left the synagogue. He passed that night at Peter's.

Saturday, December 9, AD 30 (Kislev 24)

While Jesus visited the homes of Jairus, Cornelius, and Zorobabel, the disciples baptized at Peter's house. Jesus then visited his mother, telling her that next day he would be departing. He also comforted Martha, who was deeply saddened by Mary Magdalene's relapse. Before the sabbath ended, Jesus again taught the beatitude: "Blessed are the poor in spirit." At the end of the sabbath he returned to the synagogue, inveighing against the Pharisees' teaching that he drove out devils with the help of devils (Matthew 12:31–37).

The next day Jesus, accompanied by some of his disciples, visited Jairus's family, whom he consoled and exhorted to the practice of good. They were very humble and entirely changed. They had divided their wealth into three parts, one for the poor, one for the community, and the third for themselves. Jairus's old mother was especially touched and thoroughly converted to good. The daughter did not make her appearance until called, and then came forward veiled, her whole deportment breathing humility. She had grown taller. She held herself erect, and presented the appearance of one in perfect health. Jesus visited likewise the pagan centurion Cornelius, consoled and instructed his family, and then went with him to see Zorobabel, at whose house the conversation turned upon Herod's birthday and John. Both Zorobabel and Cornelius remarked that Herod had invited all the nobility, including themselves, to Machaerus for the celebration of his birthday, and they asked Jesus whether he would permit them to go. Jesus replied that if they dared to stand aloof from the evils that might there take place, it was not forbidden them to go, although it would be better if they could excuse themselves and remain at home. They expressed their indignation at Herod's adulterous life and John's imprisonment, and hoped confidently that Herod would set him at liberty on his birthday.

Jesus next visited his mother, with whom were then stopping Susanna Alpheus, Mary, the daughter of Cleophas of Nazareth, Susanna of Jerusalem, Dinah the Samaritan, and Martha. Jesus told them that he was going away the next morning. Martha was very sad on account of Magdalene's relapse into sin and the state of demoniacal possession in which she then was. She asked Jesus whether she should go to her, but he told her to wait awhile. Magdalene was now often like one beside herself. She yielded to fits of anger and pride, struck all that came in her way, tormented her maids, and was always arrayed in the most wanton attire. I saw her striking the man that lived as master in her house, and I beheld him returning her blows with ill-treatment. At times she fell into frightful sadness, she wept and lamented. She ran about the house seeking for Jesus and crying out: "Where is the teacher? Where is he? He has abandoned me!" and then fell into convulsions like epileptic fits.

One may imagine the pain of her brother and sister at beholding one of a noble family, one so richly endowed by nature, given up to so frightful a state.

What a touching sight, that of Jesus traversing the streets of Capernaum, his robe sometimes girded up, sometimes at full length; his motions so well regulated, and yet without stiffness; his step so gentle that he seemed rather to glide than to walk; his whole appearance, though breathing simplicity, so full of majesty that his like was never before seen! There was nothing strange in his look, no irresolution in his manner. He never took a false step, never a useless one. He cast no vain glance, made no aimless turn, and yet in all his bearing there was no trace of affectation or design.

Martha and Susanna had visited their inns on the way through Galilee to Samaria, for they exercised a kind of general superintendence, the other women seeing to those established in their own respective districts. They went together to the several inns, taking with them asses laden with all kinds of household necessaries. Once when Mara the Suphanite accompanied them, the report spread among the people that Mary Magdalene now went around with the women who provided for the needs of the prophet of Nazareth and his party. The Suphanite was in figure very like Magdalene, and neither of them was very well-known on this side of the Jordan. Besides being called Mara and the ill repute her past life had gained for her, the Suphanite also had anointed Jesus at a feast given by one of the Pharisees. She was consequently, even at this early date, confounded with Magdalene, a mistake that only increased with time among those not well acquainted with the community.

The holy women took care that their inns were well supplied with beds, coverlets, linen, woollen clothes, sandals, cups, jugs of balsam, oil, etc. Although Jesus had need of little, yet he was desirous that the disciples should not be a burden to others, and should find their necessary wants supplied. In this way he deprived the Pharisees of all reasonable cause of reproach.

The Mission of the Apostles and Disciples

AT the close of the sabbath, Jesus spoke again in the synagogue, inveighing in severe terms against the wickedness of the Pharisees in saying that he drove out devils through the power of the devil. He challenged them to say whether his actions and his teachings were not in perfect harmony, whether he did not practice what he preached. But they could allege nothing against him.

In Peter's house outside the city gate, Jesus taught on the beatitude: "Blessed are the poor in spirit," and made the application against the Pharisees. After that he prepared the disciples for their approaching mission.

Jesus would not longer remain in Capernaum—the crowd was too great and too excited. Many Gergeseans also had come hither, and they wanted to follow Jesus. They were poor, were habituated to a wandering life, and thought it would be a good thing to be supported by him. Besides this they were under the impression that Jesus would, like Saul or David, cause himself to be anointed king and then establish his throne in Jerusalem. But Jesus told them to go back to their homes, to do penance, to keep the commandments, and to practice the lessons they had heard from him. His kingdom, he said, was far different from what they imagined, and no sinner should have part therein.

Sunday, December 10, AD 30 (Kislev 25)

Today there occurred—for the first time—the sending out of the disciples. At about ten o'clock in the morning, with the twelve and about thirty other disciples, Jesus left Capernaum and went north in the direction of Saphet and Hanathon, accompanied by a large crowd. Around three in the afternoon, they approached Hanathon. Here Jesus and the disciples climbed a mountain used in former times by the prophets. Jesus had taught there less than one year ago, on Tebeth 12. This time, however, the crowd did not go up the mountain. On the mountain, Jesus addressed the disciples, giving them instructions and sending them out into the world with the words found in Matthew 9:36–10:16. Each of the twelve had a small flask of oil, and Jesus taught them how to use it for anointing and also for healing. Afterward, the disciples knelt in a circle around Jesus, and he prayed and laid his hands upon the head of each of the twelve. Then he blessed the remaining disciples. After embracing one another, the disciples set off, having received indications from Jesus as to where they should go and when they should return to him. Peter, James the Less, John, Philip, Thomas, Judas, and twelve other disciples remained with him. They all came down the mountain together. At the bottom, they met up with a crowd of people returning home from Capernaum. That night Jesus stayed in Bethanat (*Matthew 11:1*).

Jesus afterward left Capernaum, accompanied by the twelve and by thirty disciples. They directed their steps northward. Crowds of people were journeying along the same way. Jesus frequently paused to instruct sometimes this, sometimes that crowd, who then turned off in the direction of their homes. In this way he arrived at about three in the afternoon at a beautiful mountain, three hours from Capernaum and not quite so far from the Jordan. Five roads branched out from it, and about as many little towns lay around it. The people who had followed Jesus thus far now took their leave, while he with his own party, having first taken some refreshment at the foot of the mountain, began to ascend the height. There was a teacher's chair upon it, from which he again instructed the apostles and disciples upon their vocation.[D26] He said that now they should show forth what they had learned. They should proclaim the advent of the kingdom, that the last chance for doing penance had arrived, that the end of John's life was very near. They should baptize, impose hands, and expel demons. He taught them how they should conduct themselves in discussions, how to recognize true from false friends, and how to confound the latter. He told them that now none should be greater than the others. In the various places to which their mission called them, they should go among the pious, should live poorly and humbly, and be burdensome to none. He told them also how to separate and how again to unite. Two apostles and some disciples should journey together, while some other disciples should go on ahead to gather together the people and announce the coming of the former. The apostles, he said, should carry with them little flasks of oil, which he taught them how to consecrate and how to use in effecting cures. Then he gave them all the other instructions recorded in the Gospels on the occasion of their mission. He made allusion to no special danger in store for them, but said only: "Today ye will everywhere be welcomed, but a time will come wherein they will persecute you!"

After that the apostles knelt down in a circle around Jesus as he prayed and laid his hands upon the head of each; the disciples he only blessed. Then they embraced and separated.

Among the directions given to the apostles, Jesus had indicated to them the place and time at which they should again join him, in order to bring him news and exchange places with the disciples that remained with him. Six of the apostles continued with him: Peter, James the Less, John, Philip, Thomas, and Judas, besides twelve of the disciples. Among the latter were the three brothers James, Sadoch, and Heliachim (Mary Heli's son), Manahem, Nathaniel (also called Little Cleophas), and several others. The other six apostles had with them eighteen disciples, among whom were Joseph Barsabbas, Joseph Barsabbas, Saturnin, and Nathaniel Chased. Nathaniel, the bridegroom of Cana, did not travel around. He attended to other affairs for the community, and like Lazarus rendered service in his own immediate circle. All shed tears on separating. The apostles who were going forth on their mission descended the mountain by the eastern route leading to the Jordan, where I saw a place situated, Leccum by name, about a quarter of an hour from the river. When Jesus came down the mountain, he was again surrounded by a crowd returning home from Capernaum.

(Follow Map 24)

Monday, December 11, AD 30 (Kislev 26)

Jesus and the disciples who were with him journeyed to a place called Hukok. Not far from there was a well, where Jesus healed a blind man and also several people who were lame. Afterward, he taught in the synagogue at Hukok, speaking of the beatitudes and telling several parables. Jesus and the disciples then stayed the night with the chief elder of the synagogue.

From the foot of the mountain Jesus started with the disciples southward from Saphet, which was situated on another high mountain, to a place called Hukok. Before reaching this place, he was met by many people who received him and the disciples with expressions of great joy.

At a fountain a blind man and several cripples were awaiting Jesus's coming, and they now implored him for help. The blind man's eyes were infected with disease. Jesus ordered him to wash his face at the fountain. When he had done so, he anointed his eyes with oil, broke off a little twig from a bush nearby, held it before his eyes, and asked whether he saw it or not. The man answered: "Yes, I see a very tall tree." Jesus anointed his eyes once more and repeated his question, whereupon the man cast himself on his knees before him, crying out joyfully: "Lord, I see mountains, trees, people! I see everything!" There was great jubilation among the people as they escorted the man back into the city. Jesus went on curing the lame and the palsied who were standing around on crutches made of light but very firm wood. Each had three feet, so that it could stand alone; and when the two were crossed together, the sick could rest the breast against them.

When the blind man and his escorts went shouting with joy into the city, many of the inhabitants, the elders of the synagogue, and the school teachers with their scholars came flocking out to meet Jesus. They were full of joy. Jesus returned with them, went into the school and gave them some instructions in parables on the eight beatitudes. He exhorted all to penance, for the kingdom was near. He explained the parables at great length. The disciples were present. Before beginning, Jesus had recommended to them strict attention, in order that they might repeat what they heard when they scattered around among the houses and villages in the environs. It was thus that they acquired in Jesus's public discourses what they, in their turn, had to teach in the country around; for the apostles along with several of the disciples scattered as usual among the environs to cure and to teach. They met again in the evening at the place indicated by Jesus and to which he himself had gone. Here they stopped with the elder of the synagogue, who placed before them fish, honey, little rolls and fruit, of which they ate.

Hukok was situated about five hours to the northwest of Capernaum, five hours southwest of the mountain upon which Jesus had given the apostles their mission, and about three hours south of Saphet. There were none but Jews in the place, and they were tolerably good people, for most of them had received John's baptism. They manufactured stuffs of fine texture, narrow scarfs of wool, tassels and fringes of silk; they knit sandals also, under which they placed two supports like heels. These sandals were flexible in the middle, and very comfortable, for they allowed the dust to fall through holes made for that purpose.

Tuesday, December 12, AD 30 (Kislev 27)

Jesus healed many sick people in Hukok. In the synagogue, he spoke of the Messiah and of the significance of prayer. He said that the Messiah was already here; indeed, that they were living at the time of the Messiah, and that he, Jesus, was proclaiming the Messiah's teachings. He taught them devotion to God in spirit and in truth. The doctors of the synagogue asked Jesus, in a friendly way, whether he himself were the Messiah, the Son of God. Jesus did not answer directly. He said that they should not inquire into his origin but consider his teachings and actions. He spoke of the will of the Father (Matthew 12:50; John 5:30). That night, Jesus and the disciples stayed again at the house of the chief elder of the synagogue.

The apostles and several of the disciples with them scattered, two by two, throughout the city and its environs. Hukok must have once been a strong fortress, for it was

Map 24: The Journey Through Middle Galilee
December 10–27, AD 30

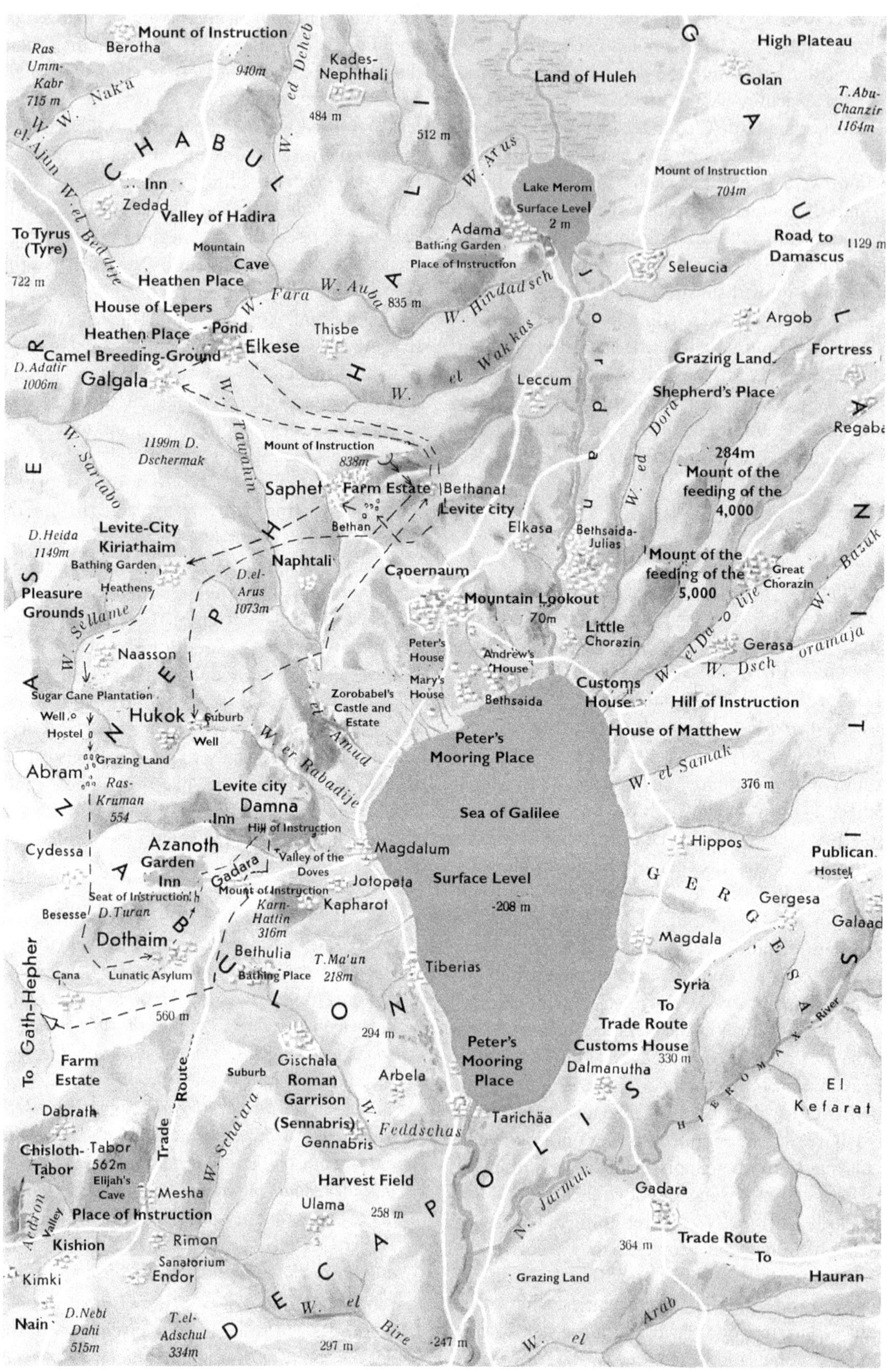

Mount of Instruction—Bethanat—Hukok—Bethanat—Galgala—Elkese—Bethan—Saphet
Kiriathaim—Plantation near Naasson—Abram—Dothaim—Azanoth—Damna

surrounded by moats now dry, and its approach was over a bridge. One could look through the gate far into the city and see its beautiful synagogue. Hukok was surrounded by verdant walks planted with trees so thick and high that, even at a short distance, its houses could not be seen. Its synagogue was extraordinarily beautiful. It was surrounded by a colonnade into which the main building could be opened for the accommodation of a more considerable crowd; opposite the entrance the wall was solid and formed a semicircle. It stood upon an open square at the end of the street upon which was the entrance. The whole city was well built and very clean. The people gathered into the synagogue. Jesus went first into two separate halls, in one healing many sick men, in the other women sick of all kinds of maladies. Many sick children were brought to him, some young enough to be carried in the arms, and he healed them. The healthy children he blessed.

In the synagogue Jesus taught of prayer and of the Messiah. He said that the Messiah had already come upon earth, that they (his hearers) were living in his time, that they were listening to his teachings. He spoke of the adoration of God in spirit and in truth, and I felt that it meant the adoration of the Father in the Holy Spirit and in Jesus Christ, for Jesus is the Truth. He is the true, the living, the incarnate God, the Son conceived of the Holy Spirit. At these words, the doctors of the synagogue humbly begged him to say who he really was, whence he came, whether they whom they looked upon as his parents were not his parents, his relatives not his relatives, whether he was really the Messiah, the Son of God. It would be well, they said, for the doctors of the Law to know positively what to think. Being placed over others, they before all others ought to know him. But Jesus answered them evasively. If he said, "I am he!" they would not believe him, but would say that he was the son of those people of whom they had spoken. They should not inquire into his origin, but should hear his doctrine and observe his actions. Whoever does the will of the Father is the Son of the Father, for the Son is in the Father and Father is in the Son, and whoever fulfills the will of the Son fulfills the will of the Father. Jesus spoke so beautifully on this subject and on that of prayer that many cried out, "Lord, thou art the Christ! Thou art the Truth!" and falling down they wished to adore him. But he repeated to them: "Adore the Father in spirit and in truth!" and he left the city with his disciples and the elder of the synagogue, at whose house they passed the night. In this suburb there was a school very well attended, but no synagogue. The Feast of Lights was still being celebrated.

Wednesday, December 13, AD 30 (Kislev 28)

This morning, again, Jesus taught in Hukok. Around midday, he set off in the direction of Bethanat. Not far from the town he was met by an old blind man, named Ctesiphon, led by two youths. Ctesiphon beseeched Jesus to have mercy on him. Jesus led him to a nearby fountain and commanded him to wash his eyes, after which Jesus anointed his forehead, temples, and eyes with oil. Ctesiphon's sight was immediately restored, and he gave profound thanks. Reaching Bethanat, Jesus taught at the synagogue, where he was well received by the people. There were no Pharisees in Bethanat.

Next day Jesus taught again in Hukok on the parable of the sower and the different ways in which the seed is received. Then he spoke of the good shepherd come to seek the lost sheep, and who would be happy to carry back even one on his shoulder. He said thus would the good shepherd do until his enemies put him to death; and thus also should his servants and his servants' servant do until the end of time. If at the end only one sheep was saved, yet would his love rest satisfied. Jesus spoke most tenderly on this point.

Jesus in Bethanat, Galgala, Elkese, and Saphet

The apostles and several of the disciples went on ahead, while Jesus with some of the others returned by the way he had come; that is, he went back to Bethanat, one hour and a half to the south of Saphet.

When within about half an hour of Bethanat, he was met by a blind man, who was led by two lovely boys in short, yellow tunics and large chip hats that shaded them from the sun. They were the children of Levites. The man was old and of honorable standing; he had long hoped for Jesus's coming. Accompanied by the boys, who had seen Jesus approaching, he hurried forward to meet him, crying out from a distance: "Jesus, thou Son of David, help me! Have mercy on me!" When he came up with him, he cast himself at his feet and said: "Lord, thou wilt certainly give me light again! I have awaited thee for so long, and for so long I have felt interiorly that thou wouldst come and cure me!" Jesus replied: "As thou hast believed, so be it done unto thee according to thy faith," and taking him to a fountain in the grove, he commanded him to wash his eyes. The man's eyes, as well as his whole forehead, were ulcerated and covered with a crust. When he had washed, the scales fell from his eyes. Then Jesus anointed them with oil, as also his forehead and temples. Sight immediately returned, and the man gave thanks. Jesus blessed him and the two boys, and predicted that they should at some future day announce the word of God.

They now drew near the city, outside which the apostles and other disciples again joined Jesus. Many of the citizens had here gathered, and when they saw the blind man coming back with his sight restored, their joy was quite extraordinary. The man's name was Ctesiphon. But he was not that blind Ctesiphon who likewise was cured, and who afterward became a disciple and went with Lazarus to Gaul.

Jesus, accompanied by the Levites and all the people, went to the synagogue, in which he delivered an instruction. The Feast of the Dedication, or the Feast of Lights as it was sometimes called, was still being celebrated, so that it was a kind of holiday. Jesus again explained the parables of the sower and of the good shepherd. The people were good and quite joyous over Jesus's coming among them. He stopped in the Levites' house near the school. There were no Pharisees in Bethanat. The Levites lived together as in a monastery and sent people out to other places.

Bethanat was once a fortified city and full of pagans, for the tribe of Naphtali, instead of exterminating them, had long held them tributary. But at this time there were no pagans in the city. They had been expelled when the temple was reestablished, when Esdras and Nehemiah had obliged the Jews to send away their pagan wives. The terrible threats that God made to his people by the prophets if they persevered in such alliances and refused to drive the pagans from the country, thereby exposing themselves to ever-present temptation to contract marriages with pagans, were fully realized; for around Tabor and in the chain between Endor and Scythopolis, where the peaks are so irregularly piled one on another, and where I saw so much gold hidden in the earth, the pagans had never been driven out, and the country had therefore become a wilderness.

Thursday, December 14, AD 30 (Kislev 29)

Jesus and his disciples made their way north toward Galgala, where Jesus taught in the synagogue. He spoke of the prophet Malachi's prophecy concerning the coming of the Messiah and his forerunner, saying that the time of fulfillment had come. Afterward, Jesus went on to the town of Elkese, the birthplace of the prophet Nahum. Here he taught and cured eight lepers at the local leper house. Later, toward evening, he went to Bethan, and visited a niece of Elizabeth, who lived there with her husband and five children. They were Essenes. The sons later became disciples and were among the original seventy-two.

From Bethanat Jesus went with the apostles and disciples northward around Saphet to Galgala, a large, beautiful place through which ran a great highway. He went with his followers to the synagogue. There were some Pharisees in this city. Jesus preached vehemently against them, explained all the passages of the prophet Malachi that spoke of the Messiah, the precursor John, and of the new, clean Sacrifice. He ended by announcing that the time for the fulfillment of these prophecies had arrived.

From Galgala Jesus went eastward to Elkese, which lay to the north of Saphet, and where the prophet Nahum was born. Here he taught for a short time and visited the leper hospital, where he cured about eight of the inmates and commanded them to show themselves to the priests in Saphet. He also taught the shepherds. I saw in the fields around Elkese grass of extraordinary height, and in it numbers of camels grazing. Jesus went likewise to a mountain containing many caves, in which dwelt pagans, whom he instructed. The whole day was spent in walking, instructing and curing, for everywhere on the roads the sick and suffering were brought to Jesus.

Toward evening he arrived at Bethan, which lay to the west under the heights of Saphet and about one hour from Bethanat. It was a little place, a colony from Bethanat, and was situated so near to the steep, western heights of Saphet that from them they could look down upon the little town. Jesus and the disciples put up here with some relatives, for the daughter of Elizabeth's sister was married at Bethan. She had five children, of whom the youngest girl was about twelve years old. The sons were already from eighteen to twenty. This family, with some others disposed like themselves, lived apart in a row of houses built near the walls of the city. Some were built in the rocks, some in the walls themselves. All belonged to the married Essenes, and the husband of Elizabeth's niece was the superior. The family owned here some property inherited from their forefathers. They were very pious people. They spoke to Jesus of John and asked him with anxiety whether or not he would soon be set at liberty. Jesus replied in words that made them very grave and sad, though without disturbing their peace of mind.

John had visited them when he came first from the source of the Jordan in the wilderness, and they had been among the first to go to his baptism. They spoke to Jesus of their sons, whom they intended soon to send to the fishery at Capernaum. Jesus replied that those fishermen, that is Peter and his companions, had begun another kind of fishing, and that their young sons also would follow him in their own good time. They did indeed join the seventy-two. Jesus taught and cured here. I heard him saying that the other disciples were then on the confines of Sidon and Tyre, and that he himself would go back to Judea. I saw that Thomas showed great pleasure at the prospect of this journey, because he anticipated opposition on the part of the Pharisees and hoped to be able to dispute with them. He expressed his sentiments to the other disciples, but they did not appear to share his satisfaction. Jesus reproved his exaggerated zeal, and told him that a time would come when his own faith would waver. But Thomas could in nowise understand his words.

Friday, December 15, AD 30 (Kislev 30)

This morning Jesus spoke in the synagogue about the second beatitude. In the afternoon he taught again, and some Pharisees from Saphet came to hear him. They invited him to Saphet for the sabbath, and Jesus accepted their invitation. He was received with much ceremony, and went straightaway to the synagogue, where a great crowd had assembled. It was not only the start of the sabbath but also the close of the Feast of Lights; at the same time, it was the New Moon Festival denoting the beginning of the month of Tebeth.

While Jesus was teaching on the beatitudes in the school at Bethan, the Pharisees of Saphet came down to invite him to their city for the sabbath. He explained before them the parable of the seed falling on different kinds of ground, but they would not understand the allusion contained in the rocky soil. They disputed the point with him, but he soon reduced them to silence. When they invited him for the sabbath, he replied that he would go with them for the sake of the lost sheep, but that both they and the Sadducees (some of whom were at Saphet) would be scandalized on his account. They replied: "Rabbi, leave that to us." Jesus responded that he knew them well, and that their unrighteousness filled the land. He went up to Saphet, followed by many from Bethan. Saphet on this side was built on so steep a part of the mountain that frequently the roof of one house was on a level with the ground floor of another. The road lay far below the houses, to which one had to mount by steps hewn in the rock. It took half an hour to climb up to the synagogue, where the mountain assumed the form of a great plateau whose northeastern declivity was not so steep. Outside the city Jesus was received with solemn ceremony by many good people. They surrounded him waving green branches and singing canticles. Then they washed his feet, as well as those of the disciples, and offered them the customary refreshments. Thus attended, Jesus reached the synagogue, where a great crowd was assembled. The Feast of the Dedication closed today, and they were celebrating that of the new moon as well as the sabbath; besides all this, the desire to see Jesus and his disciples added to the numbers present.

Saphet could boast of many Pharisees, Sadducees, scribes, and simple Levites. There was a kind of religious school here, in which youths were educated in all the Jewish liberal arts and in theology. Thomas, a couple of years before, had been a student at this school. He went now to visit one of the head teachers, a Pharisee, who expressed his wonder at seeing him in such company. But Thomas silenced him by his zealous defence of Jesus's actions and teachings. Some Pharisees and Sadducees from Jerusalem had managed to insinuate themselves into this school, and their arbitrary dealings rendered them insupportable to even the Pharisees and teachers of the place. Among them were some of those who had sent for Jesus. They addressed him in a very insinuating speech in which, alluding to his fame and his miracles, they suggested that he should raise no excitement or commotion in their city. They had been very much scandalized at the solemn reception tendered him by the people. As the sabbath had not yet begun, Jesus replied to them in the outer porch before all the people. He spoke in very strong language of the disturbance and scandal which, owing to their efforts, had been spread throughout the country. He, however, mentioned nothing in particular, though he challenged them to upbraid him with anything wherein he had violated the Law, he who had been sent by his Father for its perfect accomplishment.

While thus disputing with them, the lepers whom he had healed the day before at Elkese presented themselves to fulfill his order to go to the priests for inspection. Jesus exclaimed: "Behold how I fulfill the Law! I ordered these men to appear before you, although they had no obligation to do so, since they were made clean instantaneously by the command of God, and not by the skill of man." This encounter greatly vexed the Pharisees, who went nevertheless to examine into the cure. It was usual in such cases merely to inspect the breast. If that was clean, the whole person was judged to be the same. The Pharisees, astounded and vexed, were forced to declare these men freed from the ban of leprosy.

Besides the passages of scripture appointed for this particular sabbath, Jesus taught from Genesis, from the First Book of Kings, and likewise upon the Ten Commandments. He dwelt upon several points deduced from his texts, which both Pharisees and Sadducees felt in their hearts were thrusts at themselves. He spoke of the fulfillment of the Promises and announced the chastisement of God upon all that would not profit by his exhortations to penance. He alluded to the destruction of the temple and the ruin of many cities. He spoke of the true Law, which they did not comprehend, and of their own law of yesterday, as he denominated it, which he absolutely condemned. I understood that he meant by this latter something like the Jewish books of the present day, the Talmud, I think, because here at Saphet they were especially esteemed and studied.

The exercises of the synagogue over, Jesus and the disciples went to the house of one of the Pharisees of the place, who kept a public inn for teachers and rabbis. The other Pharisees also took part in the repast. During the meal Jesus read the Pharisees a severe lecture, because they reproached the disciples for not washing their hands before coming to table and for neglecting other observances customary before eating. He likewise checked them for their ridiculous fastidiousness respecting the serving up of the food, for they were accustomed to reprehend the servers for the slightest stain upon the dishes or their contents.

TEBETH (29 days): December 15/16, AD 30, to January 12/13, AD 31, Tebeth New Moon: December 13, AD 30 at 4:30 PM Jerusalem time

Saturday, December 16, AD 30 (Tebeth 1)

This morning Jesus healed the sick, the deaf, the blind, the palsied, and the lame. Some Pharisees and Sadducees, visiting Saphet from Jerusalem, were scandalized at what they saw. They could not tolerate such a disturbance on the sabbath and therefore began to dispute with Jesus, saying that he did not observe the Law. Jesus reduced them to silence by writing an account of their secret sins and transgressions on a wall in Old Hebrew, which only they could read. Then he asked them whether they wanted the writing to remain on the wall and become known publicly, or whether they would allow him to continue his work in peace, in which case they could efface the writing. Thoroughly frightened, they rubbed out the writing and went away to leave him to continue his work of healing the sick.

Next morning numbers of very sick persons, some of them aged, were brought and ranged in the courtyard before the house in which Jesus was stopping. It had cost their friends no little trouble to bring them from the pathless, mountainous city. Jesus began to cure them one after another. Some were deaf; others blind, palsied, lame; in a word, there were sick of all kinds among them. Jesus made use of prayer, the imposition of hands, consecrated oil, and in general of more ceremonies than usual. He spoke with the disciples, taught them to make use of this manner of curing, and exhorted the sick according to their various needs.

The Pharisees and Sadducees from Jerusalem were very much scandalized at all that they saw. They wanted to send away some of the newly arrived sick, and they began to quarrel. They would by no means tolerate such disturbance on the sabbath, and so great a tumult arose that Jesus, turning to them, inquired what they wanted. And now they began a dispute with him on the subject of his teaching, especially of his constant reference to the Father and the Son. "But," they said, "we know well whose son thou art!" Jesus replied that whoever does the will of the Father is the son of the Father. But that he who does not keep the commandments has no right to raise his voice in judgment upon others; he should rather rejoice at not being cast out of the house as an intruder. But they continued to allege all sorts of objections against his cures, to accuse him of not having washed before the meal of the preceding evening, and to repudiate his charge against them of not keeping the Law. They went so far that Jesus, to their exceedingly great terror, began to write on the wall of the house, and in letters that they alone could decipher, their secret sins and transgressions. Then he asked them whether they wanted the writing to remain upon the wall and become publicly known, or whether, effacing it, they would permit him to continue his work in peace. The Pharisees were thoroughly frightened. They rubbed out the writing and slunk away, leaving Jesus to continue his cures. These Pharisees had been guilty of embezzlement of the public funds. Legacies and donations intended for the foundation of homes for widows and orphans they had used for the erection of all kinds of magnificent buildings. Saphet was rich in such establishments, and yet there were to be found in it numbers of poor, miserable creatures.

That evening Jesus closed the instructions in the synagogue, and passed the night in the same house. There was a fountain near the synagogue. The mountain of Saphet was beautiful and green, covered with numerous trees and gardens. The roads were bordered by sweet-scented myrtles. High up on the plateau were large, four-cornered houses and solid foundations around which could be erected tent habitations. This city was largely engaged in the manufacture of vestments for the priests, and it was full of students and learned men.

Jesus in Kiriathaim and Abram

Sunday, December 17, AD 30 (Tebeth 2)

About midday, after healing people on the outskirts of Saphet, Jesus went on to Kiriathaim. Before entering the town, he blessed a group of children. Then he made his way to the synagogue, healing the sick on the way. In the synagogue Jesus again taught the beatitudes and—addressing the Levites—interpreted a passage from 1 Kings 6:15–19.

JESUS went with the disciples around the environs of Saphet and cured many sick who had been brought out of the houses and laid on the road by which he was to pass.

Early in the morning he sent one of the nephews of Joseph of Arimathea, along with Seraphia's son, to the neighboring town of Kiriathaim, about three hours from Saphet, with a commission to prepare the inn. He and the disciples left Saphet sometime after. The disciples scattered here and there on the road, while Jesus also went along teaching and healing. He went first westward between Bethan and Elkasa, after which the road turned toward the south. Somewhat beyond Elkasa—near which was a beautiful mountain—lay a little, oval lake as large as that near the baths of Bethulia. It was the source of a stream that flowed down into the valley which, southeast of Kiriathaim, declined into that of Capernaum. This valley was narrow in some parts, wide in others, and extended seven hours before reaching Capernaum.

On the way to Kiriathaim Jesus was met by some demoniacs who entreated him to help them. They told him that the disciples had not been able to relieve them, and that they thought he could do better than they. Jesus replied that if the disciples had not relieved them, it was not the fault of the disciples but their own want of faith, and he commanded them to go to Kiriathaim and remain fasting until he should deliver them. He let them wait awhile and do penance. Half an hour from Kiriathaim, Jesus was received by the Levites of the place, the school teachers accompanied by their children, and many of the good inhabitants who had come out to meet him. The two disciples who had gone on ahead to prepare the inn were also there. They received Jesus near a bathing garden, which was supplied with water conducted through a canal from that little stream of which I have spoken. The garden was full of beautiful trees, flowers, and covered walks, and enclosed by a rampart and an astonishingly dense hedge. They washed the feet of Jesus and his disciples and entertained them with the usual refreshments.

Jesus here instructed the children for a little while and gave them his blessing. It may have been nearly five o'clock when they started for the city, which lay upon a hill overlooking the valley. The whole way to the synagogue Jesus healed many sick of all kinds whom he met in the streets. In the synagogue he again taught on the beatitudes, also of the punishment of those Levites that had dared to lay their hands upon the Ark of the Covenant. And yet greater chastisements, he said, would fall upon those that would lay hands on the Son of Man, of whom the Ark was only a symbol.

Monday, December 18, AD 30 (Tebeth 3)

Jesus taught in the town park. Peter and James the Less, assisted by some other disciples, baptized about a hundred people. That evening, Jesus taught in the synagogue on the beatitudes.

While in Kiriathaim, Jesus put up at a hired inn which had been furnished with necessaries out of the common stock of the community by the two disciples sent on ahead. The food was prepared at a house in the city, where also cooking for the sick was done. The Levites ate with Jesus and the disciples. Kiriathaim was a Levitical city, and in it were no Pharisees. A couple of its families were related to Zechariah. Jesus visited them and found them very much troubled on John's account. He recalled to them the wonders that had preceded and accompanied John's birth, and spoke of his mission and wonderful life. He reminded them likewise of many circumstances attendant on the birth of Mary's son, showed them that John's fate lay in the hands of God, and that he would die when he had fulfilled his mission. Jesus prepared them in this way for John's death.

The possessed whom he had sent to Kiriathaim on the preceding day, and many other sick, accosted him near the synagogue on the subject of their cure. He healed several, but others he sent away to fulfill certain prescriptions of fasting, alms-giving, and prayer. He did this here rather than elsewhere, because the people of this place were earnest in the keeping of the Law. After that he repaired with the disciples to the garden in which he had been received, where he taught and the disciples baptized. Encamped under tents in the neighborhood were pagans awaiting Jesus's coming. They had already been in Capernaum, whence they had been ordered here. There were in all about a hundred baptized. They stood in the water around a basin. Peter and James the Less baptized, while the others laid their hands on the neophytes.

In the evening Jesus taught in the synagogue, his subject being the eight beatitudes. He spoke also of the false consolation of the false prophets who had rejected the menaces of the true whose prophecies had, nevertheless, been fulfilled. He repeated his threats against those who would not receive him who was sent by God.

Tuesday, December 19, AD 30 (Tebeth 4)

Today Jesus and his disciples went southward from Kiriathaim, toward a place called Naasson, where there was a sugar cane plantation, where Jesus paused to teach. Then he made his way to Abram, and taught there that evening. After teaching, he retired to an inn outside of the town.

Leaving Kiriathaim, Jesus went with the disciples toward the south. He was as solemnly escorted on his departure by the Levites and schoolchildren as he had been received on his entrance. The people of Kiriathaim were engaged in the transportation of goods and the manufacture of vestments for priests out of the silk that they imported from afar. On the southern declivity of the opposite side of the valley, where lay a place called Naasson, there was a sugar cane plantation whose products formed a staple of trade. Jesus ascended that height, while the disciples scattered among some of the places more to the east of the valley. Jesus taught near Naasson those whom he met coming from Capernaum, among them some idolaters. On such occasions Jesus was frequently accompanied a part of his way by crowds. I saw him curing several, among others two poor cripples who were lying on the roadside. He took them by the hand and commanded them to rise. They immediately wanted to follow him, but he forbade them to do so. He traversed another valley, arrived at a height situated before the city of Abram in the tribe of Asher, and put up at an inn outside the city, where were found beautiful gardens and pleasure grounds. There were only two disciples with Jesus when he entered the inn, the others not having yet arrived. The country here on the eastern side of the high ridges that run from Libanus down to the valley of Zebulon was rich in meadowland and very charming. Herds of cattle and camels were grazing in the high grass. Westward toward the lake, orchards were more numerous.

Abram was situated about three hours south of Kiriathaim. But Jesus, not having followed the direct route, was certainly five hours on his journey thither.

In the evening Thomas, John, and Nathaniel joined Jesus in the inn. The others were still in the neighboring towns.

Wednesday, December 20, AD 30 (Tebeth 5)

This morning the steward of the inn laid a dispute before Jesus and begged him for a decision. The dispute concerned a well, used by cattle from two different tribes. At issue was the question as to which tribe was really entitled to use the well. Jesus replied that each side should set an equal number of cattle free, and from whichever side the greater number went to the well of their own accord, this side should have the greater right to use of the well. He then employed this as an analogy for the living water that the Son of Man would give—that it would belong to those who most earnestly desired it. Then, around ten o'clock, Jesus went into Abram. On the way to the synagogue in Abram, Jesus cured many of the sick and crippled who were lying in the street. Reaching the synagogue, he taught there, but only in the Pharisees' synagogue, not in the Sadducees' synagogue. That evening, he went to an inn at the southern end of the town. This inn had been placed at the disposal of Jesus and the disciples by Lazarus.

The mountain upon which Abram was built formed in its length the boundary between Naphtali and Zebulon. The steward of the inn laid before Jesus a dispute, which he begged him to decide. It had reference to the wells in the vicinity used for watering the cattle. As the two tribes were so near each other in this place and their pasturage so extensive, altercations on the subject of the wells were frequent. The host thus addressed Jesus: "Lord, we will not let thee go until thou dost decide our quarrel." Jesus's decision was something like this: They should from each side set free an equal number of cattle, and from whichever side the greater number went of their own accord to the wells, that side should have the greater right to the said wells. Jesus drew from this circumstance matter for a profoundly significant instruction on the living water that he himself would give them, and which would belong to those that most earnestly desired it.

Around 10 o'clock the next day Jesus went into Abram, which was in two sections and on two different roads. It was like two separate villages interspersed with numerous gardens. The teachers of the school came out of the city to meet Jesus, washed his feet, and escorted him to the synagogue. On the way thither, he cured many sick and crippled whom he found lying on the street, also some old people languishing from weakness; and some demoniacs who, though not actually furious, were running about muttering to themselves like silly, vicious creatures. They came involuntarily to where Jesus was, again and again repeating the words: "Jesus of Nazareth! Jesus! Prophet! Thou Son of God! Jesus of Nazareth!" Jesus delivered them by a blessing. In the synagogue he taught of the beatitudes and from some passages of the prophet Malachi.

There were in Abram Sadducees, Pharisees, and Levites, also two synagogues, for each section of the city had its own. The Sadducees had their own special synagogue, but Jesus did not teach in it. The Pharisees conducted themselves very politely toward Jesus. His inn was distant, about a good quarter of an hour from the southern end of the city, and was one of those established by Lazarus for his convenience. The steward was a married Essene, a descendant of the family of that Zechariah who was murdered between the temple and the altar. His wife was the granddaughter of one of Anne's sisters. They had grown children, and possessed herds and meadows near that field in which Joachim had tarried before Mary's conception. Having little occupation at home, they had come hither to take charge of the inn; later on they were relieved by others. Like all the others, this inn was supplied with all kinds of necessaries, though not with superfluities. It had also its garden, its field, and its well.

There were no pagans in Abram, but down the mountain were some groups of houses inhabited by them.

The apostles and disciples whom Jesus had left near Kiriathaim came back again to the inn, as did also Andrew and Matthew. Thomas and James the Less went instead of them to Achzib in the tribe of Asher, between ten and twelve hours westward. Twenty men accompanied Andrew; some were strangers, and some had been cured and wanted to hear Jesus's instructions. The two apostles related how things had gone with them, how all had prospered with them, namely, healing, exorcising, preaching, and baptizing. Many sick and many seeking advice and consolation came to Jesus's inn. Most of them were cripples with deformed limbs, old, emaciated people, demoniacs, and infirm females, the latter of whom were in a chamber apart. The paralytics whom Jesus had healed the day before wanted to render assistance near the other sick. But he refused their help, saying that he was come to serve and not to be served.

Thursday, December 21, AD 30 (Tebeth 6)

All morning, Jesus taught and healed at the inn. He continued his healing activity and preached again at the synagogue, where the Pharisees treated him with respect.

Jesus taught and healed the whole morning, and had besides to settle a dispute concerning the wells. As the confines of Asher, Naphtali, and Zebulon here met, and the people carried on cattle raising, there arose frequent discussions on the subject of the wells. One man complained that another made use of the well that his ancestors had dug. He submitted the case to Jesus, saying that he would abide by his decision, though he did not wish to sacrifice lightly the rights of his children. Jesus decided that he should bore for a well in another field, which he pointed out to him. There he would find better and more abundant water. Between twenty and thirty Jews were baptized, among them those that had come hither with Andrew and Matthew. As there was here no brook in which they could stand, the neophytes knelt in a circle, and were baptized out of a basin with the hand. After that Jesus went into the city.

They whom Jesus cured in the city were for the most part affected with maladies similar to those already described. Their sufferings must have had some connection with the elevated situation of the city and the occupations in which they were engaged. Jesus took much notice of the children, who were standing in rows on the street corners and public squares, waiting for him. He questioned them, instructed them, and gave them his blessing. The mothers brought to him their sick little ones, and he healed them. Numbers of people from the country around had here assembled.

The Pharisees behaved most courteously to Jesus in the synagogue. They resigned the first place to him, and gave the disciples seats around their Master, before whom they laid the rolls of scripture. Jesus taught first on one of the eight beatitudes, then on the great persecutions that were to come upon himself and his followers, and lastly, of the heavy chastisement, the destruction that was to befall Jerusalem and the whole country. The Pharisees, according to their custom, interrupted him at times to ask for an explanation upon this or that point.

The people of Abram were very industrious. They prepared and sold cotton, of which wide strips moderately fine were made; they also wove something like flax. The thick stalk, after being split into fine strips, was passed over a sharp bone, or wooden instrument in order to detach the fine, long fibers. They were yellowish and shining, and were spun into the tunics worn when walking. It was neither flax nor hemp such as we have. They were engaged also in the manufacture of covers for tents and light screens of wood and matting.

Friday, December 22, AD 30 (Tebeth 7)

At a house in Abram, Jesus gave instruction on the meaning of the state of marriage to three couples, who were about to be married. He spoke of the Law, but now the situation was different, Jesus said. The time of fulfillment had come and Grace should take the place of the Law. As Jesus delivered this instruction, not only were the three bridal couples present but also their parents, relatives, and some Pharisees. That evening, while he was teaching at the synagogue, the Pharisees attacked Jesus for his teaching concerning marriage.

Jesus and the apostles spent the whole of the following morning and a part of the afternoon among some of the houses in the southern quarter of the city, teaching, consoling, reconciling enemies and exhorting them to union, charity, and peace. When a family counted many members, Jesus taught them alone; but, as a general thing, the neighbors were called in. All disputes were adjusted, all differences arranged. These visits of Jesus were mostly made to those houses in which were old, bedridden people who could not be present at the instructions in the synagogue. Some very old men received baptism in their beds. Two of them could sit upright only with support, and they were baptized out of a basin.

On the first day of his entrance into Abram, Jesus had instructed a couple for matrimony, and assisted at the nuptials. In another house there were now three other couples in expectation of the same. When the parents, the nearest relatives, and some of the Pharisees were assembled for the ceremony, Jesus instructed them upon marriage. He spoke of the wife's submission in obedience to the Law, which followed the first sin as its consequence, though the husband should honor in his wife the Promise: "The seed of the woman shall crush the head of the serpent." But now that the time of fulfillment was drawing near, Grace took the place of the Law. The wife should now obey through reverence and humility, and the husband command with love and moderation. In this instruction Jesus said that the question as to how sin had entered the world was an unnecessary one. It had come from disobedience, but salvation was to spring from faith and obedience. He alluded also to divorce, which, he said, could never take place, since husband and wife are one in the flesh. If, however, their living together was the occasion of great sins, then indeed they might separate, though without the liberty of marrying again. The Law had been made when the human race was in its infancy and in its early rude state; but now that they were no longer children and that the fullness of time had arrived, the remarrying of divorced spouses was a violation of the eternal law of nature. The privilege of separating was a concession granted when there was danger of offending God and only after a period of serious trial. Jesus delivered this instruction in the beautiful family mansion belonging to the parents of one of the bridal couples. All the young affianced were present, the brides separated from the grooms by a curtain, at one end of which Jesus stood. The parents also stood in order, the fathers on one side, the mothers on the other, while some of the disciples and Pharisees were grouped around Jesus.

This instruction on marriage gave rise to the first occasion for the Pharisees of this place to oppose Jesus. Nevertheless they did not begin their dispute at once, but waited till evening when Jesus was teaching in the synagogue upon the oppression of the children of Israel in Egypt, and developing some passages from Isaiah. Here they attacked his doctrine on marriage. With regard to the wife's submission, they found him too mild, and in respect to the divorce question, too severe. They had, they affirmed, previously consulted numerous writings on that subject, and in spite of his repeated explanations, they could not accept his teaching. Although the dispute was warmly maintained, yet were the limits of decorum never overstepped.

Next day Jesus assisted with two of the disciples at the marriage ceremony of the young couples. He even acted as witness. They were married facing the chest that contained the Law and under the open heavens, for they had opened the cupola of the synagogue. I saw that both parties allowed some drops of blood from the ring finger to fall into a glass of wine, which they then drank. They exchanged rings and went through other ceremonies. After the religious rites came the celebration of the nuptials, beginning with dance and banquet and merry-making, to all of which Jesus and the disciples were invited. The festivities took place in the beautiful public hall, which was supported by a colonnade. The bridal couples were not all from the city, but from the neighboring localities. They celebrated their nuptials here together, according to an agreement they had made to that effect when the news of Jesus's coming was announced. Some of them, indeed, had been present with their parents at his instructions in Capernaum. The people of this region were particularly good-natured and sociable. The weddings of the poorer were now celebrated with those of the rich, greatly to the advantage of the former.

I remarked that the guests brought certain presents, and that Jesus, in his own name and that of the disciples, made the young couples a gift in money. They, in their turn, sent back the money to his inn, and over and above as a present some baskets of nice wedding bread, all which Jesus caused to be distributed to the poor.

The feast began by a bridal dance in slow and measured step. The brides were veiled. The couples stood facing one another, and each bridegroom danced once with each bride. They never touched one another, but grasped the ends of the scarf that they held in their hands. The dance lasted one hour, because each groom danced once with all the brides separately, and then all danced together. Besides this, the step was very slow.

Then followed the banquet, at which the men and women were, as usual, separated. The musicians were children, little boys and girls, with crowns of wool on their heads and wreaths of the same on their arms. They played on flutes, little twisted horns, and other instruments. The banqueting tables were so placed that the guests could hear without seeing one another. Jesus went to that of the brides and related a parable, something in the style of that of the ten wise and the ten foolish virgins. He explained it in quite a homely way adapted to the occasion, though at the same time his words were full of spiritual signification. He told each how she should acquit herself of the duties of her new, domestic position and what provisions she should lay up for that. His instructions contained a spiritual sense, and were suited to the particular character and shortcomings of the one to whom they were addressed.

The banquet over, then came the game of riddles. The enigmas written on slips of paper were thrown on a board that was full of holes, through which they fell into bags. Everyone had to solve the particular enigma that had fallen into his or her bag, or else pay a forfeit. The unsolved riddles were again and again thrown on the board, and the one that was so fortunate as to solve them at last, could claim all that had been previously lost on their account. Jesus looked on during the game, making happy and instructive applications of all that took place.

At the close of the festivities, Jesus and the disciples returned to their inn outside the city, whither they were conducted with lighted torches.

Saturday, December 23, AD 30 (Tebeth 8)

After teaching again this morning in the synagogue in Abram, Jesus first visited a school for boys and youths and then a school for girls, where he taught and blessed the young people. At the service at the close of the sabbath Jesus spoke again and took leave of the people of Abram, who were deeply moved and begged him to stay. That evening, before returning to his inn, he took part in the further wedding festivities.

After Jesus had again taught in the synagogue, he visited the school of the boys and youths, whom he questioned and instructed, and then took leave of several people. After the repast, at the time generally spent in promenading on the sabbath, Jesus with two of his disciples visited a girls' school. It was, besides, a kind of embroidering establishment.

The little girls were between the ages of six and fourteen. There were a great many of them, and today they were in their fine clothes. Two doctors of the Law were present, and they too were in holiday attire, wearing broad girdles around their waists and long maniples on their sleeves. Every day they explained to the children some part of the Law. About ten widows superintended the affairs of the school. Besides instruction in reading the Law, in writing and reckoning, the girls worked at embroidery intended for sale.

Through a series of halls were extended long strips of different materials, some four feet in width, some narrower, of the breadth of a broad girdle. The finished end was always rolled up. The pattern from which the young embroiderers worked lay before them painted on a piece of stuff. It was made up of flowers and leaves and little branches and serpentine lines, all forming large figures. The material upon which they worked was woven of very fine wool, something like the light mantles worn by the three holy kings, only it was rather stronger in texture and of different colors. The children worked with fine, colored wool, also with silk, yellow being one of the principal colors. They did not use needles, but little hooks. Some also worked on white strips that were narrower than the rest. Others were engaged on girdles, upon which they embroidered certain letters. The little girls stood at their work, one next the other. Their occupation was assigned them according to their age and talent. I saw some of the little ones preparing the threads, others smoothing the wool, and others spinning. All that the embroiderers needed, such as thread and instruments, was handed them by the younger ones. On this day they were not working. While the children were showing their work to Jesus as he passed through the halls with the superintendents, the whole business of the institution was shown me in a tableau. I saw also that some of the girls embroidered figures, large and small, upon separate pieces of stuff which were private orders intended for sale, and these they showed to Jesus. The pagans exchanged all kinds of things for them.

Some of the girls lived in the house, of which two stories were given up to the business, and others came from the city. There was also a hall for instructions, and there Jesus taught and catechized the children, who held little rolls in their hands. The smallest stood in front, their mistresses behind them. The children advanced, one row at a time, to Jesus's chair. When he had blessed them and instructed them in familiar similitudes drawn from their work, he left the house, though not until they had presented him with some strips of stuff and girdles, which they sent to his inn for him. He afterward gave them to the different synagogues. Jesus then closed the exercises of the sabbath in the synagogue. The whole country around had poured into the city, which was consequently crowded with people. Several of the disciples were still going around today among the houses outside the city. Jesus took leave of all present in the synagogue and made a brief recapitulation of what he had already taught them. All were very much touched and wanted him to remain with them.

Sunday, December 24, AD 30 (Tebeth 9)

Jesus went to Dothaim. Arriving at the outskirts of town, he was met by a group of people, including some Pharisees. On the whole, however, he received a cool reception. That night, he stayed at an inn put at his disposal by Lazarus.

Before Jesus left Abram for Dothaim, he dispatched two disciples with a message to Capernaum, and two others to Cydessa. Andrew and Matthew alone remained with their Master, the others having scattered to different places.

Dothaim was built on the same mountain ridge as Abram, and may have been distant from it southward something like five hours. There was here a private inn established for Jesus and his disciples, and there he met Lazarus, who had come thither with two disciples from Jerusalem. The holy women also had journeyed with Lazarus to this inn from Jerusalem.

FROM THE SECOND CONVERSION OF MAGDALENE TO THE DELIVERY OF THE KEYS TO PETER

Jesus Teaching in Azanoth • Second Conversion of Magdalene

Monday, December 25, AD 30 (Tebeth 10)

At the inn in Dothaim, Jesus met Martha and Lazarus and some other women and disciples from Jerusalem. Martha went from Dothaim to Magdalum, to try and persuade her sister Mary Magdalene to come and hear Jesus speak the next day on a hill near Azanoth.

ABOUT an hour to the south of the inn at Dothaim lay the little town of Azanoth. It was built on an eminence upon which was a teacher's chair and, in earlier times, it had often been the scene of the prophets' preaching. Through the activity of the disciples, the report had been spread throughout the whole region that Jesus was about to deliver a great instruction in that place, and in consequence of this report, multitudes were gathered there from all Galilee. Martha, attended by her maid, had journeyed to Magdalene in the hope of inducing her to be present at the instruction, but she was received very haughtily by her sister, with whom things had come to the worst. She was, on Martha's arrival, engaged at her toilet, and sent word that she could not speak to her then. Martha awaited her sister's appearance with unspeakable patience, occupying herself meanwhile in prayer. At last the unhappy Magdalene presented herself, her manner haughty, excited, and defiant. She was ashamed of Martha's simple attire. She feared that some of her guests might see her, consequently she requested her to go away as soon as possible. But Martha begging to be allowed to rest in some corner of the house, she and her maid were conducted to a room in one of the side buildings where, either through design or forgetfulness, they were allowed to remain without food or drink. It was then afternoon.

Meanwhile Magdalene adorned herself for the banquet, at which she was seated on a richly decorated chair, while Martha and her maid were in prayer. After the revelry, Magdalene went at last to Martha, taking with her something on a little blue-edged plate and something to drink. She addressed Martha angrily and disdainfully, her whole demeanor expressive of pride, insolence, uneasiness, and interior agitation. Martha, full of humility and affection, invited Magdalene to go with her once more to the great instruction Jesus was going to deliver in the neighborhood. All Magdalene's female friends, Martha urged, those whom she had lately met, would be there and very glad to see her. She herself (Magdalene) had already testified to the esteem in which she held Jesus, and she should now gratify Lazarus and herself (Martha) by going once more to hear him preach. She would not soon again have the opportunity of hearing the wonderful prophet and at the same time of seeing all her friends in her own neighborhood. She had shown by her anointing of Jesus at the banquet at Gabara that she knew how to honor greatness and majesty. She should now again salute him whom she had once so nobly and fearlessly honored in public, etc.

It would be impossible to say how lovingly Martha spoke to her erring sister, or how patiently she endured her shamefully contemptuous manner. At last Magdalene replied: "I shall go, but not with you! You can go on ahead, for I will not be seen with one so miserably clothed. I shall dress according to my position, and I shall go with my own friends." At these words, the two sisters separated, for it was very late.

Next morning Magdalene sent for Martha to come to her room while she was making her toilet. Martha went, patient as usual and secretly praying that Magdalene might go with her and be converted. Magdalene, clothed in a fine woollen garment, was sitting on a low stool, while two of her maids were busily engaged washing her feet and arms and perfuming them with fragrant water. Her hair was divided into three parts above the ears and at the back of the head, after which it was combed, brushed, oiled, and braided. Over her fine woollen undergarment was put a green robe embroidered with large yellow flowers, and over that again a mantle with folds. Her headdress was a kind of crimped cap that rose high on the forehead. Both her hair and her cap were interwoven with numberless pearls, and in her ears were long pendants. Her sleeves were wide above the elbow, but narrow below and fastened with broad, glittering bracelets. Her robe was plaited. Her under-bodice was open on the breast and laced with shining cords.

During the toilet, Magdalene held in her hand a round, polished mirror. She wore an ornament on her breast. It was covered with gold, and encrusted with cut stones and pearls. Over the narrow-sleeved underdress she wore an upper one with a long flowing train and short, wide sleeves. It was made of changeable violet silk, and embroidered with large flowers, some in gold, others in different colors. The braids of her hair were ornamented with roses made of raw silk, and strings of pearls, interwoven with some kind of stiff transparent stuff that stood out in points. Very little of the hair could be seen through its load of ornamentation. It was rolled high around the face. Over this headdress, Magdalene wore a rich hood of fine, transparent material. It fell on the high headdress in front, shaded the cheeks, and hung low on the shoulders behind.

Martha took leave of her sister, and went to the inn near Damna, in order to tell Mary and the holy women the success she had had in her efforts to persuade Magdalene to be present at the instruction about to be given in Azanoth. With the blessed Virgin about a dozen women had come to Damna, among them Anna Cleophas, Susanna Alpheus, Susanna of Jerusalem, Veronica, Johanna Chusa, Mary Mark, Dinah, Maroni, and the Suphanite.

Tuesday, December 26, AD 30 (Tebeth 11)

Jesus made his way to the hill near Azanoth, where he had announced that he would teach. On the way, he met his mother and some of the holy women—among them were Anna Cleophas, Susanna Alpheus, Susanna of Jerusalem, Veronica, Johanna Chusa, Mary Mark, Maroni, Mara the Suphanite, and Dinah the Samaritan. Martha had succeeded in persuading Mary Magdalene to come—it had taken great patience—and she arrived with great pomp and ceremony at the hill. After healing many sick people, Jesus spoke concerning the woe that would befall the towns of Chorazin, Bethsaida, and Capernaum (Matthew 11:20). Many children who were present then began calling out: "Jesus of Nazareth! Most holy prophet! Son of David! Son of God!" Many listeners, including Magdalene, were deeply moved by this. Jesus then spoke the words recorded in Matthew 12:43. Magdalene was truly shocked. Turning to different parts of the crowd, Jesus commanded the devils to depart from all those who sought freedom from their possession. As the devils departed, many, including Mary Magdalene, sunk to the ground. Three times in all, as she took in Jesus's powerful and moving words, Mary Magdalene fell unconscious to the ground. Coming to after the third occasion, she wept bitterly and asked Martha to bring her to join the holy women. Lazarus and Martha then brought her to the inn where the holy women were staying. Meanwhile, Jesus came down to Azanoth and went to the synagogue to teach. Mary Magdalene came too. He spoke again in her direction. As he looked at her, she fell unconscious again and another devil departed from her. Later, she cast herself at his feet, begging for salvation. Jesus comforted her, saying she should repent with all her heart, and that she should have faith and hope.

Jesus, accompanied by six apostles and a number of the disciples, started from the inn at Dothaim for Azanoth. On the way, he met the holy women coming from Damna. Lazarus was among Jesus's companions on this occasion.

After Martha's departure, Magdalene was very much tormented by the devil, who wanted to prevent her going to Jesus's instruction. She would have followed his suggestions, were it not for some of her guests who had agreed to go with her to Azanoth, to witness what they called a great show. Magdalene and her frivolous, sinful companions rode on asses to the inn of the holy women near the baths of Bethulia. Magdalene's splendid seat, along with cushions and rugs for the others, followed packed on asses.

Next morning Magdalene, again arrayed in her most wanton attire and surrounded by her companions, made her appearance at the place of instruction, which was about an hour from the inn at which she was stopping. With noise and bustle, loud talk and bold staring about, they took their places under an open tent far in front of the holy women. There were some men of their own stamp in their party. They sat upon cushions and rugs and upholstered chairs, all in full view, Magdalene in front. Their coming gave rise to general whispering and murmurs of disapprobation, for they were even more detested and despised in these quarters than in Gabara. The Pharisees especially, who knew of her first remarkable conversion at Gabara and of her subsequent relapse into her former disorders, were scandalized and expressed their indignation at her daring to appear in such an assembly.

Jesus, after healing many sick, began his long and severe discourse. The details of his sermon I cannot now recall, but I know that he cried woe upon Capernaum, Bethsaida, and Chorazin. He said also that the Queen of Sheba had come from the South to hear the wisdom of Solomon, but here was one greater than Solomon. And lo, the wonder! Children that had never yet spoken, babes in their mothers' arms, cried out from time to time during the instruction: "Jesus of Nazareth! Holiest of prophets! Son of David! Son of God!" Which words caused many of the hearers, and among them Magdalene, to tremble with fear. Making allusion to Magdalene, Jesus said that when the devil has been driven out and the house has been swept, he returns with six other demons, and rages worse than before. These words terrified Magdalene. After Jesus had in this way touched the hearts of many, he turned successively to all sides and commanded the demon to go out of all that sighed for deliverance from his thralldom, but that those who wished to remain bound to the devil should depart and take him along with them. At this command, the possessed cried out from all parts of the circle: "Jesus, thou Son of God!"—and here and there people sank to the ground unconscious.

Magdalene also, from her splendid seat upon which she had attracted all eyes, fell in violent convulsions. Her companions in sin applied perfumes as restoratives, and wanted to carry her away. Desiring to remain under the empire of the evil one, they were themselves glad to profit by the opportunity to retire from the scene. But just then some persons near her cried out: "Stop, Master! Stop! This woman is dying." Jesus interrupted his discourse to reply: "Place her on her chair! The death she is now dying is a good death, and one that will vivify her!" After some time another word of Jesus pierced her to the heart, and she again fell into convulsions, during which dark forms escaped from her. A crowd gathered round her in alarm, while her own immediate party tried once again to bring her to herself. She was soon able to resume her seat on her beautiful chair, and then she tried to look as if she had suffered only an ordinary fainting spell. She had now become the object of general attention, especially as many other possessed back in the crowd had, like her, fallen in convulsions, and afterward rose up freed from the evil one. But when for the third time Magdalene fell down in violent convulsions, the excitement increased, and Martha hurried forward to her. When she recovered consciousness, she acted like one bereft of her senses. She wept passionately and wanted to go to where the holy women were sitting. The frivolous companions with whom she had come hither held her back forcibly, declaring that she should not play the fool, and they at last succeeded in getting her down the mountain. Lazarus, Martha, and others who had followed her, now went forward and led her to the inn of the holy women. The crowd of worldlings who had accompanied Magdalene had already made their way off.

Before going down to his inn, Jesus healed many blind and sick. Later on, he taught again in the school, and Magdalene was present. She was not yet quite cured, but profoundly impressed, and no longer so wantonly arrayed. She had laid aside her superfluous finery, some of which was made of a fine scalloped material like pointed lace, and so perishable that it could be worn only once. She was now veiled. Jesus in his instruction appeared again to speak for her special benefit and, when he fixed upon her his penetrating glance, she fell once more into unconsciousness and another evil spirit went out of her. Her maids bore her from the synagogue to where she was received by Martha and Mary, who took her back to the inn. She was now like one distracted. She cried and wept. She ran through the public streets saying to all she met that she was a wicked creature, a sinner, the refuse of humanity. The holy women had the greatest trouble to quiet her. She tore her garments, disarranged her hair, and hid her face in the folds of her veil. When Jesus returned to his inn with the disciples and some of the Pharisees, and while they were taking some refreshments standing, Magdalene escaped from the holy women, ran with streaming hair and uttering loud lamentations, made her way through the crowd, cast herself at Jesus's feet, weeping and moaning, and asked if she might still hope for salvation. The Pharisees and disciples, scandalized at the sight, said to Jesus that he should no longer suffer this reprobate woman to create disturbance everywhere, that he should send her away once for all. But Jesus replied: "Permit her to weep and lament! Ye know not what is passing in her"—and he turned to her with words of consolation. He told her to repent from her heart, to believe and to hope, for that she should soon find peace. Then he bade her depart with confidence. Martha, who had followed with her maids, took her again to her inn. Magdalene did nothing but wring her hands and lament. She was not yet quite freed from the power of the evil one, who tortured and tormented her with the most frightful remorse and despair. There was no rest for her—she thought herself forever lost.

Upon her request, Lazarus went to Magdalum in order to take charge of her property, and to dissolve the ties she had there formed. She owned, near Azanoth and in the surrounding country, fields and vineyards which Lazarus, on account of her extravagance, had previously sequestered.

Wednesday, December 27, AD 30 (Tebeth 12)

During the night, because of the great crowd in Azanoth, Jesus and his disciples left and made their way to Damna. In the morning, Jesus continued his teaching on a hillside near Damna. Many from Azanoth, including Mary Magdalene and the holy women, came to hear him. First, he spoke of sin, then of God's mercy and the present time of grace. He besought his listeners to accept this grace. During this discourse, he looked directly at Mary Magdalene three times, and each time she fainted. After the third time, she appeared pale and weak, as if annihilated, and was scarcely recognizable any more. Her tears flowed incessantly. Jesus came to her to comfort her. She asked him: "Lord, is there still salvation for me?" Jesus forgave her her transgressions and promised to save her from further relapses. Then he blessed her and commended her to his mother. He told her to turn to the Virgin for advice and comfort. Then Jesus said to the holy women: "Mary Magdalene has been a great sinner, but for all future time she will be a model for all penitents." This was the second—and final—conversion of Mary Magdalene.

To escape the great crowd that had gathered here, Jesus went that night with his disciples into the neighborhood of Damna, where there was an inn, as well as a lovely eminence upon which stood a chair for teaching. Next morning when the holy women came thither accompanied by

Magdalene, they found Jesus already encompassed by people seeking his aid. When his departure became known, the crowds awaiting him at Azanoth, as well as new visitors, came streaming to Damna, and fresh bands continued to arrive during the whole instruction.

Magdalene, crushed and miserable, now sat among the holy women. Jesus inveighed severely against the sin of impurity, and said that it was that vice that had called down fire upon Sodom and Gomorrha. But he spoke of the mercy of God also and of the present time of pardon, almost conjuring his hearers to accept the grace offered them. Thrice during this discourse did Jesus rest his glance upon Magdalene, and each time I saw her sinking down and dark vapors issuing from her. The third time, the holy women carried her away. She was pale, weak, annihilated as it were, and scarcely recognizable. Her tears flowed incessantly. She was completely transformed, and passionately sighed to confess her sins to Jesus and receive pardon. The instruction over, Jesus went to a retired place, whither Mary herself and Martha led Magdalene to him. She fell on her face weeping at his feet, her hair flowing loosely around her. Jesus comforted her. When Mary and Martha had withdrawn, she cried for pardon, confessed her numerous transgressions, and asked over and over: "Lord, is there still salvation for me?" Jesus forgave her sins, and she implored him to save her from another relapse. He promised so to do, gave her his blessing, and spoke to her of the virtue of purity, also of his mother, who was pure without stain. He praised Mary highly in terms I had never before heard from his lips, and commanded Magdalene to unite herself closely to her and to seek from her advice and consolation. When Jesus and Magdalene rejoined the holy women, Jesus said to them: "She has been a great sinner, but for all future time, she will be the model of penitents."

Magdalene, through her passionate emotion, her grief and her tears, was no longer like a human being, but like a shadow tottering from weakness. She was, however, calm, though still weeping silent tears that exhausted her. The holy women comforted her with many marks of affection, while she in turn craved pardon of each. As they had to set out for Nain and Magdalene was too weak to accompany them, Martha, Anna Cleophas, and Mara the Suphanite went with her to Damna, in order to rest that night and follow the others next morning. The holy women went through Cana to Nain.

Jesus and the disciples went across through the valley of the baths of Bethulia, four or five hours farther on, to Gath-Hepher, a large city that lay on a height between Cana and Sepphoris. They passed the night outside the city at an inn that was near a cave called "John's Cave."

(Follow Map 25)

Jesus in Gath-Hepher, Chisloth, and Nazareth

***Thursday, December 28, AD 30** (**Tebeth 13**)*

After staying overnight at an inn near a cave known as "the cave of John," Jesus today went to the town of Gath-Hepher, where the prophet Jonah had been born. As he approached the synagogue, he found many mothers and children awaiting him. Jesus blessed them and then went on to heal the sick. In the synagogue, he taught concerning the patriarch Joseph and spoke also of the dignity and worth of children. After visiting some homes he went to the town of Chisloth at the foot of Mount Tabor.

NEXT morning, Jesus approached Gath-Hepher. The schoolmasters and Pharisees came out to meet him and bid him welcome, though making all kinds of remonstrances, and imploring him not to disturb the peace of their city. They especially insisted upon his discountenancing the crowding around him and clamoring of women and children. He might, they said, teach quietly in their synagogue, but public disturbance they did not want to see. Jesus replied in grave and severe words that it was precisely for those that cried after him, longed for him, that he had come, and he reproached them for their dissimulation.

The Pharisees had, in fact, on hearing that Jesus was coming, issued an order that the women should not appear on the streets with their children nor should they go to meet the Nazarene with clamorous greeting. The cry of "Son of God," "Christ," was, they said, positively preposterous and scandalous, since everyone in this part of the country knew full well whence Jesus came, who were his parents, and who his brethren. The sick might assemble in front of the synagogue and allow themselves to be cured, but noise and excitement would not be tolerated.

Such were the directions given by the Pharisees, who had likewise arranged the sick around the synagogue as they thought proper, just as if it were theirs by right to order Jesus's actions. When, however, they reached the city with Jesus, to their intense chagrin they beheld the streets filled with mothers surrounded by their little ones, and some with infants in their arms. The children were stretching out their hands to Jesus and crying: "Jesus of Nazareth! Son of David! Son of God! Holiest of prophets!" The Pharisees tried to drive the women and children back, but all in vain. They came pouring out of the neighboring streets and houses, while the Pharisees, eaten with vexation, withdrew from Jesus's escort. The disciples too, who were surrounding Jesus, were somewhat timorous and frightened.

Map 25: The Third Journey to Hebron
December 27 AD 30–January 26, AD 31

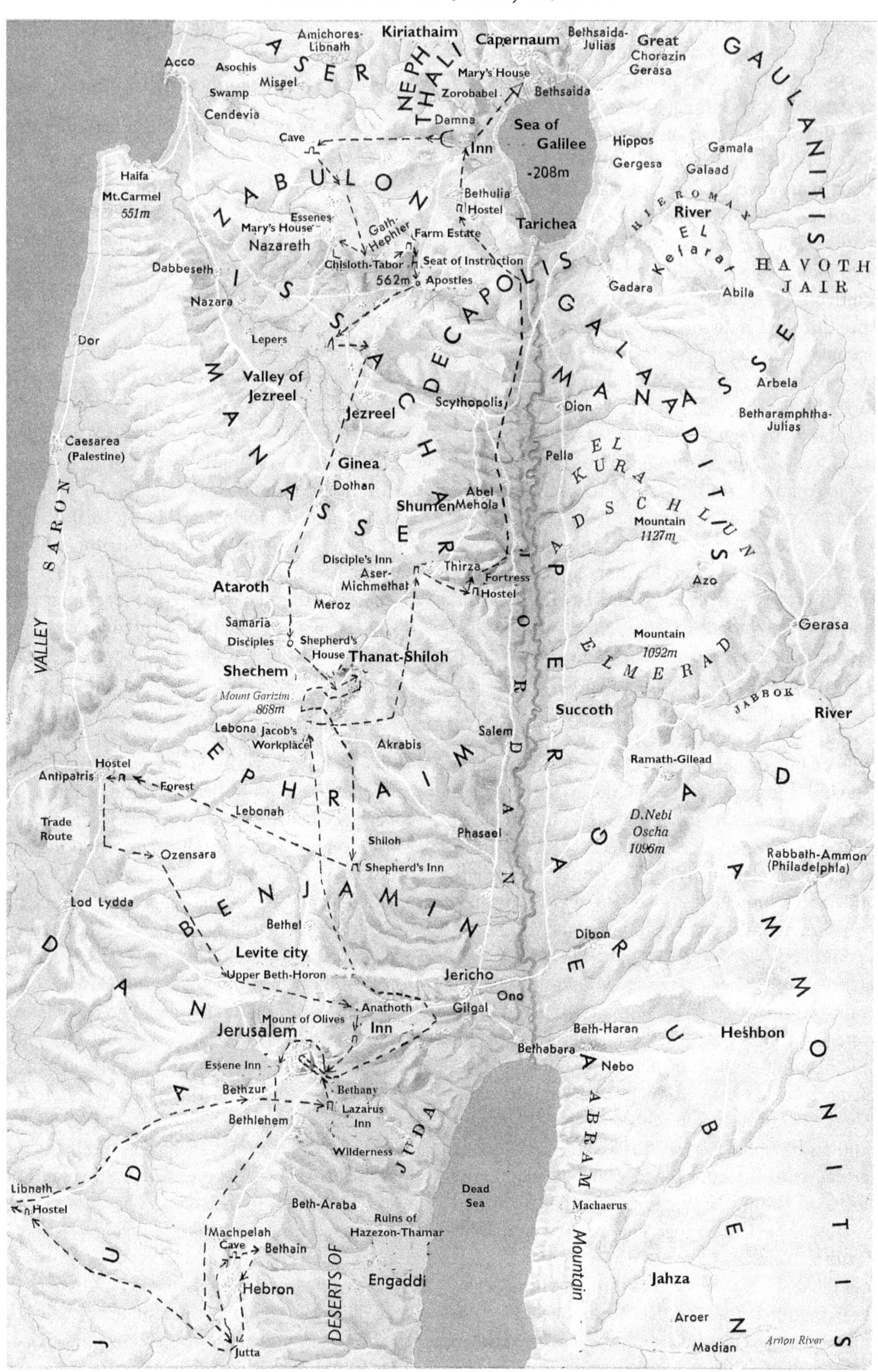

Damna—Cave of John—Gath-Hepher—Chisloth-Tabor—Nazareth—Northwest Foot of Tabor—Shunem Thanat-Shiloh—Antipatris—Ozensara—Upper Beth-Horon—Anathoth—Bethany—Mount of Olives Jutta—Machpelah—Bethain—Hebron—Jutta—Libnath—Bethzur—Bethany—Jerusalem—Lebona Aser-Michmethat—Tirzah—Bethulia—Capernaum

They would have desired a less demonstrative entrance into the city, one attended by less danger, and so they remonstrated with Jesus while attempting to drive the children back. But Jesus reproached them with their faint-heartedness. He restrained them, allowed the children to press around him, and showed himself all love and affection for them. And thus they proceeded to the court before the synagogue amid the uninterrupted shouts of the little ones: "Jesus of Nazareth! Holiest of prophets!" Even the sucklings that never yet had spoken cried out after him. They were witnesses to Jesus. They bore convincing testimony before all the people.

In front of the synagogue the children halted, the boys on one side, the girls on the other, the mothers with their infants in the rear. Jesus blessed the children and addressed some words of instruction to the mothers and their domestics who likewise had made their way thither. He said to the mothers that they should regard these last as their children. He spoke to the disciples also of the high value God sets on the child. The Pharisees were annoyed at these delays, and the sick were impatient for their cure. At last Jesus went to the latter, cured many of them, and then entered the synagogue, where he taught about the patriarch Joseph. During his discourse he took occasion to return to the dignity of children. Jesus did so because the Pharisees were complaining of what they called the disturbance.

When Jesus was leaving the synagogue, three women presented themselves before him, requesting a private interview. When he withdrew with them from the crowd, they cast themselves on their knees before him, and made their laments over their husbands, whom they begged Jesus to help. Their husbands, they said, were tormented by evil spirits, by whom they themselves were sometimes attacked. They had heard, they said, that he had helped Magdalene, and they hoped that he would likewise have pity on them. Jesus promised to visit their homes. He went first, however, with his disciples to the house of a certain Simeon, a simple-hearted man belonging to the married Essenes. He was of middle age and the son of a Pharisee of Dabrath on Tabor. Jesus and the disciples partook, in this house, of refreshments standing. Simeon was desirous of bestowing all his goods upon the community, and he spoke with Jesus to that effect.

On leaving Simeon's Jesus went as he had promised to the homes of the women, and had an interview with them and their husbands. Affairs were not just as the wives had stated, for they had thrown upon their husbands the blame of which they were themselves deserving. Jesus exhorted both parties to live in harmony, to pray, to fast, and to give alms.

After the sabbath these infirm women followed Jesus to a mountain a little to the north of Tabor where he was going to deliver a discourse. He did not remain long there. He went southward toward Chisloth, which city the holy women passed on their road to Nain, Magdalene also, when journeying with her party. On the way Jesus again instructed the apostles upon what was in store for them. He told them how they should behave when they arrived in Judea, where they would not be so well received. He gave them new directions as to their conduct, also for the imposition of hands and the driving out of the demon, and as an additional source of strength and increase of grace, he again conferred upon them his benediction.

Three youths from Egypt came to Jesus in this place. He received them as disciples, though picturing to them at the same time the hardships that awaited them. One was named Cyrinus. They had been playmates of Jesus in Egypt, and they were now about thirty years old. Their parents had ever revered the dwelling and the fountain used by the holy family as sacred memorials. The young men had visited Bethlehem and Bethany, and had gone to Dothan, to see Mary, to whom they delivered their parents' greeting.

Friday, December 29, AD 30 (Tebeth 14)

This morning Jesus received a visit from some Pharisees from Nazareth, who invited him to come there. Jesus and his disciples set off and arrived at Nazareth around midday. They went to the home of the widowed mother of his childhood friend Jonadab. Jesus then visited the sick and healed them. That evening, after teaching in the synagogue, Jesus ate at Jonadab's home and stayed there overnight.

Some Pharisees of Nazareth came to Jesus at Chisloth to invite him to his native city. Those Pharisees who, on a former occasion, wanted to hurl him from the rock, were no longer in Nazareth. The envoys told Jesus that he ought to go to his native city and there exhibit some of his signs and wonders. The people, they said, were eager to hear his doctrine; then too he could cure his fellow countrymen that were sick. But they laid down as a condition that he would not heal on the sabbath day. Jesus replied that he would go and keep the sabbath with them. He warned them, however, that they would be scandalized on his account, and as to the cures, he would condescend to their desires even if it proved to their own detriment. Upon receiving this answer, the Pharisees returned to Nazareth, whither Jesus soon followed with his disciples, whom he instructed on the way. It was noon when they arrived. Many from curiosity, others really well intentioned people, came forth from the city to meet him. They washed the feet of the newcomers and offered them some refreshments. Jesus had two disciples from Nazareth, Parmenas and Jonadab. With the widowed mother of the latter, Jesus and his companions took up their quarters. These disciples had been friends of Jesus in early youth, and had accompanied him on his first journey to Hebron after Joseph's death. He now employed them frequently in discharging commissions and errands of all kinds.

Jesus went to some sick who had implored his assistance. He knew that they believed in him and had need of his aid. But he passed by many who wanted only to test his power or who, under the pretence of a cure, were desirous only of getting a sight of him. An Essene youth, paralyzed on one side from his birth, was brought to him. He implored Jesus to cure him, and he did so on the street, as also two blind men. Then he entered certain houses wherein he cured many aged sick people, men and women. Some of them were afflicted with edema in its worst form; one woman in particular was frightfully swollen. Jesus cured, altogether, fifteen people. After that he went to the synagogue where also some sick were gathered; but he passed without curing them, and celebrated the sabbath without interruption. The reading for this sabbath was about God's speaking to Moses in Egypt, also some chapters from Ezekiel.

Saturday, December 30, AD 30 (Tebeth 15)

Today, Jesus taught in the synagogue twice, in the morning and again in the evening. In his evening sermon, he spoke of God as his heavenly Father and of the judgment that would come upon Jerusalem. He warned his disciples of the persecution they would receive, exhorting them to perseverance and faithfulness (Matthew 10:5–42). The Pharisees then began to create an uproar, calling out: "Who is he? Who does he pretend to be? Where did he get his teaching? Is he not from here? His father was a carpenter, and his relatives, brothers, and sisters are all from here!" (Matthew 13:53–56). Jesus did not reply, but continued to instruct his disciples. After further insolent remarks from the Pharisees, Jesus spoke the words recorded in Matthew 13:57–58. That night, Jesus and the disciples ate with some Essenes, the same with whom he had been last time he was in Nazareth.

Next morning Jesus again taught in the synagogue, but healed no one. At noon I saw him walking with the disciples and some good people on the road between Nazareth and Sepphoris. They entered one of the neighboring villages, as was usual on the sabbath. The road from Nazareth to Sepphoris extended toward the north and was tolerably level, but when within about a quarter of an hour from the latter place, it began to rise. I saw Jesus on this road instructing separate groups of people. The members of some households in which reigned strife and disunion cast themselves at his feet. He made peace between man and wife and reconciled neighbors, but performed no cures. The two young men who had so often desired to be received among the disciples met Jesus on this road. He asked them again whether they were willing to forsake home and parents, distribute their goods to the poor, obey blindly, and suffer persecution for his sake. Their only answer was a shrug of the shoulders as they turned away.

When returned to Nazareth, Jesus visited his parents' house. It was in perfect order, but unoccupied. He visited likewise Mary's elder sister, the mother of Mary Cleophas, who took care of the house, though she did not live in it. Jesus then went with the disciples to the synagogue, preached in sharp and severe terms, called God his heavenly Father, pronounced judgment upon Jerusalem and upon all that would not follow him, openly addressed his disciples, alluded to the persecution that awaited them, and exhorted them to fidelity and perseverance. When the Pharisees found that he did not intend to remain and that he would perform no more cures in Nazareth, they began to give utterance to their vexation, and to ask, first this one, then that one: "Who is he, then? Who does he pretend to be? Where did he get his learning? Is he not of Nazareth? His father was the carpenter. His relatives, his brothers and sisters—all belong here!" By these last words, they meant Anne's elder daughter, Mary Heli and her sons James, Heliachim, and Sadoch, all disciples of John, Mary Cleophas and her sons and daughter. Jesus made them no answer, but went on quietly instructing his disciples. Then another Pharisee, a stranger from the region of Sepphoris, more insolent than the rest, cried out: "Who, then, art thou? Hast thou forgotten that only some years before thy father's death, thou didst help him to put up partitions in my house?" Still Jesus deigned no answer. Then the Pharisees all began to shout: "Answer! Is it good manners not to answer an honorable man?" At these words, Jesus addressed his bold questioner in terms like the following: "I did indeed work on wood belonging to thee. At the same time I cast a glance upon thee, and I grieved at not being able to free thee from the hard rind of thine own heart. Thou hast now proved thyself to be what I then suspected. Thou shalt have no part in my kingdom, although I have helped thee to build up thy dwelling place upon earth." Jesus said likewise that nowhere was a prophet without honor, excepting in his own city, in his own house, among his own relatives.

But what especially irritated the Pharisees were Jesus's words to his disciples; for instance, "I send ye as lambs among wolves"; "Sodom and Gomorrha will be less severely condemned on the last day than they that refuse to receive you"; "I am not come to bring peace, but the sword."

The close of the sabbath found many waiting to be healed, but, to the great vexation of the Pharisees, Jesus cured none. Some of the people, imitating the insolence of the Pharisees in the synagogue, cried out to Jesus: "Don't you remember this? Don't you remember that?" And they recalled circumstances in which they had formerly seen him. The Pharisees remarked to him that this time he had come with fewer followers than on the preceding occasion, and they inquired whether he was not again going to take up his quarters among the Essenes. As a general thing, the Essenes did not much frequent Jesus's public instructions, and he rarely spoke of them. The enlightened among them at a later period joined the community. They never opposed his doctrine, but looked upon Jesus as the Son of God.

Jesus did, in effect, again visit those Essenes with whom he had been the last time he was in Nazareth. He and the disciples took with them a light repast, after which he taught during a part of the night. Toward ten o'clock, Peter, Matthew and James the Greater returned from the apostles in Upper Galilee. They had left the rest in the region around Seleucia to the east of Lake Merom. Andrew, Thomas and Saturnin, who had lately arrived, and another apostle, immediately started to replace those just come.

Sunday, December 31, AD 30 (Tebeth 16)

Jesus left Nazareth around one o'clock in the morning. He went toward Mount Tabor. On the way, around dawn, he healed a number of lepers. Reaching Mount Tabor, he went up to the prophet's teaching chair and, after healing the sick, spoke of the first four beatitudes and recounted some parables. Around midday Jesus gathered the twelve and all the other disciples together. After giving them instructions, he sent them out in pairs (Matthew 9:36–38; 10:5–16). Peter, John, and a few other disciples remained with him. Together, they made their way to Shunem. They got there around sunset. Here Jesus healed a mute, lame, epileptic boy. That evening, in Shunem, Jesus spoke alone with the boy's father, for it was his sin that had led to his son's condition. Jesus said that he should repent.

Jesus left Nazareth that night with his followers. He journeyed about two hours toward Tabor to the little place where recently, on his return to Capernaum after raising the youth of Nain, he had cured the leprous property holder. An instruction had been announced for the following day, which was to be delivered on a height southwest of Tabor, about half an hour from the mountain itself. Jesus stopped again with the schoolmaster of the place. The latter, counting upon Jesus's coming, had received many sick into his house. Jesus restored speech to one mute. The boy that had so cleverly delivered to Jesus the message sent by his leprous master was among the schoolmaster's pupils. Jesus spoke to him. His name was Samuel, and he afterward became a disciple.

Jesus's Instruction on the Height near Tabor, in Shunem

The Lord of the place, he whom Jesus had healed of leprosy, came to him and renewed his acts of gratitude. He pleaded for several other lepers for whom he had caused a tent to be erected on the road by which Jesus was to pass, and he likewise made overtures for applying a part of his fortune to defraying the expenses of Jesus's apostolic journeys.

It was still dawn when Jesus left the house and went out on the road where were awaiting him about five men and women. From a retired spot, a little off from the road, they cried to him for assistance. Jesus stepped to them, and they cast themselves at his feet. One of the women addressed him: "Lord, we are from Tiberias, and until now we have hesitated to implore thy help. The Pharisees told us that thou art hard and pitiless toward sinners. But we have heard of thy merciful compassion to Magdalene whom thou didst free from her miseries, and whose sins thou didst also forgive. All this gave us courage, and we have followed thee thither. Lord, have mercy on us! Thou canst heal us and purify us. Thou canst likewise forgive us our sins." The men and women were standing apart from one another. They were afflicted with leprosy and other maladies. One woman was possessed by a wicked spirit who threw her into convulsions.

Jesus took them aside, one by one, to hear the particulars of their confession, inasmuch as the detailed account would serve to increase their sorrow and repentance. He did not exact this from all, unless it was necessary. He cured those of whom we are now speaking, and forgave them their sins. They melted into tears of gratitude, and begged him to say what they should henceforth do. In reply, Jesus commanded them not to return to Tiberias, but to go to another place. I understood at that moment that Jesus himself would not go to Tiberias, and indeed I never saw him there. These people now went to the mountain to hear his instructions.

Jesus, however, turned off to the tent of the lepers, about four or five in number. He cured them, addressed to them words of admonition, commanded them to go to Nazareth and show themselves to the priests.

Jesus never lingered long over such cures, though there was never anything like precipitation in his manner. All was done with dignity and moderation, and especially without a superfluity of words. All was striking and appropriate whether he consoled or exhorted, whether he was gentle or severe. His manner was overflowing with patience and love. He went straight on with his work, but without the least hurry. Many of those that needed his help, Jesus went to meet; yes, even turning out of his way, he hastened to them, like a loving friend of men who sought to save them. From others, again, he turned away, permitting them to follow him, to sigh after him, a long time.

Valley of Esdrelon

The spot upon which Jesus now taught was a beautiful plateau where, from the stone chair, the prophets of bygone days had taught. From it one could see across the valley of Esdrelon and into the country around Megiddo. Crowds were gathered from the surrounding cities, and there were very many sick from Nazareth also, whom Jesus had not cured there, but who now were restored to health. There were some possessed, who testified to him as usual and whom he delivered. He again taught upon the first four of the eight beatitudes, and related some parables referring to penance and the coming of the kingdom. Then in most touching terms he begged his hearers to profit by the grace offered them while still they had time. The apostles listened attentively, because each in his own peculiar way was to repeat this instruction on his next mission.

Toward noon I saw Jesus gathering the apostles and disciples around him in a sequestered spot at the foot of the mountain. He sent them all out, two and two,[D27] with the exception of Peter, John, and some of the disciples who were to remain with him. They were to go in three different directions: one set into the valley of the Jordan, another into that near Dothan, and a third to the west, into the country around Jerusalem. It was on this occasion that I heard Jesus telling the apostles that they should go without purse, without scrip, girded with one garment only, and a staff in their hand. They were not to go to the pagans nor to the Samaritans, but to the lost sheep of Israel. He indicated to them how they might be received, told them where to shake the dust from their feet, and commanded them to preach penance. Jesus thus particularized because he was sending the apostles into a hostile part of the country, and because persecution threatened himself after the death of John, which was now drawing nigh. Many of the private inns had been established in this part of the Holy Land, therefore it was that the apostles had no need of money. But they that were sent to Upper Galilee and beyond the Jordan, had received some, though very little, money. And now began a new era in their apostolic career, and new regions were visited by them.

Jesus blessed them before their departure, and gave them some further instructions upon curing the sick and driving out demons. He blessed the oil also that was to be used for the sick. He notified some where they should again meet him.

After healing many more sick, Jesus bade farewell to the multitude, and accompanied by Peter, John and the disciples, journeyed southward about three hours to Shunem. Many of the people followed him, among others a man who, the last time that Jesus went from Samaria to Galilee, had entreated him to visit his sick children who were at an inn not far from Endor. This man again proffered his request to Jesus, and now it was granted.

The two demoniacal women of Gath-Hepher had followed Jesus to the instruction given on the mount, and had been delivered by the imposition of his hands. When he reached the brook Kishon, before crossing he healed a poor leper whose condition was truly forlorn and despised. He had for twenty years been reduced to this pitiable state, and someone had built him a tent hut here on the roadside. Jesus hastened to him, healed him, and told him to join the others that were going to Jerusalem to show themselves to the priests.

It was dusk when Jesus arrived in Shunem. With Peter and John, he put up at the house of the man that had invited him to visit his sick children, all of whom were in a most miserable state. One son, sixteen years old and very tall for his age, was deaf and mute. He lay flat on the ground in convulsions with contortions of the body so frightful that his head and heels met. He was perfectly lame and unable to walk. Another son was a poor idiot afraid of everything, and his two daughters also were timorous and simple. Jesus cured the deaf mute that evening. Peter and John had gone into the city. Jesus with the parents went alone into the sick boy's chamber, knelt by his bed, prayed, and supporting himself on his hands, inclined over the boy's face. He did this either to breathe into or to say something into his mouth. Then he took the boy by the hand and raised him up. The boy stood upright on his feet, and Jesus led him a few steps backward and forward. Then he took him alone into another room, made a salve out of his saliva and a little earth, took some upon his fingers and anointed his ears, and ran the first two fingers of his right hand under his tongue. Then began the boy in an unwonted, lively voice to cry: "I hear! I can speak!" The parents and servants rushed in at the sound and embraced him, weeping and shouting for joy. They cast themselves with their child on the ground before Jesus, sobbing and rocking to and fro for joy. During the evening Jesus had a private interview with the father, upon whom a great crime committed by his own father was still resting. The man asked Jesus whether the chastisement was to fall even to the fourth generation. Jesus answered that if he did penance and atoned for the crime, he might blot out its consequences.

Monday, January 1, AD 31 (Tebeth 17)

This morning, Jesus healed the brother and two sisters of the child whom he had cured yesterday. All three were feeble-minded. Laying his hands upon them, he restored them to normalcy. The three children were astounded, awaking as if from a dream. They had always believed that people wanted to kill them, and they were particularly afraid of fire. Jesus then taught on the street, and blessed and healed many children. Afterward, accompanied by Peter and John, he set off toward Samaria. They traveled quickly for the rest of the day and on through the whole night. On the way, Jesus told them that John the Baptist would soon meet his end, and that he wanted to go to Hebron to comfort the Baptist's relatives.

In the morning Jesus cured the other son and the two daughters of their idiocy. He performed the cure by the imposition of hands. When restored to sense, the children appeared to be perfectly amazed, and as if awaking from a dream. They had always thought that people wanted to kill them, and had in particular a great dread of fire. When on the day before Jesus healed the elder boy, he told (very unusual for him) the father to go out and relate to all what had taken place. The consequence was a great concourse of people, among them numbers of sick, and that morning I saw Jesus instructing the people on the street, and curing and blessing many of the children.

After that I saw him with Peter and John journeying rapidly the whole day and night through the plain of Esdrelon in the direction of Ginea. They seldom paused to rest. I heard Jesus saying on the way that John's end was approaching, and after that, his enemies would begin their pursuit of himself. But it was not lawful to expose one's self to one's enemies. I think I understood that they were going to Hebron, to console John's relatives and prevent any imprudent manifestation.

The holy women, Mary, Veronica, Susanna, Magdalene, and Mara the Suphanite, were now in Dothan near Samaria.They were stopping with Issachar, the sick husband, whom Jesus had lately healed. The holy women never went to the public inns. Martha, Dinah, Johanna Chusa, Susanna Alpheus, Anna Cleophas, Mary Mark, and Maroni went, two by two, to look after the inns and supply what was wanting. There were about twelve of these women.

Tuesday, January 2, AD 31 (Tebeth 18)

Early this morning Jesus met up with three Egyptian youths who had recently become disciples at Dothaim. After breakfasting with them, he taught the workers in the fields, speaking in parables. Jesus and the disciples then traveled on to Thanat-Shiloh.

Early the next morning, I saw Jesus and the two apostles to the south of Samaria, where he met the two Egyptian disciples and the son of Johanna Chusa coming to him from the East. These Egyptian disciples had already been over a year in Hebron, where they were studying. They had also been a long time in Bethlehem with Lazarus and other disciples that were on intimate terms with Jesus.

They were in consequence very well instructed.

Jesus and his companions some time afterward arrived at the shepherd houses where the holy women had met him after his conversation with the Samaritan at Jacob's well, and where he had cured the landlord's sick son. They here partook of some refreshment and rested a little.

Some time after I had a vision of Jesus's instructing, near a well, the laborers gathered together from the neighboring fields. He was relating to them the parable of the treasure hidden in a field, also that of the lost drachma found again. Some of his hearers laughed at the latter, saying that they had often lost more than one drachma, but they had never taken the trouble to sweep the whole house on that account. But when Jesus reproached them for their levity, and explained to them what the drachma signified and the virtue implied by that general sweeping, they became confused and laughed no more.

These laborers were occupied in threshing the grain which was lying in heaps in the fields. This they did with wooden mallets which rose and fell by means of a cylinder. Several men were employed in pushing the grain under the mallets and in sweeping it away again. The operation was carried on in a pure rocky basin hewn out of solid stone, streaked with colored veinings. A large tree shaded the spot.

Jesus continued to teach here and there in the fields, and accompanied some of the laborers to their home in Thanat-Shiloh, which was not far off. The inhabitants received him very cordially outside the city, presented refreshments, and washed his feet. They wanted to give him also a change of raiment, but he declined. He related in their synagogue the parable of the king who made a great feast.

The Beheading of John the Baptist

FOR the last two weeks Herod's guests had been pouring into Machaerus, most of them from Tiberias. It was one succession of holidays and banqueting. Near the castle was an open circular building with many seats. In it gladiators struggled with wild animals for the amusement of Herod's guests, and dancers male and female performed all kinds of voluptuous dances. I saw Salome, the daughter of Herodias, practicing them before metallic mirrors in presence of her mother.

Zorobabel and Cornelius of Capernaum were not among the guests. They had excused themselves.

For some time past, John had been allowed to go around at large within the castle precincts, and his disciples also could go and come as they pleased. Once or twice he gave a public discourse at which Herod himself was present. His release had been promised him if he would approve Herod's marriage, or, at least, never again inveigh against it. But John had always most forcibly denounced it. Herod, nevertheless, was thinking of setting him free on his own birthday, but his wife was secretly nourishing very different thoughts. Herod would have wished John to circulate freely during the festival, that the guests might see and admire the leniency of the prisoner's treatment. But scarcely had the games and banqueting begun, scarcely had vice commenced to run riot in Machaerus, when John shut himself up in his prison cell and bade his disciples retire from the city. They obeyed and withdrew to the region of Hebron, where already many were assembled.

The daughter of Herodias had been trained entirely by her mother, whose constant companion she had been from her earliest years. She was in the bloom of girlhood, her deportment bold, her attire shameless. For a long time Herod had looked upon her with lustful eyes. This the mother regarded with complacency, and laid her plans accordingly. Herodias herself had a very striking, very bold appearance, and she employed all her skill, made use of every means, to set off her charms. She was no longer young, and there was something sharp, cunning, and diabolical in her countenance that bad men love to see. In me, however, she excited disgust and aversion as would the beauty of a serpent. I can find no better comparison than this, that she reminded me of the old pagan goddesses. She occupied a wing of the castle near the grand courtyard, somewhat higher than the hall opposite in which the birthday feast was to be celebrated. From the gallery around her apartments, one could look down into that open, pillared hall. Before the latter and in Herod's courtyard, a magnificent triumphal arch had been raised. Steps led up to it, and it opened into the hall itself, which was so long that from the entrance the other end could not be descried. Mirrors and gold sparkled on all sides, flowers and green bushes everywhere met the eye. The splendor almost blinded one, for far, far back halls, and columns, and passages were blazing with torches and lamps, with transparent glittering sentences, pictures, and vases.

Herodias and her female companions, arrayed in magnificence, stood in the high gallery of her apartments, gazing upon Herod's triumphal entrance into the banqueting hall. He came attended by his guests, all arrayed in pomp and splendor. The courtyard through which he passed to the triumphal arch was carpeted and lined with choirs of singers, who saluted him with songs of joy. Around the arch were ranged boys and girls waving garlands of flowers and playing upon all kinds of musical instruments. When Herod mounted the steps to the arch of triumph, he was met by a band of dancing boys and girls, Salome in their midst. She presented him with a crown which rested on a cushion covered with sparkling ornamentation and carried by some of the children of her suite under a transparent veil. These children were clothed in thin, tightly fitting garments, and on their shoulders were imitations of wings. Salome wore a long, transparent robe, caught up here and there on the lower limbs with glittering clasps. Her arms were ornamented with gold bands, strings of pearls, and circlets of tiny feathers; her neck and breast were covered with pearls and delicate, sparkling chains. She danced for a while before Herod who, quite dazzled and enchanted, gave expression to his admiration, in which all his guests enthusiastically joined.[D28] She should, he said to her, renew this pleasure for him on the next morning.

And now the procession entered the hall, and the banquet began. The women ate in the wing of the castle with Herodias. Meantime I saw John in his prison cell kneeling in prayer, his arms outstretched, his eyes raised to heaven. The whole place around him was shining with light, but it was a very different light from that which glared in Herod's hall. The latter, compared with the former, appeared like a flame from hell. The whole city of Machaerus was illuminated by torches and, as if on fire, it cast a reflection far into the surrounding mountains.

Herod's banquet-hall opened toward that of Herodias which, as I have said, was opposite, though a little more elevated than the former. From this open side, the women feasting and enjoying themselves were reflected in one of the inclined mirrors of Herod's hall. Between pyramids of flowers and fragrant green bushes, a playing fountain jetted up in fine sprays. When all had eaten and wine had flowed freely, the guests requested Herod to allow Salome to dance again, and for this purpose they cleared sufficient space and ranged around the walls. Herod was seated on his throne surrounded by some of his most intimate associates, who were Herodians. Salome appeared with some of her dancing companions clothed in a light, transparent robe. Her hair was interwoven in part with pearls and precious stones, while another part floated around her in curls. She wore a crown and formed the central figure in the group of dancers. The dance consisted of a constant bowing, a gentle swaying and turning. The whole person seemed to be destitute of bones. Scarcely had one position been assumed when it glided into another. The dancers held wreaths and scarfs in their hands, which waved and twined around one another. The whole performance gave expression to the most shameful passions, and in it Salome excelled all her companions. I saw the devil at her side as if bending and twisting all her limbs in order to produce that abominable effect. Herod was perfectly ravished, perfectly entranced by the changing attitudes. When at the end of one of the figures Salome presented herself before the throne, the other dancers continued to engage the attention of the guests, so that only those in the immediate vicinity heard Herod saying to her: "Ask of me what thou wilt, and I will give it to thee. Yes, I swear to thee, though thou askest the half of my kingdom, yet will I give it to thee!" Salome left the hall, hurried to that of the women, and conferred with her mother. The latter directed her to ask for the head of John on a dish. Salome hastened back to Herod, and said: "I will that thou give to me at once the head of John on a dish!" Only a few of Herod's most confidential associates who were nearest the throne heard the request. Herod looked like one struck with apoplexy, but Salome reminded him of his oath. Then he commanded one of the Herodians to call his executioner, to whom he gave the command to behead John and give the head on a dish to Salome. The executioner withdrew, and in a few moments Salome followed him. Herod, as if suddenly indisposed, soon left the hall with his companions.

He was very sad. I heard his followers saying to him that he was not bound to grant such a request; nevertheless they promised the greatest secrecy, in order not to interrupt the festivities. Herod, exceedingly troubled, paced like one demented the most remote apartments of his palace, but the feast went on undisturbed.

John was in prayer. The executioner and his servant took the two soldiers on guard at the entrance of John's prison in with them. The guards bore torches, but I saw the space around John so brilliantly illuminated that their flame became dull like a light in the daytime. Salome waited in the entrance hall of the vast and intricate dungeon house. With her was a maidservant who gave the executioner a dish wrapped in a red cloth. The latter addressed John: "Herod the king sends me to bring thy head on the dish to his daughter Salome." John allowed him little time to explain. He remained kneeling, and bowing his head toward him, he said: "I know why thou hast come. Thou art my guest, one for whom I have long waited. Didst thou know what thou art about to do, thou wouldst not do it. I am ready." Then he turned his head away and continued his prayer before the stone in front of which he always prayed kneeling. The executioner beheaded him with a machine which I can compare to nothing but a fox trap. An iron ring was laid on his shoulders. This ring was provided with two sharp blades, which, being closed around the throat with a sudden pressure given by the executioner, in the twinkling of an eye severed the head from the trunk. John still remained in a kneeling posture. The head bounded to the earth, and a triple stream of blood springing up from the body sprinkled both the head and body of the saint, as if baptizing him in his own blood. The executioner's servant raised the head by the hair, insulted it, and laid it on the dish which his master held. The latter presented it to the expectant Salome. She received it joyfully, yet not without secret horror and that effeminate loathing which those given to sin always have for blood and wounds. She carried the holy head covered by a red cloth on the dish. The maid went before, bearing a torch to light the way through the subterranean passages. Salome held the dish timidly at arm's length before her, her head still laden with its ornaments turned away in disgust. Thus she traversed the solitary passages that led up to a kind of vaulted kitchen under the castle of Herodias. Here she was met by her mother, who raised the cover from the holy head, which she loaded with insult and abuse. Then taking a sharp skewer from a certain part of the wall where many such instruments were sticking, with it she pierced the tongue, the cheeks, and the eyes.[D29] After that, looking more like a demon than a human being, she hurled it from her and kicked it with her foot through a round opening down into a pit into which the offal and refuse of the kitchen were swept. Then did that infamous woman together with her daughter return to the noise and wicked revelry of the feast, as if nothing had happened. I saw the holy body of the saint, covered with the skin that he usually wore, laid by the two soldiers upon his stone couch. The men were very much touched by what they had just witnessed. They were afterward discharged from duty and imprisoned that they might not disclose what they knew of John's murder. All that had any share in it were bound to the most rigorous secrecy. The guests, however, gave John no thought. Thus his death remained a long time concealed. The report was even spread that he had been set at liberty. The festivities went on. As soon as Herod ceased to take part in them, Herodias began to entertain. Five of those that knew of John's death were shut up in dungeons. They were the two guards, the executioner and his servant, and Salome's maid who had shown some compassion for the saint. Other guards were placed at the prison door, and they in turn were at regular intervals replaced by others. One of Herod's confidential followers regularly carried food to John's cell, consequently no one had any misgiving of what had taken place.

Jesus in Thanat-Shiloh and Antipatris

Wednesday, January 3, AD 31 (Tebeth 19)

This morning Jesus taught in the synagogue. Afterward, some people from Jerusalem told him of the sudden collapse of a wall and a tower in Jerusalem two days before. As a result, a crowd of laborers, including eighteen master workers sent by Herod, had been buried beneath the falling debris (Luke 13:4). Herod's workmen had engineered the accident to stir up the people against Pontius Pilate. But their plan had backfired, resulting in their own deaths. Jesus expressed his compassion for the innocent laborers, but added that the sin of the master workers was not greater than that of the Pharisees, Sadducees, and others who labored against the kingdom of God. These later would also be buried one day under their own treacherous structures. After healing the sick, Jesus and the disciples made their way to Antipatris, where they stayed overnight in an inn. That night, during the festivities to celebrate Herod's birthday at Machaerus, John the Baptist was beheaded at the request of Herodias' daughter, Salome. After witnessing the spectacle of Salome dancing before him, Herod had said to her: "Ask what you will, and I will give it to you. Yes, I swear, even if you ask for half my kingdom, I shall give it to you." Salome hurriedly conferred with her mother, who told her to ask for the head of John the Baptist on a dish (Mark 6:17–29).

DURING the feast in Machaerus and the beheading of the Baptist, Jesus was in Thanat-Shiloh. There he heard from those that had returned from Jerusalem the catastrophe which had just occurred in the Holy City. A crowd of laborers lately engaged on a great building near the mount upon which stood the temple, along with eighteen master workmen sent thither by Herod, had been buried under the falling walls. Jesus expressed compassion for the innocent sufferers, but said that the sin of the master workmen was not greater than that of the Pharisees, the Sadducees, and all those that labored against the kingdom of God. These latter would likewise be one day buried under their own treacherous structures.

The aqueduct that had cost the lives of so many was probably a quarter of an hour in length. It was intended to conduct the water flowing from the pool of Bethesda up to the mount on which the temple stood, thus to wash down from the court to the lower ravine the blood of the slaughtered animals. Higher up on the mountain was the pool of Bethesda, which discharged the waters received from its source, the Gihon. Three vaulted aqueducts ran far in under the temple mount, and long arcades extended northward across the valley and up to the mount. Nearby stood a high tower in which, by means of wheel-work machinery, water was raised in great leathern vessels from the reservoir far below. The work had long been in progress. Being now in want of good building stone and master workmen, Pilate, acting on the advice of a member of the Sanhedrin, a Herodian in secret, had sought help from

Herod. The master workmen sent by the latter were likewise Herodians. At Herod's instigation, they designedly carried on the building in such a way that the whole structure would necessarily fall at once. By this catastrophe, they intended to embitter the Jews still more against Pilate. The foundation was broad, but hollow, and the structure arose tapering, but heavy. When the disaster happened, the eighteen Herodians were standing upon a terrace opposite the building. They had commanded the wooden scaffolding over which it had been arched to be drawn out, for that now all was solid. The poor laborers were crowded on all parts of the high arches busily working. Suddenly all split asunder, the huge walls came toppling down, and cries went up on all sides. Crash after crash was heard, and clouds of dust swept over the whole region.[D30] Many little dwellings were crushed by the falling stones, as well as a number of laborers and others at the foot of the mount. The place on which the eighteen traitors were standing, loosened by the shock, slid down with the rest, and they too were buried in the ruins. This took place shortly before the festivities at Machaerus, consequently no Roman officer or civil functionary made his appearance at the feast. Pilate became very much enraged against Herod, and thought only of revenging himself. The building was an immense undertaking, and the loss very great. Enmity arose between Pilate and Herod on account of this affair; but by the death of Jesus, that is, by the demolition of the true temple, they again became friends. The destruction of the first edifice buried the wily authors of it along with their innocent victims; that of the second brought judgment upon the whole nation.

The outlet of the pool of Bethesda was now entirely choked up, for the whole ravine was full of debris; in consequence of this, another pool was soon formed by the retarded waters.

When Pilate, greatly exasperated by what had taken place, sent some of his officers to Herod in Machaerus, the latter excused himself as absent from home.

Jesus restored sight to several blind persons in Thanat. After that he went with Peter and John through Shechem to Antipatris. Both of the apostles inquired more than once on the way whether or not he intended to stop at Aruma and other places on their route. But Jesus answered that the people of those places would not receive him, and he proceeded in the direction to Antipatris. During their journey, Jesus instructed his apostles on prayer. He made use of the similitude of a man knocking at his friend's door during the night and begging the loan of three loaves. Toward evening Jesus and his companions reached the woody region outside Antipatris, and there took lodgings at an inn.

Antipatris was situated near a little river. It was a very beautiful city recently built by Herod in honor of his father, Antipater, on the site of a little place named Kaphar-Sheba. During the war with the Maccabees, General Lysias encamped at Kaphar-Sheba, which even at that time was fortified with towers and walls. Being defeated by Judas Maccabeus, he came to terms with him here, warded off from Judea the attacks of other nations, and gave large presents for the restoration of the temple. Antipatris was six hours from the sea. It was Paul's halting place when being led a prisoner to Caesarea. The city was surrounded by uncommonly large trees, while throughout its interior were scattered gardens and magnificent walks. The whole city appeared to be clothed in verdure. The architecture was of pagan style; colonnades, under which one could walk, ran the entire length of the streets.

Thursday, January 4, AD 31 (*Tebeth 20*)

This morning Jesus entered the town of Antipatris, and visited the house of the chief magistrate, whose name was Ozias. Ozias had sent for Jesus because his daughter, Michol, about fourteen years old, was very sick. Jesus healed the girl, who was paralyzed, by anointing her with oil. She arose at Jesus's command, and she and her parents were filled with joy at this miracle. In the synagogue, Jesus told the parables of the good shepherd (John 10:1) and the wicked vine-dressers (Matthew 21:33). Afterward, he healed the sick and then set off for Ozensara, where he arrived late that evening.

When Jesus with Peter and John left the inn and entered the city, he went to the house of the chief magistrate, who was named Ozias. It was principally on account of this man that he had come hither, for his trouble was well known to Jesus. Ozias had sent a messenger out to the inn to invite Jesus to visit him, for his daughter was very sick, and Jesus returned word that he would go that very day. Ozias received him and the two apostles very reverently, washed their feet, and wanted to offer refreshments. But Jesus went straight to the invalid, while the two apostles proceeded through the city to announce the instruction about to be given in the synagogue. Ozias was a man of about forty years. His daughter was called Michol, and she may have been about fourteen. She lay stretched upon her couch, pale, wasted, and so paralyzed as to be unable to move any of her members. She could not raise or turn her head; her attendants had even to move her hands from one place to another. The mother was present and veiled. She bowed humbly before Jesus as he drew near to the maiden's couch, at one side of which she generally remained seated on a cushion in order to render assistance to her daughter. But when Jesus knelt down by the couch, for it was very low, the mother stood reverently on the opposite side, the father at the foot.

Jesus spoke with the invalid, prayed, breathed into her face, and motioned to the mother to kneel down opposite him. She obeyed. Then Jesus poured some oil that he carried with him upon the palm of his hand and, with the first two fingers of his right hand, anointed the sick maiden's forehead and temples, then the joints of both hands, allowing his own hand to rest for one moment upon them. Then he directed the mother to open Michol's long garment over the region of the stomach, which too he anointed with the oil. After that the mother raised the edge of the coverlet from her daughter's feet, and they also received the unction. Then Jesus said: "Michol, give me thy right hand and thy mother thy left!" At this command, the maiden, for the first time, raised both hands and stretched them out. Jesus continued: "Stand up, Michol!" and the pale, haggard child arose to a sitting posture and then to her feet, tottering in the unaccustomed position. Jesus and the mother led her into the open arms of the father. The mother also embraced her. They wept for joy, and all three fell at Jesus's feet. And now came in the servant-men and maids of the house, praising the Lord in accents of joy. Jesus ordered bread and grapes to be brought, and the juice of the latter to be squeezed out. He blessed both, and commanded the maiden to eat and drink a little at a time. When Michol lay upon her couch, she was clothed in a long gown of fine white wool. The piece that covered the breast was fastened upon the shoulders so that it could easily be opened. Her arms were wrapped with broad strips of the same stuff which fastened to the back. Under this gown was a covering on the back and breast like a scapular. As she arose to stand, her mother threw around her a very large, light veil.

Michol's steps were at first tottering and uncertain. She was like one who had forgotten how to walk and stand upright, and she soon lay down again even while eating. But when her young friends and playmates came in, full of shy curiosity, to see with their own eyes the cure that was now noised about, Michol arose and, trembling with emotion, tottered to meet them. Her mother led her like a child. The girls were glad and joyous. They embraced Michol and led her around. Ozias asked Jesus whether his child's malady had come upon her on account of some sin of her parents. Jesus replied: "It came through a dispensation of God." Michol's young companions also thanked Jesus, who then proceeded to the forecourt of the house where he found numbers of people waiting for him with their sick. Here too were Peter and John. Jesus cured the sick of all kinds of maladies and, followed by a crowd, went to the synagogue where the Pharisees and a great multitude were awaiting his coming. He related the parable of the shepherd. He said that he was seeking the lost sheep, that he had sent his servants also to seek them, and that he would die for his sheep. He told them likewise that he had a flock upon his mountain, that they were more secure than some others, and that if the wolf devoured any one of them, it would be owing to its own imprudence. Speaking of his mission, he related another parable. He began: "My Father has a vineyard." At these words, the Pharisees smiled derisively and looked at one another. When he had finished the whole parable, in which he described the ill-treatment the servants of his Father had received from the wicked vinedressers, and said that his Father had now sent his Son whom they would cast out and murder, they laughed in scorn and asked one another: "Who is he? What is he about? Where has his Father that vineyard? He has lost his wits! He is a fool, that's plain to be seen!" And so they went on jeering and laughing. Jesus left the synagogue with Peter and John. The Pharisees continued their insults behind his back, ascribing his miracles to sorcery and the devil.

Jesus returned with Ozias to his house, and again cured many people who were waiting in the forecourt. He took a slight repast, and accepted some bread and balsam for the journey.

Jesus cured in various ways, each one having its own signification. I cannot now, however, repeat them as I saw them. Each had reference to the meaning and the secret cause of the malady, also to the spiritual needs of the invalid. In the anointing with oil, for instance, there was a certain spiritual strength and energy denoted by the signification of the oil itself. No one of these actions was without its own peculiar meaning. With these forms, Jesus instituted all those ceremonies that the saints and priests who exercised their healing power would afterward make use of in his name. They either received them from tradition, or were used in the name of Jesus through an inspiration of the Holy Spirit. As the Son of God, in order to become man, chose the body of a most pure creature, thus to correspond to the requirements of man's nature, so did he frequently use in effecting his cures pure and simple created substances that had been blessed by his Spirit, as, for instance, oil. He afterward gave to the cured bread to eat with some juice of the grape. At other times he healed by a mere command uttered at a distance, for he had come upon earth to cure the most varied ills and that in the most varied ways. He had come to satisfy, for all that believed in him, by his own great sacrifice upon the cross, in which sacrifice were contained all pains and sorrows, all penances and satisfactions. With the various keys of his charity he first opened the fetters and bonds of temporal misery and chastisement, instructed the ignorant in all things necessary for them to know, healed all kinds of maladies, and aided the needy in every way; then with that chief key of his love, the key of the cross, he opened heaven's expiatory door as well as the door of Limbo.

Michol, Ozias's daughter, had been paralyzed from her early years, and it was a special grace that she had for so long a time been unable to move. She had been chained down by sickness during the most perilous years of her childhood, years full of danger to innocence; and in consequence of the same, her parents had an opportunity for the exercise of charity and patience. Had she been well from infancy, what would perhaps have become of both her and her parents? Had the latter not sighed after Jesus, Michol never would have been so blessed. Had they not believed in him, their daughter would never have been cured and anointed, which anointing had imparted wonderful strength and energy both to body and soul. Her sickness was a trial, a consequence of inherited sinfulness, but at the same time a loving discipline, a means of spiritual progress for Michol's soul, as well as for her parents. The patience and resignation of the parents resulted from their cooperation with grace. It brought to them the crown, the recompense of the struggle decreed for them by God, namely, the cure through Jesus of soul and body. What a grace! To be bound down by sufferings, and yet to have the spirit free for good until the Lord comes to deliver both body and soul!

Jesus conversed with Ozias, who told him about the fall of the tower of Siloam and of the unfortunate people buried under its ruins. He spoke with horror of Herod, whom some suspected of being at the bottom of the affair. Jesus remarked that greater calamities would overtake the traitors and false architects than that which had fallen upon the poor workmen. "If," he continued, "Jerusalem does not embrace the salvation offered her, the destruction of the temple will follow that of the tower." Ozias referred also to John's baptism, and expressed the hope that Herod would set him at liberty on the occasion of his birthday festival. Jesus replied that John would be freed when his time came. The Pharisees said to Jesus in the synagogue that he should be on his guard, lest Herod would imprison him with John if he went on as he was then doing. To this Jesus deigned no reply.

About five o'clock in the afternoon, Jesus left Antipatris with Peter and John and went southward to Ozensara, from four to five hours distant. A Roman garrison was stationed in Antipatris, and there were many large trunks of trees brought hither for transportation to the lake, where ship building was carried on. On their way to Ozensara they encountered many such loads of timber drawn by huge oxen and accompanied by Roman soldiers. The trees of this region also were felled and hewed for the same purpose. Jesus instructed several workmen thus employed. It was late when they reached Ozensara, a town divided into

A Water Cistern by the Way

two sections by a little river. Jesus put up here with some people whom he knew. He instructed and admonished a crowd that had collected near the inn. He had been here once before on his way to baptism. He cured and blessed the sick children.

Jesus in Beth-Horon and Bethany

Friday, January 5, AD 31 (Tebeth 21)

Jesus journeyed on from Ozensara to Beth-Horon, where he had already taught on Ab 5. This evening, at the start of the sabbath, he taught in the synagogue. Afterward he healed the sick, but the Pharisees objected to his healing on the sabbath, saying that the sabbath belonged to God. Jesus replied: "I have no other time and no other measure than the will of the Father in heaven." Afterward, when Jesus ate a meal with the Pharisees, they reproached him for allowing women of bad repute to follow him. They meant Mary Magdalene, Dinah the Samaritan, and Mara the Suphanite (Luke 8:1–3). Jesus answered: "If you knew me, you would speak differently. I have come out of compassion for sinners."

IT was about six hours from Ozensara to Beth-Horon. At some distance from the latter place, John and Peter went on ahead, leaving Jesus to follow alone. The Egyptian disciples, along with the son of Johanna Chusa, came to meet Jesus here. They brought news that the holy women were celebrating the sabbath in Machmas, which was situated in a narrow defile four hours to the north of this place. Machmas was the place at which Jesus in his twelfth year withdrew from his parents and returned to the temple. Here it was that Mary missed him and thought that he had gone on to Gophna. Not finding him at this latter place, she was filled with anxious solicitude, and made her way back to Jerusalem.

There was in Beth-Horon a Levitical school, with whose teacher the holy family was acquainted. Anne and Joachim had lodged with him on the occasion of their taking Mary to the temple; and when returning to Nazareth as Joseph's bride, Mary had again stopped at his house. Several of the disciples from Jerusalem had come hither with Joseph of Arimathea's nephews at the time of Jesus's arrival: Jesus went to the synagogue where, amid the contradictions and objections of the Pharisees, he explained the scripture appointed for that sabbath. The instruction over, he cured the sick at the inn, among them several women afflicted with an issue of blood, and blessed some sick children. The Pharisees had invited him to a dinner, and when they found him so tardy in coming, they went to call him. All things, they said, had their time and so had these cures. The sabbath belonged to God, and he had now done enough. Jesus responded: "I have no other time and no other measure than the will of the heavenly Father." When he had finished curing, he accompanied the disciples to the dinner.

During the meal the Pharisees addressed to him all kinds of reproaches; among others they alleged that he allowed women of bad repute to follow him about.[D31] These men had heard of the conversion of Magdalene, of Mara the Suphanite, and of the Samaritan. Jesus replied: "If ye knew me, ye would speak differently. I am come to have pity on sinners." He contrasted external ulcers, which carry off poisonous humors and are easily healed, with internal ones which, though full of loathsome matter, do not affect the appearance of the individual so afflicted.

Saturday, January 6, AD 31 (Tebeth 22)

Today Jesus taught and healed again on the sabbath and had to put up with the Pharisees' objections.

The Pharisees further alleged that his disciples had neglected to wash before the meal, which gave Jesus an opportunity for a timely and energetic protest against the hypocrisy and sanctimoniousness of the Pharisees themselves. When they spoke of the women of ill repute, Jesus related a parable. He asked which was the more praiseworthy, the debtor, who having a great debt, humbly implored indulgence until he could faithfully discharge it little by little; or another who, though deeply in debt, spent all he could lay his hands on in dissolute behavior and, far from thinking of paying what he owed, mocked at the conscientious debtor. Jesus related likewise the parables of the good shepherd and the vineyard, as he had done at Antipatris, but his hearers were indifferent; they did not seize the application.

Jesus and the disciples put up at the Levitical school. Upper Beth-Horon was so elevated that it could be descried from Jerusalem, but Lower Beth-Horon lay at the foot of the mountain.

Sunday, January 7, AD 31 (Tebeth 23)

Journeying on, Jesus passed through Anathoth, the birthplace of the prophet Jeremiah. He then went on to Bethany, where Mary Magdalene was now living. She had moved into the living quarters of her sister, Silent Mary, who had died on Nisan 18. Mary Magdalene set off to meet Jesus, before he arrived at Bethany. She cast herself down at his feet, shedding tears of repentance and gratitude. Jesus raised her up and spoke tenderly to her, saying that she should follow in the footsteps of her departed sister who, although she had not sinned, had done penance. At Bethany, Jesus met with his mother, who had traveled with some of the holy women to see him there. Jesus spoke with her privately about the death of John the Baptist—about which she already knew by inner revelation.

From Beth-Horon, which was six hours distant from Jerusalem, Jesus went straight on to Bethany, stopping at no place on the way excepting Anathoth. Lazarus had already returned to Bethany from Magdalum, where he had put everything in order and engaged a steward for the castle and other property. To the man who had lived with Magdalene, he had assigned a dwelling situated on the heights near Ginea and sufficient means for his support. The gift was gladly accepted.

As soon as she arrived in Bethany, Magdalene went straight to the dwelling of her deceased sister, Mary the Silent, by whom she had been very much beloved, and spent the whole night in tears. When Martha went to her in the morning, she found her weeping on the grave of her sister, her hair unbound and flowing around her.

The women of Jerusalem also had returned to their homes, all making the journey on foot. Magdalene, though exhausted by her malady and the shocks she had received, and wholly unaccustomed to such traveling, insisted upon walking like the others. Her feet bled more than once. The holy women who, since her conversion, showed her unspeakable affection, were often obliged to come to her assistance. She was pale and exhausted from weeping. She could not resist her desire to express her gratitude to Jesus, so she went over an hour's journey to meet him, threw herself at his feet, and bedewed them with repentant and grateful tears. Jesus extended his hand to her, raised her, and addressed to her words of kindness. He spoke of her deceased sister, Mary the Silent. He said that she should tread in her footsteps and do penance as she had done, although she had never sinned. Magdalene then returned home with her maid by another way.

Jesus went with Peter and John into Lazarus's garden. Lazarus came out to meet him, conducted him to the house and offered him in the hall the customary attentions, namely, washing of feet and refreshments. Nicodemus was not there, but Joseph of Arimathea was present. Jesus stayed in the house and spoke with no one excepting the members of the family and the holy women. Only with Mary did he speak of John's death, for she knew of it by interior revelation. Jesus told her to return to Galilee within a week in order to escape the annoyances of a crowded road, for Herod's guests from that part of the country would a little later be going from Machaerus to their homes.

The disciples that were going to Judea at the same time as Jesus, though not with him, stopped at the different places on the road, went into the huts on the wayside and to the shepherds in the fields, asking: "Are there any sick here whom we may cure in the name of our Master, that we may freely give to them what he has freely given to us?" Then anointing the sick with oil, they were cured.

Monday, January 8, AD 31 (Tebeth 24)

Jesus left Bethany and crossed the Mount of Olives. Weeping, he turned to those with him and said: "If this city (Jerusalem) does not accept salvation, its temple will be destroyed like this building that has tumbled down. A great number will be buried in the ruins." He referred to the recent catastrophe of the collapsing building as an example that should serve to the people as a warning (Luke 13:3–5). He visited the laborers' hospital at the southern foot of the Mount of Olives, healing the sick there and also those who had been wounded in the catastrophe. Then he went to Bethlehem and visited an inn, not far from the city gate, frequented by Essenes and other holy people. Afterward, he set off in the direction of Hebron, making his way to Zechariah's house at Jutta. Since Zechariah and Elizabeth had died, a cousin of John the Baptist lived in the house. Here Jesus met up with his mother, the holy women, and others from Jerusalem, who had traveled on ahead. They exchanged greetings. Jesus then went to the synagogue in Jutta, where he spoke of David, who had been born in Hebron.

Jerusalem Viewed from the Mount of Olives

Jesus left Bethany the next morning. He crossed the Mount of Olives to teach and heal in a neighboring place where some masons and other mechanics were encamped. It was the camping ground of the day laborers and masons engaged on the interminable buildings of the temple mount. There were some kitchens around the place in which poor women cooked the workmen's food for a trifle. There were many Galileans among the workmen, also some people who had been attracted thither by Jesus's teaching and miracles, some even whom he had cured. Some too were from Gischala, from Zorobabel the centurion's estate, and many others from a little place near Tiberias on the northern height of the valley of Magdalum. Jesus cured many sick among these people. They bemoaned to him the great misfortune that had happened about fourteen days before in the falling of that huge building, and begged him to visit several of the wounded who had barely escaped with their lives. Ninety-three people, besides the eighteen treacherous architects, had been killed. Jesus went to the wounded, whom he consoled and healed. He healed several of contusions on the head by anointing the head with oil and pressing it between his hands; and crushed hands on which splinters of bones were projecting he healed by fixing the pieces together, anointing them, and holding them in his own hands. Broken arms bound up in bandages Jesus anointed, then held the fractures in his hands, and they were made whole, so that the bandages could be removed and the arms used. The wounds of lost limbs, he closed.

I heard Jesus saying to the assembled multitude that they would have greater evils to bemoan when the sword would strike Galilee. He advised them to pay all taxes to the Emperor without murmuring, and if they had not the means to do so, they should apply to Lazarus in his name, and he would furnish what was necessary. Jesus spoke with touching kindness to these poor people. I heard them complaining that once they were able to obtain help at the pool of Bethesda, but now poor people could no longer look there for assistance—they had to languish unaided. For a long time past, they had heard of no cure at the pool.

Jesus wept as he crossed the Mount of Olives. He said, "If the city (Jerusalem) does not accept salvation, its temple will be destroyed like this building that has tumbled down. A great number will be buried in the ruins." He called the catastrophe of the aqueduct an example that should serve to the people as a warning.

Jesus went afterward to the house outside the Bethlehem gate of Jerusalem at which Mary and Joseph had lodged with him, a babe of forty days, when they were going to present him in the temple. Anne also had spent a night here when journeying to the crib, and Jesus had done the same when, in his twelfth year, he had at Machmas left his parents who were returning home and gone back to the temple. This little inn was in the hands of very devout, simple-hearted people, and it was there that the Essenes and other pious souls took lodgings. The present proprietors were the children of those that had lived there thirty years before, and there was one old man who remembered perfectly all the circumstances of those visits. They did not, however, recognize Jesus, for he had not been there for a long time. They thought perhaps he was John the Baptist, of whom even here the report was current that he had been set at liberty.

They showed Jesus in one corner of the house a doll in swaddling bands, clothed exactly as he himself had been when Mary bore him to the temple. It was lying in a crib like his own, and around it burned lights and lamps that appeared to rise out of paper horns. They said to Jesus: "Jesus of Nazareth, the great prophet, was born in Bethlehem three and thirty years ago, and was brought here by his mother. What comes from God, one may honor, and why should we not celebrate his birthday for six weeks if similar honors are paid to Herod, who is no prophet?"

These people, through their connections with Anne and other intimate friends of the holy family, as well as through the accounts of the shepherds who put up at their inn when they visited Jerusalem, were reverential believers in Jesus, Mary, and Joseph. When Jesus now made himself known to them their joy was beyond expression. They showed him every place in the house and garden hallowed by the presence of Mary, Joseph, and Anne. Jesus instructed and consoled them, and they exchanged gifts. Jesus directed one of the disciples to give them some coins while at the same time he accepted from them some bread, fruit, and honey for his journey.

They accompanied him quite a distance when, with the disciples, he left the inn and started for Hebron.

Jesus in Jutta • He Makes Known the Death of John the Baptist

Tuesday, January 9, AD 31 (Tebeth 25)

Jesus and his disciples spent the day in and around Jutta, teaching and healing. That evening, after the other women had retired, Jesus and his mother, accompanied by Peter, John, and the three sons of Mary Heli (who had been disciples of the Baptist), went into the room where John the Baptist had been born. Kneeling together with the others, on a large rug, the holy Virgin, Jesus's mother, recounted events from the Baptist's life. Then Jesus told them that John had been put to death by Herod. Stricken with grief, they shed tears of lamentation on the rug. Jesus consoled them with earnest words. He said that silence should be maintained, at least for the time being. For, with the exception of his murderers, apart from them, none knew of John the Baptist's death.

JESUS went with his companions to Jutta, the Baptist's birthplace. It was five hours' distance from the inn outside Jerusalem and one hour from Hebron. Mary, Veronica, Susanna, Johanna Chusa, Johanna Mark, Lazarus, Joseph of Arimathea, Nicodemus, and several of the disciples from Jerusalem were there awaiting Jesus. They had traveled in small parties and, having come by a shorter route from Jerusalem, had reached their destination several hours before him.

Zechariah's house was situated on a hill outside of Jutta. Both it and its surroundings, consisting of vineyards, were the inheritance of the Baptist. The son of his father's brother, likewise named Zechariah, occupied the house at this time and managed affairs. He was a Levite and an intimate friend of Luke, by whom not long before he had been visited in Jerusalem, and had then heard many particulars of the holy family. He was younger than the Baptist, of the age of the apostle John. From his early years he had been like an own child in Elizabeth's house. He belonged to that class of Levites who were most like the Essenes and who, having received from their ancestors the knowledge of certain mysteries, waited with earnest devotion for the coming of the Messiah. Zechariah was enlightened and unmarried. He received Jesus and his companions with the customary marks of respect, washing of feet and refreshments. After that Jesus repaired to the synagogue in Hebron.

It was a fast day, and on that evening began a local celebration in Jutta and Hebron. It was in memory of David's victory over Absalom who had in Hebron, as being his birthplace, first raised the standard of revolt. Numerous lamps were lighted during this feast even in the daytime, both in the synagogue and private dwellings. The people gave thanks for the interior light which had at that time led their ancestors to choose the right, and implored a continuance of that heavenly illumination, to enable them always to make choice of the same. Jesus delivered an instruction to a very large audience. The Levites showed him great esteem and affection, and he took a meal with them.

As Mary was making the journey with the women to this part of the country, she related to them many particulars connected with her former journey thither with Joseph on the occasion of her visit to Elizabeth. She showed them the spot on which Joseph had bade her farewell on his departure for home, and told them how uneasy she felt when she reflected upon what Joseph's thought would certainly be when on his return he would notice her changed condition. She visited likewise with the holy women all the places where mysteries connected with her visitation and the birth of John had occurred. She told of John's leaping for joy in his mother's womb, of Elizabeth's salutation, and of the Magnificat which she had herself uttered under the inspiration of God, and which she afterward recited every evening with Elizabeth. She told of Zechariah's being struck mute and of God's restoring his speech at the moment in which he pronounced the name of John. All these mysteries, until now unknown to them, Mary, with tears started by tender recollections, related to the holy women. They too wept at the different places, but their tears were more joyful than those of Mary, who was at the same time mourning John's death, still unknown to them. She showed them also the fountain which at her prayer had sprung up near the house, and from it they all drank.

At the family meal Jesus taught. The women were seated apart. After the meal, the blessed Virgin went with Jesus, Peter, John, and the Baptist's three disciples, James, Heliachim, and Sadoch (the sons of her eldest sister Mary Heli) into the room in which John was born. They spread out a large rug, or carpet, on the floor and all knelt or sat around it. Jesus, however, remained standing. He spoke to them of John's holiness and of his career. Then the blessed Virgin related to them the circumstances under which that rug had been made. At the time of her visit, she said, Elizabeth and herself had made it and on it John was born. It was Elizabeth's couch at the time of his birth. It was made of yellow wool, quilted and ornamented with flowers. On the upper border were embroidered in large letters passages from Elizabeth's salutation and the Magnificat. In the middle was fastened a kind of cover or pouch, into which the woman about to become a mother could have her feet buttoned up as in a sack. The upper part of this pouch formed a kind of hooded mantle that could be thrown around her. It was of yellow wool, with brown flowers, and was something like a dressing gown, the lower half being fastened to a quilted rug. I saw Mary raising the upper border before her while she read and explained the passages and prophecies embroidered on it. She told them also that she had prophesied to Elizabeth that John would see Jesus face to face only three times, and how this was verified: first, as a child in the desert when on their flight into Egypt, Jesus, Joseph, and herself had passed him, though at some distance; the second time, at Jesus's baptism; and the third, when at the Jordan he saw Jesus passing and bore witness to him.

And now Jesus disclosed to them the fact that John had been put to death by Herod. Deep grief seized upon them all. They watered the rug with their tears, especially John, who threw himself weeping on the floor. It was heartrending to behold them prostrate on the floor, sobbing and lamenting, their faces pressed upon the rug. Jesus and Mary alone were standing, one at each end. Jesus consoled them with earnest words and prepared them for still more cruel blows. He commanded silence on the matter since, with the exception of themselves, it was at present known only to its authors.

Wednesday, January 10, AD 31 (Tebeth 26)

This morning, with his disciples, Jesus visited the cave of Machpelah near the grove of Mamre where Abraham, Sarah, Isaac, and Jacob were buried. All entered the cave barefoot and stood in reverential silence. Only Jesus spoke. Then they visited the town of Bethain, where Jesus taught and healed.

Southward from Hebron was the grove of Mamre and the cave of Machpelah, where Abraham and the other patriarchs were buried. Jesus gave an instruction and cured some sick peasants who there lived isolated. The forest of Mamre was a valley full of oaks, beeches, and nut trees, that stood far apart. At the edge of the forest was the vast cave Machpelah, in which Abraham, Sarah, Jacob, Isaac, and others of the patriarchs were entombed. The cave was a double one like two cellars. Some of the tombs were hewn out in the projecting rocks, while others were formed in the rocky wall. This grotto is still held in great veneration. A flower garden and place for instruction guard its entrance. The rock was thickly clothed with vines, and higher up grain was raised. Jesus entered the grotto with the disciples, and several of the tombs were opened. Some of the skeletons were fallen to dust, but that of Abraham lay on its couch in a state of preservation. From it they unrolled a brown cover woven of camel's-hair cords thick as a man's finger. Jesus taught here. He spoke of Abraham, of the Promise and its fulfillment.

Some of the sick whom Jesus cured here were paralyzed, others consumptive, others dropsical. I saw here no possessed, though there were some simpletons and lunatics. The country around was very fertile, and the remarkably beautiful grain was already quite yellow.

The bread of these parts was excellent, and almost everyone had his own vine. The mountains terminated in plateaus upon which grain was cultivated; their sides were covered with vineyards, and in them extended wonderful caves.

When Jesus and the disciples went into the cave Machpelah, they put off their shoes outside the entrance, walked in barefoot, and stood in reverential silence around Abraham's tomb. Jesus alone spoke. From there he went an hour southeast of Hebron into the little Levitical city of Bethain, which was reached by a very steep ascent. He wrought some cures and gave an instruction in which he spoke of the Ark of the Covenant and of David, for at Bethain the Ark had once rested for fifteen days. David, on God's command, had caused the Ark to be secretly removed by night from the house of Obededon and brought hither, he himself preceding it barefoot. When he took it away again, the people were so exasperated that they almost stoned him.

There was up here near Bethain a very deep spring, from which the water was drawn in leathern bags, or bottles. The rocky soil of the roads was white, also the little pebbles on it.

Nicodemus, Joseph of Arimathea, Lazarus, the women of Jerusalem, and Mary started on their homeward journey, Lazarus going to Jerusalem, where he had to discharge a seven days' service in the temple.

Mary did not return to Bethany, but went straight to Galilee by way of Machmas, where she celebrated the sabbath at the schoolmaster's house. She had Anna Cleophas and one of Elizabeth's relatives from Sapha with her. Sapha was the birthplace of James and John. Mary had brought Elizabeth's rug with her. A servant carried it rolled up in a basket.

When speaking in Jutta to those to whom the blessed Virgin was showing the rug, Jesus referred to John's eager desire to see himself (Jesus). But John had, he said, overcome himself and longed for nothing beyond the fulfillment of his mission, which was that of precursor and preparer, not that of constant companion and fellow laborer. When a little boy he had indeed seen Jesus. When his parents were journeying with him through the desert on their flight into Egypt, their road led past the spot where John was, about the distance of an arrow shot. John was running along a brook among the high bushes. He held in his hand a little stick upon which was fastened a pennant of bark, which he waved to them as he skipped and danced for joy along the brook, until they had crossed it and were out of sight. His parents, Mary and Joseph, Jesus continued, held him up with the words: "See, John in the desert!" It was thus the Holy Spirit had led the boy to salute his Master whom he had already saluted in his mother's womb. While Jesus was relating the above, the disciples were shedding tears at the thought of John's death, and I saw again the indescribably touching scene to which he was referring. John was naked with the exception of the skin that he wore crossed over one shoulder and girded around his waist. He felt that his Savior was near and that he was athirst. Then the boy prayed, drove his little stick into the earth, and a gushing spring spouted up. John ran on some distance ahead and waited, dancing and waving his little standard at them, to see Jesus and his parents as they journeyed past the little current. Then I beheld him hurrying back to a kind of dell where a great overhanging rock formed a cave. A stream from that spring found its way into a little cavity in the dell, which John turned into a well for his own use. He remained in that cave a long time. The way of the holy family on that journey led across a portion of the Mount of Olives. One half-hour east of Bethlehem they halted to rest, and then pursued their way, the Dead Sea to their left, seven hours to the south of the city and two hours beyond Hebron, where they entered the desert in which was the boy John. I saw them stepping across the new rivulet, pausing to rest in a pleasant spot near it, and refreshing themselves with its waters. On the return journey of the holy family from Egypt, John again saw Jesus in spirit. He sprang forward exultingly in the direction of his Lord, but he did not then see him face to face, as they were separated by a distance of two hours. Jesus spoke also of John's great self-command. Even when baptizing him, he had restrained himself within the bounds exacted by the solemn occasion, although his heart was well-nigh broken by intense love and desire. After the ceremony, he was more intent upon humbling himself before him than upon gratifying his love by looking at him.

Thursday, January 11, AD 31 (Tebeth 27)

Jesus went to Hebron, where he taught in the synagogue, where the festival of the expulsion of the Sadducees from the Sanhedrin was being celebrated. He spoke out forcefully against the Sadducees for denying the resurrection of the dead. Afterward, he healed several people at their homes.

Jesus taught in the synagogue of Hebron on the occasion of a festival celebrated in memory of the expulsion from the Sanhedrin of the Sadducees who, under Alexander Jannaeus, had been the domineering party. There were three triumphal arches erected around the synagogue, and to them vine leaves, ears of corn, and all kinds of floral wreaths were brought. The people formed a procession through the streets, which were strewn with flowers, for it was likewise the beginning of the Feast of the New Moon, that of the sap's rising, and lastly that of the purification of the four-year-old trees. It was on this account that so many arches of leaves and flowers were erected. This Feast of the Expulsion of the Sadducees (who denied the resurrection) coincided very appropriately with that upon which was celebrated the return of the trees to new life.

In his discourse in the synagogue Jesus spoke very forcibly against the Sadducees and of the resurrection of the dead. Some Pharisees from Jerusalem had come hither for the feast. They did not dispute with Jesus, but behaved most courteously. He indeed experienced no contradiction here, for the people were upright and very well-disposed. He performed some cures both in the houses and before the synagogue, the cured being mostly of the working class. There were cripples, consumptives, paralytics, and simpletons, also others disturbed by certain temptations.

Jutta and Hebron were connected. Jutta was a kind of suburb joined to Hebron by a row of houses. Formerly they must have been entirely separated, for a turreted wall in ruins, as well as a little valley, ran between the two places. Zechariah's house comprised the school of Jutta. It was about a quarter of an hour from the city and was situated on a hill. Around it lay lovely gardens and vineyards, and not far off were other luxuriant vineyards in the midst of which stood a little dwelling. These vineyards likewise belonged to Zechariah. The school was adjoining the room in which John was born. I saw all that while Jesus, Mary, and the disciples were examining the rug.

Friday, January 12, AD 31 (Tebeth 28)

Jesus spent the whole day healing the sick and teaching at the entrance to the synagogue in Hebron. That evening, with the onset of the sabbath, he spoke in the synagogue about the institution of the paschal lamb. At one point in his talk, he said: "When the sun and moon are darkened, the mother brings the child to the temple to be redeemed." He also alluded to John the Baptist and spoke of the martyrdom of many of the prophets. A profound silence spread through the synagogue, affecting all deeply and causing many to shed tears. At this moment, too, several of John's relatives and friends received an interior revelation of John the Baptist's death, and many fainted from grief. Afterward, Jesus shared a meal with them and related the details of John's murder. He spoke comforting words to all present.

The next time that Jesus taught in the synagogue of Hebron the sacred edifice was thrown open on all sides, and near the entrance, placed in an elevated position, was a teacher's chair by which he stood. All the inhabitants of the city and numbers from the surrounding places were assembled, the sick lying on little beds or sitting on mats around the teacher's chair. The whole place was crowded. The festal arches were still standing and the scene was truly touching. The multitude seemed impressed and edified, and above all not a word of contradiction was heard. After the instruction Jesus cured the sick.

Jesus's discourse on this occasion was full of deep significance. The lessons from scripture were those referring to the Egyptian darkness, the institution of the paschal lamb, and the redeeming of the firstborn; there was also something from Jeremiah. Jesus gave a marvelously profound explanation of the ransom of the firstborn. I remember that he said: "When sun and moon are darkened, the mother brings the child to the temple to be redeemed." More than once he made use of the expression, "The obscuring of the sun and of the moon."

He referred to conception, birth, circumcision, and presentation in the temple as connected with darkness and light. The departure from Egypt, so full of mystery, was applied to the birth of humankind. He spoke of circumcision as an external sign which, like the obligation to ransom the firstborn, would one day be abolished. No one gainsaid Jesus; all his hearers were very quiet and attentive. He spoke likewise of Hebron and of Abraham, and came at last to Zechariah and John. He alluded to John's high dignity in terms more detailed and intelligible than ever before, namely, his birth, his life in the desert, his preaching of penance, his baptism, his faithful discharge of his mission as precursor, and lastly of his imprisonment. Then he alluded to the fate of the prophets and the high priest Zechariah, who had been murdered between the altar and the sanctuary, also the sufferings of Jeremiah in the dungeon at Jerusalem, and the persecutions endured by the others. When Jesus spoke of the murder of the first Zechariah between the temple and the altar, the relatives present thought of the sad fate of the Baptist's father, whom Herod had decoyed to Jerusalem and then caused to be put to death in a neighboring house. Jesus nevertheless had made no mention of this last fact. Zechariah was buried in a vault near his own house outside of Jutta.

As Jesus was thus speaking in an impressive and very significant manner of John and the death of the prophets, the silence throughout the synagogue grew more profound. All were deeply affected, many were shedding tears, and even the Pharisees were very much moved. Several of John's relatives and friends at this moment received an interior illumination by which they understood that the Baptist himself was dead, and they fainted away from grief. This gave rise to some excitement in the synagogue. Jesus quieted the disturbance by directing the bystanders to support those that had fainted, as they would soon revive; so they lay a few moments in the arms of their friends, while Jesus went on with his discourse.

To me there was something significant in the words, "Between the temple and the altar," as recorded of the murder of that first Zechariah. They might well be applied to John the Baptist's death since, in the life of Jesus, it also stood between the temple and the altar, for John died between the birth of Jesus and his sacrifice upon the altar of the cross. But this signification of the words did not present itself to Jesus's hearers. At the close of the instruction they who had fainted were conducted to their homes. Besides Zechariah, John's cousin, Elizabeth had a niece, her sister's daughter, married here in Hebron. She had a family of twelve children, of whom some were daughters already grown. It was these and some others who had been so deeply affected. On leaving the synagogue Jesus went with young Zechariah and the disciples to the house of Elizabeth's niece, where he had not yet been. The holy women, however, had visited her several times before their departure. Jesus had engaged to sup with her this day, but it was a very sad meal.

Jesus was in a room with Peter, John, James Cleophas, Heliachim, Sadoch, Zechariah, Elizabeth's niece and her husband. John's relatives asked Jesus in a trembling voice: "Lord, shall we see John again?" They were in a retired room, the door locked, so that no one could disturb them. Jesus answered with tears: "No!" and spoke most feelingly, but in consoling terms, of John's death. When they sadly expressed their fear that the body would be ill-treated, Jesus reassured them. He told them no, that the corpse was lying untouched, though the head had been abused and thrown into a sewer; but that too would be preserved and would one day come to light. He told them likewise that in some days Herod would leave Machaerus and the news of John's death would spread abroad; then they could take away the body. Jesus wept with his sorrowful listeners. They afterward partook of a repast which, on account of the retired situation of the apartment, the silence, the gravity, the great ardor and emotion of Jesus, made me think of the Last Supper.

I had on this occasion a vision of Mary's coming to present Jesus in the temple, which presentation took place on the forty-third day after his birth. The holy family, on account of a feast of three days, had to remain with the good people of the little inn outside the Bethlehem gate. Besides the usual offering of doves, Mary brought five little triangular plates of gold, gifts of the three kings, and several pieces of fine embroidered stuff as a present for the temple. The ass that he had pawned to one of his relatives, Joseph now sold to him. I am under the impression that the ass used by Jesus on Palm Sunday sprang from it.

Saturday, January 13, AD 31 (Tebeth 29)

This morning, after teaching in the synagogue at Jutta, Jesus healed a number of people in the neighborhood around the town. After the close of the sabbath, Joseph of Arimathea, who had come from Jerusalem, invited Jesus to heal there before returning to Galilee.

Jesus taught in Jutta also and, accompanied by about ten Levites, went to the houses in the neighborhood, in which he restored many sick to health. Neither lepers, nor raging possessed, nor great sinners male or female, appeared before him in these parts. That evening he took with the Levites a frugal meal consisting of birds, bread, honey, and fruit.

Joseph of Arimathea and several disciples were come hither in order to invite Jesus to Jerusalem, where numbers of sick were longing for him. He could, they said, come now without fear of molestation, since Pilate and Herod were in conflict with each other on the subject of the ruined aqueduct, and the Jewish magistrates likewise had their attention fixed upon the point at issue. But Jesus would not go right away, though he promised to do so before his return to Galilee.

John's female relatives celebrated the sabbath at their own home. They clothed themselves in mourning garments and sat on the ground, a stand full of lights, or lamps, being placed in the center of the apartment.

The Essenes who dwelt near Abraham's tomb came two by two to Jesus. They lived around a mountain in cells cut out of the rock. Upon the mountain was a garden which they owned.

All around Zechariah's house were very lovely gardens and remarkably high, thick rosebushes. Coming hither from Jerusalem, one could see it on the hill; about a quarter of an hour farther on and to the right rose a higher hill upon which were his vineyards, and at its foot gushed the spring that Mary had discovered. The Hebron of Abraham was not identical with that in which Jesus now was. The former lay to the south in ruins, separated from the latter by a valley. In Abraham's time, when it was still in existence, it had broad streets and houses partly hewn out of the rock. Not far from Zechariah's house was a place called Jether. I saw Mary and Elizabeth there several times.

The people of Jutta began to suspect from the words of Jesus and the mourning of the Baptist's relatives that John was no longer among the living, and soon the report of his death was whispered around.

SHEBAT (30 days): January 13/14 to February 11/12, AD 31 Shebat New Moon: January 12, at 3:45 AM Jerusalem time

Sunday, January 14, AD 31 (Shebat 1)

Today Jesus visited the grave of Zechariah. It was decided that John's body should be brought from Machaerus and buried in Jutta. Then Jesus left, escorted by about twenty friends and disciples. That evening everyone went to an inn near Libnath.

Before his departure from Jutta, Jesus visited Zechariah's tomb in company with his disciples and the nephews of the murdered man. It was not like ordinary tombs. It was more like the catacombs, consisting of a vault supported on pillars. It was a most honorable burial place for priests and prophets. It had been determined that John's body should be brought from Machaerus and here buried, therefore the vault was arranged and a funeral couch erected. It was very touching to see Jesus helping to prepare a resting place for his friend. He rendered honor to the remains of Zechariah also.

Elizabeth was not buried here, but on a high mountain, in that cave in which John had sojourned when a boy in the desert.

On Jesus's departure from Jutta, he was followed by an escort of men and women. The latter, after accompanying him the distance of an hour, took leave, but not till they had knelt and received his blessing. They wanted to kiss his feet, but Jesus would not allow it. Jesus and his disciples were now journeying toward Libnath, outside of which they stopped at an inn. The men of the escort now set out for home.

Monday, January 15, AD 31 (Shebat 2)

Today Saturnin, Joseph Barsabbas, and two other disciples arrived from Galilee at the inn near Libnath. In the evening, a group of disciples left the inn and went to Machaerus to collect John the Baptist's body.

Saturnin, Joseph Barsabbas, and two other disciples who had gone from Galilee to Machaerus, then to Jutta, and lastly had come hither in quest of Jesus, arrived today. With many expressions of grief they related the murder of the Baptist. When Herod and his family, with a numerous escort of soldiers, removed from Machaerus to Hesebon, the news of John's beheading was spread by some deserters. Some of the centurion Zorobabel's servants who had been wounded at the late disaster in Jerusalem, returning to Capernaum had also brought the news. Zorobabel had immediately imparted the frightful occurrence to Joseph Barsabbas, who was in the neighborhood—upon which he, with Saturnin and two other disciples, hastened into the region of Machaerus, where they everywhere received the same account. From Machaerus they had hurried to John's native place in order to take steps for the removal of the body. But hearing that Jesus was at the inn, they had come hither to meet him. Soon after, accompanied by the sons of Mary Heli, Joseph of Arimathea's nephews, those of Zechariah, and the sons of Johanna Chusa and Veronica, they set out for Machaerus, taking Jutta on their route. They took with them an ass laden with all that was necessary for carrying out their design. Machaerus now, with the exception of a few soldiers, was quite deserted.

Jesus tarried awhile in these parts in order not to meet Pilate who, with his wife and a retinue of fifteen persons, was on his way from Jerusalem to Appolonia. He passed through Bethzur and Antipatris. From Appolonia he embarked for Rome, to lodge a complaint against Herod.

Before his departure from Jerusalem, Pilate had held a conference with his officers upon Jesus the Galilean who performed so great miracles and who was then in the vicinity of Jerusalem. Pilate asked: "Is he followed by a crowd? Are they armed?" "No," was the answer. "He goes about with only a few disciples and people of no account whatever, people from the very lowest classes, and sometimes he goes alone. He teaches on the mountains and in the synagogues, cures the sick and gives alms. To hear his instructions, people gather from all quarters, often to the number of several thousands!" "Does he not speak against the Emperor?" asked Pilate. "No. His teachings are all on the improvement of morals. He inculcates the practice of mercy, and impresses upon his hearers to render to the Emperor that which belongs to him, and to God that which is His. But he often makes mention of a kingdom that he calls his own, and says that it is near at hand." Thereupon Pilate replied: "So long as he does not go around working his miracles with soldiers or an armed crowd, there is nothing to be feared from him. As soon as he leaves a place in which he has performed miracles and goes to another, he will be forgotten and calumniated. Indeed I hear that the Jewish priests themselves are against him. No danger is to be apprehended from him. But if he is once seen going about with armed followers, his roving must come to an end!"

Pilate had already had several encounters with the Jews, who detested him. Once he had ordered the Roman standards to be brought into the city, whereupon the Jews raised a sedition. Another time, on the occasion of a certain feast upon which the Jews were not allowed to bear arms nor to touch money, I saw Pilate's soldiers go into the temple, break open the box in which were the offerings, and carry off the contents. That was when John was still baptizing at the Jordan near Ono, and Jesus came out from the desert.

Tuesday, January 16, AD 31 (Shebat 3)

Today Jesus went from Libnath to Bethzur, where he was well received. Lazarus and some other friends from Jerusalem were already waiting for him in the inn near the synagogue.

From Libnath Jesus went to Bethzur, about ten hours to the north and two hours' distance from Jerusalem. Bethzur was a fortified place. It had citadels, ramparts and moats, which had, however, somewhat fallen to ruin, though not so much as those of Bethulia. Bethzur was certainly as large as Beth-Horon. The side by which Jesus entered was not steep, while between it and Jerusalem lay a beautiful valley. From the high points of either city the other could be seen. On the opposite side the ascent was steep and the city built with a view to ward off enemies. The Ark of the Covenant was once at Bethzur for a long time, as was publicly known.

Jesus was very well received at Bethzur. Lazarus and some others of his friends from Jerusalem were already there. The Bethzurites washed Jesus's feet, as also those of the disciples, and with sincere affection offered them an abundant supply of whatever they needed. Jesus lodged at an inn near the synagogue.

The three kings, when journeying from Jerusalem to the crib, passed near Bethzur, took some refreshments at a caravanserai, and once more saw the star in this region.

Bethzur must not be confounded with a certain Bethsoron that lay between Bethlehem and Hebron, and near which Philip baptized the servant of Queen Candace. Sometimes this place, namely, Bethsoron, is improperly called Bethzur.

Wednesday, January 17, AD 31 (Shebat 4)

Jesus healed some sick people in their homes. Then he visited a school, where he blessed the children.

In some houses of Bethzur, Jesus cured without disturbance several old people that were very sick, some of them dropsical. The inhabitants were very well-disposed, and the elders of the synagogue themselves conducted Jesus to the different houses. He taught also in the school, and I saw him blessing a great number of children, first the boys and then the girls. He greatly interested himself with them, and performed some cures among them.

John's Remains Taken from Machaerus and Buried at Jutta

WHEN Saturnin, with the disciples, reached Machaerus, they climbed the mountain on which stood Herod's castle. They carried under their arms three strong wooden bars, about a hand in breadth, a leathern cover in two parts, leathern bottles, boxes in the form of bags, rolls of linen cloths, sponges, and other similar things. The disciples best known at the castle asked the guards to be allowed to enter, but on being refused, they retraced their steps, went around the rampart and climbed upon one another's shoulders over three ramparts and two moats to the vicinity of John's prison. It looked as if God helped them, so quickly did they enter, and without disturbance. After that they descended from a round opening above the interior of the dungeons. When the two soldiers on guard at the entrance to John's cell perceived them and drew near with their torches, the disciples went boldly on to meet them, and said: "We are the disciples of the Baptist. We are going to take away the body of our master, whom Herod put to death." The soldiers offered no opposition, but opened the prison door. They were exasperated against Herod on account of John's murder, and were glad to have a share in this good work. Several of their comrades had taken flight during the last few days.

As they entered the prison the torches went out, and I saw the whole place filled with light. I do not know whether all present saw it, but I am inclined to think that they did, since they went about everything as quickly and as dexterously as if it were clear daylight. The disciples first hastened to John's body and prostrated before it in tears. Besides them, I saw in the prison the apparition of a tall, shining lady. She looked very much like the Mother of God at the time of her death. I found out later that it was Elizabeth. At first she seemed to me so natural as I watched her rendering all kinds of assistance that more than once I wondered who she could be and how she had gotten in with the disciples.

The corpse was still lying covered with the hairy garment. The disciples quickly set about making the funeral preparations. They spread out cloths upon which they laid the body, and then proceeded to wash it. They had brought with them for that purpose water in leathern bottles, and the soldiers supplied them with basins of a brownish hue. Joseph Barsabbas, James, and Heliachim took charge of the principal part of these last kind offices to the dead, the others handing what was needed and helping when necessary. I saw the apparition taking part in everything; indeed, she appeared to be the moving spirit of all, uncovering, covering, putting here, turning there, wrapping the winding-sheets—in a word, supplying each one with whatever was wanted at the moment. Her presence seemed to facilitate dispatch and order in an incredible manner. I saw them opening the body and removing the intestines, which they put into a leathern pouch. Then they placed all kinds of aromatic herbs and spices around the corpse, and bound it firmly in linen bands. It was amazingly thin, and appeared to be quite dried up.

Meanwhile, some of the other disciples gathered up a quantity of blood that had flowed on the spot upon which the head had fallen, as well as that upon which the body had lain, and put it into the empty bags that had held the herbs and spices. They then laid the body wrapped in its winding-sheet upon the leathern covers, which they fastened on top by means of a rod made for that purpose. The two light wooden bars were run into the leathern straps of the covers, which now formed a kind of box. The bars, though thin and light, showed no signs of bending under their load. The skin that John used to wear was thrown over the whole, and two of the disciples bore away the sacred remains. The others followed with the blood in the leathern bottle and the intestines in the pouch. The two soldiers left Machaerus with them. They guided the disciples through narrow passages back of the ramparts and out through that subterranean way by which John had been brought into the prison. All was done rapidly and with recollection so touching that no words can describe it.

I saw them at first with rapid steps descending the mountain in the dark. Soon, however, I saw them with a torch; two walked between the poles carrying the body on their shoulders, and the others followed. I cannot say how impressive was the sight of this procession proceeding so silently and swiftly through the darkness by the glare of their one torch. They appeared to float on the surface of the ground. How they wept when at the dawn of day they ferried across the Jordan to the place where John had first baptized and they had become his followers. They went around close to the shores of the Dead Sea, always choosing lonely paths and those that led through the desert, until they reached the valley of the shepherds near Bethlehem. Here with the remains they lay concealed in a cave until night, when they journeyed on to Jutta. Before daybreak they reached the neighborhood of Abraham's tomb. They deposited John's body in a cave near the cells of the Essenes, who guarded the precious remains all day.

Toward evening, about the hour when our Lord also was anointed and laid in the tomb (it being likewise a Friday), I saw the body brought by the Essenes to the vault wherein Zechariah and many of the prophets were reposing, and which Jesus had recently caused to be prepared for its reception.

The Baptist's relatives, male and female, were assembled in the vault with the disciples and the two soldiers who had come with the latter from Machaerus. Several of the Essenes also were present, among them some very aged people in long, white garments. These latter had provided John with the means of subsistence during his first sojourn in the desert. The women were clothed in white, in long mantles and veils. The men wore black mourning mantles, and around their necks hung narrow scarfs fringed at the ends. Many lamps were burning in the vault. The body was extended on a carpet, the winding-sheet removed, and, amid many tears, anointed and embalmed with myrrh and sweet spices. The headless trunk was, for all present, a heartrending sight. They deeply regretted not being able to look upon John's features. The ardent longings of their soul evoked him to their mental gaze such as he had appeared in the past. Each one present contributed a bundle of myrrh or other aromatic herbs. Then the disciples, having reswathed the body, laid it in the compartment hewn out for it above that of his father. The bones of the latter they had rearranged and wrapped in fresh linens.

The Essenes afterward held a kind of religious service in which they honored John not only as one of their own, but as one of the prophets promised to them. A portable altar something like a little table was placed between the two rows that they formed on either side, and one of them, with the aid of two assistants, prepared it for the ceremony. All laid little loaves on the altar, in the center of which lay a representation of a paschal lamb, over which they scattered all kinds of herbs and tiny branches. The altar was covered with a red undercloth and a white upper one. The figure of the lamb shone alternately with a red and white light, perhaps from lamps concealed under it whose glare, passing first through the red and then through the white cover, produced that effect. The priest read from rolls of writing, burned incense, blessed, and sprinkled with water. All sang as in choir. John's disciples and relatives stood around in rows and joined in the singing. The eldest delivered a speech upon the fulfillment of the prophecies, upon the signification of John's career, and made several allusions touching upon Christ. I remember that he spoke of the death of the prophets as well as that of the high priest Zechariah, who had been murdered between the temple and the altar. He said that Zechariah, the father of John, had likewise been murdered between the temple and the altar. His death signified something still higher than that of the ancient high priest, but John was the true witness in blood between the temple and the altar. By these last words, he alluded to Christ's life and death.

The ceremony of the lamb had reference to a prophetic vision that John, while still in the desert, had communicated to one of the Essenes. The vision itself referred to the Paschal Lamb, the Lamb of God, to Jesus, the Last Supper, to the Passion, and the consummation of the Sacrifice upon the cross. I do not think that they perfectly understood all this. They performed the ceremonies in a prophetic, symbolical spirit, as if they had among them at that time many endowed with the gift of prophecy.

When all was over, he who conducted the service distributed among the disciples the little loaves that had lain on the altar, and to each gave one of the little branches that had been stuck on the lamb. The other relatives likewise received branches, but not from those on the lamb. The Essenes ate the bread, after which the tomb was closed.

The holy souls among the Essenes were possessed of great knowledge and prophetic insight upon the coming of the Messiah, also of the interior signification and the reference to him of the various customs of Judaism. Four generations before the birth of the blessed Virgin, they had ceased to offer bloody sacrifices, since they knew that the coming of the Lamb of God was near.

Chastity and continence were among them a species of worship celebrated to honor the future Redeemer. In humanity they saw his temple to which he was coming, and they wished to do all in their power to preserve it pure and unsullied. They knew how often the Savior's coming had been retarded by the sins of humankind, and they sought by their own purity and chastity to satisfy for the sins of others.

All this had in some mysterious way been infused into their Order by some of the prophets, without their having, however, in Jesus's time, a perfectly clear consciousness of it. They were, as to what concerned their customs and religious observances, the precursors of the future church. They had contributed much toward the spiritual training and guidance of Mary's ancestors and other holy patriarchs. The education of John in his youth was their last great work.

Some of the most enlightened among them in Jesus's time joined the disciples. Others later on entered the community, in which, by their own long practice, they gave new impetus to the spirit of renunciation and a well-ordered life and laid the foundation for the Christian life, both eremitical and cloistered. But a great many among them who belonged not to the fruits of the tree, but to the dry wood, isolated themselves in their observances and degenerated into a sect. This sect was afterward imbued with all kinds of pagan subtleties, and became the mother of many heresies in the early days of the church.

Jesus had no particular communication with the Essenes, although there was some similarity between his customs and theirs. With a great many of them he had no more to do than with other pious and kindly disposed people. He was intimate with several of the married Essenes who were friends of the holy family. As this sect never disputed with Jesus, he never had cause to speak against them, and they are not mentioned in the Gospels, because he had nothing wherewith to censure them as he had in others. He was silent also on the great good found among them since, if he had touched upon it, the Pharisees would have immediately declared that he himself belonged to that sect.

As it had become known at Machaerus, through the domestics of Herodias, where John's head had been thrown, Johanna Chusa, Veronica, and one of the Baptist's relatives journeyed thither in order to make search for it. But until the vaulted sewer could be opened and drained, the head, which was resting on a stone projecting from the wall, could not be reached. Two months flowed by, and then many of the outbuildings and movables belonging to Herod's court at Machaerus were removed, and the whole castle was fitted up for a garrison and fortified for defense. The sewers were cleaned out and repaired, and new fortifications added to the old. During this work, I saw something very strange. Pits were dug, filled with inflammable matter, and then covered, trees being planted over them to prevent their discovery. They could be set on fire, and their explosion would kill men, overturn and scatter all things far and near like so much sand. Such pits as these were dug to quite a distance all around the walls.

There were many people engaged in carrying away the rubbish, and others gathered up the mud and slime from the sewers to enrich their fields. Among the latter were some women from Jutta and Jerusalem with their servants. They were waiting until the deep, steep sewer in which was the Baptist's holy head, should be cleaned. They prayed by night, fasted by day, and sent up ardent prayers to God that they might be enabled to find that for which they were seeking. The bottom of this sewer, on account of its being dug under the mountain, was very inclined. The whole of the lower end was already emptied and purified. To reach the upper part into which the bones from the kitchen were thrown and where the holy head was lying, the workmen had to clamber up by the stones projecting from either side. A great heap of bones obstructed this part, which was at a considerable distance from the outer entrance.

While the workmen went to take their meal, people who had been paid to do so introduced the women into the sewer which, as I have said, was cleaned out as far as that heap of bones. They prayed as they advanced that God would allow them to find the holy head, and they climbed the ascent with difficulty. Soon they perceived the head sitting upright on the neck upon one of the projecting stones, as if looking toward them, and near it shone a luster like two flames. Were it not for this light, they might easily have made a mistake, for there were other human heads in the sewer. The head was pitiful to behold: the dark-skinned face was smeared with blood; the tongue, which Herodias had pierced, was protruding from the open mouth; and the yellow hair, by which the executioner and Herodias had seized it, was standing stiff upon it. The women wrapped it in a linen cloth and bore it away with hurried steps.

Scarcely had they accomplished a part of the way when a company of Herod's soldiery, to the number of a thousand, came marching up toward the castle. They had come to replace the couple of hundreds already there on guard. The women concealed themselves in a cave. The danger past, they again set out on their journey through the mountains. On their way they came across a soldier who, having by a fall received a severe wound on the knee, was lying on the road unconscious. Here too they came up with Zechariah's nephew and two of the Essenes who had come to meet them. They laid the holy head upon the wounded soldier, who instantly recovered consciousness, arose, and spoke, saying that he had just seen the Baptist, and he had helped him. All were very much touched. They bathed his wounds in oil and wine and took him to an inn, without, however, saying anything to him about John's head. They continued their journey, always choosing the most unfrequented routes, just as had been done when John's body was conveyed to Jutta. The head was delivered to the Essenes near Hebron, and some of their sick, having been touched with it, were cured. It was then washed, embalmed with precious ointments, and with solemn ceremonies laid with the body in the tomb.

Jesus in Bethany and Jerusalem • Cure of a Man Sick for Thirty-Eight Years

Thursday, January 18, AD 31 (*Shebat 5*)

Martha, Mary Magdalene, and the widow Mary Salome, who was living in Bethany as a guest of Martha, came to meet Jesus on his way to Bethany. That evening Jesus and his friends and disciples shared a meal in Bethany. After everyone had gone to bed, Jesus went alone to pray on the Mount of Olives.

FROM Bethzur, Jesus proceeded with Lazarus and the disciples to Bethany. They stopped at several places along their route, among them at Emmaus. Jesus taught here and there on the way among the people who were busy tying up the hedges, which were already green.

Martha, Magdalene, and a widow named Salome came to meet them at almost an hour's distance from Bethany. Salome had long dwelt in Bethany with Martha. Through one of Joseph's brothers and like Susanna, she was related to the holy family. She was later on present at Jesus's sepulcher. They, Martha, Magdalene, and Salome, had been at Lazarus's inn in the desert, whence they returned at dusk to Bethany.

The four apostles and several disciples whom Jesus had sent to Tabor arrived also on this evening at Bethany. Great was their grief upon hearing now for the first time the details of John's death. Then they related what had happened to themselves. They had taught and cured, according to the instructions received from Jesus, and at one place they had been chased with stones, but without being hit by them. The last place they had visited was Saron, near Lydda.

When all in Lazarus's house had retired to rest, Jesus went in the darkness to the Mount of Olives and prayed in a solitary nook.[D32] The mount was covered with verdure and groves of noble trees. It was full of retired corners.

Magdalene occupied the little apartments of Mary the Silent's dwelling. She often sat in a very narrow little room that appeared to be formed in a tower. It was a retired corner intended for penitential exercises. She still wept freely. True, she was no longer actually sick, but from contrition and penance she had become quite pale and reduced. She looked like one crushed by sorrow.

The last two days were days of fasting. They were followed by a feast of joy, which began at the close of the sabbath and lasted for three days. The real date had fallen earlier, but for some reason the feast had been postponed. It was a feast of thanksgiving for all graces received from the deliverance of the Israelites from Egyptian bondage down to their own time. Its celebration was not confined to Jerusalem, but was observed everywhere. Numbers of the chief priests and the greatest enemies of Jesus had left Jerusalem. Since Pilate had absented himself, they had nothing to fear and a less strict guard to keep.

Jehosaphat Valley from Bethany

Friday, January 19, AD 31 (Shebat 6)

This morning Jesus and a group of disciples went to Jerusalem, first visiting the house of Johanna Chusa. Around ten in the morning, he went to the temple and taught there without arousing any opposition. After sharing a light meal with his disciples in the early afternoon at the house of Johanna Chusa, Jesus and the disciples went to the pool of Bethesda, where Jesus imparted instructions to the sick, healing a number of them. On the way out, he healed the paralyzed man who had been ill for thirty-eight years (John 5:1–15). By then, the sabbath had already begun. So Jesus went to the temple and taught there again. In the evening, around sunset, John the Baptist's body was buried at Jutta, in the vault of Zechariah, the disciples having returned from Machaerus with it the day before.

Next morning Jesus went to Jerusalem and accepted hospitality with Johanna Chusa. Neither Martha nor Magdalene was there.

Toward ten o'clock I saw Jesus in the temple. He occupied the teacher's chair in the women's porch, where he was reading and expounding the Law. All were amazed at his wisdom. No one raised the least disturbance or made objections to his teaching. Some of the priests present may not have known him, and those that did were not against him. His bitter enemies, the Pharisees and Sadducees, were for the most part absent.

About three o'clock, Jesus went with some of the disciples to the pool of Bethesda. He entered from without by a door which was closed and no longer used. This was the corner into which the poorest and most abandoned creatures were pushed; and lying in the farthest part and right next the door was a man paralyzed for thirty-eight years.[D33] He had been pressed back by the crowd to the farthest extremity of the place, and now lay in a little chamber destined for men.

When Jesus knocked at the closed door, it opened of itself. Passing along through the sick, he made his way to the hall nearest the pool where invalids of all kinds were sitting and lying, and there he taught. The disciples meanwhile distributed among the poor clothes and bread, covers and kerchiefs given them by the women for that purpose. Such attention and loving services were something quite new to these poor sick who were, for the most part, either abandoned to themselves or left to the care of servants. They were greatly touched. Jesus went about them, pausing in several different places to instruct them, and then asking whether they believed that God was able to help them, whether they wished to be cured, whether they were sorry for their sins, whether they would do penance and be baptized. When he named to some of them their sins, they trembled and cried out: "Master, thou art a prophet! Thou art certainly John!" John's death was not yet generally known, and in many places the report of his being set at liberty was current. Jesus replied in general terms as to who he really was, and cured several of them. He directed the blind to bathe their eyes in water from the pool with which he had previously mixed a little oil. Then he told them to go quietly home and not say much about their cure until after the sabbath. The disciples were at the same time curing in the other porches. All the cured were obliged to wash in the pool.

But when, on account of these cures, some excitement was beginning to arise, while now one, now another approached the pool to wash, Jesus went with John to that far-off place near the entrance where lay the poor man who had been sick for thirty-eight long years. He had been a gardener, and had formerly been engaged in the care of hedges and the raising of balsam trees. But now, so long sick and helpless, he was reduced to a state of starvation, and lay like a public beggar glad to eat the scraps left by the other sick. As he had been seen here for so many years, he was known to everyone as the incurable paralytic. Jesus spoke to him, and asked him whether or not he wanted to be cured. But he, not thinking that Jesus would cure him, but that he was asking only in a general way why he was lying there, answered that he had no help, no servant or friend to assist him down into the pool when the waters were moved.[D34] While he was creeping down, others got before him and occupied the places around the pool to which the steps led. Jesus spoke for a little while to the man, placed his sins before his eyes, excited his heart to sorrow, and told him that he should no longer live in impurity and no longer blaspheme against the temple, for it was in punishment of such sins that his sickness had come upon him. Then he consoled him by telling him that God receives all and assists all that turn again to him with contrition. The poor man, who never before had received a word of consolation, who had been allowed to lie moulding and rotting in his misery, who had often bitterly complained that no one offered him any assistance, was now deeply touched at Jesus's words. At last, Jesus said: "Arise! Take up thy bed, and walk!" But these were only the principal words of all that he said. He commanded him to go down to the pool and wash, and then told one of the disciples, who at that moment approached, to take the man to one of the little dwellings erected for the poor by Jesus's friends near the Cenacle on Mount Zion. Joseph of Arimathea had his stone-cutting shops in them.

He who had been so long paralyzed, and whose face was disfigured by skin disease, gathered together his tattered couch and went off cured to wash in the pool. He was so out of himself with joy and in such a hurry that he almost forgot to take away his bed. The sabbath had now begun, and Jesus passed out unnoticed with John by the door near the place in which the poor man had lain. The disciple who was to announce the sick man went on ahead, for the latter knew where he was to go. When therefore he issued from the buildings around the pool of Bethesda, he was met by some Jews who saw that he had been cured. Thinking that he owed the favor to the waters of the pool, they said to him: "Knowest thou not that it is the sabbath day?" He answered: "He that cured me said to me: 'Arise! Take up thy bed and walk!'" They asked him: "Who is he that said to thee: 'Take up thy bed and walk!'" But the poor man could not say, for he did not know Jesus and had never before seen him. Jesus had already left the place, and his disciples also.

What the Gospel relates in connection with this miracle, that this man saw Jesus in the temple and pointed him out as the one that had cured him; and that Jesus had in consequence a dispute with the Pharisees on the subject of healing on the sabbath day, took place upon a subsequent feast, but was recorded by John immediately after his account of the cure. I received positive information on this point.

Through those Jews that had reproached the cured man (who had been looked upon by all as incurable) for carrying his bed on the sabbath day, the report of the miracle was spread in Jerusalem after Jesus had left it. It created great excitement. The other sick who had been cured by Jesus and the disciples at the pool of Bethesda attracted little attention, for their cure was attributed to the virtue of the waters. Besides, they did not happen on the sabbath, and Jesus neither at his entrance nor his departure had been seen by the custodians or superintendents of the pool. With the exception of the sick poor, who lived in the little cells formed in the walls, there were at that time but few persons around the piscina. Those in easy circumstances had already been taken home. In these latter times, in consequence of the movement of the water being rare and mostly at sunrise, only those that had servants could be carried to the pool at the right time; and again, confidence in this manner of curing had greatly decreased. Even the pool itself was neglected, for a part of the wall on one side had gone to ruins. Only people of lively faith frequented it at that time, people such as those that among us go on pilgrimages to holy shrines.

This was the pool in which Nehemiah hid the sacred fire. A piece of the wood with which it was covered was afterward thrown aside, and later on was used for a part of Christ's cross. The pool had developed its miraculous virtue only after it had been made the depository of the sacred fire. In early times the pious sick who were endowed with the spirit of prophecy used to see an angel descend and agitate the water. Afterward very few, if any, saw that wondrous sight, and lastly the times had become such that if any did see it, they kept it to themselves. Still, at all periods, many beheld the waters agitated and bubbling. This pool, after the coming of the Holy Spirit, became the baptismal place of the apostles. It was with its agitating angel, a mystery typical of holy baptism at the time of the paschal lamb which, in turn, was a type of the Last Supper and the Redeemer's death.

After this miracle, Jesus went with the disciples into a synagogue near the temple mount, in which Nicodemus and the other friends were celebrating the sabbath. Jesus did not teach here. He prayed and listened to the reading of the holy scriptures appointed for this sabbath. They consisted of passages relating to the departure from Egypt, the journey through the Red Sea, and the prophetess Deborah. A canticle celebrating the passage through the Red Sea was sung, and in it were recounted one after another all the benefits that God had showered on the Jews, especially what regarded their worship and temple.

Mention was made of all the priestly vestments and ornaments which God had prescribed on Sinai, also of Solomon and the Queen of Sheba. This sabbath was called Beshalach, and was immediately followed by that feast of three days whose name sounds like Ennorum. It was at one and the same time the commencement, the end, and the feast of thanksgiving for all favors and for all other feasts. In the canticle thanks were given for the innumerable favors that God had shown them from the beginning; namely, for their deliverance from Egypt and the Red Sea, for the Law, the Ark of the Covenant, the Tabernacle, for the priestly vestments, and the temple, and for their wise King Solomon. They demanded also in that canticle another king as wise as he. United with this feast, which had been instituted by a prophet long before the existence of either Solomon or the temple, was a joyous festival founded by Solomon on the occasion of the presents made him by the Queen of Sheba, who was struck with admiration at his wisdom. With these gifts he had given recreation to the priests and the people. Its remembrance was perpetuated by the holiday now going on, in which everyone freely diverted himself. Since this feast could be celebrated anywhere, all the Pharisees and officers of the temple who could in any way escape availed themselves of the opportunity to visit their friends and recruit their strength for the approaching great feasts of Purim and Passover.

Abundant alms were distributed on this feast. Loaves of very fine white bread were baked and given to the poor, as a remembrance of the manna in the desert. This festival was like the Amen of the feasts, the feast of the beginning and the end.

After the service in the synagogue, Jesus went with some disciples into the temple, in which were only a few people. The Levites were coming and going, putting things in order, and filling the lamps with oil for next morning. Jesus penetrated into places not open to all, even into the vestibule of the sanctuary where stood the great teacher's chair, in order to see and speak to them. This he did upon various deep questions, and they listened for some time. Then came some of the other Levites and reproached him with his boldness in daring to enter those unusual places and at that unseasonable time. They called him a contemptible Galilean, etc. Jesus answered them very gravely, spoke of his rights, of the house of his Father, and then withdrew. They derided him, although he inspired them with secret fear. Jesus stayed that night in the city.

Saturday, January 20, AD 31 (Shebat 7)

Jesus and the disciples healed the sick this morning at the Cenacle on Mount Zion. That afternoon they ate there, and then Jesus went to the temple. Once again he was able to teach without encountering any opposition. That evening he and the disciples ate at the house of Simon the Pharisee in Bethany. Afterward, at Lazarus's castle, Jesus said goodbye to Lazarus, Martha, and Mary Magdalene.

The next morning Jesus and the apostles cured a great many sick in the side buildings of the Cenacle which, surrounded by a large court, stood upon Mount Zion. Joseph of Arimathea had rented it for his stone-cutting business. The holy women of Jerusalem were busied around the sick with all the services that tender charity would inspire. It was on account of these sufferers that Joseph of Arimathea, when recently at Hebron, had invited Jesus to Jerusalem. They were for the most part good, righteous people, acquaintances of the holy women and friends of Jesus. They had been conveyed by night into the court of the Cenacle. Jesus spent the whole morning in performing cures. He taught occasionally, sometimes by this, sometimes by that group. There were lame and blind and paralyzed, others with withered and crippled hands, others with ulcers—men, women, and children. There were also some men wounded by the overthrow of the aqueduct. Some had fractured skulls; others, broken limbs.

They were now busy in the valley of Jerusalem clearing away the rubbish. Some walls falling in had dammed up the water, and laborers were sent into the dyke to dig through the debris. In some places whole trees and large stones were thrown in to stop the course of the waters.

After Jesus had taken a slight repast with the disciples in the Cenacle, at which those that had just been cured were entertained, he and his followers went into the temple and to the public teacher's chair, near which were kept the rolls of the Law. Jesus demanded the rolls and proceeded to expound the passages appropriate to the day. They referred to the journey through the Red Sea and to Deborah, and again that Psalm treating of the feast was sung. The title is: "To sing morning or eve." All were astonished at Jesus's doctrine, and no one dared to contradict him. Some of the Pharisees alone made bold to ask: "Where didst thou study? Where didst thou receive the right to teach? How canst thou take so great a liberty?" Jesus answered them in terms so grave and severe that they had nothing to reply. Then he left the temple, and went to Bethany with his disciples and friends.

Jesus's stay in Jerusalem this time was little remarked, since his chief enemies were not there. It was only when from the great teacher's chair he closed the ceremonies of the sabbath that they paid much attention to him and again spoke here and there of the Galilean. All Jerusalem was at the time taken up with talk of the fallen aqueduct, the jealousy existing between Herod and Pilate, and the journey of the latter to Rome; even John's death was now discussed but little. Unless some particular excitement arose, the people did not talk much of Jesus. It was there as in other great cities. Occasionally indeed somebody would say: "Jesus the Galilean is now in the city" and another would reply: "If he does not come with several thousand men, he will effect nothing."

While in Bethany, Jesus went to the house of Simon, who no longer appeared in public, for he was sick, his leprosy having begun. A number of red blotches had broken out upon him. Wrapped in a large mantle, he kept himself concealed in a retired apartment. Jesus had an interview with him. Simon looked like one that is anxious not to have his malady noticed, but soon he would be unable to ward off attention. He showed himself as little as possible.

Late that night the disciples returned from Jutta, which they had left after the sabbath. They related to Jesus the circumstances of their bringing away John's body from Machaerus and its burial near his father. The two soldiers from Machaerus had come with the disciples. Lazarus took charge of them, kept them concealed, and provided for their wants.

When Jesus said to the disciples: "Let us retire to some solitude there to rest and mourn, not over John's death, but over the deplorable causes that led to it," I thought, "How will he be able to rest, for the other apostles and disciples are already gone to Mary in Capernaum." Crowds from all quarters, even from Syria and Basan, had flocked thither, and the whole country around Chorazin was covered with the tents of those that were awaiting Jesus's coming.

Jesus Delivers Prisoners in Thirza

Sunday, January 21, AD 31 (Shebat 8)

Early this morning Jesus and the disciples left Bethany. They journeyed without stopping for about eleven hours until they reached Lebona on the southern slope of Mount Garizim.

EARLY next morning, Jesus left Bethany with the six apostles and about twenty disciples. They shunned all places on the way, and journeyed without stopping eleven hours to the north, until they reached Lebona on the southern slope of Mount Garizim. Joseph before his espousals with Mary had worked here as a carpenter, and he afterward kept up friendly relations with the inhabitants. On a peak of the mountain stood a lonely fortress up to which the road from Lebona led through buildings on one side and old walls on the other. It was on this road that Joseph's workshop stood, and in it Jesus with all his disciples put up. He was, though coming unexpectedly and at a late hour, received with unusual joy and reverence. It was a Levitical family, and up further on the mountain was the synagogue.

Monday, January 22, AD 31 (Shebat 9)

Journeying further, they arrived at Thirza.

From Lebona Jesus and the disciples journeyed with rapid steps the whole of the following day through Samaria in a northwesterly direction toward the Jordan. They traversed Aser-Michmethath, tarried awhile in the inn at Aser, and then went on to the neighborhood of Thirza, about one hour from the Jordan and two from Abel-Mehola. The country around was remarkably fine. Here in Thirza, as in all other places on the way, the feast that I had seen begun in Jerusalem was right joyously commemorated. Gracefully adorned triumphal arches were erected, and public games celebrated. The actors leaped over garlands on a wager, just as our children do nowadays. Great mounds of grain and orchard fruits were heaped up in the open air for distribution among the poor.

Thirza was built in two parts, and one quarter of the city extended to within half an hour of the Jordan. The whole region was so studded with gardens and orchards that the traveler could not see the city until just within its reach. It was so broken up by gardens and commons that the quarter furthest from the Jordan looked less like a city than like some groups of houses scattered among gardens and walls. The part nearest the Jordan was the better preserved and the more compact. It was built high above a valley and rested on solid piers. A highway ran under it as under a bridge. This road was charming. From it one could see through the valley with its green trees as through a cool grotto far to the other side where the road emerged into the open air.

Water Wheel

Thirza, situated as it was on a height of moderate elevation, commanded a most beautiful view across the Jordan and into the mountain ranges beyond. To the north could be seen Jotopata, almost hidden by forests; on the right the view extended into Peraea; and across the smooth surface of the Dead Sea arose Machaerus and the country off to the west. Many a glimpse could be had of the Jordan, and here and there in its windings its waters glistened like long streaks of light as it flowed along between its verdant banks. Westward from Thirza lay a high mountain range that separated it from Dothan. Abel-Mehola lay two hours northwestward, in a deep dale more to the south than was that in which Joseph was sold by his brethren. On every side Thirza looked down upon numberless gardens and groves of fruit trees, on terraces and espaliers over which were trained balsam shrubs and paradise apples so much used by the Jews at their Feast of Tabernacles. These trees flourished only in very good and sunny positions. Besides those just mentioned, they cultivated also the sugar cane, long, yellow flax like silk, cotton, and a species of grain in whose thick stalk was stored a marrowy pith. The inhabitants were engaged in horticulture and fruit raising. Many were occupied also in preparing flax, cotton, and the sugar cane for market. The street that ran under the city was the grand military and commercial route to Tarichea and Tiberias. In many places it took the form of a tunnel between hills, as it did here in Thirza which, as I have said, rested on piers above the road.

Tuesday, January 23, AD 31 (Shebat 10)

Jesus visited the hospital and prison in Thirza and healed the sick. Later, he taught in the synagogue concerning the fifth beatitude and the parable of the prodigal son (Luke 15:11).

In the center of the city, that is, in the center of its ancient surroundings, in a large, deserted-looking space, there stood on a gentle eminence a spacious edifice with massive walls, several courtyards, and round buildings like towers in whose interior were found other courts. It was the old, ruined castle of the kings of Israel. A part had fallen to decay, but another had been fitted up as a hospital and prison. Some portions were overgrown ruins, on which were laid out gardens of all kinds. On the square before the house was a fountain whose water, by means of a wheel turned by an ass, was raised in leathern bags and poured into a great basin, from which it flowed on all sides through channels into tanks, thus supplying the city in every direction. Every quarter had its reservoir.

At this fountain five disciples from the opposite side of the Jordan joined Jesus and his followers. They were the two youths delivered from slight demoniacal possession, the two men out of whom Jesus had driven the devils into the swine, and a fifth. They had been, in accordance with Jesus's commands, proclaiming their own deliverance and the miracle of the swine in the little cities of the country of the Gerasens and in the Decapolis. They had healed in those places and had announced the approach of the kingdom of God. They embraced the disciples and washed one another's feet at the fountain. Jesus had come straight from a house outside the city where, with the other disciples, he had passed the night. These five brought him news that all his disciples whom he had sent into Upper Galilee had returned to Capernaum, and that an immense multitude of people were encamped in the district around, awaiting his coming.

Jesus now went with the disciples into the castle, sought out the superintendent of the hospital, and requested to be introduced to their quarters. The superintendent complied with his request, and Jesus went through halls and courts until he arrived at the cells and retired corners where lay the sick suffering from diseases of all kinds. He went around among them instructing, healing, and consoling. Some of the disciples were with him, helping to raise, carry, and lead the sick; others were scattered in the different corridors, performing cures and preparing the way for Jesus. In one of the courts there were several possessed in chains, who yelled and raged when Jesus entered the house. He commanded them to be silent, cured them, and drove the devils out of them. In the most distant part of the hospital were some lepers, and these too he healed. He went alone to them. The cured belonging to Thirza itself were at once taken away by their friends, not, however, before Jesus had ordered them food and drink. To the poor among them were distributed, besides, the clothing and coverlets that the disciples had brought with them to Thirza from the inn of Bezek.

Jesus visited also the abode of the sick women. It was a high, round tower with an inner court. In this court, as well as on the outside of the tower, a projecting flight of steps led from one story to another, for in the interior there was no little staircase such as we have. In the exterior apartments were women sick of all kinds of maladies. Jesus cured many. In the apartments nearest the court, from which they were separated by locked doors, women were imprisoned, some for their excesses, some on account of their bold speech, while many others of their number were innocent. In the same building many poor men underwent the rigors of grievous imprisonment, some for debt, others for having joined in a revolt, many also the victims of revenge and enmity, while others were confined merely to get them out of the way. Many of these poor creatures were quite abandoned, left to starve in their prison cells. Jesus heard bitter complaints on this subject from the sick whom he cured and from others. He indeed knew all about it, and it was principally on account of that general misery he had come.

Thirza counted numerous Pharisees and Sadducees, and among the latter were many Herodians. The prison was guarded by Roman soldiers and had a Roman superintendent. The lodgings of the guards and overseers were outside the building. Jesus, having applied to the latter for permission, was allowed to visit the part open to strangers. He listened to the prisoners' story of misery and sufferings, directed refreshments to be distributed to them, instructed and consoled them, and forgave the sins of many that confessed to him. To several of those confined for debt, as well as to many others, he promised release. To others he held out hopes of relief.

From the prison Jesus went to the Roman commander, who was not a wicked man, and spoke to him gravely and touchingly about the prisoners. He offered to discharge their debts himself, and to go part security for their innocence and good behavior. He expressed his desire also to converse with those that had for so long a time endured a more rigorous imprisonment. The commander listened very respectfully to Jesus, but explained to him that as all those prisoners were Jews who had been put into prison under very particular circumstances, he would have to speak to the Pharisees and to the Jewish authorities of the place before he could grant his request to be allowed access to them. Jesus replied that after he had taught in the synagogue he would call on him again with the Jewish authorities. Then he returned to the female prisoners, whom he consoled and advised. He received from several the avowal of their misdemeanors and promises of amendment, forgave them their sins, caused alms to be distributed among them, and promised to reconcile them with their friends.

Thus did Jesus from nine o'clock in the morning until nearly four in the afternoon labor in this abode of misery and woe, filling it with joy and consolation on a day upon which in it alone was sorrow to be found, for in the city all was jubilation. It was the first of those holidays that had been added by Solomon to the Feast of Ennorum, on account of the gifts presented by the Queen of Sheba. Jesus had beheld the sabbath of this first day celebrated the evening before at Bezek. Today the whole city, especially the most populous quarters, was alive with joy. There were triumphal arches, leaping, racing, and heaps of grain for distribution among the poor. But around that old castle, at once prison and hospital, all was still. Jesus alone had thought of its poor inmates, and he alone had brought them real joy. In the house outside the city he took with the disciples a little repast, which consisted of bread, fruit, and honey. Then he sent some of his followers to the prison with all kinds of provisions and refreshments, while he with the rest repaired to the synagogue.

The report of what Jesus had done in the hospital was

already spread throughout the whole city. Many of those that he had there cured were returned to the city and now went to the synagogue; others were assembled outside the sacred edifice, where Jesus and the apostles cured many more. In the synagogue were gathered the Pharisees and Sadducees, and many secret Herodians. Among the first-named were many of the same sect from Jerusalem who had come thither for recreation. They were full of spite and envy at Jesus's doings, which threw disgrace upon their own. In the school were present also a great many people from Bezek who had followed Jesus thither. In his instruction Jesus spoke of the feast and its signification, which was to afford an opportunity for recreation, for infusing joy into the hearts of others, and for doing good. He referred again to one of the eight beatitudes, "Blessed are the merciful." He explained the parable of the prodigal son, which he had already related to the prisoners. Then he spoke of these, as well as of the sick and their miseries, how forgotten and abandoned they were while others enriched themselves by seizing upon the funds destined for their support. He inveighed vigorously against the trustees of this establishment, some of whom were among the Pharisees present. They listened in silent rage. In recounting the parable of the prodigal son, Jesus made allusion to those that had been imprisoned on account of their misdemeanors, but who were now repentant. This he did in order to reconcile the relatives here present to some of the prisoners. All were very much touched.

Here, too, Jesus related the parable of the compassionate king and the unmerciful servant. He applied it to those that allow the poor prisoner to languish on account of an insignificant debt, while God suffers their own great indebtedness to run on.

The secret Herodians had by their trickery been the cause of the imprisonment of many poor people of this place. To this fact Jesus once vaguely alluded when, in his severe denunciation of the Pharisees, he said: "There are many indeed among you who very likely know how things fell out with John." The Pharisees railed at Jesus. They made use of expressions among themselves, such as these: "He wages war with the help of women, and goes about with them. He will get possession of no great kingdom with such warriors."

Jesus then pressed the head men among the magistrates and Pharisees to go with him to the Roman superintendent of the prison and offer to ransom the most miserable and neglected of the inmates. This proposal was made in the hearing of many, consequently the Pharisees could not refuse. When Jesus and his disciples turned off toward the residence of the superintendent, a crowd followed, sounding Jesus's praises. The superintendent was a much better man than the Pharisees, who maliciously ran up the prisoners' debts so high that, for the release of some of them, Jesus had to pay fourfold. But because he had not the money around him, he gave as a pledge a triangular coin to which hung a parchment ticket upon which he had written some words authorizing the sum to be discharged from Magdalene's property which Lazarus was about to sell. The entire proceeds were destined by Magdalene and Lazarus for the benefit of the poor, for debtors, and the relief of sinners. Magdalum was a more valuable estate than that of Bethany. Each side of the triangular coin was about three inches long, and in the center was an inscription indicating its value. To one end hung a jointed strip of metal, like two or three links of a chain, and to this the writing was fastened.

After the transaction recorded above, the superintendent ordered the poor prisoners to be brought forth. Jesus and the disciples lent their assistance in the execution of his order. Many poor creatures in tatters, half-naked and covered with hair, were dragged forth from dark holes. The Pharisees angrily withdrew. Many of the released were quite weak and sick. They lay weeping at Jesus's feet, while he consoled and exhorted them. He procured for them clothing, baths, food, lodgings, and saw to the formalities necessary to be observed in restoring them to liberty, for they had to remain under the jurisdiction of the prison and hospital a few days until their ransom was paid. A similar occurrence took place among the female prisoners. All were fed, Jesus and the disciples waiting on them, and the parable of the prodigal son was afterward related to them.

Thus was this house for once filled with joy. In it appeared to be prefigured the deliverance from Limbo of the patriarchs to whom John, after his death, had announced the near coming of the Redeemer. Jesus and the disciples spent the night once more in the house outside of Thirza.

It was this affair here in Thirza which, when reported to Herod, drew his attention more particularly upon Jesus, and called forth the remark: "Is John risen from the grave?" From this time Herod was desirous of seeing Jesus. He had indeed previously heard of him from general report and through John, but he had not thought much on the subject. Now, however, his uneasy conscience made him notice what before had passed unremarked. He was at this time living in Hesebon, where he had gathered all his soldiers around him, among them some mercenary Roman troops.

Wednesday, January 24, AD 31 (Shebat 11)

From Thirza to Capernaum, whither Jesus now proceeded with his disciples, was a journey of eighteen hours. They did not go up through the valley of the Jordan, but along the base of Mount Gilboa and across the valley of Abez, leaving Tabor on the left. They lodged at the inn on the borders of the lake near Bethulia.

Thursday, January 25, AD 31 (Shebat 12)

Around noon, Jesus arrived at an inn near Damna, where he met with his mother and some of his disciples. Their joy at seeing one another again was diminished when those who had not yet heard of the circumstances surrounding John the Baptist's death were told. After eating a meal together, everyone went on in the direction of Capernaum. That night, Jesus stayed at his mother's home.

They journeyed next day to Damna, where Jesus found Mary and several of the holy women who had arrived there before him. The other six apostles and some of the disciples had also come to Damna. The two soldiers from Machaerus, whom Lazarus had sent through Samaria, joined Jesus's followers near Azanoth.

Jesus in Capernaum and its Environs

THERE were at this time in Capernaum no fewer than sixty-four Pharisees assembled from the neighboring districts. On their way thither, they had made inquiries upon the most remarkable of Jesus's cures, and had ordered the widow of Nain with her son and witnesses from that place to be summoned to Capernaum, as well as the son of Achias, the centurion of Gischala. They had also closely interrogated Zorobabel and his son, the centurion Cornelius and his servant, Jairus and his daughters, several blind and lame that had been cured—in a word, all that had in that part of the country profited by Jesus's healing power. In every case they summoned witnesses, whom they questioned and whose answers they compared.

When, notwithstanding their malice, they were unable to construe what they heard into proofs against the truth of Jesus's miracles, they became still more enraged, and again had recourse to their old story, that he had dealings with the devil. They declared that he went about with women of bad repute, excited the people to sedition, deprived the synagogues of the alms that should flow to them, and profaned the sabbath, and they boasted that they would now put a stop to his proceedings.

Intimidated by these threats, by the ever-increasing concourse of people, and especially by the beheading of John, the relatives of Jesus were greatly troubled. They entreated him not to go to Capernaum, but to take up his residence elsewhere, and for this they named many places, such as Nain or Hebron or the cities on the other side of the Jordan. But Jesus silenced them by declaring that he would go to Capernaum, where he would both teach and cure, for as soon as he stood face to face with the Pharisees, they would cease their boasting.

When the disciples asked him what they were now to do, Jesus answered that he would tell them, and that he would give to the twelve to hold the same position to them as he himself held to the apostles. When evening came they separated. Jesus went with Mary, the women, and his relatives eastward through Zorobabel's hamlet to Mary's house in the valley of Capernaum, and the apostles and disciples departed by other routes. That night Jairus sought Jesus to relate to him the persecutions he had had to endure. Jesus calmed him. He had been discharged from his office, and now belonged entirely to Jesus.

Friday, January 26, AD 31 (Shebat 13)

Capernaum was full of visitors who had come from afar to hear Jesus. In addition, a group of sixty-four Pharisees had also gathered, having come from all around to investigate the carpenter's son from Nazareth. Jesus visited the homes of Zorobabel, Cornelius, and Jairus. Jairus had lost his position as chief elder at the synagogue and had been persecuted because of his contact with Jesus. Now Jairus committed himself wholly to the service of Jesus. Jesus then began healing and continued to heal throughout the morning. Around midday, he withdrew to a hall to preach. Then, as the sabbath began, he went to the synagogue. He had to make his way through a great crowd before he could begin to teach. When the Pharisees asked him if it was allowed to heal on the sabbath, he answered by healing a man with a withered hand (Matthew 12:9) and by driving out a devil from one who was deaf, mute, and possessed, and whose hearing and speech were immediately restored. Witnessing this, the Pharisees accused Jesus of being in league with the devil (Matthew 9:32–34). Jesus, however, defended himself with the words spoken in Matthew 12:33–37. Amid the uproar, Jesus and the disciples withdrew. That night, Jesus stayed at Peter's house.

Capernaum was full of visitors, sick and well, Jews and Gentiles. The surrounding plains and heights were covered with encampments. In the fields and mountain nooks, camels and asses were grazing; even the valleys and hills on the opposite side of the lake were alive with people waiting for Jesus. There were strangers here from all sides, from Syria, Arabia, Phoenicia, and even from Cyprus.

Jesus visited Zorobabel, Cornelius, and Jairus. The family of the last-named was entirely converted, the daughter much better than formerly, and very modest and pious. Jesus went afterward to Peter's house outside the city, and found it crowded with sick. Pagans, who had never been here before, now presented themselves. The crowd of sick was so great that the disciples had to put up a kind of scaffolding in order to afford more room for them. Not only Jesus was everywhere sought for by the sick, but the apostles and disciples also were called by them. "Art thou one of the prophet's disciples?" they cried. "Have pity on me! Help me! Take me to him!" Jesus, the apostles, and about twenty-four disciples taught and cured the whole morning. There were some possessed present, who cried after Jesus and from whom he drove the demons. No Pharisees were present, but there were among the crowd some spies and some half-disaffected.

After Jesus had performed many cures, he withdrew into a hall to preach, whither he was followed by the cured and others. Some of the apostles went on healing while the others gathered around Jesus, who again taught on the beatitudes and related several parables. Among other points, he touched upon prayer which, he said, they should never omit. He related and developed the similitude of the unjust judge who, in order to get rid of the widow ever returning to knock at his door, at last rendered her justice. If the unjust judge was thus forced to comply, will not the Father in heaven be still more merciful?

Then Jesus taught the multitude how to pray, recited the seven petitions of the Lord's Prayer, and explained the first, "Our Father, who art in heaven." [D35] Already on his journeys, he had explained several of the petitions to the disciples; now, however, he took them up as he had done the beatitudes, and made them the subject of his public instructions. Thus the prayer was all explained by degrees, repeated everywhere, and made known on all sides by the disciples. Jesus continued the eight beatitudes at the same time. In speaking of prayer, he made use of this similitude: If a child begs his father for bread, will he give him a stone? Or if asked for a fish, will he give a serpent or scorpion?

It was now toward three o'clock. Mary, aided by her sister and other women, also by the sons of Joseph's brethren from Dabrath, Nazareth, and the valley of Zebulon, had prepared in the front part of the house a meal for Jesus and the disciples. During several days they had had, on account of their great labors, no regular hours for meals. The dining room was separated from the hall in which Jesus was teaching near a court crowded with people, who could hear all that was said through the open porticos of the hall. Now when Jesus went on instructing, Mary, taking with her some relatives in order not to go through the crowd alone, approached with the intention of speaking to him and begging him to come and partake of some food. But it was impossible for her to make her way through the crowd, and so her request was passed from one to another, until it reached a man standing near Jesus. He was one of the spies of the Pharisees. As Jesus had several times made mention of his heavenly Father, the spy, not without a secret sneer, said to him: "Behold thy mother and thy brethren stand without, seeking thee." But Jesus, looking at him, said: "Who is my mother, and who are my brethren?" Then grouping the twelve and placing the disciples near them, he extended his hand over the former with the words: "Behold my mother!" and then over the latter, saying: "and these are my brethren, who hear the word of God and do it. For whosoever shall do the will of my Father who is in heaven, he is my brother, my sister, and my mother." Then he went on with his discourse, but sent his disciples in turn to take what food they needed.

After this, as he was going with the disciples to the synagogue, the sick who could still walk followed him, imploring his help. He cured them. In the outer porch of the synagogue, although the sabbath had already begun, a man stepped up to him, showed him his hand, crippled and withered, and begged to be helped. Jesus told him to wait awhile. At the same time, he was called by some people who were leading a deaf and mute possessed who was raging frightfully. Jesus commanded him to lie down quietly at the entrance of the synagogue and there wait. The possessed instantly sat down cross-legged, and bowed his head on his knees, keeping a side-glance fixed on Jesus. With the exception of an occasional slight convulsive shuddering, he remained quiet during the whole instruction.

The sabbath lesson was about Jethro giving counsel to Moses when the Israelites were encamped around Sinai, of Moses ascending the mount and receiving the Ten Commandments (Ex. 18–21), and from the prophet Isaiah the passages that record his vision of the throne of God and the seraph's purifying his lips with a burning coal (Is. 6:1–13). The synagogue was overflowing with people, and a great crowd was standing outside. The doors and windows were all thrown open, and many people were looking in from the adjacent buildings. Numbers of Pharisees and Herodians were present, all filled with rage and bitterness. The recently cured were in the synagogue, as well as all the disciples and relatives of Jesus. The citizens of Capernaum and the crowds of strangers were full of reverence and admiration for Jesus, and so the Pharisees did not dare to attack him without apparent reason. They had besides come to the synagogue more out of a desire to support one another in their vain boasting than to make any serious opposition to him, though this latter they were not able to do. They no longer cared to contradict him in public, as on such occasions his replies generally put them to shame before the people. But when Jesus withdrew, they sought by every possible means to turn the people away from him, and they set lies afloat against him.

TISSOT ILLUSTRATIONS
[SECTION D]

The Public Teaching of Jesus

⊕

Lord, I am Not Worthy [D1]

⊕

WHEN Jesus next morning, with some of the disciples, was going to the residence of the pagan officer Cornelius, which stood on a height to the north of Capernaum, he was met in the neighborhood of Peter's house by the two Jews whom Cornelius had once before sent to him. They again begged him to have pity on his servant, for Cornelius, they said, deserved the favor. He was a friend of the Jews and had built them a synagogue, reckoning it at the same time an honor to be allowed to do so. Jesus responded that he was even then on his way to Cornelius's, and he directed them to dispatch a messenger in haste to announce his coming. Before reaching Capernaum, Jesus took, just to the right of the gate, the road running between the city and the ramparts and passed the hovel of a leper living in the city wall. A short distance farther on brought Cornelius's house in sight. Upon receiving the message sent by Jesus, Cornelius had left it as if to get a glimpse of him. He knelt down and, esteeming himself unworthy to approach him or to speak with him personally, hurried off a messenger with these words: "The centurion bids me say to thee, 'Lord, I am not worthy that thou shouldst enter under my roof! Speak but one word, and my servant shall be healed. For if I, who am only a humble man dependent upon my superior, say to my servant: Do this! Do that! and he does it, how much easier will it be for thee to command thy servant to be healed and that he should be so!'" When these words were delivered to Jesus by Cornelius's messenger, he turned to those standing around and said: "Verily, I say unto ye, I have not found such faith in Israel! Know ye then! Many shall come from the east and the west and shall take place with Abraham, Isaac, and Jacob in heaven; and many of the children of God's kingdom, the Israelites, shall be cast out into exterior darkness where there shall be weeping and gnashing of teeth!" Then, turning to the servant of the centurion, he said: "Go, and as thou hast believed, so be it done to thee!" The messenger bore the words to the kneeling centurion, who inclined to the earth, arose, and hastened back to the house. As he entered, he encountered his servant, who was coming to meet him, enveloped in a mantle, his head bound in a scarf. He was not a native of the country, as was indicated by his yellowish-brown complexion. [136]

[MATTHEW 8:5–13] 5 As he entered Capernaum, a centurion came forward to him, beseeching him 6 and saying, "Lord, my servant is
lying paralyzed at home, in terrible distress." 7 And he said to him, "I will come and heal him." 8 But the centurion answered him, "Lord,
I am not worthy to have you come under my roof; but only say the word, and my servant will be healed. 9 For I am a man under authority,
with soldiers under me; and I say to one, 'Go,' and he goes, and to another, 'Come,' and he comes, and to my slave, 'Do this,' and he does it."
10 When Jesus heard him, he marveled, and said to those who followed him, "Truly, I say to you, not even in Israel have I found such faith.
11 I tell you, many will come from east and west and sit at table with Abraham, Isaac, and Jacob in the kingdom of heaven, 12 while the
sons of the kingdom will be thrown into the outer darkness; there men will weep and gnash their teeth." 13 And to the centurion Jesus
said, "Go; be it done for you as you have believed." And the servant was healed at that very moment.

IN our engraving, the centurion is represented below the Lord, and at some distance from him. His humility prevents him from going higher and approaching nearer to him, whom he beseeches to heal his servant. Beneath the arches darkening the narrow street, Christ turns towards him, and graciously grants the favor the soldier asks of him with so much faith.

The form of Jesus is draped from head to foot, as if to signify that he is not lavish of his gifts, but reserves them for those who merit them. According to one tradition, he was so beautiful, and his whole personality so full of attraction, that, as a general rule, he had to endeavor, as much as possible, to disguise and attenuate a fascination which would otherwise have gained all hearts: It did not suit his purpose to draw the multitude to him by means of a feeling of that kind; to do so would have been far beneath the divine mission he held. He wished to influence those about him by his spiritual power, by his teaching, and by his mighty works.

Healing of the Lepers at Capernaum [D2]

⊕

JESUS immediately turned back to Capernaum. As he was again passing the leper's hut, the leper himself came out and threw himself down before him. "Lord," he said, "if thou wilt, thou canst make me clean." Jesus replied: "Stretch forth thy hands!" He touched them and said: "I do will it. Be thou clean!" and the leprosy fell from the man. Jesus commanded him to present himself to the priests for inspection, to make the offering prescribed by the Law, and to speak to none other of his cure. The man went to the pharisaical priests and submitted himself to their examination as to whether he was cured or not. They became enraged, examined him rigorously, but were forced to acknowledge him cured. They had so lively a dispute with him that they almost drove him from their presence. [136]

[MARK 1:40–45] 40 And a leper came to him beseeching him, and kneeling said to him, "If you will, you can make me clean." 41 Moved with pity, he stretched out his hand and touched him, and said to him, "I will; be clean." 42 And immediately the leprosy left him, and he was made clean. 43 And he sternly charged him, and sent him away at once, 44 and said to him, "See that you say nothing to any one; but go, show yourself to the priest, and offer for your cleansing what Moses commanded, for a proof to the people." 45 But he went out and began to talk freely about it, and to spread the news, so that Jesus could no longer openly enter a town, but was out in the country; and people came to him from every quarter.

AMONG the Jews there were special laws respecting the lepers, and these sufferers were compelled to take certain precautions to protect their fellow men from coming in contact with them. On all ordinary days of the year the impure, of whom lepers were the chief, had to keep in the middle of the path or road, the undefiled passing by on either side. The rule on feast days was just the reverse, and this difference is easily explained by the desirability of leaving as clear a space as possible for circulation and traffic.

The very soil of the city of Jerusalem was considered sacred, and therefore lepers could not enter it until their recovery had been certified by the priests. The covered-in space under the gates of the town was, however, given up to them. Here they took shelter from the heat of the sun and from the rain, and were very conveniently placed for receiving alms. No doubt when it was fine, they went outside their refuge, as they do at the present day.

In our engraving, the leper is seen in the middle of an almost deserted road, and is flinging himself in the path of our Lord, to implore him to heal him.

The Resurrection of the Widow's Son at Nain [D3]

⊕

IT was almost nine in the morning when Jesus and his companions drew near to Nain and encountered the funeral procession at the gate. A crowd of Jews enveloped in mourning mantles passed out of the city gate with the corpse. Four men were carrying the coffin, in which reposed the remains upon a kind of frame made of crossed poles curved in the middle. The coffin was in shape something like the human form, light like a woven basket, with a cover fastened to the top. Jesus passed through the disciples who, formed into two rows on either side of the road, advanced to meet the coming procession, and said: "Stand still!" Then as he laid his hand upon the coffin, he said: "Set the coffin down." The bearers obeyed, the crowd fell back, and the disciples ranged on either side. The mother of the dead youth, with several of her female friends, was following the corpse. They too paused just as they were passing out of the gate a few feet from where Jesus was standing. They were veiled and showed every sign of grief. The mother stood in front shedding silent tears. Jesus said to her most kindly and earnestly: "Woman, weep not!" The grief of all present touched him, for the widow was much loved in the city on account of her great charity to orphans and the poor.

Jesus called for water and a little branch. Someone brought to a disciple, who handed them to Jesus, a little vessel of water and a twig of hyssop. Jesus took the water and said to the bearers: "Open the coffin and loosen the bands!" While this command was being executed, Jesus raised his eyes to heaven and said: "I confess to thee, O Father, Lord of heaven and earth, because thou hast hidden these things from the wise and prudent, and hast revealed them to little ones. Yea, Father, for so it hath seemed good in thy sight. All things are delivered to me by my Father, and not one knoweth the Son but the Father; neither doth anyone know the Father but the Son, and he to whom it shall please the Son to reveal him. Come to me, all you that labor and are burdened, and I will refresh you. Take up my yoke upon you, and learn of me, because I am meek and humble of heart, and you shall find rest to your souls, for my yoke is sweet and my burden light!"

When the bearers removed the cover, I saw the body wrapped like a babe in swaddling clothes and lying in the coffin. Supporting it in their arms, they loosened the bands, drew them off, uncovered the face, unbound the hands, and left about it only one linen covering. Then Jesus blessed the water, dipped the little branch into it, and sprinkled the crowd. Thereupon I saw numbers of small, dark figures like insects, beetles, toads, snakes, and little black birds issuing from many of the bystanders. The crowd became purer and brighter. Jesus then sprinkled the dead youth with the little branch, and with his hand made the sign of the cross over him, upon which I beheld a murky, black, cloud-like figure issuing from the body. Jesus said to the youth, "Arise!" [142]

[LUKE 7:11–23] 11 Soon afterward he went to a city called Nain, and his disciples and a great crowd went with him. 12 As he drew near to
the gate of the city, behold, a man who had died was being carried out, the only son of his mother, and she was a widow; and a large crowd
from the city was with her. 13 And when the Lord saw her, he had compassion on her and said to her, "Do not weep." 14 And he came and
touched the bier, and the bearers stood still. And he said, "Young man, I say to you, arise." 15 And the dead man sat up, and began to speak.
And he gave him to his mother. 16 Fear seized them all; and they glorified God, saying, "A great prophet has arisen among us!" and "God
has visited his people!" 17 And this report concerning him spread through the whole of Judea and all the surrounding country. 18 The disciples of John told him of all these things. 19 And John, calling to him two of his disciples, sent them to the Lord, saying, "Are you he who is
to come, or shall we look for another?" 20 And when the men had come to him, they said, "John the Baptist has sent us to you, saying, 'Are
you he who is to come, or shall we look for another?'" 21 In that hour he cured many of diseases and plagues and evil spirits, and on many
that were blind he bestowed sight. 22 And he answered them, "Go and tell John what you have seen and heard: the blind receive their sight,
the lame walk, lepers are cleansed, and the deaf hear, the dead are raised up, the poor have good news preached to them. 23 And blessed is
he who takes no offense at me."

The Raising of the Daughter of Jairus [D4]

⊕

THEN he passed through Aruma where he had before been. Jairus, a descendant of the Essene Chariot, dwelt in the neighboring and somewhat despised place, Phasael. He had some time previously begged Jesus to cure his sick daughter, and Jesus had promised to do so, though not just then. Although his daughter was dead, Jairus now dispatched a messenger to meet him and remind him of his promise. Jesus sent his disciples on ahead after appointing a certain place [in Jezreel] where they should again meet him, and he himself accompanied Jairus's messenger back to Phasael.

When he entered the house of Jairus, the daughter lay wrapped in the winding-sheet ready for burial, her weeping friends around her. Jesus ordered the neighbors to be called in, and the winding-sheet and linens to be loosened. Then taking the dead girl by the hand, he commanded her to arise. She did so, and stood before him. She was about sixteen years old and not good. She had no love for her father, although he prized her above all things. He was charitable and pious, and shrank not from communication with the poor and despised. That was a source of vexation to his daughter. Jesus roused her from death both of soul and body. She reformed, and some time after joined the holy women. Jesus warned those present not to speak of the miracle they had witnessed. It was through the same desire of secrecy that he had not allowed the disciples to accompany him. This was not the Jairus of Capernaum whose daughter also was, at a later period, raised from the dead by Jesus. [151]

[MARK 5:22–24] 22 Then came one of the rulers of the synagogue, Jairus by name; and seeing him, he fell at his feet, 23 and besought him, saying, "My little daughter is at the point of death. Come and lay your hands on her, so that she may be made well, and live." 24 And he went with him. And a great crowd followed him and thronged about him. [35–43] 35 While he was still speaking, there came from the ruler's house some who said, "Your daughter is dead. Why trouble the Teacher any further?" 36 But ignoring what they said, Jesus said to the ruler of the synagogue, "Do not fear, only believe." 37 And he allowed no one to follow him except Peter and James and John the brother of James. 38 When they came to the house of the ruler of the synagogue, he saw a tumult, and people weeping and wailing loudly. 39 And when he had entered, he said to them, "Why do you make a tumult and weep? The child is not dead but sleeping." 40 And they laughed at him. But he put them all outside, and took the child's father and mother and those who were with him, and went in where the child was. 41 Taking her by the hand he said to her, "Talitha cumi"; which means, "Little girl, I say to you, arise." 42 And immediately the girl got up and walked, and they were immediately overcome with amazement. 43 And he strictly charged them that no one should know this, and told them to give her something to eat.

Jesus Teaches the People by the Sea [D5]

⊕

JESUS afterward taught on the borders of the lake, not far from Peter's fishery. He had journeyed with the disciples over the mountain back of Mary's and Peter's dwellings in the direction of Bethsaida, and thence had descended to the lake. The shore near Bethsaida was steep, but at the point to which I now allude it gently sloped and afforded an easy landing place. Peter's ship and Jesus's little boat lay here. The latter was small and could at most contain fifteen men. [152]

[MARK 2:13] 13 He went out again beside the sea; and all the crowd gathered about him, and he taught them.

IN the crowd seated at the feet of Jesus and listening to him, men of many different races are to be seen. There are wealthy citizens of Tiberias, an essentially modern town at that period; there are Jews in the black and white abayeh; Africans, with loose mantles, wearing no sash or belt; women of Samaria and from the shores of the Jordan; and lastly, men from the north; for Tiberias was a halting-place for those who traveled from the north to the south, from Persia to Egypt.

Jesus Preaches in a Ship [D6]

⊕

THE shore near Bethsaida was steep, but at the point to which I now allude it gently sloped and afforded an easy landing place. Peter's ship and Jesus's little boat lay here. The latter was small and could at most contain fifteen men. A great crowd of pagans who had been at Cornelius's feast were here assembled. Jesus was instructing them and, as the throng became very great, he with some of his disciples went on board his little boat, while the rest of them and the publicans went on Peter's boat. And now from the boat he instructed the pagans on the strand, making use of the parables of the sower and the tares in the field. [154]

[MARK 4:1–2] Again he began to teach beside the sea. And a very large crowd gathered about him, so that he got into a boat and sat in it on the sea; and the whole crowd was beside the sea on the land. 2 And he taught them many things in parables.

The Calling of Matthew [D7]

⊕

JESUS meanwhile, with the disciples, continued along the shore to the right, thus passing Matthew's residence, though at a distance. A side path ran from this road to his custom office, and along it Jesus bent his steps, the disciples timidly remaining behind. Servants and publicans were out in front of the custom house, busied with all kinds of merchandise. When Matthew from the top of a little eminence beheld Jesus and the disciples coming toward him, he became confused and withdrew into his private office. But Jesus continued to approach, and from the opposite side of the road called him. Then came Matthew hurrying out, prostrated with his face on the ground before Jesus, protesting that he did not esteem himself worthy that Jesus should speak with him. But Jesus said: "Matthew, arise, and follow me!" Then Matthew arose, saying that he would instantly and joyfully abandon all things and follow him. [154]

[MATTHEW 9:9] 9 As Jesus passed on from there, he saw a man called Matthew sitting at the tax office; and he said to him, "Follow me." And he rose and followed him. [MARK 2:13–14] 13 He went out again beside the sea; and all the crowd gathered about him, and he taught them. 14 And as he passed on, he saw Levi the son of Alphaeus sitting at the tax office, and he said to him, "Follow me." And he rose and followed him.

CAPERNAUM, situated on the road from Damascus to the Mediterranean, was a much frequented halting-place, and numerous caravans, with crowds of travelers, passed through it day by day on their way to Samaria, Judea, Egypt, or, in the other direction, to Persia and the valley of the Euphrates. It was the great emporium of Eastern Galilee, and in it, as well as at other points of this border district, were stationed publicans or custom officers, who collected taxes in the name of the Imperial Treasury. Everywhere in Palestine, at the entrance ports, at the bridges, at the gates of towns, these imposts were exacted, and they weighed very heavily on the people. As a result, the collectors of the taxes were universally hated, and, as is generally the case in matters of this sort, it was the subalterns, who, though less responsible, were more easily accessible, and who came in for most of the odium. Everyone looked upon them as extortioners and tyrants on whom it seemed permissible to heap all manner of maledictions. This was especially the case in the eyes of the Jews, with whom the profession of a publican involved a sort of religious and national apostasy. To take service under Caesar, as the agent of an odious and oppressive exaction, was tacitly to recognize the domination of the foreigner, not only, as with others, to suffer it. Was not the man who could do this a mere hypocrite to call himself a son of Israel and go up to the temple to present offerings which were thus defiled?

For all that, however, there were honest men even among the publicans, who suffered from, without understanding, the popular prejudice against them. There had been some such among the disciples of John the Baptist, and he had not told them to give up their calling, but had merely urged them to pursue it honestly. In spite of this, great must have been the astonishment of the disciples when Jesus called to him a publican, named Levi bar Alpheus, or Levi, the son of Alpheus, henceforth to be known as Matthew, a name signifying "the gift of God." He himself must fully have realized the value of that gift, and his heart must have been overflowiug with gratitude. It is this feeling we have endeavored to express.

The Meal in the House of Matthew [D8]

⊕

MATTHEW received Jesus and his followers most lovingly and humbly, and washed their feet. His half brothers warmly embraced him, and then he presented his wife and children to Jesus. Jesus spoke to the mother and blessed the children, who then retired, to return no more. I have often wondered why the children whom Jesus blessed usually appeared no more. I saw Jesus seated, and Matthew on his knees before him. Jesus laid his hand upon him, blessed him, and addressed to him some words of instruction. Matthew had formerly been called Levi, but now he received the name of Matthew. The feast was a magnificent one. The table, in the form of a cross, was set in an open hall. Jesus sat in the midst of the publicans. In the intervals between the different courses, the guests arose and engaged in conversation with one another. Poor travelers passing by were supplied with food by the disciples, for the street on which the house stood led down to the ferry. [155]

[MATTHEW 9:10–13] 10 And as he sat at table in the house, behold, many tax collectors and sinners came and sat down with Jesus and his disciples. 11 And when the Pharisees saw this, they said to his disciples, "Why does your teacher eat with tax collectors and sinners?" 12 But when he heard it, he said, "Those who are well have no need of a physician, but those who are sick. 13 Go and learn what this means, 'I desire mercy, and not sacrifice.' For I came not to call the righteous, but sinners."

The Calling of Peter and Andrew [D9]

⊕

NEXT morning, when Jesus went to the lake, which was about a quarter of an hour distant from Matthew's dwelling, Peter and Andrew were upon the point of launching out on the deep to let down their nets. Jesus called to them: "Come and follow me! I will make you fishers of men!" They instantly abandoned their work, hove to their boat, and came on shore. [155]

[MATTHEW 4:18–20] 18 As he walked by the Sea of Galilee, he saw two brothers, Simon who is called Peter and Andrew his brother, casting a net into the sea; for they were fishermen. 19 And he said to them, "Follow me, and I will make you fishers of men." 20 Immediately they left their nets and followed him.

THIS time we are not told that Peter and Andrew were in their fishing boats, but that they were casting a net into the sea. This net was of the kind now called a sweep-net, and on the north of the Sea of Galilee the shores are peculiarly well adapted to this mode of fishing. Even at the present day the fishermen there show remarkable skill. They know how to hit upon the exact spot where the fish are hiding, and rarely miss their prey, which they put into a netted bag they wear round their hips, as shown in my picture. This peculiar mode of fishing from the shore explains how it was that Jesus was able to speak to the future apostles on the spot and tell them to follow him, without having to call to them from afar, and removes a certain amount of the mystery of this scene, described with a brevity so touching. In the district referred to the mountains gradually become lower, and on some parts of the shore boats can easily approach the land, while in others a beach with a gentle slope keeps them at a distance. Here and there, too, small natural harbors are sheltered by blocks of black rock peculiar to these parts, and where this is the case, the population of the shores is considerably denser than elsewhere. It was probably in a comparatively lonely part of the coast that the calling of the apostles took place. For the rest, however, there is but a narrow tract of land between the beach stretching along the valley of Galilee, and the probable site of Capernaum, which was situated on the north of the lake, near the mouth of the Jordan, that is to say near the spot where Bethsaida is supposed to have been. The shores of the lake are, on that side, cut into by five or six small harbors, where the few boats belonging to the enterprising fishermen who worked off these coasts could take shelter. Peter and his family, it would appear, were engaged together in a fishing venture.

The Calling of James and John [D10]

⊕

JESUS went on a little farther up the shore to the ship of Zebedee, who with his sons James and John was mending his nets on the ship. Jesus called the two sons to come to him. They obeyed immediately and came to land, while Zebedee remained on the ship with his servants. Then Jesus sent Peter and Andrew, James and John into the mountains where the pagans were encamped, with the order to baptize all that desired it. He himself had prepared them for it during the two preceding days. [155]

[MARK 1:19–20] 19 And going on a little farther, he saw James the son of Zebedee and John his brother, who were in their boat mending the nets. 20 And immediately he called them; and they left their father Zebedee in the boat with the hired servants, and followed him.

Jesus Sleeping during the Tempest [D11]

⊕

THAT evening when all were again assembled at Matthew's, the crowd was very great and pressed around Jesus. On that account, with the twelve apostles and Saturnin he went on board Peter's boat and commanded them to row toward Tiberias, which was on the opposite side of the lake in its greatest breadth. It looked as if Jesus wanted to escape from the crowd that pressed upon him, for he was worn out with fatigue. Three platforms surrounded the lower part of the mast, like steps one above the other. In the middle one, in one of the apartments used by the sentry, Jesus lay down and fell asleep, for he was very tired. The rowers were above him. From Jesus's resting place, although protected by a roof, there was an unobstructed view over the whole lake. When the party put out from shore, the weather was calm and beautiful, but they had scarcely reached the middle of the lake before a violent tempest arose. [156]

[MARK 4:36–38] 36 And leaving the crowd, they took him with them in the boat, just as he was. And other boats were with him. 37 And a great storm of wind arose, and the waves beat into the boat, so that the boat was already filling. 38 But he was in the stern, asleep on the cushion; and they woke him and said to him, "Teacher, do you not care if we perish?"

ON the coasts of Judea there are still to be seen boats of considerable size, which can be navigated either with oars or sails. In the narrower portion of the stern, referred to by Saint Mark as the "hinder part of the ship," there was a small cabin in which, no doubt, Jesus was asleep. The sacred text tells us that he had his head upon a pillow, a small detail which proves that the vessel was of sufficient importance to have some furniture in its cabin.

Jesus Stilling the Tempest [D12]

⊕

I THOUGHT it very strange that, although the sky was shrouded in darkness, the stars were to be seen. The wind blew in a hurricane and the waves dashed over the boat, the sails of which had been furled. I saw from time to time a brilliant light glancing over the troubled waters. It must have been lightning. The danger was imminent, and the disciples were in great anxiety when they awoke Jesus with the words: "Master! Hast thou no care for us? We are sinking!" Jesus arose, looked out on the water, and said quietly and earnestly, as if speaking to the storm: "Peace! Be still!" and instantly all became calm. The disciples were struck with fear. They whispered to one another: "Who is this man that can control the waves?" [156]

[MARK 4:39–40] 39 And he awoke and rebuked the wind, and said to the sea, "Peace! Be still!" And the wind ceased, and there was a great calm. 40 He said to them, "Why are you afraid? Have you no faith?"

The Miraculous Draught of Fishes [D13]

⊕

EVENING was now closing. Jesus told Peter to row his boat out on the lake and to cast his nets to the fish. Peter, slightly vexed, replied: "We have labored all night and have taken nothing, but at thy word I will let down the net," and he with the others entered their boats with their nets and rowed out on the lake. Jesus bade adieu to the crowd, and in his own little boat wherein were Saturnin, Veronica's son, who had arrived the day before, and some of the other disciples—he followed after Peter's. He continued to instruct them, explaining similitudes, and when out on the deep water told them where to let down the nets. Then he left them and rowed over in his little boat to the landing place near Matthew's. The fishers cast out the net, and rowed toward Chorazin, but soon they were unable to raise it. When at last, continuing to row eastward, they dragged it out of the deep into shallow water, it was so heavy that it gave way here and there. [161]

[LUKE 5:1–11] 1 While the people pressed upon him to hear the word of God, he was standing by the lake of Gennesaret. 2 And he saw two
boats by the lake; but the fishermen had gone out of them and were washing their nets. 3 Getting into one of the boats, which was Simon's,
he asked him to put out a little from the land. And he sat down and taught the people from the boat. 4 And when he had ceased speaking,
he said to Simon, "Put out into the deep and let down your nets for a catch." 5 And Simon answered, "Master, we toiled all night and took
nothing! But at your word I will let down the nets." 6 And when they had done this, they enclosed a great shoal of fish; and as their nets
were breaking, 7 they beckoned to their partners in the other boat to come and help them. And they came and filled both the boats, so that
they began to sink. 8 But when Simon Peter saw it, he fell down at Jesus's knees, saying, "Depart from me, for I am a sinful man, O Lord."
9 For he was astonished, and all that were with him, at the catch of fish which they had taken; 10 and so also were James and John, sons of
Zebedee, who were partners with Simon. And Jesus said to Simon, "Do not be afraid; henceforth you will be catching men." 11 And when
they had brought their boats to land, they left everything and followed him.

The Sermon of the Beatitudes [D14]

⊕

THERE was no teacher's chair on the mountain, only an eminence surrounded by a mound of earth. The view from the west and southwest extended over the lake and to the opposite mountains. One could even descry Mount Tabor. Crowds of people, most of them pagans that had received baptism, were encamped around. There were Jews also present. Separation between them was not so rigorously observed here, since communication between the Jews and Gentiles was greater in these parts, and on this side of the lake the latter enjoyed certain privileges. Jesus began by enumerating the eight beatitudes, and then went on to explain the first: "Blessed are the poor in spirit, for theirs is the kingdom of heaven." [163]

[MATTHEW 5:1–18] 1 Seeing the crowds, he went up on the mountain, and when he sat down his disciples came to him. 2 And he opened his mouth and taught them, saying: 3 "Blessed are the poor in spirit, for theirs is the kingdom of heaven. 4 "Blessed are those who mourn, for they shall be comforted. 5 "Blessed are the meek, for they shall inherit the earth. 6 "Blessed are those who hunger and thirst for righteousness, for they shall be satisfied. 7 "Blessed are the merciful, for they shall obtain mercy. 8 "Blessed are the pure in heart, for they shall see God. 9 "Blessed are the peacemakers, for they shall be called sons of God. 10 "Blessed are those who are persecuted for righteousness' sake, for theirs is the kingdom of heaven. 11 "Blessed are you when men revile you and persecute you and utter all kinds of evil against you falsely on my account. 12 Rejoice and be glad, for your reward is great in heaven, for so men persecuted the prophets who were before you. 13 "You are the salt of the earth; but if salt has lost its taste, how shall its saltness be restored? It is no longer good for anything except to be thrown out and trodden under foot by men. 14 "You are the light of the world. A city set on a hill cannot be hid. 15 Nor do men light a lamp and put it under a bushel, but on a stand, and it gives light to all in the house. 16 Let your light so shine before men, that they may see your good works and give glory to your Father who is in heaven. 17 "Think not that I have come to abolish the law and the prophets; I have come not to abolish them but to fulfill them. 18 For truly, I say to you, till heaven and earth pass away, not an iota, not a dot, will pass from the law until all is accomplished."

IF, on leaving Migdol, the ancient Magdalum, you turn your back on the lake, you will come to a deep gorge or ravine, flanked by the two Horns of Hattin, beyond which you will arrive at the foot of the mountains from which Jesus generally preached, and the scene of his miracle of the multiplication of the loaves. One of these mountains is that of the Beatitudes, which commands a view of the whole district. At your feet is the lake, bathing the last slopes of the Lebanon range.

The Palsied Man Let Down through the Roof [D15]

⊕

JUST at this moment a loud noise arose on the roof of the hall, and through the usual opening in the ceiling a paralytic on his bed was lowered by four men, who cried out: "Lord, have pity upon a poor sick man!" He was let down by two cords into the midst of the assembly before Jesus. [164]

[MARK 2:1–12] 1 And when he returned to Capernaum after some days, it was reported that he was at home. 2 And many were gathered together, so that there was no longer room for them, not even about the door; and he was preaching the word to them. 3 And they came, bringing to him a paralytic carried by four men. 4 And when they could not get near him because of the crowd, they removed the roof above him; and when they had made an opening, they let down the pallet on which the paralytic lay. 5 And when Jesus saw their faith, he said to the paralytic, "My son, your sins are forgiven." 6 Now some of the scribes were sitting there, questioning in their hearts, 7 "Why does this man speak thus? It is blasphemy! Who can forgive sins but God alone?" 8 And immediately Jesus, perceiving in his spirit that they thus questioned within themselves, said to them, "Why do you question thus in your hearts? 9 Which is easier, to say to the paralytic, 'Your sins are forgiven,' or to say, 'Rise, take up your pallet and walk'? 10 But that you may know that the Son of man has authority on earth to forgive sins"—he said to the paralytic—11 "I say to you, rise, take up your pallet and go home." 12 And he rose, and immediately took up the pallet and went out before them all; so that they were all amazed and glorified God, saying, "We never saw anything like this!"

The Woman with an Issue of Blood [D16]

⊕

JUST then a woman afflicted with an issue of blood, taking advantage of the darkness, made her way through the crowd, leaning on the arms of her nurses. She dwelt not far from the synagogue. The women afflicted with the same malady, though not so grievously as herself, had told her of their own cure some hours earlier. They had that day at noon, when Jesus was passing in the midst of the crowd, ventured to touch his garments, and were thereby instantly cured. Their words roused her faith. She hoped in the dusk of evening and in the throng that would gather round Jesus on leaving the synagogue, to be able to touch him unnoticed. Jesus knew her thoughts and consequently slackened his pace. The nurses led her as close to him as possible. Standing near her were her daughter, her husband's uncle, and Lea. The sufferer knelt down, leaned forward supporting herself on one hand, and with the other reaching through the crowd she touched the hem of Jesus's robe. Instantly she felt that she was healed. Jesus at the same moment halted, glanced around at the disciples, and inquired: "Who hath touched me?" To which Peter answered: "Thou askest, 'Who touched me?' The people throng and press upon thee, as thou seest!" But Jesus responded: "Someone hath touched me, for I know that virtue is gone out from me." Then he looked around and, as the crowd had fallen back a step, the woman could not longer remain hidden. Quite abashed, she approached him timidly, fell on her knees before him, and acknowledged in hearing of the whole crowd what she had done. Then she related how long she had suffered from an issue of blood, and that she believed herself healed by the touch of his garment. Turning to Jesus, she begged him to forgive her. Then Jesus addressed to her these words: "Be comforted, my daughter, thy faith hath made thee whole! Go in peace, and remain free from thy infirmity!" and she departed with her friends. She was thirty years old, very thin and pale, and was named Enue. [165]

[MARK 5:25–34] 25 And there was a woman who had had a flow of blood for twelve years, 26 and who had suffered much under many physicians, and had spent all that she had, and was no better but rather grew worse. 27 She had heard the reports about Jesus, and came up behind him in the crowd and touched his garment. 28 For she said, "If I touch even his garments, I shall be made well." 29 And immediately the hemorrhage ceased; and she felt in her body that she was healed of her disease. 30 And Jesus, perceiving in himself that power had gone forth from him, immediately turned about in the crowd, and said, "Who touched my garments?" 31 And his disciples said to him, "You see the crowd pressing around you, and yet you say, 'Who touched me?'" 32 And he looked around to see who had done it. 33 But the woman, knowing what had been done to her, came in fear and trembling and fell down before him, and told him the whole truth. 34 And he said to her, "Daughter, your faith has made you well; go in peace, and be healed of your disease."

The Blind of Capernaum [D17]

⊕

MEANWHILE two blind men with their guides were on the lookout for his coming. It seemed almost as if they scented his presence, for they followed after him, crying: "Jesus, thou Son of David, have pity on us!" At that moment Jesus went into the house of a good man who was devoted to him. The house was built in the rampart and had on the other side a door opening into the country beyond the city precincts. The disciples sometimes stopped at this house. Its owner was one of the guards in this section of the city. The blind men, however, still followed Jesus, and even into the house, crying in beseeching tones: "Have mercy on us, Son of David!" At last Jesus turned to them and said: "Do you believe that I can do this unto you?" and they answered: "Yea, Lord!" Then he took from his pocket a little flask of oil, or balsam, and poured some into a small dish, brown and shallow. Holding it and the flask in his left hand, with the right he put into the dish a little earth, mixed it up with the thumb and forefinger of the right hand, touched the eyes of the blind men with the same, and said: "May it be done unto you according to your desire!" [166]

[MATTHEW 9:27–30] 27 And as Jesus passed on from there, two blind men followed him, crying aloud, "Have mercy on us, Son of David." 28 When he entered the house, the blind men came to him; and Jesus said to them, "Do you believe that I am able to do this?" They said to him, "Yes, Lord." 29 Then he touched their eyes, saying, "According to your faith be it done to you." 30 And their eyes were opened. And Jesus sternly charged them, "See that no one knows it."

Jesus Heals a Mute Possessed Man [D18]

⊕

SOME people from the region of Sepphoris, distant relatives of Anne, brought hither a man possessed of a mute devil. His hands were bound, and they led him and pulled him along by cords tied around his body, for he was perfectly furious and oftentimes scandalous in his behavior. He was one of those Pharisees that had formed a committee to spy on the actions of Jesus. He was named Joas, and belonged to the number of those that had disputed with Jesus in an isolated school between Sepphoris and Nazareth. [166]

[MATTHEW 9:32–38] 32 As they were going away, behold, a dumb demoniac was brought to him. 33 And when the demon had been cast out, the dumb man spoke; and the crowds marveled, saying, "Never was anything like this seen in Israel." 34 But the Pharisees said, "He casts out demons by the prince of demons." 35 And Jesus went about all the cities and villages, teaching in their synagogues and preaching the gospel of the kingdom, and healing every disease and every infirmity. 36 When he saw the crowds, he had compassion for them, because they were harassed and helpless, like sheep without a shepherd. 37 Then he said to his disciples, "The harvest is plentiful, but the laborers are few; 38 pray therefore the Lord of the harvest to send out laborers into his harvest."

The Man with the Withered Hand [D19]

⊕

WHEN Jesus went to the synagogue to teach, the Pharisees laid a snare for him. In a corner of the synagogue was a poor creature with a withered hand. He had not ventured to appear before Jesus, and now held back, intimidated by the presence of the Pharisees. These latter were reproaching Jesus, asking him how he could make his appearance with a publican like Matthew. To this Jesus responded that he had come to console and convert sinners, but that no Pharisee should ever be numbered among his disciples. The Pharisees mockingly retorted: "Master, here is one for whom thou hast come. Perhaps, thou wilt heal him also." Thereupon Jesus commanded the man with the withered hand to come forward and stand in the midst of the assembly. He did so, and Jesus said to him: "Thy sins are forgiven thee!" The Pharisees, who scorned the poor man—whose reputation was not of the best—cried out: "His withered hand has never hindered him from sinning." Then Jesus grasped the hand, straightened the fingers, and said: "Use thy hand!" The man stretched out his hand, found it cured, and went away giving thanks. [167]

[MARK 3:1–5] 1 Again he entered the synagogue, and a man was there who had a withered hand. 2 And they watched him, to see whether he would heal him on the sabbath, so that they might accuse him. 3 And he said to the man who had the withered hand, "Come here." 4 And he said to them, "Is it lawful on the sabbath to do good or to do harm, to save life or to kill?" But they were silent. 5 And he looked around at them with anger, grieved at their hardness of heart, and said to the man, "Stretch out your hand." He stretched it out, and his hand was restored.

ACCORDING to an old tradition related in the Apocryphal Gospel of the Nazarenes, or of the Ebionite Christians, the man with the withered hand was a stone-cutter or mason. Saint Jerome sees in this incident a type of Judaism, in which the hand without strength had become useless and incapable of cooperating in the building of the temple of God.

The Pharisees and the Herodians Conspire against Jesus [D20]

⊕

THE Pharisees were covered with confusion and filled with wrath. They declared Jesus a sabbath-breaker against whom they would lodge an accusation, and then took their departure. In the neighborhood of the synagogue they met some Herodians with whom they consulted as to how they should lie in wait for Jesus on the next feast in Jerusalem. [167]

[MARK 3:6] 6 The Pharisees went out, and immediately held counsel with the Herodians against him, how to destroy him.

THE spot represented in our engraving is near a synagogue, and trees had been planted there to afford shelter from the sun to the doctors who frequented it to talk together. The trees chosen were cypresses, pines, and cedars, all of a more or less somber aspect, harmonizing well with and accentuating the secluded character of this place sacred to meditation. Seats were contrived in the stone walls, so that the doctors could sit at their ease.

A Woman Cries Out in a Crowd [D21]

⊕

WHEN Jesus later on addressed the people in Peter's house, among the other women present was Lea, the sister-in-law of Enue, recently cured of the issue of blood. I saw her at first, calm and sorrowful, often changing her place among the crowd, as if looking for someone, but I found out that she was in this way obeying the impulse that prompted her to proclaim aloud her reverence for Jesus. Mary and her companions entered the court that led to the hall in which Jesus was teaching. Lea, meanwhile, seeing Mary coming in, could no longer restrain herself and, as if intoxicated with joy, she cried out from among the crowd: "More blessed" (these are the exact words that I heard) "more blessed the womb that bore thee and the breasts that gave thee suck!" To which I saw Jesus quietly replying: "And far more blessed are they that hear the word of God and keep it!" [167]

[LUKE 11:27–33] 27 As he said this, a woman in the crowd raised her voice and said to him, "Blessed is the womb that bore you, and the
breasts that you sucked!" 28 But he said, "Blessed rather are those who hear the word of God and keep it!" 29 When the crowds were
increasing, he began to say, "This generation is an evil generation; it seeks a sign, but no sign shall be given to it except the sign of Jonah.
30 For as Jonah became a sign to the men of Nineveh, so will the Son of man be to this generation. 31 The queen of the South will arise at
the judgment with the men of this generation and condemn them; for she came from the ends of the earth to hear the wisdom of
Solomon, and behold, something greater than Solomon is here. 32 The men of Nineveh will arise at the judgment with this generation and
condemn it; for they repented at the preaching of Jonah, and behold, something greater than Jonah is here. 33 "No one after lighting a
lamp puts it in a cellar or under a bushel, but on a stand, that those who enter may see the light."

THE streets of the towns of Judea and Galilee are narrow, tortuous and dark; no carriages are ever seen in them; but, now and then, strings of camels laden with merchandise, or a few horsemen, pass along the wider thoroughfares, on their way through the towns, leaving the narrower ones to foot-passengers. One lane succeeds another, with many cross alleys and many gloomy corners, rendered yet darker by the arches supporting the neighboring houses. Here and there, patches of brilliant sunshine contrast vividly with the prevailing obscurity. These lanes and alleys wind backward and forward, first to the right, then to the left, and rows of houses, such as are so familiar to us in modern towns, are totally unknown. Now and then, perhaps, some tenement fallen into ruin makes the open space a little wider, and reveals a glimpse of the glowing oriental sky; but this break is succeeded by a yet more gloomy bit of street, a mere dark tunnel, formed of a series of arcades, only lighted here and there, at wide distances, by narrow openings. Our engraving represents some such spot, where a few people have gathered together in the partial shadow, where it is comparatively cool, to indulge in the never-ending gossip they are so fond of. Some sufferers, too, have grouped themselves here, in expectation of the Prophet, who is said to be going to pass soon. The women keep together, apart from the men, with whom they never mix. No doubt the Master will speak; they are all eager to hear him; their excitement is becoming greater and more intense every moment; the hope of fresh miracles is mingled with gratitude for benefits already received; the enthusiasm, when at last he who has so long been expected appears, reaches its height, and a woman in the crowd, lifting up her voice, gives utterance to what all the rest have been thinking.

Ordaining of the Twelve Apostles [D22]

⊕

IN the intervals of his public teaching and curing, Jesus, whenever he found himself alone with his apostles and disciples, prepared them for their mission. Today he led the twelve to a retired spot near the lake, placed them in the order mentioned in the Gospel, and conferred upon them the power of healing and of casting out devils. To the other disciples he gave only the power to baptize and impose hands. At the same time, he addressed to them a touching discourse in which he promised to be with them always and to share with them all that he possessed. All wept, and Jesus himself was very much moved. [168]

[MARK 3:13–19] 13 And he went up on the mountain, and called to him those whom he desired; and they came to him. 14 And he
appointed twelve, to be with him, and to be sent out to preach 15 and have authority to cast out demons: 16 Simon whom he surnamed
Peter; 17 James the son of Zebedee and John the brother of James, whom he surnamed Boanerges, that is, sons of thunder; 18 Andrew, and
Philip, and Bartholomew, and Matthew, and Thomas, and James the son of Alpheus, and Thaddeus, and Simon the Cananaean, 19 and
Judas Iscariot, who betrayed him. Then he went home.

The Two Men Possessed with Devils [D23]

⊕

WHILE he was ascending, two raging possessed higher up on the mountain were running about, darting in and out of the sepulchers, casting themselves on the ground, and beating themselves with the bones of the dead. They uttered horrible cries and appeared to be under the spell of some secret influence, for they could not flee. As Jesus drew nearer, they cried out from behind the bushes and rocks that lay a little higher up on the mountain: "Ye Powers! Ye Dominations! Come to our aid! Here comes one stronger than we!" Jesus raised his hand toward them and commanded them to lie down. They fell flat on their faces, but raising their heads again, cried out: "Jesus! Thou Son of God the Most High, what have we to do with thee? Why art thou come to torment us before the time? We conjure thee in the name of God to leave us in peace!" By this time Jesus and the disciples had reached them as they lay trembling, their whole persons horribly agitated. Jesus ordered the disciples to give them some clothing, and commanded the possessed to cover themselves. The disciples threw to them the scarfs they wore around their necks and in which they were accustomed to muffle their heads. The possessed, trembling and writhing convulsively, covered themselves, as if constrained to do so against their will, arose, and cried out to Jesus not to torture them. Jesus asked: "How many are ye?" They answered, "legion." The wicked spirits spoke always in the plural by the mouth of these two possessed. They said that the evil desires of these men were innumerable. This time the devil spoke the truth. For seventeen years these men had lived in communication with him, and in the practice of sorcery. Now and then they had suffered assaults like the present, but for the last two years they had been running, frantic, around the desert. They had been entangled in all the abominations of magic. [169]

[MATTHEW 8:28–29] 28 And when he came to the other side, to the country of the Gadarenes, two demoniacs met him, coming out of the tombs, so fierce that no one could pass that way. 29 And behold, they cried out, "What have you to do with us, O Son of God? Have you come here to torment us before the time?"

The Swine Driven into the Sea [D24]

⊕

A FEW moments after, there arose from the herds of swine sounds of grunting and raging, and from the herdsmen shouts and cries. The swine, some thousands in number, came rushing from all quarters and plunged down through the bushes on the mountainside. The herdsmen who had, at first, run after the animals, now came back to Jesus, saw the possessed who had been delivered, heard all that had happened, and then began to complain loudly of the injury done them. But Jesus replied that the salvation of these two souls was worth more than all the swine in the world. [171]

[MATTHEW 8:30–34] 30 Now a herd of many swine was feeding at some distance from them. 31 And the demons begged him, "If you cast us out, send us away into the herd of swine." 32 And he said to them, "Go." So they came out and went into the swine; and behold, the whole herd rushed down the steep bank into the sea, and perished in the waters. 33 The herdsmen fled, and going into the city they told everything, and what had happened to the demoniacs. 34 And behold, all the city came out to meet Jesus; and when they saw him, they begged him to leave their neighborhood.

The Blind and Mute Man Possessed by Devils [D25]

⊕

WHEN he went back to Capernaum, a man mute, blind, and possessed by the demon came to meet him, and Jesus cured him instantaneously. This miracle created intense astonishment, for even when approaching Jesus, the man had recovered his speech and cried out: "Jesus, thou Son of David, have mercy on me!" Jesus touched his eyes, and he saw. [174]

[MATTHEW 12:22–30] 22 Then a blind and dumb demoniac was brought to him, and he healed him, so that the dumb man spoke and saw. 23 And all the people were amazed, and said, "Can this be the Son of David?" 24 But when the Pharisees heard it they said, "It is only by Beelzebul, the prince of demons, that this man casts out demons." 25 Knowing their thoughts, he said to them, "Every kingdom divided against itself is laid waste, and no city or house divided against itself will stand; 26 and if Satan casts out Satan, he is divided against himself; how then will his kingdom stand? 27 And if I cast out demons by Beelzebul, by whom do your sons cast them out? Therefore they shall be your judges. 28 But if it is by the Spirit of God that I cast out demons, then the kingdom of God has come upon you. 29 Or how can one enter a strong man's house and plunder his goods, unless he first binds the strong man? Then indeed he may plunder his house. 30 He who is not with me is against me, and he who does not gather with me scatters.

The Exhortation to the Apostles [D26]

⊕

IN the intervals of his public teaching and curing, Jesus, whenever he found himself alone with his apostles and disciples, prepared them for their mission. Today he led the twelve to a retired spot near the lake, placed them in the order mentioned in the Gospel, and conferred upon them the power of healing and of casting out devils. To the other disciples he gave only the power to baptize and impose hands. At the same time, he addressed to them a touching discourse in which he promised to be with them always and to share with them all that he possessed. [176]

[LUKE 9:1–5] 1 And he called the twelve together and gave them power and authority over all demons and to cure diseases, 2 and he sent
them out to preach the kingdom of God and to heal. 3 And he said to them, "Take nothing for your journey, no staff, nor bag, nor bread, nor
money; and do not have two tunics. 4 And whatever house you enter, stay there, and from there depart. 5 And wherever they do not receive
you, when you leave that town shake off the dust from your feet as a testimony against them."

THROUGHOUT the whole of Palestine, and more especially in the environs of towns near the main routes of traffic and of travel, there are to be seen resting-places, where several persons can sit down comfortably together, sheltered from the heat of the sun or from the rain. Here and there, for instance, on the mountain slopes rises an isolated group of locust trees, marking some such resting-place, more than one sign indicating how many have availed themselves of it; the ground beneath the trees has become perfectly level, the rock is smooth and slippery, even worn away in parts. Many of these shelters are now the property of mosques, they probably formerly belonged to churches, and yet earlier, perhaps, to the Jews themselves. Our Lord and Savior Jesus Christ appears to have availed himself often of these spots, as places of meeting; he preached to the people from them; he multiplied the loaves and fishes; he talked with his disciples, or even sometimes retired to them alone for meditation and prayer. These secluded sites are full of attraction, not only on account of the many touching memories connected with them, but for their own natural charm. They are, as a general rule, well chosen, commanding a view of some fine landscape or set in a scene of solemn solitude. Here one can dream and meditate at one's ease, whilst all around the countless fragments of red pottery strewing the ground bear witness to the passing away of many generations.

He Sent Them Out Two by Two [D27]

⊕

TOWARD noon I saw Jesus gathering the apostles and disciples around him in a sequestered spot at the foot of the mountain. He sent them all out, two and two, with the exception of Peter, John, and some of the disciples who were to remain with him. They were to go in three different directions: one set into the valley of the Jordan, another into that near Dothan, and a third to the west, into the country around Jerusalem. It was on this occasion that I heard Jesus telling the apostles that they should go without purse, without scrip, girded with one garment only, and a staff in their hand. [196]

[LUKE 10:1] 1 After this the Lord appointed seventy others, and sent them on ahead of him, two by two, into every town and place where he himself was about to come.

Salome, Daughter of Herodias, Dancing [D28]

⊕

SALOME wore a long, transparent robe, caught up here and there on the lower limbs with glittering clasps. Her arms were ornamented with gold bands, strings of pearls, and circlets of tiny feathers; her neck and breast were covered with pearls and delicate, sparkling chains. She danced for a while before Herod who, quite dazzled and enchanted, gave expression to his admiration, in which all his guests enthusiastically joined. She should, he said to her, renew this pleasure for him on the next morning.

The dance consisted of a constant bowing, a gentle swaying and turning. The whole person seemed to be destitute of bones. Scarcely had one position been assumed when it glided into another. Mirrors and gold sparkled on all sides, flowers and green bushes everywhere met the eye. The splendor almost blinded one, for far, far back halls, and columns, and passages were blazing with torches and lamps, with transparent glittering sentences, pictures, and vases. [199]

[MARK 6:17–23] 17 For Herod had sent and seized John, and bound him in prison for the sake of Herodias, his brother Philip's wife;
because he had married her. 18 For John said to Herod, "It is not lawful for you to have your brother's wife." 19 And Herodias had a grudge
against him, and wanted to kill him. But she could not, 20 for Herod feared John, knowing that he was a righteous and holy man, and kept
him safe. When he heard him, he was much perplexed; and yet he heard him gladly. 21 But an opportunity came when Herod on his birthday gave a banquet for his courtiers and officers and the leading men of Galilee. 22 For when Herodias's daughter came in and danced, she
pleased Herod and his guests; and the king said to the girl, "Ask me for whatever you wish, and I will grant it." 23 And he vowed to her,
"Whatever you ask me, I will give you, even half of my kingdom."

The Head of John the Baptist on a Charger [D29]

⊕

SALOME held the dish timidly at arm's length before her, her head still laden with its ornaments turned away in disgust. Thus she traversed the solitary passages that led up to a kind of vaulted kitchen under the castle of Herodias. Here she was met by her mother, who raised the cover from the holy head, which she loaded with insult and abuse. Then taking a sharp skewer from a certain part of the wall where many such instruments were sticking, with it she pierced the tongue, the cheeks, and the eyes. [200]

[MARK 6:24–29] 24 And she went out, and said to her mother, "What shall I ask?" And she said, "The head of John the baptizer." 25 And
she came in immediately with haste to the king, and asked, saying, "I want you to give me at once the head of John the Baptist on a platter."
26 And the king was exceedingly sorry; but because of his oaths and his guests he did not want to break his word to her. 27 And immediately the king sent a soldier of the guard and gave orders to bring his head. He went and beheaded him in the prison, 28 and brought his
head on a platter, and gave it to the girl; and the girl gave it to her mother. 29 When his disciples heard of it, they came and took his body,
and laid it in a tomb.

SAINT Jerome relates a tradition that, when Herodias received the head of the forerunner of Christ, who had so often rebuked her for her disgraceful profligacy, she took a pin from her head-dress and gratified her hatred by piercing the tongue of her dead enemy with it.

The Tower of Siloam [D30]

⊕

DURING the feast in Machaerus and the beheading of the Baptist, Jesus was in Thanat-Shiloh. There he heard from those that had returned from Jerusalem of the catastrophe which had just occurred in the Holy City. A crowd of laborers lately engaged on a great building near the mount upon which stood the temple, along with eighteen master workmen sent thither by Herod, had been buried under the falling walls. Jesus expressed compassion for the innocent sufferers, but said that the sin of the master workmen was not greater than that of the Pharisees, the Sadducees, and all those that labored against the kingdom of God. These latter would likewise be one day buried under their own treacherous structures.

The aqueduct that had cost the lives of so many was intended to conduct the water flowing from the pool of Bethesda up to the [temple] mount, thus to wash down from the court to the lower ravine the blood of the slaughtered animals. Higher up on the mountain was the pool of Bethesda, which discharged the waters received from its source, the Gihon. Three vaulted aqueducts ran far in under the temple mount, and long arcades extended northward across the valley and up to the mount. Nearby stood a high tower in which, by means of wheel-work machinery, water was raised in great leathern vessels from the reservoir far below.

The work had long been in progress. Being now in want of good building stone and master workmen, Pilate, acting on the advice of a member of the Sanhedrin, a Herodian in secret, had sought help from Herod. The master workmen sent by the latter were likewise Herodians. At Herod's instigation, they designedly carried on the building in such a way that the whole structure would necessarily fall at once. By this catastrophe, they intended to embitter the Jews still more against Pilate.

The foundation was broad, but hollow, and the structure arose tapering, but heavy. When the disaster happened, the eighteen Herodians were standing upon a terrace opposite the building. They had commanded the wooden scaffolding over which it had been arched to be drawn out, for that now all was solid. The poor laborers were crowded on all parts of the high arches busily working. Suddenly all split asunder, the huge walls came toppling down, and cries went up on all sides. Crash after crash was heard, and clouds of dust swept over the whole region.

Jesus conversed with Ozias, who told him about the fall of the tower of Siloam and of the unfortunate people buried under its ruins. He spoke with horror of Herod, whom some suspected of being at the bottom of the affair. Jesus remarked that greater calamities would overtake the traitors and false architects than that which had fallen upon the poor workmen. "If," he continued, "Jerusalem does not embrace the salvation offered her, the destruction of the temple will follow that of the tower." [201]

[LUKE 13:1–5] 1 There were some present at that very time who told him of the Galileans whose blood Pilate had mingled with their sacrifices. 2 And he answered them, "Do you think that these Galileans were worse sinners than all the other Galileans, because they suffered thus? 3 I tell you, No; but unless you repent you will all likewise perish. 4 Or those eighteen upon whom the tower in Siloam fell and killed them, do you think that they were worse offenders than all the others who dwelt in Jerusalem? 5 I tell you, No; but unless you repent you will all likewise perish."

The Holy Women [D31]

⊕

DURING the meal the Pharisees addressed to him all kinds of reproaches; among others they alleged that he allowed women of bad repute to follow him about. These men had heard of the conversion of Magdalene, of Mara the Suphanite, and of the Samaritan. [204]

[LUKE 8:2–3] 2 and also some women who had been healed of evil spirits and infirmities: Mary, called Magdalene, from whom seven demons had gone out, 3 and Johanna, the wife of Chuza, Herod's steward, and Susanna, and many others, who provided for them out of their means.

WITH the three women named in the sacred text were also Martha, Salome, the mother of the two Zebedees, Mary Cleophas, Dinah the Samaritan, Mary the Canaanite, the mother of Mark of Jerusalem, the daughter of Jairus, and many others who had been the subjects of miracles, with some of their relations. They formed together a kind of society, which ministered to the needs of Jesus and his followers.

Jesus Goes up Alone onto a Mountain to Pray [D32]

⊕

WHEN all in Lazarus's house had retired to rest, Jesus went in the darkness to the Mount of Olives and prayed in a solitary nook. The mount was covered with verdure and groves of noble trees. It was full of retired corners. [216]

[MATTHEW 14:23] 23 And after he had dismissed the crowds, he went up on the mountain by himself to pray. When evening came, he was there alone. [LUKE 6:12] 12 In these days he went out to the mountain to pray; and all night he continued in prayer to God.

THE gospels again and again lay special stress on the fact that Jesus often withdrew from men and went apart to commune alone with his Father. Before beginning any one of the important acts of his ministry, it was his custom to seek some solitary place, in which to devote himself for a long time to prayer. This was the case before the choosing of the twelve apostles, and before his first public manifestation in Galilee. The Sermon on the Mount, which revealed him as the divine lawgiver, was also preceded by such a withdrawal into privacy; the transfiguration, that striking manifestation of the power of the Christ, intended, it would appear, to strengthen the faith of the apostles, which was to be put to such severe test by the shame of the Passion, was also prepared for by prayer. The Master again acted in a similar way before sending the disciples into the towns and villages to inaugurate their apostolic mission, and again before the mystery of the Eucharist, which Jesus presents to us as the very center of his work of sanctification here below. And lastly, on the eve of his Passion, he prayed again and again for a long time on the Mount of Olives, and the Gospel tells us that he "ofttime resorted thither" of an evening.

It was always to lofty spots that Jesus retired for prayer, and on the summits of nearly all the important mountains and hills of Palestine there is to be found the tomb of some prophet or some sanctuary set apart for prayer. These are the high places so often referred to in the Bible, where man, withdrawing from all earthly things, felt himself to be nearer to God, and in a more fitting frame of mind for intercourse with Him. With regard to our Lord himself, these prolonged and solitary prayers are to us fraught with a character of mysterious grandeur. Who shall say what ineffable communications took place between the divine when he performed the miracle of the multiplication of the loaves of bread, which was a symbol of the Son and his Father, or gauge the magnitude of the interests at stake in the all-powerful supplications of Jesus.

The Man with an Infirmity of 38 Years [D33]

⊕

ABOUT three o'clock, Jesus went with some of the disciples to the pool of Bethesda. He entered from without by a door which was closed and no longer used. This was the corner into which the poorest and most abandoned creatures were pushed; and lying in the farthest part and right next the door was a man paralyzed for thirty-eight years. He had been pressed back by the crowd to the farthest extremity of the place, and now lay in a little chamber destined for men. [216]

[JOHN 5:1–15] 1 After this there was a feast of the Jews, and Jesus went up to Jerusalem. 2 Now there is in Jerusalem by the Sheep Gate a pool, in Hebrew called Bethzatha, which has five porticoes. 3 In these lay a multitude of invalids, blind, lame, paralyzed.... 5 One man was there, who had been ill for thirty-eight years. 6 When Jesus saw him and knew that he had been lying there a long time, he said to him, "Do you want to be healed?" 7 The sick man answered him, "Sir, I have no man to put me into the pool when the water is troubled, and while I am going another steps down before me." 8 Jesus said to him, "Rise, take up your pallet, and walk." 9 And at once the man was healed, and he took up his pallet and walked. Now that day was the sabbath. 10 So the Jews said to the man who was cured, "It is the sabbath, it is not lawful for you to carry your pallet." 11 But he answered them, "The man who healed me said to me, 'Take up your pallet, and walk.'" 12 They asked him, "Who is the man who said to you, 'Take up your pallet, and walk'?" 13 Now the man who had been healed did not know who it was, for Jesus had withdrawn, as there was a crowd in the place. 14 Afterward, Jesus found him in the temple, and said to him, "See, you are well! Sin no more, that nothing worse befall you." 15 The man went away and told the Jews that it was Jesus who had healed him.

THE site of this pool is very doubtful. Traces of it are supposed to have been found near the Church of Saint Anne, where excavations have brought to light the remains of a chapel dating from the time of the Crusades. There is, however, nothing to prove the attempted identification, and we should, perhaps, be more justified in supposing that the "pool which was troubled" was situated on the south of the temple, in the so-called Ophel suburb. According to some interpreters, in fact, the word Bethesda signifies "the house of the waterfall" or "the place of the flowing of water," a name having reference to the flowing of the water from the temple reservoirs, which would place the pool on the south rather than on the north.

The priests used this water in the temple for various purposes. It is said to have acted as a purgative, and to have been of service in cases of gout, rheumatism, paralysis, and consumption. When the air bubbles were rising to the surface, and the water was lukewarm, sufferers plunged into it with all possible speed.

The *Piscina Probatica* or Pool of Bethesda [D34]

⊕

BUT when, on account of these cures, some excitement was beginning to arise, while now one, now another approached the pool to wash, Jesus went with John to that far-off place near the entrance where lay the poor man who had been sick for thirty-eight long years. He had been a gardener, and had formerly been engaged in the care of hedges and the raising of balsam trees. But now, so long sick and helpless, he was reduced to a state of starvation, and lay like a public beggar glad to eat the scraps left by the other sick. As he had been seen here for so many years, he was known to everyone as the incurable paralytic. Jesus spoke to him, and asked him whether or not he wanted to be cured. But he, not thinking that Jesus would cure him, but that he was asking only in a general way why he was lying there, answered that he had no help, no servant or friend to assist him down into the pool when the waters were moved. [217]

John 5:4] For an angel went down at a certain season into the pool, and troubled the water: whosoever then first after the troubling of the water stepped in was made whole of whatsoever disease he had.

IT is related that, a short time after the death of Jesus, Herod wished to enlarge this pool and widen the channels and reservoirs; but the spring which fed it suddenly dried up, and water did not flow from it again, till everything was restored to its original condition.

For the rest, in addition to this "Piscina Probatica," which was used for special purposes, the system of the water supply of Jerusalem was extremely well organized. On the west, at the top of the valley of Gihon, was the Birket Mamilla; lower down, the cistern now called the Birket el Sultan; then again, near to Mount Calvary, the amygdalum or Pool of Hezekiah. On the east is yet another pool, called that of the rams, which was used in the service of the temple; while, on the south of the town, was the so-called Fountain of the Holy Virgin, and the Pool of Siloam.

Moreover, every house had its cistern intended for the reception of rainwater, and wherever the nature of the surface of ground permitted the accumulation of water, in the courts and porches of houses, in open places, and at crossroads, for instance, similar reservoirs were dug out, so that plenty of water was always secured for ordinary domestic purposes.

The chief sources of supply of the town of Jerusalem, however, were the reservoirs, now known as Solomon's pools, excavated in the rock near Etham, from which great "quantities of water, following the natural slope of the mountain, flowed by way of that town and Bethlehem, accumulating in the temple reservoirs, and, with the cisterns which supplied the numerous porches, amply sufficing for every requirement.

The aqueduct through which the water flowed emptied its contents into three huge basins constructed, it is said, by Solomon, but it seems more probable that they were the work of the Canaanites and that the great king did no more than restore them, though his so doing at once led to their being called by his name. The three basins to which we are now referring were fed by the spring called the "Sealed Fountain" (fons signatus), alluded to in the Song of Solomon (4:12). Lastly, the purest water in Jerusalem, which for this reason was always used for making the unleavened bread for the Passover, was that of the well now known as the Aïn siti Mariam, and spoken of in the Bible as El Rogel. According to tradition, it was near this well that the scene occurred on the eve of the Passion, when Peter and John met the man bearing a pitcher of water (Luke 22:10).

The Lord's Prayer [D35]

⊕

AFTER Jesus had performed many cures, he withdrew into a hall to preach, whither he was followed by the cured and others. Some of the apostles went on healing while the others gathered around Jesus, who again taught on the beatitudes and related several parables. Among other points, he touched upon prayer which, he said, they should never omit. He related and developed the similitude of the unjust judge who, in order to get rid of the widow ever returning to knock at his door, at last rendered her justice. If the unjust judge was thus forced to comply, will not the Father in heaven be still more merciful? Then Jesus taught the multitude how to pray, recited the seven petitions of the Lord's Prayer, and explained the first, "Our Father, who art in heaven." Already on his journeys, he had explained several of the petitions to the disciples; now, however, he took them up as he had done the beatitudes, and made them the subject of his public instructions. Thus the prayer was all explained by degrees, repeated everywhere, and made known on all sides by the disciples. [224]

[LUKE 11:1–4] 1 He was praying in a certain place, and when he ceased, one of his disciples said to him, "Lord, teach us to pray, as John taught his disciples." 2 And he said to them, "When you pray, say: "Father, hallowed be thy name. Thy kingdom come. 3 Give us each day our daily bread; 4 and forgive us our sins, for we ourselves forgive every one who is indebted to us; and lead us not into temptation." [MATTHEW 6:5–13] 5 "And when you pray, you must not be like the hypocrites; for they love to stand and pray in the synagogues and at the street corners, that they may be seen by men. Truly, I say to you, they have received their reward. 6 But when you pray, go into your room and shut the door and pray to your Father who is in secret; and your Father who sees in secret will reward you. 7 "And in praying do not heap up empty phrases as the Gentiles do; for they think that they will be heard for their many words. 8 Do not be like them, for your Father knows what you need before you ask him. 9 Pray then like this: Our Father who art in heaven, Hallowed be thy name. 10 Thy kingdom come. Thy will be done, On earth as it is in heaven. 11 Give us this day our daily bread; 12 And forgive us our debts, As we also have forgiven our debtors; 13 And lead us not into temptation, But deliver us from evil.

The Good Samaritan

[LUKE 10: 30–37] Jesus replied and said, "A certain man was going down from Jerusalem to Jericho; and
he fell among robbers, and they stripped him and beat him, and went off leaving him half dead. 31 "And by
chance a certain priest was going down on that road, and when he saw him, he passed by on the other side.
32 "And likewise a Levite also, when he came to the place and saw him, passed by on the other side. 33 "But
a certain Samaritan, who was on a journey, came upon him; and when he saw him, he felt compassion, 34
and came to him, and bandaged up his wounds, pouring oil and wine on them; and he put him on his own
beast, and brought him to an inn, and took care of him. 35 "And on the next day he took out two denarii
and gave them to the innkeeper and said, 'Take care of him; and whatever more you spend, when I return,
I will repay you.' 36 "Which of these three do you think proved to be a neighbor to the man who fell into the
robbers' hands?" 37 And he said, "the one who showed mercy toward him." And Jesus said to him, "Go and
do the same."

They knew now that the man with the withered hand was there, and they wanted to see whether Jesus would heal him on the sabbath, that they might accuse him. This was especially the desire of those that had just come from Jerusalem. They were anxious for something to take home with them and lay before the Sanhedrin. As they could allege nothing of importance against him, and although they well knew his sentiments on the point, they always returned as if in ignorance to the same question, and to it Jesus with unwearied patience generally gave the same answer. Several of them now put the query: "Is it lawful to heal on the sabbath?" Jesus, knowing their thoughts, called the man with the withered hand, placed him in the midst of them, and said: "Is it lawful to do good on the sabbath day, or to do evil? To save life, or to destroy it?" No one answered. Then Jesus repeated the similitude of which he generally made use on such occasions: "What man shall there be among you that hath one sheep: and if the same fall into a pit on the sabbath day, will he not take hold on it and lift it up! How much better is a man than a sheep! Therefore it is lawful to do a good deed on the sabbath day." He was very much troubled at the obduracy of these men, and his angry glance penetrated to the bottom of their soul. Taking the arm of the poor man in his left hand, he stroked it down with the right, straightened out and separated the crooked fingers, and said: "Stretch out thy hand!"

The man stretched out his hand and moved it. It had become as long as the other and was perfectly cured. The whole scene was the work of an instant. The man cast himself with thanks at Jesus's feet and the people broke forth into shouts of jubilation, while the enraged Pharisees withdrew to the entrance of the synagogue to discuss what they had witnessed. Jesus next drove the devil from the possessed whom he had left waiting at the door, and instantly speech and hearing were given him. The people again shouted for joy, and the Pharisees again gave utterance to their slanderous expression: "He has a devil! He drives out one devil by the help of another!" Jesus turned toward them and said: "Who among you can convict me of sin? If the tree is good, so too is the fruit good; if the tree is evil, so also is the fruit evil, for by the fruit the tree is known. O generation of vipers, how can you speak good things, whereas you are evil! Out of the abundance of the heart the mouth speaketh."

At these words, the Pharisees set up a great cry: "We shall make an end of all this! We have had enough of this!" and one of them carried his insolence so far as to call out: "Dost thou not know that we can put thee out?" Jesus and the disciples now left the synagogue, and hurried by different routes, some to Mary's house, some to Peter's near the lake. Jesus took a repast at his mother's, and then passed the night with the twelve in Peter's house. The latter, being the more distant of the two, afforded a safer retreat.

Saturday, January 27, AD 31 (Shebat 14)

This morning, at Peter's house, the twelve and the other disciples reported their experiences from their missionary travels since Kislev 25 (Mark 6:30). Jesus listened to their doubts and to the problems they had encountered, giving practical instructions for the future. That night, Jesus and his disciples sailed across the Sea of Galilee and landed between Matthew's custom house and Little Chorazin.

The whole of the following day Jesus, the twelve apostles, and the disciples spent at Peter's healing the sick. The multitude was waiting for him and seeking him in many places, but he remained shut up in the house.

During the day Jesus called before him the apostles and disciples, two by two, as he had sent them, and received from them an account of all that had happened to them during their mission.[E1] He solved the doubts and difficulties that had arisen in certain circumstances, and instructed them how they should act in the future. He told them again that he would soon give them a new mission. The six apostles who had been laboring in Upper Galilee had been well received. They had found the people well disposed and had in consequence baptized many. The others, who had gone to Judea, had not baptized any, and here and there had experienced contradiction.

The crowd around the house becoming greater and greater, Jesus and his followers slipped away secretly. The stars shed their light down upon the little party as they hurried along the bypaths to Peter's boat. They ferried across the lake and landed between Matthew's custom house and Little Chorazin.

Sunday, January 28, AD 31 (Shebat 15)

Many people had followed Jesus from Capernaum and Bethsaida. As a result, early this morning, a large crowd had already assembled on the mountain above Matthew's custom house. They had come to hear Jesus speak. Still more people came from the surrounding area, bringing with them the sick and the possessed. In the afternoon, after healing and teaching, Jesus dismissed the crowd, saying that he would teach next morning on the mountain near Bethsaida-Julias. Jesus, the twelve, and the seventy-two disciples then withdrew to a shaded, solitary place. Jesus then gave them instruction along the lines of Matthew 10:1–42.

He arranged them in ranks as follows: the twelve apostles two by two headed by Peter and John; the older disciples formed a circle around them, and then came the younger ones according to the rank he assigned to them. He set the apostles over the disciples, saying that the former should send and call the latter, just as he sent and called the apostles.

From there they climbed the mountain at whose foot stood the custom house, for Jesus wanted to instruct the disciples in solitude. But the multitude had caught a glimpse of their departure, and the news soon spread through the tents of the encampment. The crowd near Bethsaida soon crossed, some over the lake, others further up over the Jordan bridge, and so Jesus and his party here on the mountain were again surrounded by the immense multitude. The disciples ranged the people in order, and Jesus began again his instructions on the beatitudes and prayer. He again explained the first petition of the Lord's Prayer. As the hours flew by, the crowds increased. People came from all the cities around, from Julias, Chorazin, and Gergesa, bringing with them the sick and possessed. Numbers were healed by Jesus and the disciples.

The instructions over, the multitude dispersed the next day at the place on which this sermon on the mount had been delivered. Jesus with the apostles and disciples then retired higher up the mountain to a shady, solitary spot.

Besides the twelve, there were with Jesus seventy-two disciples. Among them were the two soldiers from Machaerus and some that had not yet been formally received as disciples and had never been on a mission. The sons of Joseph's brother were there.

Jesus then instructed the disciples upon the work in store for them. He told them that they should take with them neither purse nor money nor bread, but only a staff and a pair of sandals; that wherever they were ungraciously received, they should shake the dust from their shoes. He gave them some general directions for their coming duties as apostles and disciples, called them the salt of the earth, and spoke of the light that must not be placed under a bushel, and of the city seated upon a mountain. Still he did not inform them of the full measure of persecution awaiting them.

The main point, however, of this instruction was that by which Jesus drew a definitive line between the apostles and the disciples, the former of whom were set over the latter. To them he said that they should send and call the disciples as he himself sent and called them, namely, the apostles. This they were empowered to do by virtue of their own mission. Among the disciples Jesus likewise formed several classes, setting the eldest and best instructed over the younger and more recently received. He arranged them in the following manner, the apostles, two by two, headed by Peter and John. The elder disciples formed a circle around them, and back of these the younger, according to the rank he had assigned them. Then he addressed to them words of earnest and touching instruction, and imposed hands upon the apostles as a ratification of the dignity to which he had raised them; the disciples, he merely blessed. All this was done with the greatest tranquillity. The whole scene was deeply impressive. No one offered the least resistance or showed the least sign of discontent. By this time it was evening, and Jesus with Andrew, John, Philip, and James the Less, plunged deeper into the mountains and there spent the night in prayer.

(Follow Map 26)

The Feeding of the Five Thousand

Monday, January 29, AD 31 (*Shebat 16*)

Today a large crowd of some five thousand people assembled on the mountain near Bethsaida-Julias. It was here, last Kislev 13, that Jesus had started to teach the "Sermon on the Mount." In the months since Kislev 13, Jesus had continued to teach the beatitudes and the Our Father prayer. Now Jesus taught and healed; and the apostles baptized many people. And again, the main content of Jesus's teaching was the beatitudes and the Lord's Prayer. Between four and six o'clock in the afternoon there took place the miraculous feeding of the five thousand (*John 6:5–15 and Mark 6:35–44*)*. In the evening Jesus withdrew alone* (*Matthew 14:22–23*)*, while the apostles sailed on Peter's ship back toward Bethsaida. A great storm arose on the Sea of Galilee, and there then took place the second miracle of the walking on the water* (*Matthew 14:25–33*)*, which had taken place for the first time on the night of Kislev 22–23.*

WHEN next morning Jesus and the apostles returned to the mount upon which he had already taught several times on the eight beatitudes, he found the multitude assembled. The other apostles had arranged the sick in sheltered places. Jesus and the apostles began to heal and to instruct. Many who in those days had now come for the first time to Capernaum knelt in a circle to receive baptism. The water, which had been brought for that purpose in leathern bottles, was sprinkled over them three at a time.

The mother of Jesus had come with the other women, and she now helped among the sick women and children. She did not exchange words with Jesus, but returned early to Capernaum.

Map 26: First Journey to Ornithopolis
January 27–February 19, AD 31

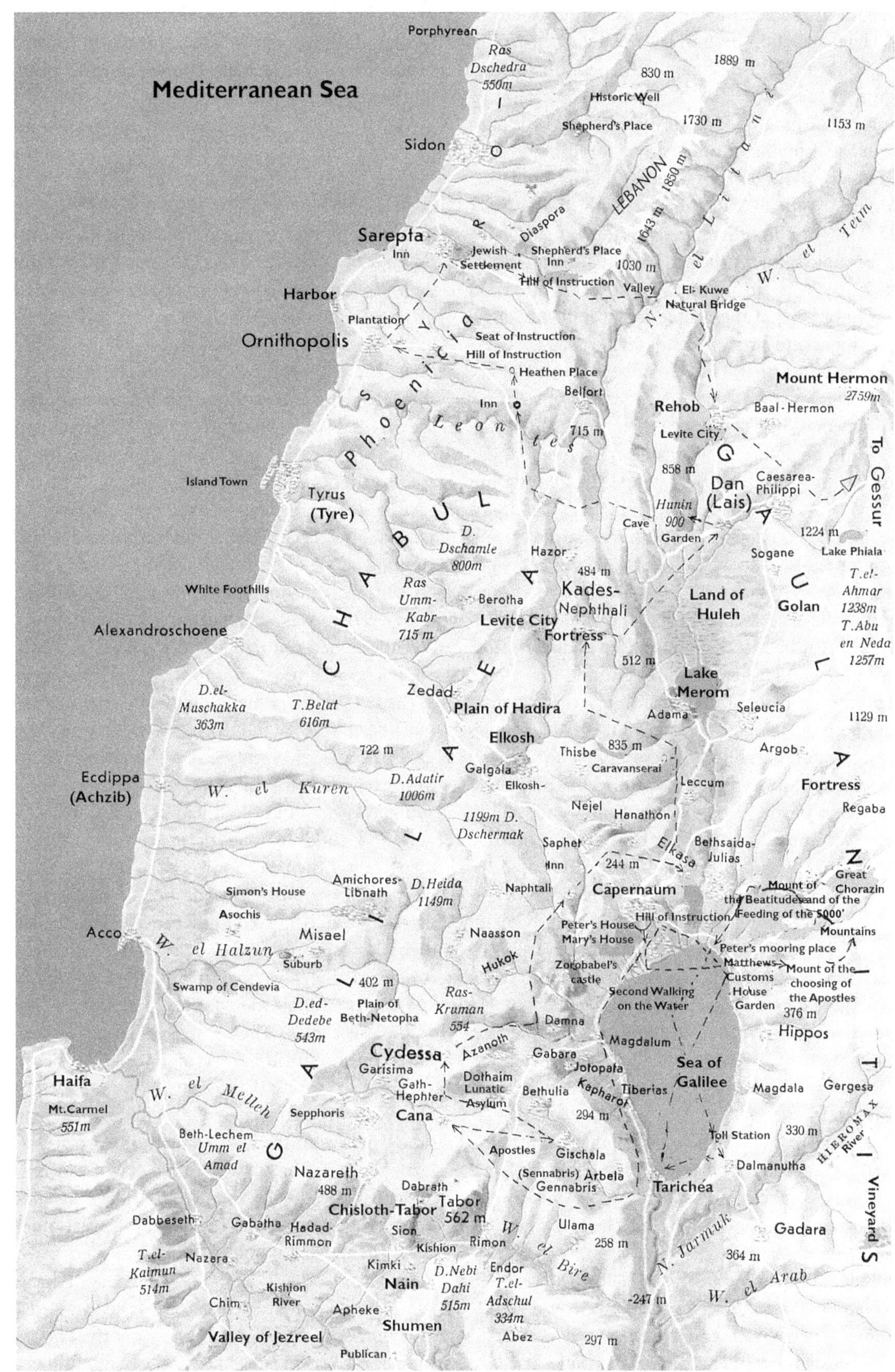

Capernaum—Mount near Matthew's Customs House—Mount of Beatitudes—Customs Place near Dalmanutha—Tarichea—Lakeshore near Matthew's Customs House—Capernaum—Hill of Instruction Cana—Cydessa—Naphtali—Elkasa—Kades-Nephthali—Dan—Hunin—Ornithopolis—Rehob

Jesus taught of the eight beatitudes and went as far as the sixth. The instruction on prayer begun at Capernaum he repeated, and explained some of the petitions of the Lord's Prayer.

Teaching and healing went on till after four o'clock, and all this time the listening crowds had had nothing to eat. They had now followed from the day before, and the scanty provisions they had brought with them were exhausted. Many among them were quite weak and languishing for nourishment. The apostles, noticing this, approached Jesus with the request that he would close the instruction in order that the people might hunt up lodgings for the night and procure food. Jesus replied: "They need not go away for that. Give them here something to eat!" Philip made answer: "Shall we go and buy two hundred pennyworth of bread and give them to eat?" This he said with some unwillingness, because he thought Jesus was about to lay upon them the fatigue of gathering up from the environs sufficient bread for all that crowd. Jesus answered: "See how many loaves you have!" and went on with his discourse. There was in the crowd a servant, who had been sent by his master with five loaves and two fishes as a present to the apostles. Andrew told this to Jesus with the words: "But what is that among so many?" Jesus ordered the loaves and fishes to be brought, and when they were laid on the sod before him he continued the explanation of the petition for daily bread. Many of the people were fainting, and the children were crying for bread. Then Jesus, in order to try Philip, asked him: "Where shall we buy bread, that these people may eat?" and Philip answered: "Two hundred pennyworth would not be sufficient for all this crowd." Jesus said: "Let the people be seated, the most famished by fifties, the others in groups of a hundred; and bring me the baskets of bread that you have at hand." The disciples set before him a row of shallow baskets woven of broad strips of bark, such as were used for bread. Then they scattered among the people, whom they arranged in fifties and hundreds all down the terraced mountain, which was clothed with grass beautiful and long. Jesus was above, the people seated below him on the mountainside.

Near the place upon which Jesus taught was a high, mossy bank, in which were several caves. On it Jesus directed a broad napkin to be spread, upon which were deposited the five loaves and two fishes. The loaves lay one upon the other on the napkin.[E2] They were long and narrow, about two inches in thickness. The crust was thin and yellow, and the inside, though not perfectly white, was close and fine. They were marked with stripes to make it more easy to break them or cut them with a knife. The fish were of a good arm's length. Their heads were somewhat projecting, not like our fish. Cut up, roasted, and ready for eating, they lay upon large leaves. Another man had brought a couple of honeycombs, and they too were laid on the napkin.

When the disciples numbered the people and seated them in fifties and hundreds as Jesus had directed, he cut the five loaves with a bone knife, and the fish, which had been split down lengthwise, he divided into crosspieces. After that he took one of the loaves in his hands, raised it on high and prayed. He did the same with one of the fish. I do not remember whether he did the same with the honey or not. Three of the disciples were at his side. Jesus now blessed the bread, the fish, and the honey, and began to break the cross-sections into pieces, and these again into smaller portions. Every portion immediately increased to the original size of the loaf, and on its surface appeared, as before, the dividing lines. Jesus then broke the individual pieces into portions sufficiently large to satisfy a man, and gave with each a piece of fish. Saturnin, who was at his side, laid the piece of fish upon the portion of bread, and a young disciple of the Baptist, a shepherd's son, who later on became a bishop, laid upon each a small quantity of honey. There was no perceptible diminution in the fish, and the honeycomb appeared to increase. Thaddeus laid the portions of bread upon which were the fish and honey in the flat baskets, which were then borne away to those in most need, who sat in the fifties and were served first.

As soon as the empty baskets were brought back, they were exchanged for full ones, and so the work went on for about two hours until all had been fed. They that had a wife and children (and these were separated from the men) found their portion so large that they could abundantly share with them. The people drank of the water that had been conveyed thither in leathern bottles. Most of them used cups formed of bark folded into the shape of a cone, and others had with them hollow gourds.

The whole affair was conducted most expeditiously and with perfect order. The apostles and disciples were, for the most part, occupied in carrying the baskets here and there and in distributing their contents. But all were silent and filled with amazement at the sight of such a multiplication. The size of the loaves was about two spans, or eighteen inches in length, and a fifth less in breadth. They were divided by ridges into twenty parts, five in length and four in breadth, so that the substance of every one of those parts increased fiftyfold, in order to feed five thousand men. The bread was a good three fingers in thickness. The fish were cut in two lengthwise. Jesus divided each half into numerous portions. It was only the two fish all the time, for it was in substance and not in number that they were most wonderfully increased.

When all had satisfied their hunger, Jesus bade the disciples to go around with the baskets and gather up the scraps, that nothing might be lost. They collected twelve baskets full. A great many of the people asked to take some of the pieces home with them as souvenirs. There were no soldiers present this time, though I was accustomed to see many at all the other great instructions. They had been called to Hesebon, where Herod was then sojourning.

When the people arose from their meal, they gathered everywhere in groups, full of wonder and admiration at this miracle of the Lord. From mouth to mouth ran the word: "This man is genuine! He is the prophet that was to come into the world! He is the Promised One!"

It was now growing dusk, so Jesus bade the disciples go to their boats and cross before him to Bethsaida; meanwhile he would take leave of the people and then follow. The disciples obeyed. Taking the baskets of bread they went down to their ships, and some of them crossed over to Bethsaida at once. The apostles and some of the older disciples remained behind a little longer and then departed on Peter's boat.

Jesus now dismissed the multitude, who were deeply moved. Scarcely had he left the spot upon which he had been teaching when the shout arose: "He has given us bread! He is our king! We will make him our king!" But Jesus disappeared into the solitude, and there gave himself up to prayer. [E3]

Jesus Walks on the Sea

PETER's boat, with the apostles and several of the disciples, was delayed during the night by contrary winds. They rowed vigorously, but were driven to the south of the proper direction. I saw that every two hours little boats with torches were sent out from either bank. They bore belated passengers to the large ships, and served in the darkness to mark their direction. As, like sentinels, they were relieved every two hours, they were here called night watches. I saw these boats changed four times while Peter's ship was being driven south of its right course.

Then Jesus walked on the sea in a direction from northeast to southwest. He was shining with light. Rays darted from him, and one could see his image reversed in the water under his feet. [E4] To walk in a direction from Bethsaida-Julias to Tiberias, almost opposite which was Peter's ship, Jesus had to pass between the two night boats that were rowing out into the sea, one from Capernaum and the other from the opposite bank. The people in these boats, seeing him walking, raised a long cry of fear and sounded a horn, for they took him for a phantom. The apostles on Peter's ship which, in order to find the true course, was guiding itself by the light from one of those boats, glanced in the direction of the sound and saw him coming toward them. He appeared to be gliding along more rapidly than in ordinary walking, and wherever he approached, the sea became calm. But a fog rested upon the water, so that he could be seen only at a certain distance. Although they had once before seen him thus walking, still the unusual and specter-like sight filled them with terror, and they uttered a great cry.

But suddenly they recalled the circumstance of Jesus's first walking on the water, and Peter, once more desirous of showing his faith, cried out again in his ardor: "Lord, if it be thou, bid me come to thee!" Jesus replied: "Come!" This time Peter ran a greater distance toward Jesus, but his faith did not yet suffice. He was already close to him when he again thought of his danger, and on the instant began to sink. He stretched out his hand and cried: "Lord, save me!" He did not, however, sink to so great a depth as the first time. [E5] Jesus again addressed to him the words: "O thou of little faith, why dost thou doubt?" When Jesus mounted the ship, all ran to cast themselves at his feet, crying: "Truly, thou art the Son of God!" Jesus reproved them for their fear and little faith, gave them a severe reprimand, and then instructed them upon the Lord's Prayer. He ordered them to steer more to the south. They now had a favorable wind and made the journey quickly, taking meanwhile a little rest in the cabin under the rower's stand around the mast. The storm on this occasion was not so violent as that of the preceding, but they had got into the current of the lake, which in the middle was very strong, and they could not get out of it.

Jesus allowed Peter to come to him on the water in order to humble him, for he knew very well that he was going to sink. Peter was very fiery and strong in believing, and in his zeal he wanted to give a testimony of his faith to Jesus and the disciples. By his sinking, he was preserved from pride. The others had not sufficient confidence to wish to follow his example and, while wondering at Peter's faith, they could see that although it excelled their own it was not yet what it ought to be.

Tuesday, January 30, AD 31 (*Shebat 17*)

At sunrise, Peter's ship landed near Dalmanutha (Mark 8:10). Here Jesus healed and continued his teaching concerning the beatitudes and the Lord's Prayer. He and the twelve then sailed over to Tarichea. After healing, he resumed teaching. It was here that he healed some children and spoke of the value of children, along the lines of Matthew 18:3–4. Toward evening he set sail again.

At sunrise Peter's ship put to on the east side of the lake at a little hamlet consisting of only a couple of rows of houses between Magdala and Dalmanutha. The hamlet belonged to the latter. It is this place that is meant when the Gospel says, "into the parts of Dalmanutha."

As soon as they perceived the approach of the ship, the inhabitants began to get all their sick ready, and they came to meet Jesus on the shore. He and the disciples healed in the streets. After that he went to a hill at a short distance beyond Dalmanutha, where all the inhabitants, Jews and pagans, assembled around him. There he taught upon the eight beatitudes and the Lord's Prayer. He also healed the sick whom they had brought with them. [E6]

Public Fountain

This little place was near the ferry, and in it the toll was paid. The people in general were occupied with the transportation of iron from the iron city of Ephron unto Basan. This was the point from which they shipped iron to all the other seaports of Galilee. From the mountains they could see over into Ephron.

From this place Jesus embarked with the apostles for Tarichea, which was situated from three to four hours south of Tiberias. The city was built on a height, a quarter of an hour from the seashore, down to which, however, were houses scattered here and there. The shore from this point to the efflux of the Jordan was bordered with a wall strong and black, upon which a road extended. It was a recently built city, very beautiful and of pagan architecture, with colonnades in front of the houses. In the marketplace was a beautiful fountain protected by a pillared roof.

Jesus went at once to this fountain and thither flocked the people with their sick, whom he healed. Numbers of women stood veiled with their children at some distance behind the men. Pharisees and Sadducees were standing around Jesus, among them some Herodians, while he discoursed upon the eight beatitudes and the Lord's Prayer. The Pharisees were not slow in bringing forward their accusations which, as ever, turned upon the same points, namely, that he frequented the society of publicans and sinners, that he attracted after him women of bad repute, that his disciples did not wash their hands before meals, that he cured upon the sabbath, etc. Jesus cut them short, and called the children to him. After curing, instructing, and blessing them, he presented them to the Pharisees with the words: "Ye must become like unto these."

Tarichea was less elevated than Tiberias. Quantities of fish were here salted and dried. Before entering the city, the traveler met large wooden frames upon which the fish lay drying.

The country in these parts was uncommonly fertile. The heights around the city were covered with terraces full of vineyards and every variety of fruit trees. The whole region as far as Tabor and the baths of Bethulia was, beyond all conception, blooming, teeming with abundance. It was most generally known as the Land of Galilee.

Toward evening Jesus left Tarichea and sailed with the disciples across the lake in a northeasterly direction. He taught while on the ship, but only of the Lord's Prayer, and this time of the fourth petition. When alone with them, Jesus always prepared his disciples for his public, more elevated teachings.

Jesus Teaches of the Bread of Life

JESUS spent the night on the ship, which was anchored on the shore between Matthew's custom office and Bethsaida-Julias.

Wednesday, January 31, AD 31 (Shebat 18)

Early this morning, Jesus and the disciples landed again between Matthew's custom house and Little Chorazin, where Jesus addressed a crowd of about a hundred people. About noon, he sailed back toward Bethsaida. On landing, he went to Peter's house. Here he was greeted by Lazarus, who had come to see him. Veronica's son Amandor and one or two others had also come. Then Jesus went to a place on the road leading into Bethsaida, where a group of people had gathered. Here he began his great teaching concerning the eucharistic bread of life, which is summarized in John 6:25–34. On this occasion, Jesus did not however say that he himself was the bread of life.

Next morning he discoursed upon the Lord's Prayer before about a hundred people, and toward midday sailed with the disciples to the region of Capernaum, where they landed unnoticed and went at once to Peter's. Here Jesus met Lazarus, who had come hither with Veronica's son and some people from Hebron.

When Jesus ascended the height behind Peter's house, over which ran the shortest route from Capernaum to Bethsaida, the multitude encamped around it followed him. Several of those present the day before at the multiplication of the loaves, and who had been seeking him ever since, asked him: "Rabbi, when camest thou hither? We have been seeking thee on both sides of the lake." Jesus, at the same time beginning his sermon, answered them: "Amen, amen, I say to you, you seek me, not because you have seen miracles, but because you did eat of the loaves, and were filled. Labor not for the meat which perisheth but for that which endureth unto life everlasting, which the Son of Man will give you. For him hath God the Father sealed." These words stand thus in the Gospel, but they are only the principal points of those that Jesus pronounced on this occasion, for he dwelt largely on the subject. The people whispered to one another: "What does he mean by the Son of Man? We are all children of man!" When upon his admonition that they should do the works of God, they asked what they should do to fulfill those works, he answered: "Believe in him whom He hath sent!" And then he gave them an instruction upon faith. They asked again what kind of a miracle he would perform that they might believe. Moses gave their fathers bread from heaven that they might believe in him, namely, the manna. What, they now asked, was Jesus going to give them. To this Jesus answered: "I say to you, Moses gave you not bread from heaven, but my Father giveth you the true bread from heaven. For the bread of God is that which cometh down from heaven and giveth life to the world."

Of this bread Jesus taught in detail, and some of them said to him: "Lord, give us always this bread!" But others objected: "His father gives us bread from heaven! How can that be? His father Joseph is already dead!" Jesus continued to teach on the same subject, dwelling upon it at great length, developing it and explaining in most precise terms. But only a few understood him. The others fancied themselves wise; they thought they knew all things.

Thursday, February 1, AD 31 (Shebat 19)

Jesus continued the teaching on the bread of life at the same place on the road leading into Bethsaida, this time saying quite plainly that he was the bread of life (John 6:35–51). Some two thousand people were present.

On the following day Jesus, from the hill behind Peter's house, continued the subject of yesterday's discourse. There were about two thousand people present, who exchanged places by turns, some coming forward, others withdrawing, that all might get a chance to hear better. Jesus also changed his position from time to time. He went from one place to another, lovingly and patiently repeating his words of instruction and refuting the same objections. Apart from the crowd were many women, veiled. The Pharisees kept moving to and fro, questioning and whispering their doubts among the people.

Today Jesus spoke out in plain words. He said: "I am the Bread of Life. He that cometh to me shall not hunger, and he that believeth in me shall never thirst. All that the Father giveth me shall come to me, and him that cometh to me, I will not cast out. Because I came down from heaven, not to do my own will, but the will of Him that sent me. Now this is the will of the Father, Who sent me: that of all that He hath given me, I should lose nothing, but should raise it up again in the last day. And this is the will of my Father that sent me: that every one who seeth the Son and believeth in him, may have life everlasting, and I will raise him up at the last day."

But there were many who did not understand him, and they said: "How can he say that he has come down from heaven? He is truly the son of the carpenter Joseph, his mother and relatives are among us, and we know even the parents of his father Joseph! He has said today that God is his Father, and then he said again that he is the Son of Man!" and they murmured. Jesus said to them: "Murmur not among yourselves. No man can come to me, except the Father, who hath sent me, draw him." Again they failed to grasp his meaning, and they asked what the words: "The Father draw him," signified. They took them quite literally. Jesus answered: "It is written in the prophets, And they shall all be taught of God. Everyone that hath heard and learned it of the Father cometh to me!"

Thereupon many of them asked: "Are we not with him? And have we not yet heard of the Father, learned of the Father?" To which Jesus made answer: "No one hath seen the Father, but he who is of God. He that believeth in me, hath everlasting life. I am the bread that cometh down from heaven, the bread of life."

Then they said again among themselves that they knew of no bread that came down from heaven, excepting the manna. Jesus explained that the manna was not the bread of life, for their fathers who had eaten it were dead. But whosoever ate of the bread that came down from heaven, should not die. He said that he was the living bread, and that he who ate thereof should live forever.

All these instructions were accompanied by full explanations and quotations from the Law and the prophets. But most of the Jews would not comprehend them. They took all literally according to the common, human acceptation, and again asked: "What meaneth these words, that we should eat him, and eternal life? Who, then, has eternal life, and who can eat of him? Enoch and Elijah have been taken away from the earth, and they say that they are not dead; nor does anyone know whither Malachi has gone, for no one knows of his death. But apart from these, all other men must die." Jesus replied by asking them whether they knew where Enoch and Elijah were and where Malachi was. As for himself, this knowledge was not concealed from him. But did they know what Enoch believed, what Elijah and Malachi prophesied? And he explained several of their prophecies.

Jesus taught no more that day. The people were in an extraordinary state of excitement; they reflected on his words and disputed their meaning among themselves. Many of the new disciples even, especially those lately received from among John's, doubted and wavered. They had swelled the number of the disciples to seventy, for up to this period Jesus had only thirty-six. The women were now about thirty-four, though the number engaged in the service of the community at last amounted to seventy. It was increased by all the stewardesses, maidservants, and directresses of the inns.

Friday, February 2, AD 31 (Shebat 20)

Still at the same place on the road into Bethsaida, Jesus taught on the same theme as the "Sermon on the Mount" (Matthew 5:3–12; 6:9–13). He spoke of the beatitudes and the Lord's Prayer. In the evening, with the start of the sabbath, he went to the synagogue. As he was teaching, he was interrupted with the question: "How can you call yourself the bread of life come down from heaven, since every one knows where you come from?" Jesus then taught again concerning the bread of life (John 6:52–59). This caused a great uproar. The Pharisees cried out: "How can he give us his body (flesh) to eat?" Jesus replied that he would give them the food of which he spoke "in its own time" (in 113 weeks).

Jesus again taught the people on the hill outside the city. He said nothing more of the bread of life, however, but confined himself to the beatitudes and the Lord's Prayer. The crowd was very great, but because most of the sick were already cured, the thronging and hurrying were less than usual. The carrying of the sick to the scene of action and their subsequent departure always gave rise to much confusion and disturbance, since everyone wanted to be first both in coming and going. All, and especially many of John's disciples, were in great expectation, eager to hear the end of the instruction begun on the previous day.

That evening as Jesus was teaching in the synagogue upon the lesson of the sabbath, some of his hearers interrupted him with the question: "How canst thou call thyself the bread of life come down from heaven, since everyone knows whence thou art?" To which Jesus answered by repeating all that he had already said on that subject.

The Pharisees again offered the same objections, and when they appealed to their father Abraham and to Moses, asking how he could call God his Father, Jesus put to them the question: "How can ye call Abraham your father and Moses your lawgiver, since ye do not follow the commandments or the example of either Abraham or Moses?" Then he placed clearly before them their perverse actions and their wicked, hypocritical life. They became confused and enraged.

Now Jesus resumed and continued his instructions on the bread of life. He said, "The bread that I will give is my flesh for the life of the world." At these words, murmurs and whispers ran through the crowd: "How can he give us his flesh to eat?" Jesus continued and taught at length as the Gospel records: "Except you eat the flesh of the Son of Man and drink his blood, you shall not have life in you. But he that eateth my flesh and drinketh my blood hath everlasting life: and I will raise him up in the last day. For my flesh is meat indeed: and my blood is drink indeed. He that eateth my flesh and drinketh my blood abideth in me and I in him. As the living Father had sent me, and I live by the Father, so he that eateth me, the same also shall live by me. This is the bread that came down from heaven. It is not bread like the manna, of which your fathers did eat, and yet died! He that eateth this bread shall live forever." Jesus then explained many passages from the prophets, especially from Malachi, and showed their accomplishment in John the Baptist, of whom he spoke at length. They asked when he would give them that food of which he spoke. He answered distinctly: "In its own time," and then, with a peculiar expression, signified a certain period in weeks. I counted as he spoke, and got: one year, six weeks, and some days. The people were very greatly agitated, and the Pharisees took care to incite them still more.

Saturday, February 3, AD 31 (Shebat 21)

Today Jesus taught in the synagogue concerning the sixth and seventh petitions of the Our Father and the first beatitude. He was questioned about his discourse of the day before on the bread of life, concerning the eating of his flesh and the drinking of his blood. He repeated in strong and precise terms all that he had said about this. Then even some of his disciples began to complain: "This saying is hard, and who can bear it?" (John 6:60). Jesus replied that they should not be scandalized, and that they would witness quite other things. He also predicted that he would be persecuted, that even his most faithful disciples would desert him, and that he would be put to death. Yet, he added, he would not desert them. His spirit would be with them (John 6:61–65). As he was leaving the synagogue, the Pharisees and certain disloyal disciples tried to detain him with further questions, but the apostles and loyal disciples surrounded him and escorted him from the synagogue amid much noise, shouting, and confusion. Jesus and his accompanying disciples then withdrew to a hill at the north end of the town. There he asked the twelve whether they too would leave him. Peter answered on behalf of all: "Lord, to whom shall we go? You have the words of eternal life. And we believe and know that you are the Holy One of God." Jesus replied: "Have I not chosen you twelve? And yet one among you is a devil"—meaning Judas Iscariot (John 6:67–71).

After that Jesus again taught in the synagogue. He explained the sixth and the seventh petitions of the Lord's Prayer, also the beatitude, "Blessed are the poor in spirit." He said that they who are learned ought not to be conscious of it, just as the rich ought not to know that they possess riches. Then the Jews murmured again and said: "Of what use would such knowledge or such riches be, if the owner did not know that he possessed either the one or the other?" Jesus answered: "Blessed are the poor in spirit!" adding that they should feel themselves poor and humble before God, from whom all wisdom comes, and apart from whom all wisdom is an abomination.

When the Jews questioned him again upon his discourse of the preceding day, that on the bread of life, on the eating of his flesh and the drinking of his blood, he repeated his former instruction in strong and precise terms. Many of his disciples murmured and said: "This saying is hard, and who can bear it?" Jesus replied that they should not be scandalized, they would witness things still more wonderful, and he predicted to them clearly that they would persecute him, that even the most faithful among them would abandon him and take to flight, and that he would fall into the arms of his enemies, who would put him to death. But, he said, he would not abandon his unfaithful disciples; his spirit would hover near them. The words, "He would run into the arms of his enemy," were not exactly those used by Jesus. It was rather that he would embrace his enemy, or be embraced by him, but I no longer remember which. It referred to the kiss and perfidy of Judas.

As the Jews were now still more scandalized, Jesus said: "If you shall see the Son of Man ascend up where he was before, what then? It is the spirit that quickeneth, the flesh profiteth nothing. The words that I have spoken to you are spirit and life. But there are some among you that believe not, therefore did I say to you: No man can come to me, unless it be given him by my Father."

These words of Jesus were greeted by jeers and murmurs throughout the synagogue. About thirty of the new disciples, principally the narrow-minded followers of John, went over to the Pharisees and began to whisper with them and express their dissatisfaction, but the apostles and the older disciples gathered more closely around Jesus. He continued to teach, and said aloud: "It is well that those men showed of whose spirit they are the children before they occasioned greater mischief."

As he was leaving the synagogue, the Pharisees and the disloyal disciples who had colleagued with them wanted to detain him in order to argue with him and demand explanations on many points. But the apostles, his disciples, and other friends surrounded him, so that he escaped their importunities, though amid shouts and confusion. Their speech was such as might be heard from the men of our own day: "Now we have it! Now we need nothing more! He has doubtless proved to every sensible man that he is himself bereft of reason. We must eat his flesh! We must drink his blood! He is from heaven! He will ascend into heaven!"

Jesus went with his followers, though by different routes, to the hill and valley north of the city near the dwellings of Zorobabel and Cornelius. When they reached a certain place, he began to instruct his disciples, and then it was that he asked the twelve whether they too were going to leave him. Peter answered for all: "Lord, to whom shall we go? Thou hast the words of eternal life. And we have believed and have known that thou art the Christ, the Son of the living God!" Jesus answered among other things: "I also have chosen you twelve, and yet one among you is a devil!"

Mary was present with other women at that last discourse of Jesus on the mountain, as well as that delivered in the synagogue. Of all the mysteries propounded in these discourses, she had long had the interior consciousness; only, just as the Second Person of the Godhead, having taken flesh in her, became man and her child, so too was this knowledge hidden, enveloped as it were in the most humble, the most reverential love of her mother-heart for Jesus. Since Jesus had now taught more plainly of these mysteries than ever before, to the scandal of those that willfully shut their eyes to the light, the meditations of Mary were directed to them. I saw her in her chamber that night praying. She had a vision, an interior contemplation of the angelical salutation, the birth, and the childhood of Jesus, of her own maternity, and of his Sonship. She contemplated her child as the Son of God, and was so overcome by humility and reverence that she melted into tears. But all these contemplations were again absorbed in the feeling of maternal love for her divine Son, just as the appearance of bread hides the Living God in the sacrament.

At the separation of the disciples from Jesus, I saw in two circles the kingdom of Christ and the kingdom of Satan. I saw the city of Satan and the Babylonian harlot with its prophets and prophetesses, its wonder-workers and apostles, all in great magnificence, more brilliant, richer, and more numerous than was the kingdom of Jesus. Kings, emperors, and even priests coursed therein with horse and chariot, and for Satan was set a magnificent throne.

But the kingdom of Christ upon earth I saw poor and insignificant, full of misery and suffering. I saw Mary as the church, and Christ on the cross. He, too, was like the church, the entrance to which was through the wound of his side.

Sunday, February 4, AD 31 (Shebat 22)

Following an invitation from Nathaniel (the bridegroom of the wedding at Cana), Jesus, the twelve apostles, and the loyal disciples set off for Cana, on the first stage of a journey through Galilee (John 7:1).

Jesus in Dan and Ornithopolis

Monday, February 5, AD 31 (Shebat 23)

While they were walking this morning in the neighborhood of Gischala, Jesus revealed to the twelve the disposition and character of each, and arranged them correspondingly in three groups or rows: in the first row—Peter, Andrew, John, James the Greater and Matthew; in the second row—Judas Thaddeus, Bartholomew, and James the Less; and in the third row—Thomas, Simon, Philip, and Judas Iscariot. Joseph Barsabbas stood at the head of the remaining disciples, nearest to the twelve, and Jesus then placed him in the second row together with Thaddeus, Bartholomew and James.

As Jesus with the apostles and disciples was making the journey from Capernaum to Cana and Cydessa, I saw him in the region of Gischala placing the twelve in three separate rows and revealing to each his own peculiar disposition and character. Peter, Andrew, John, James the Greater, and Matthew stood in the first row; Thaddeus, Bartholomew, James the Less, and the disciple Barsabbas, in the second; Thomas, Simon, Philip, and Judas Iscariot, in the third. Each heard his own thoughts and hopes revealed to him by Jesus, and all were strongly affected. Jesus delivered at the same time a lengthy discourse upon the hardships and sufferings that awaited them, and on this occasion he again made use of the expression: "Among you there is a devil."

Tuesday, February 6, AD 31 (Shebat 24)

Jesus and the disciples visited Cydessa, where many Gentiles lived.

The three different rows established no subordination among the apostles, one to another. The twelve were classed merely according to their disposition and character. Joseph Barsabbas stood foremost in the row of the disciples, and nearest to the twelve; consequently, Jesus placed him also in the second row with the apostles, and revealed to him his hopes and fears.

Wednesday, February 7, AD 31 (Shebat 25)

After healing the sick of Cydessa, Jesus taught in the synagogue. He spoke of the duration of the descent of the Son of Man into the earth's womb, saying it was the same as Jonah had endured in the whale's belly (Matthew 12:38–40). Continuing northward, Jesus then conferred new power upon the twelve and the disciples for healing the sick and exorcising the possessed. Anne Catherine saw rays of different colors streaming out from Jesus into each disciple according to his disposition.

On this journey Jesus further instructed the twelve and the disciples exactly how to proceed in the future when healing the sick and exorcising the possessed, as he himself did in such cases. He imparted to them the power and the courage always to effect, by imposition of hands and anointing with oil, what he himself could do. This communication of power took place without the imposition of hands, though not without a substantial transmission. They stood around Jesus, and I saw rays darting toward them of different colors, according to the nature of the gifts received and the peculiar disposition of each recipient. They exclaimed: "Lord, we feel ourselves endued with strength! Thy words are truth and life!" And now each knew just what he had to do in every case in order to effect a cure. There was no room left for either choice or reflection.

Thursday, February 8, AD 31 (Shebat 26)

Today Jesus taught in the synagogue at Naphtali, the birthplace of Tobias. In the evening, he arrived at Elkasa.

Friday, February 9, AD 31 (Shebat 27)

This morning Jesus healed and taught in various homes in Elkasa. As the sabbath started, he taught in the synagogue, speaking of the building of Solomon's temple. Afterward, the Pharisees invited him to a meal in the town hall. There a dispute broke out. The Pharisees complained to Jesus that his disciples did not observe the Law, for they did not wash their hands before coming to the table (Mark 7:1–13). Jesus replied with the words recorded in Mark 7:14–16. Later, Jesus explained to the disciples the nature of the Pharisees' spiritual impurity (Matthew 15:12–20).

After that Jesus with all his disciples arrived at Elkasa, a place distant from Capernaum one hour and a half. There in the synagogue he delivered the sermon of the sabbath, in which reference was made to the building of Solomon's temple. I remember that he addressed the apostles and disciples as the workmen who were to fell the cedars on the mountain and prepare them for the building. He spoke also of the interior adornment of the temple. The services over, at which many Pharisees were in attendance, Jesus was invited to dine. The meal was taken at a house of public entertainment. Many people stood around during it, to hear what Jesus was saying, and numbers of the poor were fed. The Pharisees, having remarked that the disciples had not washed their hands before coming to table, asked Jesus why his disciples did not respect the prescriptions of their forefathers, and why they did not observe the customary purifications. Jesus responded to their question by asking why they themselves did not keep the commandments, why with all their traditions they did not honor their father and mother, and he reproached them with their hypocrisy and their vain adherence to external purification. During this dispute the meal came to an end. Jesus, however, continued to address the crowd that pressed around him: "Hear ye and understand! Not that which goeth into the mouth defileth a man; but what cometh out of the mouth, this defileth a man. He that has ears to hear, let him hear!" The disciples who had remained behind in the entertainment hall told Jesus that these words of his had greatly scandalized the Pharisees. To which he responded: "Every plant that my heavenly Father hath not planted shall be rooted up! Let them alone! They are blind and leaders of the blind. And if the blind lead the blind, both fall into the pit." [E7]

Saturday, February 10, AD 31 (Shebat 28)

Jesus continued to teach in the synagogue, urging both Jews and unbelievers to become baptized. Again, the Pharisees reproached him, this time saying that his disciples did not fast regularly. Jesus replied: "The disciples eat after long labor, and then only if others are supplied. But if these latter are hungry, they give them what they have, and God blesses it." Here Jesus was referring to the feeding of the five thousand, where the disciples had given bread and fish to the hungry multitude. Then Jesus and the disciples left the town and made their way northwestward. On the way, he gave instruction concerning prayer, referring especially to the Lord's Prayer.

When on the following evening Jesus was closing the sabbath instruction, the Pharisees again reproached him on account of the irregular mode of the disciples' fasting. But Jesus retorted by charging them with their avarice and want of mercy. Among other things, he said: "The disciples eat after long labor, and then only if others are supplied. But if these latter are hungry, they give them what they have, and God blesses it." Here Jesus recalled the multiplication of the loaves, on which occasion the disciples had given their bread and fish to the hungry multitude, and he asked the Pharisees whether they would have done the same.

Sunday, February 11, AD 31 (Shebat 29)

Proceeding on further toward the northwest and continuing his discourse on prayer, Jesus with his disciples finally reached the city of Dan, also known as Lais. Here they stayed the night at an inn.

From Elkasa, Jesus went with the apostles and disciples through Kades-Nephthali to the city of Dan, called also

Lais, or Leshem. Kades-Nephthali was a stronghold and Levitical city built of black, shining stone. On the way Jesus instructed his followers, his subject always being prayer. He explained the Lord's Prayer. He told them that in the past they had not prayed worthily, but like Esau had asked for the fat of the earth; but now, like Jacob, they should petition for the dew of heaven, for spiritual gifts, for the blessing of spiritual illumination, for the kingdom according to the will of God, and not for one in accordance with their own ideas. He reminded them that even the pagans themselves did not petition for temporal goods alone, but also for those of a spiritual nature.

The city of Dan, situated at the base of a high mountain range, covered a wide extent owing to the fact that every one of its houses was surrounded by a garden. All the inhabitants were engaged in garden tillage. They raised fruits and aromatic plants of all kinds, also calamus, myrrh, balsam, cotton, and many sweet-scented herbs, which formed the staple of their trade with Tyre and Sidon. The pagans of Dan were more integrated with the Jews than in other cities. Although this region was so delightful and fertile, yet there were many sick in it.

Jesus put up with the disciples at one of his own inns situated in the heart of the city. The apostles and disciples had established it when on their last mission here. Counting the apostles, the disciples with Jesus at this time amounted to thirty.

Monday, February 12, AD 31 (Shebat 30)

In the company of Peter, John, and James the Greater, Jesus healed the sick at many homes in Dan. He was followed by an old pagan woman from Ornithopolis, who was crippled on one side. Jesus seemed to ignore her, for he was concerned solely with healing the Jews. Nevertheless, she begged him to come and heal her daughter, who was possessed. Jesus replied that it was not yet time, that he wanted to avoid giving offense, and that he would not help the pagans before the Jews. Later that afternoon, the Syrophoenician woman from Ornithopolis approached Jesus and again begged him to drive the unclean spirit out of her daughter. There then followed the exorcism of her daughter, as described in Matthew 15:21–28. Jesus asked her whether she herself wished to be healed, but the Syrophoenician woman replied that she was not worthy, and that she asked only for her daughter's cure. Then Jesus laid one hand upon her head, the other on her side, and said: "Straighten up! May it be done to you as you also will it to be done! The devil has gone out of your daughter." The woman stood upright and cried out: "O Lord, I see my daughter lying in bed well and at peace!" That evening, Jesus and the disciples dined at the home of an old man of the Nazarite sect, a friend of Lazarus and Nicodemus. It was the celebration of the New Moon festival at the start of the month of Adar.

They who had already been here and to whom consequently the inhabitants applied, led Jesus around to the different sick. The rest of the disciples scattered among the surrounding places. Peter, John, and James stayed with Jesus, who went about from house to house healing the sick. He cured the dropsical, the melancholy, the possessed, several slightly affected with leprosy, the lame, and especially numbers of blind, and others with swollen cheeks and limbs.

The blindness so prevalent came from the sting of a little insect that infested this country. Jesus pointed out an herb, with whose juice he bade them anoint their eyes in order to prevent the insect from stinging them. He gave to them also a moral application of its meaning. The swellings, which became inflamed and produced gangrene that ended in the death of many thus afflicted, were likewise caused by little insects like mildew that were blown from the trees. They were grayish black, like chimney soot, and were borne like a dense black cloud through the air. The insect bit into the skin and raised a large swelling. Jesus pointed out another insect, which was to be crushed and applied to the bite. He told them in future to make use of it in similar cases. It had fifteen little points on the back, as large as an ant's egg, and it could roll itself up into a ball.

The Syrophoenician Woman

WHILE Jesus was going from house to house in Dan healing the sick, he was perseveringly followed by an aged woman, a pagan, who was crippled on one side. She was from Ornithopolis. She remained humbly at some distance and, from time to time, implored help. But Jesus paid no attention to her, he even appeared to shun her, for he was now healing sick Jews only. A servant accompanied the woman bearing her baggage. She was clothed in the garb of a foreigner. Her dress was of striped material, the arms and neck trimmed with lace. On her head she wore a high, pointed cap, over which was tied a colored kerchief, and lastly a veil. She had at home a daughter sick and possessed, and for a long time she had been hoping for aid from Jesus. She was in Dan at the time of the apostles' mission there, and they now more than once reminded Jesus of her. But he replied that it was not yet time, that he wanted to avoid giving offense, and that he would not help the pagans before the Jews.

In the afternoon Jesus went with Peter, James, and John to the house of one of the Jewish elders of the city, a man very well disposed, a friend of Lazarus and Nicodemus, and in secret a follower of Jesus. He had contributed largely to the common fund of the holy women and to the support of the inns. He had two sons and three daughters, all of mature age, he himself being an old man far advanced in years. The children were unmarried. The sons wore their long hair parted on top of the head and allowed the beard to grow. Through the daughters' headdress, the hair could be seen similarly parted. They were Nazarites. All were clothed in white. The old father, whose beard was long and white, was led by the sons to meet Jesus, for he could not walk alone. He was shedding tears of reverential joy. The sons washed the feet of Jesus and the apostles, and presented them with refreshments, fruit and rolls. Jesus was very affable and treated the family with great confidence. He spoke to them of the journeys he was about to make, and told them that he would not show himself openly in Jerusalem at the celebration of the coming Passover. He did not remain long in the house, for the people, having found out his whereabouts, had gathered outside and in the forecourt. Jesus went out through the court and into the garden where for several hours he taught and cured between the terraced walls that supported the gardens. The pagan woman had waited long at a distance. Jesus never went near her, and she dared not approach him. From time to time, however, she repeated her cry: "Lord! Thou Son of David, have mercy on me! My daughter is grievously tormented by an impure spirit!" The disciples begged Jesus to help her. But he said: "I was not sent but to the sheep that are lost of the house of Israel." At last the woman drew nearer, ventured into the hall, cast herself down before Jesus, and cried: "Lord, help me!" Jesus replied: "It is not good to take the bread of the children and to cast it to the dogs." But she continued to entreat: "Yea, Lord! For the whelps also eat of the crumbs that fall from the table of their masters." Then Jesus said: "O woman, great is thy faith! On account of these words, help shall be given thee!" [E8]

Jesus asked her whether she herself did not want to be cured, for she was crippled on one side. But she replied that she was not worthy, and that she asked for her daughter's cure only. Then he laid one hand on her head, the other on her side, and said: "Straighten up! May it be done to thee as thou dost will! The devil has gone out of thy daughter." The woman stood upright. She was tall and thin. For some instants, she uttered not a word, and then with uplifted hands, she cried out: "O Lord, I see my daughter lying in bed well and in peace!" She was out of herself with joy. Jesus turned away with the disciples.

Jesus afterward took a repast at the house of the Nazarites. The Levites of Kedesh were present, as well as all the apostles and disciples who had again met together at the inn. It was a grand entertainment, such as had not been given for a long time, and from it abundant alms were distributed to the poor by the disciples. After all was over, Jesus returned to the inn. The Feast of the New Moon was celebrated yesterday and today.

ADAR (29 days): February 12/13 to March 12/13, AD 31 Adar New Moon: February 10 at 3:00 PM, Jerusalem time

Tuesday, February 13, AD 31 (Adar 1)

This morning, Jesus healed in the town marketplace. Among those who came to him was a relative of the Syrophoenician woman. Jesus cured his crippled arm and deaf-and-dumbness. The man who had been healed then turned to the pagans and Jews around him and began to speak prophetically: "The food that you, the children of the house, reject, we outcasts shall gather up. We shall live upon it and give thanks. What you allow to go to waste of the bread of heaven will be to us the fruit of the crumbs that we gather up." There was a great power of inspiration in his words, and much agitation arose among the crowd. Then Jesus withdrew into the mountains west of Dan. He met with the apostles and disciples, and they all spent the night there.

When Jesus on the following morning was healing and teaching under the market porticos, the pagan woman brought to Jesus one of her relatives who had come with her from Ornithopolis. He was paralyzed in the right arm besides being deaf and mute. The woman begged Jesus to cure him and also to visit her home, that they might there thank him worthily.

Jesus took the man aside from the crowd, laid his hand on the lame arm, prayed, and stretched out the arm perfectly cured. Then he moistened his ears with a little spittle, told him to raise his cured hand to his tongue, glanced upward, and prayed. The man arose, spoke, and gave thanks. Jesus stepped back with him to the pressing multitude, and the man began to speak wonderful and prophetic words. He cast himself at Jesus's feet and gave him thanks. Then turning to the Jews and pagans, he uttered menaces against Israel, named some particular places, referred to the miracles of Jesus and the obstinacy of the Jews, and said: "The food that ye, the children of the house, reject, we outcasts shall gather up. We shall live upon it, and give thanks. The fruit of the crumbs that we gather up will be to us what you allow to go to waste of the bread of heaven." His words were so wonderful, so inspired, that great agitation arose in the crowd.

Immediately after this, Jesus left the city and climbed with the apostles and disciples a mountain range to the west of Leshem. They reached a solitary height, where they found a roomy cavern containing seats cut out of the rock. Caves of this kind served as resting places for travelers. Jesus and his followers had been journeying a good two hours, and here passed the night. Jesus instructed the apostles and disciples on diverse modes of healing and the various ceremonies accompanying them, for they had asked him why he had ordered the mute man to put his own hand into his mouth, and why he had taken him aside. Jesus satisfied them on these points, instructed them again upon prayer, and praised the pagan woman who had always implored, not for temporal goods, but for the knowledge of the truth. He prescribed a certain order to be followed by them: They were to go on their missions two by two, they were all to teach the same things, they were to proclaim the last instructions that he had given them. From time to time they were to meet together in order severally to communicate all that had occurred to them. The apostles were then to impart to the disciples whatever had happened in the meantime and which ought to be known in common. They should pray together on their journeys, and speak only of the affairs of their mission.

Cave Resting-Place in the Mountains

***Wednesday, February 14, AD 31** (**Adar 2**)*

Jesus and the disciples journeyed toward Ornithopolis, where Jesus had been invited to go by the Syrophoenician woman. They stayed the night at an inn on the way.

Having resumed their route, they passed the great and very elevated city of Hammoth Dor, after which they climbed steep and toilsome heights until they reached the lofty ridge that commanded a view of the Mediterranean. They now descended the mountain for several hours, passed over a stream that flowed into the sea through the north of Tyre, and put up at an inn on the roadside, between three and four hours from Ornithopolis.

The Syrophoenician was a very distinguished lady in her native place. She had passed through these parts on her way home, and had fitted up a comfortable inn for Jesus.

The pagans came out most humbly to meet Jesus and his party, guided them to their destination, and showed them all kinds of attentions with an air at once timid and reverential. They looked upon Jesus as a great prophet.

***Thursday, February 15, AD 31** (**Adar 3**)*

Jesus healed many people this morning at a place near the inn. Then, after giving instruction concerning various passages from the prophets, he and the disciples traveled on to Ornithopolis, where their arrival had been prepared for by the Syrophoenician woman. They were given a festive reception, including a banquet at which Jesus was anointed with a flask of costly ointment by the Syrophoenician woman's daughter.

Next day Jesus and the disciples ascended a hill in the neighborhood of a little pagan city, and there found a teacher's chair. It had been in existence since the times of the early prophets, some of whom had often preached from it. The pagans had always held this place in high esteem, and today they had ornamented it by erecting a beautiful awning over the chair.

There were numbers of sick assembled on the hill, but they remained shyly at a distance, until Jesus and the disciples approached and cured many of them. Some had tumors, others were paralyzed, others wasted away, some were melancholy or half-possessed. These last, when cured, appeared as if awaking from sleep. The limbs of some were greatly swollen and inflamed. Jesus laid his hand on the swelling, which was immediately reduced and the inflammation allayed. He directed the disciples to bring a plant that grew there on the naked rock. It had large, succulent, and deeply notched leaves. He blessed one of these leaves, poured on it some water that he carried with him in a flask, and the disciples bound it, the notched side down, on the part affected.

The healing over, Jesus delivered an instruction on the vocation of the Gentiles. It was more than ordinarily impressive. He explained several passages from the prophets, and depicted the vanity of their idols. After that he went with the disciples three hours in a northwestwardly direction to Ornithopolis, which was distant from the sea three-quarters of an hour. This city, which was not very large, contained some beautiful buildings. On a height in the eastern environs stood a pagan temple.

Jesus was received with more than ordinary affection. The Syrophoenician had prepared everything for the occasion in the most sumptuous and honorable manner, but in her humility, she left to the few poor Jewish families living in the city the liberty of doing the honors of reception. The whole place resounded with the cure of her daughter, as well as with that of her own and her deaf and mute relative. The last-named, in recounting his cure, spoke of Jesus in words of inspiration. The inhabitants were ranged outside the houses. The pagans stood back humbly and closed the procession that went with green branches to meet Jesus. The Jews, about twenty in number, among them some very aged men who had to be led, also the teachers with all the children, headed the procession. The mothers and daughters followed, veiled.

A house near the school had been prepared for Jesus and the disciples. It was fitted up by the lady with beautiful carpets, furniture, and lamps. There the Jews most humbly washed the feet of Jesus and his disciples and changed their sandals and clothes, until their own were shaken, brushed, and cleaned. Jesus then went with the elders to the school and taught.

After that, a magnificent entertainment was given in a public hall, at the expense of the Syrophoenician. One could see in all the preparations, in the dishes, the delicacies, and the table furniture generally, that it was a feast given by the pagans. There were three tables much higher than those in use among the Jews, with couches correspondingly high. Some of the servings of food were very remarkable, being made up into figures representing animals, trees, mountains, and pyramids. Some others were quite deceptive, being in reality very different from what they appeared; for instance, there were all kinds of wonderful pastry, birds made out of fish, fish formed of flesh, and lambs made of spices, fruits, flour, and honey. There were also some real lambs. At one table, Jesus ate with the apostles and the oldest among the Jews; at the two others, the disciples and the rest of the Jews. The women and children were seated at a table separated from the others by a screen.

During the meal, the lady with her daughter and relatives entered to give thanks for the cures wrought among them, their servants following with presents in ornamented caskets, which they bore between them on tapestry. The daughter, veiled, stepped behind Jesus, broke a little vial of precious ointment over his head, and then modestly returned to her mother. The servants delivered the gifts (they were those of the daughter) to the disciples. Jesus returned thanks. The lady bade him welcome to her native place, and declared how happy she should be if she could only show her good will and, in spite of her unworthiness, repair even the least of the many injuries that he experienced so often from her fellow pagans. She spoke humbly and in few words, remaining all the while at a respectful distance. Jesus ordered the money that formed part of the gifts, as well as the food, to be distributed in her presence among the poor Jews.

The lady was a widow and very rich. Her husband had been dead five years. He possessed in his lifetime many large ships at sea and a great number of servants, besides much property. He owned whole villages. Not far from Ornithopolis there was a pagan settlement on a cape jutting out into the sea, all of which belonged to the lady, his widow. I think he was a large-scale merchant. His widow was held in more than ordinary esteem in Ornithopolis, where the poor Jews lived almost entirely upon her bounty. She was both intelligent and beneficent, and not without a certain degree of illumination in her pagan piety. Her daughter was twenty-four years old, tall and very beautiful. She dressed in colors and adorned her neck with chains, her arms with bracelets. Her wealth brought around her numerous suitors, and she became possessed of an evil spirit. She was afflicted with convulsions so violent that in her frenzy she would spring from her couch and try to run away; consequently she had to be guarded and even bound. But when the paroxysm was over, she became again good and virtuous. Her state caused great affliction to herself and her mother, and to both it was a subject of deep humiliation. The poor girl was obliged to live retired, and she had now endured her sufferings for several years. When the mother neared her home, she was met by her daughter who had come out for that purpose, as well as to tell her of her cure, which had taken place at the very instant in which Jesus had promised it. And, oh, her joy and wonder at seeing her once-crippled mother again a tall, graceful woman! And to hear herself distinctly and joyfully greeted by her paralyzed, deaf, and mute relative! She was filled with gratitude and reverence for Jesus, and helped to prepare everything for his reception.

The gifts that Jesus received consisted of trinkets belonging to the daughter. They had been given to her in her early years by her parents, principally by her father, whose business opened to him communications with distant lands, and whose only and well-beloved child she was. Some were jewels of ancient workmanship, objects wrought of precious metals, such as are ordinarily given to the children of the wealthy. Among them were some things that had formerly belonged to her parents' parents. There were many wonderful-looking little idols of pearls and precious stones set in gold, rare stones of great value, tiny vessels, golden animals, and figures about a finger long, the eyes and mouth formed of gems. There were also fragrant stones and amber and golden branches that looked like little live trees, laden with colored gems instead of fruit—and very, very many such things! It was a treasure in itself, for some of these objects would now be worth a thousand talers apiece. Jesus said that he would distribute them to the poor and the needy, and that his Father in heaven would reward the donors.

Friday, February 16, AD 31 (Adar 4)

Today, after healing and teaching the Jews in and around Ornithopolis, Jesus and the disciples were again guests at the home of the Syrophoenician woman. She begged Jesus to visit and help the people of Sarepta, saying: "Sarepta, whose poor widow shared all she had with Elijah, is itself now a poor widow threatened with starvation. You, the greatest of prophets, have pity on her! Forgive me, a widow and once poor, to whom you have restored all, if I may be so bold as to plead also for Sarepta." Jesus promised that he would visit the town.

On the sabbath, Jesus visited every one of the Jewish families, distributed alms, cured, and comforted. Many of these Jews were poor and abandoned. Jesus assembled them in the synagogue, where he spoke to them in terms at once deeply touching and consoling, for the poor creatures looked upon themselves as the outcast and unworthy children of Israel. He also prepared many of them for baptism. About twenty men were baptized in a bathing garden, among them the cured deaf and mute relatives of the pagan lady.

Jesus visited the Syrophoenician also, along with his disciples. She dwelt in a beautiful house surrounded by numerous courts and gardens. Jesus was received with great solemnity. The domestics in festal garments spread carpets under his feet. At the entrance of a beautiful summerhouse, which was supported on pillars, the widow and her daughter came forward veiled to meet him. They cast themselves at his feet and poured forth their thanks, in which they were joined by their cured relative, once deaf and mute. In the summerhouse were set forth odd-looking figures in pastry and fruit of all kinds on costly dishes. The vessels were of glass, which looked as if made of many colored threads that appeared to run together and cross one another, as if dissolving one into the other. Among rich Jews I have seen similar vessels, but only in small numbers. Here they seemed to be in abundance. Many such vessels were held in reserve behind curtains in the corners of the hall. They were arranged on shelves up high on the wall. The dishes were set on little tables, some round, others with corners, that could be placed together to form one large table.

Among the refreshments there were very fine dried grapes still hanging on the vine laid on those colored glass dishes, also another kind of dried fruit which arose from the branches as from a little tree. There were reeds with long, cordate leaves and fruit in form like the grape. They were perfectly white, perhaps sugared, and looked like the white part of the cauliflower. The guests snapped them off the stem, and found that they had a sweet, pleasant taste. They were raised not far from the sea, in a swampy place belonging to the Syrophoenician.

In a separate part of the hall, the pagan maidens, friends of the daughter, were standing along with the domestics. Jesus went and spoke to them. The lady very earnestly entreated Jesus on behalf of the poor people of Sarepta. She begged him to visit them as well as others in the neighborhood. She was very intelligent and had a clever way of proposing things. Her words were something to this effect: "Sarepta, whose poor widow had shared her little all with Elijah, is itself a poor widow threatened with starvation. Do thou, the greatest of prophets, have pity on her!

Forgive me, a widow and once poor, to whom thou hast restored her all, if I make bold to plead also for Sarepta." Jesus promised to do as she wished. She told him that she wanted to build a synagogue, and asked him to indicate where it should be. But I do not remember Jesus's reply.

The lady possessed large weaving and dyeing factories. In the little place near the sea and at some distance from her residence, there were great buildings on the top of which were platforms where gray and yellow stuffs were spread out. Among the gifts presented to Jesus were many little dishes and balls of amber, considered in those parts very precious.

Saturday, February 17, AD 31 (Adar 5)

After visiting a school in Ornithopolis this morning, Jesus and the disciples set off for Sarepta, the town where the widow had dwelt at the time of Elijah (1 Kings 17:10). Arriving at the Jewish settlement on the outskirts of Sarepta, they were given a joyful reception. The apostles brought bread and clothing from Sarepta to be distributed to the poor Jews in the settlement.

Jesus celebrated the close of the sabbath in the Jewish school, which was very beautifully adorned. In order to console the poor Jews, he taught that the proverb: "Our fathers have eaten sour grapes, and the teeth of the children are on edge," should no longer pass current in Israel. "Everyone that abides by the Word of God announced by me, that does penance and receives baptism, no longer bears the sins of his father." The people were extraordinarily rejoiced upon hearing these words.

On the afternoon of the following day, Jesus took leave of the lady who, in union with her daughter and cured relative, presented him with golden figures a hand in length, and provisions of bread, balsam, fruits, honey in reed baskets, and little flasks. These provisions were destined for his journey and for the poor of Sarepta. Jesus addressed words of advice to the whole family, recommended to them the poor Jews and their own salvation, and departed from the house amid the tears and reverential salutations of all. The lady had always been very enlightened and very earnest in seeking after perfection. Henceforth neither she nor her daughter went any more to the pagan temple. They observed the teachings of Jesus, joined the Jews, and sought by degrees to bring their people after them.

Several times again Jesus repeated his instructions to the disciples upon the order they were to observe and the duties they were to fulfill in their present mission. Thomas, Thaddeus, and James the Less went with some of the disciples (the others remaining with Jesus) down to the tribe of Asher. They were allowed to take nothing with them. Jesus with the nine remaining apostles, with Saturnin, Joseph Barsabbas, and another, went northward to Sarepta. Sixteen of the Jews accompanied Jesus the whole of the way, while all the rest and many of the pagans went only a part. He did not enter Sarepta, which was about two and a half hours distant from Ornithopolis, but stopped at a row of houses tolerably far from the city. They occupied the site of the spot upon which the widow of Sarepta was gathering sticks when Elijah approached the city. Some poor Jews had settled there. They were still poorer than those of Ornithopolis, who enjoyed the bounty of the Syrophoenician. Here too was an inn prepared for Jesus and his followers, and presents for the poor had been sent on in advance—all through the goodness of that lady. The inhabitants, unspeakably happy and deeply impressed, came out with the women and children to meet Jesus and to wash his feet, also those of his followers.

Sunday, February 18, AD 31 (Adar 6)

Jesus consoled and taught them. Then he proceeded on his journey a couple of hours to the east, accompanied by the sixteen men from Ornithopolis and some others from Sarepta. The country was rising, and the road uphill. On an eminence near a little pagan city, Jesus delivered an instruction to the inhabitants whom he found there awaiting him, after which he pressed on farther. Those that had followed him from Ornithopolis here took leave.

Monday, February 19, AD 31 (Adar 7)

Jesus traveled on today until he arrived at the town of Rehob.

At some distance farther on, Jesus and the disciples ascended in an easterly direction toward Mount Hermon, which forms the culminating peak of the high mountain range that bounds Upper Galilee. He crossed Hermon into an elevated valley and stopped at Rehob to the southwest at the foot of the mountain below Baal-Hermon. This last city was very large and, with its numerous pagan temples, looked down upon Rehob.

Jesus in Gessur and Nobah • Celebration of the Feast of Purim

(Follow Map 27)

Tuesday, February 20, AD 31 (Adar 8)

Leaving Rehob, Jesus walked for several hours in a northeasterly direction to Gessur, where he stayed the night with some tax collectors.

JESUS journeyed seven hours northeastward from Rehob to Gessur, where he stopped with the publicans, many of whom dwelt on the highroad leading to Damascus. Gessur was a beautiful, large city garrisoned by Roman soldiers. Jews and pagans occupied separate quarters, notwithstanding which the communications between them were very intimate. The Jews of Gessur were, on this account, held in low esteem by those of other places.

Many of the Jews and pagans of Gessur had been present at the sermon on the Mount of Beatitudes, and some of their sick were cured by the apostles who had recently visited the place. There was also a blind man who had been restored to sight at the instruction before the multiplication of the bread. The husband of Mara the Suphanite was from Gessur, but he was now residing with her at Ainon.

When Absalom was fleeing from David, he took up his abode in Gessur for a time, as his mother Maacha was the daughter of the king of the place, who was named Tholmai.

Wednesday, February 21, AD 31 (Adar 9)

This morning Jesus taught in the quarter where the tax collectors lived. An aged great-uncle of the apostle Bartholomew came to hear Jesus and invited him to dine at his home the next day.

The apostle Bartholomew, who had accompanied Jesus hither, was a descendant of that same royal house. His father had for a long time made use of the baths of Bethulia, on which account he had removed to Cana and settled in the valley of Zebulon. It was owing to this that Bartholomew had become an inhabitant of that part of the country. He still had in Gessur a very aged grand-uncle on his mother's side, a pagan and possessed of great property and riches. This old man resided in a large house in the heart of the city. He had himself conducted to the publican quarter in order to see Jesus, who was teaching on a terrace upon which the merchandise passing this way was examined, taxed, and repacked. The old uncle conversed with the apostles, especially with his nephew Bartholomew, and invited Jesus to his house to dine. All the inhabitants, men and women, Jews and pagans, attended Jesus's instructions. It was a mixed audience. Jesus also took a meal with the publicans and many others. There was considerable bustle attending it, for the publicans were putting all their goods in order to make a distribution to the poor.

Thursday, February 22, AD 31 (Adar 10)

Jesus followed the invitation and was received magnificently in the pagan style, being presented with a sumptuous meal. He healed some people in front of the house, and addressed those who were gathered there.

When Jesus entered the pagan quarter of the city, to visit Bartholomew's uncle, he was received with magnificence according to pagan style. Carpets were spread before him, and sumptuous refreshments set forth, all in accordance with pagan manners.

The pagans of Gessur adored a many-armed idol, which supported on its head a bushel measure filled with ears of wheat. Many of them inclined to Judaism, and many others to the doctrines of Jesus. Numbers of them had already been baptized either by John, or by the apostles at Capernaum.

Friday, February 23, AD 31 (Adar 11)

Today, the tax collectors with whom Jesus was staying distributed their wealth to the poor and needy. They were moved to do so by Jesus's teaching. Jesus taught at the tax collectors' custom house before a crowd of both Jews and pagans. Some Pharisees, who were visiting Gessur for the sabbath, criticized Jesus for mixing with tax collectors and pagans. That evening, he taught at the synagogue. Again a dispute arose with the Pharisees.

The publicans distributed the greater part of their wealth. On the place upon which Jesus had taught, they heaped up great quantities of corn which they afterward measured out to the poor. They likewise bestowed fields and gardens upon poor day laborers and slaves, and repaired all the wrong they had done.

When Jesus was again teaching at the custom house before the pagans and Jews, some strangers arrived, Pharisees, to celebrate here the sabbath. They reproached Jesus for lodging among the publicans and for having familiar communications with them and the pagans.

Saturday, February 24, AD 31 (Adar 12)

Today Bartholomew's great-uncle and about sixteen other elderly men were baptized by Joseph Barsabbas. After dining again with Bartholomew's great-uncle, Jesus preached in the synagogue at the close of the sabbath. Then he left Gessur, traveling to a fishing village on Lake Phiala. He arrived there late that night.

Bartholomew's uncle, along with sixteen other aged men, was baptized in a bathing garden, the water from a well of the city being conducted into the garden by a very elevated canal. Joseph Barsabbas administered the baptism. The garden had been adorned in festive style, the ceremony was most solemn, and the poor were abundantly supplied with alms, to which the old uncle largely contributed.

Jesus closed the sabbath by an instruction in the synagogue, took leave of all the people at the custom house, distributed alms to the poor, and went accompanied by a numerous retinue a distance of five hours to the fisher

Map 27: Journey to Gessur and Travels in Gaulanitis
February 19–March 19, AD 31

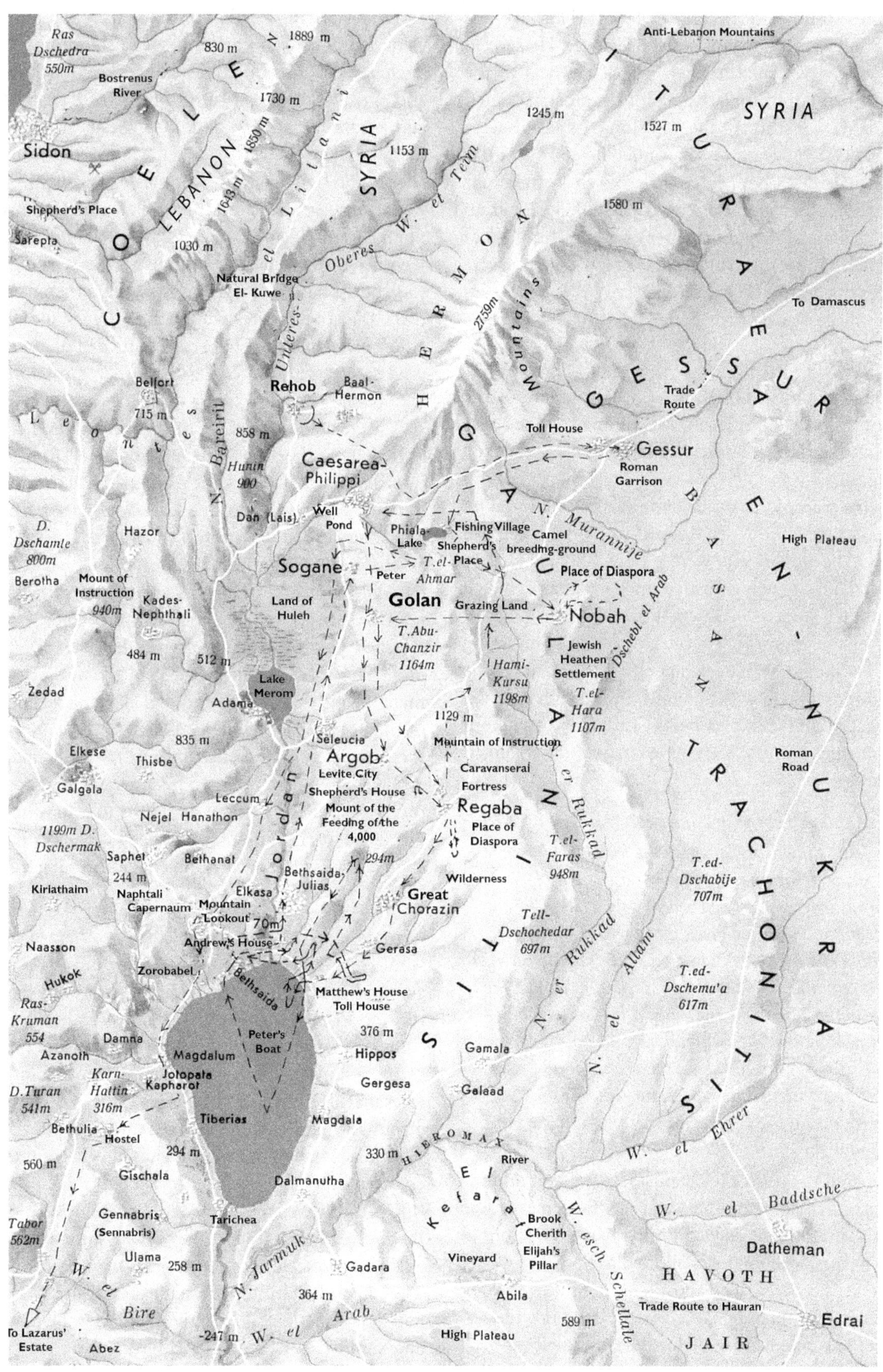

Rehob—Gessur—Lake Phiala—Nobah—Gaulon—Regaba—Caesarea-Philippi—Argob—Fortress of Regaba—Wilderness—Great Chorazin—Matthew's Customs House—Bethsaida—Mount of the Feeding of the 4,000—Bethsaida—Bethsaida-Julias—Sogane—Bethulia village on the borders of the lake of Phiala. This lake was on a plateau about three hours east of Paneas. He arrived late and lodged with the teacher in a house next to the school. The people of the place were for the most part Jews.

Lake Phiala was scarcely one hour long. Its shores were sloping, its waters clear, and its outlet flowed toward a mountain where it disappeared. There were some boats on its surface. The region was covered with fields of grain and beautiful meadows, in the latter of which numbers of asses, camels, and other cattle were grazing; there were also groves of chestnuts. On both sides of the lake lay Jewish fisher villages, each of which had its own school.

Sunday, February 25, AD 31 (*Adar 13*)

Jesus taught in the schools, and went with some of the inhabitants and the apostles into the homes of the shepherds around the lake. John the Baptist had once sojourned in this region.

From this place, Jesus with John, Bartholomew, and a disciple went three hours southward to Nobah, a city of Decapolis. The inhabitants were pagans and Jews. They dwelt apart, the city being divided into two quarters, each of which had a somewhat different name. All the cities of this part of the country were built of black, glimmering stone. Jesus taught in Nobah and in some of the little places around. John and Bartholomew were with him, the other apostles and disciples being scattered throughout the neighboring country. They stayed in an inn frequented by Pharisees.

Monday, February 26, AD 31 (*Adar 14*)

Today Jesus taught and prepared a number of people for baptism. John and Bartholomew then performed the baptism. Jesus was well received in Nobah by the people, but at a banquet given that evening in the public hall the Pharisees began to argue with him about his disciples' conduct. During the discussion, Jesus told the parable of the laborers in the vineyard (*Matthew 20:1–6*) *and also that of the rich glutton and poor Lazarus* (*Luke 16:19–31*). *Finally, he reproached the Pharisees for not having invited the poor, and sent out the disciples to round up the poor and bring them to the banquet. Today the Purim festival began.*

Jesus prepared the people for baptism, which was administered by Bartholomew. The water in these places was black and muddy, but it was purified in great, round, stone reservoirs, whence it was allowed to flow into others that were kept covered. The apostles poured into it some of the water from their drinking vessels, and Jesus blessed the whole. The people, with inclined heads, knelt for baptism around the stone basin.

The pagans of Nobah received Jesus very solemnly. They went to meet him carrying green, blooming branches, stretched cordons on either side to keep back the crowd, and spread carpets for him to walk on. These latter were laid across the streets, and, when Jesus had passed over them, they were raised quickly, carried some distance ahead, and held again in readiness for his approach. This was repeated many times, and as often did Jesus walk over them. The rabbis, who were Pharisees, received him in the Jewish quarter, where he taught in the synagogue, for it was the sabbath of the Purim festival. When all was over, there was a banquet given in the public hall. During the entertainment, the Pharisees again disputed on certain points, and reproached Jesus upon his disciples' eating fruit by the wayside and stripping the ears of wheat. [E9]

Jesus related the parable of the laborers in the vineyard, also that of the rich glutton and poor Lazarus. He reproached the Pharisees for not having, according to custom, invited the poor to the feast; whereupon they replied that their revenues were too small to allow it. Then Jesus asked whether the present entertainment had been prepared for him, and when they answered, yes, he laid on the table five large, yellow, three-cornered pieces of money attached to a little chain, saying that they might let the poor have them. Then he directed the disciples to call in many of the poor, who sat down at the table and partook of the tasty dishes. Jesus himself served them, instructing them meantime and distributing to them quantities of food. The money presented by Jesus was perhaps the customary temple tax usually paid on that day, or merely a gift usual at the time, for the people on this feast interchanged presents of fruits, bread, grain, and garments.

Tuesday, February 27, AD 31 (*Adar 15*)

On this feast of Purim they read in the synagogue the whole of the history of Esther. They did the same to the sick and aged in their own homes. Jesus also went around reading to the old people the roll of Esther, and healing some of the sick. I saw too festive games and processions of the young maidens and women, who had great privileges on this day. Once they entered the synagogue as if on an embassy, and penetrated even into the upper part. They had chosen one of their number as queen, whom they now escorted in regal robes, and presented to the priests beautiful priestly vestments. They had some games among themselves in a garden. They chose sometimes this one, again that one for queen, and in turn dethroned them. They had also a puppet which they ill-treated and then hanged, while little lads struck with hammers on boards and shouted curses. This was meant for a representation of the punishment merited by the wicked Aman.

Jesus Retreats to the Mountain at Night

When Jesus was in Galilee he often retired at night to some lofty place to pray; when he was in Judea he continued to do the same, and the Evangelists speak of the Mount of Olives as his retreat when night fell. This choice of special localities remarkable for their height and isolation is a striking peculiarity in the life of our Lord, but it was also a traditional Jewish custom to pray in elevated spots. . . . May we not suppose, in spite of the silence of the Evangelists, that in these days so near the death of the Master, the Mount of Olives was not the only height that witnessed his petitions? Near to it there was a spot from which also he could behold the beloved city and which must have attracted him more than any other, for that spot was Golgotha, where he was so soon to complete his work. May not Jesus have gone there secretly to pray and to commune with his Father in some mysterious way? We really seem justified in imagining something of the kind, for Jesus, as the Son of God as well as Son of man, could see into the future. How could his soul escape a vision, of the rising up of that cross? How could his feet help being drawn in the direction where it was so soon to be set up? [Tissot]

Jesus in Regaba and Caesarea-Philippi

Wednesday, February 28, AD 31 (Adar 16)

FROM Nobah, Jesus went to Golan. The road wound westwardly round a high mountain chain for a distance of four hours. Golan was inhabited by both Jews and pagans and was distant from the Jordan a couple of hours. Jesus tarried here only a few hours teaching and healing. Continuing his journey, he passed the city of Argob, built at a high elevation on a mountain ridge, and arrived late that night at the stronghold Regaba. He rested with his companions on the grass of a solitary place outside the city, and awaited the other apostles and disciples, fifteen in number. When these arrived, they all went with their Master to the inn established here for their accommodation. Regaba belonged to the Gergesean district. It was the most northerly of their towns, and one of the best disposed. Golan was a frontier town of the tetrarch Philip.

Thursday, March 1, AD 31 (Adar 17)

Most of the inhabitants, both Jews and pagans, were already baptized, and their sick had been healed on the Mount of Beatitudes. Jesus spent the whole day in teaching, consoling, and strengthening souls in faith, often in their homes.

Friday, March 2, AD 31 (Adar 18)

An immense crowd from the whole country around was here assembled for the sabbath, and to it was added a caravan from Arabia. This crowd of people brought with them their lame, their blind, their mute, and other sick. They pressed with such violence that Jesus left the synagogue with the disciples and retired to a mountain. Some of the disciples remained behind and endeavored, as well as they could, to bring the crowd to order.

Saturday, March 3, AD 31 (Adar 19)

Today, a crowd of people sought out Jesus on the mountain. He taught them about the Lord's Prayer, and healed many of the sick. Afterward he continued on his way with the disciples, speaking about the great trials that the future would bring.

The people followed Jesus to the mountain, where he taught of the Lord's Prayer, of prayer that should not be made with ostentation and in public places to be seen, and of the granting of prayer. He also healed many of the sick, and then returned to the synagogue in Regaba. During these last days, Jesus had spoken much upon prayer both on his journeys and in the schools. There were some disciples with him who had not been present at all the explanations of the Lord's Prayer. They said to him: "Teach us, also, to pray as thou hast taught the others!" and he again explained the Lord's Prayer, and warned them against sanctimonious prayers.

Regaba was situated very high and had a magnificent view over the lake, across Galilee, and off to Tabor. Still higher than the city, which was not very large, stood upon a rock a square building with great, steep walls, as if hewn from the rocks. It was provided with vaults and chambers, and was a home for soldiers. It was roofed by a platform upon which trees were growing. It was a citadel. From Regaba to the lake the distance was about five hours toward the southwest; to the Mount of Beatitudes, from three to four hours westward; about five hours to Bethsaida-Julias; and from seven to eight hours from the place in which Jesus drove the devil into the swine. To Caesarea-Philippi, it may have been five hours. A road for caravans ran over the high mountain between Regaba and Caesarea.

During these days Jesus spoke much of the dark future before him. Men would, he said, persecute him everywhere and even attempt his life, and once he said that his arrest was near. Since the last excitement at Capernaum, he had not spoken in public of the bread of life, nor of eating his flesh and drinking his blood. He had taught of this mystery chiefly in order to try his disciples and to get rid of the bad, whom he wished no longer to retain as his followers.

The elevated surroundings of Regaba were very lovely, though somewhat wild. Off toward the northeast, however, the country was barren and rocky. Excellent fruit, such as they had in Galilee, did not grow here, but there were quantities of grain, and on the mountains fine pasture lands. Grazing around were great herds of asses and cows. Some of the latter had very broad horns and black snouts which they carried high in the air; others bore their heads lower and their horns forward, while the horns of many others were broken off short. There were also large herds of camels, which at a distance looked quite small. They often slept standing, supported against the trees and rocks. In one quarter, in which trees like beeches were growing, I saw droves of swine. I have never seen either the Jews or the pagans prepare smoked meat, though they dried fish in the sun and salted it. Up here on the mountains there was great scarcity of water, consequently there were cisterns lower down in which the rain was caught, and the water then carried up in leathern bottles.

Sunday, March 4, AD 31 (Adar 20)

Today Jesus and the disciples arrived at Caesarea-Philippi around midday. He stayed at an inn belonging to the Pharisees, close to the synagogue.

From Regaba Jesus went with his followers to Caesarea-Philippi, where he arrived about midday. The road thither ran over mountains, and in many places it was very wild.

The situation of Caesarea was extraordinarily beautiful. It lay between five hills on one side and a mountain chain on the other. It was surrounded by groves and gardens, and was built in the pagan style of columns and arches. There were perhaps as many as seven palaces, and numbers of pagan temples. Still, the pagans dwelt apart from the Jews. In a little valley outside the city there was a very large pond, in the center of which was a little revolving building. The water welled from it into the pond and thence flowed down to the Jordan. In the pagan quarter of the city there was a very deep well over which was built a beautiful edifice. It was very deep to look down into. I think it communicated through the mountain with the source that flowed from Lake Phiala. I saw outside the city arches and vaults also through which the water flowed, as if through caves and over bridges.

Jesus was well received. They were on the watch for him, the caravan having announced his coming. Some of the relatives of the woman whom Jesus had cured of an issue of blood came out as far as the pond to meet him. He put up near the synagogue at an inn belonging to the Pharisees, and soon was surrounded by a crowd of sick and others. The apostles healed here and there. Some of the Pharisees of this place were badly disposed toward Jesus. They had formed part of the commission of Capernaum.

Monday, March 5, AD 31 (Adar 21)

Jesus cured and taught on a hill outside the city. Strangers from all quarters had brought thither their sick, and these latter were continually crying out: "Lord, command one of thy disciples to help us!" The Pharisees taunted Jesus, asking him why he went around with people so mean, why he did not associate with the learned.

Alms consisting of food and clothing were distributed by the disciples. They had been supplied by Enue (she who had been cured of the issue of blood) and her uncle, still a pagan, who dwelt in Caesarea.

Tuesday, March 6, AD 31 (Adar 22)

This morning Jesus continued his healing and teaching activity outside Caesarea-Philippi. Meanwhile some more disciples arrived, bringing the total number to about sixty. Around midday, Jesus and these disciples went to the house of Enue's uncle, who was a pagan. (It was Enue who had been cured of an issue of blood when she touched Jesus's garment at Capernaum on Kislev 16, as he was on his way to raise the daughter of Jairus from the dead.) The widow Enue and her daughter conducted Jesus to her aged uncle. Jesus spoke with Enue's uncle and the others there who desired to be baptized. They were then baptized by Saturnin, with water blessed by Jesus. At the meal that followed the baptism, Enue's twenty-one-year-old daughter approached Jesus from behind, anointing his head with a costly mixture of essence of oils.

The three apostles and all the disciples who from Ornithopolis had been sent by Jesus to Tyre, Cabul, and the tribe of Asher, met Jesus here at Caesarea as he had appointed. The meeting on such occasions is always very touching. They clasp hands and embrace. The people washed the feet of the newcomers, who immediately took part in the distribution of food and other alms, and the healing of the sick.

Jesus went afterward with all the apostles and disciples, about sixty in number, to the house of Enue's uncle, where he was received most solemnly according to pagan customs, carpets being spread for him to walk upon, and green branches and wreaths being carried. The uncle, led by Enue and her daughter, came to meet Jesus, and the women cast themselves down before him.

It was partly in answer to the prayer of this old man that Jesus had come to Caesarea. He and several other pagans wanted to be baptized, but they had scruples on the subject of circumcision. Jesus never touched upon this point in his public discourse, but he had a private interview with the uncle. In such cases, he never commanded circumcision; though, at the same time, he did not advocate its discontinuance. When pious old pagans, upon receiving baptism, told him in confidence of their trouble on this head, Jesus used to console them by telling them that if they did not wish to become Jews, they should remain as they were, but believe and practice what they heard from him. Such people then lived apart from both Judaism and paganism. They prayed, they gave alms, and became Christians without passing through Judaism. Even to the apostles, Jesus refrained from expressing himself on this point, in order not to scandalize them, so that I never remember having heard the Pharisees, who listened so closely to catch him in his words, ever accuse him on that head, no, not even at the time of his Passion.

Over the beautifully paved inner court of the old man's house an awning of white fabric was stretched, and through an opening in the center hung a wreath. Besides the trees, the whole court was adorned with garlands of flowers. Baptism was administered under the awning. Before the ceremony, Jesus gave an instruction and spoke in private with the neophytes, who opened their hearts to him. They exposed to him their whole life and made their profession of faith in him. Jesus then absolved them from their sins, and they were baptized by Saturnin in a basin of water which Jesus had previously blessed. The ceremony was followed by a grand entertainment in which all the disciples and the friends of the family took part. The meal was conducted according to pagan customs. The table was higher than those in use among the Jews, and the guests reclined upon long, raised divans, the feet turned out, and one arm resting on a cushion. The edge of the table was indented, and before each of the guests were some small dishes, though the principal servings were on large ones in the center of the table.

Enue, since her cure, was scarcely recognizable, so well and hearty had she become. She and her daughter, who was about twenty-one years old, sat at table beside their uncle. During the entertainment, they arose and withdrew for awhile. When they returned, the mother stood somewhat back while the daughter, wearing a beautiful veil and carrying a little white vase of perfume, went behind Jesus, broke it, and poured the contents over his head. Then with both hands she smoothed it right and left over his hair, and drew the part behind the ears through her hands. After that she gathered up the end of her veil, passed it over his head in order to dry it, and retired. A quantity of food was distributed to the poor outside the house.

This house was not the uncle's former residence. It was one to which he had removed with Enue, in order to avoid contact with the pagans and the frequenting of their temples; still it was not in the Jewish quarter. Enue was the daughter of either his brother or sister. She had had communications with the Jews, one of whom she had married, but he was now deceased. It was, however, from her pagan parents that she inherited all her wealth. On leaving their old home, Enue and her uncle had left behind quantities of corn, clothes, and covers for the poor.

Caesarea-Philippi was four hours east of Leshem, or Lais, whither the Syrophoenician had come to Jesus; they were consequently not one and the same city.

Wednesday, March 7, AD 31 (Adar 23)

This morning, Jesus and some disciples visited Enue's house, where they were given something to eat. Jesus directed that bread, grain, clothing, and blankets be sent to the town gate and distributed to the poor and needy. Then he went to the synagogue, where a dispute arose with the Pharisees. Following this, Jesus left Caesarea-Philippi and made his way to Argob.

During Jesus's stay in Caesarea, the pagans celebrated a feast near the fountain in the city. It had reference to the benefit they derived from the water. Incense was burned on tripods before an idol, around which was gathered a crowd of maidens wearing crowns. The idol was made up of three or four figures sitting back to back, each having its own head, hands, and feet. The arms down to the elbows were fastened to the body, but the hands were outstretched. The fountain on all sides poured out water into basins. On one side it flowed into an enclosed place in which were private halls and bathing cisterns. This was the Jews' bathing place.

When the pagan feast was over, Jesus went thither and prepared several of the Jews, who afterward received baptism from the disciples. The ceremony concluded, Jesus with several of his disciples returned to the home of Enue and her uncle and took leave of them. Humbly, reverently, and with many tears, these worthy people bade goodbye to Jesus. They had previously sent presents to the place outside the city gate where Jesus continued a while longer his instructions to the poor travelers belonging to the caravan and to others from the city. The presents consisted of bread, corn, garments, and covers, all of which with whatever else they had received, Jesus caused to be distributed among the needy. Many of the devout Jews and the newly baptized followed this example of charity. They measured out corn and distributed linen, covers, mantles and bread to the poor, for whom this was a gala day.

An Interior Room

Jesus was afterward constrained by the Pharisees, though in the most polite manner, to enter the synagogue and explain some points to them. The apostles accompanied their Master, and quite a considerable crowd was present. The Pharisees had devised all kinds of captious questions on the subject of divorce, for there were many complicated matrimonial affairs in this place, and Jesus had already reconciled some parties and set them right. The Pharisees now began to dispute maliciously with Jesus, and call him to account for all that he exacted of his disciples, for a young man in their party had complained to them of him. This young man was rich and well-educated, and he had long before pushed himself upon Jesus as his disciple. But Jesus had laid down to him several conditions, namely, that he should leave father and mother, distribute his wealth to the poor, etc. He had again, at Caesarea-Philippi, offered himself to Jesus. But he still wanted to retain his fortune and the right to administer it himself, in consequence of which Jesus had again dismissed him.[E10] The Pharisees asked Jesus why he imposed such unheard-of conditions upon people. The young man alleged diverse things that Jesus had said and called upon the apostles to witness to his statements, for they too had heard them. The apostles became embarrassed. They were not prepared for such an attack, and they knew not what to answer. The Pharisees therefore reproached Jesus with fraternizing with the ignorant only, and ascribed his sending away the young man to the fact that the latter was educated. Jesus replied to them in very severe words, and left them to resume his journey.

On leaving the city, Jesus gave instructions to the apostles and disciples, and sent them to places at a considerable distance east and northeast. They had before them a long and difficult journey to Damascus, to Arabia, and to cities which they had never yet visited. Jesus himself with two disciples, leaving Lake Phiala on the left, went to Argob, a city built on a height four hours direct from Caesarea. There he put up with the Levites near the synagogue.

Thursday, March 8, AD 31 (Adar 24)

Today Jesus taught in a public square in Argob. He also healed a number of people. In the afternoon he left Argob, traveling through a mountainous region to a shepherd community. He stayed there in an inn.

Argob was for the most part inhabited by Jews. The few pagans in it were poor and worked for them. Cotton goods were manufactured here, women, children, and men being engaged in spinning and weaving. The place suffered from want of water, which had to be carried up to the city in leathern bottles, and then poured into the cisterns. Jesus taught in a public square, healed some of the sick, and visited in their own homes some old and infirm people, whom he cured and consoled. Almost all the inhabitants had been baptized, and there were no Pharisees among them. A very distant view could be commanded from Argob. They could see far over into Upper Galilee, the Mount of Beatitudes rose before them, and the prospect down into Bethsaida-Julias was remarkably beautiful.

Jesus, with his two disciples, and escorted a part of the way by several people of Argob, started again on his journey. He crossed the mountainous district eastward toward Regaba and halted at a distance of two hours from that city, at an open cabin belonging to the inn. The caravans, which three times a year passed in this direction, often encamped in this place. Jesus was here met by four of his young disciples, who brought with them a supply of provisions. They had come from Jerusalem, taking Capernaum in their route.

Friday, March 9, AD 31 (Adar 25)

Today Jesus traveled to the stronghold of Regaba. Here a great multitude had gathered, including some Pharisees from Capernaum, who had come for the sabbath to hear Jesus preach. In the evening, Jesus taught in the crowded synagogue concerning the building of Solomon's temple (1 Kings 6–7).

From the inn Jesus went to the citadel, or stronghold of Regaba, where a great multitude—besides many from the caravan—had gathered. The citadel looked as if hewn out of a rock. Around it stood some rows of houses and a synagogue. Six of the apostles again joined Jesus here. They had been to neighboring places east of Caesarea, the others having gone to greater distances. These six were Peter, Andrew, John, James the Greater, Philip, and James the Less. There were many Pharisees here. The synagogue was so crowded that even the standing room was occupied. Jesus took his text from Jeremiah. He said that now they were eager to see and to hear him, but the time would come when they would all abandon him, mock and maltreat him.

Saturday, March 10, AD 31 (Adar 26)

Today Jesus healed many blind people in Regaba. He also drove out demons from a number of those who were possessed. The Pharisees began a violent dispute with Jesus, again bringing forward their charge that he drove out the devil through the power of Beelzebub. Jesus called them children of the father of lies, and told them that God no longer desired bloody sacrifices. I heard him speaking of the blood of the Lamb, of the innocent blood that they would soon pour out, and of which the blood of animals was only a symbol. With the sacrifice of the Lamb, he continued, their religious rites would come to an end. All they that believed in the sacrifice of the Lamb would be reconciled to God, but they to whom he was addressing himself should, as the murderers of the Lamb, be condemned. He warned his disciples in presence of the Pharisees to beware of them. This so enraged these men that Jesus and his disciples had to withdraw and hurry off into the desert. I saw among the listening crowd, some men with cudgels. Jesus had never before attacked his aggressors so boldly. He and his disciples passed the night in the desert.

Sunday, March 11, AD 31 (Adar 27)

Today they journeyed on to Chorazin. As Jesus approached the town, he healed many who were sick.

Crowds of people flocked thither, and laid their sick along the road by which Jesus was to come. On his way to the synagogue, he cured the dropsical, the lame, and the blind.

Monday, March 12, AD 31 (Adar 28)

Today in Chorazin, teaching in the synagogue, Jesus was again subject to violent attacks by the Pharisees. As he left the town, several of them even followed him. But Jesus and the disciples walked on. Then the disciples brought a pious shepherd to him who was deaf and mute. Jesus healed the shepherd in the presence of the Pharisees, so that they might see that he healed by way of prayer and faith in the heavenly Father, and not through the devil (Mark 7:31–37). Jesus and the disciples then went on to the tax-collecting place where Matthew's custom house was. After a while they withdrew from the crowd there, staying until nightfall at the foot of the Mount of Beatitudes near Bethsaida-Julias. That night, they crossed the Jordan and visited the house of Andrew in Bethsaida.

In spite of the violent attacks of the Pharisees, Jesus spoke in prophetic terms of his future Passion. He alluded to their repeated sacrifices and expiations, notwithstanding which they still remained full of sins and abomination. Then he spoke of the goat which at the Feast of Atonement was driven from Jerusalem into the desert with the sins of the people laid upon it. He said very significantly (and yet they did not understand him) that the time was drawing near when in the same way they would drive out an innocent man, one that loved them, one that had done everything for them, one that truly bore their sins. They would drive him out, he said, and murder him amid the clash of arms. At these words, a great din and jeering shouts arose among the Pharisees. Jesus left the synagogue and went out into the city. The Pharisees came to him and demanded an explanation of what he had just said, but he replied that they could not now understand it.

While Jesus was being thus pressed upon, a deaf and mute man was brought to him that he might cure him. He was a shepherd of that region, good and pious. His friends brought him to Jesus, whom they implored to lay his hand upon him. Thereupon Jesus commanded that he should be separated from the crowd. His friends obeyed, but the Pharisees followed. Jesus therefore cured him in their presence, that they might see that he healed by virtue of prayer and faith in his heavenly Father, and not through the devil. Jesus put his fingers into the ears of the mute, moistened his fingers with his own saliva and touched the man's tongue with it. Then sighing, he glanced up to heaven and said: "Be thou open!" At the same instant, the man could both hear and speak perfectly, and full of joy he gave thanks. But Jesus commanded him to refrain from talking or boasting about his cure.

The crowd becoming greater, for a caravan had just arrived, Jesus and his companions left the city and went two or three hours farther on to Matthew's custom house. But as here too the crowd was on the increase, Jesus, leaving a couple of his disciples behind, embarked with the others and rowed to Bethsaida-Julias, where they landed and remained until night in a solitary place at the foot of the Mount of Beatitudes.

Tuesday, March 13, AD 31 (Adar 29)

Today Jesus and the disciples returned to the mountain ridge above Matthew's custom house. Here Jesus delivered a discourse to the crowd and healed many (Matthew 15:29–31). He spoke the words recorded in Matthew 7:7–11. That evening the month of Nisan began. Jesus stayed overnight in Matthew's old house.

Before daylight they left Bethsaida and rowed again to the east side of the lake, where Jesus delivered a discourse on the mountain ridge beyond Matthew's custom house. There were pagans from Decapolis present, also the people belonging to the caravan. Many sick were brought up the mountain on litters and asses, and Jesus healed them. [E11]

Jesus taught of prayer, how and where it should be made, and of perseverance in it. He said: "When a child asks for bread, the father does not give it a stone, nor does he give it a serpent when it asks for a fish, or a scorpion instead of an egg." He remarked as an illustration that he knew pagans who had such confidence in God that they never petitioned for anything, but took with thanks all that was given them. "If servants and strangers have such confidence," said Jesus, "what ought not that of the children of the Father to be?" He spoke also of gratitude for restoration to health, which gratitude should be evinced by amendment of life, and of the punishment incurred by a relapse into sin. The spiritual state of those that relapse is always worse than before their cure. [E12]

NISAN (30 days): March 13/14 to April 11/12, AD 31 Nisan New Moon: March 12 at 3:15 AM Jerusalem time

Wednesday, March 14, AD 31 (Nisan 1)

By this time the crowd had become so great that Jesus was again forced to withdraw—not, however, before he had announced a great instruction to be delivered on the following day upon another mountain. This last-named mount was east of the Mount of Beatitudes, and to it flocked the multitude from all sides. The whole region around, mountains and valleys, was covered with encampments, and everywhere resounded the question: "Where is Jesus?" Jesus taught upon the seventh and the eighth beatitudes, after which, to escape the crowd, he went with the apostles and disciples on board Peter's ship. They rowed down the lake, but did not land, because the people, having secured boats, were following them. Jesus spent that night on Peter's ship.

Conclusion of the Sermon on the Mount • Feeding of the Four Thousand • The Pharisees Demand a Sign

Thursday, March 15, AD 31 (Nisan 2)

Today Jesus delivered the so-called "Sermon on the Mount" (Matthew 5:1–7; 29), signifying the conclusion of his presentation of the beatitudes, which had begun on the Mount of Beatitudes on Kislev 13. Then, toward evening, there took place the feeding of the four thousand (Matthew 15:32–39). Jesus took leave of the people, who shed tears of thanks. He made his way back to the lake with the disciples. Before they could board their ship, they were met by a group of Pharisees who demanded Jesus to show them a sign from heaven. He replied as recorded in Matthew 16:1–4, saying that, after a certain number of weeks (actually 107), they would be given the sign of Jonah (Matthew 12:40). Jesus and the disciples then boarded Peter's ship and rowed out onto the lake, where they spent the night.

NEXT morning, Jesus and his followers ascended the high mountain one hour to the northeast of Little Chorazin, and beyond that, one upon which the first multiplication of the loaves had taken place. It was in the desert to the right of Chorazin, two and a half hours west of Regaba, which was on a still higher elevation. Up where Jesus delivered the instruction there was a large level space, not far from the road by which he had lately traveled from Caesarea-Philippi to Regaba. The place was much used as a camping ground for travelers. The ruins of fortifications were found on it, and a long rocky ledge, upon which the travelers used to spread their provisions at meals. Once upon a time this region was a perfect solitude. Below this plateau were little dells and dales, in which the asses and other beasts of burden could graze. A considerable crowd was already assembled on the plateau, while others were still flocking thither from all quarters.

Here it was that Jesus concluded the eight beatitudes and delivered the so-called Sermon on the Mount. His words on this occasion were more than ordinarily forcible and impressive. Crowds of strangers and pagans were present, the whole multitude, exclusive of women and children, numbering about four thousand. Toward evening, Jesus paused in his teaching and said to John: "I have compassion on the multitudes, because they continue with me now three days, and have nothing to eat; but I will not send them away fasting lest they faint in the way." John replied: "We are far in the desert, and to bring bread this distance would be hard. Shall we gather for them the fruits and berries that are still on the trees around here?" Jesus answered by telling him to ask the other apostles how many loaves they had. The latter answered: "Seven loaves and seven little fishes." The fishes were, however, an arm in length. Upon receiving this answer, Jesus directed that the empty breadbaskets the people had brought with them, along with the loaves and fishes, should be laid upon the rocky ledge; after which he continued to teach a good half-hour. He spoke very plainly of his being the Messiah, of the persecutions that awaited him, and of his approaching imprisonment. But on that day, he said, those mountains would quake and that rock (here he pointed to the stone ledge) whereon he had announced the truth they had refused to receive, would split asunder. Then he cried woe to Capernaum, to Chorazin, and to many other places of that region. On the day of his arrest they should all become conscious of having rejected salvation. He spoke of the happiness of this region to which he had broken the bread of life, but added that the strangers passing through had carried away with them that happiness. The children of the house threw that bread under the table, while the stranger, the little whelps, as the Syrophoenician had called them, gathered up the crumbs, which were sufficient to vivify and enliven whole towns and districts. Jesus then took leave of the people. He implored them once more to do penance and amend their life, repeated his admonitions in the most forcible language, and informed them that this was the last time he would teach in those parts. The people wept. They were full of admiration at his words, although they did not comprehend them all.

After that, Jesus commanded them to take their places on the declivity around the mountain, and, as on the preceding occasion, the apostles and disciples were directed to range them in order. Jesus divided the bread and fish as before, and the disciples carried the portions round in baskets to the people on both sides of the mount. When all was over, seven baskets of scraps were gathered up and distributed to poor travelers.

During Jesus's discourse, a number of Pharisees had been standing among the crowd. Some of them left and went down into the valley before the close, while others remained long enough to hear Jesus's admonitions and to witness the multiplication of the bread. Before the people dispersed, however, these latter descended the mountain in order to confer with the others as to how they should meet Jesus on his coming down. These Pharisees numbered about twenty. Under the pretext of visiting the synagogues, they constantly followed Jesus in little bands, in order to spy out his actions. They had been in Caesarea-Philippi, in Nobah, Regaba, and Chorazin. By messengers or by word of mouth, they transmitted to Capernaum and Jerusalem all they saw and heard.

Jesus took leave of the people, who shed tears and lifted up their voices thanking and praising him. He broke away from them only with difficulty and went to the lake with the disciples, in order to cross over to the southeastern side into the region of Magdala and Dalmanutha. When about to embark just above Matthew's custom office, the Pharisees approached and, at the foot of the mountain upon which the first multiplication of the loaves had taken place, demanded from him a sign from heaven. [E13] This they did because he had spoken of frightful tremors of the earth and other signs in nature. He replied to them as is recorded in the Gospel. I heard him mention also a certain number of weeks at the end of which the sign of Jonah would be given them. This number exactly corresponded with his crucifixion and resurrection. Jesus then left them standing there and went with the apostles to Peter's ship, which the other disciples had in readiness to receive him. They rowed out into full sea and then descended the Jordan current, in which the ship needed only to be steered. They passed the night on board, praying at certain hours, and thus reached the confines of Magdala and Dalmanutha.

Friday, March 16, AD 31 (Nisan 3)

Still on board Peter's ship, Jesus taught the disciples concerning the persecution and suffering that he would endure. He warned them to beware of the Pharisees and Sadducees (Matthew 16:5–12). Around noon, they landed at Bethsaida and went to eat at Andrew's house. As Jesus was leaving the house, he healed an old blind man (Mark 8:22–26). Then Jesus and the disciples rowed back to the east side of the Sea of Galilee and went to the town of Bethsaida-Julias for the sabbath. That evening he preached in the synagogue on the deeper meaning of the commandment "Honor thy father and mother."

Next morning, getting out of the current, they rowed back to the west side of the lake, and then remarked that they had only one loaf with them.

The passage was slow, and Jesus instructed his followers on many points. He spoke of his impending captivity, of his Passion, of the persecution he should endure, and said in terms more significant than ever that he was Christ, the Messiah. They believed his words; but although they could not make them square with their simple, human way of comprehending things, and indulged in their customary views, views derived from their own experience, yet they made a note of them, and ranked them among others of a deeply significant and prophetic nature. He spoke also of his going to Jerusalem and of the persecution that would be attendant on the same. They would, he said, be scandalized on his account, and things would go so far that they would cast stones after him. Jesus said also that whoever would not renounce all his property and his relatives and follow him faithfully in his time of persecution, could not be his disciple. He spoke likewise of the journeys he still had to make and of the multiplied labors to be accomplished before his arrest. Many, he said, who had abandoned him would again return. The disciples asked whether that young man who wanted first to bury his father, would return; whether Jesus would not then receive him, for indeed he appeared to them to deserve it. But Jesus laid open to them that youth's disposition, and showed them how he clung to earthly things. I understood on this occasion that the expression "to bury one's father" was figurative, and meant "to put one's affairs in order." It was this that the young man wanted to do. He wanted to put his affairs in order, and obtain a division of the inheritance between himself and his old father, in order to secure his own share before separating from him. When Jesus spoke of the young man's hankering after temporal goods, Peter exclaimed with animation: "Thank God I have never had such thoughts since I have followed thee!" But Jesus rebuked him, saying that he should be silent on that point, until asked to speak.

When Jesus and the disciples arrived at Bethsaida they went to Andrew's to refresh themselves and there remained undisturbed and without the annoyance of a great crowd since, not knowing whither Jesus had retired, the people had dispersed. There was in Bethsaida an aged man blind from his birth, whom Jesus had hitherto refused to cure. Now, however, he was brought to him again and when Jesus and the disciples were on the point of returning to the ship, the man cried out to him for help. Jesus took him by the hand, led him outside the city, and there before his apostles and disciples touched his eyes with his tongue and with saliva, laid his hands upon them, and asked whether he saw anything. At these words, the man opened his eyes and stared around, saying: "I see people as large as trees walking about." Jesus laid his hand once more on his eyes, and bade him again look around. Now he saw perfectly. Jesus ordered him to go home and thank God, but not to go about the city boasting of his cure.

Toward evening, Jesus and his apostles rowed to the opposite shore of the lake and, having landed, took the road up the eastern bank of the Jordan to Bethsaida-Julias. On this journey the apostles and disciples who had been dispatched from Caesarea-Philippi on their mission toward the east, as they were coming down from the mountains, met Jesus and his party, and all set out together for Bethsaida-Julias.

On the way, Jesus spoke of his approaching arrest and of the dangers that threatened, whereupon the apostles implored him not to send them away any more, that they might be near him in case of need.

An inn had been prepared for them in Bethsaida-Julias. As they drew near to the city, where Jesus's coming had already been announced by the people that had gone thither for the sabbath, some of the inhabitants came out to meet them. They were received graciously and conducted to the inn for refreshments and washing of the feet. A great number of Gentiles dwelt in Bethsaida, and they now saluted Jesus from a distance.

Jesus taught in the synagogue. There were present many scribes and Pharisees from Saphet, at which place was a school for the study of science, human and divine.

All were greatly rejoiced at the sudden arrival of Jesus, who visited them now for the first time; the generality of the people were sincere in their desire to see him, but the scribes were actuated by vanity. They wished to hear the Teacher whose fame was sounded throughout the whole country, especially at Capernaum, and to judge of his merits. They were perfectly courteous, though like certain professors cold and proud in their bearing. They disputed with Jesus, putting to him questions out of the Law and the Prophets. Still there was nothing malicious in their intentions. They were moved rather by curiosity, and impelled by vanity to display their learning before the people.

Jesus read and commented upon the lesson for the sabbath, and taught upon the Fourth Commandment: "Thou shalt honor thy father and thy mother, that thy days may be long in the land." To the words, "thy days may be long in the land," he gave a most admirable and profound explanation. "That stream must dry up," he said, "which obstructs its own source." The instruction was followed by a festal entertainment, at which the school children assisted at separate tables. During it, Jesus explained the parable of the workmen in the vineyard. Julias was a modern city, not yet completed. It was very beautiful, constructed upon the pagan style with numerous arches and columns. It lay along the Jordan. On the east, where it was contiguous with the rising heights, the rear of many of the houses was hewn out of the solid rock.

Saturday, March 17, AD 31 (Nisan 4)

When Jesus, after having taught once more in the synagogue, was walking outside the city, the inhabitants stopped him to ask about the true doctrine and what they should do. He answered that they would not follow his instructions even if he gave them to them. They were, he said, inquisitive. They had already in this region heard his doctrine so often. Did they by these questions, ask another? He had even announced it openly in the synagogue. These people led Jesus to some of their newly constructed buildings, and to a place where lay stores of building materials, wood and stone. They spoke to him of the beautiful new style of architecture. Jesus embraced the opportunity to relate to them the parables of the house built upon the sand, and of the other built upon a rock (Matthew 7:24–27). He referred to the cornerstone which the builders would reject, and of the overthrow of their building (Matthew 21:42). On the way he healed several sick people, some lame, others dropsical, and a couple of possessed who were, besides, deprived of reason.

Sunday, March 18, AD 31 (Nisan 5)

From Bethsaida-Julias, Jesus with the twelve and about thirty disciples went to the country town Sogane, an hour and a half from Caesarea, where he taught and cured. Some of the inhabitants of Bethsaida-Julias escorted Jesus and his party as far as the point where the Jordan flowed into Lake Merom. The people of Sogane came crowding around Jesus, begging for an instruction. He taught and healed until toward evening, and then with his disciples went back about the distance of an hour to a mount, upon which he spent the greater part of the night in prayer.

Peter Receives the Keys of the Kingdom of Heaven

ON the way to the mount and until Jesus retired to pray, the apostles and disciples that had last returned from their several missions gave their Master a full account of all that had happened to them, all that they had seen and heard and done. He listened to everything and exhorted them to pray and hold themselves in readiness for what he was going to communicate to them. That night, Jesus withdrew alone to pray.

Monday, March 19, AD 31 (Nisan 6)

Before dawn, Jesus returned to the disciples, and they prayed together. The twelve stood around him in a circle and the other disciples around them. Jesus asked: "Who do the people say I am?" The reply to this question is recorded in Matthew 16:13–14. Then Jesus asked: "But who do you say that I am?" Peter, taking a step forward, declared: "Thou art Christ, the Son of the living God!" At this very moment the sun was rising, and Jesus spoke the words recorded in Matthew 16:17-20. He told the disciples that he was the promised Messiah, applying all the relevant passages from the prophets to himself. He announced that now the time had come for them to journey to Jerusalem for the Passover. Traveling through the day, that evening they arrived at Bethulia. Here Lazarus was waiting for Jesus. Lazarus had come to warn him that an insurrection against Pontius Pilate was planned and that this threatened to disrupt the Passover festival. The revolt would be led by Judas of Gamala, who had the support of a large number of Galileans. Lazarus said that it would therefore be advisable for Jesus to hold back from the celebrations in Jerusalem. But Jesus replied that this uprising would be the forerunner of a far greater one that would take place at a later time, meaning that which would accompany his future trial and persecution.

When before daybreak they again gathered about Jesus, the twelve stood around him in a circle. On his right were first, John, then James the Greater, and thirdly, Peter. The disciples stood outside the circle, the oldest of them nearest. Then Jesus, as if resuming the discourse of the preceding night, asked: "Who do men say that I am?" The apostles and the oldest of the disciples repeated the various conjectures of the people concerning him, as they had heard here and there in different places; some, for instance, said that he was the Baptist, others Elijah, while others again took him for Jeremiah, who had arisen from the dead. They related all that had become known to them on this subject, and then remained in expectation of Jesus's reply. There was a short pause. Jesus was very grave, and they fixed their eyes upon his countenance with some impatience. At last, he said: "And you, for whom do you take me?" No one felt impelled to answer. Only Peter, full of faith and zeal, taking one step forward into the circle, with hand raised like one solemnly affirming, exclaimed aloud and boldly, as if the voice and tongue of all: "Thou art Christ, the Son of the living God!"[E14] Jesus replied with great earnestness, his voice strong and animated: "Blessed art thou, Simon, son of Jonah, because flesh and blood hath not revealed this to thee, but my Father who is in heaven! And I say to thee: Thou art a rock, and upon this rock I will build my church, and the gates of hell shall not prevail against it. And I will give to thee the keys of the kingdom of heaven. And whatsoever thou shalt bind upon earth, it shall be bound also in heaven; and whatsoever thou shalt loose upon earth, it shall be loosed also in heaven!" Jesus made this response in a manner both solemn and prophetic. He appeared to be shining with light, and was raised some distance above the ground. Peter, in the same spirit in which he had confessed to the Godhead, received Jesus's words in their full signification. He was deeply impressed by them. But the other apostles appeared troubled. They glanced from Jesus to Peter as the latter exclaimed with such zeal: "Thou art Christ, the Son of God!" Even John allowed his anxiety to become so manifest that Jesus afterward, when walking along the road with him alone, reproved him gravely for his expression of surprise.

Jesus's words to Peter were spoken just at the moment of sunrise. The whole scene was so much the more grave and solemn, since Jesus had for that purpose retired with his disciples into the mountain and commanded them to pray. Peter alone was sensibly impressed by it. The other apostles did not fully comprehend, and still formed to themselves earthly ideas. They thought that Jesus intended to bestow upon Peter the office of high priest in his kingdom, and James told John, as they walked together, that very probably they themselves would receive places next after Peter.

Jesus now told the apostles in plain terms that he was the promised Messiah. He applied to himself all the passages to that effect found in the Prophets, and said that they must now go to Jerusalem for the Feast. They then directed their steps southwestwardly and returned to the Jordan bridge.

Peter, still profoundly impressed by Jesus's words relative to the power of the keys, drew near to him on the way to ask for information upon some points not clear to him. He was so full of faith and ardor that he fancied his work was to begin right away, for the conditions, namely, the Passion of Christ and the descent of the Holy Spirit, were as yet unknown to him. He asked therefore whether in this or that case also he could absolve from sin, and made some remarks upon publicans and those guilty of open adultery. Jesus set his mind at ease by telling him that he would later on know all things clearly, that they would be very different from what he expected, and that a new Law would be substituted for the old.

As they proceeded on their journey, Jesus began to enlighten his apostles upon what was in store for them. They should now go to Jerusalem, eat the paschal lamb with Lazarus, after which they might expect many labors, much weariness and persecution. He mentioned in general terms many circumstances of his future: namely, his raising of one of their best friends from the dead, which fact was to give rise to such fury among his enemies that he would be obliged to flee; and their going again after another year to the Feast, at which time one of them would betray him. He told them moreover that he would be maltreated, scourged, mocked, and shamefully put to death; that he must die for the sins of men, but that on the third day he would rise again. He told them all this in detail and proved it from the Prophets. His manner was very grave, but full of love. Peter was so distressed at the thought of Jesus's being maltreated and put to death that, following him, he spoke to him in private, disputing with him and exclaiming against such suffering, such treatment. No, he said, that should not be. He would rather die himself than suffer such a thing to happen! "Far be it from thee, Lord! This shall not be unto thee!" He exclaimed. But Jesus turned to him gravely and said with warmth: "Go behind me, Satan! Thou art a scandal unto me. Thou savorest not the things that are of God, but the things that are of men!" and then walked on.[E15] Peter, struck with fear, began to turn over in his mind why it was that Jesus a short time before had said not from flesh and blood but by a revelation from God he (Peter) had declared him to be the Christ; but now he called him Satan and, because he had protested against his sufferings, he reproached him with speaking not according to God, but according to human desires and considerations. Comparing Jesus's words of praise with those of his reproof, Peter became more humble and looked upon him with greater faith and admiration. He was nevertheless very much afflicted, since he became thereby only the more convinced of the reality of the sufferings awaiting Jesus.

The apostles and disciples proceeded in separate bands, each walking with the Lord by turns. He hurried on quickly, stopping nowhere, shunning the towns and villages as much as possible until nightfall, when they put up at the inn near the baths of Bethulia. Here Lazarus and some of the disciples from Jerusalem were awaiting Jesus's coming.

Lazarus had already been informed that Jesus and his disciples would eat the paschal lamb with him, and he had come hither to meet Jesus in order to warn him, the apostles, and disciples in respect to this Passover solemnity. He told them that an insurrection threatened during the Feast. Pilate wanted to levy a new tax upon the temple in order to erect a statue to the Emperor. He desired likewise certain sacrifices in his honor and that certain high titles of reverence should be publicly decreed him. The Jews were on that account ready for revolt, and a large number of Galileans had risen up against Pilate's proceedings. They were headed by a certain Judas, a Golanite, who had numerous adherents and who inveighed hotly against the servitude of his people and the Roman imposts. It would be well, Lazarus said, for Jesus to absent himself from the feast, as great disturbances might arise. Jesus, however, replied that his time was not yet come, that nothing would happen to him. This uprising was but the forerunner of a far greater one that would take place the next year when, as he said, his time would have come. Then would the Son of Man be delivered over into the hands of sinners.

(Follow Map 28)

Tuesday, March 20, AD 31 (Nisan 7)

Jesus and the disciples split up into different groups for the journey to Bethany. Jesus was accompanied by Simon, Thaddeus, Nathaniel Chased, and Joseph Barsabbas. They made rapid progress, arriving that night at Lazarus's estate near Ginea.

Jesus sent his apostles and disciples on ahead. They were divided into separate bands and were to journey by different routes. Simon and Thaddeus, Nathaniel Chased and Joseph Barsabbas, he kept with himself. Some were to go down along the Jordan, while others proceeded westward from Gerizim through Ephron, visiting on their way to the Feast some places at which they had not yet been. Lazarus journeyed with the disciples. Jesus commanded them not to go into the Samaritan cities, and gave them several directions as to their conduct. He himself went as far as Ginea, to the estate of Lazarus, where he passed the night.

Wednesday, March 21, AD 31 (Nisan 8)

Continuing their journey, Jesus and his four traveling companions reached the town of Lebonah this evening.

Thursday, March 22, AD 31 (Nisan 9)

After healing some people in Lebonah, Jesus and the four disciples traveled on to Coreae, where he healed several people.

Map 28: Journey to the Second Passover

March 20–April 1, AD 31

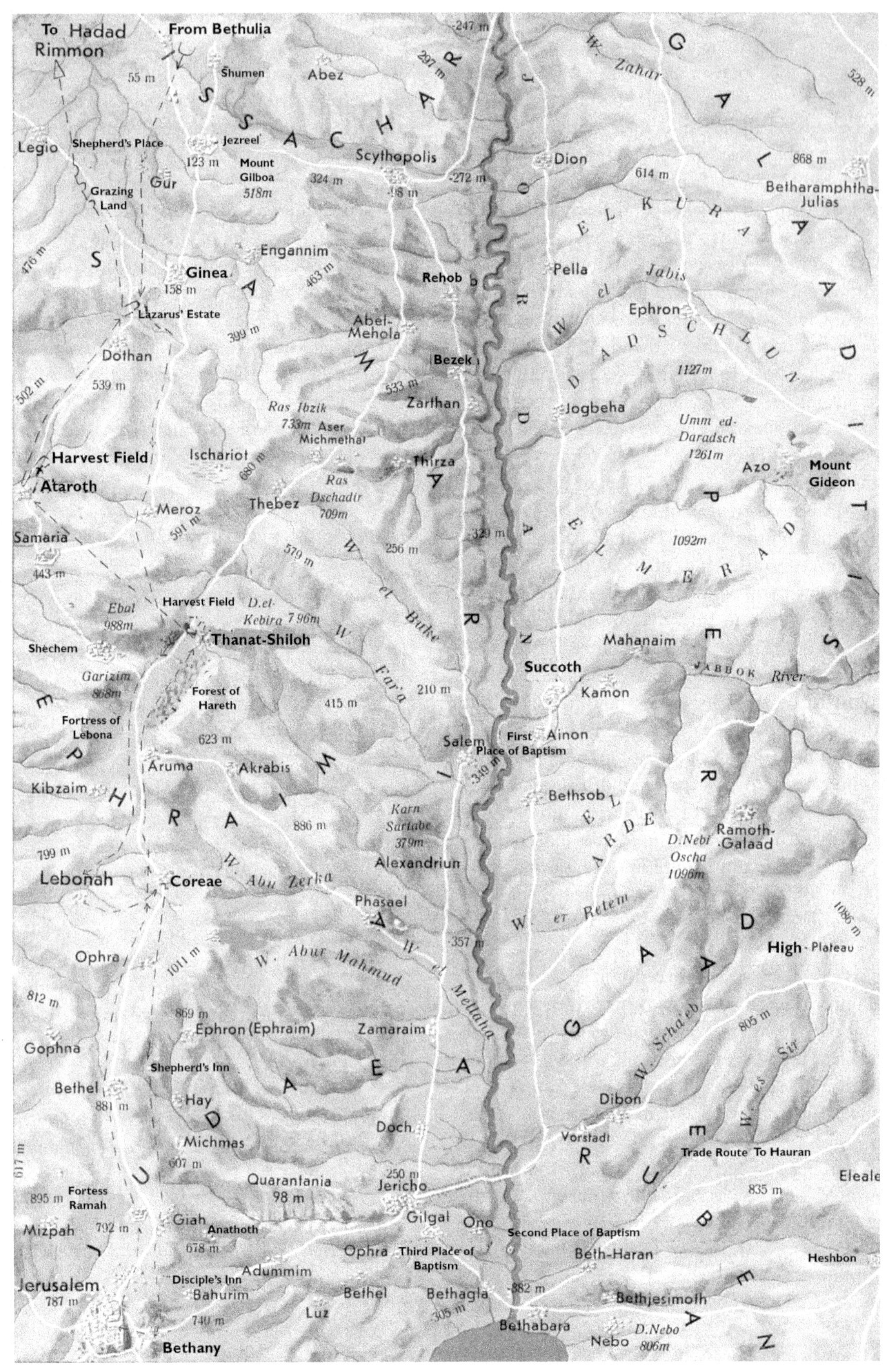

Bethulia—Lazarus's Estate near Ginea—Lebonah—Coreae—Bethany—Jerusalem—Ramah
Thanat-Shiloh—Ataroth—Lazarus's Estate near Ginea—Seleucia—Hadad-Rimmon

FROM THE SECOND PASSOVER TO THE RETURN FROM CYPRUS

Jesus in Bethany and Jerusalem

Friday, March 23, AD 31 (Nisan 10)

As Jesus and the disciples were approaching Ephron, they were met on the way by Mary Magdalene and the widow Salome, who had come together from Bethany to greet Jesus. After resting and talking with the two women, Jesus and the four disciples continued on their way. (The two women returned to Bethany by another route.) When Jesus and the disciples arrived at Bethany, they were welcomed by Lazarus. His mother, the holy Virgin, was also there, and other disciples and friends had already arrived. That evening, Jesus and all those gathered together in Bethany celebrated the sabbath in the great hall of the castle. He spoke much about the paschal lamb and about his future suffering.

ABOUT three hours from Bethany, but still in the desert, stood a solitary shepherd hut whose occupants depended for the most part on the charity of Lazarus. To this abode, Magdalene with a single companion, Mary Salome, a relative of Joseph, had come to meet Jesus. She had prepared for him some refreshments. On his approach, she hurried out and embraced his feet. Jesus rested here only a short time and then set out for Lazarus's inn, one hour from Bethany. The two women returned home by another way. Jesus found some of the disciples whom he had sent on their mission already returned and at the inn: others came later, and in Bethany all met again. Jesus did not go through Bethany, but entered Lazarus's dwelling from the rear. On his arrival, all hurried out into the court to meet him. Lazarus washed his feet, and then they passed up through the gardens. The women saluted Jesus with their veils lowered.

A very touching incident attended Jesus's arrival. The four lambs destined for the Passover solemnity were brought in at the same moment that Jesus entered. They had been separated from the flock, and turned into a little grassy park. The blessed Virgin, who also was here, and Magdalene had twined little wreaths which were to be hung around their necks. Jesus's coming was just before the commencement of the sabbath, and he celebrated it with the family in a hall. He was very grave. He read the lesson for the sabbath, and gave an instruction upon it. During the evening meal, he spoke of the paschal lamb and of his future Passion.

The insurrection broke out in Jerusalem shortly before the sabbath began, but yet without violence. Pilate, surrounded by a bodyguard, occupied an elevated position on a wall of the fortress Antonia, and all the people were gathered in the marketplace below. The fortress Antonia was built on a projecting rock at the northwest corner of the temple. If on leaving Pilate's palace one turned to the left and went through the arch past the place of flagellation, the fortress would lie on his left. Pilate's new laws, by which a tax was laid upon the temple, were read to the people. First, the tax was to be used for making an aqueduct to conduct water to the grand marketplace and to the temple; and secondly, there was question of certain honors, titles, and sacrifices to be offered to the Emperor. Immediately a great tumult arose. Loud cries and mutterings proceeded from the crowd, especially from the quarter occupied by the Galileans. Still the commotion did not reach violence. Pilate addressed some warning words to the people, and gave them time to reflect; whereupon, indignant and murmuring, they dispersed. The Herodians were in secret the prime movers and instigators of the people, yet no one could convict them of such dealings. They kept Judas Golanite under their thumb, and he had a whole sect of Galileans as his followers, to whom he constantly inveighed against paying tribute to the Emperor, and stirred up their thirst for liberty under the pretext of zeal for religion. The Herodians were exactly like the Freemasons and other secret societies of our own day. They stirred up the unthinking multitude, who knew not whither their zeal was carrying them until they paid the penalty with their blood.

Saturday, March 24, AD 31 (Nisan 11)

Jesus taught this morning and afternoon (at the close of the sabbath) in the castle. In between, he walked in the garden. Mary Magdalene followed him everywhere, full of love and contrition. She sat at his feet to take in his words. Since her final conversion, she had changed greatly in her countenance and bearing. That evening, there was a meal attended by all, including friends and disciples from Jerusalem.

On the sabbath Jesus taught at Lazarus's, and then all went to walk in the gardens. Jesus talked of his Passion and said in plain terms that he was the Christ. His words increased his hearers' reverence and admiration for him, while Magdalene's love and contrition reached their height. She followed Jesus everywhere, sat at his feet, stood and waited for him everywhere. She thought of him alone, saw him alone, knew only her Redeemer and her own sins. Jesus frequently addressed to her words of consolation.[E16] She was very greatly changed. Her countenance and bearing were still noble and distinguished, though her beauty was destroyed by her penance and tears.[E17] She sat almost always alone in her narrow penance chamber, and at times performed the lowest services for the poor and sick.

That evening there was a grand entertainment. All the friends from Jerusalem, as well as the holy women from the same place, were present at it. I saw too Heli of Hebron, the widower of one of Elizabeth's sisters, who at the Last Supper filled the office to Jesus of steward and master of the house. He had with him his son, the Levite, who now held possession of John's paternal house, and his five daughters, who were Essenes and unmarried.

Lazarus and his family were the familiar and deeply sympathetic friends of Jesus and his disciples. With their property and goods, they became the powerful helpers and supporters of the community.

Sunday, March 25, AD 31 (Nisan 12)

Around ten o'clock in the morning Jesus and the disciples crossed the Mount of Olives and went to the temple. Here Jesus taught the disciples and a crowd of people who had gathered around. However, as there were several teaching chairs set up, Jesus did not arouse too much attention. After about an hour, he and the disciples returned to Bethany. That afternoon, about fifty Galileans—followers of Judas of Gamala—were seized by Roman soldiers, as Pontius Pilate had been informed that they would try to start an insurrection. However, the people rebelled, attacking the soldiers, and managed to free the captives. Several people died in the melee.

Toward ten o'clock next morning, Jesus went with the apostles and about thirty disciples across the Mount of Olives and through Ophel to the temple. All wore the ordinary brown woollen tunic common among the Galileans, added to which Jesus had a broad cincture upon which was an inscription in letters. He attracted no attention, since bands of Galileans similarly clad were to be met in all quarters. The feast was approaching. Large encampments of huts and tents were ranged around the city, and crowds of people were circulating everywhere.

Jesus taught in the temple for a whole hour in the presence of his disciples and a large number of people. There were several teacher's chairs, from all of which instructions were given. All were so busy with preparations for the feast, and so taken up with the revolt against Pilate, that no priest of the first grade noticed Jesus, but some malicious, insignificant Pharisees approached him and asked how he dared show himself there, and how long this thing was to last, adding that they would soon put a stop to his proceedings. Jesus gave them an answer that put them to shame, and continued his discourse undisturbed, after which he returned to Bethany, and retired in the evening to the Mount of Olives.

On this day a great multitude was again assembled on the marketplace before the fortress Antonia, to speak to Pilate. But he already knew all that they had to say, for he had among them his own spies and soldiers in disguise. The Herodians had roused up Judas the Golanite and his

Fortress Antonia

Galilean followers, who went fearlessly to Pilate and told him that he should refrain from his design of touching the money belonging to the temple treasury. As many of them made use of very unbridled language, Pilate ordered his guard to attack them unexpectedly, and about fifty of them were taken prisoner. But at once the rest of the mob rushed to the rescue, freed the prisoners, and then dispersed. About five inoffensive Jews and some Roman soldiers were killed during the affray. This affair served only to increase the general discontent. Herod was in Jerusalem at this time.

Monday, March 26, AD 31 (Nisan 13)

News had spread that Jesus was in Jerusalem for the Passover, and many sick people came to the temple to be healed by him. As he was entering the temple, Jesus caught sight of the man whom he had healed at the pool of Bethesda. (He had been paralyzed for thirty-eight years.) Jesus called out to him: "See, you are well! Sin no more, that nothing worse befall you." This person had not known who had healed him. But now he made it his business to tell the Pharisees that it was Jesus who had healed him on the sabbath (John 5:14–15). Immediately the Pharisees gathered around Jesus, charging him with breaking the sabbath, but no great disturbance arose, and Jesus continued to teach concerning the Passover sacrifice. The Pharisees asked scornfully whether he—the prophet—would do them the honor of eating the paschal lamb with them. Jesus replied: "The Son of Man is himself a sacrifice for your sins!" In the end, as Jesus continued teaching, the Pharisees became so exasperated that they raised a great commotion. But Jesus managed to slip away and disappear into the crowd, returning to Bethany where preparations were underway for the feast on the following day.

On the morning of the following day, Jesus again went to the temple with all his disciples. His presence had now become known, and waiting for him in the temple court through which he had to pass were people with their sick. Already on his way thither, a man suffering from edema had been brought to him in a litter as he ascended the mount. Jesus healed him, and at the temple some others sick and gouty. In consequence of these cures, he was followed by a numerous crowd. As he drew near the temple, where they were still busy here and there clearing out and putting in order the places destined for the immolation of the lambs next day, Jesus passed the man whom he had cured at the pool of Bethesda, and who was here employed as a day laborer. Jesus turned to him and said: "Behold! Thou hast been cured. Sin no more, that something worse may not befall thee!" This man, who was well-known, had been plied with questions as to who had cured him on the sabbath day. But he did not know Jesus, whom he here saw again for the first time. Now, however, he made it his business to inform the Pharisees as they passed that this Jesus who on the preceding day had wrought so many cures, was the very one that had cured him at the pool of Bethesda. Since the cure of this man had caused great excitement and the Pharisees had been very much tried by what they termed a violation of the sabbath, they now found in it a new cause of complaint against Jesus. They gathered around his chair and again brought forward the old story of his sabbath-breaking. There was, however, no special disturbance on that day, although they were very greatly enraged.

Jesus taught two hours in the temple before a large audience. His subject was the Passover sacrifice. He said that his heavenly Father desired no bloody sacrifices from them, but rather a penitent heart, and that the paschal lamb was merely symbolical of an infinitely higher sacrifice which would soon be fulfilled. Many of his malicious enemies among the Pharisees came forward, railing at him and disputing against him. Among other things they asked in scornful words whether the prophet would do them the honor to eat the paschal lamb with them. Jesus answered: "The Son of Man is himself a sacrifice for your sins!"

That youth who had said that he would first bury his father, and to whom Jesus had responded: "Let the dead bury the dead!" was also in Jerusalem. He had repeated those words of Jesus to the Pharisees. They now reproached him with them, and asked him what he meant by them. How could one dead man bury another? Jesus answered by saying that whoever does not follow his teaching, does not do penance, and does not believe in his mission, has no life in him and is consequently dead; that whoever values goods and riches more than his salvation, whoever follows not his teachings and believes not in him, has in himself not life, but death. Such were the dispositions of this young man. He had wished to come to terms with his aged father concerning his inheritance and put the latter upon a pension; he had clung to the dead inheritance, and consequently he could have no share in the kingdom of Jesus and eternal life. It was for this reason that Jesus had told him to let the dead bury the dead while he himself turned to life. Jesus continued to teach in this strain, and reproached them severely for their covetousness. But when he warned his disciples against the leaven of the Pharisees and related the parable of the rich man and poor Lazarus, the Pharisees became so exasperated that they raised a great tumult. Jesus was forced to disappear in the crowd and make his escape, otherwise they would have taken him prisoner.

The four little lambs destined for the four sets who were to eat the Passover at Lazarus's, and which were daily washed at a fountain and adorned with fresh flowers, were taken on the evening of this day to the temple at Jerusalem. Each had, fastened to the little wreath around its neck, a ticket with the name and sign of the master of the family to which it belonged. After being washed once more, they were turned into a beautiful grassy enclosure on the temple mount.

Tuesday, March 27, AD 31 (Nisan 14)

Today, Jesus and his friends and disciples walked together on the Mount of Olives. Meanwhile, the healed man from the pool of Bethesda continued to go around telling the Pharisees that it was Jesus who had cured him. The Pharisees then determined to take Jesus into custody. In the afternoon, the slaughter of the paschal lambs in the temple began—at 3:00 PM and not at 12:30 PM as was the case on the day of the crucifixion. (On the day of the crucifixion the earlier start was occasioned by the onset of the sabbath a few hours later.)

That evening, all Jesus's friends and disciples gathered in the great hall at Lazarus's castle to share the Passover feast. During the meal, Jesus spoke of the Son of Man as the true vine and referred to his disciples as the grapes on the vine (John 15:1–8). The festivities, with singing from the Psalms, lasted until late into the night.

All the household of Lazarus performed today their purifications. Lazarus himself brought the water to be used in preparing the unleavened bread, and he also went with a servant into the different rooms. The servant carried a light and Lazarus cleaned out the corners a little. It was a ceremonial performance, after which the servant men and maids swept and cleaned thoroughly. They washed and scoured likewise the vessels and other things that were to be used in preparing the unleavened bread. All this was symbolical of the cleaning out of the old leaven. Simon the Pharisee, of Bethany, had already visited Jesus. Not long ago he appeared to be approaching the state of leprosy, but now he looked more healthy. He was a timorous follower of Jesus. The man healed at the pool of Bethesda hurried to Bethany and wherever Jesus permitted himself to be seen. He told all the Pharisees he met that it was by Jesus he had been cured, consequently they determined to take Jesus into custody and make away with him.

I saw Jesus several times walking with the disciples and other friends on the Mount of Olives, while Mary, Magdalene, and other women promenaded at some distance. I saw the disciples snapping off ears from the ripe cornfields, and here and there eating fruits and berries. Jesus gave the disciples minute instructions on prayer, warned them against hypocrisy in it, and repeated to them many things that he had before said. He likewise admonished them ever to walk by uninterrupted prayer in the presence of God, his own and their Father.

YEAR 3

YEAR 3: Nisan 15, AD 31, to Nisan 14, AD 32
March 27/28, AD 31, to April 13/14, AD 32

The Passover in Lazarus's House

THE PASCHAL lamb at this Passover was not slain in the temple at so early an hour as at the time of Christ's crucifixion, when the slaughtering began at half-past twelve o'clock, the same hour at which Jesus himself was slain upon the cross. That day was a Friday and, on account of the approaching sabbath, they began earlier. Today, however, they began about three in the afternoon. The trumpets were sounded, all was in readiness, and the people entered the temple in separate groups. The rapidity and order with which everything was done were certainly admirable. Though the crowd was great, yet no one obstructed his neighbor's way. Everyone had room to come, to slaughter, and to withdraw. The four lambs for Lazarus's household were slaughtered by the four who were to preside at the tables: namely, Lazarus, Heli of Hebron, Joseph Barsabbas, and Heliachim, the latter a son of Mary Heli and brother of Mary Cleophas. The lambs were fastened to a wooden spit that had a crosspiece, which gave them the appearance of being crucified. They were roasted upright in a bake oven. The entrails, the heart, and the liver were either replaced in the lamb or fastened to the forepart of the head. Bethphage and Bethany were reckoned as part of Jerusalem, consequently the paschal lamb could be eaten in either place.

In the evening, when the 15th of Nisan began, the paschal lamb was eaten. All were girded, new sandals on their feet, each with a staff in his hand. They began by chanting the Psalms: "Blessed be the Lord God of Israel" and "Blessed be the Lord," while with raised hands they approached the table two by two and took their place opposite one another. At the table at which Jesus sat with the apostles, Heli of Hebron presided; Lazarus was at that of his own family and friends; the disciples were at a third, presided over by Heliachim; and Joseph Barsabbas did the honors at the fourth. Thirty-six disciples here ate the paschal lamb.

After the prayer, a cup of wine was presented to the master at each table. He blessed it, sipped, and passed it round, after which he washed his hands. On the table were the paschal lamb, a dish of unleavened bread, a bowl of brown sauce, another of broth, a third filled with little branches of bitter herbs, and a fourth in which the green herbs were arranged close together in an upright position, thus giving them the appearance of actual growth. The master of each table then carved the paschal lamb and served it round among the guests, who consumed it very rapidly. They cut off pieces from the closely packed herbs, steeped them in the broth, and ate them. The master then broke one of the unleavened loaves and laid a little piece of it under the tablecloth. All was done very quickly and accompanied by prayers and passages from the scriptures. The guests stood leaning against the seats. The cup went round once more, the master again washed his hands, and laid a little bunch of bitter herbs on a morsel of bread, which he steeped and ate, all the guests following his example.

The paschal lamb had to be entirely consumed. The bones were scraped clean with ivory knives, then washed and burned. After some more chanting, the guests reclined at table in due form, to eat and drink. All kinds of elegantly prepared dishes now made their appearance, and mirth and joy prevailed. At Lazarus's house all had beautiful plates from which they ate. At Jesus's last Passover feast, however, the plates consisted of disks of bread upon which were impressed various figures. They lay in the hollow places scooped out around the table.

The women likewise stood during the Passover meal, and they too were clothed as for a journey. They sang Psalms, but observed no other ceremonies. They did not carve their lamb themselves, but portions were sent to them from another table. In the side halls of the supper room a great number of poor ate their paschal lamb. Lazarus defrayed all the expenses of their meal, and gave them presents besides.

During the supper Jesus taught and explained. He delivered an exceedingly beautiful instruction on the vine, on its cultivation, on the extermination of the bad, the planting of better shoots, and the pruning of the same after every new growth. He then turned to the apostles and disciples and told them that they were the shoots of which he spoke, that the Son of Man was the true vine, and that they must remain in him; that when he would be subjected to the wine press they must continue to make known the knowledge of the true vine, namely, himself, and plant all the vineyards with the same. The guests did not separate till very late in the night. All were deeply impressed and joyful.

Joseph Barsabbas was, with the exception of Andrew, the eldest disciple. He was married, and his family lived in the pastoral state in a row of houses between Michmethath and Iscariot. Heliachim also was married, and lived in the pastoral state on the field of Ginea. He was much older than Jesus. Jesus seldom sent these disciples into this region.

The Rich Glutton and Poor Lazarus

Wednesday, March 28, AD 31 (Nisan 15)

Early this morning Jesus and the disciples went to the temple. They stood among the crowd from sunrise until about eleven o'clock. Then there was a pause in the reception of the offerings. Jesus went up to the great teacher's chair in the court before the sanctuary. A large crowd gathered around, including many Pharisees and also the man who had been healed at the pool of Bethesda. The Pharisees accused Jesus of breaking the sabbath because he had healed this man on the sabbath. Jesus replied that the sabbath was made for humanity, not humanity for the sabbath. He then recounted the parable of the sick man and poor Lazarus. This so outraged the Pharisees that they pressed around and sent for the temple guards to take Jesus into custody. At the height of the uproar, it suddenly grew dark. Jesus looked up to heaven and said: "Father, render testimony to thy Son!" A loud noise like thunder resounded and a heavenly voice proclaimed: "This is my beloved Son in whom I am well pleased!" Jesus's enemies were terrified. The disciples then escorted Jesus from the temple to safety. They then proceeded northward from Jerusalem until they reached Ramah, where they stayed the night at an inn.

THE FEAST began very early in the temple, which was opened soon after midnight, the whole place ablaze with lamps. The people came before daybreak with their thank-offerings, consisting of all kinds of birds and animals, which were received and inspected by the priests. Besides these, there were offerings of money, stuffs, corn, oil, etc.

When morning dawned, Jesus, the disciples, Lazarus with his household, and the women, went to the temple where Jesus remained standing with his own party among the crowd. Many psalms were sung, the musicians played, sacrifices were offered, and a benediction given which all received on their knees. The people entered in bands, the gates were closed behind them, and after they had sacrificed, they left before another band entered, that no confusion might arise. Numbers, especially strangers, went to the benediction given in the synagogues of the city where there were singing and reading of the Law. Toward noon, about eleven o'clock, there was a pause in the reception of offerings. Many of the people had already dispersed. Some went to the kitchens in the women's porch where the flesh of the victims was prepared for eating, which took place in the dining halls, in which whole families were assembled. The holy women had returned earlier to Bethany.

Up to the moment at which the offerings ceased to be received, Jesus had remained standing with his party; but when the corridors were again thrown open, he went to the great teacher's chair which stood in the temple in the court before the sanctuary. A numerous crowd assembled around him, among them many Pharisees, also the man who had been cured at the pool of Bethesda. For two whole days he had related what he knew of Jesus, frequently making use of the expression that whoever could do such works as he, must be the Son of God. The Pharisees had, it is true, forbidden him to speak, but to no purpose. As on the day before Jesus had taught very boldly in the temple, the Pharisees feared that he might bring them into still greater disrepute before the people; and as all their colleagues from the country around, gathered here for the feast, brought forward complaints and lies against Jesus, they determined to seize the first opportunity to take him prisoner and pass sentence upon him. When therefore Jesus began to teach, many of them closed around him, interrupting his discourse with innumerable objections and reproaches. They asked him why he did not eat the paschal lamb with them in the temple, and whether he had today offered a thanksgiving sacrifice. Jesus referred them to the masters of the feast who had discharged that duty for him. Then they repeated the old charges, that his disciples observed not the customary usages, that they ate with unwashed hands and stole corn and fruit along the roadside, that he was never seen offering sacrifice, that six days were for labor and the seventh for rest, and yet he had healed that man on the sabbath, and that he was a sabbath-breaker. Jesus answered their charges in severe words. Of sacrifice, he said again that the Son of Man was himself a sacrifice, and that they dishonored the sacrifice by their covetousness and their slanders against their fellow men. God, Jesus went on to say, did not desire burnt offerings, but contrite hearts; their sacrifices would come to an end, but the sabbath would continue to exist. It would indeed exist, but for man's utility, for man's salvation. The sabbath was made for man, and not man for the sabbath.

Then the Pharisees questioned Jesus on the subject of the parable of poor Lazarus which he had recently related. They asked in ridicule how he knew that story so well, how he knew what Lazarus, Abraham, and the rich man had said. Had he been with the rich man in hell? Was he not ashamed of himself to impose such things upon the people? Jesus again took up this parable and taught upon it, reproaching them with their avarice, their cruelty to the poor, their self-satisfied observance of empty forms and customs, along with their total want of charity. He applied the history of the rich glutton entirely to themselves. That history is true. The glutton was well-known until his death, which was a frightful one. I saw again that the rich glutton and poor Lazarus really existed and that by their death they had become well-known throughout the country. But they did not live in Jerusalem, where later on their dwellings so-called were pointed out to pilgrims. They died in Jesus's early years, and they were much spoken of in pious families at that time. The city in which they dwelt was called Aram, or Amthar, and lay in the mountains west of the Sea of Galilee. I no longer know the whole history in detail, but I still remember this much: The rich man was very wealthy. He lived high, held the first position among his fellows, and was a distinguished Pharisee, very strict in the outward observance of the Law; but he was, on the other hand, extremely severe and merciless toward the poor. I saw him harshly reproving the poor of the place who applied to him, as to their chief magistrate, for help and support. There was a poor, wretched man in the place called Lazarus. He was full of misery and covered with ulcers, but at the same time humble and patient. Hungering for bread, he had himself carried to the house of the rich man, in order to plead the cause of the poor so rudely rebuffed. The rich man was reclining at table carousing, but Lazarus was harshly repulsed as one unclean. He lay at the gate begging for only the crumbs that fell from the rich man's table, but no one gave him to eat. The dogs, more merciful, licked his sores,[E18] which means that the pagans were more merciful than the Jews. After that Lazarus died a most beautiful and edifying death. The rich man also died, but his death was frightful. A voice was afterward heard proceeding from his tomb, and the whole country was full of the report of it.

Jesus having ended the parable by the relation of hidden truths unknown to the rest of men, the Pharisees ridiculed him, asking whether he had been with Lazarus in Abraham's bosom to hear all that talk. As the rich glutton had been a very strict, pharisaical observer of customs, it was especially irritating to the Pharisees to have this parable applied to themselves, also because it was therein implied that they did not listen to Moses and the prophets. Jesus said to them in plain words that whoever would not hear him, heard not the prophets, for they spoke of him; whoever would not hear him, heard not Moses, for he spoke of him; and even if the dead arose, they would not believe their testimony of him. But the dead should indeed arise and witness to him (this happened the next year and in that same temple, at the time of Jesus's death), and yet they, the Pharisees, would not believe. They themselves, he continued, should one day arise, and he would judge them. All that he did, his Father did in him even to the raising of the dead. Jesus spoke also of John and his testimony, of which, however, he had no need, since his own works bore a still more convincing testimony of his mission, and his Father himself bore witness to it. But they knew not God. They wanted to be saved by the scriptures, and yet they kept not the commandments. However, he would not, as he said, bring a charge against them, for Moses, who had written of him and whom they would not believe, would do that.

Jesus went on teaching many things in the midst of repeated interruptions. At last the Pharisees became so enraged that they set up a shout, pressed against him, and sent for the guard of the temple to take him into custody. At this moment, it suddenly grew dark and, when the uproar was at its height, Jesus looked up to heaven and said: "Father, render testimony to thy Son!" Instantly a dark cloud covered the heavens, a loud noise like a thunderclap resounded, and I heard a piercing voice proclaiming through the edifice: "This is my beloved Son in whom I take my delight!" Jesus's enemies were utterly dumbfounded, and gazed upward in terror. But the disciples, who were standing in a semicircle behind Jesus, began to make a move and closed round him. Thus escorted, he went without further molestation through the now-opening crowd, out by the western side of the temple, and out of the city by the corner gate near Lazarus's house. They proceeded a little further northward to Ramah.

The disciples had not heard the voice, only the thunder, for their hour was not yet come; but several of the most enraged of the Pharisees heard it. When it was again clear, they made no comment upon what had just taken place, but hurried out and sent people to seize Jesus. But he was not to be found, and the Pharisees were then incensed against themselves for being so taken by surprise as to allow him to escape.

In his instructions of these days both in the temple and at Bethany to the disciples and the crowd there assembled, Jesus alluded several times to the obligation of following him and of bearing the cross after him. "He that will save his life, shall lose it; and he that will lose his life for my sake shall find it. For what doth it profit a man if he gain the whole world, and suffer the loss of his own soul? Whoever shall be ashamed of me before this adulterous and sinful generation, of him shall the Son of Man be ashamed when he shall come in the glory of his Father, to render to everyone according to his works." Jesus added that there were some among his hearers who would not see death until they should see the kingdom of God come in all its power. At these words they mocked him. I cannot say now what Jesus meant by this. The words of the Gospel always sound to me like the mere headings of the principal doctrines, for Jesus's instructions were much more extended. His discourses that often occupied hours may there be read in a couple of minutes.

Stephen was already in communication with the disciples. On the feast upon which Jesus healed the man of Bethsaida, he became acquainted with John, and after that he went round a great deal with Lazarus. He was very slender, of an amiable disposition, and a scholar in the Holy Law. He was at this time in Bethany with several other disciples from Jerusalem, and heard Jesus's teachings.

Jesus in Ataroth and Hadad-Rimmon

Thursday, March 29, AD 31 (Nisan 16)

Leaving Ramah early this morning, Jesus and the disciples made their way to Thanat-Shiloh. Here Jesus was given a warm reception. All the Pharisees were away in Jerusalem. Today, Pontius Pilate issued an order forbidding all Galileans from leaving the city without his permission.

FROM Ramah, Jesus went with the disciples to Thanat-Shiloh near Sichar. As all the Pharisees were away at the feast in Jerusalem, Jesus was received very joyfully in Thanat. Only the aged and the infirm, the women and little children remained home from the feast, also the old shepherds with their herds. In Ramah and Thanat I saw the people going processionally through the cornfields, cutting off bunches of grain, and carrying them on a pole into their homes and synagogues. Here and there on the fields and likewise in Thanat-Shiloh, where he stayed overnight, Jesus taught and made allusion to his approaching end. He called all to himself to seek consolation, and spoke of the sacrifice most pleasing to God, namely, a contrite heart.

Friday, March 30, AD 31 (Nisan 17)

Jesus and the disciples left Thanat-Shiloh and went on to Ataroth, where Jesus taught on a hill outside of the town and healed the sick. Later, after the sabbath had begun, Jesus taught in the synagogue. During the course of the evening, he healed a widow crippled at the waist for eighteen years. She was used to going bent double, almost touching the ground. Jesus summoned her to him and laid his hand on her back, saying: "Woman, be freed from your infirmity!" She rose up straightway and gave thanks to God. An aged Pharisee, who was also a cripple and for this reason had not gone to Jerusalem, presided over the synagogue. When the healing of the crippled widow took place, he turned to the people and said: "There are six days upon which we may work. Come then and be healed, but not on the sabbath." Jesus replied: "You hypocrite! Does not everyone loose his ox or ass from the manger on the sabbath and lead it to water? And shall not this woman, a daughter of Abraham, be loosed from the bond in which Satan has bound her for eighteen years?" (Luke 13:10–17).

From Thanat-Shiloh Jesus went to Ataroth, north of the mountain near Meroz, where the Pharisees once brought him a dead man to be healed. The place was about four hours north of Thanat-Shiloh. Jesus arrived at Ataroth toward evening. He taught on a hill outside the city, to which a crowd of the aged and the sick, of women and children, followed him. All the sick, and others that were afraid before the Pharisees, now made their appearance imploring help and consolation. The Pharisees and Sadducees of Ataroth were so exasperated against Jesus that once, when they heard that he was in their neighborhood, they caused the gates of the city to be closed. Jesus taught in very severe terms, though at the same time very lovingly, and warned the poor people against the wickedness of the Pharisees. He continued to speak in plain terms of his mission, of his heavenly Father, of the persecution that would soon overtake him, of the resurrection of the dead, of the judgment, and of following him. He cured many sick: lame, blind, dropsical, sick children, and women afflicted with an issue of blood.

The disciples had prepared for their Master an inn outside Ataroth near a simple-hearted schoolteacher, an aged man, who dwelt there among the gardens. Jesus and his disciples washed their feet, took some refreshments, and repaired to the synagogue in Ataroth to celebrate the sabbath. There were assembled many who had come hither from the country around, as well as all those that had been cured. An aged Pharisee, a cripple, who had not gone to Jerusalem, presided over the synagogue. He put on great airs, though to the people he was rather an object of ridicule. The scripture lessons of the day consisted of passages referring to legal impurity contracted by childbirth, to leprosy, to Elisha's multiplication of the bread of the first fruits and the new corn, and to Naaman's cure.

Jesus had been teaching a long time when he turned to where the women were standing, and called to him a poor, crippled widow. Her daughters had conducted her into the synagogue and put her into the place she usually occupied. It never entered her mind to ask for help, although she had been sick eighteen years. She was crippled at the waist. When she walked, the upper part of her person was so bent toward the earth that she could almost have walked on her hands. Jesus addressed her as her daughters were leading her to him: "Woman, be freed from thy infirmity!" and he laid his hand on her back.[E19] She rose up straight as a candle, and began to praise God: "Blessed be the Lord God of Israel!" Then she cast herself at Jesus's feet, and all present praised God.

But the deformed old rogue was angry that such a miracle had taken place in Ataroth during the time of his sway. Not daring to expose himself to what might follow from a direct attack upon Jesus, he turned to the people and, with an air of great authority, began to find fault and say: "There are six days upon which we may labor. Come upon them and be healed, but not upon the sabbath day!" Jesus responded: "Thou hypocrite! Does not every one of you loose his ox or his ass from the manger on the sabbath day, and lead it to water? And shall not this woman, a daughter of Abraham, be loosed from the bond in which for eighteen years Satan has bound her?" The crippled Pharisee and his adherents were confounded, while the people praised God and rejoiced at the miracles.

It was truly affecting to behold the daughters and some lads belonging to her family expressing their joy around the cured woman. Yes, all the inhabitants rejoiced, for she was wealthy, beloved and esteemed in the city. It was laughable, though at the same time pitiable, to see the crippled Pharisee, instead of craving relief for himself, raging over the cure of the pious deformed woman. Jesus went on with his instruction upon the sabbath, and spoke in as severe terms as he had used in the temple on the occasion of their reproaching him with the cure of the man at the pool of Bethesda. He stayed overnight with the schoolmaster outside of Ataroth.

Saturday, March 31, AD 31 **(*Nisan 18*)**

After healing many people yesterday in Ataroth, Jesus was invited to the home of the widow whom he had healed the evening before. Later, some of the disciples were spotted plucking ears of corn as they walked. This was reported to the Pharisees and led, a few days later (Nisan 23/24), to a renewed attack on Jesus in Dothan and Capernaum (Matthew 12:1–2). After the sabbath had ended, Jesus and the disciples went to Lazarus' estate near Ginea and stayed there overnight.

The next day visited the house of the cured woman, who fed numbers of the poor and gave large alms. After that he closed the sabbath services in the synagogue, and went forward a couple of hours to an inn near Ginea.

(Follow Map 29)

Sunday, April 1, AD 31 **(*Nisan 19*)**

Jesus and the disciples journeyed to Hadad-Rimmon, where he healed the sick and taught concerning the resurrection from the dead, the last judgment, and God's mercy. Today it was learned that Pontius Pilate had ordered Judas of Gamala and many of his followers to be put to death. This was the way that Pilate took revenge for the collapse of the tower and wall that had occurred at the instigation of Herod Antipas two months before.

On the following day he and the disciples journeyed about eight hours northward through the valley of Esdrelon and across the brook Kishon to Hadad-Rimmon, leaving Endor, Jezreel, and Nain on the right. Rimon lay, at most, one hour east of Megiddo, not far from Jezreel and Nain, about three hours west of Tabor, and to the southwest about the same distance from Nazareth. It was quite an important and populous city, for a highway both military and commercial ran through it from Tiberias to the seacoast. Jesus put up at an inn outside the city. He taught all along the way and, here and there, cured shepherds and other poor sick. The subject of these instructions was the love of the neighbor. He commanded his hearers to love the Samaritans and all men. He likewise explained the parable of the compassionate Samaritan.

In Hadad-Rimmon Jesus taught chiefly upon the resurrection of the dead and judgment. He healed the sick. A great concourse of people came to his instructions. They had been in Jerusalem, but had reached it only the day after Jesus had left. The apostles and disciples taught in the surrounding places.

The day after Jesus's departure from Jerusalem, Pilate had forbidden the Galilean zealots to leave the city under

Map 29: Second Journey to Ornithopolis

April 1–25, AD 31

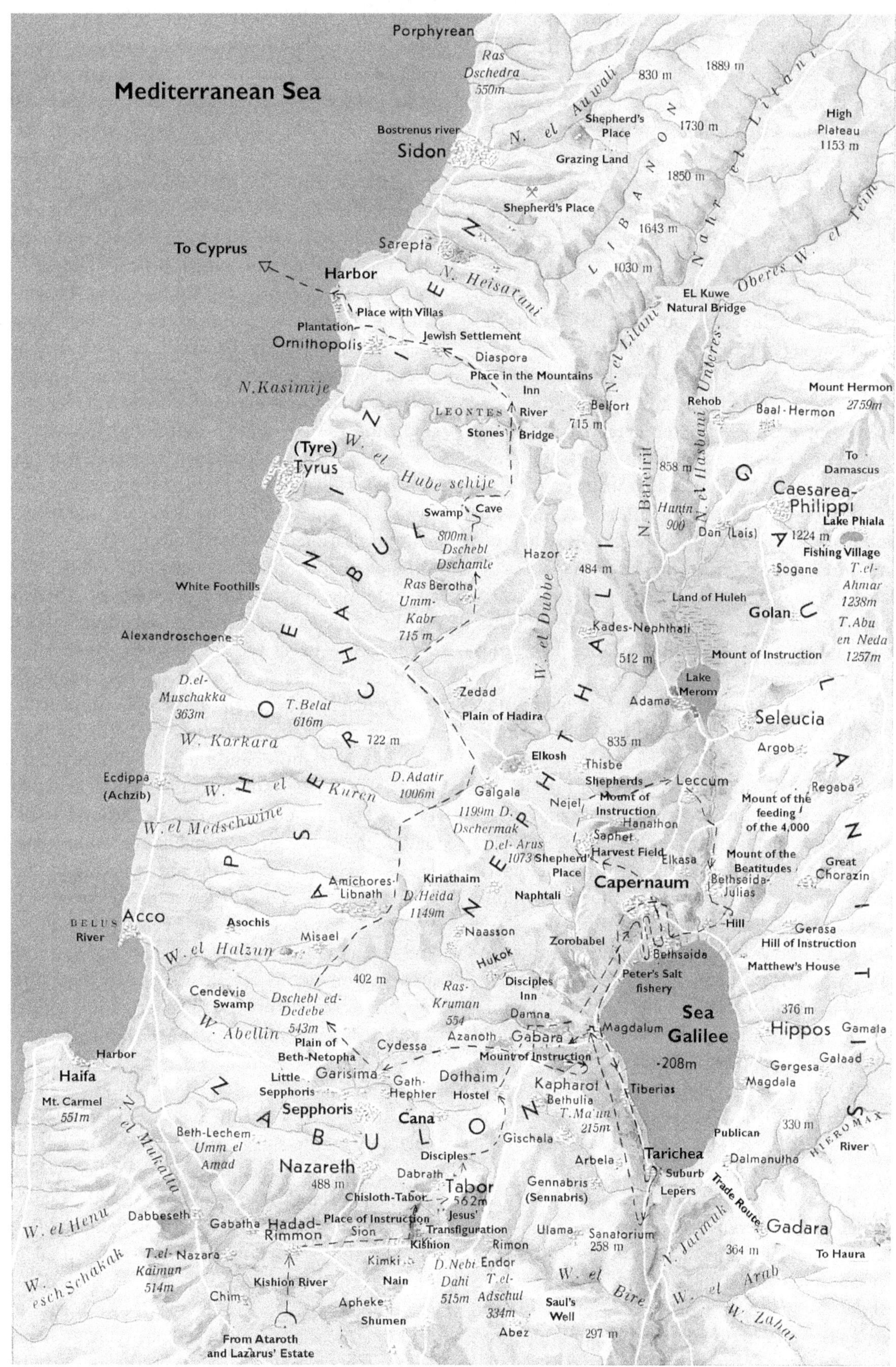

Hadad-Rimmon—Tabor—Dothaim—Capernaum—Bethsaida—Leccum—Bethsaida-Julias
Capernaum—Tarichea—Mount of Instruction near Gabara—Kapharot—Garisima
Dschebl ed-Dedebe—Dschebl Dschamle—Ornithopolis—Harbor

pain of death, although they were anxious to do so. Many of them had been arrested as hostages. Shortly after, Pilate set the latter at liberty and gave all of them permission to make their offerings at the temple and leave the city. He himself toward noon made preparations for his own departure to Caesarea. The Galileans under arrest were no less surprised than delighted at their restoration to freedom. They hurried to the temple to offer their propitiatory sacrifice, as they had incurred guilt and had not yet offered sacrifice for the same.

It was customary on this day to bring all kinds of gifts to the temple. Many purchased an animal and brought it to be sacrificed, while others (and these were the most numerous) sold such objects as they could do without and put the proceeds into the box destined for such offerings. The wealthy supplied their poorer neighbors with the means to make their offerings. I saw three different boxes for this purpose, and by each of them instructions were being given, while some of the worshippers were busy with their devotions. Others were out in the place of slaughter with their animals for sacrifice. The temple was tolerably crowded, yet not to overflowing. I saw in different places little groups of Israelites bowed down in adoration, or standing upright, or prostrate on the ground, their heads enveloped in prayer mantles.

Judas the Golanite was standing near one of the alms boxes surrounded by his followers, the Galileans whom Pilate had imprisoned and afterward released. Some of them were mere dupes, others crafty tools of the Herodians. Many of them were from Gamala, but a still greater number were from Thirza, its environs, and other places infested by Herodians. Now when these people had made the offerings of money and were lost in their devotions, turning neither to the right nor to the left, I saw about ten men stealing upon them from all sides. As they approached, they drew forth from under their mantles three-edged swords about four feet in length, with which they stabbed the nearest of the adorers. Then arose a frightful cry. The defenseless people fled confusedly in all directions, pursued by those that I had seen kneeling and enveloped in their mantles. They were Romans in disguise, and they struck down and stabbed all whom they met. Many of them pressed forward to the alms boxes, and tore out the bags of money; still they did not take all, a good part remained therein. The tumult was so great that a considerable amount of money was thrown about the temple. The Romans then hurried to the place of slaughter, and stabbed the Galileans there. I saw these Roman soldiers issuing from all corners of the edifice, even jumping in and out of the windows. As when the cry of murder was raised, all that were in the temple ran in confusion to make their escape, many harmless people belonging to Jerusalem were killed in the tumult, as well as some of the poor people that sold foods in the forecourt and the recesses of the walls. I saw some Galileans in a dark passage trying to save themselves. They had overpowered some of the Roman soldiers and wrested from them their arms. And now came Judas the Golanite into the same passage from the opposite entrance. He too was attempting to make his escape. The other Galileans took him for a Roman and pierced him with their weapons, in spite of his cries that he was Judas, for the confusion was so great, owing to the similarity of clothing between the murderers and their victims, that they indiscriminately attacked everyone they met. The massacre lasted about an hour. The inhabitants, armed with weapons, now began to crowd to the temple, whereupon the Roman soldiers hurriedly withdrew and shut themselves up in the fortress of Antonia. Pilate had already gone away, the garrison had taken possession of all points in the city capable of being defended, and all avenues of communication were seized and cut off.

I looked down the dizzy height on one side of the temple into the narrow streets below, and there I beheld frantic women and children running from house to house. They had just received the news of the murder of husbands and fathers, for many of the poor people that dwelt in the neighborhood of the temple, hucksters and day laborers, had been slain in the melee. The confusion in the temple was frightful, and the people rushed out by every loophole. Elders and superintendents, armed men and Pharisees—all came pouring out. Around were corpses, blood, and scattered coins, while the wounded and dying lay on the ground groaning and weltering in their blood. Soon appeared upon the scene the relatives of those belonging to Jerusalem that had been accidentally murdered, and lamentations, cries of indignation, rage, and anguish arose on all sides. The Pharisees and high priests were terrified, for the temple had been frightfully profaned. The priests dared not enter for fear of defilement from contamination with the dead. The feast was consequently interrupted.

I saw the corpses of the massacred Jerusalemites enveloped in winding-sheets, laid on biers, and borne away by their weeping relatives; those of the others were removed by inferior slaves. Everything else—cattle, eatables, movables of all kinds—had to be left lying in the temple, because all was now unclean. Everyone retired, excepting the guards and the workmen. The victims counted more in number than those of the overthrow of the building at the construction of the aqueduct. With the exception of the innocent people of Jerusalem, the massacred were, for the most part, adherents of Judas the Golanite, who had declaimed so zealously against the imperial tax and the contribution for the aqueduct levied, contrary to the privileges of the temple, upon the money offered in sacrifice. It was these people who had so boldly inveighed against Pilate's proposals, and who had also slain some Roman soldiers in the fray that had then taken place. Pilate, in attacking them unarmed, avenged the death of his soldiers, as well as wreaked his vengeance upon Herod for the latter's malicious overthrow of the tower. There were among the victims many from Tiberias, Golan, Upper Galilee, and Caesarea-Philippi.

Monday, April 2, AD 31 (Nisan 20)

Today Jesus spoke before a large crowd in Hadad-Rimmon.

The Transfiguration on Mount Tabor

Tuesday, April 3, AD 31 (Nisan 21)

From the inn at Hadad-Rimmon where he had been staying, Jesus went to Chisloth at the foot of Mount Tabor. Here he taught and healed. Around three o'clock in the afternoon, he went with Peter, John, and James the Greater up Mount Tabor. Around midnight, the Transfiguration took place (Matthew 17:1–8).

FROM the inn near Hadad-Rimmon, Jesus went with some of the disciples eastward to Chisloth-Tabor, which lay at the foot of Tabor toward the south, about three hours from Rimon. On the way thither he was joined, from time to time, by the disciples that were returning from their mission. At Chisloth another great multitude of travelers who had come from Jerusalem again gathered around him. He taught, and then healed the sick. In the afternoon he sent the disciples right and left around the mountain, to teach and to cure. Taking with him Peter, John, and James the Greater, he proceeded up the mountain by a footpath. They spent nearly two hours in ascent, for Jesus paused frequently at the different caves and places made memorable by the sojourn of the prophets. There he explained to them manifold mysteries and united with them in prayer. They had no provisions, for Jesus had forbidden them to bring any, saying that they should be satiated to overflowing. The view from the summit of the mountain extended far and wide. On it was a large open place surrounded by a wall and shade trees. The ground was covered with aromatic herbs and sweet-scented flowers. Hidden in a rock was a reservoir, which upon the turning of a spigot poured forth water sparkling and very cold. The apostles washed Jesus's feet and then their own, and refreshed themselves. Then Jesus withdrew with them into a deep grotto behind a rock which formed, as it were, a door to the cave. It was like the grotto on the Mount of Olives, to which Jesus so often retired to pray, and from it a descent led down into a vault.

Jesus here continued his instructions. He spoke of kneeling to pray, and told them that they should henceforth pray earnestly with hands raised on high. He taught them also the Lord's Prayer, interspersing the several petitions with verses from the Psalms; and these they recited half-kneeling, half-sitting around him in a semicircle. Jesus knelt opposite to them, leaning on a projecting rock, and from time to time interrupted the prayer with instructions wonderfully profound and sweet upon the mysteries of Creation and Redemption. His words were extraordinarily loving, like those of one inspired, and the disciples were wholly inebriated by them. In the beginning of his instruction, he had said that he would show them who he was, they should behold him glorified, that they might not waver in faith when his enemies would mock and maltreat him, when they should behold him in death shorn of all glory.

The sun had set and it was dark, but the apostles had not remarked the fact, so entrancing were Jesus's words and bearing. He became brighter and brighter, and apparitions of angelic spirits hovered around him. Peter saw them, for he interrupted Jesus with the question: "Master, what does this mean?" Jesus answered: "They serve me!" Peter, quite out of himself, stretched forth his hands, exclaiming: "Master, are we not here? We will serve thee in all things!" Jesus began again his instructions, and along with the angelic apparitions flowed alternate streams of delicious perfumes, of celestial delights and contentment over the apostles. Jesus meantime continued to shine with ever-increasing splendor, until he became as if transparent. The circle around them was so lighted up in the darkness of night that each little plant could be distinguished on the green sod as if in clear daylight. The three apostles were so penetrated, so ravished that, when the light reached a certain degree, they covered their heads, prostrated on the ground, and there remained lying.

It was about twelve o'clock at night when I beheld this glory at its height. I saw a shining pathway reaching from heaven to earth, and on it angelic spirits of different choirs, all in constant movement. Some were small, but of perfect form; others were merely faces peeping forth from the glancing light; some were in priestly garb, while others looked like warriors. Each had some special characteristic different from that of the others, and from each radiated some special refreshment, strength, delight, and light. They were in constant action, constant movement.

The apostles lay, ravished in ecstasy rather than in sleep, prostrate on their faces. Then I saw three shining figures approaching Jesus in the light. Their coming appeared perfectly natural. It was like that of one who steps from the darkness of night into a place brilliantly illuminated. Two of them appeared in a more definite form, a form more like the corporeal. They addressed Jesus and conversed with him. They were Moses and Elijah.[E20] The third apparition spoke no word. It was more ethereal, more spiritual. That was Malachi.

I heard Moses and Elijah greet Jesus, and I heard him speaking to them of his Passion and of Redemption. Their being together appeared perfectly simple and natural. Moses and Elijah did not look aged nor decrepit as when they left the earth. They were, on the contrary, in the bloom of youth. Moses—taller, graver, and more majestic than Elijah—had on his forehead something like two projecting bumps. He was clothed in a long garment. He looked like a resolute man, like one that could govern with strictness, though at the same time he bore the impress of purity, rectitude, and simplicity. He told Jesus how rejoiced he was to see him who had led himself and his people out of Egypt, and who was now once more about to redeem them. He referred to the numerous types of the Savior in his own time, and uttered deeply significant words upon the paschal lamb and the Lamb of God. Elijah was quite the opposite of Moses. He appeared to be more refined, more lovable, of a sweeter disposition. But both Elijah and Moses were very dissimilar from the apparition of Malachi, for in the former one could trace something human, something earthly in form and countenance; yes, there was even a family likeness between them. Malachi, however, looked quite different. There was in his appearance something supernatural. He looked like an angel, like the personification of strength and repose. He was more tranquil, more spiritual than the others.

Jesus spoke with them of all the sufferings he had endured up to the present, and of all that still awaited him. He related the history of his Passion in detail, point by point. Elijah and Moses frequently expressed their emotion and joy. Their words were full of sympathy and consolation, of reverence for the Savior, and of the uninterrupted praises of God. They constantly referred to the types of the mysteries of which Jesus was speaking, and praised God for having from all eternity dealt in mercy toward his people. But Malachi kept silence.

The disciples raised their heads, gazed long upon the glory of Jesus, and beheld Moses, Elijah, and Malachi. When in describing his Passion Jesus came to his exaltation on the cross, he extended his arms at the words: "So shall the Son of Man be lifted up!" His face was turned toward the south, he was entirely penetrated with light, and his robe flashed with a bluish white gleam. He, the prophets, and the three apostles—all were raised above the earth.

And now the prophets separated from Jesus, Elijah and Moses vanishing toward the east, Malachi westward into the darkness. Then Peter, ravished with joy, exclaimed: "Master, it is good for us to be here! Let us make here three tabernacles: one for thee, one for Moses, and one for Elijah!" Peter meant that they had need of no other heaven, for where they were was so sweet and blessed. By the tabernacles, he meant places of rest and honor, the dwellings of the saints. He said this in the delirium of his joy, in his state of ecstasy, without knowing what he was saying.

When they had returned to their usual waking state, a cloud of white light descended upon them, like the morning dew floating over the meadows. I saw the heavens open above Jesus and the vision of the most holy Trinity, God the Father seated on a throne. He looked like an aged priest, and at his feet were crowds of angels and celestial figures. A stream of light descended upon Jesus, and the apostles heard above them, like a sweet, gentle sighing, a voice pronouncing the words: "This is my beloved Son in whom I am well pleased. Hear ye him!"

Fear and trembling fell upon them. Overcome by the sense of their own human weakness and the glory they beheld, they cast themselves face downward on the earth. They trembled in the presence of Jesus, in whose favor they had just heard the testimony of his heavenly Father.

Wednesday, April 4, AD 31 (Nisan 22)

Early in the morning, Jesus and the three disciples came down the mountain and met up again with the other disciples. There then followed the healing of the possessed boy whom the disciples had been unable to heal (Mark 9:14–27). After healing several more people, Jesus and the disciples continued on their way until they reached Dothaim. As they walked, the three disciples who had witnessed the transfiguration asked Jesus questions concerning what he had said about the resurrection of the Son of Man and the words in the scripture about the resurrection of Elijah. Jesus answered them as recorded in Matthew 17:9–13 and Mark 9:9–13. He also taught the disciples as stated in Luke 12:22–53. In Dothaim, they met up with some other disciples who had already arrived. As these listened to the account of the healing of the possessed child whom the disciples could not heal, the question arose as to why they had been unable to do so. Jesus replied as found in Matthew 17:19–21. That evening, Jesus and the disciples were guests at a meal given by the Pharisees, who attacked them for breaking the sabbath, that is, for plucking ears of corn on the sabbath. Jesus replied in the words given in Matthew 12:2–8.

Jesus went to them, touched them, and said: "Arise, and

fear not!" They arose, and beheld Jesus alone. It was now approaching three in the morning. The gray dawn was glimmering in the heavens and the damp vapors were hanging over the country around the foot of the mountain. The apostles were silent and intimidated. Jesus told them that he had allowed them to behold the Transfiguration of the Son of Man in order to strengthen their faith, that they might not waver when they saw him delivered for the sins of the world into the hands of evildoers, that they might not be scandalized when they witnessed his humiliation, and that they might at that time strengthen their weaker brethren. He again alluded to the faith of Peter who, enlightened by God, had been the first of his followers to penetrate the mystery of his divinity, and he spoke of the rock upon which he was going to build his church. Then they united again in prayer, and by the morning light descended the northwestern side of the mountain.

While going down, Jesus talked of what had taken place, and impressed upon the disciples that they should tell no one of the vision they had seen, until the Son of Man should have risen from the dead. This command struck them. They became more timid in Jesus's presence, more reverential, and since the words: "Hear ye him!" they thought with sorrow and anguish upon their past doubts and want of faith. But as daylight advanced and they continued their descent, the wonderful impression they had received began to wear off, and they imparted to one another their surprise at the expression: "Until the Son of Man is risen from the dead." "What does that mean?" they asked one another, though they did not venture to question Jesus upon it.

They had not yet reached the foot of the mountain when Jesus was met by people coming to seek him with their sick. He healed and consoled. But the people were struck with awe at the sight of him, for there was something unusual, something supernatural and glorious in his appearance. A little lower down the mount he found assembled a crowd of people, the disciples whom he had sent out into the environs the day before, and several doctors of the Law. These people were returning home from the feast. They had met the disciples at their encampment and accompanied them thither, to wait for Jesus. Jesus saw that they and the disciples were having some kind of dispute. When they perceived Jesus, they ran forward to meet and salute him, but they were amazed at his extraordinary appearance, for the rays of his glorification were still around him. The disciples guessed from the manner of the three apostles, who followed Jesus more gravely, more timidly than usual, that something wonderful must have happened to him.

When now Jesus inquired into the subject of dispute, a man from Amthar—a city on the Galilean mountain chain, the scene of the history of Lazarus and the rich glutton—stepped forth from the crowd, threw himself on his knees before Jesus, and implored him to help his only son. The boy was a lunatic and possessed of a mute devil, who hurled him sometimes into fire, sometimes into water, and laid hold of him so roughly that he cried out with pain. The father had taken him to the disciples when they were in Amthar, but they had not been able to help him, and this was now the subject of dispute between them and the doctors of the Law. Jesus addressed them: "O unbelieving and perverse generation, how long shall I be with you? How long shall I suffer you?" and he commanded the father to bring the boy to him. The father now led the boy up by the hand. During the journey he had been obliged to carry him like a sheep flung round his neck. The child may have been between nine and ten years old. As soon as he saw Jesus, he began to tear himself frightfully, and the demon cast him to the earth, where he writhed in fearful contortions, foam pouring from his mouth. Jesus ordered him to be quiet, and he lay still. Then he asked the father how long the boy had suffered in this way. He answered: "From early childhood. Ah, if thou canst, help us! Have mercy on us!" Jesus responded: "If thou canst believe, for all things are possible to him that believes!" And the father, weeping, exclaimed: "Lord, I do believe! Help thou my unbelief!"

At these words uttered in a loud voice, the people, who had remained timidly standing at a distance, approached. Jesus raised his hand in a threatening manner toward the boy and said: "Thou mute and impure spirit, I command thee to go out of him and never again to return into him!" The spirit cried out frightfully through the boy's mouth, convulsed him violently, and went out, leaving him pale and motionless like one dead.[E21] They tried in vain to restore consciousness, and many from among the crowd called out: "He is dead! He is really dead!" But Jesus took him by the hand, raised him up well and joyous, and restored him to his father with some words of admonition. The latter thanked Jesus with tears and canticles of praise, and all the lookers-on blessed the majesty of God. This scene took place about a quarter of an hour eastward of that little place near Tabor where Jesus, the year before, had healed the leprous property holder, the one that had sent his little servant boy after him.

Jesus then proceeded on his way with the disciples. They passed near Cana, crossed the valley of the baths of Bethulia, and reached the little town of Dothaim, three hours from Capernaum. They took mostly the byways, in order to escape the multitudes returning in troops from

Jerusalem. Jesus and his disciples went in bands. Jesus walked sometimes alone, sometimes with this or that band. The apostles who had been witnesses of his transfiguration approached their Master on the way, and questioned him upon the words: "Until the Son of Man is risen from the dead," which were still for them a subject of reflection and discussion. They argued: "The scribes indeed say that Elijah must come again before the resurrection." Jesus responded: "Elijah indeed shall come and restore all things. But I say to you that Elijah is already come, and they knew him not but have done unto him whatsoever they had a mind, as it was written of him. So also the Son of Man shall suffer from them." Jesus said several other things, and the apostles understood that he was speaking of John the Baptist.

When all the disciples were again reunited around Jesus in the inn at Dothaim, they asked him why it was not in their power to free the lunatic boy from the demon. Jesus answered: "Because of your unbelief. For, amen I say to you, if you have faith as a grain of mustard seed, you shall say to this mountain, 'Remove from hence hither,' and it shall remove, and nothing shall be impossible to you. But this kind is not cast out but by prayer and fasting." Then he instructed them upon what was necessary to overcome the demon's resistance. Faith gives to action life and power, while at the same time it derives its own strength from fasting and prayer. He who fasts and prays deprives the demon that he wishes to cast out of his power, which power the exorciser attracts, as it were, into himself.

Jesus in Capernaum and its Environs

Thursday, April 5, AD 31 (Nisan 23)

This morning, after teaching in Dothaim, Jesus made his way to Capernaum. There he and the disciples were guests at a feast in honor of their homecoming. Some Pharisees were also present. These Pharisees again accused Jesus of sanctioning the violation of long-established customs, charging that the disciples had broken the sabbath, plucked corn, neglected hand-washing, and so on.

JESUS went from Dothaim by a direct route to Capernaum, where the Feast of the Homecoming was solemnly celebrated. Jesus and the disciples were invited to an entertainment in which some Pharisees also took part. When about to take their places at table, the disciple Manahem from Coreae presented himself before Jesus, and with him a young man of good education from Jericho. Jesus had already rejected the latter, but he again requested to be received among the disciples. He had applied to Manahem, because he knew him. He had large possessions in Samaria, which Jesus had told him some time before to renounce. Having arranged his affairs and divided his property among his relatives, he now returned a second time to Jesus. He had, however, reserved one estate for his own support, about which he was extremely solicitous. It was for this reason that Jesus refused his request, and he went away displeased. The Pharisees were scandalized, for they were in favor of the young man. They reproached Jesus, saying that he was destitute of charity; that he talked of the insupportable burdens imposed by the Pharisees, and yet he himself laid on others burdens equally insupportable. This young man, they continued, was educated, but Jesus favored only the ignorant. He refused men the necessaries of life, and yet sanctioned the violation of long-established customs. Once again they brought forward their old charges, sabbath-breaking, the plucking of corn, the neglect of hand-washing, etc., but Jesus confounded them.

Friday, April 6, AD 31 (Nisan 24)

This morning, at Peter's house, there occurred the exchange concerning the payment of tax (Matthew 17:24–27). Jesus told Peter that he would find a shekel in the mouth of the first fish that he would catch. Peter then went to the lake and caught a large fish, in whose mouth was a shekel. He used it to pay his and Jesus's tax. The fish was large enough to be then eaten by Jesus and the disciples for lunch. After the meal, Jesus spoke the words recorded in Mark 9:33–35. Then he went with the disciples to Capernaum. There he addressed a crowd of people at the marketplace. What he said is recorded in Mark 9:36–50 and in the entire eighteenth chapter of the Gospel of Saint Matthew. At the start of the sabbath, he went to the synagogue in Capernaum and taught there.

While Jesus was staying in Peter's house, some people from Capernaum said to Peter outside: "Does not your Master pay the tribute, the two didrachmas?" Peter answered: "Yes." And when he went into the house, Jesus said to him: "What is thy opinion, Simon? The kings of the earth, of whom do they receive tribute or custom? Of their own children, or of strangers?" Peter answered: "Of strangers," and Jesus replied: "Then the children are free! But that we may not scandalize them, go to the sea and cast in a hook; and that fish which shall first come up, take; and when thou hast opened its mouth, thou shalt find a shekel. Take that and give it to them for me and thee!" Peter went in simple faith to his fishery, let down one of the hooks kept there always ready for use, and with it drew up a very large fish. He felt in its mouth, and found an oblong yellowish coin, with which he paid the tribute for

Jesus and himself. The fish was so large that it gave the whole company a plentiful meal.

After that Jesus asked the disciples upon what subject they had been conversing on the way from Dothaim to Capernaum. They were silent, for they had been questioning who would be the greatest among them. Jesus, however, knew their thoughts, and he said: "Let him that will be the first among you, become the last, the servant of all!" [E22]

After dinner Jesus, the twelve, and the disciples went into Capernaum where a feast was being celebrated in honor of those that had returned from Jerusalem. The streets and houses were adorned with flowers and garlands. Children and old men, women and scholars, went forth to meet the returned travelers, who marched in crowds through the streets like a procession, and visited the houses of their friends and principal personages of the city. The Pharisees and many others from time to time joined Jesus and the disciples and went around with them.

Jesus visited the homes of the poor and many of his friends, and they presented to him the children, whom he blessed and to whom he made little presents. On the marketplace, on one side of which stood the old, on the other the new synagogue built by Cornelius, were houses with porticos in front. Here the school children and mothers with their little ones were assembled to salute Jesus. [E23] Jesus had been teaching in different places all along the way, and here he blessed and taught the children. He had little tunics distributed among them, the same to the rich as to the poor. They had been prepared by the stewardesses of the community and brought hither by the holy women of Jerusalem. The children received also fruit, writing tablets, and other gifts. The disciples having asked again who would be the greatest in the kingdom of heaven, Jesus called to him a wealthy lady, the wife of a merchant, who was standing with her four-year-old boy at the door of her house close by. She drew her veil and stepped forward with her boy. Jesus took him from her, and she at once went back. Then Jesus embraced the boy, stood him before him in the midst of the disciples and the crowds of children standing around, and said: "Whoever becomes not like the children, shall not enter the kingdom of heaven! Whoever receives a child in my name, receives me, yes, rather receives him that sent me. And whoever humbleth himself like this little child, he is the greatest in the kingdom of heaven." [E24]

John interrupted Jesus when he spoke of receiving in his name. The disciples had checked a certain man who, although not among their number, had nevertheless expelled the devil in Jesus's name. Jesus reproved them for so doing and continued his instruction for awhile longer. Then he blessed the boy, who was very lovely, gave him some fruit and a little tunic, beckoned to the mother, and restored her child to her with some prophetic words concerning his future, which were understood only at a later period. The child became a disciple of the apostles and was named Ignatius. He was afterward a bishop and martyr.

During the whole procession and the teaching of Jesus, a veiled lady had followed in the crowd. She seemed to be out of herself with emotion and joy. With clasped hands she frequently uttered the words half aloud, so that the women standing near her were deeply touched and moved to devotion: "Blessed the womb that bore thee! Blessed the breasts that gave thee suck! But far more blessed are they that hear the Word of God and keep it!" She spoke these words with abundant tears and a touching movement of the hands. They came from her inmost heart at every pause that Jesus made, at every striking expression that fell from his lips, and this with extraordinary emotion, love, and admiration. She took an inexpressibly childlike, absorbing interest in the life, the career, the teachings so full of love of the Redeemer. It was Lea, the wife of a malicious Pharisee belonging to Caesarea-Philippi, and sister of the deceased husband of Enue, the woman (also of Caesarea-Philippi) who had been cured of the issue of blood. She it was who, on a former occasion, had exclaimed at one of Jesus's instructions: "Blessed is the womb," etc., and to whom Jesus had replied: "But still more blessed are they that hear the Word of God and keep it!" Since then she had coupled Jesus's response with her own words of admiration. They were constantly on her lips, and had become for her a prayer of love and devotion. She had come hither to visit the holy women, and had made many rich gifts to the community.

Jesus continued to instruct at the marketplace until the sabbath began, when he repaired to the synagogue to teach. The sabbath lesson was upon the purification of the leprous, and the famine of Samaria that ceased so suddenly according to the prophetic words of Elisha.

Saturday, April 7, AD 31 (Nisan 25)

This afternoon Jesus was in Bethsaida and spoke with the disciples who had returned from their missionary journeys. Altogether about seventy disciples were gathered. As Jesus helped at the reception of the disciples, Peter said: "Lord, do you want to serve? Let us serve!" Jesus replied that he had been sent to serve. He spoke again of humility and said that whoever would be first must be the servant of all. Then he spoke of certain deeper mysteries, saying that his conception had been not human but divine, from the Holy Spirit. He spoke with great reverence of his mother, calling her the purest vessel and holiest of created beings. Also, he referred to the Fall and the ensuing separation from God. He said that now he had come to restore the relationship with God. His words were spoken with great solemnity and earnestness, so that the disciples were deeply moved.

Jesus, the apostles, and some of the disciples went next to Bethsaida, whither came also many of the other disciples, some from missions, some from their homes. Most of them came from the opposite side of the lake, from Decapolis and Gerasa. They were very much fatigued, and stood in great need of care and attention. They were affectionately received on the shore by their fellow disciples, who embraced them and served them in every way. They were conducted to Andrew's, their feet washed, baths made ready for them, fresh garments supplied, and a meal prepared.

As Jesus was very busily lending a helping hand in their service, Peter entreated him to desist. "Lord," said he, "art thou going to serve! Leave that to us." But Jesus replied that he was sent to serve, and that what was done for these disciples was done for his Father. And again his teaching turned upon humility. He that is the least, he that serves all others—he shall be the greatest. But whoever does not serve from a motive of charity, whoever lowers himself to help his neighbor, not in order to comfort a needy brother, but in order to gain distinction at that cost—he is a double-dealer, a server to the eye. He already has his reward, for he serves himself and not his brother. There were on this occasion perhaps seventy disciples present, and there were still some others in and around Jerusalem.

Jesus delivered to the apostles and disciples a deeply significant and wonderful instruction, in which he said plainly that he was not conceived by man, but by the Holy Spirit. He spoke with great reverence of his mother, calling her the purest, the holiest of creatures, a vessel of election, after whom for thousands of years the hearts of the devout had sighed and the tongues of prophets had prayed. He explained the testimony of his heavenly Father at the time of his baptism, but he made no mention of that upon Tabor. He spoke of the present time as happy and holy, since he had come, and declared that the relationship between God and man was once more restored. He referred in most profound words to the Fall of man, his separation from the heavenly Father, and to the power of Satan and the evil spirits over him. He said that, by his own birth from the purest, the most desired of virgins, the kingdom and the power of God among men had taken new life, and that by him and in him all should again become the children of God. Through him, both in the order of nature and of grace, was the bond, the bridge between God and man again established, but whoever desired to pass over that bridge must do so with him and in him, must leave behind the earthly and the pleasures of this world. He said that the power of the evil spirits over the world and humankind, as well as his share therein, was by himself brought to naught, and that all the misery arising from that diabolical influence upon nature and humankind could in his name, by interior union with him through faith and love, be crushed out. Jesus spoke of these things most earnestly and vehemently. The disciples did not comprehend all that he said, and they shuddered when he spoke of his Passion. The three apostles that had been with him on Tabor had since then been very grave and meditative.

All this took place during and after the sabbath. Some of the disciples put up in Capernaum, some at Peter's outside the city. All expenses were defrayed out of the common stock. It was almost like a religious community.

Sunday, April 8, AD 31 (Nisan 26)

Today Jesus and the disciples walked in the region north of Capernaum. Jesus paused occasionally to teach the disciples or the laborers in the fields. That evening he stayed at a shepherd settlement. He told the shepherds the parable of the lost sheep (Matthew 18:12) and spoke of the good shepherd (John 10:1).

The day after the sabbath, Jesus went with the disciples northward from Capernaum toward the mountain from which he had sent them on their first mission. He journeyed about two hours around and among the peasants who were cutting corn and among the shepherds, at one time instructing these people, at another the disciples. It was just harvest time.

The corn stood higher than a man. They cut it off at a convenient height, about half an arm long. The ears were longer and thicker than those of our corn and, that the stalks might not sink under their load, the fields were at short intervals provided with hedges of stakes. They had a kind of sickle more like a shepherd's crook than ours.

With the right hand they cut off a handful of stalks, which they held against their breast with the left, and so directed that they fell into their arms. They afterward bound them into little sheaves. It was laborious work, but they performed it very quickly. All that fell to the ground belonged to the poor gleaners who followed in the wake of the reapers.

During the pauses for rest, Jesus instructed the laborers. He questioned them as to how much they sowed, how much they reaped, to whom the corn belonged, what kind was the soil, how they worked it, etc., and around these questions he wove parables relating to sowing, to weeds, to the little grains of wheat, to the Judgment, and the consuming of the tares by fire. He taught the disciples also how they should teach, and he gave them another instruction upon teaching. He explained the spiritual signification of the harvest, called them his sowers and reapers, and told them that they must collect the seed-corn for the treasure of a coming harvest, since he would not now be with

Journey through Solitary Places

them long. The disciples became very anxious, and asked if he would not remain with them till Pentecost. Jesus said to them: "What will become of you when I am no longer with you?"

To the shepherds also Jesus introduced his discourse in many ways: "Is this your own flock? Are these sheep of several flocks? How do you guard them? Why do your sheep wander around dispersed?" etc. In this manner he put questions with which he linked his parables of the lost sheep, the good shepherd, etc.

Jesus then went to a valley that lay off toward the west and in a region more elevated than Capernaum. The mountain of Saphet was on the right. Here he journeyed through valleys and solitary places, teaching now the reapers and shepherds, now the disciples.[E25] He enumerated all the duties of a good shepherd and applied them to himself, since he was about to give his life for his sheep. He thereby indicated to the disciples how they should treat with such people whom they found in out-of-the-way districts deprived of spiritual assistance, and should sow good seed among them. These journeys of Jesus through solitary places, and his teaching full of peace and love, were deeply touching and impressive.

Monday, April 9, AD 31 (Nisan 27)

They returned by a route somewhat more to the northeast and put up at the little city of Leccum, one half-hour from the Jordan, whither the six apostles had gone on their first mission. Jesus himself had not yet been there. The inhabitants that had gone to Jerusalem for Passover had returned, and there were likewise scribes and Pharisees in the city. When the disciples visited their acquaintances, the latter related to them the circumstance of the massacre of the Galileans in the temple, but they made no mention of it to Jesus.

Tuesday, April 10, AD 31 (Nisan 28)

In Leccum, Jesus visited the aged and the sick, several of whom he healed. Then he taught at the marketplace. He spoke about marriage, making use of all kinds of analogies, including that of the son of the vineyard owner (Matthew 21:37–39). The people were deeply moved by Jesus's words. As evening approached, he went with the disciples to Bethsaida-Julias.

Leccum was a small, well-to-do place, about one half-hour from the Jordan and a couple of hours from the point at which it emptied into the lake. The inhabitants were Jews. Only on the outskirts of the place dwelt a few poor pagans in huts. They had, from time to time, remained behind from the caravans. The raising of cotton formed the chief industry here. They prepared the raw material, and spun and wove covers and various kinds of fabrics. Even the children were thus employed.

The welcome home feast for those that had returned from Jerusalem was being celebrated in Leccum, as it had just been in Capernaum. The streets were adorned with flowers and garlands of green. Those that had come home visited the houses of their friends, and the schools went out to meet them.

Jesus went into some of the houses to visit the old people, and he cured some sick. On the market square of the place in front of the synagogue, he delivered a long discourse first to the children, whom he caressed and blessed, then to the youths and maidens who, on account of the general festival, were present with their teachers. After they had gone home, he taught successively several groups of men and women, making use of all kinds of similitudes. His subject was marriage, which he treated in very beautiful and deeply significant terms. He began by saying that in human nature much evil is mixed with good, but that by prayer and renunciation the two must be separated and the evil subdued. He who follows his unbridled passions works mischief. Our works follow us and they will at some future day rise up against their author. Our body is an image of the Creator, but Satan aims at destroying that image in us. All that is superfluous brings with it sin and sickness, becomes deformity and abomination. Jesus exhorted his hearers to chastity, moderation, and prayer. Continence, prayer, and discipline have produced holy men and prophets. Jesus illustrated all this by similitudes referring to the sowing of the grain, to the clearing out of stones and weeds from the field, to its lying fallow, and to the blessing of God upon land justly acquired. In speaking of the married state, he borrowed his similitudes from the planting of the vine and the pruning of the branches. He spoke of noble offspring, of pious families, of improved vineyards, and of races exalted and ennobled. He spoke of the patriarch Abraham, of his holiness, and the alliance concluded with God in circumcision, and said that his descendants had fallen into disorders by their indulgence of unrestrained passion and their repeated marriages with the pagans. Jesus spoke also of the lord of the vineyard who had sent his son, and he recounted all that had happened to him.

The people were very much moved; many wept and felt impelled to amend their lives. Jesus gave that instruction principally because they had never been taught anything about such mysteries, and also because they lived in a very dissolute way.

Jesus taught also of the essential action of good will in prayer and renunciation, and of man's own cooperation. He said that what they deprived themselves of in food and drink and superfluous comforts, they should place with confidence in the hands of God, imploring him to allow it to benefit the poor shepherds in the wilderness and others in need. The Father in heaven would then like a true father of a family hear their prayer, if they like faithful servants shared the abundance he had given them with the poor whom they knew or whom they lovingly sought out. This was real cooperation, and God works with his true servants strong in faith. Here Jesus brought forward the example of a tree (the palm), which by love and desire as it were, but without contact, imparts fertility to its mate.

Wednesday, April 11, AD 31 (Nisan 29)

Today, in Bethsaida-Julias, there was talk of the murder of the Galileans that had occurred in the temple at Jerusalem. Jesus then spoke as recorded in Luke 13:1–5. He also referred to the parable of the unfruitful fig tree (Luke 13:6–9).

From Leccum Jesus crossed the Jordan to Bethsaida-Julias, where he taught. The welcome home feast was being celebrated here likewise. I saw Jesus with the disciples, some of the scribes and Pharisees, and other distinguished personages of Julias walking about and teaching. Here they told Jesus of the massacre of the Galileans in the temple. I heard at this time that a hundred persons belonging to Jerusalem and a hundred and fifty of the seditious followers of Judas the Golanite had been murdered. These last-named had persuaded many, perhaps forced them by threats, to go with them and offer sacrifice. The hundred Jerusalemites had united with the rebels, although they knew of their unjust determination not to pay the tax to the Emperor, and they were consequently murdered with them.

Thursday, April 12, AD 31 (Nisan 30)

Jesus and the disciples spent the whole day walking in the neighborhood surrounding the Mount of Beatitudes. That evening, they crossed the Jordan and returned to Bethsaida.

The country around Julias was extraordinarily charming, fertile, solitary, and verdant, full of grazing asses and camels. It was like a zoological garden, the abode of all kinds of birds and animals. Serpentine footpaths wound down to the harbor, and springs were abundant. The noonday sun shone full upon it and flashed on the mirror-like surface of the lake. The highroad to Julias ran nearer to the Jordan, but the country of which I speak was a solitude. Jesus and the disciples recrossed the Jordan and proceeded to Bethsaida and Capernaum. In the latter place, Jesus taught in the synagogue, for it was the sabbath. The scripture assigned for the day were passages from Moses, treating of the annual sacrifice of expiation, of that offered before the tabernacle, of the prohibition to eat the blood of animals, and of the degrees of kindred in which marriage could not be solemnized. Passages were read from Ezekiel, also, upon the sins of the city of Jerusalem.

IYYAR (29 days): April 12/13 to May 10/11, AD 31 Iyyar New Moon: April 10 at 4:30 PM, Jerusalem time

Friday, April 13, AD 31 (Iyyar 1)

After the evening sabbath sermon in the synagogue, Jesus accepted the invitation of a well-to-do Pharisee to dine with him at his house. Here took place the healing of a man with edema, which scandalized the Pharisees (Luke 14:1–14). Jesus then told the parable of the great feast (Luke 14:15–24) and asked that the poor be invited to join with them in their meal.

Jesus and the disciples were invited by one of the Pharisees to dine not far from the dwelling of Cornelius the centurion. There he found a man afflicted with edema, who begged for help. Jesus asked the Pharisees whether it was lawful to heal upon the sabbath day. They gave him no answer, so he laid his hand upon the sick man and healed him. As the poor man was retiring with many thanks, Jesus remarked to the Pharisees, as he usually did on such occasions, that not one of them would hesitate to draw out on the sabbath day his ox or his ass that had fallen into a pit. The Pharisees were scandalized, but they could make no reply.

The Pharisees had invited only their own relatives and friends, and when Jesus perceived that they had taken the best places at table for themselves, he said: "When invited to a wedding, sit not down in the first place, lest perhaps one more honorable than thou be invited also, and the host constrain thee to make room for that one, and thus bring thee to shame. But if one takes the last place and the host says, 'Friend, go up higher,' that brings with it honor. Because everyone that exalteth himself shall be humbled, and he that humbleth himself shall be exalted." Then Jesus addressed the host: "Whoever invites to his feast his relatives, friends, and rich neighbors, who will in turn invite him to theirs, has already received his reward. But whoever invites the poor, the lame, the blind, the infirm, who can make no return to him, he will happily receive his recompense at the resurrection." To this one of the guests responded: "Yes, blessed indeed will he be that shall sit at the feast in the kingdom of God!" whereupon Jesus turned to him and related the parable of the great feast.

Jesus had, by means of the disciples, caused many of the poor to be assembled at the Pharisee's. Now he asked the host whether the entertainment had been prepared for him, and on receiving an answer in the affirmative, he ordered what was left after the guests had finished to be distributed to the poor.

Saturday, April 14, AD 31 (Iyyar 2)

As usual on the sabbath, Jesus and the disciples went for a walk. They went to a deserted region between Tiberias and Magdalum and were followed by a large crowd. Jesus spoke to the crowd (Luke 14:25–33).

After that Jesus went with the disciples through the centurion Zorobabel's estate into a beautiful, solitary region between Tiberias and Magdalum. As a numerous crowd followed him, he took the opportunity to speak of renouncing all things to follow him. Whoever, he said, wanted to follow him and be his disciple must love him more than all his nearest relatives, yes, even more than himself, and must carry his cross after him. He who wanted to build a tower must first calculate the cost, otherwise he might never finish it, might make himself ridiculous. He who goes to war ought, first of all, to compare the number of his forces with those of his enemy, and if he finds it insufficient, he ought rather to sue for peace. One must renounce all things, in order to become his disciple.

Jesus Teaching on the Mountain near Gabara

Sunday, April 15, AD 31 (Iyyar 3)

Jesus sent out the disciples to invite the people to a sermon on the mountain near Gabara, which would begin on Iyyar 6.

JESUS journeyed on, teaching through the country of Galilee, and dispatched a large number of the elder disciples to invite the people to an instruction to be given on the mountain beyond Gabara. It was to begin on the following Wednesday and last several days. I heard the day indicated differently, but I knew that the coming Wednesday was meant.

Monday, April 16, AD 31 (Iyyar 4)

As Jesus arrived at the outskirts of Tarichea, several lepers called out to him. He healed them and then went on to heal many sick people who were brought to him.

A great many of the disciples rowed across the lake to the country of the Gergeseans, to Dalmanutha, and into the Decapolis. They were commissioned to invite all, for Jesus would not be with them much longer, and they were to bring back as many with them as they could. About forty disciples went on this mission. Jesus kept with him the apostles, as well as the disciples that had last returned, all of whom he continued to instruct. He went with them to Tarichea at the southern extremity of the lake. The journey to Tarichea could not be made along the lakeshore, for at two hours' distance from that place rose steep cliffs that extended off to the lake. Jesus went around Tarichea to the west, and crossed over a bridge to a place that seemed to be one of the environs of the city. The bridge spanned the stone dam which extended from Tarichea to the spot at which the Jordan flowed out of the lake. Near the bridge ran two rows of houses. Before reaching them, Jesus had to pass the abode of the lepers, where he had wrought some cures the preceding year. Being informed of his approach, these cured came out to thank him, while others, who had come hither since his last visit, now cried to him for help and he healed them. When arrived at the houses mentioned above, many sick were presented to him. They had been rowed across the lake from Dalmanutha. Jesus helped them. That dam, along with most of the houses, was overturned by the earthquake at Jesus's death. They were abandoned and never rebuilt, since the lakeshore was much changed by the catastrophe. Tiberias was in reality only half a city, being quite unfinished on one side.

Tuesday, April 17, AD 31 (Iyyar 5)

This morning, Jesus visited a sanatorium south of Tarichea and healed the sick there. Then he and the disciples went to a hostel close to the mountain where he would teach next day. Many people were already on their way to this event—so many, in fact, that the Pharisees complained to Jesus that the entire land was in disturbance.

From all quarters poured immense crowds to the mountain of Gabara, and ships full of passengers came over the lake. They brought with them tents and provisions, also sick borne in basket-litters on the backs of asses. The disciples arranged the multitude, and lent assistance everywhere.

As Jesus, with the apostles, was proceeding to Gabara, he was met by some of the Pharisees, who interrogated him as to the meaning of that great movement of the people, those multitudes hastening to the mountain. The whole country, they said, was in a state of agitation! Jesus answered by telling them that they too might, if they chose, come to hear his discourse next morning, that he had invited the multitude because he would not be among them much longer.

The holy women went to the inn at the foot of the mountain in order to provide for the wants of the disciples.

Wednesday, April 18, AD 31 (Iyyar 6)

At about ten in the morning Jesus arrived at the mountain near Gabara where the new "Sermon on the Mount" was to begin. Many Pharisees, Sadducees, and Herodians were among the people gathered there to hear him. After beginning with a prayer, Jesus began to teach about prayer and the love of one's neighbor (Matthew 5:38–6:8). He also warned against the Pharisees and false prophets. Jesus taught without interruption until evening. Then he descended the mountain to return to where he was staying. Among those who came to meet him there were Lazarus, Martha, Dinah the Samaritan, Mara the Suphanite, Maroni of Nain and his mother, Mary.

It was toward ten o'clock next day when Jesus appeared upon the mountain. The disciples had put the people in order and indicated to them how they should in certain numbers exchange places from time to time, in order to hear Jesus's discourse, for the multitude was far greater than could be accommodated within hearing distance of the teacher's chair. The people were under tents, those from the same district camping together. Each district had its own camp, the entrance to which was adorned with an arch formed of the fruits peculiar to that district and surmounted by a crown made of the most magnificent specimens. Some had grapevines and corn; others, cotton plants, sugar cane, aromatic herbs, and all kinds of fruits and berries. Every district had its own distinctive sign, adorned with flowers and beautifully arranged. The whole produced a very pleasing effect. Numbers of birds, among them pigeons and quails, had taken up their quarters in the camp and were busy picking up the scattered crumbs. They had grown so familiar, so tame, that the people fed them from their hands. A great many Pharisees, Sadducees, and Herodians, scribes and magistrates of different places were present and had taken possession of the places around Jesus's chair. They had provided themselves with comfortable seats, a kind of stool, or chair, which they had ordered to be brought for their own use.

Jesus collected his disciples close around him, to the displeasure of the Pharisees who were unwilling to see them preferred to themselves. Jesus began by prayer and calling the people to order. He bade them be attentive, because he was going to teach them what they would not learn from others, but what was at the same time necessary for their salvation. What they could not then comprehend would be repeated and explained to them later by his disciples whom he would send to them, for he himself would not be among them much longer. Then loudly and openly he warned the disciples gathered around him against the Pharisees and false prophets, and instructed the multitude upon prayer and love of the neighbor. The disciples led up the different groups in turn. The Pharisees and others versed in the Law frequently interrupted Jesus with all kinds of contradictory remarks, but he paid no attention to them. He went on with his instruction, speaking very severely against them and warning the people against them until they were greatly incensed. He performed no cures today, but ordered that the weary sick on their beds should be brought up in their turn and placed under awnings near him, that they too might hear his teaching. He sent word to them to be patient until the close of his instruction. He taught till evening without intermission, the people taking refreshment by turns. I did not see Jesus eating. He taught the great multitude so unremittingly that toward evening his voice became quite shrill and weak. At last, he went down to the inn on the plain. It had once formed part of Magdalene's property in Magdalum, and at its sale had been reserved for the use of the community.

Lazarus and Martha, Dinah and the Suphanite, Maroni of Nain, Jesus's mother, and the other Galilean women were come hither with quantities of provisions, materials for clothes, and also ready-made clothing. They had prepared a frugal meal for Jesus and the disciples, and all the rest was distributed to the poor.

Thursday, April 19, AD 31 (Iyyar 7)

Today, Jesus continued his "Sermon on the Mount." The Pharisees began to proclaim Jesus as a "disturber of the peace," saying that they had the sabbath, the festival days, and their own teaching, and that they did not need the innovations of this upstart. They threatened to complain to Herod—who would certainly put a stop to Jesus's activities. Jesus answered that he would continue to teach and heal, in spite of Herod, until his mission was complete. Eventually, the pressure of the crowd forced the Pharisees to leave so that Jesus could continue his teaching undisturbed. After the sermon had ended and the crowd had dispersed, Jesus taught the disciples concerning the character of the Pharisees and how they should conduct themselves in relation to them. That evening, as Jesus and the disciples ate together, Lazarus told of the journey the women had made to Machaerus from Hebron and Jerusalem. Indeed, one of them, Johanna Chusa, had just succeeded in recovering the head of John the Baptist from Herod's castle.

Next day Jesus continued his teaching on the mountain. He again spoke of prayer, of the love of the neighbor, of vigilance in good, of confidence in the goodness of God, and admonished the people not to allow themselves to be confounded by oppressors and calumniators.

The Pharisees today were even more disquieted. They had gathered in still larger numbers than yesterday, to dispute with Jesus. They called him an agitator of the people, a mischief-maker. They said that he enticed the people from their labor that they might follow him around the country. They had their sabbath, their festivals, and their own teaching; there was no need of his innovations. They repeated for the thousandth time the old reproaches against himself and his disciples, and ended by threatening him with Herod. They would, they said, complain to him of Jesus's actions and teaching; he already had an eye upon him, and would soon make short work of his doings. Jesus replied with severity. He said that he would, undisturbed on Herod's account, teach and heal until his mission was fulfilled. The Pharisees were so bold and violent that the people pressed forward. The confusion became great as they were pushing and treading on one another's toes, so that the Pharisees withdrew at last in great disgust.

Jesus nevertheless went on teaching in a very touching and impressive manner. As a great many of those on their return journey from Jerusalem, as well as others, had exhausted their provisions, Jesus directed the senior disciples to distribute among them bread, honey, and fish, numerous baskets of which had been brought up from the inn. The holy women had seen to its preparation. Garments, pieces of linen, covers, sandals, and little tunics for the children also were distributed to the needy. The holy women had brought all these things in abundance. They distributed them to the women, and the disciples, to the men.

Meanwhile Jesus continued to instruct the disciples alone, speaking upon the character of the Pharisees and telling them how they should, in the future, comport themselves toward them. After that he descended with them to the inn, where a meal was awaiting them.

During it Lazarus spoke of the massacre of the Galileans in the temple, of which there was much question among the disciples and the people at large. He told also of the women from Hebron, relatives of the Baptist, and of some from Jerusalem who had gone to Machaerus in search of John's head, as the sewers were being cleared out and the fortress enlarged. Lazarus himself had taken steps in the matter.

Friday, April 20, AD 31 (Iyyar 8)

This morning Jesus and the twelve apostles healed the sick who were gathered at the foot of the mountain. The remaining disciples and holy women dispensed food and clothing to the poor. This was the cause of much joy and thanksgiving. Afterward, the people dispersed to return to their home towns in time for the sabbath. Jesus and the disciples then made their way to Garisima. On the way, they passed through Kapharot. In Kapharot, some Pharisees, who were well-disposed to Jesus, warned him that Herod was out to imprison him and deal with him as he had done with John the Baptist. Jesus replied that he had nothing to fear from "the fox," and that he would do what his Father had sent him to do (Luke 13:31–33). Reaching Garisima, Jesus and the disciples went to the synagogue for the start of the sabbath.

Early on the morning of the third day, Lazarus and the holy women returned home, while Jesus and the apostles went to visit the sick whose huts and tents had been arranged, some in the neighborhood of the inn, and others in the public encampment at the foot of the mount of instruction. They cured all that were there, and did not leave the spot until all were again on their feet. The disciples busied themselves distributing among them what remained of the provisions, clothes, and unmade materials. The cured and their friends filled the air with psalms of thanksgiving. At last all took their departure, in order to reach their homes before the sabbath.

Jesus next went to Garisima, about one hour to the north of Sepphoris, on a height at the end of the valley. He sent some of the disciples on ahead to prepare the inn while he himself, on account of some sick whom he wished to visit, took a circuitous route thereto. I saw him and his party tarrying awhile in the little place Kapharot near Jotopata. The road from Capernaum to Jerusalem ran through it. Saul wandered about this part of the country shortly before his visit to the witch of Endor and his disastrous battle. It was about five hours from Kapharot to Garisima, which lay in the midst of vineyards. It enjoyed the morning and some of the noonday sun, but on the west and north it had nothing but shade.

The disciples that had been sent on in advance came a part of the way to meet Jesus, who had an inn just outside the place. They washed one another's feet and, after partaking of the customary refreshments, Jesus proceeded to the synagogue, where he taught from Leviticus and the prophet Ezekiel. He had to endure no contradiction this time, for his hearers were astonished at his knowledge of the Law and his wonderful explanations. The instruction over, he took a repast with his own followers at the inn. Some of his relatives from the region of Sepphoris were in Garisima, and they ate with them. Jesus spoke on this occasion of his approaching end.

Saturday, April 21, AD 31 (Iyyar 9)

Jesus taught the disciples openly on a hill, speaking of the lost sheep (Luke 15:3–7), the lost coin (Luke 15:8–10), and the ten virgins (Matthew 25:1–13). Some Jews from Cyprus—on their return journey there from Jerusalem—came to Jesus and told him how much the Jewish colony on Cyprus longed to hear him.

Almost a hundred disciples, along with the apostles, gathered around Jesus in Garisima for the sabbath. The two sons of Cyrinus of Cyprus, who had been baptized at Dabrath, were also here with other Jews from the same place. A great multitude of these latter were here encamped. They were returning to Cyprus from the Passover festival at Jerusalem and they listened with admiration to Jesus's teaching on the sabbath. Jesus's presence was ardently longed for in Cyprus, where there were numbers of Jews, all in a state of spiritual abandonment.

Jesus instructed the disciples in Garisima also, assembling them for this purpose on a hill. Many of them had until now served merely as messengers between the disciples dispersed in various quarters and the friends of Jesus. There were others who had for the most part been detained at home, and who in consequence had missed much of Jesus's teaching, had heard nothing of the way in which they were to conduct themselves on their missions, nor of the application and interpretation of parables. Jesus then, continuing his instruction, explained all things to these disciples in a simple and easy style, and ran quickly through all that he had taught up to the present.

Sunday, April 22, AD 31 (Iyyar 10)

This morning Jesus continued his instruction to the disciples. That afternoon, they went to a deserted region northwest of Garisima, and stayed there overnight in the mountains.

After that he went with them from four to six hours northwest from Garisima to the mountains of a very retired region, and there they passed the night. Herds of asses and camels, and flocks of sheep were grazing off in the valleys on the west side of the lofty mountain range that ran through the heart of the country. The valleys here run in a zigzag direction, like the plant known as the common club moss, or wolf's claw. There were a great many palm trees in this wilderness, also a kind of tree whose interlaced branches fell to the earth, and under which one could creep as into a hut. The shepherds of the region used to take shelter under them. Jesus and the disciples spent most of the night in prayer and instruction. Jesus repeated many of the directions he had given when first sending them out upon their earlier missions. I was especially struck on hearing that they were to possess no private purse. That was to be confided to their superior, one of whom was appointed for every ten. Jesus indicated to them the signs by which they might recognize the places in which they could effect some good, told them to shake the dust from their shoes before those that were ill-disposed, and instructed them as to how they should justify themselves when placed under arrest. They were not to be disturbed as to what they should answer, for words would then be put into their mouth, nor were they to be afraid, since their lives would not be in any danger.

I saw here and there around this region men with long staves and iron hoes. They were guarding the herds against the attacks of wild animals that came up from the seacoast.

Monday, April 23, AD 31 (Iyyar 11)

Here, in the mountains, Jesus gave his blessing to the disciples and sent them out on missionary journeys. This was the third such occasion on which they were sent out. In so doing, he laid his hands upon the apostles and the disciples of long standing, filling them with new strength.

Very early the next morning, Jesus sent the disciples and apostles out on a mission. Upon the latter, as well as upon the eldest disciples, he imposed hands, but the rest he merely blessed. By this ceremony he filled them with new strength and energy. It was not, however, priestly ordination, but only an imparting of grace and vigor to the soul. He addressed to them likewise many words on the value of obedience to superiors.

Peter and John did not remain with Jesus, but went toward the south, Peter to the country of Joppa, and John more to the east, to Judea. Some went to Upper Galilee, others into the Decapolis. Thomas received his mission to the country of the Gergeseans, whither he went with a troop of disciples, taking a circuitous route to Asach, a city situated on a height between two valleys, about nine hours from Sepphoris and one at most to the left from the road. There were a great many Jews in this city, which belonged to the Levites.

Jesus now journeyed in a northwesterly direction. With him were five apostles, each of whom had under him ten disciples. I remember having seen on this occasion Judas, James the Less, Thaddeus, Saturnin, Nathaniel, Barnabas, Azor, Mnason, and the youths from Cyprus. They accomplished on the first day six to eight hours. Several cities lay to the right and left on their road and, from time to time, some of the party would separate from their Master in order to visit them. Jesus passed Tyre on the seacoast to the left. He had indicated to the apostles and disciples a certain place where, in about thirty days, they were again to join him. He spent the night like the preceding, under some trees with his companions.

Harbor of Tyre

Jesus Journeys into the Country of Ornithopolis and Thence Takes Ship for Cyprus

Tuesday, April 24, AD 31 (Iyyar 12)

Proceeding further, around midday, Jesus and the few remaining disciples crossed the Leontes river and came to an inn. Here they were well received, and Jesus taught the people who had come to hear him.

I SAW Jesus with his followers, disciples and others, about fifty in all, journeying through a deep, mountainous ravine. It was a very remarkable-looking mountain. On two sides of it for about an hour in length were dwellings and sheds of light timber, peering into which the passer-by beheld the occupants as if in caves. Sometimes the projecting shed was covered with rushes, moss, or grassy sods. Here and there arose works something like fortifications, to prevent the landslides from the mountain from filling up the road. Here dwelt poor, outcast pagans whose duty it was to keep the road in repair and to free the region from ferocious beasts. They came to Jesus and implored his aid against these animals—long, broad-footed, spotted creatures, like immense lizards. Jesus blessed the country and commanded the animals to retire into a black swamp that was nearby. Wild orange trees grew by the roadside. It was about four hours' distance to Tyre.

Jesus here separated from his companions and, plunging deeper and deeper into the ravine, taught here and there before the caves of its inhabitants. The road led down along the clear and tolerably rapid stream Leontes which, flowing through its deep bed, emptied into the sea a couple of hours north of Tyre. The river was crossed by a high stone bridge, at the opposite end of which was a large inn, where the disciples again met Jesus.

From this place he sent several of his companions into the cities of the land of Cabul, and Judas Iscariot with some disciples to Cana near Sidon. The disciples had resigned to the care of the apostles, each to the one set over him as his superior, whatever money or goods they might happen to have with them. To Judas alone, Jesus gave a sum for himself. Jesus knew his greed for money and would not expose him to the temptation of appropriating that of others. He had remarked his anxiety on the score of money, although Judas loved to boast of his frugality and strict observance of the law of poverty. On receiving the money, he asked Jesus how much he might daily spend. Jesus answered: "He that is conscious of being so strictly temperate, needs neither rule nor direction. He bears in himself his law."

About a hundred persons were at the inn awaiting Jesus. They belonged to that same Jewish tribe whom he had already visited and consoled at Ornithopolis and near Sarepta. Some of them had come hither for the purpose of meeting him, while others belonged to this district, where they owned a synagogue. They received him and his followers humbly and joyfully, and washed their feet. They were in their holiday garments of very antique style, wore long beards, and had fur maniples hanging from their arms. They had many singular customs, and something peculiar in their manner of life, like the Essenes. The pagans too of this place were very reverential toward Jesus. They likewise held the Jews in esteem, a circumstance more common throughout this district than in Decapolis. These Jews were descendants from a natural son the patriarch Judah had had by a servant. This son, fleeing from the persecution of his brothers Her and Onan, had settled here. His family, having intermarried with the pagans of the country, did not go down with the other Israelites into Egypt and at last became quite estranged from the religion and customs of their people.

The pagans with whom these descendants of Judah had intermarried had, when Jacob—after Dinah's misfortune—was living near Samaria on Joseph's inheritance, already experienced the greatest desire to enter into marriage relations with Jacob's sons, or at least with his servant men and maids. They crossed the mountains humbly to lay before him their desire to marry amongst his followers, and of their own accord offered to receive circumcision. But Jacob would not listen to their demand. When, then, that persecuted son of Judah sought refuge among them with his family, he was very warmly received by the pagans, and his children soon united with them in marriage. How wonderful the dispensation of God! The rude desire of these Gentiles to unite with the holy race upon whom the Promise rested was not wholly frustrated, and later events brought about the ennobling of these people through the banished scion of Judah.

In spite of the great disorders arising from these mixed marriages, there was still one family among them that preserved itself pure; and it was, for the first time, instructed in the Law by Elijah, who often sojourned in this region. Solomon had given himself much trouble to unite these people again with the Jews, but without success. Still there were among them about a hundred pious souls of pure descent from Judah. Elijah had succeeded in uniting this separated branch again with Israel; and in the time of Joachim and Anne, teachers came from the country of Hebron in order to keep them to the observance of the Law. The descendants of these teachers were still living among them; and it was through them that the Syrophoenician and her people entered into relations with the Jews. They lived in sentiments of deep humility, esteeming themselves unworthy to set foot upon the Promised Land. The Cypriote Cyrinus had, when in Dabrath, spoken of them to Jesus, and the latter took occasion from this fact to discourse long and familiarly with them.

He taught at first in front of the inn, the people standing around under open arbors, or sheds. The inn belonged to the Jews or was hired by them. Afterward he taught in the synagogue, a great many pagans listening to him from outside. The synagogue was lofty and beautiful. The roof was provided with a platform around which one could walk and command a very extended view of the country.

That evening the Jews tendered Jesus at the inn a festive entertainment, at which they took the opportunity to express to him in a body their sincere gratitude for his not having despised them, for his coming to them, the lost sheep of Israel, and proclaiming to them salvation. They had kept their genealogical table in good order. They now laid it before Jesus and were deeply moved at finding that they had sprung from the same tribe as himself. It was a joyful entertainment, and at it all assisted. They spoke much of the prophets, especially of Elijah, whom they named with words of great affection, recounting his prophecies of the Messiah, also those of Malachi, and saying that the time for their fulfillment must now be near. Jesus explained everything to them, and promised to introduce them into the land of Judea. He did, in fact, later on establish them on its southern frontiers between Hebron and Gaza.

Jesus wore in this place a long, white traveling robe. He and his followers were girded and their garments tucked up, as if for a journey. They had no baggage. They carried what was necessary under the outer robe, wrapped round the body above the girdle. Some of them had staves. I never saw Jesus with any regular covering for his head; sometimes he drew over it the scarf that was usually worn around the neck.

There was in this part of the country an ugly kind of spotted animal with membranous wings, which could fly very rapidly. It was like an enormous bat, and it sucked the blood of men and animals during sleep. These animals came from the swamps up on the seashore, and did much damage. Egypt too was once infested with them. They were not real dragons, nor were they so horrible. Dragons were not so numerous, and they lived solitary in the most savage wildernesses. Fruits like nuts were gathered in these parts, some like chestnuts, and berries that hung in clusters.

Wednesday, April 25, AD 31 (*Iyyar 13*)

Today, Jesus and his few disciples—James the Less, Barnabas, Mnason, Azor, the two sons of Cyrinus and a youth from Cyprus—continued further toward Ornithopolis. They halted their journey at a small place about an hour east of Ornithopolis, where Jesus taught in the synagogue. Then they proceeded to Ornithopolis, where they went to the home of the Syrophoenician woman. Here Jesus healed some people and then took part in a feast held in his honor by the Syrophoenician woman and her daughter. Around four in the afternoon Jesus and his companions left and went to the harbor north of the city. Close to the harbor there was a synagogue, where Jesus taught. That night, as Jesus and the disciples boarded boats to set sail to Cyprus, the moon was full and the stars were shining. Altogether there were ten rowing boats, each equipped with sails (like Peter's boat on the Sea of Galilee).

From the inn, Jesus went to a seaport about three hours distant from Tyre. Alongside of the port there stretched far out into the sea, like an island, a tongue of the mountain, and on it was built the pagan city of Ornithopolis. The few, but devout, Jews of the place seemed to live in dependence upon the pagans. I saw as many as thirty pagan temples scattered here and there. Sometimes it seems to me that the port belonged to Ornithopolis. The Syrophoenician owned there so many buildings, factories for weaving and dyeing, so many ships, that I think the whole place must have been at one time subject to her deceased husband or his ancestors. She dwelt now in Ornithopolis itself, though in a kind of suburb. Back of the city arose a high mountain, and behind that lay Sidon. A little river flowed between Ornithopolis and its port. The shore between Tyre and Sidon was, with the exception of the port, but little accessible, being rough and wild. The seaport to which I have alluded was the largest between Sidon and Tyre, and the number of ships crowding its waters made it almost like a little city itself.

The property of the Syrophoenician, with its numerous buildings, courts, and gardens, looked like an immense estate. Its factories and plantations were full of workmen and slaves, whose families had their homes there. But just at present, things had come to a standstill; the former activity was not yet resumed. The lady was about to free herself from all such ties, and wished her people to choose a superior from among themselves.

Ornithopolis was situated about three hours from the little place across the river where Jesus had spent the night, but from the settlement of the poor Jews it was one and a half hours. When Jesus went straight through this place to the port, Ornithopolis lay on his left. The Jewish settlement was toward Sarepta, which received the rays of the rising sun, for on that side the mountains rose in a gentle slope. On the north it was perfectly shady. The situation was very fine. Between Ornithopolis, the Jewish settlement, and the port, there lay so many solitary buildings, so many other little settlements, that looking down upon them from above, one might think that once upon a time they were all united. Jesus had with him now only James the Less, Barnabas, Mnason, Azor, Cyrinus's two sons, and a Cypriote youth whom those last-named had brought to Jesus. All the other apostles and disciples were scattered throughout the country on missions. Judas was the last to set out. He went with his little troop to Cana the Greater.

Jesus went with his companions to the home of the Syrophoenician who, by her cured relatives, had sent him an invitation to an entertainment. A number of persons were assembled to meet him, also the poor and the crippled. Of the latter, Jesus cured many. The dwelling of the Syrophoenician with its gardens, courts, and buildings of all kinds was probably as large as Dulmen. Pieces of stuff, yellow, purple, red, and sky blue, were extended on the galleries of many of the buildings. These galleries were broad enough to permit a person's walking on them. The yellow dye was extracted from a plant which was cultivated in the neighborhood. For red and purple, they employed sea snails. I saw great beds in which they were either caught or raised, and there were other places full of slime, like frog's spawn. The cotton plant also was cultivated here, though not indigenous to this part of the country. The soil, in general, was not so fertile as that of Palestine, and around there were a great many ponds and lakes.

Gazing from the shore out upon the sea, one might imagine it to lie higher than the surrounding country, so blue does it rise toward the sky. Here and there on the shore were low trees with large, black trunks and wide-spreading branches. Their dense roots extended so far out on the water that one could walk over them to some distance from the land. The black trunks were, for the most part, hollow, and afforded a shelter for all kinds of noxious insects.

Jesus was received with solemnity. As he was reclining at table, the widow's daughter poured a flask of fragrant ointment over his head. The mother presented him with pieces of stuff, girdles, and three-cornered golden coins; the daughter, pieces of the same precious metal chained together. He did not tarry with them long, but went with his companions to the seaport, where he was solemnly received by the Jewish inhabitants and by the Cypriote Jews who were gathered there on their way back from the Passover feast. Jesus taught in the synagogue, around which a great many pagans stood listening from without.

It was by starlight that Jesus, accompanied by all the travelers, went down to the harbor and embarked. The night was clear, and the stars looked larger than they do to us. There was quite a little fleet ready to receive the travelers. One large ship of burden took the baggage, the goods and cattle, and numbers of asses. Ten galleys carrying sail were for the accommodation of the Cypriote Passover guests, Jesus, and his followers. Five of these galleys were fastened with ropes to the front and sides of the burden ship, which they drew forward after them. The remaining five formed an outer circle to these. Each of these vessels had, like Peter's boat on the Sea of Galilee, benches for the rowers raised around the mast and below these little cabins. Jesus stood near the mast of the ships that were fastened to the large one and, as they pushed off, he blessed both land and sea. Shoals of fishes swarmed after the flotilla, among them some very large ones with remarkable-looking mouths. They sported around and stretched their heads out of the water, as if hearkening to the instructions given by Jesus during the voyage.

(Follow Map 30)

Thursday, April 26, AD 31 (Iyyar 14)

The sea was calm, and the passage proceeded so rapidly that the sailors called out: "O, what an auspicious voyage! This is thanks to thee, O prophet!" Jesus stood at the mast. He bid them to be silent and to give thanks only to God. Toward evening they landed at Salamis. Here Jesus went to the synagogue in the Jewish quarter, where he healed some people who were suffering from edema.

The passage was so unusually rapid, the sea so smooth, and the weather so beautiful that the sailors, both Jews and pagans, cried out: "Oh, what an auspicious voyage! That is owing to thee, O prophet!" Jesus was standing near the mast. He commanded them silence and to give glory to the almighty God alone. Then he spoke of God, one and almighty, and of his works, of the nonexistence of the pagan divinities, of the nearness of the time, yes, even its very presence, in which the highest salvation would be given to earth, and of the vocation of the Gentiles. The whole discourse was addressed to the pagans.

The few women on the ships remained apart by themselves. Many of the passengers were quite seasick during the voyage; they lay around in retired corners and vomited violently. Jesus cured several on board his ship. Then numbers called from the other ships telling him of their needs, and he cured them from a distance.

I saw them also eating on the ships. They had fire in a metal vessel, and long, twisted strips of something, brown and clear like glue, which they dissolved in hot water. They passed the food around in portions on dishes furnished with a rim and a handle. There were several excavations like plates in each dish destined for different things, such as round cakes, vegetables, etc. The sauce was poured over it.

From Ornithopolis to Cyprus, the sea does not look so broad as below from Joppa. There one sees nothing but water.

Toward evening the ships entered the harbor of Salamis, which was very spacious and secure. It was strongly fortified with bulwarks and high walls, and the two moles that formed it ran far out into the sea. The city itself lay a good half hour inland, though one scarcely remarks the fact since the intervening space is set out with trees and covered with magnificent gardens. The ships in the harbor were numerous. That upon which Jesus was could not go close to the shore which, like a strong, high rampart, rose obliquely; besides this, the ship drew too much water to approach nearer. They cast anchor therefore at some distance. Near the shore were several small boats fastened with ropes. They approached the larger vessels, received their passengers and, by means of the ropes, drew back to the shore. In that upon which Jesus and the disciples sailed to land were some Jews who had come out to welcome and receive him.

On the shore were numerous others who, having espied the ships in the distance, had come forth from the city in solemn procession. It was customary thus to receive the Jews on their return from the Passover celebration. Those on the shore were principally old people, women, young girls, and the school children with their teachers. They had fifes, carried flying streamers, green branches, crowns on poles, and chanted songs of joy.

Cyrinus, three elder brothers of Barnabas, and some aged Jews in festive robes received Jesus and his followers,

Map 30: The Journey to Cyprus
April 26–May 30, AD 31

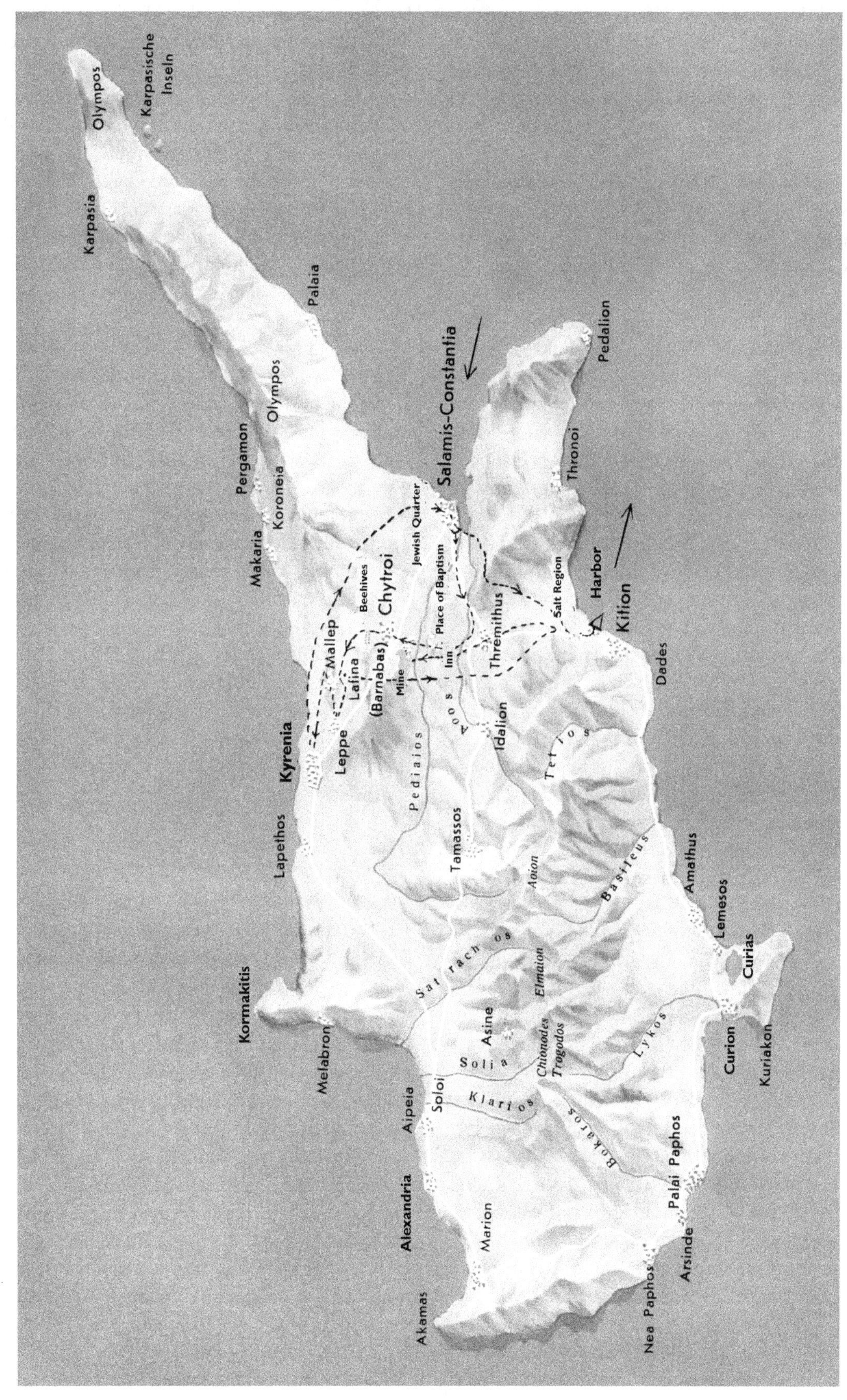

Salamis—Kythria—Mallep—Leppe—Port near Kition—Kyrenia—Mallep
Salamis—Sea Harbor of Kition

and conducted them to a lovely green terrace at some distance from the harbor. There they found carpets spread, wash basins filled with water, and on tables various dishes with refreshments. Cyrinus and his companions washed the feet of Jesus and his disciples, and presented them food to eat.

An old man, the father of Jonas, the new disciple, was now led forward. He fell weeping upon his son's neck, who presented him to Jesus, before whom he bowed low. He had been in ignorance as to what had become of his son, for they with whom he had started on the journey were come back long ago. All present were taken up with caring for the travelers returned. Many pressed through the crowd crying: "Is such a one here? Is such a one there?" and when they found their friends, they embraced them and led them away. The news of the sedition and Pilate's massacre in the temple, variously exaggerated, had already reached Cyprus, and the people were in great anxiety about their relatives.

The place in which Jesus was received was charming. Toward the west, one saw the immense city with its innumerable cupolas and towering edifices crimsoned by the fiery rays of the sun sinking huge and red below the horizon. Toward the east, the view extended over the sea to the lofty mountain ranges of Syria, which there rose up like clouds against the sky. Salamis stood in the midst of a broad plain, covered with numbers of beautiful high trees, terraces, and pleasure grounds. The soil appeared to me very friable, like dust or sand, but drinking water did not seem to be abundant. The entrance into the harbor was not open. It was guarded by fortified islands, between which were one broad and several smaller roadsteads. The little islands were fortified with semicircular towers, low and broad, through whose open windows could be observed all that was going on outside. The Jewish quarter was in the northern part of the city. When Jesus and his followers left the harbor and went one half-hour toward the city, they turned to the right and, still outside the city, went a considerable distance to the north.

When Jesus and his disciples arrived, the Jews returned from Passover were already assembled upon an open, terraced square. One of the ancients, an elder of the synagogue, was standing on an elevated point from which he could overlook all below. It reminded one of calling the muster-roll, to see whether all the soldiers were present. The elder was receiving information upon the details of their journey. He inquired whether any of them had suffered injury by the way, or had any complaints to lodge against a fellow traveler, and requested an account of what had happened in Jerusalem. Jesus and his disciples were not present at this assembly. He was solemnly welcomed by a number of venerable old Jews and from the terrace delivered an exhortation to the assembled crowd, after which they dispersed to their homes.

At the head of the two streets that formed the Jewish quarter stood the magnificent synagogue, the dwellings of the ancients and rabbis, the schools, and at some distance the hospital for the sick with a reservoir, or pond. The road leading to the city was very firm and solid, covered with fine sand, and shaded by handsome trees. On the highest point of that Jewish place of assembly there was a tree in whose strong, leafy branches one could sit as in an arbor.

Jesus and his followers were escorted by the elders to a large hall near the synagogue where they spent the night. Here Jesus cured of edema some sick who had been carried on litters into the forecourt of the inn. There was in this house a spacious lecture hall, and in it traveling rabbis were lodged. It was very handsome, built in pagan style with a colonnade around it. The interior was one immense room with tiers of seats and teachers' chairs against the walls. On the lower floor and rolled up against the walls were couches, and above them, tucked up and fastened to the wall, were tent covers that could be let down around the beds, thus forming a private alcove. One could from the outside mount to the flat roof of the hall, upon which were placed various kinds of plants in pots.

The father of Jonas, the new disciple, spent the night there, for he did not belong to the city, but Cyrinus and his sons went home.

Jesus Teaches in Salamis

Friday, April 27, AD 31 (Iyyar 15)

This morning Jesus healed the sick at the local hospital. After teaching at an open square, Jesus and the disciples ate a meal held in his honor. At the start of the sabbath, he taught in the synagogue.

ON the morning of the following day, Jesus was accompanied by the superior, a venerable old man, and some of the teachers to the hospital, a circular building enclosing a garden. In the center of the latter there was a reservoir, or pond, for bathing; but for drinking and cooking purposes, the water was collected in huge casks and purified by means of certain fruits thrown into it. Medicinal herbs were raised around the pond. The third part of the hospital was occupied by invalid females, and it was separated from the rest of the building by doors kept locked. Jesus cured some of the dropsical and gouty male patients, also such as were slightly tainted with leprosy. The newly cured followed him to the open square upon which, in the meantime, the other Jews had gathered, and where Jesus delivered an instruction first to the men. He took for his subject the gathering of the manna in the wilderness, and said that the time for the true heavenly manna of doctrine and conversion of heart had come, and that a new kind of bread from heaven was about to be given them.

This instruction over, the men withdrew and the women took their place. A great many pagan women were present, but they remained standing in the background. Jesus instructed the women in general terms, because of the pagans among them. He spoke of the one, almighty God, of the Father and Creator of heaven and earth, of the folly of polytheism, and of God's love for humankind.

After that Jesus and his followers went to dine at the superior's house, whither he had been invited along with several rabbis. It was a very large mansion of pagan architecture with forecourts, open porches, and terraces. All was here prepared for a grand entertainment. Numbers of tables were spread under the colonnade and there were arches erected and adorned with wreaths. It appeared to be a banquet intended principally for Jesus and friends returned from the Passover solemnity. The superior conducted Jesus into a side building, in which were his wife and some other women. Several doctors accompanied them. After the veiled women had with a low inclination saluted Jesus and he had said some gracious words to them, a procession of flower-crowned children appeared, playing on flutes and other instruments, to conduct Jesus to the feast. The table was ornamented with vases and bouquets. It was higher than those in use in Judea, and the other guests reclined less outstretched, closer to one another. They washed their hands. Among the various offerings was a lamb. Jesus carved it and distributed it to the guests on little round rolls. It had, however, been cut up and put together again before being placed on the table.

Then the child musicians again made their appearance. Among them were some blind children and some with other defects. They were followed by a troop of gaily dressed little girls from eight to ten years old, among them the daughter, or granddaughter of the host. All were clothed in fine, white material, somewhat glossy. The garments worn in this country were not so ample in make, not so flowing in style as those of Judea. Their hair hung down in three parts, the ends uniting into a curl, or fastened together by some kind of ornament to which hung various little trinkets, fringes, pearls, or red balls like fruit. By this arrangement, their crisp black or reddish-brown tresses were kept from streaming around. Several of the little girls carried a large crown formed of wreaths and various kinds of ornamentation. It was composed of circlets so arranged that each was firm in its own place. To the first and larger one, the second was fastened by clasps, and from the latter rose a glittering tuft, or a small flag. I do not think the wreaths were formed of natural flowers, at least not entirely; for many of the blossoms looked to me like silk, or wool intermixed with feathers and various kinds of glittering ornaments. The little girls placed this great crown like a canopy upon a high pedestal, ornamented in a similar manner, that stood behind Jesus's seat, while others brought aromatic herbs and perfumes in little dishes and alabaster vases, which they set down before him. A child belonging to the house broke one of the little flasks, poured its contents over his head, and spread it with a linen cloth over his hair, after which the children retired. The little girls went through these ceremonies with perfect composure and without speaking a word, their downcast eyes never once glancing toward the guests. Jesus very quietly received their attentions and thanked them in a few gentle, gracious words, whereupon the children—without raising their eyes—went back to the women's hall. The women ate all together.

I did not see Jesus and his disciples reclining long at table. Jesus constantly sent food and drink to the tables of the poor by his disciples, who spent most of the time serving others. After some time, Jesus himself went around from table to table, distributing food, teaching, and explaining.

After the banquet, the superior and some of the teachers went with Jesus and the disciples out to the aqueduct, which they approached from the west. The city had bad water. I saw some of those stupendous structures, like immense bridges, which contained many great reservoirs, or cisterns. Each quarter of the city had its own waterworks and reservoir. From some they had to pump the water; from others it could be drawn. The reservoir of the Jews stood apart by itself. They showed it to Jesus, complained to him of the scarcity and bad quality of the water, and wanted him to improve it. He spoke of the new reservoir in progress of construction, said that he wanted baptism to be given at it, and told them how it should be arranged.

After that they proceeded to the synagogue, for the sabbath was begun. It was an extraordinarily large and handsome edifice, lit up by numerous lamps and full of people. Around the outside ran steps and balconies from which spectators could both see and hear what was going on inside. All these places were occupied by pagans, and below they had even crowded into the interior of the synagogue, where they now stood quietly side by side with the Jews.

The instruction was on passages from the third book of Moses, treating of sacrifices and various laws, and others from Ezekiel. It began by some of the doctors reading these passages, which Jesus explained and commented upon so beautifully that all were deeply impressed. He spoke also of his own mission and its speedy accomplishment. His hearers believed him to be not only a prophet, but still more than a prophet. He must, they thought, at least be the one that was to go before the Messiah. Jesus explained to them that that precursor was John, and enumerated the signs by which they might recognize the Messiah—without, however, indicating to them clearly that he himself was the Messiah. Nevertheless, they understood him, and listened in reverence and respectful fear. After the instruction all dispersed to their homes, and Jesus went back with his followers to the house of the superior.

On the whole, Jesus was received in Salamis with extraordinary affection. The inhabitants pressed around him, all being desirous of showing him honor, for there was among them neither sect nor strife. Jesus healed several sick persons in their own homes. Jews and pagans lived here on very familiar terms, though in separate quarters. In that of the Jews there were two streets. The house of the sons of Cyrinus was a large, square building. They were engaged in commerce and owned ships. A peculiar style of architecture was predominant in Salamis. I saw numerous turrets and spires, a great deal of latticework, many latticed windows, and all kinds of ornamentation on the edifices. The people presented Jesus and the disciples on their arrival with new sandals and a change of garments. Jesus kept his only till his own were shaken and dusted; then he gave them to the poor.

Saturday, April 28, AD 31 (Iyyar 16)

This morning Jesus taught in the synagogue, which was completely full, and visited the hospital again. Then he dined as guest of honor at the house of Cyrinus. At the close of the sabbath, he taught in the synagogue concerning the Law and true sacrifice. At the same time he gave instructions to prepare those wanting to be baptized.

On the morning of the sabbath, Jesus taught again in the synagogue on the time of grace and the fulfillment of the prophecies, and that so eloquently that many of his hearers shed tears. He exhorted to penance and baptism. This instruction lasted between three and four hours.

Jesus went at the end of it with his disciples and the doctors to Cyrinus's, whither they had been invited to dine. It stood just between the Jewish and the pagan quarters. Salamis had eight streets, two of which belonged to the Jews. The little party did not go through the latter, but by a route running between the two quarters and at the rear of the houses. In this way they passed the great gates of the city. In the gateways was gathered a crowd of pagans, men, women, and children. They were very respectful and saluted Jesus and his followers timidly from a distance. They had listened to his instruction of the school, and were now come with their friends to the gates.

At the end of the street and half within the walls of the pagan quarter was the magnificent home of Cyrinus, with its courts and side buildings. As soon as the house became visible in the distance, the wife and daughters of Cyrinus were seen approaching with their servants. They saluted Jesus and his disciples. Cyrinus had five daughters, along with nieces and other young relatives. All these children bore with them presents which, after they had bowed low before Jesus, they set down at his feet on carpets which they had previously spread. The gifts consisted of bric-a-brac in all shapes and forms, some of amber, others of coral, notably a little tree of the latter mounted upon a stand. It appeared as if each child wanted to offer the dearest object in her possession, and if she could not get near enough to Jesus himself, she presented it to one of his companions.

Cyrinus's dwelling was very spacious and built in pagan style, with forecourts and outside flights of steps. On the roof was a well-arranged garden of plants growing in pots. All was adorned in festive style. The table was higher than those in ordinary use, and covered with a red cloth over which was a transparent one of glossy silk, or fine straw plaiting. The couches around the table, too, were more in accordance with pagan customs, shorter than those in use among the Jews. Besides the disciples, the guests numbered about twenty men. The women ate apart, and after dinner all took the customary sabbath promenade out to the waterworks.

From there Jesus permitted himself and his disciples to be conducted by Jonas, the new disciple, to the house of his father, which stood surrounded by gardens somewhat distant from the Jewish quarter. It was like a large farmhouse, having something of the cloister in its arrangement. The old man was an Essene, and with him dwelt, though in a separate part of the house, several old women, widowed relatives, nieces or daughters, who were somewhat differently clothed and wore white veils. The old man was humble and joyous as a child, and allowed himself to be led by his children to meet Jesus. He was at a loss as to what he should give Jesus, for he had no treasures. But he pointed around him, to himself, his sons, his daughters, as if to say: "Lord, all that we have, we ourselves are thine—and my dearest child, my son is thine!" He invited Jesus and the disciples to dine with him on the following day.

Jesus then returned to the waterworks and spoke with the superior about the arrangements for the baptismal well, which was not yet under roof and had no means of letting in water. They had first to beg or buy water from the pagans. It would have to be conveyed thither from the aqueduct which, on the plain, was about one story high with reservoirs on either side. The source of the water was in the mountain range on the west. The new baptismal well had more than four corners, and there were steps leading down into it. Around it were cavities in the form of a tray, which could be filled with water by pressing on a winch. The whole was surrounded by a rampart and nearby, for instructions, was a charming open place covered by an awning.

A great many Jews and pagans were gathered on the spot, and Jesus told them that next day he would instruct those that wanted to receive baptism. The Jews made frequent allusion to Elijah and Elisha, who likewise had been here.

Jewish women with their children had stationed themselves here and there on the way. Jesus patted the little ones in his vicinity, frequently called the others to him, and gave to all his blessing. Several pagan teachers, or mothers in yellow veils were standing apart with their little girls and boys. Jesus blessed them from afar.

After that all repaired to the synagogue for the closing exercises of the sabbath. Jesus again taught upon sacrifice, taking his texts from the third book of Moses (Leviticus) and the prophet Ezekiel. There was something marvelously sweet and impressive in his words as he showed that the Laws of Moses were now realizing their most elevated signification. He spoke of the offering of a pure heart. He said that sacrifices multiplied a thousand times could no more be of any avail, for one must purify his soul and offer his passions as a holocaust. Without rejecting anything, without condemning or abolishing any of the prescriptions of the Mosaic Law, he explained it according to its real signification, thus making it appear far more beautiful and worthy of reverence. Jesus, at the same time, prepared his hearers for the baptism and exhorted to penance, for the time was near.

His words and the tone of his voice were like living, deeply penetrating streams of light. He spoke with extraordinary calmness and power, and never very rapidly, excepting sometimes when talking with the Pharisees. At such times, his words were like sharp arrows and his voice less gentle. The tone of his ordinary voice was an agreeable tenor, perfectly pure in sound, without its counterpart in that of any human being. He could, without raising it, be distinctly heard above a great clamor.

The lessons and prayers were chanted in the synagogue on a recitative tone, in the same manner as the choral singing and Mass of the Christians, and sometimes the Jews sang alternately. Jesus read in this way the passages that he explained from holy scripture.

After Jesus's instruction, a pious old doctor of the Law began to address the assembly. He had a long, white beard, was of a meager form and kind, benevolent countenance. He did not belong to Salamis, but was a poor, traveling teacher who journeyed from place to place on the island visiting the sick, consoling the imprisoned, collecting for the poor, instructing the ignorant and little children, comforting widows, and delivering discourses in the synagogues. On this occasion, he appeared to be inspired by the Holy Spirit. He addressed the people in a speech that bore witness to Jesus, such as I never before heard in public from any one of the rabbis. He rehearsed all the benefits of almighty God to their fathers and themselves, and urged them to gratitude to him for having permitted that they should live at the coming of such a prophet, such a Teacher, to whom likewise they owed thanks for having journeyed on their account all the way from the Holy Land. He reminded them of God's mercy to their tribe (they were of the tribe of Issachar), and called upon them to do penance and amend their lives. He said that God would not treat them so severely now as he did when he punished the fabricators and adorers of the golden calf. I do not know the force of his allusion; perhaps many of their tribe had been among the idolaters. He said also marvellous things about Jesus: that he esteemed him more than a prophet, though he did not venture to say who he really was, that the fulfillment of the Promises was near, that all should consider themselves happy to hear such instructions from such lips, and to have lived at an epoch of such hope, such consolation for Israel. The people were deeply moved, and many shed tears of joy. All this took place in the presence of Jesus, who was quietly standing on one side among his disciples.

Jesus went afterward with his followers to the house of the elder, where the conversation became very animated. All present tried to prevail upon Jesus to remain among them. They quoted the words of some of the prophets relative to persecution and sufferings, which words seemed to apply to the Messiah. They trusted that such might not happen to Jesus, and asked whether he was the precursor of the Messiah. Then Jesus told them about John, and declared to them that he could not remain among them. One of those present, who had been in Palestine when Jesus was there, began to speak of the hatred of the Pharisees against him, and said some hard things about that sect. But Jesus reproached him for his severity, said a few words in their excuse, and turned the conversation to other subjects.

Sunday, April 29, AD 31 *(Iyyar 17)*

After healing some people who were then baptized by the disciples, he taught on a hill. A large crowd gathered to hear him. The Roman commandant of Salamis sent an invitation to Jesus, which Jesus accepted. At the commandants's palace Jesus answered the questions that were put to him. He emphasized that his kingdom was not of this world. The commandant was astonished at Jesus's words, at the content of his wisdom, and invited Jesus to return and speak again. Around two in the afternoon Jesus arrived at the home of the father of his disciple Jonas. Jonas's father was an Essene and lived a pious and simple life. Here Jesus gave instruction to a number of people waiting to be baptized. Barnabas, James the Less, and Azor then baptized them.

Next day, in the hospital and at the recently constructed baptismal well, Jesus prepared the people for baptism. Several in the hospital made known to him their sins, for which purpose they retired apart with him. He caused water for baptism to be put aside here in basins, and in it the sick were later on baptized by the disciples.

When Jesus arrived at the open square around the baptismal well, he found a great multitude there assembled, among them many pagans, for during the night the people had been pouring in from the surrounding country. Jesus taught under an awning. His discourse turned upon his own mission, upon penance and baptism, and he explained the Lord's Prayer.

Jesus Invited to the House of the Roman Commandant in Salamis

WHILE Jesus was delivering his instruction, a pagan soldier, or constable, made his appearance with a message to the magistrates. It was to this effect, that the Roman commandant in Salamis wished to speak with the new teacher and, consequently, invited him to his house. The soldier delivered his message rather sternly, as if he took it ill that they had not led Jesus to him at once. The magistrates transmitted it to Jesus through the disciples during a pause in the discourse. Jesus replied that he would go, and went on speaking. After his instruction, accompanied by the disciples and elders, he followed the messenger to the commandant's. They had to go a distance of half an hour, along the same way by which Jesus had come hither from the port, before reaching the principal gate of Salamis, a beautiful, high archway supported on pillars. As they passed the great walls and large gardens on the way, the pagan people and laborers looked inquisitively after Jesus, and many as he approached shyly hid behind the walls and bushes. On entering Salamis they repaired to a large open square. The houses as they passed along were lined with spectators, standing on the galleries of the courts, behind the lattices, and in the gates. On some of the street corners and under the arches were pagan women and children, ranged three by three in regular order. The women were veiled, and they bowed low to Jesus as he passed. Here and there children, sometimes too the women, stepped forward and presented to Jesus or his companions diverse little gifts, such as bunches of aromatic shrubs, little flasks of perfumes, little brown cakes, and objects in the form of stars and other things that exhaled a delicious odor. This appeared to be the custom of the country, a sign of reverential welcome. Jesus lingered a few instants near such groups, cast upon them gracious and earnest glances, and blessed them, though without touching them.

I saw idols standing here and there. They were not like those of Greece and Rome, images in human form, but like those in Sidon, Tyre, and Joppa, figures with wings, or scales. I also saw some like dolls.

As they advanced into the city, the crowd following Jesus constantly increased, and people were streaming from all sides toward the open square. In the center of the latter was a beautiful well. Steps led down into it, and through the middle of the basin the water bubbled up. It was protected by a roof supported on pillars, and surrounded by open porches, little trees, and flowers. The entrance to the well was usually closed. The people could get some of its water only by certain privileges, as it was the best in the city and thought possessed of peculiarly wholesome properties.

Opposite this well stood the commandant's palace with its colonnade. On an open balcony over which was a pillared roof sat the Roman commandant on a stone seat, watching Jesus's approach. He was dressed in military costume, a white tunic tightly fitting round the body, striped here and there with red. It descended to below the hips and ended in straps, or fringe. The lower limbs were laced. He wore a short red mantle and on his head a hat that looked to me like a shaving dish. He was a strong, robust man with a short beard, black and crisp. Behind him and on the steps of the balcony were standing Roman soldiers.

The pagans were astonished at the marks of respect he showed to Jesus, for when the latter approached, he descended from the balcony, clasped his hand in the end of a linen scarf that he held in his own, and pressed it with the other hand, in which was the other end of the scarf, at the same time bowing low before him. Then he led Jesus up to the balcony, where he put to him, most graciously, question after question. He had, he said, heard him spoken of as a wise teacher. He himself revered the Jewish Law. If all that was said of him was true, Jesus did indeed perform great wonders. Who gave him the power for such things? Was he the promised Comforter, the Messiah of the Jews? The Jews were expecting a king—was he that king? By what means would he get possession of his kingdom? Had he an army somewhere? Perhaps he was going to collect forces here in Cyprus among the Jews? Would it be long before he would show himself in all his power? The commandant put sundry questions of this kind in a tone full of respect and earnestness. His profound sympathy and reverence for Jesus were visible. Jesus answered all in vague and general terms, as he usually did when such questions were put to him by magistrates. He would, for instance, answer: "Thou sayest it! So they think. The prophets have thus declared." To the questions relative to his kingdom, to his army, he answered that his kingdom was not of this world. The kings of this world had need of warriors, but he gathered the souls of men into the kingdom of the almighty Father, the Creator of heaven and earth. In deeply significant words he touched, in passing, upon many subjects. The commandant was astounded both at his language and bearing.

He had ordered refreshments to be brought to the well in the open square, and he now invited Jesus and his disciples to follow him thither. They examined the well and partook of the refreshments, which were spread on a stone stand previously covered. There were several brown dishes with sauce of the same color, into which they dipped cakes. They partook also of sticks of confectionery, or strips of cheese, about an arm in length and two inches thick, fruit, and pastry made into figures of stars and flowers. Little jugs of wine were placed around the stand. Others, made of something with colored veining, in shape just like those of Cana only much smaller, were filled with water from the well. The commandant spoke too with marked disapprobation of Pilate, of the violence he had exercised in the temple, and of his character in general, also of the demolished aqueduct near Shiloh.

Jesus held another conversation with the commandant here at the well. He spoke of water and its different sources, some muddy, others clear, some bitter and salty, others sweet, of the great difference in its effects, of how it was conducted into the well and again distributed in conduits. From such remarks he passed to instructing both pagans and Jews upon the waters of baptism, the regeneration of humankind by penance and faith, when all would become children of God. It was an admirable instruction with something in it similar to his conversation with the Samaritan at the well. His words made a deep impression upon the commandant, who was already very well disposed toward the Jews. He wanted to hear Jesus frequently.

In Salamis the separation between Jews and pagans was not so marked. Here as in Palestine, the more enlightened Jews, and especially the followers of Jesus, ate and drank with the upper class of pagans, although always making use of separate vessels. On their return, Jesus was saluted by many of the pagans, and that still more respectfully than before, owing to the marks of honor shown him by the commandant.

Flowers in this country were extremely abundant, and artificial ones were most artistically made of colored wool, silk, and little feathers. I saw the pagan children whom Jesus blessed adorned for the most part with such flowers. The little girls were, like the boys, dressed in very short garments of thin material; the very little ones of the poor had only a cincture around the waist. The young maidens of the wealthier classes wore thin, yellow tunics richly covered with those colored woollen flowers of which I have spoken. Around the shoulders, the ends crossed over the breast, they wore a scarf of thin texture, and on their arms and head, little garlands of artificial flowers. They must have raised silkworms here, for I saw along the walls trees carefully reared whereon those insects were crawling and spinning their cocoons.

Jesus at the Home of Jonas's Father • Instruction at the Baptismal Well

WHEN Jesus visited the home of the Essene, the father of Jonas, he was accompanied by his disciples only and some of the doctors. He was received with the usual courtesies, that is, washing of the feet. The domestic arrangements were here much more simple, more like the country than those of the mansion at which Jesus had first been entertained. The family was large and belonged to the sect of Essenes, to those that married. They lived in great pur-ity, being pious and simple in their manners. The female portion were widows with children already grown, daughters of the old man, with whom they lived. Jonas the disciple was the son of a later marriage, and his mother died in giving him birth. The old man loved him so much the more as he was his only son, and he had been in great anxiety about his being absent for over a year. He had looked upon him as lost, when he received news of him through Cyrinus, whose sons had met Jonas at the Passover feast and in Dabrath near Tabor. The youth had been traveling for information, as young students often do. He had visited the most remarkable of the holy places, the Essenes in Judea, Jacob's tomb near Hebron, and that of Rachel between Jerusalem and Bethlehem. The last-named lay at that time on the direct route between these two places; now, however, it lies somewhat on one side. He had likewise visited all that was most interesting in Bethlehem, as well as Mounts Carmel and Tabor. He had heard of Jesus and had been present at one of the mountain sermons before he went into the country of the Gergeseans. After the Passover festival he had gone with the sons of Cyrinus from Dabrath to the last instruction at Gabara. It was then that Jesus received him as a disciple, in which quality he now returned home.

The entertainment was held in a garden in which were long and densely shaded arbors. An elevated green bank, covered with a cloth, served as a table. The couches too consisted of similar grassy banks covered with mats. The meal was made up of various kinds of pastry, broth, vegetables steeped in sauce, lamb's meat, fruit, and little jugs of something, all very simple. The women ate at a separate table, though they seemed more at their ease than other Jewish women. They served at table, their veils lowered, and sitting at some distance, afterward listened to the words of Jesus. On both sides of the garden there were whole rows of arbors formed of dense green foliage. I think they were intended as places for the devotional exercises of the family, which was like a perfect little Essene community. They lived by agriculture and cattle-raising, weaving, and spinning.

From this place, Jesus went with the disciples to the newly constructed baptismal well, where he prepared many Jews for baptism by a discourse in which he exhorted to penance and blessed the baptismal water. Around the central well there were some salver-shaped basins on a level with the surrounding surface. These basins were encircled by little ditches, into which the neophytes descended by a couple of steps. He who baptized stood on the edge of the basin and poured water on the head of the neophytes bowed over the same. The sponsors stood behind and imposed hands on them. By the opening or pressing of a piece of machinery in the central well, the water could be introduced into the basins and ditches. I saw Barnabas, James, and Azor baptizing by three of the basins. Before the ceremony I saw Jesus, from a flat, leathern vessel which they had brought with them from Judea, pouring a little Jordan water taken from his own place of baptism, into the basins, and then blessing the water thus mixed with it. After the baptism, not only was all this baptismal water poured again into the central well, but the basins were dried with a cloth which was then wrung out into the well. I saw the neophytes with little white mantles around their shoulders.

After that I saw Jesus going in a more westerly direction between gardens and walls, where were awaiting him several pagans who, prepared by their friend Cyrinus, were likewise desirous of baptism. He went aside with some of them whom he further instructed, and about thirty of them were baptized in the various bathing gardens around. Water was introduced into the baths for that purpose, which water Jesus blessed.

Besides the two streets belonging to the Jews, there was in the vicinity of Salamis an entire Jewish city. On one side of Salamis there was a round tower of extraordinary circumference, to which were attached all kinds of dependencies. It was like a citadel. The city possessed many temples, one of which was of uncommon dimensions, and to its terrace one could mount either by an interior or an exterior flight of steps. In the temple were found numerous columns, some so large around that in them were cut steps and little apartments wherein the people could stand on high and look down on the religious ceremonies. A couple of hours from Salamis, I saw another important city.

Westward from the city I saw a caravan of strangers approaching, who encamped under tents. They must have come from the other side of the island; indeed, on account of the direction, I was inclined to think they had come from Rome itself. They had some women with them and a great number of large, heavy oxen with broad horns and low heads. They were bound together, two by two, with long poles over their backs upon which they carried burdens. I think these strangers had come partly on account of the harvest. They brought with them merchandise which they wished to exchange for grain.

Monday, April 30, AD 31 (Iyyar 18)

This morning Jesus taught close to the place of baptism. Among the crowd—of both Jews and pagans—were some pagan philosophers. They questioned Jesus. Then, in the afternoon, Jesus visited some private homes where he healed the sick. That evening, he dined with the rabbis as their guest of honor. Later, when he and the disciples had returned to their inn, a pagan lady—her name was Mercuria—came to speak with Jesus. Mercuria confessed her sins and Jesus spoke earnestly with her. His words were full of compassion. He commanded her to renounce her way of life and told her of God the Almighty.

Next morning Jesus delivered, on the open square near the baptismal well, a lengthy instruction to both Jews and pagans. He taught of the harvest, the multiplication of the grain, the ingratitude of humankind who receive the greatest wonders of God so indifferently, and predicted for these ingrates the fate of the chaff and weeds, namely, to be cast into the fire. He said also that from one seed-corn a whole harvest was gathered, that all things came forth from One, almighty God, the Creator of heaven and earth, the Father and Supporter of all men, who would reward their good works and punish their evil ones. He showed them also how men, instead of turning to God the Father, turn to creatures, to lifeless blocks.

They pass coldly by the wonders of God, while they gaze in astonishment at the specious though paltry works of men, even rendering honor to miserable jugglers and sorcerers. Here Jesus took occasion to speak of the pagan gods, the ridiculous ideas entertained of them, the confusion existing in those ideas, the service rendered them, and all the cruelties related of them. Then he spoke of some of these gods individually, asking such questions as these: "Who is this god? Who is that other? Who was his father?" etc. To these questions he himself gave the answers, exposing in them the confused genealogies and families of their pagan divinities and the abominations connected with them, all which facts could be found, not in the kingdom of God, but only in that of the father of lies. Finally he mentioned and analyzed the various and contradictory attributes of these gods.

Although Jesus spoke in so severe and conclusive a manner, still his instruction was so agreeable, so suggestive of good thoughts to his hearers that it could rouse no displeasure. His teaching against paganism was much milder here in Salamis than it was wont to be in Palestine. He spoke too of the vocation of the Gentiles to the kingdom of God and said that many strangers from the east and from the west would get possession of the thrones intended for the children of the house, since the latter cast salvation far from them.

During a pause in the instruction, Jesus took a mouthful to eat and drink, and the people discussed among themselves what they had just heard. Meanwhile some pagan philosophers drew near to Jesus and questioned him upon some points not understood by them, also about something that had been transmitted to them by their ancestors as coming from Elijah, who had been in these parts. Jesus gave them the desired information, and then began teaching upon baptism, also of prayer, referring for his text to the harvest and their own daily bread.

Many of the pagans received most salutary impressions from Jesus's instructions and were led to reflections productive of fruit. But others, finding his words not to their liking, took their departure.

And now I saw a great number of Jews baptized at the baptismal well, the waters of which Jesus blessed. Three at a time stood round one basin. The water in the ditches reached as high as the calf of the leg.

Jesus Goes to the Jewish City

JESUS afterward went with his followers and some of the doctors to the separate Jewish city, about one half-hour to the north. He was followed by many of his late audience, and he continued to speak with several little groups. The route led over some more elevated places below which lay meadows and gardens. Here and there were rows of trees, and again some solitary ones, high and dense, up which the traveler might climb and find a shady seat. The view extended far around on several little localities and fields of golden wheat. Sometimes the road ran along broad, naked walls of rock, in which whole rows of cells had been hewn out for the field laborers.

Outside the Jewish city stood a fine inn and pleasure garden. Here Jesus's own party entered, while he bade the rest of his escort return to their homes. The disciples washed Jesus's feet, then one another's, let down their garments, and followed their Master into the Jewish city. During the foot-washing, I saw near the inn on one side of the highroad that ran along the city, long, light buildings like sheds, in which were a great number of Jewish women and maidservants busied in selecting, arranging, and carefully preserving the fruits which female slaves, or domestics, carried thither in baskets from the gardens around. The fruits were of all kinds, large and small, also berries. They separated the good from the bad, made all kinds of divisions, and even laid some wrapped in cotton on shelves one over another. Others were engaged in picking and packing cotton. I noticed all the housewives lowering their veils as soon as the men appeared on the highroad. The sheds were divided into several compartments. They looked to me like a general fruitery, where the portion intended for the tithes and that for alms were laid aside. It was a very busy scene.

Jesus went with his party to the dwelling of the rabbis near the synagogue. The eldest rabbi received him courteously, though with a tinge of stiff reserve in his manner. He offered him the customary refreshments, and said a few words upon his visit to the island and his far-famed reputation, etc. Jesus's arrival having become known, several invalids implored his help, whereupon, accompanied by the rabbis and the disciples, he visited them in their homes and cured many lame and paralyzed. The latter, with their families, followed him out of their houses, and proclaimed his praise. But he silenced them and bade them go back. On the streets he was met by mothers and their children, whom he blessed. Some carried sick children to him, and he cured them.

And so passed the afternoon away till evening, when Jesus accompanied the rabbis to an entertainment in his honor, which entertainment was likewise connected with the beginning of the harvest. The poor and the laboring people were fed at it, a custom which drew from Jesus words of commendation. They were brought from the fields in bands and seated at long tables, like benches of stone, and there served with various foods. Jesus, from time to time, waited on them himself with the disciples, and instructed them in short sentences and parables. Several of the Jewish doctors were present at the entertainment; but on the whole this company was not so well disposed, not so sincere as the Jews around Jesus's inn near Salamis. There was a tinge of pharisaism about them and, after they had become heated, they gave utterance to some offensive remarks. They asked whether he could not conveniently remain longer in Palestine, what was the real object of his visit to them, whether he intended to stay any time among them, and ended by suggesting that he should create no disturbance in Cyprus. They likewise touched upon diverse points of his doctrine and manner of acting which the Pharisees of Palestine were in the habit of rehearsing. Jesus answered them as he usually did on similar occasions, with more or less severity according to the measure of their own civility. He told them that he had come to exercise the works of mercy as the Father in heaven willed him to do. The conversation was very animated. It gave Jesus an opportunity for delivering a stern lecture in which, while commending their goodness to the poor and whatever else was praiseworthy in them, he denounced their hypocrisy. It was already late when Jesus left with his followers. The rabbis bore him company as far as the city gate.

The Pagan Priestess Mercuria • The Pagan Philosophers

WHEN Jesus had returned to the inn with the disciples, a pagan came to him and begged him to go with him to a certain garden a few steps distant, where a person in distress was waiting to implore his assistance. Jesus went with the disciples to the place indicated. There he saw standing between the walls on the road a pagan lady, who inclined low before him. He ordered the disciples to fall back a little, and then questioned the woman as to what she wanted. She was a very remarkable person, perfectly destitute of instruction, quite sunk in paganism, and wholly given up to its abominable service. One glance from Jesus had cast her into disquiet, and roused in her the feeling that she was in error, but she was without simple faith, and had a very confused manner of accusing herself. She told Jesus that she had heard of his having helped Magdalene, as also the woman afflicted with an issue of blood, of whom the latter had merely touched the hem of his garment. She begged Jesus to cure and instruct her, but then again, she said perhaps he could not cure her as she was not, like the woman with the issue, physically sick. She confessed that she was married and had three children, but that one, unknown to her husband, had been begotten in adultery. She had also intercourse with the Roman commandant. When Jesus, on the preceding day, visited the last named, she had watched him from a window and saw a halo of light around his head, which sight very powerfully impressed her. She at first thought that her emotion sprang from love for Jesus, and the idea caused her anguish so intense that she fell to the ground unconscious. When returned to herself, her whole life, her whole interior passed before her in so frightful a manner that she entirely lost her peace of mind. She then made inquiries about Jesus, and learned from some Jewish women of Magdalene's cure, also that of Enue of Caesarea-Philippi, the woman afflicted with the issue of blood. She now implored Jesus to heal her if he possibly could. Jesus told her that the faith of that afflicted woman was simple; that, in the firm belief that if she could touch only the seam of his garment she would be cured, she had approached him stealthily and her faith had saved her.

The silly woman again asked Jesus how he could have known that Enue touched him and that he healed her. She did not comprehend Jesus or his power, although she heartily longed for his assistance. Jesus rebuked her, commanded her to renounce her shameful life, and told her of God the Almighty and of his commandment: "Thou shalt not commit adultery." He placed before her all the abominations of the debauchery (against which her nature itself revolted) practiced in the impure service of her gods; and he met her with words so earnest and so full of mercy that she retired weeping and penetrated with sorrow. The lady's name was Mercuria. She was tall, and about thirty-five years old. She was enveloped in a white mantle, long and flowing in the back but rather shorter in front, which formed a cap around the head. Her other garments also were white, though with colored borders. The materials in which the pagan women dressed were so soft and clung so closely to the form that the latter could readily be traced by the eye.

Tuesday, May 1, AD 31 (Iyyar 19)

The disciples continued to baptize, while Jesus taught and healed the sick. Jesus then began to teach the pagan philosophers about the nature of their cults and the arising of false gods.

The whole morning of the following day was devoted by the disciples to baptizing at the fountain, and I saw Jesus teaching both here and at the waterworks. His instructions were given principally in parables on the harvest, the daily bread, the manna, the bread of life that was to be given them, and the one, only God. The laborers were sent to the harvest in groups, and I saw Jesus instructing them as they passed before him. The people here encamped under tents were also Jews, who had come hither especially on Jesus's account. They had brought their sick with them on beasts of burden, and now today they were placed on litters under awnings and trees in the vicinity of the place of instruction. Jesus cured about twenty lame and palsied.

On reaching the waterworks, he was accosted by several men, learned pagans, who had been present at his instructions of the preceding day. They begged for an explanation upon several points, spoke of their divinities, especially of one goddess that had risen here from the sea, and of another represented in their temple under the form of a fish. This latter was named Derketo. They questioned him also about a story circulating among the Jews and connected with Elijah. It was to this effect, that Elijah once saw a cloud rising out of the sea, which cloud was, in reality, a virgin. They would like to know, they said, where she had descended, for from her was to proceed a king. One that was to do good to the whole world. Now, according to calculation, it was time for this to happen. With this story they mixed up another concerning a star that their goddess had let fall upon Tyre, and they asked whether that could be the cloud of which they had spoken.

One of them said that there was a report current of an adventurer in Judea who was making capital of Elijah's cloud and the circumstance of the fulfillment of time, in order to proclaim himself king. Jesus gave no intimation that he was the one in question, though he said: "That man is no adventurer, nor does he proclaim what is false. Many untruths are spread against him, and thou who now sayest these things, hast joined in calumniating him. But the time has now come for the prophecies to be fulfilled." Jesus's interrogator was an evil-minded man, a great tattler. He dreamed not, when talking with Jesus, that he was in the presence of him whom he was slandering, for he had heard of Jesus only in a general way.

These men were philosophers. They had some intimation of the truth mixed up with faith in their own divinities, which they tried again to explain away by various interpretations. But all the personages and idols which they wanted to explain had, in the course of time, become so mixed up and confused in their minds that even the cloud of Elijah and the Mother of God, of whom they knew nothing at all, had to be dragged by them into the general confusion. They called their goddess Derketo the Queen of Heaven. They spoke of her as of one that had brought to earth all that it had of wisdom and pleasure. They said that her followers having ceased to acknowledge her, she prophesied to them all that would befall them in the future; also that she would plunge into the sea and reappear as a fish to be with them forever. All this, they added, had actually come to pass, etc. Her daughter, whom she had conceived in the sacred rites of paganism, was Semiramis, the wise and powerful Queen of Babylon.

How wonderful! While these men were thus speaking, I saw the whole history of these goddesses, as if they had really risen before me and were still alive. I felt impatient to disabuse the philosophers of their gross errors. They appeared to me so astonishingly silly in not seeing them themselves that I kept thinking: "Now, this is so distinct, so clear that I'll explain it all to them!" Then, again, I thought: "How dare you talk about such things! These learned men must know better than you!" and so I tormented myself during that conversation of several hours.

Jesus explained to the philosophers the confusion and absurdity of their idolatrous system. He related to them the history of Creation, of Adam and Eve, of the Fall, of Cain and Abel, of the children of Noah, the building of the Babylonian Tower, the separation of the bad and their gradual falling away into godlessness. He told them that these wicked people, in order to restore their relations with God from whom they had fallen, had invented all kinds of divinities and had by the evil one been seduced into the grossest error; nevertheless, the Promise that the seed of the woman should crush the serpent's head was interwoven with all the poetry, customs, and ceremonies of their necromantic art. It was in consequence of this faint idea they had of the Promise that so many personages had from time to time appeared with the vain design of bringing salvation to the world; but they had given to it instead still greater sins and abominations drawn from the impure source from which they themselves had sprung. He told them about the separation of Abraham's family from the rest of humankind; the education of a special race for the guarding of the Promise; the guidance, direction, and purification of the children of Israel; and he concluded by telling them about the prophets, about Elijah and his prophecies, and that the present time was to be that of their realization. Jesus's words were so simple, so convincing and impressive, that some of the philosophers were greatly enlightened, while others, returning to their mythical accounts, were again entangled in their mazes. Jesus spoke with the philosophers until nearly one o'clock. Some of them believed and reformed their lives. These men were wrapped up in their apparently learned elucidations of all sorts of foolish and perplexing questions. Jesus had, however, let a ray of light fall upon their soul, when he proved to them that to the fallen race of humankind and their history there always remained a trace, more or less correct, of God's designs upon men. He showed them how they, living as they did in a kingdom of darkness and confusion, had caught at the manifold improprieties and abominations of idolatry which, in the midst of their folly, still offered the external glamour of lost truth; but God, in his mercy toward humankind, formed from a few of the most innocent a nation from which the fulfillment of the Promise was to proceed. Then he pointed out to them that this time of grace was now arrived, that whosoever would do penance, amend his life, and receive baptism, should be born anew and become a child of God.

Before this interview with the philosophers and immediately after the baptism, Jesus had sent away Barnabas and some other disciples to Kythria, a few hours distant, where the family of Barnabas dwelt.

Wednesday, May 2, AD 31 (Iyyar 20)

Today, Jesus set off, going from field to field, instructing the workers as he went.

Jesus had with him only the disciple Jonas and another disciple from Dabrath, when he went one half hour westward from Salamis to a rich, fertile region wherein lay a little village whose inhabitants were busied with the harvest. They were chiefly Jews, for their fields lay on this side of the city. The country was very lovely, and agriculture was pursued in a manner different from ours. The grain was raised on very high ridges like ramparts, between which were grazing grounds surrounded by numerous fruit trees, olive trees, and others. They were full of cattle which, though penned up, could graze in the shade, and yet do no harm to the crops. These low meadows were likewise a sort of reservoir for dew and water. I saw a great many black cows without horns; oxen, hump-backed, heavy-footed, and very broad-horned, used as beasts of burden; numerous asses; extraordinarily large sheep with bushy tails; and, apart from the rest, herds of rams, or horned sheep. Houses and sheds lay scattered here and there. The people had a very beautiful school and a place for teaching in the open air, also a doctor of the Law among them; but on the sabbath they used to go to the synagogue in Salamis near Jesus's inn.

The road was very beautiful. As soon as ever the harvesters espied Jesus (they had already seen him in the synagogue and at the baptism), they left their work and their tools, cast off the piece of bark that they wore on their head as a protection from the sun's rays, and, hurrying in bands down from the high ridges, bowed low before him. Many of them even prostrated on the ground. Jesus saluted and blessed them, after which they returned to their labor. As Jesus drew near the school, the doctor, who had been apprised of his coming, went out with some other honorable personages to meet him. He bade him welcome, escorted him to a beautiful well, washed his feet, removed his mantle, which was then shaken and brushed, and presented him food and drink.

Jesus, with these people and others who had come from Salamis, went from field to field, here and there instructing the reapers in short parables upon sowing, harvesting, the separation of the wheat from the tares, the building of the granary, and the casting of the ill-weeds into the fire. The reapers listened to him in groups, and then returned to their work, while Jesus passed on to another band.

The men used a crooked knife in reaping. They cut off the stalk about a foot below the ear, and handed it to the women standing behind to receive it. The latter tied the ears into bundles and carried them away in baskets. I saw that many of the low ears were left standing, and that poor women came along afterward, cut them and gathered up the fallen ones as their portion. These women wore very short garments. Their waist was wound with linen bands, and their tunic tucked up around the body forming a sack, into which they put the ears they gleaned. Their arms were uncovered, the breast and neck concealed by linen bands, and the head veiled, or simply protected by a chip hat, according as they were married or maidens.

Jesus went on in this way walking and teaching for about a half-hour's distance, and then returned to the well near the school. Here he found a collation set out on a stone table for himself and companions. It consisted of a thick sauce, honey, I think, in shallow dishes; long sticks of something from which they broke off little scraps and laid them on their bread, little rolls of pastry, fruits, and little jugs of some kind of drink. The well was extremely beautiful. Back of it was a high terrace filled with trees. One had to descend many steps to get to the well cistern, which was cool and shady. The female portion of the doctor's family dwelt at some distance from the school. They were veiled when they brought the servings for the repast. Jesus gave instructions on the Lord's Prayer. In the evening the reapers assembled in the school, where Jesus explained the parables he had related to them in the fields, and taught also of the manna, of the daily bread, and of the bread from heaven. He went afterward with the doctor and others to visit the sick in their huts, and cured several of the lame and dropsical, who lay mostly in little cells built at the back of the houses. He thus visited a lady afflicted with edema. Her tiny room was only sufficiently large to accommodate her bed. It was open at her feet, thus allowing her to look out upon a little flower garden. The roof was light and could be raised to afford her a glimpse of the sky. Some men and women went with Jesus to the sick lady's hut. They removed the screen, and Jesus thus accosted the invalid: "Woman, dost thou desire to be relieved?" To which she answered humbly: "I desire what is pleasing to the prophet." Then Jesus said: "Arise! Thy faith has helped thee!" The woman arose, left her little cell, and said: "Lord, now I know thy power, for many others have tried to help me, but could not do it." She and her relatives offered thanks, and praised the Lord. Many came to see her, wondering at her cure. Jesus returned to the school.

I saw, on that day at Salamis, Mercuria the sinner walking up and down her apartments, a prey to deep sadness and disquietude. She wept, wrung her hands, and, enveloped in her veil, often threw herself on the floor in a corner. Her husband, who appeared to me not very bright, thought, like her maids, that she had lost her mind. But Mercuria was torn by remorse for her sins; her only thought, her constant dream, was how she could break loose from her bonds and join the holy women in Palestine. She had two daughters of eight and nine years, and a boy of fifteen. Her home was near to the great temple. It was large with massive walls and surrounded by servants' dwellings, pillars, terraces, and gardens. They called upon her to attend the temple, but she declined on the plea of sickness. This temple was an extraordinary building full of columns, chambers, abodes for the pagan priests, and vaults. In it stood a gigantic statue of the goddess, which shone like gold. The body was that of a fish, and the head was horned like a cow. Before it was another figure of less stature, upon whose shoulders the goddess rested her short arms, or claws. The figures stood upon a high pedestal, in which were cavities for the burning of incense and other offerings. The sacrifices in the goddess' honor consisted even of children, especially of cripples.

Mercuria's house became subsequently the dwelling of Costa, the father of St. Catherine. Catherine was born and reared in it. Her father descended from a princely race of Mesopotamia. For certain services, he was rewarded with large possessions in Cyprus. He married in Salamis a daughter of the same pagan priestly family to which Mercuria belonged. Even in her childhood, Catherine was full of wisdom, and had interior visions by which she was guided. She could not endure the pagan idols, and thrust them out of sight wherever she could. As a punishment for this, her father once put her in confinement.

The cities in these regions were not like ours, in which the houses stand apart. The buildings of those pagan cities were enormous, with terraces and massive walls in which, again, abodes for poorer people were constructed. Many of the streets were like broad ramparts, and were planted with trees. Under these thoroughfares were found the abodes of numbers of people. Great order reigned in Salamis. Each class of inhabitants had its own street. The school children also I saw for the most part in one particular street, and there were others set apart for the beasts of burden. The philosophers had one large edifice of their own. It was surrounded by courtyards, and I saw them promenading in the street that belonged to them. Wrapped in their mantles, they walked in bands four or five abreast, and spoke in turn. They always kept to one side of the street in going, and to the other in returning. This order was as a general thing observed in all the streets.

The square with the beautiful fountain, in which the commandant held his interview with Jesus, was much higher than the adjacent streets. To reach it, one had to mount a flight of steps. Around this square were arcades filled with shops. To one side was the marketplace, near which were rows of dense, pyramidal-shaped trees up which one could mount and sit in their bowerlike foliage. The commandant's palace fronted on this square.

Jesus Teaching in Kythria

Thursday, May 3, AD 31 (Iyyar 21)

During an instruction Jesus spoke the words recorded in Luke 8:18. That night he stayed at an inn near the Roman way. Today Jesus traveled further and arrived at an inn on the outskirts of Kythria, where he was greeted by the father of Barnabas.

ON the following morning, Jesus again went through the harvest fields instructing the laborers. A remarkable fog hung over the country the whole day, so dense that one could scarcely see his neighbor, and the sun glimmered through it like a white speck. The fields ran northeastwardly between the rising heights until they terminated in a point. I saw innumerable partridges, quails, and pigeons with enormous crops. I remember also to have seen a kind of thick, gray, ribbed apple, the pulp streaked with red. It grew on wide-spreading trees trained on trellises.

Jesus taught in parables of the harvest and the daily bread, and he cured several lame children who lay on sheepskins in a kind of cradle, or trough. When some of the people broke out in loud praise of his teaching, Jesus checked them with words something like these: "Whosoever hath, to him shall be given; and whosoever hath not (that also which he thinketh he hath), shall be taken away from him."

The Jews of this place had doubts upon diverse points, upon which Jesus instructed them. They feared to have no part in the Promised Land, they thought that Moses had had no need to cross the Red Sea, and that there was no reason for his wandering so long in the desert since there were other and more direct routes. Jesus met their objections with the reply that they could get possession of the kingdom of God, and that there was no need, it was true, for so long a sojourn in the desert. He challenged them, since they disapproved such proceedings in Moses, not to wander around themselves in the desert of sin, unbelief, and murmuring, but to take the shortest road by means of penance, baptism, and faith. The Jews of Cyprus had intermarried freely with the pagans, but in such contracts the latter always became converts to Judaism.

On this walk of instruction through the harvest fields, Jesus and his companions reached the highroad which, running a couple of hours to the west of Salamis, connected the port on the northwestern coast of Cyprus to that on the southeast. Here stood a very large Jewish inn, and at it Jesus and his followers stopped. Not far off stood sheds and an inn with a well for the pagan caravans. The highway was always swarming with travelers. There was no female at the inn; the women dwelt apart by themselves. Jesus had just washed his feet and taken some refreshments when the disciples, who had tarried in Salamis baptizing, arrived. Jesus's companions now numbered twenty. He continued to teach out in the open air the people coming home from their work. They brought to him some sick laborers who could no longer earn their bread. As they believed in his doctrine, Jesus cured them and bade them resume at once their daily labor.

Toward evening a caravan of Arabs arrived. They had with them, as beasts of burden, oxen yoked in couples. On two poles across their backs, they carried immense bales of goods that rose high above their heads. In narrow parts of the road they went one behind the other, still keeping their burden between them. I saw asses and camels also laden with bales of wool. These Arabs were from the region in which Jethro had dwelt. They were of a browner complexion than the Cypriotes, and had come hither with their goods in ships.

In the mining districts through which they passed, they bartered some of their goods for copper and other metals, and they were now pursuing their course southward along the highroad, in order again to embark for home. The beasts bore the heavy metal in long chests, the packages smaller than usual on account of their weight. I think the metal was in bars, or long plates. Some of it was already wrought into various vessels and kettles, which I saw in packages round and of the form of a cask. The women were exceedingly industrious. During their journey, whether walking or riding, they occupied themselves in spinning, and whenever they encamped, they set to work at weaving covers and scarfs. They could, in consequence, maintain themselves on the journey and renew their own clothing. They used for their work the wool packed on the beasts of burden. While spinning, they fastened the wool to their shoulders, spun the thread with one hand and wound it on the spindle which they turned in the other. When the spindle was full, the thread was wound off upon a bobbin that hung at their girdle.

When these people had unloaded and cared for their beasts, they saluted Jesus and begged to be permitted to hear his doctrine. He commended them for their industry and took occasion from it to ask the question, for whom was all their trouble, for whom all their labor. From this he went on to speak of the Creator and Preserver of all things, of gratitude to God, of God's mercy toward sinners and lost sheep that wander around not knowing their Shepherd. He taught them in mild and loving words. They were touched and rejoiced, and wanted to bestow all kinds of presents upon him. He blessed their children and left them. With his companions he then directed his steps more to the north toward Kythria, situated between four and five hours from this place and about six from Salamis. The way now became hilly.

I saw here in the country olive trees and cotton trees, also a plant from which I think they make a kind of silk. It did not look like our flax, but rather like hemp, and it furnishes a long, soft thread. But most conspicuous of all was a little tree with quantities of beautiful yellow flowers, most charming to behold. Its fruit was almost the same as that of the medlar, or persimmon; it appeared to me to be saffron. To the left one had a beautiful view of the mountains covered with high forests. Cypresses were numerous, also little resinous bushes of delicious fragrance. Here too among the mountains descended a little stream that in one part formed a waterfall. Still farther on and higher up, there was on one side of the mountain a forest, on the other, the naked soil over which wound a path, and on either side were caves extending into the mountain. Out of these were mined copper and some kind of white metal like silver. I saw the miners boring into them, also from above. The metal must have been smelted on the spot, and that with a certain yellow something of which there was a whole mountain in the neighborhood. The workmen kneaded the melted mass into great balls and then allowed them to dry. I heard it said on that occasion that the mountain sometimes caught fire.

After four hours' journey Jesus reached an inn more than half an hour from Kythria. All along the road mines were still to be seen. Here Jesus and his companions halted and the father of Barnabas, along with some other men, received the Lord and extended to him the usual acts of kindness. Jesus rested here and taught, after which he took a light repast with his companions.

Friday, May 4, AD 31 (Iyyar 22)

This morning Jesus visited an iron mine near Kythria. He addressed the workers and spoke the words recorded in Luke 6:31. He then entered the town and was greeted by the Jewish elders and also by two of the philosophers from Salamis. It was the start of the sabbath. Therefore, Jesus taught in the synagogue. Many pagans listened from the terrace outside. At one point, a lame rabbi called out for help, and Jesus healed him on the spot. Afterward, Jesus shared a meal at the house of Barnabas' father and stayed the night there.

Kythria lay on a low plain. Jesus approached it from the side upon which were the mines. The population was made up of Jews and pagans. All around the city stood numerous single buildings. It looked like country workshops connected by gardens and fields.

I was very much troubled at the little fruit arising from Jesus's great fatigue and labor in Cyprus. It was so small that, as the Pilgrim told me, nothing was known of that journey, no mention was made of it in scripture, not even of Paul and Barnabas's labors there. Then I had a vision concerning it, of which I remember the following details: Jesus gained five hundred and seventy souls, pagans and Jews, in Cyprus. I saw that the sinner Mercuria and her children delayed not to follow him, and that she brought with her great wealth in property and money. She joined the holy women; and at the first Christian settlements between Ophel and Bethany, made under the deacons, she contributed largely toward the buildings and the support of the brethren. I saw also that in an insurrection against the Christians (Saul not yet being converted) Mercuria was murdered. It was at the time when Saul set out for Damascus. Soon after Jesus's departure from the island, many pagans and Jews with their money and valuables left Cyprus and journeyed to Palestine, and little by little, transferred thither all their wealth. Then arose a great outcry among other members of these families who had not embraced Jesus's doctrine. They looked upon themselves as injured by the departure of their relatives, and they scoffed at Jesus as an impostor. Jews and pagans made common cause together, and considered it a crime even to speak of him. Many persons were arrested and scourged. The pagan priests persecuted those of their own belief, and forced them to offer sacrifice. The commandant who had had an interview with Jesus was recalled to Rome and deposed from his office. They even went so far as to send Roman soldiers to take possession of the ports so that no one could leave the island. They did not remain long, but on their departure they took with them some of the inhabitants.

On the way to Kythria, Jesus instructed the miners in separate bands. Some of the mines were rented by pagans; others, by Jews. The laborers looked very thin, pale, and miserable. Their nude bodies were protected in several places with pieces of brown leather, in which they were encased like turtles in their shells. Jesus took as the subject of his instruction the goldsmith, who purifies the ore in fire. The pagans and Jews were working on different sides of the road, so both could listen at the same time. There were some possessed, or grievously disturbed creatures that had to be bound with cords even when at work, and as Jesus drew near, they began to rage and cry. They published his name, and cried out to know what he wanted with them. Jesus commanded them to be silent, and they became quiet. Some Jewish miners now came forward complaining that the pagans had opened mines under the road in their district, thus encroaching upon their rights, and they begged him to decide the point between them. Then Jesus directed a hole to be bored near the boundary through the part belonging to the Jews, and the workmen came to the pagan mines. There were found heaps of white, metallic scraps, I think zinc or silver, which had tempted the pagans to overstep their limits. Jesus gave an instruction upon scandal and ill-gotten goods. The pagans were convicted, for the facts witnessed against them. But as the magistrate was not on the spot, nothing could be done, and the pagans withdrew muttering their dissatisfaction.

Kythria was a very stirring place. The inhabitants, pagans and Jews, lived on easy terms with one another as I more than once saw, though the two sects dwelt in different quarters. The pagans had several temples, and the Jews, two synagogues. Intermarriages were very frequent among them, but in such cases the pagan party always embraced Judaism.

Outside the city Jesus was met by the Jewish elders and doctors, also two of the philosophers from Salamis, who having been touched by his doctrine, had followed him thither in order to hear him again. After they had given Jesus a reception with the customary attentions, footwashing and refreshments in the house devoted to such purposes, they petitioned him for the cure of several sick persons who had been longingly awaiting his coming. Jesus accompanied his escort into the Jewish quarter where, in the street before several of the houses, about twenty invalids were lying, whom he cured. Some among them were lame. They were leaning on crutches, which were like frames resting on three feet. The cured and their relatives proclaimed the praises of Jesus, shouting after him short passages of encomium taken chiefly from the Psalms, but the disciples told them to keep quiet.

Jesus went next to the house of the elder of the synagogue where several of the literati were assembled, among them some belonging to the sect of Rechabites. These last-named wore a garb somewhat different from the other Jews, and their manners and customs were peculiarly rigorous. Of these, however, they had already laid aside many.

They had a whole street to themselves, and were especially engaged in mining. They belonged to that race that settled in Ephron, in the kingdom of Basan, in whose neighborhood also, mining was carried on. Jesus was invited by the elder to dinner, which he had ordered to be prepared for him when the sabbath was over. But as he had promised to dine with Barnabas's father, he invited all the present guests to accompany him thither, and begged the elder to entertain the poor laborers and miners after the synagogue was over with the foods prepared for the dinner.

The synagogue was filled with people, and crowds of pagans were listening on the porches outside. Jesus took his text from the third book of Moses, treating of the sacrifice of the Tabernacle, and from Jeremiah, relating to the Promise. He spoke of sacrifices living and dead, answered his hearers' questions upon the difference between them, and taught on the eight beatitudes.

There was in the synagogue a pious old rabbi who had been for a long time afflicted with edema, and who as usual had caused himself to be carried thither to his customary place. As the literati were disputing Jesus on various points, he cried aloud: "Silence! Allow me a word!" and when all were still, he called out: "Lord! Thou hast shown mercy to others. Help me, too, and bid me to come to thee!" Thereupon Jesus said to the man: "If thou dost believe, arise and come to me!" The sick man instantly arose, exclaiming: "Lord, I do believe!" He was cured. He mounted the steps to where Jesus stood, and thanked him, while the whole assembly broke forth into shouts of joy and praise. Jesus and his followers left the synagogue and went to Barnabas's dwelling. Then the master of the feast gathered together the poor and the laborers to partake of the dinner that Jesus had left them.

Paternal Home and Family of Barnabas • Jesus Teaching in the Environs of Kythria

THE father of Barnabas dwelt beyond the western limits of the city in one of the many houses there scattered. Kythria was surrounded by such dwellings, some of which, standing in clusters, formed villages. The house was quite handsome. On one side it was terraced, the walls brown as if painted in oil or smeared with resin—or was that the natural color? On these terraces were plants and foliage. Besides the terraces the house was surrounded by a colonnade, an open gallery, upon which were beautiful trees. Beyond these were vineyards and an open space full of building wood, all in good order. In it were some trunks of trees extraordinarily thick, and there were all kinds of figures made out of the wood, but all was so well arranged that one could easily walk among them. I think the wood was intended for ship building. I saw too long wagons, but not wider than the wood itself, and provided with heavy iron wheels. They were drawn by oxen yoked far apart. One can see at no great distance from Kythria a very beautiful forest of lofty trees.

The father of Barnabas was a widower. His sister with her maidservants had a house in the neighborhood; she took care of his household and provided the meals. The pagans that accompanied Jesus, as well as the philosophers from Salamis, did not recline with him at table, because it was still the sabbath; but they walked up and down in the open hall, ate from their hand and, standing under the colonnade, listened to Jesus's teaching. The meal consisted of birds and broad, flat fish, besides cakes, honey, and fruit. There were likewise dishes with pieces of meat twisted into a spiral form and garnished with all kinds of herbs. Jesus spoke of sacrifice, of the Promise, and dwelt at length upon the prophets.

During the dinner, several bands of poor, half-clad children of from four to six years old made their appearance. They had in little loosely woven baskets some kind of edible herbs, which they offered to the guests in exchange for bread or other food. They seemed to prefer that side of the table at which Jesus and his followers were reclining. Jesus stood up, emptied their baskets of the herbs, filled them from the dishes of food on the table, and blessed the little ones. This scene was very lovely, very touching.

Saturday, May 5, AD 31 (Iyyar 23)

This morning Jesus taught on a hill near Kythria. In the afternoon, he healed the sick and then preached again in the synagogue for the close of the sabbath.

Next morning Jesus taught in the rear of Barnabas's house, where there was a plot of beautiful rising ground furnished with a teacher's chair. The path leading to it from the house was through magnificent arbors of grape-vines. A large audience was gathered. Jesus first addressed the miners and other laborers, then the pagans and, lastly, a great crowd of Jews that had married into pagan families. A great many sick pagans had begged Jesus's help and permission to hear his instructions. They were mostly laborers, sick and crippled, who lay on couches near the teacher's chair. Jesus's instruction to the laborers was on the Lord's Prayer and the refining of ore by fire; that to the pagans, on the wild shoots of trees and grapevines (which had to be cut away), or the one, only God, the children of God, the son of the house and the servant, and the vocation of the Gentiles. Then he turned to the subject of mixed marriages, which were not to be countenanced lightly, though they might be tolerated through accommodation. In the latter case, however, they might be allowed only when there was a prospect of converting or perfecting one of the parties, but never merely for the gratification of sensuality. They could be suffered only when both parties were animated by a holy intention. He spoke, nevertheless, more against than for such unions, and declared them happy who had raised pure offspring in the house of the Lord. He touched upon the serious account the Jewish party would have to render, of the responsibility of rearing children in piety, of the necessity of corresponding with grace at the time of its visitation, and of penance and baptism. After that Jesus cured the sick and dined with Barnabas.

Accompanied by his friends, he next went to the opposite side of the city, where were numbers of beehives placed at an unusually great distance from one another among the large flower gardens. Nearby were a fountain and a little lake. Jesus here taught and related parables, after which all went into the city to the synagogue, where the instruction on sacrifice and the Promise was concluded.

There were at this time some learned Jews traveling through the country. They put all kinds of cunningly contrived questions to Jesus, but he soon solved them. These men seemed to be actuated by some bad design. Their questions referred to mixed marriages, to Moses and the numbers he had caused to be put to death, to Aaron, the golden calf he had ordered to be made, his punishment, etc.

Sunday, May 6, AD 31 (Iyyar 24)

Accompanied by about one hundred people, Jesus went to a place near Kythria where bees were kept. Here he taught about the Lord's Prayer and the Beatitudes.

The next day appeared to be either a feast or a fast among the Jews, for there was morning service in the synagogue, that is, prayer and preaching. That over, Jesus left the city by the north side with all his disciples and some pagan youths. His little band was joined by some Jewish doctors and several Rechabites, so that there were altogether fully one hundred men. They pursued their journey for about an hour to a place which was the principal seat of the bee-raising industry. Far off toward the rising sun stood long rows of white beehives, about the height of a man and woven, I think, of rushes or bark. They had many openings, and were placed one above another. Every group had in front of it a flowery field, and I noticed that balm grew here in abundance. Each field, or garden, was hedged in, and the whole bore the appearance of a city. One could readily recognize the pagan part of it, for here and there standing in niches were puppets with tails, like those of a fish, curving behind them into the air. They had little short paws and faces not altogether human.

The village itself consisted of many little cottages belonging to the bee proprietors, who kept there the vessels and utensils used in their branch of industry. The inn was a large building with all kinds of dependencies. Rows of sheds, or open halls, crossed one another around the courts in which were numerous trestles and long mats. The steward of this establishment provided for the needs of all that were here employed. He was a pagan. The Jews had their own halls and places for prayer. I think the wax and honey were prepared in the house and under the long sheds. It looked like a house for the general gathering in of the produce. I saw here also many of those little trees whose yellow blossoms are so beautiful. The leaves are more yellow than green, and the blossoms fall so thickly on the ground that they form, as it were, a soft carpet. Long mats were spread beneath the trees to catch them. I saw the workmen pressing the flowers to extract from them some kind of coloring matter. The little trees when young were planted in pots, and then transplanted often into the holes of rocks with earth around the roots. There were similar trees in Judea. I saw here also large plants of flax, from which they drew long threads.

Not far from Kythria, about half an hour to the north, quite a considerable stream issued from the rock, flowed first through the city, and then watered the region by which Jesus had come. In some places it flowed along freely, in others it was bridged over. I think the water supplies of the Salamis aqueducts were obtained from it. It formed at its source a real little lake. In its waters baptism was yet to be given, and I think there was some allusion made to it. The number of beautiful wildflowers in this region was surprising. All along the roads stood orange trees, fig trees, currant bushes, and grapevines.

Jesus had come here principally to be able to instruct the pagans without interruption, without disturbance from visitors. This he did all the rest of the day in the gardens and arbors of the inn. His hearers stood or lay stretched on the grass, while he instructed them on the Lord's Prayer and the eight beatitudes. When addressing the pagans, he spoke especially of the origin and abominations of their gods, of the vocation of Abraham and his separation from idolaters, and of God's guidance over the children of Israel. He spoke openly and forcibly. There were about a hundred men listening to him. After the instruction, all took refreshments in the inn, the pagans apart. The repast was made up of bread, long strips of goat cheese, honey, and fruit. The proprietor of the house was a pagan, but very humble and reserved in his manners. That evening, the pagans having retired, Jesus instructed the Jews and they prayed together. All spent the night at the inn.

Kythria was a far more stirring place than Salamis,

where all kinds of business and traffic were confined to the port and a couple of streets. Here, however, there reigned great activity. On the side by which Jesus approached the city, there was a great market where cattle and birds were exposed for sale. Near the heart of the city was another market beautiful to look upon. It was very high and all around it, as well as under its lofty arches, hung many different kinds of colored stuffs and covers. The opposite side of the city was occupied almost entirely by the workers in metal and their foundries. The hammering and pounding were so astonishingly loud that one could not hear his own words, although most of the factories were outside the city. They made all kinds of vessels, especially a kind of oval oven large and light, with a little cover and two handles near the top. In manufacturing them, the metal was first bent into shape, and then put into immense ovens, where the molten mass was blown by means of long tubes into the form of the hollow vessel required. They were yellow outside and white within. All kinds of fruit, as well as honey or syrup, were exported in them. When transported over the sea they were placed on a kind of trestle, and on land they were carried by means of poles run through the handles.

Monday, May 7, AD 31 (Iyyar 25)

Jesus continued teaching at the same place as yesterday. Meanwhile, the crowd of listeners had increased to several hundred. He spoke about the prophet Malachi. In the afternoon, he returned to the house of Barnabas's father.

The next day Jesus again taught at the apiary, the number of his hearers having increased to a couple of hundred. In most convincing terms he again explained to the pagans their errors, and represented the existence of their gods as so very pitiful that they had to explain it by all kinds of significations in order to be able even to endure them themselves. And when, continuing his discourse, he exhorted them to renounce their subtleties, their vain imaginations, their continual efforts in behalf of falsehood, and in simplicity of heart to confine their researches to God and his revelations, some of them who had come thither like traveling literati with staves in their hands, became indignant, and turning off, went murmuring upon their way. Jesus remarked at this conjuncture: "Let them go! It is better that they should do so than remain to make new gods out of what they have just heard." He uttered many prophetic words on the desolation that should one day come upon that beautiful region, its cities and temples, and of the judgment that was to fall on all those countries. He said that when idolatry should have reached its height, then would paganism come to naught, and he dwelt long on the chastisement of the Jews and the destruction of Jerusalem. The pagans took all in better part than did the Jews who, supporting themselves upon their Promises, had always some objections to bring forward. Jesus went through all the prophets with them, explained the passages relating to the Messiah, and told them that the time for their fulfillment had arrived. The Messiah would arise among the Jews, but they would not acknowledge him. They would mock and deride him, and when he would assure them he was the one whom they were expecting, they would seize him and put him to death. This language was not at all to the taste of many of his hearers, and Jesus reminded them of how they were accustomed to do with their prophets. He ended by saying that as they had treated the heralds, so too would they act toward the one whom they announced.

The Rechabites spoke with Jesus of Malachi, for whom they entertained great veneration. They told Jesus that they esteemed him an angel of God, that he had come as a child to certain pious people, that he had frequently disappeared for a time, and that no one knew whether he was now really dead or not. They dwelt at length on his prophecies of the Messiah and his new sacrifice, which Jesus explained as relating to the present and the near future.

From the apiary, Jesus went with a large company (which, however, constantly decreased on the road) back again to Barnabas's home, a journey of several hours. The greater number of his party consisted of young men belonging to the Jewish community, and who were about to embark for Jerusalem to celebrate the Feast of Pentecost. Nevertheless, they that remained with Jesus formed quite a considerable band.

From thirty to forty pagan women and maidens and about ten Jewish girls were assembled at the entrance of the gardens to do Jesus honor. They were playing on flutes and singing canticles of praise; they wore flowery wreaths and strewed green branches in the way. Here and there also they spread mats on the road over which Jesus was to pass, inclined low before him, and offered him presents of wreaths, flowers, aromatic shrubs, and little flasks of perfume. Jesus thanked them, and addressed to them some words. They followed him to the courtyard of Barnabas's house, and set their gifts down in the assembly hall. They had adorned everything with flowers and garlands. This reception, though rural and less noisy, was something similar to that tendered Jesus on Palm Sunday. His escort soon returned to their homes, for it was evening.

I was astonished at the costume of the pagan women. The young girls wore curious-looking caps, like the so-called cuckoo baskets that, when a child, I used to weave of rushes. Some were without ornament; others had a wreath twined around them from which innumerable threads with all kinds of ornamentation fell upon the forehead. The lower edge always consisted of a wreath made of worsted or feather flowers. The veil was worn under the hat, or cap. It was in two parts so that it could be opened in front, or thrown up over the hat; in the latter case, it fell behind as low as the neck. They were girdled very tightly, wore a breastpiece, and around the neck all kinds of ribbons and finery. Their lower dress was very full. It consisted of several skirts of thin material one above the other, and each about a span, or nine inches, longer than the one above it, so that the lowest of all was the longest. The arms were not entirely covered. The dress had no sleeves, only long lappets, and little wreaths were fastened round the arms. The material was of different colors: yellow, red, white, blue, some striped and others covered with flowers. Their hair fell around their shoulders like a veil. It was fastened at the ends with a tasselled string, and thus prevented from floating on the breeze. The sandals on their bare feet were bent up into a point at the toe and kept in place by means of laces. The married women's headdress was not so high as that of the young girls. It had a stiff leaf in front that screened the forehead and descended in a point as far as the nose, and thence curved up above the ears, thus exposing them to view with their pearl pendants. It was openworked and wound with braided hair, pearls, and all kinds of ornaments. They wore long mantles that hung very full in the back. The children with them had no other clothing than a band of some kind of stuff, which, passing over one shoulder, crossed the breast, and was tied around the waist, forming a covering for the middle of the body. These women had awaited Jesus fully three hours.

A repast had been prepared at Barnabas's. But the guests did not recline at table. The food was handed to each on a little board, a wooden waiter, such as had been used on the ship. Many old men were assembled here, among them the old doctor of the Law whom Jesus had cured in the synagogue. Barnabas's father was a solid, square-built old man, and one could easily see that he was accustomed to work in wood. The men of those days looked much more robust than those of the present age.

Tuesday, May 8, AD 31 (Iyyar 26)

I next saw Jesus seated in the teacher's chair at the spring outside of Kythria. He was preparing the neophytes for baptism, which the disciples conferred, first upon the Jews and then upon the pagans.

Jesus spoke here also with the Jewish doctors on the subject of circumcision. He said that it should not be imposed upon the converted pagans, unless they themselves desired it. At the same time, the Jews ought not to be expected to allow these converts entrance into the synagogue, for they should avoid scandal. But they should thank God that the pagans, having abandoned their idolatry, were awaiting the hour of salvation. Other mortifications, the circumcision of the heart and of every kind of concupiscence, could be imposed upon them. Jesus provided for their instruction and devotions apart from the Jews.

Jesus in the City of Mallep

Wednesday, May 9, AD 31 (Iyyar 27)

Jesus continued to teach at the well while the disciples baptized. Around noon, Jesus set off for Mallep, a village built by Jews for their colony. He was received there with much joy and celebration. In the synagogue Jesus taught concerning the petition "Thy kingdom come" of the Lord's Prayer.

I NOTICED some men very respectfully closing the well outside of Kythria, at which the disciples had been baptizing. The crowd that had been present at Jesus's instructions, as well as the newly baptized, were upon the point of separating for their homes. Some were standing around several Jewish travelers that had just arrived. To their questions as to Jesus's whereabouts, they received the answer: "The prophet taught here from early this morning until noon. But now he is gone with his disciples and about seven philosophers of Salamis, just baptized, to the great village of Mallep." This place was built by the Jews, therefore only Jews lived in it. It was situated on a height toward the base of a mountain chain, and commanded a wondrously beautiful view upon all sides, even as far as the sea. It had five streets, all converging toward the center where, hewn out of the rocky foundation, was a reservoir which received its water supply from the conduit of the well near Kythria. All around the reservoir were beautiful seats under shady trees, and from it stretched a magnificent view over the whole city and the surrounding country, which was teeming with fruit. Mallep was surrounded by a double entrenchment, the inner one lower than the outer. A great part of it was hewn out of the rock, and beyond it, looking like little valleys, ran ditches all around the city. On the fresh green sward, covered with lovely flowers, stood rows of the most magnificent fruit trees, under which lay the large yellow fruit in the grass, for everything here was now in full harvest. The people were busy drying the fruit that was to be sent to a distance. They manufactured also cloths, carpets, mats, and out of sapwood light, shallow cases in which to dry the fruit.

On Jesus's arrival, he was met at the gate by the doctors of the synagogue, the school children, and a crowd of people who had come to welcome him, all adorned as for a feast. The children were singing, playing on musical instruments, and carrying palm branches, the little girls going before the boys. Jesus passed through the children, blessing them as he went, and with his followers, about thirty men, was escorted by the doctors into a reception hall where the ceremony of washing the feet was performed.

Meanwhile about twenty invalids, some lame, others dropsical, were brought into the street outside the house. Jesus cured them, and directed them to follow him to the well in the heart of the city. Great was the joy of the relatives as, with the lately cured, they made their way to the place designated, where Jesus gave them an instruction upon daily bread and gratitude toward God.

From here he went to the synagogue and taught upon the petition: "Thy kingdom come." He spoke of the kingdom of God in us and of its near approach. He explained to his hearers that it was a spiritual, not an earthly kingdom, and told them how it would fare with them that cast it from them. The pagans who had followed Jesus were standing back of the Jews, for the line of separation was more strictly observed here than in pagan cities.

The instruction over, Jesus assisted at a dinner given by the doctors, after which they escorted him to the inn, which they had prepared for him and his company. A steward had been appointed to see to all things.

Thursday, May 10, AD 31 (Iyyar 28)

At the midday meal, three blind boys were led into the room where Jesus and the disciples were eating. They were playing flutes. Jesus asked them if they would like to see the light, and then—much to their joy—he healed them. As the news of this miracle spread, the whole town began to rejoice. That evening, Jesus taught again in the synagogue.

On the following day, Jesus taught again in the extraordinarily beautiful synagogue where all the people were assembled. He spoke of the sower, of different kinds of soil, of weeds, and of the grain of mustard seed, which bears fruit so large. He took his similitudes from a shrub that grew in those regions which, from a very small kernel, shoots forth a stalk thick as one's arm and almost as high as a man, and which is very useful. Its fruit was large as an acorn, red and black. Its juice when expressed was used for dyeing. The baptized pagans were not in the synagogue, but outside on the terraces listening to Jesus's words.

When Jesus was afterward taking dinner with the elders, three blind boys about ten to twelve years old were led in to him by some other children. The former were playing on flutes and another kind of instrument which they held to the mouth and touched at the same time with the fingers. It was not a fife, and it made a buzzing, humming sound like the Jew's harp. At intervals also they sang in a very agreeable manner. Their eyes were open, and it seemed as if a cataract had obscured the sight. Jesus asked them whether they desired to see the light, in order to walk diligently and piously in the paths of righteousness. They answered most joyously: "Lord, do thou help us! Help us, Lord, and we will do whatever thou commandest!" Then Jesus said: "Put down your instruments!" and he stood them before him, put his thumbs to his mouth, and passed them one after the other from the corner of the eyes to the temple above. Then he took up a dish of fruit from the table, held it before the boys, said: "Do ye see that?" blessed them, and gave them its contents. They stared around in joyful amazement, they were intoxicated with delight, and at last cast themselves weeping at Jesus's feet. The whole company were deeply touched; joy and wonder took possession of all. The three boys, full of joy, hurried with their guides out of the hall and through the streets to their parents. The whole city was in excitement. The children returned with their relatives and many others to the forecourt of the hall, singing songs of joy and playing upon their instruments, in order thus to express their thanks. Jesus took occasion from this circumstance to give a beautiful instruction on gratitude. He said: "Thanksgiving is a prayer which attracts new favors, so good is the heavenly Father."

After dinner, Jesus walked with the disciples and the pagan philosophers through the beautiful shady meadows around the city, teaching the pagan men and new disciples. The elder disciples were themselves instructing separate groups. That evening Jesus taught again in the synagogue.

Friday, May 11, AD 31 (Iyyar 29)

Today, Jesus and the disciples took a walk with seven (formerly pagan) philosophers who had received baptism. The latter asked him about the Persian king Djemschid, who had received a golden blade from God with which he had divided many lands and shed blessings everywhere. Jesus replied that Djemschid had been a leader who was wise and intelligent in things of the sense world. He spoke of Djemschid as a false type of Melchizedek, who was truly a priest and a king to whom they should turn their attention. The sacrifice of bread and wine which Melchizedek had offered would be fulfilled and perfected and would endure until the end of the world. They returned to the synagogue in Mallep for the start of the sabbath.

Next day he visited the parents of the blind boys whom he had cured. They were Jews from Arabia, from the region in which Jethro, Moses's father-in-law, had dwelt. They had a particular name. They traveled around a great deal, and had already been baptized near Capernaum. They were journeying through that part of the country at the time, and had heard Jesus's sermon on the mount. These people, that is, these two families composed of about twenty persons including the women and children, were tradesmen and manufacturers, who, as among us the Italians, the Tyrolese, and the inhabitants of the Black Forest, tarry awhile sometimes here, sometimes there, busying themselves in making clocks, mouse-traps, figures in plaster of Paris, which they sold to their neighbors, thus uniting labor and traffic. At this season they generally visited Mallep for a couple of months. Outside the city, on the north, they occupied a private inn in which they had all kinds of tools, weaving apparatus, etc. Their blind boys had, in their wanderings, to earn something by singing and playing on the flute when occasion offered. Jesus told the parents that they should no longer drag the boys around after them, but that they should remain in Mallep and attend school. He indicated to them the persons that would receive and instruct their boys, for he had already arranged all that the day before. The parents promised to do whatever he directed.

Jesus Teaching before the Pagan Philosophers • He Attends a Jewish Wedding

JESUS walked with the disciples and the seven baptized philosophers through the charming meadow valley that led from Mallep to the village of Lanifa and then, gently rising, turned southward into the mountains. From this southern side descended a brook, about three feet broad, which took its rise in the spring near Kythria. It ran in a covered bed through the mountains, then through the village Lanifa and the valley near Mallep whose surrounding moats it fed. But it was not the same water as that in the elevated fountain in the center of Mallep, although the street by which Jesus left the city, the fifth and last of the place, was that of the canal by which the beautiful reservoir was supplied. Words cannot describe the charm and quiet of this verdant valley, gently winding around and entirely shut in by the surrounding heights.

As far as Mallep lay isolated granges on either side of the road, dependent upon the village of Lanifa at the end of the valley. All was perfectly green and covered with the most beautiful flowers and fruits which here grew, some wild, some cultivated. Jesus took the road to the left, on the south side of the brook to Lanifa. He met a band of young people on their way to take ship for Jerusalem, there to celebrate Pentecost. Jesus accosted them with the command to salute Lazarus, but beyond that not to speak of him. Farther on, he crossed the brook, turned to the north, and descended again into the valley, in order to return to Mallep. On that side he came to another village, which bore the singular name of Leppe.

The harvest was now over, and the people placed together the sheaves destined for the poor.

During the whole journey Jesus taught the pagan philosophers, sometimes walking, sometimes tarrying in some lovely spot. He instructed them upon the absolute corruption of humankind before the Flood, of the preservation of Noah, of the new growth of evil, of the vocation of Abraham, and of God's guidance of his race down to the time in which the promised Consoler was to come forth from it. The pagans asked Jesus for explanations of all kinds, and brought forward many great names of ancient gods and heroes, telling him of their benevolent deeds. Jesus replied that all men possessed by nature, more or less, human kindness by which they effected many things useful and advantageous for time, but that many vices and abominations arose from such benefits. He showed them the state of degradation, the partial destruction of the nations sunk in idolatry, the ridiculous and fabulous deformity running through the history of their divinities, mixed up with demoniacal divinations and magical delusions which were woven into them as so many truths.

The philosophers made mention also of one of the most ancient of the wise kings who had come from the mountainous regions beyond India. He was called Djemschid. With a golden dagger received from God he had divided off many lands, peopled them, and shed blessing everywhere. They asked Jesus about him and the many wonders which they related of him. Jesus answered that Djsemchid, who had been a leader of the people, was a man naturally wise and intelligent in the things of sense. Upon the dispersion of men at the time of the building of the Tower of Babel, he had put himself at the head of a tribe and taken possession of lands according to certain regulations. He had fallen less deeply into evil, because the race to which he belonged was itself less corrupt. Jesus recalled to them also the fables that had been written in connection with him, and showed them that he was a false companion-picture, a false type of Melchizedek, the priest and king. Jesus told them to fix their attention on the latter and upon the descendants of Abraham, for as the stream of nations moved along, God had sent Melchizedek to the best families that he might guide them, unite them, and make ready for them countries and dwellings, in order to preserve them in their purity and, according to their worthiness or unworthiness, either hasten or retard the fulfillment of the Promise. Who Melchizedek was, he left to themselves to determine; but of him this much was true, he was an ancient type of the then far-off, but now so near grace of the Promise, and the sacrifice of bread and wine which he had offered would be fulfilled and perfected, and would endure till the end of the world.

Jesus's words upon Djemschid and Melchizedek were so clear, so indisputable, that the philosophers exclaimed in astonishment: "Master, how wise thou art! It would almost seem as if thou didst live in that time, as if thou didst know all these people even better than they knew themselves!" Jesus said to them many more things concerning the prophets, both the greater and the minor, and he dwelt especially upon Malachi. When the sabbath began, he went to the synagogue and delivered a discourse upon the passage of Leviticus referring to the jubilee year, also upon something from Jeremiah. He said that a man should cultivate his field well, so that his brother, who was to receive it from him, might see in it a proof of his affection.

SIVAN (30 days): May 11/12 to June 9/10, AD 31
Sivan New Moon: May 10 at 7:00 AM, Jerusalem time

Saturday, May 12, AD 31 (Sivan 1)

This morning Jesus continued teaching in the synagogue. He spoke of the sabbath year and the Jubilee (Leviticus 25). Then he went with a large crowd of people to the bathing gardens on the outskirts of the town. Here he taught and prepared people for baptism. James the Less and Barnabas then baptized. Many people accompanied Jesus today for the sabbath-day walk, which he took in the valley of Lanifa, before returning to the synagogue for the close of the sabbath. Afterward, he discoursed late into the night with some of the philosophers.

On the following morning Jesus continued in the synagogue his discourse on the jubilee year, the cultivation of the field, and the passages from Jeremiah. This over, he went with the disciples and, followed by many people, Jews and pagans, to a Jewish bathing garden outside the southern end of the city, the water supply to which was furnished by the Kythria aqueducts. There was a beautiful cistern in the garden and all around it were the large basins for bathing, pleasant avenues, and long shady bowers. Everything necessary for administering baptism was already prepared here. Crowds followed Jesus to an open place near the well fitted up for teaching, and among them were seven bridegrooms with their relatives and attendants.

Jesus taught of the Fall, of the perversion of Adam and Eve, of the Promise, of the degeneracy of men into the wild state, of the separation of the less corrupt, of the guard set over marriage, in order to transmit virtues and graces from father to son, and of the sanctification of marriage by the observance of the divine Law, moderation, and continency. In this way, Jesus's discourse turned upon the bride and bridegroom. To illustrate his meaning, he referred to a certain tree on the island which could be fertilized by trees at a distance, yes, even across the sea, and he uttered the words: "In the same way may hope, confidence in God, desire of salvation, humility, and chastity become in some manner the mother for the fulfillment of the Promise." This led Jesus to touch upon the mysterious signification of marriage, in that it typifies the bond of union between the Consoler of Israel and his church. He called marriage a great mystery. His words on this subject were so beautiful, so elevated, that it seems to me impossible to repeat them. He afterward taught upon penance and baptism, which expiate and efface the crime of separation, and render all worthy to participate in the alliance of salvation.

Jesus went aside also with some of the aspirants to baptism, heard their confession, forgave their sins, and imposed upon them certain mortifications and good works. James the Less and Barnabas performed the ceremony of baptism. The neophytes were principally aged men, a few pagans, and the three boys cured of blindness, who had not been baptized with their parents at Capernaum.

The sabbath over, some of the philosophers started the following questions: Whether it was necessary that God should have allowed the frightful deluge to pass over the earth? Why he permitted humankind to await so long the coming of the Redeemer? Could he not have employed other means for the same end, and send one who would restore all things? Jesus answered by explaining that that entered not into the designs of God, that he had created the angels with free will and superior faculties, and yet they had separated from him through pride and had been precipitated into the kingdom of darkness; that man, with free will, had been placed between the kingdom of darkness and that of light, but by eating the forbidden fruit he had approached nearer to the former; that man was now obliged to cooperate with God in order to receive help from him and to attract into himself the kingdom of God, that God might give it to him. Man, by eating the forbidden fruit, had sought to become like unto God; and that he might rise from his fallen state it was necessary that the Father should allow his divine Son to succor him and reconcile him again to himself. Man, in his entire being, had become so deformed that the great mercy and wonderful guidance of God were needed, to establish upon earth his kingdom, which that of darkness had driven from the hearts of men. Jesus added that this kingdom consisted not in worldly dominion and magnificence, but in the regeneration, the reconciliation of man with the Father, and in the reunion of all the good into one body.

Sunday, May 13, AD 31 (Sivan 2)

Today, again, Jesus taught at the place of baptism. Several bridegrooms were present. Jesus gave them instruction concerning marriage. They then received baptism. Afterward, Jesus accepted an invitation to dine at the house of a rabbi in the village of Leppe, west of Mallep. The bridegrooms were also invited, together with their brides-to-be. Following the meal, Jesus spoke of the sacredness of marriage. It was already dark when he and the disciples returned to Mallep to sleep.

On the following day Jesus taught again at the place of baptism. The seven bridal couples were present. Among the bridegrooms two were converted pagans who had received circumcision and espoused Jewish maidens. There were some other pagans inclined toward Judaism, who had sought and obtained permission to assist at the instructions with them.

At first Jesus spoke in general terms upon the duties of the married state, and especially upon those of wives. They should, he said, raise their eyes only to fix them upon those of their husband; at other times they should be kept lowered. He spoke, likewise, of obedience, humility, chastity, industry, and the care of their children. When the women had retired in order to prepare a repast in Leppe, Jesus instructed the men for baptism. He spoke of Elijah and of the great drought that fell upon the whole country, and of the rain cloud which, at the prayer of Elijah, had risen out of the sea. (Today there was just such another dense, white cloud of fog resting over the earth. One could not see far around him.) Jesus referred to that drought over the country as to a punishment from God for the idolatry of King Ahab. Grace and blessing likewise had withdrawn, and the drought had prevailed even in human hearts. He spoke of Elijah's concealment by the torrent of Kerith, of his being fed by the bird, of his journeying to Sarepta and his being helped by the widow, of his confounding the idolaters on Carmel, and of the uprising of the cloud by whose rain all things were refreshed. He compared this rain to baptism, and admonished his hearers to reform their lives and not, like Ahab and Jezebel, continue in sin and dryness of heart after the rain of baptism. Jesus alluded also to Segola, that pious pagan woman of Egypt who settled at Abila and performed so many good works that she at last found favor in the sight of God. Then he showed them how the pagans ought to strive to practice virtue that thereby they might attract upon themselves divine grace, for his pagan listeners knew something of Elijah and Segola.

After the baptism of the bridegrooms, Jesus and his followers, along with all the bridal parties and the rabbis, were invited by the Jewish doctor of the place to an entertainment at the village of Leppe, west of Mallep. The daughter of this doctor was the bride of a pagan philosopher of Salamis, who had there heard Jesus preach and received circumcision. The way to Leppe ran in a gently undulating course through beautiful walks like those of a garden. Near Leppe ran the highroad to the little port Kyrenia, about two miles off. The other road, upon which Jesus spoke with the traveling Arabs, led to the harbor of Lapethos more to the west. The pagans of Leppe occupied a row of houses built along the highway, and carried on commerce and other business. The Jews lived apart and had a beautiful synagogue. I saw in the pagan gardens idols like swathed puppets and, in an open square a short distance from the road and surrounded by a hedge, an idol larger than a man and with a head bearing some resemblance to that of an ox. Between the horns was something that looked like a little sheaf. The figure was squatting on its legs, its short hands dangling before it.

The entertainment at Leppe consisted of a simple meal of birds, fish, honey, bread, and fruits. The brides and bridesmaids, veiled, sat by themselves at the end of the table. They wore long, striped dresses with wreaths of colored wool and tiny feathers on their heads.

Both during and after the meal, Jesus spoke of the sanctity of marriage. He insisted on the point of each man's having but one wife, for they had here the custom of separating on trifling grounds and marrying again. On this account, he spoke very strenuously, and related the parables of the wedding feast, the vineyard, and the king's son. The groomsmen invited the passersby to share the feast and listen to Jesus's teaching. The three cured boys played on their flutes, while little girls sang and played on various instruments.

It was already dark when Jesus and his disciples returned to Mallep. From the heights along the road, the view was exceedingly beautiful. One could behold the sea, whose surface reflected a most wonderful luster. Great preparations had been made in Mallep for the nuptials of the seven bridal couples. The whole city appeared to be taking part in the feast. One would have said that all the inhabitants constituted one great brotherhood. No poor were to be seen, as they were lodged and provided for in a separate part of the city.

Mallep was built very regularly. It looked like a pancake divided into five equal parts. The five streets that divided the city converged toward the center where was an elevated place ornamented by a fountain, around which were trees and terraces. Four of these quarters, or city wards, were cut through by two cross streets, which ran in a circle around the fountain, the central point of the place. In one of these circular streets was a house in which childless widows and aged women lived together at the expense of the community, kept school, and took care of orphans. There was another house here also for lodging and entertaining poor strangers and travelers. The fifth quarter comprised the public buildings. It was cut into halves by the aqueduct that conducted the water to the fountain. In one half were the public marketplace, several inns, and an asylum for the possessed, who were not permitted here to go at large. Jesus had already cured some of them who had been led to him with the rest of the sick. In the other half stood the public house used for feasts and weddings, the top of its roof being almost on a level with the fountain near which it was. Its entrance was not facing the fountain, but on the side opposite. From the court in front, a walk about a hundred feet wide and bordered by green trees ran down through the cross streets to the forecourt of the synagogue. It was as long as about two-thirds of one of the five streets. There were other avenues leading thither from the cross streets, but they were open to the people only on feast days and by virtue of special permission.

Monday, May 14, AD 31 (Sivan 3)

Today Jesus was present at the wedding celebration of the bridegrooms and their brides. After the festivities were over, he went for a walk with the philosophers. That evening, he taught again in the synagogue concerning the significance of marriage.

Now on this day of the marriage festivities, the whole morning was spent in adorning the public feast-house. Meanwhile Jesus and his disciples retired to the inn whither came to him men and women, some seeking instruction, others advice and consolation, for in consequence of their connection with the pagans these people often had scruples and anxieties. The young affianced were longer with Jesus than the others. He spoke with the maidens alone and singly. It was something like confession and instruction. He questioned them upon their motives in entering the married state, whether they had reflected upon their posterity and the salvation of the same, which was a fruit springing from the fear of God, chastity, and temperance. Jesus found the young brides not instructed on these points.

In the public avenues, arches were erected, tapestry, wreaths of flowers, and garlands of fruits hung around, and steps and platforms raised, that the spectators might gaze from them down into the pleasure grounds below. In front of the synagogue especially an open arbor was formed of numerous beautiful little bushes and plants in boxes. Into the courts and bowers around the feast-house I saw people transporting all things, foods, etc., necessary for the entertainment. Whoever brought from the city something for this end had a right to take part in the feast. The foods were brought in a kind of long barrow, which served at the same time as tables. The various dishes, bread, little jugs, etc., stood in them and, from little side openings, could be drawn out by the guests as they reclined before them. The upper surface of the barrow was covered with a cloth, from which they ate. These barrows, or hand-carriages, were woven baskets, long and shallow, provided with a cover and side openings, as I have said, by which to get out the food. The guests reclined on mats and were supported by cushions. All these things were prepared and transported hither from various quarters.

Under the nuptial bower, a tapestried canopy was raised. Jesus and his disciples entered by special invitation. As among the bridegrooms some were converted pagans, several pagan philosophers and others of their friends took up the position assigned them not far off. The brides and bridegrooms arrived from different quarters. They were preceded by youths and maidens crowned with flowers and playing on musical instruments, accompanied by the bridemen and bridesmaids, and surrounded by their relatives, who escorted them into the nuptial bower. The bridegrooms wore long mantles and white shoes; on their cincture and the hem of their tunic were certain letters, and in their hands they carried a yellow scarf. The brides appeared in very beautiful, long, white woollen dresses embroidered with lines and flowers of gold. Their hair (some of them were golden-haired) was in the back woven into a net with pearls and gold thread and fastened at the ends with a ribbon. The veil fell over the face and down the back. On the head was a metal band with three points and a high, bent piece in front upon which the veil could be raised. They also wore little crowns of feathers or silk. Several of the veils glistened, as if made of fine silk or similar material. In their hands they carried long, golden torches, like lamps without feet. They grasped them with a scarf, either black or of some other dark color. The brides likewise wore white shoes or sandals.

During the nuptial ceremony, which was performed by the rabbis, I remarked various rites that I cannot recall in order. Rolls of parchment were read—the marriage contract, I think—and prayers. The bridal couple stepped under the canopy; the relatives cast some grains of wheat after them and uttered a blessing. The rabbi pricked both bride and bridegroom on the little finger and let some drops of the blood of each fall into a goblet of wine, which they then drank together. Then the bridegroom handed the goblet to those behind him, and it was put into a basin of water. A little of the blood was allowed to run into the palm of the hand of each. Then each reached the hand, the bride to the groom, the groom to the bride, and the blood-stained spot was rubbed. A fine white thread was then bound around the wound and rings were exchanged. I think that each had two, one for the little finger, the other large enough for the forefinger. After that an embroidered cover, or scarf, was laid over the head of the newly wedded couple. The bride took into her right hand the flambeau with the black scarf, which for a time she had resigned to her bridesmaid, and placed it in the right hand of her husband. He then passed it to the left hand and returned it to his bride, who likewise received it in her left hand, and then once more returned it to her bridesmaid. There was also a cup of wine blessed, out of which all the relatives sipped. The marriage ceremony over, the bridesmaids removed from the brides their headdress, and covered them with a veil.

It was then that I saw that the large net was woven of false hair.

Three rabbis presided at the nuptials, the whole ceremony lasting three hours. Then the brides with their attendant trains went through the embowered walk to the feast house, followed by their husbands amid the good wishes and congratulations of the bystanders. After taking some refreshments, the bridal couples went to the pleasure garden near the aqueduct, there to amuse themselves.

That evening an instruction especially intended for the newly-married was given in the synagogue. After the rabbis had spoken, they requested Jesus also to address some words of advice to the young people.

Tuesday, May 15, AD 31 (Sivan 4)

Jesus and a disciple, Mnason, accompanied by the philosophers, made their way through the fields, going from farm to farm. Here and there Jesus taught concerning the Feast of Weeks (the Jewish festival corresponding to Whitsun, seven weeks after the Passover), which was approaching. He spoke of the Feast of Weeks as a festival of remembrance of the giving of the Law to Moses on Mount Sinai.

Next day the seven bridal couples, together with all the guests and attended by musicians, went again to the feast house. The disciples of Jesus also were present, but the only part they took in the merrymaking was that of server. The brides and grooms were presented with pastry and fruit on beautiful dishes—gilded apples stuck with gilded flowers and herbs. Then came bands of children singing and playing upon instruments. They were little strangers who made their living in this way; after being rewarded, they withdrew. After that the three little musicians that had been cured by Jesus made their appearance, along with several other choirs from the city, and soon a dance in honor of the occasion was performed. It took place in a long, four-cornered arbor upon a soft and gently swaying floor. It looked as if flexible planks of some kind were laid upon a thick carpet of moss. The dancers stood in four double rows, back to back. Each pair danced, changing hands by means of a scarf, from the first place of the first row to the last of the fourth, all being soon in a serpentine movement. There was no hopping, but a graceful swaying and balancing, as if the body had no bones. The brides, as also all the other women, had their veils raised on the golden hook of their headdress. After the dance all took refreshments which had been placed on stands in each corner of the arbor. Again the music sounded, and all filed out into the garden near the fountain.

Here were exhibited, in the arbors and on the mossy grassland, various games of running, leaping, and throwing at a target. The men played by themselves, as did also the women. Little prizes were awarded and fines imposed, in the shape of money, girdles, small pieces of stuff, scarfs for the neck, etc. Whoever had nothing with which to pay his fine sent to purchase it from a peddler who, with his goods, had taken his stand not far off. Lastly, all the prizes and fines were handed over to the elder, who distributed them to the poor among the lookers-on. The brides and maidens played games in circles and in rows. Their dresses were raised to the knees, their lower limbs bound with strips of white, their veils thrown up and wound around the head back to the forehead and ear ornaments. They looked very beautiful and nimble. Each caught hold of her neighbor's girdle with the left hand, and thus formed a ring which they kept constantly revolving. With the right hand they aimed at throwing to one another and catching a yellow apple. Whoever failed to catch in her turn had to stoop, the circle still revolving, to pick it up from the ground. At last, they played in company with the men. They sat in opposite rows and threw into furrows very ripe yellow fruits, which when they met and smashed, gave rise to shouts of laughter. Toward evening, all returned in festal procession. The newly-married rode on asses gaily adorned for the occasion, the brides sitting on side-saddles. Musicians led the way and all followed, rejoicing, to the feast house at which an entertainment was awaiting them.

The bridegrooms went to the synagogue and made before the rabbis a vow to observe continence during certain festivals, binding themselves to some penance if they broke it. They promised besides to watch together on Pentecost night and spend it in prayer. From the feast house, the bridal couples were conducted to their future homes. The party that had brought the house as a dowry, stood on the threshold while the relatives led the other thither from the feast house and three times made the rounds of the premises. The wedding gifts were borne in ceremoniously, and the poor received their share.

Feast of Pentecost (Feast of Weeks, or Whitsun) • Jesus Teaches on Baptism

MALLEP was now astir in preparation for the coming feast: all were busy cleaning, scouring, and bathing. The synagogue and many of the dwellings were adorned with green branches and garlands of flowers, and the ground was strewn with blossoms. The synagogue was fumigated with delicious perfumes, and the rolls of sacred scripture were wreathed with flowers.

In the special halls set apart for the purpose in the forecourt of the synagogue the Whitsuntide loaves were baked, the flour having been previously blessed by the rabbis. Two of them were made from the wheat of that year's harvest. For the others, as also for the large, thin cakes (which were indented, that they might be more easily broken into pieces), the flour had been ordered from Judea. It was ground from the wheat raised in the field upon which Abraham had participated in the sacrifice of Melchizedek. The flour had been transported hither in long boxes. It was called the Seed of Abraham. The baking of these loaves and cakes, in which there was no leaven, had to be finished by four o'clock. There was still another kind of flour there, as well as herbs, all of which received a blessing.

Wednesday, May 16, AD 31 (Sivan 5)

Jesus taught again today about the Feast of Weeks, about the giving of the Law on Mount Sinai, and about baptism. The Feast of Weeks began that evening. There was a torchlight prayer-procession, which Jesus joined. Afterward, he retired to pray alone.

On the morning of this day Jesus gave an instruction at his inn to the baptized pagans and aged Jews. He took for his subjects the Feast of Pentecost, the Law given upon Sinai, and baptism, all of which he treated in deeply significant terms. He touched upon many passages relating to them in the prophets. He spoke also of the holy bread blessed at Pentecost, of Melchizedek's sacrifice, and of that foretold by Malachi. He said that the time for the institution of that sacrifice was drawing near, that when this feast would again come round, a new grace would have been added to baptism, and that all the baptized who would then believe in the Consoler of Israel, would share in that grace. As difficulties and objections were here raised by some who did not wish to understand his teaching, Jesus chose about fifty whom he knew to be ripe for his instructions, and sent away the others, intending to prepare them later. Taking with him those that he had selected, he left the city, went to the aqueduct nearby, and there continued his instruction. I saw them on the way sometimes standing still and with many gesticulations putting questions and raising objections; and I saw Jesus, his forefinger raised, frequently explaining something to them. In talking, they gesticulated freely with hands and fingers. As Jesus insisted upon the great grace, upon the salvation that would be conferred upon man by baptism, and by baptism alone, after the consummation of the Sacrifice of which he had spoken, some of them asked whether their present baptism possessed the same efficacy. Jesus answered, yes, if they persevered in faith and accepted that Sacrifice; for even the patriarchs, who had not received that baptism, but who had sighed after it and had had a presentiment of it in the Spirit, received grace through both that Sacrifice and that baptism.

Jesus spoke, too, of the advantages of fervent prayer during this Feast of Pentecost, which devout Jews of all times had observed and upon which they conjured God for the promised consoler of Israel.

Jesus told them many other deeply significant things which I cannot now rightly repeat. I saw that they sent, from the wedding feast, food to Jesus and his disciples at the inn to which he had returned with them toward the sabbath.

The pagans from Salamis started for home, and Jesus with the disciples accompanied them part of the way. He warned them not to return again to their worship of idols, and not to engage in business speculations, but as soon as possible to leave their country, for in it the new way would be full of obstacles for them. He directed them to different regions, among which I can recall Jerusalem, the Jewish district between Hebron and Gaza, and that near Jericho. Jesus recommended them to go to Lazarus, John Mark, the nephews of Zechariah, and to the parents of Manahem, the disciple whose sight had been restored.

Before the commencement of the sabbath exercises, the rabbis were solemnly conducted to the synagogue by the school children; the brides, by their female attendants; and the bridegrooms, by the young men. Jesus also went thither with his disciples. Divine service of this day consisted in no special explanation of scripture, only in singing and alternate reading and praying. The consecrated bread was divided into little pieces in the synagogue. It was regarded as a remedy against sickness and witchcraft. Many of the Jews, among others the seven newly-married men, spent the night in the synagogue in prayer. Many of the inhabitants of the city went in bands of ten or twelve out to the gardens and hills of the country around, and there spent the whole night in prayer. They carried a torch on the end of a pole. The disciples and baptized pagans thus passed the night, but Jesus went alone to pray.

Thursday, May 17, AD 31 (Sivan 6)

This morning Jesus took part in the ceremonies to celebrate the Feast of Weeks in the synagogue. He walked at the head of the column of rabbis as they proceeded around the synagogue blessing the land, the sea, and all regions of the earth. There then followed the reading. It had to do with the period between the exodus from Egypt and the giving of the Law on Mount Sinai on the fiftieth day after the Passover.

The women too were gathered together in the houses for the same purpose. On the day of the feast itself, the whole morning was spent in the synagogue, praying, singing, and reading the holy scriptures. They made, likewise, a kind of procession. The rabbis, with Jesus at their head and followed by crowds of the people, went processionally through the halls around the synagogue, paused several times at points that look toward different directions of the world, and pronounced a benediction over every region of land and sea. After an intermission of about two hours, they again returned to the synagogue in the afternoon, and the alternate reading and other exercises were resumed. At some of the pauses, Jesus asked: "Do ye understand this?" and then he explained different passages for them. The portions of holy scripture read were those from the departure of the Israelites through the Red Sea to the giving of the Law upon Sinai. During the reading, I saw these events in detail, and of them I can recall the following.

Vases and Vessels of the Time

VISION OF THE PASSAGE OF THE RED SEA

THE ISRAELITES were encamped on a very low strip of land, about an hour long, on the shore of the Red Sea, which was here very wide. In it were several islands of half an hour in length and from seven to fifteen minutes in breadth. Pharaoh and his army at first sought the Israelites further up the shore, and found them at last through information given by their scouts. The king thought they would easily fall into his hands, flanked, as they were, by the sea. The Egyptians were very much incensed against them on account of their carrying off with them their sacred vessels, many of their idols, and the mysteries of their religion. When the Israelites became aware of the approach of the Egyptians, they were terror-stricken. But Moses prayed and bade them trust in God and follow him. At that moment the pillar of cloud arose behind the Israelites, making so dense a veil that the Egyptians entirely lost sight of them. Then Moses stepped to the shore with his staff (which was forked at the bottom and had a knob on the upper end), prayed, and struck the water. Then appeared before each wing of the army, right and left, as if springing out of the sea, two great luminous pillars, which increased in brilliancy toward the top and terminated in a tongue of flame. At the same time, a strong wind parted the waters along the whole of the army (it was about an hour broad), and Moses proceeded by a gently inclining declivity down to the bed of the sea. The whole army followed, at least fifty men abreast. The ground was, at first setting out, somewhat slippery, but soon it became like the softest meadowland, like a mossy carpet. The pillars of fire lit the way before them, and all was as bright as day. But the most beautiful feature of the whole scene were the islands over which they shed their light. They looked like floating gardens full of the most magnificent fruits and all kinds of animals, which latter the Israelites collected and drove along before them. Without this precaution, they would have been in want of food on the other side of the sea.

The waters were not divided on either side like perpendicular walls, for they flowed off more in the form of terraces. The Hebrews went forward with hurrying, sliding steps, balancing themselves like one speeding downhill. It was toward midnight when they entered the bed of the river. The Ark containing Joseph's relics was carried in the center of the fleeing host. The pillars of light rose up out of the water. They appeared to be constantly rotating, and passed not over the islands, but around them. At a certain height they were lost in a brilliant luster. The waters did not open all at once, but before Moses's steps, leaving a wedge-formed space until the passage was completed. Near the islands, one could see by the light of the pillars the trees and fruits mirrored in the waters.

Another wonderful thing was that the Israelites crossed in three hours, whereas it would have naturally taken nine hours to do so. Higher up the shore, about six to nine hours distant, stood a city which was afterward destroyed by the waters.

About three o'clock, Pharaoh came down to the shore, but was again repulsed by the fog. Soon, however, he discovered the ford and rolled down into it with his magnificent war chariot, after which hurried his entire army. And now Moses, already on the opposite shore, commanded the waters to return to their original position. Then the fog and the fire, uniting to blind and perplex the Egyptians, all perished miserably in the waves. Next morning, upon beholding their deliverance, the Israelites chanted the praises of God. On the opposite shore, the two pillars of light united again into one of fire. I cannot do justice to the beauty of this vision.

Friday, May 18, AD 31 (Sivan 7)

Jesus and the disciples visited the homes of various people to teach, comfort, and heal. He spoke with several women about their marriage difficulties. That evening, with the beginning of the sabbath, Jesus spoke in the synagogue with tremendous power and earnestness. He spoke of the breaking of the commandments and of adultery. Afterward, he prayed alone all night.

Next day Jesus went with his disciples into two quarters of the city which he had not yet visited, and to which several persons had sent to invite him. He cured some invalids, men and women, who lay off by themselves in cells annexed to the courts of the houses, exhorted and consoled many others afflicted with melancholy and whom some secret trouble was consuming. All things were so well regulated in Mallep that every misfortune by which one's honor might be wounded could be kept secret. Several women asked Jesus how they should act. Their husbands were unfaithful to them, and yet, on account of the public scandal and severe punishment attached to such crimes, they were timid in laying a charge against them. Jesus consoled them and counselled them to patience. He told them to reflect as to whether they would have their husbands warned by himself or by his disciples, strangers in those parts, that thereby suspicion of having lodged a complaint might not fall upon them and the affair might not become known throughout the country. Many children were brought to Jesus in the different houses, to receive from him a benediction.

That afternoon, he went to a large house where, in a hall back of the court and separated from one another, numbers of distinguished men lay sick. On the other side of the court lay the women. Among these poor invalids were some melancholy and quite inconsolable, whose tears flowed unceasingly. Jesus cured about twenty of them, prescribed what they should eat and drink, and sent them to the baths. He afterward caused them all to be assembled together and taught first the women, and then the men. This lasted almost till evening, when he went to the synagogue.

Jesus Delivers a More Severe Lecture in the Synagogue

THE SCRIPTURE lessons of this day treated of God's curse upon those that transgressed his commands, of tithes, of idolatry, of the sanctification of the sabbath, etc. Jesus's words were so earnest and severe that many of his audience, penetrated with grief, sobbed and wept. The synagogue was open on all sides, and his voice rang out clear and pure like unto no other human voice. He inveighed especially against them that relied upon creatures and looked for help and comfort from human beings. He spoke of the diabolical influence of the adulterer and adulteress over each other, of the malediction of the injured spouses which falls upon the children of such intercourse, but whose guilt rests upon the adulterous parties. The people were so strongly affected that many of them, at the close of the discourse, exclaimed: "Ah, he speaks as if the Day of Judgment were already nigh!" He spoke likewise against pride, against subtle erudition and the close investigation of trifles. By this he alluded to the doings of the great school of Jewish learning here established for such Jews as would afterward add to their store of knowledge by traveling.

Saturday, May 19, AD 31 (Sivan 8)

Many came to visit Jesus at his inn. They sought comfort after the mighty speech that he had delivered the evening before. Jesus comforted and instructed many people, one of whom invited him to dine. Everyone was astonished at the remarkable effect that Jesus had in helping people right their life situations.

After this castigatory discourse many persons, sighing for relief and reconciliation with God, sought Jesus at his inn. Among them were learned men and young students belonging to the school of the place seeking advice as to how they should pursue their studies, and others troubled in mind on account of their constant communication with the pagans, with whom they carried on trade, though from a kind of necessity as their lands and workshops adjoined. The husbands of the women that had complained of them to Jesus were also among the number, as well as others guilty of similar offenses, but against whom no charge had been laid. They presented themselves individually as sinners before Jesus, cast themselves at his feet, confessed their guilt, and implored pardon. What troubled them especially was the thought that the malediction of their wives might fall upon the illegitimate, though otherwise innocent, children, and they asked whether this curse could not be counteracted or annulled. Jesus answered that it might be annulled by the sincere charity and pardon of the one that had invoked it, joined to the contrition and penance of the guilty party. Besides this, the malediction of which I speak does not extend to the soul, for the almighty Father has said: "All souls are Mine"; but it affects the body, the flesh, and temporal goods. The flesh is, however, the house, the instrument of the soul, consequently the flesh lying under such a curse causes great distress and embarrassment to the soul already oppressed with the burden of the body received with life. I saw on this occasion that the malediction varies in its baneful effects according to the intention of the one that invokes it and the disposition of the child itself. Many subject to convulsions, many possessed by the demon, owe their condition to this source. The illegitimate children themselves I generally see possessed of remarkable advantages of nature, though of an order earthly and prone to sin. They have in them something in common with those that, in early times, sprang from the union of the sons of God with the daughters of men. They are often beautiful, cunning, very reserved in disposition, agitated by eager desires and, without wishing it to appear, they would like to draw all things to themselves. They bear in their flesh the stamp of their origin, and frequently their soul goes thereby to perdition.

After hearing and exhorting these sinners individually, Jesus bade them send their wives to him. When they came, he related to each one separately the repentance of her husband, exhorted her to heartfelt forgiveness and entire forgetfulness of the past, and urged her to recall the malediction she had pronounced. If, he told them, they did not act sincerely in this circumstance, the guilt of their husband's relapse would fall upon them. The women wept and thanked and promised everything. Jesus reconciled several of these couples right away that same day. He made them come before him, interrogated them anew, as is customary at the marriage ceremony, joined their hands together, covered them with a scarf, and blessed them. The wife of one of the faithless husbands solemnly revoked the malediction that she had pronounced upon the illegitimate children. The mother of the poor little ones, who were being raised in the Jewish asylum for children, was a pagan. Standing before Jesus, the injured—but now forgiving—wife placed her hand crosswise with that of her husband over the children's heads, revoked the malediction, and blessed the children. Jesus imposed upon those guilty of adultery, as penance, alms, fasts, continence, and prayer. He who had sinned with the pagan was completely transformed. He very humbly invited Jesus to dine with him. Jesus accepted and went, accompanied by his disciples. A couple of the rabbis also were invited and they, as well as the whole city, marveled at the courtesy, for their host was known as a frivolous, worldly man who did not trouble himself much about priests and prophets. He was rich and owned landed property cultivated by servants. His house was near that hospital in which Jesus had cured the victims of melancholy. During the meal two of the little daughters of the family entered the dining hall, and poured costly perfume over Jesus's head.

After dinner Jesus and all the people went to the synagogue for the closing exercises of the sabbath. Jesus resumed his discourse of the day before, though not in terms so severe. He told his audience that God would not abandon them that call upon him. He ended by dilating on their attachment to their houses and possessions, and exhorted them, if they put faith in his teaching, to forsake the great occasion of sin in which they were living among the pagans, and among those of their own belief to practice truth in the Promised Land. Judea, he said, was large enough to harbor and support them, although at first they might have to live under tents. It was better to give up all than to lose their soul on account of their idolatry, that is, their worship of their fine houses and possessions; better to give up all than to sin through love of their own convenience. That the kingdom of God might come to them, it was necessary that they should go to meet it. They should not put their trust in their dwellings in a pleasant land, solid and magnificent though they might be, for the hand of God would fall suddenly upon them, scattering them in all directions, and overturning their mansions. He knew very well, he continued, that their virtues were more apparent than real, that they had no other basis than tepidity and the love of their own ease. They hankered after the wealth of the pagans and sought to win it by their usury, traffic, mining, and marriages, but the day would come when they would see themselves stripped of all their ill-gotten gains. Jesus warned them likewise against such marriages with the pagans as those in which both parties, indifferent to religion, enter into wedlock merely for the sake of property and money, greater freedom and the gratification of passion. All were deeply moved and impressed by Jesus's words, and many begged leave to be allowed to speak with him in private.

Sunday, May 20, AD 31 (Sivan 9)

Jesus spent the whole day visiting people at their homes. Everywhere he recommended the Jews to move from Cyprus to Palestine, prophesying future catastrophes that would take place on Cyprus.

The whole of the following day and even until late at night, was Jesus engaged visiting the different families in their homes, admonishing, consoling, and pardoning. Two women presented themselves before him lamenting to him over their illegitimate children. Jesus sent for their husbands, forgave the guilty parties, and united them once more to their lawful spouses. The children also—without understanding the ceremony, however—were received by the husbands and blessed as their own. It was harder for the wife to admit among her own the illegitimate children of her husband; she had to gain a great victory over herself. But all on this occasion did it so sincerely that they forced, so to say, their husbands to love them more and to bless children of their wives not their own. And so a general reconciliation was brought about, and scandal avoided.

Many sought comfort from Jesus on the score of his energetic admonition to them to emigrate from those pagan lands. Jesus's teaching indeed pleased them and, looking upon themselves as Jews separated from their people, they felt greatly honored by his visit to them, but they did not like the idea of following him, of leaving their homes. Here they were rich and comfortable, owned a city built by themselves, had a share in a mine, and carried on extensive trade. They enriched themselves by means of the pagans. They were not tormented by the Pharisees, not oppressed by Pilate. They were, as regards this life, in a most agreeable position, but their connection with the pagans was highly censurable. Pagan property and workshops were in their neighborhood. The pagan girls liked well to unite in marriage with the Jews, because they were not treated by them in so slavish a manner as by those of their own religion, and so they enticed the young Israelites in every way, by presents, attentions, and all kinds of allurements. When converted to Judaism, it was not from conviction, but from sordid views, and so insubordination and tepidity easily made their way into the family. The Jews of Mallep were besides less simple-hearted and hospitable than those of Palestine, their social surroundings were more studied and refined, their Jewish origin not so pure; consequently they brought forward all kinds of scruples and difficulties against Jesus's counsel to emigrate to the Holy Land. Jesus argued that their forefathers owned houses and lands in Egypt, but that they had willingly and gladly abandoned them, and he repeated once more his prediction that if they persisted in remaining, misfortune would fall upon them. The disciples, Barnabas especially, went around a great deal in the environs teaching and exhorting the people. They were less timid in his presence and laid before him all their doubts. He always had a crowd around him.

Jesus Visits the Mines near Kythria

Monday, May 21, AD 31 (Sivan 10)

Jesus and the disciples journeyed some seven hours to a miners' village near Kythria. The family of Barnabas had invited him here. He taught on the way.

FROM Mallep, Jesus, accompanied by the disciples, the disciple recently arrived from Nain and the sons of Cyrinus just come from Salamis (in all about twelve), went to a village of miners near Kythria. He took a roundabout road to it of seven hours. On the way he paused among the different bands of laborers and spoke of the path of a good life. Jesus had by the family of Barnabas and several people of Kythria been invited to this mining village because the Jewish miners of the place were celebrating a feast at which they received from their employers various presents besides their share of the harvest. Jesus took a circuitous route to the village, that he might be able to speak to his disciples without interruption and also that he might not arrive too early. During the journey, he permitted the disciple from Nain to deliver the messages and relate the news with which he had been charged; for although Jesus knew all himself, he was careful not to let it appear, lest such knowledge might be a source of annoyance or anxiety to those around him.

The disciple had left Jerusalem on the eve of Pentecost just after the money offering in the temple, and the execution of Pilate's plot. He had gone straight to Nain, thence through Nazareth to Ptolemais, and from the latter place to Cyprus. He told Jesus that his mother and the other holy women, together with John and some of the disciples, had quietly celebrated the Feast of Pentecost at Nazareth; that his mother and friends sent greetings and entreated him to stay some time in Cyprus, until minds had grown calm in his regard. The Pharisees, he continued, were already reporting that he had run away. Herod also wanted to summon him to Machaerus under pretext of conferring with him upon the subject of the prisoners freed at Thirza, but really to make him prisoner as he had done John.

The disciple told likewise of Pilate's plot on the eve of Pentecost when the Jews brought their offerings to the temple. Two friends of Jesus, relatives of Zechariah and servers in the temple, who happened to get mixed up in the tumult, lost their lives. Jesus already knew of the circumstance, and it made him very sad. The news renewed his grief, as well as that of his disciples. Pilate on the preceding evening left the city, and with some of his troops proceeded westward of the route to Joppa, where he owned a castle. He had demanded the contributions offered to the temple in honor of the feast, in order to build a very long aqueduct. On all the pillars at the entrances to the temple he had caused to be placed metal tablets on which were the head of the Emperor and, below, an inscription demanding the tax. The people were roused to indignation at the sight of these pictures, and the Herodians by means of their emissaries stirred up a band of Galileans belonging to the party of Judas the Golanite, who had been killed in the last revolt. Herod, who was at Jerusalem in secret, knew all that was transpiring. That evening the mob became perfectly infuriated. They tore down the tables, broke them in pieces, dishonored the portraits, and cast the fragments over the forum in front of the praetorium, crying: "Here is our offering money!" They then dispersed without anyone's especially resenting the act. Next morning, however, when about to leave the temple, they found the entrances beset by guards demanding the tax imposed by Pilate. When the Jews resisted and tried to force their way out, the disguised soldiers pressed out along with them and stabbed them with short swords. At that moment the alarm became general, and the two temple servers running to the scene of action lost their lives. The Jews made a brave resistance, and drove the soldiers back into the citadel of Antonia.

On the way Jesus spoke long to his disciples about the inhabitants of Mallep, their hankering after temporal goods, and how distasteful to them was the suggestion to go to Palestine. He referred to the pagan philosophers who were accompanying him, and told the disciples how they should behave toward them in Palestine when they found them actually in their midst. Jesus did this because they did not appear to accord rightly with the philosophers in the party, and were still somewhat scandalized on their account.

Toward evening they arrived at the mining village, one half hour from Kythria. It was in the neighborhood of the mines, built around a high, rocky ridge, into which the rear of many dwellings ran. Upon this ridge there were gardens and a place suited for instruction, surrounded by shady trees. Steps led up the ridge, the top of which overlooked the village. Jesus on his arrival repaired to a sort of inn where dwelt the overseer who superintended the miners, supplied them with food, and paid them their wages. The people received Jesus with manifestations of joy. All the entrances to the place and the house of the overseer were, on account of the feast, adorned with green arches and garlands of flowers. They led Jesus and his disciples into the house, washed their feet, and presented refreshments to the Lord, who then went with them to the place for teaching upon the rock. Jesus seated himself, and the crowd reclined around him. He spoke of the happiness attendant upon poverty and labor, and told them how much happier they were than the opulent Jews of Salamis, that they had fewer temptations to offend God, before whom the virtuous alone are rich. He said also that he had come in order to prove that he did not despise them, and that he loved them. He taught until night in parables on the Lord's Prayer.

Tuesday, May 22, AD 31 (Sivan 11)

Jesus taught on the village square. The disciples distributed clothes and provisions to the people. Afterward, all took part in a meal together.

Provisions of all kinds, pieces of fabric for clothing, food and grain were conveyed hither from Kythria; and on the next day came the father and brother of Barnabas, several distinguished citizens and proprietors of the mines, along with some rabbis from the same place. When the gifts already enumerated had been safely deposited in the public square of the place, where the people were assembled and seated in rows, these visitors entered also. Now began the distribution of gifts: great bowls of grain; large loaves of bread, about two feet square; honey, fruit, jugs of something, pieces of leathern clothing, covers and all kinds of furniture and utensils. The women received pieces of thick stuff like carpet, about one and a half yards square. Jesus and the disciples were present at the distribution, after which Jesus taught again on the rocky height upon which the people had assembled. He took for his subjects the laborers in the vineyard and the good Samaritan, the blessing of poverty and thanksgiving for the same, daily bread and the Lord's Prayer. After the instruction, the people had a feast under the arbors in the open air at which Jesus, the disciples, and the guests of distinction served. Little boys and girls played on flutes and sang. The meal over, they had some innocent games such as children play; for instance, running, leaping, blindfolding, hiding and seeking, etc. They danced, too, in this way: They stood in long rows, bowed here and there, crossed before one another, and then formed a ring.

In the evening, Jesus went to the mines with about ten boys of from six to eight years old. The children wore only a broad girdle with festive wreaths of woollen or feather flowers around their waist or crossed on their breast. They looked very lovely. In their own childlike way, they showed Jesus all the places in which were the best mines, and related to him all that they knew. Jesus instructed them in words full of sweetness, and made some useful application of what they told him. He likewise proposed to them enigmas and related parables. The miners were, despite their rough and dirty labor in the bowels of the earth, very cleanly in their homes and festal garments.

Wednesday, May 23, AD 31 (Sivan 12)

Today Jesus accompanied a cousin of Maroni, the widow of Nain, to the harbor at Kition, and gave him a message for his mother, and some of the apostles.

I saw Jesus and the disciples accompanying the disciple from Nain to the port about five hours distant. One group went in front and another followed, while Jesus walked between the two with the disciple and some of the others in their turn. Jesus blessed the disciple on his departure, and his fellow disciples embraced him, after which they returned to the miners' village. The disciple from Nain pursued his journey to the salt regions near Kition. The port was here not so far from the city as was that of Salamis. The sea penetrates far into the land so that the city has the appearance of being built in the midst of the waves. Not far from it rises a very high mountain, and there is a salt mine in the neighborhood. At the quay near the salt mine were only little skiffs and rafts, and a quantity of wood for the building of vessels was floating around.

Jesus Goes to Kyrenia, and Visits Mnason's Parents

Thursday, May 24, AD 31 (Sivan 13)

Early this morning Jesus and the disciples left the miners' village near Kythria. Around four in the afternoon they arrived at the family home of his disciple Mnason, three quarters of an hour from Kyrenia.

WHEN Jesus left the miners' village with the disciples, he proceeded in a northwesterly direction across the mountains to the port of Kyrenia. They left Mallep to the right, went through a portion of the valley of Lanifa, and passed near the village of Leppe. On the way Jesus rested once on a beautiful shady eminence, and there taught. Toward four in the afternoon they arrived to within about three-quarters of an hour's distance from Kyrenia, where they were received by Mnason's family and several other Jews in a garden set apart for prayer and pious reunions. This garden was a retired spot hidden away in a slope of the mountain. Mnason's family dwelt at some distance from the road, and one half-hour from Kyrenia. His father was an aged Jew, thin, stooped, and with a long beard, but withal very lively and active. He had two daughters and three sons, one son-in-law, and a daughter-in-law, and all had been living here together for about ten years. Before that they used to travel around buying and selling. They received Jesus with many expressions of joy and humility, washed the travelers' feet in a basin, and presented to them refreshments. This part of the mountain formed a large terrace full of shady walks, and comprised the sacred garden belonging to these people. Jesus taught until near evening, taking for his subjects baptism, the Lord's Prayer, and the beatitudes.

After that Jesus accompanied Mnason's brethren and his father, who was called Moses, to the house, where Mnason presented to him four children, whom he blessed. Then his mother and sisters came forward veiled, and Jesus addressed to them some words, after which the whole family took a meal together under an arbor in the open air. The table was spread with the best they had: bread, honey, birds, and fruit, the latter still hanging upon little branches. During the meal, Jesus taught. They lodged in a long arbor built of thin, light boards, the exterior entirely overgrown by green foliage. It was furnished with a row of couches.

Mnason's mother was a strong, robust woman. His father was descended from the tribe of Judah, but his ancestors had been carried off in the Babylonian Captivity and had never returned. Moses had traveled much directing caravans, had lived a long time also near the Red Sea, in Arabia; but having become impoverished, had settled in this place with his family. Mnason went to school in Mallep and later on for the sake of his studies traveled to Judea, where he met Jesus. His father with his grown-up children, Mnason being the youngest, lived in lightly built huts. They were not engaged in agriculture; they owned only a few gardens that lay back of their homes, and which were planted out in fruit trees. Having formerly, as caravan director, had much experience in the transportation of goods, the old man had established himself here as a kind of innkeeper, assistant, and commissioner for the commercial caravans that halted before Kyrenia. He owned some asses and oxen with which he conveyed small burdens received from the caravans and destined for places remote from the public road. He was like a porter who had now become an innkeeper also for others in the same business as himself. He was poor, but he had managed to maintain in his family strict Jewish discipline. For the rest, commerce did not flow toward Kyrenia, but rather to Lapethos, which lay a couple of hours westward on the grand highroad.

Friday, May 25, AD 31 (Sivan 14)

Jesus went to the synagogue in Kyrenia for the beginning of the sabbath with the disciples and with Mnason's family. There, Jesus spoke against idolatry.

Next morning Jesus taught again at the place of instruction before an audience composed of several Jews from the city and the people belonging to a little caravan. These latter were inexpressibly happy to find Jesus here, for they had already heard his instructions at Capernaum where, too, they had received baptism. On this occasion, Jesus inveighed against usury and greed of gain which made the Jews eager to enrich themselves off the pagans. He then touched upon baptism, the Lord's Prayer, and the beatitudes. Toward noon they partook of a meal in common, but Jesus did more serving and teaching around the tables than reclining at them himself.

One of Mnason's married sisters did not make her appearance, because her little daughter had died the day before. She sat closely veiled, lamenting near the corpse. The child could not (I cannot now recall on what account) be buried on that day; but on this, the next day, they were expecting the rabbis from Mallep to conduct the funeral, for it was there they had their graveyard. The child had attained a tolerably good size, although it had always been an invalid. It could neither speak nor walk with facility, but it understood all that was said to it. Mnason, who had visited his home from time to time, had spoken to Jesus about it. Jesus told him that it would soon die, and instructed him how to prepare it for death. Mnason prudently followed Jesus's directions at a time in which the mother was not present. He excited the child to faith in the Messiah, to hearty sorrow for its sins, and to the hope of salvation; he prayed with it, and anointed it with oil that Jesus had blessed. The child died a very good death. I saw it lying on a little bier near the veiled mother, just like a babe in swaddling clothes, its face covered. The casket in which it lay was shaped something like a trough. On its head was a wreath of flowers, and tiny bunches of aromatic herbs were laid closely around it. Its arms and hands also were wrapped in burial bands, but left free from the person. A little white staff rested in its arms. On the top of it was a bouquet made up of a large ear of corn, a vine leaf, a little olive branch, a rose, and foliage peculiar to the country. Several women visited the mother and mourned with her. By the child's side in the coffin they deposited playthings: two little flutes, a little crooked, spiral-shaped horn, a tiny bow spanned with a string, on top of which in a furrow lay a little wand like an arrow. In each arm, besides, the child held a short, gilded staff with a knob on top.

When the rabbis came to conduct the corpse, the coffin was closed with a light lid which, instead of being nailed, was fastened down with a cord. Four men carried it on poles. A lighted lamp in a horn-lantern was borne on a pole and was followed by a crowd of children and grown persons, who all pressed forward with no attention to order. Jesus and the disciples were standing outside the house watching the funeral. Jesus comforted the mother and relatives, and spoke of the resurrection.

All repaired to Kyrenia for the celebration of the sabbath. The city had three streets facing the sea, the middle one very wide, and these three were intersected by two others. On the opposite side, the land side, it was enclosed by a massive wall, or rampart, in whose exterior were built the houses of the few Jews belonging to the place. Their dwellings were therefore outside the city, but still enclosed by a second wall. In this way, the Jews of Kyrenia lived between the two walls of the city, entirely separate from the pagans, who had as many as ten pagan temples, or places dedicated to idols. The Jews of Kyrenia were few in number, not very rich, but still possessed of all that was necessary. In one large building they had a school and a synagogue, along with accommodations for both rabbis and teachers. It was high, and had two stories entirely distinct. They had also a beautiful, flowing fountain fed by a stream from another source. The fountain they divided, one part being used for a drinking well, the other being conducted into a delightful garden for bathing purposes.

The doctors of the Law received Jesus very respectfully at the end of the street and conducted him first to the school, and then to the synagogue. Here he found seven invalids who had caused themselves to be conveyed thither on litters, that they might listen to his instructions. There were altogether about one hundred men. The doctors allowed Jesus to teach and conduct the exercises alone. He read from Moses, passages recounting the number of the children of Israel and their different families, and from the prophet Osee a grave and severe lecture against idolatry.

In one of these passages was read the circumstance of God's commanding the prophet to marry an adulteress, the children of which marriage were to receive special names. The Jews questioned Jesus on this passage. He explained it to them. He said that the prophet, in his whole person and life, had to show forth the condition of God's covenant with the House of Israel, and that the names of the children should be expressive of God's sentence of punishment. Another lesson to be drawn from this passage was, as Jesus said, that acting under the inspiration of God, the good oftentimes united themselves to sinners in order to arrest the transmission of sin. This marriage of Osee with an adulteress and the various names of the children testified to the reiterated mercy of God and the long continuance of crime. Jesus spoke very severely. He exhorted to penance and baptism, referred to the near approach of the kingdom of God, predicted the punishment of those that repulsed it, and prophesied the destruction of Jerusalem.

While Jesus was teaching, the sick more than once cried out in the pauses of his discourse: "Lord, we believe in thy doctrine! Lord, help us!" And when they noticed that he was about to leave the synagogue, they caused themselves to be carried out before him. They were laid in the fore-court in two rows, and they continued to cry out to Jesus: "Lord, exercise upon us thy power! Do unto us, Lord, what is pleasing to thee!" But Jesus did not cure them right away. When, however, the rabbis interceded for the poor invalids, Jesus questioned the latter. "What can I do for you?" He asked. They answered: "Lord, relieve us of our infirmities! Lord, cure us!" "Believe ye that I can do it?" asked Jesus, and all cried out: "Yes, Lord! We do believe that thou canst do it!" Then Jesus ordered the rabbis to bring the rolls of the Law and to pray with him over the sick. The rabbis brought the rolls and prayed, after which Jesus commanded the disciples to impose hands upon the sick. They obeyed, laying their hands on the eyes of one, on the breast of another, and so on different parts of the body. Jesus again put the question: "Do ye believe, and do ye wish to be cured?" and again they answered: "Yes, Lord! We believe that thou canst help us!" Then said Jesus: "Rise! Your faith hath cured you!" and they arose, all seven, thanking Jesus, who ordered them to wash and purify themselves. Some among them had been very much swollen with edema. Their sickness was passed, but they were still weak and had to walk with the assistance of a staff.

Several times before in Cyprus, namely at Kythria, Mallep, and Salamis, I saw Jesus healing in that way, that is, praying with the rabbis and commanding the disciples to impose hands. As these rabbis and doctors were well-inclined, he caused them to take part like the disciples in this cure, thus to awaken in them confidence. He made use of this new way of curing in order to prepare those that took part in it for the works of the disciples, for there were a great many rabbis among the five hundred and seventy Jews whom Jesus gained in Cyprus.

Saturday, May 26, AD 31 (_Sivan 15_)

This morning Jesus taught about fifty people who were awaiting baptism. They were then baptized. At the close of the sabbath, he taught again in the synagogue at Kyrenia. Later, he returned with the disciples to Mallep.

The cured, along with other Jews from Kyrenia, were baptized at the place of instruction near Moses's dwelling. The water used for the purpose had been conveyed thither from a neighboring well, for the house lay rather high and had no spring near it. But to supply the defect, it had a reservoir in the shape of a large, copper basin buried in the earth and surrounded by a little channel lined with stone, which had an outlet into a stone trough. The water in the basin was perfectly pure, for the washing of feet, linen, etc., was all done in the channel. The stone trough was used for watering the cattle and sprinkling the garden beds. The neophytes stood in the channel and were baptized with water from the basin. First, Jesus gave an instruction on penance and purification through baptism. The men wore long, white garments with maniples and cinctures ornamented with letters. Besides the seven lately cured, there were only eight other Jews baptized. They spoke separately with Jesus, and confessed their sins. Jesus told them to take advantage of the time of grace and to accomplish the Law according to the meaning of the prophets, and not to be its slaves, for the Law was given to them, and not they to the Law. It was given to them in order to serve as a means to merit grace.

Among the newly baptized were Mnason's brothers and brother-in-law. As to his father, pious though he was, still he was an obstinate Jew and would not hear of being baptized. Mnason had all along tried, but in vain, to prepare him, and Jesus too had spoken to him that day on the same subject. The stubborn old man, however, was not to be moved. He shrugged his shoulders, shook his head, and objected with all kinds of plausible reasons in favor of circumcision, to which he held. Mnason was so troubled at his father's obstinacy that he shed tears. Jesus consoled him. He told him that his father was very old and had in consequence grown obstinate; as for the rest, however, he had always lived piously, he would weep over his blindness at another time and place, when light would dawn upon him. Jesus had blessed the baptismal water into which some from the Jordan was poured. All that remained after the baptism was carefully scooped out and buried.

During the baptism, Jesus went to a lovely garden back of the hill upon which was the place of instruction. It was full of fruit trees and fitted up with arbors, and there awaiting him were from thirty to forty Jewish women, closely veiled. They bowed low before him. Many of them were in great anxiety and dread lest their husbands, in order to follow Jesus, would forsake them, and they be left helpless. They entreated him therefore to forbid their husbands' doing such a thing. Jesus replied that if their husbands followed him, they too should go to Palestine, where they would find means of subsistence. He related to them the example of the holy women, and explained to them the character of the epoch in which they were living. The present was not the time for a life of comfort and ease, for the day was approaching upon which they ought to go forward to meet the kingdom that was drawing near and receive the Bridegroom. He spoke also of the lost drachma, and of the five wise and the five foolish virgins. The younger women begged Jesus to admonish their husbands not to visit the pagan maidens, since he had in terms so severe discussed that passage in Osee in which the prophet warns against sinning with the pagans. Most of these young women were, however, tormented with jealousy. Jesus interrogated them upon their own conduct toward their husbands, exhorted them to mildness, humility, patience, and obedience, and warned them against gossiping and making reproaches. After that he closed the sabbath exercises in the synagogue of Kyrenia, and went with his disciples back to Mallep by the shortest route.

Departure from Cyprus

Sunday, May 27, AD 31 (Sivan 16)

Jesus announced today that he would soon be leaving Cyprus to return to Palestine.

AT Mallep, Jesus delivered a long instruction at the fountain. He spoke again of the approach of the kingdom and of the obligation to go to meet it, of his own departure, and of the short time remaining to him, of the bitter consummation of his labors, and of the necessity they were under of following him and laboring with him. He alluded again to the speedy destruction of Jerusalem and the chastisement that would soon overtake all who rejected the kingdom of God, who would not do penance and amend their lives instead of clinging to their worldly goods and pleasures. Referring to the country in which they lived, where everything was so pleasant and the conveniences of life so many, Jesus compared it after all to an ornamented tomb whose interior was full of filth and corruption. Then he bade them reflect upon their own interiors, and see what lay concealed under their beautiful exteriors. He touched upon their usury, their avarice, their desire to gain which led them to communicate so freely with the pagans, their violent attachment to earthly possessions, their sanctimoniousness; and he again told them that all the magnificence and worldly conveniences that they saw around them would one day be destroyed, that the time would come in which no Israelite would there be found living. He spoke very significantly of himself and the fulfillment of the prophecies, and yet only a few comprehended his words. During this instruction the people presented themselves in bands and by turns, old men, middle-aged men, youths, women, and maidens. All were deeply touched; they wept and sobbed.

Monday, May 28, AD 31 (Sivan 17)

This morning Jesus visited some farms east of Mallep. He taught there and healed the sick, including a blind child. Later, there was a festive meal in Mallep, to which Jesus invited the poor and needy. Afterward, he taught concerning the meaning of the word "Amen." That night, he and the disciples left Mallep.

Jesus went next with some disciples and others a couple of hours to the east of Mallep, to where the occupants of several farms had begged him to come, and where he had already gone once before from Mallep. There was, nearby, a shady hill that was used as a place for instruction. The disciple of Nain also had come hither from the port of Kition, to make preparations for his departure from Cyprus.

Jesus here, as at Mallep, delivered a farewell discourse after which he went around to some huts and cured several invalids who had begged him to do so. He had already set out on his return journey to Mallep when an old peasant implored him to go to his house and take pity on his blind son. There were in the house three families of twelve persons, the grandparents, two married sons, and their children. The mother, veiled, brought the blind boy to Jesus in her arms, although it could both speak and walk. Jesus took the child into his arms, with a finger of his right hand anointed its eyes with his own saliva, blessed it, put it down on the ground, and held something before its eyes. The child grasped after it awkwardly, ran at the sound of its mother's voice, then turned to the father, and so from the arms of one to those of the other. The parents led it to Jesus, and weeping thanked him on their knees. Jesus pressed the child to his bosom and gave it back to the parents with the admonition to lead it to the true light, that its eyes, which now saw, might not be closed in darkness deeper than before. He blessed the other children also, and the whole family. The people shed tears and followed him with acclamations of praise.

In the house used for such purposes at Mallep, a feast was given, in which all took part. The poor were fed, and presents were given them. Jesus, finally, delivered a grand discourse on the word "Amen," which, he said, was the whole summary of prayer. Whoever pronounces it carelessly, makes void his prayer. Prayer cries to God; binds us to God; opens to us His mercy, and, with the word "Amen," rightly uttered, we take the asked-for gift out of His hands. Jesus spoke most forcibly of the power of the word "Amen." He called it the beginning and the end of everything. He spoke almost as if God had by it created the whole world. He uttered an "Amen" over all that he had taught them, over his own departure from them, over the accomplishment of his own mission, and ended his discourse by a solemn "Amen." Then he blessed his audience, who wept and cried after him.

Tuesday, May 29, AD 31 (Sivan 18)

Around two in the afternoon, Jesus and the disciples arrived back in Salamis. Here Jesus met again with the Roman commandant of the town, who decided to convert. The pagan priestess Mercuria also converted. Jesus discussed with her her plans to leave Cyprus and move to Palestine.

Jesus left Mallep with his disciples, Barnabas and Mnason following the next day. They left Kythria to the right and went straight on across fields, through thickets, and over mountain ridges. Jesus attempted to discharge his indebtedness at the inn with the money brought him by the disciple from Nain; but when the proprietor refused to receive it, it was distributed to the poor. All those that, either at present or in the future, were from Mallep, Kythria, or Salamis to follow Jesus into Palestine, were to go by different routes. One party was to cross over from a port northeast of Salamis; and others, who had business at Tyre, were to start from Salamis itself. The baptized pagans went, for the most part, to Gessur.

Arrived at Salamis, Jesus and his followers put up at the school in which, upon his coming to Cyprus, he had sojourned. They entered from the northwest; the aqueduct lay to the right, the Jewish city to the left. I saw them, their garments still girded, sitting in threes by the basin in the forecourt of the school. The basin was surrounded by a little channel, in which they were washing their feet. Every three made use of a long brown towel to dry their feet. Jesus did not always allow his feet to be washed by others; generally each one performed that service for himself. Here their coming had been looked for, and food was at once offered them. Jesus had here a great number of devoted adherents, and in their midst he taught for fully two hours. After that he had a long conference with the Roman commandant, who presented to him two pagan youths desirous of instruction and baptism. They confessed their sins with tears, and Jesus pardoned them. Toward evening they were privately baptized by James in the forecourt of the doctors' dwelling. These youths were to follow the philosophers to Gessur.

Mercuria also sent to beg Jesus to grant her an interview in the garden near the aqueduct. Jesus assented, and followed the servant that had delivered the message to the place designated. Mercuria came forward veiled, holding her two singularly dressed little girls by the hand. They wore only a short tunic down to the knee; the rest of their covering consisted of some kind of fine, transparent material upon which were wreaths of woollen, or feather flowers. Their arms were bare, their feet enveloped in little bands, and their hair loose. They were dressed almost like the angels that we make for representations of the crib. Jesus spoke long and graciously with Mercuria. She wept bitterly and was very much troubled at the thought of having to leave her son behind her, also because her parents lived at a distance from her younger sister, who would thus remain in the blindness of paganism. She wept also over her own sins. Jesus consoled her and assured her again of pardon. The two little girls looked at their mother in surprise, and they too began to cry and to cling to her. Jesus blessed the little ones, and went back to the school.

Mnason arrived from Kythria accompanied by one of his brothers, who wished to follow Jesus to Palestine.

Wednesday, May 30, AD 31 (Sivan 19)

At dawn, the Roman commandant bade farewell to Jesus, who then made his way to the harbor at Kition, about two hours from Salamis. After eating a meal at the harbor, Jesus and his traveling companions—now about twenty-seven in number—set off from Cyprus on board three ships.

After a farewell repast, Jesus and his disciples went to the place where, by his orders, some of the Roman commandant's people were awaiting them with asses. These they mounted. Jesus rode sidewise on a cross seat provided with a support, and by his side rode the commandant. They passed the aqueducts and, at the rear of the city, crossed the little river Padiaios. They took a narrow country road shorter than the ordinary route, which wound in a curve near the shore. During the whole of that beautiful night I saw the commandant generally at Jesus's side. In front rode a troop of twelve, then came one of nine, followed by Jesus and the commandant a little apart; another band of twelve brought up the rear. Besides this occasion and Palm Sunday, I never saw Jesus otherwise than on foot. When morning began to break and they were still three hours from the sea, the commandant, in order not to attract attention, bade adieu to Jesus. In parting, Jesus presented to him his hand, and gave him his blessing. The commandant had descended from his ass, for he wished to embrace Jesus's feet. Then he bowed low before him, withdrew a few steps, repeated his obeisance (it must have been a custom of the place), mounted his beast, and rode off. The two newly baptized pagans accompanied him. Jesus then rode on till within about an hour of the place to which he was going, when he and his party dismounted and sent back the asses with the servants. They now journeyed on through the salt hills until they reached a long building

Setting Out to Sea

where they found some mariners awaiting them. It was a quiet, solitary spot on the seashore. There were few trees around the country, but along the coast an extraordinarily long mound, or dyke, covered with moss and trees. Facing the sea were dwelling houses and open buildings belonging to the salt-works, in which poor Jewish families and some pagans dwelt. Farther on where the shore was steeper there was a little cove down to which a flight of steps led, and here were anchored three ships in readiness for the travelers. It was easy to land at this spot, and it was from this point that the salt was shipped to the cities along the coast.

Jesus was expected here, and all partook of a repast consisting of fish, honey, bread, and fruit. The water of this place was very bad, and they purified it by putting something into it, I think fruit. They kept it in jugs and leathern bottles. Seven of the Jews belonging to the ships' crew were here baptized, a basin being used for the ceremony.

Jesus went from house to house, consoling the poor occupants, bestowing alms upon them, healing the wounded, and curing the sick, who stretched out their hands pitifully toward him. First he asked whether they believed that he could cure them; and upon their answering, "Yes, Lord! We do believe!" He restored them to health. He went even to the end of the long dyke, also to the homes of the pagans, who met him looking timid and shy. Jesus blessed the poor children and gave some instructions.

The disciple from Nain had lately arrived at this place, where he awaited two other disciples. They came in good time, and then all three set out for Palestine to announce Jesus's coming.

Jesus's party counted twenty-seven men, all of whom embarked at evening twilight in three little vessels. That in which Jesus sailed was the smallest, and with him were four disciples and some rowers. Each of the vessels had in the center, rising around the mast, galleries divided into compartments which served as sleeping places. With the exception of the rowers, who took their stand above, no one of the ship's crew could be seen. I saw Jesus's little vessel sailing out ahead, and I wondered why the others took a different direction. But when it had grown quite dark, I saw them at about half an hour from the shore aground in two places, a torch raised on the mast as a sign of distress. At this sight, Jesus ordered his sailors to row back toward them. They approached one of the ships, threw out to it a rope, sailed round it, and, with it thus in tow, went to the other and did the same. The two were in this way bound to Jesus's vessel, which now they followed. Jesus rebuked the disciples on the two ill-guided vessels for having thought themselves possessed of more knowledge of the way, spoke of self-will, and of the necessity of following him. The ships had gotten caught in an eddy between two sandbanks.

(Follow Map 31)

Thursday, May 31, AD 31 (Sivan 20)

After an uneventful crossing, the three ships arrived at the bay between Akko (Ptolemais) and Haifa. Jesus and his companions landed east of Haifa, at the estuary of the river Kishon. Disciples were waiting to greet Jesus as he and the others disembarked.

The evening of the following day, just before the entrance

Map 31: Travels in Middle and Southern Galilee
May 31–June 14, AD 31

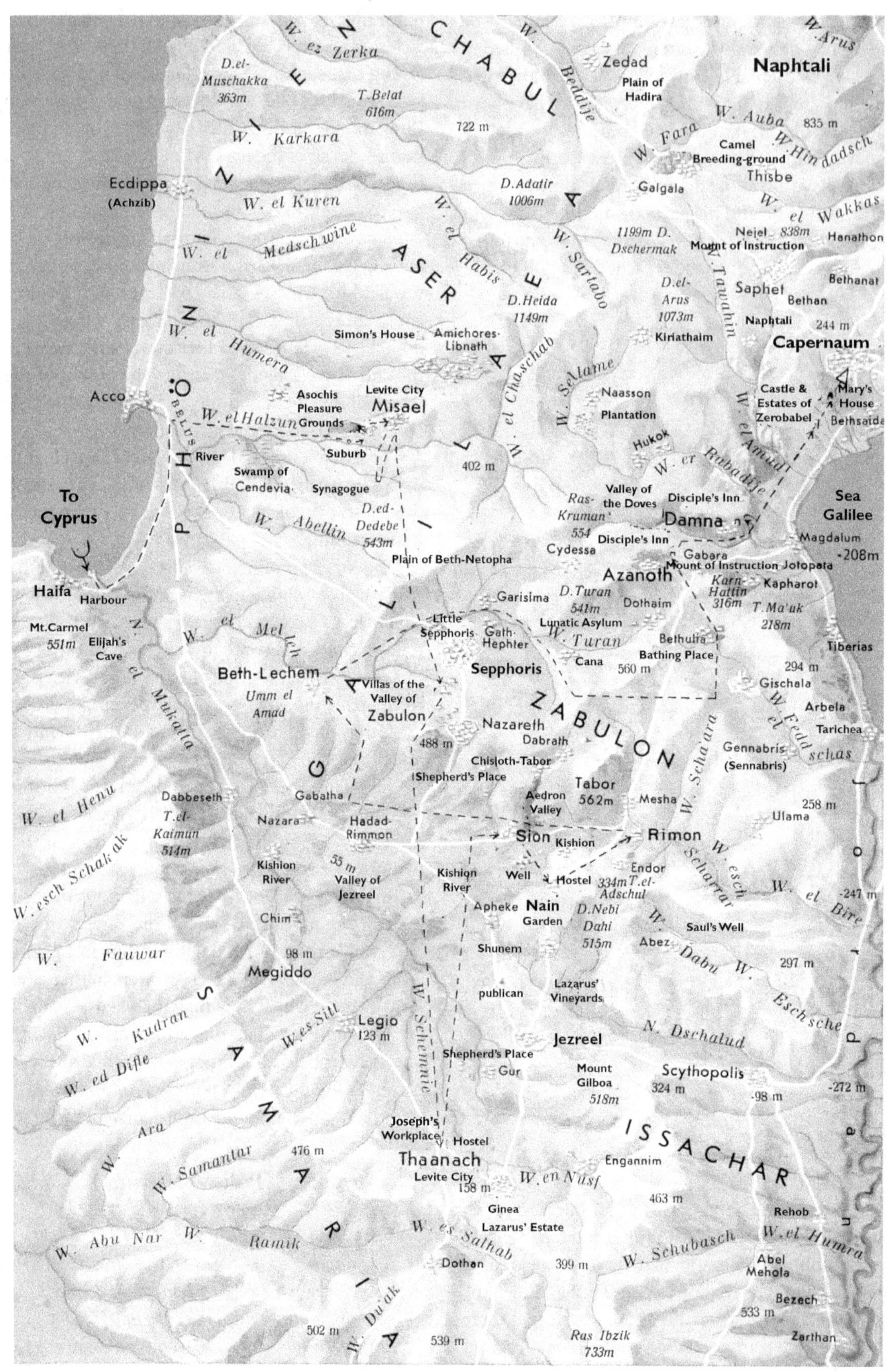

Harbor near Haifa—Misael—Place with Synagogue—Misael—Place with Villas in Zebulon Valley
Thaanach—Sion—Nain—Rimon—Beth-Lechem—Azanoth—Damna—Zorobabel—Capernaum

of the great gulf which the sea forms at the foot of Mount Carmel between Ptolemais and Haifa, I saw Jesus's three vessels rowing back again into deep water, for a little inside the gulf a struggle was going on between a large ship on one side and some smaller ones on the other. The large ship was victorious and several dead bodies were thrown out into the water. As Jesus's vessels drew near the combatants, Jesus raised his hand and blessed them, whereupon they soon separated. They did not see Jesus's vessels, for the latter were awaiting the issue at some distance from the entrance to the gulf. The dispute between the two parties had arisen in Cyprus on the subject of the cargo. The little vessels had here lain in wait for the large one. The combatants hacked away and aimed at one another from the decks with long poles. One would have thought not a soul would escape. The struggle lasted a couple of hours. At last the large ship took the smaller ones prisoner, and moved slowly off with them in tow.

Jesus landed near the mouth of the Kishon, east of Haifa, which lies on the coast. He was received on shore by several of the apostles and disciples, among them Thomas, Simon, Thaddeus, Nathaniel Chased, and Heliachim, all of whom were unspeakably delighted to embrace him and his companions. They went round the gulf for about three hours and a half, and crossed a little river that flows into the sea near Ptolemais. The long bridge across this river was like a walled street. It extended to the foot of the height behind which was the swamp of Cendevia. Having climbed this height, they proceeded to the suburbs of the Levitical city Misael, which was separated from them by a curve of that same height. This suburb faced the sea on the west, and on the south rose Carmel with its beautiful valley. Misael consisted of only one street and one inn, which extended over the height. Here, near a fountain, Jesus was met by the people in festal procession, the children singing songs of welcome. All bore palm branches, on which the dates were still hanging. Simeon from Amichores-Libnath, the "City of Waters," was here with his whole family. After his baptism, he came to Misael, for his children gave him no rest until he had again joined the Jews. He had arranged this reception for Jesus, and all at his own expense. When the procession reached the inn, nine Levites from Misael came forward to salute Jesus.

Jesus Goes from Misael, the Levitical City, Through Thaanach, Nain, Azanoth, and Damna to Capernaum

Friday, June 1, AD 31 (Sivan 21)

Jesus and the disciples went northward and crossed the river Belus. They then went eastward to the town of Misael, where Elizabeth, the mother of John the Baptist, had grown up. That evening, with the start of the sabbath, Jesus and the disciples went to the synagogue in Misael. Here Levites were responsible for the services.

To the north of the suburb and on a declivity halfway up the height lay the beautiful pleasure garden of Misael, commanding a magnificent view of the gulf. Higher up on the hill one could see the pond, or swamp, of Cendevia and Libnath, the "City of Waters," which was an hour and a half distant. It was nearer the sea, which here makes a bend into the land, than Misael, which was a couple of hours from the sea. Debbaseth was five hours to the east of the Kishon, and Nazareth about seven. Jesus walked in the garden with his disciples and related the parable of a fisherman that went out to sea to fish, and took five hundred and seventy fishes. He told them that an experienced fisherman would put into pure water the good fish found in bad, that like Elijah he would purify the springs and wells, that he would remove good fish from bad water, where the fish of prey would devour them, and that he would make for them new spawning ponds in better water. Jesus introduced into the parable also the accident that had happened on the sandbank to those that, out of self-will, had not followed the master of the vessels. The Cypriotes who had followed Jesus could not restrain their tears when they heard him speak of the laborious task of transporting fish from bad to good water. Jesus mentioned clearly and precisely the number "five hundred and seventy good fish" that had been saved, and said that that was indeed enough to pay for the labor.

He spoke of Cyprus to the Levites, who rejoiced that Jews from that country were coming hither. Many were coming also from Ptolemais, and would pass this way. There was question of measures to be taken. Jesus spoke of the danger that threatened them there, whereupon the Levites asked anxiously whether the pagans of their country would ever become so powerful as to prove dangerous. Jesus answered by an allusion to the judgment that was to fall upon the whole country, the danger that threatened himself, and the chastisement that would overtake Jerusalem. His hearers were unable to comprehend how he could again return to Jerusalem. But he said that he had still much to do before the consummation of his labors.

The Syrophoenician from Ornithopolis sent hither by some of the disciples little golden bars and plates of the same metal chained together. She was desirous to send one of her ships to Cyprus, in order to facilitate Mercuria's flight from the island.

Saturday, June 2, AD 31 (Sivan 22)

Jesus went with some Levites to visit Elizabeth's birthplace. Afterward, Jesus went to heal the sick in their homes. At the close of the sabbath, he preached in the synagogue. He taught of Samson and his deeds, as an example of a forerunner of the Messiah.

On an invitation from the Levites, Jesus accompanied them to Misael, a very ancient city, surrounded by walls and towers, in the latter of which dwelt some pagans. Elizabeth had for a long time sojourned here with her father, who exercised the functions of a Levite, and Zechariah too was once at Misael. Elizabeth was born in an isolated country house two hours from Misael in the plain of Esdrelon. The property belonged to her parents, and she afterward inherited it. In her fifth year she entered the temple. When she left it, she returned for a time to Misael and, after another period spent at the house in which she was born, she went to Zechariah's home in Judea. Jesus spoke of her and of John. He insisted in terms so significant upon John's office of precursor of the Messiah that it was easy to guess who he himself was.

While in the city, Jesus went with the Levites, to visit and cure the sick of several families. Some of the invalids were children, and several of the adults were lame. They held out to Jesus their hands enveloped in linen bands. Jesus visited Simeon also in his own house, and then proceeded to the synagogue, where he closed the sabbath exercises. Here the women stood in a kind of high tribune not far from the chair of the teacher. Jesus's teaching turned upon sacrifice for sin and upon Samson. He rehearsed the principal deeds of the latter, and spoke of him as of a saint whose life was prophetic. Samson, Jesus said, did not lose all his strength, for he had retained sufficient to do penance. His overturning of the pagan temple upon himself was owing to a special inspiration from God.

Sunday, June 3, AD 31 (*Sivan 23*)

Early this morning Judas Iscariot, Thomas, and several other disciples went to Haifa to make arrangements for the new disciples who were expected to arrive from Cyprus. Jesus went with them as far as the bridge over the river Belus. Then he turned toward the southeast and came to a place with a synagogue. Here he preached to a crowd of people who had come from all around.

Judas, who loved to execute business commissions, and Thomas, whose family owned rafts in the port and who was well-known here, went with several disciples to Haifa to make arrangements for the expected Cypriotes.

Monday, June 4, AD 31 (*Sivan 24*)

Today Jesus visited the place where Elizabeth had spent most of her youth. Some of her relatives were still living there. After healing some sick people, Jesus went to a place with a synagogue between Sepphoris and Nazareth.

Tuesday, June 5, AD 31 (*Sivan 25*)

Today Jesus traveled to Thaanach. Here he healed a Pharisee who had been part of the committee investigating Jesus and had fallen seriously ill after speaking out against him. When the Pharisees of Thaanach saw their healed colleague, they did not dare to take any steps against Jesus, who was therefore able to teach in the synagogue undisturbed. He spoke out clearly concerning the Messiah, and the Pharisees had an inkling he was referring to himself.

Jesus meanwhile, with about ten of his disciples, among them Saturnin, went on to the Levitical city of Thaanach, where he was received by the elders of the synagogue. The Pharisees here, though not open enemies of Jesus, yet were cunning and on the watch to catch him in his speech. I saw that by their own equivocal language. They said that he would undoubtedly visit their sick, and asked him whether he would extend that same charity to a man who had been in Capernaum, and who was now in a very suffering state. They thought that Jesus would refuse to see the latter, who had shown himself one of his bitterest opponents in Capernaum. His present sickness, a very singular one indeed, they supposed to be a punishment for his conduct on that occasion. He hiccoughed and vomited continually, the upper part of his body was constantly convulsed, and he was visibly pining away. He was a man between thirty and forty, and had a wife and children. When Jesus went to see him, he asked him whether he believed that he could help him. The poor man, quite dejected and ashamed of his former conduct, answered: "Yes, Lord! I do believe!" Then Jesus laid one hand on his head and the other on his breast, prayed over him, and commanded him to rise and take some nourishment. The man arose, and with tears thanked Jesus, as did likewise his wife and children. Jesus addressed some gracious and comforting words to them, but made not the slightest allusion to the man's proceedings against himself. That evening when the Pharisees beheld the cured man appear in the synagogue, they completely renounced all desire to contradict Jesus in his speech. He taught of the accomplishment of the prophecies; of John the Baptist, the precursor of the Messiah, and of the Messiah himself. His words were so significant that his hearers might readily conclude that he was alluding to himself.

Wednesday, June 6, AD 31 (*Sivan 26*)

In Thaanach, Jesus visited the carpenter's workshop where Joseph had worked. Afterward, he went south to Sion, where he taught in the synagogue. He rebuked the

Pharisees for subjugating the people with the heavy duties that they themselves did not perform.

From Thaanach, Jesus went to a carpenter shop in which Joseph had first worked after his flight from Bethlehem. It was a building wherein fully a dozen people were engaged in the manufacture of wooden articles.

They dwelt in little homes around the enclosure. The shop in which Joseph had worked was now occupied by the descendants of his master. They no longer worked at the business themselves, but employed poor people for that purpose. The goods, which consisted of thin planks, rods, grated screens, and lattice-work, were principally exported on ships. The report was still current in this place that the prophet's father had once labored here, but they no longer knew distinctly whether it was Joseph of Nazareth or not. I thought at the time: "If these people, after so short a lapse of time, know so little about these things, it is certainly not surprising that we too should know so little." Jesus delivered an instruction in the yard adjoining the workshop, taking for his subjects the love of labor and the thirst for gain.

From Thaanach, Jesus went to Sion, a horrible old place two hours west of Tabor. With its ancient citadel and synagogue, near which some Pharisees dwelt, it lay somewhat high. Below and far behind some ramparts on the banks of the Kishon, was a group of houses whose locality was not very healthful. The ramparts were so high that one could not see over them. The occupants of these houses appeared to be dependents upon those above them, by whom they were oppressed and tormented. Jesus, in his instruction given in the synagogue, inveighed against the Pharisees who imposed upon others grievous burdens that they would not themselves touch, against the oppression of the neighbor, and the thirst after power. He spoke also of the Messiah who, he said, would be very different from what they expected.

Thursday, June 7, AD 31 (Sivan 27)

Jesus visited Sion to comfort the poor and oppressed. In the morning, he healed the sick, while the disciples distributed what money and goods they had to the poor. In the afternoon, Jesus and the disciples went to Nain. Here, on Heshvan 28, he had raised the youth Martialis from the dead. Martialis's mother—the rich widow Maroni—had put one of her properties at Jesus's disposal to be used by him and his disciples as an inn. Jesus and the disciples visited this house. Martha, Mary Magdalene, Veronica, Johanna Chusa, and Mara the Suphanite were waiting there. Jesus told them of his visit to Cyprus, speaking with special warmth of the Roman commandant in Salamis.

Jesus had gone to Sion in order to console the poor, oppressed people. He visited their low, narrow, and obscure quarter of the city, and cured several poor sick in their huts, most of them gouty and paralyzed. The Pharisees banished all the sick to this miserable place, in which they could scarcely get a breath of fresh air. Jesus and the disciples gave the poor creatures presents of linen and strips of other materials.

Jesus and the disciples went from this place to Nain in about an hour and a half. Several disciples and the youth of Nain whom Jesus had raised from the dead came to meet him near the well outside the city, so that Jesus had with him now about twelve disciples, though no apostles. The disciples belonging to Jerusalem had come hither from the Holy City with some of the holy women, while others, having celebrated the Feast of Pentecost with Mary at Nazareth, awaited at Nain on their return journey the coming of Jesus. He put up at an inn prepared for him at Nain in one of the houses belonging to the widow, whom he went to see shortly after his arrival. The female portion of the family came out veiled to meet him in the portico of the inner court, and cast themselves at his feet. Jesus saluted them graciously, and accompanied them into the reception hall. There were five women present besides the widow herself; namely, Martha, Magdalene, Veronica, Johanna Chusa, and the Suphanite. They, the holy women, sat apart at the end of the hall, on a kind of raised trestle like a long, low sofa. They sat cross-legged on cushions and rugs. The seat they occupied was raised high enough to show the feet upon which it rested. The women were silent until Jesus addressed them, and then each spoke in her turn. They related what was going on at Jerusalem, and told Jesus of the snares Herod had laid for him. They became so animated in their recital that Jesus raised his finger and reproached them with their worldly solicitude and their judgments of others. Then he told them all about Cyprus, of those whom he had won to the truth, and spoke in words of love of the Roman commandant in Salamis. When the women expressed it as their opinion that it would be well if he too left the island, Jesus replied: "No. He must stay there and render service to many souls until my own work shall be accomplished. Then another will succeed him, and he too will prove himself a friend of the community."

Magdalene and the Suphanite were nothing like as beautiful as they used to be. They were pale and thin, and their eyes red from weeping. Martha was very energetic, and in business affairs very talkative. Johanna Chusa was a tall, pale, vigorous woman, grave in manner, but at the same time active. Veronica had in her deportment something very like St. Catherine; she was frank, resolute, and courageous. When the holy women were thus gathered together, they used to work industriously, sewing and preparing for the community all sorts of things, which were distributed among their private inns, or laid away in the storerooms. From these latter the apostles and disciples supplied their own needs, as well as those of the poor. When there was no special work of this kind to be done, the holy women spent their time in sewing for poor synagogues. They generally had with them their maidservants, who preceded or followed them on their journeys, and carried the various materials, sometimes in leathern pouches, sometimes attached to their girdle under their mantle. These maids wore tightly fitting bodices and short tunics. When the holy women were to remain some time at any place, their maids returned and awaited their coming at some of the inns along the route. Veronica's maid was with her a long time. She was in her service even after Jesus's death.

Friday, June 8, AD 31 (Sivan 28)

Jesus visited several people in Nain and then went to Maroni's garden. Here he gave the holy women advice about their inner life and their work serving the community of Christians.When on the sabbath Jesus repaired to the synagogue, he did not go to the teacher's chair, but stood with his disciples in the place in which traveling teachers were accustomed to stand. But after bidding him welcome and the prayers being said, the rabbis constrained him to take his place before the open rolls of scripture and to read therefrom. The sabbath lesson treated of the Levites, the murmuring of the people, the quails sent by God, and the punishment that befell Miriam; and from the prophet Zechariah, some passages referring to the vocation of the Gentiles and to the Messiah. Jesus's words were severe. He said that the pagans would occupy in the Messiah's kingdom the places of the obdurate Jews. Of the Messiah, he said that they would not recognize him as such, for he would be totally different from what they expected. Among the Pharisees were three more insolent than the others; they had been on the commission at Capernaum. The cure of the Pharisee at Thaanach had vexed them exceedingly, and they said that Jesus had effected it merely that the Pharisees of that place might connive at his doings. They recommended him to be quiet and not to disturb the sabbath with his cures. It would be just as well for him, they said, to go back whence he came and to forbear creating any excitement. Jesus replied that he would fulfill the duties of his mission, journeying and teaching until his hour had arrived. The Pharisees gave no entertainment to Jesus in Nain. They were full of spite against him, because his doctrine and charity drew after him all the poor, the miserable and the simple-hearted, whom their own severity alienated.

Saturday, June 9, AD 31 (Sivan 29)

Jesus and the disciples took a sabbath walk together through the fields around Nain. Jesus spoke earnestly with the disciples about his future. He promised them that, if they would remain true to him, his power would always be with them. Later, on the way to the synagogue for the close of the sabbath, he healed some sick people, again provoking cries of protest from the approaching Pharisees, who objected to the disturbance of the day of rest. Jesus reduced them to silence by accusing them of hypocrisy and oppression of the poor.

The season about this time in Nain was indescribably delightful. Jesus took the sabbath day's walk with the disciples, to whom he unfolded, in very earnest and confidential words, his own future. He exhorted them to remain true and faithful, for great sufferings and persecutions were in store for him. They should not, he said, be scandalized at him. He would not forsake them, neither must they abandon him, although the treatment he would receive would put their faith to the proof. The disciples were touched to tears. They went to the garden of Maroni, the widow, where too came the holy women. Jesus told them about the reconciliation that had taken place among the married couples in Mallep, and dwelt especially upon that between the couple with whom he had once taken a meal, and who had resolved to remove to Palestine. He spoke of Mercuria also, saying that she would first join the Syrophoenician, who was likewise making preparations to leave Ornithopolis. They would first go to Gessur and thence proceed further on. Already many people had left Cyprus, and a certain number would soon land at Joppa.

When Jesus left the garden with the disciples in order to close the sabbath in the synagogue, he found on his way several sick persons who had caused themselves to be carried there in litters. They stretched out their hands to him, imploring his help, and he cured them. And so he reached the synagogue whither also some others had had themselves conveyed on their beds. There was one man among them ill of the gout and terribly swollen, and there were others whom on his last journey Jesus had refused to cure because their faith was not pure. He had allowed them to continue in their sufferings that they might be brought at last to implore their cure more humbly. And now came the Pharisees, greatly incensed at Jesus's curing these invalids, for they had spread the report that he was unable to do so. They set up a great hue and cry at what they called his desecration of the sabbath. But Jesus went on with the cures until seven had been effected.

Jesus answered the infuriated Pharisees sharply, asking them whether it was forbidden to do good on the sabbath; whether they did not nourish themselves, take care of themselves, on the sabbath day; whether the curing of these sick was not in itself a sanctification of the sabbath day; whether they ought not on the sabbath day to console the afflicted; whether they should on the sabbath day retain possession of goods unjustly acquired; whether, on the sabbath day, they should leave in their affliction the widows, the orphans, and the poor whom they had oppressed and tormented during the whole week; and he upbraided them soundly for their hypocrisy and their oppression of the poor. He told them openly that, under the pretext of providing for the synagogue, which already had a superfluity of all that was necessary, they extorted the means of the poor, and in that same synagogue made the Law for them a heavy burden; but not content with that, they would now cut them off from the grace of God on the sabbath, prevent their receiving health on the sabbath, while they themselves on the sabbath feasted and drank upon what they had pitilessly wrung from them. By these words Jesus silenced the Pharisees, and all entered the synagogue. The Pharisees laid before Jesus the rolls of scripture and invited him to teach. This they did craftily in the hope of being able to convict him of error and bring a charge against him. When, then, Jesus alluded to the era of the Messiah and said that numbers of pagans would come over to the people of God at that time, they asked him mockingly whether he had not gone himself to Cyprus, in order to bring the pagans back with him. Jesus spoke likewise of the tithes, of imposing burdens on others and not carrying them one's self, and of the oppression of orphans and widows, for from Pentecost till the Feast of Tabernacles the tithes were brought to the temple. But in places remote from Jerusalem, as this was, the Levites collected them. And here it was that abuses crept in, for the Pharisees extorted the tithes from the people and converted them to their own use. It was against this that Jesus inveighed. The Pharisees were highly exasperated and on leaving the synagogue gave vent to their spleen.

Sunday, June 10, AD 31 (Sivan 30)

Jesus left Nain, going northward to Rimon, where he taught in an open place. Then he went on to Beth-Lechem, where he healed several people. Proceeding further, at sunset, he reached an inn on the outskirts of Azanoth.

From Nain, Jesus went with some of the disciples up the height this side of the Kishon. Proceeding in a northeasterly direction, they arrived at Rimon, where there was a school under the charge of some Levites. These now came to the school to meet Jesus, who gave an instruction to the youths and little boys on an open square in front of the schoolhouse. Thither also flocked many of the people who had already listened to Jesus's teachings at Nain. He explained to the children the general duties imposed by the Mosaic Law, but did not enlarge before them upon the dangers of the present time, as he was accustomed to do before his more elderly audiences. Rimon consisted of a long row of houses on a slope of the mountain. The inhabitants were mostly gardeners and vinedressers who disposed of their fruits at Nain and worked also in the gardens of that place. From Rimon, Jesus ascended the eastern side of Tabor. He was accompanied a good part of the way by the Levites who had been collecting the tithe offerings in Rimon. After a journey of about three hours he reached Beth-Lechem, a place in ruins east of the city of Dabrath. It comprised only one row of houses occupied by poor peasants, whom Jesus visited in their homes, encouraging them in their miseries and healing their sick.

Leaving Beth-Lechem, he journeyed on for about four hours through the valley in which was the well of Capernaum, and toward dusk arrived at Azanoth, where he had a private inn. Here he found friends from Capernaum awaiting him: Jairus and his daughter; the blind man of Capernaum to whom he had restored sight; the female relatives of Enue, the woman healed of an issue of blood; and Lea, the woman who had cried out to him, "Blessed is the womb that bore thee!" The women, their veils down, fell on their knees before Jesus, and he blessed them. They shed tears of joy upon beholding him again. Jairus's daughter was well and full of life, and withal quite changed, for she was now devout and modest. Jesus taught until far into the night.

TAMMUZ (29 days): June 10/11 to July 8/9, AD 31 Tammuz New Moon: June 8 at 10:00 PM, Jerusalem time

Monday, June 11, AD 31 (Tammuz 1)

After teaching in the synagogue at Azanoth, Jesus walked on to Damna, where he was greeted by Lazarus and the two nephews of Joseph of Arimathea. He spoke at length with Lazarus about accommodating those who would be arriving from Cyprus.

On the following day he went to Damna, where he had outside the city a private inn over which a relative of Joseph's family presided. Lazarus and two disciples belonging to Jerusalem were here waiting for him. Indeed, Lazarus had already been eight days in those parts attending to the real estate in land and houses of the Magdalum property, for only the household goods and similar effects belonging to Magdalene had as yet been disposed of. Jesus embraced

Lazarus, a favor he was accustomed to extend only to him and the elder apostles and disciples; to the others, he merely extended his hands. Jesus spoke of the Cypriotes, those that had accompanied him and those that were to follow later, and made some remarks as to how they should be supported. I heard on this occasion that James the Less and Thaddeus were to proceed to Gessur in order to receive and accompany the seven pagan philosophers who were to arrive there. Jesus treated Lazarus with marked confidence. On this occasion they walked alone together for a long time. Lazarus was a tall man, grave and gentle and very self-possessed in manner. Moderate in all things, even his familiar contact with others was stamped with a something that wore an air of distinction. His hair was black and he bore some resemblance to Joseph, though his features were sterner and more marked. Joseph's hair was yellow, and there was something uncommonly tender, gentle, and obliging in his whole deportment.

Tuesday, June 12, AD 31 (*Tammuz 2*)

Jesus, together with Lazarus and the disciples, visited the village belonging to the centurion Zorobabel of Capernaum where there was an inn that had been put at the disposal of Jesus and the disciples. At the inn, Jesus was met, among others, by Nathaniel of Cana. Later, Zorobabel and Cornelius came and took a walk with Jesus before they returned to Capernaum. Then Jesus and the accompanying disciples went to the house of Mary, his mother. He dined alone with her and told her of his journey to Cyprus. The holy Virgin spoke of her concern for his future. Jesus said she should think only of God's plan, which he would fulfill.

From Damna, Jesus with Lazarus, the disciples, the steward of the inn along with his son who was soon to be admitted to the number of the disciples, went almost two hours eastward to the village belonging to the centurion Zorobabel of Capernaum. It was situated on the southern side of a rocky hill which shut in the valley of Capernaum on the south, and upon which lay the centurion's gardens and vineyards. Here Jesus instructed the servants and field laborers. He took for his text the Messiah and the near coming of his kingdom, announced to them the signs enumerated by the prophets and showed how they had all been fulfilled, warned and implored them to amend their lives, and assured them that the Messiah would not appear under the form expected by the Jews, consequently only the small number of the humble and contrite would recognize him. He told them too that the Messiah would make known his doctrines by the lips of more than one, as he had formerly spoken through the mouth of many prophets. Some melancholy and possessed mutes were brought to Jesus. He laid his finger moistened with spittle under their tongues, and commanded Satan to depart, whereupon I saw some of them fall unconscious and then rise up cured, while others fell into convulsions for a short time, after which they too were restored to perfect health. All praised God and gave thanks for their cure. After that, Jesus, taking a solitary route, went to his mother's in the valley east of Capernaum, a distance of about three-quarters of an hour.

The holy women were already with the blessed Virgin, they having come from Nain by the direct road. They did not leave the house to receive Jesus, neither did Mary hurry out to meet her Son. After he had washed and let down his robe, Jesus entered the large apartment, in which several little alcoves were cut off by curtains. Mary, her head veiled and humbly inclined, stretched out to him her hand when he had first proffered his, and he graciously, though gravely, saluted her. The other women stood veiled, forming a semicircle in the rear. I have indeed seen Jesus when alone with Mary, in order to console and strengthen her, press her to his breast while conversing with her. But Mary herself, since his going forth to teach, treated him as one would treat a saint, a prophet; or as a mother might treat her son were he a pope, a bishop, or a king. Still, there was something much more noble, more holy in Mary's demeanor, though marked at the same time with indescribable simplicity. She never embraced him now, but only extended her hand when he offered his.

Some time after, I saw Jesus and Mary eating together alone. A little, low table stood between them. Jesus reclined at one side, and Mary sat at the other. On it was a fish, some bread, honey, cakes, and two little jugs. The other holy women were in the little curtained alcoves in groups of two or three, or in a side hall serving the repast of the disciples, among whom they had several relatives. Jesus told his mother about Cyprus and the souls he had there gained. She expressed her joy quietly, but asked few questions. Her words were chiefly those of maternal solicitude touching the dangers that awaited him. Jesus replied gently that he would fulfill his mission until the hour came for his return to his Father.

Arrival of the Apostles and Disciples in Capernaum

Wednesday, June 13, AD 31 (*Tammuz 3*)

Today, many disciples from Bethsaida, Capernaum, and the surrounding region came to see Jesus. They greeted him and spoke with him. News was delivered that ships had arrived from Cyprus with about two hundred Jews, who needed to be accommodated. They had arrived in Joppa, where they were met by Barnabas and Mnason.

NOT long after Jesus's return to Capernaum, there were gathered around him almost thirty disciples. Some were come from Judea with the news of the arrival at Joppa of ships bringing two hundred Cypriote Jews, who were there to be received by Barnabas, Mnason, and his brother. John, who was still at Hebron with the relatives of Zechariah, was charged with providing suitable quarters for these emigrants. The Essenes also occupied themselves with the same cares. For a time the Cypriotes were lodged in the grottoes until proper destinations could be assigned them. Lazarus and the Syrophoenician provided settlements near Ramoth-Gilead for the Jewish emigrants from the region of Ornithopolis.

Joppa from the Southwest

(Follow Map 32)

Thursday, June 14, AD 31 (Tammuz 4)

This morning Jesus and some disciples visited Peter's wife, mother-in-law, and daughter. Jesus healed some sick people. Then he went on to Capernaum, where he healed some children who later became disciples. In the afternoon, at Peter's house, Jesus met together with the disciples. He introduced them to three of the philosophers from Salamis. They had just arrived in Capernaum with James the Less and Judas Thaddeus. After dining together, Jesus and the disciples went to Andrew's house, where accounts were given of the various missionary journeys undertaken by each. (Most of the apostles, however, had not yet returned.) That evening, Jesus returned to his mother's house, where he introduced the newly converted disciples to her. Jesus and his mother had an inner accord that he should introduce his new disciples to her. This was so that, as their "spiritual mother," so to speak, she could find a place for each in her heart and in her prayers and bestow her blessing upon them.

The disciples lately come to Capernaum put up, some at Peter's outside the city, some in Bethsaida, and some at the school in the city itself. James the Less and Thaddeus came from Gessur with three of the pagan philosophers—fine, handsome young men who had received circumcision. Andrew and Simon came also with several other disciples, and the welcome they received was most touching. Jesus, according to his custom, presented the newly converted to his mother. There was a tacit understanding, an interior agreement between Jesus and Mary, that she should take the disciples into her heart, into her prayers, into her benedictions and, to a certain degree, into her very being, as her own children and the brothers of Jesus, that she should be their spiritual mother as she was his mother by nature. Mary did this with singular earnestness, while Jesus on such occasions treated her with great solemnity. There was in this ceremony of adoption something so holy, something so interior, that I am unable to express it. Mary was the vine, the ear, the flowering source of Jesus's flesh and blood.

The disciples related where they had been and all that had happened to them. In some places stones had been thrown after them, but without striking them; from others they were obliged to flee, but everywhere they were wonderfully protected. They had, too, met good people, had cured, baptized, and taught. Jesus had commanded them to go to the lost sheep of Israel only. They had likewise sought out the Jews in the pagan cities, though without meddling with the pagans excepting with such as were servants to the Jews. In Gazora, northeast of Jabes Gilead, Andrew and the disciples that accompanied him had redeemed Jewish slaves from bondage, sacrificing to this purpose all that they possessed. They asked Jesus whether they had done rightly, to which he answered in the affirmative. Jesus did not hearken to all that some of them had to say. Many of them, while eagerly and with a certain warmth of manner relating their missionary labors, Jesus interrupted with words something like these: "I know that already." To others who spoke simply and humbly, he listened for a length of time, and called upon the silent to relate what had happened to them. When they whom he had interrupted asked why he would not hear their account, Jesus answered by showing them the difference between their own and their brethren's speech. Frequently also he interrupted their narratives with parables; for instance, that of the tares sown among the good seed and which, after it had grown up, was to be burnt at the time of harvest. He said that all that had been sown would not come up. He spoke of several that had fallen away from the disciples, and exhorted those present not to place too great security in their good works, for they would still have to undergo great temptations. He recounted the parable of the lord going afar to take possession of a foreign kingdom. He gave over to his servants remaining behind a certain number of talents for which later on he required an account. This parable referred to Jesus's own journey to Cyprus and to the account he was now exacting from the disciples of their activity during his absence. As he spoke, he frequently turned first to one, then to another whose thoughts he divined, with the words: "Why art thou thinking useless thoughts?" or, "Do not think in that way!" or, "Thy thoughts are now taking a wrong direction. Think in this way, and not in that!" He read the thoughts of his hearers and reproved them accordingly.

Friday, June 15, AD 31 (*Tammuz 5*)

This morning Jesus went with some disciples to the leper hospital north of Bethsaida. Here he healed and taught. Then he returned to Peter's house, where he healed a number of sick people who had been brought there. As the sabbath began, he taught in the synagogue. He spoke out sharply against the Pharisees who were there to spy on him, and also interpreted the parable of the king's wedding feast (*Matthew 22:1–14*).

When the hour sounded the commencement of the sabbath, Jesus went with the disciples to the synagogue, where he found the Pharisees already standing around the lecture hall. But Jesus walked straight up to it, and they at once made room for him. The instruction was on Rahab and the scouts sent by Joshua to Jericho. The Pharisees were furious at what they called Jesus's audacity, and they said to one another: "Let him go on now with his talk. This evening, or when the sabbath is over, we shall hold a council and soon find means to close his lips." Jesus, knowing their malice, remarked that they were spies of a very peculiar kind, for they came not to find out the truth but to betray him and his followers. His language against them was very severe, and he spoke likewise of the destruction of Jerusalem, and the judgment in store for those of the people that would not do penance and recognize the reign of the Messiah. He introduced into his discourse also the parable of the king whose son was slain in the vineyard by the unfaithful servants. The Pharisees dared not interrupt him. All the holy women were present in the synagogue, where they had places set apart for them.

Saturday, June 16, AD 31 (*Tammuz 6*)

Jesus and some disciples visited the homes of various people in Capernaum. He healed many children who were ill, as there was an epidemic of scarlet fever. Then he visited Jairus, Zorobabel, and Cornelius. At the close of the sabbath, he returned to preach in the synagogue, addressing the Pharisees severely on account of their hypocrisy. That evening he dined at the home of Mary, his mother, the holy Virgin; also present were several apostles and disciples who had returned from their journeys.

That afternoon Jesus, at the earnest request of the parents of some sick children, went with several of the disciples to about twenty houses of Capernaum, both of the rich and of the poor, and cured a great many children, boys and girls from three to eight years old. The malady must have been a sort of epidemic, for they were all affected in pretty much the same way. The little sufferers' color was quite yellow, their throat, cheeks, and hands swollen. Their condition was similar to that attendant on many other sicknesses, scarlet fever, for instance. Jesus did not cure them all in the same way. On some he laid his hand on the parts affected, others he anointed with spittle, and over others he breathed. Many of them rose up at once. Jesus blessed them and gave them over to their parents with some words of admonition. For others, he commanded prayer and a certain kind of nursing. This was for the greater good of both children and parents.

The marketplace of Capernaum was on an eminence, and to it four streets ran. Jesus visited this part of the city and entered the home of Ignatius, whom he cured. The boy was a very lovely child of about four years. His parents were wealthy. They were engaged in the sale of brass or bronze vessels, for I saw many such standing in long corridors. For a couple of days the parents of Ignatius had begged Jesus to visit them, for he had just cured the child of their neighbor, the carpet merchant.

The market was surrounded by arcades, in which the goods of the various dealers were exposed for sale. In the center played a fountain, and at either end rose two large edifices. The Pharisees were full of wrath at these cures. Three of them went into the courtyard before Peter's house, in the porticos of which lay sick who had been transported thither, and whom Jesus was now healing. They forced their way through the crowd till they stood before him. Then they addressed him, suggesting that he should leave off curing, excite no disturbance on the sabbath, and expressed their desire to enter into an argument with him. But Jesus turned away from them saying that he had nothing to do with them, that he could not cure them, since they were incurable.

At the closing sabbath exercises that evening, Jesus again taught in the synagogue. He spoke of the murmuring of the Israelites on the news brought by the scouts sent to view the Promised Land, of the curse that fell upon them, in consequence of which they perished in the wilderness, and only their children were permitted to see the Land of Promise. He laid special stress upon malediction and benediction, of which he spoke in very energetic terms. Then he went on to speak of those that falsify the things pertaining to the kingdom of God, of those that would never enter into it, of the non-recognition of the Messiah, and of the chastisement that menaced Jerusalem and the whole country. And now two of the Pharisees, mounting the teacher's stand, began to comment upon some passages in the day's lesson, in which it was recorded that God had commanded Moses in the wilderness to cause a certain man to be stoned by all the people for having gathered sticks on the sabbath day. This fact the Pharisees cited as an argument against the cures wrought on the sabbath. Jesus responded by asking whether the health of the poor and needy was like wood destined for the fire; whether hypocrisy, lifeless and inflexible, had not in it much more of the nature of wood; and the looking out for scandal in the healing of the poor, the uncharitable fault-finding of those that had beams in their own eyes, was not a gathering of sticks—not, however, to prepare food for themselves, but to cast them as stumbling blocks in the path of truth, to use them as fuel for distilling the poison of discord and persecution. Is it not permitted to receive on the sabbath that for which we pray on the sabbath, and also to give it to others on that same day if we have it? Then Jesus explained the passages in the Law that referred to manual labor. He said that it was prohibited on the sabbath only to leave man free for the performance of spiritual exercises. How could the sabbath prevent the cure of the sick, since such cures sanctified the sabbath? In this way Jesus refuted the Pharisees and so confounded them that they had nothing more to say. Some few of his hearers were moved by his words. They reflected in silence upon what they had heard, while others put their heads together, saying: "Yes! It is he! He is the Messiah! No mere man, no prophet could teach in that way!" Significant looks were exchanged throughout the crowd generally, for the people rejoiced over the Pharisees' humiliation; some, however, obdurate at heart, joined with the latter in taking scandal.

Sunday, June 17, AD 31 (Tammuz 7)

This morning Jesus taught the disciples about their mission, work, attitudes, errors. He mentioned their future persecution and spoke at length about the parable of the workers in the vineyard (Matthew 20:1–16). That afternoon, Peter, James the Greater, and Matthew returned. All gathered in Peter's house, where they listened to Jesus's account of his journey to Cyprus.

On the evening of that day, Peter, James the Greater, and Matthew, together with some of the early disciples of John, went to salute Jesus at his mother's. Peter shed tears of joy. During the meal they took together Jesus again related the parable of the fisher, the five hundred and seventy fishes and their transportation into good water, the same upon which he had taught in Misael, also in Capernaum before the holy women and the disciples. In the same manner, all the other parables were often repeated and explained in various ways by him.

Map 32: Travels in Galilee and Gaulanitis

June 14–28, AD 31

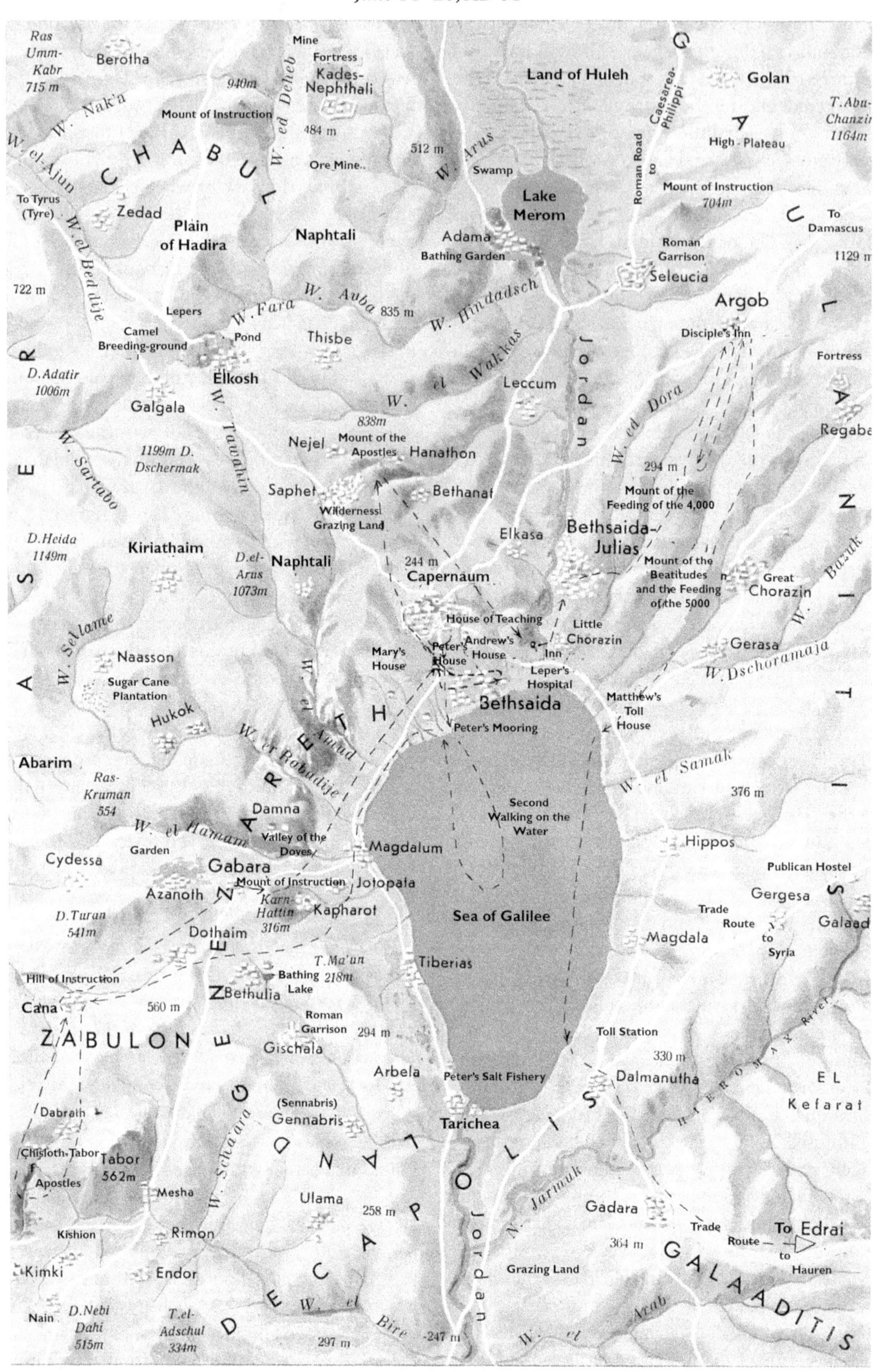

Capernaum—Bethsaida—Capernaum—Sea of Galilee—Cana—Mount of Instruction near Gabara
Capernaum—Bethsaida—Mount of Instruction near Hanathon—Bethsaida-Julias—Mount of Instruction—Argob—Matthew's Customs House—Customs Place near Dalmanutha

Monday, June 18, AD 31 (Tammuz 8)

Jesus and the disciples set sail on the Sea of Galilee. It was a beautiful day and Jesus sat at the mast and taught.

The next day he went with the apostles and disciples down to the ships. Peter's large boat and that of Jesus were bound together at some distance from the shore. They allowed them to float on the water without oar or rudder, for Jesus wanted to converse with the disciples undisturbed by the crowd. It was a beautiful day. They had stretched the sails overhead for shade, and they did not return till evening. Peter was very eager to talk, and he related with a certain complacency how much good they had effected. Jesus turned to him, and bade him to be silent. Peter, who so loved his Lord, immediately held his peace, and saw with regret that he had again been too ardent. Judas was vehemently desirous of praise, though he had not the candor to let it appear. He was on his guard more, however, that he might not be put to shame than that he might not sin.

When I consider the life of Jesus and his traveling about with his apostles and disciples, the certain conviction often forces itself upon me that, if he came now amongst us, he would encounter difficulties still greater than in his own day. How freely could he and his followers then go around teaching and healing! Apart from the Pharisees, thoroughly hardened and vainglorious as they were, no one put obstacles in his way. Even the Pharisees themselves knew not on what ground they stood with him. They did indeed know that the time of the Promise had come in which the prophecies were to be fulfilled, and they saw in him something irresistible, something holy and wonderful. How often have I seen them seated consulting the Prophets and the ancient commentaries upon them! But never would they yield assent to what they read, for they expected a Messiah very different from Jesus. They thought that he would be their friend, one of their own sect, and still they did not venture to decide upon Jesus. Even many of the disciples thought that he must certainly possess some secret power, a connection with some nation or king. They fancied that he would one day mount the throne of Jerusalem, the holy king of a holy people, that then they themselves would hold desirable positions in his kingdom and would also become holy and wise. Jesus allowed them to indulge these thoughts for awhile. Others looked upon the affair in a more spiritual sense, though not going so far as to the humiliation of the crucifixion. But very few acted through childlike, holy love and the inspiration of the Holy Spirit.

Tuesday, June 19, AD 31 (Tammuz 9)

The holy Virgin Mary and the holy women went to Cana, where Mary Cleophas was living. Jesus followed with nine apostles, Nathaniel of Cana, and a few others.

When at last all the apostles were returned from their missions, the latest arrivals being Thomas, John, and Bartholomew, Jesus went with them to Cana, whither came also the seventy disciples and the holy women from Capernaum.

Wednesday, June 20, AD 31 (Tammuz 10)

Many friends and relatives came to see Jesus in Cana. They warned him of the bitterness of the Pharisees toward him, saying that it was becoming more and more dangerous for him to continue teaching. Jesus then taught them about his mission. He said that he would do nothing except follow the will of his Father. Then, with the nine apostles and some disciples, he went to Mount Tabor, where they were reunited with the three remaining apostles—Thomas, John, and Bartholomew—who had now returned from their missionary journeys. They all went back to Cana together and dined at the house of Israel, the father of the bride at the wedding (John 2:1–11). Present were the twelve apostles, the seventy disciples who had been sent out together with the apostles on their missionary journeys, the holy women, and many other friends and relatives. It was a kind of feast of remembrance of the wedding at Cana, and it was a great joy for all to be together again.

On an eminence in the center of the city there was a teacher's chair, from which Jesus taught, taking for his subject his own mission and its accomplishment. He said that he had not come into this world to enjoy the comforts and pleasures of life, and that it was foolish to demand of him anything else than the fulfillment of his Father's will. He said in terms more significant than ever that he himself was the one so long expected, but that he would be received by only a few, and that when his work was done, he would return to his Father. He spoke warningly and entreatingly, begging his hearers most earnestly not to reject salvation and the moment of grace. He again pointed out the accomplishment of the prophecies. His teaching was so wonderful, so impressive, that the people of Cana said one to another: "He is more than a prophet! No one has ever before spoken this way in Israel!"

In the house of the father of the bride of Cana, an entertainment was given, at which the poor of the place were fed and presents bestowed upon them. Jesus and the apostles served. At the close of the feast, Jesus related the parable of the wise and the foolish virgins, explained it to his hearers, and spoke much of the near coming of the Bridegroom. It was a kind of memorial feast of the marriage at Cana, for now as then all the apostles, disciples, and friends were again assembled together. The house was garlanded with flowers, and the water urns of the first miracle were again in use. Children, bearing wreaths and pyramids of flowers, entered the festive hall playing on musical instruments. Bartholomew, Nathaniel Chased, and some of the disciples had made some beautiful mottoes relative to the spiritual nuptials of the soul with God.

Thursday, June 21, AD 31 (Tammuz 11)

Jesus went with the apostles and disciples to a hill about two hours' walk from Cana in the direction of Gabara. Jesus asked them to tell what they had experienced on their missionary journeys. He said: "Now will be seen who has loved me—and, in me, my heavenly Father—and who has spread the word of salvation and healed, not for his own sake, and not for the sake of vain renown, but on my account." As Peter spoke enthusiastically about casting out demons from those possessed, Jesus bade him to be silent and, looking up to heaven, spoke the words recorded in Luke 10:18–20. As Jesus spoke, Anne Catherine saw a cloud of light shining around him; he prayed joyfully and addressed the disciples and apostles with the words recorded in Luke 10:21–24. Later, they all proceeded to the foot of the mountain near Gabara, where they ate a meal of fish, bread, honey, and fruit. Afterward, they went up the mountain, and Jesus taught lessons related to what they had told him. Then they made their way to Capernaum, arriving there late at night.

From Cana Jesus went with all the apostles and disciples to the mount of instruction near Gabara. They walked slowly in bands, and frequently paused around Jesus to hear his words. He was very affectionate to them and often addressed them with the words: "My beloved children!" He commanded them to relate their experience, to tell how things had gone with them. The apostles spoke first. They had on the preceding days recounted some of their experience, though not all. Now each was to hear what the others had done and all that had happened to them. Jesus said to them so sweetly: "My dear little children, now will be seen who has loved me and in me my heavenly Father; who has made known the word of salvation and wrought cures in order to do my will, not his own, or not for the sake of vain renown." Thereupon they began to relate their experience: first, an apostle, and after him, the disciple that had accompanied him. This took place principally upon a hill which was about two hours from the mount of instruction and the same distance from Cana. People used to ascend it for sake of the view, which around these parts was somewhat limited.

Peter began eagerly to tell of the different kinds of possessed that had fallen in his way, his manner of treating them, and how Satan had retired before him when commanded in the name of Jesus. In his enthusiasm he had again forgotten the reproof received on board the ship. Once more he was all fire and zeal. He said that in the land of the Gergeseans, he had encountered a couple of possessed whom several others were unable to free from the demon. Here he named the unsuccessful disciples, among whom were the two Gergeseans themselves once possessed. But he, Peter, had easily expelled the devils; they had instantly submitted to him. Jesus silenced him by a look. Then raising his eyes to heaven, while all looked on in breathless expectation, he said: "I have seen Satan falling from heaven like lightning." And at the same moment, I saw a lurid light whirling and shooting through the air. Jesus reproved Peter for his too great ardor, as well as all the others that had, either in thought or word, yielded to a spirit of boasting. They should, he said, act and work in his name and by him, in humility and faith, never harboring the thought that one could do more than another. He said: "Behold, I have given you power to tread upon serpents and scorpions and upon all the might of the enemy, and nothing shall hurt you. But yet rejoice not in this, that spirits are subject to you, but rejoice in this, that your names are written in heaven." Several times he addressed them kindly and lovingly in the words: "Beloved little children," and listened to the account given by many of them. Thomas and Nathaniel received a reprimand for some negligence of which they had been guilty, but it was given with great love and sincerity.

While standing on the hill, Jesus appeared to be penetrated with joy, grave and celestial, and he held his hands raised to heaven. I saw him surrounded with splendor that fell upon him like a transparent cloud of light. He was perfectly enraptured and, in a transport of joy, he exclaimed: "I confess to thee, O Father, Lord of heaven and earth, because thou hast hidden these things from the wise and prudent, and hast revealed them to little ones. Yea, Father, for so it hath seemed good in thy sight. All things are delivered to me by my Father, and no one knoweth who the Son is but the Father, and who the Father is but the Son, and to whom the Son will reveal it!" And then turning to the disciples, he said: "Blessed are the eyes that see the things which you see! For I say to you that many prophets and kings have desired to see the things that you see, and have not seen them; and to hear the things that you hear, and have not heard them."

Having arrived at the mount beyond Gabara, Jesus

delivered an instruction in detail upon all that the apostles had related to him. He imparted to them the knowledge of many things of which they as yet knew not, and showed them wherein they had erred or acted with too little resolution. He enlightened them upon the different kinds of possession and taught them how the demon should be expelled. He spoke of all that was in store for them, of his own mission and its near accomplishment, and told them that he would shortly allow them to return to their homes to rest awhile, after which they were again to labor, to teach, and spread abroad the kingdom of God. He thanked them for their diligence and obedience, and then returned with them to Capernaum whither they arrived as night closed in. There were many others on the mountain besides the apostles and disciples.

Friday, June 22, AD 31 (*Tammuz 12*)

This morning Jesus ate with his mother. In the afternoon, he taught the apostles and disciples. Then they all went together to the synagogue in Capernaum for the sabbath. Here he taught concerning Korah and Abiram (*Numbers 16*) *and spoke of Samuel's resigning from his judicial office* (*I Samuel 12*)*. The Pharisees reproached Jesus for his disciples' failure to observe the Law. At this, Jesus again delivered a severe discourse against the Pharisees. He was interrupted by a young Pharisee suddenly crying out in a loud voice: "Truly this is the Son of God! The Holy One of Israel! He is more than a prophet!" A great commotion arose, and two Pharisees ejected the young man from the synagogue. Later, as Jesus was leaving, the young Pharisee cast himself down at his feet and begged to become a disciple. Jesus assented and introduced him to some of his disciples.*

On the following sabbath Jesus taught in the synagogue of Capernaum upon Samuel's resignation of the judicial office. His words were grave and forcible. The Pharisees felt themselves attacked on all sides, but as they could detect nothing false in Jesus's doctrine of which to accuse him, they reproached him with the trifling imperfections they had discovered in the actions of his disciples. They said that his disciples did not observe the fast rigorously, that they even stripped the ears of corn on the sabbath, and gathered fruit by the roadside and ate it, that they were rough and unclean in their clothing, that they entered the synagogues in garments covered with the dust of travel and without being decently let down, and that they were not particular about washing before meals. Thereupon Jesus delivered a discourse full of severe censure against the Pharisees, in which he depicted their conduct and actions, called them a race of vipers who imposed upon others burdens that they would by no means take upon themselves. He alluded to their sabbath promenades, their oppression of the poor, their dishonesty with regard to the tithes, their hypocrisy. They blamed, he went on to say, the mote in their neighbor's eye, while unmindful of the beam in their own, and he ended by declaring that he would continue his journeys, his teaching, and his healing, until the time for his departure from this earth. While Jesus was delivering this severe lecture a young man from among the Pharisees, rising suddenly and approaching nearer to him, lifted his hands to heaven and cried out in a loud voice: "Surely, this is the Son of God, the Holy One of Israel! He is more than a prophet!" and thus he continued to sound Jesus's praises in an inspired strain. This incident created great excitement throughout the synagogue. Two old Pharisees grasped the young man by the arm and dragged him out, he proclaiming all the while the praise of Jesus, who meantime went on with his discourse. When outside the synagogue, the young man loudly and vehemently declared to those that he found there that he had separated from the Pharisees. When Jesus left the synagogue, he cast himself at his feet and earnestly implored to be admitted among his disciples. Jesus assented on condition that he would leave father and mother, give all that he had to the poor, take up his cross, and follow him. Then some of the disciples, among whom was Mnason, took the young man off with them.

Saturday, June 23, AD 31 (*Tammuz 13*)

Jesus taught in Bethsaida this morning. In the afternoon he returned to Capernaum, where he and the disciples went to the synagogue before the close of the sabbath. Jesus taught of the need to be awake at the coming of the Son of Man (*Luke 12:35–40*)*. Then, in answer to Peter's question as to whether he spoke for everyone or only for the disciples, Jesus replied as in Luke 12:41–59. After the close of the sabbath, Jesus and some disciples were invited to dine with the Pharisees. Here, again, a dispute broke out* (*Luke 11:37–52*)*. Afterward, Jesus was approached by a young man from Nazareth who had often sought to become a disciple. Then the exchange about the good Samaritan recounted in Luke 10:25–37 took place.*

That evening Jesus closed the sabbath exercises in the synagogue. He had repaired thither with the apostles and disciples some time before the usual hour, that all might hear what he had to say to his followers and thereby understand that he had no need to teach in secret. In this instruction, he warned them against the Pharisees and false prophets, commanded them to be vigilant, explained the parable of the good and watchful servants and contrasted it with that of the slothful. As Peter during the discourse asked whether his words were meant for all his hearers or only for the disciples, Jesus now addressed himself to him. He spoke to him as if he were the master of the house, the overseer of the servants. He extolled the good householder, and at the same time condemned severely the negligent one that fulfilled not his duty.

Jesus continued to teach until the Pharisees came to close the sabbath, and when he wanted to give place to them, they very courteously addressed him with, "Rabbi, do thou explain the lesson," and laid the roll of scriptures before him. Thereupon Jesus taught, in a manner most impressive, upon Samuel's abdication of the judicial office. He quoted the words used by him on that occasion: "I am old and gray-headed"; and explained them in such a way that the Pharisees could plainly see that he was applying them to himself. He said something to this effect: "Ye have had me a long time among you, and ye are tired of me! Ye are constantly renewing your accusations, but I am always the same."

Samuel's questions to the people, "Have I committed this or that injustice against you? Have I taken any man's oxen or ass? Have I oppressed anyone?" Jesus cited as those of God and the sent of God, and the explanation that he gave of them pointed most clearly to those doctors and Pharisees who could not venture to put similar questions to the people. The clamoring of the Israelites after a king by whom, like the pagan nations, they wanted to be ruled, and their rejection of Judges, signified, Jesus said, their perverse expectation of a worldly kingdom, of a king and a Messiah surrounded by magnificence, with whom they could pass their lives in splendor and enjoyment; a Messiah who, instead of expiating their sins and disorders by his own labors, sufferings, penance, and satisfaction, would envelop them together with their filth and vices in his own rich mantle of royalty, and even reward them for their crimes.

That Samuel did not cease to pray for the nation and that by his prayer he caused thunder and lightning in the sky above them, Jesus explained as an effect of God's compassion for the good; and he assured them that the sent of God, whom instead of receiving they would reject, would likewise implore his Father's mercy for them until the end. The rain and thunder granted to prayer, Jesus explained as the signs and wonders that were to attend upon the sent of God to rouse and convert the good. They and their king, as Samuel had said, would find favor with God if they walked before him who would not reject them. Then Jesus declared to them that the righteous would receive justice and the grace of knowledge, but against the wicked, Samuel would rise up in judgment. Jesus afterward referred to David and his anointing as king in opposition to Saul, to the separation of the good from the bad, and to the destruction of Saul and his family.

The Pharisees took care not to contradict Jesus in the synagogue, that they might not (as was always the case on such occasions) be put to shame before the people. They had, however, resolved beforehand to attack him at the entertainment to which they had invited him along with the apostles and a part of the disciples. It was given in an open hall of the house belonging to the ruler of the synagogue, and there were at least twenty Pharisees present. Before taking their places at table, one of them put a large wash basin before Jesus, asking whether he did not want to wash, and he went on talking of the holy old customs and commandments of the Israelites, and called upon Jesus and his followers to observe them. But Jesus repulsed him. He told him that he saw through his trick, and wanted no water from him. When at table, they began to dispute with him upon the discourse he had delivered that day. But he convicted and confounded them in such a manner that many of them became perfectly furious, and several others were so frightened and touched that during the disputation, which they carried on walking up and down, twelve of them withdrew from their obstinate colleagues. Thus was the number of Jesus's enemies decreased.

One of the young men of Nazareth who had so often, but vainly, petitioned to be received among the disciples, here presented himself again before Jesus with the question: "Master, what must I do to possess eternal life?" Thereupon followed the scene recorded in the Gospel, and Jesus recounted the story of the compassionate Samaritan. Meanwhile the Pharisees reproached Jesus for not receiving the young man among his disciples. It was, they said, because the youth was well educated, and Jesus knew that he could not silence him so easily as he could the others. They again accused the disciples of irregular conduct, of uncleanliness, of stripping the wheat ears on the sabbath, of gathering fruit on the wayside, of eating out of time, of ill-breeding, and of many other similar things.[E26] They reproached Peter in particular with being a wrangler and quarreller like his father. Jesus defended the disciples. They might indeed be joyful, he said, as long as the Bridegroom was with them. After these words he withdrew, passing through the beautiful cemetery near the synagogue that lay in the direction of Jairus's house, and thence by the land route to Bethsaida. He prayed alone until after midnight, when he retired to his mother's. The Pharisees had hired the rabble to throw stones after the disciples, but God protected them. They knew not where Jesus had gone.

The Jews that had emigrated from Cyprus to Palestine lived at first in caves, but by degrees their settlement became a city, which received the name of Eleutheropolis.

It was situated west of Hebron and not far from the well of Samson. More than once the Jews sought to destroy the little colony, but after every attack of the kind, the inhabitants again returned. The caves lay under the city, so that in times of persecution the inhabitants could take refuge in them. In the first attack, which was made at the time of the stoning of St. Stephen, when the colony between Ophel and Bethany was destroyed, Mercuria lost her life. The people of this colony often went to the Cenacle and to the church at the pool of Bethesda, to carry thither their offerings and contributions, and at the destruction of Ophel they fled to Eleutheropolis. Joseph Barsabbas, son of Mary Cleophas and her second husband Sabbas, became the first bishop of that city, and there during a persecution he was crucified on a tree.

Jesus Instructs the New Disciples upon Prayer and the Eight Beatitudes

Sunday, June 24, AD 31 (Tammuz 14)

Jesus and the disciples went to the mountain near Hanathon. Here they were joined by some people from the neighborhood. Jesus taught about the petitions of the Lord's Prayer (Luke 11:1–4). That night Jesus, the disciples, and others—in all, some fifty people—remained in prayer on the mountain.

EARLY the next day Jesus left Mary's house with the latest received and not yet well-instructed disciples, and crossing the road between Capernaum and Bethsaida, went to that mount of instruction from which he had once dispatched the apostles on their respective missions. It was about three hours from Capernaum. On the way, he encountered Mnason and some other disciples along with the converted Pharisee from Thaanach near Nain. The last-named had been very much touched by the cure of a Pharisee at Thaanach, and still more deeply impressed by Jesus's last discourse on the mountain beyond Gabara. On the Mount of the Apostolic Mission there was a well-arranged and shaded place for holding instructions. At the foot of the mountain was a long hut in which ten poor paralytics belonging to the surrounding country lay, their limbs fearfully contorted. They were cared for by the shepherds of the district. Jesus cured and instructed them.

Here in the solitude of the mountain the disciples entreated Jesus to teach them again how to pray. He did so, repeating to them the Lord's Prayer, dwelling at length on each separate petition, and explaining it with the same examples that he had used on a former occasion: that, for instance, of the man seeking bread and persistently knocking at his friend's door until he got what he wanted; that of the child asking an egg of its father, who would surely not give it a scorpion; and, in fine, all the other illustrations he had already brought forward to show the effects of persevering prayer and the paternal relations that existed between God and man. He taught all his disciples in the same way, going over and over the same instruction with touching patience and unwearying pains, that they might be able in turn to repeat everywhere on their missions exactly the same things. He conducted these instructions to the disciples just as one would do among children, questioning them separately upon the explanations he had given, setting them right, and again explaining what they had not understood.

Monday, June 25, AD 31 (Tammuz 15)

This morning Jesus ended his teaching on prayer with a talk on the significance of the word Amen. Jesus received an invitation to go to Bethsaida-Julias. On the way, he went to an inn where the holy Virgin and some of the holy women were waiting for him. Mary was downcast and begged Jesus not to go to Jerusalem for the Feast of the Dedication of the Temple. Jesus comforted her, saying that he would complete the work of his Father, and that she should be courageous and should strengthen and encourage the others. Jesus and the disciples then continued on to Bethsaida-Julias. There he dined with the Pharisees. That evening, he taught in the synagogue.

Finally, he went over the whole prayer and gave the interpretation of the word Amen, as he had formerly done in Cyprus, saying that this word contains everything in itself, that it is the beginning and the end of prayer. Some other people and a couple of Pharisees from Bethsaida-Julias arrived while Jesus was speaking, and they too heard a part of his instruction. One of the latter invited him to dine at his house in Bethsaida-Julias, which invitation Jesus accepted.

When he and the disciples started for Bethsaida, they directed their steps to the south of the Jordan bridge. On their way they came, this side of Bethsaida, to an inn where his mother, the widow of Nain, Lea, and two other women were waiting to take leave of him, because he was now going to teach on the other side of the Jordan. Mary was very much afflicted. She had a private interview with Jesus, in which she shed abundant tears and begged him not to go to Jerusalem for the Feast of the Dedication of the Temple. She spoke so supplicatingly and in so loving a manner that I felt she must surely divine the holy destiny of her Son. Jesus supported her on his breast and consoled her gently and lovingly. He told her that he must fulfill the mission for which his Father had sent him and for which also she had become his mother, and that she must continue strong and courageous, in order to strengthen and edify the others. Then he saluted the other women, gave them his blessing, and they returned to Capernaum, while he and the disciples went on to Bethsaida-Julias, where he was received by the Pharisees. Besides those belonging to the city, there were present some others from Paneas, for it was a kind of feast day commemorative of the burning of a bad book written by the Sadducees. The Pharisees brought forward their old complaints against Jesus. When about to take his place at table, one of them pulled him by the arm, saying that he was astonished that a man who could teach so well as he should be so little mindful of holy observances as to eat without washing. Jesus responded that the Pharisees purified the outside of the cup and platter, but that within they were full of wickedness. To this the Pharisee replied by asking how he knew the state of his interior. Jesus answered that God, who formed the exterior, made also the interior, and that his eye could scan it clearly. The disciples drew Jesus to one side and begged him not to speak with too much fervor, for they might possibly be put out, but he reproved them for their cowardice.

That evening Jesus taught in the synagogue, but worked no cures, for the Pharisees had intimidated the people. They were very proud, and had here a kind of high school.

Tuesday, June 26, AD 31 (Tammuz 16)

This morning Jesus climbed the mountain northeast of Bethsaida-Julias, where the feeding of the five thousand had occurred. Besides the apostles and disciples, people from Capernaum, Caesarea Philippi, and other places had gathered together to hear him. Jesus taught for about three hours (Matthew 5:10–20; 6:1–34; 7:1–27). Then, toward evening, he went to the town of Argob and stayed there overnight at an inn.

From Bethsaida-Julias, Jesus took a northeasterly direction toward the mountain upon which the multiplication of the loaves had taken place. It was about an hour and a half from Bethsaida. There he found assembled all the apostles and disciples with many people from Capernaum, Caesarea-Philippi, and other places. He taught upon the eighth beatitude, "Blessed are ye when men hate and persecute you for the Son of Man's sake," also upon the passage "Woe to the rich, to them that are filled with the goods of this world, for in them they already have their reward; but as for you, rejoice that it is still in store for you." He spoke likewise of the salt of the earth, of the city on the mountain, of the light on the candlestick, of the fulfilling of the Law, of the hiding of good works, of prayer made in the privacy of one's chamber, and of fasting. Of the last-mentioned, Jesus said that it should be practiced joyously with anointing of the head, and not be turned into a sanctimonious parade of piety. He went on to the laying up of treasure in heaven, freedom from worldly solicitude, the impossibility of a man's serving two masters, the narrow gate, the broad road, the bad tree with its bad fruit, the wise man that built on a solid foundation, and the fool that built upon sand. This discourse lasted over three hours. During it the audience went down once to the foot of the mountain to get something to eat. Jesus continued his instruction to the apostles and disciples, exhorting them upon all those points on which he had spoken when sending them out upon former missions. He animated them to believe, to have confidence, and to persevere.

Wednesday, June 27, AD 31 (Tammuz 17)

Today Jesus taught again on the mountain where he had been yesterday. A great multitude had now assembled, and Jesus taught in part what is recorded in Luke 12. He also healed the sick and drove devils out of the possessed. The crowd was jubilant. Jesus pronounced woe upon Chorazin, Bethsaida, Capernaum (Luke 10:13–15) and also upon Jerusalem (Luke 13:34–35). Finally, he sent out the newly converted disciples, two by two. That evening, he returned to the inn at Argob.

On the next day, the number of his hearers having increased to several thousands, Jesus taught again on the mountain. On account of the caravans that traversed these parts, there were people present from all sections of the country, also many sick and possessed. The Pharisees in attendance had not come to dispute, although they received some rather severe thrusts during the discourse. Jesus's miracles were too manifest and the people too enthusiastic over him, to allow them a word. The people had food with them, and they seated themselves on the ground to partake of it. Among the cured was a blind man from Jericho, who had also been lame. One of the disciples had cured him of lameness, but had not restored his sight. He was a cousin of Manahem. The latter led him to Jesus, who restored his sight.

The new disciples, whom during these last days he had with admirable patience taught like children by question and answer, Jesus now sent out two and two with the words: "I send ye like sheep among wolves."

Thursday, June 28, AD 31 (Tammuz 18)

This morning Jesus took leave of most of the remaining apostles and disciples. Only Peter, James, John, Matthew, and a few disciples remained with him. They went to Matthew's custom house. Here several friends from Capernaum (Jairus, Zorobabel, Cornelius, and some others) were waiting for him. Jesus taught and consoled them before traveling on by boat to Dalmanutha, where he taught that evening.

One of Joseph of Arimathea's nephews arrived here from Jerusalem with the news that Lazarus was sick. Jesus kept with himself only the apostles Peter, James, John, Matthew, and some of the disciples, with whom he went to Matthew's custom office and thence by sea to Dalmanutha.

(Follow Map 33)

Friday, June 29, AD 31 (Tammuz 19)

Today, accompanied by Peter, James, and John, Jesus went to Edrai. With the beginning of the sabbath they went to the synagogue, where he taught.

Saturday, June 30, AD 31 (Tammuz 20)

Jesus taught again in the synagogue, interpreting various passages from the holy scripture (Numbers 19–21; Judges 11). He also healed many people.

Sunday, July 1, AD 31 (Tammuz 21)

Today Jesus and the three apostles journeyed further eastward in the direction of Bosra. On the way, Jesus paused to teach. He also healed the sick and the possessed.

(Follow Map 34)

Monday, July 2, AD 31 (Tammuz 22)

Bosra was a Levitical town where many pagans lived. Jesus spent some time with the Levites and then traveled further to Nobah, arriving there late at night.

Tuesday, July 3, AD 31 (Tammuz 23)

In Nobah, Jesus healed many people who were possessed. Peter, James, and John also taught and healed.

In Nobah, outside the pagan quarter of the city, dwelt a colony of sincere Rechabites. On their return from the Babylonian Captivity they found their city in the possession of the pagans, but they retook it and again reestablished themselves in it. They cherished an extraordinary hatred against the Pharisees and Sadducees, whom they shunned as much as possible. They were engaged in cattle raising, and led a very strict life. They drank no wine, excepting on certain feast days, and tenaciously held to the letter of the scripture. Jesus admonished them on this point, and gave them an instruction on the spirit of the letter. They were very humble, and took in good part all that he said. Many were baptized, among them some pagans, and a great number of possessed were delivered from the Evil One. There was a whole hospital full of these poor creatures at Nobah. Peter, James, and John cured and taught also. Jesus met no opposition in this place, and he effected a wonderful amount of good. He put up at the inn near the synagogue. Nobah was a free city which, although belonging to the Decapolis, ruled itself.

Wednesday, July 4, AD 31 (Tammuz 24)

Today Jesus and his companions traveled to a shepherd settlement called the "field of Jacob's peace," where Jesus healed some who were sick. Then, on a hill nearby, Jesus spoke to the shepherds, referring to the star of Jacob foretold by the prophet Balaam. He also spoke of the journey of the three kings from the East. After speaking of the fulfillment of John the Baptist's testimony concerning the Messiah, Jesus told the parable of the good shepherd (John 10:1–18).

From Nobah, Jesus journeyed five hours southwestwardly to the exceedingly lovely pastoral village called the "field of Jacob's peace." It received this name from the fact that it was here, when returning to Palestine and pursued by Laban, he had encamped for the first time. The mountain range of Gilead takes its rise here. The shepherds of this place were the descendants of that Eleazar, Abraham's servant, who had brought Rebecca for his master's son Isaac. Among them also were some of the posterity of those people whom Melchizedek had freed from the tyranny of Semiramis and established in these regions. They had afterward intermarried with the descendants of Eleazar. There were three beautiful wells in this place. They lay at the foot of a lovely hill all around which, as if built in a verdant rampart, were cool shepherd dwellings. At a distance one might have taken them for a mountain terrace. The oldest and most honorable among the herd owners dwelt on the hill, upon which there was likewise a place for instruction. Far around were enclosed pasture grounds for camels, asses, and sheep, each species having its own, and near the fountains were reservoirs for watering them. The shepherds dwelt in the neighborhood of the fountains, under tents that rested on solid foundations. There were long rows of mulberry trees, but the most beautiful sight of all was a long walk with palings on either side upon which ran a vine, often to the distance of two hundred paces, laden with fruit something like gourds. This walk led from the hill to Salcha and formed, as it were, one continuous arbor. Some days before, the inhabitants had celebrated a feast commemorative of the deliverance of their forefathers from the slavery of Semiramis. They attended the synagogue at Salcha, and it was from there too that teachers came to instruct them. This little village was held in respect throughout the country around, and was looked upon as a monument to Jacob's memory. Hospitality was here exercised freely. For a trifle, the Arab caravans and all other strangers were lodged and cared for by the shepherds.

Map 33: The Journey in Hauran

June 28–July 2, AD 32

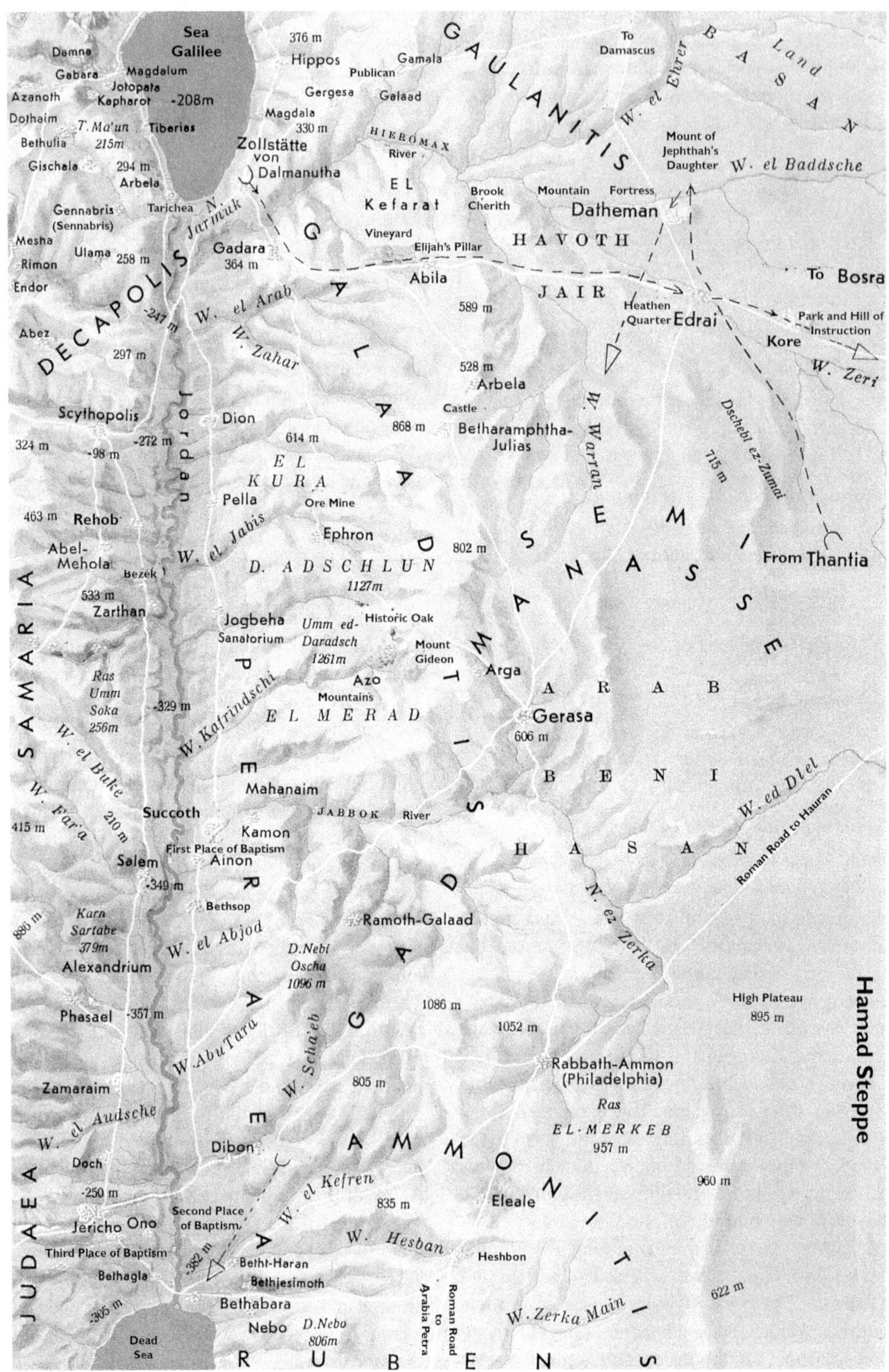

Start: Customs House of Dalmanutha—Edrai—Kore; *End*: Datheman—Terrain of Gileaditis—Bethabara

TISSOT ILLUSTRATIONS
[SECTION E]

The Public Teaching of Jesus

⊕

Jesus Commands the Apostles as They Rest [E1]

⊕

DURING the day Jesus called before him the apostles and disciples and received from them an account of all that had happened to them during their mission. He solved the doubts and difficulties that had arisen in certain circumstances, and instructed them how they should act in the future. He told them again that he would soon give them a new mission.[297]

[MARK 6:30–31] 30 The apostles returned to Jesus, and told him all that they had done and taught. 31 And he said to them, "Come away by yourselves to a lonely place, and rest a while." For many were coming and going, and they had no leisure even to eat.

The Miracle of the Loaves and Fishes [E2]

⊕

WHEN next morning Jesus and the apostles returned to the mount upon which he had already taught several times on the eight beatitudes, he found the multitude assembled. The other apostles had arranged the sick in sheltered places. Jesus and the apostles began to heal and to instruct. Many who in those days had now come for the first time to Capernaum knelt in a circle to receive baptism. Jesus taught of the eight beatitudes and went as far as the sixth. The instruction on prayer begun at Capernaum he repeated, and explained some of the petitions of the Lord's Prayer.

Teaching and healing went on till after four o'clock, and all this time the listening crowds had had nothing to eat. Jesus ordered the loaves and fishes to be brought. Near the place upon which Jesus taught was a high, mossy bank, in which were several caves. On it Jesus directed a broad napkin to be spread, upon which were deposited the five loaves and two fishes. [300]

[JOHN 6:1–14] 1 After this Jesus went to the other side of the Sea of Galilee, which is the Sea of Tiberias. 2 And a multitude followed him, because they saw the signs which he did on those who were diseased. 3 Jesus went up on the mountain, and there sat down with his disciples. 4 Now the Passover, the feast of the Jews, was at hand. 5 Lifting up his eyes, then, and seeing that a multitude was coming to him, Jesus said to Philip, "How are we to buy bread, so that these people may eat?" 6 This he said to test him, for he himself knew what he would do. 7 Philip answered him, "Two hundred denarii would not buy enough bread for each of them to get a little." 8 One of his disciples, Andrew, Simon Peter's brother, said to him, 9 "There is a lad here who has five barley loaves and two fish; but what are they among so many?" 10 Jesus said, "Make the people sit down." Now there was much grass in the place; so the men sat down, in number about five thousand. 11 Jesus then took the loaves, and when he had given thanks, he distributed them to those who were seated; so also the fish, as much as they wanted. 12 And when they had eaten their fill, he told his disciples, "Gather up the fragments left over, that nothing may be lost." 13 So they gathered them up and filled twelve baskets with fragments from the five barley loaves, left by those who had eaten. 14 When the people saw the sign which he had done, they said, "This is indeed the prophet who is to come into the world!"

The People Seek Jesus to Make Him King [E3]

⊕

JESUS now dismissed the multitude, who were deeply moved. Scarcely had he left the spot upon which he had been teaching when the shout arose: "He has given us bread! He is our king! We will make him our king!" But Jesus disappeared into the solitude, and there gave himself up to prayer. [301]

[JOHN 6:15] 15 Perceiving then that they were about to come and take him by force to make him king, Jesus withdrew again to the mountain by himself.

OUR engraving represents a portion of Galilee with the Mount of the Beatitudes, to which Jesus was in the habit of retiring. On the north can be seen the Sea of Tiberias, with Capernaum and Chorazin near the shores of the Lake Bethsaida and Magdala, with the Hauran Mountains and the Lebanon chain beyond.

Jesus Walks on the Sea [E4]

⊕

THEN Jesus walked on the sea in a direction from northeast to southwest. He was shining with light. Rays darted from him, and one could see his image reversed in the water under his feet. He appeared to be gliding along more rapidly than in ordinary walking, and wherever he approached, the sea became calm. But a fog rested upon the water, so that he could be seen only at a certain distance. Although they had once before seen him thus walking, still the unusual and specter-like sight filled them with terror, and they uttered a great cry. [301]

[MATTHEW 14:23–27] 23 And after he had dismissed the crowds, he went up on the mountain by himself to pray. When evening came, he was there alone, 24 but the boat by this time was many furlongs distant from the land, beaten by the waves; for the wind was against them. 25 And in the fourth watch of the night he came to them, walking on the sea. 26 But when the disciples saw him walking on the sea, they were terrified, saying, "It is a ghost!" And they cried out for fear. 27 But immediately he spoke to them, saying, "Take heart, it is I; have no fear."

THE incident of the apparition of Jesus walking on the sea took place, according to the gospel, in the fourth watch of the night, that is to say, about three o'clock in the morning. There had been a storm, the wind was still high, and the sky was covered with clouds. The darkness must, therefore, have been almost complete, and the disciples could not have seen far from their boat. In spite of this, they perceived the Master from afar, walking upon the waves. It is, therefore, very probable that light emanated from his body, and irradiated all around him to some extent. Hence the terror of the apostles, who took him for a spirit, and "cried out with fear." His voice alone, pronouncing his ordinary salutation, could reassure them.

Peter Walks on the Sea [E5]

⊕

BUT suddenly they recalled the circumstance of Jesus's first walking on the water, and Peter, once more desirous of showing his faith, cried out again in his ardor: "Lord, if it be thou, bid me come to thee!" Jesus replied: "Come!" This time Peter ran a greater distance toward Jesus, but his faith did not yet suffice. He was already close to him when he again thought of his danger, and on the instant began to sink. He stretched out his hand and cried: "Lord, save me!" He did not, however, sink to so great a depth as the first time. Jesus again addressed to him the words: "O thou of little faith, why dost thou doubt?" [301]

[MATTHEW 14:28–34] 28 And Peter answered him, "Lord, if it is you, bid me come to you on the water." 29 He said, "Come." So Peter got out of the boat and walked on the water and came to Jesus; 30 but when he saw the wind, he was afraid, and beginning to sink he cried out, "Lord, save me." 31 Jesus immediately reached out his hand and caught him, saying to him, "O man of little faith, why did you doubt?" 32 And when they got into the boat, the wind ceased. 33 And those in the boat worshiped him, saying, "Truly you are the Son of God." 34 And when they had crossed over, they came to land at Gennesaret.

You Follow Me for the Miracles [E6]

⊕

AS soon as they perceived the approach of the ship, the inhabitants began to get all their sick ready, and they came to meet Jesus on the shore. He and the disciples healed in the streets. After that he went to a hill at a short distance beyond Dalmanutha, where all the inhabitants, Jews and pagans, assembled around him. There he taught upon the eight beatitudes and the Lord's Prayer. He also healed the sick whom they had brought with them. When Jesus ascended the height behind Peter's house, over which ran the shortest route from Capernaum to Bethsaida, the multitude encamped around it followed him. Several of those present the day before at the multiplication of the loaves, and who had been seeking him ever since, asked him: "Rabbi, when camest thou hither? We have been seeking thee on both sides of the lake." Jesus, at the same time beginning his sermon, answered them: "Amen, amen, I say to you, you seek me, not because you have seen miracles, but because you did eat of the loaves, and were filled. Labor not for the meat which perisheth but for that which endureth unto life everlasting, which the Son of Man will give you. For him hath God the Father sealed." These words stand thus in the Gospel, but they are only the principal points of those that Jesus pronounced on this occasion, for he dwelt largely on the subject. The people whispered to one another: "What does he mean by the Son of Man? We are all children of man!" When upon his admonition that they should do the works of God, they asked what they should do to fulfill those works, he answered: "Believe in him whom He hath sent!" And then he gave them an instruction upon faith. They asked again what kind of a miracle he would perform that they might believe. [302–303]

[JOHN 6:24–32] 24 So when the people saw that Jesus was not there, nor his disciples, they themselves got into the boats and went to
Capernaum, seeking Jesus. 25 When they found him on the other side of the sea, they said to him, "Rabbi, when did you come here?" 26
Jesus answered them, "Truly, truly, I say to you, you seek me, not because you saw signs, but because you ate your fill of the loaves. 27 Do
not labor for the food which perishes, but for the food which endures to eternal life, which the Son of man will give to you; for on him has
God the Father set his seal." 28 Then they said to him, "What must we do, to be doing the works of God?" 29 Jesus answered them, "This is
the work of God, that you believe in him whom he has sent." 30 So they said to him, "Then what sign do you do, that we may see, and
believe you? What work do you perform? 31 Our fathers ate the manna in the wilderness; as it is written, 'He gave them bread from heaven
to eat.'" 32 Jesus then said to them, "Truly, truly, I say to you, it was not Moses who gave you the bread from heaven; my Father gives you the
true bread from heaven."

THE crowd, who had been dismissed by him the evening before, had returned in the morning. Having noticed that but one boat remained on the beach, and that Jesus was not there, and that his disciples had gone away without him, they hoped to find him again. Moreover, the plot to proclaim him king had not been given up during the night, and the ringleaders were seeking Jesus, and when they did not find him, they embarked for Capernaum, in boats which had come from Tiberias, in the hope of thus being able to join the prophet sooner.

The meeting represented in our picture took place, in fact, on the other side of the lake, just as Jesus was returning from Bethsaida, so that he was compelled to meet the crisis then and there. The way in which the Jews introduced the subject was naïf, and betrayed that they were to a certain extent embarrassed: "Rabbi, they said unto him, when camest thou hither?"

Curses against the Pharisees [E7]

⊕

THE services over, at which many Pharisees were in attendance, Jesus was invited to dine. The meal was taken at a house of public entertainment. Many people stood around during it, to hear what Jesus was saying, and numbers of the poor were fed. The Pharisees, having remarked that the disciples had not washed their hands before coming to table, asked Jesus why his disciples did not respect the prescriptions of their forefathers, and why they did not observe the customary purifications. Jesus responded to their question by asking why they themselves did not keep the commandments, why with all their traditions they did not honor their father and mother, and he reproached them with their hypocrisy and their vain adherence to external purification. During this dispute the meal came to an end. Jesus, however, continued to address the crowd that pressed around him: "Hear ye and understand! Not that which goeth into the mouth defileth a man; but what cometh out of the mouth, this defileth a man. He that has ears to hear, let him hear!" The disciples who had remained behind in the entertainment hall told Jesus that these words of his had greatly scandalized the Pharisees. To which he responded: "Every plant that my heavenly Father hath not planted shall be rooted up! Let them alone! They are blind and leaders of the blind. And if the blind lead the blind, both fall into the pit. [307]

[LUKE 11:37–44] 37 While he was speaking, a Pharisee asked him to dine with him; so he went in and sat at table. 38 The Pharisee was astonished to see that he did not first wash before dinner. 39 And the Lord said to him, "Now you Pharisees cleanse the outside of the cup and of the dish, but inside you are full of extortion and wickedness. 40 You fools! Did not he who made the outside make the inside also? 41 But give for alms those things which are within; and behold, everything is clean for you. 42 "But woe to you Pharisees! for you tithe mint and rue and every herb, and neglect justice and the love of God; these you ought to have done, without neglecting the others. 43 Woe to you Pharisees! for you love the best seat in the synagogues and salutations in the market places. 44 Woe to you! for you are like graves which are not seen, and men walk over them without knowing it."

The Daughter of the Syrophoenician Woman [E8]

⊕

WHILE Jesus was going from house to house in Dan healing the sick, he was perseveringly followed by an aged [Syrophoenician] woman, a pagan, who was crippled on one side. She was from Ornithopolis. She remained humbly at some distance and, from time to time, implored help. But Jesus paid no attention to her, he even appeared to shun her, for he was now healing sick Jews only. A servant accompanied the woman bearing her baggage. She was clothed in the garb of a foreigner. Her dress was of striped material, the arms and neck trimmed with lace. On her head she wore a high, pointed cap, over which was tied a colored kerchief, and lastly a veil. She had at home a daughter sick and possessed, and for a long time she had been hoping for aid from Jesus. She was in Dan at the time of the apostles' mission there, and they now more than once reminded Jesus of her. But he replied that it was not yet time, that he wanted to avoid giving offense, and that he would not help the pagans before the Jews. . . . The pagan woman had waited long at a distance. Jesus never went near her, and she dared not approach him. From time to time, however, she repeated her cry: "Lord! Thou Son of David, have mercy on me! My daughter is grievously tormented by an impure spirit!" The disciples begged Jesus to help her. But he said: "I was not sent but to the sheep that are lost of the house of Israel." At last the woman drew nearer, ventured into the hall, cast herself down before Jesus, and cried: "Lord, help me!" Jesus replied: "It is not good to take the bread of the children and to cast it to the dogs." But she continued to entreat: "Yea, Lord! For the whelps also eat of the crumbs that fall from the table of their masters." Then Jesus said: "O woman, great is thy faith! On account of these words, help shall be given thee!" [309]

[MARK 7:17–31] 17 And when he had entered the house, and left the people, his disciples asked him about the parable. 18 And he said to them, "Then are you also without understanding? Do you not see that whatever goes into a man from outside cannot defile him, 19 since it enters, not his heart but his stomach, and so passes on?" (Thus he declared all foods clean.) 20 And he said, "What comes out of a man is what defiles a man. 21 For from within, out of the heart of man, come evil thoughts, fornication, theft, murder, adultery, 22 coveting, wickedness, deceit, licentiousness, envy, slander, pride, foolishness. 23 All these evil things come from within, and they defile a man." 24 And from there he arose and went away to the region of Tyre and Sidon. And he entered a house, and would not have any one know it; yet he could not be hid. 25 But immediately a woman, whose little daughter was possessed by an unclean spirit, heard of him, and came and fell down at his feet. 26 Now the woman was a Greek, a Syrophoenician by birth. And she begged him to cast the demon out of her daughter. 27 And he said to her, "Let the children first be fed, for it is not right to take the children's bread and throw it to the dogs." 28 But she answered him, "Yes, Lord; yet even the dogs under the table eat the children's crumbs." 29 And he said to her, "For this saying you may go your way; the demon has left your daughter." 30 And she went home, and found the child lying in bed, and the demon gone. 31 Then he returned from the region of Tyre, and went through Sidon to the Sea of Galilee, through the region of the Decapolis.

THE Canaanites were the descendants of the eleven sons of Canaan, who were driven out of their country by Joshua, as a punishment, the Bible tells us, for their idolatrous customs and abominations. Defeated and despoiled of their riches, they withdrew to various countries, chiefly to Greece and Africa.

The Disciples Eat Wheat on the Sabbath [E9]

⊕

I SAW Jesus several times walking with the disciples and other friends on the Mount of Olives, while Mary, Magdalene, and other women promenaded at some distance. I saw the disciples snapping off ears from the ripe cornfields, and here and there eating fruits and berries. Jesus gave the disciples minute instructions on prayer, warned them against hypocrisy in it, and repeated to them many things that he had before said. [316]

[MARK 2:23–28] 23 One sabbath he was going through the grainfields; and as they made their way his disciples began to pluck heads of
grain. 24 And the Pharisees said to him, "Look, why are they doing what is not lawful on the sabbath?" 25 And he said to them, "Have you
never read what David did, when he was in need and was hungry, he and those who were with him: 26 how he entered the house of God,
when Abiathar was high priest, and ate the bread of the Presence, which it is not lawful for any but the priests to eat, and also gave it to
those who were with him?" 27 And he said to them, "The sabbath was made for man, not man for the sabbath; 28 so the Son of man is lord
even of the sabbath."

The Rich Young Man Went Away Sorrowful [E10]

⊕

THE Pharisees now began to dispute maliciously with Jesus, and call him to account for all that he exacted of his disciples, for a young man in their party had complained to them of him. This young man was rich and well-educated, and he had long before pushed himself upon Jesus as his disciple. But Jesus had laid down to him several conditions, namely, that he should leave father and mother, distribute his wealth to the poor, etc. He had again, at Caesarea-Philippi, offered himself to Jesus. But he still wanted to retain his fortune and the right to administer it himself, in consequence of which Jesus had again dismissed him. [321]

[MATTHEW 19:21–22] 21 Jesus said to him, "If you would be perfect, go, sell what you possess and give to the poor, and you will have treasure in heaven; and come, follow me." 22 When the young man heard this he went away sorrowful; for he had great possessions.

Jesus Heals the Blind and the Lame on the Mountain [E11]

⊕

BEFORE daylight they left Bethsaida and rowed again to the east side of the lake, where Jesus delivered a discourse on the mountain ridge beyond Matthew's custom house. There were pagans from Decapolis present, also the people belonging to the caravan. Many sick were brought up the mountain on litters and asses, and Jesus healed them. [322]

[MATTHEW 15:30–31] 30 And great crowds came to him, bringing with them the lame, the maimed, the blind, the dumb, and many others, and they put them at his feet, and he healed them, 31 so that the throng wondered, when they saw the dumb speaking, the maimed whole, the lame walking, and the blind seeing; and they glorified the God of Israel.

Jesus Discourses with his Disciples [E12]

⊕

JESUS taught of prayer, how and where it should be made, and of perseverance in it. He said: "When a child asks for bread, the father does not give it a stone, nor does he give it a serpent when it asks for a fish, or a scorpion instead of an egg." He remarked as an illustration that he knew pagans who had such confidence in God that they never petitioned for anything, but took with thanks all that was given them. "If servants and strangers have such confidence," said Jesus, "what ought not that of the children of the Father to be?" [322]

[LUKE 11:9–13] 9 And I tell you, Ask, and it will be given you; seek, and you will find; knock, and it will be opened to you. 10 For every
one who asks receives, and he who seeks finds, and to him who knocks it will be opened. 11 What father among you, if his son asks for a
fish, will instead of a fish give him a serpent; 12 or if he asks for an egg, will give him a scorpion? 13 If you then, who are evil, know how to
give good gifts to your children, how much more will the heavenly Father give the Holy Spirit to those who ask him!"

THE town of Jerusalem, with the temple area, is bounded on the east by the Valley of Jehosaphat. This valley must be crossed in going to Jericho, Bethany, or to the Jordan, so that Jesus must often have passed through it, and it was by way of it that he entered Jerusalem. The Garden of Gethsemane is situated in the north, and its grottoes and groups of olive trees often attracted the Master, who would frequently retire there for solitary prayer or for conversation with his disciples. He seldom went to the districts on the west of the Holy City, and only to those on the north on his way back from his trips to Galilee.

The Pharisees and the Sadducees Come to Tempt Jesus [E13]

⊕

JESUS took leave of the people, who shed tears and lifted up their voices thanking and praising him. He broke away from them only with difficulty and went to the lake with the disciples, in order to cross over to the southeastern side into the region of Magdala and Dalmanutha. When about to embark just above Matthew's custom office, the Pharisees approached and, at the foot of the mountain upon which the first multiplication of the loaves had taken place, demanded from him a sign from heaven. This they did because he had spoken of frightful tremors of the earth and other signs in nature. He replied to them as is recorded in the Gospel. I heard him mention also a certain number of weeks at the end of which the sign of Jonah would be given them. This number exactly corresponded with his crucifixion and resurrection. Jesus then left them standing there and went with the apostles to Peter's ship, which the other disciples had in readiness to receive him. [324]

[MATTHEW 16:1–4] 1 And the Pharisees and Sadducees came, and to test him they asked him to show them a sign from heaven. 2 He
answered them, "When it is evening, you say, 'It will be fair weather; for the sky is red.' 3 And in the morning, 'It will be stormy today, for
the sky is red and threatening.' You know how to interpret the appearance of the sky, but you cannot interpret the signs of the times. 4 An
evil and adulterous generation seeks for a sign, but no sign shall be given to it except the sign of Jonah." So he left them and departed.

The Primacy of Peter [E14]

⊕

AT last, he said: "And you, for whom do you take me?" No one felt impelled to answer. Only Peter, full of faith and zeal, taking one step forward into the circle, with hand raised like one solemnly affirming, exclaimed aloud and boldly, as if the voice and tongue of all: "Thou art Christ, the Son of the living God!" Jesus replied with great earnestness, his voice strong and animated: "Blessed art thou, Simon, son of Jonah, because flesh and blood hath not revealed this to thee, but my Father who is in heaven! And I say to thee: Thou art a rock, and upon this rock I will build my church, and the gates of hell shall not prevail against it. And I will give to thee the keys of the kingdom of heaven. And whatsoever thou shalt bind upon earth, it shall be bound also in heaven; and whatsoever thou shalt loose upon earth, it shall be loosed also in heaven!" Jesus made this response in a manner both solemn and prophetic. He appeared to be shining with light, and was raised some distance above the ground. Peter, in the same spirit in which he had confessed to the Godhead, received Jesus's words in their full signification. [326]

[MATTHEW 16:13–20] 13 Now when Jesus came into the district of Caesarea Philippi, he asked his disciples, "Who do men say that the Son of man is?" 14 And they said, "Some say John the Baptist, others say Elijah, and others Jeremiah or one of the prophets." 15 He said to them, "But who do you say that I am?" 16 Simon Peter replied, "You are the Christ, the Son of the living God." 17 And Jesus answered him, "Blessed are you, Simon Bar-Jona! For flesh and blood has not revealed this to you, but my Father who is in heaven. 18 And I tell you, you are Peter, and on this rock I will build my church, and the powers of death shall not prevail against it. 19 I will give you the keys of the kingdom of heaven, and whatever you bind on earth shall be bound in heaven, and whatever you loose on earth shall be loosed in heaven." 20 Then he strictly charged the disciples to tell no one that he was the Christ.

“Get Thee Behind Me, Satan” [E15]

⊕

HE told them moreover that he would be maltreated, scourged, mocked, and shamefully put to death; that he must die for the sins of men, but that on the third day he would rise again. He told them all this in detail and proved it from the Prophets. His manner was very grave, but full of love. Peter was so distressed at the thought of Jesus's being maltreated and put to death that, following him, he spoke to him in private, disputing with him and exclaiming against such suffering, such treatment. No, he said, that should not be. He would rather die himself than suffer such a thing to happen! "Far be it from thee, Lord! This shall not be unto thee!" He exclaimed. But Jesus turned to him gravely and said with warmth: "Go behind me, Satan! Thou art a scandal unto me. Thou savorest not the things that are of God, but the things that are of men!" and then walked on. [327]

[MATTHEW 16:21–28] 21 From that time Jesus began to show his disciples that he must go to Jerusalem and suffer many things from the elders and chief priests and scribes, and be killed, and on the third day be raised. 22 And Peter took him and began to rebuke him, saying, "God forbid, Lord! This shall never happen to you." 23 But he turned and said to Peter, "Get behind me, Satan! You are a hindrance to me; for you are not on the side of God, but of men." 24 Then Jesus told his disciples, "If any man would come after me, let him deny himself and take up his cross and follow me. 25 For whoever would save his life will lose it, and whoever loses his life for my sake will find it. 26 For what will it profit a man, if he gains the whole world and forfeits his life? Or what shall a man give in return for his life? 27 For the Son of man is to come with his angels in the glory of his Father, and then he will repay every man for what he has done. 28 Truly, I say to you, there are some standing here who will not taste death before they see the Son of man coming in his kingdom."

Magdalene at the Feet of Jesus [E16]

⊕

ON the sabbath Jesus taught at Lazarus's, and then all went to walk in the gardens. Jesus talked of his Passion and said in plain terms that he was the Christ. His words increased his hearers' reverence and admiration for him, while Magdalene's love and contrition reached their height. She followed Jesus everywhere, sat at his feet, stood and waited for him everywhere. She thought of him alone, saw him alone, knew only her Redeemer and her own sins. Jesus frequently addressed to her words of consolation. [329]

[LUKE 10:39–42] 39 And she had a sister called Mary, who sat at the Lord's feet and listened to his teaching. 40 But Martha was distracted with much serving; and she went to him and said, "Lord, do you not care that my sister has left me to serve alone? Tell her then to help me." 41 But the Lord answered her, "Martha, Martha, you are anxious and troubled about many things; 42 one thing is needful. Mary has chosen the good portion, which shall not be taken away from her."

IN the court of the house of Lazarus, Martha, the sister of him who was raised from the dead, and of Magdalene, is seen returning from an expedition to buy provisions for the Master and his disciples. A little help is needed, or would, at least be very acceptable in relieving her of her burdens, and she hopes that her sister, who has nothing to do, would come to her aid without hesitation. But Magdalene is listening to Jesus and is so profoundly absorbed in the words which are falling from the lips of her divine Guest, that nothing would induce her to move, and she is, in fact, perfectly unconscious of any thing which is going on around her. And was not this hour fraught indeed with infinite charm? Alone at the feet of the well-beloved Master in the quiet court sheltered from the heat by the stone walls, and beneath the shady olive tree, which gives forth an undefinable freshness and fragrance, she drinks in eagerly every one of his inspired words. Presently the disciples will arrive, the hour of solemn mysterious communion will be broken in upon by their greetings; farewell now to the peaceful meditation she has been so blissfully enjoying. The Master is, however, aware of all this, and he will not have her ecstasy broken in upon. She has chosen the good part, and it shall not be taken away from her. He lets his affectionate words penetrate to the very heart of the happy penitent, Martha's anxiety subsides, and again, for some little time, nothing is heard but a low whispering, broken now and then by a louder word, while the busy housekeeper silently plies her tasks, and the sweet scent from the burning roots on the hearth floats out into the court.

Many different interpretations have been given to the mysterious words of Jesus: "But one thing is needful." Some authors interpret them in far too literal a manner, and, as it appears to me, reduce them to the merest commonplace. It appears to us, therefore, infinitely preferable to adopt the more dignified rendering, which is always more in harmony with all the traditions of the Church, and to assume that Jesus meant: "But one thing is needful, the welfare of the soul, its education, its moral perfection, its well-being;" that is why it is better, like Mary, to seek all that at the feet of the Master, than to occupy herself, as Martha did, with commonplace service, which must ever be of secondary importance. Yet another interpretation of a similar kind to this has been given, less generally accepted, but perhaps even more true to the original text, namely, that Jesus praises Magdalene for having hastened at once to him, thinking of him only; for the one thing needful to man is that he should live by him, and he who gives himself up entirely to that life in Christ has chosen the better part. It is on this last-mentioned interpretation that is founded the traditional and widespread use of the names of Magdalene and Martha as typical, the former of a contemplative, the latter of an active life, and these two characters are often compared with those of John and Peter, the one resting on the bosom of the Lord, the other directing the groups of apostles. From time immemorial these names have been quoted in this connection in books on the Christian mysteries, and circulated among true believers.

The Repentant Magdalene [E17]

⊕

MAGDALENE was very greatly changed. Her countenance and bearing were still noble and distinguished, though her beauty was destroyed by her penance and tears. She sat almost always alone in her narrow penance chamber, and at times performed the lowest services for the poor and sick. [329]

THE repentant Magdalene has thrown aside the red veil of the sinner and has donned the white veil of the penitent. She wears her hair floating behind her; for it was considered a great disgrace among Jewish women to appear in public with their hair loose. They were required, even in ordinary everyday life, go hide their hair under veils or by means of bands of material of some kind. If a woman had been surprised in adultery, or was convicted of having allowed her chastity to be violated, the priest unbound her hair, in token of her shame.

Magdalene's hair was evidently very long, for she was able to use it to wipe the feet of the Master in the house of the Pharisee. Among the ancients, it was the custom for slave women to do the same; they used to wash their master's feet and dry them with their hair. The repentant Magdalene made herself in like manner the slave of Jesus, and was not afraid of letting all the world know the state of her soul. Her dress was that of women of the lowest class; her feet were shod with the sandals of the very poor; and she held herself apart, not daring to come further, thus proving alike her humility and her true penitence.

The Poor Lazarus at the Rich Man's Door [E18]

⊕

THEN the Pharisees questioned Jesus on the subject of the parable of poor Lazarus which he had recently related. They asked in ridicule how he knew that story so well, how he knew what Lazarus, Abraham, and the rich man had said. Had he been with the rich man in hell? Was he not ashamed of himself to impose such things upon the people? Jesus again took up this parable and taught upon it, reproaching them with their avarice, their cruelty to the poor, their self-satisfied observance of empty forms and customs, along with their total want of charity. He applied the history of the rich glutton entirely to themselves. That history is true. The glutton was well-known until his death, which was a frightful one. I saw again that the rich glutton and poor Lazarus really existed and that by their death they had become well-known throughout the country. But they did not live in Jerusalem, where later on their dwellings so-called were pointed out to pilgrims. They died in Jesus's early years, and they were much spoken of in pious families at that time. The city in which they dwelt was called Aram, or Amthar, and lay in the mountains west of the Sea of Galilee. I no longer know the whole history in detail, but I still remember this much: The rich man was very wealthy. He lived high, held the first position among his fellows, and was a distinguished Pharisee, very strict in the outward observance of the Law; but he was, on the other hand, extremely severe and merciless toward the poor. I saw him harshly reproving the poor of the place who applied to him, as to their chief magistrate, for help and support. There was a poor, wretched man in the place called Lazarus. He was full of misery and covered with ulcers, but at the same time humble and patient. Hungering for bread, he had himself carried to the house of the rich man, in order to plead the cause of the poor so rudely rebuffed. The rich man was reclining at table carousing, but Lazarus was harshly repulsed as one unclean. He lay at the gate begging for only the crumbs that fell from the rich man's table, but no one gave him to eat. The dogs, more merciful, licked his sores, which means that the pagans were more merciful than the Jews. [334]

[LUKE 16:19–21] 19 There was a rich man, who was clothed in purple and fine linen and who feasted sumptuously every day. 20 And at his gate lay a poor man named Lazarus, full of sores, 21 who desired to be fed with what fell from the rich man's table; moreover the dogs came and licked his sores.

The Woman with an Infirmity of Eighteen Years [E19]

⊕

THE disciples had prepared for their Master an inn outside Ataroth near a simple-hearted schoolteacher, an aged man, who dwelt there among the gardens. Jesus and his disciples washed their feet, took some refreshments, and repaired to the synagogue in Ataroth to celebrate the sabbath. There were assembled many who had come hither from the country around, as well as all those that had been cured. An aged Pharisee, a cripple, who had not gone to Jerusalem, presided over the synagogue. He put on great airs, though to the people he was rather an object of ridicule. The scripture lessons of the day consisted of passages referring to legal impurity contracted by childbirth, to leprosy, to Elisha's multiplication of the bread of the first fruits and the new corn, and to Naaman's cure.

Jesus had been teaching a long time when he turned to where the women were standing and called to him a poor, crippled widow. Her daughters had conducted her into the synagogue and put her into the place she usually occupied. It never entered her mind to ask for help, although she had been sick eighteen years. She was crippled at the waist. When she walked, the upper part of her person was so bent toward the earth that she could almost have walked on her hands. Jesus addressed her as her daughters were leading her to him: "Woman, be freed from thy infirmity!" and he laid his hand on her back. She rose up straight as a candle, and began to praise God: "Blessed be the Lord God of Israel!" Then she cast herself at Jesus's feet, and all present praised God. [336]

[LUKE 13:10–17] 10 Now he was teaching in one of the synagogues on the sabbath. 11 And there was a woman who had had a spirit of infirmity for eighteen years; she was bent over and could not fully straighten herself. 12 And when Jesus saw her, he called her and said to her, "Woman, you are freed from your infirmity." 13 And he laid his hands upon her, and immediately she was made straight, and she praised God. 14 But the ruler of the synagogue, indignant because Jesus had healed on the sabbath, said to the people, "There are six days on which work ought to be done; come on those days and be healed, and not on the sabbath day." 15 Then the Lord answered him, "You hypocrites! Does not each of you on the sabbath untie his ox or his ass from the manger, and lead it away to water it? 16 And ought not this woman, a daughter of Abraham whom Satan bound for eighteen years, be loosed from this bond on the sabbath day?" 17 As he said this, all his adversaries were put to shame; and all the people rejoiced at all the glorious things that were done by him.

The Transfiguration [E20]

⊕

IN the beginning of his instruction, he had said that he would show them who he was, they should behold him glorified, that they might not waver in faith when his enemies would mock and maltreat him, when they should behold him in death shorn of all glory. The sun had set and it was dark, but the apostles had not remarked the fact, so entrancing were Jesus's words and bearing. He became brighter and brighter, and apparitions of angelic spirits hovered around him. It was about twelve o'clock at night when I beheld this glory at its height. I saw a shining pathway reaching from heaven to earth, and on it angelic spirits of different choirs, all in constant movement. The apostles lay, ravished in ecstasy rather than in sleep, prostrate on their faces. Then I saw three shining figures approaching Jesus in the light. Their coming appeared perfectly natural. It was like that of one who steps from the darkness of night into a place brilliantly illuminated. Two of them appeared in a more definite form, a form more like the corporeal. They addressed Jesus and conversed with him. They were Moses and Elijah. The third apparition spoke no word. It was more ethereal, more spiritual. That was Malachi. [340–341]

[MARK 9:2–13] 2 And after six days Jesus took with him Peter and James and John, and led them up a high mountain apart by themselves;
and he was transfigured before them, 3 and his garments became glistening, intensely white, as no fuller on earth could bleach them. 4
And there appeared to them Elijah with Moses; and they were talking to Jesus. 5 And Peter said to Jesus, "Master, it is well that we are here;
let us make three booths, one for you and one for Moses and one for Elijah." 6 For he did not know what to say, for they were exceedingly
afraid. 7 And a cloud overshadowed them, and a voice came out of the cloud, "This is my beloved Son; listen to him." 8 And suddenly looking around they no longer saw any one with them but Jesus only. 9 And as they were coming down the mountain, he charged them to tell no
one what they had seen, until the Son of man should have risen from the dead. 10 So they kept the matter to themselves, questioning what
the rising from the dead meant. 11 And they asked him, "Why do the scribes say that first Elijah must come?" 12 And he said to them, "Elijah does come first to restore all things; and how is it written of the Son of man, that he should suffer many things and be treated with contempt? 13 But I tell you that Elijah has come, and they did to him whatever they pleased, as it is written of him."

The Possessed Boy at the Foot of Mount Tabor [E21]

⊕

WHEN now Jesus inquired into the subject of dispute, a man from Amthar—a city on the Galilean mountain chain, the scene of the history of Lazarus and the rich glutton—stepped forth from the crowd, threw himself on his knees before Jesus, and implored him to help his only son. The boy was a lunatic and possessed of a mute devil, who hurled him sometimes into fire, sometimes into water, and laid hold of him so roughly that he cried out with pain. . . . The father now led the boy up by the hand. As soon as he saw Jesus, he began to tear himself frightfully, and the demon cast him to the earth, where he writhed in fearful contortions, foam pouring from his mouth. Jesus raised his hand in a threatening manner toward the boy and said: "Thou mute and impure spirit, I command thee to go out of him and never again to return into him!" The spirit cried out frightfully through the boy's mouth, convulsed him violently, and went out, leaving him pale and motionless like one dead. They tried in vain to restore consciousness, and many from among the crowd called out: "He is dead! He is really dead!" But Jesus took him by the hand, raised him up well and joyous, and restored him to his father with some words of admonition. The latter thanked Jesus with tears and canticles of praise, and all the lookers-on blessed the majesty of God. [341]

[MARK 9:14–27] 14 And when they came to the disciples, they saw a great crowd about them, and scribes arguing with them. 15 And
immediately all the crowd, when they saw him, were greatly amazed, and ran up to him and greeted him. 16 And he asked them, "What
are you discussing with them?" 17 And one of the crowd answered him, "Teacher, I brought my son to you, for he has a dumb spirit; 18 and
wherever it seizes him, it dashes him down; and he foams and grinds his teeth and becomes rigid; and I asked your disciples to cast it out,
and they were not able." 19 And he answered them, "O faithless generation, how long am I to be with you? How long am I to bear with you?
Bring him to me." 20 And they brought the boy to him; and when the spirit saw him, immediately it convulsed the boy, and he fell on the
ground and rolled about, foaming at the mouth. 21 And Jesus asked his father, "How long has he had this?" And he said, "From childhood.
22 And it has often cast him into the fire and into the water, to destroy him; but if you can do anything, have pity on us and help us." 23
And Jesus said to him, "If you can! All things are possible to him who believes." 24 Immediately the father of the child cried out and said,
"I believe; help my unbelief!" 25 And when Jesus saw that a crowd came running together, he rebuked the unclean spirit, saying to it, "You
dumb and deaf spirit, I command you, come out of him, and never enter him again." 26 And after crying out and convulsing him terribly,
it came out, and the boy was like a corpse; so that most of them said, "He is dead." 27 But Jesus took him by the hand and lifted him up,
and he arose.

"The First Shall Be Last" [E22]

⊕

AFTER that Jesus asked the disciples upon what subject they had been conversing on the way from Dothaim to Capernaum. They were silent, for they had been questioning who would be the greatest among them. Jesus, however, knew their thoughts, and he said: "Let him that will be the first among you, become the last, the servant of all! [343]

[MARK 9:31–35] 31 For he was teaching his disciples, saying to them, "The Son of man will be delivered into the hands of men, and they will kill him; and when he is killed, after three days he will rise." 32 But they did not understand the saying, and they were afraid to ask him. 33 And they came to Capernaum; and when he was in the house he asked them, "What were you discussing on the way?" 34 But they were silent; for on the way they had discussed with one another who was the greatest. 35 And he sat down and called the twelve; and he said to them, "If any one would be first, he must be last of all and servant of all."

OUR engraving represents the terrace of a house of Bethsaida in the evening light. Palms were numerous on the shores of the lake in the time of Jesus; and between them in the distance can be seen the masts of boats, indicating the almost exclusive occupation of the inhabitants, that of fishing. In this district the houses are not built as they are in Judea, where every room has its vaulted stone roof. Here buildings consist of arcades made of stone or rubble masonry, each room having three or four such arcades, which support a number of small beams or branches of trees laid lengthwise. These beams or branches form the floor of the second storey, and are overlaid with earth, for which they form a very good foundation. This description of the mode of construction of houses in the districts where Christ taught will help us later to picture for ourselves the scene where the paralyzed man was let down through the roof, to be brought to Jesus.

Jesus and the Little Child [E23]

⊕

THE disciples having asked again who would be the greatest in the kingdom of heaven, Jesus called to him a wealthy lady, the wife of a merchant, who was standing with her four-year-old boy at the door of her house close by. She drew her veil and stepped forward with her boy. Jesus took him from her, and she at once went back. Then Jesus embraced the boy, stood him before him in the midst of the disciples and the crowds of children standing around, and said: "Whoever becomes not like the children, shall not enter the kingdom of heaven! Whoever receives a child in my name, receives me, yes, rather receives him that sent me. And whoever humbleth himself like this little child, he is the greatest in the kingdom of heaven." Then he blessed the boy, who was very lovely, gave him some fruit and a little tunic, beckoned to the mother, and restored her child to her with some prophetic words concerning his future, which were understood only at a later period. The child became a disciple of the apostles and was named Ignatius. He was afterward a bishop and martyr. [343]

[MARK 9:36–45] 36 And he took a child, and put him in the midst of them; and taking him in his arms, he said to them, 37 "Whoever receives one such child in my name receives me; and whoever receives me, receives not me but him who sent me." 38 John said to him, "Teacher, we saw a man casting out demons in your name, and we forbade him, because he was not following us." 39 But Jesus said, "Do not forbid him; for no one who does a mighty work in my name will be able soon after to speak evil of me. 40 For he that is not against us is for us. 41 For truly, I say to you, whoever gives you a cup of water to drink because you bear the name of Christ, will by no means lose his reward. 42 "Whoever causes one of these little ones who believe in me to sin, it would be better for him if a great millstone were hung round his neck and he were thrown into the sea. 43 And if your hand causes you to sin, cut it off; it is better for you to enter life maimed than with two hands to go to hell, to the unquenchable fire. 44 [No text] 45 And if your foot causes you to sin, cut it off; it is better for you to enter life lame than with two feet to be thrown into hell.

ACCORDING to a tradition, resting on no very trustworthy foundation, the child whom Jesus took on his knees, and made the text of his exhortation to his disciples, was none other than Ignatius, the future bishop of Antioch and martyr. The gospels, however, never mention the name of Ignatius, and there is absolutely nothing to prove that Ignatius of Antioch ever saw the Lord during his lifetime.

"Suffer the Little Children to Come unto Me" [E24]

⊕

JESUS visited the homes of the poor and many of his friends, and they presented to him the children, whom he blessed and to whom he made little presents. On the marketplace, on one side of which stood the old, on the other the new synagogue built by Cornelius, were houses with porticos in front. Here the school children and mothers with their little ones were assembled to salute Jesus. Jesus had been teaching in different places all along the way, and here he blessed and taught the children. He had little tunics distributed among them, the same to the rich as to the poor. They had been prepared by the stewardesses of the community and brought hither by the holy women of Jerusalem. The children received also fruit, writing tablets, and other gifts. The disciples having asked again who would be the greatest in the kingdom of heaven, Jesus called to him a wealthy lady, the wife of a merchant, who was standing with her four-year-old boy at the door of her house close by. She drew her veil and stepped forward with her boy. Jesus took him from her, and she at once went back. Then Jesus embraced the boy, stood him before him in the midst of the disciples and the crowds of children standing around, and said: "Whoever becomes not like the children, shall not enter the kingdom of heaven! Whoever receives a child in my name, receives me, yes, rather receives him that sent me. And whoever humbleth himself like this little child, he is the greatest in the kingdom of heaven." [343]

[MARK 10:13–16] 13 And they were bringing children to him, that he might touch them; and the disciples rebuked them. 14 But when Jesus saw it he was indignant, and said to them, "Let the children come to me, do not hinder them; for to such belongs the kingdom of God. 15 Truly, I say to you, whoever does not receive the kingdom of God like a child shall not enter it." 16 And he took them in his arms and blessed them, laying his hands upon them. [LUKE 18:15–17]15 Now they were bringing even infants to him that he might touch them; and when the disciples saw it, they rebuked them. 16 But Jesus called them to him, saying, "Let the children come to me, and do not hinder them; for to such belongs the kingdom of God. 17 Truly, I say to you, whoever does not receive the kingdom of God like a child shall not enter it."

JESUS is about to pass by; the fame of his benevolent works has gone before him; everybody knows how kindly he receives all who come to him. Sick children are brought go him to be healed of their sufferings, those who are well, that he may touch them and thus preserve them from all future ill. In Palestine, the women take their children to market and everywhere else with them, and, on hearing that the Master was to pass by, they hastened to him in great numbers, carrying their little ones. Crowds drew other crowds, and very soon the road would doubtless have been blocked up, making circulation impossible, so the disciples interfered, rebuking and driving back the mothers whose cries and supplications gave a certain appearance of disorder to the scene. But Jesus showed himself indulgent to the popular enthusiasm; he was always good to everybody, and all who had come to him went away healed, or rejoicing in the blessings they knew would for long afterwards accrue to them through the touch of the Prophet. The words of the text: "indigne tulit," or much displeased, show that the roughness of the disciples greatly vexed our Lord and made him very angry with his followers. It always grieved him to find himself so little understood even by his disciples, and he sometimes said to them: "Ye know not what manner of spirit ye are of."

Jesus Traveling [E25]

⊕

JESUS then went to a valley that lay off toward the west and in a region more elevated than Capernaum. The mountain of Saphet was on the right. Here he journeyed through valleys and solitary places, teaching now the reapers and shepherds, now the disciples. [345]

[JOHN 7:1–4] 1 After this Jesus went about in Galilee; he would not go about in Judea, because the Jews sought to kill him. 2 Now the Jews'
feast of Tabernacles was at hand. 3 So his brothers said to him, "Leave here and go to Judea, that your disciples may see the works you are
doing. 4 For no man works in secret if he seeks to be known openly. If you do these things, show yourself to the world."

The Scribe Stood to Tempt Jesus [E26]

⊕

ONE of the young men of Nazareth who had so often, but vainly, petitioned to be received among the disciples, here presented himself again before Jesus with the question: "Master, what must I do to possess eternal life?" Thereupon followed the scene recorded in the Gospel, and Jesus recounted the story of the compassionate Samaritan. Meanwhile the Pharisees reproached Jesus for not receiving the young man among his disciples. It was, they said, because the youth was well educated, and Jesus knew that he could not silence him so easily as he could the others. They again accused the disciples of irregular conduct, of uncleanliness, of stripping the wheat ears on the sabbath, of gathering fruit on the wayside, of eating out of time, of ill-breeding, and of many other similar things. [406]

[LUKE 10:21–28] 21 In that same hour he rejoiced in the Holy Spirit and said, "I thank thee, Father, Lord of heaven and earth, that thou
hast hidden these things from the wise and understanding and revealed them to babes; yea, Father, for such was thy gracious will. 22 All
things have been delivered to me by my Father; and no one knows who the Son is except the Father, or who the Father is except the Son and
any one to whom the Son chooses to reveal him." 23 Then turning to the disciples he said privately, "Blessed are the eyes which see what
you see! 24 For I tell you that many prophets and kings desired to see what you see, and did not see it, and to hear what you hear, and did
not hear it." 25 And behold, a lawyer stood up to put him to the test, saying, "Teacher, what shall I do to inherit eternal life?" 26 He said to
him, "What is written in the law? How do you read?" 27 And he answered, "You shall love the Lord your God with all your heart, and with all
your soul, and with all your strength, and with all your mind; and your neighbor as yourself." 28 And he said to him, "You have answered
right; do this, and you will live."

IN our engraving Jesus is seen in the Valley of the Kidron on his way from Jericho to Jerusalem, which rises up in the distant background. The spot where the Master is sitting with his disciples is a little hill, marking the last halting-place before reaching the Holy City. The mountain on the right is of chalk, scarcely covered by a scanty growth of brushwood, and on its slopes graze scattered flocks. On the left, broken here and there by grey rocks, stretch fertile districts, with soil of a reddish color, every undulation of which yields its own crop.

The Man Who Hoards

[LUKE 15–21] 15 And he said to them, "Take heed, and beware of all covetousness; for a man's life
does not consist in the abundance of his possessions." 16 And he told them a parable, saying, "The
land of a rich man brought forth plentifully; 17 and he thought to himself, 'What shall I do, for I
have nowhere to store my crops?' 18 And he said, 'I will do this: I will pull down my barns, and
build larger ones; and there I will store all my grain and my goods. 19 And I will say to my soul,
Soul, you have ample goods laid up for many years; take your ease, eat, drink, be merry.' 20 But
God said to him, 'Fool! This night your soul is required of you; and the things you have prepared,
whose will they be?' 21 So is he who lays up treasure for himself, and is not rich toward God."

Toward midday, Jesus with three of the apostles arrived at one of the fountains, where the eldest of the shepherds washed his feet and offered him fruit, honey, and bread. Jesus's coming had been expected, consequently many sick had been carried to the large house on the hill. Jesus cured them. Nearly four hundred shepherds, along with women and children, had assembled to greet him. The women's dresses were shorter than those worn in Palestine generally. Jesus gave them an instruction on the hill, speaking to them with the greatest simplicity and confidence. He reminded them of the caravan of the three kings which, two and thirty years before, had rested in this place. Then he spoke of the star that was to rise out of Jacob and of which Balaam had prophesied, of the newborn child of whom the Magi had been in search, of John, his teaching and his testimony, and concluded by saying that the promised Messiah, the Consoler, the Savior, was then in the midst of the Israelites, but that they would not recognize him. Jesus related to them also the parables of the good shepherd, the seed sown in the earth, and the harvest, for in this region there was a harvest of fruit as well as of wheat, the ears of which were extraordinarily large. He told them also of the shepherds near Bethlehem, of their finding the child even before the kings, and of the announcement made to them of it by the angels. The people fell in love with Jesus, and many of them wanted to leave all and follow him, just for the pleasure of listening to him always. But he advised them to remain at home and practice what he had taught them. From Salcha, which was almost an hour north of this place, messengers arrived with an invitation to Jesus to visit their city.

Thursday, July 5, AD 31 (Tammuz 25)

This morning Jesus visited the huts of some of the shepherds, teaching and consoling them. He then went to Salcha, arriving there around midday. He was well received. Many were baptized, the sick were healed, and children were blessed. Jesus also taught in the synagogue.

Jesus went to Salcha with the disciples. He was solemnly received at the city gate by the teachers and children in procession, and he taught in the synagogue, taking for the subject of his discourse the testimony rendered by John. Many of his hearers were baptized and cured. The children received his blessing.

Friday, July 6, AD 31 (Tammuz 26)

Before noon, Jesus and his traveling companions left Salcha and walked westward along what is called the "Way of David" on account of David's having hidden himself in this region near Mizpeh (1 Samuel 22). Jesus told his companions how Abraham had approached the promised land along David's Way and how the procession of the three holy kings had also traveled the same path. Then, after a time, they left the Way of David and went southward to the town of Thantia, arriving there at the onset of the sabbath. In the synagogue, Jesus spoke of Balaam and the star of Jacob (Numbers 24:17) and of Micah's prophecy concerning Bethlehem (Micah 5:2).

From Salcha Jesus went with his followers for about an hour and a half along the so-called Way of David which, following the windings of the valley, led down to the Jordan. This road was deep, a kind of hollow, in which water sometimes flowed. It ran through the solitudes of the mountains, and at several points along it were to be found places provided with troughs and stores of fodder for the camels, also rings for fastening them. When journeying through this country, Abraham saw a supernatural light on this road and had a vision, and when David, upon the advice of Jonathan, sought safety for his parents in the region of Mizpah, he lay concealed here with three hundred men, from which circumstance it received the name of David's Way. David here received from God a prophetic vision in which he saw the caravan of the three kings and heard, as if from the heavens open above him, melodious chanting proclaiming the praises of the promised Consoler of Israel. Malachi also, being obliged to flee after a battle, followed a mysterious light that led him to this region where, too, he lay hid for a time; and the three holy kings, giving rein to their camels upon leaving the confines of Salcha and entering this road, descended by it singing sweet hymns of thanksgiving. They then proceeded along the shore until they reached the point opposite Coreae, where they crossed the Jordan and arrived at Jerusalem through the desert beyond Anathoth. They entered the Holy City by the same gate through which Mary had passed when she went up from Bethlehem for her purification.

From David's Way, Jesus turned to the little place called Thantia, where he went immediately to the synagogue and taught, his subjects being Balaam, the star of Jacob, some passages from Micah, and Bethlehem Ephrata.

Saturday, July 7, AD 31 (Tammuz 27)

Today, in Thantia, Jesus healed several people in their homes, and the disciples baptized many converts. Jesus taught again concerning the star of Jacob, Micah's prophecy, and the journey of the three kings—all of this in relation to the coming of the Messiah.

Map 34: The Journey through Auranitis
July 2–8, AD 31

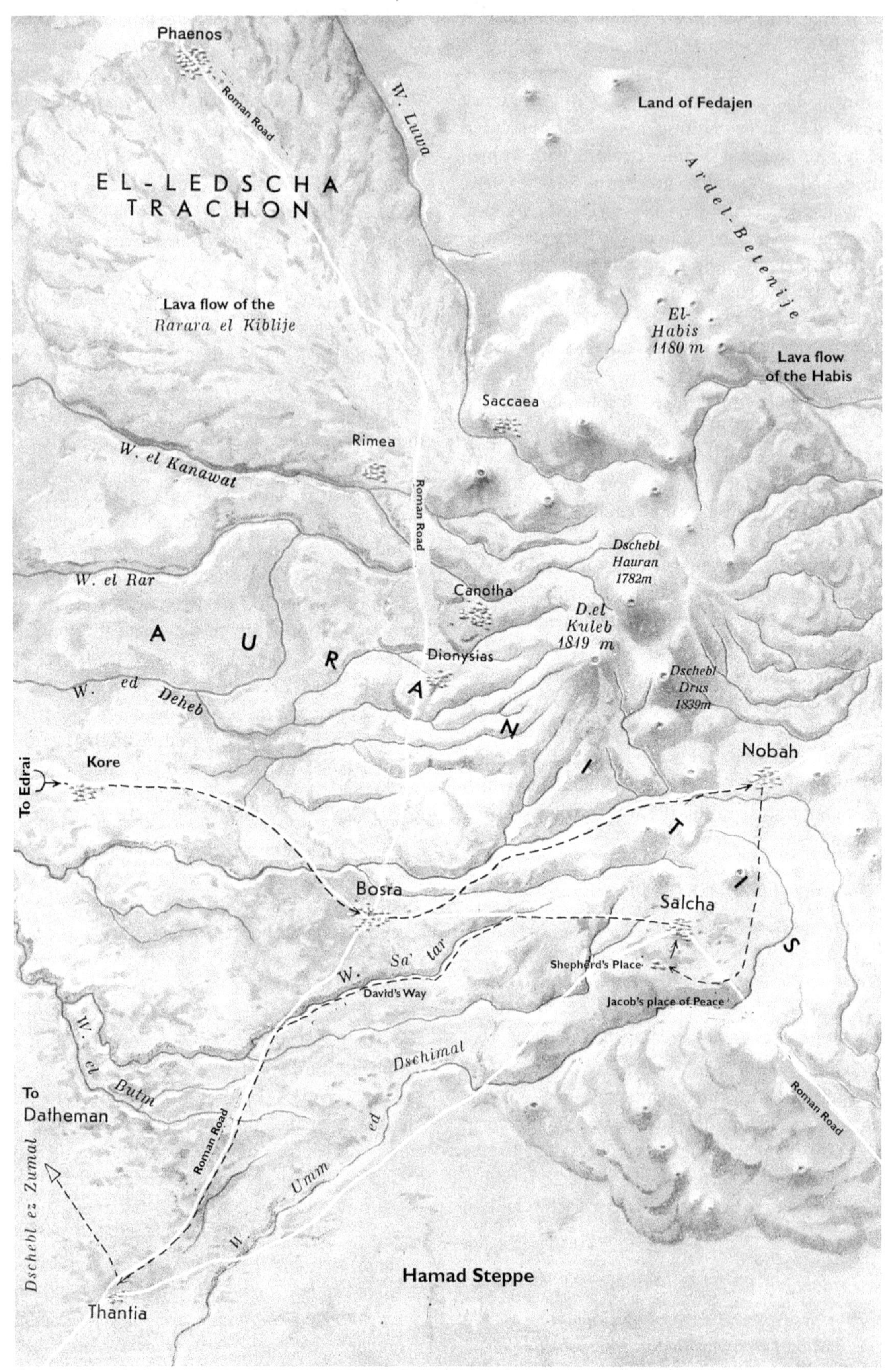

Kore—Bosra—Nobah—Jacob's Place of Peace—Shepherd's Place—Salcha—David's Way—Thantia

He next went to visit many sick in their own homes. He healed them, along with several others whom the disciples had not been able to cure. There was no organized care of the sick and the poor in Thantia. The disciples had indeed endeavored to establish something of the kind, but it was Jesus himself who effected the desired change. A great many of the people received baptism from the disciples.

Both the people and the rabbis of Thantia were pious. They were in the habit of making pilgrimages to the Way of David, and there, in fasting and prayer, crying to heaven for the coming of the Messiah. They indulged the hope of there having visions and apparitions of the Messiah who, they thought, would even come to them along that way. While Jesus was preaching, they said more than once to one another: "He speaks as if he were the Messiah himself! But no, that is not possible!" As they were under the impression that the Messiah was to come invisibly like an angel into Israel, they thought that Jesus might possibly be his herald and precursor. Jesus told them that they would perhaps recognize the Messiah when it would be too late. I saw that many from Thantia, both before and after the crucifixion, joined the community.

Upper Pool of Siloam

Sunday, July 8, AD 31 (Tammuz 28)

Jesus traveled from Thantia to Datheman, where there was a ruined citadel, used in the war of the Maccabees (1 Maccabees 5:9). Nearby was the mountain where Jephthah's daughter and her twelve maiden-companions had lamented for two months before Jephthah was put to death (Judges 11:29–40). Balaam had also been on this mountain when he was summoned by the king of Moab (Numbers 22:4–5). Jesus ascended the mountain and taught. That evening, he went to Datheman.

From Thantia Jesus journeyed four hours eastward to the ruined citadel of Datheman. Near it was the mountain that had been chosen by Jephthah's daughter upon which to mourn with her twelve young companions. Upon it were prophets and hermits, something like the Essenes. It was on this same mountain that Balaam was tarrying in solitude and meditation when summoned by the Moabite king to appear before him. He was of noble origin, his family very wealthy. From early youth, he had been filled with the spirit of prophecy, and he belonged to that nation that was ever on the lookout for the promised star, among whom were the ancestors of the three holy kings. Though a reprobate, Balaam was no sorcerer. He served the true God only, like the enlightened of other nations, but in an imperfect manner, mingling many errors with the truth. He was very young when he retired into the solitude of the mountains, and upon this one in particular he dwelt a long time. I think he had around him some other prophets, or pupils. When he returned from the Moabite king, Balak, he wished to take up his abode upon this mountain, but was prevented by divine interposition. By his scandalous counsel to the Moabites, he fell from grace, and now he wandered in despair around the desert in which at last he miserably perished.

The people of this region believed firmly in the sacred character of David's Way. They told Jesus that they would not dwell in the country beyond the Jordan where they could not dare make mention of all that had formerly been seen, all that had taken place on the Way of David.†

† This entry for Sunday, July 8, AD 31 (Tammuz 28) was the last of the daily accounts of Anne Catherine's visions that Clemens Brentano entered into his notebooks. He added: "What a pity! What a shame! Everything is lost!" Brentano wrote his entry on the evening of January 8, 1824. From then on, owing to unspeakable suffering, although she continued to live in visions of the day-by-day life of Christ, Anne Catherine was unable to communicate anything further. On January 14, she uttered the words, recorded by Clemens Brentano: "O, now I would soon be finished with relating the life of Jesus! And now I am in this wretched condition!" Within a month, however, on February 9,1824, she was dead.

According to the researches of Robert Powell, 313 days are missing from Anne Catherine's account—from where she left off (July 8, AD 31) to the period shortly before the raising of Lazarus. Historically, these 313 days run from July 9, AD 31 to May 16, AD 32. In other words, Anne Catherine's daily chronicle of Christ's ministry begins again on May 17, AD 32. All that we know of the missing period comes from the Gospel of Saint John. This may be summarized as follows: (1) Jesus was in Galilee before the Feast of Tabernacles; his brothers advised him to go to Judea (John 7:1–9); (2) Jesus attended the Feast of Tabernacles (September 19–26, AD 31) in Jerusalem (John 7:10–36); (3) On the last day of the Feast, he spoke the words: "If anyone thirst, let him come to me and drink," and the Pharisees tried to have him arrested (John 7:37–52);[F1] (4) In the temple, Jesus pardoned the woman who had committed adultery (John 8:1–11);[F2–3] (5) In the temple, Jesus referred to himself with the words: "I am the light of the world" (John 8:12). The Pharisees disputed with him and took up stones to throw at him, but Jesus hid himself and left the temple (John 8:13–59); (6) Near the pool of Siloam in Jerusalem, Jesus healed the man born blind (John 9).[F4] As this healing took place on the sabbath, i.e., between Friday evening and Saturday evening, it must have been on one of the following dates in AD 31: October 5/6, October 12/13, October 19/20, October 26/27, November 2/3, November 9/10, November 16/17, or November 23/24; (7) Jesus told the parable of the good shepherd (John 10:1–21); (8) Jesus attended the Feast of the

THE RAISING OF LAZARUS
JESUS IN THE LAND OF THE THREE KINGS

YEAR 4

Nisan 15, AD 32, to Nisan 14, AD 33
April 14/15, AD 32, to April 2/3, AD 33

(Follow Map 35)

Jesus in Bethabara and Jericho • Zacchaeus the Publican

Saturday, May 17, AD 32 (Iyyar 17)

Accompanied by Peter, James, and John, Jesus went to Bethabara, where he was joined by Matthew and another apostle. A large crowd had gathered. Jesus healed a great many people. It was here that Jesus spoke of marriage, blessed the children brought to him (Matthew 19:10–15), and advised the rich youth (Matthew 19:16–26). This last incident was followed by the exchange of words between Peter and Jesus recorded in Matthew 19:27–30. Then, toward evening, Jesus went to dine in a house where about ten of the holy women were gathered. These included Martha, her maidservant Marcella, Mary Magdalene, Mary Salome, Mary Cleophas, Veronica, and Mary Mark of Jerusalem. Jesus continued to teach.

WHEN Jesus and the apostles approached Bethabara on the Jordan, they found already assembled there an innumerable crowd of people. The whole country was full, and they were encamping under sheds and trees. Numbers of mothers with crowds of children of every age, even infants in the arms, were coming in procession. As they proceeded up the broad street to meet Jesus, the disciples who led the way wanted, on account of his great fatigue (for he had already blessed a great many), to repulse the women and children, and that even a little rudely. But Jesus checked them, and bade them bring the crowd to order. On one side of the street stood in five long rows children of all ages, one behind the other, the boys and girls apart, the latter being by far the more numerous. The mothers with infants in their arms were placed behind the fifth row. On the other side of the street stood the rest of the people, who passed in turn from the last rank to the first. Jesus now went down along the first row of children, laying his hand on their head and blessing them. He laid his hand on the head of some, on the breast of others; some he clasped to his breast, and some he held up as models to the others. He instructed them, exhorted them, encouraged them, and blessed them. When he had thus passed down one row of children, he crossed to the opposite side of the street and came up among the grown people, exhorting and instructing them, and even placing before them the example of some of the children. Then he went down the next row of children and came up, as before, among the grown people whose front ranks had been replaced by those from behind. And so it went on, until even the infants in the last row had received a loving caress and blessing. All the children blessed by Jesus received an interior grace, and later on became Christians. Jesus must have blessed fully a thousand children on this occasion, for the concourse continued during several days. He labored constantly, ever grave, mild, and gentle, with a certain secret sadness in his manner very touching to see. He taught now along the streets, now in some house into which they had pulled him by his robe. He related many parables, by which he instructed both the wise and the simple, and impressed upon the former the obligation of thankfully returning to God all that they had received from him, as he himself did.

Of the holy women, Veronica, Martha, Magdalene, and Mary Salome were gone on to Jerusalem. I saw Mary Salome with her sons, John and James the Greater, coming to Jesus and requesting that they should be allowed to sit, one at his right and the other at his left. Messengers had been sent thither by the Pharisees in Jerusalem, but many of them, being converted, remained; while others, returning in a rage to Jerusalem, repented on the way and later on became Jesus's followers.

Sunday, May 18, AD 32 (Iyyar 18)

After the close of the sabbath, Jesus with the five apostles traveled eastward from Bethabara. Not far from Nebo he was met by some people who asked him to visit a house where ten lepers lay. He went to the house and healed the lepers, instructing them to bathe in a nearby pool and to present themselves to the priests to show that they were healed. As Jesus then continued on his way, one of the lepers ran after him, cast himself down and gave thanks. (A similar incident repeated itself later on Sivan 14 and is described in Luke 17:11–19).

Dedication of the Temple in Jerusalem (November 28–December 5, AD 31), where the Pharisees tried to arrest him again (John 10:22–39); (9) He went to the place on the Jordan between Ainon and Salem, where John had first baptized (John 10:40); (10) Although not mentioned in the Gospel of Saint John, it is almost certain that Jesus attended the Feast of the Passover in Jerusalem in the month of Nisan AD 32, which started on Nisan 15, equating historically with April 14/15, AD 32, and lasted for one week. Illustrations for two other events during this period are given here. [F5–6]

Map 35: Travels in Ammonitis and Judea
May 17–Beginning of July, AD 32

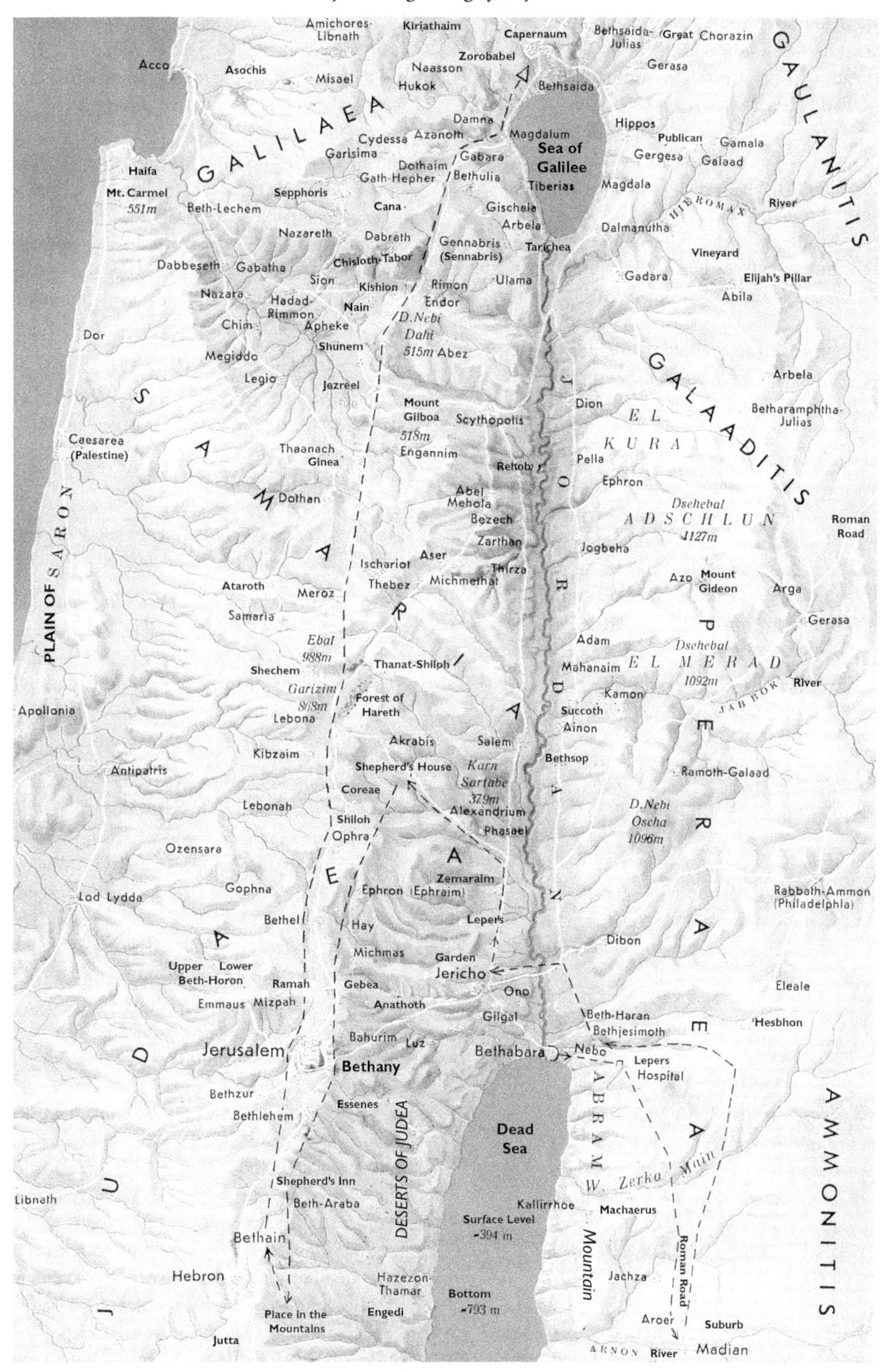

Bethabara—Hospital near Nebo—Suburb of Madian—Bethjesimoth—Jericho—Shepherd's Fields in Southern Samaria—Shepherd's House near Hebron—Place in the Mountains near Jutta—Bethain—Capernaum

Jesus left Bethabara with the apostles, and on his way he was entreated to visit a house in which lay ten lepers. The apostles, dreading contact with the leprous, went on ahead in a southerly direction, with the intention of waiting for Jesus under a tree. The lepers, enveloped in their mantles and full of sores, lay in a retired part of the house. Jesus commanded them to do something, and it seems to me that he touched one of them and then left them. The lepers one after another were taken by two people to a little pool near the house, and washed in the bathing tubs, after which they were able to present themselves to the priests as cured.

Jesus next went through another building that had a four-cornered courtyard. On either side of the latter was a covered archway, in one of which lay men, sick and crippled, and in the other, afflicted women. The beds were laid in rows of hollow places, scooped out in the ground to receive them. Another covered way on the same line cut through the middle of the house and led to a space in which the cooking and washing were done. Between this middle walk and those in which the sick lay, were grass plots. Jesus again cured several here. As he proceeded on his way, I saw following him one of the lately healed lepers proclaiming his praise. Jesus looked around, and the man fell on his face giving thanks. Further on the route, Jesus blessed many children who had been brought by their mothers to meet him.

Monday, May 19, AD 32 (Iyyar 19)

Jesus and the five apostles traveled southward in the direction of Madian. On the way, they were joined by four other apostles and several disciples.

The road traveled by Jesus and the apostles on leaving Bethabara ran on the right past Machaerus and the city of Madian.

Tuesday, May 20, AD 32 (Iyyar 20)

They did not enter Madian. Instead, they went to a Jewish settlement on the outskirts of the town. Here Jesus taught.

Wednesday, May 21, AD 32 (Iyyar 21)

Today Jesus and his traveling companions made their way northward from Madian in the direction of Jericho. They stayed the night with some shepherds.

They again approached the Jordan, made a circuit of Bethabara, and went by roundabout ways through a desert region toward Jericho.

Thursday, May 22, AD 32 (Iyyar 22)

Not far from the Jordan there was a large house where a shepherd family lived. Jesus went into the house. Here he recounted the parable of the unmerciful servant (Matthew 18:23–35) and spoke the words: "Those who say they are chaste, but who eat and drink only what pleases their appetite, are like those who try to extinguish a fire with dry wood."

As they proceeded on their journey, the disciples who had been sent out on missions returned to Jesus one after another and related to him all that they had done. He instructed them in parables, but I remember only these words of his discourse: "They who say they are chaste, but who eat and drink only what pleases their appetite, are like those who try to extinguish a fire with dry wood."

Friday, May 23, AD 32 (Iyyar 23)

Jesus and nine apostles and many disciples made their way to Bethjesimoth, where Jesus was awaited by the other apostles (Bartholomew, Judas, and another) and several disciples. With the onset of the sabbath, he taught in the synagogue at Bethjesimoth. He also healed a crippled woman. And again the Pharisees protested against healing on the sabbath.

Saturday, May 24, to Tuesday, May 27, AD 32 (Iyyar 24–27)

Jesus remained these four days in Bethjesimoth. The Pharisees tried to prevent him from going into the synagogue, but Jesus walked through them and entered the holy building, where he taught in parables.

Wednesday, May 28, AD 32 (Iyyar 28)

Today, on the way to Jericho, the apostles and disciples related their experiences and what they had done on their travels in Jesus's name. Jesus said: "Now you cling to me, because you fare well. In the time of need, you will act otherwise. Even those who bear a mantle of love toward me will let it fall and will flee." He was referring to John on the night of Gethsemane (Mark 14:51–52).

Another parable referred to the future of the twelve apostles. Jesus said: "Now ye cling to me, because ye fare well"; but they did not understand that by these words he meant the peace and beautiful instructions that they then enjoyed. "In the time of need," he continued, "ye will act otherwise. Even they whom I carry about with me like a mantle of love, will cast that mantle off and flee." These words referred to John in the garden of Gethsemane. In a little town near the Jordan, I saw a woman entreating Jesus to cure her daughter, who was covered with ulcers. Jesus told her that he would send one of the disciples to her. But she wanted him to go himself, which, however, he did not do. When he was drawing near to Jericho, the woman again approached and begged his aid. She urged that she had now renounced all that he had commanded her. Jesus, however, still repulsed her. Her child was the fruit of sin, and Jesus reproached her with a fault (it appeared to be but a small one) to which she had already clung for several years. He told her that she should not come again to him until she had freed herself from it. Then I saw the woman hurrying past the apostles and disciples toward Jericho.

Thursday, May 29, AD 32 (Iyyar 29)

Not far from Jericho, four Pharisees approached Jesus and warned him not to come, as Herod sought to kill him. Jesus replied as recorded in Luke 13:31–35. Then two brothers from Jericho came to him to ask him to divide their inheritance (Luke 12:13–34). Jesus also blessed many of the children of the city who came to see him.

Having almost reached the city, four Pharisees sent by their colleagues of Jerusalem came and warned him not to enter lest Herod would put him to death. This they did, however, not because they cared for him, but because having heard of his numerous miracles, they were afraid of him. Jesus replied that they should say to Herod, the fox, these words only: "Behold, I cast out devils and do cures today and tomorrow, and the third day I am consummated." Two of these Pharisees were converted and followed Jesus, but the other two returned in a rage to Jerusalem.

Then came to Jesus two brothers belonging to Jericho. They could not agree on the subject of their patrimony; one wanted to remain, the other desired to go away. One of them proposed that Jesus, so renowned everywhere, should divide the patrimony between them, and they had in consequence come to meet him. But he refused, saying that it was not his business. And when even John remarked to him that it was a good work, and Peter seconded the word, Jesus replied that he was not come to distribute earthly goods, but only heavenly ones. After which he took occasion to deliver a long exhortation before the rapidly increasing crowd. But the disciples as yet did not always understand him rightly. They had not yet received the Holy Spirit and so they went on expecting an earthly kingdom.

Jesus was again met by crowds of women with their children, for whom they implored a blessing. The disciples, disturbed by the recent menaces of the Pharisees and desirous of shunning such excitement, tried to drive the women back, for they were entrusted with the duty of keeping order. But Jesus commanded them to allow the children to come forward. They needed his blessing, he said, in order that they too might become his disciples. Then he blessed many of the infants at the breast and the children of ten and eleven years. Some he did not bless, but later on these again presented themselves.

SIVAN (30 days): May 29/30 to June 27/28, AD 32 Sivan New Moon: May 28 at midnight (0 hours), Jerusalem time

Friday, May 30, AD 32 (Sivan 1)

A large crowd gathered on the outskirts of Jericho to see Jesus. The chief tax collector, Zacchaeus, also wanted to see him and, because he was small in stature, climbed a sycamore tree for a better view. There then took place the exchange between Zacchaeus and Jesus as recorded in Luke 19:1–10. Then, at the start of the sabbath, Jesus and the disciples went to the synagogue. Afterward, they dined at an inn. Zacchaeus came too.

Just outside the city, which was surrounded by gardens, pleasure grounds, and villas, Jesus and his followers encountered a dense crowd composed of people from all parts of the country around. They had assembled with their sick, who were lying on litters under sheds and tents. They had been waiting for Jesus, and now they beset him and his disciples on all sides. Zacchaeus, one of the chief publicans, who dwelt outside the city, had stationed himself on the road by which Jesus had to pass. As he was short in stature, he climbed a fig tree in order to be able to see Jesus better in the crowd. Jesus looked up into the tree and said: "Zacchaeus, make haste and come down, for this day I must abide in thy house." [F7] Zacchaeus hurried down, bowed humbly to Jesus, and very much touched returned home to make preparations for receiving his honored guest. When Jesus said that he must that day enter into Zacchaeus's house, he meant into his heart, for on that day he went into Jericho itself, and not into the house of Zacchaeus. On arriving at the city gate, Jesus found none of the people assembled to welcome him, for through dread of the Pharisees they were remaining quietly in their homes. The crowd, gathered at some distance from the city, were all strangers come to implore Jesus's assistance in their various needs. He cured a blind man and a deaf mute, but some others he sent away. He blessed the children, especially the babes at the breast, and told the apostles that men must in this way be accustomed to devote their children from earliest youth to him, and that all thus blessed would follow him. Among those sent away was a woman afflicted with an issue of blood. She had come some days before with the firm resolve to implore Jesus for her cure. I heard Jesus saying to the disciples that whoever does not persevere in prayer, is not in earnest and has no faith.

As the sabbath now began, Jesus went with his apostles and disciples to the synagogue of the city and afterward to the inn. He and the apostles dined in the open refectory, the disciples in the archway. The meal consisted of little rolls, honey, and fruit. They ate standing, Jesus meantime teaching and relating parables. Every three of the apostles drank from one cup, but Jesus had one to himself. The woman that had already been twice repulsed came again to Jesus imploring help for her daughter, but with no better success than before, because she was not sincere. She had been questioning among the Pharisees of Jericho about what was said of Jesus in Jerusalem.

Zacchaeus also here presented himself to Jesus. The new disciples had already taken it ill outside the city that Jesus had accosted the ill-famed publican and even wanted to abide with him, for Zacchaeus in particular was a subject of scandal to them. Some were related to him, and they were ashamed of his remaining a publican so long and up to the present unconverted. Zacchaeus drew near the hall in which the disciples were dining, but no one wanted to have anything to do with him, no one invited him to eat. Then Jesus stepped out into the hall, beckoned Zacchaeus in, and offered him food and drink.

Saturday, May 31, AD 32 (Sivan 2)

Today, Jesus taught in the synagogue in Jericho. After the close of the sabbath, he and the apostles went to Zacchaeus's house, where they dined. Jesus told the parable of the fig tree (Luke 13:69) and other parables. He then stayed the night with Zacchaeus. It was about this time that Lazarus became deathly ill.

On the following day, when Jesus went again to the synagogue and told the Pharisees to give place to him, as he intended to read and explain the sabbath lesson, they raised a great contention, but they did not prevail. He inveighed against avarice, and cured an invalid who had been carried on a litter to the door of the synagogue. The sabbath over, Jesus went with his apostles to Zacchaeus's dwelling outside of Jericho. None of the disciples accompanied him. The woman so desirous of help for her daughter again followed Jesus on the road out to Zacchaeus's. He laid his hand on her to free her from her own bad disposition, and told her to return home, for her child was cured. During the meal, which consisted of honey, fruit, and a lamb, Zacchaeus served at table, but whenever Jesus spoke, he listened devoutly. Jesus related the parable of the fig tree in the vineyard which for three years bore no fruit, and for which the vinedresser implored one more year of indulgence. When uttering this parable, Jesus addressed the apostles as the vineyard; of himself he spoke as the owner; and of Zacchaeus as the fig tree. It was now three years since the relatives of the last-named had abandoned their dishonorable calling and followed Jesus, while he all this time had still carried on the same business, on which account he was looked upon with special contempt by the disciples. But Jesus had cast upon him a look of mercy when he called him down from the tree. Jesus spoke also of the sterile trees that produce many leaves, but no fruit. The leaves, he said, are exterior works. They make a great rustling, but soon pass away leaving no seed of good. But the fruits are that interior, efficacious reality in faith and action, with their capability of reproduction, and the prolongation of the tree's life stored away in the kernel. It seems to me that Jesus, in calling Zacchaeus down from the tree, did the same as to engage him to renounce the noise and bustle of the crowd, for Zacchaeus was like the ripe fruit which now detached itself from the tree that for three years had stood unfruitful in the vineyard. Jesus spoke, likewise, of the faithful servants who watched for the coming of their lord, and who suffered no noise that could prevent them from hearing his knock.

Sunday, June 1, to Tuesday, June 3, AD 32 (Sivan 3–5)

Jesus and the disciples stayed in Jericho.

Wednesday, June 4, AD 32 (Sivan 6)

Today Jesus and his disciples were invited to dine with the Pharisees. During the meal, they accused Jesus of breaking the Law by healing on the sabbath. Jesus replied in words similar to those recorded in Luke 14:1–24. Today, many people in Jericho were baptized by James and Bartholomew.

Thursday, June 5, AD 32 (Sivan 7)

Jesus taught in the synagogue and on the streets of Jericho. Many tax collectors and sinners came to hear him, and the Pharisees plotted against him (Luke 15:1–2). The disciples were unhappy that Jesus associated with tax collectors and sinners. Because of this, Jesus told them the parables recorded in Luke 15:3–32.

Friday, June 6, AD 32 (Sivan 8)

After healing a woman with as issue of blood this morning, Jesus taught concerning repeated and constant prayer. Later, messengers came from Bethany requesting Jesus to go there and heal Lazarus. But Jesus replied that the time was not yet ripe and that he would travel first to Samaria.

Saturday, June 7, AD 32 (Sivan 9)

Today, on the sabbath, Jesus taught and healed, going from house to house. It was the end of his stay in Jericho, and he wished to pour out the fullness of his love upon the people there.

It appeared as if Jesus was now in Jericho for the last time, and as if he wished to pour out upon it the fullness of his love. He sent the apostles and disciples two by two out into the districts around into which he himself would go no more. In Jericho itself, he went from house to house, taught in the synagogue and on the streets, and everywhere to a great concourse of people.

Sunday, June 8, AD 32 (Sivan 10)

Jesus taught and healed and also drove out demons from those possessed. He sent out the apostles and disciples.

Sinners and publicans encompassed him on all sides, and on the roads by which he had to pass lay the sick, sighing and imploring help. He taught and cured without intermission, and was so earnest, so gentle, and so tranquil.

Monday, June 9, AD 32 (Sivan 11)

About one hundred Pharisees from various places came to Jericho. Together with the local Pharisees, they questioned Jesus. Jesus replied with such powerful words that they were reduced to silence.

The disciples, on the contrary, were anxious and dissatisfied on account of Jesus's so unconcernedly exposing himself to the snares that the enraged Pharisees, of whom almost a hundred were gathered here from different parts of the country, sought to prepare for him. They sent messengers to Jerusalem to consult as to how they could take him into custody. The apostles too were in a certain dread, as if they thought that Jesus laid himself open to danger and treated with the people rather rashly. Once I saw Jesus surrounded by a great crowd seeking his help, and among them were some sick that had caused themselves to be carried to him. The disciples meanwhile kept at a distance. The palsied woman with the issue of blood whom he had already sent away more than once had caused herself to be carried to the bath of purification, or expiation, with which was connected the forgiveness of sin. She crept afterward to Jesus and touched the hem of his robe. He instantly stood still, looked after her, and healed her. The woman arose, thanked her benefactor, and returned cured to her home in the city. Jesus then taught upon persevering and repeated prayer. He said that one should never desist from his entreaties. I was thinking meantime of the great charity of the good people who had brought the woman so long a distance, carrying her here and there after the Lord, and begging the disciples to inform them whither he was going next, that they might procure for her a good place. Owing to the nature of her sickness, which was regarded as unclean, she could not rest anywhere and everywhere. She had to solicit her cure for eight days long.

Tuesday, June 10, AD 32 (Sivan 12)

Today Jesus left Jericho and went to a village about an hour north of the city. On the way, he passed two blind men sitting at the roadside and restored their sight to them (Matthew 20:29–34).

Before Jesus's departure from Jericho, messengers from Bethany brought to the disciples the news of how earnestly Martha and Magdalene were longing for his coming, as Lazarus was very sick. Jesus, however, did not go to Bethany, but to a little village north of Jericho. Here too, a crowd had assembled, and numbers of sick, blind, and crippled were awaiting his arrival. Two blind men, each with two guides, were sitting by the roadside, and when Jesus passed by they cried out after him, begging to be cured. The people tried to silence them with threats, but they followed Jesus, crying after him: "Ah, thou Son of David! Have mercy on us!" Then Jesus turned, commanded them to be led to him, and touched their eyes. They saw and followed him.[F8]

Wednesday, June 11, AD 32 (Sivan 13)

In the village north of Jericho many sick people had gathered. Jesus healed them. He also taught there.

A great tumult arose on account of the cure of these blind men, as well as of those to whom Jesus had restored sight on his entrance into Jericho. The Pharisees instituted an inquiry into the case, and interrogated the father of one of the cured as well as himself. The disciples meantime were very desirous that Jesus should go to Lazarus's, in Bethany, for there they would be in greater peace and less molested. They were in truth a little discontented, but Jesus went on curing numbers. Words cannot express how gentle and forbearing he was under such imputations, attacks, and persecutions, and how sweetly and gravely he smiled when the disciples wanted to divert him from his purpose.

Thursday, June 12, AD 32 (Sivan 14)

Not far from the village were ten lepers in a tent. Jesus healed them, but only one ran after Jesus to thank him (Luke 17:11–19). The leper who ran after Jesus later became a disciple. Shortly afterward, as they passed along, a man came out of a shepherd settlement and begged Jesus to come because his daughter had just died. Jesus, accompanied by Peter, James, and John went with the shepherd to his house. His daughter, who was about seven years old, lay dead. Looking up to heaven, Jesus placed one hand on her head and the other on her breast and prayed. The child then rose up, alive. Jesus told the apostles that—in his name—they should do as he did.

He next went in the direction of Samaria. Not far from one of the little villages along the highroad, about a hundred paces to one side, there stood a tent in which ten lepers were lying in beds. As Jesus was passing, the lepers came out and cried to him for help.[F9] Jesus stood still, but the disciples went on. The lepers, entirely enveloped in their mantles, approached—some quickly, others slowly, as their strength permitted—and stood in a circle around Jesus. He touched each one separately, directed them to present themselves to the priests, and went on his way. One of the lepers, a Samaritan and the most active of the ten, went along the same road with two of the disciples, but the others took different routes. These were not cured all at once; although able to walk, they were not made perfectly clean till about an hour afterward.

Soon after this last encounter, a father from a shepherd village a quarter of an hour to the right of the road came to meet Jesus and begged him to go back with him to the village, for his little daughter was lying dead. Jesus went with him at once, and on the way was overtaken by the cured Samaritan who, touched by his perfect cure, had hurried back to thank his benefactor. He cast himself at the feet of Jesus, who said: "Were not ten made clean? And where are the nine? Is not one found among them to return and give glory to God, but only this stranger? Arise, go thy way! Thy faith hath made thee whole!" This man later on became a disciple. Peter, John, and James the Greater were with Jesus at this time. The little girl, who was about seven years old, was already four days dead. Jesus laid one hand on her head, the other on her breast, and raising his eyes to heaven prayed, whereupon the child rose up alive. Then Jesus told the apostles that even so should they do in his name. The child's father had strong faith, and full of confidence he had awaited Jesus's coming. His wife wanted him to send word to Jesus, but he was full of hope and waited until he came. Soon after, he gave up his business to another and, when his wife died after Jesus's death, he became a disciple and acquired a distinguished name. The little girl restored to life likewise became very pious.

Friday, June 13, to Tuesday, June 17, AD 32 (Sivan 15–19)

Jesus [and the three apostles] next visited the shepherd huts that lay scattered far around, and cured many of the sick in them. He went from hut to hut all along the mountainous country in the direction of Hebron.

Wednesday, June 18, AD 32 (Sivan 20)

Today, Jesus went into the mountainous region near Hebron. Here he and Peter attended a wedding celebration in a shepherd's dwelling. Jesus then healed many weak and sickly children.

I saw Jesus alone with Peter in one of these abodes, in which a marriage was being celebrated. The bridal couple returned from the nuptial ceremony, which was performed in the school, escorted by their friends and walking under a kind of canopy. A band of little girls adorned with wreaths of colored wool led the way playing on lutes, and gaily dressed boys with similar instruments brought up the rear of the procession. A priest from Jericho was present. When the party entered the house, they were both surprised and delighted to see Jesus, who bade them not to interrupt the wedding festivities lest some might be vexed at it. The guests then drank out of little glasses. The bride retired with the women, and the children played and danced before her. Then I saw the bridegroom and the bride go to Jesus in a room set apart, where he again joined their hands with his own right and blessed their clasped hands, and gave them an instruction upon the indissolubility of marriage and the merit of continency. After that he reclined at table with Peter and the priest, while the bridegroom waited upon them. The priest, however, was angry that the most honorable places had been given to the stranger guests, Jesus and his apostles, and so he soon withdrew from the entertainment. I saw too that he hunted up some of the Pharisees, who later on unexpectedly attacked the Lord and called him to account. In the heat of their discussion, one of them pulled his mantle from his shoulder, but Jesus remained calm. As they could neither harm him nor gain a victory over him, they withdrew.

Jesus, with more than ordinary love and kindness, tarried awhile in this shepherd dwelling. The bride's parents and some others of the old shepherds who presented themselves before him, belonged to those that had visited him at the crib on the night of his birth. They began at once, in touching terms, to tell all about that night and to honor Jesus, and the younger ones related what they had heard about it from their deceased parents. They brought to Jesus some aged sick who, on account of the feebleness of old age, could no longer walk, also some sick children, and Jesus cured them all. He told the young married couple to go, after his death, to his apostles, to be baptized and instructed, and to become his followers. During the whole journey, I never saw Jesus so bright and cheerful as he was among these simple people. I saw that all who had honored him in his childhood received the grace to become Christians.

Thursday, June 19, AD 32 (Sivan 21)

From this place, Jesus took a more southerly direction into the mountainous district toward Jutta. The wedding guests formed his escort. He had with him now six apostles, including Andrew. On the way he cured a number of sick children who were very much swollen and unable to walk. The people of this region were not very good.

Friday, June 20, AD 32 (Sivan 22)

When Jesus reached a little village among the mountains near Jutta, he went straight to the synagogue to teach. The priests forbade it, and went to call assistance, but they were obliged to resign the teacher's chair to Jesus, to whom the people listened with joy.

Saturday, June 21, AD 32 (Sivan 23)

Today, on the sabbath, Jesus taught again in the village synagogue. He spoke about not being able to serve two masters (Matthew 6:24).

The disciples were eager for Jesus now to turn his steps to Nazareth, his native city, since he was always making allusion to his approaching end. But he was desirous that the good among the people here should profit by the time remaining to him, and so he did not go to Nazareth. He taught upon the words: "No man can serve two masters."

Sunday, June 22, to Tuesday, June 24, AD 32 (Sivan 24–26)

Jesus taught again in the village. He said that he had come to bring a sword (Matthew 10:34–36). The disciples were confused by this utterance, but Jesus explained to them that he meant the renunciation of all evil.

Wednesday, June 25, AD 32 (Sivan 27)

Jesus sent off most of the apostles and disciples. He left the village and went north to Bethain, where he taught under a tree.†

(Follow Map 36)

Jesus on the Way to Bethany • The Raising of Lazarus

Wednesday, July 9, AD 32 (Tammuz 11)

Jesus stayed at a little village in Samaria. His mother, accompanied by her elder sister, Mary Heli, and Mary Heli's daughter, Mary Cleophas, were on their way from Bethany to meet him and urge him to come to Bethany and heal Lazarus.

Thursday, July 10, AD 32 (Tammuz 12)

The three holy women came to Jesus today and told him of Martha and Mary Magdalene's request that he come to Bethany, as Lazarus lay seriously ill (John 11:6).

† Owing to great suffering, at this point Anne Catherine was unable to communicate anything for thirteen days. During this time it is possible that Jesus journeyed northward to Capernaum and was returning back through Samaria when Anne Catherine resumed her account. At first, she was able to communicate only fragments from the period we are now entering that leads up to the raising of Lazarus.

Friday, July 11, to Saturday, July 12, AD 32 (Tammuz 13–14)

Having talked with Jesus, the three holy women decided to stay in the little village to celebrate the sabbath there. Jesus himself went to another place with a large synagogue. Here he taught and healed and blessed some children.

Sunday, July 13, to Tuesday, July 15, AD 32 (Tammuz 15–17)

During these days Jesus taught concerning the good Samaritan (Luke 10:30–37) and the lost coin (Luke 15:8–10). He also healed the sick and blessed many children.

Wednesday, July 16, AD 32 (Tammuz 18)

Jesus, accompanied by some apostles, returned to the little village where the three holy women were waiting for him. Together they received the news of Lazarus's death. It was here that Jesus spoke the words: "Our friend Lazarus has fallen asleep" (John 11:7–13).

Thursday, July 17, AD 32 (Tammuz 19)

Toward evening, Jesus, accompanied by the three holy women and the apostles, set off for Bethany. They traveled that night by moonlight to Lazarus' country estate near Ginea. Here Martha and Mary Magdalene were waiting for him.

As Jesus had been tarrying in a little place near Samaria where too the blessed Virgin and Mary Cleophas were come to spend the sabbath, they had received the news of Lazarus's death. After this event, which happened in Bethany, his sisters left that place and went to their country house near Ginea, with the intention of there meeting Jesus and the blessed Virgin.

Friday, July 18, AD 32 (Tammuz 20)

The holy women stayed at Lazarus's estate. Jesus and the apostles went to Ginea for the sabbath. Jesus taught in the synagogue.

The remains of Lazarus were embalmed and swathed in linen bands, according to the Jewish custom, and then laid in a coffin of woven rods with a convex cover. All the apostles were again united around Jesus. They went in several bands to Ginea, where Jesus taught in the synagogue.

Saturday, July 19, AD 32 (Tammuz 21)

After the close of the sabbath, Jesus and the apostles returned to Lazarus's estate. Mary Magdalene came to meet Jesus on the way. She lamented over the death of Lazarus, saying that if Jesus had been there he would not have died. Jesus replied that his time had not yet come. They then ate at Lazarus's estate and Jesus

Map 36: The Raising of Lazarus
Beginning of July–August 6, AD 32

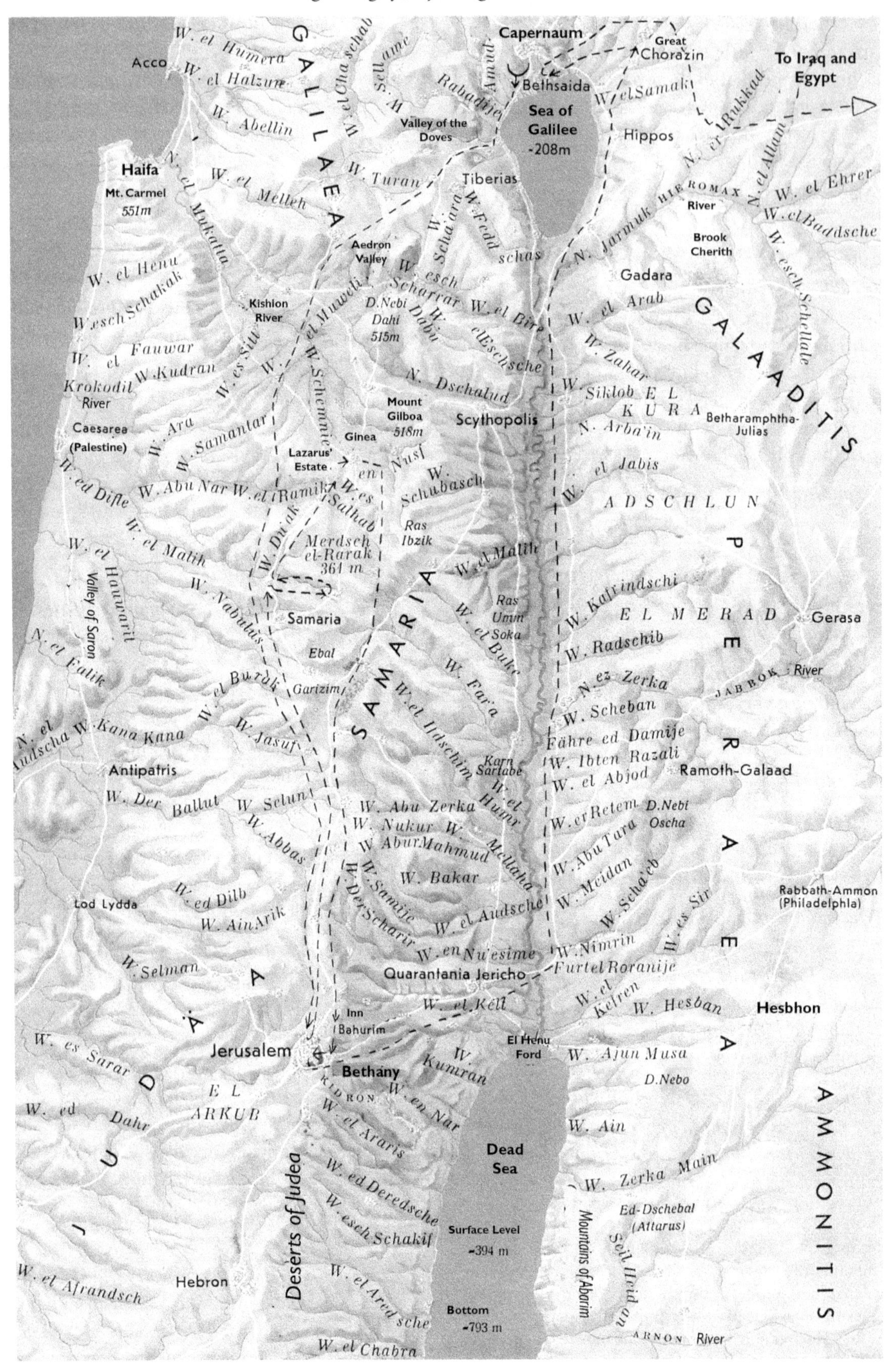

Capernaum—Jerusalem—Places near Samaria—Ginea—Lazarus's Estate near Ginea
Ginea—Inn near Bahurim—Bethany—Jerusalem—Stretch of Land in Perea
Great Chorazin—Bethsaida—In the Direction of Iraq

taught. He asked Martha and Mary Magdalene to allow all of Lazarus's effects to stay in Bethany, saying that he would come there in a few days. It was now that he told the apostles that Lazarus was dead (John 11:14–16).

After the closing exercises of the sabbath, Jesus and the apostles went out to Lazarus's country house. There they found the blessed Virgin, who had gone on before. Magdalene came to meet Jesus and to tell him of her brother's death, adding the words: "Lord, if thou hadst been here, my brother had not died!" Jesus replied that his time was not yet come and that it was well that he had died. Still he told the two sisters to allow all the effects of their brother to remain at Bethany, for that he himself would go there shortly.

Sunday, July 20, AD 32 (Tammuz 22)

This morning, the holy women set off back to Bethany. Jesus and the apostles returned to Ginea.

The holy women, therefore, set out for Bethany, while Jesus and the apostles returned to Ginea, from which they went to the inn one hour distant from Bethany. Here another messenger came to him bearing the earnest request of the sisters that he should repair to Bethany, but he still delayed to go.

Monday, July 21, AD 32 (Tammuz 23)

Today, Jesus and the apostles journeyed towards Bethany.

Tuesday, July 22, AD 32 (Tammuz 24)

Toward evening they reached the inn of a little place near Bahurim. Here Jesus taught concerning the laborers in the vineyard (Matthew 20:1–16). Mary Salome, the mother of James and John, approached him to request that her two sons be allowed to take a place beside him in his kingdom (Matthew 20:20–21).

Wednesday, July 23, AD 32 (Tammuz 25)

Jesus rebuked the disciples for their murmuring and impatience at his delaying so long to go to Bethany. He was always like one who could not give an account of his views and actions to them, because they did not understand him. In his instructions to them he was always more desirous of discovering to them their own thoughts and, on account of their earthly-mindedness, of arousing in them distrust of self than of informing them of the reasons of things that they could not comprehend.

Thursday, July 24, AD 32 (Tammuz 26)

In this little place near Bahurim there were Pharisees who reported back to Jerusalem concerning Jesus. Mary Salome again approached Jesus on account of her two sons, James and John, but he rebuked her sternly.

He still taught upon the laborers in the vineyard, and when the mother of James and John heard him speak of the near fulfillment of his mission, she thought it only proper that his own relatives should have honorable posts in his kingdom. She consequently approached him with a petition to that effect, but he sternly rebuked her.

Friday, July 25, AD 32 (Tammuz 27)

Jesus and the apostles made their way to Bethany. As he walked, Jesus taught. Mary Salome went on ahead, arriving in Bethany toward evening. She went first to Martha to tell her that Jesus was approaching. Mary Magdalene went with Mary Salome to greet him, but she returned without having spoken to him. Then Martha went to meet him. In the exchange that took place between Martha and Jesus, Jesus spoke the words: "I am the resurrection and the life" (John 11:17–27). It was dusk. Martha hurried back and spoke with Mary Magdalene, who went up to Jesus, casting herself at his feet and saying: "Lord, if you had been here, my brother would not have died." Jesus wept (John 11:28–37). Jesus then taught about death late into the night.

At last Jesus turned his steps to Bethany, continuing all along the way his instructions to the apostles. Lazarus's estate stood partly within the walls surrounding the environs of the city, and partly—that is, a portion of the garden and courtyard—outside those walls, which were now going to ruin.

Lazarus was eight days dead. They had kept him four days in the hope that Jesus would come and raise him to life. His sisters, as I have said, went to the country house near Ginea, to meet Jesus; but when they found that he was still resolved not to go back with them, they had returned to Bethany and buried their brother. Their friends, men and women from the city and from Jerusalem, were now gathered around them, lamenting the dead as was the custom. It seems to me that it was toward evening when Mary Zebedeus went in to Martha, who was sitting among the women, and said to her softly that the Lord was coming. Martha arose and went out with her into the garden back of the house. There in an arbor was Magdalene sitting alone. Martha told her that Jesus was near, for through love for Magdalene, she wanted her to be the first to meet the Lord. But I did not see Magdalene go to Jesus, for when he was alone with the apostles and disciples he did not allow women easy access to him. It was already growing dusk when Magdalene went back to the women and took Martha's place, who then went out to meet Jesus. He was standing with the apostles and some others on the confines of their garden before an open arbor. Martha spoke to Jesus and then turned back to Magdalene, who also by this time had come up. She threw herself at Jesus's feet, saying: "If thou hadst been here, he would not have died!" All present were in tears. Jesus too mourned and wept,[F10] and delivered a discourse of great length upon death. Many of the audience, which was constantly increasing outside the bower, whispered to one another and murmured their dissatisfaction at Jesus's not having kept Lazarus alive.

Saturday, July 26, AD 32 (Tammuz 28)

In the early hours of the morning, Jesus went to Lazarus's grave. He was accompanied by the apostles, seven holy women, and many other people. He went into the vault where Lazarus's tomb was. Lazarus had been dead for several days, and his corpse had lain for some days before being entombed, for it had been hoped that Jesus would come and wake him from the dead. As Jesus instructed the apostles to remove the stone from the grave, Martha said: "Lord, by this time there will be an odor, for he has been buried for four days." There then took place the raising of Lazarus from the dead, as described in John 11:38–44. After the cloths and winding-sheet had been removed, Lazarus climbed out of his coffin and came out from the tomb. He tottered on his feet and looked like a phantom. He went past Jesus through the door of the vault. His sisters and the other holy women stepped back, as if he were a ghost. Jesus followed him from the vault into the open air, went up to him, and took hold of both his hands in a gesture of friendship. A great crowd of people, who beheld Lazarus in fear and wonder, thronged around. Jesus walked with Lazarus to his house. The apostles and the holy women went with them. A great tumult arose among the crowd. Inside the house, the women went to prepare a meal, leaving Jesus and the apostles alone with Lazarus. The apostles formed a circle around Jesus and Lazarus. Lazarus kneeled before Jesus, who blessed him, laying his right hand on Lazarus' head and breathing upon him seven times. Thus, he consecrated Lazarus to his service, purifying him of all earthly connections and infusing him with the seven gifts of the Holy Spirit, which the apostles would receive only later, at Whitsun. Afterward, all dined together. Jesus taught, and Lazarus sat next to him. Because there was a great commotion outside, Jesus sent the apostles to disperse the crowd. He continued to teach that evening.

It seems to me that it was very early in the morning when Jesus went with the apostles to the tomb. Mary, Lazarus's sisters, and others, in all about seven women, were likewise there, as also a crowd of people which was constantly on the increase. Indeed, the throng presented somewhat the appearance of a tumult, as upon the day of Christ's crucifixion. They proceeded along a road upon either side of which was a thick, green hedge, then passed through a gate, after which about a quarter of an hour's distance brought them to the walled-in cemetery of Bethany. From the gate of the cemetery a road led right and left around a hill through which ran a vault. The latter was divided by railings into compartments, and the opening at the end

A Tomb of the Time

was closed by a grate. One could, from the entrance, see through the whole length of the vault and the green branches of the trees waving outside the opposite end. Light was admitted from openings above.

Lazarus's tomb was the first on the right of the entrance to the vault, down into which some steps led. It was a four-cornered, oblong cave, about three feet in depth, and covered with a flat stone. In it lay the corpse in a lightly woven coffin, and around it in the tomb there was room for one to walk. Jesus with some of the apostles went down into the vault, while the holy women, Magdalene, and Martha remained standing in the doorway. But the crowd pressed around so that many people climbed up on the roof of the vault and the cemetery walls in order to see. Jesus commanded the apostles to raise the stone from the grave.

They did so, rested it against the wall, and then removed a light cover or door that closed the tomb below that stone. It was at this point of the proceedings that Martha said: "Lord, by this time he stinketh, for he is now of four days." After that they took the lightly woven cover from the coffin, and disclosed the corpse lying in its winding sheet. At that instant Jesus raised his eyes to heaven, prayed aloud, and called out in a strong voice: "Lazarus, come forth!" At this cry, the corpse arose to a sitting posture. [F11] The crowd now pressed with so much violence that Jesus ordered them to be driven outside the walls of the cemetery. The apostles, who were standing in the tomb by the coffin, removed the handkerchief from Lazarus's face, unbound his hands and feet, and drew off the winding sheet. Lazarus, as if waking from lethargy, rose from the coffin and stepped out of the grave, tottering and looking like a phantom. The apostles threw a mantle around him. Like one walking in sleep, he approached the door, passed the Lord and went out to where his sisters and the other women had stepped back in fright as before a ghost.

Without daring to touch him, they fell prostrate on the ground. At the same instant, Jesus stepped after him out of the vault and seized him by both hands, his whole manner full of loving earnestness.

And now all moved on toward Lazarus's house. The throng was great. But a certain fear prevailed among the people; consequently the procession formed by Lazarus and his friends was not impeded in its movements by the crowd that followed. Lazarus moved along more like one floating than walking, and he still had all the appearance of a corpse. Jesus walked by his side, and the rest of the party followed sobbing and weeping around them in silent, frightened amazement. They reached the old gate, and went along the road bordered by verdant hedges to the avenue of trees from which they had started. The Lord entered it with Lazarus and his followers, while the crowd thronged outside, clamoring and shouting.

At this moment Lazarus threw himself prostrate on the earth before Jesus, like one about to be received into a religious order. Jesus spoke some words, and then they went on to the house, about a hundred paces distant.

Jesus, the apostles, and Lazarus were alone in the dining hall. The apostles formed a circle around Jesus and Lazarus, who was kneeling before the Lord. Jesus laid his right hand on his head and breathed upon him seven times. The Lord's breath was luminous. I saw a dark vapor withdrawing as it were from Lazarus, and the devil under the form of a black winged figure, impotent and wrathful, clearing the circle backward and mounting on high. By this ceremony, Jesus consecrated Lazarus to his service, purified him from all connection with the world and sin, and strengthened him with the gifts of the Holy Spirit. He made him a long address in which he told him that he had raised him to life that he might serve him, and that he would have to endure great persecution on the part of the Jews.

Up to this time, Lazarus was in his grave clothes, but now he retired to lay them aside and put on his own garments. It was at this moment that his sisters and friends embraced him for the first time, for before this there was something so corpse-like about him that it inspired terror. I saw meanwhile that Lazarus's soul, during the time of its separation from his body, was in a place peaceful and painless, lighted by only a glimmering twilight, and that while there he related to the just, Joseph, Joachim, Anne, Zechariah, John, etc., how things were going with the Redeemer on earth.

By the Savior's breathing upon him, Lazarus received the seven gifts of the Holy Spirit and was perfectly freed from connection with earthly things. He received those gifts before the apostles, for he had by his death become acquainted with great mysteries, had gazed upon another world. He had actually been dead, and he was now born again. He could therefore receive those gifts. Lazarus comprises in himself a deep significance and a profound mystery.

And now a meal was ready, and all reclined at table, upon which were many dishes and little jugs. A man served. After the meal the women entered, but remained at the lower end of the hall, to hear the teachings of Jesus. Lazarus was sitting next to him. There was a frightful noise around the house, for many had come out from Jerusalem, even the guards, and were now besetting the house. But Jesus sent the apostles out to drive off both people and guards. Jesus continued his instruction till after lamplight, and told the disciples that he was going next morning with two apostles to Jerusalem. When they placed before him the danger attending such a step, he replied that he would not be recognized, that he would not go openly. I saw them afterward taking a little sleep, leaning around against the wall.

Sunday, July 27, AD 32 (Tammuz 29)

Before daybreak, Jesus, accompanied by John and Matthew, went to Jerusalem to the house on Mount Zion where later the Last Supper would take place. This house belonged to Nicodemus. Jesus remained there for the whole day and that night. Mary Mark, Veronica, and about a dozen other friends came to visit him. He taught and consoled them. Meanwhile, a meeting of the Pharisees and high priests was being held to discuss the raising of Lazarus by Jesus. The Pharisees feared that Jesus might awaken all the dead and that this would lead to great confusion. In Bethany, a great tumult arose. Lazarus was forced to hide and the ten apostles left.

Before daybreak Jesus, accompanied by John and Matthew, who had girded up their garments somewhat differently from their usual custom, started from Bethany for Jerusalem. They went around the city and, taking byroads, reached the house in which later on the Last Supper was celebrated. There they remained quietly the whole day and the next night, Jesus instructing and confirming his friends of the city. I saw Mary Mark and Veronica in the house, and fully a dozen men. Nicodemus, to whom the house belonged, but who had gladly resigned it for the use of Jesus's friends, was not there. He had on that very day gone to Bethany to see Lazarus.

I saw also a gathering of Pharisees and high priests who had come together to discuss Jesus and Lazarus.[F12] Among other things I heard them say that they feared Jesus would raise all the dead, and then what confusion would ensue!

At noon on that day, a great tumult arose in Bethany. If Jesus had been there, they would have stoned him. Lazarus was obliged to hide, and the apostles, to slip away in different directions. All the other friends of Jesus in Bethany were likewise forced to lie in concealment. Minds became calm, however, when people took into consideration that they had no right to take action against Lazarus.

AB (30 days): July 27/28 to August 25/26, AD 32
Ab New Moon: July 26 at 5:00 AM Jerusalem time

Monday, July 28, AD 32 (Ab 1)

Jesus passed the whole night till early next morning in the house on Mount Zion. Before day he left Jerusalem with Matthew and John and fled across the Jordan, not by the route he had formerly taken on the side of Bethabara, but by another off to the northeast. It may have been toward noon when he reached the opposite shore of the Jordan. That evening the [six] apostles from Bethany joined him, and they spent the night under a great tree.

Tuesday, July 29, AD 32 (Ab 2)

Traveling on, Jesus healed a blind man, a shepherd from the region of Jericho, who immediately wanted to become a disciple. Reaching a small village, Jesus taught in a hall.

In the morning they started for a little village in the neighborhood, and on their way found a blind man lying on the roadside. He was in charge of two boys, who were not, however, related to him. He was a shepherd from the region of Jericho. He had heard from the apostles that the Lord was coming that way, and he was now crying out to him for a cure. Jesus laid his hand on his head, and the man received his sight. Then he cast off his old rags and, in his undergarment, followed Jesus to the village, where in a hall Jesus taught of following him. He said that they who wanted to do so must, as the blind man did his rags, leave all, to follow him with full use of their sight. A mantle was given to the man cured of blindness. He wanted to join Jesus at once, but he was put off till he should prove his constancy. Jesus taught here until nearly evening. There were about eight apostles with him.

Wednesday, July 30, AD 32 (Ab 3)

On the way toward a small town, Jesus passed by a fig tree that had no figs on it and cursed it, just as he did later on the way to Jerusalem on Adar 29, after his triumphant entry into Jerusalem (Matthew 21:18–20). Reaching the town, Jesus taught in the synagogue and spoke of the significance of the barren fig tree (Luke 13:6–9).

After that, as he drew near a little city, Jesus was hungry. I could not help smiling at the thought of his being hungry, for Jesus's hunger was very different from that of others. He was hungering after souls. From the last place that he had visited, some people who had not the right dispositions went with him. On the roadside stood a fig tree that bore no fruit. Jesus went up to the tree and cursed it. It withered on the instant, its leaves turning yellow, and the trunk becoming crooked. Jesus taught in the school upon the sterile fig tree. There were some malevolent doctors and Pharisees who invited Jesus to take his departure. A little stream spanned by a bridge ran by this place into the Jordan. The school was built on an eminence. Jesus and his party spent the night at an inn.

Jesus Begins His Journey into the Land of the Three Holy Kings

Thursday, July 31, AD 32 (Ab 4)

Jesus and his traveling companions made their way northward through Perea. He began to instruct the disciples regarding what they should do when he would be away. That night, Jesus stayed with some shepherds.

NEXT day, when Jesus and his companions left that last place, they took a northeasterly direction through the land of the tribe of Gad. I heard Jesus saying whither he was now about to journey. He told the apostles and disciples that they should separate from him, designated to them where they should and where they should not teach, and where they should again join him. He was now, he said, about to make an extraordinary journey. He would spend the next sabbath in Great Chorazin, then go to Bethsaida, and from there to the south into the region of Machaerus and Midian. Thence he would proceed to where Hagar had exposed Ishmael, and Jacob had set up the stone. Then he would journey to the east around the Dead Sea and on to the place upon which Melchizedek had offered sacrifice before Abraham. On this site there stands today a chapel, in which divine Service is sometimes celebrated. It is built of red stone, and overgrown with moss. Jesus declared his intention of going likewise to Heliopolis in Egypt, where he had once dwelt in childhood. There were some good people there who as children had played with him, and who had not entirely forgotten him. They were constantly asking what had become of him, but they could not believe that he of whom they heard so much was the child of their remembrance. He would return from the other side through Hebron and the valley of Jehosaphat, pass the place at which he had been baptized by John, and through the desert in which he had been tempted. He announced that his absence would be for about three months, and that his followers would be sure to find him at the end of that time at Jacob's well near Sichar, though they might meet him before that, when he would be returning through Judea. He gave them minute instructions in a long discourse, above all as to how they should during his absence conduct themselves in their missionary duties. I remember these words, that wherever they were not well received, they should shake the dust from their shoes. Matthew returned home for awhile. He was a married man. His wife was a very virtuous person and, since Matthew's vocation, they had lived in perfect continency. He was to teach in his own home, and quietly put up with the contempt of his former associates.

Friday, August 1, AD 32 (Ab 5)

Jesus wanted to hold the sabbath in the town of Great Chorazin. He dismissed most of the apostles. Then, around noon, he went into the town, accompanied by Andrew, Peter, and Philip. He taught in the synagogue.

Saturday, August 2, AD 32 (Ab 6)

This morning, Jesus taught again in the synagogue. About midday, a man from Capernaum came to him, begging him to come and heal his son, who was dangerously ill. Jesus told him to return to Capernaum where he would find that his son was well. After healing the boy from a distance, Jesus then healed many other sick people. Later, following the close of sabbath, Jesus and the apostles left the town. They crossed the Jordan on a raft formed of beams strung together. They then traveled by moonlight to Bethsaida. Here they went to Andrew's house.

Toward noon a man from Capernaum, who had been waiting for Jesus, approached him. His son, he said, was sick unto death, and he implored the Lord to go with him and cure him. But Jesus commanded him to return home, for his son was already restored to health. There were many others gathered around Jesus, some belonging to the city, and others from a distance. Some were sick and looking for a cure, others were in search of consolation. He satisfied some at once, but to others he held out the promise of future assistance.

On the evening of that sabbath, Jesus took leave of the inhabitants outside the synagogue and proceeded with several of the apostles up to where the Jordan empties into the sea, in order to cross to the other side. The ferry was higher up, and that made the journey much longer. Here they crossed on a kind of raft formed of beams laid one over another like a grating. In the center, on a raised platform, was an enclosure, like a little half-tub into which the water could not penetrate, and there the baggage of the passengers was deposited. The raft was propelled by means of long poles. The shore of the Jordan was not very high in this place, and it seems to me there were some little islands lying around in this part of the river. I saw the Lord and the three apostles traveling by moonlight. Outside of Bethsaida, as was customary at the entrance to the cities of Palestine, stood a long shed under which travelers used to ungird their garments and brush off the dust of travel before entering the city; generally some people were to be found there to wash their feet. This was the case on the arrival of the Lord and the apostles, after which they repaired to Andrew's, where they partook of a meal of honey, rolls, and grapes. Andrew was married, and his house was by no means a small one. It had a courtyard, was surrounded by walls, and was situated at one side of the city. Peter and Philip accompanied the Lord, but Andrew went on ahead. There were in all twelve men present at the meal, and at the end of it, six women came in to hear Jesus's teaching.

Sunday, August 3, AD 32 (Ab 7)

Today, Jesus visited another house in Bethsaida. Here some of the holy women had gathered. Later, Jesus and the three apostles left Bethsaida and went to a house north of the town. Here he taught a group of disciples. Then Jesus, accompanied by Andrew, Peter and Philip, traveled further, crossing back across the Jordan.

Next day, as he was leaving Bethsaida with the three apostles, he paused for awhile in a house outside the city in which were all kinds of goods and chattels peculiar to fishing. A great many men were assembled there, and Jesus gave them an instruction.

Monday, August 4, AD 32 (Ab 8)

Setting out at last, Jesus and the three apostles journeyed up the shore of the Jordan, crossed the bridge far above the ferry just mentioned, and journeyed for the whole day and night through the region known as Basan, east of the Sea of Galilee.

Tuesday, August 5, AD 32 (Ab 9)

At around five this morning, after having slept apart, Jesus and the three apostles met at a prearranged place. They then journeyed on together. As they went, Jesus taught. In the evening, they stopped at an inn, where Jesus told them of his plans for the coming journey. He said that only three disciples would accompany him: Eliud, Silas, and Eremenzear. These were three shepherd youths, sixteen, seventeen, or eighteen years of age. Jesus told the others to meet him, on his return, at Jacob's well near Shechem. He indicated when this would be (Tebeth 22). In the intervening period, the disciples were to continue their work.

I saw in a region beyond the Jordan a district covered with white sand and tiny white pebbles, several disciples in an open shepherd shed awaiting the Lord's coming. They had brought with them three youths, tall and slim. While awaiting Jesus, the disciples had gathered yellow and green berries as large as figs, also little yellow apples that grew some on bushes, others on trees, from which they broke them off with chopping sticks. The road by which Jesus and the three apostles came appeared to be not much frequented, for it was overgrown with long grass, and extended under an avenue of spreading fruit trees whose branches interlaced overhead. The apostles broke off some of the fruit and put it into their pockets, but Jesus took none. He had traveled all night through mountainous districts. The disciples who had been awaiting his coming now went forward to meet him. They pressed around him with words of salutation, but without offering their hands. In front of the shed lay a long, broad, four-cornered log, around which Jesus and the others threw themselves in a reclining posture as at table, and before each was placed a portion of the fruit just gathered. They had brought with them also little jugs containing some kind of beverage. Off in the distance lay a city and behind it rose a mountain chain. I think this region was in the land of the Amorites. From this place the road again took a downward direction. I saw Jesus and his companions journeying the whole day and, in the evening, arriving at a little scattered village. On the roadside stood an inn. The travelers entered and were soon surrounded by a crowd of inquisitive people. They had not heard much of Jesus, but they were for the most part good and simple-hearted. Jesus related to them the parable of the good shepherd, and then traveled on a short distance to another inn, at which he and his followers ate and slept. The Lord told the latter that he intended to go alone with the three youths through Chaldea and the land of Ur, Abraham's birthplace, and thence through Arabia to Egypt. The disciples should scatter here throughout the district and instruct the inhabitants; as for himself, he added, he would teach wherever he went. In fine he again told them that, at the end of three months, they would meet at the well of Jacob near Shechem. I saw Simeon, Cleophas, and Saturnin among the disciples.

(Follow Map 37)

Wednesday, August 6, AD 32 (Ab 10)

At daybreak, Jesus and the three shepherd youths parted company with the apostles and disciples, who were saddened by the departure. Andrew, Peter, and Philip returned to their homes. The remaining disciples split up and went in various directions. Jesus and his traveling companions meanwhile journeyed eastward, Jesus teaching as they went. That night, they stayed at a house. Jesus did not say who he was and was taken to be a traveling shepherd. He taught in parables but did not heal anyone.

At dawn of day Jesus bade farewell to the apostles and disciples, to each of whom he extended his hand. They were very much troubled at his taking with him only the three youths. These youths were from sixteen to eighteen years old and very different from the Jews. They were more slender and active, and wore long garments. They were like children to Jesus, whom they waited on most affectionately. Whenever they came to water, they washed his feet. They ran off on the road here and there, and came back with little rods, flowers, fruits, and berries. Jesus instructed them most lovingly and explained to them in parables all that had happened up to that time.

The parents of these youths belonged to the family of Mensor. They had come to Palestine with the caravan of the three kings and, at the departure of the same for home, had remained behind among the shepherds in the Valley of the Shepherds. They became Jews, married the daughters of the shepherds, and came into possession of meadowlands between Samaria and Jericho. The youngest of the youths was named Eremenzear and later on was called Hermas. He was the boy whom Jesus, at the prayer of his mother, had cured in the region of Shechem, after his interview with the Samaritan at Jacob's well. The next one was Sela, or Silas; and the eldest, Eliud, received in baptism the name of Siricius. They were called, also, the secret disciples, and at a later period they were associated with

Map 37: The Journey to the Kings, to Ur, and to Heliopolis
August 7, AD 32–January 7, AD 33

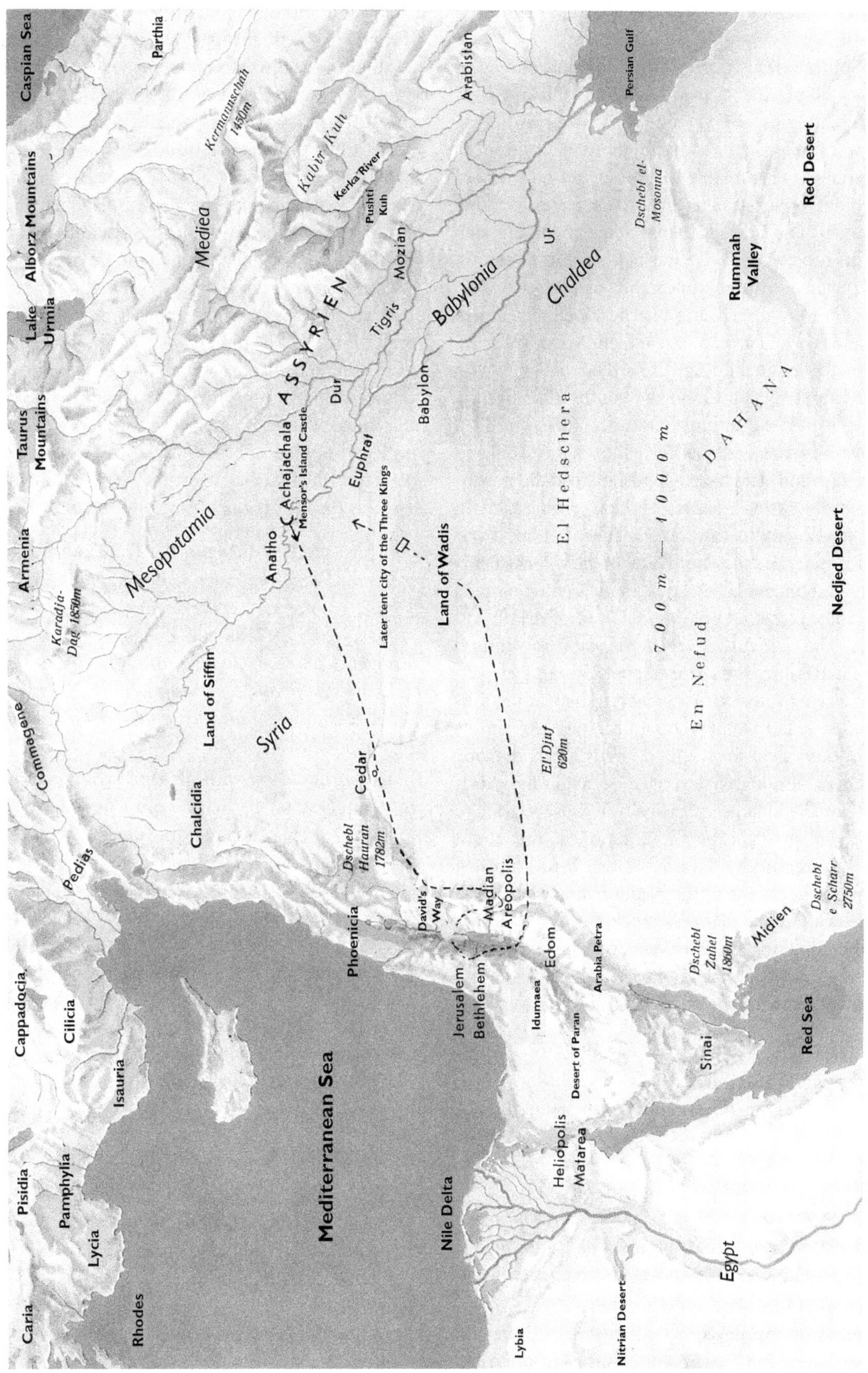

Kedar—Tent City of the Kings—Mozian—Ur—Heliopolis—Beersheba

Thomas, John, and Paul. Eremenzear wrote an account of this journey.

On this journey, Jesus wore a brownish tunic, knitted or woven, that fell around him in folds long and full; over that he had a long garment of fine white wool with wide sleeves. It was fastened at the waist by a broad girdle of the same material as the scarf that he wound around his head when sleeping. Jesus was taller than the apostles. Walking or standing, his fair, grave face rose above them. His step was firm, his bearing erect. He was neither thin nor stout, but nobly formed with an appearance of perfect health. His shoulders were broad, and his chest well developed. Exercise and traveling had strengthened his muscles, although they presented no sign of hard labor.

The road taken by Jesus and the youths after parting from the apostles was a constantly ascending one in a direction toward the east, over a white, sandy soil and through cedars and date trees. Opposite arose the mountains of Gilead. Jesus wanted to spend the coming sabbath in the last Jewish city met in this direction. I think it was called Kedar. Jesus and the youths ate on the way the fruits of the trees and berries. The youths carried pouches filled with little rolls, jugs containing some kind of drink, and staves. The Lord sometimes broke off a staff for himself from a tree in passing, and again cast it aside. His feet, otherwise bare, were protected by sandals. In the evening they went to some solitary house occupied by rude, simple people, and there slept for the night. Jesus nowhere made himself known, although he everywhere taught in beautiful parables of all kinds, but principally in those relating to the good shepherd. The people questioned him about Jesus of Nazareth, but he did not tell that it was himself. He in turn put questions to them concerning their work, their business affairs, so that they concluded he was a traveling shepherd looking around after good pasture lands, as was often the case in Jewish countries. I did not see him effect any cure nor work any miracle in these parts.

Thursday, August 7, AD 32 (Ab 11)

This morning, Jesus traveled on in a southeasterly direction. He and the three young shepherds stayed the night with some shepherds they met on the way. Anne Catherine tells that there had been a great uproar in Jerusalem about the raising of Lazarus and that Jesus had left Judea in order to be forgotten. This journey outside of Palestine, accompanied by only the three shepherd youths, was not recorded, as no apostle was present, and no one really knew where he was.

Next morning he journeyed on. He may now have still been some miles from Kedar, which was built on rising ground, the mountain chain behind it. Abraham's fatherland was in this direction, but far off toward the northeast; the land of the three kings was toward the southeast.

Some of the disciples had returned to their homes, while others had scattered around the country teaching. Zacchaeus of Jericho accompanied them awhile, after which he returned home, gave up his business, sold all that he had, bestowed the proceeds upon the poor, and went with his wife (with whom he henceforth lived in continency) to another place. The Lord told the disciples that nine weeks would pass before they should join him again.

The excitement in Jerusalem on account of Lazarus was very great. Jesus absented himself during it, that people might lose sight of him, while the conviction of the truth of this miracle disposed many to conversion. When Jesus returned he was very thin. There is no written account of this journey, since no apostle accompanied the Lord on it; perhaps too the apostles did not even know of all the places in which he had been. As well as I remember, I then saw this road for the first time.

Friday, August 8, AD 32 (Ab 12)

Today, before the onset of the sabbath, Jesus and the three youths reached the town of Kedar, one of the last towns east of Palestine where there was a Jewish settlement. Kedar was divided into a pagan and a Jewish quarter. Jesus and the youths went to the synagogue for the celebration of the sabbath. There, Jesus was held to be a prophet.

Jesus journeyed on with his three young companions to the southeast, taking byways most frequently, and spending the night, like the preceding one among the shepherds, in a solitary house. The people of these parts were good and artless. They gazed at Jesus in wonder, and loved him at once. He related to them many of the parables he was accustomed to use in Judea, and to them they listened with delight. But he neither healed nor blessed. When they asked him about Jesus of Nazareth, he answered by telling them about those that had quitted all to follow him, and then passed to parables that explained what he had said. The people thought he was a shepherd looking around for herds or meadows.

Jesus in Kedar

JESUS AND THE YOUTHS reached Kedar before the sabbath. They had not traveled by the highroad, but by roundabout ways. As it was too late to enter the city, they passed the night at a large public inn at which other wayfarers had sought shelter. There were open sheds with sleeping accommodations in the enclosure, and the whole was surrounded by a courtyard. A man, the one that superintended the establishment, unlocked the inn, after which he returned to the city. Next morning, he came out again to the inn, and then received a small sum for his services. The travelers went their several ways, but the superintendent took Jesus and his companions back with him to his own house in the city. Kedar was situated at the foot of a mountain, in a valley through which flowed a river. It consisted of an old and a new city separated by the little river, which flowed from the east and off toward Palestine. The shore was very steep, and the river was spanned by two arches very solidly built. On this side the place was poor and insignificant, and inhabited principally by Jewish shepherds who likewise engaged in the manufacture of light huts, and shepherd and stable utensils. On the opposite side Kedar presented a more opulent appearance. There were no Jews there, but only pagans. The Jewish costume was somewhat modified here, for some of the people wore a pointed cap. In the city this side of the river, there was a synagogue, and upon a square surrounded by grass plots and walks of clean white sand, played a fountain. This was the most beautiful spot in the city.

Through the Cedars on the Mountain

The Lord and the boys went with their host to the synagogue, and quietly celebrated the sabbath. At the end of the prayers, Jesus asked whether he might venture to relate something to them, and when the good people showed their willingness to listen, he recounted the parable of the prodigal son. They listened attentively, admired him greatly, but knew not who he was. He called himself a shepherd seeking the lost lambs in order to lead them into good pasture. They regarded him as a prophet and, during the rest of the day, conducted him to their houses where too he taught.

Saturday, August 9, and Sunday, August 10, AD 32 (Ab 13–14)

Jesus taught in Kedar, where he was invited to various homes. He also taught in the open by the town well.

The next day he gave an instruction at the fountain. The men and women sat at his feet, and he pressed the children to his breast. He told them about Zacchaeus climbing up the fig tree, of his leaving all and following him; of him who in the temple had said: "I thank God that I am not like the publican"; and lastly, of that other who, striking his breast, said: "Lord, be merciful to me, a poor sinner!" The inhabitants of Kedar became very fond of Jesus and thought no harm of him. They begged him to stay with them till the next sabbath and then teach again in their school, and when they asked him about Jesus of Nazareth, he related to them many things of him and his doctrine.

Monday, August 11, AD 32 (Ab 15)

This morning, Jesus was still in Kedar. The people had asked him to remain until the next sabbath and to teach in the synagogue. That evening, he went to a little village east of Kedar to which he had been invited. He stayed there overnight.

Tuesday, August 12, AD 32 (Ab 16)

This evening, he returned to Kedar.

Wednesday, August 13, AD 32 (Ab 17)

Today, Jesus and the three youths journeyed eastward to Edon. On the way, Jesus healed a bedridden married couple in their home. The couple then followed Jesus to Edon.

On leaving this place, Jesus and his traveling companions proceeded eastward from Kedar into a country of beautiful meadowlands and palm trees, and thence to Edon. On the way, he visited a house that stood off by itself, and in which both the father and mother of the family had long been bedridden with incurable maladies. Several children were going and coming around the house. All were good. Here also they asked him about Jesus of Nazareth, of whom they had heard diverse reports. Jesus answered them in a beautiful parable of a king and his son, in which he spoke of the one of whom they inquired. He told them that he would be persecuted, and that he would return to his Father's kingdom, which he would share with all those that had followed him. As Jesus spoke I had a vision of his Passion, his Ascension, his throne surrounded by all the angels and set next his Father's, meaning his dominion over the world; and, lastly, I saw the reward portioned out to his followers. I saw likewise the vision of his kingdom and the whole parable that he was relating to the people, and I saw too that he impressed upon their hearts a lasting picture of it. When he asked them whether they believed all he had told them and whether they would follow the good king, and they had protested their belief and their willingness, he promised the two old people that God would reward them by curing them and allowing them to follow him to Edon. And all of a sudden, they were restored to health and, to the astonishment of the beholders, were indeed able to follow Jesus to Edon. The man's name was Benjamin, and he was a direct descendant from Ruth. I think that Titus was either a son or a relative of this couple so suddenly cured. He was at that time between fourteen to sixteen years old. He went to Kedar and to every other place in this region in which Jesus taught, in order to hear him and to listen to others talking about him. Mark, whose birthplace was nearer Judea, was acquainted with this family, and so too was Silas.

Thursday, August 14, AD 32 (Ab 18)

This afternoon, Jesus and his traveling companions reached Edon. They went to a wedding celebration to which Jesus had been invited. It was in progress when they arrived. News of Jesus had spread from Kedar and he was received as a prophet. At the wedding feast, Jesus taught, telling of a man who had changed water into wine at a wedding in Cana. The celebration lasted late into the night.

Jesus and the three youths, on leaving that house, went on to Edon through lovely fields and meadows shaded by palm trees. Jesus carried a shepherd's crook in his right hand. In the public feast house, on a large, open square to the left of the entrance to the city, a marriage was being celebrated. The house contained a large hall, at the end of which was the kitchen. All around it were sleeping apartments, in each of which there were three beds that could be separated from one another by an ornamented screen. Although it was clear daylight, a lamp was burning in the hall. The guests, male and female, as also the bride and bridegroom, adorned with flowery wreaths, were all assembled in the same apartment. Boys were singing and playing upon flutes and other instruments. These pious people were awaiting Jesus, whom they looked upon as a prophet. They had heard of his teaching and parables in Kedar and the surrounding district, and had in consequence invited him to their wedding. They received him joyfully and reverently, washed his feet and those of his young companions, and dried them with their own garments. They took from Jesus his staff, placed it in a corner, and prepared for him a table. On it were some little rolls, a honeycomb almost a foot in length, and some red berries from the top of which they detached before eating a little circle of black leaves tipped with white. There were, too, little earthen jugs and cups on the table and some small dishes. The last mentioned looked like glazed earthenware, out of which with little spoons they put something into their drink. The guests reclined at table upon small leaning benches, and to Jesus was given the seat between the bridegroom and the bride. The women sat at the lower end. Jesus blessed the food and drink, of which all then partook.

During the meal, Jesus taught. He told the guests about that man in Judea who, at the marriage of Cana in Galilee, had changed water into wine. When the couple whom the guests had known so long as sick, but who had been restored to health, made their appearance, the amazement was great. They related all that the Lord had told them of the king and his kingdom, declared their belief in it, and said that they were as certain of having a share in that same kingdom as they were now conscious of the fact of having been cured. Jesus repeated to them the parable and told them in plain words that there was still a wall between them and the dominions of that king, but that they could force their way through it if they would overcome themselves. It was morning before the party retired to bed. The Lord and the young boys slept back of the dining hall. Before he lay down, however, he went aside and, kneeling, prayed with uplifted hands to his heavenly Father. I saw streams of light issuing from his mouth, and another stream of light, or an angelic form, descending toward him. This often happened even in full daylight when at any time Jesus retired to a solitary place to pray. I knew this about him even in my childhood, and when I saw him praying thus alone, I tried to imitate him. I saw the blessed Virgin, up to the conception of the Savior, generally standing in prayer, her hands crossed on her breast, and her eyes lowered; but after the most holy Incarnation, she generally knelt, her face raised to heaven, and her hands uplifted.

Friday, August 15, AD 32 (Ab 19)

This morning, in Edon, Jesus taught in front of the house where the wedding celebration had taken place. He taught about marriage. Then he returned to Kedar for the sabbath. That evening, until about ten o'clock, he taught in an open place for prayer, a garden next to the synagogue. Then he went into the synagogue.

Next morning, on account of the great concourse of people, Jesus taught in the open air. He settled many matrimonial affairs, for the people of this place had lost the true conception of the Law on that head. They wanted to espouse two blood relatives in succession, and they questioned Jesus on the matter. He explained to them that it was not allowed by the Mosaic Law, and they promised to refrain from such unions. It was told Jesus also that in one of the neighboring places a certain man was on the point of marrying for the sixth time, his five deceased wives being sisters of the present affianced. Jesus said that he would visit that place. He returned to Kedar for the sabbath, and taught the whole day in the school. He gave decisions upon many questions and doubts concerning the Law and marriage and reconciled some married couples that were at variance.

Saturday, August 16, AD 32 (Ab 20)

During the day, Jesus taught in the synagogue and, that evening, in the garden next to the synagogue. He spoke again about marriage.

Sunday, August 17, AD 32 (Ab 21)

This morning Jesus continued to speak in the synagogue about marriage. A divorced couple came to him. There were two groups: the husband and his relatives and the wife and her relatives. Jesus spoke with each group separately. Then the couple came together, held hands, and Jesus blessed them.

Jesus Goes to Sichar-Kedar and Teaches upon the Mystery of Marriage

Monday, August 18, AD 32 (Ab 22)

This evening Jesus visited a shepherd settlement north of Kedar. Many people went with him. It was a beautiful night and the stars shone brightly.

FROM Kedar, Jesus, with a numerous escort, wended his way northward, the country everywhere presenting a more level aspect. I saw them reach a shepherd village outside of which were open sheds, long rows of trees with interlacing branches, and huts formed of green boughs and leaves. Under one of the sheds, all partook of figs, grapes, and dates. They were still there, the night being mild and lovely, when the stars shone out in the sky and the dewdrops glittered brightly below.

Tuesday, August 19, AD 32 (Ab 23)

Jesus and the three youths went further today. In the evening, they arrived at Sichar, a little town north of Kedar. Jesus was received as a guest in the house of Eliud, whose wife had been unfaithful. Eliud knew nothing of it. Jesus spoke alone with the wife, who confessed her guilt and sank down weeping at Jesus's feet. Jesus blessed her and then spoke words of consolation to Eliud, but without mentioning his wife's infidelity.

When the rest of the party dispersed to their homes, Jesus with the three youths went around the district teaching, and arrived toward evening of the following day at the little city of Sichar-Kedar, built on the declivity of a mountain range. Some people came out to meet him. They conducted him to the public house of the city, which was something like that of Cana in Galilee, and there he found a crowd assembled. Some young married people had lost their parents by a sudden death, and they were now entertaining at this house all those who had followed the remains to the grave. In front of the house was a courtyard enclosed by a railing, and in it an arbor of skillfully woven foliage. In each of the four corners stood a stone cistern full of water out of which grew creeping plants. They were trained up on palings and then allowed to run on arches to the center of the yard, where a carved column of marble supported the verdant roof thus formed. The plants, like reeds or sedges, retained their freshness a long time. This decoration, as well as all the garlands that adorned the house, was of extraordinary beauty. In a hall just off the courtyard, Jesus's feet and those of his companions were washed, and the customary refreshments presented. Then they went to another apartment, in which a meal was in readiness. Jesus insisted upon serving at table. He handed to all the guests bread, fruit, and large pieces of honeycomb, and poured from jugs into the drinking cup of each three kinds of beverage: one was a green juice; another, some kind of yellow drink; and the third, a perfectly white fluid. Jesus taught all the time. Sichar-Kedar was the place of which Jesus had been told at the wedding feast that so many were living there in unlawful marriage relations.

Only the husband of the mourning married couple was present at the funereal feast. He was named Eliud. He had been at the marriage feast at Edon, and on his return home found that both his parents-in-law had departed this life. They had died suddenly, overcome by grief at the discovery that their daughter, Eliud's wife, was an adulteress. Eliud himself had no intimation of the fact, nor consequently of the cause of the sudden death of his parents-in-law. When the meal spoken of above was over, Jesus allowed himself to be conducted by Eliud to his home. The youths did not go with him. Jesus spoke to the wife in private. She was in great sorrow. She sank at his feet in tears, and confessed her sin. When Jesus left her, Eliud conducted him to his sleeping chamber. I saw the Lord saying some grave and touching words to him and, when Eliud left him, he prayed awhile and then went to rest.

Wednesday, August 20, AD 32 (Ab 24)

Early next morning Eliud, with a wash-basin and a green branch, went in to Jesus, who was still lying on the bed supported on his arm. He arose; Eliud washed his feet and dried them in his own garments. Then the Lord told him to conduct him to his chamber, for that he wanted in turn to wash his feet. Eliud would not hear of this. But Jesus told him gravely that if he would not yield, he would instantly leave his house, that it must be, that if he wanted to follow him he must not refuse to obey. On hearing these words, Eliud led Jesus to his bedchamber and brought him a basin of water. Jesus grasped him by the hands, gazed lovingly into his eyes, said a few words on the subject of foot washing, and then informed him that his wife was an adulteress, but penitent, and that he must pardon her. At this information Eliud fell prostrate on the ground, writhing and weeping in an excess of mental agony. Jesus turned away from him and prayed. After a little while, the first bitter struggle being over, Jesus went to him, raised him from the ground, spoke words of consolation to him, and washed his feet. When Eliud had become calm, Jesus commanded him to call his wife. He did so, and she entered the room closely veiled. Jesus took her hand, laid it in that of Eliud, blessed them both, consoled them, and raised the wife's veil. Then he dismissed them with directions to send their children to him, whom when they came he blessed and led back to their parents. From this time forward Eliud and his wife remained faithful to each other, and both made a vow of continency. On that same day, Jesus visited many other homes in order to lead their occupants from the error of their ways. I saw him going from house to house, conversing with the people upon their various affairs and thus winning their confidence.

Thursday, August 21, AD 32 (Ab 25)

This afternoon Jesus taught beneath the porch of the town hall. He spoke in parables, referring to the bees, as there were many beehives kept by the people of the town. He spoke also of the vine and the vineyard, saying that he would produce the "wine of life" from the true vine.

On the mountain near this place, Sichar-Kedar, there were whole rows of beehives. The declivity of the mountain was terraced, and on the terraces resting against the mountain stood numerous square, flat-roofed beehives about seven feet in height, the upper part ornamented with knobs. They were placed in several rows, one above the other. They were not rounded in the back, but pointed like a roof, and they could be opened from top to bottom on the shelf side. The whole apiary was enclosed by a fine trellis of woven reeds. Between these stacks of hives there were steps leading up to the terraces, and to the railings on either side bushes bearing white blossoms and berries were trained. One could mount from terrace to terrace, upon each of which were similar arrangements for bees.

When Jesus was asked by the people whence he had come he invariably answered in parables, to which they gave simple-hearted credence. Under the bower of the public house he delivered an instruction, in which he related the parable of the king's son who came to discharge all the debts of his subjects. His hearers took the parable in its literal sense and rejoiced greatly over what it promised. Jesus then turned to the parable of the debtor who, after having obtained a delay for the payment of his own great debt, insisted upon bringing before the judge the man that owed him a trifle. He told them also that his father had given him a vineyard which had to be cultivated and pruned, and that he was looking for laborers to replace the useless, lazy servants whom he was going to chase away, and who were fitting images of the branches they had neglected to prune. Then he explained to them the cutting away of the vinestock, spoke of the quantity of useless wood and foliage, and of the small number of grapes. To this he compared the hurtful elements that had, through sin, entered into man. These, he said, should be cut off and destroyed by the exercise of mortification in order that fruit might be produced. This led to some words on marriage and its precepts, as well as upon the modesty and propriety to be observed in it, after which he returned to the vine and told the people that they too ought to cultivate it. They replied quite innocently that the country was not adapted to vine culture. But Jesus responded that they ought to plant it on that side of the mountain occupied by the apiary, for that was an excellent exposure for it, and then he related a parable treating of bees. The people expressed their readiness to labor in his vineyard, if he would allow them. But he told them that he had to go and discharge the debts, that he had to see that the true vine was put into the wine press, in order to produce a life-giving wine, and to teach others how to cultivate and prepare the same. The simple-hearted people were troubled at the thought of his going away, and implored him to remain with them. But he consoled them by saying that if they believed him, he would send them one who would make them laborers in his vineyard. I saw that the inhabitants of this little place were afterward baptized by Thaddeus, and that all emigrated during a persecution.

Jesus recalled none of the prophecies, performed no miracles in this place. In spite of their moral disorders, these people were simple and childlike. Married couples living apart were again united by Jesus, and he explained to the man who, after having married five sisters was now about to espouse the sixth, that such unions were unlawful.

Friday, August 22, AD 32 (Ab 26)

This morning Jesus visited many people of the town, teaching about the cultivation of the vine and drawing analogies with marriage and alluding to his work of love, wherever it may bear fruit. That afternoon he attended a wedding which took place in the open air, in front of the synagogue. With nightfall, as the stars shone above, they held the sabbath in the synagogue.

This morning Jesus gave another instruction upon marriage. He illustrated his subject by deeply significant similitudes taken from the cultivation of the vine, the care of the vineyard, and the pruning away of the superfluous branches. I was particularly impressed by his remarkable and clearly convincing words to this effect, that wherever discord reigned in the married state and wherever marriage failed to produce good, pure fruit, the fault lay principally on the wife's side. It is for her to endure and to suffer, it is for her to form, to preserve, the fruit of marriage. By her spiritual labors and victories over self, she can perfect her own soul and the fruit of her womb, she can eradicate whatever evil there may be in it, since her whole conduct, all her actions, redound to the blessing or the ruination of her offspring. In marriage there should be no question of sensual gratification, but only of penance and mortification, of constant fear, of constant warfare against sin and sinful desires, and this warfare is best carried on by prayer and self-conquest. Such struggles against self, such victories over self on the mother's part, secure similar victories to her children. All this instruction was given by the Lord in words as wonderful for their significance as for their simplicity. He said many other things, clear and precise, on the same subject. I was so impressed by the truth of what he said and its great necessity that the thought rushed impetuously to my mind: Why is not all this put in writing! Why is there no disciple present who could write it all down, that people far and wide might know it? For in the whole of this vision I was, as it were, present among Jesus's audience, and I followed him here and there. As I was so earnestly revolving that thought, my Lord turned and addressed me in words to this effect: "I rouse charity, I cultivate the vineyard wherever it will best produce fruit. Were these things written down, they would suffer the fate of so many other writings, they would fall into oblivion, or be misinterpreted, or utterly condemned. The words that I have just spoken, as well as innumerable others that have never been written, will become more productive in effects than what has been preserved in writing. It is not the written Law that is obeyed; but they that believe, hope, and love, have everything written in their heart." The way in which Jesus taught all this, the constant use of parables by which he illustrated from the nature of the vine all that he said of marriage and, on the other hand, the borrowing from marriage apt illustrations of the cultivation of the vine—all was inexpressibly beautiful and convincing. The people questioned the Lord most simply, and he gave them answers that showed still more clearly how perfectly his similitudes explained his doctrine.

At noon the nuptial ceremony between a poor young couple took place in front of the synagogue, and at it Jesus assisted. Both were good and innocent, consequently the Lord was very kind to them. The bridal procession to the synagogue was headed by little boys of six years with wreaths on their heads and flutes in their hands, white-robed maidens carrying little baskets of flowers which they strewed on the ground, and youths playing on harps, triangles, and other musical instruments now little known. The bridegroom was dressed almost like a priest. Both he and the bride were attended by assistants who, during the ceremony, laid their hands on their shoulders. The marriage was performed by a Jewish priest, in a hall whose roof had been opened just above the bridal party. It was near the synagogue. When the stars began to appear in the sky, the sabbath exercises were celebrated in the synagogue, after which a fast that lasted until the next evening was begun.

Saturday, August 23, AD 32 (Ab 27)

Jesus taught in parables. He spoke of the prodigal son (Luke 15:11–32) and of the many rooms in his Father's house (John 14:2). He again spoke about marriage and of the importance of regarding marriage as a spiritual task, one that included the spiritual education of children. Moreover, he alluded to himself as the spouse of a bride in whom all those gathered together would be reborn.

When that was over, the wedding festivities were held in the public house used on such occasions, during which Jesus related many parables, such as that of the prodigal son and the mansions in his Father's house. The bridegroom had no house of his own. He was to make his home in that belonging to the mother of his bride. Jesus told him that, until he should receive a mansion in his Father's house, he should take up his abode under a tent in the vineyard which he himself was going to lay out on the mount of the bees.

Then he again taught on marriage, upon which he dwelt for a long time. If married people, he said, would live together modestly and chastely, if they would recognize their state as one of penance, then would they lead their children in the way of salvation, then would their state become not a means of diverting souls from their end, but one that would reap a harvest for those mansions in his Father's house. In this instruction, Jesus called himself the spouse of a bride in whom all those that should be gathered, would be born again. He alluded to the marriage feast of Cana, and told of the changing of water into wine. He always spoke of himself in the third person, as of that man in Judea whom he knew so well, who would be so bitterly persecuted, and who would finally be put to death.

The people heard all this in simple, childlike faith, and the parables were for them real facts. The bridegroom appeared to be a school teacher, for Jesus told him how he should teach by his own example. Jesus made allusion also to Ishmael, for Kedar and the country around were peopled by his descendants. They were, for the most part, shepherds, and esteemed themselves inferior to the people of Judea, of whom they spoke as of a very great nation, a chosen race. They still clung to the ancient manner of living. The owner of numerous herds lived in a large house surrounded by a moat, and in the midst of the pasture grounds by which it was encompassed stood the houses of the under-shepherds. To the well, which belonged to the head proprietor, only his own herds had a right to go, though those of his neighbors enjoyed the same privilege if there existed an agreement to that effect. Such patriarchal settlements were scattered thickly here and there, though otherwise the place was of little importance.

Sunday, August, 24, AD 32 (Ab 28)

Jesus persuaded the people of Sichar to build a house for the newly-married couple close to the hill where the beehives were placed. He instructed the couple to cultivate a vineyard behind the house, in the area reaching up to where the bees were.

Moved thereto by Jesus's words, the people determined to build for the newly-married pair a light habitation on the bee mount where, later on, the vineyard was to be laid out. Every friend in the place constructed for the tent a light wicker wall which was then covered with skins, and afterward coated with something of a viscid nature. When a piece of the work was finished, it was transported to the site for which it was destined. Each one did what was in his power, some more, some less, and they shared with one another whatever was needed. The Lord told them how all was to be done, and they listened in wonder at his knowing so much about such things. He had taught them at the marriage feast that the old and the poor should take the upper places. Jesus went with the people to the little hill in front of the bee mountain in order to choose there the best site for the vineyard. The back of the tent was to rest against the rising ground of the vineyard.

Monday, August 25, AD 32 (Ab 29)

Jesus remained in Sichar.

Tuesday, August 26, AD 32 (Ab 30)

Today began the Feast of the New Moon. It was celebrated in the evening in the synagogue. Afterward the people of Sichar gathered in the town hall to hear Jesus speak. He told them that he would not stay in Sichar, that he had no house, and that his kingdom would come later. First, he had to cultivate and water his Father's vineyard. He taught until late into the night.

As the Feast of the New Moon just now began, all returned with Jesus to the public house. He knew that, when he said that they should build a house for the newly-married pair, many had thought and said to one another: "Perhaps he has no house of his own, no place of abode. Will he, perhaps, take up his residence with these people?" Therefore it was that Jesus now told them that he was not going to stay among them, that he had no abiding place on this earth, that his kingdom was yet to come, that he had to plant his Father's vineyard, and water it with his blood upon Mount Calvary. They could not now comprehend his words, he said, but they would do so after he had watered the vineyard. Then he would come back to them from a dark country. He would send his messengers to call them, and then they would leave this place and follow him. But when he should come again for the third time, he would lead into his Father's kingdom all those who had faithfully labored in the vineyard. Their sojourning here was not to be long, therefore the house they were building was to be a light one, rather a tent that could be easily removed. Jesus next gave a long instruction upon mutual charity. They should, he said, cast their anchor in the heart of their neighbor, that the storms of the world might not separate and destroy them. He spoke again in parables of the vineyard, saying that he would remain only long enough to lay out the vineyard for the newly-married pair and teach them to plant the vines, then he would depart in order to cultivate that belonging to his Father. Jesus taught all these things in language so simple, and yet so nicely adapted to the point in question, that his hearers became more and more convinced of its truth, retaining at the same time their simplicity. He taught them to recognize in all nature, in life itself, a law hidden and holy, though now disfigured by sin. The instruction lasted till late into the night.

ELUL (29 days): August 26/27 to Sept. 23/24, AD 32
Elul New Moon: August 24 at 9:15 PM, Jerusalem time

Wednesday, August 27, AD 32 (Elul 1)

Jesus stayed on in Sichar.

When Jesus wanted to take leave of them, the people detained him. They clasped him in their arms, exclaiming: "Explain it all to us again, that we may understand it better." But he replied that they should practice what he had preached to them, and he promised to send them one who would make it all clear to them. During this assembly they partook of a slight repast, at which all drank out of the same cup.

The young man for whom the Lord had caused the house to be built was named Salathiel, and the bride's name was a word that signified "pretty," or "brunette." With the greater part of the inhabitants of the place, they were baptized by Thaddeus. The Evangelist Mark also was in this region for awhile. Thirty-five years after Christ's Ascension, Salathiel with his wife and three grown-up sons removed to Ephesus. I saw him there in company with the goldsmith Demetrius, who had once raised an insurrection against Paul, but who was afterward converted. Demetrius gave him a long account of Paul, and narrated the history of his conversion. Paul was not then at Ephesus. Salathiel, his three sons, and Demetrius went to join him, while the wife of the first-named remained behind at Ephesus in a house to which many from her own country came and resided with her. Almost all the Jews left Ephesus at this time. Salathiel and his three sons, Demetrius, Silas, and a man named Caius were all in the same ship with Paul when he suffered shipwreck near the island of Malta, and they went with him to the island. From his prison in Rome, Paul assigned to each of the three sons of Salathiel the place in which he was to labor.

Thursday, August 28, AD 32 (Elul 2)

Today Jesus visited the house where the bride's parents lived. Then he went to the place where the vineyard was to be cultivated. A trellis had already been set up. A large bunch of grapes was brought to him, and he selected five grapes. He dug up the ground, planted the grapes at a certain distance from the trellis, and showed the people how the vine should be tied in a cross to the trellis. During this he taught concerning marriage, relating everything that takes place through nature and through cultivation of the vine to reproduction and spiritual fruit. Then they went to the synagogue and Jesus taught further about marriage. He talked of the dangers of intoxication.

When Jesus went with the men to the bee mount in order to show them how to plant the vines, the site for the tent house was already marked off and an espalier erected. The men told Jesus that grapes raised in those parts were always bitter, to which Jesus responded that that was because they belonged to a poor species. They were of a bad stock, they were allowed to run wild without pruning; consequently they had the appearance only of grapes, without their sweetness. But, he added, those that he was now about to plant would be sweet. The instruction turned again upon marriage which, Jesus said, could produce pure, sweet fruit only when it was guarded by self-command, mortification, and moderation united to pain and labor.

From the young plants that he had ordered to be brought to the spot, Jesus chose five, which he laid in the ground that he had himself previously loosened, and he showed the men how to bind them to the espalier in the form of a cross. All that he said while thus engaged of the nature and training of the vine referred to the mystery of marriage and the sanctification of its fruit. When Jesus continued this instruction in the synagogue, he spoke of the obligation of continency in order to conception and, as a proof of the same, brought forward the depth of corruption into which men had fallen in this particular. Man, he said, might in this respect learn a lesson from the elephant.

(There were a few of these animals in that region.) At the close of the instruction Jesus repeated that he must now soon leave them, in order to plant and water the vine on Mount Calvary, but he would send some to teach them all things and to lead them into his Father's vineyard.

Friday, August 29, AD 32 **(*Elul 3*)**

This evening he went to the synagogue for the sabbath and taught there.

Saturday, August 30, AD 32 **(*Elul 4*)**

Today, Jesus taught again in the synagogue. He spoke of the bridegroom's house, which was delicate in construction. The bridegroom was named Salathiel. Jesus said that one should not become too attached to the earth. Why build a house for the body, when this itself was a fragile house. The house of the soul should be purified and sanctified as a temple, and should not be desecrated. He also spoke of the Messiah and how to recognize him.

When in the synagogue Jesus spoke of the kingdom and the mansions of his Father, the people asked him why he had brought nothing with him from that kingdom and why he went about so poorly clad. Jesus answered that that kingdom was reserved for such as followed him, and that no one would receive it without deserving it. He was, he said, a stranger seeking for faithful servants whom he might call into the vineyard. He had therefore built the bridegroom's house so lightly because the earth was not to be a permanent abode for his posterity and they were not to cling to it. Why should a solid habitation be constructed for the body, since it is itself only a fragile vessel? It should indeed be cared for and purified as the house of the soul, as a sacred temple, but it should not be polluted, or to the prejudice of the soul either overburdened or treated too delicately. From such discourse Jesus turned again to the house of his Father, to the Messiah, and all the signs by which he might be recognized. Among the latter he mentioned the fact that he was to be born of an illustrious race, though of simple, pious parents, and added that, according to the signs of the time, he must have already come. They should, Jesus said, attach themselves to him and observe his teachings.

Jesus next taught on the love of the neighbor and good example. Turning to the bridegroom Salathiel, he told him to allow his house to stand open, to have perfect confidence in what he had said to him, and to live piously; if he did so, God would guard his house for him and nothing would be stolen from him. Salathiel had received for his new house far more than was actually needed, for Jesus had inveighed against selfishness. They must, he said, be willing to sacrifice for God and the neighbor. The communication between Jesus and these people became more and more intimate and, in order to rescue them from the ignorance into which they had fallen, he taught under manifold similitudes upon the chastity, modesty, and self-conquest that should grace the married state. The similitudes referred to the sowing and the harvest.

Sunday, August 31, AD 32 **(*Elul 5*)**

Today Jesus spoke with a couple who wanted to marry. He told them that their plan to marry was motivated by the desire for property. They were shocked that he could read their thoughts, for they had not spoken with anyone about their secret intentions. Then they gave up their plans and believed in Jesus.

He went also to visit two parties who were about to marry notwithstanding their relationship to each other in prohibited degrees. One couple were blood relatives. Jesus summoned them into his presence and told them that their design sprang from the desire of temporal goods, and that it was not lawful. They were terrified on finding that he knew their thoughts, for no one had said anything to him about it; so they relinquished their intention. Here they washed one another's feet, and the bride wiped Jesus's feet with the end of her veil, or the upper part of her mantle. Both the man and the woman recognized Jesus by his teaching as more than a prophet. They were converted and followed him. Jesus next went out to a house in the country, in which lived a stepmother who wanted to marry her stepson, though the latter as yet did not clearly comprehend her design. Jesus made known to the son the danger in which he was, and bade him flee from the place and go labor at Salathiel's, which he obediently did. The Lord washed his feet also. The stepmother, whom Jesus gravely rebuked for her guilt, was greatly exasperated. She did no penance and went to perdition.

The people of this region must have had, through their ancestors, some special relations with the Ark of the Covenant. They asked Jesus what had become of the holy mystery contained in the Ark. He answered that humankind had received so much of it, that it had now passed into them, and that from the fact that it was no longer to be found, they might conclude that the Messiah was born. Many people of this country believed that the Messiah was put to death among the Holy Innocents.

JESUS RAISES A DEAD MAN TO LIFE

Monday, September 1, AD 32 **(*Elul 6*)**

Jesus taught further today concerning marriage. He spoke of David, who had fallen into sin on account of the superabundance of forces within him, which he should have consumed within himself. He added that nothing is lost through continence, but rather through wastefulness. This afternoon he went about one hour east of Sichar to the house of a rich herd owner who had died suddenly in one of his fields. His wife and children were very sad and had sent for Jesus, begging him to come to the funeral. He came, accompanied by the three shepherd youths, by Salathiel and his wife, and about twenty-five other people from Sichar. After sending away the people of Sichar, apart from Salathiel and his wife, Jesus spoke with the wife of the dead man, whose name was Nazor. He said that if she and her son and daughter would believe in his teaching and follow him, and if they would keep silence on the matter, Nazor would be raised to life again. For, he said, Nazor's soul had not yet passed on to be judged but was still present over the place in the field where he had died. Jesus then went with them to the field. Praying, he called Nazor back to his body, saying to those present: "When we return, Nazor will be alive and sitting upright!" They then returned to the house to find Nazor sitting upright in his coffin, wrapped in linen cloths and with his hands bound. After being freed from the wrappings, Nazor climbed out of the coffin and cast himself down at Jesus's feet. Jesus told him to wash and purify himself, stay hidden in his room, and say nothing of being raised from the dead, until he (Jesus) had left the region. Jesus and the five people with him then stayed there overnight.

ABOUT one hour to the east of Sichar stood the dwelling of a rich herd proprietor. The house was surrounded by a moat. The owner had died suddenly in a field not far from his house, and his wife and children were in great affliction. The remains were ready for interment, and the family had sent messengers into the city to beg the Lord and some others to come to the funeral. Jesus went, accompanied by his three disciples, Salathiel and his wife, and several others—about thirty in all. The corpse, ready for the grave, was placed in a broad avenue of trees before the house. The man had been struck dead in punishment of his sins, for he had seized upon part of the possessions of some shepherds who, owing to his oppressive treatment, were obliged to leave that section of the country. Shortly after the commission of this sin, he had fallen dead upon the very ground that he had unjustly appropriated. Standing in front of the corpse, Jesus spoke of the deceased. He asked of what advantage was it to him now that he had once pampered and served his body, that house which his soul had now to leave. He had, on account of that body, run his soul into debt which he neither had and which he never could discharge. The wife of the deceased was plunged in grief. She had constantly repeated before Jesus's coming: "If the Jewish king from Nazareth were here, he could raise him from the dead!" In reply to these words, Jesus said: "Yes, the Jewish king can do it. But men will persecute him on that account. They will kill him who gives life, and they will refuse to acknowledge him!" To which those around responded: "If he were among us, we would acknowledge him!"

Jesus resolved to put them to the test. He spoke of faith, and promised that the Jewish king would help them, provided they believed and practiced all that he taught. Then he separated the family of the deceased along with Salathiel and his wife from the rest of the assistants, whom he directed to withdraw, while he spoke with the wife, the daughter, and the son of the dead man. Even before the others had gone out, the wife had addressed these words to Jesus: "Lord, thou speakest as if thou thyself wert the king of the Jews!" But Jesus had motioned her to be silent. When now those others, whom he knew to be weaker in faith, had retired, Jesus told the family that if they would believe in his doctrine, if they would follow him, and if they would keep silence upon the matter, he would raise the dead man to life, for his soul was not yet judged, it was still tarrying in the field, the scene of its injustice as well as of its separation from the body. The family promised with all their heart both obedience and silence, and Jesus went with them to the field in which the man had died. I saw the state in which the soul of the deceased was. I saw it in a circle, in a sphere above the spot upon which he had died. Before it passed pictures of all its transgressions with their temporal consequences, and the sight consumed it with sorrow. I saw too all the punishments it was to undergo, and it was vouchsafed a view of the redemptive Passion of Jesus. Torn with grief, it was about to enter upon its punishment, when Jesus prayed, and called it back into the body by pronouncing the name Nazor, the name of the deceased. Then turning to the assistants, he said: "When we return, we shall find Nazor sitting up and alive!" I saw the soul at Jesus's call floating toward the body, becoming smaller, and disappearing through the mouth, at which moment Nazor rose to a sitting posture in his coffin. I always see the human soul reposing above the heart from which numerous threads run to the head.

When Jesus and his companions returned to the house they found Nazor, still enveloped in his funereal bands and his hands bound, sitting up in the coffin. His wife unbound his hands and loosened the bands. He stepped forth from the coffin, cast himself at Jesus's feet, and tried to embrace his knees. But the Lord drew back and told him that he should purify himself, should wash, and remain concealed in his chamber, that he should not speak of his resurrection until he himself had left that region. The wife then led her husband into a retired corner of the dwelling, where he washed and clothed himself. Jesus, Salathiel and his wife, and the three disciples took some food and remained at the house. The coffin was placed in the vault. The Lord taught until after nightfall.

Tuesday, September 2, AD 32 (Elul 7)

On the following morning Jesus washed the feet of the resuscitated Nazor and exhorted him for the future to think more of his soul than of his body, and to restore the ill-gotten property. After that he called the children to him, spoke of God's mercy which their father had experienced, and exhorted them to the reverence of God; then he blessed them and led them to their parents. The mother, also, Jesus conducted to the father. He presented her to him as to one returned from afar, in order that they might live together in a stricter and more God-fearing manner.

Jesus on that day taught many things relating to marriage, in similitudes. He addressed himself especially to the newly-married couple. To Salathiel he said: "Thou hast allowed thy heart to be moved by the beauty of thy wife! But think how great the beauty of the soul must be, since God sends his Son upon earth to save souls by the sacrifice of his body! Whoever serves the body, serves not the soul. Beauty inflames selfish desire, and such desire corrupts the soul. Incontinence is like a creeping plant that chokes and destroys the wheat and the vines." These last words turned the instruction again upon the subject of vine and wheat culture, and Jesus warned his hearers to keep far from their fields and vineyards two running weeds which he designated by name. At last he announced to them that on the coming sabbath he would teach in the school at Kedar, and on that occasion they would hear what they must do to become his followers and share in his kingdom. He told them, moreover, that he would then depart from that region and journey eastward to Arabia. When they asked him why he was going among those pagans, those star-worshippers, he answered that he had friends among them who had followed a star in order to greet him at his birth. These he wanted to search after, that he might invite them also into the vineyard and the kingdom of his Father, and put them on the straight road to it.

Wednesday, September 3, and Thursday, September 4, AD 32 (Elul 8–9)

An extraordinarily great multitude assembled in Kedar to meet Jesus, who now began publicly to heal crowds of sick. Sometimes while passing among those that had been brought hither by their friends, he merely pronounced the words: "Arise! Follow me!"—and they rose up cured. The wonder and admiration produced by these miracles reached such a pitch of enthusiasm that had not Jesus himself suppressed it, the whole country would have risen in one sudden transport of joy.

Friday, September 5, AD 32 (Elul 10)

Today, at noon, Jesus taught in a house in Kedar. His theme was marriage. Salathiel and his wife were there. Jesus spoke of the conditions for living together in order to become good vine. After the onset of the sabbath, Jesus spoke with a man, also called Nazor, who was responsible for the administration of the synagogue. He was a descendant of Tobias. Jesus then taught about the life of Tobias.

Salathiel and his wife were among the assembly at Kedar. Jesus once more spoke to them of the duties of the married state, and gave them detailed instructions upon the way in which they should live together in order to become a good vine (that is, one that would produce pure and excellent fruit, such as would become disciples of his apostles, saints, and martyrs). He inculcated the observance of modesty and purity, bade them in all their actions aim at purity of intention, exhorted them to prayer and renunciation, and rigorously commanded perfect continence after the period of conception. He spoke of the mutual confidence that ought to exist between husband and wife, and of the obedience of the latter to the former. The husband should not keep silence when the wife asks him questions. He ought to respect her and be indulgent toward her, since she is the weaker vessel. He should not mistrust her if he sees her talking with others, neither should she be jealous upon beholding him doing the same; still each should be careful not to give to the other cause for vexation. They should suffer no third party to come between them, and should settle their little differences themselves. He told the wife that she should become a pious Abigail, and pointed out to them a region suitable for the cultivation of wheat. They must, he said, raise a hedge around their vineyard, which hedge was to consist of the admonitions he had just given them.

Saturday, September 6, AD 32 (Elul 11)

Throughout the sabbath, Jesus taught concerning the vine, the grain, bread, and wine. He spoke of Melchizedek as a forerunner, whose sacrifice was bread and wine; in himself, however, the sacrifice had become flesh and blood. Jesus indicated clearly that he was the Messiah, and said that they should follow him.

Before leaving Kedar, Jesus gave in the synagogue another very long instruction, in which he again explained the connection existing between all the points upon which up to that time he had here taught separately. He spoke in simple, childlike allegories of the mysteries of original sin, the impure propagation of the human race, their ever-increasing corruption, the dispositions of God's grace and his guidance of the chosen people from generation to generation down to the blessed Virgin, the mystery of the Incarnation and the regeneration of fallen man from death to eternal life through the Son of the Virgin. Here he introduced the parable of the grain of wheat which had to be buried in the ground before it could spring forth into new fruit, but he was not understood by his hearers. He told them that they should follow him not for a short time only, but on a long journey that would end only at the Judgment. He spoke of the resurrection of the dead and of the Last Judgment, and he bade them watch! Then he related the parable of the slothful servants. Judgment comes like a thief in the night; death strikes at every hour. They, the Ishmaelites, were typified by the servants, and they ought to be faithful. Melchizedek, he said, was a type of himself. His sacrifice consisted of bread and wine, but in him they would be changed into flesh and blood. At last Jesus told them in plain terms that he was the Redeemer. At this revelation, many became timid and fearful, while others grew more ardent and enthusiastic in their adherence to him. He enforced upon them in particular love for one another, compassion, sympathy in joy and sorrow such as the members of the body feel for one another. The pagans from the pagan quarter of Kedar were present at this instruction, to which they listened from a distance. They had been very hostile toward the Jews, but from this time many approached them and questioned them in a friendly manner about Jesus's doctrine and miracles.

Sunday, September 7, to Monday, September 8, AD 32 (Elul 12–13)

Jesus remained in Kedar.

Jesus Reaches the First Tent City of the Star Worshippers

Tuesday, September 9, AD 32 (Elul 14)

Today, Jesus and the three shepherd youths left Kedar. About twenty people accompanied them to a place some distance from the town. Here Jesus blessed those who had accompanied them, and then those who had accompanied them returned to Kedar. This was about midday. Jesus and the young shepherds went eastward, and toward evening came to a settlement where the people lived in tents. Jesus and his traveling companions were invited to eat and stay there. Anne Catherine beheld a festival of star worship that took place there that night (it was the night after the Full Moon). The pagans cried out as the Moon rose or when other stars rose—later that night Mars rose, later still Jupiter, and then later still Saturn.

WHEN Jesus with the three youths left Kedar, Nazor, the ruler of the synagogue (who traced his origin up to Tobias), Salathiel, Eliud, and the youth Titus accompanied him a good part of the way. They crossed the river and passed through the pagan quarter of the city, in which just at that time a pagan feast was being celebrated and sacrifice was being offered in front of the temple. The road ran first eastward and then to the south through a plain that lay between two high mountain ridges, sometimes over heaths, again over yellow or white sand, and sometimes over white pebbles. At last they reached a large, open tract of country covered with verdure, in which stood a great tent among the palm trees, and around it many smaller ones. Here Jesus blessed and took leave of his escort, and then continued his journey awhile longer toward the tent city of the star worshippers. The day was on its decline when he arrived at a beautiful well in a hollow. It was surrounded by a low embankment, and near it was a drinking ladle. The Lord drank, and then sat down by the well. The youths washed his feet and he, in turn, rendered them the same service. All was done with childlike simplicity, and the sight was extremely touching. The plain was covered with palm trees, meadows, and at a considerable distance apart there were groups of tents. A tower, or terraced pyramid of pretty good size, still not higher than an ordinary church, arose in the center of the district. Here and there some people made their appearance and from a distance gazed at Jesus in surprise not unmingled with awe, but no one approached him.

Not far from the well stood the largest of the tent houses. It was surmounted by several spires, and consisted of many stories and apartments connected together by partitions, some grated, others merely of canvas. The upper part was covered with skins. Altogether it was very artistically made and very beautiful. From this tent castle five men came forth bearing branches, and turned their steps in the direction of Jesus. Each carried in his hand a branch of a different kind of fruit: One had little yellow leaves and fruit, another was covered with red berries, a third was a palm branch, one bore a vine branch full of leaves, and the fifth carried a cluster of grapes. From the waist to the knees they wore a kind of woollen tunic slit at the sides, and on the upper part of the body a jacket wide and full, made of some kind of transparent, woollen stuff, with sleeves that reached about halfway to the elbow. They were of fair complexion, had a short, black beard, and long, curling hair. On their head was a sort of spiral cap from which hung many lappets around their temples.

They approached Jesus and his companions with a friendly air, saluted them and, while presenting to them the branches they held in their hands, invited them to accompany them back to the tent. The vine branch was presented to Jesus, the one who acted as guide carrying a similar one. On entering the tent Jesus and his companions were made to sit upon cushions trimmed with tassels, and fruit was presented to them. Jesus uttered only a few words. The guests were then led through a tent corridor lined with sleeping chambers containing couch beds, and furnished with high cushions, to that part of the tent in which was the dining hall. In the center of the hall rose the pillar that supported the tent; and around it were twined garlands of leaves and fruits, vine branches, apples, and clusters of grapes—all so natural in appearance that I cannot say whether they really were natural or only painted. Here the attendants drew out a little oval table about as high as a footstool. It was formed of light leaves that could be opened quickly and its feet separated into two supports. They spread under it a colored carpet upon which were representations of men like themselves, and placed upon it cups and other table furniture. The tent was hung with tapestry, so that no part of the canvas itself could be seen.

When Jesus and the young disciples stretched themselves on the carpet around the table, the men in attendance brought cakes, scooped out in the middle, all kinds of fruits, and honey. The attendants themselves sat on low, round folding stools, their legs crossed. Between their feet they stood a little disk supported on a long leg, and on the disk they laid their plate. They served their guests themselves by turns, the servants remaining outside the tent with everything that was necessary. I saw them going to another tent and bringing thence birds, which had been roasted on a spit in the kitchen. This last-named apartment consisted merely of a mud hut in which was an opening in the roof to let out the smoke from the fire on the hearth. The birds were served up in quite a remarkable manner. They were (but I know not how it was done) covered with their feathers, and looked just as if they were alive. The meal over, the guests were escorted by five men to their sleeping rooms, and there the latter were quite amazed at seeing Jesus washing the youths' feet, which service they rendered him in return. Jesus explained to them its signification, and they resolved to practice in future the same act of courtesy.

NOCTURNAL CELEBRATION OF THE STAR WORSHIPPERS

WHEN the five men took leave of Jesus and his young companions, they all left the tent together. They wore mantles longer behind than before, with a broad flap hanging from the back of the neck. They proceeded to a temple which was built in the shape of a large four-cornered pyramid, not of stone but of very light materials such as wood and skins. There was a flight of outside steps from base to summit. It was built in a hollow that rose in terraces and was surrounded by steps and parapets. The circular enclosure was cut through by entrances to the different parts of the temple, and the entrances themselves were screened by light, ornamental hedges. Several hundred people were already assembled in the enclosure. The married women were standing back of the men; the young girls, back of them; and last of all, the children. On the steps of the pyramidal temple were illuminated globes that flashed and twinkled just like the stars of heaven, but I do not know how that was effected. They were regularly arranged, in imitation of certain constellations. The temple was full of people. In the center of the building rose a high column from which beams extended to the walls and up into the summit of the pyramid, bearing the lights by which the exterior globes were lighted. The light inside the temple was very extraordinary. It was like twilight, or rather moonlight. One seemed to be gazing up into a sky full of stars. The moon likewise could be seen, and far up in the very center of all blazed the sun. It was a most skillfully executed arrangement, and so natural that it produced upon the beholder an impression of awe, especially when he beheld by the dim light of the lower part of the temple the three idols that were placed around that central column. One was like a human being with a bird's head and a great, crooked beak. I saw the people offering to it in sacrifice all kinds of foods. They crammed into its enormous bill birds and similar things which fell down into its body and out again. Another of these idols had a head almost like that of an ox, and was seated like a human being in a squatting posture. They laid birds in its arms, which were outstretched as if to receive an infant. In it was a fire into which, through the holes made for that purpose, the worshippers cast the flesh of animals that had been slaughtered and cut up on the sacrificial table in front of it. The smoke escaped through a pipe sunk in the earth and communicating with the outer air. No flames were to be seen in the temple, but the horrible idols shone with a reddish glare in the dim light. During the ceremony, the multitude around the pyramid chanted in a very remarkable manner. Sometimes a single voice was heard, and then again a powerful chorus, the strains suddenly changing from plaintive to exultant; and when the moon and different stars shone out, they sent up shouts of enthusiastic welcome. I think this idolatrous celebration lasted till sunrise.

Wednesday, September 10, AD 32 (Elul 15)

This morning Jesus taught the pagans, reprimanding them for their sacrificial practices, saying that they should pray to the Father who had created everything. He was well received. Then he left. As he was traveling further with the three shepherd youths, he remarked to them how well he had been received by the pagans.

Before taking leave of these people on the following morning, Jesus gave them a few words of instruction. To their questions as to who he was and whither he was journeying, he answered by telling them about his Father's kingdom. He was, he said, seeking friends that had saluted him at his birth. After that he was going down to Egypt, to hunt up some companions of his childhood and to call them to follow him, as he was soon to return to his Father. He spoke to them on the subject of their idolatrous worship, for which they put themselves to so much trouble and slaughtered so many sacrifices. They should adore the Father, the Creator of all things, and instead of sacrificing victims to idols which they themselves had made, they should bestow those gifts upon their poor brethren. The abodes of the women were back of and entirely separate from the tents of the men, each of whom had many wives. They wore long garments, jewels in their ears, and headdresses in the form of a high cap. Jesus commended the separation of the women from the men. It was well, he said, for the former to stand in the background, but against a multiplicity of wives he inveighed strenuously. They should have but one wife, he said, whom they should treat as one that owed submission, though not as a slave. During this instruction, Jesus appeared to them so lovable, so much like a supernatural being, that they implored him to remain with them. They wanted to bring a wise, old priest to converse with him, but Jesus would not allow it. Then they produced some ancient manuscripts which they consulted. They were not rolls of parchment, but thick leaves, which looked as if made of bark, and upon which the writing was deeply imprinted. These leaves were very like thick leather. The pagans insisted upon the Lord's remaining and instructing them, but he refused, saying that they should follow him when he had returned to his Father, and that he would not neglect to call them at the right time.

When about to leave, Jesus wrote for them with a sharp metallic rod on the stone floor of their tent the initials of five members of his race. It looked to me like only the letters, four or five of them, entwined together, and among them I recognized an 'M'. They were deeply engraven on the stone. The pagans gazed in wonder at the inscription, for which they at once conceived great reverence. Later on they converted the stone upon which it was traced into an altar. I see it now at Rome enclosed in one of the corners of St. Peter's church, nor will the enemies of the church be able to carry it off!

Jesus would not allow any of these pagans to accompany him when he departed. He directed his steps southward with his young disciples through the widely scattered tents and passed the tower of the idols. He remarked to the youths how affectionately he had been received by these pagans for whom he had done nothing, and how maliciously the obstinate, ungrateful Jews had persecuted him, although he had loaded them with benefits. Jesus and his young companions hurried on rapidly the whole of that day. It seems to me that he still had a journey of some days, about fifty miles, before reaching the country of the kings.

JESUS ENCOUNTERS A PASTORAL TRIBE

Thursday, September 11, and Friday, September 12, AD 32 (Elul 16–17)

SHORTLY before the commencement of the sabbath I saw Jesus in the neighborhood of some shepherd tents, where he and his three young companions sat down by a fountain and washed one another's feet. Then he began to celebrate the sabbath, praying with the youths and instructing them in order that even here in a strange land, the Jews' reproaches that he did not sanctify the sabbath day might not be verified. He slept that night with the three youths in the open air by the well. There were no permanent dwellings in this place, and no women among the shepherds. They had only one temporary inn, or caravanserai, near their distant pasture grounds.

Saturday, September 13, AD 32 (Elul 18)

Next morning, the shepherds gathered around Jesus and listened to his words. He asked them whether they had not heard of some people who, three and thirty years before, had been guided by a star to Judea, to salute the newborn king of the Jews. They cried out: "Yes! Yes!" and he went on to tell them that he was now traveling in search of those men. The shepherds exhibited a childlike joy and love for Jesus. On a lovely spot surrounded by palm trees, they made for him a beautiful high seat or throne, up to which led steps covered with sod. They worked so very quickly, cutting and raising the sods with long stone, or bone knives, that the seat was soon finished. The Lord seated himself upon it, and taught in most beautiful parables. The shepherds, about forty in number, listened like little children and afterward prayed with Jesus.

That evening the shepherds took down one of their tents, and uniting it to another, formed thereby one large hall, in which they prepared for the whole party an entertainment consisting of fruit, a kind of thick pap rolled into balls, and camel's milk. When Jesus blessed the food he was about to take, they asked him why he did so, and when he explained the reason, they begged him to bless all the rest of the food, which he did. They wanted him also to leave behind him some blessed food; and when they brought him for that purpose things soft and very perishable, he called for fruits that would not decay. They brought them, and he blessed some white balls made of rice. He told them always to mix a little of the blessed provisions with their other food, which then would never spoil, and the blessing would never be taken away.

The kings already knew through dreams that Jesus was coming to see them.

A WONDERFUL GLOBE

Sunday, September 14, AD 32 (Elul 19)

Jesus taught the shepherds again today. He spoke of the creation of the world and of the Fall and of the promise of the restoration of all. During this discourse something wonderful took place. He appeared to catch a sunbeam with his right hand, and he made a luminous globe of light from it. It hung from the palm of his hand on a ray of light. While he was talking, the shepherds could see all the things he was describing in the globe of light. The Holy Trinity itself appeared there. At the end of this discourse, the globe of light disappeared, and the shepherds cast themselves down in sorrow. Jesus later taught them a wonderful prayer and how to worship God, the creator of all.

I SAW Jesus again teaching from the mossy throne. He taught about the creation of the world, the Fall of Man, and the promise of Redemption. Jesus asked whether they preserved the tradition of any Promise. But they knew only a few things connected with Abraham and David, and those were mixed up with fables. They were so simple, just like children in school. Whoever knew anything in answer to a question, said it right out. When Jesus saw how innocent and ignorant they were, he wrought a great miracle in their behalf. I cannot recall exactly what he said, but he appeared to catch with his right hand at a sunbeam from which he drew a ball like a little luminous globe, and let it hang from the palm of the same hand by a ray of light. It seemed to be large enough to contain all things, and all things could be seen in it. The good people and the disciples beheld in it everything just as the Lord related it to them, and they all stood in awe around him. I saw the most holy Trinity in the globe, and when I saw the Son in it, I did not see Jesus any longer upon earth, only an angel hovering by the globe. Once Jesus took the globe upon his hand, and again it seemed as if his hand itself was the globe, in which innumerable pictures unfolded, one from another. I heard something about the number three hundred and sixty-five, as if relating to the days of the year, connected with which also there was something in the pictures formed in the globe.

Jesus taught the shepherds a short prayer, in which occurred words like those of the Lord's Prayer, and he gave them three intentions for which they should alternately recite it. The first was to thank for Creation; the second, for Redemption; and the third, I think, was for the Last Judgment. The whole history of the Creation, the Fall, and the Redemption was unfolded in successive pictures in this globe, along with the means given to man to participate therein. I saw all things in the globe connected by rays of light with the most holy Trinity, out of whom all things proceeded, but from whom many separated miserably. The Lord gave to the shepherds an idea of Creation by the globe which sprang forth from his hand; an idea of the connection of the fallen world with the Godhead and its Redemption by the suspension of the globe from his hand by a thread; and when he held it in his hand, he gave them some idea of Judgment. He taught them likewise about the year and the days that compose it inasmuch as they are figures of this history of Creation, and then he showed by what prayers and good works they ought to sanctify the different seasons.

When the Lord concluded his instruction, the luminous globe with its varied pictures disappeared as it had come. The poor people, quite overcome by the sense of their own profound misery and the godlike dignity of their guest, showed signs of deep affliction and cast themselves, along with the three youths, prostrate on the ground, weeping and adoring. Jesus too became very sad and prostrated on the grassy mound upon which he had been sitting. The youths attempted to raise him; and when at last he arose of himself, the shepherds rose also, and standing around him timidly ventured to ask him the cause of his sadness. Jesus answered that he was mourning with those who mourned. He then took one of the hyacinths that grew wild in that region (but which were far larger and more beautiful than those we have), and asked them whether they knew the properties of that flower. When the sky is troubled, he said, it wilts, it pines as it were, and its color grows pale, and so too a cloud had passed over his own sun. He told them many other remarkable things about these flowers and their signification. I heard him also calling them by an exceedingly strange name which, I was told, corresponded to our name for it, the hyacinth.

ABOLITION OF IDOL WORSHIP

Monday, September 15, AD 32 (Elul 20)

Today, Jesus stayed with the shepherds, teaching them about their flocks and also about various herbs.

ALTHOUGH Jesus knew full well, he questioned the shepherds upon the kind of worship they practiced. He was like a good teacher who becomes a child with his children. Thereupon the good people brought to him their gods in the shape of all kinds of animals, sheep, camels, asses—all very skillful imitations of the animals themselves. They appeared to be made of metal, and were covered with skins; and, what was truly amusing, all the idols represented female animals. They were provided with long bags, in imitation of udders, to which were attached reed nipples. These bags they filled with milk, milked them at their feasts, drank, and then danced and leaped about. Everyone selected from his herd the most beautiful, the most excellent cattle, which he raised with care and looked upon as sacred. It was after these holy models that the poor idolaters made their gods, and it was with their milk that they filled the udders. When they celebrated religious services, they brought all their idols together into one tent decorated for the occasion, and then began great carousing as at a carnival. The women and children also were in attendance, and milking and eating, drinking, singing, dancing, and adoring of the idols went on vigorously. It was not the sabbath they were celebrating, but the day after.

While the pagans were relating all this to Jesus and showing him their idols, I saw the whole thing taking shape and being enacted before my eyes. The Lord explained to them what a miserable shadow of true religious service theirs was and, after some more words to that effect, ended by telling them that he himself was the chosen from the herd. He was the Lamb from whom flowed all the milk that was to nourish the soul unto salvation. Then he commanded them to abolish their zoolatry, to drive the living animals back among the herds, and the metal of which the idols were composed to be given to the poor. They should, he said, erect altars, burn upon them incense to the almighty Creator, the heavenly Father, and give thanks to him. They should moreover pray for the coming of the Redeemer, and divide their goods with their poor brethren, for not far off in the desert lived people so poor that they had not even tents to shelter them. Whatever parts of their slaughtered cattle they could not eat ought to be burned as a sacrifice, also the bread that was stale and not intended for the poor. The ashes should be sprinkled upon unproductive ground, which Jesus pointed out to them, in order to attract upon it a blessing. As he prescribed these different points he explained the reasons for observing them. Then he alluded again to the kings that had visited him. The people said, yes, they had heard that thirty-three years before, those kings had journeyed afar in search of the Savior and in the hope of finding along with him everything that could be conducive to happiness and salvation. The kings, they added, had returned to their country and changed something in their religious worship, but that was all they had ever heard about them.

Jesus next went around with these shepherds among their herds and huts, teaching them all kinds of things, even about the different herbs growing there. He promised to send someone to them soon to instruct them. He assured them that he had come on earth not merely for the Jews alone, as they in their humility thought, but for every single human being that sighed for his coming. From the little that they knew of Abraham, this poor shepherd tribe had conceived great esteem for sobriety. The three youths were impressed in a special manner by the late miracle of the luminous globe. Their relations toward the Lord were very different from those of the apostles. They served him in dependence, silence, and childlike simplicity. Unlike the apostles, they never had anything to reply to their Master. The apostles, however, held an office, whereas these youths were like poor, dependent scholars.

JESUS CONTINUES HIS JOURNEY TO THE TENT CITY OF THE KINGS

Tuesday, September 16, and Wednesday, September 17, AD 32 (Elul 21–22)

Today, Jesus and the three youths continued on their way. About twelve shepherds accompanied them. During the hottest part of the day, they rested. They made most rapid progress during the hours of darkness.

WHEN Jesus left the shepherds and pursued his journey to the land of the three kings, about twelve of them bore him company. They appeared to have some kind of a tax to pay for which they were taking with them birds in baskets. This journey was a very lonely one, for on the whole length of the route they did not meet one dwelling house. The road was, however, distinctly marked out, and there was no chance of the traveler's losing his way in the desert. Trees lined the roadside bearing edible fruits the size of figs, and here and there were found berries. At certain points, marking one day's journey, resting places were formed. They consisted of a covered well surrounded by trees, whose tops were drawn together in a large hoop, their hanging branches thus forming an arbor. These resting places were furnished with conveniences for making a fire and passing the night. During the great noonday heat, Jesus and the youths rested at one of these wells and refreshed themselves with some fruit. Each time they thus paused on their journey, Jesus and the youths washed one another's feet. The Lord never permitted any of the others to touch him. The youths, drawn by his goodness, at times treated Jesus with childlike confidence, but again, when they thought of his miracles, his divinity, they cast timid and frightened glances toward him and looked at one another. I saw too that Jesus often appeared to vanish before them, although he did not fail to direct their attention to all that they met on their way and instruct them upon the same.

They journeyed a part of the night. When they paused to rest, the youths struck fire by revolving two pieces of wood together. They had also a lantern at the end of a pole. It was open on top, and its little flame shed around a reddish glare. I do not know of what it consisted. I saw during the night wild animals running furtively about. The road ran sometimes over high mountains, not steep but gently rising. In one field I saw many rows of nut trees, and people filling sacks with the nuts that had fallen. It looked something like a gleaning. There were other trees whose leaves were gone but the fruit was still remaining, peach trees with slender trunks planted on rising ground, and another that looked almost like our laurel. Some of the resting places for travelers were under large juniper bushes whose branches were as thick as the arm of a good-sized man. They were closely grown together overhead, but thinned out below, so as to afford a delightful shelter. The greater part of the journey, however, was through a desert of white sand interspersed with places covered, some with small white pebbles, others with little polished ones like birds' eggs; and there were large beds of black stones, like the remains of fractured pipkins, or pieces of hollow pottery. Some of these fragments were provided with holes like regular rings, or handles, and the people in the country around used to come in search of them in order to utilize them as bowls and other vessels.

Thursday, September 18, AD 32 (*Elul 23*)

Today Jesus and the three youths arrived at a settlement. They were led to a house where various fruits were brought to them. Meanwhile the other shepherds, who had received some food, made their way back home. Jesus asked the people in the house about the three kings. He was told that after they had returned from Judea, they had settled in a place not far away and had erected a "tent city" around a step-pyramid. They knew that the Messiah would visit them. Of the three kings, the eldest, Mensor,† *was alive and well. Theokeno, the next in age, was bedridden, while the third, Sair, had died about nine years before. His corpse lay undecayed in a tomb built in the form of a pyramid.*

The last mountain the travelers crossed was covered with gray stones only. They found on descending its opposite side a dense hedgerow, behind which flowed a rapid stream around a piece of cultivated land. By the shore lay a ferryboat formed of the trunks of trees woven together with osiers. On this they crossed the stream, and then directed their steps to a row of huts built of sticks woven together and overlaid with moss. They had pointed roofs, and all around the central apartment were sleeping places furnished with mossy seats and couches. The occupants were modestly clothed and wore blankets around them like mantles. At some distance I saw tent buildings, much larger and stronger than any I had hitherto seen. They were raised on a stone foundation and had several stories reached by outside steps. Between the first and the second hut was a well, by which Jesus seated himself. The youths washed his feet, and then he was conducted to a house set apart for strangers. The people here were very good. They who had accompanied Jesus now left him for their homes, taking with them provisions for the way.

This region of moss cabins was of very considerable extent, and numberless dwellings such as described lay around among the meadows, fields, and gardens. The large tent palaces could not be seen from here, for they were still at quite a distance; but they were plainly visible from the descent of the mountain. The whole country was extraordinarily fruitful and charming. On the hills were numerous clusters of balsam trees, which when notched distilled a precious juice. The natives caught it in those stone vessels which looked something like iron pots, and which they found in the desert. I saw also magnificent wheat fields, the stalks as thick as reeds, vines, and roses, flowers as large and round as a child's head; and others remarkable for their great size. There were also little purling brooks clear and rapid, overarched by carefully trimmed hedges whose tops were bound together to form a bower. The flowers of these hedges were gathered with care, and those that fell into the water were caught in nets, spread here and there for that purpose, and thus preserved. At the places at which the blossoms were fished out there were gates in the hedges, which were usually kept closed. The people brought and showed to the Lord all the fruits they had.

† Anne Catherine elsewhere describes Theokeno as the eldest of the three kings, and she speaks of Mensor as the king who brought the gift of gold to the child Jesus. She said that Sair had brought incense and Theokeno myrrh, and that Mary had accepted these gifts with humble gratitude. She added that Mensor and Theokeno were baptized by the apostle Thomas three years after the ascension of Jesus. The two kings then left Chaldea and went to live on the island of Crete.

When Jesus spoke to them of those men who had followed the star, they told him that on their return from Judea to the place from which they had first noticed the star, they built on the spot a lofty temple in the form of a pyramid. Around it they erected a city of tents in which they dwelt together, although before that they had lived widely apart. They had received the assurance that the Messiah would eventually visit them, and that upon his departure they too would leave the place. Mensor, the eldest, was still alive and well; Theokeno, the second, borne down by the weakness of old age, could no longer walk. Sair, the third, had died some years previously, and his remains, perfectly preserved, lay in a tomb built in pyramidal form. On the anniversary of his death, his friends visited it, opened it, and performed certain ceremonies over the remains, near which fire was kept constantly burning.

Friday, September 19, and Saturday, September 20, AD 32 (Elul 24–25)

The people, who believed Jesus to be an envoy of the king of the Jews awaited by the kings Mensor and Theokeno, sent a messenger to Mensor to inform him of Jesus's arrival. The tent city where Mensor and Theokeno lived was only a few hours away. With the onset of the sabbath, Jesus and the three youths retired to a lonely hut where they remained until the close of the sabbath. Afterward, Jesus taught the people of the place.

They enquired of Jesus after those of the caravan that had remained behind in Palestine, and sent messengers to the tent city, a couple of hours distant, to inform Mensor that they thought they had among them an envoy of that king of the Jews so desired by him and his people.

When the hour for the sabbath approached, Jesus asked for one of the unoccupied cabins to be placed at the service of himself and his disciples, and as there were here no lamps of Jewish style, they made one for themselves and celebrated their holy exercises.

Jesus Ceremoniously Escorted by Mensor to his Tent Castle

WHEN the kings received the news of Jesus's arrival, they made great preparations for his reception. Trees were bound together so as to form covered walks, and triumphal arches erected. These latter were adorned with flowers, fruits, ornaments of all kinds, and hung with tapestry. Seven men in white, gold-embroidered mantles, long and training, and with turbans on their heads ornamented with gold and high tufts of feathers, were dispatched to the pastoral region to meet Jesus and bear to him a welcome. Jesus delivered in their presence an instruction in which he spoke of right-minded pagans who, though ignorant, were devout of heart.

The dwelling place of the kings was so commodious and so rich in ornamentation that words cannot describe it. It was more like a delightful pleasure garden than a real tent city. The principal tent looked like a large castle. It consisted of several stories raised upon a stone foundation. The lowest was formed of railings through which the eye could penetrate, and the upper ones contained the various apartments, while all around the immense building ran covered galleries and flights of steps. Similar tent castles stood around, all connected together by walks paved with colored stones ornamented with representations of stars, flowers, and similar devices. These walks, so clean and beautiful, were bordered on either side by grass plots and gardens whose beds, regularly laid out, were full of flowers, slender trees with fine leaves, such as the myrtle and dwarf laurel, and all kinds of berries and aromatic plants. In the center of the city, upon a grassy mound such as described, rose a very high and beautiful fountain of many jets. It was surmounted by a roof supported on an open colonnade around which were placed benches and other seats. The streams from the jets shot far around the central column. Back of this stood the temple, with its surrounding colonnades, containing the vaults of the kings, among which was the tomb of King Sair. This temple was open on one side, but closed on the others by the doors leading to the vaults. It was in shape a four-cornered pyramid, but the roof was not so flat as those that I saw on the early part of the Lord's journey. Spiral steps with railings ran up around the pyramid, whose summit was executed in openwork. I noticed also a tent house in one side of which youths were being educated; and on the other, but entirely separate, girls were instructed in various branches. The dwellings of the females were all together and outside of this enclosure. They lived entirely separate from the men. Words cannot say with what elegance the whole city was laid out, and with what care it was preserved in its beauty, freshness, and neatness. The buildings presented an airy appearance characterized by simplicity of taste. Beautiful gardens with seats for resting were everywhere to be met. I saw an immense cage, more like a large house than a cage, filled from top to bottom with birds; further on, I saw tents and huts in which dwelt smiths and other workmen. I saw also stables and immense meadows full of herds of camels, asses, great sheep with fine wool, also cows with small heads and large horns, very different from those of our country.

I saw no mountain in this region, only gently rising hills, not much higher than our pagan sepulchral mounds.

Down through these hills, through pipes inserted for that purpose, borings were made in search of gold. If the boring tube were brought up with gold on its point, the mine was opened in the side of the hill and the gold dug out. It was then smelted in the neighborhood of the mine in furnaces heated not with wood, but with lumps of something brown and clear, which too was dug out of the earth.

Sunday, September 21, AD 32 (Elul 26)

Today Jesus went to the tent city of Mensor and Theokeno. As he approached, Mensor came to greet him, riding on a camel, accompanied by about twenty men. They were filled with joy as they went up to Jesus. Mensor climbed down from the camel, handed Jesus his royal scepter, and cast himself down before him. Jesus gave him his hand and raised him up. Mensor asked Jesus about the king of the Jews, believing Jesus to be an envoy of that king. They all went back to the tent city, where they dined together.

Mensor, who was under the persuasion that it was only an envoy from Jesus who had arrived, set all in motion to give him as solemn a reception as if it were the king of the Jews himself who had come. He deliberated with the other chiefs and priests, and prescribed the various details of his reception. Festal garments and presents were prepared, and the roads by which he was to come magnificently decorated. All was carried forward with joyous earnestness. Mensor, mounted on a richly caparisoned camel which was laden on both sides with small chests, and attended by a retinue of twenty distinguished personages, some of whom had formed part of the caravan to Bethlehem, set out to meet Jesus who, with the three youths and seven messengers, was on his way to the tent castle. Mensor's party chanted, as they went along, a solemn, plaintive melody such as they had nightly sung during their journey to Bethlehem. Mensor, the eldest of the kings, he of the brownish complexion, wore a high, round cap ornamented with some kind of a white puffed border, and a white training mantle embroidered in gold. As a mark of honor, a standard floated at the head of the procession. It looked like a horse's tail fastened to a pole, the top of which was indented with points. The way led through an avenue across lovely meadows carpeted here and there with patches of tender white moss that glanced like dense fungus in the rays of the sun. At last, the procession reached a well covered by a verdant temple of artistically cut foliage. Here Mensor dismounted from his camel and awaited the Lord, who was seen approaching. One of the seven delegated to escort Jesus ran on before and announced his coming. The chests borne by the camels were now opened, and magnificent garments embroidered in gold, golden cups, plates, and dishes of fruit were taken out and deposited upon the carpet that was spread near the well. Mensor, bowed with age, supported by two of his retinue and attended by his train-bearer, went to meet Jesus. His whole demeanor was marked by humility. He carried in his right hand a long staff ornamented with gold and terminating in a scepter-shaped point. At a glance from Jesus he experienced, as formerly at the crib, an interior monition similar to that which had drawn him, first of the three, down upon his knees. Reaching his staff to Jesus, he now prostrated again before him, but Jesus raised him from the ground. Then the old man ordered the gifts to be brought forward and presented to Jesus, who handed them to the disciples, and they were replaced upon the camel. Jesus did indeed accept the splendid garments, though he would not consent to wear them. The camel likewise was presented to him by the old man, but Jesus thanked without accepting.

They now entered the bower. Mensor presented to the Lord fresh water into which he had poured some kind of juice from a small flask, and fruit on little dishes. In a manner inexpressibly humble, childlike, and friendly, Mensor questioned Jesus about the king of the Jews, for he still looked upon him as an envoy, though he could not explain to himself his inward emotion. His companions conversed with the youths and wept for joy when they heard from Eremenzear that he was the son of one of those followers of the kings that had remained behind and settled near Bethlehem. He was a descendant of Abraham by his second wife, Keturah. Mensor wanted Jesus to ride upon his camel when they were again starting for the tent castle, but Jesus insisted on walking, he and the young disciples heading the procession. In about an hour they reached the vast circular enclosure wherein stood Mensor's dwelling and its dependencies, and around which, in lieu of walls, was stretched white tent cloth. Under the triumphal arch before the entrance, Jesus and the disciples were met by a troop of maidens in festive attire. They came forward, two by two, carrying baskets of flowers which they strewed over the way by which he had to pass until it was entirely covered with them. The path led through an avenue of shade trees whose top branches were bound together. The maidens wore under their upper garment, which fell around them in the form of a mantle, wide white pantalets; on their feet, pointed sandals; around their heads, bands of some kind of white fabric; and on their arms and breast and around their necks were wreaths of flowers, wool, and glistening feathers.

They were clothed very modestly, though they wore no veils. The shady avenue ended at a covered bridge which led across the moat, or brook, into the large garden around which the brook ran. In front of the bridge was erected a highly ornamented triumphal arch, under which Jesus was received by five priests in white mantles with long trains. Their robes were richly adorned with lace, and from the right arm of each hung a maniple to the ground. They wore on their head a scalloped crown in the front of which was a little shield in the form of a heart, and from which rose a point. Two of them bore a fire-pan of gold, upon which they sprinkled frankincense from a golden vessel shaped like a boat. They would not allow the trains of their mantles to be held up in Jesus's presence, but tucked them up in a loop behind.

Jesus received all these honors quietly, as he afterward did those of Palm Sunday.

The magnificent garden was watered by many little streams and laid off in triangular flowerbeds by paths beautifully paved with ornamental stones. Through the center of it ran an embowered walk, likewise paved with colored stones in figures, to a second covered bridge. The trees and garden bushes were trained in all kinds of figures. I saw some cut to represent men and animals. The outside row was formed of high trees, but the inner ones were smaller, more delicate, and there were many shady resting places.

The second bridge once crossed, the way led to the middle of a large, circular place that formed the center of the surrounding enclosure. There on a mound entirely surrounded by water stood, over a well, an open edifice, like a little temple. The roof, formed of skins, was raised upon slender pillars. The whole island was one lovely garden, and opposite to it rose the large royal tent.

When Jesus crossed the second bridge, he was received by youths playing on flutes and tambourines. They dwelt near the bridge in low, four-cornered tents which stretched right and left in arches. They must have been a kind of bodyguard, for they carried short swords and stood on guard. They wore caps garnished with something like a feather horn, and they had many kinds of ornaments hanging around them, among them the representation of a large half-moon, in which was a face regularly cut out. The procession halted before the little island of the well. The king dismounted from his camel and led Jesus and the disciples to the fountain, which consisted of a wellspring with many circles of jets one above another, all made of shining metal. When a faucet was turned, the streams of water spouted far around and ran down the mound in channels, through the green hedges, and into the surrounding brook. All around the fountain were seats. The disciples washed Jesus's feet, and he theirs. A covered tent avenue ran over the bridge from the fountain to the other side of the great, circular place and up to Mensor and Theokeno's tent castle. On one side of the tent castle stood, in the spacious enclosure around the fountain island, the temple, a four-cornered pyramid. It was not so high as the tent castle and was surrounded by a colonnade, in which was found the entrance to the vaults of the deceased kings. Around the temple pyramid ran a flight of spiral steps up to the grated summit. Between the temple and the fountain island, the sacred fire was preserved in a pit covered by a metallic dome upon which was a figure with a little flag in its hand. The fire was kept constantly

Tents by a Spring

burning. It was a white flame that did not rise above the mouth of the pit. The priests frequently put into it pieces of something that they dug out of the ground.

The tent castle of the kings was several stories high. The lowest, that is, the one next above the solid foundation, was merely grated, so that one could see quite through it. It was full of little bushes and plants, and served as a garden for Theokeno, who could no longer walk. Covered steps and galleries ran around the tent castle from the ground up to the top. Here and there were openings like windows, though not symmetrically placed. The roof of the tent had several gables, all ornamented with flags, stars, and moons.

After a short time spent at the fountain, Jesus was escorted through the covered tent avenue to the castle and into the large octagonal hall. In the center rose a supporting column all around which, one above another, were little circular cavities in which various objects could be placed. The walls were hung with colored tapestry upon which were representations of flowers, and figures of boys holding drinking cups, and the floor was carpeted.

Monday, September 22, to Wednesday, September 24, AD 32 (Elul 27–29)

Mensor went with Jesus to Theokeno, who on account of weakness and old age was no longer able to walk. He rested upon an upholstered bed. Jesus visited him daily with Mensor. Mensor and Theokeno related how they had seen the star which led them to the new-born child in Bethlehem. They asked Jesus why they had lost sight of the star as they had approached Jerusalem. Jesus replied: "To test your faith, and because it should not come across Jerusalem." With this, Jesus said that he was not the envoy of the king of the Jews but was himself that king. He added that he had come for Gentiles as well as for Jews, for all who believed in him. When Mensor and Theokeno said that they wanted to follow him back to Israel, Jesus said that his kingdom was not of this world. He said that they would be much upset and their faith sorely tried if they were to see how he would be despised and mistreated.

Jesus requested Mensor to conduct him at once to Theokeno, whose rooms were in the trellised basement near the little garden. He was resting on a cushioned couch, and he took part in the meal that was served up in dishes of surpassing beauty. The food dishes were prepared very elegantly. Herbs, fine and delicate, were arranged on the plates to represent little gardens. The cups were of gold. Among the fruits was one particularly remarkable. It was yellow, ribbed, very large, and crowned by a tuft of leaves. The honeycombs were especially fine. Jesus ate only some bread and fruit, and drank from a cup that had never before been used. This was the first time that I saw him eating with pagans. I saw him teaching here whole days at a time, and but seldom taking a mouthful.

He taught during that meal and, at last, told his hosts that he was not an envoy of the Messiah, but the Messiah himself. On hearing this, they fell prostrate on the ground in tears. Mensor especially wept with emotion. He could not contain himself for love and reverence, and was unable to conceive how Jesus could have condescended to come to him. But Jesus told him that he had come for the pagans as well as for the Jews, that he was come for all who believed in him. Then they asked him whether it was not time for them to abandon their country and follow him at once to Galilee, for, as they assured him, they were ready to do so. But Jesus replied that his kingdom was not of this world, and that they would be scandalized, that they would waver in faith if they should see how he would be scorned and maltreated by the Jews. These words they could not comprehend, and they inquired how it could be that things could go so well with the bad while the good had to suffer so much. Jesus then explained to them that they who enjoy on earth have to render an account hereafter, and that this life is one of penance.

The kings had some knowledge of Abraham and David; and when Jesus spoke of his ancestors, they produced some old books and searched in them to see whether they too could not claim descent from the same race. The books were in the form of tablets opening out in a zigzag form, like sample patterns. These pagans were so childlike, so desirous of doing all that they were told. They knew that circumcision had been prescribed to Abraham, and they asked the Lord whether they too should obey this part of the Law. Jesus answered that it was no longer necessary, that they had already circumcised their evil inclinations, and that they would do so still more. Then they told him that they knew something of Melchizedek and his sacrifice of bread and wine, and said that they too had a sacrifice of the same kind, namely, a sacrifice of little leaves and some kind of a green liquor. When they offered it they spoke some words like these: "Whoever eats me and is devout, shall have all kinds of felicity." Jesus told them that Melchizedek's sacrifice was a type of the most holy Sacrifice, and that he himself was the Victim. Thus, though plunged in darkness, these pagans had preserved many forms of truth.

Either the night that preceded Jesus's coming or that which followed, I cannot now say which, all the paths and avenues to a great distance around the tent castle were brilliantly illuminated. Transparent globes with lights in them were raised on poles, and every globe was surmounted by a little crown that glistened like a star.

TISHRI (30 days): September 23/24 to October 23/24, AD 32 Tishri New Moon: September 23 at 2:00 PM Jerusalem time

Jesus in the Temple of the Kings • Feast of the Apparition of the Star

Thursday, September 25, AD 32 (Tishri 1)

Jesus visited the temple in the tent city. He also went to the tomb of Sair. Theokeno told Jesus how, according to their custom, they had placed a branch in front of the tomb; he said that a dove was often seen to settle on this branch and asked what this meant. Jesus asked Theokeno about Sair's faith. Theokeno replied: "Lord, his faith was like mine. Right up to his death, since we went to worship the king of the Jews, Sair always wanted only to think and do his will." Jesus explained to Mensor and Theokeno that the dove on the branch revealed that Sair had been baptized with the baptism of spiritual desire.

THE LORD's first visit to the temple of the kings took place by day, and he was escorted to it from the tent castle by the priests in solemn procession. They now wore high caps. From one shoulder depended ribbons with numbers of silver shields, and from the opposite arm hung the long maniple. The whole way to the temple was hung with drapery, and the priests walked barefoot. Here and there in the neighborhood of the temple women were sitting, anxious to see the Lord. They had little parasols, little canopies on poles, to shade them from the sun. When Jesus passed in the distance, they arose and bowed low to the ground. In the center of the temple rose a pillar from which chevrons extended to the four walls, and from the highest point was suspended a wheel covered with stars and globes, which was used during the religious ceremonies.

The priests showed Jesus a representation of the crib which, after their return from Bethlehem, they had caused to be made. It was exactly like that which they had seen in the star, entirely of gold, and surrounded by a plate of the same metal in the form of a star. The little child, likewise of gold, was sitting in a crib like that of Bethlehem, on a red cover. Its hands were crossed on its breast up to which from the feet it was swathed. Even the straw of the manger was represented. Behind the child's head was a little white crown, but I do not now know of what it was made. Besides this crib there was no other image in the temple. A long roll, or tablet, was hanging on the wall. It was the sacred writings, and the letters were principally formed of symbolical figures. Between the pillar and the crib stood a little altar with openings in the sides, and they sprinkled water around with a little brush, as we do holy water. I saw also a consecrated branch with which they performed all kinds of ceremonies, some little round loaves, a chalice, and a plate of the flesh of victims sacrificed. As they were showing all these things to Jesus, he enlightened them on the truth and refuted the reasons they advanced for their use.

They took him also to the tombs of King Sair and his family, which lay in the vaults in the covered way that surrounded the pyramidal temple. They looked like couches cut in the wall. The bodies lay in long, white garments, and beautiful covers hung down from their resting places. I saw their half-covered faces and their hands bare and white as snow; but I know not whether it was only their bones or whether they were still covered with dried skin, for I saw that the hands were deeply furrowed. This sepulchral vault was quite habitable, and there was a stool in each of the tombs. The priests brought in fire and burnt incense. All shed tears, especially the aged King Mensor, who wept like a child. Jesus approached the remains and spoke of the dead. Theokeno, speaking to Jesus of Sair, told him that a dove was frequently seen to alight on the branch which, according to their custom, they stuck on the door of his tomb, and he asked what it meant. Jesus in reply asked him what was Sair's belief. To this Theokeno answered: "Lord, his faith was like unto mine. After we began to honor the king of the Jews, Sair up to his death desired that all he thought and did, all that was to befall him, might ever be in accordance with the will of that king."

Thereupon Jesus informed him that the dove on the branch signified that Sair had been baptized with the baptism of desire.

Jesus drew for them on a plate the figure of the lamb resting on the Book with the Seven Seals, a little standard over its shoulder, and he bade them make one on that model and place it on the column opposite the crib.

Friday, September 26, AD 32 (Tishri 2)

Mensor and Theokeno told Jesus how they had first seen the star fifteen years before his birth. It was a vision of a virgin with a scepter in one hand and a pair of scales in the other, a beautiful ear of corn in one of the scales and a wine-grape in the other. Since returning from Bethlehem, for three days each year they had celebrated a festival in honor of Jesus, Mary, and Joseph, who had welcomed them so lovingly. That evening, as the sabbath began, Jesus and the three shepherd youths separated themselves from the others and prayed together.

Since their return from Bethlehem, the kings had every year celebrated a memorial feast of three days in honor of that upon which, fifteen years before the birth of Christ, they had for the first time seen the star containing the picture of the virgin who held in one hand a scepter, and in the other a balance with an ear of wheat in one dish and a cluster of grapes in the other. The three days were in honor of Jesus, Mary, and Joseph. They reverenced Joseph in a special manner, because he had received them so kindly and graciously. It was now time for this annual festival, but in their humility in presence of the Lord, they wanted to omit the usual religious ceremonies, and begged him to give them an instruction instead. But Jesus told them that they must celebrate their feast, lest the people in their ignorance of what had just taken place might be scandalized at the omission. I saw many things connected with their religion. They had three images in the form of animals standing around outside the temple: one was a dragon with huge jaws; another a dog with a great head; and the third was a bird with legs and neck long, almost like a stork, only that it had a peaked bill. I do not think that these images were adored as gods. They served only as symbols of certain virtues whose practice they inculcated. The dragon represented the bad, the dark principle in man's nature, which he must labor to destroy; the dog, which had reference to some star, signified fidelity, gratitude, and vigilance; and the bird typified filial love. The images embodied besides all kinds of deep, profound mysteries, but I cannot now recall them. I know well however that no idolatry, no abomination was connected with them. They were embodiments of great wisdom and humility, of deep meditation upon the wonderful things of God. They were not made of gold, but of something darker, like those fragments that were used for smelting the ore, or perhaps what remained after that process. Below the figure of the dragon I read five letters, A A S C C or A S C A S, I do not remember exactly which. The dog's name was Sur, but that of the bird I have forgotten.

The four priests delivered discourses in four different places around the temple before the men, the women, the maidens, and the youths. I saw them open the dragon's jaws and I heard them say at the same time: "If, hateful and frightful as he is, he were now alive and about to devour us, who alone could help us but the almighty God?"—and they gave to God some special name that I cannot now recall. Then they caused the wheel to be taken down from its place, put it on the altar in a track formed to receive it, and one of the priests made it revolve. There were several circles one inside the other all hung with hollow golden balls, which glittered and tinkled at every revolution, thus announcing the course of the constellations. This revolving of the wheel was accompanied by singing, the refrain being to this effect: "What would become of the world if God should cease to direct the movement of the stars?" This was followed by the offering of sacrifice before the golden Christ child in the crib, and the burning of incense. Jesus commanded them to do away with those animals for the future, and to teach mercy, love of the neighbor, and the Redemption of the human race; as for the rest, they should admire God in his creatures, give him thanks, and adore him alone. On the evening of the first of these three festivals, the sabbath began for Jesus; therefore, he withdrew with the three youths into a retired apartment of the tent castle to celebrate it. They had with them white garments almost like grave clothes. These they put on, along with a girdle, ornamented with letters and straps, which they crossed like a stole over the breast. On a table covered with red and white stood a lamp with seven burners. When in prayer, Jesus stood between two of the youths, the third behind him. No pagan was present at Jesus's celebration of the sabbath.

Saturday, September 27, AD 32 (Tishri 3)

This evening, at the close of the sabbath, Jesus went into the temple where there was an idol of a dragon. As one of the women cast herself down before this idol to worship it, Jesus said: "Why do you cast yourself down before Satan? Your faith has been taken possession of by Satan. Behold whom you worship!" Instantly there appeared before her, visible to all, a slender, redfox-colored spirit with a hideously pointed countenance. All were horrified. Jesus pointed to the spirit and indicated that it was this spirit which had woken the woman from sleep each morning before the break of day. The woman had arisen each morning and cast herself down to pray in the direction of the dragon. Jesus said: "This awoke you. However, every person also has a good angel, who should wake you, and before whom you should cast yourself down and follow his advice." All then saw a radiant figure at the woman's side. At this approach of the good angel, the satanic spirit withdrew. Like the two kings, this woman later became baptized by the apostle Thomas and received the name Serena. Later, she suffered a martyr's death.

During the whole of the sabbath, the pagans were gathered together in the enclosure around their temple, men, women, youths, and maidens—all had their respective tiers of seats. After Jesus had finished his celebration of the sabbath he went out to the pagans and then I witnessed a wonderful scene. In the center of the women's circle stood the image of the dragon. The women were very differently clothed according to their rank. The poorest wore under their long mantles only a short garment, very simple; but the more distinguished were arrayed like her whom I now saw step in front of the dragon. She was a robust-looking woman of about thirty. Under the long mantle, which she laid aside when seated, she wore a stiff, plaited tunic and a jacket very closely fitting around the neck and breast, and ornamented with glittering jewels and tiny chains. From the shoulder to the elbow hung lappets like open half-sleeves, and the rest of the arms, like the lower limbs, was covered with lace and bracelets. On her head she wore a close-fitting cap that reached down to the eyes, partly concealed the cheeks and chin, and which was formed entirely of rows of curled feathers. Above the middle of the head, bent from the forehead back, arose a kind of roll or pad through which could be seen the hair, braided and ornamented. A great many long ornamental chains hung from the ears down to the breast.

Before the priest began his instruction, the woman, attended by many others, went in front of the dragon, cast herself down and kissed the earth. She performed this action with marked enthusiasm and devotion. At this moment Jesus stepped into the middle of the circle and asked why she did that. She answered that the dragon awoke her every morning before day when she arose, turned toward the quarter in which the image stood, prostrated before her couch, and adored it. Jesus next asked: "Why dost thou cast thyself down before Satan? Thy faith has been taken possession of by Satan. It is true indeed that thou wilt be awakened, but not by Satan. It is an angel that will awake thee. Behold whom thou adorest!" At the same moment, there stood by the woman, and in sight of all present, a spirit in the form of a figure lank and reddish, with a sharp, hideous countenance. The woman shrank back in fright. Jesus, pointing to the spirit, said: "This is he that has been accustomed to awake thee, but every human being has also a good angel. Prostrate before him and follow his advice!" At these words of Jesus, all perceived a beautiful luminous figure hovering near the woman. Tremblingly she prostrated before him. So long as Satan stood beside the woman, the good angel remained behind her, but when he disappeared, the angel came forward. The woman, deeply affected, now returned to her place. She was called Cuppes. She was afterward baptized Serena by Thomas, under which name she was later on martyred and venerated as a saint.

In his instruction to the youths and maidens who were assembled in the vicinity of the bird, Jesus warned them to observe due measure in their love of both human beings and the lower animals, for there were some among them that almost adored their parents, and others that showed more affection for animals than for their fellow men.

Sunday, September 28, AD 32 (Tishri 4)

This morning Jesus went with Mensor to visit Theokeno. He bade Theokeno to arise. Taking him by the hand, Jesus raised him up, and Theokeno was able to walk. From this time on, Theokeno was no longer bedridden. Jesus then went with Mensor and Theokeno to the temple, where he taught. After teaching the people, Jesus gave instruction to the two kings and the four priests of the temple. He explained that when the good angels withdraw, Satan takes possession of a temple service. He said that they should remove the various animal idols and teach love and compassion and give thanks to the Father in heaven. Jesus now took bread and wine, which had been prepared beforehand. Having consecrated the bread and wine, he placed them upon a small altar. He prayed and blessed everyone. Mensor, Theokeno, and the four priests knelt before him with their hands folded across their chests. Jesus laid his hands upon their shoulders and prayed over them. He blessed the bread and wine and said that they should partake of it once every three months. He taught them the words of blessing to use and said that they should begin taking the communion of bread and wine at Christmas time.

On the last day of the festival, Jesus desired to deliver a discourse in the temple to the priests and kings and all the people. That the aged King Theokeno also might be among his hearers, Jesus went to him with Mensor, and commanded him to rise and accompany him. He took him by the hand and Theokeno, nothing doubting, rose up at once able to walk. Jesus led him to the temple and from that time forward he retained the use of his limbs. Jesus ordered the doors of the pyramidal temple to be opened, that all the people outside could both see and hear him. He taught sometimes outside among the men and women, the youths, the maidens, and the children, relating to them many of the parables that he had formerly recounted to the Jews. His auditors were privileged to interrupt him in order to ask questions, for he had commanded them to do so. Sometimes also he called upon a certain one to say aloud before all the others the doubts that troubled him, for he knew the thoughts of everyone. Among the questions they asked was this: Why he raised no dead to life, cured no sick, as the king of the Jews had done? Jesus answered that he did not perform such miracles among pagans, but that he would send some men who would work many wonders among them, and that through the bath of baptism they should become clean. They should, he said, until that time take his words on faith.

Jesus then gave an instruction to the priests and kings alone. He told them that whatever in their doctrine bore an appearance of truth, was a mere lie: it had only the semblance, the empty form of truth, and the demon himself gave it that form. As soon as the good angel withdraws, Satan steps forward, corrupts worship, and takes it under his own guardianship. Heretofore, Jesus continued, they had honored all those objects to which they could attach some idea of strength, and of that worship they had omitted many things after their return from Bethlehem. Now, however, he told them they should do away with those figures of animals, should melt them down: and he indicated to them the people to whom their value should be given. All their worship, all their knowledge, he said, valued nothing. They should inculcate love and mercy without the aid of those images, and thank the Father in heaven that he had so mercifully called them to the knowledge of himself. Jesus promised them that he would send one who would more fully instruct them, and he directed them to remove the wheel with its starry representations. It was as large as a carriage wheel of moderate size and had seven concentric rims, on the uppermost and the lowest of which were fastened globes from which streamed rays. The central point consisted of a larger globe, which represented the earth. On the circumference of the wheel were twelve stars, in which were as many different pictures, splendid and glittering. I saw among them one of a virgin with rays of light flashing from her eyes and playing around her mouth, while on her forehead sparkled precious stones; and another of an animal with something in its mouth that emitted sparks. But I could not see all distinctly, because the wheel was constantly revolving. The figures were not all visible at the same time, for at intervals some were hidden.

Jesus desired to leave them some bread and wine blessed by himself. The priests had, in obedience to his directions, prepared some very fine white bread like little cakes, and a small jug of some kind of red liquor. Jesus specified the shape of the vessel in which all was to be preserved. It was like a large mortar. It had two ears, a cover with a knob, and was divided into two compartments. The bread was deposited in the upper one; and in the lower one, in which there was a small door, the little jug of liquor was placed. The outside shone like quicksilver, but the inside was yellow. Jesus placed the bread and the wine on the little altar, prayed, and blessed, while the priests and the two kings knelt before him, their hands crossed on their breast. Jesus prayed over them, laid his hands on their shoulders, and instructed them how they should renew the bread, which he cut for them crosswise, giving them the words and the ceremony of benediction. This bread and wine were to be for them a symbol of Holy Communion. The kings had some knowledge of Melchizedek, and they questioned Jesus concerning his sacrifice. When he blessed the bread for them, he gave them some idea of his Passion and of the Last Supper. They should, he told them, make use of the bread and wine for the first time on the anniversary of their adoration at the crib, and after that three times in the year, or every three months, I cannot recall it exactly.

Monday, September 29, AD 32 (Tishri 5)

Jesus taught again today in the temple. He gave instruction to the women concerning prayer, saying also how they should bring up their children. Afterward, he blessed the children.

Next day Jesus again taught in the temple wherein all were gathered. He went in and out, leaving one crowd to go to another. He allowed the women and children also to come and speak to him, and he instructed the mothers how to rear their children and teach them to pray. This was the first time that I saw many children gathered together here. The boys wore only a short tunic, and the little girls, mantles. The children of the converted lady were present. She was a person of distinction and her spouse, a tall man, was near King Mensor. She had fully ten children with her. Jesus blessed them, laying his hand not on the head as he did to the children of Judea, but on the shoulder.

He instructed the people upon his mission and his approaching end, and told them that his journey into their country was unknown to the Jews. He had, he said, brought with him as companions youths that would take no scandal at what they saw and heard, and who were docile to all his words. The Jews would have taken his life, had he not made his escape. But apart from all that, he was desirous of visiting them because they had visited him, had believed in him, hoped in him, and loved him. He admonished them to thank God for not allowing them to be entirely blinded by idolatry and for giving them the true belief in himself and the grace to keep his commandments. If I do not mistake, he spoke to them also of the time of his return to his heavenly Father, when he would send to them his disciples. He told them too that he was going down into Egypt where as a child he had been with his mother, for there were some people there who had known him in his childhood. He would, however, remain quite unknown, as there were Jews there who would willingly seize him and deliver him to his enemies, but his time was not yet come.

The pagans could not understand the human foresight of Jesus. In their childlike simplicity, they mentally asked themselves: "How could they do such things to him, since he is truly God?" Jesus answered their thoughts by telling them that he was man also, that the Father had sent him to lead back all the scattered, that as a man, he could suffer and be persecuted by men when his hour would have come, and because he was a man, he could be thus intimate with them.

He warned them again to renounce all kinds of idolatry and to love one another. In speaking of his own Passion, he touched upon true compassion. They should, he said, desist from their excessive care of sick animals, and turn their love toward their fellow beings both as regards body and soul; and if there were in their neighborhood none that stood in need of assistance, they should seek at a distance for such as did, and pray for all their destitute brethren. He told them also that what they did for the needy, they did for him, and he made them understand that they were not to treat the lower animals with cruelty. They had entire tents filled with sick animals of all kinds, which they even provided with little beds. They were especially fond of dogs, of which I saw many large ones with enormous heads.

ARRIVAL OF THE LEADER OF A STRANGE TRIBE

JESUS had already taught these pagans for some time, when I saw approaching a caravan on camels. It paused and remained standing at some distance while an old man, a stranger and the leader of the tribe, dismounted and drew near. He was attended by an aged servant whom he very highly respected, and both stood still at a little distance from the assembly. No one noticed them until the Lord's discourse was ended and he, with the disciples, had retired to the tent to take some refreshment. Then the stranger was received by Mensor, and shown to a tent. He afterward went with his old servant to the priests and told them that he could not believe Jesus to be the promised king of the Jews, because he treated with them so familiarly. The Jews had as he well knew, he continued, an Ark wherein was their God, and to it no one dare approach, consequently this man could not be their God. The old servant also gave utterance to some erroneous conceptions of Mary; still both he and his master were good people. This king too had seen the wonderful star, but he had not followed it. He spoke much of his gods, whom he held in high esteem, and told how gracious they were to him, and that they brought him all kinds of good luck. He related also an incident that happened during a war which he had lately waged, and in which his gods had helped him and his old servant had brought him a certain piece of news. This king was of lighter complexion than Mensor, his clothing was shorter, and the turban round his head not so large. He was very much attached to his idols, one of which he always carried about with him on a camel. It was a figure with many arms, and with holes in its body in which could be placed the sacrifices offered it. He had some women in his caravan, which consisted of about thirty persons. As for himself, he was a very simple-minded man. He looked upon his old servant as an oracle, indeed he honored him even as a prophet. The latter had induced his master to make this journey, that he might show him, as he said, the greatest of all the gods, but Jesus did not appear to answer his expectations. What the Lord said of compassion and beneficence pleased him greatly, for he was himself very charitable. He declared that he looked upon it as the greatest crime to neglect human beings for the sake of the lower animals. A meal was afterward prepared for the stranger, but at which Jesus was not present. I did not see him even conversing with him. The king's name sounded like Acicus. The old servant was an astrologer. He was clothed like a prophet in a long robe with a girdle that had many knots around it. His turban had numerous white cords and knots pendent from it. They looked as if made of cotton, and he wore a long beard. The royal stranger and his followers were of fairer complexion than the natives of these parts, among whom they were going to sojourn for some time. The women and their other followers they had left behind near the women's tents. They had come a two days' journey. I did not see Jesus conversing with them, but I heard him say that they would come to the knowledge of the truth, and he praised the king's compassion for men. I heard names that sounded like Ormuzd and Zorosdat.

The husband of Cuppes was a son of Mensor's brother. He had, when a youth, accompanied his uncle to Bethlehem. He and Cuppes were of a yellowish-brown complexion, and both were descendants of Job.

Jesus still taught after nightfall in and around the temple. The whole place was brilliantly illuminated, the temple itself a blaze of light. The inhabitants of the whole region were gathered together, old and young, men and women. Upon the first command of Jesus, they had removed the idols. But I now saw something in the temple that I had not before noticed. Up in the roof I saw a whole firmament of shining stars, and in between were reflected little gardens and brooks and bushes, which were placed up high in the temple and illumined with lights. It was a most wonderful contrivance, and I cannot imagine how it was done.

Jesus Leaves the Tent City of the Kings and Goes to Visit Azarias, the Nephew of Mensor, in the Settlement of Atom

Tuesday, September 30, AD 32 (Tishri 6)

Before daybreak, Jesus left the tent city of the kings. Mensor begged him to remain with them, and wept profusely at Jesus's departure. Jesus and the three shepherd youths traveled far and that evening reached a shepherd settlement where they stayed that night.

JESUS left the tent city of the kings before daybreak when the lamps were still burning. They had arranged for him a festive escort such as had welcomed him, but he declined the attention and would not even accept a camel. The disciples took with them only some bread and some kind of liquor in flasks. The aged Mensor earnestly entreated Jesus to remain longer with them. He laid the crown that he wore on his turban at Jesus's feet, and offered him all that he possessed. His treasures were deposited under a grating in the floor of his tent, as in a cellar. They lay there in bars, lumps, and little heaps of grains. Mensor wept like a child.

The tears rolled like pearls down his brownish-yellow cheeks. His ancestor Job had the same complexion. It was a very delicate, shining brown, not so dark as that of the people near the Ganges. All wept and sobbed on parting.

Jesus left the city by the side upon which stood the temple, and passed the magnificent tent of the converted Cuppes, who ran forward with her children to meet him. Jesus drew the children to himself and spoke to the mother, who cast herself prostrate at his feet in tears. Mensor, the priests, and many others escorted Jesus, walking at his side two by two in turn. Jesus and the disciples carried staves. When Mensor and the priests reached home, it was already dark. Lamps were burning everywhere and all the people were gathered in and around the temple, kneeling in prayer or prostrate on the ground. Mensor announced to them that everyone who was not willing to live according to the Law of Jesus, and who did not believe in his doctrine, should leave his dominions. There were people here of a complexion still darker than Mensor. His tent city, with its temple and the burial place of the kings, was the metropolis of the star worshippers, but at some hours' distance in the surrounding district there were other tent settlements.

Jesus journeyed eastward. He took up his first night quarters in a shepherd village belonging to Mensor's tribe and at about twelve hours from his tent castle. He slept with his disciples in a circular tent, whose sleeping places were separated from one another by movable screens.

Wednesday, October 1, AD 32 (Tishri 7)

Jesus and his traveling companions left the shepherd settlement before the break of day and journeyed again for the whole day. That night they slept in a hut made of earth and moss.

Next morning Jesus left before the inhabitants were awake. I saw him arrive at a stream that was too wide to ford, in consequence of which he turned his steps northward along its banks until he came to a spot that could be easily crossed. Toward evening he arrived at some huts, built either of moss or earth, near which was an uncovered well surrounded by a rampart. Here he and his companions washed their feet and, without a reception from anyone, turned into a hut made of leafy branches and there slept during the night. This hut was round with a pointed roof. It was open on all sides and appeared to be formed of twisted branches and moss; around it was a closely woven hedge to keep off wild animals.

This region was very fruitful. I saw most beautiful fields bordered by rows of thick, shady trees, and at the corners where the trees met were dwellings, not tents like Mensor's, but round huts woven of branches. The inhabitants of this region were of a sunburnt complexion; their skin was not so rich a brown as Mensor's. They were clad very much like the first star worshippers whom Jesus had met on this journey. The women wore wide pantalets and over them a mantle. The people appeared to be engaged in weaving. From tree to tree, far apart from each other, were stretched pieces of stuff and thread, and many were busy working upon them at the same time. The whole length of the fields, the trees were trimmed in ornamental form, and seats were arranged up in the branches.

Thursday, October 2, AD 32 (Tishri 8)

Jesus and the three youths spoke with the people living at this place and accompanied them to their temple, where he taught. The name of the place was Atom and the chieftain of the people there was called Azarias. He was a son of one of Mensor's brothers. Jesus stayed that night in Azarias's house.

At the first dawn of morning, when the stars were still to be seen in the sky, several people went to the hut, but when they saw Jesus and the disciples still upon their couches, they drew back full of awe and prostrated on the ground. They had toward morning received through a courier from Mensor the news of Jesus's coming, but they did not know that he was already among them. Jesus arose, girded his white undergarment, threw on the mantle which the disciples used to carry in a bundle on their journeys, and after he had prayed with the youths and they had washed his feet, he stepped out of the hut to where the people were lying prostrate on their faces, and bade them not to be frightened at him. Then he went with them to their temple, a great, oblong building with a flat roof upon which one could walk. It had two railings on the roof, and by them I saw some people gazing at the sky through tubes. In front of the temple was the closed fountain, esteemed sacred by the natives, and a pan of coals. The latter was raised a little above the ground, so that one could see under it. All around the temple were places for the people, separated from one another by bars. The priests that I saw wore long, white garments, trimmed from top to bottom with many-colored laces, and a broad girdle with a long end upon which were glittering stones and an inscription in letters. From their shoulders hung strips of leather, to which little shields were attached. When Jesus reached the temple, he called one of the priests down from the roof where he was observing the stars. The lord of this pastoral settlement, a paternal nephew of Mensor, came forth from the temple to greet Jesus and hand to him the peace branch. Jesus took it and passed it to Eremenzear, who handed it to Silas who, in turn, gave it to Eliud. Eremenzear again received it and bore it into the temple, followed by Jesus and the rest of the party. Here they found a little round altar upon which stood a cup without a handle, something like a mortar. In it was a yellowish pap, into which Eremenzear stuck the branch. This latter was either dried or artificial. It had leaves on both sides, and it seems to me that Jesus said it would become green. The images in the temple were enveloped as with a covering, or mask of very light, stiff material. A teacher's chair had been erected in the enclosure of the temple, and there Jesus taught. He questioned his hearers, as if they were children, upon all that he said. The women stood far in the background. The people were very childlike and accepted everything willingly. Jesus spent the greater part of the day in teaching, and that night accepted hospitality from the lord of the settlement, whose dwelling consisted of several stories. It was a circular edifice with outside steps running around it. Above the door was fastened an oval shield of yellow metal, upon which were inscribed the words, "Azarias of Atom." Azarias had not been able to live upon good terms with Mensor, and hence the latter had divided with him the pasture grounds; but after Jesus's visit, he changed for the better. The interior of his dwelling was very beautiful, fitted up with fine colored carpets and tapestry, and communicating by a covered tent corridor with the apartments of his wife.

When the sabbath began, Jesus withdrew with his disciples in order to celebrate it as he had done in the tent city of the kings.

THE WONDERFUL CURE OF TWO SICK WOMEN

Friday, October 3, AD 32 (Tishri 9)

This evening, with the onset of the sabbath, Jesus and the three shepherd youths went to the hut where they had stayed on their arrival in Atom. Here they prayed together. Later, in the temple, Jesus healed one of Azarias's wives, who was afflicted with an issue of blood. He also healed a woman possessed by a devil which had made her fall hopelessly in love with a youth. The youth's name was Caisar, and he was exceptionally pure. He had long had a presentiment of the coming of salvation and joined Jesus and the three shepherd youths to accompany them on their further journey. Jesus taught in the temple throughout the night until the break of day.

WHILE Jesus was celebrating the sabbath with the disciples in the open hut in which he had passed the first night, I saw the sick wife of Azarias seeking her cure before an idol. The lady had many children, and I saw in her apartments several other women, maidservants perhaps. Back from the fireplace and in a corner between the apartments stood a slab, or table, supported on columns. On it was a beautiful pedestal pierced on all sides with holes and covered with a little ornamental roof of leaves and foliage. The pedestal supported an idol in the form of a sitting dog with a thick, flat head. It was resting upon some written pages which were fastened together with cords in the form of a book, one of its forepaws raised over it as if drawing attention to it. Above this idol arose another, a scandalous-looking figure with many arms. I saw priests bringing in fire from the pan near the temple and pouring it under the hollow figure of the sitting dog, whose eyes began to sparkle, and from his mouth and nose immediately issued fire and smoke. Two women conducted Azarias's wife (who was afflicted with an issue of blood) up to the idol and placed her upon cushions and rugs before it. Azarias himself was present. The priests prayed, burnt incense, and offered sacrifice before the idol, but all to no purpose. Flames shot forth from it, and in the dense black smoke issued horrible dog-like figures that disappeared in the air. The sick woman became perfectly miserable. She sank down faint and exhausted like one in a dying state, saying "These idols cannot help me! They are wicked spirits! They cannot longer remain here, they are fleeing from the prophet, the king of the Jews, who is amongst us. We have seen his star and have followed him! The prophet alone can help me!" After uttering these words, she fell back im-movable and, to all appearances, lifeless.

The bystanders were filled with terror. They had been under the impression that Jesus was only an envoy of the king of the Jews. They went immediately to the retired hut in which he and the disciples were celebrating the sabbath, and respectfully begged him to go to the sick woman. They told him that she had cried out that he alone could help her, and they informed him likewise of the impotence of their idols.

Jesus was still in his sabbatic robes, the disciples also, when they went to the sick woman, who was lying like one at the point of death. In earnest, vehement words, Jesus inveighed against idols and their worship. They were, he said, the servants of Satan, and all in them was bad. He reproached Azarias for this, that after his return from Bethlehem, whither as a youth he had accompanied the kings, he had again sunk so deep into the abominations of idolatry. He concluded by saying that if they would believe in his doctrine, would obey the commandments of God, and would allow themselves to be baptized, he would in three years send his apostle to them, and he would now help the lady. Then he questioned the latter, and she answered: "Yes, I do believe in thee!" All the bystanders gave him the same assurance.

The screens had been removed from around the tent, and a crowd of people were standing by. Jesus asked for a basin of water, but bade them not to bring it from their sacred fountain. He wanted only ordinary water, nor would he use their holy water sprinkler. They had to bring him a fresh branch with fine, narrow leaves. They had likewise to cover their idols, which they did with fine, white tapestry embroidered in gold. Jesus placed the water on the altar. The three disciples stood around him, one at either side, right and left, and the third behind him. One of them handed him a metal box from the wallet that they always carried with them. Several such boxes of oil and cotton were placed one above the other.

In that which the disciple handed to Jesus, there was a fine, white powder, which appeared to me to be salt. Jesus sprinkled some of it on the water, and bent low over it. He prayed, blessed it with his hand, dipped the branch into it, sprinkled the water over all around him, and extended his hand to the woman with the command to arise. She obeyed instantly, and rose up cured. She threw herself on her knees and wanted to embrace his feet, but he would not suffer her to touch him.

This cure effected, Jesus proclaimed to the crowd that there was another lady present who was much more indisposed than the first and who, notwithstanding, did not ask his help. She adored not an idol, but a man. This lady, by name Ratimiris, was married. Her malady consisted in this, that at the sight, the name, or even the thought of a certain youth, she fell into a sort of fever and became ill unto death. The youth, meanwhile, was perfectly ignorant of her state. Ratimiris, at the call of Jesus, stepped forward greatly confused. Jesus took her aside, laid before her all the circumstances both of her sickness and her sins, all which she freely acknowledged. The youth was one of the temple servers, and whenever she brought her offerings, which he was charged to receive, she fell into that sad state. After Jesus had spoken awhile with her alone, he led her again before the people, and asked her whether she believed in him and whether she would be baptized when he would send his apostle hither. When she, deeply repentant, answered that she did believe and that she would be baptized, Jesus drove the devil out of her. The evil one departed in the form of a spiral column of black vapor.

The youth's name was Caisar, and there was something of John in his appearance. He was pure and chaste, a descendant of Keturah and a relative of Eremenzear, who also was from this place. It was for this reason that on their reception Jesus had given to him the peace branch first.

Caisar spoke with the disciples, for he had long had secret presentiments of salvation. He told them several dreams he had had, among others one in which he dreamed that he had carried a great many people through water. The disciples thought that it signified perhaps that he would convert many. I saw that he accompanied Jesus on his departure. Three years after Christ's Ascension, when Thomas baptized in these parts, he returned with Thaddeus. Later on he was sent by Thomas to the bishop of a certain place where, though innocent, he was, to the great joy of his soul, crucified as a robber and criminal.

Jesus taught here until day dawned and the burning lamps went out. He commanded the people to destroy their images of the devil, and reproached them for adoring woman under a diabolical figure, and yet treating their women worse than dogs, which animals they held sacred. Toward morning Jesus retired again into the solitary house in order to celebrate the sabbath.

I was told why Jesus kept this journey so secret. I remember that he said to his apostles and disciples that he would go away for a little while only, in order that the public might lose sight of him, but they knew nothing of the journey. He had taken with him those innocent boys because they would not be scandalized at his dealings with the pagans, and would not remark things too closely. He had likewise strictly forbidden them to speak of the journey, on which account one of them said in all simplicity: "The blind man whom thou didst forbid to speak of his cure, did not remain silent, and yet thou didst not punish him!" Jesus replied: "That happened for the glory of God, but this would bear fruits of scandal." I think the Jews, and even the apostles themselves, would have been somewhat scandalized had they known that Jesus had been among the pagans.

Saturday, October 4, AD 32 (Tishri 10)

Jesus and the four youths spent the day in prayer. At the close of the sabbath, they went to the temple. Jesus taught the people and then gave instruction to the priests concerning the communion of bread and wine. He consecrated the bread and wine, and blessed the priests.

When the sabbath was over, the Lord called all together again and instructed them. He blessed some water for them and directed them to prepare for him a chalice like that used by Mensor. Here too as in the former place, he blessed for them bread and the red liquor. In the cup into which Eremenzear upon his arrival had stuck the branch in order to keep it fresh, there was a yellowish-green substance, something like pap, which consisted of the pulp of a plant from which the juice had been expressed. This juice the natives drank as something holy. I saw Jesus the whole night between Saturday and Sunday teaching in front of the temple. He himself helped to smash the idols, and he told the pagans how they should distribute the value of the metal. I saw him also, as in Mensor's land, imposing hands upon the shoulders of the priests, teaching them how to divide the blessed bread, and here as there preparing the beverage. The vessel used here, however, was larger.

Azarias later on became a priest and martyr. The two women also whom Jesus cured here were afterward martyred like Cuppes. The Lord spoke against a multiplicity of wives, and gave instructions on the married state. The wife of Azarias, as well as Ratimiris, wanted Jesus to baptize them right away. He replied that he could indeed do so, but that it would be inopportune. He must first return to the Father and send the Consoler, after which his apostles would come and baptize them. They should, he said, live in the desire of baptism and submission to his will, and such dispositions would, to those that might die in the interim, serve as baptism. Ratimiris was in fact baptized under the name of Emily by Thomas when, three years after Christ's Ascension, he visited this country accompanied by Thaddeus and Caisar. They came in a direction more from the south than did Jesus, and it was then that the kings and their people were baptized.

Jesus Goes to Sikdor, Mozian, and Ur

Sunday, October 5, AD 32 (Tishri 11)

Jesus and the four youths left Atom this morning, first traveling southward and then in an easterly direction. Toward evening they arrived at the Chaldean city of Sikdor. Here Jesus taught in the temple. He reproved them for their idolatry. He said that he was the vine whose blood would renew the world and that he was the grain of corn which would be buried in the earth and would rise again. The people here were very humble and believed that the Jews alone were the chosen people. Jesus comforted them and said that he had come for all human beings. He commanded them to destroy their idols and to give alms to the poor.

FROM Atom, Jesus went first toward the south, then eastwardly through a very fertile region cut up by rivers and canals and planted with fruit trees of various kinds, especially peaches, which grew in long rows. I heard the names Euphrates, Tigris, Chaldar, and I think Ur, the land of Abraham, and that place at which Thaddeus suffered martyrdom were not far distant. Toward evening, Jesus reached a row of flat-roofed houses occupied by Chaldeans. I heard Sikdor as the name of the place in which were established two schools, one for the priests of the country and the other for young girls. The people were not so fully clothed as those of the royal tent city. They wore only blankets over their cinctures, but they were good, and so lowly minded that they thought the Jews alone were the chosen for salvation. They had on a hill a pyramid surrounded by galleries, seats, and immense tubes pointed on high through which they observed the stars. They also predicted future events from the course of animals, and interpreted dreams. Their temple with its forecourt and fountain was oval in form, and occupied the center of the place. It contained numerous metal statues of exquisite workmanship. The principal object of note was a triangular column upon which rested three idols. The first had many feet and arms, the former not in human shape, but like the paws of animals. In its hands it held a globe, a circle, a large ribbed apple on a stem, and bunches of herbs. The face of the figure was like a sun, and its name was Mytor, or Mithras. The second was a unicorn, and it was called Asphas, or Aspax. This animal was represented in the act of using its horn in a struggle against a wild beast that was standing on the third side of the column. It had the head of an owl, a hooked beak, four legs with talons, two wings, and a tail, which last appendage ended like that of a scorpion.

Above these two animals, namely, the unicorn and the wild beast, and projecting from one of the sharp edges of the column, stood another figure, which represented the mother of all the gods. Her name was Woman, or Alpha. She was the most powerful of all their divinities, and whoever desired to obtain anything from the supreme god was obliged to plead for it through her. They called her, likewise, the Granary. Out of the figure issued a large sheaf of wheat, apparently growing, which she clasped with both hands. The head was bowed, and on the neck, bent low between the shoulders, rested a vessel of wine. Above the figure hung a crown, and above the crown were inscribed on the column two letters, or symbols, that looked to me like an 'O' or a 'W'. The lesson taught by these images was that the wheat was to become bread and that the wine was to inebriate all humankind.

There was besides in the temple a brazen altar, and what was my astonishment to see upon it, under a revolving dome, a little circular garden railed in with gold wire like a bird cage, and above it the image of a young virgin! In the center of the garden and roofed in by a little temple was a fountain with several sealed basins one above the other. In front of the fountain rose a green vine with a cluster of red grapes, which drooped over a press whose form reminded me of a cross. From the upper end of a tall stem projected a funnel-shaped, self-opening, leathern pouch with two movable arms, through which the juice of the grapes put into it could be pressed out and allowed to flow down below upon the stem. The little garden was about five or six feet in diameter. It was planted with delicate green bushes and little trees, which like the vine and its grapes looked perfectly natural. They owed this symbol to their star gazing, and they had many others that bespoke their presentiments of the blessed Mother of God. They

A Wayside Resting Place

sacrificed animals, but had a special horror of blood, which they always allowed to run off into the earth. They had likewise their sacred fire and water, their chalice of vegetable juice, and their little loaves, like the people of Atom. Jesus reproved them for their idolatry and for mixing up heavenly predictions and prognostics with Satanic errors. Their symbols, he said, had in them indeed some notions of truth, but they were discordant and filled with Satan. He explained to them the symbol of the garden enclosed. He told them that he himself was the vine whose sap, whose blood, was to quicken the world, that he himself was the grain of wheat which was to be buried in the earth thence to rise again. Jesus spoke here much more freely, much more significantly than among the Jews, for these people were humble. He comforted them by telling them that he had come for all humankind, and he commanded them to break up their idols and give their value to the poor. They showed signs of deep feeling when he was about leaving them, and threw themselves at his feet across the path in order to prevent his departure.

Monday, October 6, AD 32 (Tishri 12)

Today Jesus and his four traveling companions left Sikdor. On the way, they stopped to eat bread and honey. They traveled all night.

Some time after, I saw Jesus with the four disciples resting under a great tree that was surrounded by a hedge. It was in front of a house, from which they had been supplied with the bread and honey that they were eating. They journeyed on the whole of the night. I saw them on a plain walking sometimes over white stones, sometimes over meadows carpeted with white blossoms. On their way, they came across numbers of slender peach trees. At times the Lord paused, pointed around, and said something to the disciples. The country was intersected by numerous streams and canals. As a general thing, Jesus journeyed with extraordinary rapidity. He sometimes traveled twenty hours without interruption. His way back to Judea described a very great curve. I am always under the impression that Eremenzear wrote some details of this journey, though only a few fragments of his account escaped the fire that destroyed the rest.

Tuesday, October 7, AD 32 (Tishri 13)

They journeyed on. Today, having already crossed the Euphrates, they crossed the Tigris. In the evening, they arrived at the city of Mozian, where they stayed the night.

On the evening of the second day of their departure from Sikdor, I saw Jesus and the disciples drawing near to a city outside of which rose a hill covered with circular gardens. Most of them had a fountain in the center and were planted with fine ornamental trees and shrubbery. The way taken by the Lord ran toward the south: Babylon lay to the north. It seemed as if one would have to descend a mountainous country to reach Babylon, which lay far below. The city was built on the river Tigris, which flowed through it. Jesus entered quietly and without pausing at the gates. It was evening, but few of the inhabitants were to be seen, and no one troubled himself about him. Soon, however, I saw several men in long garments, like those worn by Abraham, and with scarfs wound round their head, coming to meet him and inclining low before him. One of them extended toward him a short, crooked staff. It was made of reed, something like that afterward presented to Christ in derision, and was called the staff of peace. The others, two by two, held across the street a strip of carpet upon which Jesus walked. When he stepped from the first to the second, the former was raised and spread before the latter to be again in readiness for use, and so on. In this way they reached a courtyard, over whose grated entrance with its idols waved a standard upon which was represented the figure of a man holding a crooked staff like that presented to Jesus. The standard was the standard of peace. They led the Lord through a building from whose gallery floated another standard. It appeared to be the temple, for all around the interior stood veiled idols and in the center was another veiled in the same way, the veil being gathered above it to form a crown. The Lord did not pause here, but proceeded through a corridor, on either side of which were sleeping apartments. At last he and his attendants reached a little enclosed garden planted with delicate bushes and aromatic shrubs, its walks paved in ornamental figures with different kinds of colored stone. In the center rose a fountain under a little temple open on all sides, and here the Lord and the disciples sat down. In answer to Jesus's request, the idolaters brought some water in a basin. The Lord first blessed it, as if to annul the pagan benediction, and then the disciples washed his feet and he theirs, after which they poured what remained into the fountain. The pagans then conducted the Lord into an open hall adjoining, in which a meal had been prepared: large yellow, ribbed apples and other kinds of fruit; honeycombs; bread in the form of thin cakes, like waffles; and something else in little, square morsels. The table upon which they were spread was very low. The guests ate standing. Jesus's coming had been announced to these people by the priests of the neighboring city. They had in consequence expected him the whole day and at last received him with so much solemnity. Abraham also had received a staff of welcome such as had been presented to Jesus.

Wednesday, October 8, AD 32 (Tishri 14)

Jesus did not enter the temple in Mozian. He taught at a well in front of the temple. He strongly reprimanded the people on account of their idolatry. He left the city and traveled throughout the night in a southerly direction, recrossing the Tigris.

The name of this city was Mozin, or Mozian. It was a sacerdotal city, but sunk deep in idolatry. Jesus did not enter the temple. I saw him teaching a crowd of people on a graded hill surrounded by a wall. It was in front of the temple and near a fountain. He reproved them severely for having fallen into idolatry even more deeply than their neighbors, showed them the abominations of their worship, and told them that they had abandoned the Law. I heard him referring to the destruction of the temple in the time of their forefathers, and speaking of Nebuchadnezzar and Daniel. He said that they should separate the believing from the spiritually blind, for there were some good souls among them, and to these he indicated whither they should go. Many of the others were stiff-necked. There was one point that they would not understand, and that was the necessity for abolishing polygamy. The women dwelt in a street to themselves at the extreme end of the city, to which, however, there was communication by shaded walks. They seemed to be held in great contempt, and after a certain age the young girls dared not appear in public. No woman of this place saw Jesus. Only the boys were present with the men.

Jesus used severe words toward these people. They were, he said, so blinded, so obstinate, that when the apostle that he was going to send would make his appearance, he would find them unprepared for baptism. Jesus would not remain longer with them. As he was leaving the city, a procession of young girls met him at the gate, chanting hymns of praise in his honor. They wore white pantalets, had garlands around their arms and necks, and flowers in their hands.

From Mozian, Jesus went with his companions across a large field to a village of pastoral tents. He sat down near the fountain, the disciples washed his feet, and some men of the place approached with the branch of welcome and gave him a glad reception. They were clad in long garments, more like Abraham than any others I had yet seen, and they possessed an astronomical pyramid. I saw no idols. These people appeared to be pure star worshippers and to belong to that race of whom some had accompanied the kings to Bethlehem. They appeared to me to be only a little band of shepherds, of whom the superior alone had a permanent dwelling. Jesus ate bread and fruit in his house standing, and drank out of a special vessel. He afterward taught at the well. When he was leaving them, the people threw themselves across his path and entreated him to remain with them.

Thursday, October 9, AD 32 (Tishri 15)

On departing from this place, Jesus traveled throughout the whole of that night and the following day. Once I saw him with the disciples taking a little rest by a fountain under a large shade tree. It was a public resting place for travelers, and there Jesus ate some bread and took a drink.

Friday, October 10, AD 32 (Tishri 16)

Traveling on, Jesus and the four youths recrossed the Euphrates. Toward evening, as the sabbath began, they arrived at Ur, the birthplace of Abraham. Here they stayed in a house and held the sabbath together in prayer.

The city to which he was going was thirty hours to the south of Mozian, but still on the Tigris. It was called Ur, or Urhi. Jesus reached it on that evening before the commencement of the sabbath. Abraham was from this region. Jesus went to a well outside the city which was surrounded by large shade trees and stone benches. Here the disciples washed the Lord's feet and then their own, lowered their girded garments, and entered the city, whose architecture struck me as different from any other I had seen in these parts. The men and women did not appear to live so much apart. There were many towers provided with galleries and tubes for observing the stars, and to them led steps both inside and outside. The people knew from the stars of the Lord's coming, consequently they had expected him and taken every stranger for him. When, therefore, Jesus's entrance into the city was noticed by some, they hurried to a large flat-roofed house which stood in a large open space, in order to give notice of his arrival. From this house, which appeared to be a school and from which waved a flag, there now issued several men in long garments of one single color, and proceeded to meet Jesus. They were girded with cinctures whose ends hung long and loose, and they wore round caps bordered by a roll of wool, or little feathers, whose strips met on top and formed a plume. The hair could be seen through them. The men prostrated before Jesus, and then led him and his companions back to the school, which consisted of one immense hall. To it flocked crowds of people. Jesus taught for a short time from an elevated seat at the top of a flight of steps, after which he was conducted to another house in which a meal had been prepared. But Jesus took only a few mouthfuls standing, and then went alone with the disciples into a retired apartment where they celebrated the sabbath.

Saturday, October 11, AD 32 (Tishri 17)

Next day he taught near a fountain on an open place upon which was a stone seat used for teaching. All the women of the place were present, and so enveloped in their narrow garments that they could scarcely walk. Their caps were like cowls, from which hung two lappets. Jesus spoke of Abraham, and made some severe remarks on the fact of their being sunk in idolatry. There were idolatrous temples here, but the idols were veiled. The Lord did not go into any of them. Thomas did not baptize these people at his first visit to them.

Sunday, October 12, AD 32 (Tishri 18)

The people of Ur accompanied Jesus this morning and strewed branches on the street in front of him as he and the four youths left the city. They journeyed westward through the day and arrived that evening at a settlement. Here Jesus strongly inveighed against the people's worship. The chief of the settlement was deaf to Jesus's teaching and became enraged, even contradicting him. The chief lived in a house full of idols. Jesus said that on the anniversary of the night on which the star had appeared to the three kings, the idols would all break, the oxen idols would bellow, the dog idols would bark, and the bird idols would squawk. This would be proof of the truth of his words. The people listened to him in disbelief. Jesus told them that this would take place throughout Chaldea in the places that he had visited.

When Jesus left Ur, the people accompanied him, strewing branches in his way. He journeyed toward the west for a long time, over a beautiful plain which toward the end became sandy, and lastly was covered with underbrush. About noon they reached a well by which they sat down to rest. The remainder of the journey was made through a wood and over cultivated land, until toward evening they arrived at a great, round building encircled by a courtyard and moat. All around stood heavy-looking houses with flat roofs. That of the great building was covered with verdure and even trees, while in the massive wall of the courtyard were the abodes of some poor people. At the fountain in the courtyard Jesus and the disciples washed their feet, as usual. And now, from the round house came forth two men in long garments profusely trimmed with laces and ribbons, and wearing feather caps on their heads. The elder of the two carried a green branch and a little bunch of berries, which he presented to Jesus, who with the disciples followed him into the building. In the center of the house was a hall, lighted from the roof, whose fireplace was reached by steps. From this circular apartment they proceeded around through irregularly shaped rooms opening one into the other, and whose end wall, concave in form, was hung with tapestry, behind which all sorts of utensils were kept. The floor was level, and like the walls covered with thick carpets. In one of these apartments Jesus and his companions took a frugal repast and drank something from vessels never before used. What the beverage was, I do not know.

After the meal, the master of the house took Jesus all around and showed him everything. The whole castle was filled with beautifully wrought idols. There were figures of all sizes, large and small, some with a head like that of an ox, others like that of a dog, and a serpent's body. One of them had many arms and heads, and into its jaws could be put all kinds of things. There were also some figures of swathed infants. Under the trees in the courtyard stood idols in the form of animals, for instance, birds looking upward, and other animals standing around. These people sacrificed animals, but they had a horror of blood, which they always allowed to run off into the earth. They had, also, the custom of distributing bread, of which the more distinguished among them received a larger portion.

Jesus taught at the fountain in the courtyard, and strongly inveighed against their diabolical worship, though his words were not taken in good part. I saw that their chief was particularly obstinate in his errors. He was irritated at Jesus, and even contradicted him. Thereupon I heard Jesus telling the people that, as a proof of the truth of his words, on the night of the anniversary of the star's appearing to the kings, the idols would fall to pieces, those that represented oxen would bellow, the dogs would bark, and the birds would scream. They listened to his predictions disdainfully and incredulously. This was what Jesus had told all whom he had visited on this journey. In all places at which he stopped on his way into the land of the pagans, he predicted that this would happen. On the holy night of Christmas, I had a vision of this whole journey from the pagan city near Kedar to the tent city of the three kings, and thence to this last pagan castle; and everywhere I saw the idols going to pieces, and heard bellowing and barking and screaming from those that represented animals. The kings I saw at prayer in their temple. Numerous lights burned around the little crib, and it seems to me there was now the figure of an ass standing by it. They, it is true, no longer revered their idols; but those in the form of animals bellowed as a sign that Jesus was really the one to whom the star had led them, a fact still doubted perhaps by some weak in faith.

In the Arabian Wilderness

Jesus Goes to Egypt, Teaches in Heliopolis, and Returns to Judea through the Desert

Monday, October 13 (Tishri 19), to Tuesday, December 30, AD 32 (Tebeth 8)

Today Jesus and the four youths set off on the long journey to Egypt, traveling westward through the Arabian desert. They traveled rapidly. In the course of this journey, which lasted some two and one-half months until the end of the year AD 32, Anne Catherine had a vision on Christmas night: she saw the journey of the Savior through Chaldea, from Kedar to the tent city of the kings, to Atom, Sikdor, Mozian, Ur, and the last Chaldean settlement. Everywhere, she saw idols broken and animal idols crying out. Historically (in AD 32) this was probably the night of December 7/8, the anniversary of the immaculate conception of the Virgin Mary, on which night the three kings had first seen the star, fifteen years before the birth of Jesus.

FROM the castle of the idols, Jesus's route now lay toward the west. He traveled quickly with his four companions, pausing nowhere, but ever hurrying on. First, they crossed a sandy desert, toiled slowly up a steep mountain ridge, pursued their way over a country covered with vegetation, then through low bushes like juniper bushes, whose branches, meeting overhead, formed a covered walk. After that they came to a stony region overrun with ivy, thence through meadows and woods until they reached a river, not rapid, but deep, over which they crossed on a raft of beams.

TEBETH (29 days): December 22/23, AD 32, to January 19/20, AD 33 Tebeth New Moon: December 21 at 10:00 AM, Jerusalem time

Wednesday, December 31, AD 32 (Tebeth 9)

Anne Catherine described the journey of Jesus and the four youths. She saw them coming from the Arabian desert and approaching Egypt; then, passing south of Mount Sinai, which they saw in the distance, they crossed the Sinai desert. She said that they traveled continuously through open, sandy desert, then crossed gently rolling hills, finally arriving in a land with more green. Then, in the evening, they arrived at the first Egyptian town. During the night, many idols fell to the ground.

It was still night when they arrived at a city built either on both sides of the river, or on one of its branches, or on a canal. It was the first Egyptian city on their route. Here, unobserved by anyone, Jesus and his companions retired under the porch of a temple, where were some sleeping places for travelers. The city appeared to me very much gone to ruin. I saw great, thick walls, massive stone houses, and many poor people. I had an interior perception that Jesus had journeyed hither by the same side of the desert by which the children of Israel had come.

Thursday, January 1, AD 33 (Tebeth 10)

This morning there was an uproar in the town when the people discovered the broken idols. Jesus and the four youths hurriedly left the town, and as they did some children ran after them calling out: "These are holy people!" Jesus traveled further westward until he and his four young disciples reached a town that evening. Before entering the town they rested by a stream. When they entered the town, it was night. They made their way through the deserted streets, and then traveled on further.

Next morning, as Jesus and the disciples were leaving the city, children ran after them crying out: "There go holy people!" The inhabitants were very much excited, inasmuch as great disturbances had happened the night before. Many of the idols had fallen from their places, and the children had been dreaming and uttering prophetic words about certain "holy people" that had entered the city.

Jesus and the disciples departed hurriedly, and plunged into the deep ravines that traversed the sandy region. That evening I saw them, not far from a city, resting and taking food at the source of a brook, the disciples having washed Jesus's feet. Nearby on a great round stone was stretched the figure of a dog in a lying posture. It had a human head, the expression of the face quite friendly. It wore a cap, like that worn by the people of the country, a band with hanging lappets notched at the ends. The figure was as large as a cow. Under a tree outside the city stood an idol whose head was like that of an ox. It had holes pierced in its body and several arms. Five streets led from the gate into the great city, and Jesus took the first to the right. It ran along the city wall, which was like a rampart on top of which were gardens and a carriage way. In the lower part of the walls were dwellings shut in by light doors of wickerwork. Jesus and his disciples passed through the city by night without speaking to anyone, or being remarked by anyone. Here too there were several idolatrous temples, and many massive buildings gone to ruins in whose walls people lived.

Friday, January 2, AD 33 (Tebeth 11)

Around four o'clock this afternoon Jesus and his traveling companions arrived at Heliopolis. Here he met some Jews who had been friends of the holy family during the time of their stay in Heliopolis. With the onset of the sabbath, Jesus was escorted to the synagogue by an aged man. In the synagogue, Jesus taught and prayed.

At a good distance from this city, the way led over an immense stone bridge across the broadest river (the Nile) that I saw on this journey. It flowed from south to north, and divided into many branches that ran in different directions. The country was low and level, and off in the distance I saw some very high buildings in form like the temples of the star worshippers, though built of stone and much higher. The soil was exceedingly fruitful, but only along the river.

About one hour's distance from that city in which Jesus as a child had dwelt with his mother (Heliopolis), he took the same road by which, with Mary and Joseph, he had entered it. It was situated on the first arm of the Nile, which flows in the direction of Judea. I saw here and there on the way people clipping the hedges, transporting rafters, and laboring in deep ditches. It was nearly evening when Jesus approached the city. Both he and the disciples had let down their garments, something that I had never seen them do before reaching their destination. Some of the laborers, as Jesus came in sight, broke off branches from the trees, hurried forward to meet him, cast themselves down before him, and presented them to him. After he had taken them in his hand, they stuck them down into the ground along the roadside. I know not how they recognized Jesus. Perhaps they knew by his garments that he was a Jew. They had been waiting and hoping for his coming, that he would free them. I saw others, however, who appeared indignant, and who ran back to the city. About twenty men surrounded Jesus as he went to the city, before which stood many trees.

Before entering, Jesus paused near a tree that was lying over on one side in such a way that its roots were being torn out of the earth, and around them was a large puddle of black water. This puddle was enclosed by a high iron grating, the bars of which were so close that one could not put his hand through. In this place an idol had sunk at the time of Mary and Joseph's flight with the child Jesus into Egypt, on which occasion the tree, too, had been uprooted. The people conducted Jesus into the city. Before it lay a large, four-cornered, perfectly flat stone, on which, among other names, was inscribed one that bore reference to the city and that ended in the syllable 'polis'. Inside the city I saw a very large temple surrounded by two courts, several high columns tapering toward the top and ornamented with numerous figures, and a great many huge dogs with human heads, all in a recumbent posture. The city showed evident signs of decay. The people led Jesus under the projection of a thick wall opposite the temple, and called to several of the citizens of the neighborhood. Then came together many Jews, young and old, among the latter some very aged men with long beards. Among the women there was one, tall and advanced in years, who pleased me especially. All welcomed Jesus respectfully, for they had been friends of the holy family at the time of their sojourn here. In the back of the projecting wall was a space, now ornamented in festal style, in which Joseph had prepared an abode for the holy family. The men who had in their childhood lived in this neighborhood with Jesus, introduced him to it. The apartment was lighted by hanging lamps.

That evening Jesus was escorted by a very aged Jew to the school, which was very ably conducted. The women took their stand back on a grated gallery, where they had a lamp to themselves. Jesus prayed and taught, for they reverently yielded precedence to him.

Saturday, January 3, AD 33 (Tebeth 12)

Today Jesus taught again in the Heliopolis synagogue.

On the following day, I saw Jesus again teaching in the synagogue. The inhabitants of this city wore white bands around their heads, their tunics were short, and only a part of their shoulders and breast was covered. The edifices were extraordinarily broad and massive, built of immense blocks of stone upon which numerous figures were carved. I saw also great figures that bore prodigious stones, some upon their neck, others on their head. The people of this country practiced the most extravagant idolatry. Everywhere were to be met idols in the form of oxen, recumbent dogs with human heads, and other animals held in peculiar veneration in special places.

Egyptian Port with Ruins

Sunday, January 4, AD 33 (Tebeth 13)

When Jesus, escorted by many of the inhabitants, left Heliopolis, he took with him a young man belonging to the city, and who now made his fifth disciple. His name was Deodatus, and that of his mother was Mira. She was that tall old lady who had, on the first evening of Jesus's arrival, been among those that welcomed him under the portico. During Mary's sojourn in Heliopolis, Mira was childless; but on the prayer of the blessed Virgin, this son was afterward given her. He was tall and slender, and appeared to be about eighteen years old. When his escort had returned to the city, I saw Jesus journeying through the desert with his five disciples. He took a direction more to the east than that taken by the holy family on their flight into Egypt. The city in which Jesus had just been was called Eliopolis (Heliopolis). The E and the L were joined back to back, something that I had never before seen, on which account I thought there was an X in the word.

Monday, January 5, AD 33 (Tebeth 14)

This evening Jesus and his five young disciples arrived at a small town in the desert, where some Jews were living. He went to the town well, where he was greeted and then escorted to a house.

Toward evening, Jesus and his disciples reached a little city in the wilderness inhabited by three different kinds of people: Jews, who dwelt in solid houses; Arabs, who lived in huts built of branches covered with skins; and still another kind. These people had drifted hither when Antiochus ravaged Jerusalem and expelled many of its inhabitants. I saw the whole affair. A pious old priest slew a Jew who had gone forward to sacrifice to the idol, overturned the altar, called all good people together and, like a hero, maintained the Law and testament of God. It was during this persecution that these good people had fled hither. I saw also the place at which they first lived. The Arabs, having joined them, were likewise expelled with them. At a still later period they, the Arabs, fell again into idolatry. As usual the Lord went to the fountain, where he was welcomed by some of the people and conducted to one of their houses.

Tuesday, January 6, AD 33 (Tebeth 15)

In this little town, Jesus was held by the Jews to be a prophet. There was no synagogue, so Jesus taught in a house. He spoke of his approaching return to the Father. They could not believe him. When Jesus left, two more youths joined him, bringing his entourage to seven. One was about twenty years old, and the other was scarcely more than twelve years of age. Before he left, Jesus blessed the children of this place.

In this house Jesus taught, for they had no school. He told them that the time was at hand when he should return to the Father, that the Jews would maltreat him, and he spoke as he had everywhere done on this journey. They could scarcely believe what they heard, and they wanted very much to retain him with them.

When he left this place, two new disciples followed him, the descendants of Mathathias. The travelers now plunged deeper into the wilderness and hurried onward day and night with but short intervals of rest.

Wednesday, January, 7 AD 33 (Tebeth 16)

Today, Jesus and his seven young disciples proceeded rapidly through the desert.

I saw them in a lovely spot of beautiful balsam hedges taking some rest at that fountain which had gushed forth for the holy family on their flight into Egypt, and with whose waters Mary had refreshed herself and bathed her child. The road by which Jesus had returned from Egypt here crossed the circuitous byway that Mary had taken on her flight thither. Mary had come by an indirect route on the west side of the desert, but Jesus had taken the eastern one which was more direct. On his journey from Arabia to Egypt, Jesus could descry on his right Mount Sinai lying off in the distance.

(Follow Map 38)

Thursday, January 8, AD 33 (Tebeth 17)

Jesus and the seven young disciples continued their journey. This evening, they arrived at the town of Beersheba where, at the town well, Jesus was received in a friendly way.

Friday, January 9, AD 33 (Tebeth 18)

This morning, Jesus taught in the large synagogue in Beersheba. He formally declared who he was and spoke of his approaching end. Afterward, he blessed some children. Then he left the town, accompanied by his seven young disciples and five youths from Beersheba. They went to Bethain, not far from Abraham's grave in the cave of Machpelah, east of Mamre. As the sabbath began, Jesus went to the synagogue in Bethain and taught there.

When Jesus reached Beersheba, he taught in the synagogue. He formally declared his identity, and spoke of his approaching end. From this place also he took with him on his departure some young men. It was about four day's journey from Beersheba to Jacob's well near Shechem, the spot appointed for Jesus and the apostles to meet again. Before the beginning of the sabbath Jesus reached a place in the valley of Mamre [Bethain] where he celebrated the sabbath in the synagogue and taught.

Saturday, January 10, AD 33 (Tebeth 19)

Today, Jesus taught again in the synagogue in Bethain. Then he went from house to house, healing the sick. Finally, at the close of the sabbath, he journeyed northward.

He likewise visited the homes of the inhabitants [of Bethain] and healed their sick. From this place to Jacob's well it may have been twenty hours at most.

Sunday, January 11, and Monday, January 12, AD 33 (Tebeth 20–21)

Jesus now traveled more by night, in order that the news of his return to Judea might not be the occasion of some sudden rising among the people. He took the route through the shepherd valleys near Jericho to Jacob's well, at which he arrived during the evening twilight.

Map 38: The Arrival at Jacob's Well
January 8–24, AD 33

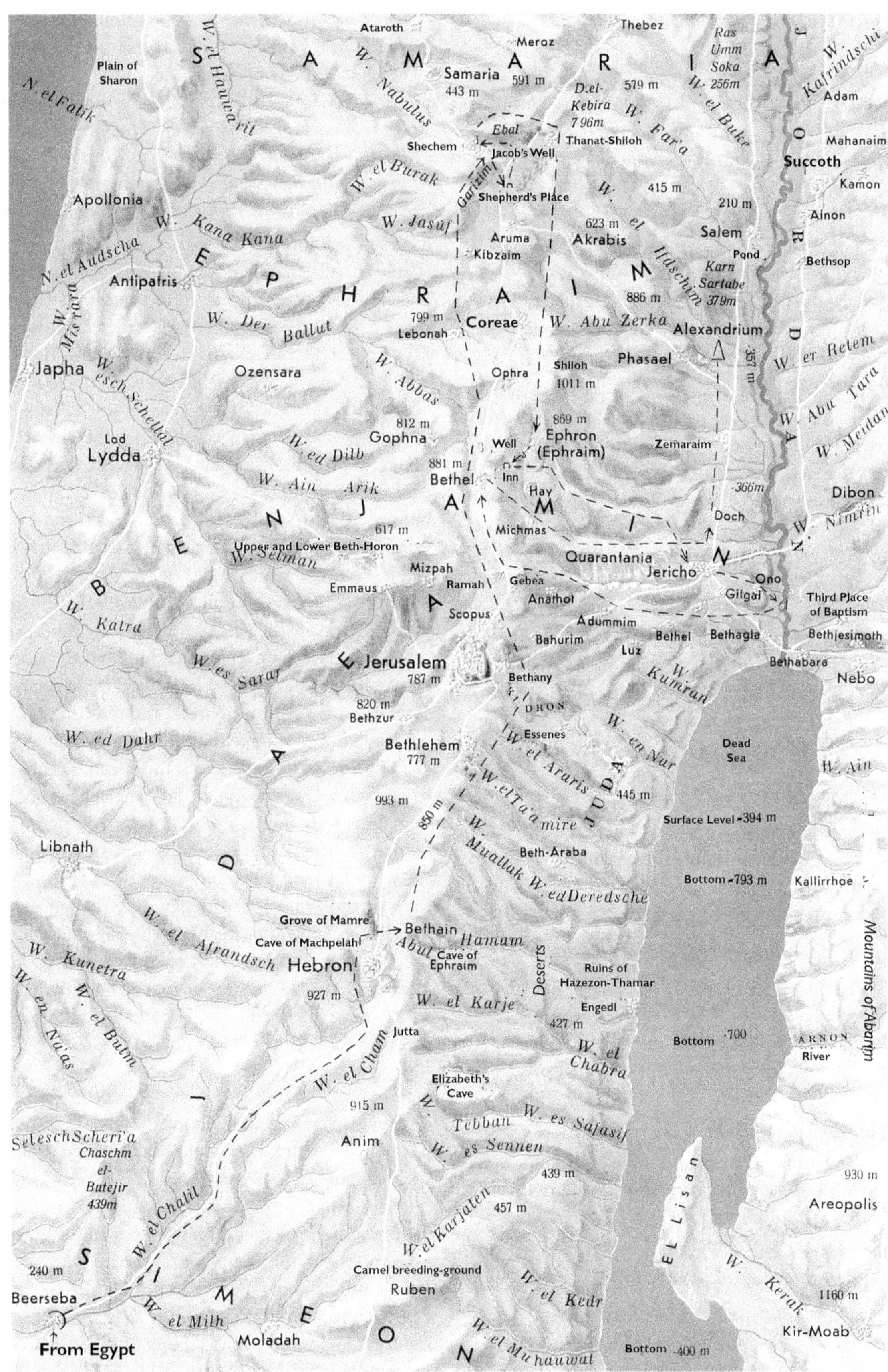

Beersheba—Bethain—Jacob's Well—Shepherd's Place in Samaria—Shechem—Ephron
Jericho—Third Place of Baptism—Bethel—Doch—Alexandrium

Tuesday, January 13, AD 33 (Tebeth 22)

Today, at daybreak, Jesus arrived at Jacob's well, accompanied by sixteen young disciples, four having joined him in Bethain. Beholding their arrival, Anne Catherine suddenly called out in ecstasy: "O, he has arrived! How joyful they are to see him! He is at Jacob's well. They are weeping for joy. They are washing his feet and also the feet of the young disciples with him. There are about twelve of them, shepherd sons, who were with him as he went to Kedar—also Peter, Andrew, John, James, Philip, and one other. They were expecting him here." Jesus and his disciples stayed the day at Jacob's well. In the evening, he spoke of his approaching path of suffering.

He had now sixteen companions, since some other youths had followed him from the valley of Mamre. In the neighborhood of the well was an inn where, in a locked place, was stored all that was necessary to contribute to the traveler's comfort when he stopped to rest. A man had the care of opening both the inn and the well. The country stretching out from Jericho to Samaria was one of indescribable loveliness. Almost the whole road was bordered by trees, the fields and meadows were green, and the brooks flowed sweetly along. Jacob's well was surrounded by beautiful grass plots and shade trees. The apostles Peter, Andrew, John, James, and Philip were here awaiting Jesus. They wept for joy at seeing him again, and washed his and the disciples' feet.

Jesus was very grave. He spoke of the approach of his Passion, of the ingratitude of the Jews, and of the judgment in store for them. It was now only three months before his Passion. I have always seen that the Feast of Easter falls at the right time when it happens late in the season.

Wednesday, January 14, AD 33 (Tebeth 23)

Early this morning, Jesus arranged to meet with the apostles and disciples at the sabbath in Shechem. Then he went with the sixteen young disciples to the settlement of the parents of the three shepherd youths—Eliud, Silas, and Eremenzear—a few hours away.

Thursday, January 15, AD 33 (Tebeth 24)

Jesus taught here and there in the settlement among the shepherds and instructed the new disciples. He wished them to stay there for the time being.

Jesus in Shechem, Ephron, and Jericho

Friday, January 16, AD 33 (Tebeth 25)

Accompanied by the three shepherd youths—Eliud, Silas, and Eremenzear—Jesus returned to Shechem, leaving the other thirteen young disciples with the shepherds at the settlement. Jesus commanded the three youths not to tell anyone where they had been with him or what had taken place on this journey. Peter and John came to meet them on the way. Six more apostles were waiting for him at the entrance to Shechem. Together, they all went to a house in the town. At the beginning of the sabbath they went to the synagogue, but Jesus did not teach or do anything to draw attention to himself.

As Jesus was journeying with the new disciples from the shepherd village, where he remained only a few hours, to Shechem, I frequently saw him standing still and giving them animated instructions. He ordered Eliud, Silas, and Eremenzear to disclose to no one where they had gone with him nor what had befallen them on that journey, and he told them some of the reasons for silence on those subjects. I saw Eremenzear holding the sleeve of Jesus's robe and begging to be allowed to write down something about it. Jesus replied that he might do so after his death, but ordered him at the same time to leave the writing with John. I cannot help thinking that a part of that writing is still in existence somewhere.

Peter and John came forward to meet the Lord on his way, and outside the gate of the city were waiting six of the other apostles. They conducted him and the disciples to a house, the master of which, though he had never before seen Jesus, gave him a cordial reception. Jesus, however, appeared not to wish to make himself publicly known, but rather to be confounded with the apostles. The feet of the newly arrived were washed, and when the sabbath began, the lamps were lighted. Jesus and his companions put on long, white garments and girdles, and after prayers went to the school, which was built on a little eminence. After that they partook of a meal prepared by their host, at which some Jews with long beards were present. The eldest of them was clothed as a priest of superior rank, and was led by attendants. Neither in the school nor at table did Jesus make himself known. The host had a false look, and it seemed to me that he was a Pharisee.

Saturday, January 17, AD 33 (Tebeth 26)

The meal over, Jesus demanded that the synagogue should be opened for him. He had, he said, listened to their teaching, but now he too would teach. He spoke of signs and miracles, which are of no avail when in spite of them people forget their own sinfulness and want of love for God. Preaching was for them more necessary than miracles. Even before the meal the apostles had besought Jesus to express himself more clearly, for they did not yet understand him. He was always talking of his approaching end, they said, but he might before it go once more to Nazareth, there to show forth his power and by miracles proclaim his mission. At this juncture also Jesus replied that miracles were useless if people were not converted by him, if after witnessing them they remained what they were before. What, he demanded, had he gained by signs and miracles, by the feeding of the five thousand, by the raising of Lazarus, since even they themselves were hankering after more. Peter and John were of one mind with their Master, but the others were dissatisfied. On the way to Shechem, Jesus had explained to Eliud, Silas, and Eremenzear why he had wrought no signs and wonders on his last journey. It was, he said, because the apostles and disciples should confirm his doctrine by miracles, of which they would perform even more than he himself had done. Jesus was displeased at the apostles' wanting to find out from the three youths where he had been and what he had done. They were very much vexed at the youths' silence on being questioned. Jesus announced to them that he was going to Jerusalem and would preach in the temple. I saw that the Jews of Shechem sent messengers to report in Jerusalem that Jesus had again appeared, for the Pharisees of Shechem were among the most dissatisfied.

Sunday, January 18, AD 33 (Tebeth 27)

The Pharisees at Shechem threatened to take Jesus into custody and deliver him to Jerusalem. Jesus replied that his time had not yet come. He said that he would go to Jerusalem of his own accord, and that he had spoken not for their benefit, but for that of his followers. Then he left Shechem, dismissing the apostles and disciples, keeping only the three "silent disciples"—Eremenzear, Eliud, and Silas—with him. Jesus and the three youths proceeded in a southeasterly direction toward Ephron. Meanwhile, his mother, the holy Virgin, who was with her friends in Bethany, had received the news of Jesus's return to Israel. Jesus sent a messenger to her requesting her to meet him at an inn southwest of Ephron.

Monday, January 19, AD 33 (Tebeth 28)

On the way to the inn, Jesus healed and comforted various people in their homes. The apostles and disciples spread out to proclaim the nearness of Jesus. That evening Jesus and the three youths arrived at Ephron (John 11:54). Jesus went to various houses and healed the sick. There was a large synagogue in Ephron, where Jesus then taught concerning his near end. He spoke of the punishment that would come upon those who refused to believe. Meanwhile, in the evening, the holy Virgin Mary, Mary Magdalene, Martha, Peter's wife and stepdaughter, Andrew's wife, Zacchaeus's wife and daughter, and two other holy women arrived at the inn they had rented between Jericho and Ephron.

Jesus had previously announced to them his return by the parents of the three disciples. On the journey from Shechem to Ephron it was very foggy, and quantities of rain fell. Jesus did not confine himself to the straight route. He went to different localities, different towns and houses, consoling the inhabitants, healing the sick, and exhorting all to follow him.[F13] The apostles and disciples likewise did not take the direct road to the places to which they were sent, but turned off into the farms and houses lying along their way in order to announce Jesus's coming. It was as if all who sighed after salvation were to be again stirred up, as if the sheep that had strayed in the forest because their shepherd had gone away were, now that he had come back, to be gathered again by the shepherd servants into one herd. When, toward evening, Jesus with the three disciples arrived at Ephron, he went into the houses, cured the sick, and called upon all to follow him to the school. This place had a large synagogue, consisting of two halls, one above and the other below. A crowd of people, men and women, some from Ephron and some from neighboring places, flocked to the instruction. The synagogue was crowded. Jesus directed a chair to be placed in the center of the hall whence he taught first the men and then the women. The latter were standing back, but the men gave place to them. Jesus taught upon the necessity of following him, upon his approaching end, and upon the chastisement that would fall on all that would not believe. Murmuring arose in the crowd, for there were many wicked souls among them.

Tuesday, January 20, AD 33 (Tebeth 29)

From Ephron Jesus dispatched the three trusty disciples to meet the holy women who, to the number of ten, had reached the rented inn near Jericho. They were the blessed Virgin, Magdalene, Martha, and two others, Peter's wife and stepdaughter, Andrew's wife, and Zacchaeus's wife and daughter. The last-mentioned was married to a very deserving disciple named Annadias, a shepherd and a relative of Silas's mother. Peter, Andrew, and John met Jesus on the road, and with them he went on to Jericho. The blessed Virgin, Magdalene, Martha, and others awaited his coming near a certain well. It was two hours before sundown when he came up with them. The women cast themselves on their knees before him and kissed his hand. Mary also kissed his hand, and when she arose, Jesus kissed hers. Magdalene stood somewhat back. At the well, the disciples washed Jesus's feet, also those of the apostles, after which all partook of a repast. The women ate alone and, when their meal was over, took their places at the lower end of the dining hall to listen to Jesus's words. He did not remain at the inn, but went with the three apostles to Jericho, where the rest of the apostles and disciples along with numerous sick were assembled. The women followed him. I saw him going into many of the houses and curing the sick, after which he himself unlocked the school and ordered a chair to be placed in the center of the hall. The holy women were present in a retired part. They had a lamp to themselves. Mary was with them. After the instruction, the holy women went back to their inn and on the following morning returned to their homes.

SHEBAT (30 days): *January 20/21 to February 18/19,* *AD 33 Shebat New Moon: January 19* *at 9:00 PM, Jerusalem time*

Wednesday, January 21, AD 33 (Shebat 1)

This morning, Jesus taught and healed in Jericho. The Virgin Mary, Peter's wife and stepdaughter, and Andrew's wife set off back to Galilee, and the other holy women also returned to their homes. There was a great throng of people in Jericho, as word had already spread that Jesus was there. The Pharisees were greatly disturbed by this and sent messengers to Jerusalem to report Jesus's presence in Jericho. Jesus, however, left the city and went to the place of baptism on the Jordan, accompanied by Peter, Andrew, and James the Less. There were many sick people waiting for him at the place of baptism. Jesus healed many, and then, as the throng of people grew, he and the apostles left and went to Bethel. They arrived in Bethel that evening and were met at an inn by Lazarus, Martha, Mary Magdalene, Nicodemus, and John Mark.

Crowds were gathered at Jericho, for Jesus's coming had been announced by the disciples. During his teaching and healing on the following day, the pressing and murmuring of the Pharisees were very great, and they sent messengers to Jerusalem to report. Jesus next went to the place of baptism on the Jordan where were lying numbers of sick in expectation of his coming. They had heard of his reappearance and had begged his aid. There were little huts and tents around, under which they could descend into the water. I saw too the basin in the little island in which he had been baptized. Sometimes it was full, but again, the water was allowed to run off. They came from all parts for this water, from Samaria, Judea, Galilee, and even from Syria. They loaded asses with large leathern sacks of it. The sacks hung on either side of the beast, and were kept together over the animal's back by hoops. Jesus cured numbers. Only John, Andrew, and James the Less were with him.

No baptisms took place at this time, only ablutions and healing. Even the baptism of John had in it more of a sacramental character than the ablutions on this occasion.

The last time that Jesus was in Jericho, many persons were healed at a bath in the city, but it was not baptism. There was at this part of the Jordan a bathing place much resorted to, which John had merely enlarged. In the middle of the well on the island in which Jesus was baptized, the pole on which he had leaned was still standing. Jesus cured many without application of water, though he poured it over the heads of the leprous, and the disciples wiped them dry.

Ruins of the Pool of Bethesda

Baptism proper came into use only after Pentecost. Jesus never baptized. The Mother of God was baptized alone at the pool of Bethesda by John after Pentecost. Before the ceremony he celebrated Holy Mass, that is, he consecrated and recited some prayers as they were accustomed to do at that time.

When the crowd became too great, Jesus went with the three apostles to Bethel, where the patriarch Jacob saw on a hill the ladder reaching from earth to heaven. It was already dark when they arrived and approached a house wherein trusty friends were awaiting them: Lazarus and his sisters, Nicodemus, and John Mark, who had come hither from Jerusalem secretly. The master of the house had a wife and four children. The house was surrounded by a courtyard in which was a fountain. Attended by two of his children, the master opened the door to the guests, whom he conducted at once to the fountain and washed their feet. As Jesus was sitting on the edge of the fountain, Magdalene came forth from the house and poured over his hair a little flat flask of perfume. She did it standing at his back, as she had often done before. I wondered at her boldness. Jesus pressed to his heart Lazarus, who was still pale and haggard. His hair was very black. A meal was spread, consisting of fruit, rolls, honeycomb, and green herbs, the usual fare in Judea. There were little cups on the table. Jesus cured the sick who were lying in a building belonging to the house. The women ate alone and afterward ranged in the lower part of the hall to hear Jesus's preaching.

Thursday, January 22, AD 33 (Shebat 2)

After healing many people in Bethel, Jesus went to a place north of Jericho, accompanied by Andrew, James the Less, and John. Jesus healed several people on the way.

Next morning Lazarus returned to Jerusalem with his companions, while Jesus with the three apostles went by a very circuitous route to the house of a son of Andrew's half-brother, whose daughter lay ill. They reached the well belonging to the house about noon. The master of the house, a robust man engaged in the manufacture of wicker screens, washed their feet and led them to his home. He had a great many children, some of them still quite small. Two grown sons from sixteen to eighteen years of age were not at home but at the fishery on the Sea of Galilee, in Andrew's dwelling place. Andrew had sent messengers to tell them that Jesus had returned, and to come to meet him at a certain place.

After a repast, the man led Jesus and the apostles to his sick daughter, a girl about twelve years old. For a long time she had been lying upon her bed perfectly pale and motionless. She had anemia, and she was also a simpleton. Jesus commanded her to arise. Then with Andrew he led her by the hand to the well, where he poured water over her head. After that, at the Lord's command, she took a bath under a tent, and returned to the house cured. She was a tall child. When Jesus with the apostles left the place, the father escorted him a part of the way.

Friday, January 23, AD 33 (Shebat 3)

Having made a detour, before the hour of the sabbath Jesus reached a little city. He took up his quarters at an inn in the city wall, and then went at once with his followers to celebrate the sabbath in the synagogue.

Saturday, January 24, AD 33 (Shebat 4)

In the synagogue this morning Jesus taught briefly. Then he healed many people. The apostles also healed and blessed the people. After the close of the sabbath, they all went to a nearby prison house in Alexandrium. Here many people were imprisoned. Jesus secured the release of about twenty-five of them. Then, together, they all traveled through the night northward along the Jordan.

Next morning he went again to the synagogue, where he prayed and delivered a short instruction. I saw a great crowd around him. They brought to him numbers of sick of diverse kinds, and he healed them. I saw that all the people of this place honored Jesus and pressed around him. The concourse was great. The apostles also cured and blessed; even the priests led the sick forward.

Bathing Place in the Jordan

I saw Jesus cure in this place a leper who had often been carried and set down on the road he was to travel, but whom he had always passed by. They had, just before Jesus's coming, brought the poor creature from a distant quarter of the city, where he dwelt in a little abode built in the wall. They brought him to Jesus sitting on a couch in a kind of litter shut in by hangings. No one went near the sick man excepting Jesus, who raised the curtain, touched the invalid, and directed that he should be taken to the bath near the city wall. When this order was executed, the scales of leprosy fell from him. He had been afflicted by a double leprosy, for that of impurity was added to the ordinary disease. The Lord healed likewise many women of an issue of blood. When he was healing in the court outside the synagogue, the crowd was so great that the people tore down the barriers and climbed upon the roof.

On leaving this place, Jesus journeyed on with the three apostles and reached a strong castle (Alexandrium) surrounded by moats, or ponds with discharging channels attached. It seemed that there were baths here, and I saw all kinds of vaults and massive walls. When Jesus manifested his intention to enter this castle, the apostles made objections to his doing so. He might, they said, rouse indignation and give occasion for scandal. Jesus rejoined that if they did not want to accompany him, they should suffer him to enter alone, and so he went in. It contained all sorts of people, some of whom appeared to be prisoners, others sick and infirm. Guards were standing at the gates, for the inmates dared not go out alone. Several always went together and attended by a guard. They were obliged to work in the country around the castle, clearing the fields and digging trenches. When Jesus with the apostles attempted to pass through the gate, the guards stopped them, but at a word from him, they respectfully allowed him to enter. The inmates assembled around him in the courtyard, where he spoke with them and separated several from the rest. From the city, which was not far off, Jesus summoned two men who appeared to be officers of the law, for they had little metallic badges hanging on straps from their shoulders. Jesus spoke with them, and it looked as if he were giving bail for those that he had separated from the rest of the inmates. Later on, I saw him leaving the castle with five and twenty of those people, and with them and the apostles traveling up the Jordan the whole night.

(Follow Map 39)

Sunday, January 25, AD 33 (*Shebat 5*)

This hurried march brought him to a little city in which he restored to their wives and children several of the prisoners lately freed. Others crossed the Jordan higher up, and then turned to the east. They were from the country of Kedar where Jesus had taught so long before his journey to the star worshippers. Jesus sent the apostles away on this road. When journeying through the valleys near Tiberias and past the well of Jacob, the three silent disciples—Silas, Eliud, and Eremenzear— and the other companions of his visit to the pagans joined Jesus.

Monday, January 26, AD 33 (*Shebat 6*)

Toward evening, Jesus and the three youths arrived in Capernaum. Here they were met by Peter, Andrew, and James the Less. Jesus went to the synagogue and taught. Many people were present. Afterward, the people on the streets of Capernaum called out: "Joseph's son is here again!"

They continued their journey a part of the night, rested only a few hours under a shed, and toward evening of the next day arrived in Capernaum. Here a young man called Sela, or Selam, was presented to Jesus. He was a cousin of the bridegroom of Kedar to whom Jesus had given the house and vineyard on the occasion of his journey to the star worshippers. It was the bridegroom who had sent Sela to Jesus, and he had been in Andrew's house awaiting his coming. He threw himself on his knees before Jesus, who imposed hands upon his shoulders and admitted him to the number of his disciples. Jesus made use of him at once, sending him to the superintendent of the school to demand the key and the roll of scriptures that had been found in the temple during the seven years that it had stood dilapidated and deprived of divine service. The last time Jesus taught here he had made use of the same roll of scriptures, which were from Isaiah. When the youth returned, Jesus and his companions went into the school and lighted the lamps. Jesus directed a space to be cleared and a pulpit with a flight of steps to be placed in it. A great crowd was gathered, and Jesus taught a long time from the roll of scriptures. The excitement in Capernaum was very great. The people assembled on the streets, and I heard the cry: "There is Joseph's son again!"

Tuesday, January 27, AD 33 (*Shebat 7*)

Jesus left Capernaum before daylight next morning, and I saw him going into Nazareth with the disciples and several of the apostles who had joined him. I saw on this occasion that Anne's house had passed into other hands. Jesus went also to Joseph's old home, now closed and unoccupied. Thence he proceeded straight to the synagogue. His appearance was the signal for great excitement among the people, who ran out in crowds. One possessed, who had a mute devil, suddenly began to shout after him: "There is Joseph's son! There is the rebel! Seize him! Imprison him!" Jesus commanded him to be silent. The man obeyed, but Jesus did not drive the devil out of him.

In the school Jesus ordered room to be made and a teacher's chair to be set for him. On this journey he acted with perfect freedom and taught openly as one having a right to do so, which proceeding greatly incensed the Jews against him. After teaching, Jesus and those with him went to an inn and stayed the night there.

Wednesday, January 28, AD 33 (*Shebat 8*)

Jesus sent the apostles on ahead to a mountain about sixteen miles south of Tiberias and then followed them there, accompanied by the remaining disciples. It was already night when he arrived at the "mount of the apostles." He found the apostles waiting for him at the top, grouped around a fire. Throughout much of the night Jesus taught, giving the apostles and disciples instructions for the next period of time.

Jesus visited many of the houses in the neighborhood of Joseph's old home, and healed and blessed the children;

Map 39: The Last Journey to Jerusalem

January 24–February 19, AD 33

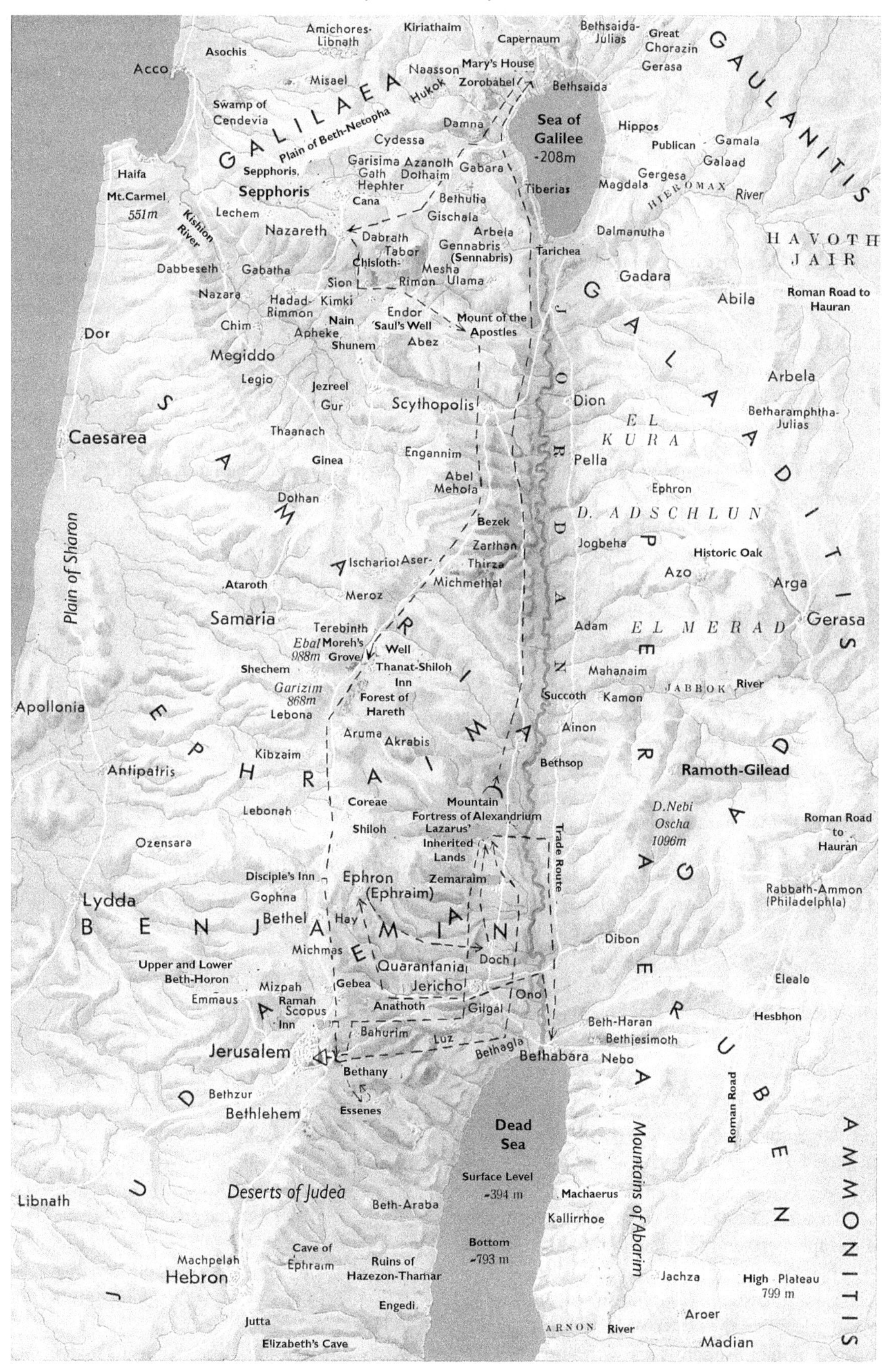

Alexandrium—Capernaum—Nazareth—Mount of the Apostles—Thanat-Shiloh—Bethany
Ensemes—Bethany—Lazarus's Property near Alexandrium—Bethabara—Ephron—Doch
Lazarus's Property near Alexandrium—Bethany—Jerusalem

whereupon the Jews who during the instruction had been tolerably quiet became extremely indignant. Jesus soon left the city, telling the apostles to meet him on the mount of the multiplication of the loaves, whither he went accompanied by the disciples only.

When they reached the mountain, it was already night, and fires were kindled on its summit. Jesus stood in the center, the apostles ranged around him, the disciples forming an outer circle. A considerable crowd had gathered. Jesus taught the whole night and until almost morning. He indicated to the apostles, pointing with his finger here and there, whither they should go on their mission of healing and teaching. It looked as if he were giving them orders as to their journeys and labors for the time just about to follow. They and many of the disciples took leave of him here, and at dawn he turned his steps southward.

Thursday, January 29, AD 33 (Shebat 9)

On this journey Jesus was implored by a father and mother to go into their house and cure their daughter who was a lunatic, pale and sick. He commanded her to arise, and she was cured.

An hour's distance from Thanat-Shiloh all the apostles, bearing green branches, came to meet Jesus. They prostrated before him and he took one of the branches in his hand. Then they washed his feet. I think this ceremony took place because they were all again reunited, and because Jesus once more appeared openly as their Master and was about to preach again everywhere. Accompanied by the apostles and disciples he went to the city, where the blessed Virgin, Magdalene, Martha, and the other holy women, except Peter's wife and step-daughter and Andrew's wife, who were still at Bethsaida, received him outside an inn. Mary had come from the region of Jericho and had here awaited Jesus. The other women also had come hither by different routes. They prepared a meal of which fifty guests partook, after which Jesus, having ordered the key to be brought, repaired to the school. The holy women and a great many people listened to his instruction.

Jesus Goes to Bethany

Friday, January 30, AD 33 (Shebat 10)

NEXT morning Jesus cured many sick of the city, although he passed before a number of houses without performing any cures. He healed also at the inn. After that he dismissed the apostles, sending some to Capernaum, and others to the place of the multiplication of the loaves. The holy women went to Bethany. Jesus himself took the same direction, and celebrated the sabbath at an inn with all the disciples whom he had brought back with him from his great journey. They hung a lamp in the middle of the hall, laid a red cover on the table and over it a white one, put on their white sabbath garments, and ranged round Jesus in the order observed at prayer. He prayed from a roll of writings. The whole party numbered about twenty.

Saturday, January 31, AD 33 (Shebat 11)

Jesus and the disciples remained at the inn for the sabbath. They prayed, and Jesus gave them instructions about what they should do.

The sabbath lamp burned the whole day, and Jesus alternately prayed and instructed the disciples in their duties. There was present a new disciple named Silvanus, whom Jesus had received in the last city. He was already thirty years old and of the tribe of Aaron. Jesus had known him from early youth, and looked upon him as his future disciple at the children's feast given by holy mother Anne when, as a boy of twelve, he returned from his teaching in the temple. It was at the same feast that he had chosen the future bridegroom of Cana.

Sunday, February 1, AD 33 (Shebat 12)

On the way to Bethany, Jesus, to continue his instructions for the benefit of the new disciples, explained to them the Lord's Prayer, spoke to them of fidelity in his service, and told them that he would now teach awhile in Jerusalem, after which he would soon return to his heavenly Father. He told them also that one would abandon him, for treason was already in his heart. All these new disciples remained faithful. On this journey, Jesus healed several lepers who had been brought out on the road. One hour from Bethany, they entered the inn at which Jesus had taught so long before Lazarus's resurrection and to which Magdalene had come forth to meet him. The blessed Virgin also was at the inn with other women, likewise five of the apostles: Judas, Thomas, Simon, James the Less, Thaddeus, John Mark, and some others. Lazarus was not there. The apostles came out a part of the way to meet the Lord at a well, where they saluted him and washed his feet, after which he gave an instruction which was followed by a meal. The women then went on to Bethany while Jesus remained at the inn with the rest of the party.

Monday, February 2, AD 33 (Shebat 13)

The five apostles and the sixteen disciples who had come with Jesus divided into two groups, one led by Judas Thaddeus and the other by James the Less. They went around the area and healed the sick. Jesus also went around healing, accompanied by the three silent disciples. Later, he went to Bethany, to the synagogue, and taught there.

Next day, instead of going straight to Bethany, he made a circuit around the adjacent country with the three silent disciples. The rest of the apostles and disciples separated into two bands, headed respectively by Thaddeus and James, and went around curing the sick. I saw them effecting cures in many different ways: by the imposition of hands, by breathing upon or leaning over the sick person, or in the case of children, by taking them on their knees, resting them on their breast and breathing upon them.

On this journey, Jesus cured a man possessed by the devil. The parents of the young man ran after Jesus just as he was entering a little village of scattered houses. He followed them into the court of their house, where he found their possessed son who, at the Lord's approach, became furious, leaping about and dashing against the walls. His friends wanted to bind him, but they could not do it, as he grew more and more rabid, flinging right and left those that approached him. Thereupon Jesus commanded all present to withdraw and leave him alone with the possessed. When they obeyed, Jesus called to the possessed to come to him. But he, heeding not the call, began to put out his tongue and to make horrible grimaces at Jesus. Jesus called him again. He came not, but, with his head twisted over his shoulder, he looked at him. Then Jesus raised his eyes to heaven and prayed.

When Jesus again commanded the possessed to come to him, he did so and cast himself full length at his feet. Jesus passed over him twice first one foot and then the other, as if treading him underfoot, and I saw rising from the open mouth of the possessed a black spiral vapor which disappeared in the air. In this rising exhalation I remarked three knots, the last of which was the darkest and strongest. These three knots were connected together by one strong thread and many finer ones. I can compare the whole thing to nothing better than to three censers one above the other, whose clouds of smoke, issuing from different openings, at last united with one another.

The possessed now lay like one dead at Jesus's feet. Jesus made over him the sign of the cross and commanded him to rise. The poor creature stood up. Jesus led him to his parents at the gate of the courtyard, and said to them: "I give you back your son cured, but I shall demand him again of you. Sin no more against him." They had sinned against him, and it was on that account that he had fallen into so miserable a condition.

Jesus now went to Bethany. The man just delivered and many others went thither also, some before Jesus, others after him. Many of those that had been cured by the apostles were likewise present in the city, and a great tumult arose when the cured everywhere proclaimed their happiness. I saw some priests go to meet Jesus and conduct him into the synagogue, where they laid before him a book of Moses from which they desired him to teach. There were many people in the school, and the holy women were in the place allotted to females.

They went afterward to the house of Simon of Bethany, the healed leper, where the women had prepared a repast in the rented hall. Lazarus was not there. Jesus and the three silent disciples spent the night at the inn near the synagogue, the apostles and other disciples at that outside Bethany; Mary and the other women stayed with Martha and Magdalene. The house in which Lazarus formerly dwelt was toward the Jerusalem side of the city. It was like a castle, surrounded by moats and bridges.

Tuesday, February 3, and Wednesday, February 4, AD 33 (Shebat 14–15)

Again, Jesus taught in the synagogue of Bethany and healed in the town.

The next morning Jesus again taught in the school where among the many disciples present were Saturnin, Nathaniel Chased, and Zacchaeus. Many sick had been brought to Bethany. In the house of Simon, the healed leper, a meal was again prepared, at which Jesus distributed all the servings to the poor and invited them to partake with the other guests. This gave rise to the report among the Pharisees and in Jerusalem that Jesus was a spendthrift who lavished upon the mob all that he could lay hands on.

While Jesus was teaching in the school, the crowds of sick, all men, were ranged in a double row of tents from the school to Simon's house. There were no lepers among them, for they showed themselves only in retired places. When Jesus approached the tents, three disciples followed him like Levites, two on either side, but a little behind him, and the third directly behind him. There was no crowd. Jesus went up along one row of tents and down by the other, curing in various ways. He merely passed by some of the sick, and exhorted others without curing them. He told them that they should change their manner of life. Some he took by the hand and commanded to rise, while others he merely touched. One man affected with edema he stroked over the head and body with his hand, and the swelling immediately went down. The water poured from his whole person in a stream of perspiration. Many of the cured threw themselves prostrate at Jesus's feet. His companions raised them and led them away. When the Lord returned to the school, he caused the cured to be seated near him, and then he taught.

Thursday, February 5, AD 33 (Shebat 16)

I saw Jesus today sending out the disciples two by two from Bethany into the country to teach and to heal. Some he told to return to Bethany, and others to Bethphage. He himself with the three silent disciples journeyed a couple of hours southward from Bethany to a little village where he healed the sick. Here I saw him going into the house of a man whom he had once cured of muteness, but who having sinned again, had now become paralyzed. His hands and fingers were quite distorted. Jesus ad-dressed to him some words of exhortation and touched him. The man arose. He healed likewise several girls who were lying pale and sick. Sometimes they lay unconscious as if dead, and again they alternately wept and laughed heartily. They were lunatics.

Friday, February 6, AD 33 (Shebat 17)

When, before the sabbath, Jesus again returned to Bethany and went to the school, I heard the Jews boasting against him that he could not yet do what God had done for the children of Israel when he rained down manna for them in the desert. They were indignant against Jesus. Jesus passed the night this time not in Bethany, but outside in the disciples' inn.

Saturday, February 7, AD 33 (Shebat 18)

Jesus taught in the synagogue.

Sunday, February 8, AD 33 (Shebat 19)

Three secret disciples came from Jerusalem to see Jesus. They reported that the high priests and Pharisees wanted to send out spies, so that they could capture him as soon as he came to Jerusalem. Jesus, accompanied by two young disciples, then left Bethany and traveled all night in a northerly direction.

While at this inn, three men came to him from Jerusalem: Obed, the son of the old man Simeon, a temple servant and a disciple in secret; the second, a relative of Veronica; and the third, a relative of Johanna Chusa. This last-mentioned became, later on, bishop of Kedar. For a time also he lived as a hermit near the date trees that, on her flight into Egypt, had bent down their fruit to Mary that she might partake of it. These disciples asked why he had so long abandoned them, why he had in other places done so much of which they knew nothing. In his answer to these questions, Jesus spoke of tapestry and other precious things which looked new and beautiful to one that had not seen them for some time. He said also that if the sower sowed his seed all at once and in one place, the whole might be destroyed by a hailstorm, and that just so the instructions and cures that were scattered far and wide would not soon be forgotten. Jesus's answers were something like the above.

These disciples brought the news that the high priests and Pharisees were going to station spies in the places round Jerusalem in order to seize him as soon as he appeared. Hearing this, Jesus took with him only his two latest disciples, Selam of Kedar and Silvanus, and traveled the whole night with them to Lazarus's estate near Ginea, where Lazarus himself was then stopping. Two days previously he was in the little city between Bethany and Bethlehem, in the neighborhood of which the three kings had rested on their journey to the latter place; but on receiving a message from Jesus, he had left and gone to his estate. Jesus knew very well that the three disciples would bring him this news from Jerusalem and that he himself would leave Bethany, therefore it was that he had already passed two nights not in Bethany, but in the disciples' inn outside.

Monday, February 9, AD 33 (Shebat 20)

Jesus arrived before dawn (it was still dark) at Lazarus's estate [south of Alexandrium] and knocked at the gate of the courtyard. It was opened by Lazarus himself who, with a light, conducted him into a large hall where were assembled Nicodemus, Joseph of Arimathea, John Mark, and Jairus, the younger brother of Obed. They ate a meal together.

Tuesday, February 10, to Saturday, February 14, AD 33 (Shebat 21–25)

I saw Jesus afterward with the two young disciples again in Bethabara, where he celebrated the sabbath.

Sunday, February 15, AD 33 (Shebat 26)

Jesus and the two young disciples went from Bethabara to Ephron. Andrew, Judas, Thomas, James the Less, Thaddeus, Zacchaeus, and seven other disciples were also present, having come hither from Bethany to meet Jesus. When Judas was about leaving Bethany, I saw the blessed Virgin earnestly exhorting him to be more moderate, to watch over himself, and not interfere in affairs as he did. In Ephron, Jesus healed the blind, the lame, the deaf and mute, who had been brought thither for that purpose. He delivered one possessed also from the power of the devil.

Monday, February 16, AD 33 (Shebat 27)

On leaving Ephron, he went to a place north of Jericho where there was an asylum for the sick and the poor. Here he restored sight to an old blind man whom once before, when engaged in healing, he had sent away, although at the same time he had restored sight to two others by anointing their eyes with salve made of clay mixed with spittle. He now cured this man by his word alone. The village was situated on his way.

Tuesday, February 17, and Wednesday, February 18, AD 33 (Shebat 28–29)

From this last place Jesus returned to Lazarus's estate near Alexandrium, and thence went with Lazarus to Bethany, whither the holy women came to meet him.

TISSOT ILLUSTRATIONS
[SECTION F]

The Public Teaching of Jesus

⊕

But No Man Laid Hands upon Him [F1]

⊕

[JOHN 7:43–47] 43 So there was a division among the people over him. 44 Some of them wanted to arrest him, but no one laid hands on
him. 45 The officers then went back to the chief priests and Pharisees, who said to them, "Why did you not bring him?" 46 The officers
answered, "No man ever spoke like this man!" 47 The Pharisees answered them, "Are you led astray, you also?" [467]

The Adulterous Woman—Jesus Writing upon the Ground [F2]

⊕

[JOHN 8:1–9] 1 But Jesus went to the Mount of Olives. 2 Early in the morning he came again to the temple; all the people came to him, and he sat down and taught them. 3 The scribes and the Pharisees brought a woman who had been caught in adultery, and placing her in the midst 4 they said to him, "Teacher, this woman has been caught in the act of adultery. 5 Now in the law Moses commanded us to stone such. What do you say about her?" 6 This they said to test him, that they might have some charge to bring against him. Jesus bent down and wrote with his finger on the ground. 7 And as they continued to ask him, he stood up and said to them, "Let him who is without sin among you be the first to throw a stone at her." 8 And once more he bent down and wrote with his finger on the ground. 9 But when they heard it, they went away, one by one, beginning with the eldest, and Jesus was left alone with the woman standing before him. [467]

The Adulterous Woman Alone with Jesus [F3]

⊕

[JOHN 8:9–11] 9 But when they heard it, they went away, one by one, beginning with the eldest, and Jesus was left alone with the woman
standing before him. 10 Jesus looked up and said to her, "Woman, where are they? Has no one condemned you?" 11 She said, "No one,
Lord." And Jesus said, "Neither do I condemn you; go, and do not sin again." 467]

The Blind Man Washes in the Pool of Siloam [F4]

⊕

[JOHN 9:6–23] 6 As he said this, he spat on the ground and made clay of the spittle and anointed the man's eyes with the clay, 7 saying to him, "Go, wash in the pool of Siloam" (which means Sent). So he went and washed and came back seeing. 8 The neighbors and those who had seen him before as a beggar, said, "Is not this the man who used to sit and beg?" 9 Some said, "It is he"; others said, "No, but he is like him." He said, "I am the man." 10 They said to him, "Then how were your eyes opened?" 11 He answered, "The man called Jesus made clay and anointed my eyes and said to me, 'Go to Siloam and wash'; so I went and washed and received my sight." 12 They said to him, "Where is he?" He said, "I do not know." 13 They brought to the Pharisees the man who had formerly been blind. 14 Now it was a sabbath day when Jesus made the clay and opened his eyes. 15 The Pharisees again asked him how he had received his sight. And he said to them, "He put clay on my eyes, and I washed, and I see." 16 Some of the Pharisees said, "This man is not from God, for he does not keep the sabbath." But others said, "How can a man who is a sinner do such signs?" There was a division among them. 17 So they again said to the blind man, "What do you say about him, since he has opened your eyes?" He said, "He is a prophet." 18 The Jews did not believe that he had been blind and had received his sight, until they called the parents of the man who had received his sight, 19 and asked them, "Is this your son, who you say was born blind? How then does he now see?" 20 His parents answered, "We know that this is our son, and that he was born blind; 21 but how he now sees we do not know, nor do we know who opened his eyes. Ask him; he is of age, he will speak for himself." 22 His parents said this because they feared the Jews, for the Jews had already agreed that if any one should confess him to be Christ, he was to be put out of the synagogue. 23 Therefore his parents said, "He is of age, ask him." [467]

Jesus Speaks near the Treasury [F5]

⊕

[JOHN 8:19–20] 19 They said to him therefore, "Where is your Father?" Jesus answered, "You know neither me nor my Father; if you knew me, you would know my Father also." 20 These words he spoke in the treasury, as he taught in the temple; but no one arrested him, because his hour had not yet come. [468]

IN the engraving Jesus is represented in the Treasury, which was identical with the space called by the Jews the Court of the Women. It had five entrances, at each of which were placed trumpet-shaped chests for offerings or treasuries, in which the offerings brought by male and female worshippers were placed, for it was the only part of the sacred building to which women were admitted. In the background can be seen the Steps of the Psalms, known as the Degrees.

Jesus Walks in the Portico of Solomon [F6]

⊕

[JOHN 10:23–31] 23 It was winter, and Jesus was walking in the temple, in the portico of Solomon. 24 So the Jews gathered round him and said to him, "How long will you keep us in suspense? If you are the Christ, tell us plainly." 25 Jesus answered them, "I told you, and you do not believe. The works that I do in my Father's name, they bear witness to me; 26 but you do not believe, because you do not belong to my sheep. 27 My sheep hear my voice, and I know them, and they follow me; 28 and I give them eternal life, and they shall never perish, and no one shall snatch them out of my hand. 29 My Father, who has given them to me, is greater than all, and no one is able to snatch them out of the Father's hand. 30 I and the Father are one." 31 The Jews took up stones again to stone him. [468]

IT was, *no doubt, in the morning that the scene in Solomon's Porch took place. This porch was on the east of the temple, leading to the Nicanor Gate, and was bounded by the Valley of Jehosaphat. It would, therefore, be in shadow in the morning, so that Jesus could walk there and teach the people without suffering from the heat of the sun as he would have done in the afternoon. This porch, as we have already stated, had two cloisters formed by two rows of columns; on the side of the Valley of Jehosaphat it was walled in, and the only openings were small windows at the top of the wall, too high up for anyone to be able to look through them into the temple. Between this supporting wall, or rampart, and the porch itself, there were shops and stables, in the latter of which were kept the animals destined to be offered in sacrifice. Now, as the space allotted to them was both low and narrow, the merchants who wished to sell their wares encroached on the porch itself, where they could have more room, and it thus became crowded with merchandise, arousing the just indignation of Jesus, to which we shall refer again further on.*

Zacchaeus in the Sycamore Awaiting the Passage of Jesus [F7]

⊕

JUST outside the city, which was surrounded by gardens, pleasure grounds, and villas, Jesus and his followers encountered a dense crowd composed of people from all parts of the country around. They had assembled with their sick, who were lying on litters under sheds and tents. They had been waiting for Jesus, and now they beset him and his disciples on all sides. Zacchaeus, one of the chief publicans, who dwelt outside the city, had stationed himself on the road by which Jesus had to pass. As he was short in stature, he climbed a fig tree in order to be able to see Jesus better in the crowd. Jesus looked up into the tree and said: "Zacchaeus, make haste and come down, for this day I must abide in thy house." Zacchaeus hurried down, bowed humbly to Jesus, and very much touched returned home to make preparations for receiving his honored guest. When Jesus said that he must that day enter into Zacchaeus's house, he meant into his heart, for on that day he went into Jericho itself, and not into the house of Zacchaeus. [471]

[LUKE 19:1–10] 1 He entered Jericho and was passing through. 2 And there was a man named Zacchaeus; he was a chief tax collector, and
rich. 3 And he sought to see who Jesus was, but could not, on account of the crowd, because he was small of stature. 4 So he ran on ahead
and climbed up into a sycamore tree to see him, for he was to pass that way. 5 And when Jesus came to the place, he looked up and said to
him, "Zacchaeus, make haste and come down; for I must stay at your house today." 6 So he made haste and came down, and received him
joyfully. 7 And when they saw it they all murmured, "He has gone in to be the guest of a man who is a sinner." 8 And Zacchaeus stood and
said to the Lord, "Behold, Lord, the half of my goods I give to the poor; and if I have defrauded any one of anything, I restore it fourfold." 9
And Jesus said to him, "Today salvation has come to this house, since he also is a son of Abraham. 10 For the Son of man came to seek and
to save the lost."

The Two Blind Men at Jericho [F8]

⊕

BEFORE Jesus's departure from Jericho, messengers from Bethany brought to the disciples the news of how earnestly Martha and Magdalene were longing for his coming, as Lazarus was very sick. Jesus, however, did not go to Bethany, but to a little village north of Jericho. Here too, a crowd had assembled, and numbers of sick, blind, and crippled were awaiting his arrival. Two blind men, each with two guides, were sitting by the roadside, and when Jesus passed by they cried out after him, begging to be cured. The people tried to silence them with threats, but they followed Jesus, crying after him: "Ah, thou Son of David! Have mercy on us!" Then Jesus turned, commanded them to be led to him, and touched their eyes. They saw and followed him. [473]

[MATTHEW 20:29–34] 29 And as they went out of Jericho, a great crowd followed him. 30 And behold, two blind men sitting by the roadside, when they heard that Jesus was passing by, cried out, "Have mercy on us, Son of David!" 31 The crowd rebuked them, telling them to be silent; but they cried out the more, "Lord, have mercy on us, Son of David!" 32 And Jesus stopped and called them, saying, "What do you want me to do for you?" 33 They said to him, "Lord, let our eyes be opened." 34 And Jesus in pity touched their eyes, and immediately they received their sight and followed him.

THE scene described in the gospel as taking place at Jericho resembled greatly many another related in the sacred text. As we have already stated, beggars collected in preference beside the main roads of traffic as they were more likely to receive liberal alms there than elsewhere. These two blind men, guessing from the crowds attending him, that the Prophet was about to pass by, cried out to attract his attention and get him to heal them. Jesus, as was his wont, was occupied in teaching the people, and did not at first appear to perceive what was required of him; the bystanders, therefore, annoyed by the noise the men were making, which prevented them from hearing the words of the Teacher rebuked them, telling them to hold their peace. But they only cried out the more, and in the end their prayer was granted.

The Healing of Ten Lepers [F9]

⊕

JESUS next went in the direction of Samaria. Not far from one of the little villages along the highroad, about a hundred paces to one side, there stood a tent in which ten lepers were lying in beds. As Jesus was passing, the lepers came out and cried to him for help. Jesus stood still, but the disciples went on. The lepers, entirely enveloped in their mantles, approached—some quickly, others slowly, as their strength permitted—and stood in a circle around Jesus. He touched each one separately, directed them to present themselves to the priests, and went on his way. One of the lepers, a Samaritan and the most active of the ten, went along the same road with two of the disciples, but the others took different routes. These were not cured all at once; although able to walk, they were not made perfectly clean till about an hour afterward.

Soon after this last encounter, a father from a shepherd village a quarter of an hour to the right of the road came to meet Jesus and begged him to go back with him to the village, for his little daughter was lying dead. Jesus went with him at once, and on the way was overtaken by the cured Samaritan who, touched by his perfect cure, had hurried back to thank his benefactor. He cast himself at the feet of Jesus, who said: "Were not ten made clean? And where are the nine? Is not one found among them to return and give glory to God, but only this stranger? Arise, go thy way! Thy faith hath made thee whole!" This man later on became a disciple. [474]

[LUKE 17:11–19] 11 On the way to Jerusalem he was passing along between Samaria and Galilee. 12 And as he entered a village, he was met by ten lepers, who stood at a distance 13 and lifted up their voices and said, "Jesus, Master, have mercy on us." 14 When he saw them he said to them, "Go and show yourselves to the priests." And as they went they were cleansed. 15 Then one of them, when he saw that he was healed, turned back, praising God with a loud voice; 16 and he fell on his face at Jesus's feet, giving him thanks. Now he was a Samaritan. 17 Then said Jesus, "Were not ten cleansed? Where are the nine? 18 Was no one found to return and give praise to God except this foreigner?" 19 And he said to him, "Rise and go your way; your faith has made you well."

IT is said to have been in the town of Jenin, or at least in its neighborhood, that the miracle of the healing of the ten lepers was performed. This town, which is situated on the northern borders of Samaria, where that province is bounded by the vast fertile plain of Esdrelon, is the granary of Syria, which yields such rich crops of every variety. It was on the usual route from the north to the south of Palestine. There were two other routes, that by way of the Jordan and the Mountains of Gilboa on the left, and that by way of Mount Carmel and the sea-coast on the right, but they were far less frequented than the Jenin way, for the numerous robbers rendered them very unsafe. It followed, therefore, that on the Jenin route many beggars and lepers collected to watch the passers-by in the hopes of alms. They were in the habit of grouping themselves about the gates of the town, assailing travelers with their deafening cries, especially if those travelers had many attendants, for they would then conclude that they were important people, likely to be liberal in their gifts. It was on such a group, in this case consisting of ten lepers, that our Lord exercised his beneficent power.

Jesus Wept [F10]

⊕

HE was standing with the apostles and some others on the confines of their garden before an open arbor. Martha spoke to Jesus and then turned back to Magdalene, who also by this time had come up. She threw herself at Jesus's feet, saying: "If thou hadst been here, he would not have died!" All present were in tears. Jesus too mourned and wept, and delivered a discourse of great length upon death. Many of the audience, which was constantly increasing outside the bower, whispered to one another and murmured their dissatisfaction at Jesus's not having kept Lazarus alive. [478]

[JOHN 11:32–35] 32 Then Mary, when she came where Jesus was and saw him, fell at his feet, saying to him, "Lord, if you had been here, my brother would not have died." 33 When Jesus saw her weeping, and the Jews who came with her also weeping, he was deeply moved in spirit and troubled; 34 and he said, "Where have you laid him?" They said to him, "Lord, come and see." 35 Jesus wept.

The Raising of Lazarus [F11]

⊕

IT seems to me that it was very early in the morning when Jesus went with the apostles to the tomb. Mary, Lazarus's sisters, and others, in all about seven women, were likewise there, as also a crowd of people which was constantly on the increase. Lazarus's tomb was the first on the right of the entrance to the vault, down into which some steps led. It was a four-cornered, oblong cave, about three feet in depth, and covered with a flat stone. In it lay the corpse in a lightly woven coffin, and around it in the tomb there was room for one to walk. Jesus with some of the apostles went down into the vault, while the holy women, Magdalene, and Martha remained standing in the doorway. But the crowd pressed around so that many people climbed up on the roof of the vault and the cemetery walls in order to see. Jesus commanded the apostles to raise the stone from the grave. They did so, rested it against the wall, and then removed a light cover or door that closed the tomb below that stone.

It was at this point of the proceedings that Martha said: "Lord, by this time he stinketh, for he is now of four days." After that they took the lightly woven cover from the coffin, and disclosed the corpse lying in its winding sheet. At that instant Jesus raised his eyes to heaven, prayed aloud, and called out in a strong voice: "Lazarus, come forth!" At this cry, the corpse arose to a sitting posture. The crowd now pressed with so much violence that Jesus ordered them to be driven outside the walls of the cemetery. The apostles, who were standing in the tomb by the coffin, removed the handkerchief from Lazarus's face, unbound his hands and feet, and drew off the winding sheet. Lazarus, as if waking from lethargy, rose from the coffin and stepped out of the grave, tottering and looking like a phantom. The apostles threw a mantle around him. Like one walking in sleep, he approached the door, passed the Lord, and went out to where his sisters and the other women had stepped back in fright as before a ghost. [479]

[JOHN 11:41–45] 41 So they took away the stone. And Jesus lifted up his eyes and said, "Father, I thank thee that thou hast heard me. 42 I knew that thou hearest me always, but I have said this on account of the people standing by, that they may believe that thou didst send me." 43 When he had said this, he cried with a loud voice, "Lazarus, come out." 44 The dead man came out, his hands and feet bound with bandages, and his face wrapped with a cloth. Jesus said to them, "Unbind him, and let him go." 45 Many of the Jews therefore, who had come with Mary and had seen what he did, believed in him.

The Evil Counsel [F12]

⊕

I SAW also a gathering of Pharisees and high priests who had come together to discuss Jesus and Lazarus. Among other things I heard them say that they feared Jesus would raise all the dead, and then what confusion would ensue! At noon on that day, a great tumult arose in Bethany. If Jesus had been there, they would have stoned him. Lazarus was obliged to hide, and the apostles, to slip away in different directions. All the other friends of Jesus in Bethany were likewise forced to lie in concealment. Minds became calm, however, when people took into consideration that they had no right to take action against Lazarus. [480]

[JOHN 11:47–53] 47 So the chief priests and the Pharisees gathered the council, and said, "What are we to do? For this man performs
many signs. 48 If we let him go on thus, every one will believe in him, and the Romans will come and destroy both our holy place and our
nation." 49 But one of them, Caiaphas, who was high priest that year, said to them, "You know nothing at all; 50 you do not understand
that it is expedient for you that one man should die for the people, and that the whole nation should not perish." 51 He did not say this of
his own accord, but being high priest that year he prophesied that Jesus should die for the nation, 52 and not for the nation only, but to
gather into one the children of God who are scattered abroad. 53 So from that day on they took counsel how to put him to death.

He Went on His Way to Ephraim [F13]

⊕

JESUS had previously announced to them his return by the parents of the three disciples. On the journey from Shechem to Ephraim it was very foggy, and quantities of rain fell. Jesus did not confine himself to the straight route. He went to different localities, different towns and houses, consoling the inhabitants, healing the sick, and exhorting all to follow him. [523]

[JOHN 11:54] 54 Jesus therefore no longer went about openly among the Jews, but went from there to the country near the wilderness, to a town called Ephraim; and there he stayed with the disciples.

THE *district near the wilderness called Ephraim, to which our Lord retired, is said to be situated near Djifneh, in the wild, shut-in mountain group bordering the Valley of Ainel-Aramiyeh, beyond which are the curious and interesting ruins of Shiloh. True harbors of refuge, the gorges and ravines, dominated by all but inaccessible mountains, clad with luxuriant verdure, can only be reached by paths suitable to goats. At daybreak the smoke from secluded mountain homes can be seen, crowning the summits of the hills, while deep down in the valleys, where the vegetation is denser, the morning mist still hovers. There, among the countless clumps, I had almost said the thickets, of pink cyclamen, Jesus could easily have found the refuge he sought. It is easy to understand the reasons for his retirement; the exasperation of the Jews against him was such that his life was in danger, and he had not yet finished his work, or, to quote his own words, "his hour had not yet come," and it did not suit him to expose himself needlessly to a violence to which it was not his intention to submit.*

www.ingramcontent.com/pod-product-compliance
Lightning Source LLC
LaVergne TN
LVHW081249100826
845148LV00009B/1176
* 9 7 8 1 5 9 7 3 1 1 4 7 2 *